BARRON'S

NEW SAT*

Ira K. Wolf, Ph.D.
President, PowerPrep, Inc.
Former High School Teacher, College Professor,
and University Director of Teacher Preparation

Brian W. Stewart, M.Ed.
Founder and President
BWS Education Consulting, Inc.

BARRON'S

*SAT is a registered trademark of the College Board, which was not involved in the production of, and does not endorse, this product.

DEDICATION

In memory of Mitchel Weiner and Samuel Brownstein, who first brought college entrance test preparation to the high school students of America.

S.W.G.

To Elaine, my wife and best friend, for all of your support and love.

I.K.W.

To Caitlin, Andrew, and Eloise for all of your love and support.

B.W.S.

ABOUT THE AUTHORS

Sharon Green started helping prepare students for the PSAT and SAT as a 13-year-old assistant at her father's college entrance tutoring course; she has never stopped since. A National Merit Scholar, she holds degrees from Harvard College, New York University School of Education, and the University of California at Berkeley. Her test preparation books, all published by Barron's, run the gamut from the California High School Proficiency Examination to the GRE. Whenever she can dig her way out from under multiple dictionaries, Sharon enjoys folk dancing, reading Jane Austen and science fiction, and watching Little League baseball.

Dr. Ira Wolf has had a long career in math education. In addition to teaching math at the high school level for several years, he was a professor of mathematics at Brooklyn College and the Director of the Mathematics Teacher Preparation program at SUNY Stony Brook.

Dr. Wolf has been helping students prepare for college entrance exams, including the PSAT, SAT, ACT, and SAT Subject Tests in Math for more than 35 years. He is the founder of PowerPrep, a test preparation company on Long Island that currently works with several hundred high school students each year.

Brian W. Stewart is the founder and president of BWS Education Consulting, Inc., a boutique tutoring and test preparation company based in Columbus, Ohio. His company has worked with thousands of students from all over the world to help them improve their test scores and earn admission to selective schools. Brian earned his A.B. in Philosophy at Princeton University and his Master's in Education at The Ohio State University. He is also the author of Barron's *ACT*, Barron's *Strategies and Practice for the New PSAT/NMSQT*, and Barron's *New SAT Reading Workbook*. You can connect with Brian at *www.bwseducationconsulting.com*.

© Copyright 2016, 2014, 2012, 2010, 2008 by Barron's Educational Series, Inc.

Previous editions © copyright 2006, 2005, 2001, 1998, 1997, 1994, 1993, 1991, 1989, 1987, 1986, 1984, 1982, 1980, 1978, 1975, 1974, 1973, 1972, 1971, 1969, 1966, 1965, 1964, 1962, 1958, 1955, 1954 by Barron's Educational Series, Inc., under the titles *How to Prepare for the SAT*, *How to Prepare for the SAT I*, and *How to Prepare for the Scholastic Aptitude Test*.

All inquiries should be addressed to:
Barron's Educational Series, Inc.
250 Wireless Boulevard
Hauppauge, NY 11788
www.barronseduc.com

ISBN: 978-1-4380-0649-9
ISBN (with CD-ROM): 978-1-4380-7572-3
ISSN (print): 1941-6180
ISSN (print with CD-ROM): 1941-6474

PRINTED IN THE UNITED STATES OF AMERICA
9 8 7 6 5 4 3 2 1

10% POST-CONSUMER WASTE
Paper contains a minimum of 10% post-consumer waste (PCW). Paper used in this book was derived from certified, sustainable forestlands.

Contents

PART ONE: GET ACQUAINTED WITH THE NEW SAT

PART TWO: PINPOINT YOUR TROUBLE SPOTS

PART THREE: THE SAT READING TEST

PART SIX: TEST YOURSELF

Preface

![striped bar]

In writing this edition of Barron's *New SAT*, we have aimed to give you the advantages on the SAT that the students we tutor and teach in classes have enjoyed for decades. Therefore, we'd like you to think of this study guide as your personal SAT tutor, because that's precisely what it is. Like any good tutor, it will work closely with you, prompting you and giving you pointers to improve your testing skills. It will help you pinpoint your trouble spots and show you how to work on them, and it will point out your strengths as well. After working with your tutor, you should see marked improvement in your performance.

Your personal tutor will be available to work with you whenever you like, for as long or short a time as you like. Working with your tutor, you can go as quickly or as slowly as you like, repeating sections as often as you need, skipping over sections you already know well. Your tutor will give you explanations, not just correct answers, when you make mistakes, and will be infinitely patient and adaptable.

Here are just a few of the things your tutor offers you:

- It takes you step by step through thousands of reading, writing and language, and mathematical questions, showing you how to solve them and how to avoid going wrong.

- It offers you dozens of clear-cut Testing Tactics and shows you how to use them to attack every question type you will find on the new SAT.

- It enables you to simulate actual testing conditions, providing you with a diagnostic test and four model tests—all with answers fully explained—each of which follows the format of the SAT.

- It provides a comprehensive review of all the math topics you need to know to do well on the SAT.

- It thoroughly prepares you for the two completely new parts of the SAT: the Writing and Language section and the optional Essay. With step-by-step lessons on English grammar and essay analysis, informational graphics drills, and sample essay prompts accompanied by a range of sample student responses, you have the tools to approach these new sections with total confidence.

- It gives you Barron's Master Word List, your best chance to acquaint yourself with the whole range of college-level vocabulary you will face on the SAT.

- It even gives you your own set of high-frequency word list flash cards in a convenient tear-out section at the back of the book. More than 200 words that have appeared regularly on previous SAT exams are presented, each with its part of speech, pronunciation, definition, and illustrative sentence. Separate the cards and carry some with you to study in spare moments. Or devise a competitive game, and use them with a partner.

No other book offers you as much. Your personal tutor embodies Barron's ongoing commitment to provide you with the best possible coaching for the SAT and every other important test you take. It has benefited from the dedicated labors of Linda Turner and other members of the editorial staff of Barron's, all of whom wish you the best as you settle down with your tutor to work on the SAT.

New SAT Format and Test Dates

SAT Format	
Total Time: 3 Hours, plus 50 minutes for the Optional Essay	
Section 1: Reading **52 Questions** *Time—65 minutes*	5 Reading Passages, including 1 paired passage
Section 2: Writing and Language **44 Questions** *Time—35 minutes*	4 Passages
Section 3: Math, No Calculator **20 Questions** *Time—25 minutes*	15 Multiple Choice, 5 Grid-in
Section 4: Math, Calculator **38 Questions** *Time—55 minutes*	30 Multiple Choice, 8 Grid-in
Optional Essay **1 Question** *Time—50 minutes*	Write an essay analyzing how the author of a given passage has made his or her argument. Evaluated on reading, analysis, and writing.

The old SAT will be in place through January 2016. The first administration of the new SAT is March 2016. You can register for the SAT at *sat.collegeboard.org*.

New SAT Test Dates		
	Registration Deadlines	
Test Dates	Regular	Late
2016 March 5 May 7 June 4	February 5 April 8 May 5	February 23 April 26 May 25
2016–2017 School Year* October 1, 2016 November 5, 2016 December 3, 2016 January 28, 2017 March 11, 2017 May 6, 2017 June 3, 2017		

*As of press time, exam dates for the 2016–2017 school year are approximate. Check *collegeboard.org* periodically to confirm the anticipated test dates and the registration and late registration deadlines.

Countdown to the SAT

The day before you take the test, don't do practice tests. Do look over all the tactics listed below so they will be fresh in your mind.

BEFORE THE TEST

If the test location is unfamiliar to you, drive there before the test day so that you will know exactly where you're going on the day you take the test.

Set out your test kit the night before. You will need your admission ticket, a photo ID (a driver's license or a non-driver picture ID, a passport, or a school ID), your calculator, four or five sharpened No. 2 pencils (with erasers), plus a map or directions showing how to get to the test center.

Get a good night's sleep so you are well rested and alert.

Wear comfortable clothes. Dress in layers. Bring a sweater in case the room is cold.

Bring an accurate watch—not one that beeps and not your cell phone—in case the room has no clock. You'll want to use the same watch or small clock that you've been using during your practice sessions.

Bring a small snack for quick energy.

Don't be late. Allow plenty of time for getting to the test site. You want to be in your seat, relaxed, before the test begins.

Pick your favorite letter from among A, B, C, and D. This is the letter you will always use when you have to make a quick guess.

DURING THE TEST

Pace yourself. Don't work so fast that you start making careless errors. On the other hand, don't get bogged down on any one question.

Feel free to skip back and forth between questions within a section.

Play the percentages: always eliminate as many of the answer choices as possible and then make an educated guess, not a random one.

If you have no idea, quickly guess your favorite letter and move on.

If you are running out of time in a section, use your last 20 seconds to fill in your favorite letter on every question you didn't get to.

Watch out for eye-catchers, answer choices that are designed to tempt you into guessing wrong.

Change answers only if you have a reason for doing so; don't change them on a last-minute hunch or whim.

Check your assumptions. Make sure you are answering the question asked and not the one you *thought* was going to be asked.

Remember that you are allowed to write anything you want in your test booklet. Make full use of it.

- Do math calculations and draw diagrams.
- Underline key words in reading passages.
- Cross out answer choices you are *sure* are wrong.
- Circle questions you want to come back to, but first make a guess.

Be careful not to make any stray marks on your answer sheet. The test is graded by a machine, and a machine cannot always tell the difference between an accidental mark and an intentionally filled-in answer.

Check frequently to make sure you are answering the questions in the right spots.

Remember that you don't have to attempt every question to do well. Just be sure to fill in answers for every question you don't attempt.

TIPS FOR THE EVIDENCE-BASED READING QUESTIONS

Read all the answer choices before you decide which is best.

Think of a context for an unfamiliar word; the context may help you come up with the word's meaning.

Break down unfamiliar words into recognizable parts—prefixes, suffixes, roots.

Consider secondary meanings of words. If none of the answer choices seems right to you, take another look. A word may have more than one meaning.

When you have a choice, tackle reading passages with familiar subjects before passages with unfamiliar ones.

Make use of the introductions to acquaint yourself with the text.

Read as rapidly as you can with understanding, but do not force yourself.

As you read the opening sentence, try to predict what the passage is about.

When you tackle the questions, use any line references given to help in the passage.

Base your answer only on what is written in the passage, not on what you know from other books or courses.

In answering questions on the paired reading passages, first read one passage and answer the questions based on it; then read the second passage and tackle the remaining questions.

On graph analysis questions, take time to evaluate the graph labels and axes. Be mindful that you will often need to integrate information from the reading passage with what is presented in the graph.

The vocabulary in context questions typically involve unusual meanings of words you know—be sure you read enough of the text in which the word appears so that you'll be able to figure exactly how the word is being used in the passage.

If you notice that a question is immediately followed by a second question that asks which lines in the passage provide evidence supporting your answer to the first question, don't waste time going over the second question's answer choices. Instead, as you answer the first question, note where you found the evidence supporting your answer choice. Mark the lines with an asterisk, or set them in brackets. Then answer the second question.

Do not hesitate to come back to questions if you are unsure; a question that initially seems confusing will often be far easier when you consider it a second time.

TIPS FOR THE MATHEMATICS QUESTIONS

Whenever you know how to answer a question directly, just do it. The tactics that are reviewed below should be used only when you need them.

Memorize all the formulas you need to know. Even though some of them are printed on the first page of each math section, during the test you do not want to waste any time referring to that reference material.

Be sure to bring a calculator for use on the long math section, but use it only when you need it. Don't use it for simple arithmetic that you can easily do in your head.

Remember that no problem requires lengthy or difficult computations. If you find yourself doing a lot of arithmetic, stop and reread the question. You are probably not answering the question asked.

Answer every question you attempt. Even if you can't solve it, you can almost always eliminate two or more choices. Often you know that an answer must be negative, but two or three of the choices are positive, or an answer must be even, and some of the choices are odd.

Unless a diagram is labeled "<u>Note</u>: Figure not drawn to scale," it is perfectly accurate, and you can trust it in making an estimate.

When a diagram has not been provided, draw one, especially on a geometry problem.

If a diagram has been provided, feel free to label it, and mark it up in any way, including adding line segments, if necessary.

Answer any question for which you can estimate the answer, even if you are not sure you are correct.

Don't panic if you see a strange symbol in a question; it will always be defined. Getting the correct answer just involves using the information given in the definition.

When a question involves two equations, the most useful thing to do is to add them or subtract them. If there are three or more, just add them.

Never make unwarranted assumptions. Do not assume numbers are positive or integers. If a question refers to two numbers, do not assume that they have to be different. If you know a figure has four sides, do not assume that it is a rectangle.

Be sure to work in consistent units. If the width and length of a rectangle are 8 inches and 2 feet, respectively, either convert the 2 feet to 24 inches or the 8 inches to two-thirds of a foot before calculating the area or perimeter.

Standard Multiple-Choice Questions

Whenever you answer a question by backsolving, start with choice (C).

When you replace variables with numbers, choose easy-to-use numbers, whether or not they are realistic.

Choose appropriate numbers. The best number to use in percent problems is 100. In problems involving fractions, the best number to use is the least common denominator.

When you have no idea how to solve a problem, eliminate all of the absurd choices before you guess. Remember, you should provide an answer to each and every question. Guess if you have to. *Bubble in an answer to every question.*

Student-Produced Response (Grid-in) Questions

Write your answer in the four spaces at the top of the grid, and *carefully* grid in your answer below. No credit is given for a correct answer if it has been gridded improperly.

Remember that the answer to a grid-in question can never be negative.

You can never grid in a mixed number—you must convert it to an improper fraction or a decimal.

Never round off your answers. If a fraction can fit in the four spaces of the grid, enter it. If not, use your calculator to convert it to a decimal (by dividing) and enter a decimal point followed by the first three decimal digits.

When gridding a decimal, do not write a zero before the decimal point.

If a question has more than one possible answer, grid in only one of them.

There is no penalty for wrong answers on grid-in questions, so you should grid in anything that seems reasonable, rather than omit a question.

TIPS FOR THE EVIDENCE-BASED WRITING AND LANGUAGE QUESTIONS

This section is all about your essay-editing skills. To edit well, you must take your time. Fortunately, this section is generally easy to finish. So use the full amount of time allowed, taking about 9 minutes per passage.

Silently *mouth out* the wording to pick up on errors. Even though you may not know the "official" grammar rule, hearing what *sounds best* can help you figure out the correct option.

Build your skills and confidence by reviewing the SAT grammar topics in Chapter 3. Grammar "pet peeves" will not be tested, but grammar rules will. Be on the lookout for some of the most common issues (punctuation, wordiness, verb tense, parallelism, subject–verb agreement, misplaced modifiers, logical comparisons, and diction/proper word usage).

Jumping to an answer without considering enough context will not work—the incorrect answers will be very tempting. If, however, you are having trouble determining what concept the question is testing, narrow down the likely issue by reviewing the answer choices to see what is different among them. "No Change" has just as much of a chance of being correct as does any other option.

On graph interpretation questions, use only the evidence in the graph and the passage. No background knowledge will be required. Carefully review the graph labels and axes to avoid making careless mistakes.

Many questions go beyond simple grammar to assess broader writing topics, like paragraph transitions, essay introductions, and argumentative evidence. As you work through the questions, be ready to shift gears between focused proofreading and general editing. Sometimes you will need only a sentence to answer the question, while other times you will need a paragraph or more. *When in doubt, check it out.*

TIPS FOR THE ESSAY

The essay prompt will not change from test to test—you will always be asked to explain how the author of a source text has made an argument.

The source text will change from test to test, but it will always be a broad argument for a general audience.

Do NOT insert your personal opinions on the topic into your response. Your job is to examine the author's argument, not to give your views on the subject.

Do NOT waste time writing about supposed flaws in the source text. These are very well-written arguments. Your job is to analyze them, not to rip them apart.

Start by taking several minutes (no more than 10) to read and take notes on the source text. Ask yourself *what* the author is arguing and *why* he or she has chosen to make that argument.

Take time to prewrite (no more than 5 minutes). Plan to show how the author makes use of *evidence, reasoning,* and *style* to make his or her case.

Start with a solid thesis, and use clear transitions and excellent organization throughout. Have variety in your sentence structure; use precise vocabulary and specific descriptions.

Write for the full 50 minutes. The essay comes last in the test—finish strong, drawing on your last reserves of energy. A longer essay (as long as it has well-written, focused material) will score better.

Write legibly—the graders are human. They can grade only what they can understand.

Watch out for spelling and grammar issues. However, don't spend so much time proofreading that you fail to develop your essay fully.

Pace yourself so that you can make all of your points and have a strong conclusion. This essay is very different from many you likely have written—don't let test day be the first time you try writing an SAT essay within the time constraints.

Acknowledgments

Page 6: From *A Handbook to Literature* by C. Hugh Holman. Copyright © 1995 by Prentice Hall, Inc.

Pages 38–39: From "3-D scans reveal secrets of extinct creatures," Alexandra Witze, *Science News*, 4 October 2014. Reprinted with permission of Science News for Students.

Pages 44–45: From "Hush, humans, We're trying to survive here," by Susan Milius, *Science News*, 21 February 2015. Reprinted with permission of Science News for Students.

Page 45: From "Highway bridge noise can disturb fish's hearing," by Susan Milius, *Science News*, 7 February 2015. Reprinted with permission of Science News for Students.

Pages 47–48: From *Civilisation* by Kenneth Clark. Copyright © 1969 by Kenneth C. Clark.

Pages 120–121: From *http://www.nlm.nih.gov/changingthefaceofmedicine/physicians/biography_26.html* (accessed July 30, 2015).

Pages 146–147: From *This Indian Country: American Indian Political Activists and the Place They Made* by Frederick E. Hoxie. Copyright © 2012, Penguin Books, New York.

Page 149: From *Take Time for Paradise* © 1989 by the Estate of A. Bartlett Giamatti.

Pages 149–150: From *City: Rediscovering the Center* by William H. Whyte. Copyright © 1988 by William H. Whyte. First published by Doubleday in 1988.

Page 709: From *Mortal Lessons: Notes on the Art of Surgery* by Richard Selzer. Copyright © 1974, 1975, 1976, 1987 by Richard Selzer.

Page 712: From *The Press and the Presidency* by John Tebbel and Sarah Miles Watts. Copyright © 1985, Oxford University Press, New York.

Page 713: From *An Analysis of the President-Press Relationship in Solo and Joint Press Conferences in the First Term of President George W. Bush, A Thesis Submitted to the Graduate Faculty of the Louisiana State University and Agricultural and Mechanical College in partial fulfillment of the requirements for the degree of Master of Mass Communication in The Manship School of Mass Communication,* by Susan Billingsley, May 2006.

Pages 716–717: From "The facts behind the frack: Scientists weigh in on the hydraulic fracturing debate," by Rachel Ehrenberg, *Science News*, 24 August 2012. Reprinted with permission of Science News for Students.

Pages 792–793: Excerpt from pp. 141–142 from *I Love Paul Revere, Whether He Rode or Not* by Richard Shenkman. Copyright © 1991 by Richard Shenkman.

ON THE CD-ROM

Practice Test 1

Practice Test 2

PART ONE
Get Acquainted with the New SAT

Introduction: Let's Look at the New SAT

- → **WHAT IS THE SAT?**
- → **THE READING TEST**
- → **THE WRITING AND LANGUAGE TEST**
- → **THE MATH TEST**
- → **CALCULATOR TIPS**
- → **THE OPTIONAL ESSAY**
- → **WINNING TACTICS FOR THE SAT**

WHAT IS THE SAT?

The SAT is a standardized exam that most high school students take before applying to college. Generally, students take the SAT for the first time as high school juniors. If they are happy with their scores, they are through. If they want to try to improve their scores, they can take the test a second or even a third time.

The SAT covers two areas: English and Math. The English Test consists of two sections: one is Evidence-Based Reading; the other, Writing and Language. In addition, there is an optional essay. Each time you take the SAT, you receive several scores and subscores. On each of the two main areas, English and Math, you receive a score between 200 and 800. You also receive a composite score, a number between 400 and 1600, which is the sum of your two area scores. If you write the optional essay, two readers will evaluate it. Each reader will award a score between 1 and 4 on each of three criteria. Those scores will be added together, so you will receive essay scores between 2 and 8 on each of three domains.

HOW DO I SIGN UP TO TAKE THE SAT?

Online: Go to *www.collegeboard.org*

Have available your social security number and/or date of birth.

Pay with a major credit card.

Note: If you are signing up for Sunday testing, or if you have a visual, hearing, or learning disability and plan to sign up for the Services for Students with Disabilities Program, you *cannot* register online. You must register by mail well in advance.

By mail: Get a copy of the SAT Program Registration Bulletin from your high school guidance office or from the College Board. (Write to College Board SAT, P.O. Box 6200, Princeton, NJ 08541-6200, or phone the College Board office in Princeton at 866-756-7346.)

Pay by check, money order, fee waiver, or credit card.

WHAT IS SCORE CHOICE?

Score Choice is the College Board's policy that enables students who take the SAT more than once to choose which scores to send to the colleges to which they are applying. Each time you take the SAT, you will receive a score report. When you are a

CAUTION

Most colleges allow you to use Score Choice; some do not. Some want to see all of your scores. Be sure to go to *http://sat.collegeboard.org/register/sat-score-choice* to check the score-use policy of the colleges to which you hope to apply.

senior and are actually applying to college, you can decide which of your score reports you want the College Board to send out.

Here's How Score Choice Works

Suppose you take the SAT in May of your junior year and again in October of your senior year, and your October scores are higher than your May scores. Through Score Choice you can send the colleges only your October scores; not only will the colleges not see your May scores, they won't even know that you took the test in May. The importance of the Score Choice policy is that it can significantly lessen your anxiety anytime you take the SAT. If you have a bad day when you take the SAT for the first time, and your scores aren't as high as you had hoped, relax: you can retake it at a later date, and if your scores improve, you will never have to report the lower scores. Even if you do very well the first time you take the SAT, you can still retake it in an attempt to earn even higher scores. If your scores do improve, terrific—those are the scores you will report. If your scores happen to go down, don't worry—you can send only your original scores to the colleges and they will never even know that you retook the test. However, if you get your best Math score on one administration of the test, say in May, and your best English score on another administration of the test, say in October, you should submit your scores from both months. Admissions officers always give you credit for your best English score and your best Math score. Just because Score Choice is available does not mean you have to use it. No matter how many times you take the SAT, because of Score Choice, you can send in only the scores that you want the colleges to see.

CHECKLIST: WHAT SHOULD I BRING TO THE TEST CENTER?

☐ admission ticket

☐ photo ID (driver's license, passport, official school photo ID)

☐ calculator (*Note:* Check the batteries the day before!)

☐ 4 or 5 sharpened No. 2 pencils (with erasers)

☐ wristwatch or small clock (not one that beeps!)

☐ map and directions to the test center

☐ sweater

☐ a drink and a small snack for quick energy

WHAT IS THE FORMAT OF THE NEW SAT?

The SAT consists of four sections that take a total of exactly 3 hours, not counting a short break between sections 2 and 3. The English part of the SAT consists of two sections: a 65-minute Evidence-Based Reading Test and a 35-minute Writing and Language Test, for a total of 100 minutes. Note that both sections consist entirely of multiple-choice questions; there is nothing to actually write on the SAT unless you stay for the optional essay. The Math part of the SAT also consists of two sections: a 55-minute section on which you are permitted to use a calculator and a 25-minute section on which calculators are not permitted, for a total of 80 minutes.

When the English and Math parts are over, students who are not writing the optional essay will hand in their test materials and leave the building. Once they leave, the students who choose to write the essay will have 50 minutes to complete that task. So for those students, the total time spent working on the SAT will be 3 hours and 50 minutes.

Of course, whether you write the essay or not, you will be in the exam room for much longer than the time required to take the test. Time is needed for you to fill out your bubble sheet and for the proctors to take attendance, pass out the exam materials, read the instructions, collect the test materials, and give you a short break in the middle of the test. So you should expect to be at the exam site for about 4 hours if you are not writing the essay and for about 5 hours if you are writing the essay.

THE READING TEST

There are 52 questions on the Reading Test of the SAT.

Below is one typical reading test format for the new SAT. You should expect to see something like the following on your test, although not necessarily in this exact order:

52-Question Reading Test (65 minutes)

Questions 1–10	U.S./world literature passage
Questions 11–21	social studies passage (with graphic)
Questions 22–31	science paired-passages
Questions 32–42	social studies passage (U.S. founding document/global conversation)
Questions 43–52	science passage (with graphic)

Two passages on your test will be accompanied by infographics—one or two tables, charts, flow maps, graphs, time lines, etc. The graphics will accompany one of the history/social studies passages and one of the science passages.

Of the 52 questions on your test, 10 will be vocabulary questions, testing relevant words and phrases whose meaning depends on the context in which they appear (2 per passage). An additional 10 will be "command of evidence" questions in which you have to decide which part of a passage supports a specific conclusion or backs up the answer choice to a previous question (2 per passage).

All of the reading questions on the new SAT directly test your skill at comprehending what you read, based on the evidence you find in the selected passages.

The questions are not necessarily arranged in order of difficulty. Instead, they generally follow the organization of the passage on which they are based. Questions about material found early in the passage precede questions about material found later. Main idea questions are likely to appear early in the question set. Questions about accompanying information graphics or questions contrasting passage pairs are likely to appear toward the end of the set. This information can help you pace yourself during the test.

Here are examples of some specific types of evidence-based reading questions you can expect.

Evidence-Based Reading

Evidence-based reading questions ask about a passage's main idea or specific details, the author's attitude about the subject, the author's logic and techniques, the implications of the discussion, or the meaning of specific words.

(The following passage is far shorter than the usual 500–750 word passages you will find on the test. It is here only to give you a quick idea of the sorts of questions you will face.)

Certain qualities common to the sonnet should be noted. Its definite restrictions make it a challenge to the artistry of the poet and call for all the technical skills at the poet's command. The more or less set rhyme patterns occurring regularly within the short
Line space of fourteen lines afford a pleasant effect on the ear of the reader and can create
(5) truly musical effects. The rigidity of the form precludes too great economy or too great prodigality of words. Emphasis is placed on exactness and perfection of expression. The brevity of the form favors concentrated expression of ideas or passion.

1. The author's primary purpose is to

    (A) contrast different types of sonnets.
    (B) criticize the limitations of the sonnet.
    (C) identify the characteristics of the sonnet.
    (D) explain the sonnet's loss of popularity as a literary form.

The first question asks you to find the author's main idea. In the opening sentence, the author says certain qualities of the sonnet should be noted. In other words, he intends to call attention to certain of its characteristics, identifying them. The correct answer is choice (C).

You can eliminate the other answers with ease. The author is upbeat about the sonnet: he doesn't say that the sonnet has limitations or that it has become less popular. You can eliminate choices (B) and (D).

Similarly, the author doesn't mention any different types of sonnets; therefore, he cannot be contrasting them. You can eliminate choice (A).

2. As used in line 4, "afford" most nearly means

    (A) spare.
    (B) exaggerate.
    (C) pay for.
    (D) provide.

The second question asks you to figure out a word's meaning from its context. Substitute each of the answer choices in the original sentence and see which word or phrase makes the most sense. Some make no sense at all: the rhyme patterns that the reader hears certainly do not *pay for* any pleasant effect. You can definitely eliminate choice (C). What is it exactly that these rhyme patterns do? The rhyme patterns have a pleasant effect on the ear of the listener; indeed, they *provide* (furnish or supply) this effect. The correct answer is choice (D).

3. The author's attitude toward the sonnet form can best be described as one of

    (A) amused toleration.
    (B) grudging admiration.
    (C) strong disapprobation.
    (D) scholarly appreciation.

The third question asks you to figure out how the author feels about his subject. All the author's comments about the sonnet are positive: he approves of this poetic form. You can immediately eliminate choice (C), *strong disapprobation* or disapproval. You can also eliminate choice (A), *amused toleration* or forbearance. The author is not simply putting up with the sonnet form in a good-humored, somewhat patronizing way; he thinks well of it.

Choice (B) is somewhat harder to eliminate. The author does seem to admire the sonnet form. However, his admiration is unforced: it is not *grudging* or reluctant. You can eliminate choice (B).

The only answer that properly reflects the author's attitude is choice (D), *scholarly appreciation.*

See Chapter 1 for tactics that will help you handle the entire range of evidence-based reading questions.

THE WRITING AND LANGUAGE TEST

There are 44 questions on the Writing and Language Test of the SAT.

Below is one typical writing and language test format for the new SAT. You should expect to see something similar to this on test day, although likely in a different order:

44-Question Writing and Language Test (35 minutes)

Questions 1–11	career-related topic
Questions 12–22	humanities
Questions 23–33	social studies
Questions 34–44	science

One or two of these will be informative/explanatory texts, one or two of these will be arguments, and one will be a narrative.

One or two passages on your test will be accompanied by an infographic—a table, chart, graph, map, or some combination of graphics.

Of the 44 questions on your test, 24 will be about expression of ideas (improving the quality of the author's message) and 20 will be about standard English conventions (grammar, usage, and mechanics). Eight questions will test your command of evidence (some with the infographics and some based on the text), and 8 questions will test words in context (e.g., determining the correct "fit" given the rhetorical goal). The writing and language questions are in a random order of difficulty.

Here are examples of particular types of writing and language questions you will find. (This is only intended to give you a brief sample of some questions—typical passages have 11 questions accompanying them.)

Properties of Water

We hear about water every day. More than 70 percent of ❶ our planets surface is covered with water. Water is a requirement for terrestrial life. Water makes up the majority of our bodies. Drink your eight glasses of water ❷ during every 24 hour period. But what makes water so special, so ubiquitous? It's a rather simple compound: ❸ 2 hydrogen atoms covalently bonded to 1 oxygen atom. However, it has several unique chemical properties that make it rather suitable for life.

1.　(A)　NO CHANGE
　　(B)　their planets
　　(C)　our planet's
　　(D)　their planets'

The first question concerns the proper use of possessive words and apostrophes. In order to be consistent with the use of "we" in the previous sentence, you should use "our." You can therefore eliminate choices (B) and (D) since they use "their." You can also eliminate choice (A). It fails to show that the "planet" possesses the "surface" because it lacks an apostrophe followed by an "s." That leaves you with choice (C) as the correct answer. It properly uses "our" to be consistent with the previous sentence and "planet's" to demonstrate that the singular planet possesses the surface.

2.　(A)　NO CHANGE
　　(B)　each day when you are awake.
　　(C)　throughout the daytime.
　　(D)　daily.

The second question is about wordiness and description. You should consider which choice gives a clear idea without unnecessary wording. Choice (D) is correct because "daily" provides the same amount of information as choices (A), (B), and (C) but does so far more concisely. Economy in writing is preferable as long as the language is clear and specific.

3. Which choice provides the most specific and relevant conclusion to the sentence?

    (A) NO CHANGE
    (B) Water has many properties that distinguish it from most substances.
    (C) In its frozen form, water is called "ice," while in its gaseous form, it is called "steam."
    (D) It is composed of a unique combination of material.

The third question asks you to choose what will be most *specific* (precise and detailed) and *relevant* (on topic) at this point in the sentence. You can eliminate choices (B) and (D) because they are far too vague. Choice (B) gives no clarification of the "properties" that distinguish water, and choice (D) provides no elaboration on the "unique combination of material" that water is. Although choice (C) is specific, you can eliminate it because it is not relevant—it fails to describe what makes water a "simple compound" as described earlier in the sentence. Choice (A) is correct since it gives both a specific scientific description and a relevant elaboration on what makes this compound relatively simple, i.e., its structure.

See Chapter 3 for an extensive grammar review and for tactics that will help you handle the whole range of writing and language questions.

THE MATH TEST

The math part of the SAT has a total of 58 questions divided into two sections, each of which has its own format.

- The 25-minute section, during which calculators may not be used, has 20 questions: 15 multiple-choice questions and 5 grid-in questions.
- The 55-minute section, during which calculators may be used, has 38 questions: 30 multiple-choice questions and 8 grid-in questions.

Multiple-Choice Questions

On the math part of the SAT, 45 of the 58 questions are multiple-choice questions. Although you have certainly taken multiple-choice tests before, the SAT uses a few different types of questions, and you must become familiar with all of them. By far, the most common type of question is one in which you are asked to solve a problem. The straightforward way to answer such a question is to do the necessary work, get the solution, look at the four choices, and choose the one that corresponds to your answer. In Chapter 5 other techniques for answering these questions are discussed, but now let's look at a few examples.

➡ **Example 1**_____

What is the average (arithmetic mean) of all the even integers between −5 and 7?

    (A) 0

    (B) $\dfrac{5}{6}$

    (C) 1

    (D) $\dfrac{6}{5}$

To solve this problem requires only that you know how to find the average of a set of numbers. Ignore the fact that this is a multiple-choice question. *Don't even look at the choices.*

- List the even integers whose average you need: –4, –2, 0, 2, 4, 6. (Be careful not to leave out 0, which *is* an even integer.)
- Calculate the average by adding the six integers and dividing by 6.

$$\frac{(-4)+(-2)+0+2+4+6}{6} = \frac{6}{6} = 1$$

- Having found the average to be 1, look at the four choices, see that 1 is choice (C), and blacken (C) on your answer sheet.

➡ Example 2

A necklace is formed by stringing 133 colored beads on a thin wire in the following order: red, orange, yellow, green, blue, indigo, violet; red, orange, yellow, green, blue, indigo, violet. If this pattern continues, what will be the color of the 101st bead on the string?

(A) orange
(B) yellow
(C) green
(D) blue

Again, you are not helped by the fact that the question, which is less a test of your arithmetic skills than of your ability to reason, is a multiple-choice question. You need to determine the color of the 101st bead, and then select the choice that matches your answer.

The seven colors keep repeating in exactly the same order.

Color:	red	orange	yellow	green	blue	indigo	violet	
Bead number:	1	2	3	4	5	6	7	
	8	9	10	11	12	13	14	etc.

- The violet beads are in positions 7, 14, 21, . . . , 70, . . . , that is, the multiples of 7.
- If 101 were a multiple of 7, the 101st bead would be violet.
- But when 101 is divided by 7, the quotient is 14 and the remainder is 3.
- Since 14 × 7 = 98, the 98th bead completes the 14th cycle, and hence is violet.
- The 99th bead starts the next cycle; it is red. The 100th bead is orange, and the 101st bead is yellow.
- The answer is (B).

> ### NOTE
> Did you notice that the solution didn't use the fact that the necklace consisted of 133 beads? This is unusual; occasionally, but not often, a problem contains information you don't need.

In contrast to Examples 1 and 2, some questions *require* you to look at all four choices in order to find the answer. Consider Example 3.

➥ Example 3_____

If a and b are both odd integers, which of the following could be an odd integer?

(A) $a + b$
(B) $a^2 + b^2$
(C) $(a + 1)(b - 1)$
(D) $\dfrac{a+1}{b-1}$

The words *Which of the following* alert you to the fact that you will have to examine each of the four choices to determine which one satisfies the stated condition, in this case that the quantity *could* be odd. Check each choice.

- The sum of two odd integers is always even. Eliminate choice (A).
- The square of an odd integer is odd; so a^2 and b^2 are each odd, and their sum is even. Eliminate choice (B).
- The product of two even integers is even. Eliminate choice (C).
- Having eliminated choices (A), (B), and (C), you know that *the answer must be* choice (D). Check to be sure: $\dfrac{a+1}{b-1}$ need not even be an integer (e.g., if a = 1 and b = 5), but it *could be*. For example, if $a = 3$ and $b = 5$, then

$$\frac{a+1}{b-1} = \frac{3+1}{5-1} = \frac{4}{4} = 1$$

which is an odd integer. The answer is **(D)**.

Another kind of multiple-choice question that appears on the SAT is the Roman numeral-type question. These questions actually consist of three statements labeled I, II, and III. The four answer choices give various possibilities for which statement or statements are true. Here is a typical example.

➥ Example 4_____

If x is negative, which of the following *must* be true?

I. $x^3 < x^2$
II. $x + \dfrac{1}{x} < 0$
III. $x = \sqrt{x^2}$

(A) I only
(B) II only
(C) I and II only
(D) II and III only

- To answer this question, examine each statement independently to determine if it is true or false.

   I. If x is negative, then x^3 is negative and so must be less than x^2, which is positive. (I is true.)

   II. If x is negative, so is $\frac{1}{x}$, and the sum of two negative numbers is negative. (II is true.)

   III. The square root of a number is never negative, and so $\sqrt{x^2}$ could not possibly equal x. (III is false.)

- Only I and II are true. The answer is **(C)**.

> ## NOTE
> You should always attempt a Roman numeral-type question. Even if you can't solve the problem completely, there should be *at least one* of the three Roman numeral statements that you *know* to be true or false. On the basis of that information, you should be able to eliminate at least one or two of the answer choices. For instance, in Example 4, if all you know for sure is that statement I is true, you can eliminate choices (B) and (D). Similarly, if all you know is that statement III is false, you can eliminate choice (D). Then, you simply guess among the remaining choices.

Grid-in Questions

On the math part of the SAT, 13 of the 58 questions are what the College Board calls student-produced response questions. Since the answers to these questions are entered on a special grid, they are usually referred to as *grid-in* questions. Except for the method of entering your answer, this type of question is probably the one with which you are most familiar. In your math class, most of your homework problems and test questions require you to determine an answer and write it down, and this is what you will do on the grid-in problems. The only difference is that, once you have figured out an answer, it must be recorded on a special grid, such as the one shown at the right, so that it can be read by a computer. Here is a typical grid-in question.

➡ **Example 5**_____

At the diner, John ordered a sandwich for \$3.95 and a soda for 85¢. A sales tax of 5% was added to his bill, and he left the waitress a \$1 tip. What was the total cost, in dollars, of John's lunch?

- Calculate the cost of the food: \$3.95 + \$0.85 = \$4.80
- Calculate the tax (5% of \$4.80): .05 × \$4.80 = \$0.24
- Add the cost of the food, tax, and tip: \$4.80 + \$0.24 + \$1.00 = \$6.04

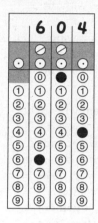

To enter this answer, you write 6.04 (*without* the dollar sign) in the four spaces at the top of the grid, and blacken the appropriate circle under each space. In the first column, under the 6, you blacken the circle marked 6; in the second column, under the decimal point, you blacken the circle with the decimal point; in the third column, under the 0, you blacken the circle marked 0; and, finally, in the fourth column, under the 4, you blacken the circle marked 4.

Always read each grid-in question very carefully. Example 5 might have asked for the total cost of John's lunch *in cents*. In that case, the correct answer would have been 604, which would be gridded in, without a decimal point, using only three of the four columns (see bottom grid).

Note that the only symbols that appear in the grid are the digits from 0 to 9, a decimal point, and a fraction bar (/). The grid does not have a minus sign, so *answers to grid-in problems can never be negative*. In Introduction to the Math Sections, in Part Five, you will learn some important tactics for answering grid-in questions and will be able to practice filling in grids. You will also learn the special rules concerning the proper way to grid in fractions, mixed numbers, and decimals that won't fit in the grid's four columns. When you take the diagnostic test, just enter your answers to the grid-in questions exactly as was done in Example 5.

NOTE

Any multiple-choice question whose answer is a positive number less than 10,000 could be a grid-in question. If Example 1 had been a grid-in question, you would have solved it in exactly the same way: you would have determined that the average of the six numbers is 1; but then, instead of looking for 1 among the five choices, you would have entered the number 1 on a grid. The mathematics is no harder on grid-in questions than on multiple-choice questions. However, if you don't know how to solve a problem correctly, it is harder to guess at the right answer, since there are no choices to eliminate.

CALCULATOR TIPS

- You must bring a calculator to the test. Some, but not all, of the questions in the 55-minute section cannot be solved without using one.
- You should use a scientific calculator. A graphing calculator is acceptable but offers no real advantage.
- *Don't* buy a new calculator the night before the SAT. If you need one, *buy one now* and become familiar with it. Do all the practice exams in this book with the calculator you plan to take to the test—probably the same calculator you use in school.
- Use your calculator when you *need* to; ignore it when you don't. Most students use calculators more than they should. You can solve many problems without doing *any* calculations—mental, written, or calculator-assisted.
- The College Board's position is that a "calculator is a tool" and that knowing when to use one and when not to use one is an important skill. Therefore, they intentionally include some questions in the calculator section on which it is better not to use your calculator.
- Throughout this book, the icon will be placed next to a problem where the use of a calculator is reasonable or recommended. As you will see, this judgment is subjective. Sometimes a question can be answered in a few seconds, with no calculations whatsoever, *if* you see the best approach. In that case, the use of a calculator is not recommended. If you don't see the easy way, however, and have to do some arithmetic, you may prefer to use a calculator.
- No SAT problem ever requires a lot of tedious calculation. However, if you don't see how to avoid calculating, just do it—*don't spend a <u>lot</u> of time looking for a shortcut that will save you a <u>little</u> time!*

THE OPTIONAL ESSAY

The optional SAT essay asks you to *analyze an argument.* This section comes at the end of the test. The argument will be on a general topic and written for a broad audience—you will not need any background knowledge on the subject to formulate your response. You will have *50 minutes* to respond to a source text and question like the following:

Sample Essay Prompt

Directions: You will be given 50 minutes to complete the assignment, including reading the source text and writing your response.

Read the following passage, and think about how the author uses:

- Evidence, such as applicable examples, to justify the argument
- Reasoning to show logical connections among thoughts and facts
- Rhetoric, like sensory language and emotional appeals, to give weight to the argument

Beauty Is in the Eye of the Beholder

1   It's entirely possible that I am a dolt. It's not out of the question that I am uncultured, uncivilized, ignorant, and misinformed. It could be that I do not understand true talent—that my personal mediocrity prevents me from the recognition of unparalleled brilliance in another. So if what I'm about to say to you reeks of blasphemy, please forgive me for my tastelessness. But, is the "Mona Lisa" really that great?

2   I love the concept of the "Western Canon." If you are unfamiliar with it, this is a de facto collection of art, music, and literature that scholars generally accept as masterpieces. The theory is that, if the world's self-proclaimed "experts" view a subjective issue with near unanimity, then the debate ceases to be subjective; it becomes a matter of certainty, a perspective that can be criticized only by the intellectual heretic.

3   Now this is where I begin to laugh. When did the people of the world become so wishy-washy as to require the assistance of the opinions of others on what is bad or good or indeterminable in its quality? Though far from Emersonian in my insistence on self-reliance, I do believe that I am more than capable of formulating opinions on my own. Truly, of the seven billion people in the world, I'd go so far as to say that I'm the best in the world at deciding what is pleasing to me.

4   Here is another qualm with the validity of the canonical process: what of those who gain fame of the least satisfying sort, which is to say, posthumously? Vincent van Gogh lived his entire life in unacknowledged anonymity. Similarly, F. Scott Fitzgerald was not enshrined by the masses until well after his death. Is this to say that the caliber of their works increased after their deaths—that they are far more adroit from the crypt? Are today's experts more expert than those of yesteryear? Of what purpose does popular opinion serve if it is a fickle, dynamic, wavering thing? Masterpieces should transcend generational trends, wouldn't you agree?

5   However, I do not question that the "Mona Lisa" resonates in its profundity with many critics. And, if somebody values da Vinci's piece at 200 million dollars, well, I am in no position to dispute this appraisal. But, to me, the "French Madame" is of minor consequence. See, she rouses nothing in my breast; she incites nothing of passion or empathy or intrigue. I see a woman—a regular woman, and nothing more.

6   I cannot help but wonder if the "Mona Lisa's" renown comes from its inherent aesthetic appeal, or more from the unusual historical incidents associated with it—it hung in Napoleon's bedroom for a time, and it was famously stolen and missing for a time. Do seemingly limitless museum-goers line up to see the "Mona Lisa" because of its artistic depth? Or, are they drawn to it because of the novelty of seeing a single painting in a room all to itself, behind bullet-proof glass?

7   Ultimately, this is the intrinsic value of art and literature and music: how it personally makes you feel. To defer to the judgments of others on the topic is to miss the entire purpose of the venture. For, if a painting leads one man to weep and another to

swoon, of what value is it to me if I feel nothing stirring inside? I am but an intruder into the trysts of others. I am crashing a soirée to which I was uninvited.

8   So go forth today and define your own canon. If your professor tells you that Ernest Hemingway revolutionized American literature, refuse to accept this at face value. Rather, read "Old Man and the Sea" and decide for yourself; see if Santiago's tribulations ignite something poignant and lasting within you. If not, cast the thing aside, for it is of no value to you. Conversely, refuse to be belittled for your interests. If a certain musician inspires you to chase your dreams, or bestows upon you an unbreakable peacefulness, or makes cloudy January days feel like warm June nights, this is your masterpiece, no matter what anybody else says. For this is how you build your very own canon, by eschewing the measuring sticks of others and gauging instead with your very own soul. Take comfort in your aptitude for the task. None is better suited than you, especially when the alternative is accepting the "because I said so" of another.

> Write a response that demonstrates how the author makes an argument to persuade his audience that artistic merit should derive from subjective preference. In your response, analyze how the author uses at least one of the features from the essay directions (or features of your own choosing) to develop a logical and persuasive argument. Be certain that your response cites relevant aspects of the source text.
>
> Your response should not give your personal opinion on the merit of the source text but, instead, show how the author crafts an argument to persuade readers.

Your essay will be evaluated by two graders, who will consider these three factors:

- **READING:** Did you properly comprehend the source? Did you show clear evidence of your understanding?
- **ANALYSIS:** Did you show how the author used *evidence, reasoning,* and *style* to make his or her argument?
- **WRITING:** Did you write a clear, organized response with appropriate word choice and proper grammar?

Each grader will evaluate your reading, analysis, and writing on a 1–4 scale; the graders' individual scores will be combined so that each of these categories will have a score from 2–8. Your score on the essay will be reported separately and will not affect your overall 400–1600 composite score.

WINNING TACTICS FOR THE SAT

You now know the basic framework of the SAT. It's time for the big question: How can you become a winner on the SAT?

- First, you have to decide just what winning is for you. For one student, winning means breaking 1000; for another, only a total score of 1400 will do. Therefore, the first thing you have to do is set *your* goal.
- Second, you must learn to pace yourself during the test. You need to know how many questions you are going to attempt to answer.
- Third, you need to understand the rewards of guessing—how *random guesses* can improve your score and how *educated guesses* can boost your scores dramatically. Educated guessing is a key strategy in helping you to reach your goal.

Here are your winning tactics for the SAT.

Set your goal.

Before you begin studying for the SAT, you should set a realistic goal for yourself. Here's what to do.

1. Establish your **baseline score**. You need to know your math, reading, and writing scores on one actual PSAT or SAT to use as your starting point.

   - If you have already taken an SAT, use your actual scores from that test.
   - If you have already taken the PSAT but have not yet taken the SAT, use your most recent actual PSAT scores.
   - If you have not yet taken an actual PSAT or SAT, do the following:

     ☐ Print out a practice test from the College Board's website.

     OR

     ☐ Get a copy of the College Board's SAT preparation booklet from your school guidance office, which will have a practice test in it.

     ☐ Find a quiet place where you can work for 3 hours without interruptions.
     ☐ Take the SAT under true exam conditions:

       Time yourself on each section.
       Take no more than a 2-minute break between sections 1 and 2 and between sections 3 and 4.
       Take a 10-minute break between sections 2 and 3.

     ☐ Follow the instructions to grade the test and convert your total raw scores on each part to a scaled score.
     ☐ Use these scores as your baseline.

2. Look up the average SAT scores for the most recent freshman class at each of the colleges to which you're thinking of applying. This information can be found online on the

colleges' websites or in a college guide, such as Barron's *Profiles of American Colleges*. You want to beat that average, if you can.

3. Now **set your goals**. Challenge yourself, but be realistic. If you earned 470 on the English portion of the PSAT, for example, you might like to get 700 on the SAT, but that's unrealistic. On the other hand, don't wimp out. Aim for 550, not 500.

General Guidelines for Setting Your Initial Goals on the English and Math Parts of the SAT

Current Score	Goal (change in score)	Current Score	Goal (change in score)
Less than 400	+100	550–590	+60
400–440	+90	600–640	+50
450–490	+80	650–690	+40
500–540	+70	700 or more	+30

TACTIC

2 Know how many questions you should attempt.

Why is it so important to set a goal? Why not just try to get the highest score you can by correctly answering as many questions as possible? The answer is that *your goal tells you how many questions you should attempt*. The most common tactical error that students make is trying to answer too many questions. Therefore, surprising as it may be, the following statement is true for almost all students:

THE BEST WAY TO INCREASE YOUR SCORE
ON THE SAT IS TO ATTEMPT FEWER QUESTIONS.

Why is slowing down and attempting fewer questions the best way to increase your score on the SAT? To understand that, you first need to know how the SAT is scored. There are two types of scores associated with the SAT: raw scores and scaled scores. First, raw scores are calculated. Each raw score is then converted to a scaled score between 200 and 800. On the SAT, every question is worth exactly the same amount: 1 raw score point. You get no more credit for a correct answer to the hardest math question than you do for the easiest. For each question that you answer correctly, you receive 1 raw score point.

# of correct answers = Raw Score

So let's see how this strategy of slowing down works in your favor.

Suppose you rush through the two Math sections, answering all 58 questions in the time allotted, and you get 39 right and 19 wrong. Then your raw score would be 39 (one point for each correct answer) and your scaled score would be about 600. That's actually not so bad for answering only two-thirds of the questions correctly. Now suppose that you slow down and use all your time to work on just 50 questions. And suppose that as a result of slowing down, being more careful, and avoiding most careless errors, you answer 42 of the 50 questions correctly and miss only 8. So far your raw score is 42. Of course, when you have 10 or 15 seconds left, you should quickly guess at the 8 questions you didn't have time for. On average, you would get 2 right and 6 wrong. So you would have 2 more raw score points, for a total of 44. Now your scaled score is about 650. WOW! You just earned an extra 50 points by attempting fewer questions and making fewer careless mistakes. So it is worth repeating: For most students:

THE BEST WAY TO INCREASE YOUR SCORE ON
THE SAT IS TO ATTEMPT FEWER QUESTIONS.

Many students prefer to think about the statement above paraphrased as follows:

THE BIGGEST MISTAKE MOST STUDENTS MAKE ON THE
SAT IS TRYING TO ANSWER TOO MANY QUESTIONS.

TACTIC

3

Know how to pace yourself.

On every section, work slowly but steadily. Always keep moving. Never get bogged down on any one question. If you get stuck, guess and move on.

TACTIC

4

Always guess.

The rule is this: if you have worked on a problem, you should be able to eliminate at least one of the choices. This is what is called an *educated* guess. You are not guessing wildly, marking answers at random. You are working on the problem, ruling out answers that make no sense. The more choices you can rule out, the better your chance is of picking the right answer and earning one more point.

You should almost always be able to rule out some answer choices. Most math questions contain at least one or two answer choices that are absurd (for example, negative choices when you know the answer must be positive). In the critical reading section, once you have read a passage, you can always eliminate some of the answer choices. Cross out any choices that you *know* are incorrect, and go for that educated guess.

Of course, if you truly have no idea, make a wild guess. Whenever you are about to run out of time, quickly guess at all of the remaining questions.

TACTIC

5

Keep careful track of your time.

Bring a watch. Even if there is a clock in the room, it is better for you to have a watch on your desk. Before you start each section, set your watch to 12:00. It is easier to know that a section will be over when your watch reads 12:25 than to have a section start at 9:37 and have to remember that it will be over at 10:02. Your job will be even easier if you have a digital stopwatch that you start at the beginning of each section; either let it count down to zero, or start it at zero and know that your time will be up after the allotted number of minutes.

TACTIC
6 Don't read the directions or look at the sample questions.

For each section of the SAT, the directions given in this book are identical to the directions you will see on your actual exam. Learn them now. Do not waste even a few seconds of your valuable test time reading them.

TACTIC
7 Remember, each question, easy or hard, is worth just 1 point.

Concentrate on questions that don't take you tons of time to answer. If interpreting graphs is easy for you but algebra is hard, do the data questions first.

TACTIC
8 Feel free to skip back and forth between questions within a section or group.

Remember that you're in charge. You don't have to answer everything in order. You can temporarily skip a question that's taking you too long and come back to it if you have time. But first make a guess and bubble it in. If you have time to come back, you can always change your answer.

TACTIC
9 In the Reading Test, read each choice before choosing your answer.

In comparison to math questions, which always have exactly one correct answer, reading questions are more subjective. You are looking for the *best* choice. Even if (A) or (B) looks good, check out the others; (C) or (D) may be better.

TACTIC
10 Make sure that you answer the question asked.

Sometimes a math question requires you to solve an equation, but instead of asking for the value of x, the question asks for the value of x^2 or $x - 5$. Similarly, sometimes a critical reading question requires you to determine the LEAST likely outcome of an action; still another may ask you to find the exception to something, as in "The author uses all of the following EXCEPT." To avoid answering the wrong question, circle or underline what you have been asked for.

TACTIC
11 Base your answers only on the information provided— never on what you think you already know.

On passage-based reading questions, base your answers only on the material in the passage, not on what you think you know about the subject matter. On data interpretation questions, base your answers only on the information given in the chart or table.

12 Remember that you are allowed to write anything you want in your test booklet.

Circle questions you skip, and put big question marks next to questions you answer but are unsure about. If you have time left at the end, you want to be able to locate those questions quickly to go over them. In reading passages, underline or put a mark in the margin next to any important point. On math questions, mark up diagrams, adding lines when necessary. And, of course, use all the space provided to solve the problem. In every section, math, reading, and writing and language, cross out every choice that you *know* is wrong. In short, write anything that will help you, using whatever symbols you like. But remember: the only thing that counts is what you enter on your answer sheet. No one but you will ever see anything that you write in your booklet.

TACTIC

13 Be careful not to make any stray pencil marks on your answer sheet.

The SAT is scored by a computer that cannot distinguish between an accidental mark and a filled-in answer. If the computer registers two answers where there should be only one, it will mark that question wrong.

TACTIC

14 Don't change answers capriciously.

If you have time to return to a question and realize that you made a mistake, by all means correct it, making sure you *completely* erase the first mark you made. However, don't change answers on a last-minute hunch or whim, or for fear you have chosen too many A's and not enough B's. In such cases, more often than not, students change right answers to wrong ones.

TACTIC

15 Use your calculator only when you need to.

Many students actually waste time using their calculators on questions that do not require them. Use your calculator whenever you feel it will help, but don't overuse it. Remember, just because the longer math section is labeled "calculator" does not mean you need to use your calculator for each question.

TACTIC

16 When you use your calculator, don't go too quickly.

Your calculator leaves no trail. If you accidentally hit the wrong button and get a wrong answer, you have no way to look at your work and find your mistake. You just have to do it all over.

TACTIC 17 — Remember that you don't have to attempt every question to do well.

You have learned about setting goals and pacing. You know you don't have to attempt all the questions to do well. It is possible to work on only half of the questions and still be in the top half of all students taking the test. Of course, you should fill in an answer for every question. After you set your final goal, pace yourself to reach it.

TACTIC 18 — Don't be nervous: if your scores aren't as high as you would like, you can always take the SAT again.

Relax. The biggest reason that some students do worse on the actual SAT than they did on their practice tests is that they are nervous. You can't do your best if your hands are shaking and you're worried that your whole future is riding on this one test. First of all, your SAT scores are only one of many factors that influence the admissions process, and many students are accepted at their first-choice colleges even if their SAT scores are lower than they had expected. But more important, because of Score Choice, you can always retake the SAT if you don't do well enough the first or second time. So, give yourself the best chance for success: prepare conscientiously and then stay calm while actually taking the test.

PART TWO
Pinpoint Your Trouble Spots

A Diagnostic Test

You are about to take a diagnostic test, which has the identical format of a real SAT. Not counting short breaks between the sections—a minute or two between Sections 1 and 2 and between Sections 3 and 4, and perhaps ten minutes between Sections 2 and 3—this test takes exactly three hours. After completing the four sections, take as long a break as you like. Then give yourself 50 minutes to write the essay in Section 5.

The diagnostic test is a multipurpose tool.

- First, it will help you identify your problem areas and skills. Take the test and evaluate your results. You will discover your strengths and weaknesses, and you will know what to study.

- Second, this test will help you design a study plan that's right for you. Use the information you get from your result to tailor a study plan to fit your particular needs. If you need extra time on a certain topic, build time in. You are in charge of your study program— make it work for you.

- Third, this test is your introduction to the format and content of the New SAT. There is nothing like working your way through actual SAT-type questions for 3 hours to teach you how much stamina you need and how much speed.

- Finally, this test is your chance to learn how to profit from your mistakes. Read the answer explanation for every question, even those you answered correctly. You'll be amazed to see how much you'll learn.

Taking this diagnostic test is the first step in your SAT preparation. Take it seriously. Good luck on this journey.

ANSWER SHEET
Diagnostic Test

Section 1: Reading

1. Ⓐ Ⓑ Ⓒ Ⓓ	14. Ⓐ Ⓑ Ⓒ Ⓓ	27. Ⓐ Ⓑ Ⓒ Ⓓ	40. Ⓐ Ⓑ Ⓒ Ⓓ
2. Ⓐ Ⓑ Ⓒ Ⓓ	15. Ⓐ Ⓑ Ⓒ Ⓓ	28. Ⓐ Ⓑ Ⓒ Ⓓ	41. Ⓐ Ⓑ Ⓒ Ⓓ
3. Ⓐ Ⓑ Ⓒ Ⓓ	16. Ⓐ Ⓑ Ⓒ Ⓓ	29. Ⓐ Ⓑ Ⓒ Ⓓ	42. Ⓐ Ⓑ Ⓒ Ⓓ
4. Ⓐ Ⓑ Ⓒ Ⓓ	17. Ⓐ Ⓑ Ⓒ Ⓓ	30. Ⓐ Ⓑ Ⓒ Ⓓ	43. Ⓐ Ⓑ Ⓒ Ⓓ
5. Ⓐ Ⓑ Ⓒ Ⓓ	18. Ⓐ Ⓑ Ⓒ Ⓓ	31. Ⓐ Ⓑ Ⓒ Ⓓ	44. Ⓐ Ⓑ Ⓒ Ⓓ
6. Ⓐ Ⓑ Ⓒ Ⓓ	19. Ⓐ Ⓑ Ⓒ Ⓓ	32. Ⓐ Ⓑ Ⓒ Ⓓ	45. Ⓐ Ⓑ Ⓒ Ⓓ
7. Ⓐ Ⓑ Ⓒ Ⓓ	20. Ⓐ Ⓑ Ⓒ Ⓓ	33. Ⓐ Ⓑ Ⓒ Ⓓ	46. Ⓐ Ⓑ Ⓒ Ⓓ
8. Ⓐ Ⓑ Ⓒ Ⓓ	21. Ⓐ Ⓑ Ⓒ Ⓓ	34. Ⓐ Ⓑ Ⓒ Ⓓ	47. Ⓐ Ⓑ Ⓒ Ⓓ
9. Ⓐ Ⓑ Ⓒ Ⓓ	22. Ⓐ Ⓑ Ⓒ Ⓓ	35. Ⓐ Ⓑ Ⓒ Ⓓ	48. Ⓐ Ⓑ Ⓒ Ⓓ
10. Ⓐ Ⓑ Ⓒ Ⓓ	23. Ⓐ Ⓑ Ⓒ Ⓓ	36. Ⓐ Ⓑ Ⓒ Ⓓ	49. Ⓐ Ⓑ Ⓒ Ⓓ
11. Ⓐ Ⓑ Ⓒ Ⓓ	24. Ⓐ Ⓑ Ⓒ Ⓓ	37. Ⓐ Ⓑ Ⓒ Ⓓ	50. Ⓐ Ⓑ Ⓒ Ⓓ
12. Ⓐ Ⓑ Ⓒ Ⓓ	25. Ⓐ Ⓑ Ⓒ Ⓓ	38. Ⓐ Ⓑ Ⓒ Ⓓ	51. Ⓐ Ⓑ Ⓒ Ⓓ
13. Ⓐ Ⓑ Ⓒ Ⓓ	26. Ⓐ Ⓑ Ⓒ Ⓓ	39. Ⓐ Ⓑ Ⓒ Ⓓ	52. Ⓐ Ⓑ Ⓒ Ⓓ

Section 2: Writing and Language

1. Ⓐ Ⓑ Ⓒ Ⓓ	12. Ⓐ Ⓑ Ⓒ Ⓓ	23. Ⓐ Ⓑ Ⓒ Ⓓ	34. Ⓐ Ⓑ Ⓒ Ⓓ
2. Ⓐ Ⓑ Ⓒ Ⓓ	13. Ⓐ Ⓑ Ⓒ Ⓓ	24. Ⓐ Ⓑ Ⓒ Ⓓ	35. Ⓐ Ⓑ Ⓒ Ⓓ
3. Ⓐ Ⓑ Ⓒ Ⓓ	14. Ⓐ Ⓑ Ⓒ Ⓓ	25. Ⓐ Ⓑ Ⓒ Ⓓ	36. Ⓐ Ⓑ Ⓒ Ⓓ
4. Ⓐ Ⓑ Ⓒ Ⓓ	15. Ⓐ Ⓑ Ⓒ Ⓓ	26. Ⓐ Ⓑ Ⓒ Ⓓ	37. Ⓐ Ⓑ Ⓒ Ⓓ
5. Ⓐ Ⓑ Ⓒ Ⓓ	16. Ⓐ Ⓑ Ⓒ Ⓓ	27. Ⓐ Ⓑ Ⓒ Ⓓ	38. Ⓐ Ⓑ Ⓒ Ⓓ
6. Ⓐ Ⓑ Ⓒ Ⓓ	17. Ⓐ Ⓑ Ⓒ Ⓓ	28. Ⓐ Ⓑ Ⓒ Ⓓ	39. Ⓐ Ⓑ Ⓒ Ⓓ
7. Ⓐ Ⓑ Ⓒ Ⓓ	18. Ⓐ Ⓑ Ⓒ Ⓓ	29. Ⓐ Ⓑ Ⓒ Ⓓ	40. Ⓐ Ⓑ Ⓒ Ⓓ
8. Ⓐ Ⓑ Ⓒ Ⓓ	19. Ⓐ Ⓑ Ⓒ Ⓓ	30. Ⓐ Ⓑ Ⓒ Ⓓ	41. Ⓐ Ⓑ Ⓒ Ⓓ
9. Ⓐ Ⓑ Ⓒ Ⓓ	20. Ⓐ Ⓑ Ⓒ Ⓓ	31. Ⓐ Ⓑ Ⓒ Ⓓ	42. Ⓐ Ⓑ Ⓒ Ⓓ
10. Ⓐ Ⓑ Ⓒ Ⓓ	21. Ⓐ Ⓑ Ⓒ Ⓓ	32. Ⓐ Ⓑ Ⓒ Ⓓ	43. Ⓐ Ⓑ Ⓒ Ⓓ
11. Ⓐ Ⓑ Ⓒ Ⓓ	22. Ⓐ Ⓑ Ⓒ Ⓓ	33. Ⓐ Ⓑ Ⓒ Ⓓ	44. Ⓐ Ⓑ Ⓒ Ⓓ

ANSWER SHEET
Diagnostic Test

Section 3: Math (No Calculator)

1. Ⓐ Ⓑ Ⓒ Ⓓ   5. Ⓐ Ⓑ Ⓒ Ⓓ   9. Ⓐ Ⓑ Ⓒ Ⓓ   13. Ⓐ Ⓑ Ⓒ Ⓓ

2. Ⓐ Ⓑ Ⓒ Ⓓ   6. Ⓐ Ⓑ Ⓒ Ⓓ   10. Ⓐ Ⓑ Ⓒ Ⓓ   14. Ⓐ Ⓑ Ⓒ Ⓓ

3. Ⓐ Ⓑ Ⓒ Ⓓ   7. Ⓐ Ⓑ Ⓒ Ⓓ   11. Ⓐ Ⓑ Ⓒ Ⓓ   15. Ⓐ Ⓑ Ⓒ Ⓓ

4. Ⓐ Ⓑ Ⓒ Ⓓ   8. Ⓐ Ⓑ Ⓒ Ⓓ   12. Ⓐ Ⓑ Ⓒ Ⓓ

16.

17.

18.

19.

20.

ANSWER SHEET
Diagnostic Test

Section 4: Math (Calculator)

1. Ⓐ Ⓑ Ⓒ Ⓓ
2. Ⓐ Ⓑ Ⓒ Ⓓ
3. Ⓐ Ⓑ Ⓒ Ⓓ
4. Ⓐ Ⓑ Ⓒ Ⓓ
5. Ⓐ Ⓑ Ⓒ Ⓓ
6. Ⓐ Ⓑ Ⓒ Ⓓ
7. Ⓐ Ⓑ Ⓒ Ⓓ
8. Ⓐ Ⓑ Ⓒ Ⓓ

9. Ⓐ Ⓑ Ⓒ Ⓓ
10. Ⓐ Ⓑ Ⓒ Ⓓ
11. Ⓐ Ⓑ Ⓒ Ⓓ
12. Ⓐ Ⓑ Ⓒ Ⓓ
13. Ⓐ Ⓑ Ⓒ Ⓓ
14. Ⓐ Ⓑ Ⓒ Ⓓ
15. Ⓐ Ⓑ Ⓒ Ⓓ
16. Ⓐ Ⓑ Ⓒ Ⓓ

17. Ⓐ Ⓑ Ⓒ Ⓓ
18. Ⓐ Ⓑ Ⓒ Ⓓ
19. Ⓐ Ⓑ Ⓒ Ⓓ
20. Ⓐ Ⓑ Ⓒ Ⓓ
21. Ⓐ Ⓑ Ⓒ Ⓓ
22. Ⓐ Ⓑ Ⓒ Ⓓ
23. Ⓐ Ⓑ Ⓒ Ⓓ
24. Ⓐ Ⓑ Ⓒ Ⓓ

25. Ⓐ Ⓑ Ⓒ Ⓓ
26. Ⓐ Ⓑ Ⓒ Ⓓ
27. Ⓐ Ⓑ Ⓒ Ⓓ
28. Ⓐ Ⓑ Ⓒ Ⓓ
29. Ⓐ Ⓑ Ⓒ Ⓓ
30. Ⓐ Ⓑ Ⓒ Ⓓ

31. [grid-in answer bubbles]
32. [grid-in answer bubbles]
33. [grid-in answer bubbles]
34. [grid-in answer bubbles]

35. [grid-in answer bubbles]
36. [grid-in answer bubbles]
37. [grid-in answer bubbles]
38. [grid-in answer bubbles]

ANSWER SHEET
Diagnostic Test

Essay

PLANNING PAGE

[START YOUR ESSAY HERE]

DIAGNOSTIC TEST

READING TEST

65 MINUTES, 52 QUESTIONS

Turn to Section 1 of your answer sheet to answer the questions in this section.

Directions: Following each of the passages (or pairs of passages) below are questions about the passage (or passages). Read each passage carefully. Then, select the best answer for each question based on what is stated in the passage (or passages) and in any graphics that may accompany the passage.

Questions 1–11 are based on the following passage.

The following passage is taken from Barchester Towers, *Anthony Trollope's novel set in the fictional cathedral town of Barchester, to which the family of Dr. Stanhope, a clergyman newly assigned to the cathedral, has just moved.*

The great family characteristic of the Stanhopes might probably be said to be heartlessness, but this want of feeling was,
Line in most of them, accompanied by so great
(5) an amount of good nature as to make itself but little noticeable to the world. They were so prone to oblige their neighbors that their neighbors failed to perceive how indifferent to them was the happiness and well-being
(10) of those around them. The Stanhopes would visit you in your sickness (provided it were not contagious), would bring you oranges, French novels, and the last new bit of scandal, and then hear of your death or your recovery
(15) with an equally indifferent composure. Their conduct to each other was the same as to the world; they bore and forbore; and there was sometimes, as will be seen, much necessity for forbearing; but their love among themselves
(20) rarely reached above this. It is astonishing how much each of the family was able to do, and how much each did, to prevent the well-being of the other four.

(The elder daughter) Charlotte Stanhope
(25) was at this time about thirty-five years old; and, whatever may have been her faults, she had none of those that belong to old young ladies. She neither dressed young, nor talked young, nor indeed looked young. She
(30) appeared to be perfectly content with her time of life, and in no way affected the graces of youth. She was a fine young woman; and had she been a man, would have been a fine young man. All that was done in the house,
(35) and was not done by servants, was done by her. She gave the orders, paid the bills, hired and dismissed the domestics, made the tea, carved the meat, and managed everything in the Stanhope household. She, and she
(40) alone, could ever induce her father to look into the state of his worldly concerns. She, and she alone, could in any degree control the absurdities of her sister. She, and she alone, prevented the whole family from falling into
(45) utter disrepute and beggary. It was by her advice that they now found themselves very unpleasantly situated in Barchester.

So far, the character of Charlotte Stanhope is not unprepossessing. But it remains to be
(50) said, that the influence that she had in her family, though it had been used to a certain extent for their worldly well-being, had not been used to their real benefit, as it might have been. She had aided her father in
(55) his indifference to his professional duties,

GO ON TO THE NEXT PAGE

counseling him that his livings were as much his individual property as the estates of his elder brother were the property of that worthy peer. She had for years past stifled every (60) little rising wish for a return to England that the reverend doctor had from time to time expressed. She had encouraged her mother in her idleness in order that she herself might be mistress and manager of the Stanhope (65) household. She had encouraged and fostered the follies of her sister, though she was always willing, and often able, to protect her from their probable result. She had done her best, and had thoroughly succeeded in spoiling (70) her brother, and turning him loose upon the world an idle man without a profession, and without a shilling that he could call his own.

Miss Stanhope was a clever woman, able to talk on most subjects, and quite indifferent as (75) to what the subject was. She prided herself on her freedom from English prejudice, and she might have added, from feminine delicacy. On religion she was a pure freethinker, and with much want of true affection, delighted to (80) throw out her own views before the troubled mind of her father. To have shaken what remained of his Church of England faith would have gratified her much; but the idea of his abandoning his preferment in the church had (85) never once presented itself to her mind. How could he indeed, when he had no income from any other source?

1. The main purpose of the passage is to

(A) explain the reasons behind a family's return to England.
(B) describe a main character's moral and intellectual temperament.
(C) analyze family dynamics in an aristocratic society.
(D) draw a contrast between a virtuous daughter and her disreputable family.

2. As used in line 3, "want" most nearly means

(A) hardship.
(B) desire.
(C) lack.
(D) necessity.

3. In lines 10–15 ("The Stanhopes would visit . . . indifferent composure"), what is the most likely reason the author inserts the parenthetic comment "(provided it were not contagious)"?

(A) To demonstrate the extreme fear of infectious disease in the period
(B) To emphasize how little the Stanhopes actually cared for their sick neighbors
(C) To commend the Stanhopes for their prudence in avoiding contagion
(D) To offer an excuse for the Stanhopes' failure to visit their friends

#6 is (C) because of the sympathy you feel for Charlotte as she cannot leave her family.

4. According to the opening paragraph, the Stanhopes' behavior to members of their family

   (A) reflected a real concern for the well-being of their close relatives.
   (B) was markedly more loving than their behavior to those outside the family.
   (C) showed the same lack of affection that typified their conduct to their neighbors.
   (D) included visiting them with books and gifts of fresh fruit when they fell ill.

5. Which choice provides the best evidence for the answer to the previous question?

   (A) Lines 1–6 ("The great . . . world")
   (B) Lines 6–10 ("They . . . them")
   (C) Lines 10–15 ("The Stanhopes . . . composure")
   (D) Lines 15–20 ("Their conduct . . . this")

6. The tone of the passage is best described as

   (A) self-righteous and moralistic.
   (B) satirical and candid.
   (C) sympathetic and sentimental.
   (D) indifferent and unfeeling.

7. On the basis of the passage, which of the following statements about Dr. Stanhope can most reasonably be made?

   (A) He is even more indolent than his wife.
   (B) He resents having surrendered his

8. Which choice provides the best evidence for the answer to the previous question?

   (A) Lines 39–41 ("She . . . concerns")
   (B) Lines 54–59 ("She had . . . peer")
   (C) Lines 59–62 ("She had . . . expressed")
   (D) Lines 77–85 ("On . . . mind")

9. The narrator indicates that the effect of Charlotte's influence on her brother's upbringing was his becoming

   (A) foolish.
   (B) lazy.
   (C) dejected.
   (D) irreverent.

10. As used in line 78, "pure" most nearly means

    (A) uncontaminated.
    (B) wholesome.
    (C) virtuous.
    (D) absolute.

11. The passage suggests that Charlotte possesses all of the following characteristics EXCEPT

    (A) an inappropriate flirtatiousness.
    (B) a lack of reverence.
    (C) a materialistic nature.
    (D) a managing disposition.

#8's answer directly correlates to #7's answer in terms of supporting evidence.

GO ON TO THE NEXT PAGE

DIAGNOSTIC TEST

Questions 12–21 are based on the following passage.

This passage is taken from Alexandra Witze's "3-D scans reveal secrets of extinct creatures," Science News, *October 4, 2014.*

[By Alexandra Witze, September 19, 2014]

Paleontologists have been trying to build 3-D visualizations of fossils since the early 20th century, when William Sollas
Line of the University of Oxford perfected a
(5) technique for grinding through a fossil sequentially. Sollas would grind away for a fraction of a millimeter, then stop and photograph the exposed fossil in exquisite detail. By repeating this process time and
(10) again—sometimes through hundreds of layers—Sollas eventually built a slice-by-slice encyclopedia of a given fossil, which he could then reconstruct as a 3-D wax model.

But his method destroyed the fossil
(15) and took a lot of time. By the 1980s, paleontologists had taken to zapping fossils in machines such as CT scanners, which send X-rays through an object to build up a three-dimensional picture of what's hidden
(20) inside. In recent years, that technology has improved enough for scientists to extract tantalizing information about fossils.

In most cases, an ordinary CT scanner will do. Researchers typically take a rock to their
(25) local hospital or university CT laboratory and adjust the settings until the X-rays penetrate at just the right energies to reveal the form encased in the rock. In more complicated cases, such as when the fossil and the rock
(30) surrounding it look stubbornly similar, the scientists might take the rock to a more sophisticated machine.

Virtual dissection

Paleontologist John Cunningham, also
(35) at the University of Bristol, regularly packs up his most precious fossils and flies with them to the Swiss Light Source in Villigen, Switzerland. That machine is a synchrotron, which accelerates electrons to nearly the
(40) speed of light. The accelerated electrons emit radiation including X-rays, which are usually used to explore questions in physics, materials science and chemistry. Unlike CT scanners, which use X-rays over a range
(45) of wavelengths, synchrotrons can produce X-rays of a single wavelength. That level of control allows scientists to manipulate the scan far more precisely and coax out detail from even the most stubborn structures
(50) hidden within rock.

Cunningham has used the Swiss synchrotron to explore some of paleontology's most controversial fossils: millimeter-sized blobs in 570-million-year-
(55) old rocks from the Doushantuo formation in southern China. Some scientists think the blobs represent embryos of some of the oldest known animals in the fossil record, which if true would be an astonishing
(60) witness to the earliest evolution of animals. But nobody could see past the surface.

Using the super-sharp insight of the synchrotron X-rays, Cunningham's team virtually dissected the blobs, revealing
(65) structures within. Those structures, some as small as a thousandth of a millimeter across, may be the nuclei of ancient cells. If so, they show that the fossil creatures had been developing differently than would be
(70) expected from early animals, and probably belong instead to a group known as protists.

The work, reported in 2011 in *Science*, underscored the power of synchrotron imaging for studying complicated fossils.

GO ON TO THE NEXT PAGE

(75) Cunningham is now looking at slightly younger fossils, embryos from about 542 million years ago—just after a diversity of animals spilled forth in the evolutionary burst known as the Cambrian explosion.

(80) The synchrotron images reveal details about how the embryos developed: One of them "might look like a worm curled up and about to hatch, or something with spines around its mouth," Cunningham says. By piecing

(85) together different fossils that represent the various stages as these embryos developed, he and his colleagues are building a more complete picture of how early animals might have been related to one another.

(90) Sometimes the scans show more than just never-before-seen details: They help paleontologists reconstruct major evolutionary changes from the past. Such insights wouldn't have been possible without

(95) the exceptional detail coming from computer scans. The discoveries are more than just pretty pictures—they divulge fundamental differences between ancient and modern life, allowing biologists to better understand how

(100) organisms evolved.

As scanning technologies and computer software get more sophisticated, 3-D reconstructions will probably gain in popularity among paleontologists. Some are

(105) already copying fossils using 3-D printers so that they can touch specimens they once only dreamed of handling.

Slicing and Dicing

Unlike older forms of analysis, which destroy the fossil and can take weeks to do, nondestructive, high-resolution scanning has become a go-to method for paleontologists interested In revealing hidden anatomies of ancient organisms.

Technique	Data Collected	Destructive?	Resolution	Scan Time
Serial grinding	Optical images of exposed surfaces	Yes	10 μm	Days to weeks
Micro-CT	X-ray attenuation images	No	1 μm	Minutes to hours
Synchrotron-based tomography	X-ray attenuation images	No	200 nm	Minutes
MRI	Distribution of light elements	No	10 μm	Minutes to days
Laser scanning	Surface images	No	50 μm	Minutes to hours

μm is the symbol for micron or micrometer, a unit of length equaling 1×10^{-6} of a meter.
nm is the symbol for nanometer, a until of length one thousandth the size of a micrometer.

GO ON TO THE NEXT PAGE

12. The purpose of sequential or serial grinding was to enable paleontologists to

    (A) dispose of redundant fossil specimens.
    (B) analyze the interior of fossil specimens.
    (C) create an encyclopedia of evolutionary theory.
    (D) avoid exposure to X-ray technology.

13. Which choice provides the best evidence for the answer to the previous question?

    (A) Lines 9–13 ("By repeating . . . model")
    (B) Lines 14–15 ("But . . . time")
    (C) Lines 15–20 ("By the 1980s . . . inside")
    (D) Lines 20–22 ("In recent . . . fossils")

14. As used in line 30, "stubbornly" most nearly means

    (A) pigheadedly.
    (B) persistently.
    (C) willfully.
    (D) perversely.

15. The author indicates that, in comparison to serial grinding, modern methods of fossil analysis have tended to be

    (A) less efficient and more expensive.
    (B) more detailed and less damaging.
    (C) less time-consuming and less reliable.
    (D) longer in duration and more destructive.

16. As used in line 48, "coax out" most nearly means

    (A) extract.
    (B) persuade.
    (C) flatter.
    (D) plead.

17. In making the assertion that "The discoveries are more than just pretty pictures," the author is attempting to

    (A) propose a hypothesis.
    (B) explain a paradox.
    (C) emphasize a point.
    (D) rephrase a question.

18. The table contains information useful to answer all of the following questions EXCEPT

    (A) Which form of analysis would be most damaging to a fossil being studied?
    (B) Of the forms of analysis listed, which is the least expensive to employ?
    (C) Which form of analysis offers the finest level of resolution?
    (D) Of the forms of analysis listed, which was the earliest to be employed?

19. Based on the table, which method of high-resolution scanning would be most appropriate for use by a paleontologist in need of speedy results?

    (A) Micro-CT
    (B) Synchrotron-based tomography
    (C) Magnetic resonance imaging (MRI)
    (D) Laser scanning

GO ON TO THE NEXT PAGE

DIAGNOSTIC TEST

20. The results of Cunningham's study of rocks from the Doushantuo formation in China can best be described as

    (A) anomalous.
    (B) definitive.
    (C) unsatisfactory.
    (D) tentative.

21. Which sentence best provides the best evidence for the answer to the previous question?

    (A) Lines 34–38 ("Paleontologist . . . Switzerland")
    (B) Lines 51–56 ("Cunningham . . . China")
    (C) Lines 65–67 ("Those . . . cells")
    (D) Lines 75–79 ("Cunningham . . . explosion")

Questions 22–32 are based on the following passage.

In this excerpt from his autobiographical Narrative of the Life of an American Slave, *the abolitionist Frederick Douglass tells how he, as a young child, learned the value of learning to read and write.*

Mr. and Mrs. Auld were both at home, and met me at the door with their little son Thomas, to take care of whom I had been
Line given. And here I saw what I had never seen
(5) before; it was a white face beaming with the most kindly emotions; it was the face of my new mistress, Sophia Auld. I wish I could describe the rapture that flashed through my soul as I beheld it. It was a new and strange
(10) sight to me, brightening up my pathway with happiness. Little Thomas was told, there was his Freddy, and I was told to take care of little Thomas; and thus I entered upon the duties of my new home with the most cheering
(15) prospect ahead.

My new mistress proved to be all she appeared when I first met her at the door—a woman of the kindest heart and feelings. She had never had a slave under her control
(20) previously to myself, and prior to her marriage she had been dependent upon her own industry for a living. She was by trade a weaver; and by constant application to her business, she had been in a good
(25) degree preserved from the blighting and dehumanizing effects of slavery. I was utterly astonished at her goodness.

I scarcely knew how to behave towards her. My early instruction was all out of place.
(30) The crouching servility, usually so acceptable a quality in a slave, did not answer when manifested toward her. Her favor was not gained by it; she seemed to be disturbed by it. She did not deem it impudent or

GO ON TO THE NEXT PAGE

(35) unmannerly for a slave to look her in the face. The meanest slave was put fully at ease in her presence, and none left without feeling better for having seen her. But alas! this kind heart had but a short time to remain such.

(40) The fatal poison of irresponsible power was already in her hands, and soon commenced its infernal work.

Very soon after I went to live with Mr. and Mrs. Auld, she very kindly commenced to

(45) teach me the A, B, C. After I had learned this, she assisted me in learning to spell words of three or four letters. Just at this point of my progress, Mr. Auld found out what was going on, and at once forbade Mrs. Auld to

(50) instruct me further, telling her that it was unlawful, as well as unsafe, to teach a slave to read. Further, he said, "If you give a slave an inch, he will take an ell. A slave should know nothing but to obey his master—to

(55) do as he is told to do. Learning would *spoil* the best slave in the world. Now," said he, "if you teach that boy (speaking of myself) how to read, there would be no keeping him. It would forever unfit him to be a slave.

(60) He would at once become unmanageable, and of no value to his master. As to him, it could do him no good, but a great deal of harm. It would make him discontented and unhappy." These words sank deep into

(65) my heart, stirred up sentiments within that lay slumbering, and called into existence an entirely new train of thought. I now understood what had been to me a most perplexing difficulty—to wit, the white man's

(70) power to enslave the black man. From that moment I understood the pathway from slavery to freedom. Though conscious of the difficulty of learning without a teacher, I set out with high hope, and a fixed purpose,

(75) at whatever cost of trouble, to learn how to read. The very decided manner with which my master spoke, and strove to impress his wife with the evil consequences of giving

me instruction, served to convince me that

(80) he was deeply sensible of the truths he was uttering. It gave me the best assurance that I might rely with the utmost confidence on the results which, he said, would flow from teaching me to read. What he most dreaded,

(85) that I most desired. What he most loved, that I most hated. That which to him was a great evil, to be carefully shunned, was to me a great good, to be diligently sought; and the argument which he so warmly urged, against

(90) my learning to read, only served to inspire me with a desire and determination to learn. In learning to read, I owe almost as much to the bitter opposition of my master, as to the kindly aid of my mistress. I acknowledge the

(95) benefit of both.

22. According to the opening paragraph, the author's initial reaction toward joining the Aulds' household was primarily one of

(A) absolute astonishment.
(B) marked pleasure.
(C) carefree nonchalance.
(D) quiet resignation.

23. To some degree, the author attributes Mrs. Auld's freedom from the common attitudes of slave owners to her

(A) abolitionist upbringing.
(B) personal wealth.
(C) experiences as a mother.
(D) concentration on her trade.

24. Which choice provides the best evidence for the answer to the previous question?

(A) Lines 4–6 ("And here . . . emotions")
(B) Lines 16–18 ("My new . . . feelings")
(C) Lines 22–26 ("She was . . . slavery")
(D) Lines 34–38 ("She did not . . . her")

GO ON TO THE NEXT PAGE

25. Which of the following best explains why the author felt his "early instruction was all out of place" (line 29)?

   (A) It failed to include instruction in reading and writing.
   (B) It did not prepare him to take adequate care of the Aulds' young son Thomas.
   (C) It had been displaced by the new instructions he received from the Aulds.
   (D) It insisted on an obsequiousness that distressed his new mistress.

26. Which choice provides the best evidence for the answer to the previous question?

   (A) Lines 19–22 ("She . . . living")
   (B) Lines 26–27 ("I . . . goodness")
   (C) Lines 30–34 ("The crouching . . . it")
   (D) Lines 40–42 ("The fatal . . . work")

27. As used in line 31, "answer" most nearly means

   (A) acknowledge.
   (B) retort.
   (C) reply.
   (D) serve.

28. By "this kind heart had but a short time to remain such" (lines 38–39), the author primarily intends to convey that Mrs. Auld

   (A) was fated to die in the near future.
   (B) was unable to keep her temper for extended periods of time.
   (C) had too much strength of will to give in to the softer emotions.
   (D) was destined to undergo a change of character shortly.

29. It can be inferred from the passage that all of the following were characteristic of Mrs. Auld at the time the author first met her EXCEPT

   (A) diligence in labor.
   (B) dislike of fawning.
   (C) disdain for convention.
   (D) benevolent nature.

30. The author's main purpose in this passage is to

   (A) describe a disagreement between a woman and her husband.
   (B) analyze the reasons for prohibiting the education of slaves.
   (C) describe a slave's discovery of literacy as a means to freedom.
   (D) portray the moral downfall of a kindhearted woman.

31. As used in line 80, "sensible" most nearly means

   (A) logical.
   (B) prudent.
   (C) intelligent.
   (D) conscious/aware.

32. The tone of the author in acknowledging his debt to his master (lines 92–95) can best be described as

   (A) sentimental and nostalgic.
   (B) cutting and ironic.
   (C) petulant and self-righteous.
   (D) resigned but wistful.

Questions 33–42 are based on the following passages.

The following passages are taken from two articles by Susan Milius, "Hush, humans, We're trying to survive here," and "Highway bridge noise can disturb fish's hearing," both published in issues of Science News *in February 2015.*

PASSAGE 1

To explore a basic question about wildlife and noise, Jesse Barber and his colleagues built what they call the phantom road.

Line Earlier studies of noise effects often
(5) compared animals near roads or other clamorous human-made features with animals in rural landscapes. This approach left questions about how much of the difference came from noise instead of from
(10) artificial lights, exhaust fumes or other non-noisy aspects. Other research teams have turned to, of all things, gas wells to try to sort out the problem—by monitoring wildlife near wells equipped with thundering
(15) compressor motors versus otherwise similar wells without the noisy equipment. In Canada's boreal forest, songbirds didn't settle as densely near the monster motors, and in a New Mexico gas field, there weren't
(20) as many bird species at the loud sites. The impact rippled onward: Because the animals found in the neighborhood changed, plants' exchange of pollen and spread of seeds would change. Noise seemed to be the cause.
(25) But for a direct test of sound effects, Barber, of Boise State University in Idaho, and his colleagues created a highway that was nothing but the noise. They broadcast recordings of cars from 15 pairs of speakers
(30) mounted in a row along a half-kilometer of

ridge near Lucky Peak State Park in Idaho. "It sounded like a highway in the woods," Barber says. "But then you get up there and there's no road."
(35) "Challenging" is his restrained word for the travails of the experiment. It took a month just to position the speakers and get the broadcast to sound realistic. And once the spectral road was running, lab members
(40) spent hours each day hiking out and back to replace batteries and take data because, of course, there was no real road to the site. But the effort was worthwhile, as revealed in the team's 2013 report in the Proceedings of the
(45) Royal Society B.
The ghostly road ran beside a major rest stop for migratory birds. Just beyond the ridge, the great Douglas fir forest of central Idaho frays into clusters of bitter cherry and
(50) chokecherry, and then the landscape opens into what small migratory birds would have every right to call challenging. They must cross miles of low-growing steppe vegetation with little cover but plenty of bird-eating
(55) raptors. Typical migrants "stop at the edge for a few days and fatten up and get ready for this dangerous and exhausting nocturnal journey," Barber says.
When the researchers turned on the
(60) speakers for four days of faux traffic, the numbers of birds stopping to rest dropped by more than a quarter on average. And during the alternating four-day stretches of silence, bird numbers bounced back. Noise
(65) matters, Barber and colleagues concluded. It can change animals' most basic stay-or-go assessments of habitat. It can prompt more than the usual number of birds on thousand-mile marathons to skip a chance to rest and
(70) refuel.

GO ON TO THE NEXT PAGE

Noise on, noise off

When speakers piped traffic noise into an Idaho forest, fewer migrating birds stopped to rest than in nearby quiet areas or when the noise was off. Yellow warblers showed a
(75) strong distaste for the noise.

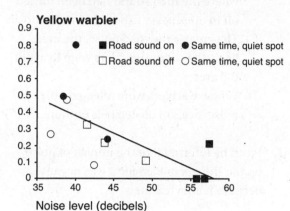

Noise level (decibels)

PASSAGE 2

Loud recordings of traffic rumbling over highway bridges can cause rock-concert hearing shifts in lab fish that normally live in Alabama streams. After two hours
(80) of broadcast traffic noise in the lab, small silvery fish called blacktail shiners (*Cyprinella venusta*) could no longer detect some important sounds as easily as fish not exposed to the highway din. Jenna Crovo of Auburn
(85) University in Alabama reported the findings January 5 at the annual meeting of the Society for Integrative and Comparative Biology.

Shiners not subjected to recordings could hear the upper peak of their species'
(90) courtship growl when tones were played at about 80 decibels. Fish subjected to traffic broadcasts didn't hear those tones until researchers played them about 10 decibels louder. Whether the threshold shift
(95) is permanent or the fish's hearing returns to normal—as often happens in human concertgoers who experience similar shifts—remains to be seen.

33. Both passages are written from the perspective of someone who is

(A) actively engaged in academic investigations of wildlife behavior.
(B) knowledgeable about research into the effects of human actions on wildlife.
(C) an active campaigner for the protection and conservation of native wildlife.
(D) a technical expert on audiological difficulties.

34. As used in line 8, "left" most nearly means

(A) abandoned.
(B) went away from.
(C) failed to answer.
(D) ceased attending.

35. The basic question about wildlife and noise that Barber and his colleagues sought to explore concerned

(A) the amount of noise produced by different wildlife species.
(B) the impact of highway construction on migratory birds.
(C) the degree to which mere noise affected wildlife populations.
(D) the difference between the effects of noise in rural and urban environments.

36. Which choice provides the best evidence for the answer to the previous question?

(A) Lines 1–3 ("To explore . . . road")
(B) Lines 4–7 ("Earlier . . . landscapes")
(C) Lines 25–28 ("But for a direct . . . noise")
(D) Lines 76–79 ("Loud recordings . . . streams")

GO ON TO THE NEXT PAGE

DIAGNOSTIC TEST

37. It is reasonable to conclude that a necessary step for the scientists conducting the research described in Passage 1 was to

   (A) isolate noise from other human-caused factors affecting wildlife behavior.
   (B) construct a road to enable their closer observation of wildlife in their native habitat.
   (C) replicate previous studies of the effects of traffic noise on animal behavior patterns.
   (D) monitor wildlife populations throughout Canada, New Mexico, and Idaho.

38. Barber's use of the word "challenging" to describe the laborious efforts involved in setting up the experiment is an example of

   (A) an understatement.
   (B) an analogy.
   (C) a simile.
   (D) a fallacy.

39. As used in line 30, "mounted" most nearly means

   (A) ascended.
   (B) installed.
   (C) launched.
   (D) increased.

40. Which statement best summarizes the information presented in the graph?

   (A) No yellow warblers stopped to rest in the areas exposed to traffic noise.
   (B) Yellow warblers strongly preferred areas where the road sound had been turned off to ones never exposed to traffic noise.
   (C) The greater the road noise, the more likely the yellow warblers were to avoid the area.
   (D) Yellow warblers were affected only by noise levels of 60 decibels or more.

41. It can be inferred that the impact of noise on the shiners in Passage 2 was negative because it affected their

   (A) sense of direction.
   (B) mating patterns.
   (C) exposure to traffic sounds.
   (D) avoidance of danger.

42. The wild birds described in the experiment in Passage 1 differed from the shiners described in the experiment in Passage 2 in that the birds were

   (A) able to avoid the noise being broadcast.
   (B) more sensitive to recorded sound.
   (C) threatened with permanent hearing loss.
   (D) less able to assess unfamiliar habitats.

GO ON TO THE NEXT PAGE

Questions 43–52 are based on the following passage.

The following passage is taken from Civilisation, *a book based on the scripts for the television series of the same name. In this excerpt, author Kenneth Clark introduces the audience to the Europe of the thirteenth to fifteenth centuries: the Gothic world.*

I am in the Gothic world, the world of chivalry, courtesy, and romance; a world in which serious things were done with a
Line sense of play—where even war and theology
(5) could become a sort of game; and when architecture reached a point of extravagance unequalled in history. After all the great unifying convictions that inspired the medieval world, High Gothic art can look
(10) fantastic and luxurious—what Marxists call conspicuous waste. And yet these centuries produced some of the greatest spirits in the history of man, amongst them St. Francis of Assisi and Dante. Behind all the fantasy of
(15) the Gothic imagination there remained, on two different planes, a sharp sense of reality. Medieval man could see things very clearly, but he believed that these appearances should be considered as nothing more than
(20) symbols or tokens of an ideal order, which was the only true reality.

The fantasy strikes us first, and last; and one can see it in the room in the Cluny Museum in Paris hung with a series of
(25) tapestries known as *The Lady with the Unicorn,* one of the most seductive examples of the Gothic spirit. It is poetical, fanciful and profane. Its ostensible subject is the four senses. But its real subject is the power
(30) of love, which can enlist and subdue all the forces of nature, including those two emblems of lust and ferocity, the unicorn and the lion. They kneel before this embodiment

of chastity, and hold up the corners of her
(35) cloak. These wild animals have become, in the heraldic sense, her supporters.

And all round this allegorical scene is what the medieval philosophers used to call *natura naturans*—nature naturing—trees,
(40) flowers, leaves galore, birds, monkeys, and those rather obvious symbols of nature naturing, rabbits. There is even nature domesticated, a little dog, sitting on a cushion. It is an image of worldly happiness
(45) at its most refined, what the French call the *douceur de vivre,* which is often confused with civilization.

We have come a long way from the powerful conviction that induced medieval
(50) knights and ladies to draw carts of stone up the hill for the building of Chartres Cathedral. And yet the notion of ideal love, and the irresistible power of gentleness and beauty, which is emblematically conveyed
(55) by the homage of these two fierce beasts, can be traced back for three centuries; we may even begin to look for it in the north portal of Chartres.

This portal was decorated in about the
(60) year 1220, and seems to have been paid for by that formidable lady, Blanche of Castile, the mother of St. Louis. Perhaps for that reason, or perhaps simply because it was dedicated to the virgin, many of the figures
(65) are women. Several of the stories depicted in the arches concern Old Testament heroines; and at the corner of the portico is one of the first consciously graceful women in western art. Only a very few years before,
(70) women were thought of as the squat, bad-tempered viragos that we see on the font of Winchester Cathedral: these were the women who accompanied the Norsemen to Iceland. Now look at this embodiment of chastity,
(75) lifting her mantle, raising her hand, turning

GO ON TO THE NEXT PAGE

her head with a movement of self-conscious
refinement that was to become mannered
but here is genuinely modest. She might be
Dante's Beatrice. In fact she represents a
(80)   saint called St. Modeste. She is still a little
austere. And when one looks at the details of
the portal—those marvelous details which
reflect the whole imaginative life of the
century—one finds figures of women whose
(85)   femininity is warmer and more accessible:
Judith kneeling and covering her head with
ashes, and Esther throwing herself at the feet
of King Holofernes. There, for almost the first
time in visual art, one gets a sense of human
(90)   rapport between man and woman.

These feelings had of course long been the
theme of the wandering poets of Provence,
the *jongleurs* and troubadours. Of the two
or three faculties that have been added to
(95)   the European mind since the civilization of
Greece and Rome, none seems to me more
inexplicable than the sentiment of ideal
or courtly love. It was entirely unknown
to antiquity. Passion, yes; desire, yes of
(100) course; steady affection, yes. But this state
of utter subjection to the will of an almost
unapproachable woman; this belief that
no sacrifice was too great, that a whole
lifetime might properly be spent in paying
(105) court to some exacting lady or suffering on
her behalf—this would have seemed to the
Romans or to the Vikings not only absurd but
unbelievable; and yet for hundreds of years it
passed unquestioned.

43.   The author distinguishes the medieval
imagination from the Gothic on the basis of
the latter's

(A) firm belief.
(B) respect for tradition.
(C) elaborateness of fancy.
(D) philosophical unity.

44.   In line 6, "point" most nearly means

(A) tip.
(B) advantage.
(C) argument.
(D) stage.

45.   The author thinks of the Unicorn tapestries
as exemplifying the essence of the Gothic
imagination because

(A) their allegorical nature derives from
medieval sources.
(B) their use as wall hangings expresses the
realistic practicality of the Gothic mind.
(C) they demonstrate the wastefulness and
extravagance of the period.
(D) they combine worldly and spiritual
elements in an allegorical celebration of
love.

46.   Which choice provides the best evidence for
the answer to the previous question?

(A) Lines 7–11 ("After all . . . waste")
(B) Lines 17–21 ("Medieval . . . reality")
(C) Lines 29–35 ("But . . . cloak")
(D) Lines 48–52 ("We have come . . .
Cathedral")

GO ON TO THE NEXT PAGE

47. By "this embodiment of chastity" (lines 33–34) the author is referring to

    (A) the unicorn.
    (B) the Gothic spirit.
    (C) St. Francis.
    (D) the lady.

48. According to lines 48–52, in the Middle Ages some members of the nobility demonstrated the depth of their faith by

    (A) designing tapestries symbolic of courtly love.
    (B) following the Franciscan ideal of living in harmony with nature.
    (C) choosing to refine their notions of worldly happiness.
    (D) hauling stones used to construct Chartres Cathedral.

49. According to the next-to-last paragraph, the figures carved on the north portal of Chartres represent

    (A) a rejection of New Testament heroines.
    (B) a marked change in the image of women.
    (C) the return to an earlier, typical perspective on women.
    (D) the artistic endeavors of Blanche of Castile.

50. Which choice provides the best evidence for the answer to the previous question?

    (A) Lines 59–62 ("This portal . . . St. Louis")
    (B) Lines 62–65 ("Perhaps . . . women")
    (C) Lines 69–78 ("Only . . . modest")
    (D) Lines 78–81 ("She might . . . austere")

51. In line 94, "faculties" most nearly means

    (A) teaching staffs.
    (B) authorizations.
    (C) modes of thought.
    (D) bodily capabilities.

52. The author indicates that the sentiment of courtly love was

    (A) historically unprecedented.
    (B) wholly theoretical.
    (C) charmingly absurd.
    (D) quickly outdated.

STOP

If there is still time remaining, you may review your answers.

WRITING AND LANGUAGE TEST

35 MINUTES, 44 QUESTIONS

Turn to Section 2 of your answer sheet to answer the questions in this section.

Directions: Questions follow each of the passages below. Some questions ask you how the passage might be changed to improve the expression of ideas. Other questions ask you how the passage might be altered to correct errors in grammar, usage, and punctuation. One or more graphics accompany some passages. You will be required to consider these graphics as you answer questions about editing the passage.

There are three types of questions. In the first type, a part of the passage is underlined. The second type is based on a certain part of the passage. The third type is based on the entire passage.

Read each passage. Then, choose the answer to each question that changes the passage so that it is consistent with the conventions of standard written English. One of the answer choices for many questions is "NO CHANGE." Choosing this answer means that you believe the best answer is to make no change in the passage.

Questions 1–11 are based on the following passage and supplementary material.

Policing Our Planet

Once completely oblivious of the damages to the environment caused by pollution, waste, and overpopulation, the world ❶ had now began to look seriously upon the depletion of our natural resources. Whether we scrutinize the harmful exhaust gases that pollute our ❷ air—carbon dioxide, sulfur dioxide, ammonia, among others— or turn to deforestation and chemical effluents, the

1. (A) NO CHANGE
    (B) has now began
    (C) has now begun
    (D) have now begun

2. (A) NO CHANGE
    (B) air, carbon dioxide sulfur dioxide, ammonia among others, or
    (C) air—carbon dioxide, sulfur dioxide, ammonia among others, or
    (D) air, carbon dioxide, sulfur dioxide, ammonia, among others—or

GO ON TO THE NEXT PAGE

Threats to the Great Lakes

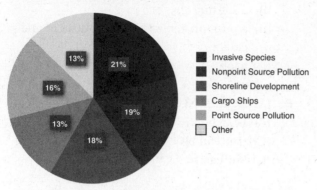

Invasive Species
Nonpoint Source Pollution
Shoreline Development
Cargo Ships
Point Source Pollution
Other

situation is clearly out of control. ❸ For example, scientists have proven that all of the threats to the Great Lakes come as a result of human activity. Furthermore, it is no longer a question limited to a certain population or government, but a matter of global concern. The recognition of its severity is undoubtedly behind the rise in demand for environmental engineers.

Environmental engineers use the ❹ principles of biology, chemistry, and engineering to develop solutions to environmental problems and consider global issues such as potable water, climate change, and sustainability. Typically, the work of an environmental engineer involves inspecting facilities for compliance with state and federal regulations, preparing and reviewing environmental investigation reports, designing projects to protect and conserve the environment, and advising corporations in regard to contamination clean-up. ❺ Unexpectedly, environmental engineers may collaborate with specialists of science, law, or business to address specific concerns such as acid rain, soil degradation, or hazardous wastes.

For those interested in pursuing a career as an environmental engineer, a bachelor's degree is a must. While a degree in environmental engineering is ❻ necessary, related fields such as

3. Which choice offers an accurate interpretation of the data in the chart?

(A) NO CHANGE
(B) For example, the vast majority of the threats to the Great Lakes comes as a result of human activity.
(C) For example, approximately 24 percent of the threats to the Great Lakes comes as a result of human activity.
(D) For example, environmental regulations have successfully negated human activity as a source of threats to the Great Lakes.

4. (A) NO CHANGE
(B) principals
(C) principle concepts
(D) principal ideas

5. Which choice provides the most logical introduction to this sentence?

(A) NO CHANGE
(B) Habitually,
(C) Other times,
(D) Possibly,

6. Which choice gives the most logical contrast with the second part of the sentence?

(A) NO CHANGE
(B) educational,
(C) preferable,
(D) adequate,

GO ON TO THE NEXT PAGE

general or civil engineering can be acceptable as well. Even then, the four-year degree is mandatory for even ❼ an entry-level position, and many employers seek out those who have differentiated themselves with previous experience, graduate degrees, and/or licensing. At the top of the list for preferred skills for candidates are strong critical thinking skills and complex problem solving, followed closely by problem sensitivity and deductive reasoning. ❽ You can be expected to have strengths in analyzing, evaluating, and interpreting highly complex data. For management or supervisor positions, a master's degree is required.

❾ Your commitment to education in environmental engineering does not go unrewarded. The median annual income is recorded at well over $80,000, and the outlook is promising. Tightening federal regulations ❿ to meet environmental safe standards and for the purpose of the cleaning of contaminated sites are expected to only stimulate the need for environmental engineers over the next decade. According to the Bureau of Labor Statistics, ⓫ environmental degradation is increasing at an exponential rate, with up to 30 percent of current species becoming extinct in the coming years. With wages climbing and job prospects high, environmental engineering seems a promising occupation for one interested in remedying the current damage and preventing further harm to our planet.

7. (A) NO CHANGE
    (B) a starting gig,
    (C) a position acquired at the outset of one's career,
    (D) a job,

8. (A) NO CHANGE
    (B) I can be
    (C) One can be
    (D) She can be

9. (A) NO CHANGE
    (B) You're commitment
    (C) One's commitment
    (D) Ones' commitment

10. (A) NO CHANGE
    (B) to meet environmentally safe standards and clean up contaminated sites is
    (C) in order to meet environmentally safe standards and in order to clean up contaminated sites are
    (D) to meeting environmentally safe standards and cleaning up contaminated sites were

11. Which choice provides the most fitting and specific justification for the argument in the sentences before and after?

    (A) NO CHANGE
    (B) job prospects for high-technology jobs are going up.
    (C) the need for environmental specialists is increasing at an alarming pace.
    (D) there are 21,100 projected job openings in environmental engineering by the year 2022.

Questions 12–22 are based on the following passage.

The Bullroarer

Apart from the drum, there is perhaps no instrument more widespread among the world's ancient cultures than the curious noisemaker known severally as the "bullroarer," ⓬ rhombus', "tundun," or "whizzing-stick." In construction and operation it is perhaps only slightly more sophisticated than the simple percussive instruments of antiquity. It is ⓭ suspicious that this instrument's significance to bygone peoples, much like the drum, was principally ritual, but perhaps also communicative. Even into modern times, tunduns were commonly used by the Australian Aboriginal cultures during ⓮ hunting and gathering on the plains of Australia.

The oldest known bullroarers were discovered in the Ukraine, and are estimated to date from the Paleolithic era, approximately 17,000 B.C., but slightly more recent bullroarers have been discovered at archeological sites on every continent ⓯ apart of Antarctica. Not surprisingly, the instrument exhibits a fairly wide variation in size, shape and ornamentation across history and cultures; but, the essential design is unmistakable: a wooden slat generally measuring between six to twenty-four inches in length affixed at one end to a length of twisted cord.

When one swings the slat by the cord in a circle around the head, the untwisting and re-twisting of the rope ⓰ caused the slat to rotate laterally. The result is a unique vibrato sound that has been likened both to an animal's roar, and the approach of a distant thunderstorm. Pitch modulation can be achieved by altering the speed of rotation, or the length of the cord. The capacity for pitch modulation has ⓱ lent credence to the idea that bullroarers could be used to communicate coded

12. (A) NO CHANGE
     (B) "rhombus,"
     (C) rhombus,
     (D) rhombus

13. (A) NO CHANGE
     (B) suspected
     (C) suspect
     (D) superstitious

14. The writer would like to express that tunduns played a role in significant transitional life events in Aboriginal culture. Which choice best conveys this idea?

     (A) NO CHANGE
     (B) the daily preparation of meals.
     (C) rites of passage and burial ceremonies.
     (D) creating fires used for both cooking and protection.

15. (A) NO CHANGE
     (B) a part of
     (C) apart from
     (D) a part from

16. (A) NO CHANGE
     (B) had caused
     (C) have been causing
     (D) cause

17. (A) NO CHANGE
     (B) lended credibility
     (C) loaned credibility
     (D) lending credence

GO ON TO THE NEXT PAGE

messages, with certain meanings attached to certain pitches. **18** This would make bullroarers, like the telegraph machines of the modern era, that transmitted Morse code messages over long distances.

Though we can only speculate on its use among preliterate peoples, some historical anthropologists have suggested that the bullroarer's ubiquity across the world's ancient cultures suggests that **19** its primary function must have been practical rather than ritual. The most common application cited by such scholars is that of long-distance communication. **20** For the reason that no scientific studies on the subject have been published, many witnesses claim that the lower audible frequencies emitted by the bullroarer can travel impressive distances, with listeners clearly discerning its sound from up to two miles away. If indeed bullroarers can be used **21** as musical instruments by early civilizations, then this usefulness would be a

18. (A) NO CHANGE
    (B) This would make bullroarers like, the telegraph machines of the modern era that transmitted Morse code messages over long distances.
    (C) This would make bullroarers like the telegraph machines of the modern era, that transmitted Morse code messages, over long distances.
    (D) This would make bullroarers like the telegraph machines of the modern era that transmitted Morse code messages over long distances.

19. (A) NO CHANGE
    (B) it's
    (C) its'
    (D) their

20. (A) NO CHANGE
    (B) Because
    (C) Since
    (D) Though

21. Which choice is most consistent with the argument in the paragraph?

    (A) NO CHANGE
    (B) to communicate over long distances with relatively high accuracy,
    (C) to discover the breeding grounds of prey to be hunted,
    (D) to symbolize the vibrancy of Aboriginal musical expression,

GO ON TO THE NEXT PAGE

logical justification as to why this instrument was invented **㉒** <u>by the greatest musician in the history of the Aboriginal peoples.</u>

22. The writer wants to express that there was NOT a single inventor of the bullroarer. Which choice best accomplishes this goal?

(A) NO CHANGE
(B) as a means to communicate easily between one group and another.
(C) independently by prehistoric peoples all over the world.
(D) for peoples in the Americas, Asia, and Australia.

GO ON TO THE NEXT PAGE

Questions 23–33 are based on the following passage.

Astrochemistry

Do ever you remember hearing in school that the sun—by far the largest body in our solar system—is composed almost entirely of the two smallest elements, **23** hydrogen, and helium. Or perhaps that the distinctive blue hues of Neptune and Uranus arise from an unusual abundance of organic methane? At the time, it may have seemed curious to you that scientists were able to make such bold hypotheses about the chemical compositions of things **24** using space-based telescopes for data-gathering; after all, we can hardly gather a gas sample from the surface of the sun. And yet we know with surprising certainty not only the composition of the bodies in our solar system, **25** from also that of many interstellar bodies, and even some intergalactic ones as well.

26 The key principle that connects astronomy and chemistry is the emission spectrum. When struck by a wave of electromagnetic radiation, every element **27** enter an "excited state," in which the electrons surrounding the nucleus "jump" to higher energy levels. Eventually, the

23. (A) NO CHANGE
    (B) hydrogen and helium.
    (C) hydrogen, and helium?
    (D) hydrogen and helium?

24. The writer wants to highlight that scientists are able to determine the chemical makeup of stars far from our solar system. Which choice would most specifically support this aim?

    (A) NO CHANGE
    (B) 93 million miles away or more;
    (C) that are a prodigious distance from Mother Earth;
    (D) capturing the imaginations of young and old alike;

25. (A) NO CHANGE
    (B) but also
    (C) also
    (D) and

26. Which choice would best introduce this paragraph?

    (A) NO CHANGE
    (B) Electromagnetic radiation is one of the major physical forces underlying the universe.
    (C) Photons are smaller than protons, representing quanta of light.
    (D) Perhaps one day, mankind will be able to move beyond observation of distant stars to exploration of faraway solar systems.

27. (A) NO CHANGE
    (B) entering
    (C) enters
    (D) entries

GO ON TO THE NEXT PAGE

complex returns to its ground state, and the excess energy is released once again as electromagnetic radiation. However, this new photon carries with it a sort of chemical "signature" called an emission spectrum, which is **28** one of the only of its kind to the element from which it was emitted.

A spectrometer is an instrument that spreads a wave of electromagnetic radiation into its component frequencies. When you look through a spectrometer at a beam of white light, **29** and you see a continuous band of colors shifting like a rainbow from red to violet. However, when a spectrometer is used to examine the flame test of, say, sodium carbonate or cobalt, the band is broken into a series of lines which represent the very specific frequencies of electromagnetic radiation that are **30** shot forth of the compound. Because emission spectra are unique to each element and constant throughout the universe, scientists are able to attach a spectrometer to a telescope, locate a celestial body, and **31** determine, the chemical composition of that body simply, by comparing the resulting spectrum to those of known compounds on Earth.

Over the past one hundred years astrochemical spectroscopy has revealed some fascinating information about our galaxy. It is because of spectroscopy, **32** however, that we know of the existence of interstellar complex organic

28. (A) NO CHANGE
    (B) partial
    (C) uniquely
    (D) specific

29. (A) NO CHANGE
    (B) and one can see
    (C) and he or she can find
    (D) you see

30. (A) NO CHANGE
    (B) emitted by
    (C) providing
    (D) linear for

31. (A) NO CHANGE
    (B) determine the chemical composition, of that body simply by comparing, the resulting spectrum to those of known compounds on Earth.
    (C) determine the chemical composition of that body simply by comparing the resulting spectrum to those of known compounds on Earth.
    (D) determine the chemical composition of that body, simply by comparing the resulting spectrum to those of known, compounds on Earth.

32. (A) NO CHANGE
    (B) on the other hand,
    (C) consequently,
    (D) for instance,

GO ON TO THE NEXT PAGE

compounds—such as ketones, aldehydes, alcohols, carboxylic acids, and even the amino acid glycine. Though it seems paradoxical that we **33** use the smallest units of matter to study the largest, astrochemical spectroscopy is sure to have a hand in our expanding knowledge of the universe for a very long time to come.

33. What would most logically follow the first part of this sentence while being consistent with the passage as a whole?

(A) NO CHANGE
(B) seek to understand the universe,
(C) look for astronomical order among the chaos,
(D) use chemistry to analyze the makeup of stars,

Questions 34–44 are based on the following passage.

Blood Ties

William Faulkner is one of the most highly recognized American authors of all time. He is celebrated for his use of "stream of consciousness" writing to give life to Southern U.S. culture, and **34** was considered one of the best people ever to put pen to paper. While *The Sound and the Fury* and *As I Lay Dying* are some of Faulkner's best known novels, his plethora of short stories are perhaps lesser known **35** because of a lack of public awareness about them. A particular short story, "Barn Burning," tells the story of Colonel Sartoris Snopes, a young protagonist who struggles to develop into his own man under his father's malevolent eyes. Colonel Sartoris, or "Sarty," is trapped in a world stricken by fear, grief, and misery. **36** While physically similar and often volatile like his father, Sarty is continually faced with the paradox of detesting the man who raised him, while also feeling an inherent fidelity to him. Sarty's personal growth is stunted by this ubiquitous inconsistency in his character.

Sarty's father, Abner, is a rigid man—set in his ways and seemingly vengeful toward everyone outside of his own family. Constantly unhappy, Abner **37** lauds anyone who surpasses him in

34. Which choice would give the most logical and specific support to the assertion made in the first sentence of the passage?

(A) NO CHANGE
(B) was thought of as a true American hero, not in the traditional, but literary sense.
(C) was revered as one of the best executors of the "stream of consciousness" style.
(D) was awarded the Nobel Prize in Literature in 1949.

35. What should be done with the underlined portion?

(A) Keep it, because it provides a relevant clarification.
(B) Keep it, because it gives specific evidentiary support.
(C) Delete it, because it repeats an assertion.
(D) Delete it, because it is inconsistent with the other information in the paragraph.

36. (A) NO CHANGE
(B) While physically similar, and often, volatile, like his
(C) While physically similar, and often volatile like his
(D) While physically similar and often, volatile like his

37. Which word would most likely capture Abner's mentality based on the context?

(A) NO CHANGE
(B) invokes
(C) despises
(D) reveres

GO ON TO THE NEXT PAGE

DIAGNOSTIC TEST

joy, health, or wealth. He is particularly fond of offending and stealing from others, and then burning the barns of those who dare to question his conduct. **38** Interestingly, Faulkner first introduces Sarty at his father's trial where he is accused of burning a local farm. It is through Sarty's inner toil **39** which the reader becomes distinctly aware of Abner's guilt. Rather than being oblivious to his father's evil disposition, Sarty wishfully, and somewhat naively, hopes that his father will **40** overcome it. The story continues not as a battle for integrity within Abner, but within Sarty, who must choose the man he is to become.

Sarty's internal conflict is **41** made more challenging by the fact that he has to remain faithful to his kin and a fear of the consequences in turning away from them. Throughout the short piece, Sarty becomes almost two separate characters, his thoughts as divided as his loyalty. On certain occasions, he is brutally ashamed of his **42** father's deceit, on others he overcompensates for his treachery by defending his father at all costs.

43 So it comes as little shock to the reader when his father decides to burn the barn of his newest employers. When enlisted to help with the crime, Sarty weighs his options, hesitant to disobey his father. Eventually, Sarty betrays his

38. (A) NO CHANGE
    (B) As a result,
    (C) For this very reason,
    (D) On the other hand,

39. (A) NO CHANGE
    (B) from
    (C) for
    (D) that

40. (A) NO CHANGE
    (B) overcome these.
    (C) overcoming this.
    (D) overcoming those.

41. (A) NO CHANGE
    (B) pretentiously made more oppressive
    (C) complicated by a desire
    (D) OMIT the underlined portion.

42. (A) NO CHANGE
    (B) fathers deceit: on others he
    (C) father's deceit; on others, he
    (D) fathers' deceit—on others, he

43. Which choice provides the best transition from the theme of the previous paragraph to the topic of this new paragraph?

    (A) NO CHANGE
    (B) Sarty has little difficulty deciding what to do
    (C) Therefore, the accumulated lies of his father surprise Sarty
    (D) Perhaps the best illustration of Sarty's divided nature is

GO ON TO THE NEXT PAGE

father by revealing the plan. This act of defiance allows Sarty to make a character transition and wholly resist the life his father has led. Sarty's story is a beautiful portrayal of **44** <u>a diverged heart</u> and its battle to follow its own path.

44. Which wording is most consistent with the passage as a whole?

(A) NO CHANGE
(B) a decisive mind
(C) a melancholy attitude
(D) unrelenting optimism

STOP

If there is still time remaining, you may review your answers.

MATH TEST (NO CALCULATOR)

25 MINUTES, 20 QUESTIONS

Turn to Section 3 of your answer sheet to answer the questions in this section.

Directions: For questions 1–15, solve each problem and choose the best answer from the given options. Fill in the corresponding circle on your answer document. For questions 16–20, solve the problem and fill in the answer on the answer sheet grid.

Notes:
- Calculators are **NOT PERMITTED** in this section.
- All variables and expressions represent real numbers unless indicated otherwise.
- All figures are drawn to scale unless indicated otherwise.
- All figures are in a plane unless indicated otherwise.
- Unless indicated otherwise, the domain of a given function is the set of all real numbers x for which the function has real values.

REFERENCE INFORMATION

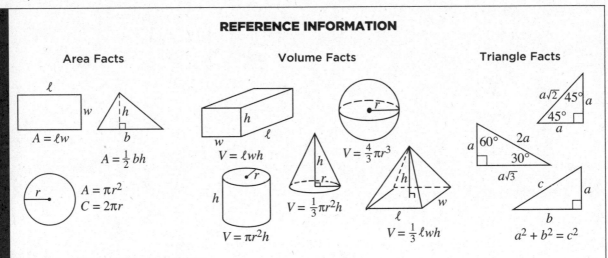

Area Facts

$A = \ell w$

$A = \frac{1}{2}bh$

$A = \pi r^2$
$C = 2\pi r$

Volume Facts

$V = \ell wh$

$V = \pi r^2 h$

$V = \frac{4}{3}\pi r^3$

$V = \frac{1}{3}\pi r^2 h$

$V = \frac{1}{3}\ell wh$

Triangle Facts

$a^2 + b^2 = c^2$

The arc of a circle contains 360°.
The arc of a circle contains 2π radians.
The sum of the measures of the angles in a triangle is 180°.

GO ON TO THE NEXT PAGE

1. If $\dfrac{5}{a-b} = 2$ and if $a = 4$, what is the value of b?

   (A) 1.5
   (B) 3
   (C) 4.5
   (D) 6.5

2. Which of the following statements is true concerning the equation below?
   $$2(x-5) = 2x - 5$$

   (A) The equation has no solutions.
   (B) The equation has one positive solution.
   (C) The equation has one negative solution.
   (D) The equation has infinitely many solutions.

3. If a small juice can contains 6 ounces of juice, how many quarts of juice are in a carton that contains 24 small cans? (1 quart = 32 ounces)

   (A) 3.5
   (B) 4
   (C) 4.5
   (D) 5

4. Let l be the line whose equation is $y = ax + b$ and let k be the line whose equation is $y = cx + d$. If l and k are distinct parallel lines, which of the following statements must be true?

   (A) $a = c$ and $b = d$
   (B) $a = c$ and $b \neq d$
   (C) $a \neq c$ and $b = d$
   (D) $a \neq c$ and $b \neq d$

5. Frank has a hot dog stand. The only things he sells are hot dogs for \$2.25 and cans of soda for \$1.25. Which of the following inequalities represents the possible number of hot dogs, h, and sodas, s, Frank could sell in a day if his gross sales for the day exceed \$100?

   (A) $2.25h + 1.25s > 100$
   (B) $2.25h + 1.25s \geq 100$
   (C) $\dfrac{2.22}{h} + \dfrac{1.25}{s} > 100$
   (D) $\dfrac{2.22}{h} + \dfrac{1.25}{s} \geq 100$

6. Line segments $\overline{AB}$ and $\overline{CD}$ are both diameters of a circle that passes through the origin of a set of coordinate axes. If $\overline{AB}$ lies on the line whose equation is $y = 2x + 3$ and if $\overline{CD}$ lies on the line whose equation is $y = 3x + 2$, what is the area of the circle?

   (A) 5π
   (B) 25π
   (C) 26π
   (D) 50π

7. If in right $\triangle ABC$ with right angle C, $\sin A = \dfrac{3}{5}$, then what is the value of $\sin B$?

   (A) $\dfrac{3}{5}$
   (B) $\dfrac{4}{5}$
   (C) $\dfrac{5}{4}$
   (D) $\dfrac{4}{3}$

GO ON TO THE NEXT PAGE

DIAGNOSTIC TEST

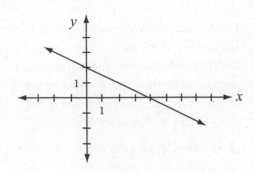

8. Which of the following is the equation of the line shown in the figure above?

(A) $y = -\frac{1}{2}x + 2$

(B) $y = \frac{1}{2}x + 2$

(C) $y = -\frac{1}{2}x + 4$

(D) $y = -2x + 4$

9. Which of the following are the solutions of the equation $4x^2 + 8x = 8$?

(A) $1 + \sqrt{2}$ and $1 - \sqrt{2}$

(B) $-1 + \sqrt{2}$ and $-1 - \sqrt{2}$

(C) $1 + \sqrt{3}$ and $1 - \sqrt{3}$

(D) $-1 + \sqrt{3}$ and $-1 - \sqrt{3}$

10. The number of cells growing in a particular Petri dish doubles every 30 minutes. If at 8:00 A.M. there were 60 cells in the dish, how many were there at noon of the same day?

(A) 60×2^4

(B) 60×4^2

(C) 60×4^4

(D) 60×4^8

11. Which of the following expressions is equivalent to $\frac{x+1}{x-1} - \frac{x-1}{x+1}$?

(A) $\frac{2}{x^2 - 1}$

(B) $\frac{2x}{x^2 - 1}$

(C) $\frac{4}{x^2 - 1}$

(D) $\frac{4x}{x^2 - 1}$

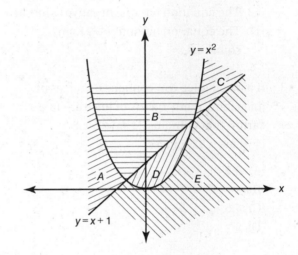

$$y \le x^2$$
$$y \ge x + 1$$

12. A pair of inequalities is shown above. Which region or regions on the graphs shown represent the solution set of the two inequalities?

(A) A and C

(B) B

(C) A, B, and C

(D) D

GO ON TO THE NEXT PAGE

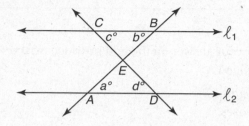

Note: Figure not drawn to scale.

13. In the figure above, lines l_1 and l_2 are parallel. Which of the following statements must be true?

(A) Triangles *AED* and *BEC* are congruent.
(B) Triangles *AED* and *BEC* are similar.
(C) Line segments $\overline{AB}$ and $\overline{CD}$ are perpendicular.
(D) $a = c$ and $b = d$

14. If a, b, c, and d are real numbers, if i is the imaginary unit, and if $(a + bi)(c + di)$ is a real number, which of the following statements must be true?

(A) $ac = bd$
(B) $ad = bc$
(C) $ac + bd = 0$
(D) $ad + bc = 0$

$$3x - 2y = 3y - 2$$
$$x + y = 10$$

15. If (x, y) is a solution of the system of equations above, what is the value of $\frac{x}{y}$?

(A) $\frac{1}{3}$

(B) $\frac{1}{2}$

(C) $\frac{2}{3}$

(D) $\frac{3}{2}$

GO ON TO THE NEXT PAGE

Grid-in Response Directions

In questions 16–20, first solve the problem, and then enter your answer on the grid provided on the answer sheet. The instructions for entering your answers follow.

- First, write your answer in the boxes at the top of the grid.
- Second, grid your answer in the columns below the boxes.
- Use the fraction bar in the first row or the decimal point in the second row to enter fractions and decimals.

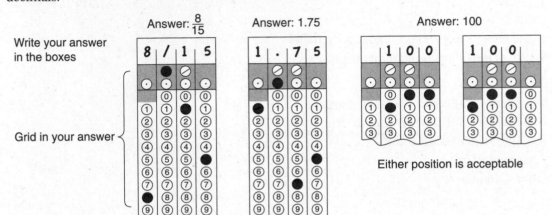

- Grid only one space in each column.
- Entering the answer in the boxes is recommended as an aid in gridding but is not required.
- The machine scoring your exam can read only what you grid, so you **must grid-in your answers correctly to get credit**.
- If a question has more than one correct answer, grid-in only one of them.
- The grid does not have a minus sign; so no answer can be negative.
- A mixed number *must* be converted to an improper fraction or a decimal before it is gridded.

    Enter $1\frac{1}{4}$ as 5/4 or 1.25; the machine will interpret 11/4 as $\frac{11}{4}$ and mark it wrong.

- **All decimals must be entered as accurately as possible.** Here are three acceptable ways of gridding

$$\frac{3}{11} = 0.272727\ldots$$

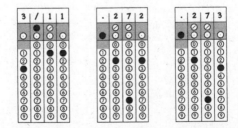

- Note that rounding to .273 is acceptable because you are using the full grid, but you would receive **no credit** for .3 or .27, because they are less accurate.

DIAGNOSTIC TEST

16. If $f(x) = x + 5$, for what value of a is $f(3a) + 2 = f(2a) + 3$?

17. If (a, b) is the vertex (turning point) of the parabola whose equation is $y = (x + 3)^2 + 3$, what is the value of $a + b$?

18. What is the value of $\left(\sqrt{x} \cdot \sqrt[3]{x}\right)^6$ when $x = 2$?

19. An amusement park has two payment options. Visitors to the park who use Plan A pay a $10 admission fee plus $3 for every ride they go on. Visitors who use Plan B pay a $20 admission fee and $1 per ride. What is the least number of rides a visitor must go on for Plan B to be less expensive?

$$x^2 + y^2 = 5$$
$$y = x^2 + 1$$

20. If (a, b) and (c, d) are the points of intersection of the circle and parabola whose equations are given above, what is the value of $a + b + c + d$?

If there is still time remaining, you may review your answers.

MATH TEST (CALCULATOR)

55 MINUTES, 38 QUESTIONS

Turn to Section 4 of your answer sheet to answer the questions in this section.

Directions: For questions 1–30, solve each problem and choose the best answer from the given options. Fill in the corresponding circle on your answer document. For questions 31–38, solve the problem and fill in the answer on the answer sheet grid.

Notes:
- Calculators **ARE PERMITTED** in this section.
- All variables and expressions represent real numbers unless indicated otherwise.
- All figures are drawn to scale unless indicated otherwise.
- All figures are in a plane unless indicated otherwise.
- Unless indicated otherwise, the domain of a given function is the set of all real numbers x for which the function has real values.

REFERENCE INFORMATION

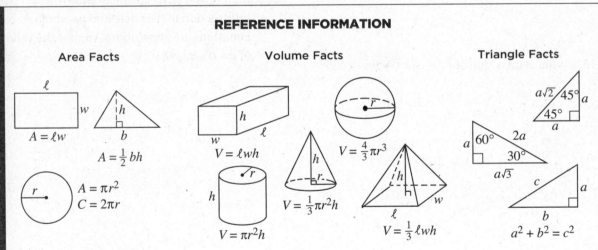

The arc of a circle contains 360°.

The arc of a circle contains 2π radians.

The sum of the measures of the angles in a triangle is 180°.

GO ON TO THE NEXT PAGE

1. A lacrosse team raised some money. The members used 74% of the money to buy uniforms, 18% for equipment, and the remaining $216 for a team party. How much money did the team raise?

   (A) $2,450
   (B) $2,500
   (C) $2,600
   (D) $2,700

Model	Number Sold (in 1,000's)
A	⊕⊕⊕⊕⊕⊕⊕⊕
B	⊕⊕⊕⊕⊕⊕⊕⊕⊕

2. If the selling price of model *B* is 60% more than the selling price of model *A*, what percent of the total sales do the sales of model *A* represent?

   (A) 25%
   (B) 36%
   (C) 40%
   (D) 50%

3. Hoover High School has 840 students, and the ratio of the number of students taking Spanish to the number not taking Spanish is 4:3. How many of the students take Spanish?

   (A) 360
   (B) 480
   (C) 560
   (D) 630

4. John was working at the registration desk of a conference that was scheduled to begin at 8:00 P.M. At 7:30, he texted the conference manager to report that only 20% of the registrants had signed in so far. At 7:45, he sent a second text stating that in the past 15 minutes, 90 additional people had signed in and that now 65% of the participants had arrived. Which of the following is closest to the total number of people who had registered for the conference?

   (A) 140
   (B) 200
   (C) 250
   (D) 450

5. Last year Jose sold a painting for $2,000. If he made a 25% profit on the sale, how much had he paid for the painting?

   (A) $1,500
   (B) $1,600
   (C) $2,400
   (D) $2,500

$$m + c < n < d - m$$

6. In the inequality above, *c* and *d* are constants. If $m = 1$ and $n = 2$ is a solution of the inequality, which of the following statements concerning *c* and *d* must be true?

   I. *cd* is negative
   II. $d - c > 2$
   III. $d + c > 2$

   (A) II only
   (B) I and II only
   (C) II and III only
   (D) I, II, and III

GO ON TO THE NEXT PAGE

D I A G N O S T I C   T E S T

<u>Questions 7 and 8 are based on the scatter plot</u>
below.

The scatter plot that shows the relationship
between a person's height at two years of age and
their height as an adult. The information provided
is for 10 people.

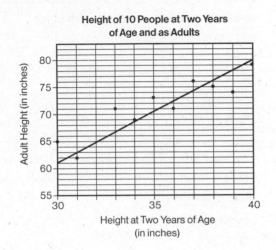

7. How many of the 10 people have an adult
   height that differs by more than 5% from the
   height predicted by the line of best fit?

   (A) 3
   (B) 4
   (C) 5
   (D) 6

8. Based on the line of best fit, which of the
   following is closest to the estimated adult
   height for a person whose height at two years
   old is 36.5 inches?

   (A) 72.5 inches
   (B) 73 inches
   (C) 74.0 inches
   (D) 74.4 inches

9. If the length and width of a rectangular
   solid are increased by 20% and the height
   is increased by 25%, by what percent is the
   volume of the solid increased?

   (A) 21.67%
   (B) 65%
   (C) 80%
   (D) 180%

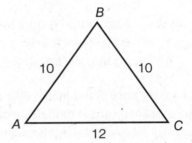

10. In the figure above, what is the value of sin A?

    (A) 0.2
    (B) 0.4
    (C) 0.6
    (D) 0.8

GO ON TO THE NEXT PAGE

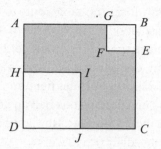

11. In the figure above, *ABCD*, *BEFG*, and *DHIJ* are squares with *AB* = 2(*DH*) and *DH* = 2(*BE*). If a point is chosen at random inside square *ABCD*, what is the probability it will be in the shaded region?

(A) $\frac{1}{2}$

(B) $\frac{5}{8}$

(C) $\frac{11}{16}$

(D) $\frac{3}{4}$

Questions 12–14 are based on the information in the following graphs.

Expenditures by the Central City School District

Expenditures per Student (in thousands of dollars)

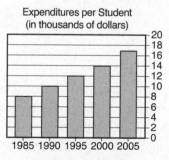

Total Expenditures (in millions of dollars)

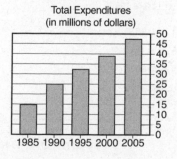

12. In 2005, 80% of the Central City School district's total expenditures came from local school taxes, and the rest came from the state government's Aid to Schools Program. If the state had reduced its aid to the district by 50%, by what percentage would local school taxes have had to be increased in order for the district to maintain the same level of expenditures?

(A) 10%
(B) 12.5%
(C) 20%
(D) 50%

13. From the graphs, it can be inferred that the number of students in the Central City School district in 1990 was closest to which of the following:

(A) 2,000
(B) 2,500
(C) 3,000
(D) 3,500

14. Based on the information in the two graphs, to the nearest hundredth of a percent, by what percent did the number of students in the Central City School district increase from 1985 to 1990?

(A) 25.00%
(B) 33.33%
(C) 50.00%
(D) 66.67%

GO ON TO THE NEXT PAGE

15. One week Susan earned $1,000, which consisted of a base salary of $475 and a 7% commission on her sales. What was the amount of her sales for that week?

(A) $36.75
(B) $75.25
(C) $6,786
(D) $7,500

16. Anthony drives the same route to work every day. Last Monday, he was able to drive at an average speed of 50 miles per hour. On Tuesday, due to heavy traffic, his average speed was only 30 miles per hour. As a result, the trip on Tuesday took half an hour longer than it did on Monday. How long, in miles, is Anthony's daily trip to work?

(A) 30
(B) 37.5
(C) 40
(D) 42.5

Questions 17 and 18 are based on the information in the graph below.

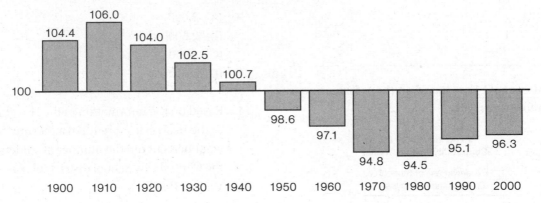

U.S. Population
Sex Ratio: 1900 to 2000
(Males per 100 females)

17. To the nearest tenth of one percent, in the year that males made up the smallest percent of the population, what percent of the population was female?

(A) 50.2%
(B) 50.6%
(C) 51.0%
(D) 51.4%

18. If in 2000 the population of the United States, to the nearest million, was 282,000,000, which of the following is closest to how many more females there were in the United States than males?

(A) 4,800,000
(B) 5,300,000
(C) 5,800,000
(D) 6,300,000

GO ON TO THE NEXT PAGE

19. If $i = \sqrt{-1}$, what is the value of i^{2016}?

    (A) $-i$
    (B) -1
    (C) 1
    (D) i

20. In 2014, Hamburger Heaven sold 20% more cheeseburgers that in 2013, and in 2014 the price of each cheeseburger they sold was 10% more than in 2013. The total income from the sale of cheeseburgers was what percent greater in 2014 than in 2013?

    (A) 20%
    (B) 22%
    (C) 30%
    (D) 32%

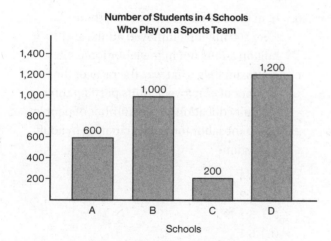

21. The bar graph above shows the number of students in four high schools who play on a school sports team. The number of students enrolled in schools *A, B, C,* and *D* are 1,500, 2,800, 550, and 3,300, respectively. In which school do the highest percent of the students play on a team?

    (A) *A*
    (B) *B*
    (C) *C*
    (D) *D*

Use the information below to answer questions 22 and 23.

At time $t = 0$, an object was launched from ground level directly upward. While the object was above the ground, its height in meters, h, after t seconds was given by the following equation: $h(t) = -4.9t^2 + 34.3t$.

22. How many seconds after it was launched did the object hit the ground?

    (A) 3
    (B) 5
    (C) 7
    (D) 9

23. For how long, to the nearest second, was the object at or above a height of 49 meters?

    (A) 1
    (B) 2
    (C) 3
    (D) 5

GO ON TO THE NEXT PAGE

DIAGNOSTIC TEST

24. If Adam can mow a large yard in 3 hours and Matthew can mow the same yard in 5 hours, when working together, how long will it take, in minutes, for the two boys to mow the yard?

(A) 92
(B) 112.5
(C) 132.5
(D) 240

25. At a summer camp, each girl is assigned to one of 48 cabins that in total can accommodate 344 campers. There are two types of cabins—small ones that can house 6 girls and large ones that can house 10 girls. Last summer even though 344 girls had registered for the camp, only 342 could come. So one of the large cabins had only 8 girls. How many more small cabins are there than large cabins?

(A) 12
(B) 16
(C) 20
(D) 24

Use the information in the following graph to answer questions 26 and 27.

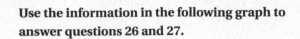

Adult Education Participation Rates in the Past 12 Months: 1991 and 1995

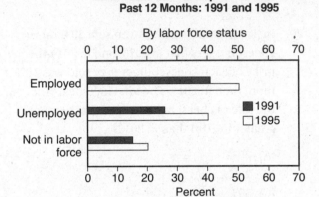

SOURCE: U.S. Department of Education

26. If, in the United States in 1995, there were 100 million employed adults and 40 million adults not in the labor force, then approximately what was the ratio of the number of employed adults participating in adult education to the number of people not in the labor force participating in adult education?

(A) 5:4
(B) 5:2
(C) 5:1
(D) 6:1

GO ON TO THE NEXT PAGE

27. Assume that in 1995 the unemployment rate was 8%, meaning that 8 out of every 100 adults in the workforce were unemployed. What percentage of adults in the labor force participated in adult education? Round your answer to the nearest whole percent.

(A) 32%

(B) 40%

(C) 49%

(D) 50%

28. When Camille, a French tourist, purchased a ring in a jewelry store in the United States, the jeweler told Camille that she had two options. She could take the ring with her, in which case he would have to charge her 6.5% sales tax, which would bring the total cost of the ring to $2,447.37. He could instead ship the ring to her home in Paris, in which case Camille wouldn't have to pay sales tax, but she would have to pay a $35 fee to cover postage and handling. How much did Camille save, rounded to the nearest dollar, by choosing to have the ring shipped to her home?

(A) $ 94

(B) $104

(C) $114

(D) $124

29. If (h, k) and r are the center and radius, respectively, of the circle whose equation is $(x + 3)^2 + (y + 4)^2 = 5$, to the nearest hundredth, what is the value of $h + k + r$?

(A) −4.76

(B) −2.00

(C) 9.24

(D) 12.00

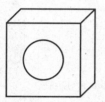

30. The volume of the nut in the diagram above is 0.2 cubic inches. If the sides of the nut's square face are 1 inch and the thickness of the nut is 0.25 inches, to the nearest hundredth of an inch what is the radius of the nut's circular hole?

(A) 0.25

(B) 0.27

(C) 0.30

(D) 0.33

GO ON TO THE NEXT PAGE

DIAGNOSTIC TEST

Grid-in Response Directions

In questions 31–38, first solve the problem, and then enter your answer on the grid provided on the answer sheet. The instructions for entering your answers follow.

- First, write your answer in the boxes at the top of the grid.
- Second, grid your answer in the columns below the boxes.
- Use the fraction bar in the first row or the decimal point in the second row to enter fractions and decimals.

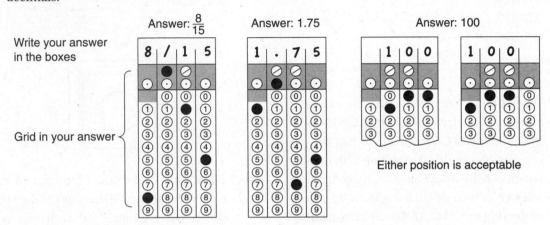

- Grid only one space in each column.
- Entering the answer in the boxes is recommended as an aid in gridding but is not required.
- The machine scoring your exam can read only what you grid, so you **must grid-in your answers correctly to get credit**.
- If a question has more than one correct answer, grid-in only one of them.
- The grid does not have a minus sign; so no answer can be negative.
- A mixed number *must* be converted to an improper fraction or a decimal before it is gridded.

  Enter $1\frac{1}{4}$ as 5/4 or 1.25; the machine will interpret 11/4 as $\frac{11}{4}$ and mark it wrong.

- **All decimals must be entered as accurately as possible.** Here are three acceptable ways of gridding

$$\frac{3}{11} = 0.272727\ldots$$

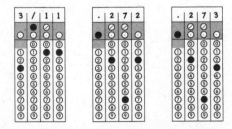

- Note that rounding to .273 is acceptable because you are using the full grid, but you would receive **no credit** for .3 or .27, because they are less accurate.

31. John received a tax refund of $900. He used 40% of it to pay some bills and used the rest to open a one-year savings certificate that paid 5% simple interest. At the end of the year, what was the value, in dollars, of the savings certificate?

32. The average (arithmetic mean) of a set of 9 numbers is 99. After one of the numbers is deleted from the set, the average of the remaining numbers is 89. What number was deleted?

33. A solid is formed by placing a pyramid on a cube. The height of the pyramid is 6 inches and the base of the pyramid is the top face of a cube whose edges are 4 inches. What is the total volume, in cubic inches, of this solid?

34. At a wedding reception, the men, women, and children could all choose either chicken, steak, or fish for their entrée. The table below shows the choices that were made.

	Men	Women	Children	Total
Chicken	17	22	30	69
Steak	15	26	37	78
Fish	32	38	10	80
Totals	64	86	77	227

What fraction of the adults did not order fish?

GO ON TO THE NEXT PAGE

DIAGNOSTIC TEST

35. If a and b are the two solutions of the equation $x^2 - 10x = 39$, what is the value of $a + b$?

36. If the base angles of an isosceles triangle measure 40°, and if the length of the congruent sides are 12, to the nearest tenth, what is the area of the triangle?

Use the following information to answer questions 37 and 38.

Michel sent Robert a check payable in euros. He asked Robert to put the money into a savings account in an American bank for one year. Robert converted the euros to dollars on a day when the exchange rate was $1.26 per euro. He used that money to purchase a one-year certificate of deposit (CD) that paid 3% interest.

37. When the CD matured exactly one year after he purchased it, Robert received $843.57. How many euros had Michel given Robert?

38. Robert sent Michel a check for the $843.57 he received when the CD matured. On the day that Michel converted the $843.57 back to euros, the exchange rate was $1.28 per euro. To the nearest euro, how much profit did Michel make on the entire transaction?

STOP

If there is still time remaining, you may review your answers.

Directions: This assignment will allow you to demonstrate your ability to skillfully read and understand a source text and write a response analyzing the source. In your response, you should show that you have understood the source, give proficient analysis, and use the English language effectively. If your essay is off-topic, it will not be scored.

Only what you write on the lined paper in your answer document will be scored—avoid skipping lines, using unreasonably large handwriting, and using wide margins in order to have sufficient space to respond. You can also write on the planning sheet in the answer document, but this will not be evaluated—no other scrap paper will be given. Be sure to write clearly and legibly so your response can be scored.

You will be given 50 minutes to complete the assignment, including reading the source text and writing your response.

Read the following passage, and think about how the author uses:

- Evidence, such as applicable examples, to justify the argument
- Reasoning to show logical connections among thoughts and facts
- Rhetoric, like sensory language and emotional appeals, to give weight to the argument

Vertical Expansion

1   It's no secret that our population is growing. From Malthusian theory, we know that any population will grow at an exponential rate, if allowed to. The larger our population gets, the faster our growth accelerates. So obviously, we need somewhere to put all of our new residents. So picture your favorite city; now, picture your favorite city, but this time, picture it in the future with the population doubled. Where did you imagine all of the new housing developments? How much more area does your new city cover? How unbearable has your morning commute into the city become? This kind of outward expansion is a problematic, antiquated model that we need to abandon for upward expansion.

2   Sure, at one time outward expansion was the only option. It wouldn't have even been particularly problematic in times of our early hunter-gatherer ancestors. City centers were still small and traveled solely by foot, so "traffic" would have been your group passing by another group also hunting mastodon, and your "morning commute" would have been however long it took you to find a berry patch you hadn't already picked over. Outward expansion was necessary as we continued to deplete the resources near our urban centers. Modern transportation nullified that need, as the necessities for life could be brought in over long distances. But as population boomed, cities had to continue expanding outward. However, this expansion model hasn't been necessary since the glorious implementation of the Otis elevator allowed us to start growing in three dimensions. It's time that architectural thinking catches up to our 21st century capabilities and needs.

3   If done correctly, vertical expansion would greatly decrease our need for cars. A "large city" would actually be made up of many "mini-communities." Each community would be a fairly self-serving network of high rises. Food would likely still need to be imported, but the people in each community would be able to walk to the grocery store. Residents would walk to work. Each community would have workers specialized in the various utilities. Each community would have a hospital, equipped with all of the staff necessary to provide medical care, all of who could walk to work. Each community would have a school, filled with teachers and students, all walking to work. The list could go on and on, but the idea is the same: each community would be its own miniature city rising high into the sky, taking up only a small plot of land. Because the residents could easily walk from home to work to wherever else they may need to go, cars would be rarely necessary. If cars weren't necessary, automobile traffic would become a thing of the past. Pollution from our cars would become a thing of the past. We would require fewer fossil fuels. We could convert parking lots to green spaces and parks. Obesity may even decline if we were to spend all of our morning commute walking up stairs, rather than sitting in a car.

4   Another, more subtle, benefit to this model is the improved sense of community that would likely result. If we were to constantly visit the same places, interact with the same people, and utilize the same businesses, we would get to know one another. This regular interaction with the same people is how hunter-gatherer groups prospered for millennia. Interpersonal tension would stay low, because as conflict would arise, people would leave their current communities and join new communities. It's not hard to imagine that an improved sense of community could even result in lower crime rates.

5   Even more important than decreasing our reliance on cars or improving sense of community, vertical expansion would preserve our farmland, and thus our food sources. If both Chicago and Indianapolis expanded their radii by fewer than 100 miles, they would spill into one another. All of the farmland between the two would be gone. It's a rather scary enigma: we expand our cities because our population is growing, yet we decrease our ability to sustain ourselves by doing so. Vertical expansion would allow for growth, without the disastrous effects on farmland, and thus our well-being.

6   So again, imagine your favorite city in the future. But this time imagine it with very little traffic. Your morning commute is a pleasant walk, rather than an hour of road rage. Everyone you pass on the sidewalk is a familiar, smiling face. Everywhere you go in the city, you feel safe and "at home." It also doesn't hurt that you're not starving because we still have farmland between cities. Now please remind me why we continue to allow this archaic expansion model to dominate.

Write a response that demonstrates how the author makes an argument to persuade an audience that vertical expansion of urban areas is a good idea. In your response, analyze how the author uses at least one of the features from the essay directions (or features of your own choosing) to develop a logical and persuasive argument. Be certain that your response cites relevant aspects of the source text.

Your response should not give your personal opinion on the merit of the source text, but instead show how the author crafts an argument to persuade readers.

ANSWER KEY
Diagnostic Test

Section 1: Reading

1.	B	14.	B	27.	D	40.	C
2.	C	15.	B	28.	D	41.	B
3.	B	16.	A	29.	C	42.	A
4.	C	17.	C	30.	C	43.	C
5.	D	18.	B	31.	D	44.	D
6.	B	19.	B	32.	B	45.	D
7.	D	20.	D	33.	B	46.	C
8.	D	21.	C	34.	C	47.	D
9.	B	22.	B	35.	C	48.	D
10.	D	23.	D	36.	C	49.	B
11.	A	24.	C	37.	A	50.	C
12.	B	25.	D	38.	A	51.	C
13.	A	26.	C	39.	B	52.	A

Number Correct _____

Number Incorrect _____

Section 2: Writing and Language

1.	C	12.	B	23.	D	34.	D
2.	A	13.	B	24.	B	35.	C
3.	B	14.	C	25.	B	36.	A
4.	A	15.	C	26.	A	37.	C
5.	C	16.	D	27.	C	38.	A
6.	C	17.	A	28.	D	39.	D
7.	A	18.	D	29.	D	40.	A
8.	C	19.	A	30.	B	41.	C
9.	C	20.	D	31.	C	42.	C
10.	B	21.	B	32.	D	43.	D
11.	D	22.	C	33.	A	44.	A

Number Correct _____

Number Incorrect _____

DIAGNOSTIC TEST

Section 3: Math (No Calculator)

1. **A**	5. **A**	9. **D**	13. **B**
2. **A**	6. **C**	10. **C**	14. **D**
3. **C**	7. **B**	11. **D**	15. **D**
4. **B**	8. **A**	12. **A**	

16. **1** 17. **0** 18. **32** 19. **6**

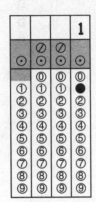

20. **4**

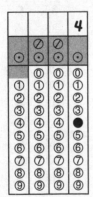

Number Correct _____

Number Incorrect _____

Section 4: Math (Calculator)

1. **D**	7. **A**	13. **B**	19. **C**	25. **C**
2. **B**	8. **B**	14. **B**	20. **D**	26. **D**
3. **B**	9. **C**	15. **D**	21. **A**	27. **C**
4. **B**	10. **D**	16. **B**	22. **C**	28. **C**
5. **B**	11. **C**	17. **D**	23. **C**	29. **A**
6. **A**	12. **B**	18. **B**	24. **B**	30. **A**

31. **567**

32. **179**

33. **96**

34. $\frac{8}{15}$ or **.533**

or

35. **10**

36. **70.9**

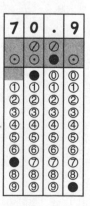

DIAGNOSTIC TEST

37. **650**   38. **9**

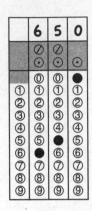

Number Correct   _____

Number Incorrect _____

SCORE ANALYSIS

Reading and Writing Test

Section 1: Reading $\dfrac{}{\text{\# correct}} = \dfrac{}{\text{raw score}}$ (A)

Section 2: Writing $\dfrac{}{\text{\# correct}} = \dfrac{}{\text{raw score}}$ (B)

To find your Reading and Writing test scores, consult the chart below: find the ranges in which your raw scores lie and read across to find the ranges of your test scores.

$$\underbrace{}_{\substack{\text{range of reading} \\ \text{test scores}}} + \underbrace{}_{\substack{\text{range of writing} \\ \text{test scores}}} = \underbrace{}_{\substack{\text{range of reading + writing} \\ \text{test scores}}} \text{(C)}$$

To find the range of your Reading and Writing Scaled Score, multiply (C) by 10.

Test Scores for the Reading and Writing Sections

Reading Raw Score	Writing Raw Score	Test Score
44–52	39–44	35–40
36–43	33–38	31–34
30–35	28–32	28–30
24–29	22–27	24–27
19–23	17–21	21–23
14–18	13–16	19–20
9–13	9–12	16–18
5–8	5–8	13–15
less than 5	less than 5	10–12

Math Test

Section 3: $\dfrac{}{\text{\# correct}} = \dfrac{}{\text{raw score}}$ (D)

Section 4: $\dfrac{}{\text{\# correct}} = \dfrac{}{\text{raw score}}$ (E)

Total Math raw score: (D) + (E) = _____

To find your Math Scaled Score, consult the chart below: find the range in which your raw score lies and read across to find the range for your scaled score.

Scaled Scores for the Math Test

Raw Score	Scaled Score	Raw Score	Scaled Score
50–58	700–800	20–25	450–490
44–49	650–690	15–19	400–440
38–43	600–640	11–14	350–390
32–37	550–590	7–10	300–340
26–32	500–540	less than 7	200–290

ANSWERS EXPLAINED

Section 1: Reading Test

1. **(B)** The passage as a whole is a portrait of Charlotte Stanhope's moral and intellectual temperament or character. Following the initial paragraph, the opening sentence of each subsequent paragraph describes some aspect of her behavior or character that the paragraph then goes on to develop. Remember, when asked to find the main idea, be sure to check the opening and summary sentences of each paragraph. Choice (A) is incorrect. The passage does not emphasize the reasons behind the Stanhopes' return to England. Choice (C) is incorrect. The passage analyzes Charlotte; it discusses the members of her family only in relationship to her. Choice (D) is incorrect. While Charlotte has her virtues, the passage stresses her faults. Likewise, while her family may not be described as admirable, nothing suggests that they are disreputable (not respectable; infamous).

2. **(C)** Think of the old rhyme "For want of a nail the shoe was lost. For want of a shoe the horse was lost." It was for *lack* of a nail that the horseshoe fell off and was lost. The Stanhopes' heartlessness reflects their *lack* of feeling. Choice (A) is incorrect. Although "want" may mean hardship, as in wishing for freedom from want, that is not how the word is used here. Choice (B) is incorrect. Although "want" may mean desire, as in expressing our wants and desires, that is not how the word is used here. Choice (D) is incorrect. Although "want" may mean necessity, as in the phrase "My wants are few," that is not how the word is used here.

3. **(B)** The Stanhopes are more interested in having the appearance of performing charitable acts than in performing the acts themselves. Thus, they are willing to visit the sick as long as in doing so they are in no danger of contracting the sickness themselves. The parenthetic comment emphasizes *how little the Stanhopes actually cared for their sick neighbors.* Choice (A) is incorrect. The Stanhopes do not avoid visiting contagious neighbors because of any extreme fear of infectious disease. They avoid these visits because they do not care enough about their sick neighbors to take the slightest risk for them. Choice (C) is incorrect. The author is not commending the Stanhopes for being careful to avoid disease. Instead, he is ironically mocking them, pointing out the hypocrisy of their "compassionately" visiting the sick as long as it costs them nothing. Choice (D) is incorrect. The author is not making an excuse for the Stanhopes' behavior. He is underscoring how heartless and uncaring they are.

4. **(C)** After describing the Stanhopes' actual indifference to the well-being of their neighbors, the opening paragraph goes on to state that "[t]heir conduct to each other was the same as to the world." In other words, their conduct to each other *showed the same lack of affection that typified their conduct to their neighbors.* Choice (A) is incorrect. The opening paragraph emphasizes the Stanhopes' heartlessness, not their concern for their relatives' well-being. Choice (B) is incorrect. The passage explicitly states that "[t]heir conduct to each other was the same as to the world." They were not more loving to one another than they were to outsiders. Choice (D) is incorrect. The passage states that the Stanhopes would visit their sick neighbors with novels and fresh oranges; it never mentions their treatment of other members of the family.

5. **(D)** The Stanhopes' "conduct to each other was the same as to the world." We already know that the Stanhopes' conduct or behavior to the world is indifferent at best. They are heartless, lacking in true sympathy for their fellows. In lines 15–20 we learn that the Stanhopes' heartlessness extends to the way they treat one another: their behavior to members of their family shows *the same lack of affection that typified their conduct to their neighbors,* for their "conduct to each other was the same as (their conduct) to the world." "(T)hey bore and forbore." In other words, they endured or put up with one another, and patiently restrained any impulses they might have had to harm one another actively, but they did nothing to promote one another's well-being.

6. **(B)** The author presents Charlotte *candidly* and openly: her faults are not concealed. The author also presents her *satirically:* her weaknesses and those of her family are mocked or made fun of. If you find the characters in a passage foolish or pompous, the author may well be writing satirically. Choice (A) is incorrect. While the author is concerned with Charlotte's moral character, he is not *moralistic* or *self-righteous* in tone; he is describing her character, not preaching a sermon against her. Choice (C) is incorrect. The author is not *sympathetic* to Charlotte's faults; his tone definitely is not *sentimental* or emotionally excessive in describing her. Choice (D) is incorrect. While the author's tone is not highly emotional, it is more appropriate to describe it as satiric than to describe it as *indifferent and unfeeling.*

7. **(D)** Charlotte is a freethinker, a person who rejects accepted opinions, especially those concerning religious belief, but her clergyman father still has something left of his Church of England faith. Not much of it remains, however, for he is troubled in mind about what he believes. Choice (A) is incorrect. There is no comparison made between the two elder Stanhopes. Both are *indolent* (lazy). Choice (B) is incorrect. Since only Charlotte could persuade her father to look after his affairs (lines 39–41), he apparently was willing to let her manage matters for him and willingly surrendered his authority. Choice (C) is incorrect. There is no evidence in the passage that Dr. Stanhope feels regret or remorse.

8. **(D)** Lines 77–85 mention the troubled mind of Dr. Stanhope and state that Charlotte would have enjoyed shaking "*what remained* of his Church of England faith." The phrase "what remained" implies that little is left of Dr. Stanhope's original religious faith.

9. **(B)** Lines 69–71 state that Charlotte "had thoroughly succeeded in spoiling her brother, and turning him loose upon the world an idle man without a profession." Young Master Stanhope has been encouraged to be *lazy* and to have no desire to work for a living. Choice (A) is incorrect. Nothing in the passage indicates that Charlotte's brother is especially *foolish.* Choice (C) is incorrect. There is nothing to suggest that being without a profession saddens Charlotte's brother or causes him to feel *dejected.* Choice (D) is incorrect. Charlotte's brother is specifically described as idle. Nothing in the passage suggests that he is *irreverent* or irreligious.

10. **(D)** By describing Charlotte as a pure freethinker, the narrator wishes to convey that she is a total or *absolute* freethinker, one who *absolutely* rejects any belief in religion. Choices (A) (*uncontaminated*), (B) (*wholesome*), and (C) (*virtuous*) make no sense as descriptive terms to apply to a freethinker.

11. **(A)** The first paragraph emphasizes that Charlotte "in no way affected the graces of youth." Her manner is that of an assured mistress of a household, not a flirt. Thus,

the passage clearly does not suggest that Charlotte's character demonstrates *an inappropriate flirtatiousness.* Choice (B) is incorrect. Charlotte is a freethinker (one who denies established beliefs) and thus lacks reverence or respect for religion. Choice (C) is incorrect. Charlotte is concerned with her family's worldly well-being and makes her father attend to his material concerns. Thus, she has a materialistic nature. Choice (D) is incorrect. Charlotte manages everything and everybody.

12. **(B)** The opening sentence states that paleontologists "have been trying to build 3-D visualizations of fossils" for years. They have been doing so "to build up a three-dimensional picture of what's hidden inside" (lines 18–20). Thus, the purpose of serial grinding was to enable paleontologists to visualize and *analyze the interior of fossil specimens.* Choice (A) is incorrect. Although serial grinding destroyed the fossil specimens, paleontologists did not grind the fossils in order to get rid of or dispose of them. Choices (C) and (D) are incorrect. Neither is suggested by the passage.

13. **(A)** Serial grinding wears away a solid fossil, layer by layer, exposing its interior. By taking photographs of each newly exposed layer, William Sollas was able to analyze what lay inside fossil specimens and, in time, to create three-dimensional models of these specimens. Only choice A supports the idea that the purpose of serial grinding was to enable paleontologists to *analyze the interior of fossil specimens.*

14. **(B)** When the fossil and rock surrounding it are stubbornly similar, they *persist* in looking so alike that ordinary CT scanners cannot differentiate between them. They are *persistently* similar, and can be distinguished from one another only by using a more sophisticated machine, such as a synchrotron. Choices (A), (C), and (D) are incorrect. *Pigheadedly, willfully,* and *perversely* all have a sense of conscious volition about them. People are described as pigheaded, willful, even perverse; fossils and rocks are not.

15. **(B)** Modern methods of fossil analysis are definitely *less damaging* to fossils than serial grinding, which totally destroys the fossil being analyzed. They are also *more detailed* than serial grinding: the level of control provided by synchrotrons, for example, "allows scientists to . . . coax out detail from even the most stubborn structures hidden within rock." Choice (A) is incorrect. Serial grinding was markedly time-consuming. In no way could it be considered more efficient than modern methods of fossil analysis. Choice (C) is incorrect. While modern methods of fossil analysis definitely are less time-consuming than serial grinding, nothing in the passage suggests that these modern methods are less reliable than Sollas's serial grinding technique. If anything, they are more reliable than serial grinding. Choice (D) is incorrect. Modern methods of fossil analysis both take less time than serial grinding did and are far less destructive of the fossils being analyzed.

16. **(A)** In coaxing out detail from difficult to analyze fossil specimens, the scientists are *extracting* information from these specimens. Choices (B) and (C) are incorrect. Although "coax" may be used in the sense of *persuade* or *flatter* ("She coaxed her father into letting her drive his car.") that is not how it is used here. Choice (D) is incorrect. To *plead* is to make an emotional appeal or to argue a point. It is not a synonym for to coax.

17. **(C)** Use the process of elimination to answer this question. A *hypothesis* is a proposed explanation made based on limited evidence as a starting point for further investigation. The assertion that "[t]he discoveries are more than just pretty pictures" is neither an explanation of anything, nor is it a starting point for any additional study. Therefore,

you can eliminate choice (A). A *paradox* is a statement that, despite apparently sound reasoning based on logical premises, leads to a seemingly illogical, self-contradictory conclusion. The assertion that "[t]he discoveries are more than just pretty pictures" is definitely not a paradox. Therefore, you can eliminate choice (B). In making the assertion, the author definitely is not rephrasing or restating a question. Therefore, you can eliminate choice (D). Only choice (C) is left. It is the correct answer. The author is emphasizing the point that the scans of fossil interior are not just pretty pictures. They are more than that. They are a source of important data for biologists, data that will help us understand how life forms have evolved.

18. **(B)** Nothing in the table indicates how much each of these forms of analysis costs to use. Therefore, it should be immediately clear that the correct answer is choice (B). You can also work out the correct answer by using the process of elimination to answer this question. Does the table contain information that would help you answer the question "Which form of analysis would be most damaging to a fossil being studied?" Yes, it indicates that serial grinding is destructive, while the other forms listed are not. You can eliminate choice (A). Does the table contain information that would help you answer the question "Which form of analysis offers the finest level of resolution?" Yes, it shows the levels of resolution for five separate techniques. The finest level of resolution clearly is offered by synchrotron-based tomography. You can eliminate choice (C). Does the table contain information that would help you answer the question "Of the forms of analysis listed, which was the earliest to be employed?" Yes, the introductory sentence that describes the table states that older forms of analysis destroy the fossil; the table lists only serial grinding as destructive. Thus, you can logically conclude that, of the forms of analysis listed, serial grinding, an older form of analysis, was the earliest technique that scientists used. You can eliminate choice (D). Only choice (B) is left. It is the correct answer.

19. **(B)** Clearly, the speediest method of high-resolution scanning listed is synchrotron-based tomography, with a scan time of only minutes.

20. **(D)** The two paragraphs describing Cunningham's work scanning rocks from the Doushantuo formation stress that Cunningham has reached no final conclusion about the nature of the blobs he is analyzing. His results are therefore best described as *tentative* (not final; provisional). Choice (A) is incorrect. Nothing in the passage suggests that Cunningham's results are *anomalous* (irregular; abnormal). Choice (B) is incorrect. Nothing in the passage suggests that Cunningham's results are *definitive* (conclusive). Further analysis is needed before Cunningham's team can come to a definite conclusion. Choice (C) is incorrect. Nothing in the passage suggests that Cunningham's results are *unsatisfactory*.

21. **(C)** This sentence describes the results of Cunningham's "virtual dissection" of the blobs, stating they *may be* the nuclei of ancient cells. Cunningham and his team are not presenting their results as a final, definitive assertion about the nature of the blobs. Instead, they are presenting a *tentative*, provisional statement of what their scans have revealed. Choice (A) is incorrect. Lines 34–38 are a general introduction to paleontologist John Cunningham as someone who uses sophisticated scanning technology. They do not mention results of any specific research. Choice (B) is incorrect. While lines 51–56 introduce the topic of Cunningham's Doushantuo research, they say nothing about the

results of his study. Choice (D) is incorrect. Lines 75–79 deal with Cunningham's work on a different, younger collection of fossils.

22. **(B)** The author describes his rapture or great joy when he first saw his new owner's smiling face. Clearly, his immediate response to the prospect of living with the Aulds was chiefly one of *marked* (distinct) *pleasure*. Choice (A) is incorrect. Though Mrs. Auld's smiling face was a new and strange sight to young Frederick, he reacted to it with sheer joy, not with *absolute astonishment*. Choice (C) is incorrect. Frederick was not *nonchalant* (blasé; unconcerned) about his new owner's response to him; he was overjoyed that she greeted him with a smile. Choice (D) is incorrect. Frederick was joyful rather than *quietly resigned* (submissive and accepting).

23. **(D)** Mrs. Auld has applied herself to her business or trade of weaving. She has *concentrated on this trade*. Because she has not owned slaves but has kept herself busy with her own work, she has been relatively unaffected by slavery and has not adopted the inhumane attitudes typical of slave owners. Choice (A) is incorrect. Nothing in the passage suggests that Mrs. Auld was brought up as an abolitionist. Choices (B) and (C) are incorrect. There is nothing in the passage to suggest that either wealth or maternal experience would have kept Mrs. Auld free of the inhumane attitudes typical of slave owners.

24. **(C)** Lines 23–26 state that "by application to her business, she [Mrs. Auld] had been in a good degree preserved from the blighting and dehumanizing effects of slavery." Involved in weaving, she worked on her own, without the help of slave labor. This saved her from contracting the typical slave owner's mentality. Choice (A) is incorrect. This sentence describes how Mrs. Auld first reacted to seeing Frederick. It does not offer an explanation of why she reacted to him so humanely. Choice (B) is incorrect. This sentence continues to describe Mrs. Auld's kind nature. It does not explain what made her so unlike other slaveholders in her initial behavior. Choice (D) is incorrect. These two sentences continue to describe Mrs. Auld's kind treatment of slaves. They do not explain what made her so unlike other slaveholders in her initial behavior.

25. **(D)** The sentences immediately following Douglass's comment about his early instruction clarify what he had been taught. He had been taught to behave in a slavish, *obsequious* fashion. However, "[h]er favor was not gained by it [crouching servility]; she seemed to be disturbed by it" (lines 32–34). In other words, the *obsequiousness* in which Douglass had been drilled *distressed his new mistress*. Choice (D) is correct. Choice (A) is incorrect. Although Douglass's early instruction failed to include reading and writing, that lack of instruction was customary. Choice (B) is incorrect. Nothing in the passage suggests that Douglass was unprepared to take adequate care of the Aulds' young son. Choice (C) is incorrect. Nothing in the passage indicates that Douglass's early instruction had been superseded by new instructions.

26. **(C)** Douglass hardly knows how to behave toward Mrs. Auld. Why is that? His "early instruction was all out of place." In other words, the ways he, as a young slave, had been taught to behave no longer fit the situation. How had he been taught to behave? He had been taught to behave like a slave, with "crouching servility," for slaves were expected to keep their heads bent low, and to put on the appearance of being happy to serve their masters. However, when he acted in this way, it did not please his mistress. Instead,

it seemed to upset her. Clearly, choice (C) provides the best evidence to explain why Douglass felt his early instruction no longer worked.

27. **(D)** Fawning and cringing did not *serve* the purpose of pleasing Mrs. Auld; such slavish behavior did not do at all in this particular situation. Choices (A), (B), and (C) are incorrect. Although *acknowledge, retort,* and *reply* all are possible synonyms for *answer,* none of them fit in the given context.

28. **(D)** According to Douglass, at the time he met her, Mrs. Auld was a kind, loving woman who had not yet had the experience of owning slaves. Thus, she had been kept free of "the blighting and dehumanizing effects of slavery" (lines 25–26). However, she now owned a slave—Douglass himself—and would inevitably be affected by her power over him. Her kind heart would cease to be kind: she *was destined to undergo a change of character* as she became corrupted by her participation in the institution of slavery. Choices (A), (B), and (C) are incorrect. They are wholly unsupported by the passage.

29. **(C)** The passage does not suggest that a *disdain* (scorn) *for convention* is typical of Mrs. Auld. Mrs. Auld was noted for "constant application to her business" (lines 23–24). This implies that *diligence* (industriousness) *in labor* was one of her characteristics. Therefore, choice (A) is incorrect. Mrs. Auld seemed "disturbed" by "crouching servility" (line 30). This implies that a *dislike of fawning* (cringing and flattering) was one of her characteristics. Therefore, choice (B) is incorrect. Mrs. Auld voluntarily began to teach young Frederick. She wished him well. This implies that a *benevolent* (kindly) *nature* was one of her characteristics. Therefore, choice (D) is incorrect.

30. **(C)** The author's purpose in this passage is to show how he discovered that learning to read was vital for him if he wanted to be free. The bulk of the passage deals with learning to read—the author's introduction to it, his master's arguments against it, his own increased determination to succeed in it. Choice (A) is incorrect. It is the cause of the disagreement between the Aulds that is central to the passage, not the existence of the disagreement. Choice (B) is incorrect. The author lists, but does not analyze, his master's reasons for forbidding his wife to teach her slave. Choice (D) may seem a possible answer, but it is too narrow in scope. Only the last two sentences of the first paragraph stress Mrs. Auld's moral downfall. The emphasis throughout the passage is on the narrator and his growing determination to be free.

31. **(D)** Douglass states that his master "was deeply sensible of the truths he was uttering." In other words, his master was highly *conscious* (mindful; aware) that he was saying the truth; he felt sure that only evil consequences would come from teaching a slave to read. Choices (A), (B), and (C) are incorrect. Although *logical, prudent,* and *intelligent* all are possible synonyms for *sensible,* none of them fit in the given context.

32. **(B)** The author's tone is strongly ironic. He knows full well that, in opposing his education, his master did not intend to benefit him. Thus, by acknowledging his "debt" to his master, the author is underlining his master's defeat. His tone is *cutting and ironic.* Choice (A) is incorrect. The author is not filled with loving sentiment and warmth when he thinks of his harsh master. Choice (C) is incorrect. The author neither whines nor congratulates himself on his own moral superiority. Choice (D) is incorrect. The author is not resigned or submissive; he certainly is not wistful or longing for the days gone by.

33. **(B)** The introductory note preceding the passages lists Susan Milius as the author of these articles. She is not mentioned in the articles as one of the academic researchers involved in these studies. It is reasonable to conclude that she is a science writer, someone *knowledgeable about research into the effects of human actions on wildlife*, but not personally involved in academic investigations. Choice (A) is incorrect. The author is not presenting the results of her own research; she is summarizing the research of others. Choice (C) is incorrect. The author is an objective reporter, not an advocate campaigning for a particular cause. Choice (D) is incorrect. Nothing in the passage suggests the author has any technical expertise in audiology.

34. **(C)** Look at the context in which "left" appears. The approach of comparing animals near roads with animals in rural settings "left questions about how much of the difference came from noise instead of from artificial lights, exhaust fumes, or other non-noisy aspects." In other words, this approach *failed to answer* or take into account such questions. Choice (A) is incorrect. The approach didn't simply *abandon* these questions; it failed to consider them. Choice (B) is incorrect. The approach didn't *go away from* these questions; it failed to raise them at all. Choice (D) is incorrect. It makes no sense in the context.

35. **(C)** Barber and his colleagues take great pains to create an environment in which the presence of noise is the single factor that affects the wildlife populations whose behavior they are studying. Thus, the basic question about wildlife and noise they sought to investigate was *the degree to which mere* (only) *noise affected wildlife populations.* Choice (A) is incorrect. The noise in question is noise produced by humans and human-made machines, not noise produced by wildlife species. Choice (B) is incorrect. Barber's team is studying the impact of noise, not the impact of highway construction. Choice (D) is incorrect. Barber's experiment took place in a wholly rural environment.

36. **(C)** Barber and his colleagues are attempting to study the effect of just noise on wildlife. Not the effect of noise and light, not the effect of noise and traffic fumes, simply the effect of noise on its own. Which statement best supports this claim? Clearly, choice (C), which states that the group "created a highway that was nothing but the noise," and that they created this phantom road so that they could directly test the effects of sound (the recorded traffic noise) on the wildlife population.

37. **(A)** In order to discover the degree to which just noise affected wildlife populations, it was necessary for Barber and his colleagues to *isolate noise from other human-caused factors affecting wildlife behavior.* Choice (B) is incorrect. Barber's team did not have to construct a physical road. What they needed was a virtual road, a highway of sound, not of asphalt or concrete. Choice (C) is incorrect. Barber's team had no need to reproduce previous studies. They needed to construct a new experiment, one that eliminated variables such as artificial lights and exhaust fumes so that they could see what effect mere noise had on wildlife behavior. Choice (D) is incorrect. They had no need to investigate wildlife populations in all three regions.

38. **(A)** By saying that "challenging" was Barber's *restrained* way of describing the travails of setting up the experiment, the author indicates that Barber's use of the word was *an understatement* (figure of speech in which a writer or speaker deliberately makes a situation seem less important or serious than it is, in process drawing attention to it). Here, by saying that setting up the experiment was "challenging," Barber calls attention

to how *extremely* hard it was to set it up. Choice (B) is incorrect. Barber is not drawing an analogy (making a comparison, typically to clarify or explain something). Choice (C) is incorrect. A simile is a figure of speech involving the comparison of one thing with another thing of a different kind. Similes are used to make descriptions more emphatic or vivid. Choice (D) is incorrect. A fallacy is a mistaken belief, often one based on unsound arguments.

39. **(B)** The speakers were mounted or *installed* (fixed in position) in a row along the ridge. The correct answer is choice B. Choice (A) is incorrect. Although *mounted* may mean *ascended,* as in "she mounted the steps," that is not how it is used here. Choice (C) is incorrect. Although *mounted* may mean *launched,* as in "they mounted an attack on the enemy," that is not how it is used here. Choice (D) is incorrect. Although *mounted* may mean *increased,* as in "our excitement mounted," that is not how it is used here.

40. **(C)** The horizontal axis of the graph indicates the noise level in decibels. The graph's vertical axis indicates the average number of birds present in the area per survey. The dark square represents the times when the road sound was turned on. From the graph you can see that when the noise level exceeded 55 decibels, the number of yellow warblers visiting the area plummeted. Indeed, on two occasions, *no* yellow warblers were spotted by observers. Thus, the statement *The greater the road noise, the more likely the yellow warblers were to avoid the area* most accurately summarizes the information presented in the graph. Choice (A) is incorrect. On one occasion, observers noted the presence of yellow warblers despite the presence of traffic noise. Choice (B) is incorrect. The graph suggests the opposite to be true. Choice (D) is incorrect. The graph clearly indicates that noise levels of roughly 55 decibels strongly affected the yellow warblers.

41. **(B)** Passage 2's first paragraph asserts that traffic noise caused the shiners to be unable to detect some important sounds. Its second paragraph makes it clear exactly what important sounds they missed: the "courtship growls" that enabled the shiners to locate mates. Thus, we can infer that the impact of noise on the shiners was negative because it interfered with their *mating patterns.* Choices (A) and (D) are incorrect. Nothing in the passage suggests that noise affected the shiners' *sense of direction* or their *avoidance of danger.* Choice (C) is incorrect. It makes no sense in the context.

42. **(A)** The birds under observation were free to fly wherever they chose; the shiners were confined to tanks in a laboratory. Unlike the shiners, the birds were *able to avoid the noise being broadcast.* Choice (B) is incorrect. Nothing in the passage suggests the birds were *more sensitive to recorded sound* than the shiners were. Choice (C) is incorrect. The author of the second passage raises the possibility that the shiners (*not* the birds) might suffer permanent hearing loss. Choice (D) is incorrect. Nothing in the passage suggests the birds were *less able to assess unfamiliar habitats.*

43. **(C)** In the opening paragraph the writer speaks of the Gothic world in terms of play and extravagance, of the fantastic and the luxurious. In other words, he speaks of it in terms of its *elaborateness of fancy* or fantasy.

44. **(D)** For architecture to reach "a point of extravagance unequalled in history" is for it to reach a *stage* or degree of lavishness and excess without an equal.

45. **(D)** The tapestries combine worldly elements (mythological beasts that symbolize lust and ferocity, wild creatures that symbolize fertility) with spiritual ones (the lady

who embodies chastity) to express "the power of love." Choice (A) is incorrect. It is unsupported by the passage. Choice (B) is incorrect. Though the Gothic imagination has a "sharp sense of reality" (line 16), it is more inclined to be playful than to be practical. Choice (C) is incorrect. Nothing in the passage suggests that wall hangings are wasteful.

46. **(C)** Why does the author think that the Unicorn tapestries exemplify the essence of the Gothic imagination? Early in the passage the author says that high Gothic art "can look fantastic and luxurious." He then goes on to say that this high Gothic fantasy can be seen in the tapestries known as *The Lady with the Unicorn.* Lines 29–35 describe the tapestry. The unicorn, a creature of fantasy, symbolizes lust; the lion symbolizes fierceness (ferocity). They are tamed by the lady, who symbolizes chastity. In this way, the tapestries *combine worldly elements* (lust and fierceness) with *spiritual elements* (chastity) *in an allegorical celebration of love.*

47. **(D)** The tapestries are known as *The Lady with the Unicorn.* In the central tapestry, the lion and the unicorn kneel before the lady, who gently, irresistibly, subdues the forces of nature.

48. **(D)** "To draw carts of stones up the hill for the building of Chartres Cathedral" is to *haul the stones used to construct the cathedral.* In doing such hard manual labor, the noble knights and ladies showed the depth of their conviction or belief.

49. **(B)** The author contrasts the graceful, unassuming figure of St. Modeste with the stubby, thickset female figures carved on the font at Winchester. Clearly the figures carved on Chartres' north portal indicate *a marked change in the image of women.* Choice (A) is incorrect. Although several of the female figures carved on the north portal of Chartres represent Old Testament heroines (Judith, Esther), nothing in the passages suggests that their presence indicates *a rejection of New Testament heroines.* Choice (C) is incorrect. The author asserts that the positive, graceful image of femininity visible on Chartres' north portal is something new: an image of human rapport between men and women appears there "for almost the first time in visual art." Therefore, the figures on the north portal do not represent a *return to an earlier, typical perspective on women.* Choice (D) is incorrect. While Blanche of Castile may have provided financial support for the north portal's decoration, the passage does not indicate she was one of the sculptors whose *artistic endeavors* created the carved figures.

50. **(C)** In lines 69–78, the author contrasts two different physical images of women—one squat and grumpy, the other graceful and serene—to make clear how very different a view of womankind the carvings at Chartres present. Choice (A) is incorrect. The sentence discusses the north portal but has no information about the carvings or about what they might represent. Choice (B) is incorrect. The sentence mentions that many of the carved figures are women but gives no additional information about them. Choice (D) is incorrect. In these lines the author describes one of the carved figures from Chartres. He provides no evidence that the carved figures at Chartres significantly differ from earlier carvings found at other historic sites.

51. **(C)** Consider the context in which "faculties" appears. "Of the two or three faculties that have been added to the European mind since the civilization of Greece and Rome, none seems to me more inexplicable than the sentiment of ideal or courtly love." The author is saying that the sentiment of courtly love was a new *mode of thought* or way of thinking about the relationship between man and woman. It was a totally new concept,

something wholly alien to classical or early medieval thinking, and the author finds himself unable to explain how it came into existence or why it took hold of people's imaginations for hundreds of years. Choices (A), (B), and (D) are incorrect. While *teaching staffs*, *authorizations*, and *bodily capabilities* are all possible definitions for *faculties* in other contexts, none of these choices works in the context here.

52. **(A)** The author plainly states that the sentiment of courtly love "was entirely unknown to antiquity." In other words, it was *historically unprecedented*. Nothing quite like this idealized "state of utter subjection to the will of an almost unapproachable woman" had occurred before. Choice (B) is incorrect. The sentiment was not *wholly theoretical*: men and women guided their actions by its dictates. Choice (C) is incorrect. Although the author indicates that the Vikings or Romans would have found the sentiment of courtly love *absurd*, and that he himself finds it inexplicable, he says nothing that would indicate he finds it in any way *charming*. Choice (D) is incorrect. The belief in courtly love "passed unquestioned" for centuries ("hundreds of years"). Clearly, it was not *quickly outdated*.

Section 2: Writing and Language Test

1. **(C)** The sentence that follows indicates that this essay is written from the present-day perspective. Choice (C) correctly uses the present perfect tense, "has now begun," and is numerically consistent with the singular subject of "world." Choices (A) and (B) improperly use "began" in the perfect tense ("began" is for the past tense), and choice (D) is plural.

2. **(A)** This choice uses dashes to set aside a parenthetical phrase, and it correctly uses commas to separate the listed items from each other. Choices (B) and (C) do not have sufficient commas breaking up the listed items. Choices (C) and (D) are inconsistent in how the parenthetical phrase starts and ends. You must both start and end a parenthetical phrase with the same sort of punctuation, like two dashes, two commas, or two parentheses.

3. **(B)** The majority of threats to the Great Lakes, according to the chart, comes from human sources like cargo ships, pollution, and development. Choice (A) is incorrect, because the "Other" sector leaves room for nonhuman threats. Choice (C) has the percentage too low. Choice (D) makes a statement about the impact of regulations that is unsupported by the information in the chart, especially since human activity still appears to have a major impact based on the data.

4. **(A)** "Principle" means "idea," while "principal" typically refers to a school administrator. Choices (B) and (D) use the school administrator spelling, and choice (C) is repetitive.

5. **(C)** The previous sentence mentions the typical work of environmental engineers, and the current sentence mentions more specialized tasks that the engineers may perform on occasion. So "other times" provides a logical transition. The collaboration among the engineers is not "unexpected," "habitual," or merely "possible," making the other choices incorrect.

6. **(C)** Since the paragraph is analyzing what those interested in pursuing careers in environmental engineering would study, it is logical that a degree in environmental engineering would be preferred. Choice (A) is not correct because the second part of

the sentence says that other fields of study are acceptable. Choices (B) and (C) do not provide a contrast with the second part of the sentence since those other acceptable fields of study would be both adequate and educational.

7. **(A)** This choice matches the more formal, professional tone of the essay. Choice (B) is too casual. Choice (C) is too wordy. Choice (D) is too vague.

8. **(C)** "One" is consistent with the third-person neutral voice used throughout the passage. Choice (A) is in the second person, and choice (B) is in the first person. Choice (D) refers too specifically only to the female gender.

9. **(C)** "One's" is consistent with the use of "one" in the last sentence of this paragraph and throughout the passage. Choices (A) and (B) use the second person "you," which is inconsistent. Choice (D) incorrectly shows plural rather than singular possession.

10. **(B)** This choice is the most concise and uses parallel phrasing. Choices (A) and (C) are too wordy. Choice (D) uses "meeting," which is incorrect to use in conjunction with "to"—one says "to meet" rather than "to meeting."

11. **(D)** The surrounding sentences state that there is an increasing demand for environmental engineers. So choice (D) is the best choice since it gives a specific statistic in support of this claim. Choice (A) is not correct because it indirectly relates to job prospects. Choices (B) and (C) are too vague.

12. **(B)** This is the only option consistent with the use of quotation marks throughout the sentence to denote a different name for this instrument.

13. **(B)** "Suspected" conveys the idea that archaeologists and historians are speculating as to the significance of the bullroarer to people from long ago. Choices (A) and (B) imply that the people of the past would have ill intent, which is not the intended meaning based on the context. Choice (D), "superstitious," could be used to characterize the overall attitudes that people in the past may themselves have had, but it would not apply to modern-day speculators on the topic.

14. **(C)** The key phrase in the question is "significant transitional life events." Choice (C) is correct because "rites of passage and burial ceremonies" certainly qualify as these types of events. Food gathering and meal preparation, as mentioned in the other choices, happen much more regularly.

15. **(C)** "Apart from" works here because it is synonymous with "except for"—the writer is expressing that bullroarers have been found throughout the world except for Antarctica. The bullroarer would not literally be a "part of" Antarctica, as in choices (A) and (B). Choice (D) gives the incorrect spelling given the needed phrasing.

16. **(D)** The surrounding verbs are in the present tense, so this verb must also be in the present tense. The other options are all in tenses other than the present.

17. **(A)** This is the only option that uses the correct present perfect tense. Choice (B) is past. Choice (C), "loaned," is always incorrect. Choice (D) is in the progressive tense.

18. **(D)** No commas are needed in this sentence because the item to which the bullroarers are compared, "the telegraph machines . . . long distances," is one item, although its description is quite long.

19. **(A)** "Its" gives the singular possessive adjective needed to refer to "bullroarer" and shows the instrument possessing a "function." Choice (B) is wrong because "it's"

means "it is." Choice (C) is wrong because "its'" is always incorrect. Choice (D) is wrong because "their" is plural.

20. **(D)** "Though" is the only option that expresses the contrast needed in the sentence. All of the other options show cause and effect.

21. **(B)** Throughout the paragraph, the focus is on how the bullroarer may have been used for the practical purpose of communication over long distances. The other options are related to other parts of the essay but not to the argument in this paragraph.

22. **(C)** If the bullroarer had been developed independently by peoples all over the world, it would definitely have had multiple inventors. Choice (A) indicates there was a single inventor. Choices (B) and (C) do not refer to the number of inventors.

23. **(D)** The sentence asks a question, so a question mark is needed, making choices (A) and (B) incorrect. Since just two items are listed, there is no need for a comma to separate them, making choice (C) incorrect and choice (D) correct.

24. **(B)** The key phrase in the question is "far from our solar system." To answer this specifically, choice (B) works best since it gives an idea of the mileage. In contrast, the other options are vague or off topic.

25. **(B)** The proper phrase is "not only . . . but also. . . ." The other options can work as transitions but not in this context given the earlier part of the sentence.

26. **(A)** The current version ties from the topic of the previous paragraph, astronomy, directly to the topic of the current paragraph, a chemistry-based explanation of the emission spectrum. Choice (B) is too broad, and choice (C) is too specific. Choice (D) is disconnected from the theme of the current paragraph.

27. **(C)** The subject of this sentence, "element," is singular. Even though the author is referring to many different elements, she is doing so one element at a time. So the singular verb "enters" is needed. Choice (A) is plural, choice (B) is progressive, and choice (D) is a noun.

28. **(D)** "Specific" in this case means "unique," stating that the particular chemical signature given off by each element is unique to it. Choice (A) is too wordy. Choice (B) is incorrect because "partial to" means "to prefer" something. Choice (C) uses an adverb instead of an adjective.

29. **(D)** This choice makes a complete, logical sentence that is consistent with the use of "you" elsewhere, unlike choices (B) and (C). Choice (A) makes the two clauses in the sentence too disconnected.

30. **(B)** Stating that radiation coming out of an item is "emitted by" that item is the most proper option. Choice (A) would work with a physical projectile. Choice (C) is too imprecise. Choice (D) uses "for" incorrectly in this context.

31. **(C)** No commas are needed in this long, descriptive phrase. The other options are too choppy.

32. **(D)** This sentence builds on the first sentence of the paragraph by giving concrete examples of some of the knowledge that spectroscopy has revealed. "For instance" makes the most sense for a transition into these examples. Choices (A) and (B) show contrast. Choice (C) shows cause and effect.

33. **(A)** The earlier part of this paragraph emphasizes that spectroscopy has used the analysis of small compounds to understand the large entity of a galaxy, making choice (A) logical. Choices (B) and (C) are too vague. Choice (D) doesn't illustrate a paradox.

34. **(D)** The first sentence of the passage refers to Faulkner's great recognition. Stating that he won the Nobel Prize would most specifically reinforce this statement. Choices (A) and (B) are too vague. Choice (C) repeats a point already made in this sentence, so inserting that choice is illogical.

35. **(C)** A "lack of public awareness" is synonymous with "lesser known." So this statement should be removed because it is repetitive. It is not inconsistent with any of the information in the paragraph, making choice (D) incorrect.

36. **(A)** Keep the entire dependent clause uninterrupted by commas by selecting "No Change." The other options make this phrase too choppy.

37. **(C)** Someone "vengeful" and "constantly unhappy" would most likely despise those who have better life situations. Choices (A) and (D) are too positive. Choice (B) is illogical since someone this self-absorbed would not look to someone else as an example.

38. **(A)** "Interestingly" makes a proper connection to the information in the previous sentence. Since Abner was someone who liked to burn barns, it is "interesting" that Faulkner emphasizes this further by having Sarty introduced at his father's barn-burning trial. There is no cause-and-effect relationship, making choices (B) and (C) incorrect. Choice (D) is incorrect because there is no contrast.

39. **(D)** "That" works because it begins an essential phrase in the sentence that cannot be set aside with commas, as would be the case with "which." The answer is not choice (B) nor (C) because it is incorrect to say "through . . . from" or "through . . . for" in a sentence like this.

40. **(A)** "It" refers to the singular "disposition." Choices (B) and (D) use plural pronouns. Choice (C) uses the improper verb "overcoming" since it is incorrect to say "will overcoming."

41. **(C)** This choice concisely expresses the idea required while maintaining the appropriate tone. Choice (A) is too wordy. Choice (B) is too stuffy in tone. Choice (D) takes away the intended meaning.

42. **(C)** The semicolon in this choice separates the two independent clauses. The apostrophe before the "s" after "father" indicates singular ownership. The comma after "others" gives a necessary break after the introductory phrase. Choice (A) creates a run-on. Choice (B) does not show possession. Choice (D) shows possession of plural fathers.

43. **(D)** The previous paragraph ends with a statement that Sarty is both ashamed of and defensive of his father, which would be associated with a "divided nature." The other options do not provide a sensible transition from the previous paragraph to the new one because they fail to introduce the duality of Sarty's personality.

44. **(A)** The passage emphasizes that Sarty is divided in his feelings toward his father. At times, Sarty detests him. At other times, he feels loyalty toward his father. This mindset is best described as a "diverged heart." Choice (B) is incorrect because Sarty is not decisive. Choice (C) is incorrect because Sarty is not consistently melancholy. Choice (D) is incorrect because Sarty is not consistently optimistic.

Section 3: Math Test (No Calculator)

1. **(A)** Multiply both sides of the given equation by $a - b$: $\dfrac{5}{a-b} = 2 \Rightarrow 5 = 2a - 2b$

   Now replace a with 4:

   $$5 = 8 - 2b$$

   So $2b = 3$ and $b = \mathbf{1.5}$.

2. **(A)** $2(x - 5) = 2x - 5 \Rightarrow 2x - 10 = 2x - 5 \Rightarrow -10 = -5$

   Since there is no value of x for which $-10 = -5$, **the equation has no solutions.**

   **A solution to the equation $2(x-5) = 2x-5$ is the x-coordinate of the point of intersection of the straight lines $y = 2(x-5)$ and $y = 2x-5$. However, since these lines are parallel (they both have a slope of 2), they do not intersect.

3. **(C)** The amount of juice in 24 6-ounce cans is $6 \times 24 = 144$ ounces, which is equivalent to $144 \div 32 = \mathbf{4.5}$ quarts.

4. **(B)** When the equation of a line is written in slope-intercept form, the slope of the line is the coefficient of x. So the slopes of lines l and k are a and c, respectively. Since parallel lines have equal slopes, $\boldsymbol{a = c}$. However, if $a = c$ and $b = d$, then l and k are the same line. Since, it is given that the lines are distinct, $\boldsymbol{b \neq d}$.

5. **(A)** The number of hot dogs that Frank sells, h, must be multiplied, not divided, by the cost of a hot dog, \$2.25. So the answer must be either choice (A) or choice (B). Since *exceeds* means greater than, not greater than or equal to, the correct sign in the inequality is >. The answer is $2.25h + 1.25s > 100$.

6. **(C)** Since all diameters pass through the center of the circle, the center is the point of intersection of the two lines on which the diameters lie:

   $$y = 2x + 3 \text{ and } y = 3x + 2 \Rightarrow 2x + 3 = 3x + 2 \Rightarrow x = 1 \Rightarrow y = 5$$

   So the center of the circle is at $(1, 5)$. Since the circle passes through the origin, $(0, 0)$, the radius, r, of the circle is the distance between those two points:

   $$r^2 = (1 - 0)^2 + (5 - 0)^2 = 1 + 25 = 26$$

   Since the formula for the area of a circle is $A = \pi r^2$, the area of the circle is $\mathbf{26\pi}$.

7. **(B)** First, draw and label triangle ABC. By Key Fact S1, $\sin = \dfrac{\text{opposite}}{\text{hypotenuse}}$, so let $BC = 3$ and $AB = 5$.

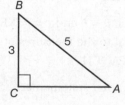

   Then either by using the Pythagorean theorem (KEY FACT J5) or by recognizing that $\triangle ABC$ is a 3-4-5 right triangle, we get that $AC = 4$. Therefore, $\sin (B) = \dfrac{4}{5}$.

8. **(A)** The equation of the line can be written in the form $y = mx + b$, where b is the y-intercept and m is the slope. Since the line crosses the y-axis at 2, $b = 2$ and the answer must be (A) or (B). Since the line has a negative slope, the answer must be A, $y = -\dfrac{1}{2}x + 1$.

** Since the line passes through (0, 2) and (4, 0), its slope $\dfrac{0-2}{4-0} = \dfrac{-2}{4} = \dfrac{-1}{2}$.

9. **(D)** The first step, which isn't required, is to divide both sides of the given equation by 4. Doing this keeps the numbers smaller and easier to work with,

$$4x^2 + 8x = 8 \Rightarrow x^2 + 2x = 2$$

Now subtract 2 from both sides to put the quadratic equation in standard form:

$$x^2 + 2x - 2 = 0$$

Looking at the answer choices should make it clear that this equation cannot be solved by factoring. So use the quadratic formula:

$$x = \frac{-2 \pm \sqrt{4-(-8)}}{2} = \frac{-2 \pm \sqrt{12}}{2} = \frac{-2 \pm 2\sqrt{3}}{2} = -1 \pm \sqrt{3}$$

So the two solutions are $-1 + \sqrt{3}$ and $-1 - \sqrt{3}$.

10. **(C)** Since the number of cells doubles every 30 minutes, it quadruples every hour. Since 4 hours elapsed from 8:00 A.M. to noon, the number of cells quadrupled 4 times. Therefore, at noon, the number of cells was $\mathbf{60 \times 4^4}$.

11. **(D)** Rewrite the original expression so that each fraction has the same denominator:

$$\frac{x+1}{x-1} - \frac{x-1}{x+1} = \frac{x+1}{x+1} \cdot \frac{x+1}{x-1} - \frac{x-1}{x-1} \cdot \frac{x-1}{x+1} = \frac{x^2+2x+1}{x^2-1} - \frac{x^2-2x+1}{x^2-1} = \frac{4x}{x^2-1}$$

**Plug in an easy-to-use number for x. If $x = 2$, then the value of the given expression is

$$\frac{2+1}{2-1} - \frac{2-1}{2+1} = 3 - \frac{1}{3} = \frac{8}{3}$$

Which of the answer choices is equal to $\dfrac{8}{3}$ when $x = 2$? Only choice (D): $\dfrac{4(2)}{(2)^2 - 1} = \dfrac{8}{3}$

12. **(A)** The solution set of the given system consists of those points that satisfy both inequalities. Such a point must lie on or above the line whose equation is $y = x + 1$, which means regions A, B, or C. The point must also lie on or below the parabola whose equation is $y = x^2$, which eliminates region B. The solution set consists of regions $\boldsymbol{A}$ **and** $\boldsymbol{C}$.

13. **(B)** Since l_1 and l_2 are parallel, $a = b$ and $c = d$ (KEY FACT I6). If the measures of two angles in one triangle are equal to the measures of two angles in another triangle, the two triangles are similar (KEY FACT J17).

Note that although each of the other statements (choices (A), (C), and (D)) *could be* true, none of them *must be* true.

14. **(D)** $(a + bi)(c + di) = ac + adi + bci + bdi^2 = ac + adi + bci - bd = ac - bd + (ad + bc)i$. For this last expression to be real, the coefficient of i must equal 0. So $\boldsymbol{ad + bc = 0}$.

15. **(D)** Since $x + y = 10$, we have that $x = 10 - y$. Replacing x by $10 - y$ in the first equation gives:

$$3(10 - y) - 2y = 3y - 2 \Rightarrow 30 - 3y - 2y = 3y - 2 \Rightarrow 32 = 8y \Rightarrow y = 4$$

Since $x + y = 10$, $x = 6$. So $\dfrac{x}{y} = \dfrac{6}{4} = \dfrac{3}{2}$.

16. **1** If $f(x) = x + 5$, then $f(3a) = 3a + 5$ and $f(2a) = 2a + 5$. Therefore,

$$f(3a) + 2 = f(2a) + 3 \Rightarrow$$
$$3a + 5 + 2 = 2a + 5 + 3 \Rightarrow$$
$$3a + 7 = 2a + 8 \Rightarrow a = \mathbf{1}$$

17. **0** If you realize that the given parabola is a translation of the parabola whose equation is $y = x^2$, the solution is immediate. The vertex of the parabola $y = x^2$ is the origin, (0, 0). The parabola $y = (x + 3)^2$ is the parabola $y = x^2$ shifted 3 units to the left; it's vertex is $(-3, 0)$. The parabola $y = (x + 3)^2 + 3$ is that parabola shifted 3 units up; its vertex is $(-3, 3)$. Finally, $-3 + 3 = \mathbf{0}$.

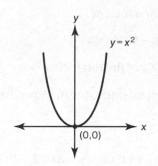 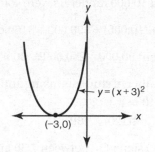 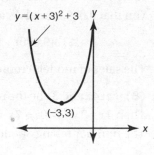

If you didn't realize that the given parabola was a translation of the parabola whose equation is $y = x^2$, you should rewrite the equation in the form

$$y = ax^2 + bx + c: \ y = (x + 3)^2 + 3 = x^2 + 6x + 12$$

Then the x-coordinate of the vertex is at $\dfrac{-b}{2a} = \dfrac{-6}{2} = -3$.

When $x = -3$, $y = (x + 3)^2 + 3 = 0 + 3 = 3$.

18. **32** This question would be trivial if you could use a calculator. You would simply type in $\left(\sqrt{2} \cdot \sqrt[3]{2}\right)^6$ and hit "enter" or the "=" button. Since this question is in the noncalculator section, though, you have to know the laws of exponents in order to simplify the given expression:

$$\left(\sqrt{x} \cdot \sqrt[3]{x}\right)^6 = \left(x^{\frac{1}{2}} \cdot x^{\frac{1}{3}}\right)^6 = \left(x^{\frac{1}{2} + \frac{1}{3}}\right)^6 = \left(x^{\frac{5}{6}}\right)^6 = x^5$$

The answer is $2^5 = \mathbf{32}$.

19. **6** Let x = number of rides someone goes on. Then the cost of using Plan A is $10 + 3x$, and the cost of using Plan B is $20 + x$. So

$$20 + x < 10 + 3x \Rightarrow 10 < 2x \Rightarrow 5 < x$$

So a person would have to go on at least 6 rides for Plan B to be less expensive.

20. **4** Solve the given system of equations. Since $y = x^2 + 1$, we have $y - 1 = x^2$. Now replace x^2 by $y - 1$ in the equation of the circle:

$$y - 1 + y^2 = 5 \Rightarrow y^2 + y - 6 = 0 \Rightarrow (y + 3)(y - 2) = 0 \Rightarrow y = -3 \text{ or } y = 2$$

Since there is no real value of x for which $x^2 + 1 = -3$, y cannot equal -3. The only possible value for y is 2. Then $x^2 + y^2 = 5 \Rightarrow x^2 + 2^2 = 5 \Rightarrow x^2 = 1 \Rightarrow x = 1$ or $x = -1$. So the two points of intersection are $(1, 2)$ and $(-1, 2)$, and $a + b + c + d = 1 + 2 + (-1) + 2 = \mathbf{4}$.

Section 4: Math Test (Calculator)

1. **(D)** Since 74% + 18% = 92%, the \$216 spent on the party represents the other 8% of the money raised. Then, if m represents the amount of money raised,

$$0.08m = 216 \Rightarrow m - 216 \div 0.08 = 2,700$$

2. **(B)** As always, with a percent problem use a simple number such as 10 or 100. Assume that model A sells for \$10; then, since 60% of 10 is 6, model B sells for \$16. The chart tells you that 9,000 model A's and 10,000 model B's were sold for a total of

$$\$10(9,000) + \$16(10,000) = \$90,000 + \$160,000 = \$250,000$$

The sales of model A represent $90,000 \div 250,000 = .36 = \mathbf{36\%}$ of the total sales.

3. **(B)** Let $4x$ and $3x$ be the number of students taking and not taking Spanish, respectively. Then $4x + 3x = 840 \Rightarrow 7x = 840 \Rightarrow x = 120$.
    The number taking Spanish is $4(120) = \mathbf{480}$.

4. **(B)** Since the 90 people who signed in between 7:30 and 7:45 represented 65% − 20% = 45% of the registrants, the total number of registrants was exactly $90 \div 0.45 = \mathbf{200}$.

5. **(B)** Jose made a 25% profit, so if he bought the painting for x, he sold it for

$$x + 0.25x = 1.25x = 2,000$$

So, $x = 2,000 \div 1.25 = 1,600$.

6. **(A)** Since $m = 1$ and $n = 2$ is a solution of the given inequality, we have $1 + c < 2 < d - 1$. So $1 + c < 2$ and $2 < d - 1$. Therefore, $c < 1$ and $3 < d$. Now examine each statement:

    - I *could be* true if c were negative, but *it doesn't have to be true.*
    - II is true. If $3 < d$ and $c < 1$, the difference between them must be greater than 2.
    - III *could be* true if, for example, $c = 0$ and $d = 4$. However, *it doesn't have to be* true if, for example, $c = -4$ and $d = 4$.

    Only statement II is true.

7. **(A)** Since 5% of 60 is 3 and 5% of 80 is 4, we are looking for the people whose adult height differs from their estimated adult height by more than 3 inches. There are three people who satisfy this condition: those whose heights at two years of ages were 30, 33, and 39 inches.

8. **(B)** The scale along the x-axis is 1 inch, therefore, the x-value of 36.5 is halfway between the lines representing 36 and 37 inches. The corresponding y-coordinate is **73.5**.

9. **(C)** If ℓ, w, and h are the dimensions of the original rectangular solid, then by KEY FACT K1, the original volume is ℓwh. The new volume is $(1.2\,\ell)(1.2x)(1.25h) = 1.8(\ell wh)$. So the new volume is **80%** more than the original volume.

**Let the original solid be a cube whose edges are 100. Then the new solid has dimensions 120, 120, and 125. The volume of the cube is $100^3 = 1,000,000$, and the volume of the new rectangular solid is $(120)(120)(125) = 1,800,000$, which is an increase of 800,000. Finally $\frac{800,000}{1,000,000} = \textbf{80\%}$.

10. **(D)** Draw in altitude $\overline{BD}$ in isosceles triangle ABC.

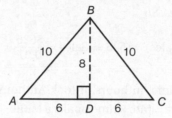

Since the altitude to the base of an isosceles triangle bisects the base, $AD = DC = 6$, and so $\triangle ADB$ is a 6-8-10 right triangle. If you don't realize that, just use the Pythagorean theorem to find BD:

$$6^2 + (BD)^2 = 10^2 \Rightarrow (BD)^2 = 10^2 - 6^2 = 100 - 36 = 64 \Rightarrow BD = 8$$

Then $\sin A = \dfrac{\text{opposite}}{\text{hypotenuse}} = \dfrac{8}{10} = 0.8$.

11. **(C)** Pick a simple value for BE, the length of a side of the smallest square, say 1. Then $DH = 2$ and $AB = 4$. So, the areas of the three squares are 1, 4, and 16, respectively. Therefore, the shaded area is $16 - 4 - 1 = 11$, and the probability that a point chosen at random inside $ABCD$ is in the shaded region is $\dfrac{11}{16}$.

12. **(B)** Surprisingly, the answer to this question does not depend on the data in the charts. Of every \$100 that the district spent in 2005, \$80 came from school taxes and \$20 came from the state. Had the state reduced its aid to the district by half (50%), the state would have reduced is contributions by \$10. To compensate for that, the district would have had to increase the portion paid by taxes from \$80 to \$90. This represents an increase of $\dfrac{10}{80} \times 100\% = \textbf{12.5\%}$.

13. **(B)** The number of students in any year can be calculated from the following equation:

(number of students) × (expenditure per student) = total expenditure

In 1990, the total expenditure was \$25,000,000, and the expenditure per student was \$10,000. So (number of students) × (\$10,000) = \$25,000,000.

Therefore, the number of students is $\dfrac{25,000,000}{10,000} = \textbf{2,500}$.

14. **(B)** As in the solution to question 13, the number of students in any year can be calculated from the equation:

(number of students) × (expenditure per student) = total expenditure

1985: (number of students) × (\$8,000) = \$15,000,000. So, the number of students was 1,975.

1990: (number of students) × ($10,000) = $25,000,000. So, the number of students was 2,500.

Finally, the number of students in the school increased from 1,875 to 2,500, an increase of 625 and a percent increase of $\frac{625}{1,875} = \frac{1}{3} = \textbf{33.33\%}$.

15. **(D)** In the given week, Susan earned $1,000 – $475 = $525 in commissions, which represented 7% of her sales. So

$$(0.07)(\text{Sales}) = \$525 \Rightarrow \text{Sales} = \frac{\$525}{0.07} = \textbf{\$7,500}$$

16. **(B)** Let x represent the time, in hours, it took Anthony to drive to work on Monday. Using the formula distance = rate × time, make a table:

	Rate	Time	Distance
Monday	50	x	$50x$
Tuesday	30	$x + 0.5$	$30x + 15$

Since the distances Anthony drove on Monday and Tuesday were the same:

$$50x = 30x + 15 \Rightarrow 20x = 15 \Rightarrow x = 15 \div 20 = 0.75$$

So the distance he drove each day was $50 \times 0.75 = \textbf{37.5 miles}$.

17. **(D)** It should be clear that the year in which males made up the smallest percent of the population was 1980, when there were the fewest number of males per 100 females. In that year, there were 94.5 males for every 100 females. So of every 194.5 people, $100 \div 194.5 = 0.514 = \textbf{51.4\%}$ of the population was female.

18. **(B)** In 2000, there were 96.3 males for every 100 females. That means of every 196.3 people, $100 \div 196.3 = 0.5094 = 50.94\%$ of the population was female. Hence 49.06% of the population was male.

- Number of females: $0.5094 \times 282,000,000 = 143,650,800$
- Number of males: $0.4906 \times 282,000,000 = 138,349,200$
- $143,650,800 - 138,349,200 = 5,301,600 \approx 5,300,000$

Note: $50.94\% - 49.06\% = 1.88\%$ and $0.0188 \times 282,000,000 = 5,301,600$.

19. **(C)** The powers of i form a repeating sequence:

$i^1 = i$ ($a^1 = a$ for *any* number)

$i^2 = -1$ (by definition)

$i^3 = -i$ $i \cdot i \cdot i = (i \cdot i)(i) = i^2 \cdot i = -1(i) = -1$

$i^4 = -1$ $i^4 = i \cdot i \cdot i \cdot i = (i \cdot i)(i \cdot i) = (-1)(-1) = 1$

$i^5 = i$ $i^5 = i^4 \cdot i = 1 \cdot i = i$

$i^6 = -1$ $i^6 = i^5 \cdot i = i \cdot i = i^2 = -1$

$i^7 = -i$ $i^7 = i^6 \cdot i = (-1)i = -i$

$i^8 = 1$ $i^8 = i^7 \cdot i = (-1)(i) = -i^2 = -(-1) = 1$

So, if n is a multiple of 4, then $i^n = 1$.

Since 2016 *is* a multiple of 4 ($2016 = 4 \times 504$), $i^{2016} = \textbf{1}$.

20. **(D)** Assume that in 2013 Hamburger Heaven sold x cheeseburgers at a price of y dollars each. Then in 2014, they sold $x + 0.20x = 1.2x$ cheeseburgers at a price of $y + 0.10y = 1.1y$ dollars each. So the total income in 2013 was xy, whereas in 2014 it was $(1.2x)(1.1y) = 1.32xy$, an increase of **32%**.

**Do exactly what was done above except replace x and y by 100. Assume that in 2013, Hamburger Heaven sold 100 cheeseburgers for \$100 each for a total of \$10,000. Then in 2014, Hamburger Heaven sold 120 cheeseburgers for \$110 each, for a total of \$13,200.

Finally, \$13,200 is \$3,200 more than \$10,000, an increase of $\dfrac{3,200}{10,000} = 0.32 = \mathbf{32\%}$.

21. **(A)** Make a table, by dividing the number who play on a team by the number in the school. In the table below, the percentages are rounded to the nearest tenth.

	A	B	C	D
Number who play on a team	600	1,000	200	1,200
Number in the school	1,500	2,800	550	3,200
Percent who play on a team	40%	35.7%	36.4%	37.5%

So school **A** has the highest percent of students who play on a team.

22. **(C)** When the object hits the ground, its height above the ground is 0. So we need to find the value of t for which $h(t) = 0$. Dividing both sides of the equation $-4.9t^2 + 34.3t = 0$ by -4.9 gives $t^2 - 7t = 0$. So $t^2 = 7t$. This equation has two solutions: $t = 0$ and $t = 7$. The object was on the ground when it was launched at $t = 0$. It was next on the ground **7** seconds later.

23. **(C)** The object was at a height of 49 meters twice, once on its way up and again on its way down. When did that occur? To answer that question, solve the equation $h(t) = -4.9t^2 + 34.3t = 49$. Dividing by -4.9 gives $t^2 - 7t = -10$ or $t^2 - 7t + 10 = 0$. Then $(t - 2)(t - 5) = 0 \Rightarrow t = 2$ or $t = 5$. So 2 seconds after the object was launched, it attained a height of 49 meters. It remained more than 49 meters off the ground for **3** seconds. At 5 seconds after the launching, it once again was exactly 49 meters off the ground.

24. **(B)** Adam works at the rate of $\dfrac{1 \text{ yard}}{3 \text{ hours}} = \dfrac{1}{3} \dfrac{\text{yard}}{\text{hour}}$. Similarly, Matthew's rate of work is $\dfrac{1}{5} \dfrac{\text{yard}}{\text{hour}}$. Together they can mow $\left(\dfrac{1}{3} + \dfrac{1}{5}\right) = \dfrac{8}{15}$ yards in one hour.

Finally,

$$1 \text{ yard} = \left(\dfrac{8}{15} \dfrac{\text{yards}}{\text{hour}}\right)(t \text{ hours}) \Rightarrow 1 = \dfrac{8}{15} t \Rightarrow t = \dfrac{15}{8}$$

So when working together, the time required for Adam and Matthew to mow the lawn is

$$\dfrac{15}{8} = 1\dfrac{7}{8} = 1.875 \text{ hours} = 1.875 \times 60 \text{ minutes} = \mathbf{112.5} \text{ minutes}$$

**If you get stuck on a problem like this, make an educated guess by eliminating the absurd choices. Since Adam can mow the lawn in 3 hours, or 180 minutes, obviously working together will take less time. Eliminate choice (D). If each boy could mow the lawn in 3 hours, together they would take 1.5 hours, or 90 minutes. Since Matthew works much slower, it will take them more than 90 minutes. Eliminate choice (A) and guess between choices (B) and (C).

25. **(C)** Let x and y represent the number of small cabins and large cabins at the camp, respectively. Ignore the fact that 2 girls didn't come; it's irrelevant. The camp has 48 cabins with a total of 344 cots for the girls to sleep on. Set up 2 equations with two unknowns:

$$x + y = 48 \quad \text{and} \quad 6x + 10y = 344$$

By multiplying the first equation by 6, we get $6x + 6y = 288$. Subtracting $6x + 6y = 288$ from $6x + 10y = 344$ gives $4y = 56$. So $y = 56 \div 4 = 14$. Since $x + y = 48$, $x = 48 - 14 = 34$. So there were $34 - 14 = $ **20** more small cabins than large ones.

**If you want to avoid the algebra, you can just reason it out. Assume there were 24 small cabins and 24 large ones; then there would be $(24 \times 6) + (24 \times 10) = 384$ cots, which is 40 more than the camp actually has. Reducing the number of large cabins by 1 and increasing the number of small cabins by 1 reduces the number of cots by $10 - 6 = 4$. Do that 10 times and the number of cots will be reduced by 40, from 384 to 344. Finally, $24 - 10 = 14$ and $24 + 10 = 34$.

26. **(D)** From the graph, we see that in 1995 50% of employed adults and 20% of adults not in the labor force participated in adult education. 50% of $100,000,000 = 50,000,000$; 20% of $40,000,000 = 8,000,000$.

$50,000,000 : 8,000,000 = 50 : 8 = 6.25 : 1$, which is closest to choice (D), **6:1**.

27. **(C)** Assume that there were 1,000 adults in the workforce, Then 80 adults were unemployed and 920 were employed. Since 50% of the employed adults and 40% of the unemployed adults participated in adult education, the number of participants was 50% of $920 + 40\%$ of $80 = 460 + 32 = 492$.

So the rate of participation was $\frac{492}{1,000} = \frac{49.2}{100} = 49.2\% \approx$ **49%**.

28. **(C)** If the price of the ring before sales tax was x dollars:

$$2,447.37 = x + 0.065x = 1.065x \Rightarrow x = 2,447.37 \div 1.065 = 2,298$$

Since Camille chose to ship the ring home, she had to pay $2,298 for the ring plus $35 for postage and handling, a total of $2,333. Finally, the amount she saved was $2447.37 - \$2,333 = \$114.37$. Rounded to the nearest dollar, she saved **$114**.

29. **(A)** The standard form for the equation of a circle whose center is the point (h, k) and whose radius r is $(x - h)^2 + (y - k)^2 = r^2$. Here, $h = -3$, $k = -4$, and $r = \sqrt{5}$.

So $h + k + r = -3 + -4 + 2.236 = $ **-4.76**.

30. **(A)** Excluding the hole in the center of the nut, the nut is a rectangular solid whose volume is $1 \times 1 \times 0.25 = 0.25$ cubic inches. Since the volume of the actual nut is 0.2 cubic inches, the volume of the circular hole is $0.25 - 0.2 = 0.05$ cubic inches. The volume of the hole is the area of its circular face times the depth of the hole:

$\pi r^2 (0.25)$, where r is the radius of the circle:

$$0.05 = 0.25\pi r^2 \Rightarrow 0.05 = 0.785 r^2 \Rightarrow r^2 = 0.05 \div 0.785 = 0.06366 \Rightarrow r = 0.2523$$

To the nearest hundredth, $r = $ **0.25**.

31. **567** John used $360 (40% of his $900 refund) to pay his bills and deposited the remaining $540 into a savings certificate that earned 5% interest per year. Since 5% of $540 is $27 ($0.05 \times 540 = 27$), at the end of the year his certificate was worth $540 + $27 = **$567**.

Since John saved 60% of his refund, the answer can be obtained in one simple calculation: $0.60 \times 900 \times 1.05 = $ **567.

32. **179** If the average of a set of 9 numbers is 99, their sum is $9 \times 99 = 891$. If deleting 1 number reduces the average of the remaining 8 numbers to 89, the sum of those 8 numbers must be $8 \times 89 = 712$. The deleted number was $891 - 712 = $ **179**.

33. **96**

- The formula for the volume of a cube is $V = e^3$, where e is the edge. So here the volume of the cube is $4^3 = 64$.

- The formula for the volume of a pyramid with a rectangular base is $V = \frac{1}{3} lwh$. Here $l = w = 4$ and $h = 6$. So the volume of the pyramid is $\frac{1}{3}(4 \times 4 \times 6) = 32$.

- Therefore, the total volume of the solid is $64 + 32 = $ **96**.

34. $\dfrac{8}{15}$ There were 150 adults at the reception (64 men and 86 women). Of those, 70 ordered fish ($32 + 38 = 70$). So $150 - 70 = 80$ adults ordered something other than fish. So, the desired fraction is $\dfrac{80}{150} = \dfrac{\mathbf{8}}{\mathbf{15}}$.

35. **10** There are several ways to solve the given quadratic equation.

- Method 1. Subtract 39 from both sides of the equation, and factor:

$$x^2 - 10x = 39 \Rightarrow x^2 - 10x - 39 = 0 \Rightarrow (x - 13)(x + 3) = 0$$

So the two solutions, a and b, are 13 and –3. Their sum is **10**.

- Method 2. Use the quadratic formula on the equation $x^2 - 10x - 39 = 0$:

$$x = \frac{10 \pm \sqrt{10^2 - 4(1)(-39)}}{2(1)} = \frac{10 \pm \sqrt{100 + 156}}{2} = \frac{10 \pm \sqrt{256}}{2} = \frac{10 \pm 16}{2}$$

$$x = \frac{10 + 16}{2} = 13 \text{ or } x = \frac{10 - 16}{2} = -3$$

- Method 3. Complete the square. Add 25 to both sides of the equation, making the left side a perfect square:

$$x^2 - 10x = 39 \Rightarrow x^2 - 10x + 25 = 39 + 25 = 64 \Rightarrow (x - 5)(x - 5) = 64$$
$$(x - 5)^2 = 64 \Rightarrow x - 5 = 8 \text{ or } x - 5 = -8 \Rightarrow x = 13 \text{ or } x = -3$$

Again, we have that the sum of the two solutions is **10**.

36: **70.9** Draw isosceles triangle PQR, and altitude $\overline{PS}$.

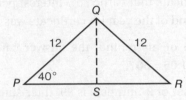

To calculate the area of $\triangle PQR$, we need to know the lengths of the base ($\overline{PR}$) and the height ($\overline{QS}$). We can use the trig ratios to find each of them.

$$\sin 40° = \frac{QS}{12} \Rightarrow QS = 12(\sin 40°) = 12(0.643) = 7.716$$

$$\cos 40° = \frac{PS}{12} \Rightarrow PS = 12(\cos 40°) = 12(0.766) = 9.192$$

Since the altitude to the base of an isosceles triangle is also a median, $SR = PS = 9.192$ and $PR = 2 \times 9.192 = 18.384$.

Finally, the area of $\triangle PQR = \frac{1}{2}(18.384)(7.716) = 70.925 \approx \textbf{70.9}$.

37. **650** The $843.57 that Robert received when the CD matured was 3% more than the amount he deposited into the CD. So if x represents the amount in dollars that Robert deposited, then $843.57 = 1.03x$. So $x = 843.57 \div 1.03 = 819$. If y represents the number of Euros that Michel gave to Robert, then $819 = 1.26y$. So $y = 819 \div 1.26 = \textbf{650}$.

38. **9** If z represents the number of euros that Michel received after converting the $843.57 he received from Robert, then $z = 843.57 \div 1.28 = 659.04$. Since the solution to question 37 shows that Michel originally gave Robert 650 euros, to the nearest euro Michel's profit was $659 - 650 = \textbf{9}$ euros.

SAT Essay Scoring

SAT Essay Scoring Rubric

	Score: 4
Reading	**Excellent:** The essay shows excellent understanding of the source. The essay shows an understanding of the source's main argument and key details and a firm grasp of how they are interconnected, demonstrating clear comprehension of the source. The essay does not misinterpret or misrepresent the source. The essay skillfully uses source evidence, such as direct quotations and rephrasing, representing a thorough comprehension of the source.
Analysis	**Excellent:** The essay gives excellent analysis of the source and shows clear understanding of what the assignment requires. The essay gives a complete, highly thoughtful analysis of the author's use of reasoning, evidence, rhetoric, and/or other argumentative elements the student has chosen to highlight. The essay has appropriate, adequate, and skillfully chosen support for its analysis. The essay focuses on the most important parts of the source in responding to the prompt.
Writing	**Excellent:** The essay is focused and shows an excellent grasp of the English language. The essay has a clear thesis. The essay has a well-executed introduction and conclusion. The essay shows a clear and well-crafted progression of thoughts both within paragraphs and in the essay as a whole. The essay has a wide range of sentence structures. The essay consistently shows precise choice of words. The essay is formal and objective in its style and tone. The essay demonstrates a firm grasp of the rules of standard English and has very few to no errors.

	Score: 3
Reading	**Skillful:** The essay shows effective understanding of the source. The essay shows an understanding of the source's main argument and key details. The essay is free of major misinterpretations and/or misrepresentations of the source. The essay uses appropriate source evidence, such as direct quotations and rephrasing, representing comprehension of the source.
Analysis	**Skillful:** The essay gives effective analysis of the source and shows an understanding of what the assignment requires. The essay decently analyzes the author's use of reasoning, evidence, rhetoric, and/or other argumentative elements the student has chosen to highlight. The essay has appropriate and adequate support for its analysis. The essay focuses primarily on the most important parts of the source in responding to the prompt.
Writing	**Skillful:** The essay is mostly focused and shows an effective grasp of the English language. The essay has a thesis, either explicit or implicit. The essay has an effective introduction and conclusion. The essay has a clear progression of thoughts both within paragraphs and in the essay as a whole. The essay has an assortment of sentence structures. The essay shows some precise choice of words. The essay is formal and objective in its style and tone. The essay demonstrates a grasp of the rules of standard English and has very few significant errors that interfere with the writer's argument.

Score: 2	
Reading	Limited: The essay shows some understanding of the source. The essay shows an understanding of the source's main argument, but not of key details. The essay may have some misinterpretations and/or misrepresentations of the source. The essay gives only partial evidence from the source, showing limited comprehension of the source.
Analysis	Limited: The essay gives partial analysis of the source and shows only limited understanding of what the assignment requires. The essay tries to show how the author uses reasoning, evidence, rhetoric, and/or other argumentative elements the student has chosen to highlight, but only states rather than analyzes their importance, or at least one part of the essay's analysis is unsupported by the source. The essay has little or no justification for its argument. The essay may lack attention to those elements of the source that are most pertinent to responding to the prompt.
Writing	Limited: The essay is mostly not cohesive and shows an ineffective grasp of the English language. The essay may not have a thesis, or may diverge from the thesis at some point in the essay's development. The essay may have an unsuccessful introduction and/or conclusion. The essay may show progression of thoughts within the paragraphs, but not in the essay as a whole. The essay is relatively uniform in its sentence structures. The essay shows imprecise and possibly repetitive choice of words. The essay may be more casual and subjective in style and tone. The essay demonstrates a weaker grasp of the rules of standard English and does have errors that interfere with the writer's argument.
Score: 1	
Reading	Insufficient: The essay shows virtually no understanding of the source. The essay is unsuccessful in showing an understanding of the source's main argument. It may refer to some details from the text, but it does so without tying them to the source's main argument. The essay has many misinterpretations and/or misrepresentations of the source. The essay gives virtually no evidence from the source, showing very poor comprehension of the source.
Analysis	Insufficient: The essay gives little to no accurate analysis of the source and shows poor understanding of what the assignment requires. The essay may show how the author uses reasoning, evidence, rhetoric, and/or other argumentative elements that the student has chosen to highlight but does so without analysis. Or many parts of the essay's analysis are unsupported by the source. The support given for points in the essay's argument are largely unsupported or off topic. The essay may not attend to the elements of the source that are pertinent to responding to the prompt. Or the essay gives no explicit analysis, perhaps only resorting to summary statements.
Writing	Insufficient: The essay is not cohesive and does not demonstrate skill in the English language. The essay may not have a thesis. The essay does not have a clear introduction and conclusion. The essay does not have a clear progression of thoughts. The essay is quite uniform and even repetitive in sentence structure. The essay shows poor and possibly inaccurate word choice. The essay is likely casual and subjective in style and tone. The essay shows a poor grasp of the rules of standard English and may have many errors that interfere with the writer's argument.

Top-Scoring Sample Student Response

In this article, the author first argues that the trajectory for human population growth is inherently unsustainable if we continue using the same techniques for accommodating growth. She then argues that, rather than maintaining our current course of action of outward expansion, we should instead shift to a more reasonable approach of vertical expansion that would better utilize the finite planetary space available. The author strengthens her position with: a hypothetical scenario depicting a continuation of our current policy and the disaster therein; a vivid description of how vertical expansion would function; the folly of continuing the same expansion approach as our hunter-gatherer ancestors; and finally with an appeal to emotion using a Utopian example of how vertical integration might ideally unfold.

First, the author relies on an established scientific principle to introduce credibility to her claim she mentions Malthusian Theory to reinforce that the rapid growth of humanity is not an issue that is going away. She then appeals to fear (perhaps the most persuasive of emotions) by calling to attention a potential doomsday scenario that is not unlikely if humanity continues attempting to accommodate its exponential growth by expanding outward. "So picture your city; now, picture your city with the population doubled. Where did you imagine all of the new housing developments?. . . How unbearable has your morning commute become?" So, from this frightful series of rhetorical questions, the author continues her compelling case that we must change our approach lest we wish to encounter both literal and figurative societal gridlock.

Next, the author details vertical integration, in action, to better illustrate how well the concept would function. Instead of growing outward (she mentions that Indianapolis and Chicago are on pace to swallow each other up), we could start growing upward. After all, the Earth only has so much surface area to use before it's exhausted; in contrast, there is little preventing humanity from constructing buildings into the heavens. This would have numerous benefits. For one, she states that the need for automobiles would be diminished. Wouldn't that be an upgrade, if we could eliminate gas costs and everything we needed were in walking distance? Also, each "mini-community" would be wholly independent (with the exception of having to import foodstuffs, which is not an insurmountable prospect given our current advanced infrastructure), with its own grocery stores and health care systems. This, she notes, would improve community cohesion and promote a greater sense of belonging. In all, it's an awfully convincing proposal.

She then again questions the wisdom of our current approach, stating that it is simply an extension of hunter-gatherer philosophy that was created in a world where the population was not 7 billion, but rather, maybe tens of thousands. Thus, it can be inferred that her point is that such an antiquated methodology of expanding outward has long since outlived its usefulness especially given technological advancement like the Otis Elevator that now permits us to build smarter. So, the day has come when we must embrace the world for what it is, and begin expanding vertically now that things like urban sprawl and shortages of natural resources are reaching pandemic proportions.

The author, in her penultimate paragraph, draws attention to the shortage of food that will result if outward expansion continues to be favored over vertical expansion. Since the world is only so big, and since only so much land is suitable for agriculture, further outward growth will continue to encroach upon the limited land that is available to be cultivated. Thus, we will be faced with the deadly paradox of countering population growth with food shortages as suburbs are built on farmland.

Finally, she concludes her argument with a Utopian image of how vertical expansion could transform our world for the better. "So again, imagine your favorite city. But this time imagine it with little traffic. Your morning commute is a pleasant walk . . . everyone is a familiar, smiling face." In all, it really ties a bow around the concept.

In conclusion, the author details her position that we must abandon our current expansion strategy in favor of vertical expansion. She appeals to the emotion of fear, reason, and the idyllic image of a Utopian society to effectively develop her argument.

PART THREE
The SAT Reading Test

The Evidence-Based Reading Test

→ **QUICK OVERVIEW**
→ **TESTING TACTICS**
→ **PRACTICE EXERCISES**
→ **ANSWERS EXPLAINED**

QUICK OVERVIEW

Here is what the new SAT Reading Test will look like:

- It will contain four single passages and one set of paired passages, for a total of 3,250 words.
- Each single passage or paired set of passages will be 500–750 words long.
- One passage will come from U.S. or world literature.
- Two passages (or one passage and one set of paired passages) will come from the natural sciences—Earth science, biology, chemistry, and physics.
- Two passages (or one passage and one set of paired passages) will come from the social sciences—anthropology, communication arts, economics, education, human geography (as opposed to physical geography), history, legal studies, linguistics, political science, psychology, and sociology.
- Some of the natural sciences and social sciences passages will be what the test-makers like to call "founding documents."
- There will be one or two graphics included in one of the history/social sciences passages and in one of the natural sciences passages. (Graphics include tables, charts, and graphs that convey information relevant to the content of the passage. To do well on the new SAT, you will need to be able not only to analyze and understand the information presented in the graphics but also to integrate that information with the information you've gathered from the text.)
- There will be 52 questions in the reading section, 10 or 11 questions on each passage or set of paired passages. Ten of these 52 questions will be vocabulary questions in which you will have to figure out a word's meaning from its context in the passage. Ten more will be command-of-evidence questions in which you have to figure out which part of the passage provides the best evidence to support your answer to a previous question.

The directions for the passage-based reading section of the SAT are minimal. They are:

> Each passage below is followed by questions based on its content. Answer all questions following a passage on the basis of what is <u>stated</u> or <u>implied</u> in that passage.

TACTICS PREVIEW

1. Make use of the introductions to acquaint yourself with the text.
2. Use the line references in the questions to be sure you've gone back to the correct spot in the passage.
3. When you have a choice, tackle passages with familiar subjects before passages with unfamiliar ones.
4. In tackling a 500–750-word reading passage, first read the passage; then read the questions.
5. Try to answer *all* the questions on a particular passage before you move on to the next.
6. Learn to spot the major reading question types.
7. When asked to find the main idea, be sure to check the opening and summary sentences of each paragraph.
8. Familiarize yourself with the technical terms used to describe a passage's organization.
9. When asked about specific details in a passage, spot key words in the question and scan the passage to find them (or their synonyms).
10. When asked to make inferences, base your answers on what the passage implies, not what it states directly.
11. When asked about an attitude or tone, look for words that convey emotions, express values, or paint pictures.
12. When asked to give the meaning of a word, look for nearby context clues.
13. When dealing with paired passages, tackle them one at a time.
14. When dealing with graph interpretation questions, use only the evidence in the graph and the passage.
15. Scan all the questions on a passage to spot the command-of-evidence questions coming up.

TACTIC
1 Make Use of the Introductions to Acquaint Yourself with the Text.

Almost every reading passage is preceded by a short introduction. Don't skip it. As you read the introductory material and tackle the passage's opening sentences, try to anticipate what the passage will be about. You'll be in a better position to understand what you read.

TACTIC
2 Use the Line References in the Questions to Be Sure You've Gone Back to the Correct Spot in the Passage.

The reading passages on the SAT tend to be long: 500–750 words. Fortunately, the lines are numbered, and the questions often refer you to specific lines in the passage by number. It takes less time to locate a line number than to spot a word or phrase. Use the line numbers to orient yourself in the text.

TACTIC 3
When You Have a Choice, Tackle Passages with Familiar Subjects Before Passages with Unfamiliar Ones.

Build on what you already know and like. It's only common sense: if you know very little about botany or are uninterested in it, you are all too likely to run into trouble reading a passage about plant life.

It is hard to concentrate when you read about something that is wholly unfamiliar to you. Give yourself a break. There will be five reading passages on your test. Start with one that interests you or that deals with a topic you know well. There is nothing wrong in skipping questions. Just remember to check the numbering of your answer sheet. You should, of course, go back to any questions you skipped and make a quick guess in the final seconds before you run out of time.

TACTIC 4
In Tackling a 500–750 Word Reading Passage, First Read the Passage; Then Read the Questions.

Try tackling the reading passages using the following technique.

1. Read as rapidly as you can with understanding, but do not force yourself. Do not worry about the time element. If you worry about not finishing the test, you will begin to take short cuts and miss the correct answer in your haste.
2. As you read the opening sentences, try to anticipate what the passage will be about. Who or what is the author talking about?
3. As you continue reading, notice in what part of the passage the author makes major points. In that way, even when a question does not point you to a particular line or paragraph, you should be able to head for the right section of the text *without* having to reread the entire passage. Underline key words and phrases—sparingly!

 TIP
Be cautious in applying this tactic. When you tackle a long passage, *if you run into real trouble understanding the material*, don't get bogged down in the text. Skip to the questions. A quick review of the questions may give you a feeling for what to look for when you return to the text.

TACTIC 5
Try to Answer *All* the Questions on a Particular Passage Before You Move on to the Next.

Don't let yourself get bogged down on any one question; you can't afford to get stuck on one question when you have ten more on the same passage to answer. Remember that the questions following each reading passage are *not* arranged in order of difficulty. If you are stumped by a tough reading question, do not give up and skip all the other questions on that passage. A tough question may be just one question away from an easy one. Skip the one that's got you stumped, but make a point of coming back to it later, after you've answered one or two more questions on the passage. Often, working through other questions on the same passage will provide you with information you can use to answer any questions that stumped you the first time around. If the question still stumps you, mark your favorite letter and move on. If you circle the problem question in your booklet, you'll be able to come back to it at the end if you still have time.

Learn to Spot the Major Reading Question Types.

Reading questions fall into certain basic types. It will definitely help you if you familiarize yourself with the major types of reading questions on the SAT.

If you can recognize just what a given question is asking you to do, you'll be better able to tell which particular reading tactic to apply.

Here are six categories of reading questions you are sure to face.

1. **MAIN IDEA** Questions that test your ability to find the central thought of a passage or to judge its significance often take the following form:

   The main point of the passage is to

   The passage is primarily concerned with

   The author's primary purpose in this passage is to

   The chief theme of the passage can be best described as

   Which of the following statements best expresses the main idea of the passage?

2. **SPECIFIC DETAILS** Questions that test your ability to understand what the author states *explicitly* are often worded:

   According to the author

   The author states all of the following EXCEPT

   According to the passage, which of the following is true of the

   According to the passage, the chief characteristic of the subject is

   Which of the following statements is (are) best supported by the passage?

   Which of the following is NOT cited in the passage as evidence of

3. **INFERENCES** Questions that test your ability to go beyond the author's explicit statements and see what these statements imply may be worded:

   It can be inferred from the passage that

   The passage suggests that the author would support which of the following views?

   The author implies that

   The author apparently feels that

   According to the passage, it is likely that

   The passage is most likely directed toward an audience of

   Which of the following statements about...can be inferred from the passage?

4. **TONE/ATTITUDE** Questions that test your ability to sense an author's or character's emotional state often take the form:

   The author's attitude to the problem can best be described as

   Which of the following best describes the author's tone in the passage?

   The author's tone in the passage is that of a person attempting to

   The author's presentation is marked by a tone of

   The passage indicates that the author experiences a feeling of

5. **VOCABULARY IN CONTEXT** Questions that test your ability to work out the meaning of words from their context often are worded:

The phrase "..." is used in the passage to mean that

As used in line 00, "..." most nearly means

As used in line 00, "..." is closest in meaning to

6. **TECHNIQUE** Questions that test your ability to recognize a passage's method of organization or technique often are worded:

Which of the following best describes the development of this passage?

In presenting the argument, the author does all of the following EXCEPT...

The relationship between the second paragraph and the first paragraph can best be described as...

During the course of the final paragraph, the narrator's focus shifts from ... to ...

7. **GRAPHICS** Questions that test your ability to interpret informational graphics and to relate that information to the accompanying passage may be worded:

Graph 1 suggests which of the following about ... in the years 2000–2010?

Do the data in the table provide support for the author's claim that ...

How does the graph support the author's point that ...

The graph following the passage offers evidence that ...

8. **COMMAND OF EVIDENCE** Questions that test your ability to identify which part of a passage provides the best evidence for the conclusions you reach are worded:

Which choice provides the best evidence for the answer to the previous question?

TACTIC

When Asked to Find the Main Idea, Be Sure to Check the Opening and Summary Sentences of Each Paragraph.

The opening and closing sentences of each paragraph are key sentences for you to read. They can serve as guideposts for you, pointing out the author's main idea.

Whenever you are asked to determine a passage's main idea, *always* check each paragraph's opening and summary sentences. Typically, in each paragraph, authors provide readers with a sentence that expresses the paragraph's main idea succinctly. Although such *topic sentences* may appear anywhere in the paragraph, experienced readers customarily look for them in the opening or closing sentences.

Note that in SAT reading passages, topic sentences are sometimes implied rather than stated directly. If you cannot find a topic sentence, ask yourself these questions:

1. Whom or what is this passage about?
2. What aspect of this subject is the author talking about?
3. What is the author trying to get across about this aspect of the subject?

Read the following reading passage and apply this tactic.

[http://www.nlm.nih.gov/changingthefaceofmedicine/physicians/biography_26.html]

Patricia E. Bath is one example of an answer to the charge that there are no Black female American scientists to include in science history textbooks and courses. Bath, an ophthalmologist and laser scientist, is an innovative research scientist and advo-
Line cate for blindness prevention, treatment, and cure. Her accomplishments include the
(5) invention of a new device and technique for cataract surgery known as laserphaco, the creation of a new discipline known as "community ophthalmology," and her appointment as the first woman chair of ophthalmology in the United States, at Drew–UCLA in 1983.

Patricia Bath's dedication to a life in medicine began in childhood, when she first
(10) heard about Dr. Albert Schweitzer's service to lepers in the Congo. . . . As a young intern shuttling between Harlem Hospital and Columbia University, she was quick to observe that at the eye clinic in Harlem half the patients were blind or visually impaired. At the eye clinic at Columbia, by contrast, there were very few obviously blind patients. This observation led her to conduct a retrospective epidemiological
(15) study, which documented that blindness among blacks was double that among whites. She reached the conclusion that the high prevalence of blindness among blacks was due to lack of access of ophthalmic care. As a result, she proposed a new discipline, known as community ophthalmology, which is now operative worldwide. Community ophthalmology combines aspects of public health, community medicine, and clinical
(20) ophthalmology to offer primary care to underserved populations. Volunteers trained as eye workers visit senior centers and daycare programs to test vision and screen for cataracts, glaucoma, and other threatening eye conditions. This outreach has saved the sight of thousands whose problems would otherwise have gone undiagnosed and untreated. By identifying children who need eyeglasses, the volunteers give these chil-
(25) dren a better chance for success in school.

In 1974 Bath joined the faculty of UCLA and Charles R. Drew University as an assistant professor of surgery (Drew) and ophthalmology (UCLA). The following year she became the first woman faculty member in the Department of Ophthalmology at UCLA's Jules Stein Eye Institute. As she notes, when she became the first woman faculty
(30) in the department, she was offered an office "in the basement next to the lab animals." She refused the spot. "I didn't say it was racist or sexist. I said it was inappropriate and succeeded in getting acceptable office space. I decided I was just going to do my work." By 1983 she was chair of the ophthalmology residency training program at Drew–UCLA, the first woman in the USA to hold such a position.
(35) Despite university policies extolling equality and condemning discrimination, Professor Bath experienced numerous instances of sexism and racism throughout her tenure at both UCLA and Drew. Determined that her research not be obstructed by the "glass ceilings," she took her research abroad to Europe. Free at last from the toxic constraints of sexism and racism, her research was accepted on its merits at the
(40) Laser Medical Center of Berlin, West Germany, the Rothschild Eye Institute of Paris, France, and the Loughborough Institute of Technology, England. At those institutions she achieved her "personal best" in research and laser science, the fruits of which are evidenced by her laser patents on eye surgery.

Bath's work and interests, however, have always gone beyond the confines of a
(45) university. In 1977, she and three other colleagues founded the American Institute
for the Prevention of Blindness, an organization whose mission is to protect, preserve, and restore the gift of sight. The AIPB is based on the principle that eyesight is
a basic human right and that primary eye care must be made available to all people,
everywhere, regardless of their economic status. Much of the work of the AIPB is done
(50) though ophthalmic assistants, who are trained in programs at major universities. The
institute supports global initiatives to provide newborn infants with protective anti-
infection eye drops, to ensure that children who are malnourished receive vitamin A
supplements essential for vision, and to vaccinate children against diseases (such as
measles) that can lead to blindness.
(55)   Dr. Bath is also a laser scientist and inventor. Her interest, experience, and research
on cataracts led to her invention of a new device and method to remove cataracts—
the laserphaco probe. When she first conceived of the device in 1981, her idea was
more advanced than the technology available at the time. It took her nearly five years
to complete the research and testing needed to make it work and apply for a patent.
(60) Today, the device is used worldwide. With the keratoprosthesis device, Dr. Bath was
able to recover the sight of several individuals who had been blind for over 30 years.

Now look at a question on this passage. It's a good example of a main idea question.

The passage primarily focuses on the

(A) influence of Patricia Bath on other scientists.
(B) recognition given to Patricia Bath for her work.
(C) experiences that influenced the work of Patricia Bath.
(D) techniques that characterize the work of Patricia Bath.

Look at the opening and/or summary sentences of paragraphs that make up the passage. "Patricia E. Bath is one example of an answer to the charge that there are no Black female American scientists to include in science history textbooks and courses." "Patricia Bath's dedication to a life in medicine began in childhood, when she first heard about Dr. Albert Schweitzer's service to lepers in the Congo." "In 1974 Bath joined the faculty of UCLA and Charles R. Drew University as an assistant professor of surgery (Drew) and ophthalmology (UCLA)." "By 1983 she was chair of the ophthalmology residency training program at Drew– UCLA, the first woman in the USA to hold such a position." "Bath's work and interests, how- ever, have always gone beyond the confines of a university." "Dr. Bath is also a laser scientist and inventor." "With the keratoprosthesis device, Dr. Bath was able to recover the sight of several individuals who had been blind for over 30 years." The passage cites experience after experience, each of which *influenced the work of Patricia Bath*. From her childhood fascina- tion with Schweitzer's work as a medical missionary, through her work at Harlem Hospital and Columbia University, to her founding of the American Institute for the Prevention of Blindness, Patricia Bath has had a vast range of experiences that have contributed to her work as a scientist. The correct answer is choice (C). Choice (A) is incorrect. The passage talks far more about influences on Patricia Bath than about Bath's influence on other scientists. Choice (B) is incorrect. Although the passage mentions recognition given to Bath, that recognition is not the passage's primary focus. Choice (D) is incorrect. The passage barely touches on specific details of craft or technique.

Certain words come up again and again in questions on a passage's purpose or main idea. Review them. It would be silly to miss an answer not because you misunderstood the passage's meaning, but because you didn't know a common question word.

KEY TERMS IN MAIN IDEA QUESTIONS

bolster (v.)	to support an idea or position
delineate	to outline or describe with care
depict	to represent or portray vividly
discredit	to disbelieve; to cause a loss of confidence in
document (v.)	to support by documentary evidence
elaborate (v.)	to add details to; to work out in minute detail
endorse	to support or approve
exemplify	to serve as an example of
illustrate	to clarify by the use of examples
refute	to prove to be false or incorrect
speculate	to reason, possibly on insufficient evidence

TACTIC
8 Familiarize Yourself with the Technical Terms Used to Describe a Passage's Organization.

Another part of understanding the author's point is understanding how the author organizes what he or she has to say. To do so, often you have to figure out how the opening sentence or paragraph is connected to the passage as a whole.

Try this question on the author's technique, based on the previous passage about Patricia Bath.

> Which of the following best summarizes the relationship of the first sentence to the rest of the passage?
>
> (A) Assertion followed by supporting evidence
> (B) Challenge followed by debate pro and con
> (C) Prediction followed by analysis
> (D) Specific instance followed by generalizations

The correct answer is choice (A). The author makes an assertion (a positive statement) about Bath's importance and then proceeds to back it up with specific details from her career.

Choice (B) is incorrect. There is no debate for and against the author's thesis or point about Bath; the only details given support that point. Choice (C) is incorrect. The author does not predict or foretell something that is going to happen; the author asserts or states positively something that is an accomplished fact. Choice (D) is incorrect. The author's opening general assertion is followed by specific details to support it, not the reverse.

KEY TERMS IN QUESTIONS ON TECHNIQUE OR STYLE

abstract (adj.)	theoretical; not concrete
analogy	similarity of functions or properties; likeness
antithesis	direct opposite
argumentative	presenting a logical argument
assertion	positive statement; declaration
cite	to refer to; to quote as an authority
concrete (adj.)	real; actual; not abstract
evidence	data presented as proof
explanatory	serving to explain
expository	concerned with explaining ideas, facts, etc.
generalization	simplification; general idea or principle
narrative (adj.)	relating to telling a story
persuasive	intended to convince
rhetorical	relating to the effective use of language
thesis	the central idea in a piece of writing; a point to be defended

TACTIC 9 — When Asked About Specific Details in a Passage, Spot Key Words in the Question and Scan the Passage to Find Them (or Their Synonyms).

In developing the main idea of a passage, a writer will make statements to support his or her point. To answer questions about such supporting details, you *must* find a word or group of words in the passage that supports your choice of answer. The words "according to the passage" or "according to the author" should focus your attention on what the passage explicitly states. Do not be misled into choosing an answer (even one that makes good sense) if you cannot find it supported in the text.

Often detail questions ask about a particular phrase or line. The SAT generally provides numbered line references to help you locate the relevant section of the passage. Occasionally it fails to do so. In such instances, use the following technique:

1. Look for key words (nouns or verbs) in the answer choices.
2. Run your eye down the passage, looking for those key words or their synonyms. (This is called *scanning*. It is what you do when you look up someone's number in the phone book.)
3. When you find a key word or its synonym, reread the sentence to make sure the test-writer hasn't used the original wording to mislead you.

A third question on the Bath passage tests you on a specific detail.

> In what way did hearing the story of Albert Schweitzer affect Bath's eventual profession?
>
> (A) It inspired her to focus on becoming a missionary in Africa.
> (B) It influenced her to write about the effects of leprosy on developing countries.
> (C) It encouraged her to consider a career in medicine.
> (D) It confirmed the feasibility of a black woman's becoming a doctor.

TIP

Be extra cautious when you scan for key words: they may be eye-catchers. Often the test-writers deliberately insert key words from the passage into *incorrect* answer choices, hoping to tempt careless readers into making a bad choice.

Looking at the question, what key words do you see? Does the name *Albert Schweitzer* leap out at you? That's great. Now scan the passage, looking for that name.

Here's the sentence in which the name Albert Schweitzer appears: "Patricia Bath's dedication to a life in medicine began in childhood, when she first heard about Dr. Albert Schweitzer's service to lepers in the Congo." Schweitzer devoted himself to serving victims of leprosy, a disease that potentially leads to nerve damage and disfigurement, and, in particular, to blindness.

What effect did hearing about Schweitzer have on Bath? It caused her to think about a medical career as something she could attain. Hearing how Schweitzer had dedicated himself to ease the suffering of lepers, Bath was encouraged *to consider a career in medicine* and determined to dedicate herself to a life in medicine. The correct answer is choice (C). Choice (A) is incorrect. Bath was inspired to focus on medicine, not on African mission work. Choice (B) is incorrect. Bath was influenced to become a medical doctor, not an author. Choice (D) is incorrect. Given the biases that black men and women faced in academia during Bath's youth, the fact that Schweitzer, a white man, successfully became a doctor would not necessarily have confirmed the feasibility (likelihood) of a black woman's sucess in doing so.

KEY TERMS IN QUESTIONS ON SPECIFIC DETAILS

aesthetic	artistic; dealing with or capable of appreciating the beautiful
allusion	an indirect reference; a casual mention
assumption	something accepted as true without proof
attribute (n.)	essential quality; characteristic
divergent	differing from another; tending to move apart
fluctuate	to shift continually; to vary irregularly
hypothetical	based on assumptions or hypotheses; supposed
incompatible	not able to exist in harmony; discordant
indicative	suggestive; pointing out (something)
inherent	firmly established by nature or habit; built-in; inborn
innate	inborn; existing from birth
innovative	novel; introducing a change; ahead of the times
misconception	mistaken idea; wrong impression
phenomenon	observable fact or occurrence; subject of scientific investigation
preclude	to make impossible; to keep from happening

TACTIC

When Asked to Make Inferences, Base Your Answers on What the Passage Implies, Not What It States Directly.

In *Language in Thought and Action*, S.I. Hayakawa defines an inference as "a statement about the unknown made on the basis of the known."

Inference questions require you to use your own judgment. You must not take anything directly stated by the author as an inference. Instead, you must look for clues in the passage that you can use in coming up with your own conclusion. You should choose as your answer a statement which is a logical development of the information the author has provided.

See how this tactic works as you read this fiction passage, taken from the novel *The Heart of the Matter* by Graham Greene.

"Imagine. Forty days in the boats!" cried Mrs. Perrot. Everything over the river was still and blank.

"The French behaved well this time at least," Dawson remarked.

Line
(5)
"They've only brought in the dying," the doctor retorted. "They could hardly have done less."

Dawson exclaimed and struck at his hand. "Come inside," Mrs. Perrot said, "The windows are netted." The stale air was heavy with the coming rains.

"There are some cases of fever," said the doctor, "but most are just exhaustion—the worst disease. It's what most of us die of in the end."

(10)
Mrs. Perrot turned a knob; music from the London Orpheum filtered in. Dawson shifted uncomfortably; the Wurlitzer organ moaned and boomed. It seemed to him outrageously immodest.

Wilson came in to a welcome from Mrs. Perrot. "A surprise to see *you*, Major Dawson."

(15)
"Hardly, Wilson." Mr. Perrot injected. "I told you he'd be here." Dawson looked across at Wilson and saw him blush at Perrot's betrayal, saw too that his eyes gave the lie to his youth.

"Well," sneered Perrot, "any scandals from the big city?" Like a Huguenot imagining Rome, he built up a picture of frivolity, viciousness, and corruption. "We bush-folk
(20) live quietly."

Mrs. Perrot's mouth stiffened in the effort to ignore her husband in his familiar part. She pretended to listen to the old Viennese melodies.

"None," Dawson answered, watching Mrs. Perrot with pity. "People are too busy with the war."

(25)
"So many files to turn over," said Perrot. "Growing rice down here would teach them what work is."

The first question based on this passage is an inference question. Note the use of the terms "suggests" and "most likely." The passage never tells you directly where the story takes place. You must put two and two together and see what you get.

The evidence in the passage suggests that the story most likely takes place

(A) on a boat during a tropical storm.
(B) at a hospital during a wartime blackout.
(C) in a small town in France.
(D) near a rice plantation in the tropics.

Go through the answer choices one by one. Remember that in answering inference questions you must go beyond the obvious, go beyond what the author explicitly states, to look for logical implications of what the author says.

The correct answer is choice (D), *near a rice plantation in the tropics*. Several lines in the passage suggest it: Perrot's reference to "bush-folk," people living in a tropical jungle or similar uncleared wilderness; Perrot's comment about the work involved in growing rice; the references to fever and the coming rains.

Choice (A) is incorrect. The people rescued have been in the boats for forty days. The story itself is not set on a boat.

Choice (B) is incorrect. Although the presence of a doctor and the talk of dying patients suggests a hospital and Dawson's comment implies that people elsewhere are concerned with a war, nothing in the passage suggests that it is set in a wartime blackout. The windows are not covered or blacked out to prevent light from getting out; instead, they are netted to prevent mosquitos from getting in. (Note how Dawson exclaims and swats his hand; he has just been bitten by a mosquito.)

Choice (C) is incorrect. Although the French are mentioned, nothing suggests that the story takes place in France, a European country not noted for uncleared wilderness or tropical rains.

KEY TERMS IN INFERENCE QUESTIONS

criterion	a standard used in judging something; a basis for comparison
excerpt	a selection from a longer work
implication	an indirect suggestion; a logical inference
imply	to suggest without stating explicitly; to mean
likelihood	probability; chance of something
plausible	appearing reasonable; apparently believable
suggestive	tending to suggest something; stimulating further thought
tentative	not definite or positive; hesitant; provisional; experimental

TACTIC

11 When Asked About an Attitude or Tone, Look for Words That Convey Emotions, Express Values, or Paint Pictures.

In figuring out the attitude or tone of an author or character, take a close look at the specific language used. Is the author using adjectives to describe the subject? If so, are they words like *fragrant, tranquil, magnanimous*—words with positive connotations? Or are they words like *fetid, ruffled, stingy*—words with negative connotations?

When we speak, our tone of voice conveys our emotions—frustrated, cheerful, critical, gloomy, angry. When we write, our images and descriptive phrases get our feelings across.

The second question on the Greene passage is a tone question. Note the question refers you to specific lines in which a particular character speaks. Those lines are repeated here so that you can easily refer to them.

"They've only brought in the dying," the doctor retorted. "They could hardly have done less."

"There are some cases of fever," said the doctor, "but most are just exhaustion—the worst disease. It's what most of us die of in the end."

The tone of the doctor's remarks (lines 4 and 5, 8 and 9) indicates that he is basically

(A) unselfish.
(B) indifferent.
(C) rich in patience.
(D) without illusions.

Note the doctor's use of "only" and "hardly," words with a negative sense. The doctor is deprecating or belittling what the French have done for the sufferers from the boats, the people who are dying from the exhaustion of their forty-day journey. The doctor is *retorting*: he is replying sharply to Dawson's positive remark about the French having behaved well. The doctor has judged the French. In his eyes, they have not behaved well.

Go through the answer choices one by one to see which choice comes closest to matching your sense of the doctor's tone.

Choice (A) is incorrect. Nothing in the passage specifically suggests selfishness or unselfishness on his part, merely irritability.

Choice (B) is incorrect. The doctor is not indifferent or uncaring. If he did not care, he would not be so sharp in challenging Dawson's innocent remark.

Choice (C) is also incorrect. The doctor is quick to counter Dawson, quick to criticize the French. Impatience, not patience, distinguishes him.

The correct answer is choice (D). The doctor is without illusions. Unlike Dawson, he cannot comfort himself with the illusion that things are going well. He has no illusions about life or death: most of us, he points out unsentimentally, die of exhaustion in the end.

When you are considering questions of attitude and tone, bear in mind the nature of the SAT. It is a standardized test aimed at a wide variety of test-takers—cosplay fans, political activists, 4-H members, computer hacks, readers of *GQ*. It is taken by Native Americans and Chinese refugees, evangelical Christians and Orthodox Jews, Buddhists and Hindus, Hispanics and blacks, New Yorkers and Nebraskans—a typically American mix.

The SAT-makers are very aware of this diversity. As members of their staff have told us, they are particularly concerned to avoid using material on the tests that might upset students (and possibly adversely affect their scores). For this reason, the goal is to be noncontroversial: to present material that won't offend *anyone*. Thus, in selecting potential reading passages, the SAT-makers tend to avoid subjects that are sensitive in favor of ones that are bland. In fact, if a passage doesn't start out bland, they may revise it and cut out the spice. One released SAT test, for example, included Kenneth Clark's comment about the "sharp wits" of Romans, but cut out his comment about their "hard heads." Another used a passage from Mary McCarthy's prickly *Memories of a Catholic Girlhood*, but cut out every reference to Catholic and Protestant interaction—and much of the humor, too.

How does this affect the sort of tone and attitude questions the SAT-makers ask? As you can see, the SAT-makers attempt to respect the feelings of minority group members. Thus, you can expect minority group members to be portrayed in SAT reading passages in a favorable light. If, for example, there had been an attitude question based on the Patricia Bath passage, it might have been worded like this:

> The author's attitude toward the scientific achievements mentioned in the passage can best be described as one of
>
> (A) incredulity.
> (B) condescension.
> (C) cool indifference.
> (D) hearty admiration.

Hearty admiration is the only possible choice.

KEY TERMS IN QUESTIONS ON ATTITUDE AND TONE

aloof	standoffish; remote in attitude
ambivalent	of two minds; unable to decide
brusque	abrupt; curt to the point of rudeness
cautionary	conveying a warning
compassionate	sympathetic; showing pity
condescension	patronizing behavior
cynical	distrustful of the motives of others; mocking
defensive	self-justifying; constantly protecting oneself from criticism
detachment	aloofness; lack of involvement; indifference
didactic	moralizing; inclined to lecture excessively
disdain	scorn; contempt; arrogance
disparaging	belittling; disapproving
dispassionate	unbiased; objective; unemotional; calm
esteem	respect; admiration
flippant	frivolously disrespectful; lacking proper seriousness
grudging	reluctant; unwilling
hypocritical	pretending to have virtues or feelings one lacks; insincere; phony
indifference	lack of concern; lack of interest
ironic	tongue in cheek; sarcastic; contrary to what was expected
judicious	sensible; showing good judgment; prudent; wise
naïve	innocent; unsophisticated
nostalgia	sentimental yearning for the past; homesickness
objective (adj.)	impartial; unbiased; neutral
optimism	hopefulness; cheerful confidence
pedantic	narrowly focused on academic trivia; excessively bookish
pessimism	negativity; lack of hopefulness; gloom
pomposity	self-importance; excessive self-esteem
prosaic	commonplace; pedestrian; ordinary
resigned (adj.)	submissive; passively accepting the inevitable
sarcasm	cutting remarks; stinging rebuke; scorn
satirical	mocking; exposing folly to ridicule
skeptical	disbelieving; doubtful; unconvinced
trite	stale; clichéd; overused
whimsical	fanciful; capricious; unpredictable

TACTIC

12 When Asked to Give the Meaning of an Unfamiliar Word, Look for Nearby Context Clues.

Every student who has ever looked into a dictionary is aware that many words have more than one meaning. A common question that appears on the new SAT tests your ability to determine the correct meaning of a word from its context. Most often the word will be a common one, and you must determine its exact meaning as used by the author. At other times, the word may be uncommon. You can determine its meaning by a careful examination of the text.

The following question based on the Patricia Bath passage asks you to determine which exact meaning of a common word is used in a particular sentence. Here is the sentence in which the word appears.

Patricia E. Bath is one example of an answer to the charge that there are no Black female American scientists to include in science history textbooks and courses.

As used in line 1, "charge" most nearly means

(A) fee.
(B) responsibility.
(C) accusation.
(D) headlong rush.

To answer this question, simply substitute each of the answer choices for the quoted word in its original context. Although a charge can be a *fee* ("an admission charge"), a *responsibility* ("the business left in her charge"), or a *headlong rush* ("a cavalry charge"), the word is used differently here.

Think of the context. What is an answer to a charge? It is a response to a claim or *accusation* that has been made with little or no proof. In this case, the claim is that there are no Black female American scientists for authors to include in science history texts. (It carries with it the suggestion that Black female scientists are not good enough to be included in such texts.) Clearly, this accusation is false. Black female American scientists exist: many of them, like physician and astronaut Mae Jemison, aerospace engineer Aprille Ericsson, and theoretical physicist Shirley Ann Jackson, have already earned a well-deserved place in science history, as has Dr. Bath. Like them, she is an example of an answer to this false accusation.

Look at the words in the immediate vicinity of the word you are defining. They will give you a sense of the meaning of the unfamiliar word.

TACTIC

When Dealing with Paired Passages, Tackle Them One at a Time.

If paired passages have you worried, relax. They are not that formidable, especially if you deal with them our way. Read the lines in italics introducing both passages. Then look at the two passages. Their lines will be numbered as if they were one *enormous* passage: if Passage 1 ends on line 42, Passage 2 will begin on line 43. However, they are two separate passages. Tackle them one at a time.

In general, these questions are organized sequentially: questions about Passage 1 come before questions about Passage 2. So, do things in order. *First* read Passage 1; then jump straight to the questions and answer all those based on Passage 1. *Next* read Passage 2; then answer all the questions based on Passage 2. (The line numbers in the questions will help you spot where the questions on Passage 1 end and those on Passage 2 begin.) *Finally*, tackle the two or three questions that refer to *both* passages. Go back to both passages as needed.

At times a couple of questions referring to *both* passages will precede the questions focusing on Passage 1. Do not let this hitch throw you. Use your common sense. You've just read the first passage. Skip the one or two questions on both passages, and head for those questions about Passage 1. Answer them. Then read Passage 2. Answer the questions on Passage 2. Finally, go back to those questions you skipped and answer them and any other questions at the end of the set that refer to both passages. Remember, however: whenever you skip from question to question, or from passage to passage, *be sure you're filling in the right circles on your answer sheet.*

TACTIC

14 When Dealing with Graph Interpretation Questions, Use Only the Evidence in the Graph and the Passage

Line graphs and bar graphs show you how one set of data relates to another. Most line and bar graphs have a horizontal axis (called the *x*-axis) and a vertical axis (called the *y*-axis). Both axes will be clearly labeled. Pay close attention to the graph labels and axes to avoid careless mistakes.

Other types of graphics you are likely to encounter on the new SAT include pie charts, flow charts, time lines, and tables.

In addition to the Khan Academy lessons about graphs, helpful online resources about the interpretation of graphics include:

"How to Read a Graph" (*http://ucatlas.ucsc.edu/howto/graph.html*)

"How do I plot points on a graph?" (*http://serc.carleton.edu/mathyouneed/graphing/plotting.html*)

"Guidelines: How to Read a Graph" (*http://sib.illinois.edu/SkillGuidelines/ReadGraph.html*)

TACTIC

15 Scan All the Questions on a Passage to Spot the Command-of-Evidence Questions Coming Up.

Ten of the reading questions on your test will be questions that test how well you are able to identify which part of a passage provides the best support for a conclusion you reach. The test-makers want you to be able not only to interpret a text correctly but also to back up your interpretation with evidence, or, in their words, to find relevant textual support.

Currently, command-of-evidence questions look like this:

> Which choice provides the best evidence for the answer to the previous question?
>
> (A) Lines 13–17 ("When . . . rights")
> (B) Lines 20–24 ("Now . . . party")
> (C) Lines 55–58 ("The time . . . victory")
> (D) Lines 65–68 ("Government . . . nation")

Thanks to the presence of the line numbers and parentheses, command-of-evidence questions are easy to spot. As you turn to the questions on a particular passage, scan the group of questions quickly to spot any command-of-evidence questions. In your booklet, circle the number of the question *immediately before* each command-of-evidence question. That's your cue to pay special attention as you answer this question. If you do it right, you'll be answering two questions, and not just one.

Here's what to do. As you answer the question *immediately before* a command-of-evidence question, note in your booklet what part of the passage helped you come up with your answer. Put a check mark in the margin next to the sentence that you think best supports the answer you chose. Next, move on to the command-of-evidence question. Look at the line numbers in the answer choices. Is the sentence you checked among the choices listed there? If it is, then that's most likely the correct answer. If not, then you need to reread the four sentences listed in the answer choices and think of how each of them might back up one of the answers to the previous question.

LONG-RANGE STRATEGIES

Are you a good reader? Do you read twenty-five or more books a year in addition to those books assigned in school? When you read light fiction, do you cover a page per minute? Do you read only light fiction, or have you begun to read "heavy" books—books on natural science, government, physics, law? Do you browse regularly through magazines and newspapers?

Faced with the above questions, students frequently panic. Used to gathering information from television and radio rather than from books, they don't know how to get back on the track. But getting back on the track is easier than they think.

Read, Read, Read!

Just do it.

There is no substitute for extensive reading as a preparation for the SAT and for college work. The only way to obtain proficiency in reading is by reading books of all kinds. As you read, you will develop speed, stamina, and the ability to comprehend the printed page. But if you want to turn yourself into the kind of reader the colleges are looking for, you must develop the habit of reading—every day.

25 Books a Year

Suppose you're an average reader; you read an ordinary book at about 300 words a minute. In 20 minutes, how many words can you read? Six thousand, right?

In a week of reading 20 minutes per day, how many words can you read? Seven days, 42,000 words.

Now get out your calculator. In 52 weeks of reading 20 minutes per day, how many words can you read? That's 52 times 42,000, a grand total of 2,184,000 words!

Now here comes the hard part. Full-length books usually contain 60,000 to 100,000 words. Say the average book runs about 75,000 words. If reading 20 minutes a day you can read 2,184,000 words in a year, how many average, 75,000-word books can you read in a year?

The answer is a little over 29. Twenty-nine books in a year. So don't panic at the thought of reading 25 books a year. Anybody can find 20 minutes a day, and if you can do that, you can read *more than* 25 books a year. The trick is always to have your book on hand, so that you don't have to waste time hunting around for it if you suddenly find yourself with some free time.

Schedule a set time for non-school reading. Make the 20-minute-a-day plan part of your life.

Upgrade What You Read

Challenge yourself. Don't limit your reading to light fiction and biography as so many high school students do. Branch out a bit. Go beyond *People* magazine. Try to develop an interest in as many fields as you can. Sample some of the quality magazines: *The New Yorker, Smithsonian, Scientific American, National Geographic, New Scientist, Science, The Economist, Science News.* In these magazines you'll find articles on literature, the natural sciences, the physical sciences, history, economics, political science, sociology, and law—the whole range of fields touched on by the SAT. If you take time to acquaint yourself with the contents of these magazines, you won't find the subject matter of the reading passages on the examination so strange.

Selected Reading List for the SAT

The reading passages you will face on the SAT are excerpts from the sorts of books and magazines your high school teachers will introduce in your junior and senior years and your college instructors will assign you to read in your freshman and sophomore years. You can get a head start on college (and on the SAT) by beginning to read college-level material now—today.

The following reading list is divided into four sections:

1. U.S. and World Literature
2. Science (biology, chemistry, physics, mathematics, geology, and astronomy)
3. Social Studies (history, political science, archaeology, and sociology)
4. U.S. Founding Documents and the Global Conversation

A few of the books on this list have been the source of passages on the New SAT.

Follow these steps in working through the list. Choose material from areas with which you feel unfamiliar. Do not worry if the first book you tackle seems difficult to you. Try working your way through a short section—the first chapter should be enough to give you a sense of what the author has to say. *Remember that this is college-level material:* it is bound to be challenging to you. Be glad you're getting a chance at it so soon.

If you get stuck, work your way up to the level of the book, taking it step by step. If E.M. Forster's novel *A Room with a View* seems hard, try reading it after you've seen the award-winning movie of the same name. If an article in the Scientific American book *The Brain* seems hard, try reading it after you've read Isaac Asimov's popular *The Human Brain.* Get introductory books on your subject from the high school library or from the Young Adults section of the local public library. Not one of these books is beyond your ability to read; you just need to fill in some background first.

(Note that books marked "M" or "TV" have been made into excellent motion pictures or television shows.)

U.S. AND WORLD LITERATURE

James Agee, *A Death in the Family*
Kingsley Amis, *Lucky Jim*
Jane Austen, *Emma*
   Lady Susan
   Pride and Prejudice (M)
James Baldwin, *Go Tell It on the Mountain*

Charlotte Bronte, *Jane Eyre*
  The Professor
  Villette
Geraldine Brooks, *People of the Book*
  Year of Wonders
Willa Cather, *My Antonia*
Joseph Conrad, *The Heart of Darkness*
Charles Dickens, *Barnaby Rudge*
  Great Expectations (M)
  Little Dorritt
  Nicholas Nickleby (TV)
  Our Mutual Friend
Margaret Drabble, *A Summer Bird-Cage*
George Eliot, *Middlemarch*
Ralph Ellison, *The Invisible Man*
William Faulkner, *Collected Stories of William Faulkner*
  Intruder in the Dust
  Sartoris
F. Scott Fitzgerald, *Babylon Revisited*
  The Great Gatsby
E.M. Forster, *A Room with a View* (M)
Elizabeth Gaskell, *Cranford*
  Sylvia's Lovers
William Golding, *Lord of the Flies*
Graham Greene, *The Heart of the Matter*
  Our Man in Havana (M)
  The Power and the Glory
  The Third Man (M)
Thomas Hardy, *Far from the Madding Crowd*
  Jude the Obscure
MacDonald Harris, *The Balloonist*
Ernest Hemingway, *A Farewell to Arms*
  For Whom the Bell Tolls (M)
  The Nick Adams Stories, "The Last Good Country"
  The Sun Also Rises
William Dean Howells, *A Modern Instance*
Henry James, *The American*
  Daisy Miller
  The Portrait of a Lady
  The Turn of the Screw
James Joyce, *Dubliners*, "Araby"
Arthur Koestler, *Darkness at Noon*
D.H. Lawrence, *Sons and Lovers*
  Women in Love (M)
C.S. Lewis, *The Screwtape Letters*
Herman Melville, *Billy Budd*
  Moby Dick (M)

Lydia Minatoya, *The Strangeness of Beauty*
George Orwell, *Animal Farm* (M)
   1984 (M)
Saki (H.H. Munro), *The Collected Short Stories*
William Makepeace Thackeray, *Vanity Fair*
Anthony Trollope, *Barchester Towers* (TV)
   The Warden (TV)
Mark Twain, *The Adventures of Huckleberry Finn*
Robert Penn Warren, *All the King's Men* (M)
Evelyn Waugh, *Brideshead Revisited* (TV)
   Men at Arms
Mary Webb, *The House in Dormer Forest*
Edith Wharton, *The Age of Innocence*
   Ethan Frome
Virginia Woolf, *Orlando*
   To the Lighthouse
Richard Wright, *Black Boy*

SCIENCE

Emily Anthes, *Frankenstein's Cat*
   Instant Egghead Guide: The Mind
Isaac Asimov, *The Human Body*
   The Human Brain
Eric T. Bell, *The Development of Mathematics*
Jeremy Bernstein, *Experiencing Science*
   Science Observed
Jacob Bronowski, *The Ascent of Man*
Brian Clegg, *Instant Egghead: Physics*
N.P. Davis, *Lawrence and Oppenheimer*
Adrian Desmond, *The Hot-Blooded Dinosaurs*
   Darwin's Sacred Cause
Gerald Durrell, *My Family and Other Animals*
   Fauna and Family
Richard Feynman, *Surely You're Joking, Mr. Feynman*
Karl von Frisch, *Animal Architecture*
George Gamow, *Mr. Tompkins* (series)
   One, Two, Three . . . Infinity
Jane Goodall, *In the Shadow of Man*
Stephen Jay Gould, *Ever Since Darwin*
Thor Hanson, *Feathers: The Evolution of a Natural Miracle*
   The Impenetrable Forest
   The Triumph of Seed
Arthur Koestler, *The Case of the Midwife Toad*
Aldo Leopold, *Sand County Almanac*
Konrad Lorenz, *King Solomon's Ring*
   On Aggression

Jonathan Miller, *The Body in Question*
Scientific American Books, *The Biosphere*
   The Brain
   Energy and Power
   Evolution
   The Ocean
   The Solar System
   Volcanoes and the Earth's Interior
James Watson, *The Double Helix*
Gary Zukav, *The Dancing Wu Li Masters*

SOCIAL STUDIES

Frederick Lewis Allen, *Only Yesterday*
Stephen Ambrose, *Rise to Globalism: U.S. Foreign Policy, 1938–1980*
Corelli Barnet, *The Desert Generals*
   The Sword Bearers
Peter Berger, *Invitation to Sociology*
Fritjof Capra, *The Turning Point*
Vincent Cronin, *Napoleon*
W.E.B. DuBois, *The Souls of Black Folk*
Will and Ariel Durant, *The Story of Civilization*
Alan Ehrenhalt, *The Great Inversion and the Future of the American City*
John Hope Franklin, *From Slavery to Freedom*
Taras Grescoe, *Bottomfeeder*
   Straphanger
J. Huizinga, *The Waning of the Middle Ages*
Iain King, *How to Make Good Decisions and Be Right All the Time*
Joseph P. Lash, *Eleanor and Franklin* (TV)
Joe McGinniss, *The Selling of the President, 1968*
Paul MacKendrick, *The Mute Stones Speak*
H. Brett Melendy, *Asians in America*
Edmund Morgan, *The Puritan Dilemma*
Steven Pinker, *The Better Angels of Our Nature*
   Words and Rules
Richard Pollenberg, *One Nation Divisible: Class, Race, Ethnicity in the U.S. Since 1938*
Alan Taylor, *The Internal Enemy: Slavery and War in Virginia, 1772–1832*
Barbara Tuchman, *A Distant Mirror*
   The Guns of August
T.H. White, *The Making of the President* (series)
Edmund Wilson, *To the Finland Station*
Virginia Woolf, *Three Guineas*

U.S. FOUNDING DOCUMENTS AND THE GREAT GLOBAL CONVERSATION

Your American history and social studies classes will introduce you to the Declaration of Independence, the Constitution, the Bill of Rights, and more. However, you can go beyond the classroom and explore a wealth of historical documents online for free. Check out the National Archives online: *http://www.archives.gov/historical-docs/*

You'll find the Gettysburg Address, the Emancipation Proclamation, the 19th Amendment (Women's Right to Vote); you'll even find Elvis Presley's letter to President Nixon, although that's unlikely to appear on the SAT.

Here is a by-no-means complete list of America's founding and foundational documents, as well as documents that are part of the worldwide conversation about the nature of civic life.

The Federalist Papers

The Gettysburg Address

The Mayflower Compact

The Northwest Ordinances

The Seneca Falls Declaration of Sentiments

Abigail Adams and John Adams, *The Letters of John and Abigail Adams*

Edmund Burke, *Reflections on the Revolution in France*

Shirley Chisholm, *Unbought and Unbossed*

Frederick Douglass, *Narrative of the Life of an American Slave*

Betty Friedan, *The Feminine Mystique*

Mahatma Gandhi, *The Story of My Experiments with Truth*

Barbara Jordan, *Barbara C. Jordan—Selected Speeches*

Martin Luther King, Jr., *I Have a Dream: Writings and Speeches That Changed the World*
   A Testament of Hope: The Essential Writings and Speeches of Martin Luther King, Jr.

Nelson Mandela, *Long Walk to Freedom*

Thomas Paine, *Common Sense*
   Rights of Man

Richard Rodriguez, *The Hunger of Memory*

Franklin Delano Roosevelt, *Great Speeches*

Elizabeth Cady Stanton, *The Solitude of Self*

Sojourner Truth, *Narrative of Sojourner Truth*

Lech Walesa, *The Struggles and the Triumph: An Autobiography*

Mary Wollstonecraft, *A Vindication of the Rights of Woman*

Malcolm X and Alex Haley, *The Autobiography of Malcolm X*

Short Passages

Try these questions based on short passages in order to familiarize yourself with some common question types.

MAIN IDEA/PURPOSE

Question 1 is based on the following passage.

The passage below is excerpted from Somerset Maugham's The Moon and Sixpence, *first published in 1919.*

> The faculty for myth is innate in the human race. It seizes with avidity upon
> any incidents, surprising or mysterious, in the career of those who have at all dis-
> tinguished themselves from their fellows, and invents a legend. It is the protest of
> *Line* romance against the commonplace of life. The incidents of the legend become the
> *(5)* hero's surest passport to immortality. The ironic philosopher reflects with a smile
> that Sir Walter Raleigh is more safely enshrined in the memory of mankind because
> he set his cloak for the Virgin Queen to walk on than because he carried the English
> name to undiscovered countries.

1. In lines 5–8, the author mentions Sir Walter Raleigh primarily to

   (A) emphasize the importance of Raleigh's voyages of discovery.
   (B) mock Raleigh's behavior in casting down his cloak to protect the queen's feet from the mud.
   (C) illustrate how legendary events outshine historical achievements in the public's mind.
   (D) distinguish between Raleigh the courtier and Raleigh the seafarer.

Question 2 is based on the following passage.

The passage below is excerpted from a text on marine biology.

> Consider the humble jellyfish. Headless, spineless, without a heart or brain, it has
> such a simple exterior that it seems the most primitive of creature. Unlike its sessile
> (attached to a surface, as an oyster is attached to its shell) relatives whose stalks cling
> *Line* to seaweed or tropical coral reefs, the free-swimming jellyfish or medusa drifts along
> *(5)* the ocean shore, propelling itself by pulsing, muscular contractions of its bell-shaped
> body. Yet beneath the simple surface of this aimlessly drifting, supposedly primitive
> creature is an unusually sophisticated set of genes, as recent studies of the invertebrate
> phylum Cnidaria (pronounced nih-DARE-ee-uh) reveal.

2. Which assertion about jellyfish is supported by the passage?

   (A) They move at a rapid rate.
   (B) They are lacking in courage.
   (C) They attach themselves to underwater rock formations.
   (D) They are unexpectedly complex.

Question 3 is based on the following passage.

The passage below is excerpted from an article on Florida's Everglades National Park.

Pioneering conservationist Marjory Stoneman Douglas called it the River of Grass. Stretching south from Lake Okeechobee, fed by the rain-drenched Kissimmee River basin, the Everglades is a water marsh, a slow-moving river of swamps and sawgrass
Line flowing southward to the Gulf of Mexico. It is a unique ecosystem, whose endur-
(5) ing value has come from its being home to countless species of plants and animals: cypress trees and mangroves, wood storks and egrets, snapping turtles and crocodiles. For the past 50 years, however, this river has been shrinking. Never a torrent, it has dwindled as engineering projects have diverted the waters feeding it to meet agricul-tural and housing needs.

3. The author of this passage cites the conservationist Marjory Stoneman Douglas in order to

   (A) present a viewpoint.
   (B) challenge an opinion.
   (C) introduce a metaphor.
   (D) correct a misapprehension.

Question 4 is based on the following passage.

The following passage is taken from a brochure for a museum exhibit.

How does an artist train his eye? "First," said Leonardo da Vinci, "learn perspective; then draw from nature." The self-taught eighteenth century painter George Stubbs followed Leonardo's advice. Like Leonardo, he studied anatomy, but, unlike Leonardo,
Line instead of studying human anatomy, he studied the anatomy of the horse. He dissected
(5) carcass after carcass, peeling away the five separate layers of muscles, removing the organs, baring the veins and arteries and nerves. For 18 long months he recorded his observations, and when he was done he could paint horses muscle by muscle, as they had never been painted before. Pretty decent work, for someone self-taught.

4. The primary purpose of the passage is to

   (A) explain a phenomenon.
   (B) describe a process.
   (C) urge a course of action.
   (D) argue against a practice.

Question 5 is based on the following passage.

The following passage is an excerpt from an article on Lady Mary Wortley Montagu, known best today for her travel writings.

In 1979, when the World Health Organization declared that smallpox had finally been eradicated, few, if any, people recollected the efforts of an eighteenth-century English aristocrat to combat the then-fatal disease. As a young woman, Lady Mary
Line Wortley Montagu had suffered severely from smallpox. In Turkey, she observed the
(5) Eastern custom of inoculating people with a mild form of the pox, thereby immunizing them, a practice she later championed in England. The Turks, she wrote home, even held house parties during which inoculated youngsters played together happily until they came down with the pox, after which they convalesced together.

5. The primary purpose of the passage is to

(A) celebrate the total eradication of smallpox.
(B) challenge the actions of Lady Mary Wortley Montagu.
(C) demonstrate that smallpox was a serious problem in the eighteenth century.
(D) call attention to a neglected historical figure.

VOCABULARY IN CONTEXT

Questions 6 and 7 are based on the following passage.

The passage below is excerpted from Somerset Maugham's The Moon and Sixpence, *first* published in 1919.

The faculty for myth is innate in the human race. It seizes with avidity upon any incidents, surprising or mysterious, in the career of those who have at all distinguished themselves from their fellows, and invents a legend. It is the protest of romance against
Line the commonplace of life. The incidents of the legend become the hero's surest passport
(5) to immortality. The ironic philosopher reflects with a smile that Sir Walter Raleigh is more safely enshrined in the memory of mankind because he set his cloak for the Virgin Queen to walk on than because he carried the English name to undiscovered countries.

6. As used in line 1, "faculty" most nearly means

(A) capacity.
(B) authority.
(C) teaching staff.
(D) branch of learning.

7. As used in line 5, "reflects" most nearly means

(A) mirrors.
(B) exhibits.
(C) muses.
(D) casts back.

Question 8 is based on the following passage.

The passage below is excerpted from a text on marine biology.

Consider the humble jellyfish. Headless, spineless, without a heart or brain, it has such a simple exterior that it seems the most primitive of creature. Unlike its sessile (attached to a surface, as an oyster is attached to its shell) relatives whose stalks cling
Line to seaweed or tropical coral reefs, the free-swimming jellyfish or medusa drifts along
(5) the ocean shore, propelling itself by pulsing, muscular contractions of its bell-shaped body. Yet beneath the simple surface of this aimlessly drifting, supposedly primitive creature is an unusually sophisticated set of genes, as recent studies of the invertebrate phylum Cnidaria (pronounced nih-DARE-ee-uh) reveal.

8. As used in line 7, "sophisticated" most nearly means

    (A) worldly.

    (B) complex.

    (C) suave.

    (D) aware.

Questions 9 and 10 are based on the following passage.

The passage below is excerpted from an article on Florida's Everglades National Park.

Pioneering conservationist Marjory Stoneman Douglas called it the River of Grass. Stretching south from Lake Okeechobee, fed by the rain-drenched Kissimmee River basin, the Everglades is a water marsh, a slow-moving river of swamps and sawgrass
Line flowing southward to the Gulf of Mexico. It is a unique ecosystem, whose enduring
(5) value has come from its being home to countless species of plants and animals: cypress trees and mangroves, wood storks and egrets, snapping turtles and crocodiles. For the past 50 years, however, this river has been shrinking. Never a torrent, it has dwindled as engineering projects have diverted the waters feeding it to meet agricultural and housing needs.

9. As used in line 4, "enduring" most nearly means

    (A) tolerating.

    (B) long-suffering.

    (C) hard-won.

    (D) lasting.

10. As used in line 8, "meet" most nearly means

    (A) encounter.

    (B) assemble.

    (C) satisfy.

    (D) join.

Question 11 is based on the following passage.

The passage below is excerpted from Willa Cather's classic novel My Antonia, *first published in 1918.*

Mrs. Harding was short and square and sturdy-looking, like her house. Every inch of her was charged with an energy that made itself felt the moment she entered a room. Her face was rosy and solid, with bright, twinkling eyes and a stubborn little chin. She
Line was quick to anger, quick to laughter, and jolly from the depths of her soul. How well
(5) I remember her laugh; it had in it the same sudden recognition that flashed into her eyes, was a burst of humor, short and intelligent. Her rapid footsteps shook her own floors, and she routed lassitude and indifference wherever she came.

11. As used in line 2, "charged with" most nearly means

   (A) accused of.
   (B) billed for.
   (C) entrusted with.
   (D) filled with.

Questions 12 and 13 are based on the following passage.

The passage below is taken from Senate History, 1964–Present, June 10, 1964, Civil Rights Filibuster Ended.

At 9:51 on the morning of June 10, 1964, Senator Robert C. Byrd completed an address that he had begun 14 hours and 13 minutes earlier. The subject was the pending Civil Rights Act of 1964, a measure that occupied the Senate for 57 working days,
Line including six Saturdays. A day earlier, Democratic Whip Hubert Humphrey, the bill's
(5) manager, concluded he had the 67 votes required at that time to end the debate.
   The Civil Rights Act provided protection of voting rights; banned discrimination in public facilities—including private businesses offering public services—such as lunch counters, hotels, and theaters; and established equal employment opportunity as the law of the land.
(10) As Senator Byrd took his seat, House members, former senators, and others—150 of them—vied for limited standing space at the back of the chamber. With all gallery seats taken, hundreds waited outside in hopelessly extended lines.
   Georgia Democrat Richard Russell offered the final arguments in opposition. Minority Leader Everett Dirksen, who had enlisted the Republican votes that made
(15) cloture a realistic option, spoke for the proponents with his customary eloquence. Noting that the day marked the 100th anniversary of Abraham Lincoln's nomination to a second term, the Illinois Republican proclaimed, in the words of Victor Hugo, "Stronger than all the armies is an idea whose time has come." He continued, "The time has come for equality of opportunity in sharing in government, in education, and
(20) in employment. It will not be stayed or denied. It is here!"
   Never in history had the Senate been able to muster enough votes to cut off a filibuster on a civil rights bill. And only once in the 37 years since 1927 had it agreed to cloture for any measure.

The clerk proceeded to call the roll. When he reached "Mr. Engle," there was no
(25) response. A brain tumor had robbed California's mortally ill Clair Engle of his ability to speak. Slowly lifting a crippled arm, he pointed to his eye, thereby signaling
his affirmative vote. Few of those who witnessed this heroic gesture ever forgot it.
When Delaware's John Williams provided the decisive 67th vote, Majority Leader Mike
Mansfield exclaimed, "That's it!" Richard Russell slumped; Hubert Humphrey beamed.
(30) With six wavering senators providing a four-vote victory margin, the final tally stood at
71 to 29. Nine days later the Senate approved the act itself—producing one of the 20th
century's towering legislative achievements.

12. As used in line 3, "occupied" most nearly means

   (A) inhabited.
   (B) engaged.
   (C) invaded.
   (D) held.

13. As used in line 5, "concluded" most nearly means
   (A) finished.
   (B) arranged.
   (C) stated.
   (D) judged.

Question 14 is based on the following passage.

The following passage is excerpted from an article in a natural history journal.

When I found out about the nesting habits of the Marbled Murrelet, I could see why
they've become endangered—it's amazing they survive at all. The only places they nest
are in old-growth redwoods or Douglas firs within thirty miles of the ocean—although
Line to call it 'nesting' is a bit of a stretch. The female lays an egg in a depression on a large
(5) branch a hundred-fifty feet or more off the ground. And that branch has to be a fair
distance below the crown of the tree, so that the egg will be concealed from above,
because the eggs and young chicks are especially susceptible to crows, jays, and other
predatory birds. Add to this the fact that adult birds mate for life, and don't nest every
year, and the odds against survival seem almost insurmountable. The only way these
(10) birds have kept going as a species is because they're extremely secretive. Even the
experts almost never actually see them in their nesting habitats. Most 'sightings'—
somewhere around ninety-five percent—are from having *heard* them.

14. In line 4, "stretch" most nearly means

   (A) expanse.
   (B) period.
   (C) elasticity.
   (D) exaggeration.

Question 15 is based on the following passage.

The following passage is excerpted from Phoenix Fire, *a novel by Tim O'Laughlin.*

Fort Bragg had once been a major fishing town, but the catch was way down from what it had been in the past. Commercial fishing was yet another casualty of unsound forestry practices that had gone unchecked for generations. The problem
Line had resulted from the massive amount of earth-moving and excavation, not to men-
(5) tion the denuded hillsides the loggers left behind. In the early days of logging, berms of soft earth had been mounded up to provide a soft landing for the huge redwoods, to keep the brittle wood from splintering when they fell. At first, no one had known the effect that the highly erosive logging practices would have on local fisheries—that the salmon and steelhead population would be decimated, as streams and rivers became
(10) warmer from their exposure to the sun, and silt covered the spawning beds. Even after scientists discovered the connection between logging and the decline of the salmon population, the legislature was horrendously slow to act to protect the fishing industry.

15. As used in line 1, "catch" most nearly means a

    (A) concealed drawback.
    (B) quantity of something caught.
    (C) device for securing motion.
    (D) desirable prospect.

Full-Length Passages

Questions 1–10 are based on the following passage.

The following passage is an excerpt from the short story "Clay" in Dubliners *by James Joyce. In this passage, tiny, unmarried Maria oversees tea for the washerwomen, all the while thinking of the treat in store for her: a night off with her younger brother and his family.*

The matron had given her leave to go out as soon as the women's tea was over and Maria looked forward to her evening out. The kitchen was spick and span: the cook said you could see yourself in the big copper boilers. The fire was nice and bright and
Line on one of the side-tables were four very big barmbracks. These barmbracks seemed
(5) uncut; but if you went closer you would see that they had been cut into long thick even slices and were ready to be handed round at tea. Maria had cut them herself.
    Maria was a very, very small person indeed but she had a very long nose and a very long chin. She talked a little through her nose, always soothingly: *"Yes, my dear,"* and *"No, my dear."* She was always sent for when the women quarreled over their tubs and
(10) always succeeded in making peace. One day the matron had said to her:
    "Maria, you are a veritable peace-maker!"
    And the sub-matron and two of the Board ladies had heard the compliment. And Ginger Mooney was always saying what she wouldn't do to the dummy who had charge of the irons if it wasn't for Maria. Everyone was so fond of Maria.

(15)   When the cook told her everything was ready, she went into the women's room and began to pull the big bell. In a few minutes the women began to come in by twos and threes, wiping their steaming hands in their petticoats and pulling down the sleeves of their blouses over their red steaming arms. They settled down before their huge mugs which the cook and the dummy filled up with hot tea, already mixed with milk
(20) and sugar in huge tin cans. Maria superintended the distribution of the barmbrack and saw that every woman got her four slices. There was a great deal of laughing and joking during the meal. Lizzie Fleming said Maria was sure to get the ring and, though Fleming had said that for so many Hallow Eves, Maria had to laugh and say she didn't want any ring or man either; and when she laughed her grey-green eyes sparkled with
(25) disappointed shyness and the tip of her nose nearly met the tip of her chin. Then Ginger Mooney lifted her mug of tea and proposed Maria's health while all the other women clattered with their mugs on the table, and said she was sorry she hadn't a sup of porter to drink it in. And Maria laughed again till the tip of her nose nearly met the tip of her chin and till her minute body nearly shook itself asunder because she knew
(30) that Mooney meant well though, of course, she had the notions of a common woman.

1. The author's primary purpose in the second paragraph is to

(A) introduce the character of a spinster.
(B) describe working conditions in a public institution.
(C) compare two women of different social classes.
(D) illustrate the value of peace-makers in society.

2. It can be inferred from the passage that Maria would most likely view the matron as which of the following?

(A) An inept administrator
(B) A benevolent superior
(C) A demanding taskmaster
(D) An intimate friend

3. Which choice provides the best evidence for the answer to the previous question?

(A) Lines 10–11 ("One day . . . peace-maker")
(B) Line 12 ("And the sub-matron . . . compliment")
(C) Lines 15–16 ("When the cook . . . bell")
(D) Lines 20–21 ("Maria superintended . . . slices")

4. It can most reasonably be inferred from the care with which Maria has cut the barmbracks (lines 4–6) that

(A) she fears the matron.
(B) she is not in a hurry to leave.
(C) it is a dangerous task.
(D) she takes pride in her work.

5. As used in line 13, "charge" most nearly means

   (A) responsibility.
   (B) accusation.
   (C) attack.
   (D) fee.

6. The language of the passage most resembles the language of

   (A) a mystery novel.
   (B) an epic.
   (C) a fairy tale.
   (D) a sermon.

7. Which choice provides the best evidence for the answer to the previous question?

   (A) Lines 2–3 ("The kitchen . . . boilers")
   (B) Lines 7–8 ("Maria . . . .chin")
   (C) Lines 16–18 ("In a few . . . arms")
   (D) Lines 25–28 ("Then Ginger . . . drink it in")

8. As used in line 30, "common" most nearly means

   (A) united.
   (B) widespread.
   (C) usual.
   (D) coarse.

9. It can be inferred from the passage that all of the following are characteristic of Maria EXCEPT

   (A) a deferential nature.
   (B) eagerness for compliments.
   (C) respect for authority.
   (D) reluctance to compromise.

10. During the course of the final paragraph, the omniscient narrator's focus shifts from

    (A) evaluation of laundry women's working conditions to reflection on personal disappointments of the main character.
    (B) depiction of an average working day to an explanation of the protagonist's importance to her community.
    (C) portrayal of interactions within a group to description of the main character's reactions to the conversation.
    (D) recounting of a current group activity to a flashback to an earlier scene.

Questions 11–20 are based on the following passage.

This passage is adapted from Frederick E. Hoxie, This Indian Country: American Indian Political Activists and the Place They Made, *published in 2012.*

Sarah Winnemucca spoke out against the morality of American expansion just as federal officials were embarking on a national campaign to "civilize" all American Indians. Of course missionaries had striven to convert and "uplift" Indian people from
Line the seventeenth century forward, but it was not until the middle of the nineteenth cen-
(5) tury, when the U.S. conquest of the continent became complete, that federal officials and the general public shifted the bulk of their attention from extending the nation's borders to creating a comprehensive system for incorporating indigenous communities into the nation. They hoped to integrate these individuals into the lower rungs of a modern industrial state.

(10) The centrality of domestic reform to the Indian civilization effort had been apparent even in prewar proposals to establish reservations, but those ideas were given new life after the Civil War by reformers such as Lydia Maria Child, who sought to extend the promise of American civilization from newly freed slaves to Indians. A former abolitionist, Child declared in 1870 that "human nature is essentially the same in all
(15) races and classes of men," adding, "My faith never wavers that men can be made just by being treated justly, honest by being dealt with honestly, and kindly by becoming objects of kindly sympathy." Women like Child and Amelia Stone Quinton, who had taught newly freed African Americans in the South immediately after the Civil War, were at the forefront of this effort. Their commitment to "all races and classes of men"
(20) inspired them to press for Indian schools and Indian citizenship. In 1879 Quinton founded the Women's National Indian Association, a forerunner of the later male-led Indian Rights Association. This activity inspired younger women, such as the anthropologist Alice Cunningham Fletcher and the popular author Helen Hunt Jackson, to join the effort.

(25) These women saw domestic reform aimed at civilization (education, traditional marriage, and individual landownership) as a solution for Native communities increasingly surrounded by land-hungry whites. Fletcher became an early advocate of replacing reservations with individual landownership and a firm supporter of the nation's growing network of boarding schools. Helen Hunt Jackson offered her prescriptions in
(30) the form of popular essays and stories. Her most famous effort was a romance set in the Mission Indian communities of southern California. Published in 1884, *Ramona* portrayed the struggle of a Christian Indian woman striving to establish a household for her pious husband and son. Jackson's account of the heroine Ramona's homemaking in the face of racial hostility and rampant lawlessness echoed the domestic images
(35) in Harriet Beecher Stowe's more famous *Uncle Tom's Cabin* and other works that illustrated the nuclear family's ability to protect individuals from hostile outsiders. For Jackson, as for Fletcher and Stowe, a civilized home managed by a Christian matron could be both a refuge from lawlessness and a vehicle for transporting its members to a better place.

(40) In 1883, with the publication of *Life among the Piutes*, Winnemucca attacked the heart of this national campaign of uplift and domestic reform. As early as 1870, she had argued from her post at Camp McDermitt that the solution to Indian suffering was "a

permanent home on [the Indians'] own native soil." Thirteen years later, in *Life among the Piutes*, she proposed the same solution. Winnemucca's angry words were hurled
(45) at a uniform set of self-serving popular attitudes and a rapidly hardening government policy: Indians represented the past, treaties were obsolete, native cultures must yield, and the incorporation of conventional American domestic behaviors was the surest recipe for civilization. Her speeches and writing, coming from an eloquent, self-confident woman, challenged that mind-set and proposed an alternative scenario in
(50) which Indian communities consolidated and progressed on their own within protected enclaves inside America's borders. Rooted in the story of herself and her family and aimed at establishing "homes to live in" for her community, the book was intended as a public testimonial that would provide a guide for Indian survival that challenged alien definitions of Native private life and civilization. The common thread of her activist
(55) career was the dignity of Indian communities and the role within them of powerful Indian women who upheld the best standards of their tribal traditions.

11. The primary purpose of the passage is to

  (A) explain that reservations are not an ideal way to uplift the Indians.
  (B) show that women share strong bonds, even though they have different backgrounds.
  (C) explain the establishment of the Women's National Indian Association.
  (D) explain one woman's resistance to a major reform movement.

12. It can most reasonably be inferred from the passage that the author would likely agree with the idea that

  (A) American Indians needed to be civilized.
  (B) the majority would inevitably have prevailed.
  (C) women authors helped bring about social and political change.
  (D) women were more effective political advocates than were men.

13. As used in line 20, "press" most nearly means

  (A) flatten.
  (B) weigh heavily.
  (C) urge insistently.
  (D) squeeze affectionately.

14. What view did domestic reformers such as Helen Hunt Jackson promote through novels, essays, and other works?

  (A) Adherence to family structure and gender roles that conformed to the dominant American culture would help Indians integrate into society more effectively.
  (B) Adherence to tribal traditions was necessary to prevent complete assimilation and to force the United States government to honor treaty obligations.
  (C) Human nature manifests itself in the same manner in all races.
  (D) The Mission Indians deserved their own reservation in southern California.

15. Which choice best provides the best evidence for the answer to the previous question?

    (A) Lines 27–29 ("Fletcher . . . schools")
    (B) Lines 29–30 ("Helen Hunt Jackson . . . stories")
    (C) Lines 31–33 ("Published . . . son")
    (D) Lines 36–39 ("For Jackson, . . . to a better place")

16. As used in line 29, "prescriptions" most nearly means

    (A) medicine to be administered.
    (B) changes to be considered.
    (C) punishments to be endured.
    (D) reforms to be instituted.

17. The role played by the Women's National Indian Association with regard to the Indian Rights Association can best be described as

    (A) adversarial.
    (B) concurrent.
    (C) cooperative.
    (D) foundational.

18. Over which major issue did Sarah Winnemucca's views clash with those of the other women reformers?

    (A) The proper form of Indian land ownership.
    (B) Use of the term "Indian."
    (C) The importance of literary works in social and political movements.
    (D) The role of women in politics.

19. *Life among the Piutes* may be most aptly characterized as

    (A) a captivating romance.
    (B) an autobiographical testimonial.
    (C) a moralizing historical novel.
    (D) a traditional Native American legend.

20. According to the passage, what was the major change that occurred in the mid-nineteenth century?

    (A) A change in United States government policy from expansion of territory to consolidation of control over people within that territory
    (B) A change in the focus of reformers from abolition to prohibition
    (C) A change in the focus of reformers from men to women
    (D) A change in Indian policy toward the United States government from cooperation to resistance

Questions 21–31 are based on the following passages.

The following passages are excerpted from works that discuss the survival of the city in our time. Passage 1 was written by the literary critic and scholar A. Bartlett Giamatti; Passage 2, by the urban planner and sociologist William H. Whyte.

PASSAGE 1

When musing on cities over time and in our time, from the first (whenever it was) to today, we must always remember that cities are artifacts. Forests, jungles, deserts, plains, oceans—the organic environment is born and dies and is reborn endlessly,
Line beautifully, and completely without moral constraint or ethical control. But cities—
(5) despite the metaphors that we apply to them from biology or nature ("The city dies when industry flees"; "The neighborhoods are the vital cells of the urban organism"), despite the sentimental or anthropomorphic devices we use to describe cities—are artificial. Nature has never made a city, and what Nature makes that may seem like a city—an anthill, for instance—only *seems* like one. It is not a city.
(10) Human beings made and make cities, and only human beings kill cities, or let them die. And human beings do both—make cities and unmake them—by the same means: by acts of choice. We enjoy deluding ourselves in this as in other things. We enjoy believing that there are forces out there completely determining our fate, natural forces—or forces so strong and overwhelming as to be like natural forces—that send
(15) cities through organic or biological phases of birth, growth, and decay. We avoid the knowledge that cities are at best works of art, and at worst ungainly artifacts—but never flowers or even weeds—and that we, not some mysterious force or cosmic bio-logical system, control the creation and life of a city.

We control the creation and life of a city by the choices and agreements we make—
(20) the basic choice being, for instance, not to live alone, the basic agreement being to live together. When people choose to settle, like the stars, not wander like the moon, they create cities as sites and symbols of their choice to stop and their agreement not to separate. Now stasis and proximity, not movement and distance, define human rela-tionships. Mutual defense, control of a river or harbor, shelter from natural forces—all
(25) these and other reasons may lead people to aggregate, but once congregated, they then live differently and become different.

A city is not an extended family. That is a tribe or clan. A city is a collection of dispa-rate families who agree to a fiction: They agree to live *as if* they were as close in blood or ties of kinship as in fact they are in physical proximity. Choosing life in an artifact,
(30) people agree to live in a state of similitude. A city is a place where ties of proximity, activity, and self-interest assume the role of family ties. It is a considerable pact, a city. If a family is an expression of continuity through biology, a city is an expression of continuity through will and imagination—through mental choices making artifice, not through physical reproduction.

PASSAGE 2

(35) It is because of this centrality [of the city] that the financial markets have stayed put. It had been widely forecast that they would move out en masse, financial work being

among the most quantitative and computerized of functions. A lot of the back-office work has been relocated. The main business, however, is not record keeping and support services; it is people sizing up other people, and the center is the place for that.

(40)   The problems, of course, are immense. To be an optimist about the city, one must believe that it will lurch from crisis to crisis but somehow survive. Utopia is nowhere in sight and probably never will be. The city is too mixed up for that. Its strengths and its ills are inextricably bound together. The same concentration that makes the center efficient is the cause of its crowding and the destruction of its sun and its light and its

(45) scale. Many of the city's problems, furthermore, are external in origin—for example, the cruel demographics of peripheral growth, which are difficult enough to forecast, let alone do anything about.

What has been taking place is a brutal simplification. The city has been losing those functions for which it is no longer competitive. Manufacturing has moved toward the

(50) periphery; the back offices are on the way. The computers are already there. But as the city has been losing functions it has been reasserting its most ancient one: a place where people come together, face-to-face.

More than ever, the center is the place for news and gossip, for the creation of ideas, for marketing them and swiping them, for hatching deals, for starting parades. This is

(55) the stuff of the public life of the city—by no means wholly admirable, often abrasive, noisy, contentious, without apparent purpose.

But this human congress is the genius of the place, its reason for being, its great marginal edge. This is the engine, the city's true export. Whatever makes this congress easier, more spontaneous, more enjoyable is not at all a frill. It is the heart of the center

(60) of the city.

21. The author's purpose in Passage 1 is primarily to

(A) identify the sources of popular discontent with cities.
(B) define the city as growing out of a social contract.
(C) illustrate the difference between cities and villages.
(D) compare cities with blood families.

22. The author cites the sentence "The neighborhoods are the vital cells of the urban organism" (line 6) as

(A) a paradox with ironic implications.
(B) a straightforward statement of scientific fact.
(C) a momentary digression from his central thesis.
(D) an example of one type of figurative language.

23. The author's attitude toward the statements quoted in lines 5–6 is

(A) approving.
(B) ambivalent.
(C) pragmatic.
(D) skeptical.

24. According to the author of Passage 1, why is an ant hill by definition unlike a city?

    (A) It can be casually destroyed by human beings.
    (B) It exists on a far smaller scale than any city does.
    (C) It is the figurative equivalent of a municipality.
    (D) It is a work of instinct rather than of imagination.

25. Mutual defense, control of waterways, and shelter from the forces of nature (line 24) are presented primarily as examples of motives for people to

    (A) move away from their enemies.
    (B) build up their supplies of armaments.
    (C) gather together in settlements.
    (D) redefine their family relationships.

26. As used in line 22, "stop" most nearly means

    (A) bring to an end.
    (B) come to a halt.
    (C) prevent.
    (D) cease.

27. By saying a city "is a considerable pact" (line 31), the author primarily stresses its

    (A) essential significance.
    (B) speculative nature.
    (C) moral constraints.
    (D) surprising growth.

28. Underlying the forecast mentioned in lines 36–39 is the assumption that

    (A) the financial markets are similar to the city in their need for quantitative data.
    (B) computerized tasks such as record keeping can easily be performed at remote sites.
    (C) the urban environment is inappropriate for the proper performance of financial calculations.
    (D) either the markets would all move or none of them would relocate.

29. As used in line 45, "scale" most nearly means

    (A) series of musical tones.
    (B) measuring instrument.
    (C) relative dimensions.
    (D) thin outer layer.

30. The author of Passage 2 differs from the author of Passage 1 in that he

(A) disapproves of relocating support services to the city's outskirts.
(B) has no patience with the harshness inherent in public life.
(C) believes that in the long run the city as we know it will not survive.
(D) is more outspoken about the city's difficulties.

31. Compared to Passage 1, Passage 2 is

(A) more lyrical and less pragmatic.
(B) more impersonal and less colloquial.
(C) more objective and less philosophical.
(D) more practical and less detached.

ANSWERS EXPLAINED

Short Passages

1. **(C)** The fact that Raleigh is remembered more for a romantic, perhaps apocryphal, gesture than for his voyages of exploration *illustrates how legendary events outshine historical achievements in the public's mind.*

2. **(D)** The final sentence of the passage maintains that, contrary to expectation, the jellyfish has a sophisticated or *complex* genetic structure. Beware of eye-catchers. Choice (B) is incorrect. "Spineless" (line 1) here means invertebrate, lacking a backbone or spinal column. It does not mean lacking in courage or cowardly.

3. **(C)** The author refers to Douglas in order to introduce Douglas's metaphoric description of the Everglades as the "River of Grass."

4. **(C)** The author is describing the process by which Stubbs taught himself to draw horses.

5. **(D)** The opening sentence of the passage states that few, if any, people recalled Lady Mary's effort to fight smallpox. Her efforts have largely been forgotten. Thus, the purpose of the passage is to *call attention to a neglected historical figure.*

6. **(A)** The human faculty for myth is the *capacity* or ability of people to invent legends.

7. **(C)** An ironic philosopher (someone who looks on the world with wry or amused detachment) might well reflect or *muse* about the irony of Raleigh's being remembered more for his romantic gesture than for his grueling voyages.

8. **(B)** The final sentence of the passage maintains that, contrary to expectation, the jellyfish has a sophisticated or *complex* genetic structure. Note the use of "Yet" here. It is a contrast signal, alerting you to be on the lookout for an antonym. The jellyfish has a simple surface, but that simple surface conceals an unusually *complex* set of genes.

9. **(D)** Enduring value is value that *lasts*. The *lasting* value of the Everglades is that it provides a habitat for endangered species.

10. **(C)** The engineering projects have diverted water away from the Everglades in order to meet or *satisfy* the water needs of Florida's farms and housing developments.

11. **(D)** In saying that "Every inch of [Mrs. Harding] was charged with an energy that made itself felt the moment she entered a room," the author is asserting that Mrs. Harding's body was *filled with* this extraordinarily vital energy. Although "charged" can mean *accused* ("charged with murder"), *billed* ("charged for shipping"), or *entrusted* ("charged with the task"), that is not how it is used here.

12. **(B)** The Civil Rights Act of 1964 was a law or measure that had *engaged* the senators (that is, kept them busy) for nearly two whole months. Although "occupied" can mean *inhabited* ("occupied an apartment"), *invaded* ("Nazis occupied Poland"), or *held* ("occupied a top position"), that is not how it is used here.

13. **(D)** Humphrey came to the conclusion or *judged* that the measure's supporters had enough votes that it would pass. Although "concluded" can mean *finished* ("the lecture concluded"), *arranged* ("they concluded a ceasefire"), or *stated* ("'That's all, Folks,' Porky Pig concluded"), that is not how it is used here.

14. **(D)** The author is emphasizing the implausibility of describing the location in which these birds lay their eggs as a proper nest. When birds nest, they find or make a secluded, safe place where they can shelter their young. The Marbled Murrelet's nesting place, however, is not particularly safe. To call what they do "nesting," therefore, is something of an *exaggeration*, stretching the definition beyond its reasonable limits. Although "stretch" can mean *expanse* ("a bumpy stretch of road"), *period* ("long stretches of time"), or *elasticity* ("the rubber band lost its stretch"), that is not how it is used here.

15. **(B)** Note that the passage opens with the statement that "Fort Bragg had once been a major fishing town." The catch referred to is the *quantity of* fish *caught* by the local fishermen. Although "catch" can mean a *concealed drawback* ("Watch out, there's a catch in it!"), *device for securing motion* ("Fasten the window catch"), or *desirable prospect* ("Prince William was quite a catch!"), that is not how it is used here.

Full-Length Passages

1. **(A)** Throughout the second paragraph, the author pays particular attention to Maria's appearance, her behavior, and her effect on others. If she had been *introduced* previously in the text, there would be no need to present these details about her at this point in the passage.

2. **(B)** The passage mentions the matron twice: once, in the opening line, where she gives Maria permission to leave work early; once, in lines 10–11, where she pays Maria a compliment. Given this context, we can logically infer that Maria views the matron positively, finding her a *benevolent* or kindly *supervisor*. Choices (A) and (C) are incorrect. Nothing in the passage suggests Maria has a negative view of the matron. Choice (D) is incorrect. Given Maria's relatively menial position, it is unlikely she and the matron would be close or intimate friends.

3. **(A)** In this sentence, the matron, Maria's supervisor at her place of employment, pays Maria a compliment, calling her a peacemaker. Maria appears to cherish this compliment. Thus, it seems likely that she would regard the matron as *a benevolent superior*.

4. **(D)** To slice loaves so neatly and invisibly takes a great deal of care. The author specifically states that Maria has cut the loaves. Not only that, he emphasizes the importance of her having done so by placing this statement at the end of the paragraph (a key position). As the subsequent paragraphs point up, Maria is hungry for compliments. Just as she takes pride in her peacemaking, she takes pride in her ability to slice barmbracks evenly.

5. **(A)** To have charge of the irons is to have the *responsibility* for looking after them. Although "charge" can mean *accusation* ("a charge of murder"), *attack* ("Charge!"), or *fee* ("a charge for admission"), that is not how it is used here.

6. **(C)** The descriptions of the bright and shiny kitchen where you "could see yourself in the big copper boilers" and of tiny, witch-like Maria with her long nose and long chin belong to the realm of the fairy tale.

7. **(B)** With her pointy nose that almost touches her pointy chin, Maria resembles a creature straight out of a fairy tale. Thus, this physical description provides the best evidence to support the answer to the previous question.

8. **(D)** From Maria's perspective, Mooney is a common woman: she is *coarse* and vulgar, liking a glass of porter (dark brown bitter beer, originally made as a drink for luggage-handlers) and drinking her tea out of a mug rather than a teacup. Although common can mean *united* ("a common defense"), *widespread* ("common knowledge"), or *usual* ("a common mistake"), that is not how it is used here.

9. **(D)** Maria helps others to compromise or become reconciled; she herself is not necessarily unwilling to compromise. Use the process of elimination to answer this question. The passage suggests that choice (A) is characteristic of Maria. She speaks soothingly and respectfully. Therefore, choice (A) is incorrect. The passage suggests that choice (B) is characteristic of Maria. Maria's response to Ginger Mooney's toast shows her enjoyment of being noticed in this way. Therefore, choice (B) is incorrect. The passage suggests that choice (C) is characteristic of Maria. Maria's obedience to the cook and to the matron shows her respect for authority. Therefore, choice (C) is incorrect.

10. **(C)** The final paragraph begins with the workers gathering for their tea. They settle down, they laugh and joke and tease Maria, who has served the sliced fruit bread. This is a *portrayal of interactions within a group*. It is followed by an account of how Maria feels about being teased and of what she thinks about Ginger Mooney, who has proposed a toast to her health. Thus, during the course of the final paragraph, the narrator's focus shifts from *portrayal of interactions within a group* to *description of main character's reactions to the conversation*.

11. **(D)** The passage focuses on the political activism of Sarah Winnemucca against the background of a national campaign to "civilize" all American Indians, showing that she rejected many of the assumptions adopted by other reformers of the day, including women reformers such as Lydia Maria Child, Amelia Stone Quinton, Alice Cunningham Fletcher, and Helen Hunt Jackson. Choice (D) is the best answer.

   Choice (A) is incorrect because it contradicts Sarah Winnemucca's view. According to the other reformers portrayed in the account, the best way to incorporate American Indians into society was through promotion of private property, the nuclear family, and cultural assimilation. Winnemucca, in contrast, felt that the United States government should honor its treaty obligations with the Indians and accord to them collective control over their own lands in protected reservations. Choice (B) conveys an idea that was one of the main assumptions of the women reformers but is not a main point of the passage. Choice (C) refers to one political accomplishment of the women reformers whose methods and goals Winnemucca criticized.

12. **(C)** The passage addresses two groups of influential reformers who were concerned about the welfare of American Indians and their place in the United States of the late nineteenth century and whose writings helped bring about needed social and political change: on the one hand, concerned non-American Indian women such as Lydia Maria Child, Amelia Stone Quinton, Alice Cunningham Fletcher, and Helen Hunt Jackson, and on the other hand, the American Indian woman activist Sarah Winnemucca. Choice (C) is the best answer.

   Choice (A) is incorrect because the passage suggests that some of the efforts to "civilize" American Indians were detrimental to them and were opposed by Winnemucca, with whose views the author generally agrees. Choice (B) is outside the scope of the passage; however, the fact that individual reformers were able to shape subsequent history suggests that no one result was inevitable. Choice (D) cannot be the correct answer because the passage, while it focuses on the effective political action of women, makes no comparison of their effectiveness with that of men.

13. **(C)** To press for Indian schools and Indian citizenship is to *urge insistently* that schools for Indians should be founded and that Indians should be granted their full rights as citizens of the United States. Choices (A), (B), and (D) are incorrect. Although press can mean *flatten* ("she pressed her slacks"), *weigh heavily* ("the heavy yoke pressed down on his shoulders"), or *squeeze affectionately* ("she pressed his hand"), that is not how it is used here.

14. **(A)** According to the passage, domestic reform formed an important part of efforts to civilize the American Indians, and women reformers such as Alice Cunningham Fletcher and Helen Hunt Jackson advocated the adoption of traditional norms, institutions, social roles prescribed by "American civilization," including monogamy and the nuclear family, on the part of native Americans. Choice (A) is the best answer. Choice (B) is incorrect because it represents the views of Winnemucca as opposed to those of Fletcher and Jackson. Choice (C) represents the views attributed to Lydia Maria Child and Amelia Stone Quinton in paragraph 2. Fletcher and Jackson may have shared these views, but that is not the focus of paragraph 3, which treats Jackson's writings. Choice (D) is incorrect because Jackson and other similar reformers favored private land ownership over the establishment of reservations.

15. **(D)** Choice (D) states explicitly the ideas conveyed by Jackson in her works regarding the prescribed roles she thought American Indian women should play. Choice (A) is incorrect because it focuses on Fletcher rather than Jackson and on schools rather than writings. Choice (B) is incorrect because it merely reports that Hunt conveyed her ideas through essays and literary works. Choice (C) is not as good an answer as choice (D) because it describes the overall plot of the 1884 novel *Ramona* without presenting the specific points that it conveys.

16. **(D)** The prescriptions in question are the recommendations that Helen Hunt Jackson provides for domestic *reform* of the Native communities. The best answer is choice (D). Choice (A) is incorrect because, as used in the passage, "prescriptions" have nothing to do with medicine, but rather are "prescribed courses of action." Choice (B) is incorrect because the changes in question are not options suggested for consideration but rather directives that are presented as obligatory. Choice (C) is incorrect because the idea of punishment does not appear in the context.

17. **(D)** The Women's National Indian Association is described as the forerunner of the Indian Rights Association, suggesting that there is a causal link between the two: the former organization led up to, or contributed to, the founding of the latter. The adjective "foundational" conveys that causal connection, for it means that the Women's National Indian Association laid the foundation or provided the basis for the Indian Rights Association. Choice (D) is the best answer. Choices (A), (B), and (C) are all incorrect because they do not capture the chronological order and causal connection between the two organizations.

18. **(A)** Choice (A) is the best answer. There are several issues regarding which of Sarah Winnemucca's views clashed with those of the other women reformers mentioned, but

the only one that appears in the answer choices is the question of *Indian land owner-ship*. The women reformers advocated private land ownership, whereas Winnemucca advocated Indian sovereignty and collective ownership of large territories, in accordance with treaties the United States government had concluded with various Native American nations. Choice (B) is incorrect because the passage never discusses the use of the term "Indian." Choice (C) is incorrect. Given that Winnemucca and the other women reformers both wrote influential works promoting their social and political agenda, they evidently shared a belief in the importance of literary works in social and political movements. Winnemucca and the other woman reformers would also have agreed that women should play an active role in politics; thus, choice (D) also is incorrect.

19. **(B)** Choice (B) is the best answer. *Life among the Piutes* has *autobiographical* elements, for it draws on Sarah Winnemucca's experience of growing up among her people under rapidly changing circumstances. It is also a *testimonial*, for it reports events of the past as she witnessed them firsthand and is meant to serve as evidence of the injustices that were done to the Piutes and other American Indians.

20. **(A)** The opening paragraph makes clear that United States government policy shifted in the mid-nineteenth century. After the United States extended control over a large part of the North American continent and secured the borders, both government officials and the American public devoted their efforts to the incorporation of Native American communities into the nation. Choice (A) is the best answer.

    Choice (B) must be incorrect because the passage does not mention prohibition, though it does mention abolition. Choice (C) is incorrect because, although the passage does mention men and women, it maintains a focus on women and does not mention any shift in focus from men to women. Choice (D) is incorrect because the passage does not focus on the policy of American Indians toward the United States government. Furthermore, all American Indians did not uniformly cooperate with the United States government prior to the mid-nineteenth century and then shift to resistance afterward.

21. **(B)** Throughout Passage 1 the author reiterates that human beings make cities, that the creation of a city is an act of choice, that a city is the result of an agreement or pact. In all these ways, he *defines the city as growing out of a social contract* by which human beings choose to bind themselves.

22. **(D)** The sentences quoted within the parenthesis are illustrations of the sort of metaphors we use in describing cities. Thus, they are examples *of one type of figurative language*.

23. **(D)** Insisting that cities are not natural but artificial, the author rejects these metaphors as inaccurate. His attitude toward the statements he quotes is clearly *skeptical* (disbelieving).

24. **(D)** An ant hill is the work of insects rather than of human beings. *It is a work of instinct rather than of imagination*, human intelligence, and choice; therefore, by the author's definition, it is not like a city.

25. **(C)** The author cites these factors as "reasons (that) may lead people to aggregate" or *gather together in settlements*.

26. **(B)** Look at the entire sentence in which "stop" appears. "When people choose to settle, like the stars, not wander like the moon, they create cities as sites and symbols of their choice to stop and their agreement not to separate." The nomads' choice to stop is their choice to cease wandering and settle down. In other words, they have chosen to *come to a halt* and put down roots. Choices (A), (C), and (D) are incorrect. Although stop can mean *bring to an end* ("Stop this racket!"), *prevent* ("Stop accidents before they happen"), or *cease* ("The rain stopped"), that is not how it is used here.

27. **(A)** The author clearly is impressed by the magnitude of the choice people make when they agree to live as if mere geographical links, "ties of proximity," can be as strong as blood relationships. In proclaiming a city "a considerable pact," he stresses the *essential significance* or weightiness of this agreement.

28. **(B)** One would predict such a mass exodus of financial firms only if one assumed that the firms could do their work just as well at distant locations as they could in the city. Thus, the basic assumption underlying the forecast is that *computerized tasks such as record keeping* (the major task of most financial institutions) *can easily be performed at remote sites.*

29. **(C)** The city's concentration of people necessitates the enormous size of its buildings. These outsized buildings destroy the scale or *relative dimensions* of the city as originally envisioned by its planners. Choices (A), (B), and (D) are incorrect. Although scale can mean a *series of musical tones* ("practicing piano scales"), a *measuring instrument* ("postage scale"), or a *thin outer layer* ("snake scales"), that is not how it is used here.

30. **(D)** The author of Passage 1 talks in terms of abstractions that keep people dwelling together in cities (the city as pact, the city as an expression of will and imagination); the author of Passage 2 openly mentions the concrete ills that threaten the city: overcrowding, overbuilding of outsized skyscrapers that block the sun, loss of businesses to the suburbs (with the attendant loss of tax revenues). Given his perspective as an urban planner and sociologist, he is inevitably moved to talk *about the city's difficulties.*

31. **(C)** The author of Passage 1 muses about the nature of the city, defining it and dwelling on its significance. He is *philosophical.* Without romanticizing the city, the author of Passage 2 discusses both its strengths and weaknesses. Though he emphasizes the importance of the city, he tries to be impartial or *objective.* Compared to Passage 1, Passage 2 is *more objective and less philosophical.*

Build Your Vocabulary 2

→ THE MASTER WORD LIST

The more you study actual SAT critical reading questions, the more you realize one thing: *the key to doing well on the critical reading portions of the SAT is a strong working vocabulary of college-level words.* And the key to building that strong working vocabulary can be summed up in one word: READ.

Read widely, read deeply, read daily. If you do, your vocabulary will grow. If you don't, it won't.

Reading widely, however, may not always help you remember the words you read. You may have the words in your passive vocabulary and be able to recognize them when you see them in a context and yet be unable to define them clearly or think of synonyms for them. In addition, unless you have already begun to upgrade your reading to the college level, reading widely also may not acquaint you most efficiently with college-level words.

What are college-level words? In going through the preceding chapter, you have examined dozens of questions modeled on those on the SAT. Some of the words in these questions have been familiar to you; others have not. Still others have looked familiar but have turned out to be defined in unexpected ways.

One of the major changes in the new SAT involves vocabulary. The new SAT has eliminated vocabulary questions involving esoteric words like, for example, "esoteric." Instead, vocabulary questions on the new SAT involve common words used in uncommon ways, as well as words with multiple meanings whose specific meaning you can uncover by examining the context in which they occur.

Here is what the test-makers say about the new vocabulary questions: "These words and phrases are neither highly obscure nor specific to any one domain. They are words and phrases whose specific meaning and rhetorical purpose are derived in large part through the context in which they are used." In other words, they are not technical jargon. They are words whose basic meaning you are likely to know, high-utility words likely to appear in many types of reading.

For this reason, in revising our Master Word List, we have eliminated many college-level vocabulary words that are unlikely to appear as question words on the new SAT and that are also unlikely to crop up in the reading passages you will find on the test. However, we have retained college-level vocabulary words that are likely to occur in the sorts of reading passages you will encounter. Even though these words will not be tested in the vocabulary-in-context questions on the test, they are important words, words you need to know on this SAT and in your future college career.

Use the vocabulary lists in this chapter to upgrade your vocabulary to a college level. They are all excellent vocabulary building tools.

Use the flash cards in the back of this book and create others for the words you want to master. Work up memory tricks to help yourself remember them. Try using them on your parents and friends. Not only will going over these words reassure you that you *do* know some SAT-type words, but also it may well help you on the actual day of the test. These words have turned up on previous tests; some of them may well turn up on the test you take.

THE MASTER WORD LIST

The Master Word List begins on the following page. *Do not let this list overwhelm you.* You do not need to memorize every word.

You can use this list as a sort of dictionary. When you come across an unfamiliar word in your reading and can't figure out its meaning from the context, look it up in the word list. The illustrative sentence may help make the word's meaning clear.

For each word, the following is provided:

1. The word (printed in heavy type).
2. Its part of speech (abbreviated).
3. A brief definition.
4. A sentence illustrating the word's use.
5. Whenever appropriate, related words are provided, together with their parts of speech.

The word lists are arranged in strict alphabetical order.

A PLAN FOR MASTERING THE ENTIRE LIST

1. Allot a definite time each day for the study of a list.
2. Devote at least one hour to each list.
3. First go through the list looking at the short, simple-looking words (7 letters at most). Mark those you don't know. In studying, pay particular attention to them.
4. Go through the list again looking at the longer words. Pay particular attention to words with more than one meaning and familiar-looking words that have unusual definitions that come as a surprise to you. Study these secondary definitions.
5. List unusual words on index cards that you can shuffle and review from time to time, along with the flash cards in this book.
6. Use the illustrative sentences in the list as models and make up new sentences of your own.

Word List 1
abate–acuity

abate V. subside; decrease, lessen. Rather than leaving immediately, they waited for the storm to *abate*. abatement, N.

abbreviate V. shorten. Because we were running out of time, the lecturer had to *abbreviate* her speech.

abdicate V. renounce; give up. When Edward VIII *abdicated* the British throne to marry the woman he loved, he surprised the entire world.

abduction N. kidnapping. The movie *Ransom* describes the attempts to rescue a multimillionaire's son after the child's *abduction* by kidnappers. abduct, V.

aberrant ADJ. abnormal or deviant. Given the *aberrant* nature of the data, we doubted the validity of the entire experiment. aberrance, aberrancy, N.

abet V. aid, usually in doing something wrong; encourage. She was unwilling to *abet* him in the swindle he had planned.

abhor V. detest; hate. She *abhorred* all forms of bigotry. abhorrence, N.

abject ADJ. wretched; lacking pride. On the streets of New York the homeless live in *abject* poverty, huddling in doorways to find shelter from the wind.

abolish V. cancel; put an end to. The president of the college refused to *abolish* the physical education requirement. abolition, N.

abominable ADJ. detestable; extremely unpleasant; very bad. Mary liked John until she learned he was dating Susan; then she called him an *abominable* young man, with *abominable* taste in women.

aboriginal ADJ. being the first of its kind in a region; primitive; native. Her studies of the primitive art forms of the *aboriginal* Indians were widely reported in the scientific journals. aborigines, N.

abortive ADJ. unsuccessful; fruitless. Attacked by armed troops, the Chinese students had to abandon their *abortive* attempt to democratize Beijing peacefully. abort, V.

abrade V. wear away by friction; scrape; erode. Because the sharp rocks had *abraded* the skin on her legs, she dabbed iodine on the scrapes and *abrasions*.

abrasive ADJ. rubbing away; tending to grind down. Just as *abrasive* cleaning powders can wear away a shiny finish, *abrasive* remarks can wear away a listener's patience. abrade, V.

abridge V. condense or shorten. Because the publishers felt the public wanted a shorter version of *War and Peace*, they proceeded to *abridge* the novel.

abscond V. depart secretly and hide. The teller who *absconded* with the bonds went uncaptured until someone recognized him from his photograph on "America's Most Wanted."

absolute ADJ. (1) complete; totally unlimited; (2) certain. Although the King of Siam was an *absolute* monarch, he did not want to behead his unfaithful wife without *absolute* evidence of her infidelity.

absolve V. pardon (an offense). The father confessor *absolved* him of his sins. absolution, N.

absorb V. (1) assimilate or incorporate; (2) suck or drink up; (3) wholly engage. During the nineteenth century, America *absorbed* hordes of immigrants, turning them into productive citizens. Can Huggies diapers *absorb* more liquid than Pampers can? This question does not *absorb* me; instead, it bores me. absorption, N.

abstain V. refrain; hold oneself back voluntarily from an action or practice. After considering the effect of alcohol on his athletic performance, he decided to *abstain* from drinking while he trained for the race. abstinence, N.

abstemious ADJ. sparing in eating and drinking; temperate. Concerned whether her vegetarian son's *abstemious* diet provided him with sufficient protein, the worried mother pressed food on him.

abstinence N. restraint from eating or drinking. The doctor recommended total *abstinence* from salted foods. abstain, V.

abstract ADJ. (1) theoretical; not concrete; (2) nonrepresentational. To him, hunger was an *abstract* concept; he had never missed a meal.

abstruse ADJ. obscure; profound; difficult to understand. Baffled by the *abstruse* philosophical texts assigned in class, Dave asked Lexy to explain Kant's *Critique of Pure Reason*.

abundant ADJ. plentiful; possessing riches or resources. At his immigration interview, Ivan listed his *abundant* reasons for coming to America: the hope of religious freedom, the prospect of employment, the promise of a more *abundant* life.

abusive ADJ. coarsely insulting; physically harmful. An *abusive* parent damages a child both mentally and physically.

abysmal ADJ. bottomless. His arrogance is exceeded only by his *abysmal* ignorance.

abyss N. enormous chasm; vast bottomless pit. Darth Vader seized the evil emperor and hurled him down into the *abyss*.

academic ADJ. (1) related to education; (2) not practical or directly useful. When Sharon applied for the faculty position, the department head inquired about her *academic* qualifications. Seismologists' studies about earthquakes are not of purely *academic* interest, for seismology is the major tool for assessing the danger of potential earthquakes.

accede v. agree. If I *accede* to this demand for blackmail, I am afraid that I will be the victim of future demands.

accelerate v. move faster. In our science class, we learn how falling bodies *accelerate*.

accentuate v. emphasize; stress. If you *accentuate* the positive and eliminate the negative, you may wind up with an overoptimistic view of the world.

accessible ADJ. easy to approach; obtainable. We asked our guide whether the ruins were *accessible* on foot.

accessory N. additional object; useful but not essential thing. She bought an attractive handbag as an *accessory* for her dress. also ADJ.

acclaim v. applaud; announce with great approval. The NBC sportscasters *acclaimed* every American victory in the Olympics and decried every American defeat. also N.

acclimate v. adjust to climate. One of the difficulties of our present air age is the need of travelers to *acclimate* themselves to their new and often strange environments.

accolade N. award of merit. In Hollywood, an "Oscar" is the highest *accolade*.

accommodate v. (1) oblige or help someone; (2) provide with housing; (3) adapt to. Mitch always tried to *accommodate* his elderly relatives. When they visited New York, he would *accommodate* them in his small apartment. His home felt cramped, but he did his best to *accommodate* himself to the situation.

accomplice N. partner in crime. Because he had provided the criminal with the lethal weapon, he was arrested as an *accomplice* in the murder.

accord N. agreement. She was in complete *accord* with the verdict.

acerbity N. bitterness of speech and temper. The meeting of the United Nations General Assembly was marked with such *acerbity* that informed sources held out little hope of reaching any useful settlement of the problem. acerbic, ADJ.

acknowledge v. recognize; admit. Although Iris *acknowledged* that the Beatles' tunes sounded pretty dated nowadays, she still preferred them to the hip-hop songs her brothers played.

acme N. top; pinnacle. His success in this role marked the *acme* of his career as an actor.

acoustics N. science of sound; quality that makes a room easy or hard to hear in. Carnegie Hall is liked by music lovers because of its fine *acoustics*.

acquiesce v. assent; agree without protesting. Although she appeared to *acquiesce* to her employer's suggestions, I could tell she had reservations about the changes he wanted made. acquiescence, N.; acquiescent, ADJ.

acquire v. obtain; get. Frederick Douglass was determined to *acquire* an education despite his master's efforts to prevent his doing so.

acquittal N. deliverance from a charge. His *acquittal* by the jury surprised those who had thought him guilty. acquit, v.

acrid ADJ. sharp; bitterly pungent. The *acrid* odor of burnt gunpowder filled the room after the pistol had been fired.

acrimonious ADJ. bitter in words or manner. The candidate attacked his opponent in highly *acrimonious* terms. acrimony, N.

acuity N. sharpness. In time his youthful *acuity* of vision failed him, and he needed glasses.

Word List 2   acumen–allegory

acumen N. mental keenness. His business *acumen* helped him to succeed where others had failed.

acute ADJ. (1) quickly perceptive; (2) keen; (3) brief and severe. The *acute* young doctor realized immediately that the gradual deterioration of her patient's once *acute* hearing was due to a chronic illness, not an *acute* one.

adage N. wise saying; proverb. There is much truth in the old *adage* about fools and their money.

adamant ADJ. hard; inflexible. Bronson played the part of a revenge-driven man, *adamant* in his determination to punish the criminals who destroyed his family. adamancy, N.

adapt v. alter; modify. Some species of animals have become extinct because they could not *adapt* to a changing environment.

addiction N. compulsive, habitual need. His *addiction* to drugs caused his friends much grief.

addle v. muddle; drive crazy; become rotten. This idiotic plan is confusing enough to *addle* anyone. addled, ADJ.

address v. direct a speech to; deal with or discuss. Due to *address* the convention in July, Brown planned to *address* the issue of low-income housing in his speech.

adept ADJ. expert at. She was *adept* at the fine art of irritating people. also N.

adhere v. stick fast. I will *adhere* to this opinion until proof that I am wrong is presented. adhesion, N.

adherent N. supporter; follower. In the wake of the scandal, the senator's one-time *adherents* quickly deserted him.

adjacent ADJ. adjoining; neighboring; close by. Philip's best friend Jason lived only four houses down the block, close but not immediately *adjacent*.

adjunct N. something added on or attached (generally nonessential or inferior). Although I don't absolutely need a second computer, I plan to buy a laptop to serve as an *adjunct* to my desktop model.

admonition N. warning. After the student protesters repeatedly rejected the dean's *admonitions*, the administration issued an ultimatum: either the students would end the demonstration at once or the campus police would arrest the demonstrators. admonish, V.

adopt V. (1) legally take a child as one's own; (2) choose to follow an approach or idea; (3) assume a position or attitude; (4) formally accept (a suggestion or report). Tom *adopted* a daughter, who told him about a new weight-loss plan that her foster mother had *adopted*. In response, Tom *adopted* a patronizing tone, saying that fad diets never worked. Was the committee's report *adopted* unanimously, or did anyone abstain?

adorn V. decorate. Wall paintings and carved statues *adorned* the temple. adornment, N.

adroit ADJ. skillful. His *adroit* handling of the delicate situation pleased his employers.

adulterate V. make impure by adding inferior or tainted substances. It is a crime to *adulterate* foods without informing the buyer; when consumers learned that Beech-Nut had *adulterated* their apple juice by mixing it with water, they protested vigorously.

advent N. arrival. Most Americans were unaware of the *advent* of the Nuclear Age until the news of Hiroshima reached them.

adversary N. opponent. The young wrestler struggled to defeat his *adversary*.

adverse ADJ. unfavorable; hostile. The recession had a highly *adverse* effect on Father's investment portfolio: he lost so much money that he could no longer afford the butler and the upstairs maid. adversity, N.

adversity N. unfavorable fortune; hardship; a calamitous event. According to the humorist Mark Twain, anyone can easily learn to endure *adversity*, as long as it is another man's.

advocacy N. support; active pleading on something's behalf. No threats could dissuade Bishop Desmond Tutu from his *advocacy* of the human rights of black South Africans.

advocate V. urge; plead for. The abolitionists *advocated* freedom for the slaves. also N.

aesthetic ADJ. artistic; dealing with or capable of appreciation of the beautiful. The beauty of Tiffany's stained glass appealed to Esther's *aesthetic* sense. aesthete, N.

affable ADJ. easily approachable; warmly friendly. Accustomed to cold, aloof supervisors, Nicholas was amazed at how *affable* his new employer was.

affected ADJ. artificial; pretended; assumed in order to impress. His *affected* mannerisms—his "Harvard" accent, air of boredom, use of obscure foreign words—annoyed us: he acted as if he thought he was too good for his old high school friends. affectation, N.

affinity N. kinship. She felt an *affinity* with all who suffered; their pains were her pains.

affirmation N. positive assertion; confirmation; solemn pledge by one who refuses to take an oath. Despite Tom's *affirmations* of innocence, Aunt Polly still suspected he had eaten the pie.

affliction N. state of distress; cause of suffering. Even in the midst of her *affliction*, Elizabeth tried to keep up the spirits of those around her.

affluence N. abundance; wealth. Foreigners are amazed by the *affluence* and luxury of the American way of life.

afford V. (1) have enough money to pay for; (2) provide. Although Phil is not sure he can *afford* a membership at the yoga studio, he wants to sign up because of the excellent training the studio *affords*.

aftermath N. consequences; outcome; upshot. People around the world wondered what the *aftermath* of China's violent suppression of the student protests would be.

agenda N. items of business at a meeting. We had so much difficulty agreeing upon an *agenda* that there was very little time for the meeting.

agent N. means or instrument; personal representative; person acting in an official capacity. "I will be the *agent* of America's destruction," proclaimed the beady-eyed villain, whose *agent* had gotten him the role. With his face, he could never have played the part of the hero, a heroic F.B.I. *agent*.

aggrandize V. increase or intensify. The history of the past quarter century illustrates how a President may *aggrandize* his power to act aggressively in international affairs without considering the wishes of Congress.

aggregate V. gather; accumulate. Before the Wall Street scandals, dealers in so-called junk bonds managed to *aggregate* great wealth in short periods of time. aggregation, N.

aggressor N. attacker. Before you punish both boys for fighting, see whether you can determine which one was the *aggressor*.

agility N. nimbleness. The *agility* of the acrobat amazed and thrilled the audience.

agitate V. stir up; disturb. Her fiery remarks *agitated* the already angry mob.

agnostic N. one who is skeptical of the existence or knowability of a god or any ultimate reality. *Agnostics* say we can neither prove nor disprove the existence of god; we simply just can't know. also ADJ.

alacrity N. cheerful promptness. Eager to get away to the mountains, Phil and Dave packed up their ski gear and climbed into the van with *alacrity*.

alias N. an assumed name. John Smith's *alias* was Bob Jones. also ADV.

alienate V. make hostile; separate. Her attempts to *alienate* the two friends failed because they had complete faith in each other.

alimentary ADJ. supplying nourishment. The *alimentary* canal in our bodies is so named because digestion of foods occurs there. When asked for the name of the digestive tract, Sherlock Holmes replied, "*Alimentary*, my dear Watson."

alimony N. payments made to an ex-spouse after divorce. Because Tony had supported Tina through medical school, on their divorce he asked the court to award him $500 a month in *alimony*.

allay V. calm; pacify. The crew tried to *allay* the fears of the passengers by announcing that the fire had been controlled.

allege V. state without proof. Although it is *alleged* that she has worked for the enemy, she denies the *allegation* and, legally, we can take no action against her without proof. allegation, N.

allegiance N. loyalty. Not even a term in prison could shake Lech Walesa's *allegiance* to Solidarity, the Polish trade union he had helped to found.

allegory N. story in which characters are used as symbols; fable. *Pilgrim's Progress* is an *allegory* of the temptations and victories of man's soul. allegorical, ADJ.

Word List 3   alleviate–anomalous

alleviate V. relieve. This should *alleviate* the pain; if it does not, we shall have to use stronger drugs.

alliteration N. repetition of beginning sound in poetry. "The furrow followed free" is an example of *alliteration.*

allocate V. assign. Even though the Red Cross had *allocated* a large sum for the relief of the sufferers of the disaster, many people perished.

allude V. refer indirectly. Try not to mention divorce in Jack's presence because he will think you are *alluding* to his marital problems with Jill.

allure V. entice; attract. *Allured* by the song of the sirens, the helmsman steered the ship toward the reef. also N.

allusion N. indirect reference. When Amanda said to the ticket scalper, "One hundred bucks? What do you want, a pound of flesh?," she was making an *allusion* to Shakespeare's *Merchant of Venice.*

aloft ADV. upward. The sailor climbed *aloft* into the rigging. To get into a loft bed, you have to climb *aloft.*

aloof ADJ. apart; reserved. Shy by nature, she remained *aloof* while all the rest conversed.

altercation N. noisy quarrel; heated dispute. In that hot-tempered household, no meal ever came to a peaceful conclusion; the inevitable *altercation* might even end in blows.

altruistic ADJ. unselfishly generous; concerned for others. In providing tutorial assistance and college scholarships for hundreds of economically disadvantaged youths, Eugene Lang performed a truly *altruistic* deed. altruism, N.

amalgamate V. combine; unite in one body. The unions will attempt to *amalgamate* their groups into one national body.

amass V. collect. The miser's aim is to *amass* and hoard as much gold as possible.

ambidextrous ADJ. capable of using either hand with equal ease. A switch-hitter in baseball should be naturally *ambidextrous.*

ambience N. environment; atmosphere. She went to the restaurant not for the food but for the *ambience.*

ambiguous ADJ. unclear or doubtful in meaning. His *ambiguous* instructions misled us; we did not know which road to take. ambiguity, N.

ambivalence N. the state of having contradictory or conflicting emotional attitudes. Torn between loving her parents one minute and hating them the next, she was upset by the *ambivalence* of her feelings. ambivalent, ADJ.

ambulatory ADJ. able to walk; not bedridden. Juan was a highly *ambulatory* patient; not only did he refuse to be confined to bed, but he insisted on riding his skateboard up and down the halls.

ameliorate V. improve. Many social workers have attempted to *ameliorate* the conditions of people living in the slums.

amenable ADJ. readily managed; willing to be led. Although the ambassador was usually *amenable* to friendly suggestions, he balked when we hinted that he should waive his diplomatic immunity and pay his parking tickets.

amend V. correct; change, generally for the better. Hoping to *amend* his condition, he left Vietnam for the United States.

amiable ADJ. agreeable; lovable; warmly friendly. In *Little Women*, Beth is the *amiable* daughter whose loving disposition endears her to all who know her.

amicable ADJ. politely friendly; not quarrelsome. Beth's sister Jo is the hot-tempered tomboy who has a hard time maintaining *amicable* relations with those around her. Jo's quarrel with her friend Laurie finally reaches an *amicable* settlement, but not because Jo turns amiable overnight.

amity N. friendship. Student exchange programs such as the Experiment in International Living were established to promote international *amity*.

amnesia N. loss of memory. Because she was suffering from *amnesia*, the police could not get the young girl to identify herself.

amnesty N. pardon. When his first child was born, the king granted *amnesty* to all in prison.

amoral ADJ. nonmoral. The *amoral* individual lacks a code of ethics; he cannot tell right from wrong. The immoral person can tell right from wrong; he chooses to do something he knows is wrong.

amorous ADJ. moved by sexual love; loving. "Love them and leave them" was the motto of the *amorous* Don Juan.

amorphous ADJ. formless; lacking shape or definition. As soon as we have decided on our itinerary, we shall send you a copy; right now, our plans are still *amorphous*.

amphibian ADJ. able to live both on land and in water. Frogs are classified as *amphibian*. also N.

ample ADJ. abundant. Bond had *ample* opportunity to escape. Why did he let us catch him?

amplify V. (1) broaden or clarify by expanding; (2) intensify; make stronger. Charlie Brown tried to *amplify* his remarks, but he was drowned out by jeers from the audience. Lucy was smarter: she used a loudspeaker to *amplify* her voice.

amputate V. cut off part of body; prune. Though the doctors had to *amputate* his leg to prevent the spread of cancer, the young athlete refused to let the loss of a limb keep him from participating in sports.

anachronistic ADJ. having an error involving time in a story. The reference to clocks in *Julius Caesar* is *anachronistic*: clocks did not exist in Caesar's time. anachronism, N.

analogous ADJ. comparable. She called our attention to the things that had been done in an *analogous* situation and recommended that we do the same.

analogy N. similarity; parallelism. A well-known *analogy* compares the body's immune system with an army whose defending troops are the lymphocytes or white blood cells.

anarchist N. person who seeks to overturn the established government; advocate of abolishing authority. Denying she was an *anarchist*, Katya maintained she wished only to make changes in our government, not to destroy it entirely. anarchy, N.

ancestry N. family descent. David can trace his *ancestry* as far back as the seventeenth century, when one of his *ancestors* was a court trumpeter somewhere in Germany. ancestral, ADJ.

anchor V. secure or fasten firmly; be fixed in place. We set the post in concrete to *anchor* it in place. anchorage, N.

anecdote N. short account of an amusing or interesting event. Rather than make concrete proposals for welfare reform, President Reagan told *anecdotes* about poor people who became wealthy despite their impoverished backgrounds.

anemia N. condition in which blood lacks red corpuscles. The doctor ascribes her tiredness to *anemia*. anemic, ADJ.

anesthetic N. substance that removes sensation with or without loss of consciousness. His monotonous voice acted like an *anesthetic*; his audience was soon asleep. anesthesia, N.

anguish N. acute pain; extreme suffering. Visiting the site of the explosion, the governor wept to see the *anguish* of the victims and their families.

angular ADJ. sharp-cornered; stiff in manner. Mr. Spock's features, though *angular*, were curiously attractive, in a Vulcan way.

animated ADJ. lively; spirited. Jim Carrey's facial expressions are highly *animated*: when he played Ace Ventura, he looked practically rubber-faced.

animosity N. active enmity. He incurred the *animosity* of the ruling class because he advocated limitations of their power.

annex V. attach; take possession of. Mexico objected to the United States' attempts to *annex* the territory that later became the state of Texas.

annihilate V. destroy. The enemy in its revenge tried to *annihilate* the entire population.

annotate V. comment; make explanatory notes. In explanatory notes following each poem, the editor carefully *annotated* the poet's more esoteric references.

annul V. make void. The parents of the eloped couple tried to *annul* the marriage.

anomalous ADJ. abnormal; irregular. He was placed in the *anomalous* position of seeming to approve procedures which he despised.

Word List 4   anomaly–articulate

anomaly N. irregularity. A bird that cannot fly is an *anomaly*.

anonymity N. state of being nameless; anonymousness. The donor of the gift asked the college not to mention him by name; the dean readily agreed to respect his *anonymity*.

anonymous ADJ. having no name. She tried to ascertain the identity of the writer of the *anonymous* letter.

antagonism N. hostility; active resistance. Barry showed his *antagonism* toward his new stepmother by ignoring her whenever she tried talking to him. antagonistic, ADJ.

antecede v. precede. The invention of the radiotelegraph *anteceded* the development of television by a quarter of a century.

anthology N. book of literary selections by various authors. This *anthology* of science fiction was compiled by the late Isaac Asimov. anthologize, v.

anthropoid ADJ. manlike. The gorilla is the strongest of the *anthropoid* animals. also N.

anthropologist N. a student of the history and science of mankind. *Anthropologists* have discovered several relics of prehistoric man in this area.

anticlimax N. letdown in thought or emotion. After the fine performance in the first act, the rest of the play was an *anticlimax*. anticlimactic, ADJ.

antidote N. medicine to counteract a poison or disease. When Marge's child accidentally swallowed some cleaning fluid, the local poison control hotline instructed Marge how to administer the *antidote*.

antipathy N. aversion; dislike. Tom's extreme *antipathy* for disputes keeps him from getting into arguments with his temperamental wife. Noise in any form is *antipathetic* to him. Among his other *antipathies* are honking cars, boom boxes, and heavy metal rock.

antiquated ADJ. old-fashioned; obsolete. Philip had grown so accustomed to editing his papers on word processors that he thought typewriters were too *antiquated* for him to use.

antiseptic N. substance that prevents infection. It is advisable to apply an *antiseptic* to any wound, no matter how slight or insignificant. also ADJ.

antithesis N. contrast; direct opposite of or to. Stagnation is the *antithesis* of growth.

apathy N. lack of caring; indifference. A firm believer in democratic government, she could not understand the *apathy* of people who never bothered to vote. apathetic, ADJ.

apocalyptic ADJ. prophetic; pertaining to revelations. The crowd jeered at the street preacher's *apocalyptic* predictions of doom. The *Apocalypse* or *Book of Revelations* of Saint John prophesies the end of the world as we know it and foretells marvels and prodigies that signal the coming doom.

apocryphal ADJ. untrue; made up. To impress his friends, Tom invented *apocryphal* tales of his adventures in the big city.

apolitical ADJ. having an aversion or lack of concern for political affairs. It was hard to remain *apolitical* during the Vietnam War; even people who generally ignored public issues felt they had to take political stands.

appall v. dismay; shock. We were *appalled* by the horrifying conditions in the city's jails.

apparatus N. equipment. Firefighters use specialized *apparatus* to fight fires.

appease v. (1) pacify or soothe; (2) relieve. Tom and Jody tried to *appease* the crying baby by offering him one toy after another, but he would not calm down until they *appeased* his hunger by giving him a bottle.

application N. (1) request; (2) act of putting something to use; (3) diligent attention; (4) relevance. Jill submitted her scholarship *application* to the financial aid office. Martha's research project is purely academic; it has no practical *application*. Pleased with how well Tom had whitewashed the fence, Aunt Polly praised him for his *application* to the task. Unfortunately, John's experience in book publishing had little or no *application* to the e-publishing industry.

apposite ADJ. appropriate; fitting. He was always able to find the *apposite* phrase, the correct expression for every occasion.

appraise v. estimate value of. It is difficult to *appraise* the value of old paintings; it is easier to call them priceless. appraisal, N.

appreciate v. (1) be thankful for; (2) increase in worth; (3) be thoroughly conscious of. Little Orphan Annie truly *appreciated* the stocks Daddy Warbucks gave her, which *appreciated* in value considerably over the years. While I *appreciate* the skill and craftsmanship that went into Lucian Freud's paintings, I still dislike them.

apprehension N. (1) fear of future evil; (2) understanding; (3) arrest (of a criminal). Despite the *apprehension* many people feel about black bears, these bears are generally more afraid of humans than humans are of them. Our *apprehension* of the present inevitably is based upon our understanding of the past. Inspector Javert's lifelong ambition was to bring about the *apprehension* and imprisonment of Jean Valjean.

apprenticeship N. time spent as a novice learning a trade from a skilled worker. As a child, Pip had thought it would be wonderful to work as Joe's *apprentice*; now he hated his *apprenticeship* and scorned the blacksmith's trade.

approbation N. approval. She looked for some sign of *approbation* from her parents, hoping her good grades would please them.

appropriate v. acquire; take possession of for one's own use. The ranch owners *appropriated* the lands that had originally been set aside for the Indians' use.

apropos PREP. with reference to; regarding. I find your remarks *apropos* of the present situation timely and pertinent. also ADJ. and ADV.

aptitude N. fitness; talent. The counselor gave him an *aptitude* test before advising him about the career he should follow.

aquatic ADJ. pertaining to water. Paul enjoyed *aquatic* sports such as scuba diving and snorkeling.

arable ADJ. fit for growing crops. The first settlers wrote home glowing reports of the New World, praising its vast acres of *arable* land ready for the plow.

arbiter N. a person with power to decide a dispute; judge. As an *arbiter* in labor disputes, she has won the confidence of the workers and the employers.

arbitrary ADJ. capricious; randomly chosen; tyrannical. Tom's *arbitrary* dismissal angered him; his boss had no reason to fire him. He threw an *arbitrary* assortment of clothes into his suitcase and headed off, not caring where he went.

arbitrator N. judge. Because the negotiating teams had been unable to reach a contract settlement, an outside *arbitrator* was called upon to mediate the dispute between union and management. arbitration, N.

arcane ADJ. secret; mysterious; known only to the initiated. Secret brotherhoods surround themselves with *arcane* rituals and trappings to mystify outsiders. So do doctors. Consider the *arcane* terminology they use and the impression they try to give that what is *arcane* to us is obvious to them.

archaeology N. study of artifacts and relics of early mankind. The professor of *archaeology* headed an expedition to the Gobi Desert in search of ancient ruins.

archaic ADJ. antiquated. "Methinks," "thee," and "thou" are *archaic* words that are no longer part of our normal vocabulary.

archetype N. prototype; primitive pattern. The Brooklyn Bridge was the *archetype* of the many spans that now connect Manhattan with Long Island and New Jersey.

archives N. public records; place where public records are kept. These documents should be part of the *archives* so that historians may be able to evaluate them in the future.

ardent ADJ. intense; passionate; zealous. Katya's *ardor* was contagious; soon all her fellow demonstrators were busily making posters and handing out flyers, inspired by her *ardent* enthusiasm for the cause. ardor, N.

arduous ADJ. hard; strenuous. Her *arduous* efforts had sapped her energy.

arid ADJ. dry; barren. The cactus has adapted to survive in an *arid* environment.

aristocracy N. hereditary nobility; privileged class. Americans have mixed feelings about hereditary *aristocracy*: we say all men are created equal, but we describe particularly outstanding people as natural *aristocrats*.

aromatic ADJ. fragrant. Medieval sailing vessels brought *aromatic* herbs from China to Europe.

arousal N. awakening; provocation (of a response). On *arousal*, Papa was always grumpy as a bear. The children tiptoed around the house, fearing they would *arouse* his anger by waking him up.

arrest V. stop or slow down; catch someone's attention. Slipping, the trapeze artist plunged from the heights until a safety net luckily *arrested* his fall. This near-disaster *arrested* the crowd's attention.

arrogance N. pride; haughtiness. Convinced that Emma thought she was better than anyone else in the class, Ed rebuked her for her *arrogance*.

articulate ADJ. effective; distinct. Her *articulate* presentation of the advertising campaign impressed her employers. also V.

articulate V. (1) express (an idea) clearly; (2) pronounce distinctly. A skilled impromptu debater must be able to *articulate* her ideas clearly and fluently. A speech therapist helps patients *articulate* sounds.

Word List 5   artifact–avalanche

artifact N. object made by human beings, either handmade or mass-produced. Archaeologists debated the significance of the *artifacts* discovered in the ruins of Asia Minor but came to no conclusion about the culture they represented.

artifice N. deception; trickery. The Trojan War proved to the Greeks that cunning and *artifice* were often more effective than military might.

artisan N. manually skilled worker; craftsman, as opposed to artist. A noted *artisan*, Arturo was known for the fine craftsmanship of his inlaid cabinets.

artless ADJ. without guile; open and honest. Sophisticated and cynical, Jack could not believe Jill was as *artless* and naive as she appeared to be.

ascendancy N. controlling influence; domination. Leaders of religious cults maintain *ascendancy* over their followers by methods that can verge on brainwashing.

ascertain V. find out for certain. Please *ascertain* her present address.

ascetic ADJ. practicing self-denial; austere. The wealthy, self-indulgent young man felt oddly drawn to the strict, *ascetic* life led by members of some monastic orders. also N.

asinine ADJ. stupid. "What an *asinine* comment!" said Bob contemptuously. "I've never heard such a stupid remark."

aspire V. seek to attain; long for. Because he *aspired* to a career in professional sports, Philip enrolled in a graduate program in sports management. aspiration, N.

assail V. assault. He was *assailed* with questions after his lecture.

assent V. agree; accept. It gives me great pleasure to *assent* to your request.

assert V. (1) declare or state with confidence; (2) put oneself forward boldly. Malcolm *asserted* that if Reese quit acting like a wimp and *asserted* himself a bit more, he'd improve his chances of getting a date. assertion, N.

assessment N. evaluation; judgment. Your high school record plays an important part in the admission committee's *assessment* of you as an applicant.

assiduous ADJ. diligent. He was *assiduous*, working at this task for weeks before he felt satisfied with his results. assiduity, N.

assimilate V. absorb; cause to become homogeneous. The manner in which the United States was able to *assimilate* the hordes of immigrants during the nineteenth and early twentieth centuries will always be a source of pride to Americans. The immigrants eagerly *assimilated* new ideas and customs; they soaked them up, the way plants soak up water.

assuage V. (1) ease or lessen (pain); (2) satisfy (hunger); (3) soothe (anger). Jilted by Jane, Dick tried to *assuage* his heartache by indulging in ice cream. One gallon later, he had *assuaged* his appetite but not his grief.

assumption N. (1) something taken for granted; (2) taking over or taking possession of. The young princess made the foolish *assumption* that the regent would not object to her *assumption* of power. assume, V.

assurance N. (1) promise or pledge; (2) certainty; self-confidence. When Guthrie gave Guinness his *assurance* that rehearsals were going well, he spoke with such *assurance* that Guinness felt relieved. assure, V.

astronomical ADJ. enormously large or extensive. The government seems willing to spend *astronomical* sums on weapons development.

astute ADJ. wise; shrewd; keen. John Jacob Astor made *astute* investments in land, shrewdly purchasing valuable plots throughout New York City.

asylum N. place of refuge or shelter; protection. The refugees sought *asylum* from religious persecution in a new land.

asymmetric ADJ. not identical on both sides of a dividing central line. Because one eyebrow was set markedly higher than the other, William's face had a particularly *asymmetric* appearance.

atheistic ADJ. denying the existence of God. His *atheistic* remarks shocked the religious worshippers.

atlas N. a bound volume of maps, charts, or tables. Embarrassed at being unable to distinguish Slovenia from Slovakia, George W. finally consulted an *atlas*.

atone V. make amends for; pay for. He knew no way in which he could *atone* for his brutal crime.

atrocity N. brutal deed. In time of war, many *atrocities* are committed by invading armies.

atrophy V. waste away. After three months in a cast, your calf muscles are bound to *atrophy*; you'll need physical therapy to get back in shape. also N.

attain V. achieve or accomplish; gain. The scarecrow sought to *attain* one goal: he wished to obtain a brain.

attentive ADJ. (1) alert and watchful; (2) considerate; thoughtful. Spellbound, the *attentive* audience watched the final game of the tennis match, never taking their eyes from the ball. A cold wind sprang up; Stan's *attentive* daughter slipped a sweater over his shoulders without distracting his attention from the game.

attenuate V. make thin; weaken. By withdrawing their forces, the generals hoped to *attenuate* the enemy lines.

attest V. testify, bear witness. Having served as a member of the Grand Jury, I can *attest* that our system of indicting individuals is in need of improvement.

attribute N. essential quality. His outstanding *attribute* was his kindness.

attribute V. ascribe; explain. I *attribute* her success in science to the encouragement she received from her parents.

attrition N. gradual decrease in numbers; reduction in the work force without firing employees; wearing away of opposition by means of harassment. In the 1960s urban churches suffered from *attrition* as members moved from the cities to the suburbs. Rather than fire staff members, church leaders followed a policy of *attrition*, allowing elderly workers to retire without replacing them.

atypical ADJ. not normal. The child psychiatrist reassured Mrs. Keaton that playing doctor was not *atypical* behavior for a child of young Alex's age. "Yes," she replied, "but not charging for house calls!"

audacious ADJ. daring; bold. Audiences cheered as Luke Skywalker and Princess Leia made their *audacious*, death-defying leap to freedom, escaping Darth Vader's troops. audacity, N.

audit N. examination of accounts. When the bank examiners arrived to hold their annual *audit*, they discovered the embezzlements of the chief cashier. also V.

auditory ADJ. pertaining to the sense of hearing. Audrey suffered from *auditory* hallucinations: she thought Elvis was speaking to her from the Great Beyond.

augment V. increase; add to. Armies *augment* their forces by calling up reinforcements; teachers *augment* their salaries by taking odd jobs.

august ADJ. impressive; majestic. Visiting the palace at Versailles, she was impressed by the *august* surroundings in which she found herself.

auspicious ADJ. favoring success. With favorable weather conditions, it was an *auspicious* moment to set sail. Thomas, however, had doubts about sailing: a paranoid, he became suspicious whenever conditions seemed *auspicious*.

austere ADJ. (1) forbiddingly stern; (2) severely simple and unornamented. The headmaster's *austere* demeanor tended to scare off the more timid students, who never visited his study willingly. The room reflected the man, *austere* and bare, like a monk's cell, with no touches of luxury to moderate its *austerity*.

authenticate V. confirm as genuine. After a thorough chemical analysis of the pigments and canvas, the experts were prepared to *authenticate* the painting as an original Rembrandt.

authoritarian ADJ. subordinating the individual to the state; completely dominating another's will. The leaders of the *authoritarian* regime ordered the suppression of the democratic protest movement. After years of submitting to the will of her *authoritarian* father, Elizabeth Barrett ran away from home with the poet Robert Browning.

authoritative ADJ. having the weight of authority; peremptory and dictatorial. Impressed by the young researcher's well-documented presentation, we accepted her analysis of the experiment as *authoritative*.

autocratic ADJ. having absolute, unchecked power; dictatorial. Someone accustomed to exercising authority may become *autocratic* if his or her power is unchecked. Dictators by definition are *autocrats*. Bosses who dictate behavior as well as letters can be *autocrats* too.

automaton N. robot; person performing a task mechanically. The assembly line job called for no initiative or intelligence on Homer's part; on automatic pilot, he pushed button after button like an *automaton*.

autonomous ADJ. self-governing. Although the University of California at Berkeley is just one part of the state university system, in many ways Cal Berkeley is *autonomous*, for it runs several programs that are not subject to outside control. autonomy, N.

auxiliary ADJ. helper, additional or subsidiary. To prepare for the emergency, they built an *auxiliary* power station. also N.

avalanche N. great mass of falling snow and ice. The park ranger warned the skiers to stay on the main trails, where they would be in no danger of being buried beneath a sudden *avalanche*.

Word List 6   avarice–blare

avarice N. greediness for wealth. King Midas is a perfect example of *avarice*, for he was so greedy that he wished everything he touched would turn to gold.

avenge V. take vengeance for something (or on behalf of someone). Hamlet vowed he would *avenge* his father's murder and punish Claudius for his horrible crime.

averse ADJ. reluctant; disinclined. The reporter was *averse* to revealing the sources of his information.

aversion N. firm dislike. Bert had an *aversion* to yuppies; Alex had an *aversion* to punks. Their mutual *aversion* was so great that they refused to speak to one another.

avert V. (1) prevent; (2) turn away. Hitting the brakes, the vigilant driver was able to *avert* what seemed like an inevitable collision. She *averted* her eyes from the dead opossum on the highway.

avid ADJ. greedy; eager for. *Avid* for pleasure, Abner partied with great *avidity*. avidity, N.

avocation N. secondary or minor occupation. His hobby proved to be so fascinating and profitable that gradually he abandoned his regular occupation and concentrated on his *avocation*.

avow V. declare openly. Lana *avowed* that she never meant to steal Debbie's boyfriend, but no one believed her *avowal* of innocence.

awe N. solemn wonder. The tourists gazed with *awe* at the tremendous expanse of the Grand Canyon.

axiom N. self-evident truth requiring no proof. Before a student can begin to think along the lines of Euclidean geometry, he must accept certain principles or *axioms*.

babble V. chatter idly. The little girl *babbled* about her doll. also N.

baffle V. frustrate; perplex. The new code *baffled* the enemy agents.

balk V. foil or thwart; stop short; refuse to go on. When the warden learned that several inmates were planning to escape, he took steps to *balk* their attempt. However, he *balked* at punishing them by shackling them to the walls of their cells.

banal ADJ. hackneyed; commonplace; trite; lacking originality. The hack writer's worn-out clichés made his comic sketch seem *banal*. He even resorted to the *banality* of having someone slip on a banana peel!

bane N. cause of ruin; curse. Lucy's little brother was the *bane* of her existence: his attempts to make her life miserable worked so well that she could have poisoned him with ratsbane for having such a *baneful* effect.

baroque ADJ. highly ornate. Accustomed to the severe lines of contemporary buildings, the architecture students found the flamboyance of *baroque* architecture amusing. also N. They simply didn't go for *baroque*.

barren ADJ. desolate; fruitless and unproductive; lacking. Looking out at the trackless, *barren* desert, Indiana Jones feared that his search for the missing expedition would prove *barren*.

barricade N. hastily put together defensive barrier; obstacle. Marius and his fellow students hurriedly improvised a rough *barricade* to block police access to the students' quarter. Malcolm and his brothers *barricaded* themselves in their bedroom to keep their mother from seeing the hole in the bedroom floor. also V.

beam N. ray of light; long piece of metal or wood; course of a radio signal. V. smile radiantly. If a *beam* of light falls on you, it illuminates you; if a *beam* of iron falls on you, it eliminates you. (No one feels like *beaming* when crushed by an iron *beam*.)

beeline N. direct, quick route. As soon as the movie was over, Jim made a *beeline* for the exit.

befuddle V. confuse thoroughly. His attempts to clarify the situation succeeded only in *befuddling* her further.

begrudge V. resent. I *begrudge* every minute I have to spend attending meetings; they're a complete waste of time.

beguile V. mislead or delude; pass time. With flattery and big talk of easy money, the con men *beguiled* Kyle into betting his allowance on the shell game. Broke, he *beguiled* himself during the long hours by playing solitaire.

belabor V. explain or go over excessively or to a ridiculous degree; attack verbally. The debate coach warned her student not to bore the audience by *belaboring* her point.

belated ADJ. delayed. He apologized for his *belated* note of condolence to the widow of his friend and explained that he had just learned of her husband's untimely death.

belie V. contradict; give a false impression. His coarse, hard-bitten exterior *belied* his inner sensitivity.

belittle V. disparage or depreciate; put down. Parents should not *belittle* their children's early attempts at drawing, but should encourage their efforts. Barry was a put-down artist: he was a genius at *belittling* people and making them feel small.

belligerent ADJ. quarrelsome. Whenever he had too much to drink, he became *belligerent* and tried to pick fights with strangers. belligerence, N.

bemoan V. lament; express disapproval of. The widow *bemoaned* the death of her beloved husband. Although critics *bemoaned* the serious flaws in the author's novels, each year his latest book topped the best-seller list.

bemused ADJ. confused; lost in thought; preoccupied. Jill studied the garbled instructions with a *bemused* look on her face.

benefactor N. gift giver; patron. Scrooge later became Tiny Tim's *benefactor* and gave him gifts.

beneficial ADJ. helpful; useful. Tiny Tim's cheerful good nature had a *beneficial* influence on Scrooge's once-uncharitable disposition.

beneficiary N. person entitled to benefits or proceeds of an insurance policy or will. In Scrooge's will, he made Tiny Tim his *beneficiary*: everything he left would go to young Tim.

benevolent ADJ. generous; charitable. Mr. Fezziwig was a *benevolent* employer, who wished to make Christmas merrier for young Scrooge and his other employees.

benign ADJ. (1) kindly; favorable; (2) not malignant. Though her *benign* smile and gentle bearing made Miss Marple seem a sweet little old lady, in reality she was a tough-minded, shrewd observer of human nature. We were relieved that Tom's tumor turned out to be *benign*. benignity, N.

bent ADJ; N. determined; natural talent or inclination. *Bent* on advancing in the business world, the secretary-heroine of *Working Girl* has a true *bent* for high finance.

bequeath V. leave to someone by a will; hand down. Though Maud had intended to *bequeath* the family home to her nephew, she died before changing her will. bequest, N.

berate V. scold strongly. He feared she would *berate* him for his forgetfulness.

berserk ADV. frenzied. Angered, he went *berserk* and began to wreck the room.

beseech V. beg; plead with. The workaholic executive's wife *beseeched* him to spend more time with their son.

besiege V. surround with armed forces; harass (with requests). When the bandits *besieged* the village, the villagers holed up in the town hall and prepared to withstand a long siege. Members of the new administration were *besieged* with job applications from people who had worked on the campaign.

betray V. (1) be unfaithful; (2) reveal (unconsciously or unwillingly). The spy *betrayed* his country by selling military secrets to the enemy. When he was taken in for questioning, the tightness of his lips *betrayed* his fear of being caught.

biased ADJ. slanted; prejudiced. Because the judge played golf regularly with the district attorney's father, we feared he might be *biased* in the prosecution's favor. bias, N.

bicameral ADJ. two-chambered, as a legislative body. The United States Congress is a *bicameral* body.

bicker V. quarrel. The children *bickered* morning, noon, and night, exasperating their parents.

biennial ADJ. every two years. Seeing no need to meet more frequently, the group held *biennial* meetings instead of annual ones. Plants that bear flowers *biennially* are known as *biennials*.

bigotry N. stubborn intolerance. Brought up in a democratic atmosphere, the student was shocked by the *bigotry* and narrowness expressed by several of his classmates.

bizarre ADJ. fantastic; violently contrasting. The plot of the novel was too *bizarre* to be believed.

bland ADJ. soothing or mild; agreeable. Jill tried a *bland* ointment for her sunburn. However, when Jack absent-mindedly patted her on the sunburned shoulder, she couldn't maintain a *bland* disposition.

blare N. loud, harsh roar or screech; dazzling blaze of light. I don't know which is worse: the steady *blare* of a boom box deafening your ears or a sudden *blare* of flashbulbs dazzling your eyes.

Word List 7   blasé–cacophonous

blasé ADJ. bored with pleasure or dissipation. Although Beth was as thrilled with the idea of a trip to Paris as her classmates were, she tried to act super cool and *blasé*, as if she'd been abroad hundreds of times.

blasphemy N. irreverence; sacrilege; cursing. In my father's house, the Dodgers were the holiest of holies; to cheer for another team was to utter words of *blasphemy*. blasphemous, ADJ.

blatant ADJ. flagrant; conspicuously obvious; loudly offensive. To the unemployed youth from Dublin, the "No Irish Need Apply" placard in the shop window was a *blatant* mark of prejudice.

bleak ADJ. cold or cheerless; unlikely to be favorable. The frigid, inhospitable Aleutian Islands are *bleak* military outposts. It's no wonder that soldiers assigned there have a *bleak* attitude toward their posting.

blighted ADJ. suffering from a disease; destroyed. The extent of the *blighted* areas could be seen only when viewed from the air.

blithe ADJ. gay; joyous; carefree. Without a care in the world, Beth went her *blithe*, lighthearted way.

bluff ADJ. rough but good-natured. Jack had a *bluff* and hearty manner that belied his actual sensitivity; he never let people know how thin-skinned he really was.

bluff N. pretense (of strength); deception; high cliff. Claire thought Lord Byron's boast that he would swim the Hellespont was just a *bluff;* she was astounded when he dove from the high *bluff* into the waters below. also V.

blunder N. error. The criminal's fatal *blunder* led to his capture. also V.

blurt V. utter impulsively. Before she could stop him, he *blurted* out the news.

bluster V. blow in heavy gusts; threaten emptily; bully. "Let the stormy winds *bluster*," cried Jack, "we'll set sail tonight." Jill let Jack *bluster*: she wasn't going anywhere, no matter what he said.

bode V. foreshadow; portend. The gloomy skies and the sulphurous odors from the mineral springs seemed to *bode* evil to those who settled in the area.

bogus ADJ. counterfeit; not authentic. The police quickly found the distributors of the *bogus* twenty-dollar bills.

bohemian ADJ. unconventional (in an artistic way). Gertrude Stein ran off to Paris to live an eccentric, *bohemian* life with her writer friends. Oakland was not *bohemian*: it was too bourgeois, too middle-class.

boisterous ADJ. violent; rough; noisy. The unruly crowd became even more *boisterous* when he tried to quiet them.

bolster V. support; reinforce. The debaters amassed file boxes full of evidence to *bolster* their arguments.

bolt N. door bar; fastening pin or screw; length of fabric. The carpenter shut the workshop door, sliding the heavy metal *bolt* into place. He sorted through his toolbox for the nuts and *bolts* and nails he would need. Before he cut into the *bolt* of canvas, he measured how much fabric he would need.

bolt V. dash or dart off; fasten (a door); gobble down. Jack was set to *bolt* out the front door, but Jill *bolted* the door. "Eat your breakfast," she said, "don't *bolt* your food."

booming ADJ. (1) deep and resonant; (2) flourishing, thriving. "Who needs a microphone?" cried the mayor in his *booming* voice. Cheerfully he *boomed* out that, thanks to him, the city's economy was *booming*. boom, V.

boon N. blessing; benefit. The recent rains that filled our empty reservoirs were a *boon* to the whole community.

boorish ADJ. rude; insensitive. Though Mr. Collins constantly interrupted his wife, she ignored his *boorish* behavior, for she had lost hope of teaching him courtesy.

boundless ADJ. unlimited; vast. Mike's energy was *boundless*: the greater the challenge, the more vigorously he tackled the job.

bountiful ADJ. abundant; graciously generous. Thanks to the good harvest, we had a *bountiful* supply of food, and we could be as *bountiful* as we liked in distributing food to the needy.

bourgeois ADJ. middle class; selfishly materialistic; dully conventional. Technically, anyone who belongs to the middle class is *bourgeois*, but, given the word's connotations, most people resent it if you call them that.

boycott V. refrain from buying or using. To put pressure on grape growers to stop using pesticides that harmed the farm workers' health, Cesar Chavez called for consumers to *boycott* grapes.

braggart N. boaster. Modest by nature, she was no *braggart*, preferring to let her accomplishments speak for themselves.

brandish V. wave around; flourish. Alarmed, Doctor Watson wildly *brandished* his gun until Holmes told him to put the thing away before he shot himself.

bravado N. swagger; assumed air of defiance. The *bravado* of the young criminal disappeared when he was confronted by the victims of his brutal attack.

brawn N. muscular strength; sturdiness. It takes *brawn* to become a champion weightlifter. brawny, ADJ.

brazen ADJ. insolent. Her *brazen* contempt for authority angered the officials.

breach N. breaking of contract or duty; fissure or gap. Jill sued Jack for *breach* of promise, claiming he had broken his promise to marry her. They found a *breach* in the enemy's fortifications and penetrated their lines. also V.

breadth N. width; extent. We were impressed by the *breadth* of her knowledge.

brevity N. conciseness. *Brevity* is essential when you send a telegram or cablegram; you are charged for every word.

brittle ADJ. easily broken; difficult. My employer's self-control was as *brittle* as an egg-shell. Her *brittle* personality made it difficult for me to get along with her.

browse V. graze; skim or glance at casually. "How now, brown cow, *browsing* in the green, green grass." I remember lines of verse that I came across while *browsing* through the poetry section of the local bookstore.

brunt N. main impact or shock. Tom Sawyer claimed credit for painting the fence, but the *brunt* of the work fell on others. However, he bore the *brunt* of Aunt Polly's complaints when the paint began to peel.

brusque ADJ. blunt; abrupt. Was Bruce too *brusque* when he brushed off Bob's request with a curt "Not now!"?

buffet N. table with food set out for people to serve themselves; meal at which people help themselves to food that's been set out. Please convey the soufflé on the tray to the *buffet*. (*Buffet* rhymes with tray.)

buffet V. slap; batter; knock about. To *buffet* something is to rough it up. (*Buffet* rhymes with Muffett.) Was Miss Muffett *buffeted* by the crowd on the way to the buffet tray?

bulwark N. earthwork or other strong defense; person who defends. The navy is our principal *bulwark* against invasion.

bungle V. mismanage; blunder. Don't botch this assignment, Bumstead; if you *bungle* the job, you're fired!

buoyant ADJ. (1) able to float; (2) cheerful and optimistic. When the boat capsized, her *buoyant* life jacket kept Jody afloat. Scrambling back on board, she was still in a *buoyant* mood, certain that despite the delay she'd win the race.

bureaucracy N. over-regulated administrative system marked by red tape. The Internal Revenue Service is the ultimate *bureaucracy*: taxpayers wasted so much paper filling out IRS forms that the IRS *bureaucrats* printed up a new set of rules requiring taxpayers to comply with the Paperwork Reduction Act.

burgeon V. grow forth; send out buds. In the spring, the plants that *burgeon* are a promise of the beauty that is to come.

burlesque V. give an imitation that ridicules. In *Spaceballs*, Rick Moranis *burlesques* Darth Vader of *Star Wars*, outrageously parodying Vader's stiff walk and hollow voice.

burnish V. make shiny by rubbing; polish. The maid *burnished* the brass fixtures until they reflected the lamplight.

bustle V. move about energetically; teem. David and the children *bustled* about the house getting in each other's way as they tried to pack for the camping trip. The whole house *bustled* with activity.

buttress V. support; prop up. The attorney came up with several far-fetched arguments in a vain attempt to *buttress* his weak case. also N.

cache N. hiding place. The detectives followed the suspect until he led them to the *cache* where he had stored his loot. He had *cached* the cash in a bag for trash: it was a hefty sum.

cacophonous ADJ. discordant; inharmonious. Do the students in the orchestra enjoy the *cacophonous* sounds they make when they're tuning up? I don't know how they can stand the racket. cacophony, N.

Word List 8   cajole–chary

cajole V. coax; wheedle. Diane tried to *cajole* her father into letting her drive the family car. cajolery, N.

calamity N. disaster; misery. As news of the *calamity* spread, offers of relief poured in to the stricken community.

calculated ADJ. deliberately planned; likely. Lexy's choice of clothes to wear to the debate tournament was carefully *calculated*. Her conventional suit was one *calculated* to appeal to the conservative judges.

caliber N. ability; quality. The scholarship committee searched for students of high *caliber*, ones with the intelligence and ability to be a credit to the school.

callous ADJ. hardened; unfeeling. He had worked in the hospital for so many years that he was *callous* to the suffering in the wards. callus, N.

callow ADJ. youthful; immature; inexperienced. As a freshman, Jack was sure he was a man of the world; as a sophomore, he made fun of freshmen as *callow* youths. In both cases, his judgment showed just how *callow* he was.

cameo N. shell or jewel carved in relief; star's special appearance in a minor role in a film. Don't buy *cameos* from the street peddlers in Rome: the workmanship is wretched. Did you catch Bill Murray's *cameo* in *Little Shop of Horrors*? He was on-screen so briefly that if you blinked you missed him.

camouflage V. disguise; conceal. In order to rescue Han Solo, Princess Leia *camouflaged* herself in the helmet and cloak of a space bandit.

candor N. frankness; open honesty. Jack can carry *candor* too far: when he told Jill his honest opinion of her, she nearly slapped his face. candid, ADJ.

cantankerous ADJ. ill humored; irritable. Constantly complaining about his treatment and refusing to cooperate with the hospital staff, he was a *cantankerous* patient.

capacious ADJ. spacious. In the *capacious* rotunda of the railroad terminal, thousands of travelers lingered while waiting for their train.

capacity N. (1) greatest amount or number that something can hold; (2) amount that something can produce; (3) power to understand or to perform; (4) specified position. This thermos container has a one-liter *capacity*. Management has come up with a plan to double the factory's automobile production *capacity*. I wish I had the mental *capacity* to understand Einstein's theory of relativity. Rima traveled to Japan in her *capacity* as director of the Country Dance & Song Society.

capricious ADJ. unpredictable; fickle; fanciful. The storm was *capricious*: it changed course constantly. Jill was *capricious*, too: she changed boyfriends almost as often as she changed clothes. caprice, N.

caption N. title; chapter heading; text under illustration. The *captions* that accompany *The Far Side* cartoons are almost as funny as the pictures. also V.

captivate V. charm or enthrall. Bart and Lisa were *captivated* by their new nanny's winning manner.

cardinal ADJ. chief. If you want to increase your word power, the *cardinal* rule of vocabulary-building is to read.

caricature N. exaggerated picture or description; distortion. The cartoonist's *caricature* of President Bush grossly exaggerated the size of the president's ears. also V.

carnivorous ADJ. meat-eating. The lion's a *carnivorous* beast. A hunk of meat makes up his feast. A cow is not a *carnivore*. She likes the taste of grain, not gore.

carping ADJ. finding fault. A *carping* critic is a nitpicker: he loves to point out flaws. If you don't like this definition, feel free to *carp*.

castigate V. criticize severely; punish. When the teacher threatened that she would *castigate* the mischievous boys if they didn't behave, they shaped up in a hurry.

casualty N. serious or fatal accident. The number of automotive *casualties* on this holiday weekend was high.

cataclysm N. violent upheaval; deluge. The Russian Revolution was a political and social *cataclysm* that overturned czarist society. cataclysmic, ADJ.

catalyst N. agent which brings about a chemical change while it remains unaffected and unchanged. Many chemical reactions cannot take place without the presence of a *catalyst*.

catastrophe N. calamity; disaster. The 1906 San Francisco earthquake was a *catastrophe* that destroyed most of the city. A similar earthquake striking today could have even more *catastrophic* results.

categorical ADJ. without exceptions; unqualified; absolute. Though the captain claimed he was never, never sick at sea, he finally had to qualify his *categorical* denial: he was "hardly ever" sick at sea.

cater to V. supply something desired (whether good or bad). The chef was happy to *cater to* the tastes of his highly sophisticated clientele. Critics condemned the movie industry for *catering to* the public's ever-increasing appetite for violence.

catharsis N. Release of repressed emotional tensions. She blurted out her feelings but felt no *catharsis*, no flood of relief; instead, she merely felt embarrassed at having made a scene.

catholic ADJ. wide-ranging in interests. Her musical tastes are surprisingly *catholic*: she enjoys everything from the Anonymous Four to Lady Gaga.

caucus N. private meeting of members of a party to select officers or determine policy. At the opening of Congress, the members of the Democratic Party held a *caucus* to elect the Majority Leader of the House and the Party Whip.

causal ADJ. implying a cause-and-effect relationship. The psychologist maintained there was a *causal* relationship between the nature of one's early childhood experiences and one's adult personality. causality, N.

caustic ADJ. burning; sarcastically biting. The critic's *caustic* comments angered the actors, who resented his cutting remarks.

cavil V. make frivolous objections. It's fine when you make sensible criticisms, but it really bugs me when you *cavil* about unimportant details. also N.

cede V. yield (title, territory) to; surrender formally. Eventually the descendants of England's Henry II were forced to *cede* their French territories to the King of France.

celebrated ADJ. famous; well-known. Neil deGrasse Tyson is a *celebrated* American astrophysicist and popularizer of science. Director of the Hayden Planetarium, he gained fame as host of the radio show *Star Talk* and the television show *Cosmos*. celebrity, N.

censor N. overseer of morals; person who reads to eliminate inappropriate remarks. Soldiers dislike having their mail read by a *censor* but understand the need for this precaution. also V.

censorious ADJ. critical. *Censorious* people delight in casting blame.

censure V. blame; criticize. The senator was *censured* for behavior inappropriate to a member of Congress. also N.

centrifugal ADJ. radiating; departing from the center. Many automatic drying machines remove excess moisture from clothing by *centrifugal* force.

centripetal ADJ. tending toward the center. Does *centripetal* force or the force of gravity bring orbiting bodies to the earth's surface?

cerebral ADJ. pertaining to the brain or intellect. The heroes of *Dumb and Dumber* were poorly equipped for *cerebral* pursuits.

ceremonious ADJ. marked by formality. Ordinary dress would be inappropriate at so *ceremonious* an affair.

certitude N. certainty. Though there was no *certitude* of his getting the job, Lou thought he had a good chance of doing so.

cessation N. stoppage. The airline's employees threatened a *cessation* of all work if management failed to meet their demands. cease, V.

cession N. yielding to another; ceding. The *cession* of Alaska to the United States is discussed in this chapter.

chagrin N. vexation (caused by humiliation or injured pride); disappointment. Embarrassed by his parents' shabby, working-class appearance, Doug felt their visit to his school would bring him nothing but *chagrin*. Someone filled with *chagrin* doesn't grin: he's too mortified.

chameleon N. lizard that changes color in different situations. Like the *chameleon,* he assumed the political thinking of every group he met.

champion V. support militantly. Martin Luther King, Jr., won the Nobel Peace Prize because he *championed* the oppressed in their struggle for equality.

chaotic ADJ. in utter disorder. He tried to bring order into the *chaotic* state of affairs. chaos, N.

charismatic ADJ. compellingly charming; magnetic. The late Steve Jobs, former CEO of Apple, who commanded a rock-star-like following, was more than once called "the model of a *charismatic* leader."

charlatan N. quack; pretender to knowledge. When they realized that the Wizard didn't know how to get them back to Kansas, Dorothy and her companions were indignant that they'd been duped by a *charlatan.*

chary ADJ. cautious; sparing or restrained about giving. A prudent, thrifty, New Englander, DeWitt was as *chary* of investing money in junk bonds as he was *chary* of paying people unnecessary compliments.

Word List 9   chasten–comeuppance

chasten V. discipline; punish in order to correct. Whom God loves, God *chastens.*

chastise V. punish. "Spare the rod and spoil the child" was Miss Watson's motto: she relished whipping Huck with a birch rod to *chastise* him.

chauvinist N. blindly devoted patriot. A *chauvinist* cannot recognize any faults in his country, no matter how flagrant they may be. Likewise, a male *chauvinist* cannot recognize his bias in favor of his own sex, no matter how flagrant that may be. chauvinistic, ADJ.

check V. (1) stop motion; (2) curb or restrain. Thrusting out her arm, Grandma *checked* Bobby's lunge at his sister. "Young man," she said, "you'd better *check* your temper."

checkered ADJ. marked by changes in fortune. During his *checkered* career he had lived in palatial mansions and in dreary boardinghouses.

chicanery N. trickery; deception. Those sneaky lawyers misrepresented what occurred, made up all sorts of implausible alternative scenarios to confuse the jurors, and in general depended on *chicanery* to win the case.

chide V. scold. Grandma began to *chide* Steven for his lying.

chimerical ADJ. fantastically improbable; highly unrealistic; imaginative. As everyone expected, Ted's *chimerical* scheme to make a fortune by raising ermines in his backyard proved a dismal failure.

chisel V. (1) swindle or cheat; (2) cut with a chisel. That crook *chiseled* me out of a hundred dollars when he sold me that "marble" statue he'd *chiseled* out of some cheap hunk of rock.

chivalrous ADJ. courteous; faithful; brave. *Chivalrous* behavior involves noble words and good deeds.

chronic ADJ. long established as a disease. The doctors were finally able to attribute his *chronic* headaches and nausea to traces of formaldehyde gas in his apartment.

chronicle V. report; record (in chronological order). The gossip columnist was paid to *chronicle* the latest escapades of the socially prominent celebrities. also N.

cipher N. secret code. Lacking his code book, the spy was unable to decode the message sent to him in *cipher.*

cipher N. nonentity; worthless person or thing. She claimed her ex-husband was a total *cipher* and wondered why she had ever married him.

circuitous ADJ. roundabout. To avoid the traffic congestion on the main highways, she took a *circuitous* route. circuit, N.

circumlocution N. indirect or roundabout expression. He was afraid to call a spade a spade and resorted to *circumlocutions* to avoid direct reference to his subject.

circumscribe V. limit; confine. School regulations *circumscribed* Elle's social life: she hated having to follow rules that limited her activities.

circumspect ADJ. prudent; cautious. As the trial date draws near, defendants and their lawyers become increasingly *circumspect* about their comments, for fear that reports of what they have said might prejudice the outcome.

circumvent V. outwit; baffle. In order to *circumvent* the enemy, we will make two preliminary attacks in other sections before starting our major campaign.

cite V. (1) refer to or quote, especially to justify a position; (2) praise; (3) summon someone before a court. When asked to support her position on the need to vaccinate children against polio, Rosemary *cited* several reports of dangerous new outbreaks of this once nearly eliminated disease. The mayor *cited* the volunteers of Hook & Ladder Company 1 for their heroism in extinguishing the recent fire. Although Terry was *cited* for contempt of court, he never went to jail.

civil ADJ. (1) having to do with citizens or the state; (2) courteous and polite. Although Internal Revenue Service agents are *civil* servants, they are not always *civil* to suspected tax cheats.

clamor N. noise. The *clamor* of the children at play outside made it impossible for her to take a nap. also V.

clemency N. disposition to be lenient; mildness, as of the weather. The lawyer was pleased when the case was sent to Judge Smith's chambers because Smith was noted for her *clemency* toward first offenders.

clench V. close tightly; grasp. "Open wide," said the dentist, but Clint *clenched* his teeth even more tightly than before.

cliché N. (1) phrase dulled in meaning by repetition; (2) trite theme. In writing your SAT essay, avoid using *clichés* like "sadder but wiser" and "old as the hills." Once a novel item on restaurant menus, blackened seafood dishes are now just another gastronomic *cliché*.

clientele N. body of customers. The rock club attracted a young, stylish *clientele*.

climactic ADJ. relating to the highest point. When he reached the *climactic* portions of the book, he could not stop reading. climax, N.

clip N. section of filmed material. Phil's job at Fox Sports involved selecting *clips* of the day's sporting highlights for later broadcast. also V.

clique N. small exclusive group. Fitzgerald wished that he belonged to the *clique* of popular athletes and big men on campus who seemed to run Princeton's social life.

clout N. great influence (especially political or social). Gatsby wondered whether he had enough *clout* to be admitted to the exclusive club.

coagulate V. thicken; congeal; clot. Even after you remove the pudding from the burner, it will continue to *coagulate* as it stands; therefore, do not overcook the pudding, lest it becomes too thick.

coalesce V. combine; fuse. The brooks *coalesce* into one large river. When minor political parties *coalesce*, their *coalescence* may create a major coalition.

coalition N. partnership; league; union. The Rainbow *Coalition* united people of all races in a common cause.

coddle V. to treat gently. Don't *coddle* the children so much; they need a taste of discipline.

codify V. arrange (laws, rules) as a code; classify. We need to take the varying rules and regulations of the different health agencies and *codify* them into a national health code.

coercion N. use of force to get someone to obey. The inquisitors used both physical and psychological *coercion* to force Joan of Arc to deny that her visions were sent by God. coerce, V.

cogent ADJ. convincing. It was inevitable that David chose to go to Harvard: he had several *cogent* reasons for doing so, including a full-tuition scholarship. Katya argued her case with such *cogency* that the jury had to decide in favor of her client.

cogitate V. think over. *Cogitate* on this problem; the solution will come.

cognitive ADJ. having to do with knowing or perceiving; related to the mental processes. Though Jack was emotionally immature, his *cognitive* development was admirable; he was very advanced intellectually.

cognizance N. knowledge. During the election campaign, the two candidates were kept in full *cognizance* of the international situation.

cohere V. stick together. Solids have a greater tendency to *cohere* than liquids.

cohesion N. tendency to keep together. A firm believer in the maxim "Divide and conquer," the evil emperor, by means of lies and trickery, sought to disrupt the *cohesion* of the federation of free nations.

coin V. (1) make coins; (2) invent or fabricate. Mints *coin* good money; counterfeiters *coin* fakes. Slanderers *coin* nasty rumors; writers *coin* words. A neologism is an expression that's been newly *coined*.

coincidence N. two or more things occurring at the same time by chance. Was it just a *coincidence* that John and she had chanced to meet at the market for three days running, or was he deliberately trying to seek her out? coincidental, ADJ.

collaborate V. work together. Three writers *collaborated* in preparing this book.

collate V. examine in order to verify authenticity; arrange in order. They *collated* the newly found manuscripts to determine their age.

collateral N. security given for loan. The sum you wish to borrow is so large that it must be secured by *collateral*.

colloquial ADJ. pertaining to conversational or common speech. Some of the less formal reading passages on the SAT have a *colloquial* tone that is intended to make them more appealing to students.

collusion N. conspiring in a fraudulent scheme. The swindlers were found guilty of *collusion*.

colossal ADJ. huge. Radio City Music Hall has a *colossal* stage.

comeuppance N. rebuke; deserts. After his earlier rudeness, we were delighted to see him get his *comeuppance*.

Word List 10   commandeer–confound

commandeer V. to draft for military purposes; to take for public use. The policeman *commandeered* the first car that approached and ordered the driver to go to the nearest hospital.

commemorate V. honor the memory of. The statue of the Minute Man *commemorates* the valiant soldiers who fought in the Revolutionary War.

commensurate ADJ. equal in extent. Your reward will be *commensurate* with your effort.

commiserate V. feel or express pity or sympathy for. Her friends *commiserated* with the widow.

commodious ADJ. spacious and comfortable. After sleeping in small roadside cabins, they found their hotel suite *commodious*.

communal ADJ. held in common; of a group of people. When they were divorced, they had trouble dividing their *communal* property.

compact N. agreement; contract. The signers of the Mayflower *Compact* were establishing a form of government.

compact ADJ. tightly packed; firm; brief. His short, *compact* body was better suited to wrestling than to basketball.

comparable ADJ. similar. People whose jobs are *comparable* in difficulty should receive *comparable* pay.

compatible ADJ. harmonious; in harmony with. They were *compatible* neighbors, never quarreling over unimportant matters. compatibility, N.

compelling ADJ. overpowering; irresistible in effect. The prosecutor presented a well-reasoned case, but the defense attorney's *compelling* arguments for leniency won over the jury.

compensatory ADJ. making up for; repaying. Can a *compensatory* education program make up for the inadequate schooling he received in earlier years?

compile V. assemble; gather; accumulate. We planned to *compile* a list of the words most frequently used on SAT examinations.

complacency N. self-satisfaction; smugness. Full of *complacency* about his latest victories, he looked smugly at the row of trophies on his mantelpiece. complacent, ADJ.

complement N. (1) something that completes or fills up; (2) number or quantity needed to make something complete. During the eighteenth century, fashionable accessories became an important *complement* to a lady's attire; without her proper fan and reticule, her outfit was incomplete. Gomer had the usual *complement* of eyes and ears, two of each.

complement V. complete; consummate; make perfect. The waiter recommended a glass of port to *complement* the cheese.

complementary ADJ. serving to complete something. John and Lisa's skills are *complementary*: he's good at following a daily routine, while she's great at improvising and handling emergencies. Together they make a great team.

compliance N. (1) readiness to yield; (2) conformity in fulfilling requirements. Bullheaded Bill was not noted for easy *compliance* with the demands of others. As an architect, however, Bill recognized that his design for the new school had to be in *compliance* with the local building code.

compliant ADJ. yielding. Because Joel usually gave in and went along with whatever his friends desired, his mother worried that he might be too *compliant*.

complicity N. participation; involvement. You cannot keep your *complicity* in this affair secret very long; you would be wise to admit your involvement immediately.

component N. element; ingredient. I wish all the *components* of my stereo system were working at the same time.

composure N. mental calmness. Even the latest work crisis failed to shake her *composure*.

compound N. (1) something composed of the union of separate parts or elements; (2) walled-in area containing separate buildings. As a chemical *compound*, a water molecule contains one oxygen and two hydrogen atoms linked by covalent bonds. The Kennedy *Compound* consists of three houses on six fenced-in acres of waterfront property on Cape Cod in Hyannis Port, Massachusetts.

compound V. (1) make up into a whole; (2) combine ingredients; (3) make something bad worse. "The flavor of American life was *compounded* of risk, spontaneity, independence, initiative, drift, mobility, and opportunity." (Daniel Boorstin) Before pharmacies existed, doctors *compounded* their own medicines, using a mortar and pestle to grind the ingredients. Trying to run or hide away from your fears only *compounds* the problem; the only way to overcome fear is to tackle the problem head-on.

comprehensive ADJ. thorough; inclusive. This book provides a *comprehensive* review of verbal and math skills for the SAT.

comprise v. include; consist of. If the District of Columbia were to be granted statehood, the United States of America would *comprise* fifty-one states, not just fifty.

compromise v. (1) adjust or settle by making mutual concessions; (2) endanger the interests or reputation of. Sometimes the presence of a neutral third party can help adversaries *compromise* their differences. Unfortunately, you're not neutral; therefore, your presence here *compromises* our chances of reaching an agreement. also N.

compute v. reckon; calculate. He failed to *compute* the interest, so his bank balance was not accurate. computation, N.

concede v. admit; yield. Despite all the evidence Monica had assembled, Mark refused to *concede* that she was right.

conceit N. (1) vanity or self-love; (2) whimsical idea; extravagant metaphor. Although Jack was smug and puffed up with *conceit*, he was an entertaining companion, always expressing himself in amusing *conceits* and witty turns of phrase.

concentration N. (1) action of focusing one's total attention; (2) gathering of people or things close to one another; (3) relative amount of a substance (in a mixture, solution, volume of space, etc.). As Ty filled in the bubbles on his answer sheet, he frowned in *concentration*. Oakland has one of the largest *concentrations* of Tagalog speakers in California. Fertilizers contain high *concentrations* of nitrogen to help promote the growth of crops.

concentric ADJ. having a common center. The target was made of *concentric* circles.

conception N. (1) beginning; (2) forming of an idea. From its *conception* in 2005, the research project ran into serious problems. I had no *conception* of how serious the problems had grown until I visited the project in 2015.

concerted ADJ. (1) mutually agreed on; (2) done together. All the Girl Scouts made a *concerted* effort to raise funds for their annual outing. When the movie star appeared, his fans let out a *concerted* sigh.

concession N. (1) something granted in response to a demand; (2) acknowledgment; (3) preferential rate; (4) right granted to use land, property, etc., for a specific purpose. Before they could reach an agreement, both sides had to make certain *concessions*. Signing up for marital counseling is not a *concession* of failure; it is a commitment to do your best to make the marriage a success. The government intended its recent tax *concessions* to help subsidize homeowners through lower tax rates. California's Shell Oil Company was granted the parking *concession* for the 1915 World's Fair.

conciliatory ADJ. reconciling; soothing. She was still angry despite his *conciliatory* words. conciliate, v.

concise ADJ. brief and compact. When you define a new word, be *concise*: the shorter the definition, the easier it is to remember.

conclusive ADJ. decisive; ending all debate. When the stolen books turned up in John's locker, we finally had *conclusive* evidence of the identity of the mysterious thief.

concoct v. prepare by combining; make up in concert. How did the inventive chef ever *concoct* such a strange dish? concoction, N.

concord N. harmony; agreement between people or things. Watching Tweedledum and Tweedledee battle, Alice wondered at their lack of *concord*.

concrete ADJ. (1) physical or material in nature, as opposed to abstract; (2) real; (3) specific. The word "boy" is *concrete*; the word "boyhood" is abstract. Unless the police turn up some *concrete* evidence of his guilt, we have no case against him. I don't have time to listen to vague pitches; come up with a *concrete* proposal, and then we can talk.

concur v. (1) express agreement with an opinion; (2) happen together. Justice Sotomayor wrote a minority opinion because she did not *concur* with the reasoning of her fellow justices. Sunday was both Mother's Day and Sally's graduation: it was a happy coincidence that the two events *concurred*.

condemn v. (1) censure; (2) sentence; (3) force or limit to a particular state. In *My Cousin Vinnie*, Vinnie's fiancée *condemned* Vinnie for mishandling his cousin Tony's defense. If Vinnie didn't do a better job defending Tony, the judge would *condemn* Tony to death, and Vinnie would be *condemned* to cleaning toilets for a living.

condense v. (1) make more compact or dense; (2) shorten or abridge; (3) reduce into a denser form. If you squeeze a slice of Wonder Bread, taking out the extra air, you can *condense* it into a pellet the size of a sugar cube. If you cut out the unnecessary words from your essay, you can *condense* it to a paragraph. As the bathroom cooled down, the steam from the shower *condensed* into droplets of water.

condescend v. act conscious of descending to a lower level; patronize. Though Jill had been a star softball player in college, when she played a pickup game at the park she never *condescended* to her less experienced teammates. condescension, N.

condone v. overlook; forgive; give tacit approval; excuse. Unlike the frail widow, who indulged her only son and *condoned* his minor offenses, the boy's stern uncle did nothing but scold.

conducive ADJ. contributive; tending to. Rest and proper diet are *conducive* to good health.

confine v. shut in; restrict. The terrorists had *confined* their prisoner in a small room. However, they had not chained him to the wall or done anything else to *confine* his movements further. confinement, N.

confirm v. corroborate; verify; support. I have several witnesses who will *confirm* my account of what happened.

confiscate v. seize; commandeer. The army *confiscated* all available supplies of uranium.

conformity N. (1) state of obeying regulations, standards; (2) behavior that matches the behavior of most others in a group. In *conformity* with the by-laws of the society, I am calling for a special election. Be grateful for the oddballs who defy convention and break through the culture of *conformity* to go their own unique way.

confound v. confuse; puzzle. No mystery could *confound* Sherlock Holmes for long.

Word List 11   confrontation–corrosive

confrontation N. act of facing someone or something; encounter, often hostile. Morris hoped to avoid any *confrontations* with his ex-wife, but he kept on running into her at the health club. How would you like to *confront* someone who can bench press 200 pounds? confront, v., confrontational, ADJ.

congenial ADJ. pleasant; friendly. My father loved to go out for a meal with *congenial* companions.

congenital ADJ. existing at birth. Were you born stupid, or did you just turn out this way? In other words, is your idiocy *congenital* or acquired? Doctors are able to cure some *congenital* deformities such as cleft palates by performing operations on infants.

conglomeration N. mass of material sticking together. In such a *conglomeration* of miscellaneous statistics, it was impossible to find a single area of analysis.

congruent ADJ. in agreement; corresponding. In formulating a hypothesis, we must keep it *congruent* with what we know of the real world; it cannot disagree with our experience.

conjecture v. surmise; guess. Although there was no official count, the organizers *conjectured* that more than 10,000 marchers took part in the March for Peace. also N.

conjure v. summon a devil; practice magic; imagine or invent. Sorcerers *conjure* devils to appear. Magicians *conjure* white rabbits out of hats. Political candidates *conjure* up images of reformed cities and a world at peace.

connivance N. assistance; pretense of ignorance of something wrong; permission to offend. With the *connivance* of his friends, he plotted to embarrass the teacher. connive, v.

connoisseur N. person competent to act as a judge of art, etc.; a lover of an art. She had developed into a *connoisseur* of fine china.

connotation N. suggested or implied meaning of an expression. Foreigners frequently are unaware of the *connotations* of the words they use.

conscientious ADJ. scrupulous; careful. A *conscientious* editor, she checked every definition for its accuracy.

consecrate v. dedicate; sanctify. We shall *consecrate* our lives to this noble purpose.

consensus N. general agreement. Every time the garden club members had nearly reached a *consensus* about what to plant, Mistress Mary, quite contrary, disagreed.

consistency N. (1) absence of contradictions; (2) dependability; (3) degree of thickness. Sherlock Holmes judged puddings and explanations on their *consistency*: he liked his puddings without lumps and his explanations without improbabilities. Show up every day and do your job: *consistency* in performance is the mark of a good employee. If the pea soup is too thick, add some stock until it reaches the *consistency* you want.

consolidation N. unification; process of becoming firmer or stronger. The recent *consolidation* of several small airlines into one major company has left observers of the industry wondering whether room still exists for the "little guy" in aviation. consolidate, v.

conspicuous ADJ. easily seen; noticeable; striking. Janet was *conspicuous* both for her red hair and for her height.

conspiracy N. treacherous plot. Brutus and Cassius joined in the *conspiracy* to kill Julius Caesar. conspire, v.

constituent N. supporter. The congressman received hundreds of letters from angry *constituents* after the Equal Rights Amendment failed to pass.

constraint N. compulsion; repression of feelings. There was a feeling of *constraint* in the room because no one dared to criticize the speaker. constrain, v.

construe v. explain; interpret. If I *construe* your remarks correctly, you disagree with the theory already advanced.

contagion N. infection. Fearing *contagion,* they took great steps to prevent the spread of the disease.

contaminate v. pollute. The sewage system of the city so *contaminated* the water that swimming was forbidden.

contemporary N. person belonging to the same period. Though Charlotte Brontë and George Eliot were *contemporaries,* the two novelists depicted their Victorian world in markedly different ways. also ADJ.

contempt N. scorn; disdain. The heavyweight boxer looked on ordinary people with *contempt,* scorning them as weaklings who couldn't hurt a fly. We thought it was *contemptible* of him to be *contemptuous* of people for being weak.

contend v. (1) argue earnestly; (2) struggle in rivalry. Sociologist Harry Edwards *contends* that some colleges exploit young African American athletes, supporting them as athletes *contending* against one another in sports, but failing to support them as students working toward a degree.

contention N. (1) angry disagreement; (2) point made in a debate or argument; (3) competition. Some people are peacemakers; others seek out any excuse for quarrels and *contention*. It is our *contention* that, if you follow our tactics, you will boost your score on the SAT. Through his editor, Styron learned that he was in *contention* for the National Book Award.

contentious ADJ. quarrelsome. Disagreeing violently with the referees' ruling, the coach became so *contentious* that they threw him out of the game.

contest V. dispute. The defeated candidate attempted to *contest* the election results.

context N. writings preceding and following the passage quoted. Because these lines are taken out of *context*, they do not convey the message the author intended.

contingent ADJ. dependent on; conditional. Caroline's father informed her that any raise in her allowance was *contingent* on the quality of her final grades. contingency, N.

contingent N. group that makes up part of a gathering. The New York *contingent* of delegates at the Democratic National Convention was a boisterous, sometimes rowdy lot.

contract V. (1) compress or shrink; (2) establish by agreement; (3) incur an obligation; (4) catch a disease. Warm metal expands; cold metal *contracts*. During World War II, Germany *contracted* an alliance with Italy and Japan. To pay for his college education, James *contracted* a debt of $20,000. If you think you have *contracted* an infectious disease, see your doctor.

contrived ADJ. forced; artificial; not spontaneous. Feeling ill at ease with his new in-laws, James made a few *contrived* attempts at conversation and then retreated into silence.

controvert V. oppose with arguments; attempt to refute; contradict. The witness's testimony was so clear and her reputation for honesty so well-established that the defense attorney decided it was wiser to make no attempt to *controvert* what she said.

convene V. assemble. Because much needed legislation had to be enacted, the governor ordered the legislature to *convene* in special session by January 15.

convention N. social or moral custom; established practice. Flying in the face of *convention*, George Sand shocked society by taking lovers and wearing men's clothes.

conventional ADJ. ordinary; typical. His *conventional* upbringing left him wholly unprepared for his wife's eccentric family.

converge V. approach; tend to meet; come together. African American men from all over the United States *converged* on Washington to take part in the historic Million Men march.

converse N. opposite. The inevitable *converse* of peace is not war but annihilation.

converse V. chat; talk informally. Eva was all ears while Lulu and Lola *conversed*. Wasn't it rude of her to eavesdrop on their *conversation*? conversation, N.

convert N. one who has adopted a different religion or opinion. On his trip to Japan, though the President spoke at length about the virtues of American automobiles, he made few *converts* to his beliefs. also V.

conviction N. judgment that someone is guilty of a crime; strongly held belief. Even her *conviction* for murder did not shake Peter's *conviction* that Harriet was innocent of the crime.

convoluted ADJ. coiled around; involved; intricate. The new tax regulations are so *convoluted* that even accountants have trouble following their twists and turns.

copious ADJ. plentiful. She had *copious* reasons for rejecting the proposal.

corollary N. consequence; accompaniment. Brotherly love is a complex emotion, with sibling rivalry its natural *corollary*.

corporeal ADJ. bodily; material. The doctor had no patience with spiritual matters: his job was to attend to his patients' *corporeal* problems, not to minister to their souls.

correlation N. mutual relationship. He sought to determine the *correlation* that existed between ability in algebra and ability to interpret reading exercises. correlate, V., N.

corroborate V. confirm; support. Though Huck was quite willing to *corroborate* Tom's story, Aunt Polly knew better than to believe either of them.

corrode V. destroy by chemical action. The girders supporting the bridge *corroded* so gradually that no one suspected any danger until the bridge suddenly collapsed. corrosion, N.

corrosive ADJ. eating away by chemicals or disease. Stainless steel is able to withstand the effects of *corrosive* chemicals. corrode, V.

Word List 12   cosmopolitan–defiance

cosmopolitan ADJ. sophisticated. Her years in the capitol had transformed her into a *cosmopolitan* young woman highly aware of international affairs.

countenance N. face. When Jose saw his newborn daughter, a proud smile spread across his *countenance*.

countenance V. approve; tolerate. He refused to *countenance* such rude behavior on their part.

countermand v. cancel; revoke. The general *countermanded* the orders issued in his absence.

counterpart N. a thing that completes another; things very much alike. Night and day are *counterparts*, complementing one another.

coup N. highly successful action or sudden attack. As the news of his *coup* spread throughout Wall Street, his fellow brokers dropped by to congratulate him.

couple v. join; unite. The Flying Karamazovs *couple* expert juggling and amateur joking in their nightclub act.

covenant N. agreement. We must comply with the terms of the *covenant*.

covert ADJ. secret; hidden; implied. Investigations of the Central Intelligence Agency and other secret service networks reveal that such *covert* operations can get out of control.

craftiness N. slyness; trickiness. In many Native American legends, the coyote is the clever trickster, the embodiment of *craftiness*. crafty, N.

credence N. belief. Do not place any *credence* in his promises.

credibility N. believability. Because the candidate had made some pretty unbelievable promises, we began to question the *credibility* of everything she said.

credo N. creed. I believe we may best describe his *credo* by saying that it approximates the Golden Rule.

credulity N. belief on slight evidence; gullibility; naivete. Con artists take advantage of the *credulity* of inexperienced investors to swindle them out of their savings. credulous, ADJ.

creed N. system of religious or ethical belief. Any loyal American's *creed* must emphasize love of democracy.

criterion N. standard used in judging. What *criterion* did you use when you selected this essay as the prizewinner? criteria, PL.

crux N. crucial point. This is the *crux* of the entire problem: everything centers on its being resolved.

cryptic ADJ. mysterious; hidden; secret. Thoroughly baffled by Holmes's *cryptic* remarks, Watson wondered whether Holmes was intentionally concealing his thoughts about the crime.

culminate v. attain the highest point; climax. George Bush's years of service to the Republican Party *culminated* in his being chosen as the Republican candidate for the presidency. His subsequent inauguration as President of the United States marked the *culmination* of his political career.

culpable ADJ. deserving blame. Corrupt politicians who condone the activities of the gamblers are equally *culpable*.

cumulative ADJ. growing by addition. Vocabulary building is a *cumulative* process: as you go through your flash cards, you will add new words to your vocabulary, one by one.

cursory ADJ. casual; hastily done. Because a *cursory* examination of the ruins indicates the possibility of arson, we believe the insurance agency should undertake a more extensive investigation of the fire's cause.

curtail v. shorten; reduce. When Herb asked Diane for a date, she said she was really sorry she couldn't go out with him, but her dad had ordered her to *curtail* her social life.

cynical ADJ. skeptical or distrustful of human motives. *Cynical* from birth, Sidney was suspicious whenever anyone gave him a gift "with no strings attached." cynic, N.

daunt v. intimidate; frighten. "Boast all you like of your prowess. Mere words cannot *daunt* me," the hero answered the villain.

dauntless ADJ. bold. Despite the dangerous nature of the undertaking, the *dauntless* soldier volunteered for the assignment.

dawdle v. loiter; waste time. We have to meet a deadline so don't *dawdle*; just get down to work.

deadlock N. standstill; stalemate. Because negotiations had reached a *deadlock*, some of the delegates had begun to mutter about breaking off the talks. also v.

dearth N. scarcity. The *dearth* of skilled labor compelled the employers to open trade schools.

debacle N. sudden downfall; complete disaster. In the *Airplane* movies, every flight turns into a *debacle*, with passengers and crew members collapsing, engines falling apart, and carry-on baggage popping out of the overhead bins.

debilitate v. weaken; enfeeble. Michael's severe bout of the flu *debilitated* him so much that he was too tired to go to work for a week.

debunk v. expose as false, exaggerated, worthless, etc; ridicule. Pointing out that he consistently had voted against strengthening anti-pollution legislation, reporters *debunked* the candidate's claim that he was a fervent environmentalist.

decadence N. decay. The moral *decadence* of the people was reflected in the lewd literature of the period.

decelerate v. slow down. Seeing the emergency blinkers in the road ahead, he *decelerated* quickly.

decimate v. kill, usually one out of ten. We do more to *decimate* our population in automobile accidents than we do in war.

decipher v. interpret secret code. Lacking his code book, the spy was unable to *decipher* the scrambled message sent to him from the KGB.

decorum N. propriety; orderliness and good taste in manners. Even the best-mannered students have trouble behaving with *decorum* on the last day of school. decorous, ADJ.

decoy N. lure or bait. The wild ducks were not fooled by the *decoy.* also V.

decrepit ADJ. worn out by age. The *decrepit* car blocked traffic on the highway. decrepitude, N.

decry V. express strong disapproval of; disparage. The founder of the Children's Defense Fund, Marian Wright Edelman, strongly *decries* the lack of financial and moral support for children in America today.

deducible ADJ. derived by reasoning. If we accept your premise, your conclusions are easily *deducible.*

deface V. mar; disfigure. If you *deface* a library book, you will have to pay a hefty fine.

defame V. harm someone's reputation; malign; slander. If you try to *defame* my good name, my lawyers will see you in court. If rival candidates persist in *defaming* one another, the voters may conclude that all politicians are crooks. defamation, N.

default N. failure to act. When the visiting team failed to show up for the big game, they lost the game by *default.* When Jack failed to make the payments on his Jaguar, the dealership took back the car because he had *defaulted* on his debt. default, V.

defeatist ADJ. attitude of one who is ready to accept defeat as a natural outcome. If you maintain your *defeatist* attitude, you will never succeed. also N.

defection N. desertion. The children, who had made him an idol, were hurt most by his *defection* from our cause.

defer V. (1) delay till later; (2) exempt temporarily. In wartime, some young men immediately volunteer to serve; others *defer* making plans until they hear from their draft boards. During the Vietnam War, many young men, hoping to be *deferred,* requested student *deferments.*

defer V. give in respectfully; submit. When it comes to making decisions about purchasing software, we must *defer* to Michael, our computer guru; he gets the final word. Michael, however, can *defer* these questions to no one; only he can decide.

deference N. (1) courteous regard for another's wishes; (2) respect owed to a superior. In *deference* to the minister's request, please do not take photographs during the wedding service. As the Bishop's wife, Mrs. Proudie expected the wives of the lesser clergy to treat her with due *deference.*

defiance N. refusal to yield; resistance. When John reached the "terrible two's," he responded to every parental request with howls of *defiance.* defy, V.

Word List 13   definition–detrimental

definition N. (1) statement of a word's exact meaning; (2) clarity of sound or image being reproduced; (3) distinctness of outlines, boundaries. This word list

gives three *definitions* for the word "*definition.*" The newest flat screen monitors have excellent resolution and amazing color *definition.* The gym's fitness program includes specific exercises to improve *definition* of the abdominal muscles.

definitive ADJ. final; complete. Carl Sandburg's *Abraham Lincoln* may be regarded as the *definitive* work on the life of the Great Emancipator.

deflect V. turn aside. His life was saved when his cigarette case *deflected* the bullet.

deft ADJ. neat; skillful. The *deft* waiter uncorked the champagne without spilling a drop.

defunct ADJ. dead; no longer in use or existence. The lawyers sought to examine the books of the *defunct* corporation.

defuse V. (1) remove the fuse of a bomb; (2) reduce or eliminate a threat. Police negotiators are trained to *defuse* dangerous situations by avoiding confrontational language and behavior.

degenerate V. become worse; deteriorate. As the fight dragged on, the champion's style *degenerated* until he could barely keep on his feet.

delete V. erase; strike out. Less is more: if you *delete* this paragraph, your whole essay will have greater appeal.

deleterious ADJ. harmful. If you believe that smoking is *deleterious* to your health (and the Surgeon General certainly does), then quit!

deliberate V. consider; ponder. Offered the new job, she asked for time to *deliberate* before she told them her decision.

delineate V. portray; depict; sketch. Using only a few descriptive phrases, Austen *delineates* the character of Mr. Collins so well that we can predict his every move. delineation, N.

delude V. deceive. His mistress may have *deluded* herself into believing that he would leave his wife and marry her.

deluge N. flood; rush. When we advertised the position, we received a *deluge* of applications.

delusion N. false belief; hallucination. Don suffers from *delusions* of grandeur: he thinks he's a world-famous author when he's published just one paperback book.

delve V. dig; investigate. *Delving* into old books and manuscripts is part of a researcher's job.

demagogue N. person who appeals to people's prejudice; false leader of people. He was accused of being a *demagogue* because he made promises that aroused futile hopes in his listeners.

demean V. degrade; humiliate. Standing on his dignity, he refused to *demean* himself by replying to the offensive letter. If you truly believed in the dignity of labor, you would not think it would *demean* you to work as a janitor.

demeanor N. behavior; bearing. His sober *demeanor* quieted the noisy revelers.

demur V. object (because of doubts, scruples); hesitate. When offered a post on the board of directors, David *demurred*: he had scruples about taking on the job because he was unsure he could handle it in addition to his other responsibilities.

demystify V. clarify; free from mystery or obscurity. Helpful doctors *demystify* medical procedures by describing them in everyday language, explaining that a myringotomy, for example, is an operation involving making a small hole in one's eardrum.

denigrate V. blacken. All attempts to *denigrate* the character of our late president have failed; the people still love him and cherish his memory.

denizen N. inhabitant or resident; regular visitor. In *The Untouchables*, Eliot Ness fights Al Capone and the other *denizens* of Chicago's underworld. Ness's fight against corruption was the talk of all the *denizens* of the local bars.

denotation N. meaning; distinguishing by name. A dictionary will always give us the *denotation* of a word; frequently, it will also give us the connotations. denote, V.

denouement N. outcome; final development of the plot of a play. The play was childishly written; the *denouement* was obvious to sophisticated theatergoers as early as the middle of the first act.

denounce V. condemn; criticize. The reform candidate *denounced* the corrupt city officers for having betrayed the public's trust. denunciation, N.

depict V. portray. In this sensational exposé, the author *depicts* Beatle John Lennon as a drug-crazed neurotic. Do you question the accuracy of this *depiction* of Lennon?

deplete V. reduce; exhaust. We must wait until we *deplete* our present inventory before we order replacements.

deplore V. regret; disapprove of. Although I *deplore* the vulgarity of your language, I defend your right to express yourself freely.

depose V. dethrone; remove from office. The army attempted to *depose* the king and set up a military government.

deposition N. testimony under oath. He made his *deposition* in the judge's chamber.

depravity N. extreme corruption; wickedness. The *depravity* of Caligula's behavior came to sicken even those who had willingly participated in his earlier, comparatively innocent orgies.

deprecate V. express disapproval of; protest against; belittle. A firm believer in old-fashioned courtesy, Miss Post *deprecated* the modern tendency to address new acquaintances by their first names. deprecatory, ADJ.

depreciate V. lessen in value. If you neglect this property, it will *depreciate*.

depredation N. plundering. After the *depredations* of the invaders, the people were penniless.

derelict ADJ. abandoned; negligent. The *derelict* craft was a menace to navigation. Whoever abandoned it in the middle of the harbor was *derelict* in living up to his responsibilities as a boat owner. also N.

deride V. ridicule; make fun of. The critics *derided* his pretentious dialogue and refused to consider his play seriously. derision, N.

derivative ADJ. unoriginal; derived from another source. Although her early poetry was clearly *derivative* in nature, the critics thought she had promise and eventually would find her own voice.

derogatory ADJ. expressing a low opinion. I resent your *derogatory* remarks.

desolate ADJ. unpopulated. After six months in the crowded, bustling metropolis, David was so sick of people that he was ready to head for the most *desolate* patch of wilderness he could find.

desolate V. rob of joy; lay waste to; forsake. The bandits *desolated* the countryside, burning farms and carrying off the harvest.

despise V. look on with scorn; regard as worthless or distasteful. Mr. Bond, I *despise* spies; I look down on them as mean, *despicable*, honorless men, whom I would wipe from the face of the earth with as little concern as I would scrape dog droppings from the bottom of my shoe.

despondent ADJ. depressed; gloomy. To the dismay of his parents, William became seriously *despondent* after he broke up with Jan; they despaired of finding a cure for his gloom. despondency, N.

despot N. tyrant; harsh, authoritarian ruler. How could a benevolent king turn overnight into a *despot*?

destitute ADJ. extremely poor. Because they had no health insurance, the father's costly illness left the family *destitute*.

desultory ADJ. aimless; haphazard; digressing at random. In prison Malcolm X set himself the task of reading straight through the dictionary; to him, reading was purposeful, not *desultory*.

detachment N. (1) emotional remoteness; (2) group sent away (on a military mission, etc.); (3) process of separation. Psychoanalysts must maintain their professional *detachment* and stay uninvolved with their patients' personal lives. The plane transported a *detachment* of Peace Corps volunteers heading for their first assignment abroad. Retinal *detachment*, in which the retina and optic nerve separate, causes severe vision loss.

determination N. (1) firmness of purpose; (2) calculation; (3) decision. Nothing could shake his *determination* that his children would get the best education that money could buy. Thanks to my calculator, my *determination* of the answer to the problem took only seconds. In America's system of government, the president and Congress must heed the Supreme Court's *determination* of constitutional issues.

deterrent N. something that discourages; hindrance. Does the threat of capital punishment serve as a *deterrent* to potential killers? deter, V.

detraction N. slandering; aspersion. He is offended by your frequent *detractions* of his ability as a leader.

detrimental ADJ. harmful; damaging. The candidate's acceptance of major financial contributions from a well-known racist ultimately proved *detrimental* to his campaign, for he lost the backing of many of his early grassroots supporters. detriment, N.

Word List 14   deviate–disengage

deviate V. turn away from (a principle, norm); depart; diverge. Richard never *deviated* from his daily routine: every day he set off for work at eight o'clock, had his sack lunch (peanut butter on whole wheat) at 12:15, and headed home at the stroke of five.

devious ADJ. roundabout; erratic; not straightforward. The Joker's plan was so *devious* that it was only with great difficulty we could follow its shifts and dodges.

devise V. think up; invent; plan. How clever he must be to have *devised* such a devious plan! What ingenious inventions might he have *devised* if he had turned his mind to science and not to crime.

devoid ADJ. lacking. You may think her mind is a total void, but she's actually not *devoid* of intelligence. She just sounds like an airhead.

devout ADJ. pious. The *devout* man prayed daily.

dexterous ADJ. skillful. The magician was so *dexterous* that we could not follow him as he performed his tricks.

diabolical ADJ. devilish. "What a fiend I am, to devise such a *diabolical* scheme to destroy Gotham City," chortled the Joker gleefully.

diagnosis N. art of identifying a disease; analysis of a condition. In medical school Margaret developed her skill at *diagnosis*, learning how to read volumes from a rapid pulse or a hacking cough. diagnose, V.; diagnostic, ADJ.

dichotomy N. split; branching into two parts (especially contradictory ones). Willie didn't know how to resolve the *dichotomy* between his ambition to go to college and his childhood longing to run away and join the circus. Then he heard about Ringling Brothers Circus College, and he knew he'd found the perfect school.

dictum N. authoritative and weighty statement; saying; maxim. University administrations still follow the old *dictum* of "Publish or perish." They don't care how good a teacher you are; if you don't publish enough papers, you're out of a job.

didactic ADJ. teaching; instructional. Pope's lengthy poem *An Essay on Man* is too *didactic* for my taste: I dislike it when poets turn preachy and moralize.

differentiate V. distinguish; perceive a difference between. Tweedledum and Tweedledee were like two peas in a pod; not even Mother Tweedle could *differentiate* the one from the other.

diffidence N. shyness. You must overcome your *diffidence* if you intend to become a salesperson.

diffuse ADJ. (1) both wordy and poorly organized; (2) spread out (as opposed to concentrated). If you pay authors by the word, you're tempting them to produce *diffuse* books instead of concise ones. When a cloud covers the sun, the lighting is *diffuse*, or spread evenly across the entire sky overhead.

digression N. wandering away from the subject. Nobody minded when Professor Renoir's lectures wandered away from their official theme; his *digressions* were always more fascinating than the topic of the day. digress, V.

dilapidated ADJ. ruined because of neglect. The *dilapidated* old building needed far more work than just a new coat of paint. dilapidation, N.

dilatory ADJ. delaying. If you are *dilatory* in paying bills, your credit rating may suffer.

dilemma N. problem; choice of two unsatisfactory alternatives. In this *dilemma,* he knew no one to whom he could turn for advice.

dilettante N. aimless follower of the arts; amateur; dabbler. He was not serious in his painting; he was rather a *dilettante*.

diligence N. steadiness of effort; persistent hard work. Her employers were greatly impressed by her *diligence* and offered her a partnership in the firm. diligent, ADJ.

dilute V. make less concentrated; reduce in strength. She preferred to *dilute* her coffee with milk.

diminution N. lessening; reduction in size. Old Jack was as sharp at eighty as he had been at fifty; increasing age led to no *diminution* of his mental acuity.

din N. continued loud noise. The *din* of the jackhammers outside the classroom window drowned out the lecturer's voice. also V.

dint N. means; effort. By *dint* of much hard work, the volunteers were able to place the raging forest fire under control.

dire ADJ. disastrous. People ignored her *dire* predictions of an approaching depression.

disabuse V. correct a false impression; undeceive. I will attempt to *disabuse* you of your impression of my client's guilt; I know he is innocent.

disaffected ADJ. disloyal. Once the most loyal of Gorbachev's supporters, Sheverdnaze found himself becoming increasingly *disaffected*.

disapprobation N. disapproval; condemnation. The conservative father viewed his daughter's radical boyfriend with *disapprobation.*

disarray N. a disorderly or untidy state. After the New Year's party, the once orderly house was in total *disarray.*

disavowal N. denial; disclaiming. His *disavowal* of his part in the conspiracy was not believed by the jury. disavow, v.

disband V. dissolve; disperse. The chess club *disbanded* after its disastrous initial season.

discernible ADJ. distinguishable; perceivable. The ships in the harbor were not *discernible* in the fog. discern, v.

discerning ADJ. mentally quick and observant; having insight. Though no genius, the star was sufficiently *discerning* to tell her true friends from the countless phonies who flattered her.

disclose V. reveal. Although competitors offered him bribes, he refused to *disclose* any information about his company's forthcoming product. disclosure, N.

discombobulated ADJ. confused; discomposed. The novice square dancer became so *discombobulated* that he wandered into the wrong set.

discomposure N. agitation; loss of poise. Perpetually poised, Agent 007 never exhibited a moment's *discomposure.*

disconcert V. confuse; upset; embarrass. The lawyer was *disconcerted* by the evidence produced by her adversary.

disconsolate ADJ. sad. The death of his wife left him *disconsolate.*

discord N. conflict; lack of harmony. Watching Tweedledum battle Tweedledee, Alice wondered what had caused this pointless *discord.*

discordant ADJ. (1) disagreeable to the ear; (2) not in harmony. Nothing is quite so *discordant* as the sound of a junior high school orchestra tuning up. Viewers disagree wildly about the merits of *Game of Thrones*, as the highly *discordant* comments on Facebook make obvious.

discount V. (1) minimize the significance of; (2) reduce in price. Be prepared to *discount* what he has to say about his ex-wife; he is still very bitter about the divorce. Sharon waited to buy a bathing suit until Macy's fall sale, when the department store *discounted* the summer fashions.

discourse N. formal discussion; conversation. The young Plato was drawn to the Agora to hear the philosophical *discourse* of Socrates and his followers. also v.

discredit V. defame; destroy confidence in; disbelieve. The campaign was highly negative in tone; each candidate tried to *discredit* the other.

discrepancy N. lack of consistency; difference. The police noticed some *discrepancies* in his description of the crime and did not believe him.

discrete ADJ. separate; unconnected. The universe is composed of *discrete* bodies.

discretion N. prudence; ability to adjust actions to circumstances. Use your *discretion* in this matter and do not discuss it with anyone. discreet, ADJ.

discriminating ADJ. (1) treating people of different classes unequally; (2) able to see subtle differences. The firm was accused of *discriminating* hiring practices that were biased against women. A superb interpreter of Picasso, she was sufficiently *discriminating* to judge the most complex works of modern art. discrimination, N.

disdain V. view with scorn or contempt. In the film *Funny Face*, the bookish heroine *disdained* fashion models for their lack of intellectual interests. also N.

disenfranchise V. deprive of a civil right. The imposition of the poll tax effectively *disenfranchised* poor Southern blacks, who lost their right to vote.

disengage V. uncouple; separate; disconnect. A standard movie routine involves the hero's desperate attempt to *disengage* a railroad car from a moving train.

Word List 15   disgruntle–dutiful

disgruntle V. make discontented. The passengers were *disgruntled* by the numerous delays. •

dishearten V. discourage; cause to lose courage or hope. His failure to pass the bar exam *disheartened* him.

disinclination N. unwillingness. Some mornings I feel a great *disinclination* to get out of bed.

disingenuous ADJ. lacking genuine candor; insincere. Now that we know the mayor and his wife are engaged in a bitter divorce fight, we find their earlier remarks regretting their lack of time together remarkably *disingenuous.*

disinterested ADJ. unprejudiced. Given the judge's political ambitions and the lawyers' financial interest in the case, the only *disinterested* person in the courtroom may have been the court reporter.

dismantle V. take apart. When the show closed, they *dismantled* the scenery before storing it.

dismay V. discourage; frighten. The huge amount of work she had left to do *dismayed* her. also N.

dismiss V. (1) let go from employment (2) refuse to accept or consider. To cut costs, the store manager *dismissed* all the full-time workers and replaced them with part-time employees at lower pay. Because Tina believed in Tony's fidelity, she *dismissed* the notion that he might be having an affair.

disparage v. belittle. A doting mother, Emma was more likely to praise her son's crude attempts at art than to *disparage* them.

disparate ADJ. basically different; unrelated. Unfortunately, Tony and Tina have *disparate* notions of marriage: Tony sees it as a carefree extended love affair, while Tina sees it as a solemn commitment to build a family and a home.

disparity N. difference; condition of inequality. Their *disparity* in rank made no difference at all to the prince and Cinderella.

dispassionate ADJ. calm; impartial. Known in the company for his cool judgment, Bill could impartially examine the causes of a problem, giving a *dispassionate* analysis of what had gone wrong, and go on to suggest how to correct the mess.

dispatch N. (1) speediness; prompt execution; (2) message sent with all due speed. Young Napoleon defeated the enemy with all possible *dispatch;* he then sent a *dispatch* to headquarters informing his commander of the great victory. also V.

dispel v. scatter; drive away; cause to vanish. The bright sunlight eventually *dispelled* the morning mist.

disperse v. scatter. The police fired tear gas into the crowd to *disperse* the protesters. dispersion, N.

disputatious ADJ. argumentative; fond of arguing. Convinced he knew more than his lawyers, Alan was a *disputatious* client, ready to argue about the best way to conduct the case. disputant, N.

disquiet v. make uneasy or anxious. Holmes's absence for a day, slightly *disquieted* Watson; after a week with no word, however, Watson's uneasiness about his missing friend had grown into a deep fear for his safety. disquietude, N.

dissemble v. disguise; pretend. Even though John tried to *dissemble* his motive for taking modern dance, we all knew he was there not to dance but to meet girls.

disseminate v. distribute; spread; scatter (like seeds). By their use of the Internet, propagandists have been able to *disseminate* their pet doctrines to new audiences around the globe.

dissent v. disagree. In the recent Supreme Court decision, Justice Sotomayor *dissented* from the majority opinion. also N.

dissertation N. formal essay. In order to earn a graduate degree from many of our universities, a candidate is frequently required to prepare a *dissertation* on some scholarly subject.

dissident ADJ. dissenting; rebellious. In the purge that followed the student demonstrations at Tiananmen Square, the government hunted down the *dissident* students and their supporters. also N.

dissimulate v. pretend; conceal by feigning. Although the governor tried to *dissimulate* his feelings about the opposing candidate, we all knew he despised his rival.

dissolution N. (1) breaking of a union; (2) decay; termination. Which caused King Lear more suffering: the *dissolution* of his kingdom into warring factions or the *dissolution* of his aged, failing body?

dissonance N. discord. Composer Charles Ives often used *dissonance*—clashing or unresolved chords—for special effects in his musical works.

dissuade v. persuade not to do; discourage. Since Tom could not *dissuade* Huck from running away from home, he decided to run away with him. dissuasion, N.

distant ADJ. reserved or aloof; cold in manner. His *distant* greeting made me feel unwelcome from the start. (secondary meaning)

distinction N. (1) honor; (2) contrast; discrimination. A holder of the Medal of Honor, George served with great *distinction* in World War II. He made a *distinction*, however, between World War II and Vietnam, which he considered an immoral conflict.

distort v. twist out of shape. It is difficult to believe the newspaper accounts of the riots because of the way some reporters *distort* and exaggerate the actual events. distortion, N.

diverge v. vary; go in different directions from the same point. The spokes of the wheel *diverge* from the hub.

divergent ADJ. differing; deviating. Since graduating from medical school, the two doctors have taken *divergent* paths, one going on to become a nationally prominent surgeon, the other dedicating himself to a small family practice in his hometown. divergence, N.

diverse ADJ. differing in some characteristics; various. The professor suggested *diverse* ways of approaching the assignment and recommended that we choose one of them. diversity, N.

diversion N. act of turning aside; pastime. After studying for several hours, he needed a *diversion* from work. divert, V.

diversity N. variety; dissimilitude. The *diversity* of colleges in this country indicates that many levels of ability are being cared for.

divulge v. reveal. No lover of gossip, Charlotte would never *divulge* anything that a friend told her in confidence.

docile ADJ. obedient; easily managed. As *docile* as he seems today, that old lion was once a ferocious, snarling beast. docility, N.

doctrinaire ADJ. unable to compromise about points of doctrine; dogmatic; unyielding. Weng had hoped that the student-led democracy movement might bring about change in China, but the repressive response of the *doctrinaire* hard-liners crushed his dreams of democracy.

doctrine N. (1) teachings, in general; (2) particular principle (religious, legal, etc.) taught. He was so committed to the *doctrines* of his faith that he was unable to evaluate them impartially. The Monroe *Doctrine* declared the Western Hemisphere off-limits to European attempts at colonization.

document V. (1) create a detailed record; (2) provide written evidence to support statements. As a young photographer, Johnny Seal *documented* the Occupy Oakland demonstrations in his hometown. Sue kept all the receipts from her business trip in order to *document* her expenses for the Internal Revenue Service. also N.

dogmatic ADJ. opinionated; arbitrary; doctrinal. We tried to discourage Doug from being so *dogmatic* but never could convince him that his opinions might be wrong.

domineer V. rule over tyrannically. Students prefer teachers who guide, not ones who *domineer*.

dormant ADJ. sleeping; lethargic; latent. At fifty her long-*dormant* ambition to write flared up once more; within a year she had completed the first of her great historical novels.

downcast ADJ. disheartened; sad. Cheerful and optimistic by nature, Beth was never *downcast* despite the difficulties she faced.

drudgery N. menial work. Cinderella's fairy godmother rescued her from a life of *drudgery*.

dubious ADJ. (1) uncertain; suspicious; (2) causing doubt to arise; of doubtful quality. I am *dubious* about the value of the changes the College Board is making in the SAT. Many critics of the SAT contend that the test is of *dubious* worth: they doubt the test accurately predicts which students will succeed in college.

dumbfound V. astonish. Egbert's perfect 1600 on his SAT exam *dumbfounded* his classmates, who had always found him to be perfectly dumb.

dupe N. someone easily fooled. While the gullible Watson often was made a *dupe* by unscrupulous parties, Sherlock Holmes was far more difficult to fool. also V.

duplicity N. double-dealing; hypocrisy. When Tanya learned that Mark had been two-timing her, she was furious at his *duplicity*.

duration N. length of time something lasts. Because she wanted the children to make a good impression on the dinner guests, Mother promised them a treat if they'd behave for the *duration* of the meal.

dutiful ADJ. respectful; obedient. When Mother told Billy to kiss Great-Aunt Hattie, the boy obediently gave the old woman a *dutiful* peck on her cheek.

Word List 16   dwarf–engage

dwarf V. cause to seem small. The giant redwoods and high cliffs *dwarfed* the elegant Ahwahnee Hotel, making it appear a modest lodge rather than an imposing hostelry.

dwindle V. shrink; reduce. The food in the lifeboat gradually *dwindled* away to nothing; in the end, they ate the ship's cook.

dynamic ADJ. energetic; vigorously active. The *dynamic* aerobics instructor kept her students on the run; she was a little *dynamo*.

ebullient ADJ. showing excitement; overflowing with enthusiasm. Amy's *ebullient* nature could not be repressed; she was always bubbling over with excitement. ebullience, N.

eccentric ADJ. (1) irregular; (2) odd; whimsical; bizarre. The comet veered dangerously close to the earth in its *eccentric* orbit. People came up with some *eccentric* ideas for dealing with the emergency: someone even suggested tieing a knot in the comet's tail!

eccentricity N. oddity; idiosyncrasy. Some of his friends tried to account for his rudeness to strangers as the *eccentricity* of genius.

eclectic ADJ. composed of elements drawn from disparate sources. His style of interior decoration was *eclectic*: bits and pieces of furnishings from widely divergent periods, strikingly juxtaposed to create a unique decor. eclecticism, N.

eclipse V. darken; extinguish; surpass. The new stock market high *eclipsed* the previous record set in 1995.

ecologist N. a person concerned with the interrelationship between living organisms and their environment. The *ecologist* was concerned that the new dam would upset the natural balance of the creatures living in Glen Canyon.

economy N. (1) national condition of monetary supply, goods production, etc.; (2) prudent management of resources; (3) efficiency or conciseness in use of words, etc. The president favors tax cuts to stimulate the *economy*. I need to practice *economy* when I shop: no more impulse buying for me! Reading the epigrams of Pope, I admire the *economy* of his verse: in few words he conveys worlds of meaning.

ecstasy N. rapture; joy; any overpowering emotion. When Allison received her long-hoped-for letter of acceptance from Harvard, she was in *ecstasy*. ecstatic, ADJ.

edict N. decree (especially issued by a sovereign); official command. The emperor issued an *edict* decreeing that everyone should come see him model his magnificent new clothes.

edify V. instruct; correct morally. Although his purpose was to *edify* and not to entertain his audience, many of his listeners were amused rather than enlightened.

effectual ADJ. able to produce a desired effect; valid. Medical researchers are concerned because of the development of drug-resistant strains of bacteria; many once useful antibiotics are no longer *effectual* in curing bacterial infections.

effervescence N. inner excitement or exuberance; bubbling from fermentation or carbonation. Nothing depressed Sue for long; her natural *effervescence* soon reasserted itself. Soda that loses its *effervescence* goes flat. effervescent, ADJ. effervesce, V.

effete ADJ. lacking vigor; worn out; sterile. Is the Democratic Party still a vital political force, or is it an *effete*, powerless faction, wedded to outmoded liberal policies?

efficacy N. power to produce desired effect. The *efficacy* of this drug depends on the regularity of the dosage. efficacious, ADJ.

egotistical ADJ. excessively self-centered; self-important; conceited. Typical *egotistical* remark: "But enough of this chit-chat about you and your little problems. Let's talk about what's really important: *Me!*"

egregious ADJ. notorious; conspicuously bad or shocking. She was an *egregious* liar; we all knew better than to believe a word she said. Ed's housekeeping was *egregious*: he let his dirty dishes pile up so long that they were stuck together with last week's food.

elaboration N. addition of details; intricacy. Tell what happened simply, without any *elaboration.* elaborate, V.

elated ADJ. overjoyed; in high spirits. Grinning from ear to ear, Bonnie Blair was clearly *elated* by her fifth Olympic gold medal. elation, N.

elicit V. draw out by discussion. The detectives tried to *elicit* where he had hidden his loot.

eloquence N. expressiveness; persuasive speech. The crowds were stirred by Martin Luther King's *eloquence.* eloquent, ADJ.

elucidate V. explain; enlighten. He was called upon to *elucidate* the disputed points in his article.

elusive ADJ. evasive; baffling; hard to grasp. Trying to pin down exactly when the contractors would be finished remodeling the house, Nancy was frustrated by their *elusive* replies. elude, V.

emancipate V. set free. At first, the attempts of the Abolitionists to *emancipate* the slaves were unpopular in New England as well as in the South.

embargo N. ban on commerce or other activity. As a result of the *embargo*, trade with the colonies was at a standstill.

embark V. commence; go on board a boat or airplane; begin a journey. In devoting herself to the study of gorillas, Dian Fossey *embarked* on a course of action that was to cost her her life.

embed V. enclose; place in something. Tales of actual historical figures like King Alfred have become *embedded* in legends.

embellish V. (1) make more beautiful; (2) make a story more interesting by adding (generally fictitious) details. The costume designer *embellished* the leading lady's ball gown with yards and yards of ribbon and lace. The producer *embellished* his account of his

Hollywood years with a list of all the starlets who had been madly in love with him.

embody V. personify; make concrete; incorporate. The Wright Spirit Award honors an individual who, through artistic, architectural, scholarly, professional, or other endeavors *embodies* the spirit of the architect Frank Lloyd Wright.

embrace V. (1) hug; (2) adopt or espouse; accept readily; (3) encircle; include. Clasping Maid Marian in his arms, Robin Hood *embraced* her lovingly. In joining the outlaws in Sherwood Forest, she had openly *embraced* their cause. The Encyclopedia of the Middle Ages *embraces* a wide variety of subjects, with articles on everything from agricultural implements to zodiac signs.

embroil V. throw into confusion; involve in strife; entangle. He became *embroiled* in the heated discussion when he tried to arbitrate the dispute.

embryonic ADJ. undeveloped; rudimentary. The CEO reminisced about the good old days when the computer industry was still in its *embryonic* stage and start-up companies were founded in family garages.

emend V. correct; correct by a critic. The critic *emended* the book by selecting the passages which he thought most appropriate to the text.

emendation N. correction of errors; improvement. Please initial all the *emendations* you have made in this contract.

eminent ADJ. high; lofty. After his appointment to this *eminent* position, he seldom had time for his former friends.

empathy N. ability to identify with another's feelings, ideas, etc. What made Ann such a fine counselor was her *empathy*, her ability to put herself in her client's place and feel his emotions as if they were her own. empathize, V.

empirical ADJ. based on experience. He distrusted hunches and intuitive flashes; he placed his reliance entirely on *empirical* data.

emulate V. imitate; rival. In a brief essay, describe a person you admire, someone whose virtues you would like to *emulate*.

encipher V. encode; convert a message into code. One of Bond's first lessons was how to *encipher* the messages he sent to Miss Moneypenny so that none of his other lady friends could decipher them.

encompass V. surround. A moat, or deep water-filled trench, *encompassed* the castle, protecting it from attack.

encroachment N. gradual intrusion. The *encroachment* of the factories upon the neighborhood lowered the value of the real estate.

encumber V. burden. Some people *encumber* themselves with too much luggage when they take short trips.

endemic ADJ. prevailing among a specific group of people or in a specific area or country. This disease is *endemic* in this part of the world; more than 80 percent of the population are at one time or another affected by it.

endorse V. approve; support. Everyone waited to see which one of the rival candidates for the city council the mayor would *endorse*.

enduring ADJ. lasting; surviving. Keats believed in the *enduring* power of great art, which would outlast its creators' brief lives.

energize V. invigorate; make forceful and active. Rather than exhausting Maggie, dancing *energized* her.

enfranchise V. to admit to the rights of citizenship (especially the right to vote). Although Blacks were *enfranchised* shortly after the Civil War, women did not receive the right to vote until 1920.

engage V. (1) pledge to do something (especially, to marry); (2) hire someone to perform a service; (3) attract and keep (attention); (4) induce someone to participate; (5) take part in; (6) attack (an enemy). When Tony and Tina became *engaged*, they decided to *engage* a lawyer to write up a pre-nuptial agreement. Tony's job *engages* him completely. When he's focused on work, not even Tina can *engage* him in conversation. Instead, she *engages* in tennis matches, fiercely *engaging* her opponents.

Word List 17 engaging–execrable

engaging ADJ. charming; attractive. Everyone liked Nancy's pleasant manners and *engaging* personality.

engender V. cause; produce. To receive praise for real accomplishments *engenders* self-confidence in a child.

engross V. occupy fully. John was so *engrossed* in his studies that he did not hear his mother call.

enhance V. increase; improve. You can *enhance* your chances of being admitted to the college of your choice by learning to write well; an excellent essay can *enhance* any application.

enigma N. puzzle; mystery. "What *do* women want?" asked Dr. Sigmund Freud. Their behavior was an *enigma* to him. enigmatic, ADJ.

enmity N. ill will; hatred. At Camp David, President Carter labored to bring an end to the *enmity* that prevented the peaceful coexistence of Egypt and Israel.

enormity N. hugeness (in a bad sense). He did not realize the *enormity* of his crime until he saw what suffering he had caused.

ensemble N. group of (supporting) players; organic unity; costume. As a dancer with the Oakland Ballet, Benjamin enjoyed being part of the *ensemble*. Having acted with one another for well over a decade, the cast members have developed a true sense of *ensemble*: they work together seamlessly. Mitzi wore a charming two-piece *ensemble* designed by Donna Karan.

entail V. require; necessitate; involve. Building a college-level vocabulary will *entail* some work on your part.

enterprising ADJ. full of initiative. By coming up with fresh ways to market the company's products, Mike proved himself to be an *enterprising* businessman.

entitlement N. right to claim something; right to benefits. While Bill was *entitled* to use a company car while he worked for the firm, the company's lawyers questioned his *entitlement* to the vehicle once he'd quit his job.

entity N. real being. As soon as the Charter was adopted, the United Nations became an *entity* and had to be considered as a factor in world diplomacy.

entrepreneur N. businessman; contractor. Opponents of our present tax program argue that it discourages *entrepreneurs* from trying new fields of business activity.

enumerate V. list; mention one by one. Huck hung his head in shame as Miss Watson *enumerated* his many flaws.

enunciate V. speak distinctly. Stop mumbling! How will people understand you if you do not *enunciate*?

ephemeral ADJ. short-lived; fleeting. The mayfly is an *ephemeral* creature: its adult life lasts little more than a day.

epic N. long heroic poem, or similar work of art. Kurosawa's film *Seven Samurai* is an *epic* portraying the struggle of seven warriors to destroy a band of robbers. also ADJ.

episodic ADJ. loosely connected; divided into incidents. Though he tried to follow the plot of *Gravity's Rainbow*, John found the novel too *episodic*; he enjoyed individual passages, but had trouble following the work as a whole.

epitome N. perfect example or embodiment. Singing "I am the very model of a modern Major-General," in *The Pirates of Penzance*, Major-General Stanley proclaimed himself the *epitome* of an officer and a gentleman.

equanimity N. calmness of temperament; composure. Even the inevitable strains of caring for an ailing mother did not disturb Bea's *equanimity*.

equilibrium N. balance. After the divorce, he needed some time to regain his *equilibrium*.

equitable ADJ. fair; impartial. I am seeking an *equitable* solution to this dispute, one that will be fair and acceptable to both sides.

equity N. fairness; justice. Our courts guarantee *equity* to all.

equivocal ADJ. ambiguous; intentionally misleading. Rejecting the candidate's *equivocal* comments on tax reform, the reporters pressed him to state clearly where he stood on the issue. equivocate, v.

equivocate v. lie; mislead; attempt to conceal the truth. No matter how bad the news is, give it to us straight. Above all, don't *equivocate*.

erode v. eat away. The limestone was *eroded* by the dripping water until only a thin shell remained. erosion, N.

erratic ADJ. odd; unpredictable. Investors become anxious when the stock market appears *erratic*.

erroneous ADJ. mistaken; wrong. I thought my answer was correct, but it was *erroneous*.

erudite ADJ. learned; scholarly. Unlike much scholarly writing, Huizinga's prose was entertaining as well as *erudite*, lively as well as learned.

esoteric ADJ. hard to understand; known only to the chosen few. *The New Yorker* short stories often include *esoteric* allusions to obscure people and events: the implication is, if you are in the in-crowd, you'll get the reference; if you come from Cleveland, you won't.

espouse v. adopt; support. She was always ready to *espouse* a worthy cause.

esteem v. respect; value. Jill *esteemed* Jack's taste in music, but she deplored his taste in clothes.

estranged ADJ. separated; alienated. The *estranged* wife sought a divorce. estrangement, N.

ethnic ADJ. relating to races. Intolerance between *ethnic* groups is deplorable and usually is based on lack of information.

ethos N. underlying character of a culture, group, etc. Seeing how tenderly ordinary Spaniards treated her small daughter made author Barbara Kingsolver aware of how greatly children were valued in the Spanish *ethos*.

etymology N. study of word parts. A knowledge of *etymology* can help you on many English tests: if you know what the roots and prefixes mean, you can determine the meanings of unfamiliar words.

euphoria N. feeling of great happiness and well-being (sometimes exaggerated). Delighted with her SAT scores, sure that the university would accept her, Allison was filled with *euphoria*. euphoric, ADJ.

evanescent ADJ. fleeting; vanishing. Brandon's satisfaction in his new job was *evanescent*, for he immediately began to notice its many drawbacks. evanescence, N.

evasive ADJ. not frank; eluding. Your *evasive* answers convinced the judge that you were withholding important evidence. evade, v.

evenhanded ADJ. impartial; fair. Do men and women receive *evenhanded* treatment from their teachers, or, as recent studies suggest, do teachers pay more attention to male students than to females?

evocative ADJ. tending to call up (emotions, memories). Scent can be remarkably *evocative*: the aroma of pipe tobacco *evokes* the memory of my father; a whiff of talcum powder calls up images of my daughter as a child.

exacerbate v. worsen; embitter. The latest bombing *exacerbated* England's already existing bitterness against the IRA, causing the prime minister to break off the peace talks abruptly.

exacting ADJ. extremely demanding. Cleaning the ceiling of the Sistine Chapel was an *exacting* task, one that demanded extremely meticulous care on the part of the restorers. exaction, N.

exasperate v. vex. Johnny often *exasperates* his mother with his pranks.

exceptionable ADJ. objectionable. Do you find the punk rock band Green Day a highly *exceptionable*, thoroughly distasteful group, or do you think they are exceptionally talented performers?

excerpt N. selected passage (written or musical). The cinematic equivalent of an *excerpt* from a novel is a clip from a film. also v.

excise v. cut away; cut out. When you *excise* the dead and dying limbs of a tree, you not only improve its appearance but also enhance its chances of bearing fruit. excision. N.

exclaim v. cry out suddenly. "Watson! Behind you!" Holmes *exclaimed*, seeing the assassin hurl himself on his friend.

exculpate v. clear from blame. He was *exculpated* of the crime when the real criminal confessed.

execrable ADJ. very bad. The anecdote was in such *execrable* taste that it revolted the audience.

Word List 18   execute–falter

execute v. (1) put into effect; (2) carry out; (3) put to death (someone condemned by law). The United States Agency for International Development is responsible for *executing* America's development policy and foreign assistance. The ballet master wanted to see how well Margaret could *execute* a pirouette. Captured by the British while gathering military intelligence, Nathan Hale was tried and *executed* on September 22, 1776. execution, N.

exegesis N. explanation; interpretation, especially of a biblical text. The minister based her sermon on her *exegesis* of a difficult passage from the book of Job. exegetical, ADJ.

exemplary ADJ. serving as a model; outstanding. At commencement the dean praised Ellen for her *exemplary* behavior as class president.

exemplify v. serve as an example of; embody. For a generation of balletgoers, Rudolf Nureyev *exemplified* the ideal of masculine grace.

exempt ADJ. not subject to a duty, obligation. Because of his flat feet, Foster was *exempt* from serving in the armed forces. also v.

exertion N. effort; expenditure of much physical work. The *exertion* spent in unscrewing the rusty bolt left her exhausted.

exhaustive ADJ. thorough; comprehensive. We have made an *exhaustive* study of all published SAT tests and are happy to share our research with you.

exhilarating ADJ. invigorating and refreshing; cheering. Though some of the hikers found tramping through the snow tiring, Jeffrey found the walk on the cold, crisp day *exhilarating*.

exhort V. urge. The evangelist *exhorted* all the sinners in his audience to repent. exhortation, N.

exigency N. urgent situation. In this *exigency,* we must look for aid from our allies.

exodus N. departure. The *exodus* from the hot and stuffy city was particularly noticeable on Friday evenings.

exonerate V. acquit; exculpate. The defense team feverishly sought fresh evidence that might *exonerate* their client.

exorbitant ADJ. excessive. The people grumbled at his *exorbitant* prices but paid them because he had a monopoly.

exotic ADJ. not native; strange. Because of his *exotic* headdress, he was followed in the streets by small children who laughed at his strange appearance.

expansive ADJ. (1) outgoing and sociable; (2) broad and extensive; able to increase in size. Mr. Fezziwig was in an *expansive* humor, cheerfully urging his guests to join in the Christmas feast. Looking down on his *expansive* paunch, he sighed: if his belly *expanded* any further, he'd need an *expansive* waistline for his pants.

expatriate N. exile; someone who has withdrawn from his native land. Henry James was an American *expatriate* who settled in England.

expedient ADJ. suitable; practical; politic. A pragmatic politician, he was guided by what was *expedient* rather than by what was ethical. expediency, N.

expedite V. hasten. Because we are on a tight schedule, we hope you will be able to *expedite* the delivery of our order. The more *expeditious* your response is, the happier we'll be.

expenditure N. (1) payment or expense; (2) output. When you are operating on an expense account, you must keep receipts for all your *expenditures*. If you don't save your receipts, you won't get repaid without the *expenditure* of a lot of energy arguing with the firm's accountants.

expertise N. specialized knowledge; expert skill. Although she was knowledgeable in a number of fields, she was hired for her particular *expertise* in computer programming.

explicate V. explain; interpret; clarify. Harry Levin *explicated* James Joyce's often bewildering novels with such clarity that even *Finnegan's Wake* seemed comprehensible to his students.

explicit ADJ. totally clear; definite; outspoken. Don't just hint around that you're dissatisfied: be *explicit* about what's bugging you.

exploit N. deed or action, particularly a brave deed. Raoul Wallenberg was noted for his *exploits* in rescuing Jews from Hitler's forces.

exploit V. make use of, sometimes unjustly. Cesar Chavez fought attempts to *exploit* migrant farmworkers in California. exploitation, N. exploitative, ADJ.

expository ADJ. explanatory; serving to explain. The manual that came with my iPhone was no masterpiece of *expository* prose: its explanations were so garbled that I couldn't even figure out how to synchronize my contacts. exposition, N.

exposure N. (1) risk, particularly of being exposed to disease or to the elements; (2) unmasking; act of laying something open. *Exposure* to sun and wind had dried out her hair and weathered her face. She looked so changed that she no longer feared *exposure* as the notorious Irene Adler, one-time antagonist of Sherlock Holmes.

expropriate V. take possession of. He questioned the government's right to *expropriate* his land to create a wildlife preserve.

expurgate V. clean; remove offensive parts of a book. The editors felt that certain passages in the book had to be *expurgated* before it could be used in the classroom.

extant ADJ. still in existence. Although the book is out of print, some copies are still *extant*. Unfortunately, all of them are in libraries or private collections; none are for sale.

extent N. degree; magnitude; scope. What is the *extent* of the patient's injuries? If they are not too *extensive*, we can treat him on an outpatient basis.

extenuate V. weaken; mitigate. It is easier for us to *extenuate* our own shortcomings than those of others.

extol V. praise; glorify. The president *extolled* the astronauts, calling them the pioneers of the Space Age.

extraneous ADJ. not essential; superfluous. No wonder Ted can't think straight! His mind is so cluttered up with *extraneous* trivia, he can't concentrate on the essentials.

extrapolation N. projection; conjecture. Based on their *extrapolation* from the results of the primaries on Super Tuesday, the networks predicted that Jeb Bush would be the Republican candidate for the presidency. extrapolate, V.

extricate V. free; disentangle. Icebreakers were needed to *extricate* the trapped whales from the icy floes that closed them in.

extrinsic ADJ. external; not essential; extraneous. A critically acclaimed *extrinsic* feature of the Chrysler Building is its ornate spire. The judge would not admit the testimony, ruling that it was *extrinsic* to the matter at hand.

extrovert N. person interested mostly in external objects and actions. A good salesman is usually an *extrovert*, who likes to mingle with people.

exuberance N. overflowing abundance; joyful enthusiasm; flamboyance; lavishness. I was bowled over by the *exuberance* of Amy's welcome. What an enthusiastic greeting!

exult V. rejoice. We *exulted* when our team won the victory.

fabricate V. (1) manufacture or build; (2) make up to mislead or deceive. Motawi Tileworks *fabricates* distinctive ceramic tiles in the Arts and Crafts style. The defense lawyer accused the arresting officer of *fabricating* evidence against her client.

facade N. (1) front (of building); (2) superficial or false appearance. The ornate *facade* of the church was often photographed by tourists, who never bothered to walk around the building to view its other sides. Susan seemed super-confident, but that was just a *facade* she put on to hide her insecurity.

facile ADJ. ready or fluent; superficial. Words came easily to Jonathan: he was a *facile* speaker and prided himself on being ready to make a speech at a moment's notice.

facilitate V. help bring about; make less difficult. Rest and proper nourishment should *facilitate* the patient's recovery.

facility N. (1) natural ability to do something with ease; (2) ease in performing; (3) something (building, equipment) set up to perform a function. Morgan has always displayed a remarkable *facility* for playing basketball. Thanks to years of practice, he handles the ball with such *facility* that as a twelve-year-old he can outplay many students at the university's recreational *facility*.

facsimile N. copy. Many museums sell *facsimiles* of the works of art on display.

faction N. party; clique; dissension. The quarrels and bickering of the two small *factions* within the club disturbed the majority of the members.

faculty N. (1) inherent mental or physical power; (2) teaching staff. As he grew old, Professor Twiggly feared he might lose his *faculties* and become unfit to teach. Once he'd lost his *faculties*, he'd no place on the *faculty*.

fallacious ADJ. false; misleading. Paradoxically, *fallacious* reasoning does not always yield erroneous results: even though your logic may be faulty, the answer you get may nevertheless be correct. fallacy, N.

fallible ADJ. liable to err. I know I am *fallible*, but I feel confident that I am right this time.

falter V. hesitate. When told to dive off the high board, she did not *falter*, but proceeded at once.

Word List 19   fanaticism–forensic

fanaticism N. excessive zeal; extreme devotion to a belief or cause. When Islamic fundamentalists demanded the death of Salman Rushdie because his novel questioned their faith, world opinion condemned them for their *fanaticism*.

fancy N. notion; whim; inclination. Martin took a *fancy* to paint his toenails purple. Assuming he would outgrow such *fanciful* behavior, his parents ignored his *fancy* feet. also ADJ.

farce N. broad comedy; mockery. Nothing went right; the entire interview degenerated into a *farce*. farcical, ADJ.

fastidious ADJ. difficult to please; squeamish. Bobby was such a *fastidious* eater that he would eat a sandwich only if his mother first cut off every scrap of crust.

fatalism N. belief that events are determined by forces beyond one's control. With *fatalism*, he accepted the hardships that beset him. fatalistic, ADJ.

fathom V. comprehend; investigate. I find his motives impossible to *fathom*; in fact, I'm totally clueless about what goes on in his mind.

faze V. disconcert; dismay. No crisis could *faze* the resourceful hotel manager.

feasible ADJ. practical. Is it *feasible* to build a new stadium for the Yankees on New York's West Side? Without additional funding, the project is clearly unrealistic.

feign V. pretend. Bobby *feigned* illness, hoping that his mother would let him stay home from school.

feint N. trick; shift; sham blow. The boxer was fooled by his opponent's *feint* and dropped his guard. also V.

felicitous ADJ. apt; suitably expressed; well chosen. He was famous for his *felicitous* remarks and was called upon to serve as master-of-ceremonies at many a banquet.

felicity N. happiness; appropriateness (of a remark, choice, etc.). She wrote a note to the newlyweds wishing them great *felicity* in their wedded life.

felon N. person convicted of a grave crime. A convicted *felon* loses the right to vote.

feral ADJ. not domestic; wild. Abandoned by their owners, dogs may revert to their *feral* state, roaming the woods in packs.

ferment N. agitation; commotion. With the breakup of the Soviet Union, much of Eastern Europe was in a state of *ferment*.

fervor N. glowing ardor; intensity of feeling. At the protest rally, the students cheered the strikers and booed the dean with equal *fervor*.

fester V. rankle; produce irritation or resentment. Joe's insult *festered* in Anne's mind for days, and made her too angry to speak to him.

fiasco N. total failure. Tanya's attempt to look sophisticated by taking up smoking was a *fiasco*: she lit the filter, choked when she tried to inhale, and burned a hole in her boyfriend's couch.

fickle ADJ. changeable; faithless. As soon as Romeo saw Juliet, he forgot all about his old girlfriend Rosaline. Was Romeo *fickle*?

fictitious ADJ. imaginary. Although this book purports to be a biography of George Washington, many of the incidents are *fictitious*.

fidelity N. loyalty. Iago wickedly manipulates Othello, arousing his jealousy and causing him to question his wife's *fidelity*.

figment N. invention; imaginary thing. Was he hearing real voices in the night, or were they just a *figment* of his imagination?

figurative ADJ. not literal, but metaphorical; using a figure of speech. "To lose one's marbles" is a *figurative* expression; if you're told that Jack has lost his marbles, no one expects you to rush out to buy him a replacement set.

finale N. conclusion. It is not until we reach the *finale* of this play that we can understand the author's message.

finesse N. delicate skill. The *finesse* and adroitness with which the surgeon wielded her scalpel impressed all the observers in the operating room.

fitful ADJ. spasmodic; intermittent. After several *fitful* attempts, he decided to postpone the start of the project until he felt more energetic.

flabbergasted ADJ. astounded; astonished; overcome with surprise. In the film *Flubber,* the hero invents a remarkable substance whose amazing properties leave his coworkers *flabbergasted*. flabbergast, V.

flag V. droop; grow feeble. When the opposing hockey team scored its third goal only minutes into the first quarter, the home team's spirits *flagged*. flagging, ADJ.

flagrant ADJ. conspicuously wicked; blatant; outrageous. The governor's appointment of his brother-in-law to the State Supreme Court was a *flagrant* violation of the state laws against nepotism (favoritism based on kinship).

flair N. talent. She has an uncanny *flair* for discovering new artists before the public has become aware of their existence.

flamboyant ADJ. ornate. Modern architecture has discarded *flamboyant* trimming on buildings and emphasizes simplicity of line.

flaunt V. display ostentatiously. Mae West saw nothing wrong with showing off her considerable physical charms, saying, "Honey, if you've got it, *flaunt* it!"

fledgling ADJ. inexperienced. The folk dance club set up an apprentice program to allow *fledgling* dance callers a chance to polish their skills. also N.

flinch V. hesitate, shrink. He did not *flinch* in the face of danger but fought back bravely.

flippant ADJ. lacking proper seriousness. When Mark told Mona he loved her, she dismissed his earnest declaration with a *flippant* "Oh, you say that to all the girls!" flippancy, N.

flounder V. struggle and thrash about; proceed clumsily or falter. Up to his knees in the bog, Floyd *floundered* about, trying to regain his footing. Bewildered by the new software, Flo *floundered* until Jan showed her how to get started.

flourish V. grow well; prosper; decorate with ornaments. The orange trees *flourished* in the sun.

flout V. reject; mock. The headstrong youth *flouted* all authority; he refused to be curbed.

fluctuate V. waver; shift. The water pressure in our shower *fluctuates* wildly; you start rinsing yourself off with a trickle and, two minutes later, a blast of water nearly knocks you down.

fluency N. smoothness of speech. He spoke French with *fluency* and ease.

fluster V. confuse. The teacher's sudden question *flustered* him and he stammered his reply.

flux N. flowing; series of changes. While conditions are in such a state of *flux*, I do not wish to commit myself too deeply in this affair.

foible N. weakness; slight fault. We can overlook the *foibles* of our friends; no one is perfect.

foil N. contrast. In *Star Wars*, dark, evil Darth Vader is a perfect *foil* for fair-haired, naïve Luke Skywalker.

foil V. defeat; frustrate. In the end, Skywalker is able to *foil* Vader's diabolical schemes.

foment V. stir up; instigate. Cheryl's archenemy Heather spread some nasty rumors that *fomented* trouble in the club. Do you think Cheryl's foe meant to *foment* such discord?

foolhardy ADJ. rash. Don't be *foolhardy*. Get the advice of experienced people before undertaking this venture.

forbearance N. patience. Be patient with John. Treat him with *forbearance*: he is still weak from his illness.

foreboding N. premonition of evil. Suspecting no conspiracies against him, Caesar gently ridiculed his wife's *forebodings* about the Ides of March.

forensic ADJ. suitable to debate in courts of law. In her best *forensic* manner, the lawyer addressed the jury. forensics, N.

Word List 20   foreshadow–germinal

foreshadow v. give an indication beforehand; portend; prefigure. In retrospect, political analysts realized that Yeltsin's defiance of the attempted coup *foreshadowed* his emergence as the dominant figure of the new Russian republic.

foresight N. ability to foresee future happenings; prudence. A wise investor, she had the *foresight* to buy land just before the current real estate boom.

forestall v. prevent by taking action in advance. By setting up a prenuptial agreement, the prospective bride and groom hoped to *forestall* any potential arguments about money in the event of a divorce.

forgo v. give up; do without. Determined to lose weight for the summer, Ida decided to *forgo* dessert until she could fit into a size eight again.

formality N. ceremonious quality; something done just for form's sake. The president received the visiting heads of state with due *formality*: flags waving, honor guards standing at attention, anthems sounding at full blast. Signing this petition is a mere *formality*; it does not obligate you in any way.

formidable ADJ. inspiring fear or apprehension; difficult; awe inspiring. In the film *Meet the Parents,* the hero is understandably nervous around his fiancee's father, a *formidable* CIA agent.

forsake v. desert; abandon; renounce. No one expected Foster to *forsake* his wife and children and run off with another woman.

forte N. strong point or special talent. I am not eager to play this rather serious role, for my *forte* is comedy.

forthright ADJ. outspoken; straightforward; frank. Never afraid to call a spade a spade, she was perhaps too *forthright* to be a successful party politician.

fortitude N. bravery; courage. He was awarded the medal for his *fortitude* in the battle.

fortuitous ADJ. accidental; by chance. Though he pretended their encounter was *fortuitous*, he'd actually been hanging around her usual haunts for the past two weeks, hoping she'd turn up.

forum N. place of assembly to discuss public concerns; meeting for discussion. The film opens with a shot of the ancient *Forum* in Rome, where several senators are discussing the strange new sect known as Christians. At the end of the movie, its director presided over a *forum* examining new fashions in filmmaking.

foster v. rear; encourage. According to the legend, Romulus and Remus were *fostered* by a she-wolf who raised the abandoned infants with her own cubs. also ADJ.

founder v. (1) fail completely; (2) sink. Unfortunately, the peace talks *foundered* when the two parties could not reach a compromise. After hitting the sub-merged iceberg, the *Titanic* started taking in water rapidly and soon *foundered.*

founder N. person who establishes (an organization, business). Among those drowned when the *Titanic* sank was the *founder* of the Abraham & Strauss department store.

frail ADJ. weak. The delicate child seemed too *frail* to lift the heavy carton. frailty, N.

franchise N. (1) right granted by authority; (2) right to vote; (3) business licensed to sell a product in a particular territory. The city issued a *franchise* to the company to operate surface transit lines on the streets for ninety-nine years. For most of American history women lacked the right to vote: not until the early twentieth century was the *franchise* granted to women. Stan owns a Carvel's ice cream *franchise* in Chinatown.

frantic ADJ. wild. At the time of the collision, many people became *frantic* with fear.

fraternize v. associate in a friendly way. After the game, the members of the two teams *fraternized* as cheerfully as if they had never been rivals.

fraudulent ADJ. cheating; deceitful. The government seeks to prevent *fraudulent* and misleading advertising.

fret v. to be annoyed or vexed. To *fret* over your poor grades is foolish; instead, decide to work harder in the future.

friction N. (1) rubbing against; (2) clash of wills. If it were not for the *friction* between the tires and the pavement, driving a car would be like sliding all over an ice rink. The *friction* between Aaron Burr and Alexander Hamilton intensified over time until it culminated in their famous duel.

frigid ADJ. intensely cold. Alaska is in the *frigid* zone.

frivolous ADJ. lacking in seriousness; self-indulgently carefree; relatively unimportant. Though Nancy enjoyed Bill's *frivolous*, lighthearted companionship, she sometimes wondered whether he could ever be serious. frivolity, N.

frugality N. thrift; economy. In economically hard times, anyone who doesn't learn to practice *frugality* risks bankruptcy. frugal, ADJ.

fruition N. bearing of fruit; fulfillment; realization. After years of saving and scrimping, her dream of owning her own home finally came to *fruition.*

frustrate v. thwart; defeat. Constant partisan bickering *frustrated* the governor's efforts to convince the legislature to approve his proposed budget.

fugitive ADJ. fleeting or transitory; roving. The film brought a few *fugitive* images to her mind, but on the whole it made no lasting impression upon her.

fundamental ADJ. basic; primary; essential. The committee discussed all sorts of side issues without ever getting down to addressing the *fundamental* problem.

furor N. frenzy; great excitement. The story of her embezzlement of the funds created a *furor* on the Stock Exchange.

furtive ADJ. stealthy; sneaky. Noticing the *furtive* glance the customer gave the diamond bracelet on the counter, the jeweler wondered whether he had a potential shoplifter on his hands.

fusion N. union; blending; synthesis. So-called rockabilly music represents a *fusion* of country music and blues that became rock and roll.

futile ADJ. useless; hopeless; ineffectual. It is *futile* for me to try to get any work done around here while the telephone is ringing every thirty seconds. futility, N.

gainsay V. deny. Even though it reflected badly upon him, he was too honest to *gainsay* the truth of the report.

galvanize V. stimulate by shock; stir up; revitalize. News that the prince was almost at their door *galvanized* the ugly stepsisters into a frenzy of combing and primping.

gamut N. entire range. In a classic put-down of actress Katharine Hepburn, the critic Dorothy Parker wrote that the actress ran the *gamut* of emotion from A to B.

garbled ADJ. mixed up; jumbled; distorted. A favorite party game involves passing a whispered message from one person to another until, by the time it reaches the last player, the message is totally *garbled*.

garner V. gather; store up. In her long career as an actress, Katharine Hepburn *garnered* many awards, including the coveted Oscar.

garrulous ADJ. loquacious; wordy; talkative. My Uncle Henry is the most *garrulous* person in Cayuga County: he can outtalk anyone I know. garrulity, N.

gauche ADJ. clumsy; coarse and uncouth. Compared to the sophisticated young ladies in their elegant gowns, tomboyish Jo felt *gauche* and out of place.

gaudy ADJ. flashy; showy. The newest Trump skyscraper is typically *gaudy*, covered in gilded panels that gleam in the sun.

generality N. vague statement. This report is filled with *generalities*; be more specific in your statements.

generalization N. (1) broad, general statement derived from specific instances; (2) vague, indefinite statement. It is foolish to make *generalizations* based on insufficient evidence: that one woman defrauded the welfare system of thousands of dollars does not mean all welfare recipients are cheats. I would rather propose solutions to problems than make vague *generalizations*.

generate V. cause; produce; create. In his first days in office, President Obama managed to *generate* a new mood of optimism; we just hoped he could *generate* some new jobs.

generic ADJ. characteristic of an entire class or species. Sue knew so many computer programmers who spent their spare time playing fantasy games that she began to think that playing Dungeons & Dragons was a *generic* trait.

genesis N. beginning; origin. Tracing the *genesis* of a family is the theme of *Roots*.

geniality N. cheerfulness; kindliness; sympathy. This restaurant is famous and popular because of the *geniality* of the proprietor who tries to make everyone happy.

genre N. particular variety of art or literature. Both a short story writer and a poet, Langston Hughes proved himself equally skilled in either *genre*.

germane ADJ. pertinent; bearing upon the case at hand. The judge refused to allow the testimony to be heard by the jury because it was not *germane* to the case.

germinal ADJ. pertaining to a germ; creative. Such an idea is *germinal*; I am certain that it will influence thinkers and philosophers for many generations.

Word List 21   germinate–homage

germinate V. cause to sprout; sprout. After the seeds *germinate* and develop their permanent leaves, the plants may be removed from the cold frames and transplanted to the garden.

gist N. essence. She was asked to give the *gist* of the essay in two sentences.

glacial ADJ. like a glacier; extremely cold. Never a warm person, when offended John could seem positively *glacial*.

glaring ADJ. highly conspicuous; harshly bright. *Glaring* spelling or grammatical errors in your resumé will unfavorably impress potential employers.

glib ADJ. fluent; facile; slick. Keeping up a steady patter to entertain his customers, the kitchen gadget salesman was a *glib* speaker, never at a loss for a word.

gloat V. express evil satisfaction; view malevolently. As you *gloat* over your ill-gotten wealth, do you think of the many victims you have defrauded?

glossary N. brief explanation of words used in the text. I have found the *glossary* in this book very useful; it has eliminated many trips to the dictionary.

gloss over V. explain away. No matter how hard he tried to talk around the issue, President Bush could not *gloss over* the fact that he had raised taxes after all.

goad V. urge on; spur; incite. Mother was afraid that Ben's wild friends would *goad* him into doing something that would get him into trouble with the law. also N.

graduated ADJ. (1) arranged by degrees (of height, difficulty, etc.); (2) marked out with lines (for measuring). Margaret loved her *graduated* set of Russian hollow wooden dolls; she spent hours happily putting the smaller dolls into their larger counterparts. We measured the liquid to the nearest milliliter in a *graduated* cylinder.

grandeur N. impressiveness; stateliness; majesty. No matter how often he hiked through the mountains, David never failed to be struck by the *grandeur* of the Sierra Nevada range.

graphic ADJ. (1) pertaining to visual art; (2) relating to visual images; (3) vividly portrayed. The illustrator Jody Lee studied the *graphic* arts at San Francisco's Academy of Art. In 2016 the SAT will include reading questions that require students to interpret *graphic* information from charts and diagrams. The description of the winter storm was so *graphic* that you could almost feel the hailstones.

grapple V. wrestle; come to grips with. He *grappled* with the burglar and overpowered him.

grate V. make a harsh noise; have an unpleasant effect; shred. The screams of the quarreling children *grated* on her nerves.

gratify V. please. Lori's parents were *gratified* by her successful performance on the SAT.

gravity N. seriousness. We could tell we were in serious trouble from the *gravity* of the principal's expression.

grievance N. cause of complaint. When her supervisor ignored her complaint, she took her *grievance* to the union.

grouse V. complain; fuss. Students traditionally *grouse* about the abysmal quality of "mystery meat" and similar dormitory food.

grotesque ADJ. fantastic; comically hideous. On Halloween people enjoy wearing *grotesque* costumes.

grudging ADJ. unwilling; reluctant; stingy. We received only *grudging* support from the mayor despite his earlier promises of aid.

grueling ADJ. exhausting. The marathon is a *grueling* race.

guile N. deceit; duplicity; wiliness; cunning. Iago uses considerable *guile* to trick Othello into believing that Desdemona has been unfaithful.

guileless ADJ. without deceit. He is naïve, simple, and *guileless;* he cannot be guilty of fraud.

guise N. appearance; costume. In the *guise* of a plumber, the detective investigated the murder case.

gullible ADJ. easily deceived. Overly *gullible* people have only themselves to blame if they fall for con artists repeatedly. As the saying goes, "Fool me once, shame on you. Fool me twice, shame on *me.*"

hackneyed ADJ. commonplace; trite. When the reviewer criticized the movie for its *hackneyed* plot, we agreed; we had seen similar stories hundreds of times before.

halting ADJ. hesitant; faltering. Novice extemporaneous speakers often talk in a *halting* fashion as they grope for the right words.

hamper V. obstruct. The new mother didn't realize how much the effort of caring for an infant would *hamper* her ability to keep an immaculate house.

haphazard ADJ. random; unsystematic; aimless. In place of a systematic family policy, America has a *haphazard* patchwork of institutions and programs created in response to immediate crises.

harass V. to annoy by repeated attacks. When he could not pay his bills as quickly as he had promised, he was *harassed* by his creditors.

harbor V. provide a refuge for; hide. The church *harbored* illegal aliens who were political refugees.

hardy ADJ. sturdy; robust; able to stand inclement weather. We asked the gardening expert to recommend particularly *hardy* plants that could withstand our harsh New England winters.

haughtiness N. pride; arrogance. When she realized that Darcy believed himself too good to dance with his inferiors, Elizabeth took great offense at his *haughtiness*.

hazardous ADJ. dangerous. Your occupation is too *hazardous* for insurance companies to consider your application.

headlong ADJ. hasty; rash. The slave seized the unexpected chance to make a *headlong* dash across the border to freedom.

headstrong ADJ. stubborn; willful; unyielding. Because she refused to marry the man her parents had chosen for her, everyone scolded Minna and called her a foolish, *headstrong* girl.

heckler N. person who harasses others. The *heckler* kept interrupting the speaker with rude remarks. heckle, v.

heed V. pay attention to; consider. We hope you *heed* our advice and get a good night's sleep before the test. also N.

heedless ADJ. not noticing; disregarding. He drove on, *heedless* of the danger warnings placed at the side of the road.

heinous ADJ. atrocious; hatefully bad. Hitler's *heinous* crimes will never be forgotten.

heresy N. opinion contrary to popular belief; opinion contrary to accepted religion. Galileo's assertion that the earth moved around the sun directly contradicted the religious teachings of his day; as a result, he was tried for *heresy*. heretic, N.

heterodox ADJ. unorthodox; unconventional. To those who upheld the belief that the earth did not move, Galileo's theory that the earth circled the sun was disturbingly *heterodox*.

heterogeneous ADJ. dissimilar; mixed. This year's entering class is a remarkably *heterogeneous* body:

it includes students from forty different states and twenty-six foreign countries, some the children of billionaires, others the offspring of welfare families. heterogeneity, N.

heyday N. time of greatest success; prime. In their *heyday,* the San Francisco Forty-Niners won the Super Bowl two years running.

hiatus N. gap; interruption in duration or continuity; pause. During the summer *hiatus,* many students try to earn enough money to pay their tuition for the next school year.

hierarchy N. arrangement by rank or standing; authoritarian body divided into ranks. To be low man on the totem pole is to have an inferior place in the *hierarchy.*

hinder V. (1) slow down or make (something) difficult; (2) prevent. Although the operation was successful, an infection *hindered* the recovery of the patient, who remained hospitalized for an additional week. Gordon was determined not to let anyone *hinder* him from achieving his goal.

hoard V. stockpile; accumulate for future use. Whenever there are rumors of a food shortage, many people are tempted to *hoard* food. also N.

hoax N. trick; deception; fraud. In the case of Piltdown man, a scientific forgery managed to fool the experts for nearly half a century, when the *hoax* was finally unmasked. also V.

homage N. honor; tribute. In her speech she tried to pay *homage* to a great man.

Word List 22 homogeneous–implement

homogeneous ADJ. of the same kind. Because the student body at Elite Prep was so *homogeneous,* Sara and James decided to send their daughter to a school that offered greater cultural diversity. homogenize, V.

horde N. crowd. Just before Christmas the stores are filled with *hordes* of shoppers.

host N. great number; person entertaining guests; animal or plant from which a parasite gets its nourishment. You must attend to a *host* of details if you wish to succeed as *host* of a formal dinner party. Leeches are parasites that cling to their *hosts* and drink their *hosts'* blood.

hostility N. unfriendliness; hatred. A child who has been the sole object of his parents' affection often feels *hostility* toward a new baby in the family, resenting the newcomer who has taken his place.

humane ADJ. marked by kindness or consideration. It is ironic that the *Humane* Society sometimes must show its compassion toward mistreated animals by killing them to put them out of their misery.

humility N. humbleness of spirit. Despite his fame as a Nobel Prize winner, Bishop Tutu spoke with a *humil-*

ity and lack of self-importance that immediately won over his listeners.

husband V. use sparingly; conserve; save. Marathon runners must *husband* their energy so that they can keep going for the entire distance.

hybrid N. mongrel; mixed breed. Mendel's formula explains the appearance of *hybrids* and pure species in breeding. also ADJ.

hyperbole N. exaggeration; overstatement. As far as I'm concerned, Apple's claims about the new computer are pure *hyperbole*: no machine is that good!

hypercritical ADJ. excessively exacting. You are *hypercritical* in your demands for perfection; we all make mistakes.

hypocritical ADJ. pretending to be virtuous; deceiving. It was *hypocritical* of Martha to say nice things about my poetry to me and then make fun of my verses behind my back. hypocrisy, N.

hypothetical ADJ. based on assumptions or hypotheses; supposed. Suppose you are accepted by Harvard, Stanford, and Brown. Which one would you choose to attend? Remember, this is only a *hypothetical* situation. hypothesis, N.

iconoclastic ADJ. attacking cherished traditions. Deeply *iconoclastic,* Jean Genet deliberately set out to shock conventional theatergoers with his radical plays.

ideology N. system of ideas of a group. For people who had grown up believing in the communist *ideology,* it was hard to adjust to capitalism.

idiom N. expression whose meaning as a whole differs from the meanings of its individual words; distinctive style. The phrase "to lose one's marbles" is an *idiom*: if I say that Joe lost his marbles, I'm not asking you to find some for him. I'm telling you *idiomatically* that he's crazy.

idiosyncrasy N. individual trait, usually odd in nature; eccentricity. One of Richard Nixon's little *idiosyncrasies* was his liking for ketchup on cottage cheese. One of Hannibal Lecter's little *idiosyncrasies* was his liking for human flesh. idiosyncratic, ADJ.

ignoble ADJ. unworthy; base in nature; not noble. Sir Galahad was so pure in heart that he could never stoop to perform an *ignoble* deed.

ignominy N. deep disgrace; shame or dishonor. To lose the Ping-Pong match to a trained chimpanzee! How could Rollo stand the *ignominy* of his defeat? ignominious, ADJ.

illicit ADJ. illegal. The defense attorney maintained that his client had never performed any *illicit* action.

illuminate V. brighten; clear up or make understandable; enlighten. Just as a lamp can *illuminate* a dark room, a perceptive comment can *illuminate* a knotty problem.

illusion N. misleading vision. It is easy to create an optical *illusion* in which lines of equal length appear different.

illusory ADJ. deceptive; not real. Unfortunately, the costs of running the lemonade stand were so high that Tom's profits proved *illusory*.

imbalance N. lack of balance or symmetry; disproportion. To correct racial *imbalance* in the schools, school boards have bussed black children into white neighborhoods and white children into black ones.

immaculate ADJ. spotless; flawless; absolutely clean. Ken and Jessica were wonderful tenants and left the apartment in *immaculate* condition when they moved out.

imminent ADJ. near at hand; impending. Rosa was such a last-minute worker that she could never start writing a paper until the deadline was *imminent*.

immobility N. state of being unable to move. Peter's fear of snakes shocked him into *immobility*; then the use of his limbs returned to him, and he bolted from the room.

immune ADJ. resistant to; free or exempt from. Fortunately, Florence had contracted chicken pox as a child and was *immune* to it when her baby broke out in spots.

immutable ADJ. unchangeable. All things change over time; nothing is *immutable*.

impair V. injure; hurt. Drinking alcohol can *impair* your ability to drive safely; if you're going to drink, don't drive.

impartial ADJ. not biased; fair. Knowing she could not be *impartial* about her own child, Jo refused to judge any match in which Billy was competing.

impassable ADJ. not able to be traveled or crossed. A giant redwood had fallen across the highway, blocking all four lanes: the road was *impassable*.

impasse N. predicament from which there is no escape; deadlock. The negotiators reported they had reached an *impasse* in their talks and had little hope of resolving the deadlock swiftly.

impassive ADJ. without feeling; imperturbable; stoical. Refusing to let the enemy see how deeply shaken he was by his capture, the prisoner kept his face *impassive*.

impeach V. charge with crime in office; indict. The angry congressman wanted to *impeach* the president for his misdeeds.

impeccable ADJ. faultless. The uncrowned queen of the fashion industry, Diana was acclaimed for her *impeccable* taste.

impecunious ADJ. without money. Though Scrooge claimed he was too *impecunious* to give alms, he easily could have afforded to be charitable.

impede V. hinder; block; delay. A series of accidents *impeded* the launching of the space shuttle.

impediment N. hindrance; stumbling-block. She had a speech *impediment* that prevented her speaking clearly.

impel V. drive or force onward. A strong feeling of urgency *impelled* her; if she failed to finish the project right then, she knew that she would never get it done.

impenetrable ADJ. not able to be pierced or entered; beyond understanding. How could the murderer have gotten into the locked room? To Watson, the mystery, like the room, was *impenetrable*.

impending ADJ. nearing; approaching. The entire country was saddened by the news of his *impending* death.

imperative ADJ. absolutely necessary; critically important. It is *imperative* that you be extremely agreeable to Great-Aunt Maud when she comes to tea: otherwise she might not leave you that million dollars in her will. also N.

imperceptible ADJ. unnoticeable; undetectable. Fortunately, the stain on the blouse was *imperceptible* after the blouse had gone through the wash.

imperial ADJ. like an emperor; related to an empire. When hotel owner Leona Helmsley appeared in ads as Queen Leona standing guard over the Palace Hotel, her critics mocked her *imperial* fancies.

imperious ADJ. domineering; haughty. Jane rather liked a man to be masterful, but Mr. Rochester seemed so bent on getting his own way that he was actually *imperious*!

impervious ADJ. impenetrable; incapable of being damaged or distressed. The carpet salesman told Simone that his most expensive brand of floor covering was warranted to be *impervious* to ordinary wear and tear. Having read so many negative reviews of his acting, the movie star had learned to ignore them, and was now *impervious* to criticism.

impetuous ADJ. violent; hasty; rash. "Leap before you look" was the motto suggested by one particularly *impetuous* young man.

impetus N. incentive; stimulus; moving force. A new federal highway program would create jobs and give added *impetus* to our economic recovery.

impiety N. irreverence; lack of respect for God. When members of the youth group draped the church in toilet paper one Halloween, the minister reprimanded them for their *impiety*. impious, ADJ.

implausible ADJ. unlikely; unbelievable. Though her alibi seemed *implausible*, it in fact turned out to be true.

implement N. piece of equipment. We now own so many rakes, hoes, and hedge clippers that we need a tool shed in which to store all our gardening *implements*.

implement V. put into effect. The mayor was unwilling to *implement* the plan until she was sure it had the governor's backing.

Word List 23   implicate–indices

implicate V. incriminate; show to be involved. Here's the deal: if you agree to take the witness stand and *implicate* your partners in crime, the prosecution will recommend that the judge go easy in sentencing you.

implication N. (1) something hinted at or suggested; (2) likely consequence; (3) close involvement. When Miss Watson said that she hadn't seen her purse since the last time Jim was in the house, her *implication* was that Jim had taken it. This had potentially serious *implications* for Jim. If his *implication* in a theft were proved, he'd be thrown into jail.

implicit ADJ. understood but not stated. Jack never told Jill he adored her; he believed his love was *implicit* in his actions.

imply V. suggest a meaning not expressed; signify. When Aunt Millie said, "My! That's a big piece of pie, young man!" was she *implying* that Bobby was being a glutton in helping himself to such a huge piece?

imponderable ADJ. not able to be determined precisely. Psychology is not a precise science; far too many *imponderable* factors play a part in determining human behavior.

import N. importance; meaning. To Miss Manners, proper etiquette was a matter of great *import*. Because Tom knew so little about medical matters, it took a while for the full *import* of the doctor's words to sink in.

impotent ADJ. weak; ineffective. Although he wished to break the nicotine habit, he found himself *impotent* to resist the craving for a cigarette.

impoverished ADJ. poor. The loss of their farm left the family *impoverished* and without hope.

impregnable ADJ. invulnerable. Until the development of the airplane as a military weapon, the fort was considered *impregnable*.

impromptu ADJ. without previous preparation; off the cuff; on the spur of the moment. The judges were amazed that she could make such a thorough, well-supported presentation in an *impromptu* speech.

impropriety N. improperness; unsuitableness. Because of the *impropriety* of the punk rocker's slashed T-shirt and jeans, the management refused to admit him to the hotel's very formal dining room.

improvident ADJ. thriftless. He was constantly being warned to mend his *improvident* ways and begin to "save for a rainy day." improvidence, N.

improvise V. compose on the spur of the moment. She would sit at the piano and *improvise* for hours on themes from Bach and Handel.

imprudent ADJ. lacking caution; injudicious. It is *imprudent* to exercise vigorously and become overheated when you are unwell.

impudence N. impertinence; insolence. Kissed on the cheek by a perfect stranger, Lady Catherine exclaimed, "Of all the nerve! Young man, I should have you horse-whipped for your *impudence*."

impunity N. freedom from punishment or harm. A 98-pound weakling can't attack a beachfront bully with *impunity*: the poor, puny guy is sure to get mashed.

imputation N. accusation; charge; reproach. Paradoxically, the guiltier he was of the offense with which he was charged, the more he resented the *imputation*.

inadvertently ADV. unintentionally; by oversight; carelessly. Judy's great fear was that she might *inadvertently* omit a question on the exam and mismark her whole answer sheet.

inalienable ADJ. not to be taken away; nontransferable. The Declaration of Independence asserts that all people possess certain *inalienable* human rights that no powers on earth can take away.

inane ADJ. silly; senseless. There's no point to what you're saying. Why are you bothering to make such *inane* remarks?

inarticulate ADJ. speechless; producing indistinct speech. He became *inarticulate* with rage and uttered sounds without meaning.

inaugurate V. start; initiate; install in office. The airline decided to *inaugurate* its new route to the Far East with a special reduced fare offer. inaugural, ADJ.

incapacitate V. disable. During the winter, many people were *incapacitated* by respiratory ailments.

incentive N. spur; motive. Mike's strong desire to outshine his big sister was all the *incentive* he needed to do well in school.

inception N. start; beginning. She was involved with the project from its *inception*.

incessant ADJ. uninterrupted; unceasing. In a famous TV commercial, the frogs' *incessant* croaking goes on and on until eventually it turns into a single word: "Bud-weis-er."

incidence N. rate of occurrence; particular occurrence. Health professionals expressed great concern over the high *incidence* of infant mortality in major urban areas.

incidental ADJ. not essential; minor. The scholarship covered his major expenses at college and some of his *incidental* expenses as well.

incipient ADJ. beginning; in an early stage. I will go to sleep early for I want to break an *incipient* cold.

incisive ADJ. cutting; sharp. His *incisive* remarks made us see the fallacy in our plans.

incite V. arouse to action; goad; motivate; induce to exist. In a fiery speech, Mario *incited* his fellow students to go out on strike to protest the university's anti-affirmative action stand.

inclined ADJ. tending or leaning toward; bent. Though I am *inclined* to be skeptical, the witness's manner *inclines* me to believe his story. also V.

inclusive ADJ. tending to include all. The comedian turned down the invitation to join the Players' Club, saying any club that would let him in was too *inclusive* for him.

incoherence N. unintelligibility; lack of logic or relevance. "This essay makes no sense at all," commented the teacher, giving it an F because of its *incoherence*.

incompatible ADJ. (1) so opposed in nature as to be unable to coexist; (2) unable to work together in combination. He was a staunch Republican; she, a fervent Democrat. Their political views were clearly *incompatible*, and yet they remained good friends despite their differences. The Dragon Naturally Speaking dictation program worked on my PC but was *incompatible* with my iMac.

incongruous ADJ. not fitting; absurd. Dave saw nothing *incongruous* about wearing sneakers with his tuxedo; he couldn't understand why his date took one look at him and started to laugh. incongruity, N.

inconsequential ADJ. insignificant; unimportant. Brushing off Ali's apologies for having broken the wineglass, Tamara said, "Don't worry about it; it's *inconsequential*."

inconsistency N. state of being self-contradictory; lack of uniformity or steadiness. How are lawyers different from agricultural inspectors? While lawyers check *inconsistencies* in witnesses' statements, agricultural inspectors check *inconsistencies* in Grade A eggs. inconsistent, ADJ.

incontrovertible ADJ. indisputable; not open to question. Unless you find the evidence against my client absolutely *incontrovertible*, you must declare her not guilty of this charge.

incorporate V. introduce something into a larger whole; combine; unite. Breaking with precedent, President Truman ordered the military to *incorporate* blacks into every branch of the armed services. also ADJ.

incorrigible ADJ. not correctable. Though Widow Douglass hoped to reform Huck, Miss Watson called him *incorrigible* and said he would come to no good end.

incredulous ADJ. withholding belief; skeptical. When Jack claimed he hadn't eaten the jelly doughnut, Jill took an *incredulous* look at his smeared face and laughed. incredulity, N.

increment N. increase. The new contract calls for a 10 percent *increment* in salary for each employee for the next two years.

incriminate V. accuse. The evidence gathered against the racketeers *incriminates* some high public officials as well.

incumbent ADJ. (1) obligatory; (2) currently holding an office. It is *incumbent* upon all *incumbent* elected officials to keep accurate records of expenses incurred in office. also N.

indefatigable ADJ. tireless. Although the effort of taking out the garbage tired Wayne out for the entire morning, when it came to partying, he was *indefatigable*.

indelible ADJ. not able to be erased. The *indelible* ink left a permanent mark on my shirt. Young Bill Clinton's meeting with President Kennedy made an *indelible* impression on the youth.

indeterminate ADJ. uncertain; not clearly fixed; indefinite. That interest rates shall rise appears certain; when they will do so, however, remains *indeterminate*.

indicative ADJ. suggestive; implying. A lack of appetite may be *indicative* of a major mental or physical disorder.

indices N. PL. signs; indications. Many college admissions officers believe that SAT scores and high school grades are the best *indices* of a student's potential to succeed in college. N. SG. index.

Word List 24   indifferent–insolvent

indifferent ADJ. (1) unmoved or unconcerned by; (2) mediocre. Because Ann felt no desire to marry, she was *indifferent* to Carl's constant proposals. Not only was she *indifferent* to him personally, but she felt that, given his general silliness, he would make an *indifferent* husband.

indigenous ADJ. native. Cigarettes are made of tobacco, a plant *indigenous* to the New World.

indigent ADJ. poor; destitute. Someone who is truly *indigent* can't even afford to buy a pack of cigarettes. [Don't mix up *indigent* and *indigenous*. See previous sentence.]

indignation N. anger at an injustice. He felt *indignation* at the ill-treatment of helpless animals.

indiscretion N. lack of tactfulness or sound judgment. Terrified that the least *indiscretion* could jeopardize his political career, the novice politician never uttered an unguarded word. indiscreet, ADJ.

indiscriminate ADJ. (1) not marked by making careful distinctions; (2) done at random. Mother disapproved of Junior's *indiscriminate* television viewing; she wished he'd be a little more discriminating in his choice of shows. The newspaper editorial denounced the terrorists for their *indiscriminate* killing of civilians.

indisputable ADJ. too certain to be disputed. In the face of these *indisputable* statements, I withdraw my complaint.

indoctrinate V. instruct in a doctrine or ideology. Cuban-Americans resisted sending Elian Gonzalez back to Cuba because he would be *indoctrinated* there with Communist principles.

indomitable ADJ. unconquerable; unyielding. Focusing on her game despite all her personal problems, tennis champion Steffi Graf proved she had an *indomitable* will to win.

indubitable ADJ. unable to be doubted; unquestionable. Auditioning for the chorus line, Molly was an *indubitable* hit: the director fired the leading lady and hired Molly in her place!

induce V. (1) move someone to do something by persuasion; (2) bring about; (3) conclude through inductive reasoning. After their quarrel, Tina said nothing could *induce* her to talk to Tony again. Drinking a glass of warm milk before bedtime can help *induce* sleep. Rather than indulging in vain speculation, Isaac Newton attempted to *induce* principles from observations. inducement, N.

indulgent ADJ. humoring; yielding; lenient. Jay's mom was excessively *indulgent*: she bought him every Nintendo cartridge and video game on the market. She *indulged* Jay so much, she spoiled him rotten.

industrious ADJ. diligent; hard-working. Look busy when the boss walks by your desk; it never hurts to appear *industrious*. industry, N.

ineffectual ADJ. not effective; weak. Because the candidate failed to get across his message to the public, his campaign was *ineffectual*.

inefficacious ADJ. not effective; unable to produce a desired result. All Lois's coaxing and urging was *inefficacious*: Clark still refused to join her and Superman for dinner. inefficacy, N.

inept ADJ. lacking skill; unsuited; incompetent. The *inept* glovemaker was all thumbs.

inequity N. unfairness. In demanding equal pay for equal work, women protest the basic *inequity* of a system that gives greater financial rewards to men.

inert ADJ. (1) chemically inactive; (2) lacking power to move. If you surround hot metals with chemically *inert* argon, you can protect the metals from potential oxidation by oxygen in the air. "Get up, you lazybones," she cried to her husband, who lay in bed *inert*. inertia, N.

inevitable ADJ. unavoidable. Though death and taxes are both supposedly *inevitable*, some people avoid paying taxes for years.

inexorable ADJ. relentless; unyielding; implacable. After listening to the pleas for clemency, the judge was *inexorable* and gave the convicted man the maximum punishment allowed by law.

infallible ADJ. unerring. Jane refused to believe the pope was *infallible*, reasoning, "All human beings are capable of error. The pope is a human being. Therefore, the pope is capable of error."

infamous ADJ. notoriously bad. Charles Manson and Jeffrey Dahmer are both *infamous* killers.

infer V. deduce; conclude. From the students' glazed looks, it was easy for me to *infer* that they were bored out of their minds. inference, N.

infinitesimal ADJ. exceedingly small; so small as to be almost nonexistent. Making sure everyone was aware she was on an extremely strict diet, Melanie said she would have only an *infinitesimal* sliver of pie.

inflated ADJ. exaggerated; pompous; enlarged (with air or gas). His claims about the new product were *inflated*; it did not work as well as he had promised.

influx N. flowing into. The *influx* of refugees into the country has taxed the relief agencies severely.

informal ADJ. absence of ceremony; casual. The English teacher preferred *informal* discussions to prepared lectures.

infraction N. violation (of a rule or regulation); breach. When Dennis Rodman butted heads with that referee, he committed a clear *infraction* of NBA rules.

infuriate V. enrage; anger. Her big brother's teasing always *infuriated* Margaret; no matter how hard she tried to keep her temper, he always got her goat.

ingenious ADJ. clever; resourceful. Franchising was an *ingenious* way to grow a new company in a new industry: rather than having the company pay the salesmen, the salesmen, as franchise owners, would pay the company. ingenuity, N.

inherent ADJ. firmly established by nature or habit. Katya's *inherent* love of justice caused her to champion anyone she considered treated unfairly by society.

inhibit V. (1) restrain; (2) retard or prevent. Only two things *inhibited* him from taking a punch at Mike Tyson: Tyson's left hook, and Tyson's right jab. The protective undercoating on my car *inhibits* the formation of rust.

inimical ADJ. unfriendly; hostile; harmful; detrimental. I've always been friendly to Martha. Why is she so *inimical* to me?

inimitable ADJ. matchless; not able to be imitated. We admire Auden for his *inimitable* use of language; he is one of a kind.

initiate V. begin; originate; receive into a group. The college is about to *initiate* a program in reducing math anxiety among students.

injurious ADJ. harmful. Smoking cigarettes can be *injurious* to your health.

inkling N. hint. This came as a complete surprise to me as I did not have the slightest *inkling* of your plans.

innate ADJ. inborn. Mozart's parents soon recognized young Wolfgang's *innate* talent for music.

innocuous ADJ. harmless. An occasional glass of wine with dinner is relatively *innocuous* and should have no ill effect on you.

innovation N. change; introduction of something new. Although Richard liked to keep up with all the latest technological *innovations*, he didn't always abandon tried and true techniques in favor of something new. innovate, V.

innovative ADJ. novel; introducing a change. The establishment of our SAT computer database has enabled us to come up with some *innovative* tactics for doing well on the SAT.

inopportune ADJ. untimely; poorly chosen. A rock concert is an *inopportune* setting for a quiet conversation.

inordinate ADJ. unrestrained; excessive. She had an *inordinate* fondness for candy, eating two or three boxes in a single day.

insatiable ADJ. not easily satisfied; unquenchable; greedy. David's appetite for oysters was *insatiable*: he could easily eat four dozen at a single sitting.

inscrutable ADJ. impenetrable; not readily understood; mysterious. Experienced poker players try to keep their expressions *inscrutable*, hiding their reactions to the cards behind a so-called "poker face."

insightful ADJ. discerning; perceptive. Sol thought he was very *insightful* about human behavior, but he was actually clueless as to why people acted the way they did.

insinuate V. hint; imply; creep in. When you said I looked robust, did you mean to *insinuate* that I'm getting fat?

insipid ADJ. lacking in flavor; dull. Flat prose and flat ginger ale are equally *insipid*: both lack sparkle.

insolence N. impudent disrespect; haughtiness. How dare you treat me so rudely! The manager will hear of your *insolence*. insolent, ADJ.

insolvent ADJ. bankrupt; unable to repay one's debts. Although young Lord Widgeon was *insolvent*, he had no fear of being thrown into debtors' prison, for he was sure that if his creditors pressed him for payment his wealthy parents would repay what he owed. insolvency, N.

Word List 25   instigate–jargon

instigate V. urge; start; provoke. Rumors of police corruption led the mayor to *instigate* an investigation into the department's activities.

insubordination N. disobedience; rebelliousness. At the slightest hint of *insubordination* from the sailors of the *Bounty*, Captain Bligh had them flogged; finally, they mutinied.

insubstantial ADJ. lacking substance; insignificant; frail. His hopes for a career in acting proved *insubstantial*; no one would cast him, even in an *insubstantial* role.

insularity N. narrow-mindedness; isolation. The *insularity* of the islanders manifested itself in their suspicion of anything foreign. insular, ADJ.

insuperable ADJ. insurmountable; unbeatable. Though the odds against their survival seemed *insuperable*, the Apollo 13 astronauts reached earth safely.

insurgent ADJ. rebellious. Because the *insurgent* forces had occupied the capital and had gained control of the railway lines, several of the war correspondents covering the uprising predicted a rebel victory.

insurmountable ADJ. overwhelming; unbeatable; insuperable. Faced by almost *insurmountable* obstacles, the members of the underground maintained their courage and will to resist.

insurrection N. rebellion; uprising. In retrospect, given how badly the British treated the American colonists, the eventual *insurrection* seems inevitable.

intangible ADJ. not able to be perceived by touch; vague. Though the financial benefits of his Oxford post were meager, Lewis was drawn to it by its *intangible* rewards: prestige, intellectual freedom, the fellowship of his peers.

integral ADJ. complete; necessary for completeness. Physical education is an *integral* part of our curriculum; a sound mind and a sound body are complementary.

integrate V. make whole; combine; make into one unit. We hope to *integrate* the French, Spanish, and Italian programs into a combined Romance languages department.

integrity N. (1) uprightness; (2) wholeness. Lincoln, whose personal *integrity* has inspired millions, fought a civil war to maintain the *integrity* of the Republic, that these United States might remain undivided for all time.

intellect N. higher mental powers. If you wish to develop your *intellect*, read the great books.

interim N. meantime. The company will not consider our proposal until next week; in the *interim*, let us proceed as we have in the past.

interminable ADJ. endless. Although his speech lasted for only twenty minutes, it seemed *interminable* to his bored audience.

intermittent ADJ. periodic; on and off. The outdoor wedding reception had to be moved indoors to avoid the *intermittent* showers that fell on and off all afternoon.

interrogate V. question closely; cross-examine. Knowing that the Nazis would *interrogate* him about his background, the secret agent invented a cover story that would help him meet their questions.

intervene V. (1) come between in order to prevent or alter; (2) occur between (events, periods of time). If two good friends get into a fight, don't try to *intervene*: if you do, they may gang up on you. Spring break *intervened*, and Johnny headed to Fort Lauderdale for a short vacation before classes started again.

intimacy N. closeness, often affectionate; privacy; familiarity. In a moment of rare *intimacy*, the mayor allowed the reporters a glimpse of his personal feelings about his family. intimate, ADJ.

intimate V. (1) hint, suggest; (2) make known. Was Dick *intimating* that Jane had bad breath when he asked if she'd like a breath mint? We were taken by surprise when the principal *intimated* his decision to eliminate the after-school program.

intimidate V. frighten. I'll learn karate and then those big bullies won't be able to *intimidate* me anymore.

intractable ADJ. unruly; stubborn; unyielding. Charlie Brown's friend Pigpen was *intractable*: he absolutely refused to take a bath.

intransigence N. refusal of any compromise; stubbornness. The negotiating team had not expected such *intransigence* from the striking workers, who rejected any hint of a compromise. intransigent, ADJ.

intrepid ADJ. fearless. For her *intrepid* conduct nursing the wounded during the war, Florence Nightingale was honored by Queen Victoria.

intricate ADJ. complex; knotty; tangled. Philip spent many hours designing mazes so *intricate* that none of his classmates could solve them. intricacy, N.

intrinsic ADJ. essential; inherent; built-in. Although my grandmother's china has little *intrinsic* value, I shall always cherish it for the memories it evokes.

introspective ADJ. looking within oneself. Though young Francis of Assisi led a wild and worldly life, even then he had *introspective* moments during which he examined his soul.

introvert N. one who is introspective; inclined to think more about oneself. Uncommunicative by nature and disinclined to look outside himself, he was a classic *introvert*.

intrude V. trespass; enter as an uninvited person. She hesitated to *intrude* on their conversation.

intuition N. immediate insight; power of knowing without reasoning. Even though Tony denied that anything was wrong, Tina trusted her *intuition* that something was bothering him. intuitive, ADJ.

inundate V. (1) overwhelm; (2) flood; submerge. This semester I am *inundated* with work: You should see the piles of paperwork flooding my desk. Until the great dam was built, the waters of the Nile used to *inundate* the river valley like clockwork every year.

invalidate V. weaken; destroy. The relatives who received little or nothing sought to *invalidate* the will by claiming that the deceased had not been in his right mind when he had signed the document.

inveterate ADJ. deep-rooted; habitual. An *inveterate* smoker, Bob cannot seem to break the habit, no matter how hard he tries.

invigorate V. energize; stimulate. A quick dip in the pool *invigorated* Meg, and with renewed energy she got back to work.

invincible ADJ. unconquerable. Superman is *invincible*.

invulnerable ADJ. incapable of injury. Achilles was *invulnerable* except in his heel.

iota N. very small quantity. She hadn't an *iota* of common sense.

irksome ADJ. annoying; tedious. He found working on the assembly line *irksome* because of the monotony of the operation he had to perform. irk, V.

ironic ADJ. resulting in an unexpected and contrary outcome. It is *ironic* that his success came when he least wanted it.

irony N. hidden sarcasm or satire; use of words that seem to mean the opposite of what they actually mean. Gradually his listeners began to realize that the excessive praise he was lavishing on his opponent was actually *irony*; he was in fact ridiculing the poor fool.

irrational ADJ. illogical; lacking reason; insane. Many people have such an *irrational* fear of snakes that they panic at the sight of a harmless garter snake.

irreconcilable ADJ. incompatible; not able to be resolved. Because the separated couple were *irreconcilable*, the marriage counselor recommended a divorce.

irrefutable ADJ. indisputable; incontrovertible; undeniable. No matter how hard I tried to find a good comeback for her argument, I couldn't think of one: her logic was *irrefutable*.

irrelevant ADJ. not applicable; unrelated. No matter how *irrelevant* the patient's mumblings may seem, they give us some indications of what he has on his mind.

irremediable ADJ. incurable; uncorrectable. The error she made was *irremediable*; she could see no way to repair it.

irreparable ADJ. not able to be corrected or repaired. Your apology cannot atone for the *irreparable* damage you have done to her reputation.

irreproachable ADJ. blameless; impeccable. Homer's conduct at the office party was *irreproachable*; even Marge didn't have anything bad to say about how he behaved.

irresolute ADJ. uncertain how to act; weak. Once you have made your decision, don't waver; a leader should never appear *irresolute*.

irrevocable ADJ. unalterable; irreversible. As Sue dropped the "Dear John" letter into the mailbox, she suddenly had second thoughts and wanted to take it back, but she could not: her action was *irrevocable*.

jargon N. language used by a special group; technical terminology; gibberish. The computer salesmen at the store used a *jargon* of their own that we simply couldn't follow; we had no idea what they were jabbering about.

Word List 26 jeopardize–magnanimous

jeopardize V. endanger; imperil; put at risk. You can't give me a D in chemistry: you'll *jeopardize* my chances of getting into M.I.T. jeopardy, N.

jocular ADJ. said or done in jest. Although Bill knew the boss hated jokes, he couldn't resist making one *jocular* remark.

jollity N. gaiety; cheerfulness. The festive Christmas dinner was a merry one, and old and young alike joined in the general *jollity*.

jovial ADJ. good-natured; merry. A frown seemed out of place on his invariably *jovial* face.

jubilation N. rejoicing. There was great *jubilation* when the armistice was announced. jubilant, ADJ.

judicious ADJ. sound in judgment; wise. At a key moment in his life, he made a *judicious* investment that was the foundation of his later wealth.

juncture N. crisis; joining point. At this critical *juncture,* let us think carefully before determining the course we shall follow.

justification N. good or just reason; defense; excuse. The jury found him guilty of the more serious charge because they could see no possible *justification* for his actions.

kindle V. (1) start a fire; (2) inspire. One of the first things Ben learned in the Boy Scouts was how to *kindle* a fire by rubbing two dry sticks together. Her teacher's praise for her poetry *kindled* a spark of hope inside Maya.

kindred ADJ. related; belonging to the same family. Tom Sawyer and Huck Finn were *kindred* spirits, born mischief makers who were always up to some new tomfoolery.

knotty ADJ. (1) intricate; difficult; (2) tangled. What to Watson had been a *knotty* problem, to Sherlock Holmes was simplicity itself. Santiago uses a detangling spray before he tries to comb his perennially *knotty* hair.

kudos N. honor; glory; praise. The singer complacently received *kudos* from his entourage on his performance.

laborious ADJ. demanding much work or care; tedious. In putting together his dictionary of the English language, Doctor Johnson undertook a *laborious* task.

labyrinth N. (1) something very intricate or bewildering in structure; (2) place made up of twisting passages and blind alleys. Conflicting rules from New York's Health, Transportation, and Sanitation agencies create a *labyrinth* of regulations that make it almost impossible for food trucks to get a permit. Hiding from Injun Joe, Tom and Becky soon lost themselves in the *labyrinth* of secret underground caves. labyrinthine, ADJ.

lackadaisical ADJ. lacking purpose or zest; halfhearted; languid. Because Gatsby had his mind more on his love life than on his finances, he did a very *lackadaisical* job of managing his money.

lackluster ADJ. dull. We were disappointed by the *lackluster* performance.

laconic ADJ. brief and to the point. Many of the characters portrayed by Clint Eastwood are *laconic* types: strong men of few words.

lament V. grieve; express sorrow. Even advocates of the war *lamented* the loss of so many lives in combat. also N. lamentation, N.

lampoon V. ridicule. This article *lampoons* the pretensions of some movie moguls. also N.

latent ADJ. (1) potential but undeveloped; (2) dormant; hidden. Polaroid pictures are popular at parties because you can see the *latent* photographic image gradually appear before your eyes. Sometimes *latent* tuberculosis becomes active years later.

lateral ADJ. coming from the side. In order to get good plant growth, the gardener must pinch off all *lateral* shoots.

latitude N. freedom from narrow limitations. I think you have permitted your son too much *latitude* in this matter.

laud V. praise. The NFL *lauded* Boomer Esiason's efforts to raise money to combat cystic fibrosis. laudable, laudatory, ADJ.

lavish ADJ. generous; openhanded; extravagant; wasteful. Her wealthy suitors wooed her with lavish gifts. also V.

lax ADJ. careless. We dislike restaurants where the service is *lax* and inattentive.

legacy N. a gift made by a will. Part of my *legacy* from my parents is an album of family photographs.

legend N. explanatory list of symbols on a map. The *legend* at the bottom of the map made it clear which symbols stood for rest areas along the highway and which stood for public camp sites. (secondary meaning)

leniency N. mildness; permissiveness. Considering the gravity of the offense, we were surprised by the *leniency* of the sentence.

lethal ADJ. deadly. It is unwise to leave *lethal* weapons where children may find them.

lethargic ADJ. drowsy; dull. The stuffy room made her *lethargic*: she felt as if she was about to nod off.

levity N. lack of seriousness; lightness. Stop giggling and wriggling around in the pew: such *levity* is improper in church.

levy V. impose (a fine); collect (a payment). Crying "No taxation without representation," the colonists demonstrated against England's power to *levy* taxes.

lexicon N. dictionary. I cannot find this word in any *lexicon* in the library.

liability N. drawback; debts. Her lack of an extensive vocabulary was a *liability* that she was eventually able to overcome.

liaison N. (1) contact keeping parts of an organization in communication; go-between; (2) secret love affair. As the *liaison* between the American and

British forces during World War II, the colonel had to ease tensions between the leaders of the two armies. Romeo's romantic *liaison* with Juliet ended in tragedy.

libel N. defamatory statement; act of writing something that smears a person's character. If Batman wrote that the Joker was a dirty, rotten, mass-murdering criminal, could the Joker sue Batman for *libel*?

liberator N. one who sets free. Simon Bolivar, who led the South American colonies in their rebellion against Spanish rule, is known as the great *liberator*. liberate, v.

likelihood N. state of being likely to happen. Mastering these vocabulary words increases the *likelihood* of your doing well on the SAT.

linger v. (1) loiter or dawdle; (2) continue or persist. Hoping to see Juliet pass by, Romeo *lingered* outside the Capulet house for hours. Though Mother made stuffed cabbage on Monday, the smell *lingered* around the house for days.

linguistic ADJ. pertaining to language. Exposed to most modern European languages in childhood, she grew up to be a *linguistic* prodigy.

loath ADJ. reluctant; disinclined. Fearing for their son's safety, the overprotective parents were *loath* to let him go on the class trip.

loathe v. detest. Booing and hissing, the audience showed how much they *loathed* the wicked villain.

lofty ADJ. very high. Though Barbara Jordan's fellow students used to tease her about her *lofty* ambitions, she rose to hold one of the highest positions in the land.

log N. (1) record of a voyage or flight; (2) record of day to day activities. "Flogged two seamen today for insubordination" wrote Captain Bligh in the *Bounty's log*. To see how much work I've accomplished recently, just take a look at the number of new files listed on my computer *log*.

loquacious ADJ. talkative. Though our daughter barely says a word to us these days, put a phone in her hand and see how *loquacious* she can be: our phone bills are out of sight! loquacity, N.

lucid ADJ. easily understood; clear; intelligible. Ellen makes an excellent teacher: her explanations of technical points are *lucid* enough for a child to grasp.

lucrative ADJ. profitable. He turned his hobby into a *lucrative* profession.

lurid ADJ. wild; sensational; graphic; gruesome. Do the *lurid* cover stories in the *Enquirer* actually attract people to buy that trashy tabloid?

machinations N. evil schemes or plots. Fortunately, Batman saw through the wily *machinations* of the Riddler and saved Gotham City from destruction by the forces of evil.

magnanimous ADJ. generous; great-hearted. Philanthropists by definition are *magnanimous*; misers, by definition, are not. Cordelia was too *magnanimous* to resent her father's unkindness to her; instead, she generously forgave him. magnanimity, N.

Word List 27 magnate–misapprehension

magnate N. person of prominence or influence. Growing up in Pittsburgh, Annie Dillard was surrounded by the mansions of the great steel and coal *magnates* who set their mark on that city.

magnitude N. (1) greatness of extent; (2) great importance; (3) size. Seismologists use the Richter scale to measure the *magnitude* of earthquakes. Mexico's Bicentennial Celebration was an event of such *magnitude* that it had a lasting positive impact on the country's economy. When students work with very large numbers (millions and billions), they need to understand the *magnitude* of these numbers.

malefactor N. evildoer; criminal. Mighty Mouse will save the day, hunting down *malefactors* and rescuing innocent mice from peril.

malevolent ADJ. wishing evil. Iago is a *malevolent* villain who takes pleasure in ruining Othello.

malicious ADJ. hateful; spiteful. Jealous of Cinderella's beauty, her *malicious* stepsisters expressed their spite by forcing her to do menial tasks. malice, N.

malign v. speak evil of; bad-mouth; defame. Putting her hands over her ears, Rose refused to listen to Betty *malign* her friend Susan.

malignant ADJ. injurious; tending to cause death; aggressively malevolent. Though many tumors are benign, some are *malignant*, growing out of control and endangering the life of the patient.

malleable ADJ. (1) capable of being shaped by pounding; (2) impressionable. Gold is a *malleable* metal, easily shaped into bracelets and rings. Fagin hoped Oliver was a *malleable* lad, easily shaped into a thief.

mammal N. a vertebrate animal whose female suckles its young. Many people regard the whale as a fish and do not realize that it is a *mammal*.

mammoth ADJ. gigantic; enormous. To try to memorize every word on this vocabulary list would be a *mammoth* undertaking; take on projects that are more manageable in size.

mandate N. order; charge. In his inaugural address, the president stated that he had a *mandate* from the people to seek an end to social evils such as poverty. also v.

mandatory ADJ. obligatory; compulsory. It is *mandatory* that, before graduation, all students must pass the swimming test.

manifest ADJ. evident; visible; obvious. Digby's embarrassment when he met Madonna was *manifest*: his ears turned bright pink, he kept scuffing one shoe in the dirt, and he couldn't look her in the eye.

manifesto N. declaration; statement of policy. The *Communist Manifesto* by Marx and Engels proclaimed the principles of modern communism.

manipulate V. operate with one's hands; control or play upon (people, forces, etc.) artfully. Jim Henson understood how to *manipulate* the Muppets. Madonna understands how to *manipulate* men (and publicity).

marked ADJ. noticeable or pronounced; targeted for vengeance. He walked with a *marked* limp, a souvenir of an old I.R.A. attack. As British ambassador, he knew he was a *marked* man, for he knew the Irish Republican Army wanted him dead.

marred ADJ. damaged; disfigured. She had to refinish the *marred* surface of the table. mar, v.

marshal V. put in order. At a debate tournament, extemporaneous speakers have only a minute or two to *marshal* their thoughts before they address their audience.

marsupial N. one of a family of mammals that nurse their offspring in a pouch. The most common *marsupial* in North America is the opossum.

martial ADJ. warlike. The sound of *martial* music inspired the young cadet with dreams of military glory.

martyr N. one who voluntarily suffers death for his or her religion or cause; great sufferer. By burning her at the stake, the English made Joan of Arc a *martyr* for her faith. Mother played the *martyr* by staying home cleaning the house while the rest of the family went off to the beach.

material ADJ. (1) made of physical matter; (2) unspiritual; (3) important. Probing the mysteries of this *material* world has always fascinated physicist George Whitesides. Reporters nicknamed Madonna the *Material* Girl because, despite her name, she seemed wholly uninterested in spiritual values. Lexy's active participation made a *material* difference to the success of the fund-raiser.

materialism N. preoccupation with physical comforts and things. By its nature, *materialism* is opposed to idealism, for where the materialist emphasizes the needs of the body, the idealist emphasizes the needs of the soul.

matrix N. point of origin; array of numbers or algebraic symbols; mold or die. Some historians claim the Nile Valley was the *matrix* of Western civilization.

maverick N. rebel; nonconformist. To the masculine literary establishment, George Sand with her insistence on wearing trousers and smoking cigars was clearly a *maverick* who fought her proper womanly role.

maxim N. proverb; a truth pithily stated. Aesop's story of the hare and the tortoise illustrates the *maxim* "Slow and steady wins the race."

meager ADJ. scanty; inadequate. Still hungry after his *meager* serving of porridge, Oliver Twist asked for a second helping.

mediate V. settle a dispute through the services of an outsider. King Solomon was asked to *mediate* a dispute between two women, each of whom claimed to be the mother of the same child.

mediocre ADJ. ordinary; commonplace. We were disappointed because he gave a rather *mediocre* performance in this role.

meditation N. reflection; thought. She reached her decision only after much *meditation*.

medium N. (1) means of doing something; (2) substance in which an organism lives; (3) form or material employed by an artist, author, or composer. M.I.T.'s use of the Internet as a *medium* of education has transformed the university into a global enterprise. Ty's experiment involved growing bacteria in a nutrient-rich *medium*. Johnny's favorite artistic *medium* is photography; he hopes to become a photojournalist.

mendacious ADJ. lying; habitually dishonest. Distrusting Huck from the start, Miss Watson assumed he was *mendacious* and refused to believe a word he said.

menial ADJ. suitable for servants; lowly; mean. Her wicked stepmother forced Cinderella to do *menial* tasks around the house while her ugly stepsisters lolled around painting their toenails.

mentor N. teacher. During this very trying period, she could not have had a better *mentor*, for the teacher was sympathetic and understanding.

mercenary ADJ. interested in money or gain. Andy's every act was prompted by *mercenary* motives: his first question was always "What's in it for me?"

mercurial ADJ. capricious; changing; fickle. Quick as quicksilver to change, he was *mercurial* in nature and therefore unreliable.

merger N. combination (of two business corporations). When the firm's president married the director of financial planning, the office joke was that it wasn't a marriage, it was a *merger*.

metamorphosis N. change of form; major transformation. The *metamorphosis* of caterpillar to butterfly is typical of many such changes in animal life. metamorphose, v.

metaphor N. implied comparison. "He soared like an eagle" is an example of a simile; "He is an eagle in flight," is a *metaphor*.

methodical ADJ. systematic. An accountant must be *methodical* and maintain order among his financial records.

meticulous ADJ. excessively careful; painstaking; scrupulous. Martha Stewart was a *meticulous* housekeeper, fussing about each and every detail that went into making up her perfect home.

metropolis N. large city. Every evening the terminal is filled with thousands of commuters going from this *metropolis* to their homes in the suburbs.

microcosm N. small world; the world in miniature. The small village community that Jane Austen depicts serves as a *microcosm* of English society in her time, for in this small world we see all the social classes meeting and mingling.

migrant ADJ. changing its habitat; wandering. *Migrant* workers return to the Central Valley each year at harvest time. also N.

migratory ADJ. wandering. The return of the *migratory* birds to the northern sections of this country is a harbinger of spring. migrate, V.

milieu N. environment; means of expression. Surrounded by smooth preppies and arty bohemians, the country boy from Smalltown, USA, felt out of his *milieu*. Although he has produced excellent oil paintings and lithographs, his proper *milieu* is watercolor.

militant ADJ. combative; bellicose. Although at this time he was advocating a policy of neutrality, one could usually find him adopting a more *militant* attitude. also N.

minute ADJ. extremely small. The twins resembled one another closely; only *minute* differences set them apart.

minutiae N. petty details. She would have liked to ignore the *minutiae* of daily living.

misapprehension N. error; misunderstanding. To avoid *misapprehension*, I am going to ask all of you to repeat the instructions I have given.

Word List 28   miscellany–neophyte

miscellany N. mixture of writings on various subjects. This is an interesting *miscellany* of nineteenth-century prose and poetry.

mischance N. ill luck. By *mischance*, he lost his week's salary.

misconception N. mistaken idea. "Sir, you are suffering from a *misconception*. I do not wish to marry you in the least!"

misconstrue V. interpret incorrectly; misjudge. She took the passage seriously rather than humorously because she *misconstrued* the author's ironic tone.

misdemeanor N. minor crime. The culprit pleaded guilty to a *misdemeanor* rather than face trial for a felony.

miserly ADJ. stingy; mean. Transformed by his vision on Christmas Eve, mean old Scrooge ceased being *miserly* and became a generous, kind old man.

misgivings N. doubts. Hamlet described his *misgivings* to Horatio but decided to fence with Laertes despite his foreboding of evil.

mishap N. accident. With a little care you could have avoided this *mishap*.

misrepresent V. give a false or incorrect impression, often deliberately; serve unsatisfactorily as a representative. In his job application, Milton *misrepresented* his academic background; he was fired when his employers discovered the truth. The reformers accused Senator Gunbucks of *misrepresenting* his constituents and claimed he took bribes from the NRA.

mitigate V. appease; moderate. Nothing Jason did could *mitigate* Medea's anger; she refused to forgive him for betraying her.

mnemonic ADJ. pertaining to memory. He used *mnemonic* tricks to master new words.

mobile ADJ. movable; not fixed. The *mobile* blood bank operated by the Red Cross visited our neighborhood today. mobility, N.

mock V. ridicule; imitate, often in derision. It is unkind to *mock* anyone; it is stupid to *mock* anyone significantly bigger than you. mockery, N.

mode N. prevailing style; manner; way of doing something. The rock star had to have her hair done in the latest *mode*: frizzed, with occasional moussed spikes for variety. Henry plans to adopt a simpler *mode* of life: he is going to become a mushroom hunter and live off the land.

modicum N. limited quantity. Although his story is based on a *modicum* of truth, most of the events he describes are fictitious.

modulate V. tone down in intensity; regulate; change from one key to another. Always singing at the top of her lungs, the budding Brunhilde never learned to *modulate* her voice.

molecule N. the smallest particle (one or more atoms) of a substance, having all the properties of that substance. In chemistry, we study how atoms and *molecules* react to form new substances.

mollify V. soothe. The airline customer service representative tried to *mollify* the angry passenger by offering her a seat in first class.

momentous ADJ. very important. When Marie and Pierre Curie discovered radium, they had no idea of the *momentous* impact their discovery would have upon society.

momentum N. quantity of motion of a moving body; impetus. The car lost *momentum* as it tried to ascend the steep hill.

monarchy N. government under a single ruler. Though England today is a *monarchy*, there is some question whether it will be one in twenty years, given the present discontent at the prospect of Prince Charles as king.

monetary ADJ. pertaining to money. Jane held the family purse strings: she made all *monetary* decisions affecting the household.

monolithic ADJ. solidly uniform; unyielding. Knowing the importance of appearing resolute, the patriots sought to present a *monolithic* front.

monotony N. sameness leading to boredom. What could be more deadly dull than the *monotony* of punching numbers into a computer hour after hour?

monumental ADJ. massive. Writing a dictionary is a *monumental* task.

mores N. conventions; moral standards; customs. In America, Benazir Bhutto dressed as Western women did; in Pakistan, however, she followed the *mores* of her people, dressing in traditional veil and robes.

moribund ADJ. dying. Hearst took a *moribund*, failing weekly newspaper and transformed it into one of the liveliest, most profitable daily papers around.

motif N. theme. This simple *motif* runs throughout the entire score.

multifaceted ADJ. having many aspects. A *multifaceted* composer, Roger Davidson has recorded original pieces that range from ragtime tangos to choral masses.

multilingual ADJ. having many languages. Because Switzerland is surrounded by France, Germany, Italy, and Austria, many Swiss people are *multilingual*.

multiplicity N. state of being numerous. He was appalled by the *multiplicity* of details he had to complete before setting out on his mission.

mundane ADJ. worldly as opposed to spiritual; everyday. Uninterested in philosophical or spiritual discussions, Tom talked only of *mundane* matters such as the daily weather forecast or the latest basketball results.

muse V. ponder. For a moment he *mused* about the beauty of the scene, but his thoughts soon changed as he recalled his own personal problems. also N.

mushroom V. expand or grow rapidly. Between 1990 and 1999, the population of Silicon Valley *mushroomed*; with the rapidly increasing demand for housing, home prices skyrocketed as well.

muster V. gather; assemble. Washington *mustered* his forces at Trenton. also N.

mutability N. ability to change in form; fickleness. Going from rags to riches, and then back to rags again, the bankrupt financier was a victim of the *mutability* of fortune.

muted ADJ. silent; muffled; toned down. Thanks to the thick, sound-absorbing walls of the cathedral, only *muted* traffic noise reached the worshippers within.

myriad N. very large number. *Myriads* of mosquitoes from the swamps invaded our village every twilight. also ADJ.

mystify V. bewilder purposely. When doctors speak in medical jargon, they often *mystify* their patients, who have little knowledge of medical terminology.

nadir N. lowest point. Although few people realized it, the Dow-Jones averages had reached their *nadir* and would soon begin an upward surge.

narrative ADJ. related to telling a story. A born teller of tales, Tillie Olsen used her impressive *narrative* skills to advantage in her story "I Stand Here Ironing." narrate, V.

nascent ADJ. incipient; coming into being. If we could identify these revolutionary movements in their *nascent* state, we would be able to eliminate serious trouble in later years.

nebulous ADJ. (1) vague; (2) like a cloud. Phil and Dave tried to come up with a clear, intelligible business plan, not some hazy, *nebulous* proposal. A nebula is an interstellar cloud of dust, hydrogen, helium, and other ionized gases; such clouds are by definition *nebulous*.

nefarious ADJ. very wicked. The villain's crimes, though various, were one and all *nefarious*.

negate V. (1) cancel out; nullify; (2) deny the truth of. A sudden surge of adrenalin can *negate* the effects of fatigue: there's nothing like a good shock to wake you up. I disagree with you strongly on many points, but I won't try to *negate* your viewpoint.

negligence N. neglect; failure to take reasonable care. Tommy failed to put back the cover on the well after he fetched his pail of water; because of his *negligence*, Kitty fell in.

negligible ADJ. so small, trifling, or unimportant that it may be easily disregarded. Because the damage to his car had been *negligible*, Michael decided he wouldn't bother to report the matter to his insurance company.

nemesis N. someone seeking revenge. Abandoned at sea in a small boat, the vengeful Captain Bligh vowed to be the *nemesis* of Fletcher Christian and his fellow mutineers.

neologism N. new or newly coined word or phrase. As we invent new techniques and professions, we must also invent *neologisms* such as "microcomputer" and "astronaut" to describe them.

neophyte N. recent convert; beginner. This mountain slope contains slides that will challenge experts as well as *neophytes*.

Word List 29   nepotism–opus

nepotism N. favoritism (to a relative). John left his position with the company because he felt that advancement was based on *nepotism* rather than ability.

neutral ADJ. impartial; not supporting one side over another. Reluctant to get mixed up in someone else's quarrel, Bobby tried to remain *neutral,* but eventually he had to take sides.

nicety N. subtlety; precision; minute distinction; fine point. This word list provides illustrative sentences for each entry word; it cannot, however, explain all the *niceties* of current English usage.

nomenclature N. terminology; system of names. Sharon found Latin word parts useful in translating medical *nomenclature*: when her son had to have a bilateral myringotomy, she figured out that he just needed a hole in each of his eardrums to end the earaches he had.

nominal ADJ. in name only; trifling. He offered to drive her to the airport for only a *nominal* fee.

nonchalance N. indifference; lack of concern; composure. Cool, calm, and collected under fire, James Bond shows remarkable *nonchalance* in the face of danger.

noncommittal ADJ. neutral; unpledged; undecided. We were annoyed by his *noncommittal* reply for we had been led to expect definite assurances of his approval.

notable ADJ. conspicuous; important; distinguished. Normally *notable* for his calm in the kitchen, today the head cook was shaking, for the *notable* chef Julia Child was coming to dinner.

notoriety N. disrepute; ill fame. To the starlet, any publicity was good publicity: if she couldn't have a good reputation, she'd settle for *notoriety*. notorious, ADJ.

novelty N. (1) something new; (2) newness. First marketed in 1977, home computers were no longer a *novelty* by 1980. After the first couple of months at college, Johnny found that the *novelty* of living in a dormitory had worn off. novel, ADJ.

novice N. beginner. Even a *novice* at working with computers can install voice recognition software by following the easy steps outlined in the user's manual.

nuance N. shade of difference in meaning or color; subtle distinction. Jody gazed at the Monet landscape for an hour, appreciating every subtle *nuance* of color in the painting.

nullify V. to make invalid. Once the contract was *nullified,* it no longer had any legal force.

nurture V. nourish; educate; foster. The Head Start program attempts to *nurture* pre-kindergarten children so that they will do well when they enter public school. also N.

nutrient N. nourishing substance. As a budding nutritionist, Kim has learned to design diets that contain foods rich in important basic *nutrients*.

obdurate ADJ. stubborn. He was *obdurate* in his refusal to listen to our complaints.

objective ADJ. (1) not influenced by personal feelings or prejudices; (2) able to be perceived by the senses. Andrea loved her little son so much that it was impossible for her to be *objective* about his behavior. Nurses gather *objective* data about a patient by taking the patient's temperature or measuring the patient's height and weight.

objective N. goal; aim. Morgan's *objective* is to play basketball so well that he can be a starter on the varsity team.

obligatory ADJ. binding; required. It is *obligatory* that books borrowed from the library be returned within two weeks.

oblique ADJ. indirect; slanting (deviating from the perpendicular or from a straight line). Casting a quick, *oblique* glance at the reviewing stand, the sergeant ordered the company to march "*Oblique* Right."

obliterate V. destroy completely. The tidal wave *obliterated* several island villages.

oblivion N. obscurity; forgetfulness. After a decade of popularity, Hurston's works had fallen into *oblivion*; no one bothered to read them anymore.

oblivious ADJ. inattentive or unmindful; wholly absorbed. Deep in her book, Nancy was *oblivious* to the noisy squabbles of her brother and his friends.

obnoxious ADJ. offensive; objectionable. A sneak and a tattletale, Sid was an *obnoxious* little brat.

obscure ADJ. dark; vague; unclear. Even after I read the poem a fourth time, its meaning was still *obscure*. obscurity, N.

obscure V. (1) make unclear; (2) conceal. At times he seemed purposely to *obscure* his meaning, preferring mystery to clarity. We had hoped to see Mount Rainier, but Seattle's ever-present cloud cover *obscured* our view.

obsessive ADJ. related to thinking about something constantly; preoccupying. Ballet, which had been a hobby, began to dominate his life: his love of dancing became *obsessive*. obsession, N.

obsolete ADJ. no longer useful; outmoded; antiquated. The invention of the pocket calculator made the slide rule used by generations of engineers *obsolete*.

obstinate ADJ. stubborn; hard to control or treat. We tried to persuade him to give up smoking, but he was *obstinate* and refused to change. Blackberry stickers are the most *obstinate* weeds I know: once established in a yard, they're extremely hard to root out. obstinacy, N.

obtuse ADJ. blunt; stupid. Because Mr. Collins was too *obtuse* to take a hint, Elizabeth finally had to tell him that she wouldn't marry him if he were the last man on earth.

obviate V. prevent; make unnecessary. In the twentieth century, people believed electronic communications would *obviate* the need for hard copy; they envisioned a paperless society.

odyssey N. long, eventful journey. The refugee's journey from Cambodia was a terrifying *odyssey*.

offensive ADJ. attacking; insulting; distasteful. Getting into street brawls is no minor matter for professional boxers, who are required by law to restrict their *offensive* impulses to the ring.

officious ADJ. meddlesome; excessively pushy in offering one's services. Judy wanted to look over the new computer models on her own, but the *officious* salesman kept on butting in with "helpful" advice until she was ready to walk out of the store.

oligarchy N. government by a privileged few. One small clique ran the student council: what had been intended as a democratic governing body had turned into an *oligarchy*.

ominous ADJ. threatening. Those clouds are *ominous*; they suggest a severe storm is on the way.

omnipotent ADJ. all-powerful. Under Stalin, the Soviet government seemed *omnipotent*: no one dared defy the all-powerful State.

omnipresent ADJ. universally present; ubiquitous. The Beatles are a major musical force, whose influence is *omnipresent* in all contemporary popular music.

omniscient ADJ. all-knowing. I may not be *omniscient*, but I know a bit more than you do, young man!

onerous ADJ. burdensome. He asked for an assistant because his work load was too *onerous*.

onset N. beginning; attack. Caught unprepared by the sudden *onset* of the storm, we rushed around the house closing windows and bringing the garden furniture into shelter. Caught unprepared by the enemy *onset*, the troops scrambled to take shelter.

onus N. burden; responsibility. The emperor was spared the *onus* of signing the surrender papers; instead, he relegated the assignment to his generals.

opaque ADJ. (1) not transparent; (2) hard to understand or explain. The *opaque* window shade kept the sunlight out of the room. The language of the federal income tax forms was so *opaque* that I had to turn to an accountant for help. opacity, N.

opportune ADJ. timely; well-chosen. Sally looked at her father struggling to balance his checkbook; clearly this would not be an *opportune* moment to ask him for a raise in her allowance.

opportunist N. individual who sacrifices principles for expediency by taking advantage of circumstances. Joe is such an *opportunist* that he tripled the price of bottled water at his store as soon as the earthquake struck. Because it can break water pipes, an earthquake is, to most people, a disaster; to Joe, it was an *opportunity*.

optimist N. person who looks on the good side. The pessimist says the glass is half empty; the *optimist* says it is half full.

optimum ADJ. most favorable. If you wait for the *optimum* moment to act, you may never begin your project. also N.

optional ADJ. not obligatory; left to one's choice. Most colleges require applicants to submit SAT scores; at some colleges, however, submitting SAT scores is *optional*.

opulence N. extreme wealth; luxuriousness; abundance. The glitter and *opulence* of the ballroom took Cinderella's breath away. opulent, ADJ.

opus N. work. Although many critics hailed his Fifth Symphony as his greatest work, he did not regard it as his major *opus*.

Word List 30   oracular–pathetic

oracular ADJ. prophetic; uttered as if with divine authority; mysterious or ambiguous. Like many others who sought divine guidance from the *oracle* at Delphi, Oedipus could not understand the enigmatic *oracular* warning he received.

orator N. public speaker. The abolitionist Frederick Douglass was a brilliant *orator* whose speeches brought home to his audience the evils of slavery.

ordeal N. severe trial or affliction. June was so painfully shy that it was an *ordeal* for her to speak up when the teacher called on her in class.

ordinance N. decree. Passing a red light is a violation of a city *ordinance*.

orient V. get one's bearings; adjust. Philip spent his first day in Denver *orienting* himself to the city.

orientation N. act of finding oneself in society. Freshman *orientation* provides the incoming students with an opportunity to learn about their new environment and their place in it.

orthodox ADJ. traditional; conservative in belief. Faced with a problem, he preferred to take an *orthodox* approach rather than shock anyone. orthodoxy, N.

oscillate V. vibrate pendulumlike; waver. It is interesting to note how public opinion *oscillates* between the extremes of optimism and pessimism.

ostensible ADJ. apparent; professed; pretended. Although the *ostensible* purpose of this expedition is to discover new lands, we are really interested in finding new markets for our products.

ostentatious ADJ. showy; pretentious; trying to attract attention. Donald Trump's latest casino in Atlantic City is the most *ostentatious* gambling palace in the East: it easily outglitters its competitors. ostentation, N.

ostracize V. exclude from public favor; ban. As soon as the newspapers carried the story of his connection with the criminals, his friends began to *ostracize* him. ostracism, N.

outmoded ADJ. no longer stylish; old-fashioned. Unconcerned about keeping in style, Lenore was perfectly happy to wear *outmoded* clothes as long as they were clean and unfrayed.

outspoken ADJ. candid; blunt. The candidate was too *outspoken* to be a successful politician; he had not yet learned to weigh his words carefully.

outstrip V. surpass; outdo. Jesse Owens easily *outstripped* his white competitors to win the gold medal at the Olympic Games.

outwit V. outsmart; trick. By disguising himself as an old woman, Holmes was able to *outwit* his pursuers and escape capture.

overbearing ADJ. bossy and arrogant; decisively important. Certain of her own importance, and of the unimportance of everyone else, Lady Bracknell was intolerably *overbearing* in her manner. "In choosing a husband," she said, "good birth is of *overbearing* importance; compared to that, neither wealth nor talent signifies."

overt ADJ. open to view. According to the United States Constitution, a person must commit an *overt* act before he may be tried for treason.

overwrought ADJ. extremely agitated; hysterical. When Kate heard the news of the sudden tragedy, she became too *overwrought* to work and had to leave the office early.

pacifist N. one opposed to force; antimilitarist. During the war, though the *pacifists* refused to bear arms, they nevertheless served in the front lines as ambulance drivers and medical corpsmen.

pacify V. soothe; make calm or quiet; subdue. Dentists criticize the practice of giving fussy children sweets to *pacify* them.

pact N. agreement; treaty. Tweedledum and Tweedledee made a *pact* not to quarrel anymore.

painstaking ADJ. showing hard work; taking great care. The new high-frequency word list is the result of *painstaking* efforts on the part of our research staff.

pall V. grow tiresome. The study of word lists can eventually *pall* and put one to sleep.

palliate V. lessen the violence of (a disease); alleviate; moderate intensity; gloss over with excuses. Not content merely to *palliate* the patient's sores and cankers, the researcher sought a means of wiping out the disease. palliative, ADJ.

palpable ADJ. tangible; easily perceptible; unmistakable. The patient's enlarged spleen was *palpable*: even the first year medical student could feel it.

pandemonium N. wild tumult. When the ships collided in the harbor, *pandemonium* broke out among the passengers.

panoramic ADJ. related to an unobstructed and comprehensive view. From Inspiration Point we had a magnificent *panoramic* view of the Marin headlands and San Francisco Bay. panorama, N.

pantomime N. acting without dialogue. Artists in *pantomime* need no words to communicate with their audience; their only language is gesture. also V.

parable N. short, simple story teaching a moral. Let us apply to our own conduct the lesson that this *parable* teaches.

paradigm N. model; example; pattern. Pavlov's experiment in which he trains a dog to salivate on hearing a bell is a *paradigm* of the conditioned-response experiment in behavioral psychology. Barron's *How to Prepare for College Entrance Examinations* was a *paradigm* for all the SAT-prep books that followed.

paradox N. something apparently contradictory in nature; statement that looks false but is actually correct. Richard presents a bit of a *paradox*, for he is a card-carrying member of both the National Rifle Association and the relatively pacifist American Civil Liberties Union.

paragon N. model of perfection. Her fellow students disliked Lavinia because Miss Minchin always pointed her out as a *paragon* of virtue.

parallelism N. state of being parallel; similarity. Although the twins were separated at birth and grew up in different adoptive families, a striking *parallelism* exists between their lives.

parameter N. boundary; limiting factor; distinguishing characteristic. According to feminist Andrea Dworkin, men have defined the *parameters* of every subject; now women must redefine the limits of each field.

paramount ADJ. foremost in importance; supreme. Proper nutrition and hygiene are of *paramount* importance in adolescent development and growth.

paraphernalia N. equipment; odds and ends. His desk was cluttered with paper, pen, ink, dictionary and other *paraphernalia* of the writing craft.

paraphrase V. restate a passage in one's own words while retaining thought of author. In 250 words or less, *paraphrase* this article. also N.

parasite N. animal or plant living on another; toady; sycophant. The tapeworm is an example of the kind of *parasite* that may infest the human body.

pariah N. social outcast. If everyone ostracized singer Mariah Carey, would she then be Mariah the *pariah*?

parity N. equality in status or amount; close resemblance. Unfortunately, some doubt exists whether women's salaries will ever achieve *parity* with men's.

parochial ADJ. narrow in outlook; provincial; related to parishes. Although Jane Austen sets her novels in small rural communities, her concerns are universal, not *parochial*.

parody N. humorous imitation; spoof; takeoff; travesty. The show *Forbidden Broadway* presents *parodies* spoofing the year's new productions playing on Broadway.

partial ADJ. incomplete; having a liking for something. In this issue we have published only a *partial* list of contributors because we lack space to acknowledge everyone. I am extremely *partial* to chocolate eclairs.

partiality N. inclination; bias. As a judge, not only must I be unbiased, but I must also avoid any evidence of *partiality* when I award the prize.

partisan ADJ. one-sided; prejudiced; committed to a party. On certain issues of principle, she refused to take a *partisan* stand, but let her conscience be her guide. Rather than joining forces to solve our nation's problems, the Democrats and Republicans spend their time on *partisan* struggles. also N.

partition V. divide into parts. Before their second daughter was born, Jason and Lizzie decided each child needed a room of her own, and so they *partitioned* a large bedroom into two small but separate rooms. also N.

passive ADJ. not active; acted upon. Mahatma Gandhi urged his followers to pursue a program of *passive* resistance as he felt that it was more effective than violence and acts of terrorism.

passport N. legal document identifying the bearer as a citizen of a country and allowing him or her to travel abroad. In arranging your first trip abroad, be sure to allow yourself enough time to apply for and receive your *passport*: you won't be allowed to travel without one.

patent ADJ. open for the public to read; obvious. It was *patent* to everyone that the witness spoke the truth. also N.

pathetic ADJ. causing sadness, compassion, pity; touching. Everyone in the auditorium was weeping by the time he finished his *pathetic* tale about the orphaned boy.

Word List 31 pathological–platitude

pathological ADJ. related to the study of disease; diseased or markedly abnormal. Jerome's *pathological* fear of germs led him to wash his hands a hundred times a day. pathology, N.

pathos N. tender sorrow; pity; quality in art or literature that produces these feelings. The quiet tone of *pathos* that ran through the novel never degenerated into the maudlin or the overly sentimental.

patronize V. (1) support; (2) act superior toward; (3) be a customer of. Penniless artists hope to find some wealthy art-lover who will *patronize* them. If some condescending wine steward *patronized* me because he saw I knew nothing about fine wine, I'd refuse to *patronize* his restaurant.

pecuniary ADJ. pertaining to money. Seldom earning enough to cover their expenses, folk dance teachers work because they love dancing, not because they expect any *pecuniary* reward.

pedagogy N. teaching; art of education. Though Maria Montessori gained fame for her innovations in *pedagogy,* it took years before her teaching techniques were common practice in American schools.

pedantic ADJ. showing off learning; bookish. Leavening his decisions with humorous, down-to-earth anecdotes, Judge Walker was not at all the *pedantic* legal scholar. pedant, pedantry, N.

pedestrian ADJ. ordinary; unimaginative. Unintentionally boring, he wrote page after page of *pedestrian* prose.

peerless ADJ. having no equal; incomparable. The reigning operatic tenor of his generation, Luciano Pavarotti was *peerless* to his admirers: no one could compare with him.

penchant N. strong inclination; liking. Dave has a *penchant* for taking risks: one semester he went steady with three girls, two of whom were stars on the school karate team.

penitent ADJ. repentant. When he realized the enormity of his crime, he became remorseful and *penitent.* also N.

pensive ADJ. dreamily thoughtful; thoughtful with a hint of sadness; contemplative. The *pensive* lover gazed at the portrait of his beloved and deeply sighed.

penury N. severe poverty; stinginess. When his pension fund failed, George feared he would end his days in *penury.* He became such a penny pincher that he turned into a closefisted, *penurious* miser.

perceptive ADJ. insightful; aware; wise. Although Maud was a generally *perceptive* critic, she had her blind spots: she could never see flaws in the work of her friends.

peremptory ADJ. demanding and leaving no choice. From Jack's *peremptory* knock on the door, Jill could tell he would not give up until she let him in.

perennial N. something that is continuing or recurrent. These plants are hardy *perennials* and will bloom for many years. also ADJ.

perfunctory ADJ. superficial; not thorough; lacking interest, care, or enthusiasm. The auditor's *perfunctory* inspection of the books overlooked many errors. Giving the tabletop only a *perfunctory* swipe with her dust cloth, Betty promised herself she'd clean it more thoroughly tomorrow.

peripheral ADJ. (1) outer; (2) of minor importance. We lived, not in central London, but in one of those *peripheral* suburbs that spring up on the outskirts of a great city. The struggles, challenges, dysfunctions, dreams and accomplishments of families in the past are not *peripheral* to historical inquiry, but central to it. periphery, N.

permeable ADJ. penetrable; porous; allowing liquids or gas to pass through. If your jogging clothes weren't made out of *permeable* fabric, you'd drown in your own perspiration (figuratively speaking).

permeate V. pass through; spread. The odor of frying onions *permeated* the air.

pernicious ADJ. very destructive. Crack cocaine has had a *pernicious* effect on urban society: it has destroyed families, turned children into drug dealers, and increased the spread of violent crimes.

perpetrate V. commit an offense. Only an insane person could *perpetrate* such a horrible crime.

perpetual ADJ. everlasting. Ponce de Leon hoped to find the legendary fountain of *perpetual* youth.

perpetuate V. make something last; preserve from extinction. Some critics attack *The Adventures of Huckleberry Finn* because they believe Twain's book *perpetuates* a false image of Blacks in this country. In environments where resources are unstable, large numbers of organisms are produced quickly on the chance that some will survive to *perpetuate* the species.

persevere V. persist; endure; strive. Despite the church's threats to excommunicate him for heresy, Galileo *persevered* in his belief that the earth moved around the sun.

perspicacious ADJ. having insight; penetrating; astute. "Absolutely brilliant, Holmes!" cried Watson, as Holmes made yet another *perspicacious* deduction. perspicacity, N.

pertinent ADJ. to the point; relevant. Virginia Woolf's words on women's rights are as *pertinent* today as they were when she wrote them nearly a century ago.

perturb V. disturb greatly. The thought that electricity might be leaking out of the empty lightbulb sockets *perturbed* my aunt so much that at night she crept about the house screwing fresh bulbs in the vacant spots. perturbation, N.

peruse V. read with care. After the conflagration that burned down her house, Joan closely *perused* her home insurance policy to discover exactly what benefits her coverage provided her. perusal, N.

pervasive ADJ. pervading; spread throughout every part. Despite airing them for several hours, Martha could not rid her clothes of the *pervasive* odor of mothballs that clung to them. pervade, V.

perverse ADJ. stubbornly wrongheaded; wicked and perverted. When Jack was in a *perverse* mood, he would do the opposite of whatever Jill asked him. When Hannibal Lecter was in a *perverse* mood, he ate the flesh of his victims. Jack acted out of *perversity*. Hannibal's act proved his *perversion*.

pessimism N. belief that life is basically bad or evil; gloominess. Considering how well you have done in the course so far, you have no real reason for such *pessimism* about your final grade.

petrify V. turn to stone. His sudden, unexpected appearance shocked her into immobility: she was *petrified*.

petty ADJ. trivial; unimportant; very small. She had no major complaints to make about his work, only a few *petty* quibbles that were almost too minor to state.

petulant ADJ. touchy; peevish. If you'd had hardly any sleep for three nights and people kept phoning and waking you up, you'd sound pretty *petulant*, too.

phenomena N. observable facts; subjects of scientific investigation. We kept careful records of the *phenomena* we noted in the course of these experiments.

philanthropist N. lover of mankind; doer of good. In his role as *philanthropist* and public benefactor, John D. Rockefeller, Sr., donated millions to charity; as an individual, however, he was a tight-fisted old man.

philistine N. narrow-minded person, uncultured and exclusively interested in material gain. A *philistine* knows the price of everything, but the value of nothing.

phlegmatic ADJ. calm; not easily disturbed. The nurse was a cheerful but *phlegmatic* person, unexcited in the face of sudden emergencies.

phobia N. morbid fear. Her fear of flying was more than mere nervousness; it was a real *phobia*.

physiological ADJ. pertaining to the science of the function of living organisms. To understand this disease fully, we must examine not only its *physiological* aspects but also its psychological elements.

piety N. religious devotion; godliness. The nuns in the convent were noted for their *piety*; they spent their days in worship and prayer.

pious ADJ. devout; religious. The challenge for church people today is how to be *pious* in the best sense, that is, to be devout without becoming hypocritical or sanctimonious.

pique V. provoke or arouse; annoy. "I know something *you* don't know," said Lucy, trying to *pique* Ethel's interest.

pitfall N. hidden danger; concealed trap. Her parents warned young Sophie against the many *pitfalls* that lay in wait for her in the dangerous big city.

pithy ADJ. concise; meaningful; substantial; meaty. While other girls might have gone on and on about how uncool Elton was, Liz summed it up in one *pithy* remark: "He's bogus!"

pivotal ADJ. crucial; key; vital. The new "smart weapons" technology played a *pivotal* role in the quick resolution of the war with Iraq.

placate V. pacify; conciliate. The store manager tried to *placate* the angry customer, offering to replace the damaged merchandise or to give back her money right away.

placid ADJ. peaceful; calm. Looking at the storm-tossed waters of the lake, Bob wondered how people had ever come to call it Lake *Placid*.

plagiarize V. steal another's ideas and pass them off as one's own. The teacher could tell that the student had *plagiarized* parts of his essay; she could recognize whole paragraphs straight from *Barron's Book Notes*. plagiarism, N.

platitude N. trite remark; commonplace statement. In giving advice to his son, old Polonius expressed himself only in *platitudes*; every word out of his mouth was commonplace.

Word List 32   plausible–pretentious

plausible ADJ. having a show of truth but open to doubt; specious. Your mother made you stay home from school because she needed you to set up her new iPhone 6? I'm sorry, you'll have to come up with a more *plausible* excuse than that.

pliable ADJ. flexible; yielding; adaptable. In remodeling the bathroom, we have replaced all the old, rigid lead pipes with new, *pliable* copper tubing.

pliant ADJ. flexible; easily influenced. Pinocchio's disposition was *pliant*; he was like putty in his tempters' hands.

plight N. condition, state (especially a bad state or condition); predicament. Many people feel that the federal government should do more to alleviate the *plight* of the homeless. Loggers, unmoved by the *plight* of the spotted owl, plan to continue logging whether or not they ruin the owl's habitat.

plummet V. fall sharply. Stock prices *plummeted* as Wall Street reacted to the crisis in the economy.

plutocracy N. society ruled by the wealthy. From the way the government caters to the rich, you might think our society is a *plutocracy* rather than a democracy.

poignancy N. quality of being deeply moving; keenness of emotion. Watching the tearful reunion of the long-separated mother and child, the social worker was touched by the *poignancy* of the scene. poignant, ADJ.

polarize V. split into opposite extremes or camps. The abortion issue has *polarized* the country into pro-choice and anti-abortion camps. polarization, N.

polemical ADJ. aggressive in verbal attack; disputatious. Lexy was a master of *polemical* rhetoric; she should have worn a T-shirt with the slogan "Born to Debate."

politic ADJ. expedient; prudent; well advised. Even though he was disappointed by the size of the bonus he was offered, he did not think it *politic* to refuse it.

pomposity N. self-important behavior; acting like a stuffed shirt. Although the commencement speaker had some good things to say, we had to laugh at his *pomposity* and general air of parading his own dignity. pompous, ADJ.

ponderous ADJ. (1) very heavy, and possibly awkward because of its heaviness; (2) tedious and lacking fluency or grace. The elephant is *ponderous*, his trumpet call most thunderous. He cannot gallop, jump, or trot. The reason is he weighs a lot. Do you think this rhyme is clever, or do you find it a bit *ponderous*?

pore V. study industriously; ponder; scrutinize. Determined to become a physician, Beth spent hours *poring* over her anatomy text.

posterity N. descendants; future generations. We hope to leave a better world to *posterity*.

posthumous ADJ. after death (as of child born after father's death or book published after author's death). The critics ignored his works during his lifetime; it was only after the *posthumous* publication of his last novel that they recognized his great talent.

postulate N. essential premise; underlying assumption. The basic *postulate* of democracy, set forth in the Declaration of Independence, is that all men are created equal.

potent ADJ. powerful; persuasive; greatly influential. Looking at the expiration date on the cough syrup bottle, we wondered whether the medication would still be *potent*. potency, N.

potential ADJ. expressing possibility; latent. The cello teacher viewed every new pupil as a *potential* Yo-Yo Ma. also N.

practicable ADJ. feasible. The board of directors decided that the plan was *practicable* and agreed to undertake the project.

practical ADJ. based on experience; useful. He was a *practical* man, opposed to theory.

practitioner N. someone engaged in a profession (law, medicine). In need of a hip replacement, Carl sought a *practitioner* with considerable experience performing this particular surgery.

pragmatic ADJ. practical (as opposed to idealistic); concerned with the practical worth or impact of something. This coming trip to France should provide me with a *pragmatic* test of the value of my conversational French class.

pragmatist N. practical person. No *pragmatist* enjoys becoming involved in a game he can never win.

preamble N. introductory statement. In the *Preamble* to the Constitution, the purpose of the document is set forth.

precarious ADJ. uncertain; risky. Saying the stock would be a *precarious* investment, the broker advised her client against purchasing it.

precedent N. something preceding in time that may be used as an authority or guide for future action. If I buy you a car for your sixteenth birthday, your brothers will want me to buy them cars when they turn sixteen, too; I can't afford to set such an expensive *precedent*. The law professor asked Jill to state which famous case served as a *precedent* for the court's decision in *Brown II*.

precept N. practical rule guiding conduct. "Love thy neighbor as thyself" is a worthwhile *precept*.

precipitate ADJ. rash; premature; hasty; sudden. Though I was angry enough to resign on the spot, I had enough sense to keep myself from quitting a job in such a *precipitate* fashion.

precipitate V. throw headlong; hasten. The removal of American political support appears to have *precipitated* the downfall of the Marcos regime.

précis N. concise summing up of main points. Before making her presentation at the conference, Ellen wrote up a neat *précis* of the major elements she would cover.

precise ADJ. exact. If you don't give me *precise* directions and a map, I'll never find your place.

preclude V. make impossible; eliminate. The fact that the band was already booked to play in Hollywood on New Year's Eve *precluded* their accepting the New Year's Eve gig in London they were offered.

precocious ADJ. advanced in development. Listening to the grown-up way the child discussed serious topics, we couldn't help remarking how *precocious* she was. precocity, N.

predator N. creature that seizes and devours another animal; person who robs or exploits others. Not just cats, but a wide variety of *predators*—owls, hawks, weasels, foxes—catch mice for dinner. A carnivore is by definition *predatory*, for he *preys* on weaker creatures.

predecessor N. former occupant of a post. I hope I can live up to the fine example set by my late *predecessor* in this office.

predetermine V. predestine; settle or decide beforehand; influence markedly. Romeo and Juliet believed that Fate had *predetermined* their meeting. Bea gathered estimates from caterers, florists, and stationers so that she could *predetermine* the costs of holding a catered buffet. Philip's love of athletics *predetermined* his choice of a career in sports marketing.

predicament N. tricky or dangerous situation; dilemma. Tied to the railroad tracks by the villain, Pauline strained against her bonds. How would she escape from this terrible *predicament*?

predilection N. partiality; preference. Although Ogden Nash wrote all sorts of poetry over the years, he had a definite *predilection* for limericks.

predispose V. give an inclination toward; make susceptible to. Oleg's love of dressing up his big sister's Barbie doll may have *predisposed* him to become a fashion designer. Genetic influences apparently *predispose* people to certain forms of cancer.

preeminent ADJ. outstanding; superior. The king traveled to Boston because he wanted the *preeminent* surgeon in the field to perform the operation.

preempt V. head off; forestall by acting first; appropriate for oneself; supplant. Hoping to *preempt* any attempts by the opposition to make educational reform a hot political issue, the candidate set out her own plan to revitalize the public schools. preemptive, ADJ.

prelude N. introduction; forerunner. I am afraid that this border raid is the *prelude* to more serious attacks.

premeditate V. plan in advance. She had *premeditated* the murder for months, reading about common poisons and buying weed killer that contained arsenic.

premise N. assumption; postulate. Based on the *premise* that there's no fool like an old fool, P. T. Barnum hired a ninety-year-old clown for his circus.

preposterous ADJ. absurd; ridiculous. When he tried to downplay his youthful experiments with marijuana by saying he hadn't inhaled, we all thought, "What a *preposterous* excuse!"

prerogative N. privilege; unquestionable right. The president cannot levy taxes; that is the *prerogative* of the legislative branch of government.

presentiment N. feeling something will happen; anticipatory fear; premonition. Saying goodbye at the airport, Jack had a sudden *presentiment* that this was the last time he would see Jill.

prestige N. impression produced by achievements or reputation. Many students want to go to Harvard College not for the education offered but for the *prestige* of Harvard's name.

presumptuous ADJ. overconfident; impertinently bold; taking liberties. Matilda thought it was somewhat *presumptuous* of the young man to have addressed her without first having been introduced. Perhaps manners were freer here in the New World.

pretentious ADJ. ostentatious; pompous; making unjustified claims; overly ambitious. None of the other prize winners are wearing their medals; isn't it a bit *pretentious* of you to wear yours?

Word List 33   pretext–prudent

pretext N. excuse. He looked for a good *pretext* to get out of paying a visit to his aunt.

prevail V. induce; triumph over. He tried to *prevail* on her to type his essay for him.

prevalent ADJ. widespread; generally accepted. A radical committed to social change, Reed had no patience with the conservative views *prevalent* in the America of his day.

prevaricate V. lie. Some people believe that to *prevaricate* in a good cause is justifiable and regard such a statement as a "white lie."

prey N. target of a hunt; victim. In *Stalking the Wild Asparagus*, Euell Gibbons has as his *prey* not wild beasts but wild plants. also V.

privation N. hardship; want. In his youth, he knew hunger and *privation*.

probe V. explore with tools. The surgeon *probed* the wound for foreign matter before suturing it. also N.

problematic ADJ. doubtful; unsettled; questionable; perplexing. Given the way building costs have exceeded estimates for the job, whether the arena will ever be completed is *problematic*.

proclivity N. inclination; natural tendency. Watching the two-year-old voluntarily put away his toys, I was amazed by his *proclivity* for neatness.

procrastinate V. postpone; delay or put off. Looking at four years of receipts and checks he still had to sort through, Bob was truly sorry he had *procrastinated* for so long and not finished filing his taxes long ago.

prod V. poke; stir up; urge. If you *prod* him hard enough, he'll eventually clean his room.

prodigal ADJ. wasteful; reckless with money. Don't be so *prodigal* spending my money; when you've earned some money yourself, you can waste it as much as you want! also N.

prodigious ADJ. marvelous; enormous. Watching the champion weight lifter heave the weighty barbell to shoulder height and then boost it overhead, we marveled at his *prodigious* strength.

prodigy N. marvel; highly gifted child. Menuhin *was a prodigy*, performing wonders on his violin when he was barely eight years old.

profane V. violate; desecrate; treat unworthily. The members of the mysterious Far Eastern cult sought to kill the British explorer because he had *profaned* the sanctity of their holy goblet by using it as an ashtray. also ADJ.

profound ADJ. deep; not superficial. Freud's remarkable insights into human behavior caused his fellow scientists to honor him as a *profound* thinker. profundity, N.

profusion N. (1) abundant quantity; (2) lavish expenditure. Along the Mendocino coast, where there is enough moisture, wildflowers flourish in great *profusion*. Polly tried to win friends by her *profusion* in throwing extravagant parties.

prognosis N. forecasted course of a disease; prediction. If the doctor's *prognosis* is correct, the patient will be in a coma for at least twenty-four hours.

proletarian N. member of the working class; blue collar person. "Workers of the world, unite! You have nothing to lose but your chains" is addressed to *proletarians*, not preppies. So is *Blue Collar Holler*. proletariat, N.

proliferation N. rapid growth; spread; multiplication. Times of economic hardship inevitably encourage the *proliferation* of countless get-rich-quick schemes. proliferate, V.

prolific ADJ. abundantly fruitful. My editors must assume I'm a *prolific* writer: they expect me to revise six books this year!

prologue N. introduction (to a poem or play). In the *prologue* to *Romeo and Juliet*, Shakespeare introduces the audience to the feud between the Montagues and the Capulets.

prolong V. make longer; draw out; lengthen. In their determination to discover ways to *prolong* human life, doctors fail to take into account that longer lives are not always happier ones.

prominent ADJ. conspicuous; notable; sticking out. Have you ever noticed that Prince Charles's *prominent* ears make him look like the big-eared character in *Mad* comics?

promote V. help to flourish; advance in rank; publicize. Founder of the Children's Defense Fund, Marian Wright Edelman ceaselessly *promotes* the welfare of young people everywhere.

prompt V. (1) bring about or cause an action or feeling; (2) cue someone to speak. Being cast as the lead in the school play *prompted* Dan to consider acting as a career. Unfortunately, he had trouble remembering his lines: the stage manager had to *prompt* him from the wings.

prone ADJ. (1) inclined to; (2) prostrate. She was *prone* to sudden fits of anger during which she would lie *prone* on the floor, screaming and kicking her heels.

propagate V. multiply; spread. Since bacteria *propagate* more quickly in unsanitary environments, it is important to keep hospital rooms clean.

propensity N. natural inclination. Convinced of his own talent, Sol has an unfortunate *propensity* to belittle the talents of others.

prophetic ADJ. foretelling the future. I have no magical *prophetic* powers; when I predict what will happen, I base my predictions on common sense. prophesy, V.

propitiate V. appease. The natives offered sacrifices to *propitiate* the gods.

propitious ADJ. favorable; fortunate; advantageous. Chloe consulted her horoscope to see whether Tuesday would be a *propitious* day to dump her boyfriend.

proponent N. supporter; backer; opposite of opponent. In the Senate, *proponents* of the universal health care measure lobbied to gain additional support for the controversial legislation.

propriety N. fitness; correct conduct. Miss Manners counsels her readers so that they may behave with due *propriety* in any social situation and not embarrass themselves.

prosaic ADJ. dull and unimaginative; matter-of-fact; factual. Though the ad writers came up with an original way to publicize the product, the head office rejected it for a more *prosaic*, ordinary slogan.

proselytize V. convert to a religion or belief. In these interfaith meetings, there must be no attempt to *proselytize; we* must respect all points of view.

prosperity N. good fortune; financial success; physical well-being. Promising to stay together "for richer, for poorer," the newlyweds vowed to be true to one another in *prosperity* and hardship alike.

protégé N. person receiving protection and support from a patron. Born with an independent spirit,

Cyrano de Bergerac refused to be a *protégé* of Cardinal Richelieu.

protocol N. diplomatic etiquette. We must run this state dinner according to *protocol* if we are to avoid offending any of our guests.

prototype N. original work used as a model by others. The National Air and Space Museum displays the Wright brothers' first plane, the *prototype* of all the American aircraft that came after.

protract V. prolong. Seeking to delay the union members' vote, the management team tried to *protract* the negotiations endlessly.

protrude V. stick out. His fingers *protruded* from the holes in his gloves. protrusion, N.

provident ADJ. displaying foresight; thrifty; preparing for emergencies. In his usual *provident* manner, he had insured himself against this type of loss.

provincial ADJ. (1) pertaining to a province; (2) limited in outlook; unsophisticated. As *provincial* governor, Sir Henry administered the Queen's law in his remote corner of Canada. Caught up in local problems, out of touch with London news, he became sadly *provincial*.

provisional ADJ. tentative. Kim's acceptance as an American Express card holder was *provisional*: before issuing her a card, American Express wanted to check her employment record and credit history.

provocative ADJ. arousing anger or interest; annoying. In a typically *provocative* act, the bully kicked sand into the weaker man's face. provocation, N.; provoke, V.

prowess N. extraordinary ability; military bravery. Performing triple axels and double lutzes at the age of six, the young figure skater was world famous for her *prowess* on the ice.

proximity N. nearness. Blind people sometimes develop a compensatory ability to sense the *proximity* of objects around them.

proxy N. authorized agent. Please act as my *proxy* and vote for this slate of candidates in my absence.

prudent ADJ. cautious; careful. A miser hoards money not because he is *prudent* but because he is greedy. prudence, N.

Word List 34   prune–rebuke

prune V. cut away; trim. With the help of her editor, she was able to *prune* her overlong manuscript into publishable form.

pseudonym N. pen name. Samuel Clemens's *pseudonym* was Mark Twain.

psyche N. soul; mind. It is difficult to delve into the *psyche* of a human being.

puerile ADJ. childish; immature. Throwing tantrums! You should have outgrown such *puerile* behavior years ago.

punitive ADJ. punishing. He asked for *punitive* measures against the offender.

puny ADJ. insignificant; tiny; weak. Our *puny* efforts to stop the flood were futile.

purge V. remove or get rid of something unwanted; free from blame or guilt; cleanse or purify. When the Communist government *purged* the party to get rid of members suspected of capitalist sympathies, they sent the disloyal members to labor camps in Siberia.

purported ADJ. alleged; claimed; reputed or rumored. The *purported* Satanists sacrificing live roosters in the park turned out to be a party of Shriners holding a chicken barbecue.

quadruped N. four-footed animal. Most mammals are *quadrupeds*.

quagmire N. soft, wet, boggy land; complex or dangerous situation from which it is difficult to free oneself. Up to her knees in mud, Myra wondered how on earth she was going to extricate herself from this *quagmire*.

quail V. cower; lose heart. The Cowardly Lion was afraid that he would *quail* in the face of danger.

quaint ADJ. odd; old-fashioned; picturesque. Her *quaint* clothes and old-fashioned language marked her as an eccentric.

qualified ADJ. limited; restricted. Unable to give the candidate full support, the mayor gave him only a *qualified* endorsement.

qualms N. misgivings; uneasy fears, especially about matters of conscience. I have no *qualms* about giving this assignment to Helen; I know she will handle it admirably.

quandary N. dilemma. When both Harvard and Stanford accepted Laura, she was in a *quandary* as to which school she should attend.

quarantine N. isolation of person or place to prevent spread of infection. We will have to place this house under *quarantine* until we determine the exact nature of the disease. also V.

quarry N. victim; object of a hunt. The police closed in on their *quarry*.

quarry V. dig into. They *quarried* blocks of marble out of the hillside. also N.

quell V. extinguish; put down; quiet. Miss Minchin's demeanor was so stern and forbidding that she could *quell* any unrest among her students with one intimidating glance.

quench V. douse or extinguish; assuage or satisfy. No matter how much water the hiker drank, she could not *quench* her thirst.

query N. inquiry; question. In her column "Ask Beth," the columnist invites young readers to send her their *queries* about life and love.

quibble N. minor objection or complaint. Aside from a few hundred teensy-weensy *quibbles* about the set, the script, the actors, the director, the costumes, the lighting, and the props, the hypercritical critic loved the play. also V.

quiescent ADJ. at rest; dormant; temporarily inactive. After the massive eruption, fear of Mount Etna was great; people did not return to cultivate the rich hillside lands until the volcano had been *quiescent* for a full two years. quiescence, N.

quintessence N. purest and highest embodiment. Gandhi maintained that to befriend someone who regards himself as your enemy is the *quintessence* of true religion.

quixotic ADJ. idealistic but impractical. Constantly coming up with *quixotic*, unworkable schemes to save the world, Simon has his heart in the right place, but his head somewhere in the clouds.

quizzical ADJ. teasing; bantering; mocking; curious. When the skinny teenager tripped over his own feet stepping into the bullpen, Coach raised one *quizzical* eyebrow, shook his head, and said, "Okay, kid. You're here, let's see what you've got."

quorum N. number of members necessary to conduct a meeting. The senator asked for a roll call to determine whether a *quorum* was present.

rabid ADJ. like a fanatic; furious. He was a *rabid* follower of the Dodgers and watched them play whenever he could go to the ballpark.

rally V. call up or summon (forces, vital powers, etc.); revive or recuperate. Washington quickly *rallied* his troops to fight off the British attack. The patient had been sinking throughout the night, but at dawn she *rallied* and made a complete recovery.

ramble V. wander aimlessly (physically or mentally). Listening to the teacher *ramble*, Judy wondered whether he'd ever get to his point.

ramification N. branching out; subdivision. We must examine all the *ramifications* of this problem.

ramify V. divide into branches or subdivisions. When the plant begins to *ramify*, it is advisable to nip off most of the new branches.

rampant ADJ. growing in profusion; unrestrained. The *rampant* weeds in the garden choked the flowers until they died.

rancor N. bitterness; hatred. Thirty years after the war, she could not let go of the past and was still consumed with *rancor* against the foe.

random ADJ. without definite purpose, plan, or aim; haphazard. Although the sponsor of the raffle claimed all winners were chosen at *random*, people had their suspicions when the grand prize went to the sponsor's brother-in-law.

rant V. rave; talk excitedly; scold; make a grandiloquent speech. When he heard that I'd totaled the family car, Dad began to *rant* at me like a complete madman.

rapacious ADJ. excessively greedy; predatory. The *rapacious* brigands stripped the villagers of all their possessions. rapacity, N.

rapport N. emotional closeness; harmony. In team teaching, it is important that all teachers in the group have good *rapport* with one another.

rapt ADJ. absorbed; enchanted. Caught up in the wonder of the storyteller's tale, the *rapt* listeners sat motionless, hanging on his every word.

ratify V. approve formally; confirm; verify. Party leaders doubted that they had enough votes in both houses of Congress to *ratify* the constitutional amendment.

ratiocination N. reasoning; act of drawing conclusions from premises. While Watson was a man of average intelligence, Holmes was a genius, whose gift for *ratiocination* made him a superb detective.

rationale N. fundamental reason or justification; grounds for an action. Her need to have someplace to hang her earring collection was Dora's *rationale* for piercing fifteen holes in each ear.

rationalize V. give a plausible reason for an action in place of a true, less admirable one; offer an excuse. When David told gabby Gabrielle he couldn't give her a ride to the dance because he had no room in the car, he was *rationalizing*; actually, he couldn't stand being cooped up in a car with anyone who talked as much as she did.

raucous ADJ. harsh and shrill; disorderly and boisterous. The *raucous* crowd of New Year's Eve revelers got progressively noisier as midnight drew near.

rave N. overwhelmingly favorable review. Though critic John Simon seldom has a good word to say about most contemporary plays, his review of *All in the Timing* was a total *rave*.

raze V. destroy completely. Spelling is important: to raise a building is to put it up; to *raze* a building is to tear it down.

reactionary ADJ. recoiling from progress; politically ultraconservative. Opposing the use of English in worship services, *reactionary* forces in the church fought to reinstate the mass in Latin.

realm N. kingdom; field or sphere. In the animal *realm*, the lion is the king of beasts.

rebuff V. snub; beat back. She *rebuffed* his invitation so smoothly that he did not realize he had been snubbed. also N.

rebuke V. scold harshly; criticize severely. No matter how sharply Miss Watson *rebuked* Huck for his misconduct, he never talked back but just stood there like a stump. also N.

Word List 35   rebuttal–renounce

rebuttal N. refutation; response with contrary evidence. The defense lawyer confidently listened to the prosecutor sum up his case, sure that she could answer his arguments in her *rebuttal*.

recalcitrant ADJ. obstinately stubborn; determined to resist authority; unruly. Which animal do you think is more *recalcitrant*, a pig or a mule?

recant V. disclaim or disavow; retract a previous statement; openly confess error. Those who can, keep true to their faith; those who can't, *recant*. Hoping to make Joan of Arc *recant* her sworn testimony, her English captors tried to convince her that her visions had been sent to her by the Devil.

recapitulate V. summarize. Let us *recapitulate* what has been said thus far before going ahead.

recast V. reconstruct (a sentence, story, etc.); fashion again. Let me *recast* this sentence in terms your feeble brain can grasp: in words of one syllable, you are a fool.

receptive ADJ. quick or willing to receive ideas, suggestions, etc. Adventure-loving Huck Finn proved a *receptive* audience for Tom's tales of buried treasure and piracy.

recession N. withdrawal; retreat; time of low economic activity. The slow *recession* of the flood waters created problems for the crews working to restore power to the area. recede, V.

recipient N. receiver. Although he had been the *recipient* of many favors, he was not grateful to his benefactor.

reciprocal ADJ. mutual; exchangeable; interacting. The two nations signed a *reciprocal* trade agreement.

reciprocate V. repay in kind. If they attack us, we shall be compelled to *reciprocate* and bomb their territory. reciprocity, N.

reconcile V. correct inconsistencies; become friendly after a quarrel. Each month when we try to *reconcile* our checkbook with the bank statement, we quarrel. However, despite these monthly lovers' quarrels, we always manage to *reconcile*.

reconnaissance N. survey of enemy by soldiers; reconnoitering. If you encounter any enemy soldiers during your *reconnaissance*, capture them for questioning.

recount V. (1) narrate or tell; (2) count over again. A born storyteller, my father loved to *recount* anecdotes about his early years in New York. Because the vote for class president was so close, we had to *recount* all the ballots before we were sure that Johnny was the winner.

recourse N. resorting to help when in trouble. The boy's only *recourse* was to appeal to his father for aid.

recrimination N. countercharges. Loud and angry *recriminations* were her answer to his accusations.

rectify V. set right; correct. You had better send a check to *rectify* your account before American Express cancels your credit card.

rectitude N. uprightness; moral virtue; correctness of judgment. The Eagle Scout was a model of *rectitude*.

recuperate V. recover. The doctors were worried because the patient did not *recuperate* as rapidly as they had expected.

recurrent ADJ. occurring again and again. Richard's *recurrent* asthma attacks disturbed us, and we consulted a physician.

redress N. remedy; compensation. Do you mean to tell me that I can get no *redress* for my injuries? also V.

redundant ADJ. superfluous; repetitious; excessively wordy. The bottle of wine I brought to Bob's was certainly *redundant*: how was I to know Bob owned a winery? In your essay, you repeat several points unnecessarily; try to be less *redundant* in the future. redundancy, N.

reflect V. (1) think seriously about; (2) represent faithfully; (3) show a physical image; (4) create a good or bad impression. Mr. Collins *reflected* on Elizabeth's rejection of his proposal. Did it *reflect* her true feelings, he wondered. Looking at his image *reflected* in the mirror, he refused to believe that she could reject such a fine-looking man. Such behavior *reflected* badly upon her.

refrain V. abstain from; resist. N. chorus. Whenever he heard a song with a lively chorus, Sol could never *refrain* from joining in on the *refrain*.

refute V. disprove. The defense called several respectable witnesses who were able to *refute* the false testimony of the prosecution's sole witness. refutation, N.

regime N. method or system of government. When the French mention the Old *Regime*, they refer to the government existing before the revolution.

regimen N. prescribed diet and habits. I doubt whether the results warrant our living under such a strict *regimen*.

rehabilitate V. restore to proper condition. We must *rehabilitate* those whom we send to prison.

reimburse V. repay. Let me know what you have spent and I will *reimburse* you.

reiterate V. repeat. He *reiterated* the warning to make sure everyone understood it.

rejoinder N. retort; comeback; reply. When someone has been rude to me, I find it particularly satisfying to come up with a quick *rejoinder*.

rejuvenate V. make young again. The charlatan claimed that his elixir would *rejuvenate* the aged and weary.

relegate V. banish to an inferior position; delegate; assign. After Ralph dropped his second tray of drinks that week, the manager swiftly *relegated* him to a minor post cleaning up behind the bar.

relent V. give in. When her stern father would not *relent* and allow her to marry Robert Browning, Elizabeth Barrett eloped with her suitor. relentless, ADJ.

relevant ADJ. pertinent; referring to the case in hand. How *relevant* Virginia Woolf's essays are to women writers today! It's as if Woolf in the 1930s foresaw our current literary struggles. relevancy, N.

relic N. (1) surviving remnant; (2) memento. Egypt's Department of Antiquities prohibits tourists from taking mummies and other ancient *relics* out of the country. Mike keeps his photos of his trip to Egypt in a box with other *relics* of his travels.

relinquish V. give up something with reluctance; yield. Denise never realized how hard it would be for her to *relinquish* her newborn son to the care of his adoptive parents. Once you get used to fringe benefits like expense account meals and a company car, it's very hard to *relinquish* them.

relish V. savor; enjoy. Watching Peter enthusiastically chow down, I thought, "Now there's a man who *relishes* a good dinner!" also N.

remediable ADJ. reparable. Let us be grateful that the damage is *remediable*.

remedial ADJ. curative; corrective. Because he was a slow reader, he decided to take a course in *remedial* reading.

reminiscence N. recollection. Her *reminiscences* of her experiences are so fascinating that she ought to write a book.

remiss ADJ. negligent. The guard was accused of being *remiss* in his duty when the prisoner escaped.

remission N. temporary moderation of disease symptoms; cancellation of a debt; forgiveness or pardon. Though the senator had been treated for cancer, his symptoms were in *remission*, and he was considered fit enough to handle the strains of a presidential race.

remnant N. remainder. I suggest that you wait until the store places the *remnants* of these goods on sale.

remonstrance N. protest; objection. The authorities were deaf to the pastor's *remonstrances* about the lack of police protection in the area. remonstrate, V.

remorse N. guilt; self-reproach. The murderer felt no *remorse* for his crime.

remunerative ADJ. compensating; rewarding. I find my new work so *remunerative* that I may not return to my previous employment. remuneration, N.

render V. deliver; provide; represent. He *rendered* aid to the needy and indigent.

renegade N. deserter; traitor. Because he had abandoned his post and joined forces with the Indians, his fellow officers considered the hero of *Dances with Wolves* a *renegade*. also ADJ.

renege V. deny; go back on. He *reneged* on paying off his debt.

renounce V. abandon; disown; repudiate. Even though she knew she would be burned at the stake as a witch, Joan of Arc refused to *renounce* her belief that her voices came from God. renunciation, N.

Word List 36   renovate–retrograde

renovate V. restore to good condition; renew. We *renovated* our kitchen, replacing the old cabinets and countertop and installing new appliances.

renown N. fame. For many years an unheralded researcher, Barbara McClintock gained international *renown* when she won the Nobel Prize in Physiology and Medicine. renowned, ADJ.

reparable ADJ. capable of being repaired. Fortunately, the damage to our car was *reparable*, and after two weeks in the shop it looks brand new.

repeal V. revoke; annul. What would the effect on our society be if we decriminalized drug use by *repealing* the laws against the possession and sale of narcotics?

repel V. (1) drive away; (2) disgust. In the game *Zombie Attack*, your goal is to *repel* the zombie hordes, driving them away from Gotham City. At first, the Beast's ferocious appearance *repelled* Beauty, but she came to love the tender heart hidden behind that beastly exterior.

repellent ADJ. driving away; unattractive. Mosquitoes find the odor so *repellent* that they leave any spot where this liquid has been sprayed. also N.

repercussion N. result or impact (of an event, etc.); rebound; reverberation. The brothers' quarrel had serious *repercussions*, for it led to their estrangement.

repertoire N. list of works of music, drama, etc., a performer is prepared to present. The opera company decided to include *Madame Butterfly* in its *repertoire* for the following season.

replenish V. fill up again. Before she could take another backpacking trip, Carla had to *replenish* her stock of freeze-dried foods.

replete ADJ. filled to the brim or to the point of being stuffed; abundantly supplied. The movie star's memoir was *replete* with juicy details about the love life of half of Hollywood.

replica N. copy. Are you going to hang this *replica* of the Declaration of Independence in the classroom or in the auditorium?

reprehensible ADJ. deserving blame. Shocked by the viciousness of the bombing, politicians of every party uniformly condemned the terrorists' *reprehensible* deed.

repress V. restrain; crush; oppress. Anne's parents tried to curb her impetuosity without *repressing* her boundless high spirits.

reprieve N. temporary stay. During the twenty-four-hour *reprieve*, the lawyers sought to make the stay of execution permanent. also V.

reprimand V. reprove severely; rebuke. Every time Ermengarde made a mistake in class, she was afraid that Miss Minchin would *reprimand* her and tell her father how badly she was doing in school. also N.

reprisal N. retaliation. I am confident that we are ready for any *reprisals* the enemy may undertake.

reprise N. musical repetition; repeat performance; recurrent action. We enjoyed the soprano's solo in Act I so much that we were delighted by its *reprise* in the finale.

reproach V. express disapproval or disappointment. He never could do anything wrong without imagining how the look on his mother's face would *reproach* him afterwards. reproachful, ADJ.

reprove V. censure; rebuke. Though Aunt Bea at times had to *reprove* Opie for inattention in church, she believed he was at heart a God-fearing lad.

repudiate V. (1) refuse to have anything to do with; (2) reject as untrue or unauthorized; (3) refuse to pay. Angered by Cordelia's refusal to express her love for him in flattering words, King Lear *repudiates* his daughter, disinheriting her. The lawyer maintained that this new evidence would *repudiate* the allegations against her client. On separating from Tony, Tina announced that she would *repudiate* all debts incurred by her soon-to-be ex-husband.

repugnant ADJ. loathsome; hateful. Whereas some people like earthworms, others find them *repugnant* and view them with disgust.

repulsion N. (1) distaste; (2) act of driving back. Hating bloodshed, she viewed war with *repulsion*. Even defensive battles distressed her, for the *repulsion* of enemy forces is never accomplished bloodlessly.

reputable ADJ. respectable. If you want to buy antiques, look for a *reputable* dealer; far too many dealers today pass off fakes as genuine antiques.

reputed ADJ. supposed. Though he is the *reputed* father of the child, no one can be sure. repute, N.

requisite N. necessary requirement. Many colleges state that a student must offer three years of a language as a *requisite* for admission.

rescind V. cancel. Because of the public outcry against the new taxes, the senator proposed a bill to *rescind* the unpopular financial measure.

resentment N. indignation; bitterness; displeasure. Not wanting to appear a sore loser, Bill tried to hide his *resentment* of Barry's success.

reserve N. (1) backup supply; (2) body of troops not part of the regular military forces; (3) place set aside for specific purpose; (4) formal but distant manner. Australia supplies much of the world's uranium from its abundant uranium *reserves*. Reluctant to enlist in the regular army, Don considered joining the *reserves*. On their African safari, Tom and Susan visited some fascinating big game *reserves*. Although Mark's air of *reserve* attracted some girls, it put off Judy, who felt his aloofness showed a lack of warmth.

residue N. remainder; balance. In his will, he requested that after payment of debts, taxes, and funeral expenses, the *residue* be given to his wife. residual, ADJ.

resigned ADJ. accepting one's fate; unresisting; patiently submissive. *Resigned* to his downtrodden existence, Bob Cratchit was too meek to protest Scrooge's bullying. resignation, N.

resilient ADJ. elastic; having the power of springing back. Highly *resilient*, steel makes excellent bedsprings. resilience, N.

resolution N. (1) firmness of purpose; (2) formal expression of intent; (2) solving of a problem. Nothing could shake Philip's *resolution* that his children would get the best education that money could buy. The symphony board passed a *resolution* to ban cell phone use during concerts. Friar Laurence hoped for a peaceful *resolution* of the conflict between the feuding Montagues and Capulets.

resolve N. determination; firmness of purpose. How dare you question my *resolve* to take up sky-diving! Of course I haven't changed my mind!

resolve V. (1) decide; (2) settle; solve. Holmes *resolved* to travel to Bohemia to *resolve* the dispute between Irene Adler and the king.

responsiveness N. state of reacting readily to appeals, orders, etc. The audience cheered and applauded, delighting the performers by its *responsiveness*.

restitution N. reparation; indemnification. He offered to make *restitution* for the window broken by his son.

restraint N. moderation or self-control; controlling force; restriction. Control yourself, young lady! Show some *restraint*!

resumption N. taking up again; recommencement. During summer break, Don had not realized how much he missed university life; at the *resumption* of classes, however, he felt marked excitement and pleasure. resume, V.

resurge V. rise again; flow to and fro. It was startling to see the spirit of nationalism *resurge* as the Soviet Union disintegrated into a loose federation of ethnic and national groups. resurgence, N.

retain V. keep; employ. Fighting to *retain* his seat in Congress, Senator Foghorn *retained* a new manager to head his reelection campaign.

retaliation N. repayment in kind (usually for bad treatment). Because everyone knew the Princeton Band had stolen Brown's mascot, the whole Princeton student body expected some sort of *retaliation* from Brown. retaliate, V.

retentive ADJ. able to retain or keep; able to remember. Priding herself on her *retentive* memory, she claimed she never forgot a face.

reticence N. reserve; uncommunicativeness; inclination to silence. Fearing his competitors might get advance word about his plans from talkative staff members, Hughes preferred *reticence* from his employees to loquacity. reticent, ADJ.

retort N. quick sharp reply. Even when it was advisable for her to keep her mouth shut, she was always ready with a quick *retort*. also V.

retract V. (1) withdraw; (2) draw back. When I saw how Fred and his fraternity brothers had trashed the frat house, I decided to *retract* my offer to let them use our summer cottage for the weekend. Startled, the crab *retracts* its claws; then, scuttling backwards, it withdraws. retraction, N.

retrench V. cut down; economize. In order to be able to afford to send their children to college, they would have to *retrench*. retrenchment, N.

retribution N. vengeance; compensation; punishment for offenses. The evangelist maintained that an angry deity would exact *retribution* from the sinners.

retrieve V. recover; find and bring in. The dog was intelligent and quickly learned to *retrieve* the game killed by the hunter.

retroactive ADJ. taking effect before its enactment (as a law) or imposition (as a tax). Because the new pension law was *retroactive* to the first of the year, even though Martha had retired in February she was eligible for the pension.

retrograde V. go backwards; degenerate. instead of advancing, our civilization seems to have *retrograded* in ethics and culture. also ADJ.

Word List 37   retrospective–sedentary

retrospective ADJ. looking back on the past. The Museum of Graphic Arts is holding a *retrospective* showing of the paintings of Michael Whelan over the past two decades.

reverent ADJ. respectful; worshipful. Though I bow my head in church and recite the prayers, sometimes I don't feel properly *reverent*. revere, V.

revert V. relapse; backslide; turn back to. Most of the time Andy seemed sensitive and mature, but occasionally he would *revert* to his smart-alecky, macho, adolescent self.

revoke V. cancel; retract. Repeat offenders who continue to drive under the influence of alcohol face having their driver's licenses permanently *revoked*.

revulsion N. sudden violent change of feeling; reaction. Many people in this country who admired dictatorships underwent a *revulsion* when they realized what Hitler and Mussolini were trying to do.

rhetoric N. art of effective communication; insincere language. All writers, by necessity, must be skilled in *rhetoric*.

rhetorical ADJ. pertaining to effective communication; insincere in language. To win his audience, the speaker used every *rhetorical* trick in the book.

rig V. fix or manipulate. The ward boss was able to *rig* the election by bribing people to stuff the ballot boxes with ballots marked in his candidate's favor.

rigid ADJ. (1) unable to bend; (2) not easily changed; (3) unwilling to change (beliefs, opinions). Deacon Dobbs wore a *rigid* white plastic collar that chafed his neck. His church maintained *rigid* rules concerning women's roles within the congregation, and Dobbs was far too *rigid* in his beliefs to challenge the church's teachings.

rigor N. severity. Many settlers could not stand the *rigors* of the New England winters.

rigorous ADJ. severe; harsh; demanding; exact. Disliked by his superiors, the officer candidate in *An Officer and a Gentleman* endured an extremely *rigorous* training program.

rote N. repetition. He recited the passage by *rote* and gave no indication he understood what he was saying.

rousing ADJ. lively; stirring. "And now, let's have a *rousing* welcome for TV's own Roseanne Barr, who'll lead us in a *rousing* rendition of 'The Star-Spangled Banner.'"

rudimentary ADJ. (1) limited to the basics; (2) imperfectly developed. Although my grandmother's English vocabulary was limited to a few *rudimentary* phrases, she always could make herself understood. Echidnas lack external ears; their tails are, at best, *rudimentary*. They dine on a diet of termites and ants, with beetle larvae supplementary.

ruminate V. chew over and over (mentally, or, like cows, physically); mull over; ponder. Unable to digest quickly the baffling events of the day, Reuben *ruminated* about them until four in the morning.

ruse N. trick; stratagem. You will not be able to fool your friends with such an obvious *ruse*.

rustic ADJ. pertaining to country people; uncouth. The backwoodsman looked out of place in his *rustic* attire.

ruthless ADJ. pitiless; cruel. Captain Hook was a dangerous, *ruthless* villain who would stop at nothing to destroy Peter Pan.

sadistic ADJ. inclined to cruelty. If we are to improve conditions in this prison, we must first get rid of the *sadistic* warden.

sagacious ADJ. perceptive; shrewd; having insight. My father was a *sagacious* judge of character: he could spot a phony a mile away. sagacity, N.

sage N. person celebrated for wisdom. Hearing tales of a mysterious Master of All Knowledge who lived in the hills of Tibet, Sandy was possessed with a burning desire to consult the legendary *sage*. also ADJ.

salient ADJ. protruding; strikingly conspicuous; jumping. Good readers quickly grasp the *salient* and significant points of a passage; indeed, the ideas almost leap out at them, demanding their attention.

salubrious ADJ. promoting good health; healthful. The health resort advertised the *salubrious* properties of the waters of its famous hot springs.

salutary ADJ. tending to improve; beneficial; wholesome. The punishment had a *salutary* effect on the boy, as he became a model student.

salvage V. rescue from loss. All attempts to *salvage* the wrecked ship failed. also N.

sanction V. (1) approve; (2) impose a penalty on. Nothing will convince me to *sanction* the engagement of my daughter to such a worthless young man. The board has no legal authority to *sanction* members as a way to enforce the ethics code.

sanctuary N. refuge; shelter; shrine; holy place. The tiny attic was Helen's *sanctuary* to which she fled when she had to get away from the rest of her family.

sanguine ADJ. cheerful; hopeful. Let's not be too *sanguine* about the outcome of the election; we may still lose.

sarcasm N. scornful remarks; stinging rebuke. Though Ralph pretended to ignore the mocking comments of his supposed friends, their *sarcasm* wounded him deeply.

sardonic ADJ. cynically mocking; sarcastic. Dorothy Parker's wry couplet, "Men seldom make passes at girls who wear glasses," epitomizes her *sardonic* wit.

satire N. form of literature in which irony, sarcasm, and ridicule are employed to attack vice and folly. *Gulliver's Travels*, which is regarded by many as a tale for children, is actually a bitter *satire* attacking man's folly.

satirical ADJ. mocking. The humor of cartoonist Gary Trudeau often is *satirical;* through the comments of the Doonesbury characters, Trudeau ridicules political corruption and folly.

saturate V. soak thoroughly. *Saturate* your sponge with water until it can't hold any more.

savor V. enjoy; have a distinctive flavor, smell, or quality. Relishing his triumph, the actor especially *savored* the chagrin of the critics who had predicted his failure.

savory ADJ. tasty; pleasing, attractive, or agreeable. Julia Child's recipes enable amateur chefs to create *savory* delicacies for their guests.

scanty ADJ. (1) meager, insufficient; (2) revealing (of clothing). Thinking his helping of food was *scanty,* Oliver Twist asked for more. A *scanty* bikini top may be all right for the beach, but not for the office.

schematic ADJ. relating to an outline or diagram; using a system of symbols. In working out the solution to this logic puzzle, you may find it helpful to construct a simple *schematic* diagram outlining the order of events.

schism N. division; split. His reforms led to a *schism* in the church and the establishment of a new sect opposing the old order.

scruple V. fret about; hesitate, for ethical reasons. Fearing that her husband had become involved in an affair, she did not *scruple* to read his diary. also N.

scrupulous ADJ. (1) conscientious and extremely thorough; (2) careful to behave in an ethical and morally right way. Although Alfred is *scrupulous* in fulfilling his duties at work, he is less conscientious about meeting his obligations at home. Betsy was far too *scrupulous* to try to steal away another girl's boyfriend.

scrutinize V. examine closely and critically. Searching for flaws, the sergeant *scrutinized* every detail of the private's uniform.

seasoned ADJ. experienced. Though pleased with her new batch of rookies, the basketball coach wished she had a few more *seasoned* players on the team.

secession N. withdrawal. The *secession* of the Southern states provided Lincoln with his first major problem after his inauguration. secede, v.

seclusion N. isolation; solitude. One moment she loved crowds; the next, she sought *seclusion*. seclude, v.

secrete V. (1) hide away; (2) produce and release a substance into an organism. The pack rat *secretes* odds and ends in its nest; the pancreas *secretes* insulin in the islets of Langerhans.

sect N. separate religious body; faction. As university chaplain, she sought to address universal religious issues and not limit herself to concerns of any one *sect*.

sectarian ADJ. relating to a religious faction or subgroup; narrow-minded; limited. Far from being broad-minded, the religious leader was intolerant of new ideas, paying attention only to purely *sectarian* interests. sect. N.

secular ADJ. worldly; not pertaining to church matters; temporal. The church leaders decided not to interfere in *secular* matters.

sedate ADJ. calm and composed; dignified. To calm the agitated pony, we teamed him with a *sedate* mare who easily accepted the harness.

sedentary ADJ. requiring sitting. Sitting all day at the computer, Sharon grew to resent the *sedentary* nature of her job.

Word List 38   sedition–sporadic

sedition N. resistance to authority; insubordination. His words, though not treasonous in themselves, were calculated to arouse thoughts of *sedition*.

seemly ADJ. proper; appropriate. Lady Bracknell did not think it was *seemly* for Ernest to lack a proper family: no baby abandoned on a doorstep could grow up to be a fit match for *her* daughter.

seismic ADJ. pertaining to earthquakes. The Richter scale is a measurement of *seismic* disturbances.

sentinel N. sentry; lookout. Though camped in enemy territory, Bledsoe ignored the elementary precaution of posting *sentinels* around the encampment.

serenity N. calmness; placidity. The sound of air raid sirens pierced the *serenity* of the quiet village of Pearl Harbor.

servile ADJ. slavish; cringing. Constantly fawning on his employer, humble Uriah Heap was a *servile* creature.

servitude N. slavery; compulsory labor. Born a slave, Frederick Douglass resented his life of *servitude* and plotted to escape to the North.

sever V. cut; separate. The released prisoner wanted to begin a new life and *sever* all connections with his criminal past. Dr. Guillotin invented a machine that could neatly *sever* an aristocratic head from its equally aristocratic body. Unfortunately, he couldn't collect any *severance* pay. severance, N.

severity N. harshness; intensity; sternness; austerity. The *severity* of Jane's migraine attack was so great that she took to her bed for a week.

sham V. pretend. He *shammed* sickness to get out of going to school. also N.

shirk V. avoid (responsibility, work, etc.); malinger. Brian has a strong sense of duty; he would never *shirk* any responsibility.

shoddy ADJ. inferior; trashy; cheap. Grumbling, "They don't make things the way they used to," Grandpa complained about the *shoddy* workmanship nowadays.

shrewd ADJ. clever; astute. A *shrewd* investor, he took clever advantage of the fluctuations of the stock market.

shun V. keep away from. Cherishing his solitude, the recluse *shunned* the company of other human beings.

simile N. comparison of one thing with another, using the word "like" or "as." "My love is like a red, red rose" is a *simile*.

simplistic ADJ. oversimplified. Though Jack's solution dealt adequately with one aspect of the problem, it was *simplistic* in failing to consider various complications that might arise.

simulate V. feign. He *simulated* insanity in order to avoid punishment for his crime.

singular ADJ. unique; extraordinary; odd. Though the young man tried to understand Father William's *singular* behavior, he still found it odd that the old man incessantly stood on his head. singularity, N.

sinister ADJ. evil; conveying a sense of ill omen. Aware of the Penguin's *sinister* purpose, Batman wondered how he could save Gotham City from the ravages of his evil enemy.

skeptic N. doubter; person who suspends judgment until the evidence supporting a point of view has been examined. I am a *skeptic* about the new health plan; I want some proof that it can work. skepticism, N.

skimp V. provide scantily; live very economically. They were forced to *skimp* on necessities in order to make their limited supplies last the winter.

slacken V. slow up; loosen. As they passed the finish line, the runners *slackened* their pace.

slander N. defamation; utterance of false and malicious statements. Considering the negative comments politicians make about each other, it's a wonder that more of them aren't sued for *slander*. also V.

slovenly ADJ. untidy; careless in work habits. Unshaven, sitting around in his bathrobe all afternoon, Gus didn't seem to care about the *slovenly* appearance he presented. The dark ring around the bathtub and the spider webs hanging from the beams proved what a *slovenly* housekeeper she was.

sluggish ADJ. slow; lazy; lethargic. After two nights without sleep, she felt *sluggish* and incapable of exertion.

slur V. speak indistinctly; mumble. When Sol has too much to drink, he starts to *slur* his words: "Washamatter? Cansh you undershtand what I shay?"

slur N. insult to one's character or reputation; slander. Polls revealed that the front-runner's standing had been badly damaged by the *slurs* and innuendoes circulated by his opponent's staff. also V.

sobriety N. moderation (especially regarding indulgence in alcohol); seriousness. Neither falling-down drunks nor stand-up comics are noted for *sobriety*. sober, ADJ.

solemnity N. seriousness; gravity. The minister was concerned that nothing should disturb the *solemnity* of the marriage service. solemn, ADJ.

solicit V. request earnestly; seek. Knowing she needed to have a solid majority for the budget to pass, the mayor telephoned all the members of the city council to *solicit* their votes.

solicitous ADJ. worried; concerned. Dora was delicate, David knew, and he was very *solicitous* about her health during her pregnancy.

soliloquy N. talking to oneself. Dramatists use the *soliloquy* as a device to reveal a character's innermost thoughts and emotions.

solitude N. state of being alone; seclusion. Much depends on how much you like your own company. What to one person seems fearful isolation to another is blessed *solitude*.

soluble ADJ. (1) able to be dissolved; (2) able to be explained. Sugar is *soluble* in water; put a sugar cube in water, and it will quickly dissolve. Thanks to Sherlock Holmes, the Mystery of the Missing Sugar Cube proved to be *soluble* after all.

solution N. (1) act of solving (a problem, difficult situation, etc.); (2) liquid mixture whose components are uniformly distributed. If you get a foreign object in your eye, one possible *solution* to the problem is to try to flush the object out of your eye with clean water or a saline *solution*.

solvent ADJ. (1) able to dissolve; (2) able to pay all debts. Sol was perpetually broke until he invented

Glu-Off, whose *solvent* power was strong enough to dissolve Crazy Glue. It proved so popular that Sol is finally *solvent*.

solvent N. substance that dissolves another. Dip a cube of sugar into a cup of water; note how the water acts as a *solvent*, causing the cube to break down.

somber ADJ. (1) gloomy, depressing; (2) dark, drab. From the doctor's grim expression, I could tell he had *somber* news. Dull brown and charcoal gray are pretty *somber* colors; can't you wear something bright?

sophisticated ADJ. worldly-wise and urbane; complex. When Sophie makes wisecracks, she thinks she sounds *sophisticated*, but instead she sounds sophomoric. A few years ago the new IBM laptop with the butterfly keyboard and the built-in quad-speed fax modem seemed the height of computer *sophistication*.

sophistry N. seemingly plausible but fallacious reasoning. Instead of advancing valid arguments, he tried to overwhelm his audience with a flood of *sophistries*.

sophomoric ADJ. immature; half-baked, like a sophomore. Even if you're only a freshman, it's no compliment to be told your humor is *sophomoric*. The humor in *Dumb and Dumber* is *sophomoric* at best.

sovereign ADJ. (1) efficacious; (2) supreme or paramount; (3) self-governing. Professor Pennywhistle claimed his panacea was a *sovereign* cure for all chronic complaints. In medicine the *sovereign* task of the doctor is to do no harm. Rebelling against the mother country, the onetime colony now proclaimed itself a *sovereign* state. also N.

sparse ADJ. not thick; thinly scattered; scanty. No matter how carefully Albert combed his hair to make it look as full as possible, it still looked *sparse*.

spatial ADJ. relating to space. NASA is engaged in an ongoing program of *spatial* exploration. Certain exercises test your sense of *spatial* relations by asking you to identify two views of an object seen from different points in space.

specious ADJ. seemingly reasonable but incorrect; misleading (often intentionally). To claim that, because houses and birds both have wings, both can fly, is extremely *specious* reasoning.

spectrum N. colored band produced when a beam of light passes through a prism. The visible portion of the *spectrum* includes red at one end and violet at the other.

speculate V. (1) form a theory about something, often without sufficient evidence; (2) assume a financial risk in hopes of gain. Students of the stock market *speculate* that the seeds of the financier's downfall were planted when he *speculated* heavily in junk bonds.

spendthrift N. someone who wastes money. Easy access to credit encourages people to turn into *spendthrifts* who shop till they drop.

spontaneity N. lack of premeditation; naturalness; freedom from constraint. When Anne and Amy met, Amy impulsively hugged her new colleague, but Anne drew back, unprepared for such *spontaneity*. The cast over-rehearsed the play so much that the eventual performance lacked any *spontaneity*. spontaneous, ADJ.

sporadic ADJ. occurring irregularly. Although you can still hear *sporadic* outbursts of laughter and singing outside, the big Halloween parade has passed; the party's over until next year.

Word List 39   spurious–succinct

spurious ADJ. false; counterfeit; forged; illogical. The antique dealer hero of Jonathan Gash's mystery novels gives the reader tips on how to tell *spurious* antiques from the real thing. Natasha's claim to be the lost heir of the Romanoffs was *spurious*: the only thing Russian about her was the vodka she drank!

squander V. waste. If you *squander* your allowance on candy and comic books, you won't have any money left to buy the new box of crayons you want.

stagnant ADJ. (1) motionless; (2) not advancing. Mosquitoes commonly breed in ponds of *stagnant* water. When the economy is *stagnant*, even college graduates struggle to find work. stagnate, V.

stalemate N. deadlock. Negotiations between the union and the employers have reached a *stalemate*; neither side is willing to budge from previously stated positions.

stamina N. strength; staying power. I doubt that she has the *stamina* to run the full distance of the marathon race.

stanza N. division of a poem. Do you know the last *stanza* of "The Star-Spangled Banner"?

static ADJ. unchanging; lacking development. Why watch chess on TV? I like watching a game with action, not something *static* where nothing seems to be going on.

statute N. law enacted by the legislature. The *statute* of limitations sets the limits on how long you have to take legal action in specific cases.

steadfast ADJ. loyal; unswerving. Penelope was *steadfast* in her affections, faithfully waiting for Ulysses to return from his wanderings.

stealth N. slyness; sneakiness; secretiveness. Fearing detection by the sentries on duty, the scout inched his way toward the enemy camp with great *stealth*.

stem V. check the flow. The paramedic used a tourniquet to *stem* the bleeding from the slashed artery.

stem from V. arise from. Milton's problems in school *stemmed from* his poor study habits.

stereotype N. fixed and unvarying representation; standardized mental picture, often reflecting prejudice. Critics object to the character of Jim in *The Adventures of Huckleberry Finn* because he seems to reflect the *stereotype* of the happy, ignorant slave.

stifle   v. suppress; extinguish; inhibit. Halfway through the boring lecture, Laura gave up trying to *stifle* her yawns.

stigma   N. token of disgrace; brand. I do not attach any *stigma* to the fact that you were accused of this crime; the fact that you were acquitted clears you completely.

stigmatize   v. brand; mark as wicked. I do not want to *stigmatize* this young offender for life by sending her to prison.

stint   N. supply; allotted amount; assigned portion of work. He performed his daily *stint* cheerfully and willingly. also v.

stint   v. be thrifty; set limits. "Spare no expense," the bride's father said, refusing to *stint* on the wedding arrangements.

stipend   N. pay for services. There is a nominal *stipend* for this position.

stipulate   v. make express conditions; specify. Before agreeing to reduce American military forces in Europe, the president *stipulated* that NATO inspection teams be allowed to inspect Soviet bases.

stock   ADJ. (1) regularly available for sale at a store; (2) used so regularly that it becomes trite; (3) indicating a conventional character type. Rather than ordering custom-made cabinets, Sharon saved money by purchasing *stock* units. In your college interview, avoid giving *stock* answers to the interviewer's questions: you don't want to bore her to tears. The characters of the *commedia dell' arte* usually represent fixed social types, *stock* characters, such as foolish old men, sneaky servants, and boastful military officers.

stoic   ADJ. impassive; unmoved by joy or grief. I wasn't particularly *stoic* when I had my flu shot; I squealed like a stuck pig. also N.

stolid   ADJ. unruffled; impassive; dull. Marianne wanted a romantic, passionate suitor like Willoughby, not a *stolid*, unimaginative one like Colonel Brandon.

stratagem   N. deceptive scheme. Though Wellington's forces seemed in full retreat, in reality their withdrawal was a *stratagem* intended to lure the enemy away from its sheltered position.

stratify   v. divide into classes; be arranged into strata. As the economic gap between the rich and the poor increased, Roman society grew increasingly *stratified*.

stratum   N. layer of earth's surface; layer of society. Neither an elitist nor a reverse snob, Mitch had friends from every social *stratum*.

strident   ADJ. loud and harsh; insistent. Whenever Sue became angry, she tried not to raise her voice; she had no desire to appear *strident*.

stringent   ADJ. severe; rigid; constricted. Fearing the rapid spread of the SARS virus, the Canadian government imposed *stringent* quarantine measures.

studied   ADJ. not spontaneous; deliberate; thoughtful. Given Jill's previous slights, Jack felt that the omission of his name from the guest list was a *studied* insult.

stupefy   v. make numb; stun; amaze. Disapproving of drugs in general, Laura refused to take sleeping pills or any other medicine that might *stupefy* her. stupefaction, N.

stymie   v. present an obstacle; stump. The detective was *stymied* by the contradictory evidence in the robbery investigation. also N.

suavity   N. urbanity; polish. The elegant actor is particularly good in roles that require *suavity* and sophistication.

subdued   ADJ. less intense; quieter. Bob liked the *subdued* lighting at the restaurant because he thought it was romantic. I just thought it was dimly lit.

subjective   ADJ. occurring or taking place within the subject; unreal. Your analysis is highly *subjective;* you have permitted your emotions and your opinions to color your thinking.

subjugate   v. conquer; bring under control. Alexander the Great conquered most of the known world of his time, first *subjugating* the Persians under Darius, then defeating the armies of India's King Porus.

sublime   ADJ. exalted or noble and uplifting; utter. Lucy was in awe of Desi's *sublime* musicianship, while he was in awe of her *sublime* naiveté.

submissive   ADJ. yielding; timid. When he refused to permit Elizabeth to marry her poet, Mr. Barrett expected her to be properly *submissive*; instead, she eloped!

subordinate   ADJ. occupying a lower rank; inferior; submissive. Bishop Proudie's wife expected all the *subordinate* clergy to behave with great deference to the wife of their superior.

subsequent   ADJ. following; later. In *subsequent* lessons, we shall take up more difficult problems.

subside   v. (1) settle down; (2) sink to a lower level. The doctor assured Johnny's parents that their son's fever would eventually *subside*. Once the floodwaters *subsided*, the Greens set about assessing the damage to their waterlogged house.

subsidiary   N. something secondary in importance or subordinate; auxiliary. The Turner Broadcasting System is a wholly owned *subsidiary* of AOL Time Warner. First deal with the critical issues, then with the *subsidiary* ones. also ADJ.

subsidy   N. direct financial aid by government, etc. Without this *subsidy*, American ship operators would not be able to compete in world markets.

subsistence N. means needed to support life; existence. Farming those barren, depleted fields, he raised barely enough food for his family's *subsistence*.

substantial ADJ. ample; solid; in essentials. The generous scholarship represented a *substantial* sum of money.

substantiate V. establish by evidence; verify; support. You should provide all documentation you have available to *substantiate* your claim that you were the victim of identity theft, as well as copies of all bills, invoices, and other correspondence establishing the losses you are claiming.

substantive ADJ. real, as opposed to imaginary; essential; solidly based; substantial. Bishop Tutu received the Nobel Peace Prize in recognition of his *substantive* contributions to the peace movement in South Africa.

subterfuge N. deceitful stratagem; trick; pretense. Hiding from his pursuers, the fugitive used every *subterfuge* he could think of to get them off his track.

subtlety N. perceptiveness; ingenuity; delicacy. Never obvious, she expressed herself with such *subtlety* that her remarks went right over the heads of most of her audience. subtle, ADJ.

subversive ADJ. tending to overthrow; destructive. At first glance, the notion that styrofoam cups may actually be more ecologically sound than paper cups strikes most environmentalists as *subversive*.

succinct ADJ. brief; terse; compact. Don't bore your audience with excess verbiage: be *succinct*.

Word List 40   succumb–terminology

succumb V. yield; give in; die. I *succumb* to temptation whenever I see chocolate.

suffragist N. advocate of voting rights (for women). In recognition of her efforts to win the vote for women, Congress authorized coining a silver dollar honoring the *suffragist* Susan B. Anthony.

summation N. act of finding the total; summary. In his *summation*, the lawyer emphasized the testimony given by the two witnesses.

summit N. (1) utmost height or pinnacle; (2) highest point (of a mountain, etc.) The *summit* of the amateur mountain climber's aspirations was someday to reach the *summit* of Mount Everest.

superficial ADJ. (1) on the surface; (2) not thorough. Justin's fall left him with *superficial* scrapes and bruises that healed quickly. To revise a textbook properly, you must do more than make a few *superficial* changes to the manuscript.

superfluous ADJ. (1) unnecessary; (2) excessive; overabundant. Betsy lacked the heart to tell June that the wedding present she brought was *superfluous*; she

and Bob had already received five toasters. Please try not to include so many *superfluous* details in your report; just give me the facts. superfluity, N.

superimpose V. place over something else. The filmmakers *superimposed* the credits over the movie's opening scene.

supersede V. cause to be set aside; replace; make obsolete. The new bulk mailing postal regulation *supersedes* the old one. If you continue to follow the old regulation, your bulk mailing will be returned to you.

supposition N. hypothesis; the act of supposing. I based my decision to confide in him on the *supposition* that he would be discreet. suppose, V.

suppress V. stifle; overwhelm; subdue; inhibit. Too polite to laugh in anyone's face, Roy did his best to *suppress* his amusement at Ed's inane remark.

surmise V. suspect; guess; imagine. I *surmise* that Suzanne will be late for this meeting; I've never known her to be on time. also N.

surmount V. overcome. Could Helen Keller, blind and deaf since childhood, *surmount* her physical disabilities and lead a productive life?

surpass V. exceed. Her SAT scores *surpassed* our expectations.

surrogate N. substitute. For a fatherless child, a male teacher may become a father *surrogate*.

surveillance N. watching; guarding. The FBI kept the house under constant *surveillance* in the hope of capturing all the criminals at one time.

susceptible ADJ. (1) impressionable; easily influenced; (2) having little resistance, as to a disease; receptive to. Said the patent medicine man to his very *susceptible* customer: "Buy this new miracle drug, and you will no longer be *susceptible* to the common cold."

sustain V. (1) live through; (2) keep up. Stuart *sustained* such heavy losses in the stock market that he could no longer *sustain* his jet-setting life style.

sustenance N. means of support, food, nourishment. In the tropics, the natives find *sustenance* easy to obtain, due to all the fruit trees.

swerve V. deviate; turn aside sharply. The car *swerved* wildly as the driver struggled to regain control of the wheel.

symbiosis N. interdependent relationship (between groups, species), often mutually beneficial. Both the crocodile bird and the crocodile derive benefit from their *symbiosis*: pecking away at food particles embedded in the crocodile's teeth, the bird receives nourishment; the crocodile, meanwhile, receives proper dental hygiene. symbiotic, ADJ.

symmetry N. (1) arrangement of parts so that balance is obtained; (2) state of having pleasing proportions. Something lopsided by definition lacks *symmetry*. In choreographing, we strive for *symmetry*, so that a movement performed by one couple will balance a similar movement performed by another pair.

synoptic ADJ. providing a general overview; summary. The professor turned to the latest issue of *Dissertation Abstracts* for a *synoptic* account of what was new in the field. synopsis, N.

synthesis N. (1) combination of different parts (ideas, styles, genres) to create a connected whole; (2) chemical production of a more complex substance from simpler ones; (3) electronic production of sounds. Combining their owners' Catholicism with their own West African beliefs, Haitian slaves created a *synthesis* now known as Voodoo. The *synthesis* of aspirin involves the reaction of salicylic acid and acetic anhydride in the presence of a catalyst. Using digital tools, musicians mix sounds from different instruments, creating a *synthesis* of new musical sounds. synthesize, V.

synthetic ADJ. (1) made by combining different substances; (2) (of an action or emotion) not genuine. Tires, once manufactured from rubber plants, nowadays are made from *synthetic* materials pro-duced from crude oil. Although the dean strongly condemned the actions of the campus police, we felt his outrage was *synthetic*: he took no action against the police for their brutal treatment of the demonstrators.

table V. set aside a resolution or proposal for future consideration. Because we seem unable to agree on this issue at the moment, let us *table* the motion for now and come back to it at a later date.

tacit ADJ. understood; not put into words. We have a *tacit* agreement based on only a handshake.

taciturn ADJ. habitually silent; talking little. The stereotypical cowboy is a *taciturn* soul, answering lengthy questions with "Yep" or "Nope."

tactile ADJ. pertaining to the organs or sense of touch. His callused hands had lost their *tactile* sensitivity.

taint V. contaminate; cause to lose purity; modify with a trace of something bad. One speck of dirt on your utensils may contain enough germs to *taint* an entire batch of preserves.

tangential ADJ. peripheral; only slightly connected; digressing. Despite Clark's attempts to distract her with *tangential* remarks, Lois kept on coming back to her main question: why couldn't he come out to dinner with Superman and her?

tangible ADJ. able to be touched; real; palpable. Although Tom did not own a house, he had several *tangible* assets—a car, a television, a PC—that he could sell if he needed cash.

tantalize V. tease; torture with disappointment. Tom *tantalized* his younger brother, holding the ball just too high for Jimmy to reach.

tantamount ADJ. equivalent in effect or value. Because so few Southern blacks could afford to pay the poll tax, the imposition of this tax on prospective voters was *tantamount* to disenfranchisement for black voters.

tautology N. unnecessary repetition. "Joyful happiness" is an illustration of *tautology*.

tedious ADJ. boring; tiring. The repetitious nature of work on the assembly line made Martin's job very *tedious*. tedium, N.

temerity N. boldness; rashness. Do you have the *temerity* to argue with me?

temper V. (1) make something less intense or extreme; (2) toughen (steel, glass) by heating and then cooling. Not even her supervisor's grumpiness could *temper* Nancy's enthusiasm for her new job. Heated in a forge and then *tempered*, stainless steel blades hold an edge well.

temperament N. characteristic frame of mind; disposition; emotional excess. Although the twins look alike, they differ markedly in *temperament*: Todd is calm, but Rod is excitable.

temperate ADJ. restrained; self-controlled; moderate in respect to temperature. Try to be *temperate* in your eating this holiday season; if you control your appetite, you won't gain too much weight.

temporize V. act evasively to gain time; avoid committing oneself. Ordered by King John to drive Robin Hood out of Sherwood Forest, the sheriff *temporized*, hoping to put off any confrontation with the outlaw band.

tenacious ADJ. holding fast. I had to struggle to break his *tenacious* hold on my arm.

tenacity N. firmness; persistence. Jean Valjean could not believe the *tenacity* of Inspector Javert. Here all Valjean had done was to steal a loaf of bread, and the inspector had pursued him doggedly for twenty years!

tender V. offer; extend. Although no formal charges had been made against him, in the wake of the recent scandal the mayor felt he should *tender* his resignation.

tenet N. doctrine; dogma. The agnostic did not accept the *tenets* of their faith.

tensile ADJ. capable of being stretched. Mountain climbers must know the *tensile* strength of their ropes.

tentative ADJ. (1) hesitant; (2) not fully worked out or developed. Unsure of his welcome at the Christmas party, Scrooge took a *tentative* step into his nephew's drawing room. Phil had a *tentative* plan for organizing the camping trip; he just needed to think through a few more details before he was ready to share his ideas.

tenuous ADJ. thin; rare; slim. The allegiance of our allies is based on such *tenuous* ties that we have little hope they will remain loyal.

tenure N. holding of an office; time during which such an office is held. A special recall election put a sudden end to Gray Davis's *tenure* in office as governor of California.

termination N. end. Though the time for *termination* of the project was near, we still had a lot of work to finish before we shut up shop. terminate, v.

terminology N. terms used in science or art. In talking to patients, doctors should either avoid medical *terminology* altogether or take time to explain the technical terms they use.

Word List 41   terrestrial–ulterior

terrestrial ADJ. earthly (as opposed to celestial); pertaining to the land. In many science fiction films, alien invaders from outer space plan to destroy all *terrestrial* life.

terse ADJ. concise; abrupt; pithy. There is a fine line between speech that is *terse* and to the point and speech that is too abrupt.

thematic ADJ. relating to a unifying motif or idea. Those who think of *Moby Dick* as a simple adventure story about whaling miss its underlying *thematic* import.

theoretical ADJ. (1) not practical or applied; (2) hypothetical. Bob was better at applied engineering and computer programming than he was at *theoretical* physics and math. While I can still think of some *theoretical* objections to your plan, you've convinced me of its basic soundness.

therapeutic ADJ. curative. Now better known for its racetrack, Saratoga Springs first gained attention for the *therapeutic* qualities of its famous "healing waters." therapy, N.

thesis N. (1) statement advanced as a premise to be supported; (2) long essay. In her speech, Lexy made a convincing argument, supporting her *thesis* with statistics as well as anecdotal evidence. In graduate school, she wrote a doctoral *thesis*, which was later published to great reviews.

thespian ADJ. pertaining to drama. Her success in the school play convinced her she was destined for a *thespian* career. also N.

thrifty ADJ. careful about money; economical. A *thrifty* shopper compares prices before making major purchases.

thrive V. prosper; flourish. Despite the impact of the recession on the restaurant trade, Philip's cafe *thrived*.

thwart V. prevent; frustrate; oppose and defeat. Batman searched for a way to *thwart* the Joker's evil plan to destroy Gotham City.

timidity N. lack of self-confidence or courage. If you are to succeed as a salesman, you must first lose your *timidity* and fear of failure.

timorous ADJ. fearful; demonstrating fear. His *timorous* manner betrayed the fear he felt at the moment.

tirade N. extended scolding; denunciation; harangue. The cigar smoker went into a bitter *tirade*, denouncing the anti-smoking forces that had succeeded in banning smoking from most planes and restaurants.

titanic ADJ. gigantic. *Titanic* waves beat against the majestic S.S. *Titanic*, driving it against the concealed iceberg.

title N. right or claim to possession; mark of rank; name (of a book, film, etc.). Though the penniless Duke of Ragwort no longer held *title* to the family estate, he still retained his *title* as head of one of England's oldest families.

tonic ADJ. invigorating; refreshing. The tart homemade ginger ale had a *tonic* effect on Kit: she perked right up. also N.

topography N. physical features of a region. Before the generals gave the order to attack, they ordered a complete study of the *topography* of the region.

torpor N. lethargy; sluggishness; dormancy. Throughout the winter, nothing aroused the bear from his *torpor*: he would not emerge from hibernation until spring. torpid, ADJ.

toxic ADJ. poisonous. We must seek an antidote for whatever *toxic* substance he has eaten. toxicity, N.

tract N. (1) region of land (often imprecisely described); (2) pamphlet. The king granted William Penn a *tract* of land in the New World. Penn then printed a *tract* in which he encouraged settlers to join his colony.

tractable ADJ. docile; easily managed. Although Susan seemed a *tractable* young woman, she had a stubborn streak of independence that occasionally led her to defy the powers-that-be when she felt they were in the wrong.

traduce V. expose to slander. His opponents tried to *traduce* the candidate's reputation by spreading rumors about his past.

trajectory N. path taken by a projectile. The police tried to locate the spot from which the assassin had fired the fatal shot by tracing the *trajectory* of the bullet.

tranquillity N. calmness; peace. After the commotion and excitement of the city, I appreciate the *tranquillity* of these fields and forests.

transgression N. violation of a law; sin. Although Widow Douglass was willing to overlook Huck's *transgressions*, Miss Watson refused to forgive and forget.

transient ADJ. momentary; temporary; staying for a short time. Lexy's joy at finding the perfect Christmas gift for Phil was *transient*; she still had to find presents for the cousins and Uncle Bob. Located near the airport, this hotel caters to a largely *transient* trade. transience, N.

transition N. going from one state of action to another. During the period of *transition* from oil heat to gas heat, the furnace will have to be shut off.

transitory ADJ. impermanent; fleeting. Fame is *transitory*: today's rising star is all too soon tomorrow's washed-up has-been. transitoriness, N.

transmute V. change; convert to something different. He was unable to *transmute* his dreams into actualities.

transparent ADJ. permitting light to pass through freely. The blue Caribbean waters were so *transparent* that we could clearly see the colorful tropical fish darting through the coral reefs. John's pride in his son is *transparent*; no one who sees the two of them together can miss it.

transport N. strong emotion. Margo was a creature of extremes, at one moment in *transports* of joy over a vivid sunset, at another moment in *transports* of grief over a dying bird. also V.

traumatic ADJ. pertaining to an injury caused by violence. In his nightmares, he kept on recalling the *traumatic* experience of being wounded in battle.

travail N. painful physical or mental labor; drudgery; torment. Like every other high school student she knew, Sherry hated the yearlong *travail* of cramming for the SAT. also V.

treatise N. article treating a subject systematically and thoroughly. He is preparing a *treatise* on the Elizabethan playwrights for his graduate degree.

trenchant ADJ. forceful and vigorous; cutting. With his *trenchant* wit, Rich cuts straight to the heart of the matter, panning a truly dreadful play.

trepidation N. fear; nervous apprehension. As she entered the office of the dean of admissions, Sharon felt some *trepidation* about how she would do in her interview.

trespass V. unlawfully enter the boundaries of someone else's property. The wicked baron flogged any poacher who *trespassed* on his private hunting grounds. also N.

tribute N. tax levied by a ruler; mark of respect. The colonists refused to pay *tribute* to a foreign despot.

trifling ADJ. trivial; unimportant. Why bother going to see a doctor for such a *trifling*, everyday cold?

trigger V. set off. John is touchy today; say one word wrong and you'll *trigger* an explosion.

trite ADJ. hackneyed; commonplace. The *trite* and predictable situations in many television programs turn off many viewers, who, in turn, turn off their sets.

trivial ADJ. unimportant; trifling. Too many magazines ignore newsworthy subjects and feature *trivial* affairs. trivia, N.

truculence N. aggressiveness; ferocity. Tynan's reviews were noted for their caustic attacks and general tone of *truculence*. truculent, ADJ.

tumult N. commotion; riot; noise. She could not make herself heard over the *tumult* of the mob.

turbulence N. state of violent agitation. Warned of approaching *turbulence* in the atmosphere, the pilot told the passengers to fasten their seat belts.

turmoil N. great commotion and confusion. Lydia running off with a soldier! Mother fainting at the news! The Bennet household was in *turmoil*.

tycoon N. wealthy leader. John D. Rockefeller was a prominent *tycoon*.

tyranny N. oppression; cruel government. Frederick Douglass fought against the *tyranny* of slavery throughout his life.

ubiquitous ADJ. being everywhere; omnipresent. That Christmas "The Little Drummer Boy" seemed *ubiquitous;* David heard the tune everywhere.

ulterior ADJ. unstated; hidden; more remote. Suspicious of altruistic gestures, he looked for an *ulterior* motive behind every charitable deed.

Word List 42   ultimate–verity

ultimate ADJ. final; not susceptible to further analysis. Scientists are searching for *ultimate* truths.

unaccountable ADJ. inexplicable; unreasonable or mysterious. I have taken an *unaccountable* dislike to my doctor: "I do not love thee, Doctor Fell. The reason why, I cannot tell."

unanimity N. complete agreement. We were surprised by the *unanimity* with which members of both parties accepted our proposals. unanimous, ADJ.

unassailable ADJ. not subject to question; not open to attack. Penelope's virtue was *unassailable*; while she waited for her husband to come back from the war, no other man had a chance.

underlying ADJ. fundamental; lying below. The *underlying* cause of the student riot was not the strict curfew rule but the moldy cafeteria food. Miss Marple seems a sweet little old lady at first, but there's an iron will *underlying* that soft and fluffy facade.

undermine V. weaken; sap. The recent corruption scandals have *undermined* many people's faith in the city government. The recent torrential rains have washed away much of the cliffside; the deluge threatens to *undermine* the pillars supporting several houses at the edge of the cliff.

underscore V. emphasize. Addressing the jogging class, Kim *underscored* the importance to runners of good nutrition.

unequivocal ADJ. plain; obvious; unmistakable. My answer to your proposal is an *unequivocal* and absolute "No."

unerringly ADJ. infallibly. My teacher *unerringly* pounced on the one typographical error in my essay.

unfathomable ADJ. incomprehensible; impenetrable. Unable to get to the bottom of the mystery, Watson declared it was *unfathomable*.

uniformity N. sameness; monotony. At *Persons* magazine, we strive for *uniformity* of style; as a result, all our writers wind up sounding exactly alike.

unimpeachable ADJ. blameless and exemplary. Her conduct in office was *unimpeachable* and her record is spotless.

unique ADJ. without an equal; single in kind. You have the *unique* distinction of being the only student whom I have had to fail in this course.

universal ADJ. characterizing or affecting all; present everywhere. At first, no one shared Christopher's opinions; his theory that the world was round was met with *universal* disdain.

unkempt ADJ. disheveled; uncared for in appearance. Jeremy hated his neighbor's *unkempt* lawn: he thought its neglected appearance had a detrimental effect on neighborhood property values.

unmitigated ADJ. unrelieved or immoderate; absolute. After four days of *unmitigated* heat, I was ready to collapse from heat prostration. The congresswoman's husband was an *unmitigated* jerk: not only did he abandon her, he took her campaign funds, too!

unobtrusive ADJ. inconspicuous; not blatant. Reluctant to attract notice, the governess took a chair in a far corner of the room and tried to be as *unobtrusive* as possible.

unpalatable ADJ. distasteful; disagreeable. "I refuse to swallow your conclusion," said she, finding his logic *unpalatable*.

unprecedented ADJ. novel; unparalleled. For a first novel, Margaret Mitchell's novel *Gone with the Wind* was an *unprecedented* success.

unravel V. disentangle; solve. With equal ease Miss Marple *unraveled* tangled balls of yarn and baffling murder mysteries.

unrequited ADJ. not reciprocated. Suffering the pangs of *unrequited* love, Olivia rebukes Cesario for his hardheartedness.

untenable ADJ. indefensible; not able to be maintained. Wayne is so contrary that, the more *untenable* a position is, the harder he'll try to defend it.

unwarranted ADJ. unjustified; groundless; undeserved. Your assumption that I would accept your proposal is *unwarranted*, sir; I do not want to marry you at all. We could not understand Martin's *unwarranted* rudeness to his mother's guests.

unwieldy ADJ. awkward; cumbersome; unmanageable. The large carton was so *unwieldy* that the movers had trouble getting it up the stairs.

unwitting ADJ. unintentional; not knowing. She was the *unwitting* tool of the swindlers.

upshot N. outcome. The *upshot* of the rematch was that the former champion proved that he still possessed all the skills of his youth.

urbane ADJ. suave; refined; elegant. The courtier was *urbane* and sophisticated. urbanity, N.

usurp V. seize another's power or rank. The revolution ended when the victorious rebel general succeeded in his attempt to *usurp* the throne.

utopia N. ideal place, state, or society. Fed up with this imperfect universe, Don would have liked to run off to Shangri-la or some other imaginary *utopia*. utopian, ADJ.

vacillate V. waver; fluctuate. Uncertain which suitor she ought to marry, the princess *vacillated*, saying now one, now the other. The big boss likes his people to be decisive: when he asks you for your opinion, whatever you do, don't *vacillate*. vacillation, N.

valedictory ADJ. pertaining to farewell. I found the *valedictory* address too long; leave-taking should be brief.

valid ADJ. logically convincing; sound; legally acceptable. You're going to have to come up with a better argument if you want to convince me that your reasoning is *valid*.

validate V. confirm; ratify. I will not publish my findings until I *validate* my results.

valor N. bravery. He received the Medal of Honor for his *valor* in battle.

vantage N. position giving an advantage. They fired upon the enemy from behind trees, walls, and any other point of *vantage* they could find.

vapid ADJ. dull and unimaginative; insipid and flavorless. "*Bor*-ing!" said Jessica, as she suffered through yet another *vapid* lecture about Dead White Male Poets.

vaporize V. turn into vapor (steam, gas, fog, etc.). "Zap!" went Super Mario's atomic ray gun as he *vaporized* another deadly foe.

vehement ADJ. forceful; intensely emotional; with marked vigor. Alfred became so *vehement* in describing what was wrong with the Internal Revenue Service that he began jumping up and down and frothing at the mouth. vehemence, N.

velocity N. speed. The train went by at considerable *velocity*.

venerable ADJ. deserving high respect. We do not mean to be disrespectful when we refuse to follow the advice of our *venerable* leader.

venerate V. revere. In Tibet today, the common people still *venerate* their traditional spiritual leader, the Dalai Lama.

vent N. a small opening; outlet. The wine did not flow because the air *vent* in the barrel was clogged.

vent V. (1) make known (opinions, feelings); (2) give off; (3) give emotional release to. At the city council meeting, homeowners *vented* their opinions about the proposed new factory in their residential neighborhood. The homeowners claimed that the factory would *vent* gases into the air, creating unpleasant smells. Exasperated, the factory owner *vented* his anger, ranting at his critics.

venturesome ADJ. bold. A group of *venturesome* women were the first to scale Mt. Annapurna.

veracity N. truthfulness. Asserting his *veracity*, young George Washington proclaimed, "Father, I cannot tell a lie!"

verbalize V. put into words. I know you don't like to talk about these things, but please try to *verbalize* your feelings.

verbiage N. pompous array of words. After we had waded through all the *verbiage*, we discovered that the writer had said very little.

verbose ADJ. wordy. Someone mute can't talk; someone *verbose* can hardly stop talking.

verge N. border; edge. Madame Curie knew she was on the *verge* of discovering the secrets of radioactive elements. also V.

verity N. quality of being true; lasting truth or principle. Did you question the *verity* of Kato Kaelin's testimony about what he heard the night Nicole Brown Simpson was slain? To the skeptic, everything was relative: there were no eternal *verities* in which one could believe.

Word List 43   vernacular–zealot

vernacular N. living language; natural style. Cut out those old-fashioned thee's and thou's and write in the *vernacular*. also ADJ.

versatile ADJ. having many talents; capable of working in many fields. She was a *versatile* athlete, earning varsity letters in basketball, hockey, and track.

verve N. energy in expressing ideas, especially artistically; liveliness. In his rhymes, Seuss writes with such *verve* and good humor that adults as well as children delight in the adventures of *The Cat in the Hat*.

vestige N. trace; remains. We discovered *vestiges* of early Indian life in the cave. vestigial, ADJ.

vex N. annoy; distress. Please try not to *vex* your mother; she is doing the best she can.

viable ADJ. (1) having a reasonable chance of success; (2) capable of living or growing into something living. The plan to build a new stadium, though lacking a few details, is *viable* and stands a good chance of winning popular support. By definition, a fetus is *viable* once it has reached the stage of being capable of living, under normal conditions, outside the uterus or womb.

vicarious ADJ. acting as a substitute; done by a deputy. Though Violet was too meek to talk back to anybody, she got a *vicarious* kick out of Rita's sharp retorts.

vie V. contend; compete. Politicians *vie* with one another, competing for donations and votes.

vigilance N. watchfulness. Eternal *vigilance* is the price of liberty.

vignette N. picture; short literary sketch. The *New Yorker* published her latest *vignette*.

vigor N. active strength. Although he was over seventy years old, Jack håd the *vigor* of a man in his prime. vigorous, ADJ.

vilify V. slander. Waging a highly negative campaign, the candidate attempted to *vilify* his opponent's reputation. vilification, N.

vindicate V. clear from blame; exonerate; justify or support. The lawyer's goal was to *vindicate* her client and prove him innocent on all charges. The critics' extremely favorable reviews *vindicate* my opinion that *The Madness of King George* is a brilliant movie.

vindictive ADJ. out for revenge; malicious. I think it's unworthy of Martha to be so *vindictive*; she shouldn't stoop to such petty acts of revenge.

virtual ADJ. in essence; for practical purposes. She is a *virtual* financial wizard when it comes to money matters.

virtue N. goodness, moral excellence; good quality. *Virtue* carried to extremes can turn into vice: humility, for example, can degenerate into servility and spinelessness.

virulent ADJ. extremely poisonous; hostile; bitter. Laid up with a *virulent* case of measles, Vera blamed her doctors because her recovery took so long. In fact, she became quite *virulent* on the subject of the quality of modern medical care.

visionary ADJ. produced by imagination; fanciful; mystical. She was given to *visionary* schemes that never materialized. also N.

vital ADJ. vibrant and lively; critical; living, breathing. The *vital*, highly energetic first aid instructor stressed that it was *vital* in examining accident victims to note their *vital* signs.

vivacious ADJ. animated; lively. She had always been *vivacious* and sparkling.

vociferous ADJ. clamorous; noisy. The crowd grew *vociferous* in its anger and threatened to take the law into its own hands.

vogue N. popular fashion. Jeans are the *vogue* on college campuses.

volatile ADJ. (1) changeable; (2) explosive; (3) evaporating rapidly. The political climate today is extremely *volatile*: no one can predict what the electorate will do next. Maria Callas's temper was extremely *volatile*: the only thing you could predict was that she was sure to blow up. Acetone is an extremely *volatile* liquid: it evaporates instantly.

volition N. act of making a conscious choice. She selected this dress of her own *volition*.

voluble ADJ. fluent; glib; talkative. The excessively *voluble* speaker suffers from logorrhea: he runs off at the mouth a lot!

voluminous ADJ. bulky; large. A caftan is a *voluminous* garment; most people wearing one look as if they're draped in a small tent.

vulnerable ADJ. susceptible to wounds. His opponents could not harm Achilles, who was *vulnerable* only in his heel.

waive V. give up a claim or right voluntarily; refrain from enforcing; postpone considering. Although, technically, prospective students had to live in Piedmont to attend high school there, occasionally the school *waived* the residence requirement in order to enroll promising athletes.

wake N. trail of ship or other object through water; path of something that has gone before. The *wake* of the swan gliding through the water glistened in the moonlight. Reporters and photographers converged on South Carolina in the *wake* of the hurricane that devastated much of the eastern seaboard.

wane V. decrease in size or strength; draw gradually to an end. The verb "wax," which means to grow in size, is an antonym for *wane*. As it burns, does a wax candle *wane*?

wanton ADJ. unrestrained; willfully malicious; unchaste. Pointing to the stack of bills, Sheldon criticized Sarah for her *wanton* expenditures. In response, Sarah accused Sheldon of making an unfounded, *wanton* attack.

warrant V. (1) give adequate grounds for; (2) give a warranty for a product. No matter how irritated Warren was, that did not *warrant* his rudeness to his mother's guests. The Honda dealership *warranted* the condition of our new van.

warranty N. guarantee; assurance by seller. The purchaser of this automobile is protected by the manufacturer's *warranty* that the company will replace any defective part for five years or 50,000 miles.

wary ADJ. very cautious. The spies grew *wary* as they approached the sentry.

watershed N. crucial dividing point. The invention of the personal computer proved a historic *watershed*, for it opened the way to today's Information Age.

wax V. increase; grow. With proper handling, his fortunes *waxed* and he became rich.

weather V. endure the effects of weather or other forces. Reporters wondered whether Governor Gray Davis would *weather* his latest political challenge and remain in office, or whether he would be California's first governor to be recalled.

whimsical ADJ. capricious; fanciful. In *Mrs. Doubtfire*, the hero is a playful, *whimsical* man who takes a notion to dress up as a woman so that he can look after his children, who are in the custody of his ex-wife. whimsy, N.

willful ADJ. intentional; headstrong. Donald had planned to kill his wife for months; clearly, her death was a case of deliberate, *willful* murder, not a crime of passion committed by a hasty, *willful* youth unable to foresee the consequences of his deeds.

wily ADJ. cunning; artful. If coyotes are supposed to be such sneaky, *wily* creatures, how does Road Runner always manage to outwit Wile E. Coyote?

withdrawn ADJ. introverted; remote. Rebuffed by his colleagues, the initially outgoing young researcher became increasingly *withdrawn*.

wither V. shrivel; decay. Cut flowers are beautiful for a day, but all too soon they *wither*.

withhold V. refuse to give; hold back. The tenants decided to *withhold* a portion of the rent until the landlord kept his promise to renovate the building.

withstand V. stand up against; successfully resist. If you can *withstand* all the peer pressure in high school to cut classes and goof off, you should survive college just fine.

witless ADJ. foolish; idiotic. If Beavis is a half-wit, then Butthead is totally *witless*.

witticism N. witty saying; wisecrack. I don't mean any criticism, but that last *witticism* totally hurt my feelings.

woe N. deep, inconsolable grief; affliction; suffering. Pale and wan with grief, Wanda was bowed down beneath the burden of her *woes*.

worldly ADJ. engrossed in matters of this earth; not spiritual. You must leave your *worldly* goods behind you when you go to meet your Maker.

wrath N. anger; fury. She turned to him, full of *wrath*, and said, "What makes you think I'll accept lower pay for this job than you get?"

wry ADJ. twisted; with a humorous twist. We enjoy Dorothy Parker's verse for its *wry* wit.

xenophobia N. fear or hatred of foreigners. *Xenophobia* is directed against foreign people, not necessarily against foreign products: even *xenophobes* patronize Chinese restaurants and buy Japanese TVs.

yen N. longing; urge. She had a *yen* to get away and live on her own for a while.

yield V. give in; surrender. The wounded knight refused to *yield* to his foe.

yield N. amount produced; crop; income on investment. An experienced farmer can estimate the annual *yield* of his acres with surprising accuracy. also V.

zeal N. eager enthusiasm. Katya's *zeal* was contagious; soon all her fellow students were busily making posters, inspired by her ardent enthusiasm for the cause. zealous, ADJ.

zealot N. fanatic; person who shows excessive zeal. Though Glenn was devout, he was no *zealot*; he never tried to force his beliefs on his friends.

PART FOUR
The SAT Writing and Language Test

The Evidence-Based Writing and Language Test

3

The new SAT Writing and Language Test is a part of the "Evidence-Based Reading and Writing" half of the test. The writing test is set up as follows:

- 1 section with 4 passages
- 35 minutes long
- 11 questions per passage, with 44 questions total
- Questions in a random order of difficulty

In this chapter, you will find:

- An overview of the new SAT Writing and Language Test
- Reviews of the key grammar knowledge and graph analysis skills for the new SAT Writing and Language Test
- 13 Writing and Language test strategies
- "Putting It All Together" with "Small-Picture" and "Big-Picture" example problems and explanations
- In-depth practice for the types of questions and passages you will encounter:

  – Standard English conventions questions: sentence structure, conventions of usage, and conventions of punctuation
  – Expression of ideas questions: development, organization, and effective language use
  – Four passage types: careers, humanities, social studies/history, science

NEW SAT WRITING AND LANGUAGE TEST OVERVIEW

On the new SAT Writing and Language Test, you will find passages and questions like the ones below. Read the directions and note the format. Then try the questions. Detailed solutions follow.

> **Directions:** The passages below are accompanied by several questions, some of which refer to an underlined portion in the passage and some of which refer to the passage as a whole. Some questions ask you to determine how the expression of ideas can be improved. Other questions ask you to determine the best sentence structure, usage, or punctuation given the context. A passage or question may have an accompanying graphic that you will need to consider as you choose the best answer.
>
> Choose the best answer to each question, considering what will optimize the writing quality and make the writing follow the conventions of standard written English. Some questions have a "NO CHANGE" option that you can pick if you believe the best choice is to leave the underlined portion as it is.

STAY-AT-HOME PARENTS, IN MILLIONS

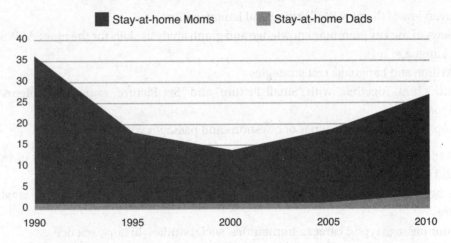

Working From Home

A customer sales representative, still in her pajamas, takes a call and assists a customer with resetting a cellular device. A nutrition consultant e-mails a limited-time 30% off coupon from his smartphone to his most valued clients while watching his favorite show on television. **❶** Prior to arranging meetings on behalf of his company, a packed lunch is prepared by a marketing assistant for his daughter's consumption. A graphic designer spends hours a day on her personal PC creating eye-catching brand logos without ever stepping foot outside. An often-overlooked change in a workforce evermore reliant on technology is

1. (A) NO CHANGE
   (B) A packed lunch is made upstairs prior to the arrangement of company meetings, a task that the marketing assistant completed.
   (C) A marketing assistant packs his daughter's lunch before heading upstairs to arrange meetings on behalf of his company.
   (D) A marketing assistant, prior to the arranging of his company meetings upstairs, packed up his daughter's lunch.

the increasing number of employees who find themselves staying at home during the workday. **2**

While it is true that online work-from-home scamming reached a peak in 2010 and 2011, there **3** is a swarm of legitimate jobs being reeled into the domestic sphere. Some jobs have adopted a hybrid model, bringing in a small number of employees to run a daily office and encouraging others to do what they can at home. **4** A hybrid model involves a combination of two different ways of doing things. Other companies have drastically cut expenses by running their businesses entirely without a physical address. Government corporations have invested in **5** protected federally owned computers to lend to their at-home employees; those who may only have to visit the office once a week but spend the majority of their workday at home completing billing, payroll, or data entry. Online selling sensations like Etsy are emerging regularly to undertake entrepreneurial ambitions in a work-from-home

2. Which choice, if inserted here, would best use the data from the chart to support the claim in the previous sentence?

(A) From 1990 to 2000, the number of stay-at-home moms declined, while the number of stay-at home dads remained steady.

(B) From 1995 to 2005, the number of stay-at-home moms increased slightly, while the number of stay-at home dads remained steady.

(C) From 1990 to 2010, the number of stay-at-home moms somewhat declined, while the number of stay-at home dads slightly increased.

(D) From 2000 to 2010, the number of stay-at-home moms and stay-at-home dads both increased.

3. (A) NO CHANGE
   (B) are a swarm
   (C) was a swarm
   (D) were swarms

4. Should the underlined sentence be kept or deleted?

(A) Kept. It provides a necessary clarification of a concept from the previous sentence.

(B) Kept. It provides expanded details as to how the workplace of the future is making seismic shifts.

(C) Deleted. It contradicts information found elsewhere in the passage.

(D) Deleted. It unnecessarily repeats an idea already discussed in the paragraph.

5. (A) NO CHANGE

(B) protected, federally owned computers to lend to their at-home employees—those

(C) protected, federally, owned computers to lend to they're at home employees: those

(D) protected federally owned computers to lend there to at home employees, those

atmosphere. **6** Even professions that rely heavily on having a central location, like law and medicine, are encouraging the "busywork" to be done outside the office.

Flexibility and comfort are just the tip of the iceberg; there is also money to be made **7** and superfluous expenses to be cut. For parents or those caring for elderly, sick, or disabled family members, working from home may be the only way to bring in an income. And for those barely making it financially in their traditional jobs, the at-home trend can mean an indispensable second income. **8** Some employment websites are reporting more than a 25% increase in remote or virtual job listings each year, and Flexjobs testifies that the majority of at-home workers are more profitable than their in-office counterparts.

Employees say it means **9** fewer money spent on gas and daycare. Employers brag that they can reduce real estate, diminish employee turnover, **10** and end the practice of employees disregarding their attendance obligations. Let's not forget the benefit of at-home tax breaks for those who do choose to make a living from their own home. **11** On the consumer side, home workers are suggesting that decreased stress and increased productivity allow them to provide better services. It may be too early to say, but it seems like a win-win.

6. Where is the most logical place to insert the phrase "inspiring both the employed and unemployed" into the previous sentence?

   (A) Before "online"
   (B) Before "Etsy"
   (C) Before "to undertake"
   (D) Before "work-from-home"

7. (A) NO CHANGE
   (B) with the extra accompanying expenses.
   (C) and items cut.
   (D) and extra expenses that are clearly unneeded to be eliminated.

8. (A) NO CHANGE
   (B) Some employment websites, are reporting more than a 25% increase in remote or virtual job listings
   (C) Some employment websites are reporting more than a 25% increase, in remote or virtual, job listings
   (D) Some employment websites are reporting more than: a 25% increase in remote or virtual job listings

9. (A) NO CHANGE
   (B) the fewest
   (C) less
   (D) lesser

10. (A) NO CHANGE
    (B) and annihilate absence.
    (C) and making a lack of attendance a distant memory.
    (D) and cut absenteeism.

11. (A) NO CHANGE
    (B) On the side of consumers, suggestions from home workers include
    (C) Suggestions from the home workers based on the side of consumers include the idea
    (D) In the consumer side, workers from home have been suggesting

Answers Explained

1. **(C)** This question involves the proper ordering of words. It is not just a matter of what you say but how you say it. To communicate as clearly as possible, generally place the subject earlier in the sentence and the verb later. Choice (C) is the only choice that puts the words in the most logical sequence—which is packing what and what that person does thereafter. Choice (A) incorrectly uses the passive voice on top of having the words in a jumbled sequence. Choice (B) doesn't clarify who made the lunch until the very end of the sentence. Choice (D) confuses the order of events, discussing what the assistant did later before discussing what he did first.

2. **(D)** The new SAT Writing and Language Test will have questions that call upon you to draw proper conclusions about quantitative information presented in graphs and charts. Typically, you will need to determine what conclusions are justifiable based on the data. The correct answer is choice (D) because in 2000, both the number of stay-at-home moms and the number of stay-at-home dads were lower than they were in 2010. This data support the claim in the previous sentence that there is an "increasing number of employees who find themselves staying at home during the workday." Choices (A), (B), and (C) make accurate statements based on the data in the graph, but they do not support the claim made in the previous sentence.

3. **(A)** This question tests your ability to determine whether something is consistent with the text with respect to verb tense and subject-verb agreement. Choice (A) is correct because the sentence as a whole is in the present tense ("While it is true" establishes that this sentence is from the present-day perspective; the verb "reached" refers to a previous event). The subject "swarm" is singular and requires a singular verb "is." The other choices are incorrect either because they use the past tense—choices (C) and (D)—or because they use a plural verb—choices (B) and (D).

4. **(D)** The new SAT will have questions that ask you to determine whether a given sentence will add or detract from the essay. This sentence needs to be removed. The point it makes—giving a definition of a hybrid—has already been made in the previous sentence, where we can infer what the hybrid model is based on the example of "bringing in a small number of employees to run a daily office and encouraging others to do what they can at home." Choices (A) and (B) are incorrect because both of these options recommend keeping this repetitive sentence. Choice (C) is not correct because this sentence merely repeats an idea already given in the previous sentence—it does not contradict information found elsewhere in the essay.

5. **(B)** Punctuation questions are now a major component of the SAT Writing and Language Test. Choice (B) correctly places a dash between the two clauses since a dash can provide a heavy pause. Choice (A) is incorrect because a semicolon in a context like this needs to have an independent clause (i.e., a complete sentence) both before and after it. Although what follows the semicolon is rather long, it is not a complete sentence. The SAT will also assess your understanding of commonly confused words. Choice (C) is incorrect because it uses "they're," which means "they are." Choice (D) is incorrect because it uses "there," which refers to a place.

6. **(C)** Be prepared to solve placement questions involving words, phrases, sentences, and paragraphs on the SAT Writing and Language Test. You might find it helpful to write an "A," "B," "C," and "D" in the spots where they would go in the sentence. Then think

through what makes the most sense as you try placing the phrase into the different potential spots. Choice (C) is correct because it clarifies the groups of people who are inspired to undertake entrepreneurial activities. Choice (A) is incorrect because a transitional word or phrase would be needed between "unemployed" and "online." Choice (B) is wrong because the insertion interrupts the example of Etsy as an online selling sensation. Choice (D) is not correct because describing a "work-from-home atmosphere" as "employed" or "unemployed" is illogical.

7. **(A)** This answer is correct because it concisely expresses the idea that there are too many expenses and is parallel to the phrase "money to be made." Choice (B) is not right because "extra" and "accompanying" are repetitive. Choice (C) is incorrect because the intended meaning is changed by the deletions. Choice (D) is not the answer because it is way too wordy. Be sure to look out for wording that is repetitive or off topic.

8. **(A)** Comma placement is a major topic on the SAT Writing and Language Test. Sometimes less is more when it comes to commas. Choice (B) incorrectly places a comma between the subject "websites" and the verb "are." Choice (C) breaks up the phrase "increase in." Choice (D) places a colon where it would cause too abrupt of a pause since colons need to come after independent clauses. Choice (A) is correct. Although the phrase "more than a 25% increase in remote or virtual job listings" is rather long, it is a unified statement with no extra information that needs to be set aside with commas.

9. **(C)** Word choice is a frequent topic on the SAT Writing and Language Test. Trust your instincts on questions like these so that you don't overthink them. "Fewer" is typically used with items that can be counted one at a time (like "fewer cars" or "fewer dogs"). "Less" is typically used with items that cannot be counted (like "less anger" or "less rain"). In reference to money in a general sense, "less" should be used ("fewer" is used in reference to things like quantities of coins or dollar bills since they are easily countable), making choice (C) correct. Choices (A) and (B) are incorrect because these both use "few" in some way. Choice (D) is not right because "less" is used when comparing the different amounts of an item, while "lesser" is used when talking about two different items (e.g., "less time today" vs. "the lesser of two evils").

10. **(D)** This question focuses on wordiness and proper tone. Choice (D) is correct because it conveys the idea concisely and maintains the tone of the essay. Both Choices (A) and (C) are far too wordy. Choice (B) is incorrect because "annihilate" means "utterly defeat" something, which would give this too much of a confrontational, militaristic tone even though the wording in choice (B) is concise. Sometimes it can be helpful to try the words in sentences of your own. You would "cut" absence, not "annihilate" it.

11. **(A)** This question tests a variety of grammar issues. Choice (A) is correct because it is concise, has an appropriate pause with the comma after the introductory phrase, uses the preposition "on" correctly in conjunction with "the side," and parallels the introductory sentence's use of "employees" as the subject. Choice (B) is incorrect because is literally means that the "suggestions" are on the side of consumers rather than the home workers, which makes for an illogical comparison. Choice (C) is far too wordy. Choice (D) incorrectly uses the preposition in the phrase "In the consumer side" when it should say "on the consumer side." When it comes to the proper use of prepositions—like "on," "in," "about," and "from"—trust your instincts to pick what sounds appropriate given common practice.

- Sentence Basics

  - Wordiness
  - Parallelism
  - Modifier Placement
  - Logical Comparisons
  - Coordination and Subordination
  - Verb Use and Tense

- Singular and Plural Agreement
- Diction (Proper Wording)
- Punctuation

  - Commas
  - Semicolons
  - Colons
  - Dashes
  - Apostrophes

- Quantitative Graph Analysis

SENTENCE BASICS

A **sentence** expresses a complete thought with both a subject and a predicate, i.e., a subject and a verb. A subject is a noun—a person, place, or thing—or a pronoun. The predicate includes a verb—a word that expresses an *action*, such as "is," "were," "do," "drove," "eat," or "sat." Here are some examples of complete sentences:

> Who won the game?
> The sky is falling.
> The flag is waving in the wind.
> Don went to see the latest movie at the theater last night.

A **sentence fragment** expresses an incomplete thought with only a subject or a predicate. Here are some examples of sentence fragments:

> Need the latest results from the survey.
> To my house.
> A cup of coffee with my breakfast.
> The United Kingdom of Great Britain and Northern Ireland, also known as the U.K.

Here are some possible ways the above sentence fragments can be fixed:

> **You** need the latest results from the survey.
> **Go** to my house.
> **I like** a cup of coffee with my breakfast.
> The United Kingdom of Great Britain and Northern Ireland **is** also known as the U.K.

A **_run-on sentence_** *consists of two or more complete sentences that are <u>not</u> joined together with appropriate punctuation or transitions.* Here are some examples of run-on sentences. Can you figure out where the first sentence ends?

> Dan worked diligently on his computer his son read a book.
> You don't take out the trash, I will be very angry.
> The forecast was for a tornado, we headed to the basement.
> It was a long time ago, an ocean covered what is now a modern city.

Here are some possible ways the above run-ons can be fixed:

> Dan worked diligently on his computer **while** his son read a book.
> <u>If</u> you don't take out the trash, I will be very angry.
> The forecast was for a **<u>tornado; we</u>** headed to the basement.
> **<u>A long time ago,</u>** an ocean covered what is now a modern city.

PRACTICE

Determine if each of the following is a complete sentence, a sentence fragment, or a run-on sentence. Correct the fragments and run-ons to make them complete sentences.

1. A beautiful day in the neighborhood.

2. Watch where you are going.

3. I can't believe I forgot my calculator, how am I going to do my math homework?

4. The cars driving down the freeway.

5. Thomas Jefferson, president of the United States of America.

6. You were wrong to leave litter on the pavement.

7. While walking slowly to the entryway, the lady careful to avoid missteps.

8. I am done.

9. Finish your vegetables there are people starving elsewhere.

10. Who's coming over to dinner?

ANSWERS WITH POSSIBLE CORRECTIONS

1. Fragment. **<u>It is a</u>** beautiful day in the neighborhood.

2. Complete sentence—the subject (you) is implied rather than directly stated.

3. Run-on. I can't believe I forgot my **<u>calculator; how</u>** am I going to do my math homework?

4. Fragment. The cars **<u>are</u>** driving down the freeway.

5. Fragment. Thomas Jefferson **<u>was the</u>** president of the United States of America.

6. Complete sentence.

7. Fragment. While walking slowly to the entryway, the lady **<u>is</u>** careful to avoid missteps.

8. Complete sentence.

9. Run-on. Finish your vegetables—there are people starving elsewhere.

10. Complete sentence.

Wordiness

Quality writing demands clear descriptions, but a longer sentence is not necessarily a better one. Repetitive and irrelevant wording must be removed.

Incorrect	Correct
I am going to run for the distance of 3 miles.	I am going to run for ~~the distance of~~ 3 miles. (A mile is widely known to be a unit of distance, so this wording is extra.)
Teachers who educate people often have to work long hours grading papers and planning lessons.	Teachers ~~who educate people~~ often have to work long hours grading papers and planning lessons. (A teacher by definition educates people, so this information is unnecessary.)
Quantitative easing, the process in which a central bank increases the money supply, can be used to stimulate the economy.	Fine as is. Since "quantitative easing" is a specialized term, clarifying its meaning is helpful.

PRACTICE

Cross out the unnecessary wording or leave the sentence unchanged if it is fine.

1. What is the largest and most enormous animal at the zoo?

2. There was nothing like going for a hike on a beautiful summer afternoon.

3. Please order a pizza that is crunchy, crispy, and crusty.

4. When you write, be sure to be concise and to avoid wordiness.

5. The admissions rates at selective schools to which it is challenging to earn acceptance continue to decline.

6. Elizabeth Cochrane Seaman had the pen name "Nellie Bly."

7. Owen Willans Richardson, a winner of the Nobel Prize, was a great physicist.

8. When the earthquake occurred, an event that resulted in the earth shaking, we sought refuge away from potentially falling debris.

9. My neighbor's house, which is where my neighbors have their residence, is very close to mine.

10. Toronto, Canada, features the CN tower—a structure with communications technology, an observatory, and a restaurant.

ANSWERS WITH POSSIBLE CORRECTIONS

1. What is the largest ~~and most enormous~~ animal at the zoo?

2. Fine as is.

3. Please order a pizza that is crunchy~~, crispy, and crusty~~.

4. When you write, be sure to be concise ~~and to avoid wordiness~~.

5. The admissions rates at selective schools ~~to which it is challenging to earn acceptance~~ continue to decline.

6. Fine as is.

7. Fine as is.

8. When the earthquake occurred~~, an event that resulted in the earth shaking~~, we sought refuge away from potentially falling debris.

9. My neighbor's house~~, which is where my neighbors have their residence,~~ is very close to mine.

10. Fine as is.

Parallelism

Excellent writing requires more than just the necessary information. The information must be presented in a way that is consistent, flowing, and parallel.

Incorrect	Correct*
Eating sandwiches and to drink milk are my lunchtime mainstays.	Eating sandwiches and **drinking** milk are my lunchtime mainstays.
Neither the dog or the cat made a mess.	Neither the dog **nor** the cat made a mess.
Respond to the essay question quickly and with thoroughness.	Respond to the essay question quickly and **thoroughly**.

*These sentences can be fixed in multiple ways.

PRACTICE

Make changes to each sentence, if needed, to make it parallel.

1. Driving the sports car is both exhilarating and relaxed.

2. In the gym, on the field, and the classroom, Hannah acted like a true champion.

3. Either you win, or you lose.

4. In the adventure movie, they ran through the forest, fought fierce predators, and stopping the evil villains.

5. Swimming is to my father what gardening was to my grandfather—a healthful hobby.

ANSWERS WITH POSSIBLE CORRECTIONS

1. Driving the sports car is both exhilarating and **relaxing**.

2. In the gym, on the field, and **in** the classroom, Hannah acted like a true champion.

3. Fine as is.

4. In the adventure movie, they ran through the forest, fought fierce predators, and **stopped** the evil villains.

5. Fine as is.

Modifier Placement

Place descriptions in logical spots in the sentence so that the object of discussion is clear. Clarify vague or dangling modifiers.

Incorrect	Correct*
The student's work was subpar, not complete all the requirements.	The student's work was subpar, **because he did** not complete all the requirements.
My friend pensively enjoyed his dinner, chewing quietly.	My friend, **chewing quietly,** pensively enjoyed his dinner.
Once the movie was over, unsatisfied about the ending was I.	Once the movie was over, **I was** unsatisfied about the ending.
When driving through the city, many pedestrians jaywalked.	**Many pedestrians jaywalked when I was** driving through the city.
Michael Jordan is regarded as the best basketball player of all time, winner of 6 World Championships.	Michael Jordan, **winner of 6 World Championships,** is regarded as the best basketball player of all time.
After eating the whole pizza, ready to take a nap was John.	**After he ate the whole pizza, John was ready to take a nap.** (This places "John" in a more logical spot.)
About to get out of bed, the covers were removed.	About to get out of bed, **he removed the covers.** (This clarifies who was ready to get out of bed.)

*These sentences can be fixed in multiple ways.

PRACTICE

Make changes to each sentence, if needed, to make the modifiers clear.

1. Almost, the writer finished all the pages of the manuscript.

2. When swimming through the lake, a giant fish was seen jumping.

3. Although only a short book, Sam found *Animal Farm* tough to finish.

4. Upon receiving the notice of losing his job, the desk was cleared.

5. The brand new phone was covered under the cell phone plan I found online, which cost only $30.

ANSWERS WITH POSSIBLE CORRECTIONS

1. The writer finished **almost** all the pages of the manuscript. (Put "almost" next to "all the pages" so there is no doubt that the sentence is referring to the pages, not to the writer herself or to the act of finishing.)

2. When swimming through the lake, **I saw a giant fish jumping.** (This clarifies who saw the fish—the fish didn't see itself jumping.)

3. Although only a short book, ***Animal Farm* was tough for Sam to finish.** (The book is *Animal Farm*, not Sam.)

4. Upon receiving the notice of losing his job, **he cleared his desk.** (This clarifies who is clearing the desk.)

5. The brand new phone, **which cost only $30,** was covered under the cell phone plan I found online. (Clarify that the phone costs $30—"online" wouldn't make sense to be $30.)

Logical Comparisons

Make sure that the sentence compares the correct number and types of things so that the comparison is logical.

Incorrect	Correct*
Your locker is always neater than me.	Your locker is always neater than **mine.** (Compare a locker to a locker, not a locker to a person.)
The president of the steel company is more qualified than the computer company.	The president of the steel company is more qualified than **the president of** the computer company. (Compare a president to a president, not a president to a company.)
My sister is better than everybody at solving differential equations.	My sister is better than everybody **else** at solving differential equations. (Clarify that the sister is not a part of the group to which she is being compared.)

*These sentences can be fixed in multiple ways.

PRACTICE

Make changes to each sentence, if needed, to make the comparison logical.

1. It is clear that the carnival in my hometown is better than any carnival.

2. Out of everyone in my city, I am better at solving crossword puzzles.

3. Your tires are flatter than John's.

4. The coach of the Tigers is better than the Lions.

5. My résumé is better than any job applicant.

ANSWERS WITH POSSIBLE CORRECTIONS

1. It is clear that the carnival in my hometown is better than any **other** carnival. (Clarify that the hometown carnival is not being compared to itself.)

2. Out of everyone in my city, I am **the best** at solving crossword puzzles. (Since there are certainly at least 3 people in an entire city, use the superlative "best" instead of the comparative "better.")

3. Fine as is. "John's" indicates that the tires belong to John without having to explicitly name them.

4. The coach of the Tigers is better than the **coach of the** Lions. (Compare one coach to another coach. You could also say, "The coach of the Tigers is better than that of the Lions" or " . . . better than the Lions'.")

5. My résumé is better than **that of** any **other** job applicant. (Clarify that the résumé is being compared to the individual résumés of other job applicants and that the writer is not comparing his own résumé to itself.)

Coordination and Subordination

Parts of sentences must coordinate and subordinate. In other words, the parts of sentences must be joined by logical connecting words.

Incorrect	Correct*
The newspaper delivery didn't come, and we watched television news.	The newspaper delivery didn't come, **so** we watched television news.
She finished her homework, she is going to play video games.	**Since** she finished her homework, she is going to play video games.
Mary loves to go for bike rides, and she loves the wind rushing through her hair.	Mary loves to go for bike rides, **for** she loves the wind rushing through her hair.

*These sentences can be fixed in multiple ways.

PRACTICE

Make changes to each sentence, if needed, to make the sentence have proper coordination and subordination.

1. He either told the truth, and he told a lie.

2. The forecast was for sunshine, you should still have an umbrella.

3. Rather than buying a new watch, she should fix the one she has.

4. The alarm goes off, it makes a loud sound.

5. The weather was fine; it snowed, nor hailed.

ANSWERS WITH POSSIBLE CORRECTIONS

1. He either told the truth **or** told a lie. ("Either" and "or" go together.)

2. **Even if** the forecast was for sunshine, you should still have an umbrella.

3. Fine as is.

4. **Whenever** the alarm goes off, it makes a loud sound.

5. The weather was fine; it **neither** snowed nor hailed. (Neither goes with nor.)

Verb Use and Tense

This table summarizes some of the basic conjugation patterns of verbs.

Past	Present	Future
He was	He is	He will
They were	They are	They will
She tasted	She tastes	She will taste
We washed	We wash	We will wash
Past Perfect	**Present Perfect**	**Future Perfect**
I had been	I have been	I will have been
They had been	They have been	They will have been
She had tasted	She has tasted	She will have tasted
We had washed	We have washed	They will have washed

Although many verbs follow a simple pattern, quite a few verbs have irregular conjugations, particularly for the past and past perfect forms. These irregular verbs are often called "strong" verbs since they form a past tense without the aid of the "-ed" ending as with "weak" verbs. This table shows a sampling of irregular verbs you might encounter.

Common Irregular Verbs

Present Tense (I am)	Past Tense (I was)	Past Participle (What comes after "have" in the present perfect; I have been)
Become	Became	Become
Begin	Began	Begun
Bring	Brought	Brought
Choose	Chose	Chosen
Do	Did	Done
Draw	Drew	Drawn
Drink	Drank	Drunk
Drive	Drove	Driven
Fly	Flew	Flown
Get	Got	Gotten
Go	Went	Gone
Grow	Grew	Grown
Have	Had	Had
Hear	Heard	Heard
Know	Knew	Known
Lay (i.e., place)	Laid	Laid
Lead	Led	Led
Lie (i.e., recline)	Lay	Lain
Light	Lit	Lit
Ride	Rode	Ridden
Ring	Rang	Rung
Rise	Rose	Risen
Run	Ran	Run
See	Saw	Seen
Shine	Shone	Shone
Show	Showed	Shown
Sing	Sang	Sung
Sink	Sank	Sunk
Swim	Swam	Swum
Swing	Swung	Swung
Take	Took	Taken
Wake	Woke	Woken
Wear	Wore	Worn

Be sure that the tense, mood, and voice of all verbs are properly used.

Incorrect	Correct*
In the 19th century, Phillip has been a naval officer before he becomes a pirate.	In the 19th century, Phillip had been a naval officer before he became a pirate. (This was in the 19th century, so it took place in the past. Use the past perfect, "had been," to indicate that an event preceded another past event, "became.")
The gift was purchased by you.	You purchased the gift. (Use active voice rather than passive voice.)
If he was winning, he would be much more satisfied.	If he were winning, he would be much more satisfied. (Use the subjunctive mood to indicate situations that are contrary to fact.)

*These sentences can be fixed in multiple ways.

PRACTICE

Make changes to each sentence, if needed, to correct the verb use.

1. If I was able to type more quickly, I would already be done with my assignment.

2. Three years ago, she went on vacation and visits her relatives.

3. My requirement is that everyone is punctual.

4. Before he won the Olympics, he had been practicing for years.

5. The contest was won by the team.

ANSWERS WITH POSSIBLE CORRECTIONS

1. If I **were** able to type more quickly, I would already be done with my assignment. (Use the subjunctive mood to demonstrate that this is contrary to fact.)

2. Three years ago, she went on vacation and **visited** her relatives. (Put everything in the past tense for consistency.)

3. My requirement is that everyone **be** punctual. (This is expressing a demand, so use "be" rather than "is.")

4. Fine as is. It states what happened at a particular moment in the past (winning the Olympics), followed by mentioning what was done over a span of time beforehand (practicing for years).

5. **The team won the contest.** (Use active voice, not passive voice.)

Singular and Plural Agreement

Matching subjects and verbs would be easy if they were always placed next to one another. On the SAT, determining correct number agreement among nouns, pronouns, adjectives, and verbs will often be challenging. The following table includes some examples.

Incorrect	Correct*
The pilot who has flown many planes are captaining our flight.	The pilot who has flown many planes is captaining our flight. ("Pilot" is the singular subject.)
Either the table or the chair need to be fixed.	Either the table or the chair needs to be fixed. (When using "either . . . or," treat each item in the pair as a unique object. In this case, each item will be fixed separately.)
The union of carpenters advocate for better pay.	The union of carpenters advocates for better pay. (The subject is the singular group "union" not the "carpenters.")
Each person need to perform their best if we are going to succeed.	Each person needs to perform his or her best if we are going to succeed. (The sentence refers to each person individually. Collective words like "each," "anyone," and "everybody" are singular.)
Every dress for the bridesmaids were the same.	Every dress for the bridesmaids was the same. (This is another example of a collective word. "Every" is referring to each dress by itself, so a singular verb is needed.)
If you need to find a book, one should seek assistance from a librarian.	If you need to find a book, you should seek assistance from a librarian. (Keep the pronouns consistent. The sentence could also be changed to "If one needs to find a book, one should.")
Andy and Tanner were thrilled to drive on his boat.	Andy and Tanner were thrilled to drive on Andy's boat. (The pronoun "his" is vague. The pronoun needs to be clarified so we know whose boat it is.)

*These sentences can be fixed in multiple ways.

PRACTICE

Correct the sentence—not all sentences need to be fixed. There are multiple ways the sentences can be completed. So when you are reviewing the solutions, make sure that you at least understand why the given solution is correct.

1. Anyone who assembles comic book collections probably enjoy superheroes.

2. A gathering of the wise sages are taking place in the castle.

3. The flock of geese have 30 birds.

4. How many cookies is there in the jar?

5. If one wishes to find a good job, you should work on your networking skills.

6. The secretary general of the United Nations were well-respected in the international community.

7. Will the guy who forgot their microscope in the lab please pick it up later?

8. A charcoal grill—considered by many a staple of summer cooking—is what I use to cook hamburgers.

9. Jennifer and Debby couldn't wait to go see her new dog.

10. Because it is not provided at the testing center, a watch and a snack are two things you should take with you.

ANSWERS WITH POSSIBLE CORRECTIONS

1. Anyone who assembles comic book collections probably **enjoys** superheroes. ("Anyone" is a singular collective word.)

2. A gathering of the wise sages **is** taking place in the castle. ("Gathering" is singular.)

3. The flock of geese **has** 30 birds. ("Flock" is singular.)

4. How many cookies **are** there in the jar? ("Cookies" is plural.)

5. If **you wish** to find a good job, you should work on your networking skills. (Be consistent in the use of either "you" or "one." Either would work in this sentence as long as it is done consistently.)

6. The secretary general of the United Nations **was** well-respected in the international community. ("Secretary" is singular.)

7. Will the guy who forgot **his** microscope in the lab please pick it up later? ("His" is needed to match up with "guy.")

8. Fine as is. "Grill" matches with "is."

9. Jennifer and Debby couldn't wait to go see **Jennifer's** new dog. (Either "Jennifer's" or "Debby's" would be fine. The "her" is unclear, so a specific name is needed.)

10. Because **they are** not provided at the testing center, a watch and a snack are two things you should take with you. (Be sure you look at the entire sentence before jumping to a conclusion. "A watch and a snack" is plural and needs "they" to refer to it.)

Diction (Proper Wording)

The SAT will assess your abilities to distinguish between commonly confused words and to recognize proper idiomatic expressions. This table clarifies the correct usage of many commonly confused words.

Confused Words	General Rules	Examples of Proper Use
Accept vs. Except	*accept*: receive *except*: excluding	My teacher will <u>accept</u> my work, <u>except</u> when it is late.
Affect vs. Effect	*affect:* typically a verb *effect*: typically a noun	The biggest <u>effect</u> of the policy was how it <u>affected</u> immigration.
Allude vs. Elude	*allude:* indirectly refer to *elude*: escape from	The novelist <u>alluded</u> to how the robber could <u>elude</u> the police.
Amount vs. Number	*amount:* usually not countable *number*: usually countable	It took a great <u>amount</u> of courage to round up the necessary <u>number</u> of votes.
Beside vs. Besides	*beside:* next to *besides:* in addition to	<u>Besides</u> riding the roller coaster, I am going to ride the carousel <u>beside</u> the park entrance.
Between vs. Among	*between*: comparing one thing at a time, typically just two objects *among*: comparing nondistinct items or comparing three or more objects	Keeping this <u>between</u> you and me, I think she has <u>among</u> the most lovely smiles I have ever seen. ("You" and "me" are mentioned one at a time, whereas "smiles" is not mentioning the individual smiles.)
Choose vs. Chose	*choose*: present tense *chose*: past tense	After I <u>chose</u> poorly last time I went to the restaurant, I will be much more careful what I <u>choose</u> today.
Complement vs. Compliment	*complement*: complete something *compliment*: flattery	When the coach recognized how my skills <u>complemented</u> those of my teammates, she gave me a very nice <u>compliment</u>.
Elicit vs. Illicit	*elicit*: evoke or obtain *illicit*: illegal	The detective tried to <u>elicit</u> information from the witnesses about the <u>illicit</u> activity in their neighborhood.

Confused Words	General Rules	Examples of Proper Use
Have vs. Of	*have*: verb (action word) *of*: preposition (connecting word)	I would <u>have</u>. **NOT** "I would <u>of</u>."
I vs. Me	*I*: subject *me*: object	I love it when my friend talks to <u>me</u>.
Its vs. It's	*its*: possession *it's*: "it is"	It's important that when you purchase a phone, you are certain to check <u>its</u> warranty.
Less/much vs. Fewer/many	*less/much*: usually not countable *fewer/many*: usually countable	There is <u>less</u> anger and <u>much</u> contentment. There are <u>fewer</u> criminals and <u>many</u> law-abiding citizens.
Lie vs. Lay	*lie*: recline (present tense) *lay*: place (present tense)	<u>Lay</u> the pillow on the bed before you <u>lie</u> down to go to sleep.
Lose vs. Loose	*lose*: suffer a loss *loose*: not tight fitting	If your pants are too <u>loose</u>, you may <u>lose</u> your wallet.
Principal vs. Principle	*principal*: high-ranking person or primary *principle*: rule or belief	Our high school <u>principal</u> is very serious about following his <u>principles</u>.
Than vs. Then	*than*: for comparisons *then*: for time	I had more time back <u>then</u> but less time <u>than</u> I probably will have next year.
There vs. Their vs. They're	*there*: place *their*: possession *they're*: "they are"	When we travel over <u>there</u> to our friends' house, <u>their</u> hospitality is remarkable. In fact, <u>they're</u> the best hosts I know.
To vs. Too vs. Two	*to*: connecting preposition *two*: number *too*: comparisons	Go <u>to</u> the store, buy <u>two</u> apples, and be sure they aren't <u>too</u> old.
Your vs. You're	*your*: possession *you're*: "you are"	<u>You're</u> on the way to <u>your</u> house.
Which vs. That	*which*: nonrestrictive (extra information) *that*: restrictive (essential information)	The house <u>that</u> was on fire burned to the ground, <u>which</u> was unfortunate.

Confused Words	General Rules	Examples of Proper Use
Who vs. Whom	*who*: subject *whom*: object (use "who" when you would use "he," and use "whom" when you would use "him")	<u>Who</u> is going to the movie? From <u>whom</u> did you purchase the ticket?
Whose vs. Who's	*whose*: possession *who's*: "who is"	<u>Who's</u> going to determine <u>whose</u> bike that is?
Your vs. You're	*your*: possession *you're*: "you are"	<u>You're</u> very nice; you must have learned that from <u>your</u> parents.

The following is a list of common idiomatic expressions.

at a high rate	in advance	in opposition to
at the outset	in agony	in origin
at a disadvantage	in bulk	in other words
at all costs	in character	in particular
at any rate	in charge of	in practice
at least	in code	in preparation for
at length	in collaboration with	in principle
at play	in command of	in private
at the beginning	in common	in public
at the expense of	in conclusion	in pursuit of
at times	in confidence	in quantity
at work	in confusion	in question
by all means	in conjunction with	in reality
by chance	in connection with	in recognition of
by check	in contact with	in relation to
by definition	in contrast to	in reply to
by force	in fear of	in reserve
by hand	in contrast with	in residence
by mistake	in control of	in response to
by no means	in danger	in retrospect
by process of	in demand	in return
by request	in detail	in secret
by surprise	in doubt	in self-defense
by way of	in effect	in silence
for a change	in error	in suspense
for certain	in essence	in tears
for granted	in exchange for	in terms of
for hire	in existence	in the absence of
for lack of	in fact	in the course of
for the good of	in fairness	in the event of
for the sake of	in favor of	in the interests of
from experience	in general	in the lead
from memory	in good faith	in the making
in a hurry	in memory of	in the mood for
in abundance	in mind	in the name of
in addition to	in moderation	in the wrong

in theory	on file	to an extent
in time for	on fire	to date
in trouble	on good terms	to excess
in tune with	on hand	to the satisfaction of
in turmoil	on impulse	under consideration
in turn	on leave	under cover of
in vain	on loan	under discussion
in view of	on no account	under pressure
of the opinion	on occasion	under strain
on the record	on order	under stress
on a trip	on purpose	with regard to
on a regular basis	on reflection	within reason
on account of	on the move	within limits
on average	out of context	without delay
on behalf of	out of duty	without fail
on board	out of order	without precedent
on display	out of the question	without question

PRACTICE

Choose the better option based on the context of the sentence.

1. Pigs [(A) that or (B) which] fly are a rare occurrence.

2. My mother was [(A) of or (B) in] the opinion that my art project was amazing.

3. [(A) Between or (B) Among] all the people in our city, she was chosen to carry the Olympic torch.

4. Mind [(A) your or (B) you're] manners when you take someone on a date.

5. I am going to [(A) lie or (B) lay] my teddy bear down in bed next to me before I take a nap.

6. When spring break comes, my friends and I are going [(A) on or (B) in] a trip.

7. At the oil change, my car needs [(A) its or (B) it's] brake fluid checked.

8. From [(A) who or (B) whom] did you receive that award?

9. The doctor was [(A) under or (B) within] stress before the major transplant operation.

10. My alarm clock has a louder sound [(A) then or (B) than] my cellphone timer.

ANSWERS

1. (A) that
2. (A) of
3. (B) Among
4. (A) your
5. (B) lay

6. (A) on
7. (A) its
8. (B) whom
9. (A) under
10. (B) than

PUNCTUATION

The old SAT had very little focus on punctuation—on the new SAT, it is highly emphasized. Although there are many specific punctuation rules, the most important guidelines for the grammar tested on the SAT are given in the tables that follow.

Commas

General Guideline	Appropriate Use
Separate a phrase (dependent clause) from a complete sentence (independent clause).	Once you have completed your homework, you may watch your favorite television show.
Join two complete sentences when there is a transitional word, like the "FANBOYS": *for, and, nor, but, or, yet,* and *so.*	The shark seemed excited about all the fish in the water, but the scuba divers were worried about all the activity.
Separate extra information (parenthetical phrases) from the rest of the sentence.	My history textbook, which I have had since the beginning of the year, occupies a special shelf in my locker.
Separate items in a list with commas.*	My favorite forms of punctuation include commas, semicolons, and dashes.
Do not use commas to separate parts of a sentence if everything in the sentence is needed to make it clear and logical.	A car that is speeding away from the police poses a danger to the community. (In this case, you must specify that a speeding car is the type of car that is a danger to the community. So a comma must not be used.)
Just because a sentence is long does not mean that it needs a comma. Look more at the structure of the sentence than at its length.	The European Organization for Nuclear research has used its world-class particle accelerators to make significant strides in particle physics.
A clarifying phrase (appositive) needs to be separated with commas. The name is sufficient to know who the person is, so commas are needed to separate the description. If the description is too vague to narrow down the item precisely, then no commas should separate descriptive phrases.	George Washington, the first President of the United States, has the U.S. capital named after him. (Alternatively, consider a sentence like this: *"President George Washington was elected."* The title "President" is not specific enough to narrow it down. However, the title "first President of the United States" is specific enough in the example above, so this phrase needs to be separated.)

*The SAT has traditionally preferred the serial or "Oxford" comma (i.e., having a comma between the second-to-last and last items in a list). Since there is not a universally accepted rule about whether the serial comma should be used, it is extremely unlikely that the SAT would include a test question about it.

PRACTICE

Insert commas as needed.

1. It is impossible to dust the shelves vacuum the floor and clean the windows in time for the party.

2. Ashley who is a big fan of comic books loved watching the latest action movie.

3. The man who lives in the apartment above me makes quite a bit of noise when he walks around.

4. Yes I would be happy to help.

5. The buckeye tree the state tree of Ohio can grow as tall as 60 feet.

6. While surfing the Internet John found that Sprinkles his missing pet cat had been found in a nearby city.

7. Reading the newspaper will help you become up to speed on current events.

8. When I go backpacking I will hike through Maine New Hampshire and Vermont.

9. I was responsible for making the huge mess so I cleaned it up.

10. Although he did not study for very long he still managed to do quite well on the quiz.

ANSWERS

1. It is impossible to dust the shelves, vacuum the floor, and clean the windows in time for the party. (Separate the three different items with commas.)

2. Ashley, who is a big fan of comic books, loved watching the latest action movie. (Since the subject, "Ashley," is already clear, the phrase "who is a big fan of comic books" can be set aside with commas.)

3. The man who lives in the apartment above me makes quite a bit of noise when he walks around. (No commas are needed because the phrase "who lives in the apartment above me" is essential to identifying the man.)

4. Yes, I would be happy to help. (A small break is needed after an introductory word like this.)

5. The buckeye tree, the state tree of Ohio, can grow as tall as 60 feet. (The phrase "the state tree of Ohio" could be removed and still leave a fully functional sentence. The phrase gives extra information and can therefore be set aside.)

6. While surfing the Internet, John found that Sprinkles, his missing pet cat, had been found in a nearby city. (Separate the introductory phrase from the rest of the sentence with a comma, and separate the clarification of "Sprinkles" with commas. The cat has already been clearly identified by name, so the description can be set apart.)

7. Reading the newspaper will help you become up to speed on current events. (No commas are needed because the phrase "Reading the newspaper" acts as the subject and because "become up to speed on current events" gives a complete, unified description

of what will happen if you read the paper. Nothing extra can be set aside in this sentence.)

8. When I go backpacking, I will hike through Maine, New Hampshire, and Vermont. (The introductory phrase "When I go backpacking" needs to be separated from the complete sentence (independent clause) that immediately follows. Also, the names of the states need to be separated from one another as they are listed as three unique items.)

9. I was responsible for making the huge mess, so I cleaned it up. (The comma is used to provide a break before the FANBOYS words when they provide transitions between two complete sentences—"so" is one of these words.)

10. Although he did not study for very long, he still managed to do quite well on the quiz. (The comma provides a break between the introductory dependent clause and the independent clause that follows.)

Semicolons

General Guideline	Appropriate Use
You can use a semicolon to separate two complete, related sentences.	I am excited to go to the amusement park; I can't wait to ride the big roller coaster.
Use a semicolon to separate items in a list when at least one of the items has a comma or commas within it.	John's rock band traveled to New York, Boston, and Hartford in the Northeast; Chicago, Columbus, and Cleveland in the Midwest; and Orlando, Charleston, and Birmingham in the South.

PRACTICE

Insert a semicolon or semicolons where needed.

1. I love to play basketball it is my favorite sport.

2. When you go shopping, please buy sugar, flour, and butter at the grocery antacid, bandages, and a thermometer at the pharmacy and a hammer, a screwdriver, and some sandpaper from the hardware store.

3. When you pick up the phone, be sure that you have turned off the music.

4. Mitchell wrote an excellent poem he had it published in a journal.

5. As the human resources officer was immersed in making changes to the employee manual, he neglected to enforce the polices already on the books.

ANSWERS

1. I love to play basketball; it is my favorite sport. (Separate the two independent clauses, i.e., complete sentences, with the semicolon so that it is not a run-on sentence. Keep in mind that a period, dash, or comma with a transitional word such as "because" could work here as well.)

2. When you go shopping, please buy sugar, flour, and butter at the grocery; antacid, bandages, and a thermometer at the pharmacy; and a hammer, a screwdriver, and some sandpaper from the hardware store. (Since the listed items have commas within them, use semicolons to separate each major item so that the sentence is clear.)

3. When you pick up the phone, be sure that you have turned off the music. (A semicolon is not needed here since there is a dependent clause before the comma, i.e., not a complete sentence, and an independent clause, i.e., complete sentence, after the comma.)

4. Mitchell wrote an excellent poem; he had it published in a journal. (The two independent clauses need to be separated with strong punctuation. A period, dash, or comma with a transitional word like "so" could work here as well.)

5. As the human resources officer was immersed in making changes to the employee manual, he neglected to enforce the polices already on the books. (Although this is a long sentence, its structure is a dependent clause before the comma and an independent clause after the comma. So it does not need a semicolon.)

Colons

General Guideline	Appropriate Use
Use a colon after a complete sentence to set off a list.	When you go to the store, please pick up the following items: soap, gum, and batteries.
Use a colon after a complete sentence to set off a clarification.	We were shocked to learn who the true villain in the film was: the seemingly friendly storekeeper.

PRACTICE

Insert a colon where needed.

1. I always put these items into my coffee milk, sugar, and honey.

2. My history teacher brings history to life with stimulating activities, guest speakers, and discussions about controversial topics.

3. Be sure to put the two essential herbs into the pasta basil and oregano.

4. She's been to many interesting places, including Egypt, Brazil, and Vietnam.

5. He finally achieved his goal he was elected president of his class.

ANSWERS

1. I always put these items into my coffee: milk, sugar, and honey. (Put the colon before listing the items. A dash could also work.)

2. My history teacher brings history to life with stimulating activities, guest speakers, and discussions about controversial topics. (Even though there is a list, there is no need for a colon since the word "with" provides the transition into the list.)

3. Be sure to put the two essential herbs into the <u>pasta: basil</u> and oregano. (Put the colon before the clarifying list of what the herbs are. A dash could also work.)

4. She's been to many interesting places, including Egypt, Brazil, and Vietnam. (Even though there is a list, the word "including" provides the transition into it, making a colon unnecessary.)

5. He finally achieved his <u>goal: he</u> was elected president of his class. (Although there must be a complete sentence before a colon, it is also fine to have a complete sentence after it. A semicolon or dash would work here as well.)

Dashes

A dash, —, is longer than a hyphen. In contrast, a hyphen, -, is used to make compound words.

General Guideline	Appropriate Use
Although other punctuation can often work, the dash can provide variety in your writing when you need to indicate an interruption or change of thought.	Be careful when crossing that street—it is not very safe. (In this case, a colon or semicolon could work instead of the dash.)
A dash can be used to interrupt a sentence and provide a change of voice.	We lost the game—hardly a surprise given our terrible effort—but at least our dreadful season was over.
Dashes can set off a parenthetical phrase. If you start with a dash at one end of the phrase, you need to use a dash at the other end for consistency.	Test anxiety—something that affects many students—can be managed by setting realistic expectations for test performance.

PRACTICE

Insert a dash or dashes where needed.

1. To do well on the SAT, be sure to work on improving several key skills reading comprehension, quantitative reasoning, and essay editing.

2. Some of the best things in life sunshine, fresh air, and starlit nights are completely free.

3. Authenticity in your college application essay is vital demonstrate originality in your writing and in your thought process.

4. As you read the textbook, pay close attention to the details that your teacher may ask about on the upcoming quiz.

5. Now that we have *finally* arrived at our hotel take a deep breath we can finally go for a swim!

ANSWERS

1. To do well on the SAT, be sure to work on improving several key <u>skills—reading</u> comprehension, quantitative reasoning, and essay editing. (The dash gives a long pause before the list of the skills. A colon would work as well.)

2. Some of the best things in <u>life—sunshine, fresh air, and starlit nights—are</u> completely free. (The dashes set aside a parenthetical phrase.)

3. Authenticity in your college application essay is <u>vital—demonstrate</u> originality in your writing and in your thought process. (The dash gives a long pause between the two complete sentences. A semicolon would work well too.)

4. As you read the textbook, pay close attention to the details that your teacher may ask about on the upcoming quiz. (There is no need for a dash in this sentence. The comma provides a pause after the introductory phrase, and the independent clause "pay close . . . quiz" does not need any interruption.)

5. Now that we have *finally* arrived at our <u>hotel—take a deep breath—we</u> can finally go for a swim! (The dashes set aside a sudden change of thought.)

Apostrophes

General Guideline	Appropriate Use
Use an apostrophe before the "s" to indicate that a singular entity possesses something.	The toy's instructions were rather confusing.
Use an apostrophe after the "s" to indicate that a plural entity possesses something.	All players' equipment must be within the rules.
Use an apostrophe to indicate a contraction with pronouns (they're, it's, you're, who's) and no apostrophe to indicate possession (their, its, your, whose).	It's a good idea to talk to your doctor if you're concerned that friends shared their cold when you visited them. No matter whose cold it was, they're going to be glad that you found out if you show its symptoms. Who's going to argue with that?
Use an apostrophe before the "s" to indicate possession after a noun that is already plural.	The women's restroom is next to the men's.

PRACTICE

Pick which option is correct.

1. (A) <u>Your</u> or (B) <u>You're</u> actions speak louder than words.

2. Three (A) <u>pig's</u> or (B) <u>pigs'</u> houses were attacked by the wolf.

3. (A) <u>Oranges'</u> or (B) <u>Oranges</u> are a delicious fruit for juice.

4. Chris had no trouble fixing the (A) <u>computer's</u> or (B) <u>computers'</u> screen.

5. The (A) <u>children's</u> or (B) <u>childrens'</u> playground had some enormous slides and swings.

6. My (A) <u>cats</u> or (B) <u>cat's</u> nails need to be trimmed.

7. (A) <u>Who's</u> or (B) <u>Whose</u> responsible for telling me who is coming to the meeting?

8. One of the simplest forms of poker is (A) <u>five-card</u> or (B) <u>five-cards'</u> draw.

9. (A) <u>Its</u> or (B) <u>It's</u> a great afternoon to read a good book.

10. (A) <u>Caitlin and Hannahs'</u> or (B) <u>Caitlin's and Hannah's</u> individual résumés were both impressive.

ANSWERS

1. **(A) <u>Your</u>** actions speak louder than words. (Show possession since the "actions" belong to "you.")

2. Three **(B) <u>pigs'</u>** houses were attacked by the wolf. (There are three pigs, so make the possession plural by placing the apostrophe after "pigs.")

3. **(B) <u>Oranges</u>** are a delicious fruit for juice. (There is no need for an apostrophe here, as "Oranges" is the subject of the sentence. This word is not showing possession.)

4. Chris had no trouble fixing the **(A) <u>computer's</u>** screen. (It is a singular computer given that it says "screen" later on, so use an apostrophe followed by an "s" to demonstrate possession.)

5. The **(A) <u>children's</u>** playground had some enormous slides and swings. (Since "children" is already plural, use an apostrophe followed by an "s" to indicate possession.)

6. My **(B) <u>cat's</u>** nails need to be trimmed. (The cat possesses its nails, so an apostrophe is needed.)

7. **(A) <u>Who's</u>** responsible for telling me who is coming to the meeting? (Use the contraction "who's" since this is the same as "who is.")

8. One of the simplest forms of poker is **(A) <u>five-card</u>** draw. (There is no need for apostrophes here since "five-card" indicates a description, not a possession.)

9. **(B) <u>It's</u>** a great afternoon to read a good book. ("It's" stands in for "it is," which is what this sentence requires.)

10. **(B) <u>Caitlin's and Hannah's</u>** individual résumés were both impressive. (This is a tricky one. Since Caitlin and Hannah have individual résumés, the individual ownership of their respective résumés needs to be established. So, put an apostrophe and an "s" after each name.)

A totally new part of the SAT Writing and Language Test will be the analysis of graphs. You can expect that a few questions will assess your ability to determine what claims can be made based on the information in a graph. The graphs can take a variety of forms—several possible presentations are given below. When you encounter graph analysis questions, keep these tips in mind:

- These questions will be about your quantitative reasoning, not about your mastery of grammar.
- Look carefully at the key/legend, axis labels, and units. Allow yourself enough time to become acquainted with the graph's organization.
- Since the questions will usually ask you to pick an accurate interpretation of the graph, take a glance at what the choices are generally stating so that you have a feel for what they are after. Then, as best as you can, try to come up with an answer of your own before jumping to a given answer.

PRACTICE

Determine whether the following claims are supported or not supported based on the information in the graph.

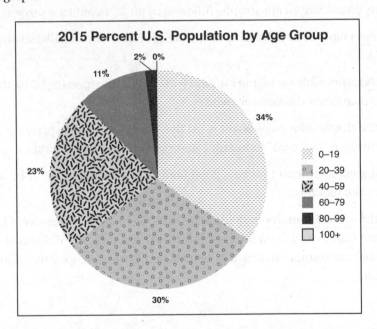

Source: *http://www.census.gov/population/international/data/worldpop/tool_population.php*

1. *Supported or NOT Supported*: The majority of the 2015 U.S. population is under 40 years of age.

2. *Supported or NOT Supported*: It is about three times as likely that a randomly selected U.S. citizen is in his or her 40s or 50s as it is that he or she is in his or her 60s or 70s.

3. *Supported or NOT Supported*: Women represent a slight minority of the overall U.S. population.

1. Supported. Adding the 0–19 age group and the 20–39 age group gives us 34% + 30% for a total of 64%, which is clearly a majority of the population.

2. NOT Supported. 40–59 year olds represent 23% of the population, and 60–79 year olds represent 11% of the population. 23 is not three times 11. Instead, 23 is closer to twice 11, making this claim incorrect.

3. NOT Supported. The graph gives information only about the relative percentages of age groups. No information is given about gender breakdown. So this claim cannot be justified based on the information in the graph.

PRACTICE

Determine whether the following claims are supported or not supported based on the information in the graph.

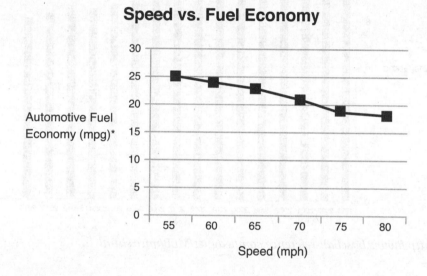

Speed vs. Fuel Economy

Source: *http://www.mpgforspeed.com*

1. *Supported or NOT Supported*: Automotive speed and fuel economy, when considering speeds between 55 and 80 miles per hour, have an inverse relationship.

2. *Supported or NOT Supported*: An increase in wind speed causes a proportional decrease in fuel efficiency because of an increase in wind resistance and friction.

3. *Supported or NOT Supported*: A car like one tested by the researchers who made this graph will likely have a fuel efficiency of approximately 22 miles per gallon at a speed of approximately 77 miles per hour.

ANSWERS

1. Supported. The graph shows a steady decline in fuel efficiency as automotive speed increases, making for an inverse relationship.

2. NOT Supported. Although this is an accurate scientific statement, it is outside the scope of the information presented in the graph. So the graph cannot make an accurate claim about the statement.

3. NOT Supported. Read the statement closely—if it had said 67 miles per hour instead of 77, the statement would be correct. At 77 miles per hour, the fuel efficiency is close to 18 miles per gallon.

PRACTICE

Determine whether the following claims are supported or not supported based on the information in the graph.

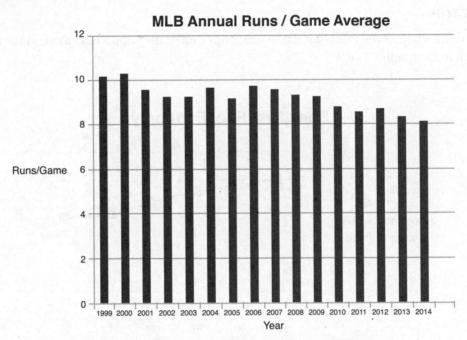

Source: *http://www.baseball-reference.com/leagues/MLB/misc.shtml*

1. *Supported or NOT Supported*: Between 2012 and 2014, there was approximately a 20 percent decrease in the average runs per game in Major League Baseball.

2. *Supported or NOT Supported*: There was a steady decline in the average runs per game in Major League Baseball from 1999 to 2014.

3. *Supported or NOT Supported*: From 1999 to 2014, the average runs per game in Major League Baseball declined by approximately one-fifth.

ANSWERS

1. NOT Supported. There is only a half of a run decrease on average during this span, which does not approach a 20 percent decrease.

2. NOT Supported. Although there is an overall decline, the decline is not steady—it goes up a bit in the mid-2000s before going down again.

3. Supported. It decreases from approximately 10 to approximately 8, making a decrease of 10 − 8 = 2, which is one-fifth of the original amount of 10.

PRACTICE

Determine whether the following claims are supported or not supported based on the information in the graph.

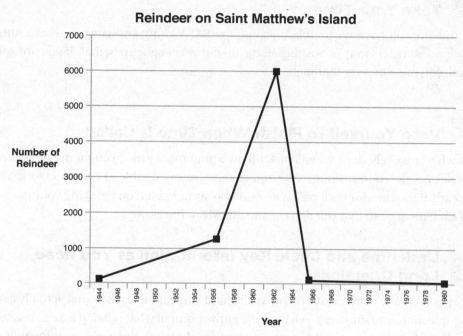

Reindeer on Saint Matthew's Island

Source: *http://www.gi.alaska.edu/AlaskaScienceForum/article/when-reindeer-paradise-turned-purgatory*

1. *Supported or NOT Supported*: An increase in human habitation on Saint Matthew's Island caused the decline in reindeer population between 1963 and 1980.

2. *Supported or NOT Supported*: Between 1957 and 1963, the increase in reindeer population on Saint Matthew's Island was more than fourfold.

3. *Supported or NOT Supported*: In 1974, there were definitely no reindeer on Saint Matthew's Island.

ANSWERS

1. NOT Supported. Nothing in the graph gives us any information about human habitation, so we cannot make this conclusion.

2. Supported. The value in 1957 is around 1,300–1,400, and the value in 1963 is a little over 6,000. So the increase was more than fourfold since 1,350 × 4 = 5,400, and 6,000 is greater than 5,400.

3. NOT Supported. 1974 is not one of the five labeled points on the graph. So although we can estimate the number of reindeer, we cannot make an accurate statement about the exact number of reindeer on the island at that time.

STRATEGY

1 Take Your Time

Most students will have no trouble finishing the SAT Writing and Language test. Although your fellow test takers may be rushing along, do not get caught up in that. If you are going to edit well, you must be very thorough.

STRATEGY

2 Pace Yourself to Finish When Time Is Called

It is much more likely that you will pick up on a grammar issue if you do the questions one time well as opposed to rushing to the end so that you can double-check your work. You will have nearly 9 minutes for each passage—you may want to plan on checking your pace at the end of each passage so that you don't go too quickly or too slowly.

STRATEGY

3 Underline and Circle Key Information as You Read Long Questions

If you miss even one word on one of the writing and language questions that actually asks you a direct question, you may very well miss the entire point of what is being asked. Take advantage of the fact that you can write all over the test. So underline and circle anything that seems especially important as you read through the questions.

STRATEGY

4 Try to "Hear" as You Read by Silently Mouthing Things

One of the best ways to edit a paper is to hear what is written as opposed to reading it only visually. Mouthing what is written will help you pick up on a variety of things, such as necessary pauses for punctuation, parallel phrasing, and proper idiom usage. Hearing the words will help you tap into your intuitive knowledge about what *sounds right* in the English language. You simply need to answer the question correctly; there is no need to justify why you have chosen your answer. Do be careful that while hearing it, you are not too casual in your tone. The SAT Writing and Language test will be more formal, so the style may at times differ from the way you may talk informally. For example, "I knew it was she" is correct while "I knew it was her" is not. While the writing you find will be more formal, it will not be stuffy. For example, you should say, "The teacher tried to stop the fight," as opposed to "The teacher endeavored to terminate the belligerence."

STRATEGY

5 Think About the Meaning

Many writing errors involve small-scale issues, like punctuation and subject-verb agreement. Other errors will involve large-scale issues, like conforming to a given writing objective or making an appropriate transition. As a result, it is essential that you focus not only on looking for minor grammar errors but also carefully consider how you can make the meaning of what is written as logical as possible. The SAT Writing and Language test is more about *editing* than just *proofreading*, so be sure you consider the big picture.

6 Consider Relevant Context

You must consider the context surrounding potential grammar issues to analyze a number of possible problems, such as logical transitions, tense agreement, and tone consistency. Sometimes you may need to read quite a bit beyond what is highlighted in the question so that your answer will be consistent with what follows. When in doubt about whether a selection is consistent with the rest of the passage, take the time to check it out.

7 Consider Reading the Passage Through Once Before Answering the Questions

With nearly 9 minutes per passage and a little under 1 minute per question, you should have plenty of time to work through the problems. Rather than having time at the end of the Writing and Language test to double-check and possibly do nothing, you can instead use your time to read the passage with an eye on its overall flow and meaning. This will enable you to do well on questions involving big-picture analysis of the passage and proper transitions.

8 Try to Create Your Own Answer Before Looking at the Choices

All of the choices on the SAT Writing and Language test will be well written, and many will be quite persuasive. Prior to jumping into the choices, do your best to come up with a general idea of what you think the answer should be. This will put you in control rather than letting the test control you. If you are having trouble developing an idea for an answer, use the differences among the choices to pinpoint the type of error in question. That way, you can at least narrow down your thoughts before making a decision.

9 Do Not Hesitate to Come Back to Questions

If you are having difficulty figuring out the answer to a question, let your subconscious mind take over while you consciously move on to other problems. While you are working through the other problems, your subconscious mind will likely piece together what makes the most sense on the problem you skipped. Then, with fresh eyes, you can come back to the question you previously skipped, and it will likely seem much easier than before.

10 Use Similarities Among the Answers to Eliminate Choices

If you have a multiple-choice question with these choices, what is the answer?

(A) %
(B) %
(C) $
(D) %

The answer is choice (C), because it is different from the other options. Similarly, if you have an SAT Writing and Language question with choices like these,

(A) Additionally
(B) Also
(C) In contrast
(D) Moreover

you can use the similarities among the answers to eliminate possibilities. "Additionally," "also," and "moreover" mean that you are giving further discussion or examples along the same lines as before. However, "in contrast" means you have something that is the opposite of what came previously. So the answer must be choice (C). This technique can be particularly helpful in sorting out wordiness, punctuation, and transitions, among other things. Use this technique as a useful supplement to thinking through the question, not as your primary approach.

 STRATEGY
11 If You Must Guess, Be Smart About It

There is no penalty for guessing on questions as there was in the past. So be certain you have filled in an answer for every question. Instead of picking a random answer, keep the following tips in mind:

- The SAT will often have a few of the same answer choices in a row. Do not avoid picking an answer choice simply because you have used it on the previous question.
- "No Change" has just as much of a chance of being right as do the other options. Do not feel that you must make edits to every single question.
- Once you have made a thoughtful decision, don't second-guess. Read the context, consider the answers carefully, and pick the best option. If you have done these things, be comfortable picking your answer and moving on.

 STRATEGY
12 Realize That These Are Grammar Rules, Not Merely Grammar Preferences

You have likely had a teacher who has had certain "pet peeves" about how you should write your essays. Maybe you have had a teacher who insisted you use only the formal third person voice in your essays; maybe your teacher marked off points for starting sentences with "but" or "because." The SAT does not care about such things. Any issues you encounter will be clear problems. The answers will be based on widespread English practice, not the personal preferences of particular editors. As a result, don't overthink what you encounter on the SAT Writing and Language test.

 STRATEGY
13 Give the SAT the Benefit of the Doubt

The College Board has invested tremendous resources into making the SAT error free. Do not waste time looking for mistakes on the test, because it is <u>extremely</u> unlikely there will be any. Instead, realize that this is a well-crafted assessment that demands you demonstrate your editing skills. The questions are not about whether what is given is true—they are simply about what is grammatically correct. The questions do not have tricks or gimmicks. If you are picking an answer because of some trick (e.g., thinking the SAT always prefers short answers), you will be incorrect. If you pick an answer because it represents well-written English, you will be right.

PUTTING IT ALL TOGETHER

The questions on the SAT Writing and Language test include small-picture questions about punctuation, tense, and wordiness as well as big-picture questions about fine-tuning the structure and logic of the essays. These question types come in a random sequence. For the sake of practice, let's try some small-picture questions in isolation and then some big-picture questions. For the following small-picture questions, make sure you are silently mouthing out the wording, looking at the surrounding context, and thinking about what makes the most sense. Don't rush through these—be very patient and thorough to do your best.

Small-Picture Question Practice

The Romani People

It comes as a rather disturbing ❶ <u>surprise and shock</u> that even in contemporary ethnic dialogue the term "Gypsy" remains in remarkably common employ. Disregarding for the moment the ❷ <u>word's</u> historically contumelious overtones, it has been so broadly misapplied throughout the past several centuries that "Gypsy" now refers to no fewer than eight discrete ethnic groups spread across half of the world. The term itself is seldom used within the migrant communities of Europe; ❸ <u>they are</u> an exonym of English origin, and evolved from the mistaken belief that the nomadic Romani people, who arrived in Britain at the end of the 16th century, had ❹ <u>immigrated</u> from Egypt ("Gypcien" being a dialectical permutation of "Egyptian"). "Gypsy" is a word that signifies not only ignorance but also the ❺ <u>global indifference of the community toward the person of Romani backgrounds.</u>

The perpetuation of the Romani's nomadic lifestyle throughout the centuries ❻ <u>has been</u> integral in preserving their culture. Formal efforts to sedentarize, assimilate and—occasionally—expel or eliminate the Romani have followed them since the Middle Ages and remain prevalent in Europe today. Capturing and enslaving Romani refugees was common practice within the Byzantine Empire and remained technically legal in Moldavia and

1. (A) NO CHANGE
   (B) surprise
   (C) shocking surprise
   (D) OMIT the underlined portion.

2. (A) NO CHANGE
   (B) words
   (C) word is
   (D) words'

3. (A) NO CHANGE
   (B) they were
   (C) it is
   (D) it was

4. (A) NO CHANGE
   (B) integrated
   (C) emanated
   (D) emigrated

5. (A) NO CHANGE
   (B) community of Romani people with indifference toward the global backgrounds.
   (C) indifference of the global community toward the Romani people.
   (D) backgrounds of Romani indifference toward the community of which it is global.

6. (A) NO CHANGE
   (B) have been
   (C) had been
   (D) were

Wallachia up until the unification of Romania in 1859. **7** In, Western Europe, antiziganism, achieved a particular vogue during the mid-18th century. In Austria and Switzerland, Romani were forbidden from owning horses and wagons, wearing traditional Romani clothing, speaking the Romani language, and marrying another person of Romani descent. **8** Just as those in England and Spain, where Romani families were frequently separated by the State and male Romani children were conscripted by the military. Up until 1977, in Norway it was not uncommon for the State to forcibly sterilize Romani immigrants. Most infamously of all, the Romani were among the groups targeted by the Nazis in the Holocaust.

Paradoxically, it may be that the very persecutional precedents that sought to eliminate the Romani were also the forces that encouraged and necessitated **9** their continuous migration, thus obstructing their gradual genetic and cultural assimilation. Today, hostility toward the Romani remains widespread throughout Europe in the **10** form for racism with educational segregation. The Czech Republic in particular has received international criticism for a law passed in 1992 that denied Romani permanent residents Czech citizenship. The law was superficially revised in 1999, **11** also citizenship remains a contentious issue for the Romani. Repatriation raids of Romani encampments in 2005 and 2011 resulted in the deportation of Romani refugees **12** en masse from Germany and France.

7. (A) NO CHANGE
   (B) In Western Europe antiziganism, achieved
   (C) In Western, Europe, antiziganism achieved
   (D) In Western Europe, antiziganism achieved

8. (A) NO CHANGE
   (B) Similar laws were enforced in England and Spain,
   (C) Just like the laws England and Spain,
   (D) Similarly for the English and Spanish laws,

9. (A) NO CHANGE
   (B) they're
   (C) its
   (D) its'

10. (A) NO CHANGE
    (B) form of racism and also by the form of educational segregation.
    (C) racist and educational forming of segregation.
    (D) forms of racism and educational segregation.

11. (A) NO CHANGE
    (B) for
    (C) but
    (D) because

12. (A) NO CHANGE
    (B) in mass
    (C) with mass
    (D) massively

Answers Explained

1. **(B)** Since "surprise" and "shock" mean virtually the same thing, choices (A) and (C) are repetitive. Although one could argue that "shock" has more of a negative connotation than "surprise," the word "disturbing" that comes immediately before this underlined portion already expresses the negativity, making "shock" repetitive. Choice (D) is not correct because without including wording here, the phrase "It comes as a rather disturbing that even" is missing a needed transition or clarification between "disturbing" and "that." Choice (B) is correct because it expresses the intended idea concisely and precisely.

2. **(A)** Determine what the "word" is referring to in order to see if it is singular or plural. Based on the context in the previous sentences, the word in question is "Gypsy," which is just one word. Also, it is showing possession of the word "overtones," so use the singular, possessive form of "word," which is "word's." Choice (B) uses the plural noun form of "word." Choice (C) changes the meaning so it is no longer about possession. Choice (D) is the plural possessive form of "word."

3. **(C)** This is a pronoun agreement question. The pronoun must refer to the earlier "term" mentioned in the sentence, which is singular. So, the pronoun must be "it," making choices (A) and (B) incorrect. The question also involves making the verb tense consistent. Choice (D) is not right because it uses the past tense, which is inconsistent with the present tense used earlier in the sentence.

4. **(D)** This is an example of a commonly confused word problem. When one moves *from* one country, that is called "emigration." When one moves *into* a country, that is called "immigration." The Romani people are described as going from Egypt, so choice (D) works and choice (A) is not. Choice (B) is wrong because to "integrate" means to combine things from parts to a whole, which does not describe the process of leaving a country. Choice (C) is not the answer because although "emanated" means "to emerge or spread out from," it is typically applied to ideas or phenomena (e.g., "the smell emanated" or "happiness emanated"). So "emanated" does not make sense in reference to people leaving a country.

5. **(C)** These choices have virtually the same wording but shift the word order. Choice (C) is correct, because it is the only choice that logically continues the statement made earlier in the sentence, that the word "signifies not only ignorance but also. . . ." It is logical to pair "indifference" with "ignorance," as both are negative attributes. It is not logical to make such a pairing with "community" in choice (B) or with "backgrounds" in choice (D). Choice (A) is not correct because there is not a singular "person" but rather many "people" of Romani backgrounds to which the author refers.

6. **(A)** This question assesses both verb tense and subject-verb agreement. Choice (A) is correct, because the subject of the sentence is "perpetuation," which is singular. Notice the long description of "perpetuation": "of the Romani's nomadic lifestyle throughout the centuries." Be careful not to mistake the words in this descriptive prepositional phrase for the subject of the sentence. Choices (B) and (D) are incorrect, because they require a plural subject. Choice (C) is incorrect, because "had been" is used for something that took place before another past action. The paragraph is discussing long-standing issues that the Romani have faced all the way to the present day. Therefore, the present perfect "has been" is needed instead.

7. **(D)** Comma placement is a major small-picture question on the SAT. If you silently mouth this out, you may be able to detect that a breath is needed between "Europe" and "antiziganism." To be more precise, a comma is needed between these two words because "in Western Europe" functions as an introductory dependent clause, and "antiziganism" begins an independent clause that follows. A comma should be used to separate an introductory dependent clause from an independent clause. Choice (A) places an unneeded break right after "in" and "antiziganism," interrupting the flow of the sentence. Choice (B) places a comma between the subject, "antiziganism," and the verb, "achieved." When the subject and verb are right next to one another like this, do not break them up with a comma. Choice (C) breaks up the unified item "Western Europe" with a comma.

8. **(B)** It is important to be clear when making comparisons so that the reader knows precisely what is being compared. It is also important to use proper prepositions (words like "of," "from," and "to") to connect words. Choice (B) is correct, because it clearly states that the laws were similar. It also uses proper phrasing with the prepositions and other wording. Choice (A) is incorrect because "those" is too vague—this word must be specified so that the comparison is clear. (On questions like this, do not worry about whether the information in the corrections is true—the SAT will assess only the proper grammar and usage. So if a pronoun needs to be clarified, go ahead and use the wording provided by the clarification.) Choice (C) needs an "of" between "laws" and "England." Choice (D) is not right because the commonly accepted phrase is "similar to," not "similarly for."

9. **(A)** Match the pronoun with the word for which it stands. Choice (A) is correct because "their" properly refers to the plural Romani people and their possession of the "continuous migration." Choice (B) is incorrect because "they're" equates to "they are." Choices (C) and (D) are not right because "the Romani people" is plural, not singular. Also, be mindful that "its'" will always be incorrect—the correct possessive form of "it" is "its."

10. **(D)** Make sure that words agree in terms of singular and plural number. Choice (D) is correct because it clarifies that there are plural "forms" of both "racism" and "educational segregation." Choice (A) is not right because the proper expression is "form of," not "form for." Choice (B) is incorrect because the word "also" is unnecessary given that there is already an "and" in the phrase to give the needed connection. Choice (C) confuses the meaning, stating that there is a creation or "forming" of segregation that is paradoxically both racist and educational, changing the author's original intent.

11. **(C)** This question asks you to determine which transitional word is most effective. Look at what comes before and after the transition to see what sort of logical relationship the transition should express. In this case, what comes before states that an anti-Romani law was somewhat revised. What comes after states that the Romani continue to have difficulty with citizenship recognition. The relationship is therefore one of contrast, so "but" (choice (C)) makes the most sense. Choices (A), (B), and (D) do not show a contrast.

12. **(A)** Sometimes you will need to recognize proper English expressions—the more widely you have read well-written books and articles, the easier questions like these will be for you. The correct expression is "en masse," which means "in a group." The refugees were deported all at once from Germany and France. Choices (B), (C), and (D) describe the size of physical objects, not the deportation of a group of people.

Big-Picture Question Practice

On the following types of questions, be sure you *really focus on what the question is asking.* Rarely will these test issues of grammar. They will instead test concepts like your understanding of whether something should be added or deleted, where a sentence or paragraph should be placed, and whether a sentence accomplishes a specific goal of the author. Carefully underline and circle these questions as you read them to ensure you fully grasp what is asked. Also, try to create your own idea of what the answer is before jumping into the choices.

Into the Abyss

How much do we truly know about our planet? Satellites and advances in aerial photography have made it so few terrestrial areas go unmarked or unexplored. ❶ But what about the seven-tenths of Earth's surface that is ocean? In fact, very little is known.

❷ The United States' Ocean Observatories Initiative, or OOI, is taking off in hopes of uncovering a few more of the planet's mysteries. The project consists of the prized observatory, the *Cabled Array*, and six other smaller observatories that will be scattered around the world's oceans to measure physical, chemical, geological, and biological phenomena. The *Cabled Array*

1. The author wants to insert a sentence at this point that builds on the idea that humanity has widespread access to information about terrestrial areas. Which choice best accomplishes the author's objective?

   (A) The circumference of Earth is approximately 25,000 miles around the equator, slightly larger than it would be if measured along lines of longitude.

   (B) In comparison, we know very little about the outer reaches of space and the great depths of the seas.

   (C) In fact, most of the world's land is available for viewing by anyone in the world with Internet access.

   (D) It all started when Ferdinand Magellan successfully circumnavigated Earth in the 1500s.

2. Which of these sentences, if inserted at this point, would best introduce the topic of the current paragraph and provide a logical transition from the previous one?

   (A) We know more about the surfaces of the ocean than what lies beneath.

   (B) A new $385 million project is set to change that.

   (C) A global consortium of countries is working to "stem the tide" of misinformation.

   (D) Approximately $254 million dollars has been invested in terrestrial earthquake research in the past year alone.

itself will be just off the coasts of Oregon and Washington. ❸ The six other observatories—*Pioneer, Endurance, Irminger Sea, Argentine Basin, Southern Ocean,* and *Ocean Station Papa*—will be powered by battery, sun, and wind but transmit data via satellite.

(1) Using torpedo-shaped ocean gliders that travel long distances through the sea, OOI will sample sunlight penetration, element concentrations, pressure, temperature, etc. (2) A particular focus of the underwater observatories is to monitor the drastic changes that occur with the movement of tectonic plates or where the continental shelf abruptly ends. (3) Altogether, some 800+ instruments will collect data and funnel it back to Rutgers University, where it will then be made available to the public. ❹

3. Which option, if inserted here, gives the most specific description as to how the *Cabled Array* would function?

(A) and uses the very latest oceanic observation technology

(B) gathering information on underwater tectonic movements, which serves as data for a tsunami warning system since tsunamis originate with deep sea geological abnormalities

(C) the two most northwestern states in the contiguous Continental United States, homes to both spectacular scenery in National Parks and cutting-edge technology companies

(D) organized around a submarine cable and linked to seventeen junction boxes that distribute power and signals to the unit's instruments, which will then collect and return data

4. The author wishes to insert the following sentence into the preceding paragraph.

"In addition to the gliders, some observatories will employ propeller-driven autonomous underwater vehicles, or AUVs, that can 'swim' in strong currents."

Where should it be placed?

(A) Before sentence 1
(B) Before sentence 2
(C) Before sentence 3
(D) After sentence 3

OOI is clouded with the ambiguity and uncertainty that undoubtedly follow a project of this sort—groundbreaking and colossal. Yet, it turns out that the project isn't exactly pioneering; **❺** Canada has been operating a similar facility since 2006 and has had its own share of ups and downs. Hopefully, the U.S. can learn from the decade of **❻** experience. Some are already predicting serious flaws. While Canada's significantly smaller project is overseen by five researchers, OOI has employed only four researchers to manage an initiative that is almost eight times larger. Other detractors argue that the lack of scientific oversight during construction is bound to result in failure. Still, many anticipate the wealth of knowledge and new discoveries that will certainly follow underwater monitoring— **❼** friend or foe of OOI, that is something to be excited about.

5. The author is considering deleting the underlined part of the sentence and adjusting the punctuation in the sentence by changing the semicolon that immediately precedes it to a period. Should the author make this deletion?

(A) Yes. The underlined part distracts from the primary focus on what the United States has done.

(B) Yes. The underlined part gives information that is inconsistent with what comes later in the essay.

(C) No. The underlined part provides a relevant elaboration on the first part of the sentence.

(D) No. The underlined part gives specific details as to how the OOI will function successfully.

6. Which option most effectively joins the two sentences at this point?

(A) experience; however some

(B) experience, but some

(C) experience and some

(D) experience, with some

7. The author wants to end the essay on a positive note that is tied to the argument of this paragraph. Which option best accomplishes the author's objective?

(A) NO CHANGE

(B) the consensus of scientists and policy makers can only be characterized as optimistic.

(C) the OOI is designed to gather data about oceanic activities.

(D) with such a large staff operating the OOI, expectations for success couldn't be higher.

Answers Explained

1. **(C)** We need a sentence that shows that humans have wide access to information about areas on Earth. Choice (C) best accomplishes this objective since it states that most anyone in the world with access to the Internet can look at a picture of most any spot on Earth. Choice (A) is quite specific, but it does not direct support to the notion that humans have wide access to information about terrestrial areas. Choice (B) makes an irrelevant statement about space and the seas. Choice (D) talks about what one man did long ago but does not directly express that humans have wide access to information about Earth.

2. **(B)** To answer this question, determine the topic of the current paragraph and also consider what would provide a clear transition from the previous paragraph. The current paragraph focuses on an in-depth description of the U.S. Ocean Observatories Initiative. Choice (B) introduces this topic well, because it gives us a fact about the project that would spark our interest—the significant monetary investment the project requires. Choice (B) also transitions well from the previous paragraph. The previous paragraph states that very little is known about the ocean and the OOI project with a 385 million dollar investment would likely do much to increase our knowledge of the seas. Choice (A) is incorrect because although this loosely connects to the previous paragraph, it does not give a strong introduction to the topic of this paragraph. Choice (C) is not right because it contradicts the fact that the OOI is being implemented by just the United States, not by a global group of countries. The correct answer is not choice (D) because the amount of money invested in terrestrial earthquake research is irrelevant to introducing a paragraph about a project that will provide data on the oceans.

3. **(D)** The key word in this question is "specific"—not only must the wording be specific, but it must clearly communicate how this device would work. Choice (D) accomplishes all of this because it gives precise details about how the *Cabled Array* will be organized, powered, and programmed. Choice (A) is extremely vague. Choice (B) is specific but does not focus on how the *Cabled Array* would function—instead, it focuses on how the array could help with tsunami warnings. Choice (C) is also specific, but it does not accomplish the task in the question. Instead, it highlights the positive characteristics of Oregon and Washington.

4. **(B)** On questions involving placement of sentences or paragraphs, it can be helpful to write down the potential placements of the choices in the passage. You can write an "A" where choice (A) would go, a "B" where choice (B) would go, and so on. This will help you stay organized as you think through the question. Sentence 1 mentions the "gliders," so it makes sense to put this sentence before sentence 2 because the insert's introductory phrase, "In addition to the gliders," transitions from sentence 1 into the discussion that follows. Choice (A) does not work, because it would be illogical to start the paragraph by referring to the gliders if the author had not yet clarified what the gliders were. Choice (C) is not correct because putting the insert at this point interrupts the flow between sentences 2 and 3. Choice (D) is not the answer because sentence 3 already gives a solid conclusion to the paragraph, summarizing what the project will do "altogether."

5. **(C)** On this type of a question, stop and think first about whether or not the phrase should be deleted. Then think why or why not this should be the case. Doing this will help you avoid choosing one of the wrong answer choices. This part of the sentence

should remain because it gives a specific elaboration on how the OOI project "isn't exactly pioneering" because another country, Canada, has done it previously. Without this statement, the first part of the sentence lacks clear evidence supporting its claim. Choices (A) and (B) are incorrect because leaving this part of the sentence in is helpful. Choice (D) is not correct because it gives us no information specific to the functions of the OOI, instead focusing on what Canada did with its version of this type of project.

6. **(B)** Be prepared to encounter questions that ask you to combine sentences and phrases effectively. These questions typically involve a grasp of transitions (words like "and," "but," and "because") and of punctuation. Attack this by considering the logical relationship between the two sentences. The first sentence is optimistic, while the second sentence is pessimistic. Because of this, a transition that marks a contrast is necessary. Choices (C) and (D) do not provide contrasting words, and choice (C) lacks a comma before the "and." Both choices (A) and (B) have contrasting words. However, the punctuation in choice (A) is incorrect, since a comma is needed after "however" when it follows a semicolon in this context. Choice (B) has both a logical transition, "but," and proper punctuation.

7. **(A)** With questions about the conclusion of the essay, it can often be helpful to first skim through the passage or at least look over the topic sentences of the different paragraphs. Since the Writing and Language section is generally easy to finish, in all likelihood you will have the time you need to gather the necessary information to answer the question correctly. In this case, the paragraph provides most of the necessary context. The sentences before this mention what both "detractors" and more optimistic people think about the possible success or failure of the OOI project. To end the paragraph in a positive way, state that the most likely outcomes of the OOI are things that everyone will find exciting, no matter their attitude toward the OOI. Choice (B) is inconsistent with what the author has said about there being mixed opinions on the OOI, so it is incorrect. Choice (C) is not correct because it is too neutral in its tone. Choice (D) is not the answer because the author has already stated that the OOI has a relatively small research staff.

PRACTICE PASSAGES

On the SAT Writing and Language test, you will have 4 passages from the following different content areas: careers, history and social studies, humanities, and science. One of each of these passage categories is presented below, giving you the same number of passages and questions you will have on the actual SAT Writing and Language test. Detailed answer explanations follow each passage.

The Doctor Is In

According to the United States Department of Labor, the 2012 median pay for veterinarians ❶ were approximately $85,000 annually, with the top ten percent earning more than $140,000. The job outlook is about average, so Doctors of Veterinary Medicine have to compete for jobs ❷ by differentiating themselves through past experience and specialization. Although private practice is expected to grow with more pet owners attending regular visits and animal medical care expanding into cancer treatments and organ transplants, the number of graduating veterinarian students is higher than ever—a trend that ❸ continue to keeps jobs scarce.

Prospective veterinarians should pursue a ❹ bachelors degree in an area of science like biology, chemistry, or animal science and maintain a high G.P.A. to gain admission into a veterinary program, ❺ where they will spend three years in classrooms and labs, followed by a year in clinical rotations. After completing the doctorate, veterinarians have to pass federal and state licensing examinations before being allowed to practice. Still, even with accredited licensing, many veterinarians choose to enter one-year internships so they can later compete for higher-paying positions.

❻ Eventually, vets will research, diagnose, and treat medical conditions of pets, livestock, and other animals. Some will specialize in companion animals and work in private clinics and hospitals, while others will choose to work with farm animals or in research facilities. These vets usually travel back and forth between offices

1. (A) NO CHANGE
   (B) has been approximately
   (C) had been approximately
   (D) was approximately

2. Which choice would most logically complete the sentence?
   (A) NO CHANGE
   (B) as people in a wide variety of professions must do on a regular basis.
   (C) by considering what other career paths may be most interesting to them.
   (D) with research scientists, project engineers, and computer specialists, all of whom have technical expertise.

3. (A) NO CHANGE
   (B) continues to keep
   (C) continue to keep
   (D) continues to keeping

4. (A) NO CHANGE
   (B) bachelors'
   (C) bachelor's
   (D) bachelor is

5. (A) NO CHANGE
   (B) that
   (C) which
   (D) in

6. (A) NO CHANGE
   (B) Eventually, vets will research diagnose, and treat
   (C) Eventually vets will research diagnose and treat
   (D) Eventually vets will research, diagnose and treat

and farms or ranches to care for and perform surgeries on livestock. Those involved in food safety and inspection may spend their workdays in slaughterhouses and food-processing plants in an effort to prevent the spread of disease. Many others choose to stay at the university and teach. ❼ Irregardless of the work environment a veterinarian chooses, the job resembles that of a normal physician in its expanse; it is interdisciplinary, unpredictable, and constantly changing with new medical discoveries.

A rare ❽ acception to the usual veterinarian routines may be best exemplified in someone like Luke Gamble, a British vet who founded Worldwide Veterinary Services and Mission Rabies to support global initiatives to help animals ❾ in need. Besides being a surgeon in his own practice, Gamble often volunteers in India and South Africa, going so far as to document his research on television and in books. A quick look at Gamble's website ❿ shows the skill with which Gamble is able to create a visually appealing introduction to his work. Certainly, the glamour and excitement associated with Gamble's daily life in veterinary medicine and research is far from typical, but that doesn't make it any less ⓫ enthralling.

7. (A) NO CHANGE
   (B) With regards
   (C) Regarding
   (D) Regardless

8. (A) NO CHANGE
   (B) acceptance
   (C) exception
   (D) exceptance

9. (A) NO CHANGE
   (B) that require the assistance of humankind.
   (C) which demand help of the global community.
   (D) OMIT the underlined portion and end the selection with a period.

10. Which choice would most specifically elaborate on the range of Gamble's medical capabilities?
    (A) NO CHANGE
    (B) provides users with videos, links to articles, blog pieces, and helpful graphics.
    (C) gives interesting insights on his multitudinous hobbies and passions.
    (D) reveals a practice that expands from pet rabbits to wild lions.

11. Which of the following alternatives to the underlined word would NOT work?
    (A) fascinating
    (B) riveting
    (C) impulsive
    (D) captivating

Answers Explained

1. **(D)** Make sure the verb is consistent with the number of the subject. The subject is "pay," which is singular, making choice (A) incorrect. Also, the tense needs to be in the past because this refers to the pay in a past year, 2012. So, choice (D) is needed since "was" gives the past tense. Choice (B) is in the present perfect (e.g., *has/have been*—something that is continuing through the present or has recently been completed), and choice (C) is in the past perfect (e.g., *had been*—typically to indicate that the event took place prior to another past event).

2. **(A)** Choice (A) logically completes the sentence because it gives specific ways that Doctors of Veterinary Medicine can better compete for limited jobs. Choice (B) is too vague, choice (C) is irrelevant, and choice (D) is illogical since veterinarians would most likely not be in direct competition for jobs with people in these fields.

3. **(B)** Choice (B) is numerically consistent with the singular subject, "number," and uses the correct infinitive form of the verb, "to keep." Choice (C) uses the plural verb "continue," and choices (A) and (D) use incorrect forms of "keep."

4. **(C)** The degree belongs to a single person, so put the apostrophe before the "s." Choice (A) would work if you were using "bachelors" as a subject, but it does not show possession. Choice (B) would be accurate for multiple bachelors, and choice (D) incorrectly uses the verb "is" in a way that changes the original meaning away from possession.

5. **(A)** Since this refers to the physical locations of classes and labs and since the veterinary program would have a physical location, "where" would make sense. Choices (B), (C), and (D) use improper prepositions to make the needed connection. "In which" could work instead of "where," but this is not an option.

6. **(A)** Choice (A) is the only option to give a needed break after the introductory word "Eventually" and also to clearly break up the different verbs that state what vets will do. Choice (B) does not have a needed comma between the separate actions "research" and "diagnose," and choices (C) and (D) lack a comma after the introductory word "Eventually."

7. **(D)** Choice (D) uses the proper idiomatic expression, "regardless of." Choice (A) is not a word, choice (B) would need the word "to" immediately following it instead of "of" to be correct, and choice (C) could work if the "of" immediately following were deleted, but not in its current form. Choices (B) and (C) can work grammatically in other contexts, like "regarding the latest assignment" or "regardless of his intentions."

8. **(C)** Choice (C) uses the correct word "exception" to indicate that this is an unusual case. Choice (A) is not a word, choice (B) does not fit the needed definition given the context, and choice (D) is also not a word.

9. **(A)** Choice (A) expresses the necessary idea most concisely. Choices (B) and (C) are too wordy, and choice (D) would remove a key clarification of what these global initiatives would accomplish.

10. **(D)** Choice (D) best accomplishes this task because it shows that Gamble's veterinary practice ranges from being able to treat small rabbits to large lions. Choices (A) and (B) focus on his skill in website design, not on the range of his capabilities. Choice (C) is far too vague.

11. **(C)** Be sure you picked up on the word NOT in the question. The current word, "enthralling," means extremely interesting. Choices (A), (B), and (D) all are synonymous with this word. Choice (C), "impulsive," is associated with unconscious desires rather than something that consciously interests people.

Maslow's Hierarchy and Violence

[1]

There are many issues involved in trying to explain how the people who commit vicious crimes are created. Are they formed by society? Is violent behavior genetically encoded in ❶ his or her DNA? Or was there some sort of trauma in their lives that causes them to behave this way? One theory attempts to explain the evolution of murder ❷ to it's ancient origins through what we describe as the modern day serial killer by applying Maslow's Hierarchy of Needs to the psychology of a murderer.

[2]

Improvements in farming and taxes on alcohol eventually helped people gain enough money to feed themselves, ❸ and allowed them to focus on the next level of needs: safety needs. We usually have little awareness of this type of need, except for in times of emergency. ❹ Emergencies can come any place, any time, and people need to be prepared for them. Beginning around the mid-19th century, murders moved to a new stage of evolution. Throughout this period they dealt primarily with maintaining domestic security. People were frequently compelled to defend their homes by force, as the majority of the population ❺ hold only precarious ownership of their house and a meager income.

[3]

The first level of Maslow's pyramid involves the basic biological needs. These include food, water, and oxygen, and are necessary to carry out the ❻ fundamentally body functions that keep us alive. In the 18th century, the majority of crimes and murders that were recorded involved obtaining food. Poverty and starvation ran rampant in this era of history, so it follows that this first level of physiological needs would be particularly emphasized and perhaps motivate someone to kill. ❼

1. (A) NO CHANGE
   (B) its
   (C) one's
   (D) their

2. (A) NO CHANGE
   (B) to its
   (C) from it's
   (D) from its

3. (A) NO CHANGE
   (B) but
   (C) or
   (D) with

4. The writer is considering deleting the underlined portion. Should it be kept or deleted?

   (A) Kept, because it clarifies an important concept.
   (B) Kept, because it builds on the argument in the previous sentence.
   (C) Deleted, because it makes an unnecessary point.
   (D) Deleted, because it diverges from the theme of the previous sentence.

5. (A) NO CHANGE
   (B) held
   (C) holded
   (D) helded

6. (A) NO CHANGE
   (B) fundamentally bodily
   (C) fundamental bodily
   (D) fundamental body

7. The writer is considering moving paragraph 3 to a different point in the essay. Where would it best be placed?

   (A) Where it currently is
   (B) Before paragraph 1
   (C) Before paragraph 2
   (D) After paragraph 4

[4]

In the late 19th century, laws were passed which allowed parishes to pave and clean streets and build suburbs. These communities were safer and more permanent than those at the beginning of the century, enabling people to move on to their third level of **8** needs, and—by extension—to new motives for murder. This third level includes love, affection and sexual needs. In regards to the evolution of murder, no sexually motivated murders were recorded in Europe prior to the 19th-century, when "Jack the Ripper" emerged **9** between many similarly violent deviants.

[5]

It took a while for the fourth level of Maslow's hierarchy—esteem needs—to come around as a murder motivation. Murder and serial killing motivated by this level began around the mid-20th century when the majority of Western society had more or less **10** become a better place in which to reside. It's theorized that a killer's reason for committing this variety of murder often involves a desire to stand out, become famous, or to be recognized by society. **11**

8. (A) NO CHANGE
   (B) needs; by extension to
   (C) needs and by extension, to
   (D) needs: by extension to

9. (A) NO CHANGE
   (B) among
   (C) within
   (D) throughout

10. Which choice would be most closely and specifically tied to the points made previously in the essay?

    (A) NO CHANGE
    (B) found Maslow to be an insightful engineering mind.
    (C) secured physiological, safety, and love needs.
    (D) undergone wide-ranging poverty in the aftermath of World War II.

11. Which sentence, if inserted at this point, would provide the most logical conclusion to the paragraph and relevantly expand on the point made in the previous sentence?

    (A) Society will one day come to understand the widespread influence of Maslow's psychological theories.
    (B) Murderers use a variety of weapons to carry out their nefarious plans, including guns, knives, and ropes.
    (C) If society did more to feed the hungry, then perhaps gruesome murders would be a thing of the past.
    (D) This may explain why they frequently commit multiple murders, which they believe will distinguish them from other criminals.

Answers Explained

1. **(D)** "Their" is consistent with the plural "they" and "the people" earlier in the paragraph. Choices (A), (B), and (C) all refer to things in a singular way.

2. **(D)** The proper idiomatic phrase is "evolution from," making choices (A) and (B) incorrect. Also, "its" as in choice (D) is the possessive form of "it," while "it's" means "it is," making choice (C) incorrect.

3. **(A)** "And" gives an appropriate transition between the first and second parts of this sentence, since the improvements in farming and taxes on alcohol both helped people gain money *and* allowed them to focus on their safety. Choice (B) ("but") shows a contrast, choice (C) ("or") shows that only one of these consequences would happen, and choice (D) ("with") changes these two separate ways of helping people into a single item, thereby changing the original meaning to an improper phrase, "with allowed them."

4. **(C)** The description of emergencies gives vague, irrelevant, and unneeded information about the broad characteristics of emergencies. This statement is unnecessary and should be removed, making choice (C) correct and choices (A) and (B) incorrect. Choice (D) is not correct because it continues with the same theme of "emergency" from the previous sentence, albeit giving irrelevant information about it.

5. **(B)** "Held" is consistent with the past tense of this sentence. Choice (A) is in the present tense, and choices (C) and (D) use incorrect forms of "hold."

6. **(C)** Even though "bodily" ends in "ly," it is an adjective describing the noun "functions." "Fundamental" is also describing "functions," so it too must be in the adjective form. Choices (A) and (B) incorrectly use the adverb form "fundamentally." Choice (D) incorrectly uses the noun "body" to describe another noun.

7. **(C)** The overall structure of the essay is to first introduce the topic of Maslow's Hierarchy and then to chronologically and sequentially present the different levels of Maslow's pyramid as they relate to murder psychology. Paragraph 3 analyzes the first level of Maslow's pyramid, so it makes sense to insert it before Paragraph 2. If the paragraph were left where it currently is (choice (A)), it would make Paragraph 2's placement illogical, since Paragraph 2 refers to the "next level of needs"—it makes no sense to refer to the "next" level of needs without mentioning the first level of needs. Choice (B) would not work, because the general introduction of Paragraph 1 would not make sense following Paragraph 3. Choice (D) would illogically place paragraph 3, which describes the first level of Maslow's pyramid, well after the other levels in the pyramid have been sequentially discussed.

8. **(A)** Choice (A) correctly sets off the parenthetical phrase "by extension" using dashes. Choice (B) doesn't work because there must be a complete sentence before and after a semicolon. Choices (C) and (D) do not set aside "by extension" using punctuation like dashes or commas.

9. **(B)** "Among" correctly means "out of" as it is used in this context. Choice A, "between," is used when comparing things considered one at a time. Choices (C) and (D) do not work because it is illogical to state that a murderer could emerge "within" or "throughout" many similarly minded people.

10. **(C)** Choice (C) gives specific examples of needs that have been analyzed previously in the passage. It is not choice (A) because the passage has not focused on the relative quality of living conditions. It is not choice (B) because Maslow did not have an engineering mind but rather a psychological mind. It is not choice (D) because the passage did not make claims about poverty in the years following World War II.

11. **(D)** The point made in the previous sentence is that killers may want to commit murders in order to become famous. Choice (D) logically ties in to this theme by giving a possible justification as to why people commit serial murder—they want to be recognized for their uniqueness. Choice (A) is not correct because it is too vague. Choice (B) is not correct because it fails to tie in to the murderers' likely motivation. Choice (C) is not correct because this makes an irrelevant, off-topic point.

Folklore

Think traditions. Think stories, dances, jokes, and old fairy tales. ❶ <u>Why is this the case?</u> Think about ways of living and expressing oneself—maybe through language, or cooking, or laughing, or rituals. The Center for Folklore Studies at Ohio State University defines it this way: "Folklore may be seen as the products of human work and thought that have developed within a limited community and that are communicated directly from generation to generation, usually orally, with the author or creator unknown." The University of North Carolina's Folklore program at Chapel Hill "focuses attention on those expressive realms that communities ❷ <u>inflame</u> with cultural meaning and through which they give voice to the issues and concerns that they see as central to their being." ❸ Technically only a discipline since the end of the 19th century, folklore is as old as humanity, and has as much to do with the present as it does with the past.

Number of Universities Offering Folklore Degrees / Concentrations

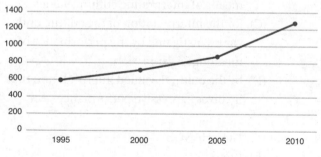

1. Which of the following choices would most logically connect the introductory sentences to the sentences that follow?

   (A) NO CHANGE
   (B) But, don't stop there.
   (C) Life is what we make of it.
   (D) Think about the economy.

2. (A) NO CHANGE
   (B) infuse
   (C) imply
   (D) infer

3. The author would like to insert a statement at this point in the essay to demonstrate the increasing interest in folklore scholarship. Which statement would be best supported by the information in the graph?

   (A) In fact, if the number of universities offering folklore degrees and concentrations increases between 2010 and 2015 at the same rate as it did between 2000 and 2005, there will be approximately 2,000 schools in 2015 that offer such programs.
   (B) In fact, if the number of universities offering folklore degrees and concentrations increases between 2010 and 2015 at the same rate as it did between 1995 and 2005, there will be approximately 1,800 schools in 2015 that offer such programs.
   (C) In fact, if the number of universities offering folklore degrees and concentrations increases between 2010 and 2015 at the same rate as it did between 2005 and 2010, there will be approximately 1,700 schools in 2015 that offer such programs.
   (D) In fact, if the number of universities offering folklore degrees and concentrations increases at the same rate between 2010 and 2015 as it did between 1995 and 2010, there will be approximately 1,400 schools in 2015 that offer such programs.

Folklorists—regardless of their focus within the wide, interdisciplinary field of Folklore—often **4** uses a similar approach and methodology, called "ethnographic fieldwork." This means the folklorist's job is not confined to a desk, a university, **5** or a museum; instead, the work is participatory and engaging, often in real-world settings in the expressive realms of festival, narrative, faith, art, architecture, and food, **6** as such. Naturally, this work overlaps with that of anthropologists, sociologists, feminists, historians, and cultural studies, race, class, and literature scholars. Digging into the lifestyles **7** atop a community, the study of folklore questions and imagines how artistic forms of expression may be used as spaces of reflection, resistance, autonomy, and identity.

Ruth Benedict, perhaps one of the best known women anthropologists and folklorists, studied under Franz Boas—the so-named "Father of Anthropology"—and is credited with helping to transition the study of folklore from the confinements of the historical and the vernacular, **8** to the performance of expression as a means of interpreting culture and values. Another prominent folklorist, Richard Bauman, is widely celebrated in performance studies, linguistics, and folkloristics. His work on language ideology examines how people's ideas about **9** their language affect their linguistic practices; and, along with other scholars of folklore, Bauman is part of the shift to verbal art and the moment of performance.

4. (A) NO CHANGE
   (B) uses a similarly
   (C) use a similar
   (D) use a similarly

5. (A) NO CHANGE
   (B) or a museum, instead, the
   (C) or a museum, instead the
   (D) or a museum instead: the

6. Which wording would best express the idea that there are further settings in which folklorists can conduct their work?

   (A) NO CHANGE
   (B) which comes as no surprise.
   (C) sparingly.
   (D) among others.

7. (A) NO CHANGE
   (B) within
   (C) from which
   (D) to

8. (A) NO CHANGE
   (B) with the performance of expression by means of interpreting cultural values.
   (C) for the interpretation of the culture and values instigated by the performance of meaningful expression.
   (D) by the cultural, valued interpretation that involves expressive performance.

9. (A) NO CHANGE
   (B) there
   (C) one's
   (D) ones'

By looking at the breadth of research of a couple folklorists, **10** you will learn about the scholarly qualifications of these researchers. A folklorist may enter a city or village or subculture, and begin to participate in that population's day-to-day life. Possibly, **11** he or she may end up studying a story, a joke, a dance, a dish, or even a child's game—an apparently trivial practice that, when looked at closely, turns out to be substantial in meaning.

10. Which choice gives the most logical and relevant conclusion to this sentence?

    (A) NO CHANGE
    (B) you will begin to understand the definition of folklore.
    (C) you can come to see the expanse of the field.
    (D) you will find contrasting, if not conflicting viewpoints.

11. (A) NO CHANGE
    (B) it
    (C) you
    (D) they

Answers Explained

1. **(B)** The sentences both before and immediately after the underlined portion hook the reader's interest on the topic of folklore. Choice (B) provides a good transition from talking about this theme in more general terms to talking about more specific themes. Choice (A) doesn't work because the sentence that follows does not explain why someone would have these thoughts. Choices (C) and (D) are irrelevant to the theme of the surrounding sentences.

2. **(B)** "Infuse" captures the intended meaning of "fill"—these expressive activities fill communities with cultural meaning. Choice (A), "inflame," is too negative; choice (C), "imply," means to suggest; and choice (D), "infer," means to pick up on the implicit meaning of something.

3. **(C)** Between 2005 and 2010, there is a rough increase of about 400 along the y-axis. So, if the number of universities offering folklore increases at the same rate as this between 2010 and 2015, there will be approximately 1,700 schools in 2015 that offer such programs. Choices (A), (B), and (D) do not make conclusions supported by the trends in the presented data.

4. **(C)** "Use" is the needed plural form of the verb, matching the plural subject "Folklorists." This makes choices (A) and (B) incorrect, since they use the singular "uses." Choice (C) also correctly uses the adjective "similar" rather than the adverb "similarly," as in choice (D), to describe the noun "approach."

5. **(A)** A semicolon provides a needed break between the two independent clauses, making choice (A) correct. Choices (B) and (C) are run-on sentences. Choice (D) is incorrect because a longer pause is needed before the transitional word "instead" rather than after it.

6. **(D)** Stating "among others" implies that even though a variety of settings is mentioned—festival, narrative, faith, etc.—there would be even more that are not mentioned. "As such," choice (A), means in the exact sense of the word, which does not work. Choice (B) does nothing to convey that there are further settings, and choice (C) would, if anything, make it seem like there were fewer such settings.

7. **(B)** "Within" is the proper word to use in this context, since people live within a community, not "atop" it (choice (A)), "from which" it (choice (C)), or "to" it (choice (D)).

8. **(A)** Choice (A) uses the correct transitional word to start off the phrase, since the proper wording is "from" one thing "to" another. Also, choice (A) is parallel to the structure of the previous part of the sentence. Choices (B), (C), and (D) do not use the proper initial transitional word.

9. **(A)** "Their" is the possessive plural word needed to describe how the language belonged to the plural people. Choice (B) uses the spelling of "there," which generally refers to places. Choice (C) is singular, and choice (D) is not a word.

10. **(C)** Choice (C) gives the best conclusion to this sentence, not only because it connects to the mention of "breadth" in research by mentioning the "expanse" of the field but because it introduces the presentation of diverse research methodologies that folklorists use. Choice (A) focuses too narrowly on the qualifications of the folklorists rather than on what they would actually do. Choice (B) doesn't work because folklore was

defined earlier in the passage, and what follows this sentence doesn't define folklore but identifies the different ways folklorists can conduct research. Choice (D) doesn't work because although folklorists surely have some differing views on important topics, that is not what is emphasized in this paragraph.

11. **(A)** "He or she" functions as a singular, gender-neutral way to identify the subject and works because the writer is referring to "a folklorist" in the previous sentence and continues to do so in this sentence. Choice (B) refers to things, not people. Choice (C) is in the second person, and choice (D) is plural.

Age of the Drone

Could robots soon be delivering your mail? Allow me to set the scene: you're coming home from school, walking toward your front door, and **①** bam a flying robot drops your oldest sister's just-ordered DVD collection on your head. It may not be as farfetched as it sounds. Today is the age of the drone, also known as the unmanned aerial vehicle (UAV), and it's only a matter of time before it becomes an everyday occurrence.

② Throughout the years of the past, drones have been controlled remotely and, most often, used for military services and special operations. In World War II, it became common practice **③** to use drones to fly attack missions. By the early 2000s, more than 50 countries had operating military drones. In recent years, **④** we've seen drones move into other fields such as photography, surveillance, search and rescue, security, and policing. And they aren't stopping there. **⑤** In fact, researchers project that between 2015 and 2030, the economic impact of drones will roughly triple.

As technology advances, an increasing number of autonomous drones are being designed for everyday services. Recently, Amazon announced its plan to use small, pilotless aircraft to deliver the majority of its packages. The end goal—although, still far off—is to be able to get goods to Amazon

Projected Economic Impact of UAV Industry, U.S.

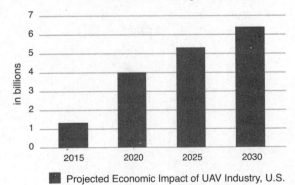

■ Projected Economic Impact of UAV Industry, U.S.

1. (A) NO CHANGE
   (B) bam—a flying robot drops your oldest sister's just-ordered DVD collection on your head.
   (C) bam, a flying robot drops, your oldest sisters just-ordered DVD collection on your head.
   (D) bam: a flying robot drops your oldest sisters' just-ordered DVD collection on your head.

2. (A) NO CHANGE
   (B) In the past years of history,
   (C) In the decades of the past,
   (D) Historically,

3. (A) NO CHANGE
   (B) in use
   (C) for the using
   (D) while use

4. (A) NO CHANGE
   (B) we've saw
   (C) we have sawed
   (D) we had saw

5. Which choice represents an accurate interpretation of the information in the graph?

   (A) NO CHANGE
   (B) In fact, researchers project that between 2015 and 2020, the economic impact of drones will roughly quintuple.
   (C) In fact, researchers project that between 2015 and 2030, the economic impact of drones will roughly double.
   (D) In fact, researchers project that between 2015 and 2025, the economic impact of drones will roughly quadruple.

customers in approximately 30 minutes from the time they are ordered. **⑥** Unmanned aerial vehicles are clearly safe for the majority of uses for which they are intended. To help with the more temporary obstacles—birds, strong winds, or you attempting to unlock your front door—will be on-the-ground human operators. Yet, **⑦** drone engineers and roboticists have their way, these human operators won't be necessary for long.

Amazon isn't the only company replacing parts of its labor force with drones. Aurizon, Australia's largest rail company, uses drones to survey **⑧** its entire transport infrastructure. When a job is too dirty, too dangerous, or too inaccessible, Aurizon utilizes a drone **⑨** in order to maximize its corporate bond valuation. With more than 2,600 kilometers of railway to inspect, it is not just safer, but more cost-effective to send a drone. In fact, company leaders are so confident in the implementation of microdrones, they are predicting a 50% **⑩** extermination in operational failures.

While all of this sounds promising, it's hard to take in from the currently droneless day to day we live in. **⑪** And NASA believes that is to change rather quickly; representatives have estimated that drones will be a billion dollar business in the United States within the next ten years. Ready or not, here they come.

6. The writer wants to address the reader's potential objection that using UAVs will be unsafe. Which option would most clearly and specifically accomplish this goal?

(A) NO CHANGE
(B) With their multiyear track record of safe use in this way, consumers and safety advocates have little cause for alarm.
(C) These microdrones will be programmed with destinations before liftoff and use navigation systems to avoid permanent obstacles like buildings and trees.
(D) It is highly unlikely that drone usage will result in a gradual decline in societal norms for moral behavior.

7. (A) NO CHANGE
(B) if drone engineers and roboticists have their way,
(C) drone engineers and roboticists,
(D) if they have their way,

8. (A) NO CHANGE
(B) it's
(C) its'
(D) it is

9. Which choice gives the most logical justification for using a drone based on the rest of the sentence?

(A) NO CHANGE
(B) instead of employing outside janitorial services.
(C) that is a machine controlled by a man.
(D) rather than risk the safety of its employees.

10. (A) NO CHANGE
(B) decrease
(C) less
(D) fewness

11. (A) NO CHANGE
(B) To
(C) But
(D) With

Answers Explained

1. **(B)** An interruption is needed after "bam" since this comes as an abrupt end to the sequence of events with the surprising drone delivery coming immediately after. A dash can provide the needed pause. Choice (A) does not have the necessary pauses after "bam," and choice (C) has an unnecessary comma after "drops" and lacks an apostrophe in "sisters." While choice (D) correctly uses a colon, it incorrectly places an apostrophe after "sisters," which would not work because if one refers to the oldest sister, it can only be a singular person.

2. **(D)** "Historically" is the most concise option—choices (A), (B), and (C) express the same idea as choice (D), but do so using many more words.

3. **(A)** The proper phrase is "common . . . to use," making choice (A) correct. Choice (B) can work in other contexts, like "the bathroom is in use," but choices (C) and (D) are idiomatically incorrect.

4. **(A)** The present perfect tense, "we've seen" as a substitute for "we have seen," works because this states that this shift has happened in recent years, which means it would likely continue up to the present day. Choices (B), (C), and (D) use the incorrect conjugation of "to see," as "saw" is used as the past tense form of the verb, not a present or past perfect form.

5. **(D)** In 2015, the economic impact of drones is around 1.25 billion dollars, and in 2025, it is around 5 billion dollars. Choice (D) correctly states that between 2015 and 2025 the economic impact would roughly quadruple, since $1.25 \times 4 = 5$. Choices (A), (B), and (C) do not accurately reflect the quantitative information in the graph.

6. **(C)** Choice (C) does the best job in giving *clear and specific* ways that the researcher can address the notion that UAV usage will be unsafe. Since they will have preprogrammed destinations and the capability to avoid obstacles, they will be quite safe to operate. Choices (A) and (B) are too vague, and choice (D) is off topic.

7. **(B)** Without using "if" to start the phrase, the sentence as a whole would be illogical, making choices (A) and (C) incorrect. Choice (D) is too vague with "they"—the pronoun needs to be clarified in this case since it is unclear precisely to what it is referring.

8. **(A)** The "its" correctly refers to the singular company's ownership of an infrastructure. "It's," choice B, is the same as "it is." "Its'," choice (C), is never correct. "It is," choice (D), expresses action rather than ownership.

9. **(D)** The previous part of the sentence emphasizes how many jobs could be unsafe or filthy for humans to do; therefore, "rather than risk the safety of its employees" would logically follow since a drone could provide clean and safe access to otherwise dangerous and dirty places. Choice (A) focuses on just the economic benefits. Choice (B) focuses only on cleanliness, ignoring the safety and inaccessibility concerns. Choice (C) simply defines what a drone is.

10. **(B)** All of these choices mean "go down" or "less" in some way; however, "decrease" is most appropriately used in conjunction with concrete numbers and percentages. Choice (A), "extermination," is too violent; choice (C), "less," is generally used with noncountable items; and choice (D), "fewness," is not a word.

11. **(C)** The previous sentence and the current sentence have a contrasting relationship with one another—the first sentence states that we are not used to drones, and the current sentence states that this could very well change in the near future. "But" is the only one of these words that expresses a contrast.

SAT Essay

4

WHAT IS THE SAT ESSAY?

The SAT Essay is an optional part of the SAT that requires you to demonstrate understanding and analysis of an argument. You will not need to have any specific background knowledge—you only need to focus on what is given in the source text. The rubric and general question will remain identical from test to test, but the source text will change, although it will consistently be a high-quality argument on a general topic intended for a broad audience of readers. The essay comes at the end of the SAT.

HOW IS THE NEW SAT ESSAY DIFFERENT FROM THE OLD SAT ESSAY?

Old SAT Essay	New SAT Essay
25 minutes.	50 minutes.
Comes at the beginning of the test.	Comes at the end of the test.
Required—directly affects your composite SAT score.	Optional—does not affect your composite SAT score.
Use examples from your own experiences, observations, and reading.	Analyze only the source text presented to you.
Not a right or wrong answer.	Must interpret the source text accurately.
Graded holistically from 1 to 6 by two graders for a total score between 2 and 12.	Scored by two graders from 1 to 4 in three categories: Reading, Analysis, and Writing. Category scores are then combined and reported separately (i.e., 2–8 for Reading, 2–8 for Analysis, and 2–8 for Writing).
Creativity and speed more important. Must quickly produce examples and your argument.	Analysis and focus more important. Can take more time for source reading and prewriting.

HOW IS THIS CHAPTER ORGANIZED?

- **A SAMPLE PROMPT** to familiarize you with the essay format
- **A SAMPLE RESPONSE** with the general essay rubric so you understand how the essay is scored
- **SKILL-BUILDING LESSONS AND PRACTICE** in the major components of the SAT Essay: Reading, Analysis, and Writing
- **10 KEY STRATEGIES FOR SAT ESSAY WRITING SUCCESS**
- **PUTTING IT ALL TOGETHER** with a sample prompt, reading notes, prewrite, and response
- **SAMPLE ESSAYS OF DIFFERENT QUALITY** so that you can learn what it takes to earn a particular score
- **MORE SAMPLE ESSAY PROMPTS FOR PRACTICE**

SAMPLE PROMPT

Review the following sample prompt, directions, and format.

Directions: This assignment will allow you to demonstrate your ability to skillfully read and understand a source text and write a response analyzing the source. In your response, you should show that you have understood the source, give proficient analysis, and use the English language effectively. If your essay is off-topic, it will not be scored.

Only what you write on the lined paper in your answer document will be scored—avoid skipping lines, using unreasonably large handwriting, and using wide margins in order to have sufficient space to respond. You can also write on the planning sheet in the answer document, but this will not be evaluated—no other scrap paper will be given. Be sure to write clearly and legibly so your response can be scored.

You will be given 50 minutes to complete the assignment, including reading the source text and writing your response.

Read the following passage, and think about how the author uses:

- Evidence, such as applicable examples, to justify the argument
- Reasoning to show logical connections among thoughts and facts
- Rhetoric, like sensory language and emotional appeals, to give weight to the argument

Life: Pass It On

1   I have been called many things throughout the course of life—some fit for publication, and others a little less . . . savory, we'll say. Yet, despite my host of titles, Saint is something with which I will never be confused. This is not to say that I'm unconcerned with being a good person. Rather, it's more an indictment of my laziness; when doing nothing is often so much easier than doing the right thing, inaction is an appealing choice.

2   So, when I stumble across one of those rare ways to make a difference that manages to coincide with my penchant for convenience, I'm anxious to oblige—especially if my sole obligation is to checkmark a box at the DMV once every five years when I renew my driver's license. Really, that's the extent of my hassle. Besides, I already have to go there, anyway.

3   If you have a driver's license, I expect that you are aware that this is the process by which one registers as an organ donor (at least in the majority of states). No monetary sacrifice, no extensive paperwork, and really no time at all are required on your part. Just a checkmark. ✔

4   Yet, it may surprise you that only 40% of American adults have registered; that's only two out of every five. This statistic is particularly jarring when it is contrasted with another: 95% of Americans strongly support organ donation (according to a 2005 Gallup poll). That is every 19 out of 20 people, which is a figure that positively dwarfs the number who have actually registered.

5   My question to you is a simple one: why? When such a vast majority is fervently in favor of the concept, and when the societal benefits absolutely eclipse the (lack of) personal costs involved, why is such a depressing minority willing to check that tiny box?

6   Two out of five. Now, if you are part of that 40%, I salute you. But, should you fall in that silent majority, my plea today is on your behalf. (And if you fall into neither group and don't have a driver's license in the first place, feel free to carry on at your pedestrian leisure.) You have the opportunity to save several lives and improve several more—just with a casual flick of the wrist. Convenience isn't the issue; check the box, then pat yourself on the back. Good deed for the day, just like that.

7   So if it's not a matter of convenience, then what? Is it fear? I was 18 when I first registered to be a donor. This was also the first time in my life that I was required to acknowledge my own mortality, and I recall it was quite surreal. When I die? When, not if?! But you don't understand, I can't die yet! I haven't even gone to senior prom! But I reflected on this decision to be a donor, and it was really quite simple: I will die when I die, whether I admit my mortality on my driver's license or not; burying my head in the sand would not deter the inevitable.

8   Moreover, contrary to tabloid sensationalism, no organ donor has ever been declared dead prematurely; donors are actually subject to more post-mortem testing than non-donors just to ensure that this scenario never occurs. Thus, you are far more likely to be buried alive as a non-donor than to be declared dead as a donor. Roll that around in your head for a moment.

9   Ultimately, though, I expect that people are so reluctant to register primarily because of the anonymity of the people one would be saving. When dealing with strangers, the whole concept is more abstract and impersonal, because you haven't seen the suffering of those you would help. You haven't spoken to these people and listened to the infinite gratitude of those who have been saved, or to the despair of those who pass away before an organ can be procured. But, I have; I worked in transplant centers in my first job out of college, and, if there was one thing that I learned, it's that those in need are just like you and me. So, should the day come when I need an organ (and it could for all of us), I hope somebody would be willing to do something as simple as check a box to save my life.

Write a response that demonstrates how the author makes an argument to persuade an audience that it makes sense to become a registered organ donor. In your response, analyze how the author uses at least one of the features from the essay directions (or features of your own choosing) to develop a logical and persuasive argument. Be certain that your response cites relevant aspects of the source text.

Your response should not give your personal opinion on the merit of the source text but instead show how the author crafts an argument to persuade readers.

SAMPLE RESPONSE

How will you be evaluated on the SAT Essay? Essay graders use a general rubric like this:

SAT Essay Rubric

Each of the two graders will use a similar rubric to this one, grading your essay from 1 to 4 for each category, and then the two graders' individual scores will be combined to give you category scores between 2 and 8. Your score on the Essay will be reported separately and will not affect your overall SAT composite score.

	Score: 4
Reading	Excellent: The essay shows excellent understanding of the source. The essay shows an understanding of the source's main argument and key details and a firm grasp of how they are interconnected, demonstrating clear comprehension of the source. The essay does not misinterpret or misrepresent the source. The essay skillfully uses source evidence, such as direct quotations and rephrasing, representing a thorough comprehension of the source.
Analysis	Excellent: The essay gives excellent analysis of the source and shows clear understanding of what the assignment requires. The essay gives a complete, highly thoughtful analysis of the author's use of reasoning, evidence, rhetoric, and/or other argumentative elements the student has chosen to highlight. The essay has appropriate, adequate, and skillfully chosen support for its analysis. The essay focuses on the most important parts of the source in responding to the prompt.
Writing	Excellent: The essay is focused and shows an excellent grasp of the English language. The essay has a clear thesis. The essay has a well-executed introduction and conclusion. The essay shows a clear and well-crafted progression of thoughts both within paragraphs and in the essay as a whole. The essay has a wide range of sentence structures. The essay consistently shows precise choice of words. The essay is formal and objective in its style and tone. The essay demonstrates a firm grasp of the rules of standard English and has very few to no errors.

	Score: 3
Reading	Skillful: The essay shows effective understanding of the source. The essay shows an understanding of the source's main argument and key details. The essay is free of major misinterpretations and/or misrepresentations of the source. The essay uses appropriate source evidence, such as direct quotations and rephrasing, representing comprehension of the source.
Analysis	Skillful: The essay gives effective analysis of the source and shows an understanding of what the assignment requires. The essay decently analyzes the author's use of reasoning, evidence, rhetoric, and/or other argumentative elements the student has chosen to highlight. The essay has appropriate and adequate support for its analysis. The essay focuses primarily on the most important parts of the source in responding to the prompt.
Writing	Skillful: The essay is mostly focused and shows an effective grasp of the English language. The essay has a thesis, either explicit or implicit. The essay has an effective introduction and conclusion. The essay has a clear progression of thoughts both within paragraphs and in the essay as a whole. The essay has an assortment of sentence structures. The essay shows some precise choice of words. The essay is formal and objective in its style and tone. The essay demonstrates a grasp of the rules of standard English and has very few significant errors that interfere with the writer's argument.

Score: 2

Reading	Limited: The essay shows some understanding of the source.
	The essay shows an understanding of the source's main argument, but not of key details.
	The essay may have some misinterpretations and/or misrepresentations of the source.
	The essay gives only partial evidence from the source, showing limited comprehension of the source.
Analysis	Limited: The essay gives partial analysis of the source and shows only limited understanding of what the assignment requires.
	The essay tries to show how the author uses reasoning, evidence, rhetoric, and/or other argumentative elements the student has chosen to highlight, but only states rather than analyzes their importance, or at least one part of the essay's analysis is unsupported by the source.
	The essay has little or no justification for its argument.
	The essay may lack attention to those elements of the source that are most pertinent to responding to the prompt.
Writing	Limited: The essay is mostly not cohesive and shows an ineffective grasp of the English language. The essay may not have a thesis, or may diverge from the thesis at some point in the essay's development.
	The essay may have an unsuccessful introduction and/or conclusion. The essay may show progression of thoughts within the paragraphs, but not in the essay as a whole. The essay is relatively uniform in its sentence structures. The essay shows imprecise and possibly repetitive choice of words.
	The essay may be more casual and subjective in style and tone. The essay demonstrates a weaker grasp of the rules of standard English and does have errors that interfere with the writer's argument.

Score: 1

Reading	Insufficient: The essay shows virtually no understanding of the source.
	The essay is unsuccessful in showing an understanding of the source's main argument. It may refer to some details from the text, but it does so without tying them to the source's main argument.
	The essay has many misinterpretations and/or misrepresentations of the source.
	The essay gives virtually no evidence from the source, showing very poor comprehension of the source.
Analysis	Insufficient: The essay gives little to no accurate analysis of the source and shows poor understanding of what the assignment requires.
	The essay may show how the author uses reasoning, evidence, rhetoric, and/or other argumentative elements that the student has chosen to highlight but does so without analysis.
	Or many parts of the essay's analysis are unsupported by the source.
	The support given for points in the essay's argument are largely unsupported or off topic.
	The essay may not attend to the elements of the source that are pertinent to responding to the prompt.
	Or the essay gives no explicit analysis, perhaps only resorting to summary statements.
Writing	Insufficient: The essay is not cohesive and does not demonstrate skill in the English language. The essay may not have a thesis. The essay does not have a clear introduction and conclusion. The essay does not have a clear progression of thoughts. The essay is quite uniform and even repetitive in sentence structure.
	The essay shows poor and possibly inaccurate word choice. The essay is likely casual and subjective in style and tone. The essay shows a poor grasp of the rules of standard English and may have many errors that interfere with the writer's argument.

What does a good response look like? Here is an example of a top-scoring response to the sample prompt. As you read, think about how the student demonstrated his/her skill in Reading, Analysis, and Writing. When you finish, review the aspects of an essay that scored a 4 in all of these areas. What do you think? Did the writer do an exceptional job in each aspect?

RESPONSE WITH SCORES OF 4/4 READING, 4/4 ANALYSIS, AND 4/4 WRITING

In a whimsical and intimate voice, the writer tackles a very sobering issue. "*Life*: Pass It On" forcefully contends for more organ donors by presenting its argument in a journal-like letter to those who have failed "to check that tiny box." Although statistics are utilized, the writer relies more emphatically on a personal appeal to potential donors, alluding to the convenience, harmlessness, and morality in the decision to donate organs after death. The evidence, reasoning, and plea to the reader arise from the writer's own experience, and are accompanied by a chummy and likeable affectation. It is through this friendly writer-reader exchange that the piece drives home its ultimate goal: to bridge the gap between strangers and advocate for compassion toward others in a potentially life-or-death situation.

First, let us acknowledge the writer's relatability. The essay begins with a brutally honest self-reflection: the writer is no "Saint." And let's face it: laziness is something we can all relate to. Yet, despite the author's lack of philanthropy, he is amiable and even kindhearted. In the author's reflection on his mortality, the reader is able to stop and recall a similar moment—or perhaps, have that moment for the very first time. And suddenly, the reader is participating in a direct dialogue with the writer—a dialogue so cordial that it allows the writer to pose baffling questions to the reader him/herself. If the reader is one of the 60% who failed to check that box, he/she is instantly questioning his own motives. This very approachable style of writing proves effective in the buildup of the argument for organ donation.

Initially, the writer testifies—through his own usual passiveness—the utter convenience of becoming an organ donor; it boils down to "Just a checkmark." Since you need not enter sainthood to mark this box, it is free game for all, the writer argues. Next, the passage deals with the possibility of fear, alleviating it with a personal anecdote that is simultaneously dramatic, comical, and yet recognizable. Again, the reader is aligned with the writer in mortality, "I will die when I die." Though, this indication may seem trivial, it is the author's intent to leap nonchalantly over the irrelevant fear of death, safely bringing his reader along. Then, the writer appeals to the reader morally, insisting that if "you" had only seen the power behind that checkmark, you'd surely have signed up without a second thought. These techniques are exerted in an effort to unite reader and writer, while refuting any counterarguments—the author simply cannot find a good reason *not* to be an organ donor.

The dichotomy between registered donors and those who "*strongly support* organ donation" is equally effective in setting the foundation for the author's argument. The figures don't add up, and the writer appeals to the reader by asking for his opinion on such a wide contrast. Saving lives is easy, he argues; in fact, it takes just "a casual flick of the wrist." Once the writer enlists the readers to disregard inconvenience and fear in their interpretation of the stark statistics, it comes down to the author's opinion on the previously unanswered question. Anonymity and impersonality are, for the writer, at the heart of the lagging organ donors. Here, the reasoning stands that author has experience with transplant survivors (and those corpses failed by the numerous unchecked boxes), and is, therefore, in a position of authority to declare that they are "just like you and me."

Now, who wouldn't want to help (especially when you could be on the other end of it)? The case for more organ donors is made via an intimate plea to the reader—the writer and reader, once strangers, are now companionable; it is this hospitable demeanor that encourages the uncertain to check the box and do a part in saving lives. Experts, in-depth statistics, and quotes are hardly needed because the writer allows the reader to make his own call while presenting a somewhat infallible argument: if Americans support it, it is time we show our support. By being relatable and divulging personal insight, the writer effectively asserts his position for increased organ donation.

> The following mini-lessons and practice exercises are designed to help you sharpen your skills in *Reading, Analysis, and Writing* so that you can perform your very best on the SAT Essay.

READING SKILL BUILDING

To demonstrate reading skill on the SAT Essay, you must go beyond merely restating what the author has said. Instead, you must *paraphrase* the author's argument, putting things in your own words. Let's examine some examples of good and bad paraphrasing of a couple of famous historical documents.

Preamble to the U.S. Constitution

"We the people of the United States, in order to form a more perfect union, establish justice, insure domestic tranquility, provide for the common defense, promote the general welfare, and secure the blessings of liberty to ourselves and our posterity, do ordain and establish this Constitution for the United States of America."

TERRIBLE PARAPHRASING: "The United States needs to have justice, tranquility, defense, welfare and posterity." This sentence merely takes wording from the selection without seeing the big picture.

GOOD PARAPHRASING: "The U.S. Constitution will provide the foundational elements for a long-lasting, successful governmental structure." This sentence concisely summarizes the general ideas expressed in the selection.

Abraham Lincoln's Gettysburg Address

"Four score and seven years ago our fathers brought forth on this continent, a new nation, conceived in Liberty, and dedicated to the proposition that all men are created equal.

Now we are engaged in a great civil war, testing whether that nation, or any nation so conceived and so dedicated, can long endure. We are met on a great battle-field of that war. We have come to dedicate a portion of that field, as a final resting place for those who here gave their lives that that nation might live. It is altogether fitting and proper that we should do this.

But, in a larger sense, we can not dedicate—we can not consecrate—we can not hallow—this ground. The brave men, living and dead, who struggled here, have consecrated it, far above our poor power to add or detract. The world will little note, nor long remember what we say here, but it can never forget what they did here. It is for us the living, rather, to be dedicated here to the unfinished work which they who fought here have thus far so nobly advanced. It is rather for us to be here dedicated to the great task remaining before us—that from these honored dead we take increased devotion to that cause for which they gave the last full measure of devotion—that we here highly resolve that these dead shall not have died in vain—that this nation, under God, shall have a new birth of freedom—and that government of the people, by the people, for the people, shall not perish from the earth."

TERRIBLE PARAPHRASING: "A while ago the country happened. There was a civil war and a lot of bad things took place. We cannot dedicate this ground here. People shall not perish from the earth." This statement gives key wording from the passage but fails to demonstrate a correct understanding of what is written.

GOOD PARAPHRASING: "Those who perished on this battlefield fought for human freedom and equality. It is our solemn obligation to honor their memory by continuing to fight for the ideals for which they so nobly sacrificed." This statement puts the essence of what is expressed into the student's own words.

Now, let's practice paraphrasing the type of source text you will see on the actual SAT.

Essay Paraphrasing Example

The following SAT Essay Prompt is broken down paragraph by paragraph. Read each paragraph and try to put the author's argument into your own words as concisely as possible. After each paragraph, review the example of a well-crafted paraphrased sentence about the overall meaning of that paragraph.

When Did Music Become Optional?

Paragraph 1

A man taking an elevator up twenty-one floors, a woman on hold with her insurance company, a car of seventeen-year-olds driving to a high school football game, a hungry family walking into a Italian restaurant—what do all of these instances have in common? They'd be utterly unbearable without music. The importance of music can best be surmised through the understanding that every culture since the beginning of time has made music. Long before writing and reading and mathematics, there were instruments and voices and melodies. Music is as old as humanity, and its diminution in schools is intolerable, *for everybody*.

PARAPHRASED SUMMARY: *Universally used by cultures and peoples throughout history to make otherwise dull experiences enjoyable, music should not have been deemphasized in school.*

Paragraph 2

The argument for music could rest alone on the joy it brings. Name one person who detests music—not a type of music, but music as a whole. You cannot. No person exists. And if he or she did, I would wager that he or she was merely not exposed to enough music to adequately testify. Music, in its beauty and breadth, transcends communication and brings people together, evoking emotion and boosting social behavior. In short, music is pleasurable. And, its pleasures are only intensified by its versatility. We listen and play music to help ourselves think, relax, and let loose. We use music to express ourselves and interact with others. We go to music to mourn, to celebrate, to unite, and even to resist. It is a language that is not limited by language, and its delights are truly empowering.

PARAPHRASED SUMMARY: *Anyone fully exposed to the joys of music undoubtedly finds that it gives him or her an endless variety of ways to express feelings and enjoy life.*

Paragraph 3

Still, when it comes to education and the training of our future generations, many will demand more than joy and empowerment as the rationale for the inclusion of music programs in public school curriculums. They will not be disappointed. President Obama's PCAH (President's Committee on Arts & Humanities) found in its landmark study, Reinvesting in Arts Education, that there is a direct link between arts education and achievement in other subjects, identifying inventiveness, resourcefulness, and imagination as key strengths of the arts-instructed. A 1999 article, "The Importance of Music in Early Childhood," advocated for music education in learning of language, mathematics, and social studies. Music—readily available and easily engaged—is a powerful memory trigger that can be approached via "play," beginning in delight but ending in knowledge.

PARAPHRASED SUMMARY: *Far from being a mere means to pleasure, music study is linked to improved performance in a variety of academic areas.*

Paragraph 4

The advantages of music don't stop there. Musically-educated students are more likely to be involved in extracurricular activities and volunteer in their communities. They are less likely to have discipline problems or use alcohol, tobacco, and illicit drugs. A 1998 study reported that high school music students have more positive attitudes toward school and less classroom friction. The College Entrance Examination Board found students in music programs scored higher on the verbal and math sections of the SAT. Rather than music programs taking away from other subjects, they are known to enhance students' academic abilities across the board while building confidence and creativity. Schools with music programs, regardless of demographics, see higher graduation rates than those without.

PARAPHRASED SUMMARY: *The positive impact of music education goes far beyond the classroom—it can lead to decreased juvenile delinquency, more positive life outlooks, and improved test scores and graduation rates.*

Paragraph 5

With cuts in education funding, music programs are usually the last to be added and the first to go. District administrators argue that, with 80% of schools facing dramatic budget cuts since 2008, they have little choice; they can only afford to keep those subjects which are tested. Yet, this mindset that the arts, and music more specifically, are "extras" is damaging and quite simply, incorrect. Music itself improves education and stimulates learning in those highly-regarded STEM (Science, Technology, Engineering, and Mathematics) courses that continue to get preferential treatment. And parents aren't fooled either: in a recent Harris Poll, 93% of Americans named the arts as vital in a well-rounded education. Moreover, Concordia University is conducting research to confirm that instrumental training produces long-lasting changes in brain structure that prove more beneficial in adulthood than long-forgotten Biology or Calculus classes.

PARAPHRASED SUMMARY: *Instead of being seen as the first thing on the budget chopping block, music should be rightly appreciated as a foundational component of a high quality, well-rounded education.*

Paragraph 6

It is time that we considered the removal of Music programs in the public curriculum equal to the removal of English programs—unthinkable. If we continue to treat the arts as secondary rather than core, we will continue to see drops in standardized test scores in all subjects and witness our youth fail to compete with internationally-educated peers. Countries like Japan and the Netherlands, who continue to outperform the U.S. in the Mathematics and Sciences, have mandatory arts programs; by acknowledging the fundamental obligation to expose every youth to music, art, and foreign language, they reap the reward in overall academic excellence. Not to mention, *who are we to take away the joy of music?*

PARAPHRASED SUMMARY: *The U.S. should follow the examples of other countries that have embraced music as an untouchable component of their school curriculum.*

Now, practice paraphrasing this source text on your own, paragraph by paragraph. This passage will also be used in the Analysis and Writing sections.

Books: A Lost Art

1   It is not solely nostalgia for the good ol' days when you finished a great book and passed on your copy—dog-eared, coffee stained, and splattered with notes—to a friend who would add her own thoughts and pass it to another that has book lovers resenting the age of the e-book (though certainly this is part of it). Instead, book lovers argue that the severed relationship between reader and print book in the current technologically-inclined generation is more worrying and encompassing than most imagine. It is not just the literary crowd, devotedly attached to their overflowing bookshelves, who have a stake in the disappearance of hard-copies, but also small business owners, editing and publishing firms, and even the general public.

2   With the e-book's conquest over traditional hardcovers and paperbacks, *Publishers Weekly* released a report of a steady decrease in print sales, with 2012 sales down 9% from those in 2011. Meanwhile, after the disastrous closing of Borders and the plummet of sales suffered by Barnes and Noble, *Business Insider* suggested that bookstores, large and small, were doomed. The convenience and low cost of e-books has many hesitant to drive out to a store that may or may not have what they are looking for. Yet, it isn't just the enthusiastic reader trying to reverse the trend of disappearing bookstores. Are we truly ready to give up the retail experience—shelves upon shelves of

your favorites, quiet nooks to cuddle up in, children's reading hour, a latte and a stack of magazines—in its entirety? In February 2015, *U.S. News and World Report* directly connected the suspension in economic recovery to the decline of small businesses. If their research is conclusive, it is not just the unique shopping experience or quirky atmospheres of independent bookstores at risk.

3   Likewise, dwindling print sales means unpredictability in the publishing and edit-ing industries, where professionals are trying hard to keep up with erratic consumer trends. The rise in e-books, self-publishing, and the Amazon empire has made rev-enues more unstable than ever. With bookselling drifting more and more to the online market, publishing will also turn digital, and the implications for traditional publishing companies are grave. Publishers wonder how quickly it will take for their jobs to follow the tendencies of print books and become gradually obsolete. And how long will it take writers, competing for quick sales, to turn to direct online publishing to boost their own prospects for success?

4   If the evidence of failing small businesses and unhinged bookselling industries isn't enough to favor the printed, in-hand book, then perhaps an account by *The Atlantic* released in late 2014 will be; data shows that the number of American nonreaders has tripled since the 1980s. With the fading of the hard-copy, reading itself has plummeted, undoubtedly in favor of the savvy digital distractions that make up our on-the-go e-lifestyles. Certainly, there are many factors contributing to America's abandonment of literature, but it stands that e-books are failing to keep the public's nose in a book. Perhaps, the e-book age has discouraged having books on hand, visiting the library on the weekends, and telling stories before bedtime. Could it be that once frequent readers have lost the love for stories that they once had when they could feel them in their hands, turn their pages, and never have to plug them in or interrupt them for an email alert? When asked why she neglected reading after thirty years, one mother of three answered, "I grew up around books—we had hundreds. When I got older, I used to spend Saturday mornings at a coffee shop down the street reading for hours. Somewhere along the way, life got faster and I lost it."

5   Possibly, few can relate to Jason Epstein's declaration in his 2001 *Book Business*: "A civi-lization without retail bookstores is unimaginable. Like shrines and other sacred meet-ing places, bookstores are essential artifacts of human nature. The feel of a book taken from the shelf and held in the hand is a magical experience, linking writer to reader." But surely, it is not just the Epsteins of the world who understand the value of a literate, engaged public. What's next to go, libraries?

Paragraph 1 Paraphrase: _____

_____

_____

_____

Paragraph 2 Paraphrase: _____

_____

_____

_____

Paragraph 3 Paraphrase: _____

_____

_____

_____

Paragraph 4 Paraphrase: _____

_____

_____

_____

Paragraph 5 Paraphrase: _____

_____

_____

_____

ANALYSIS SKILL BUILDING

The SAT Essay is not a book report; it requires you to *analyze* the argument of the source text. You need not only to understand what the author has said—you must also articulate *why* the author has used certain evidence, reasoning, and stylistic approaches to make his or her argument. The following charts display some of the major methods that an author can use to persuade his or her audience:

Evidence

Type of Evidence	What Is It?	What Could It Look Like in the Argument?
Statistics	Information from scientific studies and popular polls, based on observation and presented using numbers.	"According to a recent study of how teachers allocate their time in classroom management, approximately 15 percent of students in the class monopolize most of a teacher's time as far as class discipline, while the other 85 percent is more compliant."
Authoritative Observation and Opinion	The author cites credible sources to give support to an argument. (Sometimes referred to as "ethos" from the Ancient Greeks.)	"According to the President of the American Association for Retired Persons, retired people are more interested in continuing to work part-time than they have been in the past."
Anecdote	The author uses personal stories to convey observations about a topic. Usually these are directly from the author's perspective, but the author could retell anecdotes from other people.	"The early start time for high school is a major problem for students. When I was of high school age, I found it exceedingly difficult to fall asleep before midnight, despite my best efforts to go to bed around 10 PM. When the alarm clock woke me up at 6 AM, I was exhausted and certainly not in the best frame of mind to learn."
Historical Allusion	The author makes reference to historical information. This could take the form of citing facts, referring to common historical knowledge, or making interpretations.	"It is well known that a major consequence of the U.S. Civil War was the end of slavery. How can it be that slavery still exists in our country to this day?"
Current Events and Media	This can go beyond mere quotations from authoritative sources and refer to newsworthy events with which the reader will likely be familiar.	"The tightening of security for the upcoming Olympic games is a necessary evil in today's society. In order to have secure gatherings, we must sacrifice some of our personal privacy and freedoms."

Reasoning

Reasoning in argument is often referred to as "logos" by Aristotle and the Ancient Greeks.

Type of Reasoning	What Is It?	What Could It Look Like in the Argument?
Contrast	Looking at a given situation and demonstrating how it is different from another situation.	"Requiring people to vote is in no way like requiring people to observe the speed limit. If people do not vote, it will not directly lead to the potential property damage and loss of life that a speeding motorist could cause."
Reciprocity	Appealing to the idea of justice and fairness by arguing that obligations should be mutual.	"If society refuses to make the necessary investments in early childhood education, why would underserved young children feel an obligation as adults to help fund the retirements and medical care of those who ignored them in their time of need?"
Consistency	Using the idea that a good intellectual position cannot be contradictory.	"People are completely opposed to testing experimental medicines and cosmetics on their own pets; yet, these same people seem to have no trouble purchasing medicines and cosmetics that have been tested on other animals, albeit ones that don't live with them. It seems that "out of sight, out of mind" is all too true when it comes to animal testing."
Cause and Effect	Showing how one event will directly lead to another. This can be done on a small scale with examples or on a large scale in the essay as a whole.	"Once the federal government increases the automotive mileage requirements for new vehicles, car manufacturers will have no choice but to create ways that car performance can be preserved without harming the environment."
Comparison and Analogy	Drawing parallels between different situations.	"Modern-day educators who dismiss the pedagogical value of comic books are like the bitter skeptics in the 1800s who argued that novel writing would cause social upheaval."
Rhetorical Question	Asking a question to the readers without expecting an answer in order to emphasize a point.	"Isn't everything fair in love and war?" "Don't all parents want what is best for their children?"

Style and Persuasion

Emotional appeal and style in argument are often referred to as "pathos" by Aristotle and the Ancient Greeks.

Type of Persuasion	What Is It?	What Could It Look Like in the Argument?
Sensory Language	Using language that appeals to the five senses, particularly sight, to illustrate an idea.	"Imagine a subway system free of litter, where you can sit without first having to clean your seat, and where you can inhale without feeling like you're in a restroom."
Emotional Appeal	Appealing to the reader's sense of love, duty, fear, greed, pride, and many more potential feelings to make a point.	"Sure—we could allocate less money to space exploration. But do we really want to be known as the generation that stopped dreaming of the heavens because we were too busy worrying about our pocketbooks?"
Attack	Showing why the views with which the author disagrees are unsound.	"I cannot help but notice that many of the same people who oppose giving women the opportunity to break through the 'glass ceiling' into management positions in major corporations also believe that women shouldn't have the opportunity to work in the first place."
Humor	Using jokes, irony, or sarcasm to engage the reader.	"An end to social prejudice will happen on the day that you can walk into a high school cafeteria and find nobody sitting in cliques."
Formal Language	Establishing the author's authority by using scholarly or sophisticated language.	"To make such an argument entails a *post hoc ergo propter hoc* logical fallacy, since correlation does not imply causation."
Informal Language	The author's using more approachable language to relate to his or her readers.	"There is no need to be fancy— give me some *good ol' down home cooking* any day!"
Inclusive/Exclusive Language	Encouraging the reader to identify with (inclusive) or want to separate from (exclusive) particular ideas.	"There are those of us who believe that if we work hard, we can achieve our dreams; and then there are some people who believe that the only way to get an advantage is to take advantage of others."

Practice

To become comfortable analyzing the arguments of an author, you need to be able to identify how the author is making his or her arguments. The examples that follow can all be labeled as at least one of the types of argument methodologies in the tables above. For fun, these examples are all on the topic of whether or not teenagers should be able to sleep in later. Label the type of methodology next to the example.

EXAMPLES

1. Can you imagine the danger if sleepy teenagers were allowed to drive their cars during rush hour?

2. A lack of sleep among teenagers may account for the increased preponderance of insomnia and narcolepsy due to a lack of uninterrupted REM dream states.

3. What could possibly better determine how much sleep a body needs than the body itself?

4. Some countries like the U.S. look at napping as a waste of time, while others fully embrace the afternoon siesta.

5. Depriving teenagers of sleep is like depriving a car of oil changes and maintenance—without the opportunity to recover, both will fall apart.

6. There are those who believe that unless people are completely busy every second, they are wasting their time. We know that without adequate rest, time spent being busy will simply be time spent being unproductive.

7. Imagine if teenagers could force adults to get up at a mandatory hour every single day, no matter the unique needs of the adults in question. Just as adults are able to choose their jobs and lifestyles based on their body clocks, teenagers should have the same freedom to structure their schedules in accordance with their bodily rhythms.

8. The U.S. Surgeon General recently stated that a later start to the school day could have a marked positive impact on student learning outcomes.

9. Young people are asked to make healthy choices when it comes to drugs, sex, and nutrition. Yet when it comes to sleep, parents often encourage decidedly unhealthy habits.

10. Imagine yourself as a troubled teenager, burdened throughout the day with adults telling you how to behave. Your one refuge is your bed, where your soft pillow comforts your weary head at the end of a long, long day.

11. Once, when I took the SAT, I stayed up late partying the night before the test. My score was atrocious. The next time I took the test, I got a good night's sleep every day of the week before test day. Unsurprisingly, my score increased by over 200 points.

12. If you forget to wear your pajamas, next day you'll probably go bananas.

13. Those opposed to adequate sleep may not realize that sleep deprivation is a method used by torturers to produce confessions.

14. According to the Centers for Disease Control, approximately 43% of young adults ages 18–25 have reported involuntarily falling asleep during the day within the past month. (*http://www.cdc.gov/features/dssleep/*)

15. If students are able to sleep as much as their bodies truly need, they will be able to achieve their full academic potential since they will be able to devote their full attention to their studies. If students can achieve their full academic potential, the country will have a far stronger workforce in the decades to come.

16. A noted Frenchman once said, "Some people talk in their sleep. Lecturers talk while other people sleep."

17. Most people have heard that the tanker captain who crashed his ship into the reef last week, causing the oil spill, had been working a triple shift. This is the sort of thing that can happen when people are sleep-deprived.

18. Young people today have many more potential distractions that keep them from sleeping well than those from past generations. Fifty years ago, there was no texting, tweeting, or messaging.

KEY

1. Emotional appeal
2. Formal Language, authoritative observation, or cause and effect
3. Rhetorical question
4. Contrast
5. Comparison and analogy
6. Inclusive/exclusive language
7. Reciprocity or consistency
8. Authoritative observation and opinion
9. Consistency or comparison
10. Sensory language
11. Anecdote
12. Informal language
13. Attacks or emotional appeal
14. Statistics
15. Cause and effect
16. Humor
17. Current events
18. Historical allusion

Now, identify the type(s) of persuasive device(s) in the numbered examples in a sample SAT Source Text (the same one from the practice exercise from Reading Skill Building above). These examples do not constitute every possible example of analysis in the text below but merely a sample.

Books: A Lost Art

It is not solely nostalgia for the [1] good ol' days when you finished a great book and passed on your copy—[2] dog-eared, coffee stained, and splattered with notes—to a friend who would add her own thoughts and pass it to another that has book lovers resenting the age of the e-book (though certainly this is part of it). Instead, book lovers argue that the severed relationship between reader and print book in the [3] current technologically-inclined generation is more worrying and encompassing than most imagine. It is not just the literary crowd, devotedly attached to their overflowing bookshelves, who have a stake in the disappearance of hard-copies, but also small business owners, editing and publishing firms, and even the general public.

With the e-book's conquest over traditional hardcovers and paperbacks, *Publishers Weekly* released a report of a steady decrease in print sales, with [4] 2012 sales down 9% from those in 2011. Meanwhile, after the disastrous closing of Borders and the plummet of sales suffered by Barnes and Noble, [5] *Business Insider* suggested that bookstores, large and small, were doomed. The convenience and low cost of e-books has many hesitant to drive out to a store that may or may not have what they are looking for. Yet, it isn't just the enthusiastic reader trying to reverse the trend of disappearing bookstores. [6] Are we truly ready to give up the retail experience—shelves upon shelves of your favorites, quiet nooks to cuddle up in, children's reading hour, a latte and a stack of magazines—in its entirety? In February 2015, *U.S. News and World Report* directly connected the suspension in economic recovery to the decline of small businesses. If their research is conclusive, it is not just the unique shopping experience or quirky atmospheres of independent bookstores at risk.

Likewise, dwindling print sales means unpredictability in the publishing and editing industries, where professionals are trying hard to keep up with erratic consumer trends. The rise in e-books, self-publishing, and the Amazon empire has made revenues more unstable than ever. [7] With bookselling drifting more and more to the online market, publishing will also turn digital, and the implications for traditional publishing companies are grave. Publishers wonder how quickly it will take for their jobs to follow the tendencies of print books and become gradually obsolete. And how long will it take writers, competing for quick sales, to turn to direct online publishing to boost their own prospects for success?

If the evidence of failing small businesses and unhinged bookselling industries isn't enough to favor the printed, in-hand book, then perhaps an account by *The Atlantic* released in late 2014 will be; data shows that the number of American nonreaders has tripled since the 1980s. With the fading of the hard-copy, reading itself has plummeted, undoubtedly in favor of the [8] savvy digital distractions that make up our on-the-go e-lifestyles. Certainly, there are many factors contributing to America's abandonment of literature, but it stands that e-books are failing to keep the public's nose in a book. Perhaps, the e-book age has discouraged having books on hand, visiting the library on the weekends, and telling stories before bedtime. Could it be that once frequent readers have lost the love for stories that they once had when they could feel them in their hands, turn their pages, and never have to plug them in or interrupt them for an email alert? [9] When asked why she neglected reading after thirty years, one mother of three answered, "I grew up around books—we had hundreds. When I got older, I used to spend Saturday mornings at a coffee shop down the street reading for hours. Somewhere along the way, life got faster and I lost it."

Possibly, few can relate to Jason Epstein's declaration in his 2001 *Book Business*: "A civilization without retail bookstores is unimaginable. [10] Like shrines and other sacred meeting places, bookstores are essential artifacts of human nature. The feel of a book taken from the shelf and held in the hand is a magical experience, linking writer to reader." But surely, it is not just the Epsteins of the world who understand the value of a literate, engaged public. What's next to go, libraries?

YOUR ANSWERS

1. _____

2. _____

3. _____

4. _____

5. _____

6. _____

7. _____

8. _____

9. _____

10. _____

SOLUTIONS

1. Informal language
2. Sensory language
3. Current events
4. Statistics
5. Authoritative opinion
6. Rhetorical question and sensory language
7. Cause and effect
8. Formal language
9. Anecdote
10. Comparison/analogy and authoritative opinion

WRITING SKILL BUILDING

In addition to having a command of English grammar, your essay should demonstrate excellent writing skills by having the following four elements:

1. A clear thesis
2. Good progression of ideas
3. Variety in wording and sentence structure
4. Precise communication with well-chosen words

Let's examine each of these elements of good writing:

1 Thesis

The thesis of your essay is a clear statement of your central claim that previews your argument. Read the following examples to see what poor and good theses in response to questions would look like.

QUESTION: Should the penny coin be eliminated?

POOR THESIS: "It is very important that the penny coin be eliminated for many reasons." There is no preview of the author's argument.

GOOD THESIS: "Since it costs more to manufacture a penny than a penny itself is worth, it is time that to abandon this antiquated relic, making the nickel the smallest unit of hard currency." This gives a clear idea of where the author is going to take the argument.

QUESTION: Should textbooks be replaced with tablet computers?

POOR THESIS: "I really think that textbooks are bad and that tablet computers are much better because they will improve upon what we can do in school." This uses many words to say virtually nothing, and "improve" is too vague.

GOOD THESIS: "Because of long-term cost savings, ease of transport, and opportunities for more interactive learning, tablet computers should replace textbooks in schools." Using virtually the same number of words as the previous thesis, this statement is far more clear as to how tablet computers will make education better.

QUESTION: Should students not be permitted to use cell phones in school?

POOR THESIS: "There are many pros and cons to the important issue of whether cellular phones provide a salubrious solution to learning." This uses a big word, "salubrious," (i.e., "health-giving), in a poor attempt to impress the reader. Also, it takes no position on the question.

GOOD THESIS: "While cellular phones provide a possible vehicle for independent research and dynamic learning, their potential to distract students from instruction is too great; as a result, students should be prohibited from using cellular phones in school." This statement provides a strong idea of the author's position and the major points that the author will make.

2 Progression

Your essay must be organized in a logical, sequential manner. A reader should be able to outline your argument easily. The following mini-essays give you an idea of *what* not *to do* and *what to do* in order to demonstrate progression of thoughts.

Topic: Should high school students be able to leave school for lunch?

Poor Progression	Good Progression
Try to follow the writer's argument. How does it advance?	*Try to follow the writer's argument. How does it advance?*
Lunch is a very important thing for students to have the freedom to enjoy on their own. I love to eat lunch with my friends and family instead of eating at school. As the second meal of the day, lunch is sometimes the only meal that many students are sure to have each day, so it is really important that they can eat it how they want. A couple of weeks ago, my friends and I went out to eat at a restaurant and we had a really good time there. My teachers get to leave school for lunch, so I don't see why on earth we can't do that either. Who are the principal and school board to boss us around and take away our freedoms? School lunches may be nutritious, but I for one would much rather eat whatever I want whenever I want to do so. Some of the restaurants close to my school are pretty inexpensive—that is important for people who don't have a lot of pocket money. Poverty is a major issue nationwide and worldwide. If you take away the freedom to have lunch on your own, what's next? Will we not be able to have freedom of speech, press, and religion? I look forward to lunch more than any time during the school day. It is therefore proven that lunch needs to be open for students.	Students should be given the opportunity to leave school for lunch for three major reasons. First, when students become adults, they will have such freedom. In order to prepare students for the world of work, they should begin learning responsibility at a young age. Second, students will benefit from having a break from the monotony of school. Having the opportunity to get off school grounds and recharge will build student morale and empower students to be more focused when they return from their meal. Finally, giving students the chance to leave school for lunch will likely encourage more physical activity, as many students will walk home or to a nearby restaurant. With obesity an increasingly menacing issue for young people, students should be encouraged to have a dedicated time each day when they have the chance to walk around. Many people are rightly concerned that some students cannot be trusted to act appropriately with this freedom; rather than letting a few bad apples spoil the barrel, schools should prohibit troublemakers from leaving the school grounds, while allowing responsible students the freedom to make their own choices.
It's difficult to see the layers of the argument, isn't it?	*Did you notice how the writer uses transition words like "First" and "Finally" to alert the reader of the progression?*

3 Variety

On the new SAT Writing, you will likely find it most challenging to avoid repeating yourself in two major areas: transition words (both in the general structure of your essay and in your analysis of the given prompt), and argumentative words. These tables give you more variety in how you can express these ideas.

Examples of Transitional Words		
First	Generally speaking	Going forward
Then	Of course	Now
Next	Initially	In fact
In summary	Since	At last
Overall	In turn	By allowing
Undeniably	Therefore	Furthermore
More so	However	Meanwhile
Lastly	Perhaps	Simultaneously
Finally	From this point forward	Subsequently
Additionally	At times	Specifically
Hence	For example	On the contrary
Thus	Again	Accordingly
From here on out	Nonetheless	That is to say
As a result of	Throughout	Suddenly

Examples of Argumentative Words		
Argue	Allows	Rely
Argument	Contemplate	Acknowledge
Prove	Enable	Connect
Show	Define	Concede
Illustrate	Consider	Enlist
Appeal	Complex	Effectively
Depict	Cite	Reason
Builds	Reference	Plea
Present	Provide	Maintain
Employ	Questions	Persuade
Insist	Display	Convince

4 Precision

Show your command of the English language by using *precise* words to express your ideas. Here are some examples of imprecise and precise responses to given questions.

QUESTION: How are you feeling today?

IMPRECISE RESPONSE: I am feeling pretty decent. Pretty ok, more or less.

PRECISE RESPONSE: I feel physically rested, intellectually contemplative, and socially extroverted.

QUESTION: How was that movie you just watched?

IMPRECISE RESPONSE: The movie had several bad qualities about it that made me not find it very pleasing.

PRECISE RESPONSE: While the movie attempted to fit the drama genre, the acting was so amateurish that the film was more of a comedy.

QUESTION: What are you looking for in a college?

IMPRECISE RESPONSE: I would like to go to a college where I will be happy, learn cool things, have some pretentious and multitudinous experiences, and make friends with interesting people.

PRECISE RESPONSE: I want to attend a college that is close to a major city, yet is self-contained, has opportunities for independent research and study abroad, and has a large international student body so I can learn about other cultures outside of the classroom.

Let's now examine a top-scoring response to the "Books: A Lost Art" passage for examples of the **thesis**, **progression**, **variety**, and **precision**:

> **Prompt:** Write a response that demonstrates how the author makes an argument to persuade an audience that traditional book publishing is valuable. In your response, analyze how the author uses at least one of the features from the essay directions (or features of your own choosing) to develop a logical and persuasive argument. Be certain that your response cites relevant aspects of the source text.
>
> Your response should not give your personal opinion on the merit of the source text, but instead show how the author crafts an argument to persuade readers.

RESPONSE

In response to the growing issue of "the disappearance of hardcopies" the author of the article, "Books: A Lost Art", makes the argument that traditional book publishing is valuable. **The author effectively persuades the audience by utilizing published research, rhetorical questions, and powerful word choice.**

> **THESIS**
>
> This sentence clearly states the writer's position and previews her argument. It should typically be stated in the first or second paragraph so the reader understands what the writer will argue.

Throughout the article the author strategically inserts published research to help bring merit to the idea that the diminishing publication of hard-copy books and closing of local bookstores is not only an issue for book lovers, "but also small business owners, publishing and editing firms, and the general public." The author **shares** a finding from a February 2015, *U.S. News and World Report* that "directly connected the suspension in economic recovery to the decline of small businesses." This powerful statement insinuates that the consumer does crave the retail experience of the past over the current electronic lifestyle we have created. The author continues to **influence** the audience by examining research of dwindling book sales by introducing a report from *Publishers Weekly* that states there is "a steady decrease in print sales, with 2012 sales down 9% from those in 2011." From this piece of statistical information the author is better able to **explain** to the audience the growing issues facing publishers and editors including: erratic consumer trends, job loss, and writer instability. By **highlighting** the major issues small businesses and publishing firms face today the author is able to **support the claim** that traditional book publishing is valuable beyond just pleasing the avid reader.

> **VARIETY**
>
> The highlighted words in this paragraph give five different ways that the writer has referred to argumentative techniques without repeating herself.

To help balance the hard-fact approach of introducing the audience to research, the author also engages the audience by using rhetorical questions to help elicit an emotional response. **Awakening an emotional response in the audience persuades the readers to see value in traditional book publishing because it helps connect the individual to the big picture problem.** For example, the question, "Are we truly ready to give up the retail experience—shelves upon shelves of your favorites, quiet nooks to cuddle up in, children's reading hour, a latte and a stack of magazines—in its entirety?" paints a vivid picture in the mind of the readers and helps transport them to a moment in time that they enjoyed. Now that the audience is in a positive space, it would seem almost unfathomable to them to give up the bookstore experience, which is the ultimate goal of the author. The author continues to push the audience's emotional level when in the final sentence asks, "What's next to go, libraries?" Strategically placing this question at the very end of the article delivers a final punch to the audience that really makes them think about the value of traditional book publishing. This is because, for many, libraries are a staple in the community that have been around for decades and many could not comprehend an end to libraries, but the author makes sure to emphasize the possibility of this if traditional book publishing ceases to exist.

> **PRECISION**
>
> The writer uses precise language to communicate her analysis of the source text.

Finally, the author uses powerful word choice throughout the article in order to persuade the audience to see the value in traditional book publishing. It is important for the author to use meaningful words in the article so that the audience quickly grasps the dire situation with decreasing traditional book publish-

> **PROGRESSION**
>
> The writer has used logical transitions to introduce the body paragraphs, and each paragraph ties directly to the thesis.

ing. An example of this is in the opening sentence of the second paragraph when the author states "with the e-book's conquest over traditional hardcovers and paperbacks." This sentence helps the audience quickly understand—from the use of the word "conquest"—that e-books have purposefully taken over traditional books. And as the author continues to explain in the article, dominance of the e-book has many consequential effects for different types of businesses. If the author chose a less powerful word or rearranged the sentence, the audience might not fully understand the severity of the situation caused by increasing e-books in the market.

As the digital age continues to grow at rapid rates many traditional businesses, including the book publishing industry, continue to dwindle. Understanding the value of keeping traditional book publishing, the author is able to persuade the audience to the same understanding by using published research, rhetorical questions, and powerful word choice throughout the article.

Now that we have a better grasp of the fundamentals, let's move on to the Essay Writing Strategies.

TEN KEY STRATEGIES FOR SAT ESSAY WRITING SUCCESS

1. **KEEP YOUR PERSONAL OPINIONS TO YOURSELF!** Unlike many essays you have written, this is not a persuasive opinion piece. One of the most significant errors students will make on the SAT Essay will be inserting their own views on a topic and criticizing the argument provided. The task is to analyze *how the author makes his or her argument*, not to make your own argument on the topic.

2. **LOOK FOR WHAT IS GOOD IN THE ARGUMENT—DON'T RIP IT APART.** The source text you will analyze will be a well-written argument for a general audience. There will likely be no major argumentative fallacies in the piece, and the assignment does not ask you to find problems in the source. So, instead of critiquing the source text as you read, carefully take it all in and look for the skillful ways in which the author uses evidence, reasoning, and rhetoric to make his or her argument.

3. **THE PROMPT WILL NOT CHANGE, WHILE THE SOURCE TEXT WILL. KNOW THE QUESTION, FORMAT, AND DIRECTIONS AHEAD OF TIME.** You will always need to read the source text carefully, looking for how the author builds an argument. You will always need to write a response that describes and analyzes how the author makes this argument. You will always have 50 minutes to do all of this. With the source text changing with each essay, prepare yourself by being completely familiar with what stays consistent with each SAT essay.

4. **ALLOW ENOUGH TIME TO READ THE PASSAGE WELL.** You will be tempted to rush through reading the passage, but don't—if you don't fully understand the argument, you will not be able to produce a good response. Time invested up front in the initial reading will pay major dividends when you write an essay that accurately and thoroughly analyzes the source text.

5. **READ *ACTIVELY*!** While reading the source text, ask yourself this two part question over and over: *What is the author saying and why?* "What" the author is saying aligns with the "Reading" component of the essay rubric, and "why" aligns with the "Analysis" component of the rubric. Here are some more specific things to focus on as you read:

- Paraphrase: What is the author generally saying? What is the thesis?
- Intention: Why might the author have argued this?
- Tone: Is it informal or formal? Why?
- Perspective: Is it first, second, or third person? Why?
- Structure: Is the essay structured chronologically? Does it move general observations to specific illustrations? Does the essay illustrate the pros and cons of an idea? Does it gradually "discover" a general conclusion? Why has the author structured the essay in this way?
- Style: What kind of wording does the author use? How about imagery and sensory appeal? Why was this done?
- Evidence: How does the author support his or her claims? Are there examples, evidence, statistics, or anecdotes? Why was this evidence chosen?

6. **DETERMINE YOUR PREFERRED PREWRITING METHOD.** Figure out the best way to organize your thoughts for the essay, and do so before the actual test so you don't just "wing it." Here are three major ways you might want to prewrite:

- **Outline:** Write a step-by-step outline of what you are going to argue in each body paragraph and what examples you will use. This is a good approach if you sometimes go on tangents when you write, and you appreciate having a clear plan before you begin.
- **Plan your general points:** After reading the text, jot down the 3–4 major points you are going to make in the essay. As you write your body paragraphs, frequently go back to the text to find support for your claims.
- **Get going:** If you have a difficult time determining the overall structure and thesis of your argument ahead of time, you may want to start by writing your body paragraphs, leaving a few lines blank at the beginning of your essay for the introduction that you will write later. As you write the body paragraphs, be mindful of the general points you are arguing. With 5–10 minutes remaining, write your conclusion and go back to the beginning of your response and write your introductory paragraph. If you plan on doing this approach, be certain to practice it ahead of time so you allow adequate time to have a well-developed introduction and a clear thesis.

7. **STAY FOCUSED.** The graders will look to see whether you have a clear thesis and whether you are able to sustain your argument all the way through your essay. Be sure you have a well-constructed introduction and conclusion and that you are explicit in stating your claims. You don't have time for digressions. Make it as easy as possible for the graders to understand and follow your argument so that they can give you the best score.

8. **DETERMINE HOW YOU WANT TO PACE YOURSELF.** Review the following chart and fill in the last column with your personal plan for timing. You can make a solid determination without writing an entire essay simply by practicing the reading and prewriting steps and noting how long these two steps take.

Part of the Process	Range of Times	How to Decide	How Much Time Will I Take for Each Part?
Reading the Source	4–10 minutes	Are you are a faster or slower reader? Be sure you take the time to understand the source text fully. If you are going to spend more time prewriting, you may want to spend less time with the initial reading, and vice versa.	
Prewriting	1–5 minutes	If you need to have a clear outline to stay focused as you write, take the time to prewrite well. If you stay focused without a detailed outline, devote more time to writing your response.	
Writing the Essay	35–45 minutes	The response is handwritten, so be mindful of how quickly you are physically able to write. Factor in how much time you want to devote to reading and prewriting.	
Editing	0–5 minutes	Do you generally make quite a few spelling/grammar errors that need to be fixed? If so, allow enough time to proofread. If you are generally careful in your initial writing, devote less time to editing and focus on writing a more in-depth response.	

Be sure your total time adds up to 50 minutes!

As you practice writing SAT essays, you will learn what pacing plan works best for you.

9. **DON'T LET THE PERFECT BE THE ENEMY OF THE GOOD!** The SAT graders realize that you are a high school student writing a challenging essay along with doing hours of multiple-choice questions. They don't expect perfection. You will certainly want to minimize grammar and spelling errors, but you should not devote so much time to proofreading that you sacrifice the development of your argument.

10. **BUILD YOUR ARGUMENT ANALYSIS SKILLS OVER THE LONG TERM.** There is a great deal you can do besides working through practice SAT essays to improve your skills for test day. Here are some ideas:

   ■ Read and analyze editorial and opinion articles from major newspapers and magazines:

   - *New York Times*
   - *Wall Street Journal*
   - *Washington Post*
   - *L. A. Times*
   - *The Atlantic*
   - *The Economist*

   - *Legal Affairs*
   - *The New Republic*
   - *Sports Illustrated Writers*
   - *Popular Science*
   - *Scientific American*
   - *Discover*

- Debate with your friends on current events and other issues. The more you practice argumentation, the more easily you will recognize its structure.
- Become an active reader and commenter on blog discussions.
- Make a habit of not taking things on face value. If you are watching the news, ask why the information is being presented as it is. If you are watching a commercial, question the use of evidence and make note of emotional appeals. Be an active, rather than passive, consumer of information.

PUTTING IT ALL TOGETHER

Let's go step by step through everything you will need to do to write a successful essay.

First, let's actively read the prompt. Know the directions ahead of time so you can focus your energy on actively reading the source text. The types of thoughts/notes you could have while reading are given after the prompt.

Directions: This assignment will allow you to demonstrate your ability to skillfully read and understand a source text and write a response analyzing the source. In your response, you should show that you have understood the source, give proficient analysis, and use the English language effectively. If your essay is off-topic, it will not be scored.

Only what you write on the lined paper in your answer document will be scored—avoid skipping lines, using unreasonably large handwriting, and using wide margins in order to have sufficient space to respond. You can also write on the planning sheet in the answer document, but this will not be evaluated—no other scrap paper will be given. Be sure to write clearly and legibly so your response can be scored.

You will be given 50 minutes to complete the assignment, including reading the source text and writing your response.

Read the following passage, and think about how the author uses:

- Evidence, such as applicable examples, to justify the argument
- Reasoning to show logical connections among thoughts and facts
- Rhetoric, like sensory language and emotional appeals, to give weight to the argument

The History Major

1   I am sure you have heard by now—news trickles fast down the steep façade of the ivory tower. Perhaps, you've already packed up my room, taken my portrait off the mantel, and relayed my unfortunate accident to the intrusive Mr. and Mrs. Duta ("a rare condition," "such ill-fated tragedy," "nonetheless, Swanson's Home for the Irresponsibly Insane provides the very best care"). Or, you've called the Dean, pleaded for immediate intervention (surely, the choice should belong to those whose pockets dwindle every semester), and sabotaged my class schedule so that I inadvertently end up at the College of Science and Technology once again. And so, it is with utmost austerity that I beg for your ear; fear not, I am no lost cause.

2   The Liberal Arts education is far from obsolete. Despite the rumors of late, you need not worry that your son will end up unemployed and homeless, pining over unheeded art in shadowy bars with rickety tabletops and flyer-covered walls. Nor must you relinquish hopes for a charming daughter-in-law and animated, curly-haired grandchildren. What I mean to say is that liberal arts graduates are well-suited—in some ways, even better suited—for success and happiness than their narrowed, specializing counterparts. Not only are our skills coveted in graduate school and the workforce, but we are also more adaptable and likely to move up rank in our careers. The breadth of study emphasized in a liberal arts education provides an exemplary foundation for a variety of professional fields and career paths, while molding open-minded, curious problem solvers. *Mom and Dad*, I implore you to reconsider my cosmopolitan ambitions and reinstate my place at the dinner table.

3   A third of all Fortune 500 CEOs possess liberal arts degrees. LEAP, or Liberal Education & America's Promise, is an initiative launched by the Association of American Colleges & Universities to emphasize the importance of a 21st Century liberal education for individuals and a nation "dependent on economic creativity and democratic vitality." According to LEAP's recent national survey, 93% of employers say that "a demonstrated capacity to think critically, communicate clearly, and solve complex problems is more important than undergraduate major." You've guessed it—these three skill sets are the unifying objective of liberal arts programs nationwide.

4   Furthermore, these skills are timelessly useful and valuable; in a quickly evolving world, they are the few ingenuities that will neither be replaced nor outdated. Whether students decide on graduate education, law or medical school, or dive right into the job hunt, a broad and diverse interdisciplinary education provides the analytical, research, and independent judgment training necessary to gain an edge on other applicants. Acquisition of self-understanding, accompanied by a respect for others and an aptitude for clear expression, shapes leaders in a variety of work environments from government to business to education. The lucrative liberal arts education results in a life-long learner who asks difficult questions, presents information intelligibly, and makes coherent arguments across disciplines. *Is this not what you want for your baby boy?*

5   Even more intriguing is the evidence that a liberal arts education spawns happier individuals. With a capacity to understand and enjoy humanity's achievements, my artsy cohort and I will be more likely to spend time appreciating literature, music, art, and even witty conversation, and to participate in our communities and global politics. An active and engaged life is indeed something to be happy about. According to Robert Harris's *On the Purpose of a Liberal Education*, in addition to teaching students how to think, learn, and see things whole, a liberal education also enhances students' faith and wisdom, with their gained knowledge begetting increased pleasure.

6   Let us not forget Leonard da Vinci, Michelangelo, or America's own, Benjamin Franklin, who made their marks on society not with one expertise, but with a legion of talents— renaissance men of the highest degree. It is the cultivated mind of the multifarious and enlightened that I endeavor toward with my decision to declare a History major. If I manage to avoid the fate of the shaggy-haired drifter of your nightmares, I could turn out to be brilliant (or mediocre with a steady job and varied interests).

Write a response that demonstrates how the author makes an argument to persuade an audience that a liberal arts education is valuable. In your response, analyze how the author uses at least one of the features from the essay directions (or features of your own choosing) to develop a logical and persuasive argument. Be certain that your response cites relevant aspects of the source text.

Your response should not give your personal opinion on the merit of the source text, but instead show how the author crafts an argument to persuade readers.

Active Reading Notes

This is a detailed paragraph-by-paragraph summary of the essay's argument. These are the types of things you can think about and make notes of while reading the source text:

1. Draws you in—at first you're not sure what the author is talking about

    a. Seems like something dramatic, like suicide

    b. The dramatization plays to your emotions and draws you in

    c. After the first paragraph dramatization, the author announces that he is talking about choosing to get a liberal arts education

2. The fact that it's written as a sort of letter to the parents causes you to put yourself in the author's shoes

    a. This is a particularly effective technique with this topic because this is a topic about which many students probably have argued, or will argue, with their parents

3. Considers possible objections to the liberal arts education

    a. Graduates end up unemployed

        i. Combats this with facts:

            1. 1/3 of Fortune 500 CEOs have liberal arts degrees
            2. 93% of employers say the very skills a liberal arts education strives to provide are more important than a major

4. Appeals to anxieties many students may have

    a. Not finding a job in the future

    b. Happiness in the future

        i. There is evidence that those with liberal arts educations may tend to be happier
        ii. Cites *On the Purpose of a Liberal Education*

            1. Enhances students' faith and wisdom

                a. Leads to increased pleasure

5. Compares getting a liberal arts education to being a renaissance man and references some of the greats—who wouldn't want to be like them?

Then, you can spend time prewriting your essay. The following is a rough prewrite for this essay; the author summarizes the theme of each of her body paragraphs.

- Author uses persuasive techniques.
- We empathize with him as teenagers.
- Explain how he addresses objections.
- Analyze how he appeals to reader anxieties.
- Examine renaissance man argument.

Now, review an excellent response to this essay that builds upon the above reading notes and prewrite.

Full Top-Scoring Essay Response

This author uses a wide variety of persuasive techniques in his essay to craft an extremely well thought-out argument for why liberal arts educations are useful. He considers possible objections to his argument, which he combats with facts. He very purposely evokes certain emotions in the reader, such as empathy and anxiety. He proceeds to alleviate these anxieties with facts that make the reader want to pursue a liberal arts education, before wrapping up the argument by comparing the liberal arts educated to renaissance men.

The author is mindfully persuasive from the very beginning, introducing the topic with a dramatization that draws the reader in. The description of the family cleaning out the author's room out and taking the author's picture off of the mantel makes the reader think that something tragic has happened. The author then shocks the reader by announcing that the "tragedy" that has taken place was simply his choice to pursue a liberal arts education. The author seems to have carefully chosen such an introduction to get the reader to think that such a "tragedy" is extremely trivial; this is the author's first step in his persuasion.

The author also seems to have carefully chosen to write this essay as a mock address to his parents. It seems as if the purpose for this choice was to put the reader in the author's shoes. This is a seamless transition for the reader, as many students have had, or will have, similar arguments with their parents. This forces the reader to feel empathy, making the author's attempt at persuasion more effective.

After the initial dramatization, the author goes on to consider some possible objections to a liberal arts education. For instance, the author alludes to the parents expressing concern that their child will end up unemployed after college. The author's rebuttal to such concerns is twofold. First, he uses tongue-in-cheek humor to brush off such concerns, by assuring his parents that he will not end up homeless. Second, and more effectively, he uses facts to the contrary. For instance, he states that 1/3 of Fortune 500 CEOs have liberal arts degrees.

Another technique used in the argument is appealing to the reader's own anxieties. Many students worry that they won't find jobs in today's competitive job market. The author eases this anxiety by assuring the reader that 93% of employers say that they care more that an employee possess the skills that a liberal arts education strives to foster than about the particular major the employee chose. Another thing that many young people worry about is whether or not they'll be happy in the future. The author assures the reader that many liberal arts degree recipients tend to be happier than their peers. He cites *On the Purpose of a Liberal Education* as saying that a liberal arts education can increase faith and wisdom, which leads to an increase in pleasure.

Finally, the author compares getting a liberal arts education to being a renaissance man. Both the liberal arts educated and the people we tend to think of as renaissance men are well-versed in a wide array of disciplines. He cites Leonardo da Vinci, Michelangelo, and Ben Franklin, forcing the reader to consider why someone wouldn't strive to be like these greats.

In conclusion, the author begins his argument by first hinting that something tragic has happened to him. When he reveals that this "tragedy" was choosing a liberal arts path, this forces the reader to think, "how disastrous can such a decision really be?" Once the reader is feeling fairly neutral on the subject matter, the author begins persuading. He uses a variety of techniques, such as appealing to the emotions of the reader and considering possible objections. He also backs up his argument with facts about how job and happiness prospects are very good for those with liberal arts educations. Finally, he allows the reader to compare what they could be with a liberal arts education to some of the great renaissance men. Overall, the argument was very well developed, owing much of its effectiveness to the success of evoking chosen emotions in the reader.

SCORING: READING = 4, ANALYSIS = 4, WRITING = 4

EXPLANATION: The response demonstrates an excellent grasp of the source text's argument, primarily using paraphrase to show understanding. The writer's response is well structured and focused on analysis of the text's use of evocation of emotions. The essay has a well-developed introduction and conclusion. The author's word choice is precise, and there is a variety of sentence structure. Underneath the central umbrella of emotional evocation, the response analyzes how and why the author of the source does this, citing (among other things) how readers can relate to arguments with parents, how the author uses humor, and how the author hooks the audience in the introduction.

SAMPLE ESSAYS

Now, let us examine a variety of responses to a given prompt, each response having a different score.

> Read the following passage, and think about how the author uses:
>
> - Evidence, such as applicable examples, to justify the argument
> - Reasoning to show logical connections among thoughts and facts
> - Rhetoric, like sensory language and emotional appeals, to give weight to the argument

The Importance of Studying Philosophy

1 Consider the work that you most enjoy doing. How do you figure out what to do when complications arise? Relationships with family members, friends, and others enrich our lives. What makes those relationships go well? Many forms of recreation contribute to living a good life. But is there any ultimate meaning or purpose to these temporary activities, or even to life itself? Studying philosophy equips us with the skills needed to understand these and many other important questions.

2   "Philosophy" literally means the love of wisdom. It involves striving to understand the most fundamental questions about life and all other disciplines. It provides us with the opportunity to engage ideas, to learn from great minds throughout history, and to contribute to our understanding of the world and ourselves. Studying philosophy builds our abilities to break down concepts, such as love and justice, to understand them, to communicate ideas effectively, and to discover good reasons that help us know what beliefs to accept. It enables us to have the *summum bonum*, or the highest good, through the pursuit of what is true, good, and beautiful.

3   Training in philosophy helps us to make progress in working through otherwise intractable problems. There are some issues about which there has been ongoing debate, such as God's existence, immortality, and abortion. How do we handle these topics? We might avoid them, sweeping them under the rug, either in our interactions with others or even in our own minds. Other times, we resort to name-calling, getting emotionally heated, or personal attacks. In the case of slavery, such responses led to an American civil war! These approaches only make matters worse, generating more heat than light and leading to hurt feelings, broken relationships, or worse. Taking a philosophical approach, however, focuses our attention on the issue at hand to understand it, to learn about different views, and to explore the reasoning behind those views, getting to the heart of the matter. This provides the possibility of finding resolution and implementing solutions. Regardless of how much disagreement remains, through respect for one another, we can maintain friendships and work together toward the common goal of learning more about what is true. If everyone consistently followed this path, imagine how much better our world would be!

4   The skills developed through studying philosophy train us to clear up confusions. Sometimes, when two people are discussing a significant life issue, they talk past one another and use the same terms in different ways. Learning to analyze concepts helps us to step back and clarify what we mean by the terms we use, to realize the assumptions we are making in holding certain views, and to make important distinctions. Through this process, we may discover that we did not even have a disagreement with someone, but that we were simply emphasizing different aspects of the same idea. Take, for example, the concept of equality. Most people recognize that this is an important value to uphold. But what do we mean by it in a certain context? We could be referring to people having equal value, equal opportunities, equal outcomes, or equal treatment. Then, how does something like equal treatment apply in matters of friendship, for example? Answering that question requires a further investigation into the nature of friendship. Learning to make key distinctions and clarifications like this in philosophy improves our ability to think well and in turn to live wisely.

5   Another way in which we can recognize the importance of philosophy is by considering how we have acquired the fruits of science and technology. The advances made in medicine, transportation, communications, and so forth have been remarkable. But certain philosophical ideas have made modern science possible, such as that there are laws by which matter and energy operate over time and throughout space. In Isaac Newton's great work, *Mathematical Principles of Natural Philosophy*, it was through philosophical reflection about his observations that led him to revolutionary scien-

tific ideas. Questions about how to best explain what we observe, what the laws of nature are, or what science itself is, are issues explored in philosophy of science. Does philosophy involve working through difficult concepts and abstract arguments? Yes, but it's doable as we learn from others, standing on the shoulders of those who have gone before us. It is also well worth the effort, as it improves our understanding of the mundane to the most profound issues, and helps us know how to put that knowledge to good use.

Write a response that demonstrates how the author makes an argument to persuade an audience that a study of philosophy is worthwhile. In your response, analyze how the author uses at least one of the features from the essay directions (or features of your own choosing) to develop a logical and persuasive argument. Be certain that your response cites relevant aspects of the source text.

Your response should not give your personal opinion on the merit of the source text but instead show how the author crafts an argument to persuade readers.

EXAMPLE 1: READING = 1, ANALYSIS = 1, WRITING = 1

In "The Importance of Studying Philosophy" the author argues that studying philosophy is very important. Philosophy can help solve wars and by making new discoveries in science.

Philosophy or "the love of wisdom," "focuses our attention on the issue at hand in an attempt to understand it, to consider different views, and to explore the reasoning behind those views, get to the heart of the matter." It could be used in slavery and the civil war to think through people's problems and stop fights because both sides could respect each other and want a better world.

Philosophy is also important because it answers big questions and even helped Isaac Newton write his book *Mathematics Principles of Natural Philosophy* in which "it was through philosophical refelction about his observations that he was able to revolutionize scientific ideas." So, without philosophy we wouldn't probably have science or math either.

In this argument the writer shows that philosophy is important by showing it could have stopped slavery and also because it helps scientists. Now everyone who didn't know it was important will definitely know it is.

EXPLANATION: This response misinterprets the general argument of the source, giving no clear analysis. The writing is disorganized and has numerous errors.

EXAMPLE 2: READING = 2, ANALYSIS = 2, WRITING = 2

The passage argues that philosophy is important by defining it and showing its advantages to all aspects of life. It is most likely addressing high school students who are entering college and may not know what philosophy is or how it relates to them. The author builds an argument for philosophy by making it easier to understand and really explaining to the students what philosophy can do for them.

The author uses rhetorical questions to build the argument. For instance: "But is there any ultimate meaning or purpose to these temporary activities, or even to life itself?" Another example is when she asks how we handle God's existence, immortality, and abortion. These questions may seem really deep for a high school student and make them think about the meaning behind their lives in ways they haven't before. The author therefore attracts a readership by making philosophy interesting and accessible.

The author also uses a famous scientist, Isaac Newton who is known by his audience for his work in gravity and laws of motion, to really hone in the fact that philosophy has influenced important people and important discoveries. This is important because now students who may have not been convinced earlier will see that philosophy makes really great thinkers, and may want to study it themselves.

The pursuit of "what is true, good, and beautiful" is philosophy and now the readers can know a lot about it when going to college. Through rhetorical questioning and references to Isaac Newton the author successfully builds a good argument for the study of philosophy. Because philosophy is "well worth the effort, as it improves our understaning of the mundane to the most profound issues, and helps us know how to put that knowledge to good use," it is a major we might all take seriously.

EXPLANATION: The response shows a better grasp of the point of the argument than does the example that received 1s and gives some limited analysis, such as that about the use of rhetorical questions. The writing style is simplistic with some noticeable errors.

EXAMPLE 3: READING = 3, ANALYSIS = 3, WRITING = 3

The argument in "The Importance of Studying Philosophy" can be found eponymously. The author of the argument takes an informal, yet informative approach to his audience, possibly anybody considering studying philosophy or more generally concerned with its merits. He uses a series of open-ended questions, philosophical possibilities, and even a historical figure to point out the significance philosophy has had and will continue to have on our world.

In defining philosophy as "the love of wisdom," the writer is able to peak the interests of those who crave answers, knowledge for its own sake, and purpose in life. This crowd will be intrigued by the questions posed to begin the piece, possibly taking a moment to consider deeper meanings in their own lives. The reader is left to wonder *how do I approach problems, how do I foster relationships, what is the meaning of my life*, and other esoteric questions. With this foundation the writer begins his argument.

"Name-calling, intense emotions, or personal attacks" are the examples given in regard to common ways of solving problems. Is there another way? Yes, the writer argues. By "taking a philosophical approach," we can "focus," "explore," and get to "the heart of the matter." Here, the author effectively builds an argument by allowing the reader to imagine the possibilities of philosophy. As an example of a major event that could have had very different implications if approached philosophically, the author names the American civil war. Take a moment, he seems to say, to imagine if we had all been trained to approach slavery and state formation with an eye "toward the common goal of learning more about what is true."

The possibilities evolve for philosophers when they are trained to "clear up confusions." Again the author uses a general social issue, that of equality, to imagine the many disagreements that are not disagreements at all, but merely "different aspects of the same idea." Here the argument for philosophy gains power in that it has the ability to make important discintcions and investigate the bigger questions of life. The writer even ventures to appeal to the reader once again, stating that this kind of thinking allows us to "live wisely."

Lastly, the writer reasons that the significance of philosophy can be depicted through its past triumphs, take that of Isaac Newton, the author of *Mathematical Principles of Natural Philosophy* and a very famous physicist. Here, the passage works to prove the need for philosophy in showing its worth in other fields of "science and technology." The writer allows the reader to imagine the world without Newton and the numerous other inventors, philosphers, innovators, scientists, etc. who utilized philosophical reflection in their contributions to society. Here, we are able to see the significance of philosophy in a much broader context, again providing indisputable evidence of the importance of this particular field of study. Philosophy, the writer argues, is tough, but necessary.

EXPLANATION: This response represents a decent interpretation of the argument, providing some quality analysis, such as examining how the author taps into questions about the meaning of life that many readers are likely to have. The essay is decently written, with some use of precise vocabulary and only a couple of spelling errors.

EXAMPLE 4: READING = 2, ANALYSIS = 3, WRITING = 4

Let us ponder the worth of philosophical reflection—philosophize philosophy if you will. Perhaps, it is a field you have never heard of, or perhaps you are only vaguely aware of it. More likely, you categorize it as many do: multifaceted and morally rewarding, yet utterly useless in the job market. Many deliberate on philosophy in an archaic way, imagining old, bearded men withering away in silence and deep contemplation. If nothing else, philosophy is viewed as outdated—I mean everything has already been thought up, hasn't it? Besides, it seems rather futile, and financially impractical, to spend one's days lost in thought, even if the reward is a greater understanding of life. "The Importance of Studying Philosophy" is a magnificent attempt to revive a dying major of study.

When is the last time you took a moment to think about the why's? Why do you go to school everyday? Why do you play sports or an instrument or participate in the student council? Why must you get into that beloved higher institution and earn employment with a big firm? Why do you pray, or not pray? Why do you fear death when it is inevitable? These are all philosophical questions that, albeit important, may seem circuitous and without answers. Better yet, what good would it do you to spend time on these questions? This is the question the author sets out to answer.

Confirming the importance of philosophy via its expansive definition, broad implications, and wide reach, the author effectively builds a case that philosophy yields better people and, thus, a better world. Conversationally and, perhaps didactically, the writer shows philosophy's pertinence to everybody's life. In highly politicized debates and humanity's biggest questions, we have failed over and over to take a philosophical approach that could encourage a diplomatic compromise. The author is not satisfied. If only we would have realized the worth of abstract thinking, we could have spent our days over tea and conversation, seeking truth and progress rather than dabbling in war after war.

What's more is our failure to think critically and theoretically has left us incapable of expressing ourselves. And without communication, we fall to pieces. We mind as well spend our days arguing over synonymous terms, never bothering to say what we mean or hear what the other side is intending. "The Importance of Studying Philosophy" builds a steady argument for the skills acquired in those fields that focus on complex thinking and out-of-the-box approaches to life's most immediate disasters. Do you not wish to be educated? Do you not wish to have knowledge and wisdom to share and expand? Do you fail to see the importance of theoretical imagining in alternative solutions to social and political issues? Philosophy can provide the training to make this all real, improving you and the world in which you live and prosper.

It is not just lofty talk. Philosophy has had its moments. Imagine how it is has affected the sciences and mathematics as well as the social sciences. Imagine how it has initiated some of life's most prominent figures and their irreplaceable contributions to society. Imagine the author's example—Isaac Newton—without a predetermined nature in reflection of his individual observations. You cannot, if not only because that name would mean nothing without that paramount tendency. The author's case for philosophy becomes most lucid in this example, highlighting how philosophy is truly invaluable. Some of the world's best thinkers—Aristotle, Galileo, Freud—have their roots in philosophy, and look what it has done for society. Philosophy is far from obsolete; in fact, in today's ever-changing digital world, it is more necessary than ever.

EXPLANATION: This response shows a great grasp of sentence variety, vocabulary, and diction. However, it fails to show a close reading of the passage, rarely citing specific points and never directly quoting the text. The student does analyze parts of the author's argument and shows an in-depth understanding of the author's intentions but fails (by ignoring the reading itself) to show a clear analysis of the entire argument. It fails to note evidence, reasoning, and persuasive elements; instead it begins to make an argument of its own.

EXAMPLE 5: READING = 4, ANALYSIS = 2, WRITING = 3

The author of "The Importance of Studying Philosophy" begins with questions that make the reader think deeply about the meaning of life in order to eventually make the argument that philosophy is important. For example, how do we solve problems, make relationships go well, or give purpose to our hobbies and pursuits. The writer then goes on to define philosophy and consider its applications for "fundamental questions," "abilities to break down concepts," and "reasons behind our own beliefs." The author is showing just how applicable philosophy is, and showing that its significance is far-reaching.

Next, the author delves into the training, i.e. education, in philosophical thinking that allows students to think about "intractable problems" such as "God's existence, immortality, and abortion." She describes how many times hostile and biased approaches to life's ongoing debates just reap worse consequences, and ultimately, she concludes, a philosophical approach would prove better. Philsophy is successfully presented as a way "of finding resolution and implementing solutions." It can be, if recognized adequately, a way to change the world.

In the following paragraph, the author goes on to dissect "confusions" and how philosophy could provide ways of helping people clearly express themselves and make distinctions between obscure concepts. In the author's example of equality, she shows that although it is a term everyone can agree on, it has versatile meanings that could potentially cause disputes if not approached correctly and coherently. Again, the answers lay in philosophical reasoning: "Learning to make key distinctions and clarifications like this in philosophy improves our ability to think well and, in turn, live wisely." This paragraph continues to show how people use philosophy to think critically and approach complex problems.

In conclusion, the author examines how philosophy has influenced other fields of study like "science and technology [. . .] medicine, transportation, communications, and so forth" in order to satisfy the reader's need to see philosophy in action. Isaac Newton is an example of an influential figure who used philosophy for the betterment of mankind. His training in philosophy allowed him to work in other fields, again proving the value of philosophy. Surely, philosophy is beneficial in its expanse into other careers and interests; critical thinking is useful no matter what one decides to study.

The author is able to finish with a casual afterthought: philosophy is difficult, but worth it. Because of it's signification in thinking abstractly, solving problems and influencing other fields of study, it is indeed important to study.

EXPLANATION: This response shows a very close reading. The student is capable of understanding the structure and the argument of the author, but does not analyze it beyond a superficial level. The student also uses good vocabulary but transitions from informal to formal tones and writes some badly structured sentences, such as this one that should end in a question mark: "For example, how do we solve problems, make relationships go well, or give purpose to our hobbies and pursuits."

EXAMPLE 6: READING = 4, ANALYSIS = 4, WRITING = 4

Who is in favor of thoughtful consideration, complex problem solving, and intelligent debate? Everyone is. More so, these skills have vast implications for society as a whole. In "The Importance of Studying Philosophy," the writer builds a contention for the study of philosophy on the grounds that it leads to peaceful resolution, allows us to consider other perspectives, and yields knowledge in other discourses. By making philosophy relevant, and even appealing, to each and every person, the writer effectively proves its worth, noting historical examples of its extensive and significant impact.

TIP

The thesis statement in this excellent response is underlined.

Beginning with a series of relatable life activities followed by abstract and ambiguous questions, the writer challenges the reader to deliberate on how philosophy could benefit his or her life. Rather than remaining an abstruse field of study, philosophy becomes tangible, and even necessary. This technique enables the writer to encapsulate a wide audience before going into a more thorough discussion of philosophy's far-reaching consequences for humanity. Through the language of "knowledge," "wisdom," and "purpose," the writer not only makes it clear that everyone benefits from the efforts of philosophers, but also hints at the allure of studying philosophy oneself.

Since philosophy involves the "most fundamental questions about life" and empowers us to have the "highest good," it is not only relevant to everyone but supremely rewarding. It is in this way that the writer works to define the study of philosophy and depict it as a peaceful alternative approach to some of life's most difficult conflicts. From "God's existence, immortality, and abortion" to slavery and equality, we all have a card in the game, the writer argues. In the example of the Civil War—an infamously catastrophic historical event that everyone is familiar with—the writer invites the reader to consider what might have happened had the powers at hand taken a philosophical approach instead. In this way, the reader is made to see the practical power of this type of thinking.

Next, the writer moves onto instances that may be more manifold than a fundamental disagreement. There are many ways to disagree, and sometimes, it isn't as clear cut as yes and no. The writer illustrates through the concept of equality just how multifaceted social issues can truly be. The technique of asking several questions (what do we mean, what exactly are we referencing, how does it apply) effectively defends the breadth of such issues and supports the need for philosophical examination. It is through the skills developed in a Philosophy education, the author concedes, that one is equipped to "think well" and "live wisely."

Lastly, the author appeals to philosophy's influence among other disciplines. Modern science, the author posits, would not be possible without philosophy. Any left doubting the field's worth are persuaded by its influence on Sir Isaac Newton—a household name that epitomizes advancement in the fields of physics and mathematics. By citing such a well-known scientist, the writer successfully postulates that the world would not be where it is today without the rigor of philosophical reflection. It is easy, then, for the reader to imagine how essential the study of philosophy may be to "medicine, transportation, communications" among other disciplines.

The author most notably informs the reader of the infinite advantages of philosophy. The author's straightforward presentation allows a clear and logical transition from the purpose of philosophy to its application in thoughtful resolution of politicized issues, in differing particularities of the same idea, and in fields of science and technology. Yet, the argument, at times, fails to be complex in itself. Ultimately, the writer succeeds in building a defense for the study of philosophy through an exploration of its many assets, but does so without mentioning why anyone might disagree or question the importance of philosophy to begin with. Nonetheless, through historical examples and obscure concepts, the worth of philosophy is clearly proven, and the attentive reader may just consider it as an intended major.

EXPLANATION: This is an outstanding response all around. The word choice is elevated, there is a great deal of sentence variety, and the essay is tightly focused on its central claim. The author completely understands the given source, and seamlessly incorporates analysis throughout, such as pointing out that the reference to a famous scientist from the past like Newton would help readers see the powerful influence of philosophy on a variety of practical fields.

Now that you have read several sample responses, see how well you understand the SAT Essay evaluation process by **scoring responses to the following source text and prompt:**

Read the following passage, and think about how the author uses:

- Evidence, such as applicable examples, to justify the argument
- Reasoning to show logical connections among thoughts and facts
- Rhetoric, like sensory language and emotional appeals, to give weight to the argument

---

The Last Amateurs

1   A man owns a factory that produces an item consumed regularly by hundreds of millions of captive customers. As his product is a cultural staple, the factory earns billions of dollars every year, and the man becomes extravagantly wealthy. Yet, while this golden empire flourishes, the factory workers toil day after day without compensation, nary a cent passing from the owner's pockets to their own. They labor on, resigned to destitution, cognizant of the corporeal cost of their existence.

2   You've been to this sweatshop. You've yelled at the workers to come on, implored them to dig deep, demanded that they give 110 percent today. And God bless them, they oblige, ravaging their bodies in tune to our feral cheers. We are enablers, you and I; we are hypocrites blinded by our naïveté. We are college sports fans. And now we must expunge our fanatical sins.

3   It's difficult to conceptualize how such an economic injustice can persist in these United States of Free Market Capitalism, but the NCAA has managed to perpetuate exactly that with their iron-fisted control over major collegiate athletics. Consider that the NCAA and participating universities earned 6 billion dollars last year. Consider that NCAA president Mark Emmert earned 1.7 million dollars last year without ever taking the field. Or that Alabama football coach Nick Saban earned 6.9 million without ever getting tackled, while Vanderbilt athletic director David Williams earned 3.2 million.

4   Conversely, though the athletes are bringing in the dollars (again, six billion of them annually), they see none of the profits. NCAA supporters will point to the academic scholarships that the athletes receive in return for the services, as if being forced to accept a lesser compensation still constitutes a sufficient payment for services rendered. Moreover, though these athletes receive full academic scholarships, they don't receive "cost of living" scholarships, which is to say that the schools don't even give them enough money to survive without personal expense. Superstar basketball player Shabazz Napier—who was the face of a national championship team as he filled arenas, sold thousands of over-priced jerseys, and enticed corporate sponsors to spend millions on commercial advertising during nationally-televised games—claims that he often went to bed hungry before he made it to the NBA. Though Shabazz earned tens of millions of dollars in revenue for the NCAA and the University of Connecticut, he was not even given enough to eat. Surely, none can argue that this is a just exchange.

5   Here is the real kicker: this life of paucity isn't voluntary, but rather a form of indentured servitude; football and basketball players are barred from playing in the NFL and NBA until they are 3 three and 1 one years removed from high school, respectively. They are forced to play college ball before being allowed to earn a living. This is akin to the corporate world saying, "Sorry, Bill Gates; though your Microsoft idea is revolutionary and will redefine technology as we know it, we really feel like you need to stay in college for three more years before you can start to monetize. But, in the meantime, how about you let us keep the billions in Microsoft profits, and we'll pay your $50,000 tuition in return?" So yes, you can point to the free education for athletes, but let us not be so gullible as to confuse complimentary with compulsory.

6   In addition, what happens when a world-class athlete suffers a debilitating injury while biding his or her time and playing for the NCAA for free? Consider the case of former South Carolina running back Marcus Lattimore. Marcus was physically ready to be a star NFL player during his junior season, but he was prohibited from doing so. During this time, Marcus suffered a gruesome knee injury; despite rehabilitation, he has never really been the same, and his earning potential is mere decimal points of what it once was. To be blunt, Marcus' career was ruined while the NCAA profited from his free labor. In a society that hangs its hat on the level playing field of free free-market principles, it is baffling that such a travesty is permitted to continue.

Write a response that demonstrates how the author makes an argument to persuade an audience that college athletes should be paid. In your response, analyze how the author uses at least one of the features from the essay directions (or features of your own choosing) to develop a logical and persuasive argument. Be certain that your response cites relevant aspects of the source text.

Your response should not give your personal opinion on the merit of the source text, but instead show how the author crafts an argument to persuade readers.

SAMPLE A

In "The Last Amateurs" the author builds and argument to convince the readers that college athletes need more reimbursement than just scholarships. The author employs a variety of devices to make his or her point. The author uses logical comparison and appeals to emotion to persuade the reader.

By using comparisons, the author forces the reader to think about college athletics in a related, but different way than they are used to. The initial comparison of college athletes as near enslaved sweat shop workers, introduces the reader to the idea that the current NCAA system might have something very, very wrong with it. While obviously the college athlete isn't locked in a factory making pennies while the big business prospers with no chance at moving up, the reality isn't that far off. College athletes put in many many hours and are not even permitted to be paid those pennies. They are awarded scholarships that pay for their education, but nothing else.

A second comparison the author uses is comparing a college athlete to Bill Gates and software. He says the current system is the same as if someone had said Bill Gates HAD to stay in college even though he could have been successful without his degree. No one questions that Bill Gates in no one needed to stay in school to be immensely successful, so it leads the reader to wonder: why do we force athletes to go to college before playing professionally?

A last strategy the author uses is appeals to emotion. Appeals to emotion allow a reader to feel connected not only with the problem, but with specific people hurt by the current NCAA system. Shabazz Napier is a perfect example. He made a ton of money for the NCAA but told new reporters that he would often go to bed hungry before he went to the NBA. The idea of such a talent being forced to go hungry before he's able to make money from his gift is unsettling to just about any reader.

Another appeal the author makes is through Marcus Lattimore. Marcus had a very promising career but was injured while playing in college. This destroyed his earning potential for later in life. Most readers can relate an experience where they felt they were wronged and the Lattimore example is no exception. Had he been able to go straight to the NFL he could have made money before getting hurt. He also would not have le the NCAA profit of his labor, while receiving no pay, and have his career be ruined overall.

The author of "The Last Amateurs" uses a variety of devices to convince the audience of his point. The two most important are comparisons and appeals to emotions of the reader. These allow him to reach a wide audience an convince them in many ways.

How would you score Sample A?

Reading: _____ /4   Analysis: _____ /4   Writing: _____ /4

SAMPLE B

The author of "The Last Amateurs" argues that college athletes should be paid for their "work." He divides his argument into two sections. These are an extended comparison and specific examples of players who had been harmed by current NCAA regulations.

The author begins the piece with a descriptive paragraph about people working in a sweat-shop. He says "the factory workers toil day after day without compensation." Later, the reader is led to realize that the sweat shop workers represent college athletes. The author says that sports fans are partially at fault for creating the demand and that we must "expunge our fanatical sins."

The argument is then moved into a discussion of economics and the injustices that arise from the current system. The United States is supposed to follow the ideas of free market, laissez faire capitalism; however, the author argues that the NCAA has managed control collegiate athletes to the point that they are breaking with those American ideals. Specifically, he mentions how much the NCAA, and various higher ups made in the last year while the actual athletes made nothing.

Next, the author discusses issues related to college athletes receiving scholarships as compensation. He says that while athletes get full academic scholarships, they don't receive "cost of living" scholarships. The author uses Shabazz Napier as an example of someone who made a lot of money for the NCAA as the "face of a national championship team" but yet "often went to bed hungry before he made it to the NBA." This is a man who reportedly made the NCAA and University of Connecticut "tens of millions of dollars."

As the author says, "the real kicker" is that the athletes aren't necessarily participating in this system on voluntary terms, but rather are committed to a form of indentured servitude. Athletes must be a certain amount of years (one for basketball, three for football) prior to playing professionally. Essentially, they aren't allowed to make their own money, until giving the NCAA due diligence.

The last point the author brings up is this: what happens to college athletes if they get hurt while playing for free? Marcus Lattimore could have been a star NFL running back during his junior year of college. However, due to NCAA regulations, he wouldn't have been allowed. He suffered a knee injury that made his future earning potential "mere decimal points of what it once was." The author states that "Marcus' career was ruined while the NCAA profited from his free labor." He sums up his whole argument with the following statement: "In a society that hangs its hat on the level playing field of free market principles, it is baffling that such a travesty is permitted to continue."

How would you score Sample B?

Reading: _____/4   Analysis: _____/4   Writing: _____/4

SAMPLE C

In the essay "The Last Amateurs," the author attempts to convince the reader that college athletes deserve greater compensation than mere "athletic scholarships." The author presents facts to inform readers of policies in place by the NCAA that he finds unfair to the athletes. The author the passage persuades the reader to his point of view through the use of allegory, and emotional appeals through specific examples.

The author begins the passage with an allegory that eventually leads the reader to compare college athletes to sweat shop workers. He draws many similarities between the factory's products, and the "product" created by college athletes. Through terms like "culture staple" the reader is led to see the clear link between the two ideas. The author continues to say that the "gold empire flourishes" while the workers "toil day after day without compensation." The media has recently sensationalized the effects of sweat shop labor and as such this would be an example near and dear to the hearts of many readers. By introducing the comparison at the beginning of the essay, the author is able to allow the reader to subconsciously mull the idea over as he makes other points. He later specifically cites the incomes of college athletic coaches and directors while pointing out that the athletes receive no, or little, compensation. With even a basic level of analysis, the reader can clearly see the parallels the author intends between sweat shop labor and college athletics.

Throughout the passage, the author uses specific examples to his advantage. By providing named examples, the author forces the reader to feel closer to the subjects and thus his overall topic. This closeness creates a bond with a PERSON rather than a statistical examples. As people are more relatable than numbers, the author makes the reader feel sympathy and empathy with those he perceives as hurt by the system.

The first issue the author brings up is compensation for athletes. This issue is explained through the example of Shabazz Napier. Napier made, possibly, millions of dollars for the NCAA but has reported often going to bed hungry prior to going professional. As the reader begins to wonder, "why stay in college? Why not go pro immediately?" The author explains that basketball players are required to be at least one year removed from high school before playing in the NBA: ensuring that the NCAA will make profits off of them for at least one year.

The requirement of athletes to play college ball, for at least a period, is a perfect segue into the second example and problem. Marcus Lattimore exemplifies the issue of compensation and injury among college athletes. Athletics have a risk and reward system deeply ingrained in them. There is the possibility of fame and fortune, but also the very real risk that a person could be injured and end their career. By requiring athletes to play at a college level, they are risking their futures with no chance of reward.

This is exactly what happened with Lattimore. Lattimore suffered a knee injury that decimated his earning potential. Because these are "student-athletes" the NCAA is in no way required to pay workers comps for these injuries, or to allow the STUDENT-athletes to keep their scholarships. This system causes many to drop out as they cannot afford college without their scholarships. Had Lattimore been permitted to go straight to the NFL, he would have had the opportunity to earn more money and receive compensation following his injury.

The author crafts a very persuasive argument against the NCAA's current system. He uses allegory and emotional appeals through specific examples to expertly build a position that seems irrefutable. Shabazz Napier and Marcus Lattimore are real people whom the reader can easily empathize with. Overall, the author of "The Last Amateurs" is successful in his attempt to convince readers of his opinion.

How would you score Sample C?
Reading: _____/4   Analysis: _____/4   Writing: _____/4

SAMPLE D

The NCAA is one of the worst institutions imagineable. In a modernized, free world, it is almost impossible to comprehend how an institution so akin to slavery could exist. The author of "The Last Amateurs" agrees with me that attention needs to be called to the atrocities rendered by the NCAA.

The NCAA last year alone earned 6 BILLION dollars. Guess how much of that individual athletes saw: none. However in that same year the NCAA president earned 1.7 million, Alabama football coach Nick Saban earned 6.9 million, and Vanderbilt AD David Williams earned 3.2 million. College athletes who risk their physical and mental health every time they step on the field ought to be given something more than a "scholarship" for their dedication.

Personally, I think it would be much better if basketball and football had a minor system more akin to what baseball already has. This way, athletes aren't forced to earn money for a corporation like the NCAA while receiving almost nothing for their investment. In the minor system, athletes can earn at least some wages while working their way up to the majors. Had Shabazz Napier had the opportunity to play minor league basketball, he wouldn't have gone to bed hungry while training to play in the majors.

Having a minor league system also eliminates the problem of injury in college athletics. People, obviously, still get injured in the minor league BUT as they are employees of the team, the owners are forced to pay workers compensation for those injuries. In the NCAA system, it's more of a "too bad, so sad" situation when a student-athlete gets hurt. They can have their scholarship revoked along with their entire future. This was the case as the author states with Marcus Lattimore who got hurt in college when he could have just gone to the NFL, and even if he had gotten hurt, he would have gotten workers comp.

Overall, there needs to be a change in the current NCAA system as the owners gain more and more while the college athlete is left to work away for the man and possibly earn nothing. The author of "The Last Amateurs" does a great job of drawing attention to the fact that there needs to be a change to the current NCAA system.

> **How would you score Sample D?**
>
> Reading: _____/4   Analysis: _____/4   Writing: _____/4

Scoring and Explanations

Note: There are two graders for a reason—people often grade the same essay differently. The graders will be thoroughly trained in the rubric and very familiar with example responses, but the makers of the SAT realize that smart people can often disagree. So, if your grading differs slightly from the grading below, it's not a big problem. It's more important that you are able to distinguish a low-scoring essay from a high-scoring essay in terms of the writer's ability to relate information (reading), interpret it (analysis), and compose the response with skill (writing).

SAMPLE A: 4-4-3

This response shows an excellent understanding of the source's argument, evidence, and rhetoric. It provides a clear thesis and logical structure while returning to the text often to cite details and evidence. Moreover, the student understands the implications of the evidence and reasoning and is able to express clearly why the author chose to use those techniques. However, the writing isn't always precise, and it includes some errors.

SAMPLE B: 4-2-3

Student B shows an excellent reading of the source but ultimately fails to give a successful analysis. While understanding the argument itself and summarizing it effectively, Student B only gives partial analysis of the author's intention and ends up stating rather than analyzing the comparisons and anecdotes provided in the source. The writing is fairly focused and logical, but without variety or complex progression.

SAMPLE C: 4-4-4

Overall, this response is excellent in the areas of Reading, Analysis, and Writing. The student states a clear thesis, provides a logical and structured analysis of the source text, and gives an exceptional rephrasing of the argument itself. Through an effective understanding of the argument, a clear understanding of how the argument was built, and precise and varied language, this response earns a top score.

SAMPLE D: 2-2-3

The reader shows some understanding of the source and the source's arguments, but only gives partial evidence. The reader has a limited understanding of what the assignment requires, creating an independent argument rather than evaluating the author's argument. At times, evidence and reasoning are highlighted but not analyzed for their importance within the argument. While the essay fails to give a pertinent thesis, it shows an effective grasp of language and is clearly written with some precision and few significant errors.

SAMPLE ESSAY PROMPTS WITH SAMPLE TOP-SCORING RESPONSES

The directions are the same from essay to essay, so only the last bit of the directions is printed with each sample essay. You can use these examples in a variety of ways.

- Read through the prompts and sample responses to internalize the test format and what a good response will look like.
- Work on annotating the source text.
- Work on interpreting how the author of the source text uses analysis (reasoning, evidence, and rhetoric) to make his or her argument.
- Try different prewriting methods.
- Try responding to the essay in the given amount of time and compare your response to the top-scoring response provided.

Read the following passage, and think about how the author uses:

- Evidence, such as applicable examples, to justify the argument
- Reasoning to show logical connections among thoughts and facts
- Rhetoric, like sensory language and emotional appeals, to give weight to the argument

Healthy Pets, Literally

1   When, in 1956, Fred Gipson introduced a shaggy yellow dog with a soprano bark and a heart as gold as his fur, kids around the nation begged their parents for their own loyal daredevil. From the imposing bear to the vicious wild hogs and the rabid wolf, every family was in dire need of an Old Yeller, lest they risk the great perils of nature. *Lions, Tigers, and Bears! Oh my!* If a stray pup could convert Travis's rancor, surely there was a pet out there to soften their own parents' rigid distastes. How many forlorn youth lost that battle on the irrelevant premise that they did not live on a cattle ranch in the 1860's, we may never know. What we do know is that their arguments were seriously hindered by a circumscribed vision of what it means to own a pet.

2   Subterfuges aside, our imminent death via heinous wild animal is not the only reason for having a furry friend. On the contrary, research shows that animal companionship supports mental and physical health, increasing life expectancy despite the lack of tyrannous flora or fauna. *Take that mom!* Pets are associated with lower blood pressure, lower triglyceride and cholesterol levels, and a reduced risk of heart disease. Pet owners are known to be more active, less anxious, and get this, more socially adept. Similarly, pets can improve relationship bonds and unite families around a shared responsibility.

3   Word has it that even the presence of a pet—not to mention, cuddles and kisses—gives off a calming effect that fights depression and feelings of loneliness. Studies have found that pet owners release higher levels of feel-good brain chemicals like serotonin and dopamine when petting or stroking their pets. These hormones are associated with joy, confidence, and a sense of purpose. No wonder Travis fell victim so quickly to the charms of his beloved confidante.

4   Perhaps, the familiar label, "a man's best friend," fails to do justice to the devotion of a furry family member. Although it is likely to be more reflective of myself and my lagging social skills, I currently have zero comrades who attribute so valuably to my wellbeing. There remains a chance, however, that with an addition of a pet, my social interactions would soar and I could find the faultless friend—*still doubtful*. Not to worry, pet owners on the whole have better self-esteem and are more easily able to build relationships with others.

5   Thus far, my case has been limited to generalities, proven but slightly ambiguous; shall we turn to the professionals? According to articles by James E. Gern, MD, homes with pets turn out far less children with allergies and asthma. The celebrated doc found that being around dingy, dirty cats and dogs from a young age boosted children's immune systems, contributing to declined risk for hay fever and eczema, among other discomforts. Research at the State University of New York at Buffalo expanded the benefits to include the elderly and unwell. Patients being treated for hypertension cut blood pressure in half just by the addition of a pet to their homes. More so, those delightful hormones released by the presence of animals that we discussed earlier act as natural pain relievers—hence the innumerable programs that bring animals into hospitals to visit the sick. Possibly because of the anesthetic value and the tendency to ward off loneliness, pet owners who have suffered from a heart attack recover faster and live longer than those without pets.

6   If my argument has even now failed to convince your rigid parents, then maybe you are destined to grow up without your own Old Yeller. Certainly, there are other ways to live a healthy, fulfilling life surrounded by those who love you unconditionally—I just cannot think of them at the moment. As for myself, I am making up for years of youthful solitude by adopting two dogs, a cat, six fish, and a turtle. To you, dear mother and father, enjoy your chronic pain and feeble immunity.

Write a response that demonstrates how the author makes an argument to persuade an audience that having pets can bring major benefits to their owners. In your response, analyze how the author uses at least one of the features from the essay directions (or features of your own choosing) to develop a logical and persuasive argument. Be certain that your response cites relevant aspects of the source text.

   Your response should not give your personal opinion on the merit of the source text, but instead show how the author crafts an argument to persuade readers.

Sample Top-Scoring Student Response

While it isn't hard to convince most people that pets are great, this author has no trouble making the argument that they're also healthy for their owners. The bulk of this author's argument is made up by science, using medical facts as well as testimonial from experts and research. There are also several minor components to the argument such as appeal to emotions and personal anecdote. All of these elements combine for an effective persuasion.

The author begins her persuasion for pets with an appeal to the reader's emotions, in particular nostalgia, with her Old Yeller example. Most people can relate to begging their parents to get a pet sometime during childhood, often to no avail. Certainly most people remember crying at the end of Old Yeller when the beloved dog died.

Nostalgia can only take an argument so far, however. After this initial call on emotions, the author resorts to science. Few want to argue with medicine, making this an effective technique. She states that people with pets have increased physical health. They have lower blood pressure, lower triglyceride levels, lower cholesterol levels, lower risk of heart disease, and they're more active. She also asserts that those with pets have better mental health. She notifies the reader that those with pets have less anxiety, depression, loneliness, and they have better social skills as well as stronger relationships. She backs these medical claims for increased mental health with chemistry—pets cause us to release serotonin and dopamine, neurotransmitters which cause us to feel "joy, confidence, and a sense of purpose." The author also alludes to pets causing owners to be more responsible when she says " . . . pets can improve relationship bonds and unite families around a shared responsibility." While she doesn't come out and say that pets force owners to be more responsible, it can be read between the lines.

But the author doesn't want us to just take her word for it, so she also includes evidence from experts to back up her claims. For instance, she cites James E. Gern, MD as saying pet owners have fewer cases of allergies, asthma and eczema. Gern suggests that this could be because being exposed to "dirty" pets improves immune function. Providing a potential mechanism for this benefit makes the reader more likely to believe it. The author also cites research from the State University of New York at Buffalo that states that pets can help to cut blood pressure in half in the hypertensive, increase levels of the aforementioned neurotransmitters that may act as natural pain relievers, and also have helped heart attack victims to both recover faster and live longer.

Another, albeit lesser, persuasive technique the author uses is firsthand information. The author states, somewhat jokingly, that she was never allowed to have a pet, and she has less than adequate social skills. While correlation does not equal causation, and it's a stretch to say that her lack of social skills was caused by her lack of furry friends during her childhood, we cannot rule it out either.

Finally, the author ends her argument with reverse logic. She extrapolates that if owning pets is responsible for all of these benefits, not having pets will result in the opposite of these benefits: "chronic pain and feeble immunity." While the author certainly meant this with a note of sarcasm, it doesn't hurt her argument.

In conclusion, the author makes a convincing argument for why owning a pet can be healthy. She begins her persuasion by appealing to nostalgia with her Old Yeller example and reminding the reader of feelings they had during childhood. She then provides many medical reasons for owning a pet, which she backs up with expert testimony. She also peppers the argument with some sarcastic humor that contributes very slightly. Overall, she makes the reader want to go out and buy a puppy.

Read the following passage, and think about how the author uses:

- Evidence, such as applicable examples, to justify the argument
- Reasoning to show logical connections among thoughts and facts
- Rhetoric, like sensory language and emotional appeals, to give weight to the argument

You Get What You Pay For

1   Finding a job directly out of college is, for many, a catch-22. Employers want experience, and graduates are hard-pressed to gain the experience needed to, well, gain experience. As a remedy, universities are encouraging internships, opportunities to enter the workforce temporarily and train in a position of interest. The idea is that both sides will come out the better—the intern strengthening his or her resume and building a strong social network, the employer expanding its workforce and investing in a prospective employee. But now, more students are questioning exactly who is getting their money's worth when many internships are unpaid. Rather than doubting the value of experience, they wonder at its fairness and practicality. Internships, when paid, are not only more valuable, but also more meaningful.

2   After all, it is a small minority of college students who can afford to work for free. A certain incongruity exists when those students, who have the least connections and need the most help breaking into the job market, are also those who have to pass up internships to earn cash for food, gas, and books. First-generation college students from low-income families are particularly frustrated at the prospect of unpaid work. Between adjusting to campus life and difficult coursework, there is little time to spare. What is left must be devoted to bookstore clerking, restaurant serving, pizza delivering, and other rent-paying positions, even when it would be better spent in on-the-job training.

3   There is conflict too, when interns are doing the same work as entry-level employees who enjoy a salary for their efforts. According to the Fair Labor Standards Act, internships can legally only go unpaid when the work is similar to training in an educational environment and does not give immediate advantage to the employer. These stipulations have students asking, "Then, what's the point?" If the work is not directly benefiting the employer, and the student isn't being paid, the situation seems much more like a lose-lose. The lack of reward for each party paints a dismal picture—one with interns failing to perform at high standards and employers hesitant to offer permanent employment.

4   Instead, internships, when requiring investment by both parties, are more likely to result in job matching. According to a survey by the National Association of Colleges

and Employers, paid internships markedly increase a student's chances of landing a job by graduation, while unpaid internships give little or no edge. Statistics of that same survey find starting annual salaries of those with paid intern experience some $15,000 higher than those with unpaid work. Not only are students profiting, but employers are finding employees more valuable after their paid on-the-job training. When the stakes are raised, everybody is coming out on top.

5   Then there are the naysayers. *Forbes* answered the "mantra" of pro-payers with a simple solution: let the individuals decide for themselves. If it were only that simple. Do students, in dire need of a bullet point or two under the subheading "experience," have a choice with the current 11% unemployment rate for recent graduates that *Forbes* reports? Critics concede that all experience is valuable, and so it must be left to the student to decide whether or not to take an internship based on pay rate, or lack thereof. Clearly, they add, the requirement to offer only paid internships will discourage many corporations from offering them at all, and limited opportunities will only further harm the untested, job-seeking graduates. Yet if these unpaid prospects are doing so little to enhance their job search, why should students express concern over their depletion? Additionally, if companies are forced to offer internships only under paid circumstances, aren't they more likely to provide substantial training to new talent, and offer permanent employment to those who meet their expectations?

6   Work experience in a market that expects experience at the entry-level is thus hard to come by. Student's yearning to expand their skills and marketability should not be met with meaningless, unpaid work, particularly when so many families are financially strapped with tuition, housing, and living expenses. The opportunity cost of committing time, effort, and aptitude to a prospective career must be acknowledged with fair pay and genuine likelihood for extended employment. While students hone their skills, employers relish in a skillful and productive workforce generation after generation. The key to a successful internship lies in its potential reward for both parties.

Write a response that demonstrates how the author makes an argument to persuade an audience that internships should be paid. In your response, analyze how the author uses at least one of the features from the essay directions (or features of your own choosing) to develop a logical and persuasive argument. Be certain that your response cites relevant aspects of the source text.

    Your response should not give your personal opinion on the merit of the source text, but instead show how the author crafts an argument to persuade readers.

Sample Top-Scoring Student Response

In response to the current market difficulties surrounding young people and job opportunities, the author argues first that internships are essential for young people, but secondly that unpaid internships are inherently unfair, and that they furthermore provide little benefit for either the employer or the intern. Instead, she argues first through the introduction of a *Catch 22* paradox that establishes the importance of internships in general, and then through statistical evidence and an appeal against those that support unpaid internships that the establishment of *paid* (rather than unpaid) internships would be most advantageous for both employers and interns.

As stated, the author begins her persuasive approach with the use of a *Catch22* paradox to emphasize the need for internships." Employers want experience, and graduates are hard-pressed to gain the experience needed to, well, gain experience," she asserts in her opening paragraph. The primary point here is that the requirement to attain entry-level employment is often previous entry-level employment. Thus, the author seems to call to attention the rhetorical question: *if I need a job to get a job, what in the world am I supposed to do?* However, the author states that all is not lost; this is where the concept of the internship is introduced to fill this paradoxical void. With an internship, young people can attain that work experience before they begin to apply for full-time employment upon graduation. Nonetheless, not just *any type* of internship will do. After all, many college students can't afford the opportunity cost of working for free. Thus, these internships must be paid to accommodate not just students who can afford to work for free, but rather *all students*, the author posits. "A certain incongruity exists when those students who have the least connections . . . are also those who have to pass up internships to earn cash for gas, money, and books."

In addition, the author relies on the concreteness of statistical evidence to lend additional credence to her perspective. According to a report from *Forbes*, the author states that the unemployment rate is currently 11%. Her point here is that, when one out of every nine prospective applicants is unable to attain work, something must be done to remedy this shortfall. Again, this is another example that is introduced in order to strengthen the argument in favor of internships; if these 11% had had the opportunity to complete an internship before hitting the open market, they would certainly be stronger applicants, and also would have a connection and an "in" with that employer with whom they interned. Furthermore, the author introduces a statistic that epitomizes the value of paid rather than unpaid internship: according to a survey by the National Association of Colleges and Employers, those with paid intern experience commanded starting annual salaries that were a whopping *$15,000* higher than those with unpaid experience. Thus, the employees with paid experience benefit tremendously, and the employers evidently feel that they benefit from employing a paid intern, as well; otherwise, the additional compensation would not be as pronounced. Now, as Mark Twain famously stated, there are "lies, damned lies, and statistics," but this is an awfully convincing figure to support her position.

Finally, the author strengthens her own position by *weakening* that of her opposition. Again, she calls attention to a *Forbes* reference, but this time, she doesn't agree with the assessment. *Forbes* states that the *invisible hand* of the market should dictate whether or not an internship should be paid or unpaid. In essence, *Forbes'* point is that, if people are completing *unpaid* internships of their own volition, then they must feel that there is still benefit to be had from the opportunity. The author doesn't dispute that young people are willing to offer free labor, but she argues that—based on her points already stated—these unpaid internships aren't achieving anything. Thus, though two parties might enter into a consensual agreement, that doesn't necessarily constitute a *productive* agreement.

In conclusion, the author argues that internships fulfill a void in society, but only if they are of the paid variety. She supports her position by offering a *Catch-22* paradox, statistical evidence, and by attacking the position of her opposition.

_____

_____

_____

_____

_____

_____

_____

_____

_____

_____

_____

_____

_____

_____

_____

_____

_____

_____

Additional Prompts for Practice

How can you use these prompts? Here are some ideas:

- Practice your reading and analytical skills as you annotate the source texts.
- Work on your prewriting.
- Write full responses and have a teacher, parent, or friend review your work and give suggestions for improvement.

Directions: You will be given 50 minutes to complete the assignment, including reading the source text and writing your response.

Read the following passage, and think about how the author uses:

- Evidence, such as applicable examples, to justify the argument
- Reasoning to show logical connections among thoughts and facts
- Rhetoric, like sensory language and emotional appeals, to give weight to the argument

Education Reimagined

1   Since 2012—the year of Massive Open Online Courses (MOOCs)—the discourse on the success of open online education and its implications for traditional colleges has been mixed, and often conflicting. While some raved that e-learning platforms would dismantle and revolutionize the university overnight, others doubted their maturation and assimilation into the job market. In response to the influx of online learning platforms that offer free content, President Obama called upon online learning as a key ingredient in redefining higher education, stating colleges must, "embrace innovative new ways to prepare our students for a 21st-century economy and maintain a high level of quality without breaking the bank." Although open online courses have failed to transform higher education in the abrupt manner that many reformers predicted, the current push for discernible and accessible digital credentials from accredited institutions will be a turning point in education.

2   The open educational movement really took off in 2008; and, within just a few short years, providers like Coursera, Udacity, and edX emerged among hundreds of other self-paced, virtual education platforms, including the immensely popular Khan Academy, that offer quality learning at a great price, *free*. Now, students could enjoy learning outside of a formal education environment with asynchronous and unconstrained access to free content. And many took advantage. Coursera, associated with Stanford University, boasts that it currently offers more than 1,000 free courses. Udacity, similarly connected with Stanford, specializes in vocational courses for professionals who can choose to pay a fee for a certificate of completion to submit to employers. MIT and Harvard introduced edX, a nonprofit provider that now has more than three million users. Then, in November 2012, the University of Miami launched the first high school MOOC to assist students in preparing for the SAT.

3   As programs expanded and quality increased, many speculated that MOOCs would be the vanguard for a reduction in rising costs of higher education that could potentially replace the business model of education. Others pointed to the meager 10% completion rate common among MOOCs and the unceasing admission rates and rising tuition costs in traditional universities, and chalked open online education up to a fleeting fad. Thus far, neither prediction has manifested, but the former is seemingly more indicative of current trends than the latter. Stanford celebrates several courses that have "graduated" over 20,000 students; and, as distance education moves toward reputable degree-granting, these numbers will soar. In collaborative e-platforms, more students than ever are watching video lectures, participating in discussion boards, engaging in peer-review exercises, and taking up interactive blogging. Imagine unlimited access to a college education for anyone who can get in front of a computer screen.

4   The prophesized revolution will come with the next step in open online courses: the reconception of education. Students are failing to turn to the cheaper, more convenient online platform because it is yet to lead to jobs. More than a broad, encompassing education for personal growth and intellectual stimulation, students are paying for degrees that get jobs. A lag with employers is expected and understandable; the conventional diploma is well-tested and time-honored, so naturally employers are skeptical of change. Moreover, ways to recognize and measure quality in online education had to be established. But now, as online education becomes accredited and archives make it easy for employers to see students' work and achievements, open online education is in position to overtake its predecessor. Digital credentials and reputable degrees and/or certificates mean that employers can not only rest assured that employees have extensive training and knowledge, but will also, for the first time, be able to effortlessly glimpse academic accomplishments, rather than try to decipher the meaningless acronyms on standardized transcripts.

5   While it is still unlikely to happen overnight, employer-friendly online platforms are already working to bridge the gap. Acknowledgement and recognition of accredited virtual education leaves a lot of questions for the traditional university model. If students are afforded quality education at unbeatable costs without having to move on campus *and* are competing for first-rate jobs, there will be little incentive to attend the expensive, corporeal universities where memories created are only outshone by debt accumulated. Higher education will soon become accessible for the masses and "college" will look very different, for students, instructors, and employers.

Write a response that demonstrates how the author makes an argument to persuade an audience that MOOCs represent a turning point in education. In your response, analyze how the author uses at least one of the features from the essay directions (or features of your own choosing) to develop a logical and persuasive argument. Be certain that your response cites relevant aspects of the source text.

Your response should not give your personal opinion on the merit of the source text, but instead show how the author crafts an argument to persuade readers.

Read the following passage, and think about how the author uses:

- Evidence, such as applicable examples, to justify the argument
- Reasoning to show logical connections among thoughts and facts
- Rhetoric, like sensory language and emotional appeals, to give weight to the argument

Promoting Dignity: Freedom from Trafficking

1. "Congratulations!" we exclaim, after hearing of a baby's birth, a joyful time of celebration. Regardless of who people are, where they come from, or what stage of life they are in, human beings have great worth and dignity. From the beginning of the Universal Declaration of Human Rights, the international community recognizes this reality. The idea that people have inherent rights just in virtue of the fact that they are human beings is based in the inherent moral value of human beings. Human trafficking, however, which involves exploiting someone for financial gain, is a direct attack on human dignity. Therefore, we must work together to create a world free of such exploitation.

2. It is estimated that nearly 21 million people worldwide are victims of forced labor or sexual exploitation. Human trafficking is a modern day form of slavery, in which victims typically are kept in unsanitary conditions and endure physical, sexual, and psychological harms. The average age at which people are trafficked is about 13 years old, and they are sometimes brutally violated many times a day. Traffickers use force, fraud, deception, or coercion in order to use other people for the purpose of making money for themselves. Victims' inability to escape leads to self-destructive behaviors, including attempted suicide.

3. Achieving freedom from trafficking first requires promoting awareness of the signs of it in order to help prevent becoming a victim. Experienced traffickers have subtle tactics to lure people by getting to know them gradually, happening to show up at the same places as the one being targeted, and making attractive offers of good jobs, marriage, or a "better life." One former perpetrator recounted how many times he heard young ladies say that "it can't happen to me," and yet they gradually became desensitized in environments where, despite earning money at first and receiving many compliments, they end up with shattered lives. Some signs that someone is being trafficked include working excessively long hours, having high security measures around the place of employment or living, being fearful or anxious, showing signs of abuse, and having a lack of control of possessions, money, and identification.

4   Creating a world free from trafficking also includes not contributing to it. The Super Bowl is said to be the single largest human trafficking incident in the United States, where traffickers take advantage of so many men being out of town at a hotel with a festive atmosphere and lowered inhibitions. There are, however, many ways to have a great time without using and abusing other people's sons and daughters. Bringing trafficking to an end does not just involve our behavior though; it also includes changing the attitudes and ideas that lead to such behaviors, stimulating the demand for it. Instead of viewing others as objects for one's own gratification, we must recognize them as whole persons with minds, wills, and emotions. Each person has intrinsic moral worth and so is deserving of respect and kindness, not degradation and humiliation. According to the U.S. Department of State Office to Monitor and Combat Trafficking in Persons, an end to human trafficking "can only be achieved by rejecting long-held notions that regard commercial sex as a 'boys will be boys' phenomenon, and instead sending the clear message that buying sex is wrong." Leaders, they argued, "must foster the belief that it is everyone's responsibility to reduce the demand for sex trafficking."

5   In addition to not becoming a victim or a perpetrator, protecting people from trafficking requires that we take positive steps to stop it from happening. At the governmental level, it is important to enact laws that carry with them penalties proportional to the seriousness of the crimes of human trafficking, the enforcement of which will bring people to justice and actually deter them from committing such crimes in the first place. At the individual level, we need to be aware of our surroundings, notice the signs of trafficking, and report suspicious activities to the appropriate authorities. A final essential component involves groups of people forming organizations to educate the public, help identify victims and provide aftercare for those that are rescued from enslavement, and contribute toward the elimination of demand for trafficked victims.

6   It is commonly thought that slavery ended long ago. Let us work together so that one day we can hold that belief truly.

Write a response that demonstrates how the author makes an argument to persuade an audience that human trafficking must come to an end. In your response, analyze how the author uses at least one of the features from the essay directions (or features of your own choosing) to develop a logical and persuasive argument. Be certain that your response cites relevant aspects of the source text.

Your response should not give your personal opinion on the merit of the source text, but instead show how the author crafts an argument to persuade readers.

Read the following passage, and think about how the author uses:

- Evidence, such as applicable examples, to justify the argument
- Reasoning to show logical connections among thoughts and facts
- Rhetoric, like sensory language and emotional appeals, to give weight to the argument

The Hunt for Success

1   Ask parents what they want most for their children and many will answer success. By "success," they may mean happiness, financial stability, good health, etc. Chances are, they mean a combination of these things and many more. Perhaps, success is not a concept that falls to easy measurement or simple understanding because of its tendency to particularity; it is different for every individual—there is no one recipe. So then, without a clear definition of success let alone an apprehensible path toward its fulfillment, how is one to choose a field of study, a major, and eventually a career?

2   According to *Forbes* magazine, more than half of Americans are unhappy at work, with disconsolation hitting a record high in 2010. Fifty-two percent of people report feeling disengaged at work, while eighteen percent say they downright hate their jobs. *Business Insider* complicates the statistics further by asking the working public whether they chose a passion or a paycheck, and whether these two are incompatible. The argument only gains complexity when one considers how much fulfillment comes from the pay itself: would the unfulfilled be bigger fans of their current jobs if the salary was higher, or do they, regardless of pay, need to feel pride in what they spend forty hours a week or more doing? With so many falling short of self-realization, surely there needs to be more attention paid to what makes up a successful career.

3   The answer to choosing the right career lies in the nuances of success itself. Just as there is no one definition of success, there is no one path to it, and one will rarely find success by sitting around thinking about it. Furthermore, it can be equally futile to weigh everything in the name of one small part of the plethora that makes up success: there are plenty of wealthy men and women who do not consider their work fulfilling, just like there are many who don't consider themselves successful despite their contentment at work. The fact is, one does not know the best career path for them until they feel it, see it, hear it. This balance, particular to an individual's personal needs and priorities, is found most often through action.

4   In Lindsey Pollak's *Getting from College to Career*, she suggests that career-hunters "follow every rainbow," a tip that involves finding and exploring every opportunity that comes one's way. From job shadowing to career fairs to campus ads to online resumes,

Pollak asserts that the potential paths to one's dream job are innumerable, so every angle and every avenue should be pursued. Her work as a career expert has allowed her to interview thousands of people who boast that they found success in a fulfilling and engaging career; their paths are as many as their number. Some cite a family friend, a coincidental conversation with a stranger, an employment agency, or a referral as the reason behind their success. Yet, all successful stories have this in common: action.

5   Many universities have caught on and are beginning to implement programs that encourage, or even mandate, action throughout a student's undergraduate study. These initiatives often include study abroad, research experiences, internships, community outreach, career fairs, and senior project fairs—all with the goal of bolstering one's exploration of opportunities and exposing one's talents to prospective employers. When students are able to expand their interests and experiences by trying new things and meeting new people, they are likewise expanding their career search. Not only are students more likely to find employment, they are more likely to be engaged, challenged, and enriched by their work. While universities are undeniably attempting to improve their career placement rates, they are simultaneously doing something much more important—changing the lives of their students.

6   With the evidence for action so overwhelming, one must ask if the university is really the best place to start. College applications indeed ask students for their intended majors, and with many undergraduate degrees taking five and even six years to complete, it would appear that students are expected to come into the university with some sort of direction. High schools—which are presumed to prepare students for the workforce, military, and/or college—must take on some of this responsibility in order to ensure the success of future generations. Seventeen-year-olds with an idea of where their interests lie and what makes them happy, albeit uncommon, undoubtedly have the advantage in exploring meaningful opportunities.

Write a response that demonstrates how the author makes an argument to persuade an audience that schools should do more to help students determine what they want to do for their careers. In your response, analyze how the author uses at least one of the features from the essay directions (or features of your own choosing) to develop a logical and persuasive argument. Be certain that your response cites relevant aspects of the source text.

Your response should not give your personal opinion on the merit of the source text, but instead show how the author crafts an argument to persuade readers.

Read the following passage, and think about how the author uses:

- Evidence, such as applicable examples, to justify the argument
- Reasoning to show logical connections among thoughts and facts
- Rhetoric, like sensory language and emotional appeals, to give weight to the argument

The Customer Is Always Right

1   The dormitories are ten stories high, bounded by ovals of forest green lawn and narrow brick walkways. The recreation center is enclosed by six thousand square feet of unblemished glass and equipped with no less than thirteen pools, one hundred and fifty-seven treadmills, and a full time massage therapist. The football stadium is unmatched, sitting thrice the number of fans as enrolled students. Campus night life, with all its shining neon lights and immaculate dance floors, is a tropical haven for the lonesome and homesick. And the admission brochure brags aimlessly that university students are "making the impossible possible." So it goes. College is a business, eighteen-year-old students (and their preferably wealthy parents) the consumers. As appealing as it all sounds, the current university model is failing the student in arguably the most important ways.

2   Take Psychology 101, now offered on Thursdays at 1 P.M. because lethargic and fetid students stopped coming on Fridays, and the remaining sleepwalkers were hesitant to enroll in a course before 11 A.M. Next, consider Instructor Evaluation Day, the next-to-last class meeting where a semester's worth of interpretive intelligence and deliberation culminates in a 1 to 5 rating; 1 being "I wish I would have taken this course at the community college down the street and passed" and 5 being "the professor is such a hunk that I totally clicked the chili pepper on ratemyprofessor.com." Dare we mention exams, when 79% of the class failed so miserably that a curve was fabricated to soothe exasperated parents and riled department chairs? Failing, after all, leads to transfers and drop-outs, which of course means less money, and *can this shrinking department really afford any more cuts?*

3   So, where did it all go wrong? Long before admission offices began hiring the top marketing students and graphic designers to *sell* their respective universities, there was the idea of a college education being somewhat unsettling, something to push and challenge and stimulate and unearth the dissenter within. Prior to softened grades and political correctness, classrooms were marked by tough student-instructor exchange, passionate intellectual debates, and an eagerness to expand thinking. Today, the university model mass produces graduates who can unequivocally repeat facts, memorize definitions, and reference experts (at least for a semester at a time), but fails to truly engage, ripen, or educate its *customers.*

4   Currently, the government rewards universities for innovative research; so, it is hardly surprising that this is where professors direct their focus. Professors, busy with research and ceaseless publishing, have little time to teach. Frequently, teaching is left to inexperienced graduate students who are just as occupied with research and thesis or doctorate writing. And so, the students suffer. On the other end, students are less concerned with notable faculty and demanding curriculum, and more interested in impressing employers. Employers are most enthralled with rankings and selectivity. Meanwhile, colleges, in order to be desirable, must keep enrollment low (i.e., be selective) and, therefore, must charge students more to keep revenue high. And so the student-consumer cycle continues with its first-rate communal bathrooms and seventeen cafeterias, including a Chik-fil-A and, get this, a Starbucks.

5   Almost half of college graduates show no improvement in critical thinking, reasoning, and writing skills according to *Academically Adrift*, a recent book that explores the stagnant and, at times, utterly ineffective U.S. collegiate system. Critical thinking and deductive reasoning aren't the only areas in which the university is failing either: the *Wall Street Journal* asserts that four of every ten college graduates don't have the skills needed to manage white-collar work, with less than 2 out of 5 employers finding recent graduate interviewees ready for the workforce. Indeed, the high-points of the American university don't seem to include progression, preparedness, or professionalization.

6   Are we to give up hope and abandon college education? Not exactly. Yet the paradox of the current student-consumer university is something that cannot go on unaddressed. If U.S. students fail to compete, it won't be long before other job-seekers take advantage of our stupor. One proposal suggests that common tests be given upon admission and graduation to see which colleges are doing their job and which are not. Acknowledging the complexity of testing graduates from a myriad of majors, others turn to the government to back programs that encourage quality graduates. Whichever alternatives we pursue, teaching must regain the foreground.

Write a response that demonstrates how the author makes an argument to persuade an audience that college is changing for the worst as it becomes increasingly consumerist. In your response, analyze how the author uses at least one of the features from the essay directions (or features of your own choosing) to develop a logical and persuasive argument. Be certain that your response cites relevant aspects of the source text.

Your response should not give your personal opinion on the merit of the source text, but instead show how the author crafts an argument to persuade readers.

Read the following passage, and think about how the author uses:

- Evidence, such as applicable examples, to justify the argument
- Reasoning to show logical connections among thoughts and facts
- Rhetoric, like sensory language and emotional appeals, to give weight to the argument

Poor Potential

"Give me your tired, your poor,
Your huddled masses yearning to breathe free,
The wretched refuse of your teeming shore.
Send these, the homeless, tempest-tost to me,
I lift my lamp beside the golden door!"

—from "The New Colossus," the Statue of Liberty

1   Howard Schultz, billionaire CEO of Starbucks, grew up in a government housing complex before attending the University of Northern Michigan on a football scholarship. Oprah Winfrey was born into a poor Mississippi family, but worked tirelessly to gain a scholarship to Tennessee State University, where she became the first African American TV correspondent in the state at age 19. Founder of Oracle—one of the largest technology companies in the world—Larry Ellison was born to a poor mother in Brooklyn, NY, and raised by an aunt who passed away during his sporadic college years, when he alternated classes with odd jobs. Ben Carson, the first surgeon to successfully separate conjoined twins at the head, grew up in Detroit under the care of a poor, single mother who had never finished the third grade but encouraged her sons to read. What all these public figures have in common is that the world, as we know it, would not exist without their contribution, and their contribution would be null and void without efforts to diversify the university.

2   For those without the resources, college may seem like an ambiguous dream floating dangerously out of reach on the words *scholarship*, *grant*, and *financial aid*. The battle to gain support from working class parents and time to study in a backdrop that demands all free hands is, for many, just the beginning to academic success and the chance for a brighter future. Then, there is admission, where these same underprivileged students are measured against more affluent peers who benefit from more time devoted to academics, superior school systems, costly tutoring, opportunities to job shadow and intern, and a myriad of networking contacts via their prosperous parents. While one of these advantages is sufficient to forge an insurmountable gap of inequality, the combination of them leaves students in tremendous discordance as they fill out applications. Hence, the very real need for consideration of socioeconomic diversity as a factor in college admissions.

3   The grounds for socioeconomic diversity within the university lie on the axiom of the American Dream itself, the ethos of freedom, opportunity, and prosperity for all who are willing to work for it in a nation devoid of substantial barriers. Where would the world be without the Winfreys and Ellisons, and those innumerable innovators, scholars, artists, and philanthropists who were left out of the spare list that begins this essay? The National Association for College Admissions Counseling failed to list class or economic-status in their 2011 article "Factors of Admission Decision." Yet, *The New York Times* found in 2014 that socioeconomic affirmative action not only opened doors for students from low-income and under-resourced high schools, but also effectively promoted racial, ethnic, and religious diversity.

4   Catherine B. Hill, the president of Vassar College in New York, calls for increased resources for financial aid, saying, "If higher education in America is to continue to contribute to equal opportunity and economic mobility, not only do its leaders need to make more places available across the entire system, the highly selective institutions need to do their fair share by educating a more socioeconomically diverse student body." It is not lack of talent, but finite resources that deter access. Hill's research found that the shortage of low-income students at the nation's most select universities wasn't based on scarcity of student competency, but scarcity of university funds and awareness. Opportunity and diversity within the U.S. post-secondary education system rely on the incorporation of socioeconomics into the admissions process.

5   Others argue that admissions should be blind to class, race, and gender; just as historical preference to white, wealthy males is wrong, so is the "reverse discrimination" implied in favoring another group. The argument allows that merit-based admissions will lead to the best quality of students and promote fairness. Yet, the danger in evaluating students by virtue of rigorous high school coursework and standardized testing is in its blindness to disadvantage—that life-long penal sentence of choosing the wrong parents; a debilitating condition which obscures the talent of even the most prodigious. Furthermore, in a merit-based model, even those highly-qualified, low-income students who gain admission are more likely to decline it without apt resources provided. It is time that our system does more to ensure outlook, or risk crippling the next Ben Carson.

Write a response that demonstrates how the author makes an argument to persuade an audience that socioeconomic diversity should have an impact on college admissions. In your response, analyze how the author uses at least one of the features from the essay directions (or features of your own choosing) to develop a logical and persuasive argument. Be certain that your response cites relevant aspects of the source text.

Your response should not give your personal opinion on the merit of the source text, but instead show how the author crafts an argument to persuade readers.

PART FIVE
The SAT Math Test

Introduction to the Math Test

PART FIVE consists of this Introduction and two extremely important chapters. Chapter 5 presents several important strategies that can be used on many of the mathematics questions that appear on the SAT. Chapter 6 contains a complete review of the mathematics you need to know in order to do well on the SAT, as well as hundreds of sample problems.

FIVE TYPES OF TACTICS

Five different types of tactics are discussed in this book.

1. General Tactics. In the Introduction you learned many basic tactics used by all good test takers. These include: never waste time reading directions; read each question carefully; pace yourself; don't get bogged down on any one question; eliminate as many choices as you can before guessing, *but always guess*; don't leave any question unanswered. These tactics apply to all four sections of the SAT.
2. In Chapter 1 you learned the important tactics needed for handling the questions in the reading test.
3. In Chapter 3 you learned tactics for handling the different types of writing skills questions, and in Chapter 4 you learned strategies for writing a good essay.
4. In Chapter 5 you will find all of the tactics that apply to the mathematics sections of the SAT. Specific strategies are presented to deal with each type of multiple-choice and grid-in question found on the SAT test.
5. In Chapter 6 you will learn or review all of the mathematics that is needed for the SAT, and you will master the tactics and key facts that apply to each of the different mathematical topics.

Using these tactics will enable you to answer more quickly many problems that you already know how to do. The greatest value of these tactics, however, is that they will allow you to answer correctly, or make educated guesses on, problems that you *do not know how to do.*

WHEN TO STUDY CHAPTER 6

How much time you initially devote to Chapter 6 should depend on how good your math skills are. If you are an excellent student who consistently earns A's in math, you can initially skip the instructional parts of Chapter 6. If, however, while taking the model tests in Part Six, you find that you keep making mistakes on certain types of problems (averages, percentages, geometry, etc.) or if you are spending too much time on them, you should then study the appropriate sections of Chapter 6. Even if your math skills are excellent, and you don't need the review, you should do the sample questions in those sections; they are an excellent source of additional SAT questions. If you know that your math skills are not very good, it is advisable to review the material in Chapter 6, including working out the problems, *before* tackling the model tests in Part Six.

No matter how good you are in math, *you should carefully read and do the sample problems in Chapter 5.* For many of these problems, two solutions are given: the most direct mathematical solution and a solution using one or more of the special tactics taught in these chapters.

AN IMPORTANT SYMBOL

Throughout the book, the symbol "⇒" is used to indicate that one step in the solution of a problem follows *immediately* from the preceding one, and that no explanation is necessary. You should read:

$$2x = 12 \Rightarrow x = 6$$

as "$2x = 12$ *implies that* $x = 6$," or, "*since* $2x = 12$, then $x = 6$."

Here is a sample solution, using ⇒, to the following problem:

What is the value of $3x^2 - 7$ when $x = -5$?

$$x = -5 \Rightarrow x^2 = (-5)^2 = 25 \Rightarrow 3x^2 = 3(25) = 75 \Rightarrow$$
$$3x^2 - 7 = 75 - 7 = \mathbf{68}$$

When the reason for a step is not obvious, ⇒ is not used: rather, an explanation is given, often including a reference to a KEY FACT from Chapter 6. In many solutions, some steps are explained, while others are linked by the ⇒ symbol, as in the following example:

➡ Example _____

In the diagram at the right, if $w = 30$, what is z?

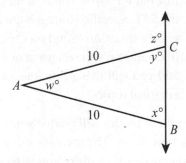

- By KEY FACT J1, $w + x + y = 180$.
- Since $\triangle ABC$ is isosceles, $x = y$ [KEY FACT J5].
- Therefore, $w + 2y = 180 \Rightarrow 30 + 2y = 180 \Rightarrow 2y = 150 \Rightarrow y = 75$.
- Finally, since $y + z = 180$ [KEY FACT I2], $75 + z = 180 \Rightarrow z = \mathbf{105}$.

SEVEN IMPORTANT HEADINGS

In Chapters 5 and 6, you will see seven headings that will appear either in the text or in the margins. They will indicate valuable information and will help to guide you as you study this book. Here is a brief explanation of each heading.

TACTIC
1

A useful strategy for attacking a certain type of problem.

Some TACTICS give you advice on how to handle multiple-choice questions, regardless of the subject matter. Others point out ways to handle specific subject matter, such as finding averages or solving equations, regardless of the type of problem.

Key Fact

An important mathematical fact that you should commit to memory because it comes up often on the SAT.

REFERENCE FACT

A basic mathematical fact that is included in the "Reference Information" that appears on the first page of every math section.

HELPFUL HINT

A useful idea that will help you solve a problem more easily or avoid a pitfall.

CAUTION: A warning of a potential danger. Often a CAUTION points out a common error or a source of careless mistakes.

 CALCULATOR SHORTCUT

A method of using your calculator, even when it is unnecessary, to help you get an answer faster than you otherwise might. Often this heading will signal an unusual or nonstandard way of using your calculator that you might not think of.

 CALCULATOR HINT

Often, a way of using your calculator to get an answer that you could get more quickly without the calculator if you only knew how. CALCULATOR HINTS allow you to use your calculator to get answers to questions on which you would otherwise have to make a wild guess.

USE OF THE CALCULATOR

Before doing any of the work in Part Three and the model tests in Part Four, you should reread the short discussion in Part One on the use of calculators on the SAT. As you do the sample problems in this book, always have available the calculator you intend to take to the SAT, and use it whenever you think it will be helpful. Throughout the rest of the book, whenever the use of a calculator is recommended, the icon 🖩 has been placed next to the example or question. Remember:

■ In the 25-minute math section, you may NOT use a calculator.
■ In the 55-minute math section, many—but definitely not all—of the questions do require the use of a calculator.

Because students' mathematical knowledge and arithmetic skills vary considerably, the decision as to when to use a calculator is highly subjective. Consider the following rather easy problem. Would you use a calculator?

What is the average (arithmetic mean) of 301, 303, and 305?

Let's analyze the four possibilities:

1. Some students would use their calculators twice: first to add, 301 + 303 + 305 = 909, and then to divide, 909 ÷ 3 = 303.
2. Others would use their calculators just once: to add the numbers; these students would then divide mentally.
3. Others would not use their calculators at all, because they could add the three numbers mentally faster than they could on a calculator. (Just say to yourself: 300, 300, and 300 is 900; and 1 + 3 + 5 is 9 more.)
4. Finally, others would do no calculations whatsoever. They would realize that the average of any three consecutive odd integers is the middle one: 301, **303**, 305.

> **NOTE:** The more the calculator was used, the *longer* it took to solve the problem. Use your calculator only when it will really save you time or if you think you will make a mistake without it.

MEMORIZE IMPORTANT FACTS AND DIRECTIONS

At the beginning of each math section, you will see the following directions and notes.

Directions: For each multiple-choice question, solve each problem and choose the best answer from the given choices. Fill in the corresponding circle on your answer document. For each grid-in question, solve the problem and fill in the answer on the answer sheet grid.

Notes:
■ Calculators **ARE NOT PERMITTED** in Section 3. Calculators **ARE PERMITTED** in Section 4.
■ All variables and expressions represent real numbers unless indicated otherwise.
■ All figures are drawn to scale unless indicated otherwise.
■ All figures are in a plane unless indicated otherwise.
■ Unless indicated otherwise, the domain of a given function is the set of all real numbers x for which the function has real values.

Immediately preceding Question 16 in Section 3 and Question 31 in Section 4, you will see the following set of instructions.

Grid-in Response Directions

First solve the problem, and then enter your answer on the grid provided on the answer sheet. The instructions for entering your answers follow.

- First, write your answer in the boxes at the top of the grid.
- Second, grid your answer in the columns below the boxes.
- Use the fraction bar in the first row or the decimal point in the second row to enter fractions and decimals.

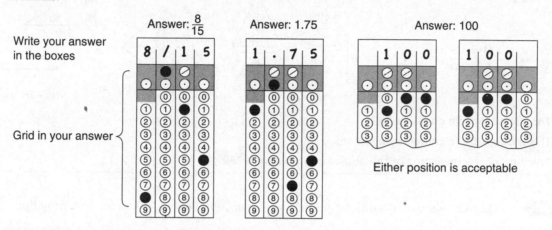

Answer: $\frac{8}{15}$ Answer: 1.75   Answer: 100

Write your answer in the boxes

Grid in your answer

Either position is acceptable

- Grid only one space in each column.
- Entering the answer in the boxes is recommended as an aid in gridding but is not required.
- The machine scoring your exam can read only what you grid, so you **must grid-in your answers correctly to get credit**.
- If a question has more than one correct answer, grid-in only one of them.
- The grid does not have a minus sign; so **no answer can be negative**.
- A mixed number *must* be converted to an improper fraction or a decimal before it is gridded.

  Enter $1\frac{1}{4}$ as 5/4 or 1.25; the machine will interpret 11/4 as $\frac{11}{4}$ and mark it wrong.

- **All decimals must be entered as accurately as possible.** Here are three acceptable ways of gridding

$$\frac{3}{11} = 0.272727\ldots$$

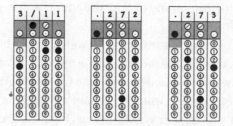

- Note that rounding to .273 is acceptable because you are using the full grid, but you would receive **no credit** for .3 or .27, because they are less accurate.

On the first page of every mathematics section of the SAT, a box labeled "Reference Information" contains several basic math facts and formulas. In each math section of every model test in this book, you will find the exact same information.

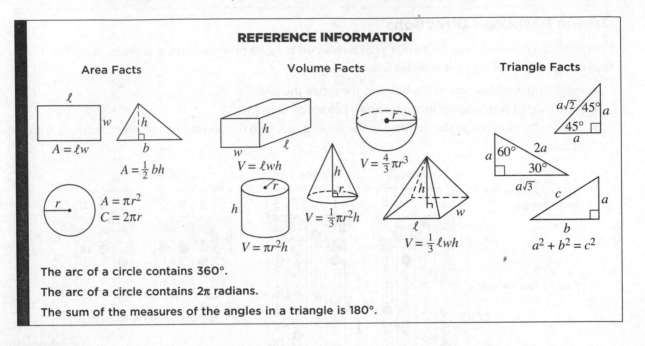

REFERENCE INFORMATION

Area Facts

$A = \ell w$

$A = \frac{1}{2} bh$

$A = \pi r^2$
$C = 2\pi r$

Volume Facts

$V = \ell wh$

$V = \pi r^2 h$

$V = \frac{1}{3}\pi r^2 h$

$V = \frac{4}{3}\pi r^3$

$V = \frac{1}{3}\ell wh$

Triangle Facts

$a^2 + b^2 = c^2$

The arc of a circle contains 360°.

The arc of a circle contains 2π radians.

The sum of the measures of the angles in a triangle is 180°.

HELPFUL HINT

As your prepare for this test, memorize the directions for each section. *When you take the SAT, do not waste even one second reading directions.*

The College Board's official guide, *SAT Preparation Booklet*, offers the following tip:

The test does not require you to memorize formulas. Commonly used formulas are provided in the test booklet at the beginning of each mathematical section.

If you interpret this to mean "Don't bother memorizing the formulas provided," this is terrible advice. It may be reassuring to know that, if you should forget a basic geometry fact, you can look it up in the box headed "Reference Information," but you should decide right now that you will never have to do that. During the test, you don't want to spend any precious time looking up facts that you can learn now. All of these "commonly used formulas" and other important facts are presented in Chapter 6. As you learn and review these facts, you should commit them to memory.

ENTERING YOUR ANSWERS ON THE ANSWER SHEET

On multiple-choice questions, once you determine which answer choice you believe is correct, blacken the corresponding oval on the answer sheet. For grid-in questions the situation is a little more complicated.

For each math seciton, the answer sheet will have one blank grid for each grid-in question. Each one will look exactly like the grid on the next page. After solving a problem, the first step is to write the answer in the four boxes at the top of the grid. You then blacken the appropriate oval under each box. For example, if your answer to a question is 2.45, you write 2.45 at the top of the grid, one digit or symbol in each box, and then in each column blacken the oval that contains the number or symbol you wrote at the top of the column. (See the grid on the next page.) This is not difficult; but there are some special rules concerning grid-in questions, so let's go over them before you practice gridding-in some numbers.

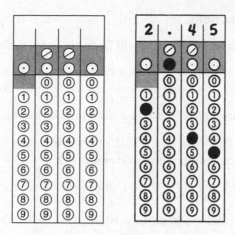

1. **THE ANSWER TO EVERY GRID-IN QUESTION IS A POSITIVE NUMBER OR ZERO.** The only symbols that appear in the grid are the digits 0 to 9, a decimal point, and a slash (/), used to write fractions. Note that there is no negative sign.

2. **BE AWARE THAT YOU WILL RECEIVE CREDIT FOR A CORRECT ANSWER NO MATTER WHERE YOU GRID IT.** For example, the answer 17 could be gridded in any of three positions:

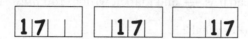

Neverthelesss, try to consistently *write all your answers* the way numbers are usually displayed—*to the right, with blank spaces at the left.*

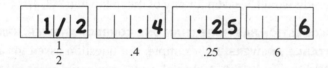

3. **DO NOT ROUND OFF ANY ANSWER UNLESS YOU ARE SPECIFICALLY TOLD TO DO SO.**

- For example, suppose the answer to a question is .148. If the question asks what is the value to the nearest hundredth, you must enter .15. You will receive no credit if you entered .148. On the other hand, if the question did not ask you to round off your answer, you will receive no credit for entering .15 since you could enter .148, which is more accurate.

- If a decimal answer will not fit in the grid, enter a decimal point in the first column, followed by the first three digits. For example, if your answer is 0.454545..., enter it as .454. You would receive credit if you rounded it to .455, but don't. You might occasionally make a mistake in rounding, whereas you'll *never* make a mistake if you just copy the first three digits. *Note:* If the correct answer has more than two decimal digits, *you must use all four columns of the grid.* You will receive *no credit* for .4 or .5 or .45. (These answers are not accurate enough.)

4. **NEVER WRITE A 0 BEFORE THE DECIMAL POINT.** The first column of the grid doesn't even have a 0 in it. If the correct answer is 0.3333..., you must grid it as .333. You can't grid 0.33, and 0.3 is not accurate enough.

5. **NEVER REDUCE FRACTIONS.**

- If your answer is a fraction that will fit in the grid, such as $\frac{2}{3}$ or $\frac{4}{18}$ or $\frac{6}{34}$, *just enter it*. Don't waste time reducing it or converting it to a decimal.

- If your answer is a fraction that won't fit in the grid, do not attempt to reduce it; use your calculator to *convert it to a decimal*. For example, $\frac{24}{65}$ won't fit in a grid— it would require five spaces: 2 4 / 6 5. Don't waste even a few seconds trying to reduce it; just divide on your calculator, and enter .369.

  Unlike $\frac{24}{65}$, the fraction $\frac{24}{64}$ can be reduced—to $\frac{12}{32}$, which doesn't help, or to $\frac{6}{16}$ or $\frac{3}{8}$, either of which could be entered. *Don't do it!* Reducing a fraction takes time, and you might make a mistake. You won't make a mistake if you just use your calculator: $24 \div 64 = .375$.

6. **BE AWARE THAT YOU CAN NEVER ENTER A MIXED NUMBER.** If your answer is $2\frac{1}{2}$, you *cannot* leave a space and enter your answer as 2 1/2. Also, if you enter $\boxed{2\ 1\ /\ 2}$, the machine will read it as $\frac{21}{2}$ and mark it wrong. You *must* enter $2\frac{1}{2}$ as the improper fraction $\frac{5}{2}$ or as the decimal 2.5.

7. **FULL CREDIT IS GIVEN FOR ANY EQUIVALENT ANSWER. USE THESE GUIDELINES TO ENTER YOUR ANSWER IN THE SIMPLEST WAY.** If your answer is $\frac{6}{9}$, you should enter 6/9. (However, credit would be given for any of the following: 2/3, 4/6, 8/12, .666, .667.)

8. **IF A GRID-IN QUESTION HAS MORE THAN ONE CORRECT ANSWER, GRID IN ONLY ONE OF THE ACCEPTABLE ANSWERS.** For example, if a question asked for a positive number less than 100 that was divisible by both 5 and 7, you could enter *either* 35 *or* 70, but not both. Similarly, if a question asked for a number between $\frac{3}{7}$ and $\frac{5}{9}$, you could enter any *one* of more than 100 possibilities: fractions such as $\frac{1}{2}$ and $\frac{4}{9}$ or *any* decimal between .429 and .554—.43 or .499 or .52, for example.

9. **BE SURE TO ENTER AN ANSWER FOR EVERY GRID-IN QUESTION.** Remember that since there is no penalty for an incorrect answer, *never* leave out any question on the SAT. If you are running out of time, just grid in any number, such as 1, in each grid when you have 10 seconds left.

10. **BE SURE TO GRID EVERY ANSWER VERY CAREFULLY.** The computer does not read what you have written in the boxes; it reads only the answer in the grid. If the correct answer to a question is 100 and you write 100 in the boxes, but accidentally grid in 200, you get *no* credit.

11. **WRITE EACH ANSWER IN THE BOXES.** If you know that the answer to a question is 100, can you just grid it in and not bother writing it on top? Yes, you will get full credit, and so some SAT guides recommend that you don't waste time writing the answer. This is terrible advice. *Write each answer in the boxes.* It takes less than 2 seconds per answer to do this, and it definitely cuts down on careless errors in gridding. Equally important,

if you go back to check your work, it is much easier to read what's in the boxes on top than what's in the grid.

12. **NOTE THE LIMITATIONS OF THE GRID.** Be aware that the smallest number that can be gridded is 0; the largest is 9999. No number greater than 100 can have a decimal point. The largest number less than 100 that can be gridded is 99.9; the smallest number greater than 100 that can be gridded is 101.

PRACTICE IN GRIDDING-IN NUMBERS

Now, check your understanding of these guidelines. Use the empty numbered grids that follow to show how you would enter these answers.

1. 123

2. $\dfrac{7}{11}$

3. $2\dfrac{3}{4}$

4. $\dfrac{8}{30}$

5. 1.1111...

6. 0

7. $\dfrac{48}{80}$

8. $\dfrac{83}{100}$

9. $\dfrac{19}{15}$

10. $3\dfrac{5}{18}$

1.
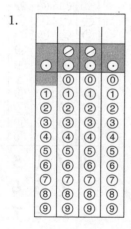

2.
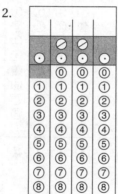

3.
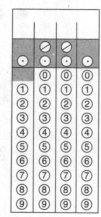

4.
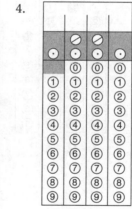

5.
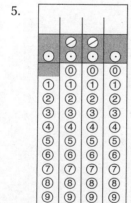

6.
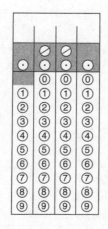

7.

8.

9. 10.

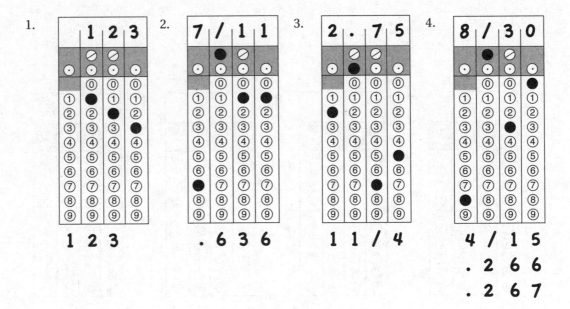

Solutions

Each grid shows the recommended answer. Other acceptable answers, if any, are written below each grid.

1.   **1 2 3**

1 2 3

2.   **7 / 1 1**

. 6 3 6

3.   **2 . 7 5**

1 1 / 4

4.   **8 / 3 0**

4 / 1 5
. 2 6 6
. 2 6 7

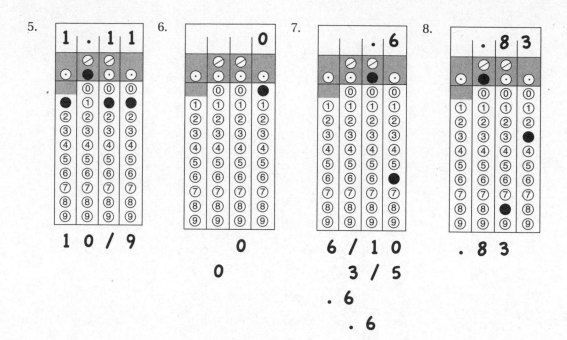

5.   6.   7.   8.

10/9   0   6/10   .83

0   3/5

.6

.6

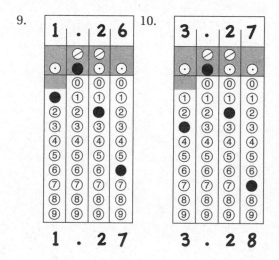

9.   10.

1.27   3.28

If you missed even one of these, go back and reread the rules for gridding. *You <u>never</u> want to solve a problem correctly but get no credit because you didn't grid it properly.* Whenever you practice grid-in problems, actually grid in the answers. Make sure you understand all of these rules *now*. When you actually take the SAT, don't even look at the instructions for gridding.

Math Strategies and Tactics

5

Most of the questions in the two mathematics sections of the SAT are multiple-choice questions. In this chapter, you will learn the important strategies that will help you answer these questions. As a bonus, most of these tactics can also be used on the grid-in questions. However, as invaluable as these tactics are, use them only when you need them.

The first four tactics deal with the best ways of handling diagrams.

TACTIC 1. Draw a diagram.
TACTIC 2. If a diagram has been drawn to scale, trust it.
TACTIC 3. If a diagram has not been drawn to scale, redraw it.
TACTIC 4. Add a line to a diagram.

To implement these tactics, you need to be able to draw line segments and angles accurately, and also to be able to look at segments and angles and accurately estimate their measures. Let's look at three variations of the same problem.

NOTE

If you know how to solve a problem and are confident that you can do so accurately and reasonably quickly, **JUST DO IT!**

a. If the diagonal of a rectangle is twice as long as the shorter side, what is the degree measure of the angle the diagonal makes with the longer side?

b. In the rectangle at the right, what is the value of x?

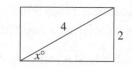

c. In the rectangle at the right, what is the value of x?

For the moment, let's ignore the correct mathematical way to solve this problem. You should be able to look at the diagram in (b) and "see" that x is about 30, *certainly* between 25 and 35. In (a), however, you aren't given a diagram, and in (c) the diagram is useless because it hasn't been drawn

Note: Figure not drawn to scale

to scale. In both of these cases, you should be able to draw a diagram that looks just like the one in (b); then you can look at *your* diagram and "see" that the measure of the angle in question is about 30°.

If this were a multiple-choice question, and the choices were as follows:

(A) 15   (B) 30   (C) 45   (D) 60

you would, of course, choose **30 (B)**. If the choices were

(A) 20   (B) 25   (C) 30   (D) 35

you would be a little less confident, but you should still choose **30**, here **(C)**.

If this were a grid-in problem, you would be much less certain of your answer, but should surely bubble in 30, rather than guess a "strange" number such as 28 or 31.

By the way, *x* is *exactly* 30. A right triangle in which one leg is half the hypotenuse must be a 30-60-90 triangle, and that leg is opposite the 30° angle [see KEY FACT J11].

But how can you know the value of *x* just by looking at the diagram in (b)? In this section, you will learn not only how to look at *any* angle and know its measure within 5 or 10°, but also how to draw any angle with the same accuracy. You will also learn how to draw line segments of the correct lengths, so that your diagrams won't be as bad as the one in (c). Do you see what is wrong with that diagram? The diagonal is *labeled* 4 and one of the sides is *labeled* 2, but the diagonal, *as drawn*, is only slightly longer than the side, not nearly twice as long.

Consider the following example:

➡ Example 1

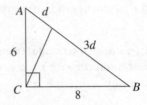

In the figure above, what is the value of *d*?

(A) 2
(B) 2.5
(C) 3
(D) 3.5

 Solution. Since there is no note indicating that the diagram has not been drawn to scale, you can trust it [see TACTIC 2].

- Clearly, *d* is less than *AC*, which is 6; but all four choices are less than 6, so that doesn't help.
- Actually, it looks as though *d* is less than *half* of *AC*.
- So assume *d* < 3 and eliminate choices (C) and (D).

You could now guess between choices A and B; but if you measure, you'll *know* which is right. However, there's a problem—on the SAT, you are *not* allowed to use a ruler, a compass, or a protractor. So how can you measure anything? *Use the back of your answer sheet!*

Turn your answer sheet over, place one corner of it on point A, and with your pencil make a small mark to indicate length d. Now use this "ruler" to measure AC. Put a dot on AC d units from A; slide the answer sheet, mark off a second segment of length d, and do this once more. The third mark is well past C, so $3d$ is more than 6; that is, $d > 2$. Eliminate (A). The answer is **2.5 (B)**.

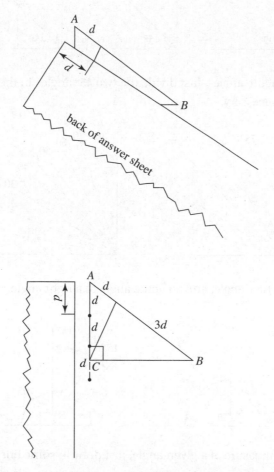

Finally, erase the dot or mark you made on the back of your answer sheet, so it won't confuse you if you need to make a new "ruler" for another question. Also, there should be no stray pencil marks anywhere on the answer sheet when you hand it in.

To answer this question without TACTIC 2, use the Pythagorean theorem to get that $AB = 10$ (or recognize that this is a 6-8-10 right triangle) and then solve the equation: $d + 3d = 10 \Rightarrow d = \mathbf{2.5}$.

To take full advantage of TACTICS 1, 2, and 3, you need to be able to measure angles as well as line segments. Fortunately, this is very easy. In fact, you should be able to *look* at any angle and know its measure within 5–10°, and be able to *draw* any angle accurately within 10°. Let's see how.

First, you should easily recognize a 90° angle and can probably draw one freehand, or you can always just trace the corner of your answer sheet.

Second, to draw a 45° angle, just bisect a 90° angle. Again, you can probably do this free-hand. If not, or to be more accurate, draw a right angle, mark off the same distance on each side, draw a square, and then draw in the diagonal.

Third, to draw other acute angles, just divide the two 45° angles in the above diagram with as many lines as are necessary.

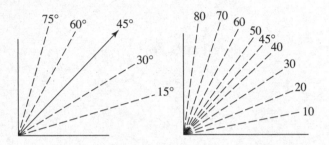

Finally, to draw an obtuse angle, add an acute angle to a right angle.

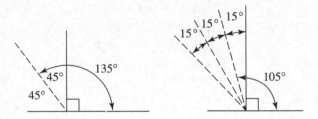

Now, to estimate the measure of a given angle, just draw in some lines.

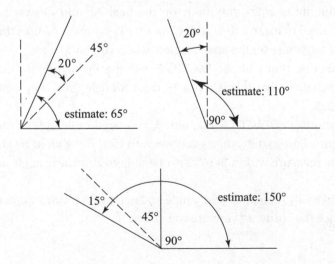

To test yourself, estimate the measure of each angle shown below. The answers follow written upside down.

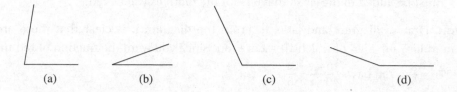

(a)   (b)   (c)   (d)

Answers: (a) 80° (b) 20° (c) 115° (d) 160°.
Did you come within 10° on each one?

TESTING TACTICS

TACTIC

1   **Draw a Diagram.**

On any geometry question for which a figure is not provided, draw one (as accurately as possible) in your test booklet. Drawings should not be limited, however, to geometry questions; there are many other questions on which drawings will help. Whether you intend to solve a problem directly or to use one of the tactics described in this chapter, drawing a diagram is the first step.

A good drawing requires no artistic ability. Usually, a few line segments are sufficient. Let's consider some examples.

➡ **Example 2**_____

What is the area of a rectangle whose length is twice its width and whose perimeter is equal to that of a square whose area is 1?

Solution. Don't even think of answering this question until you have drawn a square and a rectangle and labeled each of them: each side of the square is 1; and if the width of the rectangle is w, its length (ℓ) is $2w$.

$1 \quad P = 4 \qquad w \quad P = 6w$

Now, write the required equation and solve it:

$$6w = 4 \Rightarrow w = \frac{4}{6} = \frac{2}{3} \Rightarrow 2w = \frac{4}{3}.$$

The area of the rectangle $= \ell w = \left(\frac{4}{3}\right)\left(\frac{2}{3}\right) = \frac{8}{9}$.

➡ **Example 3**_____

      A jar contains 10 red marbles and 30 green ones. How many red marbles
      must be added to the jar so that 60% of the marbles will be red?

Solution. Draw a diagram and label it. From the diagram it is clear that there are now
$40 + x$ marbles in the jar, of which $10 + x$ are red. Since you want the fraction of red marbles
to be $60\% \left(= \dfrac{3}{5} \right)$, you have $\dfrac{10+x}{40+x} = \dfrac{3}{5}$.

Cross-multiplying gives:

$$5(10 + x) = 3(40 + x) \Rightarrow$$

$$50 + 5x = 120 + 3x \Rightarrow 2x = 70 \Rightarrow x = \mathbf{35}$$

Of course, you could have set up the equation and solved it without the diagram, but the
drawing makes the solution easier and you are less likely to make a careless mistake.

➡ **Example 4**_____

      Tony drove 8 miles west, 6 miles north, 3 miles east, and 6 more miles
      north. How far was Tony from his starting place?

      (A) 13
      (B) 17
      (C) 19
      (D) 21

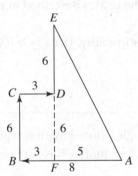

Solution. Draw a diagram. Now, extend line segment $\overline{ED}$ until it intersects $\overline{AB}$ at F [see
TACTIC 4]. Then, $\triangle AFE$ is a right triangle whose legs are 5 and 12 and, therefore, its hypotenuse is **13 (A)**.

    [If you drew the diagram accurately, you could get the right answer by measuring!]

➡ **Example 5**_____

By how many degrees does the angle formed by the hour hand and the minute hand of a clock increase from 1:27 to 1:28?

Solution. Draw a simple picture of a clock. The hour hand makes a complete revolution, 360°, once every 12 hours. Therefore, in 1 hour it goes through 360° ÷ 12 = 30°, and in 1 minute it advances through 30° ÷ 60 = 0.5°. The minute hand moves through 30° every 5 minutes and 6° each 1 minute. Therefore, in the minute from 1:27 to 1:28 (or any other minute), the *difference* between the hands increases by 6 – 0.5 = **5.5** degrees. [Note that it was not necessary, and would have been more time-consuming to determine the angles between the hands at 1:27 and 1:28 (see TACTIC 10: Don't do more than you have to).]

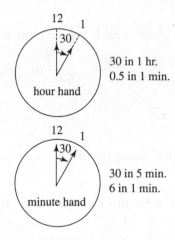

30 in 1 hr.
0.5 in 1 min.

hour hand

30 in 5 min.
6 in 1 min.

minute hand

TACTIC 2
If a Diagram Is Drawn to Scale, Trust It, and Use Your Eyes.

Remember that every diagram that appears on the SAT has been drawn as accurately as possible *unless* you see "<u>Note</u>: Figure not drawn to scale" written below it.

For figures that are drawn to scale, the following are true: line segments that appear to be the same length *are* the same length; if an angle clearly looks obtuse, it *is* obtuse; and if one angle appears larger than another, you may assume that it *is* larger.

Try Examples 6 and 7, which have diagrams that have been drawn to scale. Both of these examples would be classified as hard questions. On an actual SAT, questions of comparable difficulty would be answered correctly by at most 20–35% of the students taking the exam. After you master TACTIC 2, you should have no trouble with problems like these.

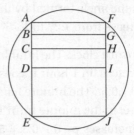

In the figure above, $\overline{EF}$, not shown, is a diagonal of rectangle *AFJE* and a diameter of the circle. *D* is the midpoint of $\overline{AE}$, *C* is the midpoint of $\overline{AD}$, and *B* is the midpoint of $\overline{AC}$.

If *AE* is 8 and the radius of the circle is 5, what is the area of rectangle *BGHC*?

(A) 4
(B) 6
(C) 8
(D) 12

Solution. Since there is no note indicating that the diagram has not been drawn to scale, you can trust it.

- The area of rectangle *BGHC* is the product of its width, *BC*, and its length, *BG*.
- $AE = 8 \Rightarrow AD = 4 \Rightarrow AC = 2 \Rightarrow BC = 1$.
- $\overline{BG}$ *appears* to be longer than $\overline{AD}$, which is 4, and shorter than $\overline{AE}$, which is 8. Therefore, *BG is* more than 4 and *is* less than 8.
- Then, the area of *BGHC* is more than $1 \times 4 = 4$ and less than $1 \times 8 = 8$.
- The only choice between 4 and 8 is **6**. The answer is **(B)**.

Note that you never used the fact that the radius of the circle is 5, information that is necessary to actually *solve* the problem. You were able to answer this question *merely by looking at the diagram*. Were you just lucky? What if the four choices had been 4, 5, 6, and 8, so that there were two choices between 4 and 8, not just one? Well, you could have eliminated 4 and 8 and guessed, or you could have looked at the diagram even more closely. *BG appears* to be about the same length as *CE*, which is 6. If *BG is* 6, then the area of *BGHC is* exactly 6. How can you be sure? Measure the lengths!

On the answer sheet make two small pencil marks to indicate length *BG*:

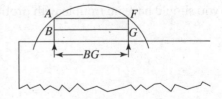

Now, use that length to measure *CE*:

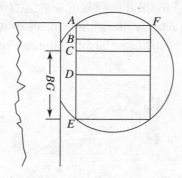

The lengths *are* the same. *BG is* 6; the area *is* 6. It's not a guess after all.

Mathematical Solution. Diameter $\overline{EF}$, which is 10, is also the hypotenuse of right triangle *EAF*. Since leg $\overline{AE}$ is 8, $\overline{AF}$, the other leg, is 6 (either you recognize this as a 6-8-10 triangle, or you use the Pythagorean theorem). Since *BG = AF, BG is* 6, and the area *is* **6**.

If Example 6 had been a grid-in problem instead of a multiple-choice question, you could have used TACTIC 2 in exactly the same way, but you would have been less sure of your answer. If, based on a diagram, you know that the area of a rectangle is about 6 or the measure of an angle is about 30°, you can almost always pick the correct choice, but on a grid-in you can't be certain that the area isn't 6.2 or the angle 31°. Nevertheless, if you can't solve a problem directly, you should always grid in a "simple" number that is consistent with the diagram.

Now try using TACTIC 2 on Examples 7 and 8.

➡ **Example 7** _____

In the figure to the right, what is the value of *x*?

(A) 95
(B) 125
(C) 135
(D) 145

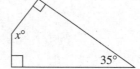

➡ **Example 8** _____

In the figure to the right, what is the value of *x – y*?

(A) –15
(B)   0
(C) 15
(D) 30

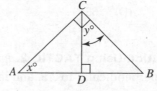

Solution 7 Using TACTIC 2. Since the diagram is drawn to scale, trust it. Look at x: it appears to be *about* $90 + 50 = 140$. In this case, using TACTIC 2 did not get you the exact answer. It only enabled you to narrow down the choices to (C) and (D). At this point, you would guess—unless, of course, you know the following mathematical solution.

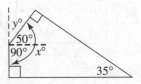

Mathematical Solution 7. The sum of the measures of the four angles in *any* quadrilateral is 360° (KEY FACT K1). Then

$$360 = 90 + 90 + 35 + x = 215 + x \Rightarrow x = 360 - 215 = \mathbf{145} \quad \textbf{(D)}$$

Solution 8 Using TACTIC 2. In the diagram, x and y look about the same, so assume they are. Certainly, neither one is 30° or even 15° greater than the other. Therefore, $x - y = \mathbf{0}$ **(C)**

Mathematical Solution 8. The sums of the measures of the three angles in triangles *ABC* and *CBD* are equal (they are both 180°). Then

$$90 + \mathrm{m}\angle B + x = 90 + \mathrm{m}\angle B + y \Rightarrow x = y \Rightarrow x - y = \mathbf{0} \quad \textbf{(B)}$$

Now try Examples 9–11, in which the diagrams are drawn to scale, and you need to find the measures of angles. Even if you know that you can solve these problems directly, practice TACTIC 2 and estimate the answers. The correct mathematical solutions without using this tactic are also given.

➡ **Example 9**_____

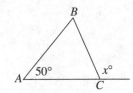

If, in the figure above, $AB = AC$, what is the value of x?

(A) 135
(B) 125
(C) 115
(D) 65

Solution Using TACTIC 2. *Ignore the information in the question.* Just "measure" x. Draw *DC* perpendicular to *AB*, and let *EC* divide right angle *DCA* into two 45° angles, $\angle DCE$ and $\angle ACE$.

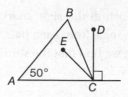

Now, $\angle DCB$ is about half of $\angle DCE$, say 20–25°. Therefore, your estimate for x should be about 110 (90 + 20) or 115 (90 + 25). Choose **(C)**.

Mathematical Solution. Since $\triangle ABC$ is isosceles, with $AB = AC$, the other two angles in the triangle, $\angle B$ and $\angle C$, each measure 65°. Therefore,

$$x + 65 = 180 \Rightarrow x = \mathbf{115}$$

➤ **Example 10** _____

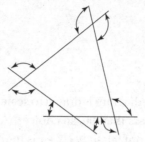

In the figure above, what is the sum of the measures of all of the marked angles?

(A)   360°
(B)   540°
(C)   720°
(D)   900°

Solution Using TACTIC 2. Make your best estimate of each angle, and add up the values. The four choices are so far apart that, even if you're off by 15° or more on some of the angles, you'll get the right answer. The sum of the estimates shown below is 690°, so the correct answer *must* be **720° (C)**.

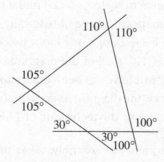

Mathematical Solution. Each of the eight marked angles is an exterior angle of the quadrilateral. If we take one angle from each pair, their sum is 360° (KEY FACT K3); so, taking both angles at each vertex, we find that the sum of the measures is 360° + 360° = **720°**.

➡ **Example 11** _____

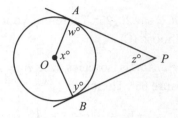

In the diagram above, rays $\overrightarrow{PA}$ and $\overrightarrow{PB}$ are tangent to circle O. Which of the following is equal to z?

(A) x

(B) $180 - x$

(C) $w + x + y$

(D) $\dfrac{w+x+y}{3}$

Solution Using TACTIC 2. The diagram is drawn to scale, so trust it. In the figure, x is clearly greater than 90 and z is clearly less than 90, so choices (A) and (C) are surely wrong. Also, it appears that w and y are each about 90, so $w + x + y$ is more than 270. So choice (D) is greater than $\dfrac{270}{3} = 90$ and could not be equal to z.

The answer must be **(B)**.

Mathematical Solution. Tangents to a circle are perpendicular to the radii drawn to the points of contact, so w and y both equal 90. The sum of the four angles in a quadrilateral is 360°, so $w + x + y + z = 360$. Then $90 + x + 90 + z = 360 \Rightarrow x + z = 180 \Rightarrow z = \mathbf{180 - x}$ **(B)**.

TACTIC
3
If a Diagram Is *Not* Drawn to Scale, Redraw It to Scale, and Then Use Your Eyes.

For figures that have not been drawn to scale, you can make *no* assumptions. Lines that look parallel may not be; an angle that appears to be obtuse may, in fact, be acute; two line segments may have the same length even though one looks twice as long as the other.

In the examples illustrating TACTIC 2, all of the diagrams were drawn to scale and could be used to advantage. When diagrams have not been drawn to scale, you must be much more careful. TACTIC 3 tells you to redraw the diagram *as accurately as possible*, based on the information you are given, and then to apply the technique of TACTIC 2.

> **CAUTION:** Redrawing a diagram, even roughly, takes time. Do this only when you do not see an easy direct solution to the problem.

HELPFUL HINT

In order to redraw a diagram to scale, you first have to ask yourself, "What is wrong with the original diagram?" If an angle is marked 45°, but in the figure it looks like a 75° angle, redraw it. If two line segments appear to be parallel, but you have not been told that they are, redraw them so that they are clearly *not* parallel. If two segments appear to have the same length, but one is marked 5 and the other 10, redraw them so that the second segment is twice as long as the first.

➡ **Example 12** _____

In △*ACB*, what is the value of *x*?

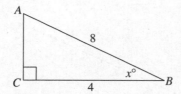

Note: Figure not drawn to scale

(A) 75
(B) 60
(C) 45
(D) 30

Solution. In what way is this figure not drawn to scale? *AB* = 8 and *BC* = 4, but in the figure $\overline{AB}$ is *not* twice as long as $\overline{BC}$. Redraw the triangle so that $\overline{AB}$ *is* twice as long as $\overline{BC}$.

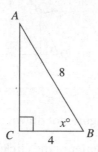

Now, just look: *x* is about **60 (B)**.

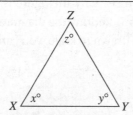 **Mathematical Solution.** In fact, *x* is exactly 60. If the hypotenuse of a right triangle is twice the length of one of the legs, the triangle is a 30-60-90 triangle, and the angle formed by the hypotenuse and that leg is 60° (see Section 6-J).

➡ **Example 13** _____

Note: Figure not drawn to scale

In △*XYZ* at the right, if *XY* < *YZ* < *ZX*, then which of the following *must* be true?

(A) *x* < 60
(B) *z* < 60
(C) *y* < *z*
(D) *x* < *z*

Solution. As drawn, the diagram is useless. The triangle looks like an equilateral triangle, even though the question states that $XY < YZ < ZX$. Redraw the figure so that the condition is satisfied (that is, $\overline{ZX}$ is clearly the longest side and $\overline{XY}$ the shortest).

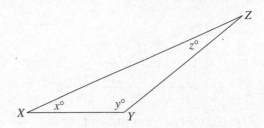

From the redrawn figure, it is clear that y is the largest angle (eliminate choice (C)) and $z < x$ (eliminate (D) as well). Both x and z appear to be less than 60, but only one answer can be correct. Since $z < x$, if only one of these angles is less than 60, it must be z. Therefore, $z < 60$ **(B)** *must* be true.

➡ Example 14

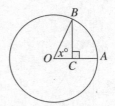

Note: Figure not drawn to scale

In the figure above, O is the center of the circle. If $OA = 4$ and $BC = 2$, what is the value of x?

(A) 15
(B) 30
(C) 45
(D) 60

Solution Using TACTIC 3. Do you see why the figure isn't drawn to scale? $\overline{BC}$, which is 2, looks almost as long as $\overline{OA}$, which is 4. Redraw the diagram, making sure that $\overline{BC}$ is only one-half as long as $\overline{OA}$. With the diagram drawn to scale, you can see that x is approximately **30 (C)**.

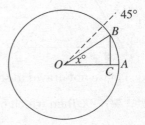

Mathematical Solution. Since $\overline{OB}$ is a radius, it has the same length as radius $\overline{OA}$, which is 4. Then $\triangle BCO$ is a right triangle in which the hypotenuse is twice as long as one leg. This can occur *only* in a 30-60-90 triangle, and the angle opposite that leg measures 30°. Therefore, $x = 30$.

TACTIC 4

Add a Line to a Diagram.

Occasionally, after staring at a diagram, you still have no idea how to solve the problem to which it applies. It looks as though there isn't enough given information. In this case, it often helps to draw another line in the diagram.

➡ **Example 15** _____

In the figure to the right, Q is a point on the circle whose center is O and whose radius is r, and $OPQR$ is a rectangle. What is the length of diagonal $\overline{PR}$?

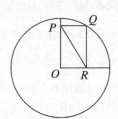

(A) r

(B) r^2

(C) $\dfrac{r^2}{\pi}$

(D) $\dfrac{r\sqrt{2}}{\pi}$

Solution. If, after staring at the diagram and thinking about rectangles, circles, and the Pythagorean theorem, you're still lost, don't give up. Ask yourself, "Can I add another line to this diagram?" As soon as you think to draw in $\overline{OQ}$, the other diagonal, the problem becomes easy. In a rectangle, the two diagonals are congruent. Since $\overline{OQ}$ is a radius, $OQ = PR = r$ **(A)**.

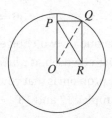

TACTIC 5

Test the Choices, Starting with (B) or (C).

TACTIC 5, often called *backsolving*, is useful when you are asked to solve for an unknown and you understand what needs to be done to answer the question, but you want to avoid doing the algebra. The idea is simple: test the various choices to see which one is correct.

NOTE: On the SAT the answers to virtually all numerical multiple-choice questions are listed in either increasing or decreasing order. Consequently, (B) and (C) are the middle values; and in applying TACTIC 5, *you should always start with one of them.* For example, assume that choices (A), (B), (C), and (D) are given in increasing order. Try (C). If it works, you've found the answer. If C doesn't work, you should now know whether you need to test a larger number or a smaller one, and that information permits you to eliminate one or two more choices. If (C) is too small, you need a larger number, so (A) and (B) are out; the answer is (D). If (C) is too large, you can eliminate (D), which is even larger.

Example 16 illustrates the proper use of TACTIC 5.

➥ Example 16 _____

If the average (arithmetic mean) of 2, 7, and x is 12, what is the value of x?

    (A) 9
    (B) 12
    (C) 21
    (D) 27

Solution. Use TACTIC 5. Test choice (C): $x = 21$.

- Is the average of 2, 7, and 21 equal to 12?
- No: $\dfrac{2+7+21}{3} = \dfrac{30}{3} = 10$, which is *too small*.
- Eliminate (C); also, since, for the average to be 12, x must be *greater* than 21, eliminate (A) and (B).
- The answer is **(D)**.

Every problem that can be solved using TACTIC 5 can be solved directly, often in less time. Therefore, we stress: *if you are confident that you can solve a problem quickly and accurately, just do so.*

Here is the direct method for solving Example 16, which is *faster* than backsolving. (See Section 9-E on averages.) If you know this method, you should use it and save TACTIC 5 for problems that you can't easily solve directly.

Direct Solution. If the average of three numbers is 12, their sum is 36. Then

$$2 + 7 + x = 36 \Rightarrow 9 + x = 36 \Rightarrow x = \mathbf{27}$$

Some tactics allow you to eliminate one or two choices so that you can make an educated guess. On problems where TACTIC 5 can be used, it *always* leads you to the right answer. The only reason not to use it on a particular problem is that you can easily solve the problem directly.

Now try applying TACTIC 5 to Examples 17 and 18.

➥ Example 17 _____

If the sum of five consecutive even integers is 740, what is the largest of these integers?

    (A) 156
    (B) 152
    (C) 146
    (D) 144

 Solution. Use TACTIC 5. Test choice (C): 146.

- If 146 is the largest of the five integers, the integers are 146, 144, 142, 140, and 138. Quickly add them on your calculator. The sum is 710.
- Since 710 is too small, eliminate (C) and (D).
- If you noticed that the amount by which 710 is too small is 30, you should realize that each of the five numbers needs to be increased by 6; therefore, the largest is **152 (B)**.
- If you didn't notice, just try 152, and see that it works.

This solution is easy, and it avoids having to set up and solve the required equation:

$$n + (n+2) + (n+4) + (n+6) + (n+8) = 740$$

➡ Example 18

A competition offers a total of $250,000 in prize money to be shared by the top three contestants. If the money is to be divided among them in the ratio of 1:3:6, what is the value of the largest prize?

(A) $ 25,000
(B) $ 75,000
(C) $100,000
(E) $150,000

 Solution. Use TACTIC 5. Test choice (C): $100,000.

- If the largest prize were $100,000, the second largest would be $50,000 (they are in the ratio of 6:3 = 2:1). The third prize would be much less than $50,000, so all three would add up to less than $200,000.
- Eliminate (A), (B), and (C).
- The answer is **(D)**.

Again, TACTIC 5 lets you avoid the algebra if you can't do it or just don't want to. Here is the correct solution. By TACTIC D1 the three prizes are x, $3x$, and $6x$. Therefore,

$$x + 3x + 6x = \$250{,}000 \Rightarrow 10x = \$250{,}000$$

So, $x = \$25{,}000$ and $6x = \textbf{\$150,000}$.

➡ Example 19

If $2\sqrt{2x+1} + 5 = 8$, then $x =$

(A) $-\dfrac{1}{8}$

(B) 0

(C) $\dfrac{5}{8}$

(D) 1

Solution. Since plugging in 0 is much easier than plugging in $\dfrac{5}{8}$, start with B. If $x = 0$, the left-hand side of the equation is $2\sqrt{1} + 5$, which is equal to 7 and so is too small. Eliminate (A) and (B), and try something bigger. Still preferring whole numbers to fractions, try choice (D). If $x = 1$, then $2\sqrt{2(1)+1} + 5 = 2\sqrt{3} + 5 \approx 8.46$.

Since that's too big, eliminate (D). The answer must be **(C)** $\dfrac{5}{8}$.

Again, remember: no matter what the choices are, backsolve *only* if you can't easily do the algebra. Many students would do this problem directly:

$$2\sqrt{2x+1} + 5 = 8 \Rightarrow 2\sqrt{2x+1} = 3 \Rightarrow \sqrt{2x+1} = \frac{3}{2}.$$

So, $2x+1=\left(\dfrac{3}{2}\right)^2=\dfrac{9}{4} \Rightarrow 2x=\dfrac{5}{4} \Rightarrow x=\dfrac{5}{8}$ and save backsolving for an even harder problem. You have to determine which method is better for you.

For some multiple-choice questions on the SAT, you *have to* test the various choices. On these problems you are not really backsolving (there is nothing to solve!); rather you are testing whether a particular choice satisfies a given condition.

Examples 20 and 21 are two such problems. In Example 20, you are asked for the *largest* integer that satisfies a certain condition. Usually, some of the smaller integers offered as choices also satisfy the condition, but your job is to find the largest one.

➡ Example 20_____

What is the largest integer, n, such that $\dfrac{112}{2^n}$ is an integer?

(A) 2
(B) 3
(C) 4
(D) 5

 Solution. Since you want the *largest* value of n for which $\dfrac{112}{2^n}$ is an integer, start by testing 5, choice D, the largest of the choices.

- Is $\dfrac{112}{2^5}$ an integer? No: $\dfrac{112}{2^5} = \dfrac{112}{32} = 3.5$.

Eliminate (D) and try (C).

- Is $\dfrac{112}{2^4}$ an integer? Yes: $2^4 = 16$, and $\dfrac{112}{16} = 7$.

- The answer is **4 (C)**.

It doesn't matter whether any of the smaller choices work (you need the *largest*), although in this case they *all* do.

Surprisingly, on a problem that asks for the *smallest* number satisfying a property, you should also start with (D), because the choices for these problems are usually given in decreasing order.

It is also better to start with (D) on questions such as Example 21, in which you are asked "which of the following...?" The right answer is *rarely* one of the first choices.

Sometimes a question asks which of the four choices satisfies a certain condition. Usually, in this situation there is no way to answer the question directly. Rather, you must look at the choices and test each of them until you find one that works. At that point, stop—none of the other choices could be correct. There is no particular order in which to test the choices, but it makes sense to test the easier ones first. For example, it is usually easier to test whole numbers than fractions and positive numbers than negative ones.

➡ **Example 21** _____

Which of the following is NOT equivalent to $\frac{3}{5}$?

(A) 60%

(B) 0.6

(C) $\frac{3}{7} \times \frac{7}{5}$

(D) $\frac{3}{7} \div \frac{7}{5}$

 Solution. Here, you have to test each of the choices until you find one that satisfies the condition that it is *not* equal to $\frac{3}{5}$. If, as you glance at the choices to see if any would be easier to test than the others, you happen to notice that 60% = 0.6, then you can immediately eliminate choices (A) and (B), since it is impossible that both are correct.

- Test choice (C). $\frac{3}{7} \times \frac{7}{5} = \frac{3}{5}$.

- You now know that **(D)** must be the correct answer. In fact, $\frac{3}{7} \div \frac{7}{5} = \frac{3}{7} \times \frac{5}{7} = \frac{15}{49} \neq \frac{3}{5}$.

TACTIC

6 Replace Variables with Numbers.

Mastery of TACTIC 6 is critical for anyone developing good test-taking skills. This tactic can be used whenever the four choices in a multiple-choice math question involve the variables in the question. There are three steps:

1. Replace each variable with an easy-to-use number.
2. Solve the problem using those numbers.
3. Evaluate each of the four choices with the numbers you picked to see which choice is equal to the answer you obtained.

Examples 22 and 23 illustrate the proper use of TACTIC 6.

➡ **Example 22** _____

If a is equal to b multiplied by c, which of the following is equal to b divided by c?

(A) $\frac{a}{bc}$

(B) $\frac{ab}{c}$

(C) $\frac{a}{c}$

(D) $\frac{a}{c^2}$

Solution.

- Pick three easy-to-use numbers that satisfy $a = bc$: for example, $a = 6$, $b = 2$, $c = 3$.
- Solve the problem with these numbers: $b \div c = \dfrac{b}{c} = \dfrac{2}{3}$.
- Check each of the four choices to see which one is equal to $\dfrac{2}{3}$:

(A) $\dfrac{a}{bc} = \dfrac{6}{(2)(3)} = 1$: NO.

(B) $\dfrac{ab}{c} = \dfrac{(6)(3)}{3} = 6$: NO.

(C) $\dfrac{a}{c} = \dfrac{6}{3} = 2$: NO.

(D) $\dfrac{a}{c^2} = \dfrac{6}{3^2} = \dfrac{6}{9} = \dfrac{2}{3}$: YES!

- The answer is **(D)**.

➡ **Example 23** _____

If the sum of four consecutive odd integers is s, then, in terms of s, what is the greatest of these integers?

(A) $\dfrac{s-12}{4}$

(B) $\dfrac{s-6}{4}$

(C) $\dfrac{s+6}{4}$

(D) $\dfrac{s+12}{4}$

Solution.

- Pick four easy-to-use consecutive odd integers: say, 1, 3, 5, 7. Then s, their sum, is 16.
- Solve the problem with these numbers: the greatest of these integers is 7.
- When $s = 16$, the four choices are $\dfrac{s-12}{4} = \dfrac{4}{4}$, $\dfrac{s-6}{4} = \dfrac{10}{4}$, $\dfrac{s+6}{4} = \dfrac{22}{4}$, and $\dfrac{s+12}{4} = \dfrac{28}{4}$.
- Only $\dfrac{28}{4}$, choice **(D)**, is equal to 7.

Of course, Examples 22 and 23 can be solved without using TACTIC 6 *if your algebra skills are good*. Here are the solutions.

Solution 22. $a = bc \Rightarrow b = \dfrac{a}{c} \Rightarrow b \div c = \dfrac{a}{c} \div c = \dfrac{a}{c^2}$.

Solution 23. Let n, $n+2$, $n+4$, and $n+6$ be four consecutive odd integers, and let s be their sum. Then:

$$s = n + (n+2) + (n+4) + (n+6) = 4n + 12$$

Therefore:

$$n = \dfrac{s-12}{4} \Rightarrow n+6 = \dfrac{s-12}{4} + 6 = \dfrac{s-12}{4} + \dfrac{24}{4} = \dfrac{s+12}{4}$$

The important point is that, if you are uncomfortable with the correct algebraic solution, you can use TACTIC 6 and *always* get the right answer. Of course, even if you can do the algebra, you should use TACTIC 6 if you think you can solve the problem faster or will be less likely to make a mistake. With the proper use of the tactics in this chapter, you can correctly answer many problems that you may not know how to solve mathematically.

Example 24 is somewhat different. You are asked to reason through a word problem involving only variables. Many students find problems like these mind-boggling. Here, the use of TACTIC 6 is essential.

HELPFUL HINT

Replace the variables with numbers that are easy to use, not necessarily ones that make sense. *It is perfectly OK to ignore reality.* **A school can have five students, apples can cost $10 each, trains can go 5 miles per hour or 1000 miles per hour—it doesn't matter.**

➡ Example 24

If a school cafeteria needs c cans of soup each week for each student, and if there are s students in the school, for how many weeks will x cans of soup last?

(A) $\dfrac{cx}{s}$

(B) $\dfrac{xs}{c}$

(C) $\dfrac{s}{cx}$

(D) $\dfrac{x}{cs}$

Solution.

- Replace c, s, and x with three easy-to-use numbers. If a school cafeteria needs 2 cans of soup each week for each student, and if there are 5 students in the school, how many weeks will 20 cans of soup last?
- Since the cafeteria needs $2 \times 5 = 10$ cans of soup per week, 20 cans will last for 2 weeks.
- Which of the choices equals 2 when $c = 2$, $s = 5$, and $x = 20$?
- The four choices become: $\dfrac{cx}{s} = 8$, $\dfrac{xs}{c} = 50$, $\dfrac{s}{cx} = \dfrac{1}{8}$, $\dfrac{x}{cs} = 2$.

The answer is (**D**).

Even though Example 24 is more abstract than Examples 22 and 23, it too can be solved directly and more quickly *if* you can manipulate the variables.

Algebraic Solution 24. If each week the school needs c cans for each of the s students, then it will need cs cans per week. Dividing cs into x gives the number of weeks that x cans will last: $\dfrac{x}{cs}$.

Now, practice TACTIC 6 on the following problems.

➦ Example 25

Nadia will be x years old y years from now. How old was she z years ago?

(A) $x + y + z$
(B) $x + y - z$
(C) $x - y - z$
(D) $y - x - z$

➦ Example 26

If $a = b + \dfrac{1}{2}$, $b = 2c + \dfrac{1}{2}$, and $c = 3d + \dfrac{1}{2}$, which of the following is an

expression for d in terms of a?

(A) $\dfrac{a-2}{6}$

(B) $\dfrac{2a-3}{6}$

(C) $\dfrac{2a-3}{12}$

(D) $\dfrac{3a-2}{18}$

➦ Example 27

Anne drove for h hours at a constant rate of r miles per hour. How many miles did she go during the final 20 minutes of her drive?

(A) $\dfrac{hr}{3}$

(B) $3rh$

(C) $\dfrac{hr}{20}$

(D) $\dfrac{r}{3}$

Solution 25. Assume Nadia will be 10 in 2 years. How old was she 3 years ago? If she will be 10 in 2 years, she is 8 now and 3 years ago was 5. Which of the choices equals 5 when $x = 10$, $y = 2$, and $z = 3$? Only $x - y - z$ **(C)**.

Solution 26. Let $d = 1$. Then $c = 3\dfrac{1}{2}$, $b = 7\dfrac{1}{2}$, and $a = 8$. Which of the choices equals 1 when $a = 8$? Only $\dfrac{a-2}{6}$ **(A)**.

Solution 27. If Anne drove at 60 miles per hour for 2 hours, how far did she go in the last 20 minutes?

Since 20 minutes is $\dfrac{1}{3}$ of an hour, she went $20\left(\dfrac{1}{3}\text{ of }60\right)$ miles.

Only $\frac{r}{3}$ **(D)** = 20 when $r = 60$ and $h = 2$.

Notice that h is irrelevant. Whether Anne had been driving for 2 hours or 20 hours, the distance she covered in her last 20 minutes would be the same.

7   Choose an Appropriate Number.

TACTIC 7 is similar to TACTIC 6 in that you pick a convenient number. However, here no variable is given in the problem. TACTIC 7 is especially useful in problems involving fractions, ratios, and percents.

➡ Example 28

At Central High School each student studies exactly one foreign language. Three-fifths of the students take Spanish, and one-fourth of the remaining students take Italian. If all of the others take French, what <u>percent</u> of the students take French?

(A) 15
(B) 20
(C) 25
(D) 30

> **HELPFUL HINT**
>
> In problems involving fractions, the best number to use is the least common denominator of all the fractions. In problems involving percents, the easiest number to use is 100. (See Sections 6-B and 6-C.)

Solution. The least common denominator of $\frac{3}{5}$ and $\frac{1}{4}$ is 20, so assume that there are 20 students at Central High. (Remember that the number you choose doesn't have to be realistic.) Then the number of students taking Spanish is $12\left(\frac{3}{5}\text{ of }20\right)$. Of the remaining 8 students, $2\left(\frac{1}{4}\text{ of }8\right)$ take Italian. The other 6 take French. Finally, 6 is **30%** of 20.

The answer is **(D)**.

➡ Example 29

From 2013 to 2014 the number of boys in the school chess club decreased by 20%, and the number of girls in the club increased by 20%. The ratio of girls to boys in the club in 2014 was how many times the ratio of girls to boys in the club in 2013?

(A) $\frac{2}{3}$

(B) $\frac{4}{5}$

(C) $\frac{5}{4}$

(D) $\frac{3}{2}$

Solution. This problem involves percents, so try to use 100. Assume that in 2013 there were 100 boys and 100 girls in the club. Since 20% of 100 is 20, in 2014 there were 120 girls (a 20% increase) and 80 boys (a 20% decrease). See the following chart:

Year	Number of Girls	Number of Boys	Ratio of Girls to Boys
2013	100	100	$\frac{100}{100} = 1$
2014	120	80	$\frac{120}{80} = \frac{3}{2}$

The chart shows that the 2013 ratio of 1 was multiplied by $\frac{3}{2}$. The answer is **(D)**.

Here are two more problems where TACTIC 7 is useful.

➥ Example 30

In a particular triathlon the athletes cover $\frac{1}{24}$ of the total distance by swimming, $\frac{1}{3}$ of it by running, and the rest by bike. What is the ratio of the distance covered by bike to the distance covered by running?

(A) 15:8
(B) 8:5
(C) 5:8
(D) 8:15

➥ Example 31

From 2012 to 2013 the sales of a book decreased by 80%. If the sales in 2014 were the same as in 2012, by what percent did they increase from 2013 to 2014?

(A) 100%
(B) 120%
(C) 400%
(D) 500%

Solution 30. The least common denominator of the two fractions is 24, so assume that the total distance is 24 miles. Then, the athletes swim for 1 mile and run for 8 $\left(\frac{1}{3} \text{ of } 24\right)$ miles. The remaining 15 miles they cover by bike. Therefore, the required ratio is **15:8 (A)**.

Solution 31. Use TACTIC 7, and assume that 100 copies were sold in 2012 (and 2014). Sales dropped by 80 (80% of 100) to 20 in 2013 and then increased by 80, from 20 back to 100, in 2014. The percent increase was

$$\frac{\text{actual increase}}{\text{original amount}} \times 100\% = \frac{80}{20} \times 100\% = 400\% \quad \textbf{(C)}$$

Eliminate Absurd Choices, and Guess.

Of course, whenever you have no idea how to solve a problem, you guess. First be sure to eliminate all the absurd choices.

During the course of an SAT, you will probably find at least a few multiple-choice questions that you have no idea how to solve. Before taking a wild guess look at the choices. Often one or two of the answers are absurd. Eliminate them and then *guess*. Occasionally, three of the choices are absurd. When this occurs, your answer is no longer a guess!

What makes a choice absurd? Lots of things. Even if you don't know how to solve a problem, even with very hard ones, you may realize that:

- the answer must be positive, but some of the choices are negative;
- the answer must be even, but some of the choices are odd;
- the answer must be less than 100, but some choices exceed 100;
- a ratio must be less than 1, but some choices are greater than or equal to 1.

Let's look at several examples. In a few of them the information given is intentionally insufficient to solve the problem, but you will still be able to determine that some of the answers are absurd. In each case the "solution" provided will indicate which choices you should have eliminated. At that point you would simply guess. Remember: on the SAT when you decide to guess, don't agonize. Just make your choice and then move on.

➡ Example 32 _____

A region inside a semicircle of radius r is shaded. What is the area of the shaded region?

(A) $\frac{1}{4}\pi r^2$

(B) $\frac{1}{3}\pi r^2$

(C) $\frac{1}{2}\pi r^2$

(D) $\frac{2}{3}\pi r^2$

Solution. You may have no idea how to find the area of the shaded region, but you should know that, since the area of a circle is πr^2, the area of a semicircle is $\frac{1}{2}\pi r^2$. Therefore, the area of the shaded region must be *less than* $\frac{1}{2}\pi r^2$, so eliminate (C) and (D). On an actual problem that includes a diagram, if the diagram is drawn to scale, you may be able to make an educated guess between (A) and (B). If not, just choose one or the other.

➥ Example 33 _____

The average of 5, 10, 15, and x is 20. What is x?

(A) 20
(B) 25
(C) 45
(D) 50

Solution. If the average of four numbers is 20, and three of them are less than 20, the other one must be greater than 20. Eliminate (A). If you further realize that, since 5 and 10 are *a lot* less than 20, x will probably be *a lot* more than 20, eliminate (B), as well. Then guess either (C) or (D).

➥ Example 34 _____

If 25% of 220 equals 5.5% of w, what is w?

(A)   55
(B)   100
(C)   110
(D)   1000

Solution. Since 5.5% of w equals 25% of 220, which is surely greater than 5.5% of 220, w must be *greater* than 220. Eliminate (A), (B), and (C)! The answer *must* be **(D)**!

Example 34 illustrates an important point. *Even if you know how to solve a problem*, if you immediately see that three of the four choices are absurd, just pick the remaining choice and move on.

➥ Example 35 _____

A prize of $27,000 is to be divided in some ratio among three people. What is the largest share?

(A) $18,900
(B) $13,500
(C) $ 8100
(D) $ 5400

Solution. If the prize were divided equally, each share would be worth $9000. If it is divided unequally, the largest share is surely *more than* $9000, so eliminate (C) and (D). In an actual question, you would be told what the ratio is, and that information should enable you to eliminate (A) or (B). If not, you would just guess.

➡ Example 36

A jar contains only red and blue marbles. The ratio of the number of red marbles to the number of blue marbles is 5:3. What percent of the marbles are blue?

(A) 37.5%

(B) 50%

(C) 60%

(D) 62.5%

Solution. Since there are 5 red marbles for every 3 blue ones, there are fewer blue ones than red ones. Therefore, *fewer than half* (50%) of the marbles are blue. Eliminate (B), (C), and (D). The answer is **(A)**.

Now use TACTIC 8 on each of the following problems. Even if you know how to solve them, don't. Practice this technique, and see how many choices you can eliminate *without* actually solving.

➡ Example 37

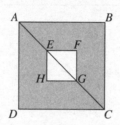

In the figure above, diagonal $\overline{EG}$ of square *EFGH* is one-half of diagonal $\overline{AD}$ of square *ABCD*. What is the ratio of the area of the shaded region to the area of *ABCD*?

(A) $\sqrt{2}$:1

(B) 3:4

(C) $\sqrt{2}$:2

(D) 1:2

➡ Example 38

Jim receives a commission of 25¢ for every $20.00 worth of merchandise he sells. What percent is his commission?

(A) $1\frac{1}{4}$%

(B) $2\frac{1}{2}$%

(C) 5%

(D) 25%

➡ Example 39

From 2000 to 2010, Michael's weight increased by 25%. If his weight was W kilograms in 2010, what was it in 2000?

(A) $1.25W$

(B) $1.20W$

(C) $.80W$

(D) $.75W$

➡ Example 40

The average of 10 numbers is −10. If the sum of six of them is 100, what is the average of the other four?

(A) −100

(B) −50

(C)   50

(D) 100

➡ Example 41

What is 3% of 4%?

(A) 0.12%

(B) 1.2%

(C) 7%

(D) 12%

➡ Example 42

If $f(x) = 4x^2 + 2x^4$, what is the value of $f(-2)$?

(A) −48

(B) −32

(C)   0

(D) 48

Solution 37. Obviously, the shaded region is smaller than square $ABCD$, so the ratio must be less than 1. Eliminate (A) ($\sqrt{2} > 1.4$). Also, from the diagram, it is clear that the shaded region is more than half of square $ABCD$, so the ratio is greater than 0.5. Eliminate (D). Since $3:4 = 0.75$ and $\sqrt{2}:2 \approx 0.71$, (B) and (C) are too close to tell which is right just by looking. So guess. The answer is **(B)**.

Solution 38. Clearly, a commission of 25¢ on $20 is quite small. Eliminate (D), and guess one of the small percents. If you realize that 1% of $20 is 20¢, then you know the answer is a little more than 1%, and you should guess (A) (maybe (B), but definitely not (C)). The answer is **(A)**.

Solution 39. Since Michael's weight increased, his weight in 2000 was *less than W*. Eliminate (A) and (B), and guess. The answer is **(C)**.

Solution 40. Since the average of all 10 numbers is negative, so is their sum. However, the sum of the first six is positive, so the sum (and the average) of the others must be negative. Eliminate (C) and (D). The answer is **(B)**.

Solution 41. Since 3% of a number is just a small part of it, 3% of 4% must be *much less* than 4%. Eliminate (C) and (D), and probably (B). The answer is **(A)**.

Solution 42. Any nonzero number raised to an even power is positive, so $4x^2 + 2x^4$ is positive. Eliminate (A), (B), and (C). The answer is **(D)**.

9   Subtract to Find Shaded Regions.

Whenever part of a figure is white and part is shaded, the straightforward way to find the area of the shaded portion is to find the area of the entire figure and then subtract from it the area of the white region. Of course, if you are asked for the area of the white region, you can, instead, subtract the shaded area from the total area. Occasionally, you may see an easy way to calculate the shaded area directly, but usually you should subtract.

➡ **Example 43**

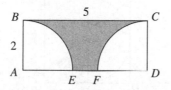

In the figure above, $ABCD$ is a rectangle, and $\widehat{BE}$ and $\widehat{CF}$ are arcs of circles centered at A and D. What is the area of the shaded region?

(A) $10 - \pi$
(B) $2(5 - \pi)$
(C) $2(5 - 2\pi)$
(D) $6 + 2\pi$

Solution. The entire region is a 2×5 rectangle whose area is 10. Since each white region is a quarter-circle of radius 2, the combined area of these regions is that of a semicircle of radius 2: $\frac{1}{2}\pi(2)^2 = 2\pi$. Therefore, the area of the shaded region is $10 - 2\pi = \mathbf{2(5 - \pi)}$ **(B)**.

The idea of subtracting a part from the whole works with line segments as well as areas.

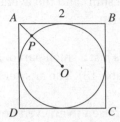

In the figure above, the circle with center O is inscribed in square $ABCD$. Line segment $\overline{AO}$ intersects the circle at P. What is the length of $\overline{AP}$?

(A) $2 - \sqrt{2}$

(B) $1 - \dfrac{\sqrt{2}}{2}$

(C) $2\sqrt{2} - 2$

(D) $\sqrt{2} - 1$

Solution. First use TACTIC 4 and draw some lines. Extend $\overline{AO}$ to form diagonal $\overline{AC}$.

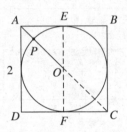

Then, since $\triangle ADC$ is an isosceles right triangle, $AC = 2\sqrt{2}$ (KEY FACT J8) and AO is half of that, or $\sqrt{2}$. Then draw in diameter $\overline{EF}$ parallel to $\overline{AD}$. Since the diameter is 2 ($EF = AD = 2$), the radius is 1. Finally, subtract: $AP = AO - PO = \boldsymbol{\sqrt{2} - 1}$ **(D)**.

   Note: If you don't realize which lines to add and/or you can't reason a question like this one out, you can still make an educated guess. Use TACTIC 2: trust the diagram. Since $AB = 2$, then $AE = 1$, and AP is less than 0.5.

   With your calculator evaluate each choice. (A) and (C) are both greater than 0.5. Eliminate them, and guess either (B) or (D). Since choice (B) is a lot less than 0.5, (D) is the better guess

TACTIC
10

Don't Do More Than You Have To.

In Example 5 on page 383, you were asked, "By how many degrees does the angle formed by the hour hand and the minute hand of a clock increase from 1:27 to 1:28?" If you look at the solution, you will see that we didn't have to calculate either angle. This is a common situation. *Look for shortcuts.* Since a problem can often be solved in more than one way, you should always look for the easiest method. Consider the following examples.

➡ Example 45 _____

If $5(3x - 7) = 20$, what is $3x - 8$?

It's not difficult to solve for x:

$$5(3x - 7) = 20 \Rightarrow 15x - 35 = 20 \Rightarrow 15x = 55 \Rightarrow$$

$$x = \frac{55}{15} = \frac{11}{3}$$

But it's too much work. Besides, once you find that $x = \frac{11}{3}$, you still have to multiply to get $3x$: $3\left(\frac{11}{3}\right) = 11$, and then subtract to get $3x - 8$: $11 - 8 = \mathbf{3}$.

Solution. The key is to recognize that you don't need x. Finding $3x - 7$ is easy (just divide the original equation by 5), and $3x - 8$ is just 1 less:

$$5(3x - 7) = 20 \Rightarrow 3x - 7 = 4 \Rightarrow 3x - 8 = \mathbf{3}$$

➡ Example 46 _____

If $7x + 3y = 17$ and $3x + 7y = 19$, what is the average (arithmetic mean) of x and y?

The obvious way to do this is to first find x and y by solving the two equations simultaneously and then to take their average. If you are familiar with this method, try it now, before reading further. If you work carefully, you should find that $x = \frac{31}{20}$ and $y = \frac{41}{20}$, and their average is $\frac{\frac{31}{20} + \frac{41}{20}}{2} = \frac{9}{5}$ or **1.8**. This method is not too difficult; but it is quite time-consuming.

Look for a shortcut. Is there a way to find the average without first finding x and y? Absolutely! Here's the best way to do this.

 Solution. Add the two equations:

$$\begin{array}{r} 7x + 3y = 17 \\ + \; 3x + 7y = 19 \\ \hline 10x + 10y = 36 \end{array}$$

Divide each side by 10: $\qquad x + y = 3.6$

Calculate the average: $\qquad \dfrac{x+y}{2} = \dfrac{3.6}{2} = \mathbf{1.8}$

When you learn TACTIC 16, you will see that adding two equations, as was done here, is the standard way to attack problems such as this on the SAT.

TACTIC
11 Pay Attention to Units.

Often the answer to a question must be in units different from those used in the given data. As you read the question, <u>underline</u> exactly what you are being asked. Do the examiners want hours or minutes or seconds, dollars or cents, feet or inches, meters or centimeters? On multiple-choice questions an answer with the wrong units is almost always one of the choices.

➡ **Example 47** _____

At a speed of 48 miles per hour, how many minutes will be required to drive 32 miles?

(A) $\dfrac{2}{3}$

(B) $\dfrac{3}{2}$

(C) 40

(D) 2400

Solution. This is a relatively easy question. Just be attentive. Since $\dfrac{32}{48} = \dfrac{2}{3}$, it will take $\dfrac{2}{3}$ of an *hour* to drive 32 miles. Choice A is $\dfrac{2}{3}$; but that is *not* the correct answer because you are asked how many *minutes* will be required. (Did you underline the word "minutes" in the question?) The correct answer is $\dfrac{2}{3}$ (60) = **40 (C)**.

Note that you could have been asked how many *seconds* would be needed, in which case the answer would be 40(60) = 2400 (D).

➡ **Example 48** _____

The wholesale price of potatoes is usually 3 pounds for $1.79. How much money, in cents, did a restaurant save when it was able to purchase 600 pounds of potatoes at 2 pounds for $1.15?

Solution. For 600 pounds the restaurant would normally have to buy 200 3-pound bags for 200 × $1.79 = $358. On sale, it bought 300 2-pound bags for 300 × $1.15 = $345. Therefore, the restaurant saved 13 dollars. *Do not* grid in 13. If you underline the word "cents" you won't forget to convert the units: 13 dollars is **1300** cents.

You already know that you can use a calculator on the longer math section of the SAT. (See Chapter 5 for a complete discussion of calculator usage.) The main reason to use a calculator is that it enables you to do arithmetic more quickly and more accurately than you can by hand on *problems that you know how to solve*. (For instance, in Example 48, you should use your calculator to multiply 200×1.79.) The purpose of TACTIC 12 is to show you how to use your calculator to get the right answer to *questions that you do not know how to solve or you cannot solve*.

➡ **Example 49**_____

If $x^2 = 2$, what is the value of $\left(x+\dfrac{1}{x}\right)\left(x-\dfrac{1}{x}\right)$?

(A) 1
(B) 1.5
(C) $1 + \sqrt{2}$
(D) $2 + \sqrt{2}$

Solution. The College Board would consider this a hard question, and most students would either take a wild guess or, worse, spend time working on it, and still miss it. The best approach is to realize that $\left(x+\dfrac{1}{x}\right)\left(x-\dfrac{1}{x}\right)$ is a product of the form

$$(a + b)(a - b) = a^2 - b^2$$

Therefore:

$$\left(x+\frac{1}{x}\right)\left(x-\frac{1}{x}\right) = x^2 - \frac{1}{x^2} = 2 - \frac{1}{2} = \textbf{1.5 (B)}$$

If you didn't see this solution, you could still solve the problem by writing $x = \sqrt{2}$ and then trying to multiply and simplify $\left(\sqrt{2}+\dfrac{1}{\sqrt{2}}\right)\left(\sqrt{2}-\dfrac{1}{\sqrt{2}}\right)$. It is likely, however, that you would make a mistake somewhere along the way.

 The better method is to *use your calculator*. $\sqrt{2} \approx 1.414$ and $\dfrac{1}{\sqrt{2}} \approx 0.707$, so

$$\left(\sqrt{2}+\frac{1}{\sqrt{2}}\right)\left(\sqrt{2}-\frac{1}{\sqrt{2}}\right) \approx (1.414 + 0.707)(1.414 - 0.707) = (2.121)(0.707) = 1.499547$$

Clearly, choose **1.5**, the small difference being due to the rounding off of $\sqrt{2}$ as 1.414.

➡️ **Example 50**_____

If a and b are positive numbers, with $a^3 = 3$ and $a^5 = 12b^2$, what is the ratio of a to b?

🖩 **Solution.** This is another difficult question that most students would just guess the answer. If you think to divide the second equation by the first, however, the problem is not too bad:

$$\frac{a^5}{a^3} = \frac{12b^2}{3} = 4b^2 \quad \text{and} \quad \frac{a^5}{a^3} = a^2$$

Then

$$a^2 = 4b^2 \Rightarrow \frac{a^2}{b^2} = 4 \Rightarrow \frac{a}{b} = \mathbf{2}$$

🖩 If you don't see this, you can still solve the problem with your calculator:

$$a = \sqrt[3]{3} \approx 1.44225 \Rightarrow a^5 = (1.44225)^5 \approx 6.24026 \Rightarrow b^2 = \frac{6.24026}{12} \approx 0.52$$

$$\Rightarrow b \approx \sqrt{0.52} \approx 0.7211$$

So, $\dfrac{a}{b} \approx \dfrac{1.44225}{0.7211} = 2.00007.$

Grid in 2.

➡️ **Example 51**_____

What is the value of $\dfrac{1 + \dfrac{7}{5}}{1 - \dfrac{5}{7}}$?

Solution. There are two straightforward ways to do this: (i) multiply the numerator and denominator by 35, the LCM of 5 and 7, and (ii) simplify and divide:

(i) $\quad \dfrac{35\left(1 + \dfrac{7}{5}\right)}{35\left(1 - \dfrac{5}{7}\right)} = \dfrac{35 + 49}{35 - 25} = \dfrac{84}{10} = \mathbf{8.4}$

(ii) $\quad \dfrac{1 + \dfrac{7}{5}}{1 - \dfrac{5}{7}} = \dfrac{\dfrac{12}{5}}{\dfrac{2}{7}} = \dfrac{\overset{6}{\cancel{12}}}{5} \times \dfrac{7}{\underset{1}{\cancel{2}}} = \dfrac{42}{5} = \mathbf{8.4}$

🖩 However, if you don't like working with fractions, you can easily do the arithmetic on your calculator. Be sure you know how *your* calculator works. Be sure that when you evaluate the given complex fraction you get 8.4.

If this had been a multiple-choice question, the four choices would probably have been fractions, in which case the correct answer would be $\dfrac{42}{5}$. If you had solved this with your calculator, you would then have had to use the calculator to determine which of the fractions offered as choices was equal to 8.4.

TACTIC 13 — Know When *Not* to Use Your Calculator.

Don't get into the habit of using your calculator on every problem involving arithmetic. Since many problems can be solved more easily and faster without a calculator, learn to use your calculator only when you need it (see Chapter 5).

➡ Example 52

> John had $150. He used 85% of it to pay his electric bill and 5% of it on a gift for his mother. How much did he have left?

Solution. Many students would use their calculators on each step of this problem.

Electric bill:	$150 × .85 = $127.50
Gift for mother:	$150 × .05 = $7.50
Total spent:	$127.50 + $7.50 = $135
Amount left:	$150 − $135 = **$15**

Good test-takers would have proceeded as follows, finishing the problem in less time than it takes to calculate the first percent: John used 90% of his money, so he had 10% left; and 10% of $150 is **$15**.

TACTIC 14 — Systematically Make Lists.

When a question asks "how many," often the best strategy is to make a list of all the possibilities. It is important that you make the list in a *systematic* fashion so that you don't inadvertently leave something out. Often, shortly after starting the list, you can see a pattern developing and can figure out how many more entries there will be without writing them all down.

Even if the question does not specifically ask "how many," you may need to count some items to answer it; in this case, as well, the best plan may be to make a list.

Listing things systematically means writing them in numerical order (if the entries are numbers) or in alphabetical order (if the entries are letters). If the answer to "how many" is a small number (as in Example 53, below), just list all possibilities. If the answer is a large number (as in Example 54), start the list and write enough entries to enable you to see a pattern.

➡ Example 53

> The product of three positive integers is 300. If one of them is 5, what is the least possible value of the sum of the other two?

Solution. Since one of the integers is 5, the product of the other two is 60 (5 × 60 = 300). Systematically, list all possible pairs, (*a*, *b*), of positive integers whose product is 60, and check their sums. First, let *a* =1, then 2, and so on.

a	*b*	*a* + *b*
1	60	61
2	30	32
3	20	23
4	15	19
5	12	17
6	10	16

The answer is **16**.

➡ Example 54

A palindrome is a number, such as 93539, that reads the same forward and backward. How many palindromes are there between 100 and 1000?

Solution. First, write down
the numbers in the 100's   101, 111, 121, 131, 141,
that end in 1:   151, 161, 171, 181, 191
Now write the numbers   202, 212, 222, 232, 242,
beginning and ending in 2:   252, 262, 272, 282, 292

By now you should see the pattern: there are 10 numbers beginning with 1, and 10 beginning with 2, and there will be 10 beginning with 3, 4, ..., 9 for a total of 9 × 10 = **90** palindromes.

➡ Example 55

In how many ways can Al, Bob, Charlie, Dan, and Ed stand in a line if Bob must be first and either Charlie or Dan must be last?

Solution. Represent the five boys as A, B, C, D, and E. Placing Charlie last, you see that the order is B __ __ __ C. Systematically fill in the blanks with A, D, and E. Write all the three-letter "words" you can in alphabetical order so you don't accidentally skip one.

A D E
A E D
D A E
D E A
E A D
E D A

There are 6 possibilities when C is last. Clearly, there will be 6 more when D is last. Therefore, there are **12** ways in all to satisfy the conditions of the problem.

See Section P in Chapter 6 for additional examples and for another method of solving these problems using the counting principle.

Trust All Grids, Graphs, and Charts.

Figures that show the grid lines of a graph are *always* accurate, whether or not the coordinates of the points are given. For example, in the figure below, you can determine each of the following:

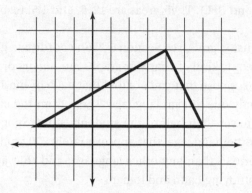

- the lengths of all three sides of the triangle;
- the perimeter of the triangle;
- the area of the triangle;
- the slope of each line segment.

➡ **Example 56** _____

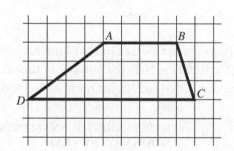

In the grid above, what is the area of quadrilateral *ABCD*?

(A) 19.5
(B) 21
(C) 25.5
(D) 27

Solution. $\overline{AB}$ and $\overline{CD}$ are parallel (they're both horizontal), so *ABCD* is a trapezoid. If you know that the formula for the area of a trapezoid is $A = \frac{1}{2}(b_1 + b_2)h$, use it. By counting boxes, you see that

$$b_1 = CD = 9, \ b_2 = AB = 4, \text{ and } h = 3$$

Therefore, the area is $\frac{1}{2}(9+4)(3) = $ **19.5 (A).**

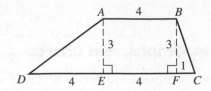

If you don't know the formula, use $\overline{AE}$ and $\overline{BF}$ to divide *ABCD* into a rectangle *(ABFE)* and two right triangles *(AED* and *BFC)*. Their areas are 12, 6, and 1.5, respectively, for a total area of **19.5**.

For sample problems using grids, see Section 6-N on coordinate geometry.

SAT problems that use any kind of charts or graphs are *always* drawn accurately and can be trusted. For example, suppose that you are told that each of the 1000 students at Central High School studies exactly one foreign language. Then, from the circle graph that follows, you may conclude that fewer than half of the students study Spanish, but more students study Spanish than any other language; that approximately 250 students study French; that fewer students study German than any other language; and that approximately the same number of students are studying Latin and Italian.

FOREIGN LANGUAGES STUDIED BY
1000 STUDENTS AT CENTRAL HIGH SCHOOL

From the bar graph that follows, you know that in 2001 John won exactly three tournaments, and you can calculate that from 2000 to 2001 the number of tournaments he won decreased by 50% (from 6 to 3), whereas from 2001 to 2002 the number increased by 300% (from 3 to 12).

NUMBER OF TENNIS TOURNAMENTS
JOHN WON BY YEAR

➡ **Example 57**

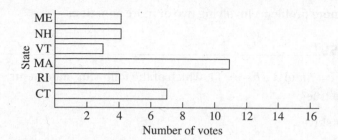

The chart above depicts the number of electoral votes assigned to each of the six New England states. What is the average (arithmetic mean) number of electoral votes, to the <u>nearest tenth</u>, assigned to these states?

(A) 5.0

(B) 5.5

(C) 6.0

(D) 6.5

 Solution. Since you can trust the chart to be accurate, the total number of electoral votes for the six states is

$$4 + 4 + 3 + 11 + 4 + 7 = 33$$

and the average is $33 \div 6 = $ **5.5 (B)**.

Several different types of questions concerning bar graphs, circle graphs, line graphs, and various charts and tables can be found in Section 6-O.

TACTIC
16 Add Equations.

When a question involves two equations that do not have exponents, either add the equations or subtract them. If there are three or more equations, add them.

HELPFUL HINT

Very often, answering a question that involves two or more equations does _not_ require you to solve the equations. Remember TACTIC 10: Do not do any more than is necessary.

➡ **Example 58**

If $3x + 5y = 14$ and $x - y = 6$, what is the average of x and y?

(A) 2.5

(B) 3

(C) 3.5

(D) 5

Solution. Add the equations:

$$3x + 5y = 14$$
$$+ \quad x - y = 6$$
$$\overline{4x + 4y = 20}$$

Divide each side by 4: $\quad x + y = 5$

The average of x and y is their sum divided by 2: $\quad \dfrac{x+y}{2} = \dfrac{5}{2} = $ **2.5**

The answer is **(A)**.

Note that you *could have* actually solved for x and y [$x = 5.5$, $y = -0.5$], and then taken their average. However, that would have been time-consuming and unnecessary.

Here are two more problems involving two or more equations.

➡ **Example 59**_____

If $a - b + c = 7$ and $a + b - c = 11$, which of the following statements MUST be true?

  I. a is positive
  II. $b > c$
  III. $bc < 0$

(A) I only
(B) II only
(C) III only
(D) I and II only

➡ **Example 60**_____

If $a - b = 1$, $b - c = 2$, and $c - a = d$, what is the value of d?
(A) -3
(B) -1
(C) 1
(D) 3

Solution 59. Start by adding the two equations:

$$\begin{array}{r} a - b + c = 7 \\ + \; a + b - c = 11 \\ \hline 2a = 18 \end{array}$$

Therefore, $a = 9$. (I is true.)

Replace a by 9 in each equation to obtain two new equations:

$9 - b + c = 7 \Rightarrow -b + c = -2 \Rightarrow b = c + 2$
and
$9 + b - c = 11 \Rightarrow b - c = 2 \Rightarrow b = c + 2$

Since $b = c + 2$, then $b > c$. (II is true.)

As long as $b = c + 2$, however, there are no restrictions on b *and* c: if $b = 2$ and $c = 0$, $bc = 0$; if $b = 4$ and $c = 2$, then $bc > 0$. (III is false.)

   The answer is **(D)**.

Solution 60. Add the three equations:

$$\begin{array}{r} a - b = 1 \\ b - c = 2 \\ + \; c - a = d \\ \hline 0 = 3 + d \Rightarrow d = \mathbf{-3} \end{array}$$

The answer is **(A)**.

Multiple-Choice Questions

1. In 1995, Diana read 10 English books and 7 French books. In 1996, she read twice as many French books as English books. If 60% of the books that she read during the 2 years were French, how many English and French books did she read in 1996?

   (A) 16
   (B) 26
   (C) 32
   (D) 48

2. In the figure below, if the radius of circle O is 10, what is the length of diagonal $\overline{AC}$ of rectangle $OABC$?

   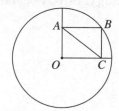

   (A) $\sqrt{2}$
   (B) $\sqrt{10}$
   (C) $5\sqrt{2}$
   (D) 10

3. In the figure below, vertex Q of square $OPQR$ is on a circle with center O. If the area of the square is 8, what is the area of the circle?

   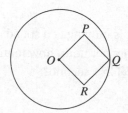

   (A) 8π
   (B) $8\pi\sqrt{2}$
   (C) 16π
   (D) 32π

4. In the figure below, $ABCD$ is a square and AED is an equilateral triangle. If $AB = 2$, what is the area of the shaded region?

   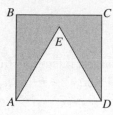

   (A) $\sqrt{3}$
   (B) 2
   (C) $4 - 2\sqrt{3}$
   (D) $4 - \sqrt{3}$

5. If $5x + 13 = 31$, what is the value of $\sqrt{5x+31}$?

   (A) $\sqrt{13}$
   (B) $\sqrt{\dfrac{173}{5}}$
   (C) 7
   (D) 13

6. At Nat's Nuts a $2\frac{1}{4}$-pound bag of pistachio nuts costs $6.00. At this rate, what is the cost, in cents, of a bag weighing 9 ounces? (<u>Note</u>: 1 pound = 16 ounces)

   (A)　24
   (B)　150
   (C) 1350
   (D) 2400

7. If $12a + 3b = 1$ and $7b - 2a = 9$, what is the average (arithmetic mean) of a and b?

   (A) 0.1
   (B) 0.5
   (C) 1
   (D) 2.5

8. Jessica has 4 times as many books as John and 5 times as many as Karen. If Karen has more than 40 books, what is the least number of books that Jessica can have?

(A) 220
(B) 210
(C) 205
(D) 200

9. What is the largest integer, n, that satisfies the inequality $n^2 + 8n - 3 < n^2 + 7n + 8$?

(A) 5
(B) 7
(C) 10
(D) 11

10. If $a < b$ and c is the sum of a and b, which of the following is the positive difference between a and b?

(A) $2a - c$
(B) $2b - c$
(C) $c - 2b$
(D) $c - a + b$

11. If w widgets cost c cents, how many widgets can you get for d dollars?

(A) $\dfrac{100dw}{c}$

(B) $\dfrac{dw}{100c}$

(C) $\dfrac{dw}{c}$

(D) cdw

12. If 120% of a is equal to 80% of b, which of the following is equal to $a + b$?

(A) $1.5a$
(B) $2a$
(C) $2.5a$
(D) $3a$

13. Which of the following numbers can be expressed as the product of three different integers greater than 1?

    I. 25
    II. 36
    III. 45

(A) I only
(B) II only
(C) III only
(D) II and III only

14. What is the average of $4y + 3$ and $2y - 1$?

(A) $3y + 1$
(B) $3y + 2$
(C) $3y + 3$
(D) $3y + 4$

15. If x and y are integers such that $x^3 = y^2$, which of the following CANNOT be the value of y?

(A) 1
(B) 8
(C) 16
(D) 27

16. What is a divided by $a\%$ of a?

(A) $\dfrac{a}{100}$

(B) $\dfrac{100}{a}$

(C) $\dfrac{a^2}{100}$

(D) $\dfrac{100}{a^2}$

17. If an object is moving at a speed of 36 kilometers per hour, how many meters does it travel in 1 second?

(A) 10
(B) 36
(C) 100
(D) 360

18. For what value of x is $8^{2x-4} = 16^x$?

(A) 2
(B) 4
(C) 6
(D) 8

19. On a certain Russian-American committee, $\frac{2}{3}$ of the members are men, and $\frac{3}{8}$ of the men are Americans. If $\frac{3}{5}$ of the committee members are Russians, what fraction of the members are American women?

(A) $\frac{3}{20}$

(B) $\frac{11}{60}$

(C) $\frac{1}{4}$

(D) $\frac{2}{5}$

20. If $x\%$ of y is 10, what is y?

(A) $\frac{10}{x}$

(B) $\frac{100}{x}$

(C) $\frac{1000}{x}$

(D) $\frac{x}{10}$

Grid-in Questions

21. In writing all of the integers from 1 to 300, how many times is the digit 1 used?

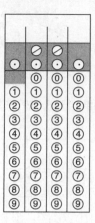

22. If $a + 2b = 14$ and $5a + 4b = 16$, what is the average (arithmetic mean) of a and b?

23. In the figure below, the area of circle O is 12. What is the area of the shaded sector?

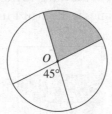

Note: Figure not drawn to scale

24. At a certain university, $\frac{1}{4}$ of the applicants failed to meet minimum standards and were rejected immediately. Of those who met the standards, $\frac{2}{5}$ were accepted.

If 1200 applicants were accepted, how many applied?

25. How many integers between 1 and 1000 are the product of two consecutive integers?

Answer Key

1. **D**	6. **B**	11. **A**	16. **B**
2. **D**	7. **B**	12. **C**	17. **A**
3. **C**	8. **A**	13. **B**	18. **C**
4. **D**	9. **C**	14. **A**	19. **A**
5. **C**	10. **B**	15. **C**	20. **C**

21. `1 6 0`

22. `5 / 2` or `2 . 5`

23. `1 2 / 8` or `3 / 2` or `1 . 5`

24. `4 0 0 0`

25. `3 1`

Answer Explanations

Note: For many problems, an alternative solution, indicated by two asterisks (**), follows the first solution. In this case, one of the solutions is the direct mathematical one and the other is based on one of the tactics discussed in this chapter.

1. **(D)** Use TACTIC 1: draw a diagram representing a pile of books or a bookshelf.

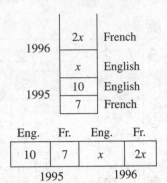

In the 2 years the number of French books Diana read was $7 + 2x$, and the total number of books was $17 + 3x$. Then 60% or $\dfrac{3}{5} = \dfrac{7+2x}{17+3x}$. To solve, cross-multiply:

$$35 + 10x = 51 + 9x \Rightarrow x = 16$$

In 1996, Diana read 16 English books and 32 French books, a total of **48** books.

2. **(D)** If you can't solve this problem, use TACTIC 2: trust the diagram. $\overline{AC}$ is clearly longer than $\overline{OC}$, and very close to radius $\overline{OE}$ (measure them).

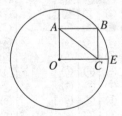

Therefore, AC must be about 10. Either by inspection or with your calculator, check the choices. They are approximately as follows:

(A) $\sqrt{2} = 1.4$

(B) $\sqrt{10} = 3.1$

(C) $5\sqrt{2} = 7$

(D) 10

The answer must be **10**.

The answer *is* **10. The two diagonals are equal, and diagonal $\overline{OB}$ is a radius.

3. **(C)** As in question 2, if you get stuck trying to answer this, use TACTIC 2: look at the diagram.

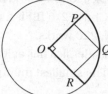

Square *OPQR*, whose area is 8, takes up most of the quarter circle, so the area of the quarter circle is certainly between 11 and 14. The area of the whole circle is 4 times as great: between 44 and 56. Check the choices. They are approximately as follows:

(A) $8\pi = 25$
(B) $8\pi\sqrt{2} = 36$
(C) $16\pi = 50$
(D) $32\pi = 100$

The answer is clearly **16π**.

 Use TACTIC 4: draw in line segment $\overline{OQ}$. Since the area of the square is 8, each side is $\sqrt{8}$, and diagonal $\overline{OQ}$ is $\sqrt{8} \cdot \sqrt{2} = \sqrt{16} = 4$. But $\overline{OQ}$ is also a radius, so the area of the circle is $\pi(4)^2 = $ **16π.

4. **(D)** Use TACTIC 9: subtract to find the shaded area. The area of square *ABCD* is 4. The area of $\triangle AED$ is $\dfrac{2^2\sqrt{3}}{4} = \dfrac{4\sqrt{3}}{4} = \sqrt{3}$ (see Section 6-J). Then the area of the shaded region is **$4 - \sqrt{3}$**.

 Use TACTIC 2: trust the diagram. The area of the square is 4 and the white area clearly takes up less than half of the square. So the white area is less than 2, and the shaded area is more than 2, but definitely less than 3. Only choice (D) ($4 - \sqrt{3}$**) works.

5. **(C)** Use TACTIC 10: don't do more than you have to. In particular, don't solve for *x*. Here $5x + 13 = 31 \Rightarrow 5x = 18$. So, $\sqrt{5x+31} = \sqrt{18+31} = \sqrt{49} = $ **7**.

6. **(B)** This is a relatively simple ratio, but use TACTIC 11 and make sure you get the units right. You need to know that there are 100 cents in a dollar and 16 ounces in a pound.

$$\frac{\text{price}}{\text{weight}} : \frac{6 \text{ dollars}}{2.25 \text{ pounds}} = \frac{600 \text{ cents}}{36 \text{ ounces}} = \frac{x \text{ cents}}{9 \text{ ounces}}$$

Now cross-multiply and solve: $36x = 5400 \Rightarrow x = $ **150**.

7. **(B)** Use TACTIC 16, and add the two equations to get

$$10a + 10b = 10 \Rightarrow a + b = 1 \Rightarrow$$

$$\frac{a+b}{2} = \frac{1}{2} = \textbf{0.5}$$

Remember TACTIC 10: don't do more than you have to. In particular, do *not* solve for *a* and *b*.

8. **(A)** Use TACTIC 5: backsolve. Since you want the least number, start with the smallest answer, (D). If Jessica had 200 books, Karen would have 40; but Karen has more than 40, so 200 is too small. Neither 205 (C) nor 210 (B) is a multiple of 4, so John wouldn't have a whole number of books. Finally, **220** works.

   Since Karen has at least 41 books, Jessica has at least 205. But Jessica's total must be a multiple of 4 and 5, hence of 20. The smallest multiple of 20 greater than 205 is **220.

9. **(C)** Use TACTIC 5: backsolve (using your calculator). Test the choices, starting with (D) (since you want the largest value):

$$11^2 + 8(11) - 3 = 121 + 88 - 3 = 206$$

and

$$11^2 + 7(11) + 8 = 121 + 77 + 8 = 206$$

The two sides are equal. When $n = $ **10**, however, the left-hand side is smaller:

$$100 + 80 - 3 = 177 \quad \text{and} \quad 100 + 70 + 8 = 178$$

**$n^2 + 8n - 3 < n^2 + 7n + 8 \Rightarrow n < 11$.

10. **(B)** Use TACTIC 6. Pick simple values for a, b, and c. Let $a = 1$, $b = 2$, and $c = 3$. Then $b - a = 1$. Only choice (B), **$2b - c$**, is equal to 1 when $b = 2$ and $c = 3$.

   **$c = a + b \Rightarrow a = c - b$.

   So, $b - a = b - (c - b) = $ **$2b - c$**.

11. **(A)** Use TACTIC 6: replace variables with numbers. If 2 widgets cost 10 cents, then widgets cost 5 cents each; and for 3 dollars, you can get 60 widgets. Which of the choices equals 60 when $w = 2$, $c = 10$, and $d = 3$?

   Only $\dfrac{100dw}{c}$.

   **Convert d dollars to $100d$ cents, and set the ratios equal: $\dfrac{\text{widgets}}{\text{cents}} = \dfrac{w}{c} = \dfrac{x}{100d}$.

   Multiply both sides by $100d$: $x = \dfrac{100dw}{c}$.

12. **(C)** Use TACTIC 7: choose appropriate numbers. Since 120% of 80 = 80% of 120, let $a = 80$ and $b = 120$. Then $a + b = 200$. Which of the choices equals 200 when $a = 80$? Only **$2.5a$**.

13. **(B)** Treat the number in each of the three Roman numeral choices as a separate true/false question.

   - Could 25 be expressed as the product of three different integers greater than 1? No, 25 has only two positive factors greater than 1 (5 and 25), and so clearly cannot be the product of three different positive factors. (I is false.)
   - Could 36 be expressed as the product of three different positive factors? Yes, $36 = 2 \times 3 \times 6$. (**II is true.**)
   - Could 45 be expressed as the product of three different integers greater than 1? No, the factors of 45 that are greater than 1 are 3, 5, 9, 15, and 45; no three of them have a product equal to 45. (III is false.)

   Only II is true.

14. **(A)** To find the average, add the two quantities and divide by 2:

$$\frac{(4y+3)+(2y-1)}{2}=\frac{6y+2}{2}=3y+1$$

**Use TACTIC 6. Let $y = 1$. Then $4y + 3 = 7$ and $2y - 1 = 1$. The average of 7 and 1 is $\frac{7+1}{2} = 4$. Of the five choices, only $3y + 1$ is equal to 4 when $y = 1$.

15. **(C)** Use TACTIC 5: test the choices. When there is no advantage to starting with any particular choice, start with (D). Could $y = 27$? Is there an integer x such that $x^3 = 27^2 = 729$? Use your calculator to evaluate $\sqrt[3]{729}$ or test some numbers: $10^3 = 1000$—too large; $9^3 = 729$ works.

 Try choice (C): 16. Is there an integer x such that $x^3 = 16^2 = 256$? No: $5^3 = 125$, $6^3 = 216$, so 5 and 6 are too small; but $7^3 = 343$, which is too large. Alternatively, use your calculator to see that $\sqrt[3]{256}$ is not an integer.
The answer is **16**.

16. **(B)** $a \div (a\% \text{ of } a) = a \div \left(\frac{a}{100} \times a\right) = a \div \left(\frac{a^2}{100}\right) = a \times \frac{100}{a^2} = \frac{100}{a}$

**Use TACTICS 6 and 7: replace a by a number; use 100 since the problem involves percents.

$$100 \div (100\% \text{ of } 100) = 100 \div 100 = 1$$

Test each choice; which one equals 1 when $a = 100$?

A and B: $\frac{100}{100} = 1$.

Eliminate (C) and (D); and test (A) and (B) with another value, 50, for a:

$$50 \div (50\% \text{ of } 50) = 50 \div (25) = 2$$

Now, only $\dfrac{\mathbf{100}}{\boldsymbol{a}}$ works: $\frac{100}{50} = 2$.

17. **(A)** Set up a ratio:

$$\frac{\text{distance}}{\text{time}} = \frac{36 \text{ kilometers}}{1 \text{ hour}} = \frac{36,000 \text{ meters}}{60 \text{ minutes}} = \frac{36,000 \text{ meters}}{3600 \text{ seconds}} = \mathbf{10} \text{ meters/second}$$

**Use TACTIC 5: Test choices, starting with 100, choice (C):

100 meters/second = 6000 meters/minute =
360,000 meters/hour = 360 kilometers/hour

Not only is that result too big, but it is too big by a factor of 10. The answer is **10**, choice (A).

18. **(C)** Use TACTIC 5: backsolve, using your calculator. Let $x = 4$: then $8^{2(4)-4} = 8^4 = 4096$, whereas $16^4 = 65{,}536$. Eliminate (A) and (B), and try a larger value.

Let $x = 6$: then

$$8^{2(6)-4} = 8^8 = 16{,}777{,}216$$

and

$$16^6 = 16{,}777{,}216$$

**$8^{2x-4} = 16^x \Rightarrow (2^3)^{2x-4} = (2^4)^x$.

Then $3(2x-4) = 4x \Rightarrow 6x - 12 = 4x$ and so $2x = 12 \Rightarrow x = \mathbf{6}$.

19. **(A)** Use TACTIC 7: choose appropriate numbers. The LCM of all the denominators is 120, so assume that the committee has 120 members.

Then there are $\frac{2}{3} \times 120 = 80$ men and 40 women. Of the 80 men, $30 \left(\frac{3}{8} \times 80 \right)$ are Americans. Since there are $72 \left(\frac{3}{5} \times 120 \right)$ Russians, there are $120 - 72 = 48$ Americans of whom 30 are men, so the other 18 are women.

Finally, the fraction of American women is $\frac{18}{120} = \frac{3}{20}$, as illustrated in the Venn diagram below.

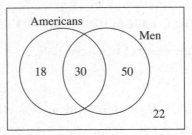

20. **(C)** Use TACTICS 6 and 7. Since 100% of 10 is 10, let $x = 100$ and $y = 10$. When $x = 100$, choices (C) and (D) are each 10. Eliminate (A) and (B), and try some other numbers: 50% of 20 is 10.

Of (C) and (D), only $\dfrac{1000}{x} = 20$ when $x = 50$.

21. **160** Use TACTIC 14. Systematically list the numbers that contain the digit 1, writing as many as you need to see the pattern. Between 1 and 99 the digit 1 is used 10 times as the units digit (1, 11, 21, ..., 91) and 10 times as the tens digit (10, 11, 12, ..., 19) for a total of 20 times. From 200 to 299, there are 20 more times (the same 20 but preceded by 2). Finally, from 100 to 199 there are 20 more plus 100 numbers where the digit 1 is used in the hundreds place. The total is $20 + 20 + 20 + 100 = \mathbf{160}$.

22. $\frac{5}{2}$ **or 2.5** Use TACTIC 10: don't do more than is necessary. You don't need to solve this system of equations; you don't need to know the values of a and b, only their average. Use TACTIC 17. Add the two equations:

$$6a + 6b = 30 \Rightarrow a + b = 5$$

Then, $\frac{a+b}{2} = \frac{5}{2}$ or **2.5**.

23. $\frac{12}{8}$ **or** $\frac{3}{2}$ **or 1.5** The shaded sector is $\frac{45}{360} = \frac{1}{8}$ of the circle, so its area is $\frac{1}{8}$ of 12: $\frac{12}{8}$ or $\frac{3}{2}$ or **1.5**. (Note that, since $\frac{12}{8}$ fits in the grid, it is not necessary to reduce it or to convert it to a decimal. See Chapter 5.)

**If you didn't see that, use TACTIC 3 and redraw the figure to scale by making the angle as close as possible to 45°. It is now clear that the sector is $\frac{1}{8}$ of the circle (or very close to it).

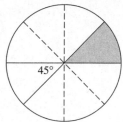

24. **4000** Use TACTIC 7: choose an appropriate number. The LCD of $\frac{1}{4}$ and $\frac{2}{5}$ is 20, so *assume* that there were 20 applicants. Then $\frac{1}{4}(20) = 5$ failed to meet the minimum standards. Of the remaining 15 applicants, $\frac{2}{5}$, or 6, were accepted, so 6 of every 20 applicants were accepted. Set up a proportion:

$$\frac{6}{20} = \frac{1200}{x} \Rightarrow 6x = 24{,}000 \Rightarrow x = \mathbf{4000}$$

25. **31** Use TACTIC 14. List the integers systematically: $1 \times 2, 2 \times 3, \ldots, 24 \times 25, \ldots$. You don't have to multiply and list the products $(2, 6, 12, \ldots, 600, \ldots)$; you just have to know when to stop. The largest product less than 1000 is $31 \times 32 = 992$, so there are **31** integers.

Reviewing Mathematics

6

This chapter reviews the topics that you need to know to excel on the mathematics part of the SAT. The College Board lists the following four content areas: Heart of Algebra, Problem Solving and Data Analysis, Passport to Advanced Math, and Additional Topics in Math. These headings aren't too useful for students preparing for the SAT. So in this chapter, we have divided the math content into 20 concise sections:

- **5 SECTIONS ON ARITHMETIC:** basic facts; fractions and decimals; percents; ratios and proportions; averages.
- **3 SECTIONS ON ALGEBRA:** polynomials; solving equations and inequalities; word problems.
- **6 SECTIONS ON GEOMETRY:** Lines and angles; triangles; quadrilaterals; circles; solid geometry; coordinate geometry.
- **6 SECTIONS ON MISCELLANEOUS TOPICS:** probability, sequences; interpretation of charts and graphs; functions; basic trigonometry; basics of complex numbers.

In each of these sections you will review the basic definitions, key facts, and tactics that you will need to answer SAT-type questions on that topic correctly.

No topic, however, really belongs to only one category. Percent problems are discussed in the arithmetic sections, but on the SAT you need to be able also to use percents in many of the data interpretation qeustions. Most algebra problems involve arithmetic, as well; many geometry problems need algebra to solve them; and several of the problems in the miscellaneous topics sections require a knowledge of arithmetic and/or algebra.

At the end of each section is a set of exercises that consists of a variety of multiple-choice and grid-in questions, similar to actual SAT questions, that utilize the concepts covered in the section. You should use whichever TACTICS and KEY FACTS from that section that you think are appropriate. If you've mastered the material in the section, you should be able to answer most of the questions. If you get stuck, you can use the various strategies you learned in Chapter 5; but then you should carefully read the solutions that are provided, so that you understand the correct mathematical way to answer the question. In the solutions some references are made to the TACTICS from Chapter 5, but the major emphasis here is on doing the mathematics properly.

Finally, one small disclaimer is appropriate. This is not a mathematics textbook—it is a *review* of the essential facts that you need to know to do well on the SAT. Undoubtedly, you have already learned most, if not all, of them. If, however, you find some topics with which you are unfamiliar or on which you need more information, get a copy of Barron's *E-Z Arithmetic*, *E-Z Algebra*, and/or *E-Z Geometry*. For additional practice on SAT-type questions, see Barron's *Math Workbook for the SAT*.

ARITHMETIC

To do well on the SAT, you need to be comfortable with most topics of basic arithmetic. The first five sections of this chapter provide you with a review of the arithmetic concepts you need to know. Note that you should do almost no arithmetic by hand. In particular, you should never do long division, lengthy multiplications, or other tedious calculations. No question in the noncalculator section will require such calculations. For any question in the calculator section that does require such calculations, you should, of course, use your calculator.

The solutions to many of the mathematics questions on the SAT depend on your knowing the KEY FACTS in these sections. Be sure to review them all.

6-A BASIC ARITHMETIC CONCEPTS

A **set** is a collection of "things" that have been grouped together in some way. Those "things" are called the **elements** or **members** of the set, and we say that the "thing" is in the set. For example:

- If A is the set of former presidents of the United States, then John Adams *is an element of A*.
- If B is the set of vowels in the English alphabet, then *i is a member of B*.
- If C is the set of prime numbers, then 17 *is in C*.

The symbol for "is an element (or member) of" is $\in$, so we can write "$17 \in C$."

The **union** of two sets, X and Y, is the set consisting of all the elements that are in X or in Y or in both. Note that this definition includes the elements that are in X *and* Y. The union is represented as $X \cup Y$. Therefore, $a \in X \cup Y$ if and only if $a \in X$ or $a \in Y$.

The **intersection** of two sets, X and Y, is the set consisting only of the elements that are in both X and Y. The intersection is represented as $X \cap Y$. Therefore, $b \in X \cap Y$ if and only if $b \in X$ and $b \in Y$.

In describing a set of numbers, we usually list the elements inside a pair of braces. For example, let X be the set of prime numbers less than 10, and let Y be the set of odd positive integers less than 10.

$$X = \{2, 3, 5, 7\} \qquad Y = \{1, 3, 5, 7, 9\}$$
$$X \cup Y = \{1, 2, 3, 5, 7, 9\}$$
$$X \cap Y = \{3, 5, 7\}$$

The **solution set** of an equation is the set of all numbers that satisfy the equation.

➥ Example 1 _____

If A is the solution set of the equation $x^2 - 4 = 0$ and B is the solution set of the equation $x^2 - 3x + 2 = 0$, how many elements are in the union of the two sets?

Solution. Solving each equation (see Section 6-G if you need to review how to solve a quadratic equation), you get $A = \{-2, 2\}$ and $B = \{1, 2\}$. Therefore, $A \cup B = \{-2, 1, 2\}$. There are **3** elements in the union.

Let's start our review of arithmetic by discussing the most important sets of numbers and their properties. On the SAT the word *number* always means "real number," a number that can be represented by a point on the number line.

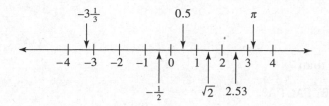

Signed Numbers

The numbers to the right of 0 on the number line are called **positive**, and those to the left of 0 are **negative**. Negative numbers must be written with a *negative sign* (–2); positive numbers can be written with a *plus sign* (+2) but are usually written without it (2). All numbers can be called **signed numbers**.

> ### Key Fact A1

For any number *a*, exactly one of the following is true:

- *a* is negative.
- *a* = 0.
- *a* is positive.

The **absolute value** of a number *a*, denoted as |*a*|, is the distance between *a* and 0 on the number line. Since 3 is 3 units to the right of 0 on the number line and –3 is 3 units to the left of 0, both have absolute values of 3:

- $|3| = 3$
- $|-3| = 3$

➡ Example 2 _____

What is the value of $||3| - |-5||$?

(A) –8
(B) –2
(C) 2
(D) 8

Solution. $||3| - |-5|| = |3 - 5| = |-2| = 2$ **(C).**

> ### Key Fact A2

For any number *a* and positive number *b*:

- $|a| = b \Rightarrow a = b$ or $a = -b$
- $|a| < b \Rightarrow -b < a < b$
- $|a| > b \Rightarrow a < -b$ or $a > b$

➥ Example 3 _____

How many integers satisfy the inequality $|x| < \pi$?

(A) 3
(B) 4
(C) 7
(D) More than 7

Solution. By KEY FACT A2,

$$|x| < \pi \Rightarrow -\pi < x < \pi \Rightarrow -3.14 < x < 3.14$$

There are **7** integers that satisfy this inequality: –3, –2, –1, 0, 1, 2, 3. Choice **(C)** is correct.

Arithmetic is basically concerned with the addition, subtraction, multiplication, and division of numbers. Column 3 of the table below shows the terms used to describe the results of these operations.

Operation	Symbol	Result	Example	
Addition	+	*Sum*	16 is the sum of 12 and 4.	$16 = 12 + 4$
Subtraction	–	*Difference*	8 is the difference of 12 and 4.	$8 = 12 - 4$
Multiplication*	×	*Product*	48 is the product of 12 and 4.	$48 = 12 \times 4$
Division	÷	*Quotient*	3 is the quotient of 12 and 4.	$3 = 12 \div 4$

*Multiplication can be indicated also by a dot, parentheses, or the juxtaposition of symbols without any sign: $2^2 \cdot 2^4$, 3(4), 3(x + 2), 3a, 4abc.

Given any two numbers *a* and *b*, you can *always* find their sum, difference, product, and quotient (with a calculator, if necessary), except that we can *never divide by zero*:

- $0 \div 7 = 0$
- $7 \div 0$ is meaningless.

➥ Example 4 _____

What is the sum of the product and the quotient of 7 and 7?

Solution. Product: $7 \times 7 = 49$. Quotient: $7 \div 7 = 1$. Sum: $49 + 1 = $ **50**.

Key Fact A3

For any number *a*: $a \times 0 = 0$. Conversely, if the product of two or more numbers is 0, *at least one* of them must be 0.

- If $ab = 0$, then $a = 0$ or $b = 0$.
- If $xyz = 0$, then $x = 0$ or $y = 0$ or $z = 0$.

➥ Example 5 _____

What is the product of all the integers from –3 to 6?

Solution. Before reaching for your calculator, think. You are asked for the product of 10 numbers, one of which is 0. Then, by KEY FACT A3, the product is **0**.

The product and the quotient of two positive numbers or two negative numbers are positive; the product and the quotient of a positive number and a negative number are negative.

×	+	−
+	+	−
−	−	+

÷	+	−
+	+	−
−	−	+

$6 \times 3 = 18$	$6 \times (-3) = -18$	$(-6) \times 3 = -18$	$(-6) \times (-3) = 18$
$6 \div 3 = 2$	$6 \div (-3) = -2$	$(-6) \div 3 = -2$	$(-6) \div (-3) = 2$

To determine whether a product of more than two numbers is positive or negative, count the number of negative factors.

Key Fact A5

- The product of an *even* number of negative factors is positive.
- The product of an *odd* number of negative factors is negative.

➡ Example 6

If the product of 10 numbers is positive, what is the greatest number of them that could be negative?

(A)   0
(B)   5
(C)   9
(D) 10

Solution. Since by KEY FACT A5, the product of 10 negative numbers is positive, all **10** of the numbers could be negative **(D)**.

Key Fact A6

The *reciprocal* of any nonzero number a is $\frac{1}{a}$.

The product of any number and its reciprocal is 1: $a\left(\frac{1}{a}\right) = 1$.

Key Fact A7

- The sum of two positive numbers is positive.
- The sum of two negative numbers is negative.
- To find the sum of a positive and a negative number, find the difference of their absolute values and use the sign of the number with the larger absolute value.

$$6 + 2 = 8 \qquad (-6) + (-2) = -8$$

To calculate either 6 + (–2) or (–6) + 2, take the difference, 6 – 2 = 4, and use the sign of the number whose absolute value is 6:

$$6 + (-2) = 4 \qquad (-6) + 2 = -4$$

Key Fact A8

The sum of any number and its opposite is 0: $a + (-a) = 0$.

Many properties of arithmetic depend on the relationships between subtraction and addition and between division and multiplication. Subtracting a number is the same as adding its opposite, and dividing by a number is the same as multiplying by its reciprocal.

$$a - b = a + (-b) \qquad a \div b = a\left(\frac{1}{b}\right)$$

Many problems involving subtraction and division can be simplified by changing them to addition and multiplication problems, respectively.

Key Fact A9

To subtract signed numbers, change the problem to an addition problem by changing the sign of what is being subtracted, and then use KEY FACT A7.

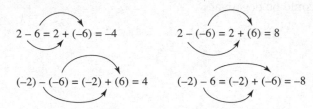

$$2 - 6 = 2 + (-6) = -4 \qquad 2 - (-6) = 2 + (6) = 8$$
$$(-2) - (-6) = (-2) + (6) = 4 \qquad (-2) - 6 = (-2) + (-6) = -8$$

In each case, the minus sign was changed to a plus sign, and either the 6 was changed to –6 or the –6 was changed to 6.

 CALCULATOR HINT

All arithmetic involving signed numbers can be accomplished on *any* calculator, but not all calculators handle negative numbers in the same way. Be sure you know how to enter negative numbers and how to use them on *your* calculator.

Integers

The *integers* are {... , –4, –3, –2, –1, 0, 1, 2, 3, 4, ...}.
The *positive integers* are {1, 2, 3, 4, 5, ...}.
The *negative integers* are {..., –5, –4, –3, –2, –1}.
Note: The integer 0 is neither positive nor negative. Therefore, if an SAT question asks how many positive numbers have a certain property, and the only numbers with that property are –2, –1, 0, 1, and 2, the answer is 2.

Consecutive integers are two or more integers, written in sequence, each of which is 1 more than the preceding integer. For example:

$$22, 23 \quad 6, 7, 8, 9 \quad -2, -1, 0, 1 \quad n, n+1, n+2, n+3$$

➥ Example 7

If the sum of three consecutive integers is less than 75, what is the greatest possible value of the smallest of the three integers?

Solution. Let the numbers be n, $n+1$, and $n+2$. Then

$$n + (n+1) + (n+2) = 3n + 3 \Rightarrow 3n + 3 < 75 \Rightarrow 3n < 72 \Rightarrow n < 24$$

The most n can be is **23**. (See Section 6-G for help in solving inequalities like this one.)

Of course, you don't *need* to do the algebra (see Chapter 5, TACTIC 7). Try three consecutive integers near 25, say 24, 25, 26. Their sum is 75, which is *slightly* too big (the sum needs to be *less* than 75), so the numbers must be **23**, 24, 25.

> **CAUTION:** Never assume that *number* means *integer*. 3 is the only integer between 2 and 4, but there are infinitely many numbers between 2 and 4, including 2.5, 3.99, $\frac{10}{3}$, π, and $\sqrt{10}$.

➥ Example 8

If $2 < x < 4$ and $3 < y < 7$, what is the largest integer value of $x + y$?

Solution. If x and y are integers, the largest value is $3 + 6 = 9$. However, although $x + y$ is to be an integer, neither x nor y must be. If $x = 3.8$ and $y = 6.2$, then $x + y = \mathbf{10}$.

The sum, the difference, and the product of two integers are *always* integers; the quotient of two integers may be, but is not necessarily, an integer. The quotient $23 \div 10$ can be expressed as $\frac{23}{10}$ or $2\frac{3}{10}$ or 2.3. If the quotient is to be an integer, we can also say that the quotient is 2 and there is a **remainder** of 3.

 CALCULATOR SHORTCUT

The standard way to find quotients and remainders is to use long division; but on the SAT, you *never* do long division: you use your calculator. To find the remainder when 100 is divided by 7, divide on your calculator: $100 \div 7 = 14.285714\ldots$ This tells you that the quotient is 14. (Ignore everything to the right of the decimal point.) To find the remainder, multiply: $14 \times 7 = 98$, and then subtract: $100 - 98 = \mathbf{2}$.

The way we express the answer depends on the question. For example, if \$23 are to be divided among 10 people, each one will get \$2.30 (2.3 dollars); but if 23 books are to be divided among 10 people, each one will get 2 books and 3 will be left over (the remainder).

➥ Example 9

If a is the remainder when 999 is divided by 7, and b is the remainder when 777 is divided by 9, what is the remainder when a is divided by b?

Solution.

$999 \div 7 = 142.714...$; $7 \times 142 = 994$; $999 - 994 = 5 = a$.

$777 \div 9 = 86.333...$; $9 \times 86 = 774$; $777 - 774 = 3 = b$.

Finally, when 5 is divided by 3, the quotient is 1 and the remainder is **2**.

➡ Example 10 _____

How many positive integers less than 100 have a remainder of 3 when divided by 7?

Solution. To have a remainder of 3 when divided by 7, an integer must be 3 more than a multiple of 7. For example, when 73 is divided by 7, the quotient is 10 and the remainder is 3: $73 = 10 \times 7 + 3$. Just take the multiples of 7 and add 3:

$$\underline{0} \times 7 + 3 = 3; \qquad \underline{1} \times 7 + 3 = 10; \qquad \underline{2} \times 7 + 3 = 17; \ldots; \qquad \underline{13} \times 7 + 3 = 94$$

There are **14** positive integers less than 100 that have a remainder of 3 when divided by 7. If a and b are integers, the following four terms are synonymous:

a is a **divisor** of b. a is a **factor** of b.

b is **divisible** by a. b is a **multiple** of a.

All these statements mean that, when b is divided by a, there is no remainder (or, more precisely, the remainder is 0). For example:

3 is a divisor of 12.   3 is a factor of 12.

12 is divisible by 3.   12 is a multiple of 3.

Key Fact A10

Every integer has a finite set of factors (or divisors) and an infinite set of multiples.

The factors of 12: $-12, -6, -4, -3, -2, -1, 1, 2, 3, 4, 6, 12$

The multiples of 12: $\ldots, -48, -36, -24, -12, 0, 12, 24, 36, 48, \ldots$

The only positive divisor of 1 is 1. Every other positive integer has at least two positive divisors: 1 and itself, and possibly many more. For example, 6 is divisible by 1 and 6, as well as by 2 and 3; whereas 7 is divisible only by 1 and 7. Positive integers, such as 7, that have exactly two positive divisors are called **prime numbers** or **primes**. Here are the first several primes:

$$2, 3, 5, 7, 11, 13, 17, 19, 23, 29$$

Memorize this list—it will come in handy. Note that 1 is *not* a prime.

Key Fact A11

Every integer greater than 1 that is not a prime can be written as a product of primes.

To find the prime factorization of any integer, find any two factors: if they're both primes, you are done; if not, factor them. Continue until each factor has been written in terms of primes.

A useful method is to make a *factor tree*.

For example, here are the prime factorizations of 108 and 240:

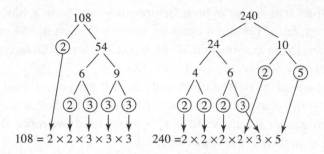

$$108 = 2 \times 2 \times 3 \times 3 \times 3 \qquad 240 = 2 \times 2 \times 2 \times 2 \times 3 \times 5$$

➥ Example 11

For any positive integer a, let $\lceil a \rfloor$ denote the smallest prime factor of a.
Which of the following is equal to $\lceil 35 \rfloor$?

    (A) $\lceil 10 \rfloor$
    (B) $\lceil 15 \rfloor$
    (C) $\lceil 45 \rfloor$
    (D) $\lceil 55 \rfloor$

Solution. Check the first few primes; 35 is not divisible by 2 or 3, but is divisible by 5, so 5 is the *smallest* prime factor of 35, and $\lceil 35 \rfloor = 5$. Now check the four choices: $\lceil 10 \rfloor = 2$, $\lceil 15 \rfloor = 3$, and $\lceil 45 \rfloor = 3$. Only $\lceil \mathbf{55} \rfloor = 5$. The answer is **(D)**.

The ***least common multiple*** **(LCM)** of two or more integers is the smallest positive integer that is a multiple of each of them. For example, the LCM of 6 and 10 is 30. Infinitely many positive integers are multiples of both 6 and 10, including 60, 90, 180, 600, 6000, and 66,000,000, but 30 is the smallest one.

The ***greatest common factor*** **(GCF)** or ***greatest common divisor*** **(GCD)** of two or more integers is the largest integer that is a factor of each of them. For example, the only positive integers that are factors of both 6 and 10 are 1 and 2, so the GCF of 6 and 10 is 2. For small numbers, you can often find the GCF and LCM by inspection. For larger numbers, KEY FACTS A12 and A13 are useful.

Key Fact A12

The product of the GCF and LCM of two numbers is equal to the product of the two numbers.

Key Fact A13

> ### HELPFUL HINT
>
> It is usually easier to find the GCF than the LCM. For example, you may see immediately that the GCF of 36 and 48 is 12. You can then use KEY FACT A12 to find the LCM: since GCF × LCM = 36 × 48:
>
> $$\text{LCM} = \frac{\overset{3}{\cancel{36}} \times 48}{\underset{1}{\cancel{12}}} = 3 \times 48 = 144.$$

To find the GCF or LCM of two or more integers, first get their prime factorizations.

- The GCF is the product of all the primes that appear in each of the factorizations, using each prime the smallest number of times it appears in any factorization.
- The LCM is the product of all the primes that appear in any of the factorizations, using each prime the largest number of times it appears in any factorization.

    For example, let's find the GCF and LCM of 108 and 240. As we saw:

$$108 = 2 \times 2 \times 3 \times 3 \times 3 \quad \text{and} \quad 240 = 2 \times 2 \times 2 \times 2 \times 3 \times 5$$

■ **GCF.** The primes that appear in both factorizations are 2 and 3. Since 2 appears twice in the factorization of 108 and 4 times in the factorization of 240, we take it twice; 3 appears 3 times in the factorization of 108, but only once in the factorization of 240, so we take it just once. The GCF = $2 \times 2 \times 3 = $ **12**.

■ **LCM.** We take one of the factorizations and add to it any primes from the other that are not yet listed. We'll start with $2 \times 2 \times 3 \times 3 \times 3$ (108) and look at the primes from 240. There are four 2's; we already wrote two 2's, so we need two more; there is a 3, but we already have that; there is a 5, which we need.

$$\text{The LCM} = (2 \times 2 \times 3 \times 3 \times 3) \times (2 \times 2 \times 5) = 108 \times 20 = \textbf{2160}$$

➡ **Example 12** _____

What is the smallest number that is divisible by both 34 and 35?

Solution. You are being asked for the LCM of 34 and 35.

 By KEY FACT A12, the LCM = $\frac{34 \times 35}{\text{GCF}}$. The GCF, however, is 1 since no number greater than 1 divides evenly into both 34 and 35. The LCM is $34 \times 35 = $ **1190**.

The **_even numbers_** are all the multiples of 2: {..., –4, –2, 0, 2, 4, 6, ...}.
The **_odd numbers_** are all the integers not divisible by 2: {..., –5, –3, –1, 1, 3, 5, ...}.
Note:

■ The terms _odd_ and _even_ apply only to integers.
■ Every integer (positive, negative, or 0) is either odd or even.
■ 0 is an even integer; it is a multiple of 2 ($0 = 0 \times 2$).
■ 0 is a multiple of _every_ integer ($0 = 0 \times n$).
■ 2 is the only even prime number.

Key Fact A14

The tables below summarize three important facts:

1. **If two integers are both even or both odd, their sum and difference are even.**
2. **If one integer is even and the other odd, their sum and difference are odd.**
3. **The product of two integers is even unless both of them are odd.**

+ and –	even	odd		×	even	odd
even	even	odd		even	even	even
odd	odd	even		odd	even	odd

Exponents and Roots

Repeated addition of the same number is indicated by multiplication:

$$17 + 17 + 17 + 17 + 17 + 17 + 17 = 7 \times 17$$

Repeated multiplication of the same number is indicated by an exponent:

$$17 \times 17 \times 17 \times 17 \times 17 \times 17 \times 17 = 17^7$$

In the expression 17^7, 17 is called the **base** and 7 is the **exponent**.

On the SAT, most of the exponents you will encounter are positive integers; these are defined in KEY FACT A15. Occasionally you may see an exponent that is zero or negative or is a fraction; these exponents are defined later in KEY FACT A20.

Key Fact A15

For any number b: $b^1 = b$.

For any number b and integer $n > 1$: $b^n = b \times b \times \cdots \times b$, where b is used as a factor n times.

(i) $2^5 \times 2^3 = (2 \times 2 \times 2 \times 2 \times 2) \times (2 \times 2 \times 2) = 2^8 = 2^{5+3}$.

(ii) $\dfrac{2^5}{2^3} = \dfrac{2 \times 2 \times 2 \times 2 \times 2}{2 \times 2 \times 2} = 2 \times 2 = 2^2 = 2^{5-3}$.

(iii) $(2^2)^3 = (2 \times 2)^3 = (2 \times 2) \times (2 \times 2) \times (2 \times 2) = 2^6 = 2^{2 \times 3}$.

(iv) $2^3 \times 7^3 = (2 \times 2 \times 2) \times (7 \times 7 \times 7) = (2 \times 7)(2 \times 7)(2 \times 7) = (2 \times 7)^3$.

(v) $\dfrac{2^3}{7^3} = \dfrac{2 \times 2 \times 2}{7 \times 7 \times 7} = \dfrac{2}{7} \times \dfrac{2}{7} \times \dfrac{2}{7} = \left(\dfrac{2}{7}\right)^3$.

These five examples illustrate the five important laws of exponents given in KEY FACT A16.

Key Fact A16

HELPFUL HINT

Memorize these laws of exponents; they are very useful.

For any numbers b and c and positive integers m and n:

(i) $b^m b^n = b^{m+n}$ (ii) $\dfrac{b^m}{b^n} = b^{m-n}$ (iii) $(b^m)^n = b^{mn}$ (iv) $b^m c^m = (bc)^m$ (v) $\dfrac{b^m}{c^m} = \left(\dfrac{b}{c}\right)^m$

> **CAUTION:** In (i) and (ii) the bases are the same, and in (iv) the exponents are the same. None of these rules applies to expressions such as $2^5 \times 3^4$, in which both the bases and the exponents are different.

➥ Example 13 _____

If $2^x = 32$, what is x^2?

HELPFUL HINT

Write out the first ten powers of 2 and memorize them.

Solution. To solve $2^x = 32$, just count (and keep track of) how many 2's you need to multiply to get 32: $2 \times 2 \times 2 \times 2 \times 2 = 32$, so $x = 5$ and $x^2 = $ **25**.

➥ Example 14 _____

If $3^a \times 3^b = 3^{100}$, what is the average (arithmetic mean) of a and b?

Solution. Since $3^a \times 3^b = 3^{a+b}$, you can see that $a + b = 100 \Rightarrow \dfrac{a+b}{2} = $ **50**.

The next KEY FACT is an immediate consequence of KEY FACTS A4 and A5.

For any positive integer n:

(i) $0^n = 0$.

(ii) If a is positive, a^n is positive.

(iii) If a is negative, a^n is positive if n is even, and negative if n is odd.

➡ **Example 15** _____

Which of the following statements is (are) true?

  I. $-2^{10} > 0$

  II. $-(-2)^{10} > 0$

  III. $2^{10} - (-2)^{10} > 0$

  (A) None
  (B) I only
  (C) III only
  (D) I and III only

Solution.

■ Since 2^{10} is positive, -2^{10} is negative. (I is false.)

■ Since $(-2)^{10}$ is positive, $-(-2)^{10}$ is negative. (II is false.)

■ Since $(-2)^{10} = 2^{10}$, $2^{10} - (-2)^{10} = 0$. (III is false.)

None of the statements is true. Choice **(A)** is correct.

Squares and Square Roots

The exponent that appears most often on the SAT is 2. It is used to form the square of a number, as in πr^2 (the area of a circle), $a^2 + b^2 = c^2$ (the Pythagorean theorem), or $x^2 - y^2$ (the difference of two squares). Therefore, it is helpful to recognize the **perfect squares**, numbers that are the squares of integers. The squares of the integers from 0 to 15 are as follows:

x	0	1	2	3	4	5	6	7
x^2	0	1	4	9	16	25	36	49

x	8	9	10	11	12	13	14	15
x^2	64	81	100	121	144	169	196	225

There are two numbers that satisfy the equation $x^2 = 9$: $x = 3$ and $x = -3$. The positive number, 3, is called the **square root** of 9 and is denoted by the symbol $\sqrt{9}$.

Clearly, each perfect square has a square root: $\sqrt{0} = 0$, $\sqrt{36} = 6$, $\sqrt{81} = 9$, and $\sqrt{144} = 12$. It is an important fact, however, that *every* positive number has a square root.

For any positive number a, there is a positive number b that satisfies the equation $b^2 = a$. That number is called the square root of a, and we write $b = \sqrt{a}$.

Therefore, for any positive number a: $\sqrt{a} \times \sqrt{a} = (\sqrt{a})^2 = a$.

The only difference between $\sqrt{9}$ and $\sqrt{10}$ is that the first square root is an integer, while the second one isn't. Since 10 is a little more than 9, we should expect that $\sqrt{10}$ is a little more than $\sqrt{9}$, which is 3. In fact, $(3.1)^2 = 9.61$, which is close to 10; and $(3.16)^2 = 9.9856$, which is very close to 10, so $\sqrt{10} \approx 3.16$. Square roots of integers that aren't perfect squares can be approximated as accurately as we wish, and by pressing the $\sqrt{\ }$ key on our calculators we can get much more accuracy than is needed for the SAT. Actually, most answers involving square roots use the square root symbol.

➡ **Example 16** _____

What is the circumference of a circle whose area is 10π?

(A) 10π

(B) $\pi\sqrt{10}$

(C) $2\pi\sqrt{10}$

(D) $\pi\sqrt{20}$

Solution. See Section 6-L for the formulas for the area and circumference of a circle. Since the area of a circle is given by the formula $A = \pi r^2$, then

$$\pi r^2 = 10\pi \Rightarrow r^2 = 10 \Rightarrow r = \sqrt{10}$$

Since the circumference is given by the formula $C = 2\pi r$, then $C = \mathbf{2\pi\sqrt{10}}$ **(C).**

For any positive numbers a and b:

$$\sqrt{ab} = \sqrt{a} \times \sqrt{b} \quad \text{and} \quad \sqrt{\frac{a}{b}} = \frac{\sqrt{a}}{\sqrt{b}}.$$

CAUTION: $\sqrt{a+b} \neq \sqrt{a} + \sqrt{b}$.

For example: $\sqrt{9+16} = \sqrt{25} = 5$, but $\sqrt{9} + \sqrt{16} = 3 + 4 = 7$.

CAUTION: Although it is always true that $(\sqrt{a})^2 = a$, $\sqrt{a^2} = a$ is *not* true if a is negative:

$$\sqrt{(-5)^2} = \sqrt{25} = 5, \textit{ not } -5.$$

In the same way that we write $b = \sqrt{a}$ to indicate that $a^2 = b$, we write

$b = \sqrt[3]{a}$ to indicate that $b^3 = a$,

and

$b = \sqrt[4]{a}$ to indicate that $b^4 = a$.

For example,

$$\sqrt[3]{64} = 4 \text{ because } 4^3 = 64$$

and

$$\sqrt[4]{16} = 2 \text{ because } 2^4 = 16$$

So far, the only exponents we have considered have been positive integers. We now expand our definition to include other numbers as exponents.

Key Fact A20

- For any real number $a \neq 0$: $a^0 = 1$.
- For any real number $a \neq 0$: $a^{-n} = \dfrac{1}{a^n}$.
- For any *positive* number a and positive integer n: $a^{\frac{1}{n}} = \sqrt[n]{a}$.

Here are some examples to illustrate the definitions in KEY FACT A20:

$$4^0 = 1, \qquad 4^{-3} = \frac{1}{4^3} = \frac{1}{64}, \qquad 4^{\frac{1}{2}} = \sqrt{4} = 2$$

$$8^0 = 1, \qquad 8^{-1} = \frac{1}{8^1} = \frac{1}{8}, \qquad 8^{\frac{1}{3}} = \sqrt[3]{8} = 2$$

Key Fact A21

REMEMBER

All exponents satisfy the basic laws of exponents.

The laws of exponents given in KEY FACT A16 are true for *any* exponents, not just positive integers.

For example:

(i) $\quad 2^{-4} \times 2^4 = 2^{-4+4} = 2^0 = 1$

(ii) $\quad \dfrac{2^3}{2^5} = 2^{3-5} = 2^{-2} = \dfrac{1}{2^2} = \dfrac{1}{4}$

(iii) $\quad \left(2^{-6}\right)^{\frac{1}{2}} = 2^{(-6)\frac{1}{2}} = 2^{-3} = \dfrac{1}{2^3} = \dfrac{1}{8}$

(iv) $\quad \left(2^3\right)^{\frac{1}{6}} = 2^{\frac{3}{6}} = 2^{\frac{1}{2}} = \sqrt{2}$

(v) $\quad 2^{\frac{3}{4}} = 2^{3\left(\frac{1}{4}\right)} = \left(2^3\right)^{\frac{1}{4}} = 8^{\frac{1}{4}} = \sqrt[4]{8}$

➥ Example 17 _____

What is the value of $5^{\frac{1}{5}} \times 5^{\frac{2}{5}} \times 5^{\frac{3}{5}} \times 5^{\frac{4}{5}}$?

Solution. $5^{\frac{1}{5}} \times 5^{\frac{2}{5}} \times 5^{\frac{3}{5}} \times 5^{\frac{4}{5}} = 5^{\left(\frac{1}{5}+\frac{2}{5}+\frac{3}{5}+\frac{4}{5}\right)} = 5^{\frac{10}{5}} = 5^2 = \mathbf{25}$

PEMDAS

When a calculation requires performing more than one operation, it is important to carry the operations out in the correct order. For decades students have memorized the sentence "$\underline{P}$lease $\underline{E}$xcuse $\underline{M}$y $\underline{D}$ear $\underline{A}$unt $\underline{S}$ally," or just the acronym, PEMDAS, to remember the proper order of operations. The letters stand for:

- $\underline{P}$arentheses: first do whatever appears in parentheses, following PEMDAS within the parentheses also if necessary.
- $\underline{E}$xponents: next evaluate all terms with exponents.
- $\underline{M}$ultiplication and $\underline{D}$ivision: then do all multiplications and divisions *in order from left to right*—do *not* multiply first and then divide.
- $\underline{A}$ddition and $\underline{S}$ubtraction: finally, do all additions and subtractions *in order from left to right*—do *not* add first and then subtract.

Here are some worked-out examples.

1. $12 + 3 \times 2 = 12 + 6 = 18$ [Multiply before you add.]
   $(12 + 3) \times 2 = 15 \times 2 = 30$ [First add in the parentheses.]
2. $12 \div 3 \times 2 = 4 \times 2 = 8$ [Just go from left to right.]
   $12 \div (3 \times 2) = 12 \div 6 = 2$ [Multiply first.]
3. $5 \times 2^3 = 5 \times 8 = 40$ [Do the exponent first.]
   $(5 \times 2)^3 = 10^3 = 1000$ [Multiply first.]
4. $4 + 4 \div (2 + 6) = 4 + 4 \div 8 = 4 + .5 = 4.5$
   [Do parentheses first, then division.]
5. $100 - 2^2(3 + 4 \times 5) = 100 - 2^2(23) = 100 - 4(23) = 100 - 92 = 8$
   [Do parentheses first (using PEMDAS), then the exponent, then multiplication.]

 CALCULATOR SHORTCUT

Almost every scientific and graphing calculator automatically follows PEMDAS. Test each of these calculations on *your* calculator. Be sure you know whether or not you need to use parentheses or to put anything in memory as you proceed.

There is one situation when you shouldn't start with what's in the parentheses. Consider the following two examples.

(i)   What is the value of $7(100 - 1)$?
Using PEMDAS, you would write $7(100 - 1) = 7(99)$; and then, multiplying on your calculator, you would get **693**. But you can do the arithmetic more quickly in your head if you think of it this way: $7(100 - 1) = 700 - 7 = 693$.

(ii)   What is the value of $(77 + 49) \div 7$?
If you followed the rules of PEMDAS, you would first add: $77 + 49 = 126$, and then divide: $126 \div 7 = \mathbf{18}$. This is definitely more difficult and time-consuming than mentally calculating $\frac{77}{7} + \frac{49}{7} = 11 + 7 = 18$.

Both of these examples illustrate the very important distributive law.

For any real numbers *a*, *b*, and *c*:

Many students use
the distributive law
with multiplication
but forget about it
with division. Don't
make that mistake.

- $a(b + c) = ab + ac$
- $a(b - c) = ab - ac$

and, if $a \neq 0$,

- $\dfrac{b+c}{a} = \dfrac{b}{a} + \dfrac{c}{a}$

- $\dfrac{b-c}{a} = \dfrac{b}{a} - \dfrac{c}{a}$

➡ **Example 18** _____

If $a = 3(x - 7)$ and $b = 3x - 7$, what is the value of $a - b$?

(A) -28

(B) -14

(C) 0

(D) $3x - 14$

Solution. $a - b = 3(x - 7) - (3x - 7) = 3x - 21 - 3x + 7 = -21 + 7 = \mathbf{-14}$ **(B)**

➡ **Example 19** _____

The proper use of
the distributive law
is essential in the
algebra review in
Section 6-F.

What is the average (arithmetic mean) of 3^{10}, 3^{20}, and 3^{30}?

(A) 3^{20}

(B) 3^{30}

(C) 3^{60}

(D) $3^9 + 3^{19} + 3^{29}$

Solution. $\dfrac{3^{10}+3^{20}+3^{30}}{3} = \dfrac{3^{10}}{3} + \dfrac{3^{20}}{3} + \dfrac{3^{30}}{3} = \dfrac{3^{10}}{3^1} + \dfrac{3^{20}}{3^1} + \dfrac{3^{30}}{3^1} = \mathbf{3^9 + 3^{19} + 3^{29}}$ **(D)**

Inequalities

The number *a* is **greater than** the number *b*, denoted as $a > b$, if *a* is to the right of *b* on the number line. Similarly, *a* is **less than** *b*, denoted as $a < b$, if *a* is to the left of *b* on the number line. Therefore, if *a* is positive, $a > 0$; and if *a* is negative, $a < 0$. Clearly, if $a > b$, then $b < a$.

KEY FACT A23 gives an important alternative way to describe *greater than* and *less than*.

Key Fact A23

- For any numbers *a* and *b*: $a > b$ means that $a - b$ is positive.
- For any numbers *a* and *b*: $a < b$ means that $a - b$ is negative.

For any numbers *a* and *b*, exactly one of the following is true:

$$a > b \quad \text{or} \quad a = b \quad \text{or} \quad a < b$$

The symbol ≥ means *greater than or equal to* and the symbol ≤ means *less than or equal to*. The statement "$x \geq 5$" means that x can be 5 or any number greater than 5; the statement "$x \leq 5$" means that x can be 5 or any number less than 5.

The statement "$2 < x < 5$" is an abbreviation for the statement "$2 < x$ and $x < 5$." It means that x is a number between 2 and 5 (greater than 2 and less than 5).

KEY FACTS A25 and A26 give some important information about inequalities that you need to know for the SAT.

Key Fact A25 The Arithmetic of Inequalities

■ **Adding a number to an inequality or subtracting a number from the inequality preserves the inequality.**

If $a < b$, then $a + c < b + c$ and $a - c < b - c$.

$$3 < 7 \Rightarrow 3 + 100 < 7 + 100 \quad (103 < 107)$$
$$3 < 7 \Rightarrow 3 - 100 < 7 - 100 \quad (-97 < -93)$$

■ **Adding inequalities in the same direction preserves them.**

If $a < b$ and $c < d$, then $a + c < b + d$.
$$3 < 7 \text{ and } 5 < 10 \Rightarrow 3 + 5 < 7 + 10 \quad (8 < 17)$$

■ **Multiplying or dividing an inequality by a positive number preserves the inequality.**

If $a < b$, and c is positive, then $ac < bc$ and $\dfrac{a}{c} < \dfrac{b}{c}$.

$$3 < 7 \Rightarrow 3 \times 100 < 7 \times 100 \quad (300 < 700)$$
$$3 < 7 \Rightarrow 3 \div 100 < 7 \div 100 \quad \left(\frac{3}{100} < \frac{7}{100}\right)$$

■ **Multiplying or dividing an inequality by a negative number reverses the inequality.**

If $a < b$, and c is negative, then $ac > bc$ and $\dfrac{a}{c} > \dfrac{b}{c}$.

$$3 < 7 \Rightarrow 3 \times (-100) > 7 \times (-100) \quad (-300 > -700)$$
$$3 < 7 \Rightarrow 3 \div (-100) > 7 \div (-100) \quad \left(-\frac{3}{100} > -\frac{7}{100}\right)$$

■ **Taking negatives reverses an inequality.**

If $a < b$, then $-a > -b$, and if $a > b$, then $-a < -b$.
$$3 < 7 \Rightarrow -3 > -7 \quad \text{and} \quad 7 > 3 \Rightarrow -7 < -3$$

■ **If two numbers are each positive or each negative, taking reciprocals reverses an inequality.**

If a and b are both positive or both negative and $a < b$, then $\dfrac{1}{a} > \dfrac{1}{b}$.

$$3 < 7 \Rightarrow \frac{1}{3} > \frac{1}{7} \quad \text{and} \quad -7 < -3 \Rightarrow \frac{1}{-7} > \frac{1}{-3}$$

HELPFUL HINT

Be sure you understand KEY FACT A25; it is very useful. Also, review the important properties listed in KEY FACTS A26–A28.

■ If $0 < x < 1$, and a is positive, then $xa < a$.
For example, $0.85 \times 19 < 19$.

■ If $0 < x < 1$, and m and n are integers with $m > n > 1$, then $x^m < x^n < x$.
For example, $\left(\dfrac{1}{2}\right)^5 < \left(\dfrac{1}{2}\right)^2 < \dfrac{1}{2}$.

■ If $0 < x < 1$, then $\sqrt{x} > x$.
For example, $\sqrt{\dfrac{3}{4}} > \dfrac{3}{4}$.

■ If $0 < x < 1$, then $\dfrac{1}{x} > x$. In fact, $\dfrac{1}{x} > 1$.
For example, $\dfrac{1}{0.2} > 1 > 0.2$.

■ 0 is the only number that is neither positive nor negative.
■ 0 is smaller than every positive number and greater than every negative number.
■ 0 is an even integer.
■ 0 is a multiple of every integer.
■ For every number a: $a + 0 = a$ and $a - 0 = a$.
■ For every number a: $a \times 0 = 0$.
■ For every integer n: $0^n = 0$.
■ For every number a (including 0): $a \div 0$ and $\dfrac{a}{0}$ are *meaningless expressions*.
(They are *undefined*.)
■ For every number a other than 0: $0 \div a = \dfrac{0}{a} = 0$.
■ 0 is the only number that is equal to its opposite: $0 = -0$.
■ If the product of two or more numbers is 0, at least one of the numbers is 0.

■ For any number a: $1 \times a = a$ and $\dfrac{a}{1} = a$.
■ For any integer n: $1^n = 1$.
■ 1 is a divisor of every integer.
■ 1 is the smallest positive integer.
■ 1 is an odd integer.
■ 1 is the only integer with only one divisor. It is not a prime.

Multiple-Choice Questions

1. For how many positive integers, a, is it true that $a^2 \leq 2a$?

   (A) None
   (B) 1
   (C) 2
   (D) More than 2

2. If $0 < a < b < 1$, which of the following is (are) true?

   I. $a - b$ is negative.

   II. $\dfrac{1}{ab}$ is positive.

   III. $\dfrac{1}{b} - \dfrac{1}{a}$ is positive.

   (A) I only
   (B) II only
   (C) I and II only
   (D) I, II, and III

3. If a and b are negative, and c is positive, which of the following is (are) true?

   I. $a - b < a - c$

   II. If $a < b$, then $\dfrac{a}{c} < \dfrac{b}{c}$.

   III. $\dfrac{1}{b} < \dfrac{1}{c}$

   (A) I only
   (B) II only
   (C) III only
   (D) II and III only

4. At 3:00 A.M. the temperature was 13° below zero. By noon it had risen to 32°. What was the average hourly increase in temperature?

   (A) $\left(\dfrac{19}{9}\right)^{\circ}$

   (B) $\left(\dfrac{19}{6}\right)^{\circ}$

   (C) 5°
   (D) 7.5°

5. If $(7^a)(7^b) = \dfrac{7^c}{7^d}$, what is d in terms of a, b, and c?

   (A) $\dfrac{c}{ab}$

   (B) $c - a - b$

   (C) $a + b - c$

   (D) $c - ab$

6. If p and q are primes greater than 2, which of the following *must* be true?

   I. $p + q$ is even.
   II. pq is odd.
   III. $p^2 - q^2$ is even.

   (A) I only
   (B) I and II only
   (C) I and III only
   (D) I, II, and III

Questions 7 and 8 refer to the following definition.

For any positive integer n, $\tau(n)$ represents the number of positive divisors of n.

7. Which of the following is (are) true?

   I. $\tau(5) = \tau(7)$

   II. $\tau(5) \cdot \tau(7) = \tau(35)$

   III. $\tau(5) + \tau(7) = \tau(12)$

   (A) I only
   (B) I and II only
   (C) I and III only
   (D) I, II, and III

8. What is the value of $\tau(\tau(\tau(12)))$?

   (A) 2
   (B) 3
   (C) 4
   (D) 6

9. Which of the following is equal to $(7^8 \times 7^9)^{10}$?

   (A) 7^{27}
   (B) 7^{82}
   (C) 7^{170}
   (D) 49^{720}

10. How many integers are greater than $-\pi$ and less than $\sqrt{2}$?

   (A) 3
   (B) 4
   (C) 5
   (D) 6

11. If $0 < x < 1$, which of the following lists the numbers in increasing order?

   (A) $\sqrt{x}, x, x^2$
   (B) $x^2, x, \sqrt{x}$
   (C) $x^2, \sqrt{x}, x$
   (D) $x, x^2, \sqrt{x}$

Grid-in Questions

12. At Ben's Butcher Shop 99 pounds of chopped meat is being divided into packages each weighing 2.5 pounds. How many pounds of meat are left when there isn't enough to make another whole package?

13. Maria has two electronic beepers. One of them beeps every 4 seconds; the other beeps every 9 seconds. If they are turned on at exactly the same time, how many times during the next hour will both beepers beep at the same time?

14. If $-7 \leq x \leq 7$ and $0 \leq y \leq 12$, what is the greatest possible value of $y - x$?

15. If x is an integer less than 1000 that has a remainder of 1 when it is divided by 2, 3, 4, 5, 6, or 7, what is one possible value of x?

18. What is the greatest prime factor of 132?

16. What is the value of $2^4 \div 2^{-4}$?

19. If the product of four consecutive integers is equal to one of the integers, what is the largest possible value of one of the integers?

17. What is the value of $|(-2-3)-(2-3)|$?

20. If x and y are positive integers, and $(13^x)^y = 13^{13}$, what is the average (arithmetic mean) of x and y?

Answer Key

1. **C**   4. **C**   7. **B**   10. **C**
2. **C**   5. **B**   8. **B**   11. **B**
3. **D**   6. **D**   9. **C**

12. **1.5**

13. **100**

14. **19**

15. **421**

or 841

16. **256**

17. **4**

18. **11**

19. **3**

20. **7**

Answers Explained

1. **(C)** Since a is positive, divide both sides of the given inequality by a:

$$a^2 \leq 2a \Rightarrow a \leq 2 \Rightarrow a = 1 \text{ or } 2$$

   There are two positive integers that satisfy the given inequality.

2. **(C)**
   - Since $a < b$, $a - b$ is negative. (I is true.)
   - Since a and b are positive, so is their product, ab; and the reciprocal of a positive number is positive. (II is true.)
   - $\frac{1}{b} - \frac{1}{a} = \frac{a-b}{ab}$. Since the numerator, $a - b$, is negative and the denominator, ab, is positive, the value of the fraction is negative. (III is false.)

3. **(D)**
   - Since b is negative and c is positive, $b < c \Rightarrow -b > -c \Rightarrow a - b > a - c$. (I is false.)
   - Since c is positive, dividing by c preserves the inequality. (II is true.)
   - Since b is negative, $\frac{1}{b}$ is negative, and so is less than $\frac{1}{c}$, which is positive. (III is true.)

4. **(C)** In the 9 hours from 3:00 A.M. to noon, the temperature rose $32 - (-13) = 32 + 13 = 45°$. Therefore, the average hourly increase was $45 \div 9 = 5°$.

5. **(B)** $(7^a)(7^b) = 7^{a+b}$, and $\frac{7^c}{7^d} = 7^{c-d}$. Therefore:

$$a + b = c - d \Rightarrow a + b + d = c \Rightarrow d = c - a - b$$

6. **(D)** All primes greater than 2 are odd, so p and q are odd, and $p + q$ is even. (I is true.) The product of two odd numbers is odd. (II is true.) Since p and q are odd, so are their squares, and so the difference of the squares is even. (III is true.)

7. **(B)** Since 5 and 7 have two positive factors each, $\tau(5) = \tau(7)$. (I is true.) Since 35 has four divisors (1, 5, 7, and 35) and $\tau(5) \cdot \tau(7) = 2 \times 2 = 4$, II is true. The value of $\tau(12)$ is 6, which is *not* equal to $2 + 2$. (III is false.)

8. **(B)** Since $\tau(12) = 6$, $\tau(\tau(\tau(12))) = \tau(\tau(6))$. Since $\tau(6) = 4$, then $\tau(\tau(6)) = \tau(4) = 3$.

9. **(C)** First, multiply inside the parentheses: $7^8 \times 7^9 = 7^{17}$; then raise to the 10th power: $(7^{17})^{10} = 7^{170}$.

10. **(C)** There are five integers (1, 0, –1, –2, –3) that are greater than –3.14 ($-\pi$) and less than 1.41 ($\sqrt{2}$).

11. **(B)** For any number, x, between 0 and 1: $x^2 < x$ and $x < \sqrt{x}$.

12. **1.5** Divide: $99 \div 2.5 = 39.6$. The butchers can make 39 packages, weighing a total of $39 \times 2.5 = 97.5$ pounds, and have $99 - 97.5 = 1.5$ pounds of meat left over.

13. **100** Since 36 is the LCM of 4 and 9, the beepers will beep together every 36 seconds. One hour = 60 minutes = 3600 seconds, and so the simultaneous beeping will occur 100 times.

14. **19** To make $y - x$ as large as possible, let y be as large as possible (12), and subtract the smallest amount possible ($x = -7$): $12 - (-7) = 19$.

15. **421 or 841** The LCM of 2, 3, 4, 5, 6, 7 is 420, so 420 is divisible by each of these integers, and there will be a remainder of 1 when 421 is divided by any of them. One more than any multiple of 420 will also work.

16. **256** $2^4 \div 2^{-4} = \dfrac{2^4}{2^{-4}} = 2^{4-(-4)} = 2^{4+4} = 2^8 = 256$

17. **4** $|(-2-3)-(2-3)| = |(-5)-(-1)| = |-5+1| = |-4| = 4$

18. **11** The easiest way to find the greatest prime factor of 132 is to find its prime factorization: $132 = 2 \times 2 \times 3 \times 11$, so 11 is the greatest prime factor.

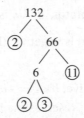

19. **3** If all four integers were negative, their product would be positive, and so could not equal one of them. If all four integers were positive, their product would be much greater than any of them (even $1 \times 2 \times 3 \times 4 = 24$). Therefore, the integers must include 0, in which case their product *is* 0. The four possibilities are: –3, –2, –1, 0; –2, –1, 0, 1; –1, 0, 1, 2; and 0, 1, 2, 3. Therefore, the largest possible value of one of the integers is 3.

20. **7** Since $13^{13} = (13^x)^y = 13^{xy}$, then $xy = 13$. The only positive integers whose product is 13 are 1 and 13. Their average is $\dfrac{1+13}{2} = 7$.

Several questions on the SAT involve fractions and/or decimals. In this section we will review all of the important facts on these topics that you need to know for the SAT.

When a whole is *divided* into n equal parts, each part is called *one-nth* of the whole, written as $\frac{1}{n}$. For example, if a pizza is cut (*divided*) into eight equal slices, each slice is one-eighth $\left(\frac{1}{8}\right)$ of the pizza; a day is *divided* into 24 equal hours, so an hour is one-twenty-fourth $\left(\frac{1}{24}\right)$ of a day; and an inch is one-twelfth $\left(\frac{1}{12}\right)$ of a foot.

- If Sam slept for 5 hours, he slept for five-twenty-fourths $\left(\frac{5}{24}\right)$ of a day.

- If Tom bought eight slices of pizza, he bought eight-eighths $\left(\frac{8}{8}\right)$ of a pie.

- If Joe's shelf is 30 inches long, it measures thirty-twelfths $\left(\frac{30}{12}\right)$ of a foot.

Numbers such as $\frac{5}{24}$, $\frac{8}{8}$, and $\frac{30}{12}$, in which one integer is written over a second integer, are called *fractions*. The center line is the fraction bar. The number above the bar is called the *numerator*, and the number below the bar is the *denominator*.

CAUTION: The denominator of a fraction can *never* be 0.

- A fraction such as $\frac{5}{24}$, in which the numerator is less than the denominator, is called a *proper fraction*. Its value is less than 1.

- A fraction such as $\frac{30}{12}$, in which the numerator is more than the denominator, is called an *improper fraction*. Its value is greater than 1.

- A fraction such as $\frac{8}{8}$, in which the numerator and denominator are the same, is also an *improper fraction*, but it is equal to 1.

It is useful to think of the fraction bar as a symbol for division. If three pizzas are divided equally among eight people, each person gets $\frac{3}{8}$ of a pizza. If you actually use your calculator to divide 3 by 8, you get $\frac{3}{8} = 0.375$.

Key Fact B1

Every fraction, proper or improper, can be expressed in decimal form (or as a whole number) by dividing the numerator by the denominator. For example:

$$\frac{3}{10} = 0.3 \qquad \frac{3}{4} = 0.75 \qquad \frac{5}{8} = 0.625 \qquad \frac{3}{16} = 0.1875$$

$$\frac{8}{8} = 1 \qquad \frac{11}{8} = 1.375 \qquad \frac{48}{16} = 3 \qquad \frac{100}{8} = 12.5$$

Note: Any number beginning with a decimal point can be written with a 0 to the left of the decimal point. In fact, some calculators will express $3 \div 8$ as .375, whereas others will print 0.375.

Unlike the examples above, when most fractions are converted to decimals, the division does not terminate after two, three, or four decimal places; rather it goes on forever with some set of digits repeating itself.

$$\frac{2}{3} = 0.666666... \qquad \frac{3}{11} = 0.272727... \qquad \frac{5}{12} = 0.416666... \qquad \frac{17}{15} = 1.133333...$$

 CALCULATOR SHORTCUT

On the SAT, *never* do long division to convert a fraction to a decimal. Use your calculator. You will never have to do this on the noncalculator section.

On the SAT, *you do not need to be concerned with this repetition.* On grid-in problems you just enter as much of the number as will fit in the grid; and on multiple-choice questions, all numbers written as decimals terminate.

Although on the SAT you will have occasion to convert fractions to decimals (by dividing), you will not have to convert decimals to fractions.

Comparing Fractions and Decimals

Key Fact B2

To compare two decimals, follow these rules:

- Whichever number has the greater number to the left of the decimal point is greater: since 11 > 9, 11.001 > 9.896; and since 1 > 0, 1.234 > 0.8. (Recall that, if a decimal has no number to the left of the decimal point, you may assume that a 0 is there, so 1.234 > .8).

- If the numbers to the left of the decimal point are equal (or if there are no numbers to the left of the decimal point), proceed as follows:

  1. If the numbers do not have the same number of digits to the right of the decimal point, add zeros at the end of the shorter one until the number of digits is equal.

  2. Now, compare the numbers, *ignoring* the decimal point itself.

For example, to compare 1.83 and 1.823, add 0 at the end of 1.83, forming 1.830. Now, *thinking of them as whole numbers,* compare the numbers, ignoring the decimal point:

$$1830 > 1823 \Rightarrow 1.830 > 1.823$$

Key Fact B3

To compare two fractions, use one of the following two methods:

- Use your calculator to convert them to decimals. Then apply KEY FACT B2. This *always* works.

  For example, to compare $\frac{1}{3}$ and $\frac{3}{8}$, write $\frac{1}{3} = 0.3333...$ and $\frac{3}{8} = 0.375$.

  Since $0.375 > 0.333$, $\frac{3}{8} > \frac{1}{3}$.

- Use the fact that $\dfrac{a}{b} < \dfrac{c}{d}$ if and only if $ad < bc$.

For example, $\dfrac{1}{3} < \dfrac{3}{8}$ because $(1)(8) < (3)(3)$.

 CALCULATOR HINT

You can always use your calculator to compare two numbers: fractions, decimals, or integers. By KEY FACT A21, $a > b$ means $a - b$ is positive, and $a < b$ means $a - b$ is negative. Therefore, to compare two numbers, just subtract them. For example,

$$1.83 - 1.823 = .007 \Rightarrow 1.83 > 1.823, \quad .2139 - .239 = -.0251 \Rightarrow .2139 < .239,$$

$$\frac{1}{3} - \frac{3}{8} = -\frac{1}{24} \Rightarrow \frac{1}{3} < \frac{3}{8}, \quad -6 - (-7) = 1 \Rightarrow -6 > -7.$$

Key Fact B4

When comparing fractions, there are three situations in which it is faster *not* to use your calculator to convert fractions to decimals (although, of course, that will work).

1. The fractions have the same positive denominator. Then the fraction with the larger numerator is greater. Just as \$9 are more than \$7, and 9 books are more than 7 books, 9 tenths is more than 7 tenths: $\dfrac{9}{10} > \dfrac{7}{10}$.

2. The fractions have the same numerator. Then, if the denominators are positive, the fraction with the smaller denominator is greater. If you divide a cake into five equal pieces, each piece is larger than a piece you would get if you divided the cake into 10 equal pieces: $\dfrac{1}{5} > \dfrac{1}{10}$, and similarly $\dfrac{3}{5} > \dfrac{3}{10}$.

3. The fractions are so familiar or easy to work with that you already know the answer. For example, $\dfrac{3}{4} > \dfrac{1}{5}$ and $\dfrac{11}{20} > \dfrac{1}{2}$.

Key Fact B5

KEY FACTS B2, B3, and B4 apply to *positive* decimals and fractions. Clearly, any positive number is greater than any negative number. For negative decimals and fractions, use KEY FACT A25, which states that, if $a > b$, then $-a < -b$.

$$\frac{1}{2} > \frac{1}{5} \Rightarrow -\frac{1}{2} < -\frac{1}{5} \quad \text{and} \quad .83 > .829 \Rightarrow -.83 < -.829$$

➥ **Example 1**

Which of the following lists the fractions $\frac{2}{3}$, $\frac{5}{8}$, $\frac{7}{11}$, and $\frac{13}{20}$ in order from least to greatest?

(A) $\frac{2}{3}$, $\frac{5}{8}$, $\frac{7}{11}$, $\frac{13}{20}$

(B) $\frac{5}{8}$, $\frac{7}{11}$, $\frac{13}{20}$, $\frac{2}{3}$

(C) $\frac{5}{8}$, $\frac{13}{20}$, $\frac{7}{11}$, $\frac{2}{3}$

(D) $\frac{13}{20}$, $\frac{7}{11}$, $\frac{5}{8}$, $\frac{2}{3}$

Solution. On your calculator convert each fraction to a decimal, writing down the first few decimal places:

$$\frac{2}{3} = 0.666 \quad \frac{5}{8} = 0.625 \quad \frac{7}{11} = 0.636 \quad \text{and} \quad \frac{13}{20} = 0.65$$

It is now easy to order the decimals:

$$0.625 < 0.636 < 0.650 < 0.666$$

The answer is $\frac{5}{8}$, $\frac{7}{11}$, $\frac{13}{20}$, $\frac{2}{3}$ **(B)**.

Equivalent Fractions

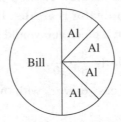

If Bill and Al shared a pizza, and Bill ate $\frac{1}{2}$ and Al ate $\frac{4}{8}$, they had exactly the same amount of the pizza. We express this idea by saying that $\frac{1}{2}$ and $\frac{4}{8}$ are *equivalent fractions*: that is, they have the exact same value.

Note: If you multiply both the numerator and the denominator of $\frac{1}{2}$ by 4, you get $\frac{4}{8}$; and if you divide both the numerator and the denominator of $\frac{4}{8}$ by 4, you get $\frac{1}{2}$.

This illustrates the next KEY FACT.

Two fractions are equivalent if multiplying or dividing both the numerator and the denominator of the first fraction *by the same number* gives the second fraction.

Consider the following two cases.

1. Are $\frac{3}{8}$ and $\frac{45}{120}$ equivalent? There is a number that, when multiplied by 3 gives 45, and there is a number that, when multiplied by 8, gives 120. By KEY FACT B6, if these numbers are the same, the fractions are equivalent. They *are* the same number: $3 \times 15 = 45$ and $8 \times 15 = 120$.

2. Are $\frac{2}{3}$ and $\frac{28}{45}$ equivalent? Since $2 \times 14 = 28$, but $3 \times 14 \neq 45$, the fractions are *not* equivalent. Alternatively, $28 \div 14 = 2$, but $45 \div 14 \neq 3$.

 CALCULATOR SHORTCUT

To determine whether two fractions are equivalent, convert them to decimals by dividing. For the fractions to be equivalent, the two quotients must be the same.

➡ **Example 2** _____

Which of the following is NOT equivalent to $\frac{15}{24}$?

(A) $\frac{45}{72}$

(B) $\frac{60}{96}$

(C) $\frac{5}{8}$

(D) $\frac{3}{5}$

Solution. Since $\frac{15}{24} = 0.625$, just check each choice until you find the one that is NOT equal to 0.625. Each of $\frac{45}{72}$, $\frac{60}{96}$, and $\frac{5}{8}$ is equal to 0.625. Only $\frac{3}{5}$ **(D)** does not equal $0.625 \left(\frac{3}{5} = 0.6 \right)$.

A fraction is in *lowest terms* if no positive integer greater than 1 is a factor of both the numerator and the denominator. For example, $\frac{9}{20}$ is in lowest terms, since no integer greater than 1 is a factor of both 9 and 20; but $\frac{9}{24}$ is not in lowest terms, since 3 is a factor of both 9 and 24.

Every fraction can be *reduced* to lowest terms by dividing the numerator and the denominator by their greatest common factor (GCF). If the GCF is 1, the fraction is already in lowest terms.

➡ **Example 3**_____

For any positive integer n, $n!$ means the product of all the integers from 1 to n. What is the value of $\dfrac{6!}{8!}$?

(A) $\dfrac{1}{56}$

(B) $\dfrac{1}{48}$

(C) $\dfrac{1}{8}$

(D) $\dfrac{1}{4}$

Solution. Assume that you don't see the easy way, shown below, to do this. On your calculator quickly multiply or use the ! key:

$$6! = 1 \cdot 2 \cdot 3 \cdot 4 \cdot 5 \cdot 6 = 720$$
$$8! = 1 \cdot 2 \cdot 3 \cdot 4 \cdot 5 \cdot 6 \cdot 7 \cdot 8 = 40{,}320$$

You are now faced with reducing $\dfrac{720}{40{,}320}$. Don't do it; just use your calculator to divide:

$\dfrac{720}{40{,}320} = 0.0178\ldots$, and now test the choices, starting with (C).

$\dfrac{1}{8} = 0.125$, which is too large. Eliminate (C) and (D), which is even larger, and try (A) or (B).

In fact, $\dfrac{1}{56} = 0.0178\ldots$ Choice **(A)** is correct. Here's the easy solution:

$$\frac{6!}{8!} = \frac{\overset{1}{\cancel{6 \times 5 \times 4 \times 3 \times 2 \times 1}}}{8 \times 7 \times \underset{1}{\cancel{6 \times 5 \times 4 \times 3 \times 2 \times 1}}} = \frac{1}{8 \times 7} = \frac{1}{56}$$

This solution takes only a few seconds, but the calculator solution is simple enough and can surely be done in less than a minute.

HELPFUL HINT

Any whole number can be treated as a decimal: 7 = 7.0.

Arithmetic Operations with Decimals

On the SAT, *all* decimal arithmetic (including whole numbers) that you can't easily do in your head should be done on your calculator. This shortcut saves time and avoids careless errors. If you know that $12 \times 12 = 144$ and that $1.2 \times 1.2 = 1.44$, fine; but if you're not sure, use your calculator rather than your pencil. You should even use your calculator to multiply 0.2×0.2 if there's any chance that you would get 0.4 instead of 0.04 as the answer.

You should *not* have to use your calculator to multiply or divide any decimal number by a power of 10, because multiplying and dividing by 10 or 100 or 1000 is a calcuation you should be able to do easily in your head.

Key Fact B8

To multiply any decimal or whole number by a power of 10, move the decimal point as many places to the right as there are 0's in the power of 10, filling in with 0's if necessary.

$$1.35 \times 10 = 13.5 \qquad 1.35 \times 100 = 135$$
$$1.35 \times 1000 = 1350$$

$$23 \times 10 = 230 \qquad 23 \times 100 = 2300$$
$$23 \times 1,000,000 = 23,000,000$$

Key Fact B9

To divide any decimal or whole number by a power of 10, move the decimal point as many places to the left as there are 0's in the power of 10, filling in with 0's if necessary.

$$67.8 \div 10 = 6.78 \qquad 67.8 \div 100 = 0.678$$
$$67.8 \div 1000 = 0.0678$$

$$14 \div 10 = 1.4 \qquad 14 \div 100 = 0.14$$
$$14 \div 1,000,000 = 0.000014$$

On the SAT, you *never* have to round off decimal answers. On grid-ins just enter the number, putting in as many digits after the decimal point as fit. For example, enter 3.125 as $\boxed{3}.\boxed{1}\boxed{2}$ and .1488 as $\boxed{.}\boxed{1}\boxed{4}\boxed{8}$. However, you do have to know how to round off, because *occasionally* there is a question about that procedure.

Key Fact B10

To *round off* a decimal number to any place, follow these rules, which are fully explained with examples in the table below.

- **Keep all of the digits to the left of the specified place.**
- **In that place, keep the digit if the next digit is < 5, and increase that digit by 1 if the next digit is ≥ 5. (*Note:* 9 increased by 1 is 10: put down the 0 and carry the 1.)**
- **If there are still digits to the left of the decimal point, change them to 0's and eliminate the decimal point and everything that follows it.**
- **If you are at or beyond the decimal point, stop: don't write any more digits.**

For example, here is how to round off 3815.296 to any place.

Round to the Nearest:	Procedure	Answer
thousand	The digit in the thousands place is 3; since the next digit (8) is ≥ 5, increase the 3 to a 4; fill in the 3 places to the left of the decimal point with 0's.	4000
hundred	The digit in the hundreds place is 8; keep everything to the left of it, and keep the 8 since the next digit (1) is < 5; fill in 0's to the left of the decimal point.	3800
ten	The digit in the tens place is 1; keep everything to the left of it, and increase the 1 to a 2 since the next digit (5) is ≥ 5; fill in 0's to the left of the decimal point.	3820
one	The digit in the ones place is 5; keep everything to the left of it, and keep the 5 since the next digit (2) is < 5; there are no more places to the left of the decimal point, so stop.	3815
tenth	The digit in the tenths place is 2; keep everything to the left of it, and increase the 2 to a 3 since the next digit (9) is ≥ 5; you are beyond the decimal point, so stop.	3815.3
hundredth	The digit in the hundredths place is 9; keep everything to the left of it, and, since the next digit (6) is ≥ 5, increase the 9 to a 10; put down the 0 and carry a 1 into the tenths place: 0.29 becomes 0.30; since you are beyond the decimal point, stop.	3815.30

➥ **Example 4**_____

When 423,890 is rounded off to the nearest thousand, how many digits will be changed?

(A) 1
(B) 2
(C) 3
(D) 4

Solution. When 423,890 is rounded off to the nearest thousand, **3** digits are changed: 424,000 **(C).**

Arithmetic Operations with Fractions

Key Fact B11

To multiply two fractions, multiply their numerators and multiply their denominators.

$$\frac{3}{5} \times \frac{4}{7} = \frac{3 \times 4}{5 \times 7} = \frac{12}{35}$$

To multiply a fraction by any other number, write that number as a fraction whose denominator is 1.

$$\frac{3}{5} \times 7 = \frac{3}{5} \times \frac{7}{1} = \frac{21}{5} \qquad \frac{3}{4} \times \pi = \frac{3}{4} \times \frac{\pi}{1} = \frac{3\pi}{4}$$

TACTIC B1 **Before multiplying fractions, reduce. You may reduce by dividing any numerator and any denominator by a common factor.**

➡ **Example 5**_____

Express the product $\frac{3}{4} \times \frac{8}{9} \times \frac{15}{16}$ in lowest terms.

Solution. If you just multiply the numerators and denominators (with a calculator, of course), you get $\frac{360}{576}$, which is a nuisance to reduce. Also, dividing on your calculator won't help, since your answer is supposed to be a fraction in lowest terms. It is better to use TACTIC B1 and reduce first:

$$\frac{\overset{1}{\cancel{3}}}{4} \times \frac{\overset{1}{\cancel{8}}}{\underset{\underset{1}{\cancel{3}}}{\cancel{9}}} \times \frac{\overset{5}{\cancel{15}}}{\underset{2}{\cancel{16}}} = \frac{1 \times 1 \times 5}{4 \times 1 \times 2} = \frac{5}{8}$$

TACTIC B2 **When a problem requires you to find a fraction of a number, multiply.**

➡ **Example 6**_____

If $\frac{4}{7}$ of the 350 sophomores at Adams High School are girls, and $\frac{7}{8}$ of the girls play on a team, how many sophomore girls do NOT play on a team?

 Solution. There are $\frac{4}{7} \times 350 = 200$ sophomore girls.

Of these, $\frac{7}{8} \times 200 = 175$ play on a team. Then, $200 - 175 = $ **25** do not play on a team.

How should you multiply $\frac{4}{7} \times 350$? If you can do this mentally, you should:

$$\frac{4}{\cancel{7}} \times \overset{50}{\cancel{350}} = 200$$
$$\underset{1}{}$$

The next step, however, requires you to multiply $\frac{7}{8}$ by 200, and more likely than not you don't *immediately* see that 200 divided by 8 is 25 or that 7 times 25 equals 175:

$$\frac{7}{\overset{}{\underset{1}{8}}} \times \overset{25}{\cancel{200}} = 175$$

For any step that you can't do instantly, you should use your calculator:

$$(4 \div 7) \times 350 \times (7 \div 8) = 175.$$

 CALCULATOR HINT

If you are going to use your calculator on a problem, don't bother reducing anything. Given the choice of multiplying $\frac{48}{128} \times 80$ or $\frac{3}{8} \times 80$, you would prefer the second option, but for your *calculator* the first one is just as easy.

The *reciprocal* of any nonzero number, x, is the number $\frac{1}{x}$. The reciprocal of the fraction $\frac{a}{b}$ is the fraction $\frac{b}{a}$.

Key Fact B13

To divide any number by a fraction, multiply the number by the reciprocal of the fraction.

$$20 \div \frac{2}{3} = \frac{\overset{10}{\cancel{20}}}{1} \times \frac{3}{\underset{1}{\cancel{2}}} = 30 \qquad \frac{3}{5} \div \frac{2}{3} = \frac{3}{5} \times \frac{3}{2} = \frac{9}{10}$$

$$\sqrt{2} \div \frac{2}{3} = \frac{\sqrt{2}}{1} \times \frac{3}{2} = \frac{3\sqrt{2}}{2}$$

➡ **Example 7**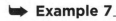

In the meat department of a supermarket, 100 pounds of chopped meat was divided into packages, each of which weighed $\frac{4}{7}$ pound. How many packages were there?

Solution. $100 \div \frac{4}{7} = \frac{\overset{25}{\cancel{100}}}{1} \times \frac{7}{\underset{1}{\cancel{4}}} = \mathbf{175}$

Key Fact B14

To add or subtract fractions with the same denominator, add or subtract the numerators and keep the denominator.

$$\frac{4}{9}+\frac{1}{9}=\frac{5}{9} \quad \text{and} \quad \frac{4}{9}-\frac{1}{9}=\frac{3}{9}=\frac{1}{3}$$

To add or subtract fractions with different denominators, first rewrite the fractions as equivalent fractions with the same denominator.

$$\frac{1}{6}+\frac{3}{4}=\frac{2}{12}+\frac{9}{12}=\frac{11}{12}$$

Note: The *easiest* denominator to find is the product of the denominators ($6 \times 4 = 24$, in this example), but the *best* denominator to use is the *least common denominator*, which is the least common multiple (LCM) of the denominators (12 in this case). Using the least common denominator minimizes the amount of reducing that is necessary to express the answer in lowest terms.

Key Fact B15

If $\frac{a}{b}$ is the fraction of the whole that satisfies some property, then $1 - \frac{a}{b}$ is the fraction of the whole that does *not* satisfy it.

➡ **Example 8**

In a jar, $\frac{1}{2}$ of the marbles are red, $\frac{1}{4}$ are white, and $\frac{1}{5}$ are blue.

What fraction of the marbles are neither red, white, nor blue?

Solution. The red, white, and blue marbles constitute

$$\frac{1}{2}+\frac{1}{4}+\frac{1}{5}=\frac{10}{20}+\frac{5}{20}+\frac{4}{20}=\frac{19}{20}$$

of the total, so

$$1-\frac{19}{20}=\frac{20}{20}-\frac{19}{20}=\mathbf{\frac{1}{20}}$$

of the marbles are neither red, white, nor blue.

➡ **Example 9**

Ali ate $\frac{1}{3}$ of a cake and Jason ate $\frac{1}{4}$ of it. What fraction of the cake was still uneaten?

➡ **Example 10**

Ali ate $\frac{1}{3}$ of a cake and Jason ate $\frac{1}{4}$ of what was left. What fraction of the cake was still uneaten?

CAUTION: Be sure to read questions carefully. In Example 9, Jason ate $\frac{1}{4}$ of the cake. In Example 10, however, he ate only $\frac{1}{4}$ of the $\frac{2}{3}$ that was left after Ali had her piece.

He ate $\frac{1}{\overset{}{\underset{2}{4}}} \times \overset{1}{\frac{2}{3}} = \frac{1}{6}$ of the cake.

Solution 9. $\frac{1}{3} + \frac{1}{4} = \frac{4}{12} + \frac{3}{12} = \frac{7}{12}$ of the cake was eaten, and $1 - \frac{7}{12} = \frac{5}{12}$ was uneaten.

Solution 10. $\frac{1}{3} + \frac{1}{6} = \frac{2}{6} + \frac{1}{6} = \frac{3}{6} = \frac{1}{2}$ of the cake was eaten, and the other $\frac{1}{2}$ was uneaten.

Complex Fractions

A **complex fraction** is a fraction, such as $\dfrac{1 + \frac{1}{6}}{2 - \frac{3}{4}}$, that has one or more fractions in its numerator or denominator or both.

Key Fact B16

There are two ways to simplify a complex fraction:

1. **Multiply *every* term in the numerator and denominator by the least common multiple of all the denominators that appear in the fraction.**
2. **Simplify the numerator and the denominator, and divide.**

To simplify $\dfrac{1 + \frac{1}{6}}{2 - \frac{3}{4}}$, multiply each term by 12, the LCM of 6 and 4:

$$\frac{12(1) + \overset{2}{\cancel{12}}\left(\frac{1}{\cancel{6}}\right)^{1}}{12(2) - \overset{3}{\cancel{12}}\left(\frac{3}{\cancel{4}}\right)_{1}} = \frac{12 + 2}{24 - 9} = \frac{14}{15}$$

or write

$$\frac{1 + \frac{1}{6}}{2 - \frac{3}{4}} = \frac{\frac{7}{6}}{\frac{5}{4}} = \frac{7}{\cancel{6}_{3}} \times \frac{\overset{2}{\cancel{4}}}{5} = \frac{14}{15}$$

 CALCULATOR SHORTCUT

Remember that, on the calculator section of the SAT, if you ever get stuck on a fraction problem, you can always convert the fractions to decimals and do all the work on your calculator.

EXERCISES ON FRACTIONS AND DECIMALS

Multiple-Choice Questions

1. A French class has 12 boys and 18 girls. Boys are what fraction of the class?

   (A) $\frac{2}{5}$

   (B) $\frac{3}{5}$

   (C) $\frac{2}{3}$

   (D) $\frac{3}{4}$

2. For how many integers, a, between 30 and 40 is it true that $\frac{5}{a}$, $\frac{8}{a}$, and $\frac{13}{a}$ are all in lowest terms?

   (A) 1
   (B) 2
   (C) 3
   (D) 4

3. $\frac{1}{4}$ is the average (arithmetic mean) of $\frac{1}{5}$ and what number?

   (A) $\frac{1}{20}$

   (B) $\frac{3}{10}$

   (C) $\frac{1}{3}$

   (D) $\frac{9}{20}$

4. If $\frac{3}{11}$ of a number is 22, what is $\frac{6}{11}$ of that number?

   (A) 11
   (B) 12
   (C) 33
   (D) 44

5. What fractional part of a week is 98 hours?

   (A) $\frac{24}{98}$

   (B) $\frac{1}{2}$

   (C) $\frac{4}{7}$

   (D) $\frac{7}{12}$

6. $\frac{5}{8}$ of 24 is equal to $\frac{15}{7}$ of what number?

   (A) 7
   (B) 15
   (C) $\frac{7}{225}$

   (D) $\frac{225}{7}$

7. Which of the following is less than $\frac{5}{9}$?

   (A) $\frac{5}{8}$

   (B) $\frac{21}{36}$

   (C) $\frac{25}{45}$

   (D) $\frac{55}{100}$

8. Which of the following is (are) greater than x when $x = \frac{9}{11}$?

   I. $\frac{1}{x}$

   II. $\frac{x+1}{x}$

   III. $\frac{x+1}{x-1}$

   (A) I only
   (B) II only
   (C) I and II only
   (D) I, II, and III

9. Which of the following statements is true?

(A) $\dfrac{3}{8} < \dfrac{4}{11} < \dfrac{5}{13}$

(B) $\dfrac{4}{11} < \dfrac{3}{8} < \dfrac{5}{13}$

(C) $\dfrac{5}{13} < \dfrac{4}{11} < \dfrac{3}{8}$

(D) $\dfrac{4}{11} < \dfrac{5}{13} < \dfrac{3}{8}$

10. If $a = 0.99$, which of the following is (are) less than a?

   I. $\sqrt{a}$

   II. a^2

   III. $\dfrac{1}{a}$

(A) None
(B) I only
(C) II only
(D) III only

11. For the final step in a calculation, Paul accidentally divided by 1000 instead of multiplying by 1000. What should he do to his answer to correct it?

(A) Multiply it by 1000.
(B) Multiply it by 100,000.
(C) Multiply it by 1,000,000.
(D) Square it.

Grid-in Questions

12. One day at Central High School, $\dfrac{1}{12}$ of the students were absent, and $\dfrac{1}{5}$ of those present went on a field trip. If the number of students staying in school was 704, how many students are enrolled at Central High?

13. What is a possible value of x if $\dfrac{3}{5} < \dfrac{1}{x} < \dfrac{7}{9}$?

14. If $7a = 3$ and $3b = 7$, what is the value of $\dfrac{a}{b}$?

15. If $A = \{1, 2, 3\}$, $B = \{2, 3, 4\}$, and C is the set consisting of all the fractions whose numerators are in A and whose denominators are in B, what is the product of all of the numbers in C?

Answer Key

1.	**A**	3.	**B**	5.	**D**	7.	**D**	9.	**B**	11.	**C**
2.	**C**	4.	**D**	6.	**A**	8.	**C**	10.	**C**		

12.

9	6	0	

13.

1	.	3	3

$$1.28 < x < 1.67$$

14.

9	/	4	9

or

.	1	8	3

15.

1	/	6	4

or

.	0	1	5

Answers Explained

1. **(A)** The class has 30 students, of whom 12 are boys. The boys make up $\frac{12}{30} = \frac{2}{5}$ of the class.

2. **(C)** If a is even, then $\frac{8}{a}$ is *not* in lowest terms, since both a and 8 are divisible by 2. The only possibilities are 31, 33, 35, 37, and 39, but $\frac{5}{35} = \frac{1}{7}$ and $\frac{13}{39} = \frac{1}{3}$, so only 31, 33, and 37 (that is, 3 integers) remain.

3. **(B)** The average of $\frac{1}{5}$ and another number, x, is $\dfrac{\frac{1}{5} + x}{2} = \frac{1}{4}$.

   Multiplying both sides by 2 yields

   $$\frac{1}{5} + x = \frac{1}{2} \Rightarrow x = \frac{1}{2} - \frac{1}{5} = \frac{5}{10} - \frac{2}{10} = \frac{3}{10}$$

4. **(D)** Don't bother writing an equation for this one; just think. You know that $\frac{3}{11}$ of the number is 22, and $\frac{6}{11}$ of a number is twice as much as $\frac{3}{11}$ of it: $2 \times 22 = 44$.

5. **(D)** There are 24 hours in a day and 7 days in a week, so there are $24 \times 7 = 168$ hours in a week: $\frac{98}{168} = \frac{7}{12}$.

6. **(A)** If x is the number,

   $$\frac{15}{7}x = \frac{5}{\cancel{8}} \times \overset{3}{\cancel{24}} = 15$$

   Then, $\frac{15}{7}x = 15$, which means (dividing by 15) that $\frac{1}{7}x = 1$, so $x = 7$.

7. **(D)** Use your calculator: $\frac{5}{9} = 0.555555....$ Choice (C) is also equal to 0.555555...; choices (A) and (B) are both greater; only $\frac{55}{100} = 0.55$ is less.

8. **(C)**
   - The reciprocal of a number less than 1 is greater than 1. (I is true.)
   - $\frac{x+1}{x} = 1 + \frac{1}{x}$, which is greater than 1. (II is true.)
   - When $x = \frac{9}{11}$, $x + 1$ is positive, whereas $x - 1$ is negative. Then $\frac{x+1}{x-1}$ is negative, and hence less than 1. (III is false.)

9. **(B)** Use your calculator to convert each fraction to a decimal:

   $$\frac{4}{11} = 0.3636..., \quad \frac{3}{8} = 0.375, \quad \frac{5}{13} = 0.3846....$$

   This is the correct order.

10. **(C)**
- Since $a < 1$, then $\sqrt{a} > a$. (I is false.)
- Since $a < 1$, then $a^2 < a$. (II is true.)
- The reciprocal of a number less than 1 is greater than 1. (III is false.)

11. **(C)** Multiplying the incorrect answer by 1000 would undo the final division Paul made—the point at which he should have multiplied by 1000. Then, to correct his error, he would have to multiply again by 1000. In all, he should multiply by $1000 \times 1000 = 1,000,000$.

12. **960** If s is the number of students enrolled, $\frac{1}{12}s$ is the number who were absent, and $\frac{11}{12}s$ is the number who were present. Since $\frac{1}{5}$ of those present went on a field trip, $\frac{4}{5}$ of them stayed in school. Therefore,

$$704 = \frac{\overset{1}{\cancel{4}}}{5} \times \frac{11}{\underset{3}{\cancel{12}}}s = \frac{11}{15}s$$

$$s = 704 \div \frac{11}{15} = 704 \times \frac{15}{11} = 960.$$

13. **1.28 < x < 1.67** Since $\frac{3}{5} = .6$ and $\frac{7}{9} = .777...$, $\frac{1}{x}$ can be any number between .6 and .777. If $\frac{1}{x} = .7 = \frac{7}{10}$, then $x = \frac{10}{7}$ or 1.42; if $\frac{1}{x} = .75 = \frac{3}{4}$, then $x = \frac{4}{3}$ or 1.33; and so on.

14. $\frac{9}{49}$ **or .183** Since $7a = 3$ and $3b = 7$, then $a = \frac{3}{7}$ and $b = \frac{7}{3}$. So

$$\frac{a}{b} = \frac{3}{7} \div \frac{7}{3} = \frac{3}{7} \times \frac{3}{7} = \frac{9}{49} \text{ or } .183$$

15. $\frac{1}{64}$ **or .015** Nine fractions are formed:

$$\frac{1}{2}, \frac{1}{3}, \frac{1}{4}, \frac{2}{2}, \frac{2}{3}, \frac{2}{4}, \frac{3}{2}, \frac{3}{3}, \frac{3}{4}$$

When you multiply, the three 2's and the three 3's in the numerators cancel with the three 2's and three 3's in the denominators. Then, the numerator is 1 and the denominator is $4 \times 4 \times 4 = 64$. Grid in $\frac{1}{64}$ or .015.

HELPFUL HINT

A percent is just a fraction whose denominator is 100:

$x\% = \dfrac{x}{100}$.

The word *percent* means "hundredth." The symbol "%" is used to express the word *percent*. For example, "17 percent" means "17 hundredths" and can be written with a % symbol, as a fraction, or as a decimal:

$$17\% = \frac{17}{100} = 0.17$$

Key Fact C1

To convert a percent to a decimal, or a percent to a fraction, follow these rules:

1. **To convert a percent to a decimal, drop the % symbol and move the decimal point two places to the left, adding 0's if necessary. (Remember: it is assumed that there is a decimal point to the right of any whole number.)**
2. **To convert a percent to a fraction, drop the % symbol, write the number over 100, and reduce.**

$$25\% = 0.25 = \frac{25}{100} = \frac{1}{4} \qquad 100\% = 1.00 = \frac{100}{100}$$

$$12.5\% = 0.125 = \frac{12.5}{100} = \frac{125}{1000} = \frac{1}{8}$$

$$1\% = 0.01 = \frac{1}{100} \qquad \frac{1}{2}\% = 0.5\% = 0.005 = \frac{.5}{100} = \frac{1}{200}$$

$$250\% = 2.50 = \frac{250}{100} = \frac{5}{2}$$

Key Fact C2

To convert a decimal to a percent, or a fraction to a percent, follow these rules:

1. **To convert a decimal to a percent, move the decimal point two places to the right, adding 0's if necessary, and add the % symbol.**
2. **To convert a fraction to a percent, first convert the fraction to a decimal, then do step 1.**

$$0.375 = 37.5\% \qquad 0.3 = 30\% \qquad 1.25 = 125\% \qquad 10 = 1000\%$$

$$\frac{3}{4} = 0.75 = 75\% \qquad \frac{1}{3} = 0.33333\ldots = 33.333\ldots\% = 33\frac{1}{3}\%$$

$$\frac{1}{5} = 0.2 = 20\%$$

You should be familiar with the following basic conversions:

$\frac{1}{2} = 50\%$	$\frac{1}{10} = 10\%$	$\frac{6}{10} = \frac{3}{5} = 60\%$
$\frac{1}{3} = 33\frac{1}{3}\%$	$\frac{2}{10} = \frac{1}{5} = 20\%$	$\frac{7}{10} = 70\%$
$\frac{2}{3} = 66\frac{2}{3}\%$	$\frac{3}{10} = 30\%$	$\frac{8}{10} = \frac{4}{5} = 80\%$
$\frac{1}{4} = 25\%$	$\frac{4}{10} = \frac{2}{5} = 40\%$	$\frac{9}{10} = 90\%$
$\frac{3}{4} = 75\%$	$\frac{5}{10} = \frac{1}{2} = 50\%$	$\frac{10}{10} = 1 = 100\%$

Knowing these conversions can help you to solve many problems more quickly. For example, the fastest way to find 25% of 32 is to know that $25\% = \frac{1}{4}$, and that $\frac{1}{4}$ of 32 is 8, *not* to use your calculator.

It is important to keep in mind, however, that *any* problem involving percents can be done on your calculator: to find 25% of 32, write 25% as a decimal and multiply: $32 \times .25 = 8$. Here is another example of mental math being much faster than calculator math. Since $10\% = \frac{1}{10}$, to take 10% of a number, just divide by 10 by moving the decimal point one place to the left: 10% of 60 is 6. Also, since 5% is half of 10%, then 5% of 60 is 3 (half of 6); and since 30% is 3 times 10%, then 30% of 60 is 18 (3×6).

Practice this shortcut, because improving your ability to do mental math will add valuable points to your score on the SAT.

Solving Percent Problems

Now, consider these three questions:

   (i) What is 45% of 200?
  (ii) 90 is 45% of what number?
 (iii) 90 is what percent of 200?

Each question can be answered easily by using your calculator, but you must first set the question up properly so that you know what to multiply or divide. In each case, there is one unknown; call it x. Now, just translate each sentence, replacing "is" by "=" and the unknown by x.

   (i) $x = 45\%$ of $200 \Rightarrow x = 0.45 \times 200 = 90$
  (ii) $90 = 45\%$ of $x \Rightarrow 90 = 0.45x \Rightarrow x = 90 \div 0.45 = 200$

 (iii) $90 = x\%$ of $200 \Rightarrow 90 = \dfrac{x}{\cancel{100}_{1}}(\cancel{200}^{2}) \Rightarrow x = 45$

Many students have been taught to answer questions such as these by writing this proportion:

$$\frac{is}{of} = \frac{percent}{100}$$

To use this method, think of *is, of,* and *percent* as variables. In each percent problem you are given two variables and asked to find the third, which you label x. Of course, you then solve the equation by cross-multiplying.

For example, the three problems solved above could be handled as follows:

   (i) <u>What is</u> 45% of 200? (Let x = the *is* number.)

$$\frac{x}{200} = \frac{45}{100} \Rightarrow 100x = 45(200) = 9000 \Rightarrow x = 90$$

  (ii) 90 is 45% <u>of what number</u>? (Let x = the *of* number.)

$$\frac{90}{x} = \frac{45}{100} \Rightarrow 9000 = 45x \Rightarrow x = 200$$

 (iii) 90 is <u>what %</u> of 200? (Let x = the *percent*.)

$$\frac{90}{200} = \frac{x}{100} \Rightarrow 200x = 9000 \Rightarrow x = 45$$

Example 1

Brian gave 20% of his baseball cards to Scott and 15% to Adam. If he still had 520 cards, how many did he have originally?

 Solution. Originally, Brian had 100% of the cards (all of them). After he gave away 35% of them, he had 100% – 35% = 65% of them left. Then 520 is 65% of what number?

$$520 = .65x \Rightarrow x = 520 \div .65 = \mathbf{800}$$

Example 2

After Michael gave 110 baseball cards to Sally and 75 to Heidi, he had 315 left. What percent of his cards did Michael give away?

 Solution. Michael gave away a total of 185 cards and had 315 left. Therefore, he started with 185 + 315 = 500 cards. Then 185 is what percent of 500?

$$185 = \frac{x}{\cancel{100}_{1}}(\cancel{500}^{5}) \Rightarrow 5x = 185 \Rightarrow x = 185 \div 5 = \mathbf{37}$$

Michael gave away 37% of his cards.

Since *percent* means "hundredth," the easiest number to use in any percent problem is 100:

$$a\% \text{ of } 100 = \frac{a}{100}(100) = a$$

> **Key Fact C3**

For any positive number a: $a\%$ of 100 is a.

For example, 11.2% of 100 is 11.2; 500% of 100 is 500; and $\frac{1}{2}\%$ of 100 = $\frac{1}{2}$.

TACTIC

 In any problem involving percents, use the number 100.

Example 3

In 2000 the populations of town A and town B were the same. From 2000 to 2010, however, the population of town A increased by 60% while the population of town B decreased by 60%. In 2010, the population of town B was what percent of the population of town A?

(A) 25%
(B) 36%
(C) 40%
(D) 60%

Solution. In your math class, you would let x be the population of town A in 2000 and then proceed to set up an algebra problem. *Don't do that on the SAT.* Assume that the populations of both towns were 100 in 2000. Then, since 60% of 100 is 60, in 2010 the populations were

$100 + 60 = 160$ (town A) and $100 - 60 = 40$ (town B). Then, in 2010, town B's population was $\frac{40}{160} = \frac{1}{4} = 25\%$ of town A's. Choice **(A)** is correct.

Since $a\%$ of b is $\frac{a}{100}(b) = \frac{ab}{100}$, and $b\%$ of a is $\frac{b}{100}(a) = \frac{ba}{100}$, KEY FACT C4 follows.

Key Fact C4

For any positive numbers a and b: $a\%$ of $b = b\%$ of a.

Percent Increase and Decrease

Key Fact C5

The *percent increase* of a quantity is $\dfrac{\text{actual increase}}{\text{original amount}} \times 100\%$.

The *percent decrease* of a quantity is $\dfrac{\text{actual decrease}}{\text{original amount}} \times 100\%$.

For example:

■ If the price of a DVD player rises from \$80 to \$100, the actual increase is \$20, and the percent increase is

$$\frac{\overset{1}{\cancel{20}}}{\underset{4}{\cancel{80}}} \times 100\% = \frac{1}{4} \times 100\% = 25\%$$

■ If a \$100 DVD player is on sale for \$80, the actual decrease in price is \$20, and the percent decrease is

$$\frac{20}{\cancel{100}} \times \cancel{100}\% = 20\%$$

Note that the percent increase in going from 80 to 100 is not the same as the percent decrease in going from 100 to 80.

Key Fact C6

If $a < b$, the percent increase in going from a to b is *always* greater than the percent decrease in going from b to a.

Key Fact C7

■ To increase a number by $k\%$, multiply it by $(1 + k\%)$.
■ To decrease a number by $k\%$, multiply it by $(1 - k\%)$.

For example:

■ The value of a \$1600 investment after a 25% increase is \$1600(1 + 25%) = \$1600(1.25) = \$2000.

■ If the investment then loses 25% of its value, it is worth $2000(1 − 25%) = $2000(.75) = $1500.

Note that, after a 25% increase followed by a 25% decrease, the value is $1500, $100 less than the original amount.

 Example 4_____

From 2013 to 2014, the number of applicants to a college increased 15% to 5060. How many applicants were there in 2013?

(A) 759
(B) 4301
(C) 4400
(D) 5819

 Solution. The number of applicants in 2013 was 5060 ÷ 1.15 = **4400**   **(C)**.

Note: Some students find percent problems like Example 4 to be harder than other types. Now, you should be able to solve them correctly. If, however, you get stuck on a problem like this on the SAT, you still should answer it. In Example 4, since the number of applicants increased from 2013 to 2014, the number in 2013 was clearly fewer than 5060, so eliminate (D). Also, 759 (A) is much too small, leaving only (B) and (C) as reasonable choices. Therefore, do not make a wild guess—make an educated one. This situation, in which some of the choices are absurd, is commonplace on the SAT. (See TACTIC 8.)

CALCULATOR SHORTCUT

If a number is the result of increasing another number by k%, then, to find the original number, divide by $(1 + k$%). Also, if a number is the result of decreasing another number by k%, then to find the original number, divide it by $(1 - k$%).

CAUTION: Percents over 100%, which come up most often on questions involving percent increases, are confusing for many students. Be sure you understand that 100% of a particular number is that number, 200% of a number is 2 times the number, and 1000% of a number is 10 times the number. For example, if the value of an investment rises from $1000 to $5000, the investment is now worth 5 times, or 500%, as much as it was originally; but there has been only a *400%* increase in value:

$$\frac{\text{actual increase}}{\text{original amount}} \times 100\% = \frac{4000}{1000} \times 100\% = 4 \times 100\% = 400\%.$$

➡ **Example 5**_____

The population of a town doubled every 10 years from 1980 to 2010. What was the percent increase in population during this time?

Solution. The population doubled 3 times from, say, 100 to 200 to 400 to 800. Therefore, the population in 2010 was 8 times the population in 1980, but this was an increase of 700 people, or **700%**.

Multiple-Choice Questions

1. Charlie bought a $60 radio on sale at 5% off. How much did he pay, including 5% sales tax?

   (A) $57.00
   (B) $57.75
   (C) $59.85
   (D) $60.00

2. If a is a positive number, 400% of a is what percent of $400a$?

   (A) 0.1
   (B) 1
   (C) 10
   (D) 100

3. What percent of 50 is b?

   (A) $\dfrac{b}{2}$
   (B) $\dfrac{50}{b}$
   (C) $\dfrac{2}{b}$
   (D) $2b$

4. At Harry's Discount Hardware everything is sold for 20% less than the price marked. If Harry buys tool kits for $80, what price should he mark them if he wants to make a 20% profit on his cost?

   (A) $96
   (B) $100
   (C) $120
   (D) $125

5. 9 is $\dfrac{1}{3}$% of what number?

   (A) .27
   (B) 3
   (C) 300
   (D) 2,700

6. Mr. Howard was planning on depositing a certain amount of money each month into a college fund for his children. He then decided not to make any contributions during June and July. To make the same annual contribution that he had originally planned, by what percent should he increase his monthly deposits?

   (A) $16\dfrac{2}{3}$%
   (B) 20%
   (C) 25%
   (D) $33\dfrac{1}{3}$%

7. During his second week on the job, Jason earned $110. This represented a 25% increase over his earnings of the previous week. How much did he earn during his first week of work?

   (A) $82.50
   (B) $85.00
   (C) $88.00
   (D) $137.50

8. What is 10% of 20% of 30%?

   (A) 0.006%
   (B) 0.6%
   (C) 6%
   (D) 60%

9. If 1 micron = 10,000 angstroms, then 100 angstroms is what percent of 10 microns?

   (A) 0.001%
   (B) 0.01%
   (C) 0.1%
   (D) 1%

10. On a test consisting of 80 questions, Marie answered 75% of the first 60 questions correctly. What percent of the other 20 questions did she need to answer correctly for her grade on the entire exam to be 80%?

    (A) 87.5%
    (B) 90%
    (C) 95%
    (D) 100%

Grid-in Questions

11. A jar contains 2000 marbles. If 61.5% of them are red, 27.2% of them are white, and 10% of them are blue, how many are neither red, white, nor blue?

12. If 25 students took an exam and 4 of them failed, what percent of them passed?

13. There are twice as many girls as boys in an English class. If 30% of the girls and 45% of the boys have already handed in their book reports, what percent of the students have not yet handed in their reports?

14. During a sale a clerk was putting a new price tag on each item. On one radio, he accidentally raised the price by 15% instead of lowering the price by 15%. As a result the price on the tag was $45 too high. What was the original price, in dollars, of the radio?

15. If a person has an income of $100,000, what percent of his income does he pay in federal income tax if the tax rate is as given below?

    15% of the first $30,000 of income,

    28% of the next $30,000 of income, and

    31% of all income in excess of $60,000.

16. The price of a can of soup was increased by 20%. How many cans can be purchased for the amount of money that used to buy 300 cans?

```
    ⊘  ⊘
⊙  ⊙  ⊙  ⊙
   ⓪  ⓪  ⓪
①  ①  ①  ①
②  ②  ②  ②
③  ③  ③  ③
④  ④  ④  ④
⑤  ⑤  ⑤  ⑤
⑥  ⑥  ⑥  ⑥
⑦  ⑦  ⑦  ⑦
⑧  ⑧  ⑧  ⑧
⑨  ⑨  ⑨  ⑨
```

17. An art dealer bought a painting for $1000 and later sold it for $10,000. By what percent did the value of the painting increase?

```
    ⊘  ⊘
⊙  ⊙  ⊙  ⊙
   ⓪  ⓪  ⓪
①  ①  ①  ①
②  ②  ②  ②
③  ③  ③  ③
④  ④  ④  ④
⑤  ⑤  ⑤  ⑤
⑥  ⑥  ⑥  ⑥
⑦  ⑦  ⑦  ⑦
⑧  ⑧  ⑧  ⑧
⑨  ⑨  ⑨  ⑨
```

18. Jar B has 20% more marbles than jar A. What percent of the marbles in jar B have to be moved to jar A in order that the number of marbles in each jar will be the same?

```
    ⊘  ⊘
⊙  ⊙  ⊙  ⊙
   ⓪  ⓪  ⓪
①  ①  ①  ①
②  ②  ②  ②
③  ③  ③  ③
④  ④  ④  ④
⑤  ⑤  ⑤  ⑤
⑥  ⑥  ⑥  ⑥
⑦  ⑦  ⑦  ⑦
⑧  ⑧  ⑧  ⑧
⑨  ⑨  ⑨  ⑨
```

19. Wendy drew a square. She then erased it and drew a second square whose sides were 3 times the sides of the first square. The area of the second square is k% greater than the area of the first square. What is k?

```
    ⊘  ⊘
⊙  ⊙  ⊙  ⊙
   ⓪  ⓪  ⓪
①  ①  ①  ①
②  ②  ②  ②
③  ③  ③  ③
④  ④  ④  ④
⑤  ⑤  ⑤  ⑤
⑥  ⑥  ⑥  ⑥
⑦  ⑦  ⑦  ⑦
⑧  ⑧  ⑧  ⑧
⑨  ⑨  ⑨  ⑨
```

20. In a large jar full of jelly beans, 30% of them are red, and 40% of the red jelly beans are cherry. If 25% of the non-cherry-flavored red jelly beans are raspberry, what percent of all the jelly beans are either cherry or raspberry?

```
    ⊘  ⊘
⊙  ⊙  ⊙  ⊙
   ⓪  ⓪  ⓪
①  ①  ①  ①
②  ②  ②  ②
③  ③  ③  ③
④  ④  ④  ④
⑤  ⑤  ⑤  ⑤
⑥  ⑥  ⑥  ⑥
⑦  ⑦  ⑦  ⑦
⑧  ⑧  ⑧  ⑧
⑨  ⑨  ⑨  ⑨
```

Answer Key

1. **C**   3. **D**   5. **D**   7. **C**   9. **C**
2. **B**   4. **C**   6. **B**   8. **B**   10. **C**

11. **2 6**

12. **8 4**

13. **6 5**

14. **1 5 0**

15. **2 5 . 3**

16. **2 5 0**

17. **9 0 0**

18. **8 . 3 3** or **2 5 / 3**

19. **8 0 0**

20. **1 6 . 5**

Answers Explained

1. **(C)** Since 5% of 60 is 3, Charlie saved $3, and thus paid $57 for the radio. He then had to pay 5% sales tax on the $57: .05 × 57 = 2.85, so the total cost was $57 + $2.85 = $59.85.

2. **(B)** 400% of $a = 4a$, which is 1% of $400a$.

3. **(D)** If b is x% of 50, then $\dfrac{b}{50} = \dfrac{x}{100} \Rightarrow 100b = 50x \Rightarrow x = 2b$.

4. **(C)** Since 20% of 80 is 16, Harry wants to get $96 for each tool kit he sells. What price should the tool kits be marked so that, after a 20% discount, the customer will pay $96? If x represents the marked price, then

$$0.80x = \$96 \Rightarrow x = \$96 \div .80 = \$120$$

5. **(D)** $9 = \dfrac{\frac{1}{3}}{100}\, x = \dfrac{1}{300}\, x \Rightarrow x = 9 \times 300 = 2700$

6. **(B)** Assume that Mr. Howard was going to contribute $100 each month, for an annual total of $1200. Having decided not to contribute for 2 months, he would have to contribute the $1200 in 10 monthly deposits of $120 each. This is an increase of $20, and a percent increase of $\dfrac{\text{actual increase}}{\text{original amount}} = \dfrac{20}{100} = 20\%$.

7. **(C)** To find Jason's earnings during his first week, divide his earnings of the second week by 1.25: $110 ÷ 1.25 = $88.

**If you let x represent Jason's earnings during the first week, then

$$x + 0.25x = 110 \Rightarrow 1.25x = 110$$

and so, as above, $x = 110 \div 1.25 = 88$.

8. **(B)** 10% of 20% of 30% = .10 × .20 × .30 = 0.006 = 0.6%.

9. **(C)** 1 micron = 10,000 angstroms $\Rightarrow$ 10 microns = 100,000 angstroms; then, dividing both sides by 1000 gives 100 angstroms = $\dfrac{1}{1000}$ (10 microns); and $\dfrac{1}{1000} = 0.001 = 0.1\%$.

10. **(C)** To earn 80% on the entire exam, Marie needs to correctly answer 64 questions (80% of 80). So far, she has answered 45 questions correctly (75% of 60). Therefore, on the last 20 questions she needs 64 – 45 = 19 correct answers; and $\dfrac{19}{20} = 95\%$.

11. **26** Since 61.5 + 27.2 + 10 = 98.7, then 98.7% of the marbles are red, white, or blue, and the other 100% – 98.7% = 1.3% are some other colors. Therefore:

$$1.3\% \text{ of } 2000 = 0.013 \times 2000 = 26$$

12. **84** If 4 of the 25 students failed, then the other 21 students passed, and $\dfrac{21}{25} = 0.84 = 84\%$.

13. **65** Assume that there are 100 boys and 200 girls in the class. Then, 45 boys (45% of 100) and 60 girls (30% of 200) have handed in their reports. Then, 105 of the 300 students have handed in the reports, and 300 – 105 = 195 have not. What percent of 300 is 195?

$$\dfrac{195}{300} = 0.65 = 65\%$$

14. **150** If p represents the original price, the radio was priced at $1.15p$ instead of $.85p$. Since this was a $45 difference:

$$45 = 1.15p - .85p = 0.30p \Rightarrow p = 45 \div .30 = 150$$

15. **25.3** A person with a $100,000 income would pay 15% of $30,000 plus 28% of $30,000 plus 31% of $40,000:

$$(.15 \times 30,000) + (.28 \times 30,000) + (.31 \times 40,000) = 4,500 + 8,400 + 12,400 = 25,300$$

and 25,300 is 25.3% of 100,000.

16. **250** Assume that a can of soup used to cost $1 and that it now costs $1.20 (20% more). Then 300 cans of soup used to cost $300. How many cans costing $1.20 each can be bought for $300?

$$300 \div 1.20 = 250$$

17. **900** The increase in the value of the painting was $9000, and

$$\text{percent increase} = \frac{\text{actual increase}}{\text{original cost}} \times 100\% = \frac{9000}{1000} \times 100\% = 900\%$$

18. **8.33 or $\frac{25}{3}$** Assume that there are 100 marbles in jar A and 120 in jar B. You may already see that, if 10 marbles are moved, each jar will contain 110. If not, let x be the number of marbles to be moved, and solve the equation:

$$120 - x = 100 + x \Rightarrow 20 = 2x \Rightarrow x = 10$$

Finally, 10 is what percent of 120?

$$\frac{10}{120} = \frac{1}{12} = 8\frac{1}{3}\%$$

19. **800** Assume that the sides of the first square were 1 inch long, so that the area was 1 square inch. Then, the sides of the second square were 3 inches long, and its area was 9 square inches, an increase of 8 square inches or 800%.

20. **16.5** Since 40% of the red jelly beans are cherry, 60% of the red jelly beans are not cherry. Also, 25% of 60% is 15%, so 15% of the red jelly beans are raspberry and 40% are cherry, for a total of 55%. Therefore, the raspberry and cherry jelly beans constitute 55% of the 30% of the jelly beans that are red. Finally, 55% of 30% is 16.5%.

6-D RATIOS AND PROPORTIONS

A *ratio* is a fraction that compares two quantities that are measured in the *same* units. One quantity is the numerator of the fraction, and the other quantity is the denominator.

For example, if there are 4 boys and 16 girls on the debate team, the ratio of the number of boys to the number of girls on the team is 4 to 16, or $\frac{4}{16}$, often written as 4:16. Since a ratio is a fraction, it can be reduced or converted to a decimal or a percent. The following are different ways to express the same ratio:

$$4 \text{ to } 16, \quad 4{:}16, \quad \frac{4}{16} \qquad\qquad 2 \text{ to } 8, \quad 2{:}8, \quad \frac{2}{8}$$

$$1 \text{ to } 4, \quad 1{:}4, \quad \frac{1}{4} \qquad\qquad 0.25, \quad 25\%$$

CAUTION: Saying that the ratio of boys to girls on the team is 1:4 does *not* mean that $\frac{1}{4}$ of the team members are boys. It means that, for each boy on the team there are 4 girls, so, of every 5 members of the team, 4 are girls and 1 is a boy. Boys, therefore, make up $\frac{1}{5}$ of the team, and girls $\frac{4}{5}$.

Key Fact D1

If a set of objects is divided into two groups in the ratio of *a:b*, then the first group contains $\frac{a}{a+b}$ of the objects and the second group contains $\frac{b}{a+b}$ of the objects.

➡ **Example 1** _____

Last year, the ratio of the number of math tests John passed to the number of math tests he failed was 7:3. What percent of his math tests did John pass?

Solution. John passed $\frac{7}{7+3} = \frac{7}{10}$ = **70%** of his math tests.

➡ **Example 2** _____

If 45% of the students at a college are male, what is the ratio of male students to female students?

Reminder: In problems involving percents, the best number to use is 100.

Solution. Assume that there are 100 students. Then, 45 of them are male, and 55 of them (100 – 45) are female.

The ratio of males to females is $\frac{45}{55} = \frac{9}{11}$.

If we know how many boys and girls there are in a club, then, clearly, we know not only the ratio of boys to girls, but also several other ratios. For example, if the club has 7 boys and 3 girls, the ratio of boys to girls is $\frac{7}{3}$, the ratio of girls to boys is $\frac{3}{7}$, the ratio of boys to members is $\frac{7}{10}$, the ratio of members to girls is $\frac{10}{3}$, and so on.

However, if we know a ratio, we *cannot* determine from that fact alone how many objects there are. For example, if a jar contains only red and blue marbles, and if the ratio of red marbles to blue marbles is 3:5, there *may be* 3 red marbles and 5 blue marbles, but *not necessarily*. There may be 300 red marbles and 500 blue ones, since the ratio 300:500 reduces to 3:5. In the same way, all of the following are possibilities for the distribution of the marbles:

Red	6	12	33	51	150	3000	**3x**
Blue	10	20	55	85	250	5000	**5x**

The important thing to observe is that the number of red marbles can be *any* multiple of 3, as long as the number of blue marbles is the *same* multiple of 5.

Key Fact D2

If two numbers are in the ratio of *a:b*, then, for some number *x*, the first number is *ax* and the second number is *bx*. If the ratio is in lowest terms, and if the quantities must be integers, then *x* is also an integer.

TACTIC

 In any ratio problem, write the letter *x* after each number and use some given information to solve for *x*.

➡ **Example 3**

If the ratio of boys to girls at a school picnic is 5:3, which of the following CANNOT be the number of children at the picnic?

(A) 24
(B) 40
(C) 96
(D) 150

Solution. If $5x$ and $3x$ are the number of boys and the number of girls, respectively, at the picnic, then the number of children present is $5x + 3x = 8x$. Therefore, the number of children must be a multiple of 8. Only **150 (D)** is not divisible by 8.

Note: Assume that the ratio of the number of pounds of cole slaw to the number of pounds of potato salad consumed at the school picnic was 5:3. Then, it is possible that a total of exactly 150 pounds of these foods was eaten: 93.75 pounds of cole slaw and 56.25 pounds of potato salad. In Example 3, however, 150 isn't a possible answer because there has to be a *whole number* of boys and girls.

➡ Example 4 _____

The measures of the two acute angles of a right triangle are in the ratio of 5:13. What is the measure of the larger acute angle?

Solution. Let the measure of the smaller angle be $5x$ and the measure of the larger angle be $13x$. Since the sum of the measures of the two acute angles of a right triangle is 90° (KEY FACT J3):

$$5x + 13x = 90 \Rightarrow 18x = 90 \Rightarrow x = 5$$

Therefore, the measure of the larger angle is $13 \times 5 = $ **65°**.

Ratios can be extended to three or four or more terms. For example, we can say that the ratio of freshmen to sophomores to juniors to seniors in the school band is 6:8:5:8, which means that for every 6 freshmen in the band there are 8 sophomores, 5 juniors, and 8 seniors.

Note: TACTIC D1 applies to extended ratios, as well.

➡ Example 5 _____

Frannie's Frozen Yogurt sells three flavors: vanilla, chocolate, and coffee. One day, Frannie sold 240 cones, and the ratio of vanilla to chocolate to coffee was 8:17:15. How many chocolate cones were sold that day?

Solution. Let $8x$, $17x$, and $15x$ be the number of vanilla, chocolate, and coffee cones sold, respectively. Then:

$$8x + 17x + 15x = 240 \Rightarrow 40x = 240 \Rightarrow x = 6$$

The number of chocolate cones sold was $17 \times 6 = $ **102**.

> **Key Fact D3**

KEY FACT D1 applies to extended ratios, as well. If a set of objects is divided into three groups in the ratio $a{:}b{:}c$, then the first group contains $\dfrac{a}{a+b+c}$ of the objects, the second $\dfrac{b}{a+b+c}$, and the third $\dfrac{c}{a+b+c}$.

➡ Example 6 _____

If the ratio of vanilla to chocolate to coffee cones sold at Frannie's was 8:17:15 on a particular day, what percent of the cones sold were chocolate?

Solution. Chocolate cones made up $\dfrac{17}{8+17+15} = \dfrac{17}{40} = $ **42.5%** of the total.

A jar contains a number of red (R), white (W), and blue (B) marbles. Suppose that R:W = 2:3 and W:B = 3:5. Then, for every 2 red marbles, there are 3 white ones, and for those

3 white ones, there are 5 blue ones. Then, R:B = 2:5, and we can form the extended ratio R:W:B = 2:3:5.

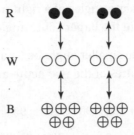

If the ratios were R:W = 2:3 and W:B = 4:5, however, we couldn't combine them as easily. From the diagram below, we see that for every 8 reds there are 15 blues, so R:B = 8:15.

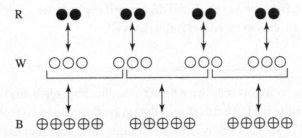

To see this without drawing a picture, we write the ratios as fractions: $\frac{R}{W} = \frac{2}{3}$ and $\frac{W}{B} = \frac{4}{5}$.

Then, we multiply the fractions:

$$\frac{R}{\cancel{W}} \times \frac{\cancel{W}}{B} = \frac{2}{3} \times \frac{4}{5} = \frac{8}{15} \quad \text{so} \quad \frac{R}{B} = \frac{8}{15}$$

Not only does this give us R:B = 8:15, but also, if we multiply both W numbers, $3 \times 4 = 12$, we can write the extended ratio: R:W:B = 8:12:15.

➡ **Example 7** _____

Jar A and jar B each contain 70 marbles, all of which are red, white, or blue.

In jar A, R:W = 2:3 and W:B = 3:5.
In jar B, R:W = 2:3 and W:B = 4:5.

What is the total number of white marbles in the two jars?

Solution. From the discussion immediately preceding this example, in jar A the extended ratio R:W:B is 2:3:5, which implies that the white marbles constitute $\frac{3}{2+3+5} = \frac{3}{10}$ of the total:

$$\frac{3}{\cancel{10}} \times \overset{7}{\cancel{70}} = 21$$

In jar B the extended ratio R:W:B is 8:12:15, so the white marbles are $\frac{12}{8+12+15} = \frac{12}{35}$ of the total:

$$\frac{12}{\cancel{35}} \times \overset{2}{\cancel{70}} = 24$$

Finally, there is a total of 21 + 24 = **45** white marbles.

A *proportion* is an equation that states that two ratios are equivalent. Since ratios are just fractions, any equation, such as $\frac{4}{6} = \frac{10}{15}$, in which each side is a single fraction is a proportion.

Usually the proportions encountered on the SAT involve one or more variables.

TACTIC D2

Solve proportions by cross-multiplying: if $\frac{a}{b} = \frac{c}{d}$, then $ad = bc$.

Several problems on the SAT can be solved by setting up proportions. These problems are usually quite easy and are among the first few in a section.

➥ **Example 8** _____

If $\frac{3}{7} = \frac{x}{84}$, what is the value of x?

 Solution. Cross-multiply: $3(84) = 7x \Rightarrow 252 = 7x \Rightarrow x = \mathbf{36}$

➥ **Example 9** _____

If $\frac{x+2}{17} = \frac{x}{16}$, what is the value of $\frac{x+6}{19}$?

Solution. Cross-multiply: $16(x + 2) = 17x \Rightarrow 16x + 32 = 17x \Rightarrow x = 32$, so

$$\frac{x+6}{19} = \frac{32+6}{19} = \frac{38}{19} = \mathbf{2}$$

➥ **Example 10** _____

A state law requires that on any field trip the ratio of the number of chaperones to the number of students must be at least 1:12. If 100 students are going on a field trip, what is the minimum number of chaperones required?

 Solution. Let x represent the number of chaperones required, and set up a proportion:

$$\frac{\text{number of chaperones}}{\text{number of students}} = \frac{1}{12} = \frac{x}{100}$$

Cross-multiply: $100 = 12x \Rightarrow x = 8.33$. This, of course, is *not* the answer since, clearly, the number of chaperones must be a whole number. Since x is greater than 8, you know that 8 chaperones will not be enough. The answer is **9**.

A *rate* is a fraction that compares two quantities that are measured in *different* units. The word *per* often appears in rate problems: miles per hour, dollars per week, cents per ounce, children per classroom, and so on.

TACTIC
D3   **Set rate problems up just like ratio problems. Then, solve the proportions by cross-multiplying.**

➡️ **Example 11** _____

Sharon read 24 pages of her book in 15 minutes. At this rate, how many pages can she read in 40 minutes?

 Solution. Handle this rate problem exactly like a ratio problem. Set up a proportion and cross-multiply:

$$\frac{\text{pages}}{\text{minutes}} = \frac{24}{15} = \frac{x}{40} \Rightarrow 15x = 40 \times 24 = 960 \Rightarrow x = \mathbf{64}$$

When the denominator in the given rate is 1 unit (1 minute, 1 mile, 1 dollar), the problem can be solved by a single division or multiplication. Consider Examples 12 and 13.

➡️ **Example 12** _____

If Jack types at the rate of 35 words per minute, how long will he take to type 987 words?

➡️ **Example 13** _____

If Jack types at the rate of 35 words per minute, how many words can he type in 85 minutes?

To solve, set up the proportions and cross-multiply.

Solution 12. $\dfrac{\text{words typed}}{\text{minutes}} = \dfrac{35}{1} = \dfrac{987}{x} \Rightarrow 35x = 987 \Rightarrow x = \dfrac{987}{35} = \mathbf{28.2}$ minutes

Solution 13. $\dfrac{\text{words typed}}{\text{minutes}} = \dfrac{35}{1} = \dfrac{x}{85} \Rightarrow x = 35 \times 85 = \mathbf{2975}$ words

Notice that, in Example 12, all that was done was to divide 987 by 35, and in Example 13, 35 was multiplied by 85. If you realize that, you don't have to introduce x and set up a proportion. You must know, however, whether to multiply or divide. If you're not absolutely positive which is correct, write the proportion; then you can't go wrong.

> **CAUTION:** In rate problems it is essential that the units in both fractions be the same.

➧ Example 14

If three apples cost 50¢, how many apples can you buy for $20?

Solution. You have to set up a proportion, but it is *not* $\frac{3}{50} = \frac{x}{20}$. In the first fraction, the denominator represents *cents*, whereas in the second fraction, the denominator represents *dollars*. The units must be the same. You can change 50 cents to 0.5 dollar, or you can change 20 dollars to 2000 cents:

$$\frac{3}{50} = \frac{x}{2000} \Rightarrow 50x = 6000 \Rightarrow x = \mathbf{120} \text{ apples}$$

On the SAT, you might see a rate problem that involves only variables. These problems are handled in exactly the same way.

➧ Example 15

If a apples cost c cents, how many apples can be bought for d dollars?

(A) $\dfrac{100d}{ac}$

(B) $\dfrac{ad}{100c}$

(C) $\dfrac{c}{100ad}$

(D) $\dfrac{100ad}{c}$

Solution. First change d dollars to $100d$ cents; then set up the proportion and cross-multiply:

$$\frac{\text{apples}}{\text{cents}} = \frac{a}{c} = \frac{x}{100d} \Rightarrow 100ad = cx \Rightarrow x = \frac{\mathbf{100ad}}{\mathbf{c}} \quad \textbf{(D)}$$

Most students find questions such as these very difficult. Be sure to do all the exercises at the end of this section, but also see TACTIC 6 in Chapter 5 for another way to handle these problems.

Notice that in rate problems, as one quantity increases or decreases, so does the other. If you are driving at 45 miles per hour, the more hours you drive, the further you go; if you drive fewer miles, less time is required.

Rate problems are examples of ***direct variation***. We say that one variable is ***directly proportional*** to a second variable if their quotient is a constant. If y is directly proportional to x, there is a constant k, such that $\frac{y}{x} = k$.

When two quantities vary directly, as one quantity increases (or decreases), so does the other. The constant is the rate of increase or decrease. In Example 11, the number of pages Sharon reads varies directly with the number of minutes she reads. Sharon's rate of reading is 1.6 pages per minute.

The quotient $\dfrac{\text{pages}}{\text{minutes}}$ is constant: $\dfrac{24}{15} = 1.6$ and $\dfrac{64}{40} = 1.6$.

➡ Example 16 _____

If p is directly proportional to q, and if $q = 12$ when $p = 8$, then what is the value of p when $q = 15$?

Solution. Since p and q are directly proportional, the quotient $\frac{p}{q}$ is a constant, so $\frac{8}{12} = \frac{p}{15}$. Cross-multiply:

$$12p = 8 \times 15 = 120 \Rightarrow p = \mathbf{10}$$

In some problems, however, as one quantity increases, the other decreases. These problems *cannot* be solved by setting up a proportion. Consider Examples 17 and 18, which look similar but must be handled differently.

➡ Example 17 _____

A hospital needs 150 pills to treat 6 patients for a week. How many pills does it need to treat 10 patients for a week?

➡ Example 18 _____

A hospital has enough pills on hand to treat 10 patients for 14 days. How long will the pills last if there are 35 patients?

Solution 17. Example 16 is a standard rate problem. The more patients there are, the more pills are needed.

The *ratio* or *quotient* remains constant:

$$\frac{150}{6} = \frac{x}{10} \Rightarrow 6x = 1500 = x = \mathbf{250}$$

In Example 18, the situation is different. With more patients, the supply of pills will last for a shorter period of time; if there were fewer patients, the supply would last longer. It is not the ratio that remains constant; it is the *product*.

Solution 18. We are told that the hospital has enough pills to last for $10 \times 14 = 140$ patient-days:

$$140 \text{ patient-days} = (10 \text{ patients}) \times (14 \text{ days})$$
$$140 \text{ patient-days} = (20 \text{ patients}) \times (7 \text{ days})$$
$$140 \text{ patient-days} = (70 \text{ patients}) \times (2 \text{ days})$$

To solve Example 18, write:

$$140 \text{ patient-days} = (35 \text{ patients}) \times (d \text{ days}) \Rightarrow d = \frac{140}{35} = \mathbf{4}$$

HELPFUL HINT

Be sure you understand the definitions of direct variation and indirect variation.

Problems like this one are examples of **inverse variation**. We say that one variable is **inversely proportional** to a second variable if their product is a constant. If y is inversely proportional to x, there is a constant k such that $xy = k$.

➡ **Example 19** _____

      If p is inversely proportional to q^2, and if $q = 2$ when $p = 6$, what is the value of
      p when $q = 6$?

Solution. Since p and q^2 are inversely proportional, the product pq^2 is a constant, so

$$6 \times 2^2 = p \times 6^2 \Rightarrow 24 = 36p \Rightarrow p = \frac{24}{36} = \frac{2}{3}$$

In Example 18, the number of patients varies inversely with the number of days that the
supply of pills lasts. The product, patients $\times$ days, is constant. Notice that, as the number of
patients increases from 10 to 20 to 70, the number of days the supply of pills lasts decreases,
from 14 to 7 to 2.

➡ **Example 20** _____

      If 15 workers can paint a certain number of houses in 24 days, how many days
      will 40 workers take, working at the same rate, to do the same job?

Solution. Clearly, the more workers there are, the less time will be required. This is an
example of inverse variation, so multiply. The job takes:

          (15 workers) $\times$ (24 days) = 360 worker-days

Then (40 workers) $\times$ (d days) = 360 worker-days.

$$40d = 360 \Rightarrow d = \mathbf{9}$$

This job will take **9** days.

Multiple-Choice Questions

1. If $\frac{2}{3}$ of the workers in an office are nonsmokers, what is the ratio of smokers to nonsmokers?

   (A) 2:5
   (B) 1:2
   (C) 3:5
   (D) 2:3

2. If 80% of the applicants to a program were rejected, what is the ratio of the number accepted to the number rejected?

   (A) $\frac{1}{5}$

   (B) $\frac{1}{4}$

   (C) $\frac{2}{5}$

   (D) $\frac{4}{5}$

3. The measures of the three angles in a triangle are in the ratio 1:1:2. Which of the following *must* be true?

   I. The triangle is isosceles.
   II. The triangle is a right triangle.
   III. The triangle is equilateral.

   (A) None
   (B) I only
   (C) II only
   (D) I and II only

4. What is the ratio of the circumference of a circle to its radius?

   (A) $\frac{\pi}{2}$

   (B) $\sqrt{\pi}$

   (C) π

   (D) 2π

5. If $a:b = 3:5$ and $a:c = 5:7$, what is the value of $b:c$?

   (A) 21:35
   (B) 21:25
   (C) 25:21
   (D) 35:21

6. In the diagram below, $b:a = 7:2$. What is $b - a$?

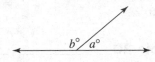

   (A) 20
   (B) 70
   (C) 100
   (D) 110

7. If x is a positive number and $\frac{x}{3} = \frac{12}{x}$, then $x =$

   (A) 3
   (B) 4
   (C) 6
   (D) 12

8. A snail can move i inches in m minutes. At this rate, how many feet can it move in h hours?

   (A) $\frac{5hi}{m}$

   (B) $\frac{60hi}{m}$

   (C) $\frac{hi}{12m}$

   (D) $\frac{5m}{hi}$

9. Barbra can grade t tests in $\frac{1}{x}$ hours. At this rate, how many tests can she grade in x hours?

   (A) tx

   (B) tx^2

   (C) $\frac{1}{t}$

   (D) $\frac{x}{t}$

10. If 500 pounds of mush will feed 20 pigs for a week, for how many days will 200 pounds of mush feed 14 pigs?

(A) 4
(B) 5
(C) 6
(D) 7

Grid-in Questions

11. John can read 72 pages per hour. At this rate, how many pages can he read in 72 minutes?

12. If $3a = 2b$ and $3b = 5c$, what is the ratio of a to c?

13. If $\dfrac{3x-1}{25} = \dfrac{x+5}{11}$, what is the value of x?

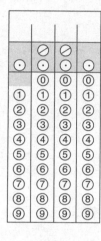

14. Three associates agreed to split the profit of an investment in the ratio of 2:5:8. If the profit was $3000, what is the difference between the largest share and the smallest?

15. If y is inversely proportional to x, and $y = 8$ when $x = 4$, what is the value of y when $x = 5$?

Answer Key

1. **B**	3. **D**	5. **C**	7. **C**	9. **B**
2. **B**	4. **D**	6. **C**	8. **A**	10. **A**

11. **8 6 . 4**

12. **1 0 / 9** or **1 . 1 1**

13. **1 7**

14. **1 2 0 0**

15. **3 2 / 5** or **6 . 4**

Answers Explained

1. **(B)** Of every 3 workers, 2 are nonsmokers, and 1 is a smoker. Then, the ratio of smokers to nonsmokers is 1:2.

2. **(B)** If 80% of the applicants were rejected, 20% were accepted, and the ratio of accepted to rejected is $20:80 = 1:4 = \dfrac{1}{4}$.

3. **(D)** It is worth remembering that, if the ratio of the measures of the angles of a triangle is 1:1:2, then the angles are 45-45-90 (see Section 6-J). Otherwise, the first step is to write

$$x + x + 2x = 180 \Rightarrow 4x = 180 \Rightarrow x = 45$$

   - Since two of the angles have the same measure, the triangle is isosceles. (I is true.)
   - Also, since one of the angles measures 90°, the triangle is a right triangle. (II is true.)
   - Statement III, of course, is false.

4. **(D)** By definition, π is the ratio of the circumference to the diameter of a circle (see Section 6-L), so

$$\pi = \frac{C}{d} = \frac{C}{2r} \Rightarrow 2\pi = \frac{C}{r}$$

5. **(C)** Since $\dfrac{a}{b} = \dfrac{3}{5}$, $\dfrac{b}{a} = \dfrac{5}{3}$, then $\dfrac{b}{\not a} \times \dfrac{\not a}{c} = \dfrac{5}{3} \times \dfrac{5}{7} \Rightarrow \dfrac{b}{c} = \dfrac{25}{21}$

   Alternatively, you could write equivalent ratios with the same value for a:

$$a:b = 3:5 = 15:25 \quad \text{and} \quad a:c = 5:7 = 15:21$$

   Then, when $a = 15$, $b = 25$ and $c = 21$.

6. **(C)** Let $b = 7x$ and $a = 2x$. Then

$$7x + 2x = 180 \Rightarrow 9x = 180 \Rightarrow x = 20 \Rightarrow b = 140$$
$$\text{and } a = 40 \Rightarrow b - a = 140 - 40 = 100$$

7. **(C)** To solve a proportion, cross-multiply:

$$\frac{x}{3} = \frac{12}{x} \Rightarrow x^2 = 36 \Rightarrow x = 6$$

8. **(A)** Set up the proportion, keeping track of units:

$$\frac{x \text{ feet}}{h \text{ hours}} = \frac{12x \text{ inches}}{60h \text{ minutes}} = \frac{i \text{ inches}}{m \text{ minutes}} \Rightarrow \frac{x}{5h} = \frac{i}{m} \Rightarrow x = \frac{5hi}{m}$$

9. **(B)** Barbra grades at the rate of

$$\frac{t \text{ tests}}{\frac{1}{x} \text{ hours}} = \frac{tx \text{ tests}}{1 \text{ hour}}$$

   Since she can grade tx tests each hour, in x hours she can grade $x(tx) = tx^2$ tests.

10. **(A)** Since 500 pounds will last for 20 pig-weeks or 140 pig-days, 200 pounds will last for

$$\frac{200}{500} \times 140 \text{ pig-days} = 56 \text{ pig-days, and } \frac{56 \text{ pig-days}}{14 \text{ pigs}} = 4 \text{ days}$$

11. **86.4** Set up a proportion:

$$\frac{72 \text{ pages}}{1 \text{ hour}} = \frac{72 \text{ pages}}{60 \text{ minutes}} = \frac{x \text{ pages}}{72 \text{ minutes}}$$

and cross-multiply:

$$72 \times 72 = 60x \Rightarrow 5184 = 60x \Rightarrow x = 86.4$$

12. $\dfrac{10}{9}$ **or 1.11** Multiplying each equation to get the same coefficient of b gives

$$9a = 6b \text{ and } 6b = 10c \Rightarrow 9a = 10c \Rightarrow \frac{a}{c} = \frac{10}{9} \text{ or } 1.11$$

13. **17** Cross-multiplying gives

$$11(3x - 1) = 25(x + 5) \Rightarrow 33x - 11 = 25x + 125 \Rightarrow 8x = 136 \Rightarrow x = 17$$

14. **1200** The shares are $2x$, $5x$, and $8x$, and their sum is 3000:

$$2x + 5x + 8x = 3000 \Rightarrow 15x = 3000 \Rightarrow x = 200$$

so $8x - 2x = 6x = 1200$.

15. $\dfrac{32}{5}$ **or 6.4** If y is inversely proportional to x, there is a constant k such that $xy = k$, so

$k = (8)(4) = 32$. Thus $32 = 5y$, and $y = \dfrac{32}{5}$ or 6.4.

The **average** of a set of n numbers is the sum of those numbers divided by n:

$$\text{average} = \frac{\text{sum of the } n \text{ numbers}}{n}$$

or simply

$$A = \frac{\text{sum}}{n}$$

If you took three math tests so far this year and your grades were 80, 90, and 76, to calculate your average, you would add the three grades and divide by 3:

$$\frac{80+90+76}{3} = \frac{246}{3} = 82$$

The technical name for average is "arithmetic mean," and on the SAT those words always appear in parentheses—for example, "What is the average (arithmetic mean) of 80, 90, and 76?"

Very often on the SAT, you are not asked to find an average; rather, you are given the average of a set of numbers and asked to provide some other information. The key to solving all of these problems is to first find the sum of the numbers. Since $A = \frac{\text{sum}}{n}$, multiplying both sides by n yields this equation: sum = nA.

> **HELPFUL HINT**
>
> On the SAT you can ignore the words "arithmetic mean." They simply mean "average."

TACTIC
E1
If you know the average, A, of a set of n numbers, multiply A by n to get their sum.

> **HELPFUL HINT**
>
> Most SAT problems involving averages can be solved using TACTIC 1.

➡️ **Example 1** _____

One day a delivery-truck driver picked up 25 packages whose average (arithmetic mean) weight was 14.2 pounds. What was the total weight, in pounds, of all the packages?

 Solution. Use TACTIC E1: 25 × 14.2 = **355**.

NOTE: You do not know how much any individual package weighed or how many packages weighed more or less than 14.2 pounds. All you know is the total weight.

➡️ **Example 2** _____

John took five English tests during the first marking period, and his average (arithmetic mean) was 85. If his average after the first three tests was 83, what was the average of his fourth and fifth tests?

(A) 85
(B) 87
(C) 88
(D) 90

📟 **Solution.**

- Use TACTIC E1: On his five tests John earned 5 × 85 = 425 points.
- Use TACTIC E1 again: On the first three tests he earned 3 × 83 = 249 points.
- Subtract: On his last two tests he earned 425 – 249 = 176 points.
- Calculate his average on his last two tests: $\frac{176}{2} = \mathbf{88}$ **(C)**.

NOTE: You cannot determine John's grade on even one of the five tests.

Key Fact E1

If all the numbers in a set are the same, then that number is the average.

Key Fact E2

If the numbers in a set are not all the same, then the average must be greater than the smallest number and less than the largest number. Equivalently, at least one of the numbers is less than the average and at least one is greater.

If Mary's test grades are 85, 85, 85, and 85, her average is 85. If Bob's test grades are 76, 83, 88, and 88, his average must be greater than 76 and less than 88. What can we conclude if, after taking five tests, Ellen's average is 90? We know that she earned exactly 5 × 90 = 450 points, and that either she got 90 on every test or at least one grade was less than 90 and at least one was over 90. Here are a few of the thousands of possibilities for Ellen's grades:

(a) 90, 90, 90, 90, 90
(b) 80, 90, 90, 90, 100
(c) 83, 84, 87, 97, 99
(d) 77, 88, 93, 95, 97
(e) 50, 100, 100, 100, 100

Key Fact E3

Assume that the average of a set of numbers is *A*. If a number, *x*, is added to the set and a new average is calculated, then the new average will be less than, equal to, or greater than *A*, depending on whether *x* is less than, equal to, or greater than *A*, respectively.

➥ Example 3

Let n be an integer greater than 1, let a = the average (arithmetic mean) of the integers from 1 to n, and let b = the average of the integers from 0 to n. Which of the following could be true?

I. $a = b$

II. $a < b$

III. $a > b$

(A) I only

(B) II only

(C) III only

(D) II and III only

Solution 1. Since a is the average of the integers from 1 to n, a is surely greater than 1. You are told that b is the average of those same n numbers and 0. Since the extra number, 0, is less than a, b must be less than a. Only Statement **III (C)** is true.

Solution 2. Clearly, the sum of the $n + 1$ integers from 0 to n is the same as the sum of the n integers from 1 to n. Since that sum is positive, dividing by $n + 1$ yields a smaller quotient than dividing by n (KEY FACT B4).

If in Example 3 $n = 12$, then you could calculate each average as follows:

$$0 + 1 + 2 + 3 + 4 + 5 + \mathbf{6} + 7 + 8 + 9 + 10 + 11 + 12 = 78 \quad \text{and} \quad \frac{78}{13} = 6$$

$$1 + 2 + 3 + 4 + 5 + \mathbf{6} + \mathbf{7} + 8 + 9 + 10 + 11 + 12 = 78 \quad \text{and} \quad \frac{78}{12} = 6.5$$

Notice that the average of the 13 *consecutive* integers 0, 1,...,12 is the *middle integer*, **6**, and the average of the 12 *consecutive* integers 1, 2,...,12 is the *average of the two middle integers*, **6** and **7**. This is a special case of KEY FACT E4.

Key Fact E4

Whenever n numbers form an arithmetic sequence (one in which the difference between any two consecutive terms is the same): (i) if n is odd, the average of the numbers is the middle term in the sequence; and (ii) if n is even, the average of the numbers is the average of the two middle terms. Whether n is odd or even, the average of the n numbers is equal to the average of the first and last numbers.

For example, in the arithmetic sequence 6, 9, 12, 15, 18, the average is the middle number, 12; and in the sequence 10, 20, 30, 40, 50, 60, the average is 35, the average of the two middle numbers—30 and 40. Note that 12 is the average of 6 and 18, and that 35 is the average of 10 and 60.

➥ Example 4

On Thursday, 20 of the 25 students in a chemistry class took a test, and their average (arithmetic mean) was 80. On Friday, the other 5 students took the test, and their average (arithmetic mean) was 90. What was the average for the entire class?

(A) 82
(B) 84
(C) 85
(D) 88

HELPFUL HINT

Without doing any calculations, you should immediately realize that, since the grade of 80 is being given more weight than the grade of 90, the average will be closer to 80 than to 90—certainly *less than* 85.

 Solution. The class average is calculated by dividing the sum of all 25 test grades by 25.

- The first 20 students earned a total of: $20 \times 80 = 1600$ points
- The other 5 students earned a total of: $5 \times 90 = 450$ points
- Add: altogether the class earned: $1600 + 450 = 2050$ points
- Calculate the class average: $\dfrac{2050}{25} = $ **82 (A)**

Notice that the answer to Example 4 is *not* 85, which is the average of 80 and 90. The averages of 80 and 90 were earned by different numbers of students, and so the two averages must be given different weights in the calculation. For this reason, 82 is called a ***weighted average***.

Key Fact E5

To calculate the weighted average of a set of numbers, multiply each number in the set by the number of times it appears, add all the products, and divide by the total number of numbers in the set.

 The solution to Example 4 should look like this:

$$\frac{20(80)+5(90)}{25} = \frac{1600+450}{25} = \frac{2050}{25} = 82$$

Problems involving *average speed* will be discussed in Section 6-H, but we mention them briefly here because they are closely related to problems on weighted averages.

➥ Example 5

For the first 3 hours of her trip, Susan drove at 50 miles per hour. Then, because of construction delays, she drove at only 40 miles per hour for the next 2 hours. What was her average speed, in miles per hour, for the entire trip?

Solution. This is just a weighted average:

$$\frac{3(50)+2(40)}{5} = \frac{150+80}{5} = \frac{230}{5} = 46$$

Note that in each of the above fractions the numerator is the total distance traveled and the denominator the total time the trip took. This is *always* the way to find an average speed. Consider the following slight variation of Example 5.

➥ Example 5A

> For the first 100 miles of her trip, Susan drove at 50 miles per hour. Then, because of construction delays, she drove at only 40 miles per hour for the next 120 miles. What was her average speed, in miles per hour, for the entire trip?

 Solution. This is not a *weighted* average. Here you immediately know the total distance: 220 miles. To get the total time, find the time for each portion and add: the first 100 miles took 100 ÷ 50 = 2 hours, and the next 120 miles took 120 ÷ 40 = 3 hours. The average speed was $\frac{220}{5}$ = **44** miles per hour.

Notice that in Example 5, since Susan spent more time traveling at 50 than at 40 miles per hour, her average speed was closer to 50; in Example 5a, however, she spent more time driving at 40 than at 50 miles per hour, so her average speed was closer to 40.

Three other terms associated with averages are *median, mode*, and *range*.

- In a set of n numbers arranged in increasing order, the *median* is the middle number (if n is odd), or the average of the two middle numbers (if n is even).
- In any set of numbers, the *mode* is the number that appears most often.
- In any set of numbers, the *range* is the difference between the greatest and least numbers.

➥ Example 6

> During a 10-day period, Olga received the following number of phone calls each day: 2, 3, 9, 3, 5, 7, 7, 11, 7, 6. What is the average (arithmetic mean) of the median, mode, and range of this set of data?

Solution. The first step is to write the data in increasing order: 2, 3, 3, 5, 6, 7, 7, 7, 9, 11.

- The median is 6.5, the average of the middle two numbers.
- The mode is 7, the number that appears more often than any other.
- The range is 11 − 2 = 9
- The average of the median, mode, and range is $\frac{6.5+7+9}{3} = \frac{22.5}{3} = \mathbf{7.5}$.

The median is actually a special case of a measure called a *percentile*. In the same way that the median divides a set of data into two roughly equal groups, percentiles divide a set of data into 100 roughly equal groups. P_{63}, the 63rd percentile, for example, is a number with the property that 63% of the data in the group is less than or equal to that number and the rest of the data is greater than that number. Clearly, percentiles are mainly used for large groups of data—it doesn't make much sense to talk about the 63rd percentile of a set of data with 5 or 10 or 20 numbers in it. When you receive your SAT scores in the mail, you will receive a percentile ranking for each of your scores. If you are told that your Math score is at the 63rd percentile, that means that your score was higher than the scores of approximately 63% of all SAT test takers (and, therefore, that your score was lower than those of approximately 37% of SAT test takers).

From the definition of percentile, it follows that the median is exactly the same as the 50th percentile. Another term that is often used in analyzing data is *quartile*. There are three quartiles, Q_1, Q_2, and Q_3, which divide a set of data into four roughly equal groups. Q_1, Q_2, and Q_3 are called the first, second, and third quartiles and are equal to P_{25}, P_{50}, and P_{75}, respectively.

So, if M represents the median, then $M = Q_2 = P_{50}$. A measure that is sometimes used to show how spread out the numbers in a set of data are is the ***interquartile range***, which is defined as the difference between the first and third quartiles: $Q_3 - Q_1$.

The interquartile range shows where the middle half of all the data lies. The interquartile range can be graphically illustrated in a diagram called a ***boxplot***. A boxplot extends from the smallest number in the set of data (S) to the largest number in the set of data (L) and has a box representing the interquartile range. The box, which begins and ends at the first and third quartiles, also shows the location of the median (Q_2). The box may be symmetric about the median, but does not need to be, as is illustrated in the two boxplots, below. The upper boxplot shows the distribution of math SAT scores for all students who took the SAT in 2010, while the lower boxplot shows the distribution of math scores for the students at a very selective college.

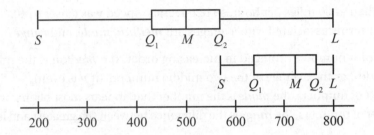

➡ Example 7_____

Twelve hundred 18-year-old boys were weighed, and their weights, in pounds, are summarized in the following boxplot.

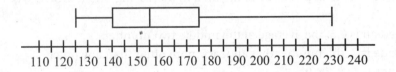

If the 91st percentile of the weights is 200 pounds, approximately how many of the students weigh less than 140 pounds or more than 200 pounds?

(A) 280

(B) 350

(C) 410

(D) 470

Solution. From the boxplot, we see that the first quartile is 140. So, approximately 25% of the boys weigh less than 140. And since the 91st percentile is 200, approximately 9% of the boys weigh more than 200. So 25% + 9% = 34% of the 1,200 boys fall within the range we are considering. Finally, 34% of 1,200 = 0.34 × 1,200 = 408, or approximately **410 (C)**.

In statistics the ***standard deviation*** is a useful measure that takes a kind of average of how far each piece of data is from the mean. In a distribution in which much of the data is near the mean, the standard deviation tends to be smaller; when the data is more spread out, the standard deviation tends to be larger. You would never have to calculate a standard deviation on the SAT, but it is instructive to see how to do it.

Assume a group consists of n numerical pieces of data.

(STEP 1) Find the mean of the n numbers.

(STEP 2) Calculate the difference between each of the n pieces of data and the mean.

(STEP 3) Square each of the n differences.

(STEP 4) Take the average of the n squared differences.

(STEP 5) Take the square root of the average just calculated.

➡ Example 8

Find the standard deviation of the following five pieces of data:

$$10, 20, 30, 50, 65$$

Solution.

- The sum of the five numbers is 175, so the mean is $175 \div 5 = 35$.
- Calculate the squares of the differences of each number from the mean:

$$(10 - 35)^2 = (-25)^2 = 625; (20 - 35)^2 = (-15)^2 = 225; (30 - 35)^2 = (-5)^2 = 25;$$
$$(50 - 35)^2 = (15)^2 = 225; (65 - 35)^2 = (30)^2 = 900$$

- The sum of the five squared differences is 2000, so their average is $2000 \div 5 = 400$.
- Finally, the standard deviation is 20, the square root of 400.

Even though you will not have to calculate a standard deviation, here are a few facts about standard deviations you should know:

- A standard deviation cannot be negative.
- The only way a standard deviation can be 0 is if all the pieces of data are the same.
- Adding or subtracting a constant to each piece of data does not change the standard deviation. For example, the standard deviation of the set {13, 23, 33, 53, 68} is 20, since each number in the set is 3 more than each number in the set of data in Example 8.
- Multiplying or dividing each piece of data in a set by a factor greater than 1, multiplies or divides, respectively, the value of the standard deviation by the same factor. For example, the standard deviation of the set {20, 40, 60, 100, 130} is 40, since each number in the set is two times each number in the set of data in Example 8.

Multiple-Choice Questions

1. Justin's average (arithmetic mean) on four tests is 80. What grade does he need on his fifth test to raise his average to 84?

   (A) 84
   (B) 92
   (C) 96
   (D) 100

2. Judy's average (arithmetic mean) on four tests is 80. Assuming she can earn no more than 100 on any test, what is the least she can earn on her fifth test and still have a chance for an 85 average after seven tests?

   (A) 60
   (B) 70
   (C) 75
   (D) 80

3. Adam's average (arithmetic mean) on four tests is 80. Which of the following CANNOT be the number of tests on which he earned exactly 80 points?

   (A) 1
   (B) 2
   (C) 3
   (D) 4

4. If $a + b = 3(c + d)$, which of the following is the average (arithmetic mean) of a, b, c, and d?

   (A) $\dfrac{c+d}{4}$
   (B) $\dfrac{3(c+d)}{8}$
   (C) $\dfrac{3(c+d)}{4}$
   (D) $c + d$

5. If the average (arithmetic mean) of 5, 6, 7, and w is 8, what is the value of w?

   (A) 12
   (B) 14
   (C) 16
   (D) 24

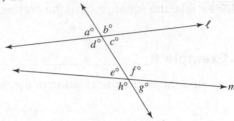

6. In the diagram above, lines ℓ and m are *not* parallel. If A represents the average (arithmetic mean) of the measures of all eight angles, which of the following is true?

   (A) $A = 45°$
   (B) $45° < A < 90°$
   (C) $A = 90°$
   (D) $90° < A < 180°$

7. What is the average (arithmetic mean) of 2^{10} and 2^{20}?

   (A) 2^{15}
   (B) $2^5 + 2^{10}$
   (C) $2^9 + 2^{19}$
   (D) 2^{29}

8. Let M be the median, and m the mode, of the following set of numbers: 10, 70, 20, 40, 70, 90. What is the average (arithmetic mean) of M and m?

   (A) 55
   (B) 60
   (C) 62.5
   (D) 65

9. Which of the following is the average (arithmetic mean) of $x^2 - 10$, $30 - x^2$, and $6x + 10$?

(A) $2x + 10$
(B) $2x + 30$
(C) $3x + 15$
(D) $6x + 10$

Grid-in Questions

10. The average (arithmetic mean) weight of the students in the French Club is 150 pounds, and the average weight of the students in the Spanish Club is 130 pounds. If no one is a member of both clubs, if the average weight of all the students is 142 pounds, and if there are 30 members in the French Club, how many members are there in the Spanish Club?

11. If $10a + 10b = 35$, what is the average (arithmetic mean) of a and b?

12. What is the average (arithmetic mean) of the measures of the five angles in a pentagon?

Answer Key

1. **D** 3. **C** 5. **B** 7. **C** 9. **A**
2. **C** 4. **D** 6. **C** 8. **C**

10.

| | | 2 | 0 |

11. 1 . 7 5 or 7 / 4

12. 1 0 8

Answers Explained

1. **(D)** Use TACTIC E1. For Justin's average on five tests to be 84, he needs a total of $5 \times 84 = 420$ points. So far, he has earned $4 \times 80 = 320$ points. Therefore, he needs a grade of 100 points on the fifth test.

2. **(C)** Use TACTIC E1. So far, Judy has earned 320 points. She can survive a low grade on test 5 if she gets the maximum possible on both the sixth and seventh tests. Assume she gets two 100's. Then her total for tests 1, 2, 3, 4, 6, and 7 will be 520. For her seven-test average to be 85, she needs a total of $7 \times 85 = 595$ points. Therefore, she needs at least $595 - 520 = 75$ points.

3. **(C)** Adam could not have earned exactly 80 on three tests. If he did, his average for those three tests would clearly be 80; and since adding the fourth score didn't change his average, KEY FACT E3 tells us that his fourth score must also be 80. Therefore, it is *not* possible for him to have earned exactly 80 on each of three tests.

   Alternative solution. Could Adam have earned a total of 320 points with exactly:

1 grade of 80?	Lots of ways; 80, 40, 100, 100, for instance.
2 grades of 80?	Yes; 80, 80, 60, 100, for instance.
4 grades of 80?	Sure: 80, 80, 80, 80.
3 grades of 80?	No! If $80 + 80 + 80 + x = 320$, then $x = 80$, as well.

4. **(D)** Calculate the average:
   $$\frac{a+b+c+d}{4} = \frac{3(c+d)+c+d}{4} = \frac{3c+3d+c+d}{4} = \frac{4c+4d}{4} = c + d$$

5. **(B)** Use TACTIC E1. The sum of the four numbers is $4 \times 8 = 32$. Then
   $$5 + 6 + 7 + w = 32 \Rightarrow 18 + w = 32 \Rightarrow w = 14$$

6. **(C)** $a + b + c + d = 360$ and $w + x + y + z = 360$ (see Section 6-I); so the sum of the measures of all eight angles is $360° + 360° = 720°$, and their average, A, is $720° \div 8 = 90°$.

7. **(C)** The average of 2^{10} and 2^{20} is $\dfrac{2^{10} + 2^{20}}{2} = \dfrac{2^{10}}{2} + \dfrac{2^{20}}{2} = 2^9 + 2^{19}$.

   (See Section 6-A if you had trouble with the exponents.)

   Alternative solution. Use your calculator and estimate: 2^{10} is about 1000 and 2^{20} is about 1,000,000. Their average is about 500,000. None of the wrong choices is even close.

8. **(C)** Arrange the numbers in increasing order: 10, 20, 40, 70, 70, 90. The median, M, is the average of the middle two numbers: $\dfrac{40 + 70}{2} = 55$; the mode, m, is 70, the number that appears most frequently. The average of M and m, therefore, is the average of 55 and 70, which is 62.5.

9. **(A)** Find the sum of the three expressions, and divide by 3:

$$(x^2 - 10) + (30 - x^2) + (6x + 10) = 6x + 30 \text{ and } \frac{6x + 30}{3} = 2x + 10$$

   Alternative solution. If you get bogged down in the algebra, use TACTIC 6 from Chapter 5. Choose an easy number for x: 1, for example. Then, the three numbers become –9, 29, and 16, whose average is 12. Only (A) has a value of 12 when $x = 1$. This is also an easy way to check your answer, if you use the first solution.

10. **20** Let x = number of students in the Spanish Club, and write the weighted average:

$$142 = \frac{30(150) + x(130)}{30 + x}$$

   Cross-multiply:

$$142(30 + x) = 30(150) + 130x \Rightarrow$$
$$4260 + 142x = 4500 + 130x \Rightarrow$$
$$12x = 240 \Rightarrow x = 20$$

11. **1.75 or $\dfrac{7}{4}$** Since $10a + 10b = 35$, dividing both sides of the equation by 10 gives $a + b = 3.5$. Therefore, the average of a and b is

$$3.5 \div 2 = 1.75 \text{ or } \frac{7}{4}$$

12. **108** The average of the measures of the five angles is the sum of their measures divided by 5. The sum is $(5 - 2) \times 180 = 3 \times 180 = 540$ (see Section 6-K), so their average is $540 \div 5 = 108$.

ALGEBRA

For the SAT you need to know only a small part of the algebra normally taught in high school. Sections 6-F, 6-G, and 6-H review the topics that you need for the SAT.

6-F POLYNOMIALS

Even though the terms *monomial, binomial, trinomial,* and *polynomial* are not used on the SAT, you must be able to work with simple polynomials, and the use of these terms will make it easy to discuss the important concepts.

A **monomial** is any number or variable or product of numbers and variables. Each of the following is a monomial:

$$3 \quad -4 \quad x \quad y \quad 3x \quad -4xyz \quad 5x^3 \quad 1.5xy^2 \quad a^3b^4$$

The number that appears in front of the variable or variables in a monomial is called the **coefficient**. The coefficient of $5x^3$ is 5. If there is no number, the coefficient is 1 or –1, because x means $1x$ and $-ab^2$ means $-1ab^2$.

On the SAT, you are often asked to evaluate a monomial for specific values of the variables.

➡ Example 1 _____

What is the value of $-3a^2b$ when $a = -4$ and $b = 0.5$?

Solution. Rewrite the expression, replacing the letters a and b by the numbers –4 and 0.5, respectively. Make sure to write each number in parentheses. Then evaluate: $-3(-4)^2(0.5) = -3(16)(0.5) = $ **–24**.

CAUTION: Be sure you follow PEMDAS: handle exponents before the other operations. In Example 1, you *cannot* multiply –4 by –3, get 12, and then square 12.

A **polynomial** is a monomial or the sum of two or more monomials. Each monomial that makes up the polynomial is called a **term** of the polynomial. Each of the following is a polynomial:

$$2x^2 \quad 2x^2 + 3 \quad 3x^2 - 7 \quad x^2 + 5x - 1$$
$$a^2b + b^2a \quad x^2 - y^2 \quad w^2 - 2w + 1$$

The first polynomial in the above list is a monomial; the second, third, fifth, and sixth polynomials are called **binomials** because each has two terms; the fourth and seventh polynomials are called **trinomials** because each has three terms. Two terms are called **like terms** if they have exactly the same variables and exponents; they can differ only in their coefficients: $5a^2b$ and $-3a^2b$ are like terms, whereas a^2b and b^2a are not.

The polynomial $3x^2 + 4x + 5x + 2x^2 + x - 7$ has six terms, but some of them are like terms and can be combined:

$$3x^2 + 2x^2 = 5x^2 \quad \text{and} \quad 4x + 5x + x = 10x$$

Therefore, the original polynomial is equivalent to the trinomial $5x^2 + 10x - 7$.

The only terms of a polynomial that can be combined are like terms.

To add two polynomials, first enclose each one in parentheses and put a plus sign between them; then erase the parentheses and combine like terms.

To add, subtract, multiply, and divide polynomials, use the usual laws of arithmetic. To avoid careless errors, write each polynomial in parentheses before performing any arithmetic operations.

➡ **Example 2**

What is the sum of $5x^2 + 10x - 7$ and $3x^2 - 4x + 2$?

Solution. $(5x^2 + 10x - 7) + (3x^2 - 4x + 2)$
$= 5x^2 + 10x - 7 + 3x^2 - 4x + 2$
$= (5x^2 + 3x^2) + (10x - 4x) + (-7 + 2)$
$= \mathbf{8x^2 + 6x - 5}$

To subtract two polynomials, enclose each one in parentheses, change the minus sign between them to a plus sign, and change the sign of every term in the second parentheses. Then use KEY FACT F2 to add them: erase the parentheses and combine like terms.

CAUTION: Make sure you get the order right in a subtraction problem.

➡ **Example 3**

Subtract $3x^2 - 4x + 2$ from $5x^2 + 10x - 7$.

Solution. Be careful. Start with the second polynomial and subtract the first:

$$(5x^2 + 10x - 7) - (3x^2 - 4x + 2) =$$
$$(5x^2 + 10x - 7) + (-3x^2 + 4x - 2) = \mathbf{2x^2 + 14x - 9}$$

➡ **Example 4**

What is the average (arithmetic mean) of $5x^2 + 10x - 7$, $3x^2 - 4x + 2$, and $4x^2 + 2$?

Solution. As in any average problem, add and divide:

$$(5x^2 + 10x - 7) + (3x^2 - 4x + 2) + (4x^2 + 2) = 12x^2 + 6x - 3$$

and by the distributive law (KEY FACT A22):

$$\frac{12x^2 + 6x - 3}{3} = \mathbf{4x^2 + 2x - 1}$$

Key Fact F4

To multiply monomials, first multiply their coefficients, and then multiply their variables by adding the exponents (see Section 6-A).

➡ **Example 5** _____

What is the product of $3xy^2z^3$ and $-2x^2y$?

Solution. $(3xy^2z^3)(-2x^2y) = 3(-2)(x)(x^2)(y^2)(y)(z^3) = \mathbf{-6x^3y^3z^3}$

All other polynomials are multiplied by using the distributive law.

Key Fact F5

To multiply a monomial by any polynomial, just multiply each term of the polynomial by the monomial.

➡ **Example 6** _____

What is the product of $2a$ and $3a^2 - 6ab + b^2$?

Solution. $2a(3a^2 - 6ab + b^2) = \mathbf{6a^3 - 12a^2b + 2ab^2}$

On the SAT, you could be asked to multiply two binomials.

Key Fact F6

To multiply two binomials, use the so-called FOIL method, which is really nothing more than the distributive law. Multiply each term in the first parentheses by each term in the second parentheses and simplify by combining terms, if possible.

$$(2x - 7)(3x + 2) = (2x)(3x) + (2x)(2) + (-7)(3x) + (-7)(2) =$$

First terms   Outer terms Inner terms   Last terms

$$6x^2 + 4x - 21x - 14 = 6x^2 - 17x - 14$$

➡ **Example 7** _____

What is the value of $(x - 2)(x + 3) - (x - 4)(x + 5)$?

Solution. First, multiply both pairs of binomials:

$$(x - 2)(x + 3) = x^2 + 3x - 2x - 6 = x^2 + x - 6$$
$$(x - 4)(x + 5) = x^2 + 5x - 4x - 20 = x^2 + x - 20$$

Now, subtract: $(x^2 + x - 6) - (x^2 + x - 20) = x^2 + x - 6 - x^2 - x + 20 = \mathbf{14}$

HELPFUL HINT

If you memorize the products in KEY FACT F7, you won't have to multiply the binomials out each time you need them.

The three most important binomial products on the SAT are these:

- $(x - y)(x + y) = x^2 + xy - yx - y^2 = x^2 - y^2$
- $(x - y)^2 = (x - y)(x - y) = x^2 - xy - yx + y^2 = x^2 - 2xy + y^2$
- $(x + y)^2 = (x + y)(x + y) = x^2 + xy + yx + y^2 = x^2 + 2xy + y^2$

➥ Example 8

If $a - b = 17.5$ and $a + b = 10$, what is the value of $a^2 - b^2$?

Solution. Section 6-G reviews the methods used to solve such a pair of equations; but even if you know how to solve them, *you should not do so here*. You don't need to know the values of a and b to answer this question. The moment you see $a^2 - b^2$, you should think $(a - b)(a + b)$. Then:

$$a^2 - b^2 = (a - b)(a + b) = (17.5)(10) = \mathbf{175}$$

➥ Example 9

If $x^2 + y^2 = 36$ and $(x + y)^2 = 64$, what is the value of xy?

Solution. Here, $64 = (x + y)^2 = x^2 + 2xy + y^2 = x^2 + y^2 + 2xy = 36 + 2xy$. Therefore:

$$2xy = 64 - 36 = 28 \Rightarrow xy = \mathbf{14}$$

On the SAT, the only division of polynomials you will have to do is to divide a polynomial by a monomial. You will *not* have to do long division of polynomials.

To divide a polynomial by a monomial, use the distributive law. Then simplify each term by reducing the fraction formed by the coefficients to lowest terms and applying the laws of exponents.

➥ Example 10

What is the quotient when $32a^2b + 12ab^3c$ is divided by $8ab$?

Solution. By the distributive law,

$$\frac{32a^2b + 12ab^3c}{8ab} = \frac{32a^2b}{8ab} + \frac{12ab^3c}{8ab}$$

Now reduce each fraction: $\mathbf{4a + \dfrac{3}{2}\,b^2c}$

On the SAT, the most important way to use the three formulas in KEY FACT F7 is to recognize them in reverse. In other words, whenever you see $x^2 - y^2$, you should realize that it can be rewritten as $(x - y)(x + y)$. This process, which is the reverse of multiplication, is called *factoring*.

Example 11

If $x^2 - y^2 = 14$ and $x - y = 7$, what is the value of $x + y$?

Solution. Since $x^2 - y^2 = (x - y)(x + y)$, you have $14 = 7(x + y) \Rightarrow x + y = 2$.

Note that you could solve for x and y ($x = 4.5$, $y = -2.5$) and then add; but you shouldn't because that would take much more time.

To *factor* a polynomial, you must find other polynomials whose product is the original polynomial. For example, since $2x(3x - 5) = 6x^2 - 10x$, then $2x$ and $3x - 5$ are each factors of $6x^2 - 10x$; and since $(a - b)(a + b) = a^2 - b^2$, then $(a - b)$ and $(a + b)$ are factors of $a^2 - b^2$.

On the SAT, you will have to do almost no factoring. Occasionally, an SAT will have a question which requires you to solve a very simple quadratic equation such as $x^2 - x - 6 = 0$. Often you can solve it by inspection since the roots will be two small integers. At worst you will have to factor:

$$x^2 - x - 6 = 0 \Rightarrow (x - 3)(x + 2) = 0 \Rightarrow x - 3 = 0 \text{ or } x + 2 = 0 \Rightarrow x = 3 \text{ or } x = -2$$

On the SAT there will be some questions that require you to simplify algebraic expressions. In that case, you will probably have to do some simple factoring.

Key Fact F9

To factor a polynomial, the first step is *always* to use the distributive property to remove the greatest common factor of all the terms.

For example:

$$6xy + 8yz = 2y(3x + 4z) \quad \text{and} \quad x^3 + x^2 + x = x(x^2 + x + 1)$$

Key Fact F10

To factor a trinomial use trial and error to find the binomials whose product is the given trinomial.

For example:

$$x^2 + 4x + 4 = (x + 2)(x + 2) \text{ (see KEY FACT F7)}$$
$$x^2 - 3x - 10 = (x - 5)(x + 2)$$
$$2x^2 + 18x + 16 = 2(x^2 + 9x + 8) = 2(x + 8)(x + 1)$$

➡ Example 12 _____

Which of the following is equivalent to $\dfrac{3x^2-12}{x^2-4x+4}$?

(A) $\dfrac{3(x+2)}{x-2}$

(B) $\dfrac{3(x+4)}{x-4}$

(C) $\dfrac{3x+2}{x-2}$

(D) $\dfrac{6}{4x-4}$

Solution.

$$\frac{3x^2-12}{x^2-4x+4} = \frac{3(x^2-4)}{(x-2)(x-2)} = \frac{3(x-2)(x+2)}{(x-2)(x-2)} = \frac{3(x+2)}{x-2} \quad \textbf{(A)}$$

In Example 12, when $x = 3$, the value of $\dfrac{3x^2-12}{x^2-4x+4}$ is

$$\frac{3(3)^2-12}{3^2-4(3)+4} = \frac{27-12}{9-12+4} = \frac{15}{1} = 15$$

Only choice (A) is 15 when $x = 3$: $\dfrac{3(3+2)}{3-2} = \dfrac{3(5)}{1} = 15$

Note that this method does not depend on the choice of x. You can verify, for example, that, if $x = 5$, the original expression and the correct answer are both equal to 7.

Although the coefficient of any term in a polynomial can be a fraction, such as $\dfrac{2}{3}x^2 - \dfrac{1}{2}x$, the variable itself cannot be in the denominator. An expression such as $\dfrac{3+x}{x^2}$, which has a variable in the denominator, is called an ***algebraic fraction***. Fortunately, you should have no trouble with algebraic fractions since they are handled just like regular fractions. The rules that you reviewed in Section 6-B for adding, subtracting, multiplying, and dividing fractions apply also to algebraic fractions.

HELPFUL HINT

If you ever get stuck trying to simplify an algebraic expression, just plug in a number and test the answers.

➡ Example 13 _____

What is the sum of the reciprocals of x^2 and y^2?

Solution. To add $\dfrac{1}{x^2} + \dfrac{1}{y^2}$, you need a common denominator, which is $x^2 y^2$.

Multiply the numerator and denominator of $\dfrac{1}{x^2}$ by y^2 and the numerator and denominator of $\dfrac{1}{y^2}$ by x^2:

$$\frac{1}{x^2} + \frac{1}{y^2} = \frac{y^2}{x^2 y^2} + \frac{x^2}{x^2 y^2} = \frac{x^2+y^2}{x^2 y^2}$$

Multiple-Choice Questions

1. If $a^2 - b^2 = 21$ and $a^2 + b^2 = 29$, which of the following could be the value of ab?

   I. -10

   II. $5\sqrt{2}$

   III. 10

   (A) I only

   (B) II only

   (C) III only

   (D) I and III only

2. What is the average (arithmetic mean) of $x^2 + 2x - 3$, $3x^2 - 2x - 3$, and $30 - 4x^2$?

   (A) $\dfrac{8x^2 + 24}{3}$

   (B) $\dfrac{24 - 4x}{3}$

   (C) -12

   (D) 8

3. If $a^2 + b^2 = 4$ and $(a - b)^2 = 2$, what is the value of ab?

   (A) 1

   (B) 2

   (C) 3

   (D) 4

4. If $\dfrac{1}{a} + \dfrac{1}{b} = \dfrac{1}{c}$ and $ab = c$, what is the average (arithmetic mean) of a and b?

   (A) 0

   (B) $\dfrac{1}{2}$

   (C) 1

   (D) $\dfrac{c}{2}$

5. If $x \neq 2$ and $x \neq -2$, which of the following is equivalent to $\dfrac{x^3 + 3x^2 - 10x}{2x^2 - 8}$?

   (A) $\dfrac{x(x-5)}{2(x-2)}$

   (B) $\dfrac{x(x+5)}{2(x+2)}$

   (C) $\dfrac{x(x-5)}{2(x+2)}$

   (D) $\dfrac{x(x+5)}{2(x-2)}$

Grid-in Questions

6. What is the value of $\dfrac{a^2 - b^2}{a - b}$ when $a = 17.9$ and $b = 19.7$?

7. If $x^2 - y^2 = 28$ and $x - y = 8$, what is the average (arithmetic mean) of x and y?

8. What is the value of
$(2x + 3)(x + 6) - (2x - 5)(x + 10)?$

10. If $\left(\dfrac{1}{a} + a\right)^2 = 100$, what is the value of $\dfrac{1}{a^2} + a^2?$

9. What is the value of
$x^2 + 12x + 36$ when $x = 64?$

Answer Key

1. **D**   2. **D**   3. **A**   4. **B**   5. **B**

6. 3 7 . 6   7. 1 . 7 5   8. 6 8   9. 4 9 0 0   10. 9 8

Answers Explained

1. **(D)** Add the two equations:

$$2a^2 = 50 \Rightarrow a^2 = 25 \Rightarrow b^2 = 4$$

Then, $a = 5$ or -5 and $b = 2$ or -2. The only possibilities for the product ab are -10 and 10. (Only I and III are true.)

2. **(D)** To find the average, take the sum of the three polynomials and then divide by 3. The sum is $(x^2 + 2x - 3) + (3x^2 - 2x - 3) + (30 - 4x^2) = 24$, and $24 \div 3 = 8$.

3. **(A)** Start by squaring $a - b$: $(a - b)^2 = a^2 - 2ab + b^2$. Then

$$2 = 4 - 2ab \Rightarrow 2ab = 2 \Rightarrow ab = 1$$

4. **(B)** $\dfrac{1}{c} = \dfrac{1}{a} + \dfrac{1}{b} = \dfrac{a+b}{ab} = \dfrac{a+b}{c} \Rightarrow 1 = a + b \Rightarrow \dfrac{a+b}{2} = \dfrac{1}{2}$

5. **(B)** $\dfrac{x^3 + 3x^2 - 10x}{2x^2 - 8} = \dfrac{x(x^2 + 3x - 10)}{2(x^2 - 4)} = \dfrac{x(x+5)\cancel{(x-2)}}{2(x+2)\cancel{(x-2)}} = \dfrac{x(x+5)}{2(x+2)}$

6. **37.6** $\dfrac{a^2 - b^2}{a - b} = \dfrac{\cancel{(a-b)}(a+b)}{\cancel{a-b}} = a + b = 17.9 + 19.7 = 37.6$

7. **1.75** Since $x^2 - y^2 = (x - y)(x + y)$, we have:

$$28 = (x - y)(x + y) = 8(x + y) \Rightarrow x + y = 28 \div 8 = 3.5$$

Finally, the average of x and y is

$$\frac{x+y}{2} = \frac{3.5}{2} = 1.75$$

8. **68** First, multiply out both pairs of binomials:

$$(2x + 3)(x + 6) = 2x^2 + 15x + 18 \quad \text{and} \quad (2x - 5)(x + 10) = 2x^2 + 15x - 50$$

Now subtract:

$$(2x^2 + 15x + 18) - (2x^2 + 15x - 50) = 18 - (-50) = 68$$

Alternative solution. Note that, since this is a grid-in question, the answer must be a (positive) number. All of the x's must cancel out. Therefore, the answer will be the same no matter what x is, so pick a simple value for x. If $x = 0$: $(3)(6) - (-5)(10) = 18 - (-50) = 68$; if $x = 4$: $(11)(10) - (3)(14) = 110 - 42 = 68$.

9. **4900** Of course, you can do this problem on your calculator; but you can do it quicker if you recognize that $x^2 + 12x + 36 = (x + 6)^2$. The value is $(64 + 6)^2 = 70^2 = 4900$.

10. **98** $100 = \left(\dfrac{1}{a} + a\right)^2 = \dfrac{1}{a^2} + 2 + a^2 \Rightarrow \dfrac{1}{a^2} + a^2 = 98$

6-G SOLVING EQUATIONS AND INEQUALITIES

The most important thing to remember when solving an *equation* is that you can manipulate the equation in any way, as long as *you do the same thing to both sides*. For example, you may always add the same number to each side, subtract the same number from each side, multiply or divide each side by the same number (except 0), square each side, take the square root of each side (if the quantities are positive), or take the reciprocal of each side. These comments apply to inequalities, as well, but here you must be very careful because some procedures, such as multiplying or dividing by a negative number and taking reciprocals, reverse inequalities (see KEY FACT A25).

Linear Equations and Inequalities

Equations and inequalities that have only one variable and no exponents can be solved using the simple six-step method outlined in the solution of Example 1.

➡️ **Example 1** _____

If $\frac{1}{2}x + 3(x - 2) = 2(x + 1) + 1$, what is the value of x?

Solution. Follow the steps outlined in the following table.

Step	What to Do	Example 1
1	Get rid of fractions and decimals by multiplying both sides by the lowest common denominator (LCD).	Multiply each term by 2: $x + 6(x - 2) = 4(x + 1) + 2$.
2	Get rid of all parentheses by using the distributive law.	$x + 6x - 12 = 4x + 4 + 2$.
3	Combine like terms on each side.	$7x - 12 = 4x + 6$.
4	By adding or subtracting, get all the variables on one side.	Subtract $4x$ from each side: $3x - 12 = 6$.
5	By adding or subtracting, get all the plain numbers on the other side.	Add 12 to each side: $3x = 18$.
6	Divide both sides by the coefficient of the variable.*	Divide both sides by 3: $x = 6$.

*If you start with an inequality and in Step 6 you divide by a negative number, remember to reverse the inequality (see KEY FACT A25).

Solving the equation in Example 1 is harder than solving most equations on the SAT, because it requires all six steps. On the SAT that rarely happens. Think of the six steps as a list of questions that must be answered. Ask whether each step is necessary. If it is, do it; if it isn't, move on to the next one.

Let's look at Example 2, which does not require all six steps.

➥ **Example 2**_____

For what real number n is it true that $3(n - 20) = n$?

(A)   0
(B)   10
(C)   20
(D)   30

Solution. Do each of the six steps that are necessary.

Step	Question	Yes/No	What to Do
1	Are there any fractions or decimals?	No	
2	Are there any parentheses?	Yes	Get rid of them: $3n - 60 = n$
3	Are there any like terms to combine?	No	
4	Are there variables on both sides?	Yes	Subtract n from each side: $2n - 60 = 0$
5	Is there a plain number on the same side as the variable?	Yes	Add 60 to each side: $2n = 60$
6	Does the variable have a coefficient?	Yes	Divide both sides by 2: $n = 30$

**TACTIC
G1**

Memorize the six steps *in order*, and use this method whenever you have to solve this type of equation or inequality.

➥ **Example 3**_____

Three brothers divided a prize as follows. The oldest received $\frac{2}{5}$, the middle brother received $\frac{1}{3}$, and the youngest received the remaining \$120. What was the value, in dollars, of the prize?

Solution. If x represents the value of the prize, then

$$\frac{2}{5}x + \frac{1}{3}x + 120 = x$$

Solve this equation using the six-step method.

Step	Question	Yes/No	What to Do
1	Are there any fractions or decimals?	Yes	Get rid of them: multiply by 15.* $\overset{3}{\cancel{15}}\left(\dfrac{2}{\underset{1}{\cancel{5}}}x\right) + \overset{5}{\cancel{15}}\left(\dfrac{1}{\underset{1}{\cancel{3}}}x\right) + 15(120) = 15(x)$ $6x + 5x + 1800 = 15x$
2	Are there any parentheses?	No	
3	Are there any like terms to combine?	Yes	Combine them: $11x + 1800 = 15x$
4	Are there variables on both sides?	Yes	Subtract $11x$ from each side: $1800 = 4x$
5	Is there a plain number on the same side as the variable?	No	
6	Does the variable have a coefficient?	Yes	Divide both sides by 4: $x = 450$

*Multiply by 15 since it is the LCM of the two denominators, 3 and 5.

Sometimes on the SAT, you are given an equation with several variables and asked to solve for one of them in terms of the others.

TACTIC
G2

When you have to solve for one variable in terms of the others, treat all of the others as if they were numbers, and apply the six-step method.

➡ **Example 4**_____

If $a = 3b - c$, what is the value of b in terms of a and c?

Solution. To solve for b, treat a and c as numbers and use the six-step method with b as the variable.

Step	Question	Yes/No	What to Do
1	Are there any fractions or decimals?	No	
2	Are there any parentheses?	No	
3	Are there any like terms to combine?	No	
4	Are there variables on both sides?	No	Remember: the only variable is b.
5	Is there a plain number on the same side as the variable?	Yes	Remember: you're considering c as a number, and it is on the same side as b, the variable. Add c to both sides: $a + c = 3b$.
6	Does the variable have a coefficient?	Yes	Divide both sides by 3: $b = \dfrac{a+c}{3}$

Sometimes when solving equations, you may see a shortcut. For example, to solve $7(w - 3) = 42$, you can save time if you start by dividing both sides by 7, getting $w - 3 = 6$, rather than using the distributive law to eliminate the parentheses. Similarly, if you have to solve a proportion such as $\frac{x}{7} = \frac{3}{5}$, it is easier to cross-multiply, getting $5x = 21$, than to multiply both sides by 35 to get rid of the fractions (although that's exactly what cross-multiplying accomplishes). Other shortcuts will be illustrated in the problems at the end of the section. If you spot such a shortcut, use it; but if you don't, be assured that the six-step method *always* works.

➡ **Example 5**

If $x - 4 = 11$, what is the value of $x - 8$?

(A) -15
(B) -7
(C) 7
(D) 15

Solution. Going immediately to Step 5, add 4 to each side of the equation: $x = 15$. But this is *not* the answer. You need the value, not of x, but of $x - 8$: $15 - 8 = \mathbf{7}$ **(C)**.

As in Example 5, on the SAT you are often asked to solve for something other than the simple variable. In Example 5, you could have been asked for the value of x^2, $x + 4$, $(x - 4)^2$, and so on.

TACTIC
G3

As you read each question on the SAT, circle in your test booklet what you are looking for. Then you will always be sure to answer the question that is asked.

On the SAT, you could have to solve an equation such as $3\sqrt{x} - 1 = 5$, which involves a radical. Proceed normally, treating the radical as the variable and using whichever of the six steps are necessary until you have a radical equal to a number. Then raise each side to the same power. For example, if the radical is a square root, square both sides; if the radical is a cube root, cube both sides.

➡ **Example 6**

If $3\sqrt{x} - 1 = 5$, what is the value of x?

Solution.
- Add 1 to each side: $\qquad 3\sqrt{x} = 6$
- Divide each side by 3: $\qquad \sqrt{x} = 2$
- Now square each side: $\qquad \left(\sqrt{x}\right)^2 = 2^2 \Rightarrow x = \mathbf{4}$

➥ Example 7_____

If $4(\sqrt{x}+1) = \sqrt{x}+25$, what is the value x?

Solution.

- Get rid of the parentheses: $4\sqrt{x}+4 = \sqrt{x}+25$
- Subtract $\sqrt{x}$ from each side: $3\sqrt{x}+4 = 25$
- Subtract 4 from each side: $3\sqrt{x} = 21$
- Divide each side by 3: $\sqrt{x} = 7$
- Square each side: $x = 7^2 = \mathbf{49}$

➥ Example 8_____

If $\sqrt[3]{x} - 4 = 1$, what is the value of x?

Solution.

- Add 4 to each side: $\sqrt[3]{x} = 5$

- Cube each side: $\left(\sqrt[3]{x}\right)^3 = 5^3 \Rightarrow x = \mathbf{125}$

➥ Example 9_____

If $2x - 5 = 98$, what is the value of $2x + 5$?

Solution. First, circle what you are asked for (the value of $2x + 5$), and then look at the question carefully. The best approach is to observe that $2x + 5$ is 10 more than $2x - 5$, so the answer is **108** (10 more than 98). Next best would be to do only one step of the six-step method, and add 5 to both sides: $2x = 103$. Now, add 5 to both sides: $2x + 5 = 103 + 5 = \mathbf{108}$. The *worst* method would be to divide $2x = 103$ by 2, get $x = 51.5$, and then use that value to calculate $2x + 5$.

HELPFUL HINT

Very often, solving the given equation is *not* the quickest way to answer a question.

➥ Example 10 _____

If w is an integer, and the average (arithmetic mean) of 3, 4, and w is less than 10, what is the greatest possible value of w?

Solution.

- Set up the inequality: $\dfrac{3+4+w}{3} < 10$
- Get rid of fractions: $3 + 4 + w < 30$
- Combine like terms: $7 + w < 30$
- Subtract 7 from both sides: $w < 23$

Since w is an integer, the most it can be is **22**.

The six-step method also works when there are variables in denominators.

⇒ **Example 11** _____

For what value of x is $\dfrac{4}{x}+\dfrac{3}{5}=\dfrac{10}{x}$?

Solution. Multiply each side by the LCD, $5x$:

$$5x\left(\frac{4}{x}\right)+5x\left(\frac{3}{5}\right)=5x\left(\frac{10}{x}\right)\Rightarrow 20+3x=50$$

Now solve normally:

$$20+3x=50\Rightarrow 3x=30\Rightarrow x=\mathbf{10}$$

⇒ **Example 12** _____

If x is positive, and $y=5x^2+3$, which of the following is an expression for x in terms of y?

(A) $\sqrt{\dfrac{y}{5}-3}$

(B) $\sqrt{\dfrac{y-3}{5}}$

(C) $\dfrac{\sqrt{y-3}}{5}$

(D) $\dfrac{\sqrt{y}-3}{5}$

Solution. The six-step method works only when there are no exponents. So, treat x^2 as a single variable, and use the method as far as you can:

$$y=5x^2+3\Rightarrow y-3=5x^2\Rightarrow \frac{y-3}{5}=x^2$$

Now take the square root of each side: $x=\sqrt{\dfrac{y-3}{5}}$ **(B)**

> **CAUTION:** Doing the same thing to each *side* of an equation does *not* mean doing the same thing to each *term* of the equation. Study Examples 13 and 14 carefully.

⇒ **Example 13** _____

If $\dfrac{1}{a}=\dfrac{1}{b}+\dfrac{1}{c}$, what is a in terms of b and c?

Note: You *cannot* just take the reciprocal of each term; the answer is *not* $a=b+c$. Here are two solutions.

Solution 1. First add the fractions on the right-hand side:

$$\frac{1}{a}=\frac{1}{b}+\frac{1}{c}=\frac{b+c}{bc}$$

Now, take the reciprocal of *each side*: $a=\dfrac{bc}{b+c}$

Solution 2. Use the six-step method. Multiply each term by abc, the LCD:

$$abc\left(\frac{1}{a}\right) = abc\left(\frac{1}{b}\right) + abc\left(\frac{1}{c}\right) \Rightarrow bc = ac + ab = a(c+b) \Rightarrow a = \frac{bc}{c+b}$$

➥ Example 14 _____

If $a > 0$ and $a^2 + b^2 = c^2$, what is a in terms of b and c?

Note: You *cannot* take the square root of each term and write $a + b = c$.

Solution. $a^2 + b^2 = c^2 \Rightarrow a^2 = c^2 - b^2$. Now, take the square root of *each side*:

$$a = \sqrt{a^2} = \sqrt{c^2 - b^2}$$

➥ Example 15 _____

If $a = b(c + d)$, what is d in terms of a, b, and c?

(A) $\dfrac{a}{b} - c$

(B) $\dfrac{a}{bc}$

(C) $\dfrac{a}{bc} - b$

(D) $\dfrac{a-c}{b}$

Solution. Use the six-step method:

$$a = b(c + d) \Rightarrow a = bc + bd \Rightarrow a - bc = bd \Rightarrow d = \frac{a-bc}{b}$$

Now what? This answer isn't one of the choices. It is, however, *equivalent* to one of the choices. Use the distributive law to divide each term in the numerator by b:

$$\frac{a-bc}{b} = \frac{a}{b} - \frac{bc}{b} = \frac{a}{b} - c \quad \textbf{(A)}$$

HELPFUL HINT

On a multiple-choice question, if your answer is not among the four choices, check to see whether it is *equivalent* to one of the choices.

On the SAT, most of the equations that you will have to solve do not involve exponents. Of those equations that do have exponents, the ones you will see most often are quadratic equations. Quadratic equations are equations that can be written in the form $ax^2 + bx + c = 0$, where a, b, and c are real numbers and $a \neq 0$.

The easiest quadratic equations to solve are those that have no x-term, that is, those in which $b = 0$ as in the following three examples.

➥ Example 16 _____

If x is a positive number and $x^2 + 4 = 125$, what is the value of x?

Solution. When there is an x^2-term, but no x-term, just take the square root:

$$x^2 + 4 = 125 \Rightarrow x^2 = 121 \Rightarrow x = \sqrt{121} = \textbf{11}$$

➡ **Example 16a** _____

If x is a positive number and $x^2 + 5 = 125$, what is the value of x?

Solution. This is exactly like Example 16, except now $x^2 = 120$. So $x = \sqrt{120}$. Even though 120 is not a perfect square, $\sqrt{120}$ can be simplified.

Since $120 = 4 \times 30$, we have that $x = \sqrt{120} = \sqrt{4} \times \sqrt{30} = \mathbf{2\sqrt{30}}$.

 CALCULATOR SHORTCUT

If you can easily simplify a square root, that's great; but on the SAT, you never have to. The answers to grid-in problems don't involve square roots, and if the answer to a multiple-choice question turns out to be $\sqrt{120}$, you can use your calculator to see which of the four choices is equal to 10.95.

➡ **Example 16b** _____

If x is a positive number and $x^2 + 6 = 125$, what is the value of x?

Solution. Again, this is exactly like Example 16, except now $x^2 = 119$. Not only isn't 119 a perfect square, $\sqrt{119}$ can't be simplified. So $x = \mathbf{\sqrt{119}}$.

The next easiest quadratic equations to solve are those that have no constant term, that is, those in which $c = 0$. In Example 17 below, $a = 2$, $b = -3$, and $c = 0$.

➡ **Example 17** _____

What is the largest value of x that satisfies the equation $2x^2 - 3x = 0$?

Solution. When an equation has an x^2-term and an x-term but no constant term, solve it by factoring out the x and using the fact that, if the product of two numbers is 0, one of them must be 0 (KEY FACT A3):

$$2x^2 - 3x = 0 \Rightarrow x(2x - 3) = 0.$$

So, $x = 0$ or $2x - 3 = 0 \Rightarrow$
$$x = 0 \text{ or } 2x = 3 \Rightarrow$$
$$x = 0 \text{ or } x = 1.5$$

So the largest value of x that satisfies the given equation is **1.5**.

Solving quadratic equations in which a, b, and c are all nonzero requires more sophisticated techniques. The two most common methods are factoring and using the quadratic formula. The easier method is factoring *if you immediately see how to factor the given expression.*

➡ **Example 18** _____

If x is a positive number and $x^2 - 2x = 15$, what is the value of x?

Solution. First rewrite the given equation in the form $x^2 - 2x - 15 = 0$. See if you can factor $x^2 - 2x - 15$. Hopefully, you quickly realize that $x^2 - 2x - 15 = (x - 5)(x + 3)$. Then

$$(x - 5)(x + 3) = 0 \Rightarrow (x - 5) = 0 \text{ or } (x + 3) = 0 \Rightarrow x = 5 \text{ or } x = -3$$

So the positive number that satisfies the given equation is **5**.

Unfortunately, even if $ax^2 + bx + c$ can be factored, you may not immediately see how to do it. What's worse is that most quadratic expressions can't be factored.

None of the following expressions are factorable:

$$x^2 - 2x - 16; \quad x^2 - 2x - 17; \quad x^2 - 2x - 18; \quad x^2 - 2x - 19; \quad x^2 - 2x - 20$$

So how do you solve an equation such as $x^2 - 2x - 20 = 0$? Use the quadratic formula.

Key Fact G1

Quadratic Formula

If a, b, and c are real numbers with $a \neq 0$ and if $ax^2 + bx + c = 0$, then

$$x = \frac{-b \pm \sqrt{b^2 - 4ac}}{2a}$$

Recall that the symbol $\pm$ is read "plus or minus" and that $x = \dfrac{-b \pm \sqrt{b^2 - 4ac}}{2a}$ is an abbreviation for $x = \dfrac{-b + \sqrt{b^2 - 4ac}}{2a}$ or $x = \dfrac{-b - \sqrt{b^2 - 4ac}}{2a}$.

As you can see, a quadratic equation has two solutions, usually referred to as **roots**, both of which are determined by the quadratic formula.

The expression $b^2 - 4ac$ that appears under the square root symbol is called the **discriminant** of the quadratic equation. As explained in KEY FACT G2, the discriminant provides valuable information about the nature of the roots of a quadratic equation. If we let D represent

the discriminant, an alternative way to write the quadratic formula is $x = \dfrac{-b \pm \sqrt{D}}{2a}$. The

following examples illustrate the proper use of the quadratic formula.

First, let's look at a different solution to Example 18.

➡ Example 19 _____

What are the roots of the equation $x^2 - 2x - 15 = 0$?

Solution. Here $a = 1$, $b = -2$, $c = -15$ and $D = b^2 - 4ac = (-2)^2 - 4(1)(-15) = 4 + 60 = 64$

$$\text{So } x = \frac{-(-2) \pm \sqrt{64}}{2(1)} = \frac{2 \pm 8}{2} \Rightarrow$$

$$x = \frac{2 + 8}{2} = 5 \quad \text{or} \quad x = \frac{2 - 8}{2} = -3$$

➥ **Example 20** _____

What are the roots of the equation $x^2 = 10x - 25$?

Solution. First, rewrite the equation in the form $ax^2 + bx + c = 0$:

$$x^2 - 10x + 25 = 0$$

Then $a = 1$, $b = -10$, $c = 25$ and $D = b^2 - 4ac = (-10)^2 - 4(1)(25) = 100 - 100 = 0$

$$\text{So } x = \frac{-(-10) \pm \sqrt{0}}{2(1)} = \frac{10 \pm 0}{2} \Rightarrow$$

$$x = \frac{10 + 0}{2} = 5 \quad \text{or} \quad x = \frac{10 - 0}{2} = 5$$

Notice that since $10 + 0 = 10$ and $10 - 0 = 10$, the two roots are each equal to 5. Some people would say that the equation $x^2 - 10x + 25 = 0$ has only one root; it is better to say that the equation has two equal roots.

➥ **Example 21** _____

What are the roots of the equation $2x^2 - 4x - 1 = 0$?

Solution. $a = 2$, $b = -4$, $c = -1$ and $D = b^2 - 4ac = (-4)^2 - 4(2)(-1) = 16 + 8 = 24$

$$\text{So } x = \frac{-(-4) \pm \sqrt{24}}{2(2)} = \frac{4 \pm 2\sqrt{6}}{4} \Rightarrow$$

$$x = \frac{4 + 2\sqrt{6}}{4} = 1 + \frac{1}{2}\sqrt{6} \quad \text{or} \quad x = \frac{4 - 2\sqrt{6}}{4} = 1 - \frac{1}{2}\sqrt{6}$$

➥ **Example 22** _____

What are the roots of equation $x^2 - 2x + 2 = 0$.

Solution. $a = 1$, $b = -2$, $c = 2$ and $D = b^2 - 4ac = (-2)^2 - 4(1)(2) = 4 - 8 = -4$

Since there is no real number whose square root is -4, we often say that this equation "has no solutions" or "has no roots." However, what we mean is that this equation "has no *real* roots." Continuing with the quadratic formula, we get:

$$x = \frac{-(-2) \pm \sqrt{-4}}{2(1)} = \frac{2 \pm 2i}{2} = 1 \pm i \Rightarrow$$

$$x = 1 + i \quad \text{or} \quad x = 1 - i$$

See Section 6-T for a discussion of the imaginary unit i and complex numbers.

Examples 19–22, above, illustrate the facts about the discriminant, D, that are summarized in Key Fact G2.

If a, b, and c are real numbers with $a \neq 0$, if $ax^2 + bx + c = 0$, and if $D = b^2 - 4ac$, then

Value of Discriminant	Nature of the Roots
$D = 0$	2 equal roots
$D > 0$	2 unequal real roots
$D < 0$	2 unequal complex roots that are conjugates of each other

Exponential Equations

Occasionally, on an SAT you will have to solve an equation in which the variables are in the exponents. The way to handle an equation of this type is to use the laws of exponents.

➡ **Example 23**

If $2^{x+3} = 32$, what is the value of 3^{x+2}?

Solution. How many 2's do you have to multiply together to get 32? If you don't know that the answer is 5, just multiply and keep track. Count the 2's on your fingers as you say to yourself, "2 times 2 is 4, times 2 is 8, times 2 is 16, times 2 is 32." Then

$$2^{x+3} = 32 = 2^5 \Rightarrow x + 3 = 5 \Rightarrow x = 2$$

Therefore, $x + 2 = 4$, and $3^{x+2} = 3^4 = 3 \times 3 \times 3 \times 3 = \mathbf{81}$.

If both sides of an equation have variables in the exponents, you have to rewrite both exponentials with the same base.

➡ **Example 24**

If $4^{w+3} = 8^{w-1}$, what is the value of w?

Solution. Since it is necessary to have the same base on each side of the equation, write $4 = 2^2$ and $8 = 2^3$. Then

$$4^{w+3} = (2^2)^{w+3} = 2^{2(w+3)} = 2^{2w+6}$$

and

$$8^{w-1} = (2^3)^{w-1} = 2^{3(w-1)} = 2^{3w-3}$$

Therefore, $2^{2w+6} = 2^{3w-3} \Rightarrow 2w + 6 = 3w - 3 \Rightarrow w = \mathbf{9}$.

Systems of Linear Equations

A *system of equations* is a set of two or more equations involving two or more variables. A solution consists of a value for each variable that will simultaneously satisfy each equation.

The equations $x + y = 10$ and $x - y = 2$ each have lots of solutions (infinitely many, in fact). Some of them are given in the following tables.

$$x + y = 10$$

x	5	**6**	4	1	1.2	10	20
y	5	**4**	6	9	8.8	0	–10
$x+y$	10	10	10	10	10	10	10

$$x - y = 2$$

x	5	**6**	2	0	2.5	19	40
y	3	**4**	0	–2	.5	17	38
$x-y$	2	2	2	2	2	2	2

However, only one pair of numbers, $x = 6$ and $y = 4$, satisfies both equations simultaneously: $6 + 4 = 10$ and $6 - 4 = 2$. These numbers, then, are the only solution of the *system of equations* $\begin{cases} x+y=10 \\ x-y=2 \end{cases}$.

The above is called a *system of linear* equations because the graph of each equation is a line. If you graph the lines whose equations are $x + y = 10$ and $x - y = 2$, they will intersect at the point $(6, 4)$. In an algebra course you learn several ways to solve systems of linear equations. On the SAT, the most useful way is to add or subtract (usually add) the equations. Examples 25 and 26 demonstrate this method, and Example 27 shows another way to handle some systems of equations.

TACTIC

G4

To solve a system of equations, first try to add or subtract them. If there are more than two equations, add them.

➡ **Example 25** _____

If the sum of two numbers is 10 and their difference is 2, what is their product?

Solution. Letting x and y represent the two numbers, first write the two equations: $x + y = 10$ and $x - y = 2$. Now add them:

$$
\begin{array}{r}
x + y = 10 \\
+\ x - y = 2 \\
\hline
2x\quad = 12 \Rightarrow x = 6
\end{array}
$$

Replacing x by 6 in $x + y = 10$ yields $y = 4$. The product, xy, is **24**.

➡ **Example 26** _____

If $3a + 5b = 10$ and $5a + 3b = 30$, what is the average (arithmetic mean) of a and b?

(A) 2.5

(B) 4

(C) 5

(D) 20

Solution. Add the two equations:

$$3a + 5b = 10$$
$$+ 5a + 3b = 30$$
$$\overline{8a + 8b = 40}$$

Divide both sides by 8:

$$a + b = 5$$

The average of a and b is:

$$\frac{a+b}{2} = \frac{5}{2} = \mathbf{2.5} \quad \textbf{(A)}$$

Note: It is not only unnecessary but also a waste of time to first solve for a and b ($a = 7.5$ and $b = -2.5$) and then take the average of the two numbers.

For additional examples of the proper use of TACTIC G4, see the examples following TACTIC 16 in Chapter 5.

Occasionally on the SAT, it is as easy, or easier, to solve a system of equations by substitution.

HELPFUL HINT

On the SAT, some problems involving systems of equations do *not* require you to solve the systems. These problems often ask for something other than the value of each variable. Read the questions very carefully, circle what you need, and do not do more than is required.

TACTIC **G5**

If one of the equations in a system of equations consists of a single variable equal to some expression, substitute that expression for the variable in the other equation.

➡ **Example 27** _____

If $x + y = 10$ and $y = x - 2$, what is the value of xy?

Solution. This is essentially the same problem as Example 25. However, since here the second equation states that a single variable (y) is equal to some expression ($x - 2$), substitution is a more efficient method than adding. Replace y by $x - 2$ in the first equation: $x + y = 10$ becomes $x + (x - 2) = 10$. Then

$$2x - 2 = 10 \Rightarrow 2x = 12 \Rightarrow x = 6$$

To find the value of y, replace x by 6 in either of the original equations:

$$6 + y = 10 \Rightarrow y = 4 \text{ or } y = 6 - 2 = 4$$

Finally, $xy = (6)(4) = \mathbf{24}$.

Solving Linear-Quadratic Systems

A question on the SAT could ask you to solve a system of equations in which one, or even both, of the equations are quadratic. The next example illustrates this.

➡ **Example 28** _____

To solve the system $\begin{cases} y = 2x - 1 \\ y = x^2 - 2x + 2 \end{cases}$, use the substitution method. Replace the y in the second equation by $2x - 1$:

$$2x - 1 = x^2 - 2x + 2 \Rightarrow x^2 - 4x + 3 = 0 \Rightarrow$$

$$(x - 3)(x - 1) = 0 \Rightarrow x = 3 \text{ or } x = 1$$

If $x = 3$, then $y = 2(3) - 1 = 5$; and if $x = 1$, then $y = 2(1) - 1 = 1$.
So there are two solutions: $x = 3$, $y = 5$ and $x = 1$, $y = 1$.

Solving the system of equations in Example 28 is equivalent to determining the points of intersection of the line $y = 2x - 1$ and the parabola $y = x^2 - 2x + 2$. Those points are (1, 1) and (3, 5).

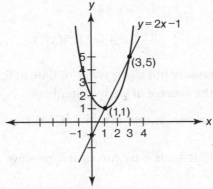

So an alternative method of solving the system of equations in Example 28 is to graph them. If you have a graphing calculator, you can graph the given line and parabola and then determine their points of intersection. Which solution is preferable? This is a personal decision. If your algebra skills are strong, solving the system graphically offers no advantage. If, on the other hand, your algebra skills are weak and your facility with the calculator is good, you could avoid the algebra and use your calculator.

Multiple-Choice Questions

1. If $4x + 12 = 36$, what is the value of $x + 3$?

   (A) 3

   (B) 6

   (C) 9

   (D) 12

2. If $4x + 13 = 7 - 2x$, what is the value of x?

   (A) $-\dfrac{10}{3}$

   (B) -1

   (C) 1

   (D) $\dfrac{10}{3}$

3. If $ax - b = c - dx$, what is the value of x in terms of a, b, c, and d?

   (A) $\dfrac{b+c}{a+d}$

   (B) $\dfrac{c-b}{a-d}$

   (C) $\dfrac{b+c-d}{a}$

   (D) $\dfrac{c-b}{a+d}$

4. If $\dfrac{1}{3}x + \dfrac{1}{6}x + \dfrac{1}{9}x = 33$, what is the value of x?

   (A) 18

   (B) 27

   (C) 54

   (D) 72

5. If $17 - 2\sqrt{x} = 14$, what is the value of x?

   (A) $\dfrac{9}{4}$

   (B) $\dfrac{29}{4}$

   (C) 36

   (D) 196

6. If $32^{a+b} = 16^{a+2b}$, then $a =$

   (A) b

   (B) $2b$

   (C) $3b$

   (D) $b + 2$

7. If the average (arithmetic mean) of $3a$ and $4b$ is less than 50, and a is twice b, what is the largest integer value of a?

   (A) 10

   (B) 11

   (C) 19

   (D) 20

8. If $\dfrac{1}{a-b} = 5$, then $a =$

   (A) $b + 5$

   (B) $b - 5$

   (C) $b + \dfrac{1}{5}$

   (D) $b - \dfrac{1}{5}$

9. If $x = 3a + 7$ and $y = 9a^2$, what is y in terms of x?

   (A) $(x - 7)^2$

   (B) $3(x - 7)^2$

   (C) $\dfrac{(x-7)^2}{3}$

   (D) $(x + 7)^2$

10. Which of the following is a solution of $3|x + 1| - 5 = -2$?

    (A) -2

    (B) 1

    (C) $\dfrac{4}{3}$

    (D) 2

Grid-in Questions

11. If $x - 4 = 9$, what is the value of $x^2 - 4$?

12. If $7x + 10 = 44$, what is the value of $7x - 10$?

13. If $3x - 4 = 9$, what is the value of $(3x - 4)^2$?

14. If $x^{-3} = \dfrac{1}{4x}$, what is one possible value of x?

15. If $x^2 + 3 < 4$ and $2x^2 + 3 > 4$, what is one possible value of x?

Answer Key

1. **C**   3. **A**   5. **A**   7. **C**   9. **A**
2. **B**   4. **C**   6. **C**   8. **C**   10. **A**

11.

	1	6	5

12.

		2	4

13.

	8	1	

14.

			2

15.

	.	7	5

.707 < x < 1

Answers Explained

1. **(C)** The easiest method is to recognize that $x + 3$ is $\frac{1}{4}$ of $4x + 12$, and, therefore, equals $\frac{1}{4}$ of 36, which is 9. If you don't see that, solve normally:

$$4x + 12 = 36 \Rightarrow 4x = 24 \Rightarrow x = 6 \Rightarrow x + 3 = 9$$

2. **(B)** Add $2x$ to each side: $6x + 13 = 7$. Subtract 13 from each side: $6x = -6$. Divide by 6: $x = -1$.

3. **(A)** Treat a, b, c, and d as constants, and use the six-step method to solve for x:

$$ax - b = c - dx \Rightarrow ax - b + dx = c \Rightarrow$$
$$ax + dx = c + b \Rightarrow x(a + d) = b + c \Rightarrow$$
$$x = \frac{b+c}{a+d}$$

4. **(C)** Multiply both sides by 18, the LCD:

$$18\left(\frac{1}{3}x + \frac{1}{6}x + \frac{1}{9}x\right) = 18(33) \Rightarrow$$

$$6x + 3x + 2x = 594 \Rightarrow 11x = 594 \Rightarrow x = 54$$

Mentally, it's easier not to multiply 18×33; leave it in that form and divide by 11:

$\dfrac{18 \times \overset{3}{\cancel{33}}}{\underset{1}{\cancel{11}}} = 18 \times 3 = 54$. Since you have a calculator, however, you might as well use it.

5. **(A)** $17 - 2\sqrt{x} = 14 \Rightarrow -2\sqrt{x} = -3 \Rightarrow 2\sqrt{x} = 3 \Rightarrow \sqrt{x} = \frac{3}{2} \Rightarrow x = \frac{9}{4}$

6. **(C)** $32^{a+b} = (2^5)^{a+b} = 2^{5a+5b}$, and $16^{a+2b} = (2^4)^{a+2b} = 2^{4a+8b}$. Therefore:

$$5a + 5b = 4a + 8b \Rightarrow a + 5b = 8b \Rightarrow a = 3b$$

7. **(C)** Since $a = 2b$, then $2a = 4b$. Therefore, the average of $3a$ and $4b$ is the average of $3a$ and $2a$, which is $2.5a$. Therefore, $2.5a < 50 \Rightarrow a < 20$, so the largest integer value of a is 19.

8. **(C)** Take the reciprocal of each side:

$$a - b = \frac{1}{5}, \text{ so } a = b + \frac{1}{5}$$

9. **(A)** If $x = 3a + 7$, then $x - 7 = 3a$ and $a = \frac{x-7}{3}$. Therefore

$$y = 9a^2 = 9\left(\frac{x-7}{3}\right)^2 = \overset{1}{\cancel{9}} \frac{(x-7)^2}{\underset{1}{3^2}} = (x-7)^2$$

10. **(A)** $3|x + 1| - 5 = -2 \Rightarrow 3|x + 1| = 3 \Rightarrow |x + 1| = 1 \Rightarrow x + 1 = 1$ or $x + 1 = -1 \Rightarrow x = 0$ or $x = -2$

The equation has two solutions, 0 and -2, but 0 is not a choice. The answer is -2.

11. **165** $x - 4 = 9 \Rightarrow x = 13 \Rightarrow x^2 = 169$, and so $x^2 - 4 = 165$.

12. **24** Subtracting 20 from each side of $7x + 10 = 44$ gives $7x - 10 = 24$. If you don't see that, subtract 10 from each side, getting $7x = 34$. Then subtract 10 to get $7x - 10 = 24$. The worst alternative is to divide both sides of $7x = 34$ by 7 to get $x = \dfrac{34}{7}$; then you have to multiply by 7 to get back to 34, and then subtract 10.

13. **81** Be alert. Since you are given the value of $3x - 4$, and want the value of $(3x - 4)^2$, just square both sides: $9^2 = 81$. If you don't see that, you'll waste time solving $3x - 4 = 9$, getting that $x = \dfrac{13}{3}$, only to use that value to calculate that $3x - 4$ is equal to 9, which you aready knew.

14. **2** $x^{-3} = \dfrac{1}{4x} \Rightarrow 4x(x^{-3}) = 1 \Rightarrow 4x^{-2} = 1$. So,

$$x^{-2} = \frac{1}{4} \Rightarrow \frac{1}{x^2} = \frac{1}{4} \Rightarrow x^2 = 4 \Rightarrow x = 2 \text{ or } x = -2$$

Since -2 cannot be entered in a grid, the only acceptable solution is 2.

15. **.707 < x < 1** $x^2 + 3 < 4 \Rightarrow x^2 < 1$, and $2x^2 + 3 > 4 \Rightarrow 2x^2 > 1 \Rightarrow x^2 > .5$. Grid in any number between $\sqrt{.5} \approx .707$ and 1.

6-H WORD PROBLEMS

A typical SAT has several word problems, covering almost every math topic for which you are responsible. In this chapter you have already seen word problems on consecutive integers in Section 6-A, fractions and percents in Sections 6-B and 6-C, ratios and proportions in Section 6-D, and averages in Section 6-E. Later in this chapter you will see word problems involving circles, triangles, and other geometric figures. A few of these problems can be solved just with arithmetic, but most of them require basic algebra.

To solve word problems algebraically, you must treat algebra as a foreign language and learn to translate "word for word" from English into algebra, just as you would from English into French or Spanish or any other foreign language. When translating into algebra, you use some letter (often x) to represent the unknown quantity you are trying to determine. It is this translation process that causes difficulty for some students. Once the translation is completed, solving is easy using the techniques already reviewed.

Consider the pairs of questions in Examples 1 and 2. The first ones in each pair (1A and 2A) would be considered very easy, whereas the second ones (1B and 2B) would be considered harder because they require you first to translate the word problem into algebraic equations.

➡ Example 1A

What is 4% of 4% of 40,000?

➡ Example 1B

In a lottery, 4% of the tickets printed can be redeemed for prizes, and 4% of those tickets have values in excess of $100. If the state prints 40,000 tickets, how many of them can be redeemed for more than $100?

➡ Example 2A

If $x + 7 = 2(x - 8)$, what is the value of x?

➡ Example 2B

In 7 years Erin will be twice as old as she was 8 years ago. How old is Erin now?

Once you translate the words into arithmetic expressions or algebraic equations, Examples 1A as are 1B are identical, as are 2A and 2B. The problem that many students have is doing the translation. It really isn't very difficult, and you'll learn how. First, though, look over the following English-to-algebra "dictionary."

English Words	Mathematical Meaning	Symbol
Is, was, will be, had, has, will have, is equal to, is the same as	Equals	=
Plus, more than, sum, increased by, added to, exceeds, received, got, older than, farther than, greater than	Addition	+
Minus, fewer, less than, difference, decreased by, subtracted from, younger than, gave, lost	Subtraction	−
Times, of, product, multiplied by	Multiplication	×
Divided by, quotient, per, for	Division	$\div$, $\frac{a}{b}$
More than, greater than	Inequality	>
At least	Inequality	≥
Fewer than, less than	Inequality	<
At most	Inequality	≤
What, how many, etc.	Unknown quantity	x (or some other variable)

Let's use this "dictionary" to translate some phrases and sentences.

1. The <u>sum</u> of 5 and some number <u>is</u> 13.　　　　　　　$5 + x = 13$
2. John <u>was</u> 2 years <u>younger than</u> Sam.　　　　　　$J = S - 2$
3. Bill has <u>at most</u> $100.　　　　　　　　　　　　$B \leq 100$
4. The <u>product</u> of 2 and a number <u>exceeds</u> that number by 5 (is 5 more than).　　　　　　　　　　　　$2n = n + 5$

In translating a statement, you first must decide what quantity the variable will represent. Often, this is obvious. Other times there is more than one possibility.

Let's translate and solve the two examples at the beginning of this section, and then look at a few new ones.

➡ Example 1B _____

In a lottery, 4% of the tickets printed can be redeemed for prizes, and 4% of those tickets have values in excess of $100. If the state prints 40,000 tickets, how many of them can be redeemed for more than $100?

 Solution. Let x be the number of tickets worth more than $100. Then

$$x = 4\% \text{ of } 4\% \text{ of } 40{,}000 = 0.04 \times 0.04 \times 40{,}000 = \mathbf{64},$$

which is also the solution to Example 1A.

➡ Example 2B

In 7 years Erin will be twice as old as she was 8 years ago. How old is Erin now?

Solution. Let x be Erin's age now; 8 years ago she was $x - 8$ and 7 years from now she will be $x + 7$. Then,

$$x + 7 = 2(x - 8)$$

and

$x + 7 = 2(x - 8) \Rightarrow x + 7 = 2x - 16 \Rightarrow 7 = x - 16 \Rightarrow x = \mathbf{23}$, which is also the solution to Example 2A.

➡ Example 3

The product of 2 and 8 more than a certain number is 10 times that number. What is the number?

Solution. Let x represent the unknown number. Then

$$2(8 + x) = 10x$$

and

$$2(8 + x) = 10x \Rightarrow 16 + 2x = 10x \Rightarrow 8x = 16 \Rightarrow x = \mathbf{2}$$

➡ Example 4

If the sum of three consecutive integers is 20 more than the middle integer, what is the smallest of the three?

Solution. Let n represent the smallest of the three consecutive integers. Then the middle integer is $n + 1$ and the largest is $n + 2$. So

$$n + (n + 1) + (n + 2) = 20 + (n + 1)$$

and

$$n + n + 1 + n + 2 = 20 + n + 1 \Rightarrow 3n + 3 = 21 + n \Rightarrow 2n + 3 = 21 \Rightarrow 2n = 18 \Rightarrow n = \mathbf{9}$$

(Note: The integers are 9, 10, and 11. Their sum is 30, which is 20 more than 10, the middle integer.)

Most algebraic word problems on the SAT are not very difficult. If, after studying this section, you still get stuck on a question, don't despair. Use the tactics that you learned in Chapter 5. In each of Examples 3 and 4, if you had been given choices, you could have backsolved; and if the questions had been grid-ins, you could have used trial and error (effectively, backsolving by making up your own choices). Here's how.

 Alternative Solution to Example 3. Pick a starting number and test (using your calculator, if necessary).

Try 10: $8 + 10 = 18$ and $2 \times 18 = 36$, but $10 \times 10 = 100$, which is *much too big*.

Try 5: $8 + 5 = 13$ and $2 \times 13 = 26$, but $10 \times 5 = 50$, which is *still too big*.

Try 2: $8 + 2 = 10$ and $2 \times 10 = 20$, and $10 \times 2 = 20$. That's it.

Alternative Solution to Example 4. You need three consecutive integers whose sum is 20 more than the middle one. Obviously, 1, 2, 3 and 5, 6, 7 are too small; neither one even adds up to 20.

Try 10, 11, 12: $10 + 11 + 12 = 33$, which is 22 more than 11—a bit too much.
Try 9, 10, 11: $9 + 10 + 11 = 30$, which *is* 20 more than 10.

Of course, if you can do the algebra, that's usually the best way to handle these problems. On grid-ins you might have to backsolve with several numbers before zooming in on the correct answer; also, if the correct answer was a fraction, such as $\frac{13}{5}$, you might never find it. In the rest of this section, the proper ways to set up and solve various word problems are stressed.

Age Problems

In problems involving ages, remember that "years ago" means you need to subtract, and "years from now" means you need to add.

➥ Example 5 _____

In 1980, Judy was 3 times as old as Adam, but in 1984 she was only twice as old as he was. How old was Adam in 1990?

(A)   8
(B)   12
(C)   14
(D)   16

Solution. Let x be Adam's age in 1980, and fill in the table below.

Year	Judy	Adam
1980	$3x$	x
1984	$3x + 4$	$x + 4$

Now translate: Judy's age in 1984 was twice Adam's age in 1984:

$$3x + 4 = 2(x + 4)$$
$$3x + 4 = 2x + 8 \Rightarrow x + 4 = 8 \Rightarrow x = 4$$

Adam was 4 in 1980. However, 4 is *not* the answer to this question. Did you remember to circle what you're looking for? The question *could have* asked for Adam's age in 1980 (choice (A)) or 1984 (choice (B)) or Judy's age in any year whatsoever (choice (C) is 1980); but it didn't. It asked for *Adam's age in 1990*. Since he was 4 in 1980, then 10 years later, in 1990, he was **14** **(C)**.

HELPFUL HINT

In all word problems on the SAT, remember to circle what you're looking for. Don't answer the wrong question!

HELPFUL HINT

It is often very useful to organize the data from a word problem in a table.

Distance Problems

All distance problems involve one of three variations of the same formula:

$$\text{distance} = \text{rate} \times \text{time} \qquad \text{rate} = \frac{\text{distance}}{\text{time}} \qquad \text{time} = \frac{\text{distance}}{\text{rate}}$$

These are usually abbreviated as $d = rt$, $r = \dfrac{d}{t}$, and $t = \dfrac{d}{r}$.

➡ **Example 6** _____

How much longer, in <u>seconds</u>, is required to drive 1 mile at 40 miles per hour than at 60 miles per hour?

Solution. The time to drive 1 mile at 40 miles per hour is given by

$$t = \frac{1 \text{ mile}}{40 \text{ miles per hour}} = \frac{1}{40} \text{ hour} = \frac{1}{40} \times \overset{3}{\underset{2}{60}} \text{ minutes} = \frac{3}{2} \text{ minutes} = 1\frac{1}{2} \text{ minutes}$$

The time to drive 1 mile at 60 miles per hour is given by

$$t = \frac{1 \text{ mile}}{60 \text{ miles per hour}} = \frac{1}{60} \text{ hour} = 1 \text{ minute}$$

The difference is $\dfrac{1}{2}$ minute = **30** seconds.

Note that this solution used the time formula given but required only arithmetic, not algebra. Example 7 requires an algebraic solution.

➡ **Example 7** _____

Mark drove to a meeting at 60 miles per hour. Returning over the same route, he encountered heavy traffic, and was able to drive at only 40 miles per hour. If the return trip took 1 hour longer, how many miles did he drive each way?

(A)   2
(B)   3
(C)   120
(D) 240

Solution. Let x represent the number of hours Mark took to go, and make a table.

	Rate	Time	Distance
Going	60	x	$60x$
Returning	40	$x+1$	$40(x+1)$

Since Mark drove the same distance going and returning:

$$60x = 40(x+1) \Rightarrow 60x = 40x + 40 \Rightarrow 20x = 40 \Rightarrow x = 2$$

Now be sure to answer the correct question. Choices (A) and (B) are the *times*, in hours, for going and returning, rspectively; choices (C) and (D) are the distances each way and round-trip, respectively. You could have been asked for any of the four. If you circle what you're looking for, you won't make a careless mistake. Mark drove **120** miles each way, and so the correct answer is **(C)**.

The d in the formula $d = rt$ stands for distance, but it could represent any type of work that is performed at a certain rate, r, for a certain amount of time, t. Example 7 need not be about distance. Instead of driving 120 miles at 60 miles per hour for 2 hours, Mark could have read 120 pages at a rate of 60 pages per hour for 2 hours, or planted 120 flowers at the rate of 60 flowers per hour for 2 hours, or typed 120 words at a rate of 60 words per minute for 2 minutes.

This section concludes with a miscellaneous collection of word problems of the type that you may find on the SAT. Some of them are similar to problems already discussed in preceding sections.

➡ Example 8 _____

At 8:00 P.M., the hostess of the party remarked that only $\dfrac{1}{4}$ of her guests had arrived so far, but that, as soon as 10 more showed up, $\dfrac{1}{3}$ of the guests would be there. How many people were invited?

Solution. Let x represent the number of people invited. First, translate the first sentence of the problem into algebra: $\dfrac{1}{4}x + 10 = \dfrac{1}{3}x$. Then, use the six-step method of Section 6-G to solve the equation.
Multiply each term by 12: $3x + 120 = 4x$.
Subtract $3x$ from each side: $x = \mathbf{120}$.

➡ Example 9 _____

In a family of three, the father weighed 5 times as much as the child, and the mother weighed $\dfrac{3}{4}$ as much as the father. If the three of them weighed a total of 390 pounds, how much did the mother weigh?

In this problem it is easier to let x represent the weight of the child, and $5x$ the weight of the father, than to let x represent the weight of the father, and $\dfrac{1}{5}x$ the weight of the child.

The worst choice would be to let x represent the weight of the mother; in that case, since the mother's weight is $\dfrac{3}{4}$ that of the father's, his weight would be $\dfrac{4}{3}$ of hers.

Solution. Let x = weight of the child; then $5x$ = weight of the father, and $\dfrac{3}{4}(5x)$ = weight of the mother. Since their combined weight is 390:

$$x + 5x + \frac{15}{4}x = 390$$

 Multiply by 4 to get rid of the fraction:

$$4x + 20x + 15x = 1560$$

Combine like terms and then divide:

$$39x = 1560 \Rightarrow x = 40$$

The child weighed 40 pounds, the father weighed $5 \times 40 = 200$ pounds, and the mother weighed $\dfrac{3}{4}(200) = \mathbf{150\ pounds}$.

➥ Example 10 _____

A teacher wrote three consecutive odd integers on the board. She then multiplied the first by 2, the second by 3, and the third by 4. Finally, she added all six numbers and got a sum of 400. What was the smallest number she wrote?

Solution. Let n be the first odd integer she wrote. Since the difference between any two consecutive odd integers is 2 (3, 5, 7, 9, etc.), the next consecutive odd integer is $n + 2$ and the third is $n + 4$. The required equation is

$$n + (n + 2) + (n + 4) + 2n + 3(n + 2) + 4(n + 4) = 400$$

 Simplifying gives

$$n + n + 2 + n + 4 + 2n + 3n + 6 + 4n + 16 = 400 \Rightarrow$$
$$12n + 28 = 400 \Rightarrow 12n = 372 \Rightarrow n = \mathbf{31}$$

Multiple-Choice Questions

1. In the afternoon, Judy read 100 pages at the rate of 60 pages per hour; in the evening, when she was tired, she read another 100 pages at the rate of 40 pages per hour. In pages per hour, what was her average rate of reading for the day?

   (A) 45
   (B) 48
   (C) 50
   (D) 55

2. If the sum of five consecutive integers is S, what is the largest of those integers in terms of S?

   (A) $\dfrac{S-10}{5}$

   (B) $\dfrac{S+5}{4}$

   (C) $\dfrac{S-5}{2}$

   (D) $\dfrac{S+10}{5}$

3. A jar contains only red, white, and blue marbles. The number of red marbles is $\dfrac{4}{5}$ the number of white ones, and the number of white ones is $\dfrac{3}{4}$ the number of blue ones. If there are 470 marbles in all, how many of them are blue?

   (A) 150
   (B) 184
   (C) 200
   (D) 210

4. As a fundraiser, the Key Club was selling two types of candy: lollipops at 40 cents each and chocolate bars at 75 cents each. On Monday, the members sold 150 candies and raised 74 dollars. How many lollipops did they sell?

   (A) 75
   (B) 90
   (C) 96
   (D) 110

5. On a certain project the only grades awarded were 75 and 100. If 85 students completed the project and the average of their grades was 85, how many earned 100?

   (A) 34
   (B) 40
   (C) 45
   (D) 51

6. Aaron has 3 times as much money as Josh. If Aaron gives Josh $50, Josh will then have 3 times as much money as Aaron. How much money do the two of them have together?

   (A) $ 75
   (B) $100
   (C) $125
   (D) $150

7. If $\dfrac{1}{2}x$ years ago Jason was 12, and $\dfrac{1}{2}x$ years from now he will be $2x$ years old, how old will he be $3x$ years from now?

   (A) 18
   (B) 24
   (C) 30
   (D) 54

8. Two printing presses working together can complete a job in 2.5 hours. Working alone, press A can do the job in 10 hours. How many hours will press B take to do the job by itself?

(A) $3\frac{1}{3}$

(B) 4

(C) 5

(D) $6\frac{1}{4}$

9. Henry drove 100 miles to visit a friend. If he had driven 8 miles per hour faster than he did, he would have arrived in $\frac{5}{6}$ of the time he actually took. How many <u>minutes</u> did the trip take?

(A) 120
(B) 125
(C) 144
(D) 150

10. Since 1970, when Martin graduated from high school, he has gained 2 pounds every year. In 2000 he was 40% heavier than in 1970. What percent of his 2015 weight was his 2000 weight?

(A) 80
(B) 85
(C) 87.5
(D) 90

Grid-in Questions

11. What is the greater of two numbers whose product is 900, if the sum of the two numbers exceeds their difference by 30?

12. The number of shells in Fred's collection is 80% of the number in Phil's collection. If Phil has 80 more shells than Fred, how many do they have altogether?

13. Karen played a game several times. She received $5 every time she won and had to pay $2 every time she lost. If the ratio of the number of times she won to the number of times she lost was 3:2, and if she won a total of $66, how many times did she play this game?

14. Each of the 10 players on the basketball team shot 100 free throws, and the average number of baskets made was 75. When the highest and lowest scores were eliminated, the average number of baskets for the remaining 8 players was 79. What is the smallest number of baskets anyone could have made?

15. In an office there was a small cash box. One day Ann took half of the money plus $1 more. Then Dan took half of the remaining money plus $1 more. Stan then took the remaining $11. How many dollars were originally in the box?

Answer Key

1. **B**	3. **C**	5. **A**	7. **D**	9. **D**
2. **D**	4. **D**	6. **B**	8. **A**	10. **C**

11. **60**

12. **720**

13. **30**

14. **18**

15. **50**

Answers Explained

1. **(B)** Judy's average rate of reading is determined by dividing the total number of pages she read (200) by the total amount of time she spent reading. In the afternoon she read for $\frac{100}{60} = \frac{5}{3}$ hours, and in the evening for $\frac{100}{40} = \frac{5}{2}$ hours, for a total time of

$$\frac{5}{3} + \frac{5}{2} = \frac{10}{6} + \frac{15}{6} = \frac{25}{6} \text{ hours}$$

Her average rate was $200 \div \frac{25}{6} = 200 \times \frac{6}{25} = 48$ pages per hour.

2. **(D)** Let the five consecutive integers be n, $n + 1$, $n + 2$, $n + 3$, $n + 4$. Then:

$$S = n + n + 1 + n + 2 + n + 3 + n + 4 = 5n + 10 \Rightarrow 5n = S - 10 \Rightarrow n = \frac{S-10}{5}$$

Choice (A), $\frac{S-10}{5}$, is the *smallest* of the integers; the *largest* is

$$n + 4 = \frac{S-10}{5} + 4 = \frac{S-10}{5} + \frac{20}{5} = \frac{S+10}{5}$$

3. **(C)** If there are b blue marbles, there are $\frac{3}{4}b$ white ones, and $\frac{4}{5}\left(\frac{3}{4}b\right) = \frac{3}{5}b$ red ones.

Then, $470 = b + \frac{3}{4}b + \frac{3}{5}b = b\left(1 + \frac{3}{4} + \frac{3}{5}\right) = \frac{47}{20}b$, so $b = 470 \div \frac{47}{20} = 470 \times \frac{20}{47} = 200$.

4. **(D)** If x represents the number of chocolate bars sold, then the number of lollipops sold is $150 - x$. You must use the same units, so you can write 75 cents as 0.75 dollar or 74 dollars as 7400 cents. Avoid the decimals: x chocolates sold for $75x$ cents and $(150 - x)$ lollipops sold for $40(150 - x)$ cents. Therefore:

$$7400 = 75x + 40(150 - x) = 75x + 6000 - 40x = 6000 + 35x \Rightarrow 1400 = 35x \Rightarrow x = 40$$

and $150 - 40 = 110$.

5. **(A)** Let x represent the number of students earning 100; then $85 - x$ is the number of students earning 75. Then:

$$85 = \frac{100x + 75(85 - x)}{85} = \frac{100x + 6375 - 75x}{85} = \frac{25x - 6375}{85} \Rightarrow$$

$$7225 = 25x - 6375 \Rightarrow 850 = 25x \Rightarrow x = 34$$

6. **(B)**

	Josh	Aaron
At the beginning	x	$3x$
After the gift	$x + 50$	$3x - 50$

After the gift, Josh will have 3 times as much money as Aaron:

$$x + 50 = 3(3x - 50) \Rightarrow x + 50 = 9x - 150$$

So, $8x = 200 \Rightarrow x = 25$.

Therefore, Josh has $25 and Aaron has $75, for a total of $100.

7. **(D)** Since $\frac{1}{2}x$ years ago Jason was 12, he is now $12 + \frac{1}{2}x$; and $\frac{1}{2}x$ years from now, he will be $12 + \frac{1}{2}x + \frac{1}{2}x = 12 + x$. At that time he will be $2x$ years old, so $12 + x = 2x \Rightarrow x = 12$.

Thus, he is now $12 + 6 = 18$, and $3x$, or 36, years from now he will be $18 + 36 = 54$.

8. **(A)** Let x represent the number of hours press B would take working alone.

	Press A Alone	Press B Alone	Together
Part of job that can be completed in 1 hour	$\frac{1}{10}$	$\frac{1}{x}$	$\frac{1}{2.5}$
Part of job that can be completed in 2.5 hours	$\frac{2.5}{10}$	$\frac{2.5}{x}$	1

- Write the equation: $\quad \frac{2.5}{10} + \frac{2.5}{x} = 1$
- Multiply each term by $10x$: $\quad 2.5x + 25 = 10x$
- Subtract $2.5x$ from each side: $\quad 25 = 7.5x$
- Divide each side by 7.5: $\quad x = 3\frac{1}{3}$ hours

9. **(D)** Let t represent the time, in hours, and r the rate, in miles per hour, that Henry drove. Then

$$t = \frac{100}{r} \quad \text{and} \quad \frac{5}{6}t = \frac{100}{r+8}$$

Multiply the second equation by $\frac{6}{5}$:

$$\frac{\cancel{6}^{1}}{\cancel{5}^{1}}\left(\frac{\cancel{5}^{1}}{\cancel{6}^{1}}t\right) = \frac{6}{5}\left(\frac{100}{r+8}\right) \Rightarrow t = \frac{600}{5r+40}, \quad \text{so} \quad \frac{100}{r} = \frac{600}{5r+40}$$

Cross-multiply:

$$500r + 4000 = 600r \Rightarrow 100r = 4000 \Rightarrow r = 40$$

Henry drove at 40 miles per hour, and the trip took $100 \div 40 = 2.5$ hours $= 150$ minutes. (Had he driven at 48 miles per hour, the trip would have taken 125 minutes, which is $\frac{5}{6}$ of 150 minutes.)

10. **(C)** Let x represent Martin's weight in 1970. By 2000, he had gained 60 pounds (2 pounds per year for 30 years) and was 40% heavier:

$$60 = 0.40x \Rightarrow x = 60 \div 0.4 = 150$$

In 2000, he weighed 210 pounds, and 15 years later, in 2015, he weighed 240:

$$\frac{210}{240} = \frac{7}{8} = 87.5\%$$

11. **60** Let x be the greater and y the smaller of the two numbers; then

$$(x + y) = 30 + (x - y) \Rightarrow y = 30 - y \Rightarrow 2y = 30 \Rightarrow y = 15$$

and, since $xy = 900$, $x = 900 \div 15 = 60$.

12. **720** If x represents the number of shells in Phil's collection, then Fred has $.80x$ shells. Since Phil has 80 more shells than Fred:

$$x = .80x + 80 \Rightarrow .20x = 80$$

So, $x = 80 \div .20 = 400$.

Then Phil has 400 shells and Fred has $(.80) \times 400 = 320$ shells: a total of 720 shells.

13. **30** Use TACTIC D1: write the letter x after each number in the ratio. Karen won $3x$ times and lost $2x$ times, and thus played a total of $5x$ games. Since she got \$5 every time she won, she received $\$5(3x) = \$15x$. Also, since she paid \$2 for each loss, she paid out $\$2(2x) = \$4x$. Therefore, her net winnings were $\$15x - \$4x = \$11x$, which you are told was \$66. Then, $11x = 66 \Rightarrow x = 6$, and so $5x = 30$.

14. **18** Since the average for all 10 players was 75, the total number of baskets made was $10 \times 75 = 750$. Also, since 8 of the players had an average of 79, they made a total of $8 \times 79 = 632$ baskets. The other 2 players, therefore, made $750 - 632 = 118$ baskets. The most baskets that the player with the highest number could have made was 100, so the player with the lowest number had to have made at least 18.

15. **50** You can avoid some messy algebra by working backwards. Put back the \$11 Stan took; then put back the extra \$1 that Dan took. There is now \$12 in the box, which means that, when Dan took his half, he took \$12. Put that back. Now there is \$24 in the box. Put back the extra \$1 that Ann took. The box now has \$25, so before Ann took her half, there was \$50.

Algebraic solution. Assume that there were originally x dollars in the box. Ann took $\frac{1}{2}x + 1$, leaving $\frac{1}{2}x - 1$. Dan then took $\frac{1}{2}$ of that plus \$1 more; he took

$$\frac{1}{2}\left(\frac{1}{2}x - 1\right) + 1 = \frac{1}{4}x - \frac{1}{2} + 1 = \frac{1}{4}x + \frac{1}{2}$$

Then Stan took \$11. Since together they took all x dollars:

$$x = \left(\frac{1}{2}x + 1\right) + \left(\frac{1}{4}x + \frac{1}{2}\right) + 11 = \frac{3}{4}x + 12\frac{1}{2}$$

Therefore, $12\frac{1}{2} = \frac{1}{4}x \Rightarrow x = 50$.

GEOMETRY

Although the SAT now has fewer questions specifically on plane geometry than in the past, there is an increased emphasis on solid geometry and coordinate geometry. Be sure to review all of the geometry topics in this chapter—any of them could be the basis for an SAT question. To underline the importance of geometry on the SAT further note that *every one of the 15 Reference Facts that are given to you at the beginning of each math section is a geometry fact.* All of that notwithstanding, you need to know far less geometry than you learned in your geometry class and, of course, there are no proofs! In the next six sections, there are plenty of sample multiple-choice and grid-in problems for you to solve, and they will show you exactly how these topics are treated on the SAT.

6-1 LINES AND ANGLES

On the SAT, lines are usually referred to by lowercase letters, typically k, ℓ, and m. If P and Q are any points on line ℓ, we can also refer to ℓ as $\overleftrightarrow{PQ}$. In general, we have the following notations:

- $\overleftrightarrow{PQ}$ represents the **line** that goes through P and Q:

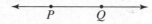

- $\overrightarrow{PQ}$ represents a **ray**; it consists of point P and all the points on $\overleftrightarrow{PQ}$ that are on the same side of P as Q:

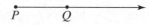

- $\overline{PQ}$ represents a **line segment** (often referred to simply as a **segment**); it consists of points P and Q and all the points on $\overleftrightarrow{PQ}$ that are between them:

- PQ represents the **length** of segment $\overline{PQ}$.

If $\overline{AB}$ and $\overline{PQ}$ have the same length, we say that $\overline{AB}$ and $\overline{PQ}$ are **congruent,** and write $\overline{AB} \cong \overline{PQ}$. We can also write $AB = PQ$.

NOTE

$\overline{AB} \cong \overline{PQ}$ means exactly the same thing as $AB = PQ$.

An **angle** is formed by the intersection of two line segments, rays, or lines. The point of intersection is called the **vertex**.

An angle can be named by three points: a point on one side, the vertex, and a point on the other side. When there is no possible ambiguity, the angle can be named just by its vertex. For example, in the diagram below we can refer to the angle on the left as $\angle B$ or $\angle ABC$. To talk about $\angle E$, on the right, however, would be ambiguous; $\angle E$ might mean $\angle DEF$ or $\angle FEG$ or $\angle DEG$.

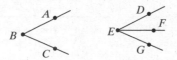

On geometry questions on the SAT, angles are always measured in degrees. The degree measure of ∠ABC is represented by m∠ABC. If ∠P and ∠Q have the same measure, we say that they are ***congruent*** and write ∠P ≅ ∠Q. In the diagram below, ∠A and ∠B are right angles. Therefore, m∠A = 90° and m∠B = 90°, so m∠A = m∠B and ∠A ≅ ∠B. In equilateral triangle PQR, m∠P = m∠Q = m∠R = 60°, and ∠P ≅ ∠Q ≅ ∠R.

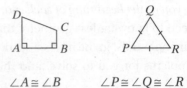

∠A ≅ ∠B   ∠P ≅ ∠Q ≅ ∠R

Key Fact I1

Angles are classified according to their degree measures.

- An *acute* angle measures less than 90°.
- A *right* angle measures 90°.
- An *obtuse* angle measures more than 90° but less than 180°.
- A *straight* angle measures 180°.

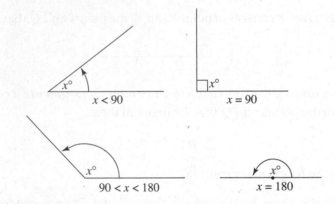

Key Fact I2

If two or more angles form a straight angle, the sum of their measures is 180°.

KEY FACT I2 is one of the facts provided in the "Reference Information" at the beginning of each math section.

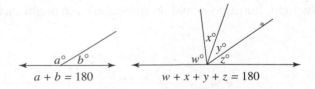

➡️ **Example 1** _____

In the figure below, R, S, and T are all on line ℓ. What is the average (arithmetic mean) of a, b, c, d, and e?

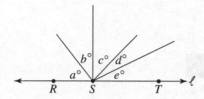

Solution. Since $\angle RST$ is a straight angle, by KEY FACT I2, the sum of a, b, c, d, and e is 180, and so their average is $\dfrac{180}{5} = \mathbf{36}$.

In the figure below, since $a + b + c + d = 180$ and $e + f + g = 180$, $a + b + c + d + e + f + g = 180 + 180 = 360$.

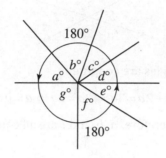

It is also true that in the diagram below $u + v + w + x + y + z = 360$, even though none of the angles forms a straight angle.

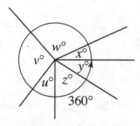

Key Fact I3

The sum of the measures of all the angles around a point is 360°.

NOTE: This fact is particularly important when the point is the center of a circle, as will be seen in Section 6-L.

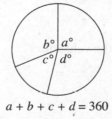

$a + b + c + d = 360$

REFERENCE FACT

KEY FACT I3 is one of the facts provided in the "Reference Information" at the beginning of each math section.

When two lines intersect, four angles are formed. The two angles in each pair of opposite angles are called *vertical angles*.

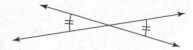

NOTE

Key Fact I4 means that if ∠A and ∠B are vertical angles, then m∠A = m∠B.

Key Fact I4

Vertical angles are congruent.

➡ **Example 2** _____

In the figure below, what is the value of a?

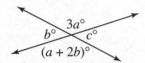

Solution. Because vertical angles are congruent:

$$a + 2b = 3a \Rightarrow 2b = 2a \Rightarrow a = b$$

For the same reason, $b = c$. Therefore, a, b, and c are all equal. Replace each b and c in the figure with a, and add:

$$a + a + 3a + a + 2a = 360 \Rightarrow 8a = 360 \Rightarrow a = \mathbf{45}$$

Consider these vertical angles:

By KEY FACT I4, $a = c$ and $b = d$.
By KEY FACT I2, $a + b = 180$, $b + c = 180$, $c + d = 180$, and $a + d = 180$.
It follows that, if any of the four angles is a right angle, all the angles are right angles.

➡ **Example 3** _____

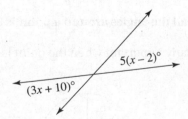

In the figure above, what is the value of x?

(A)   6
(B)   8
(C)   10
(D) 20

Solution. Since vertical angles are congruent:

$$3x + 10 = 5(x - 2) \Rightarrow 3x + 10 = 5x - 10 \Rightarrow 3x + 20 = 5x \Rightarrow 20 = 2x \Rightarrow x = \mathbf{10} \quad \textbf{(C)}.$$

In the figures below, line ℓ divides $\angle ABC$ into two congruent angles, and line k divides line segment $\overline{DE}$ into two congruent segments. Line ℓ is said to **bisect** the angle, and line k **bisects** the line segment. Point M is called the **midpoint** of segment $\overline{DE}$.

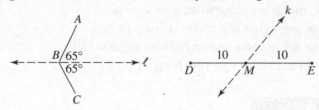

➡ **Example 4** _____

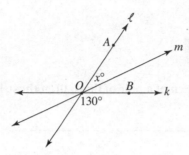

In the figure above, lines k, ℓ, and m intersect at O. If line m bisects $\angle AOB$, what is the value of x?

Solution. Here, $m\angle AOB + 130 = 180 \Rightarrow m\angle AOB = 50$; and since $\angle AOB$ is bisected, $x = \mathbf{25}$. Two lines that intersect to form right angles are said to be **perpendicular**.

Two lines that never intersect are said to be **parallel**. Consequently, parallel lines form no angles. However, if a third line, called a **transversal**, intersects a pair of parallel lines, eight angles are formed, and the relationships among these angles are very important.

Key Fact 15

If a pair of parallel lines is cut by a transversal that is perpendicular to the parallel lines, all eight angles are right angles.

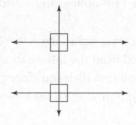

Key Fact 16

If a pair of parallel lines is cut by a transversal that is *not* perpendicular to the parallel lines:

- Four of the angles are acute, and four are obtuse.
- All four acute angles are congruent: $a = c = e = g$.
- All four obtuse angles are congruent: $b = d = f = h$.
- The sum of any acute angle and any obtuse angle is 180°: for example, $d + e = 180$, $c + f = 180$, $b + g = 180$, ...

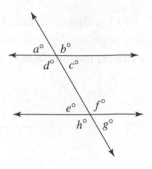

Key Fact 17

If a pair of lines that are not parallel is cut by a transversal, *none* of the statements listed in KEY FACT 16 is true.

Key Fact 18

If a line is perpendicular to each of a pair of lines, then these lines are parallel.

➡ **Example 5** _____

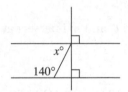

Note: Figure not drawn to scale

What is the value of x in the figure above?

    (A)   40
    (B)   50
    (C)   140
    (D)   It cannot be determined from the information given.

Solution. Despite the fact that the figure has not been drawn to scale, the little squares assure you that the vertical line is perpendicular to both of the horizontal ones, so these lines are parallel. Therefore, the sum of the 140° obtuse angle and the acute angle marked $x°$ is 180°: $x + 140 = 180 \Rightarrow x = \mathbf{40\ (A)}$.

NOTE: If the two little squares indicating right angles were not in the figure, the answer would be (D): "It cannot be determined from the information given." You are not told that the two lines that look parallel are actually parallel; and since the figure is not drawn to scale, you certainly cannot make that assumption. If the lines are not parallel, then $140 + x$ is *not* 180, and x cannot be determined.

➡ **Example 6** _____

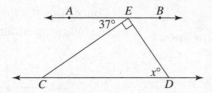

In the figure above, $\overrightarrow{AB}$ is parallel to $\overrightarrow{CD}$. What is the value of x?

Solution. Let y be the measure of $\angle BED$. Then by KEY FACT I2:

$$37 + 90 + y = 180 \Rightarrow 127 + y = 180 \Rightarrow y = 53$$

Since $\overrightarrow{AB}$ is parallel to $\overrightarrow{CD}$ by KEY FACT I6, $x = y \Rightarrow x = \mathbf{53}$.

➡ **Example 7** _____

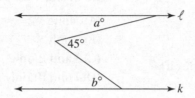

In the figure above, lines ℓ and k are parallel. What is the value of $a + b$?

(A) 45
(B) 60
(C) 135
(D) It cannot be determined from the information given.

Solution. If you were asked for the value of either a or b, the answer would be (D)—neither one can be determined; but if you are clever, you can find the value of $a + b$. Draw a line parallel to ℓ and k through the vertex of the angle. Then, looking at the top two lines, you see that $a = x$, and looking at the bottom two lines, you have $b = y$. Therefore, $a + b = x + y = \mathbf{45}$ (**A**).

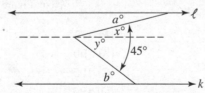

Alternative solution. Draw a different line and use a fact from Section 6-J on triangles. Extend one of the line segments to form a triangle. Since ℓ and k are parallel, the measure of the bottom angle in the triangle equals a. Now, use the fact that the sum of the measures of the three angles in a triangle is 180° or, even easier, that the given 45° angle is an exterior angle, and so is equal to the sum of a and b.

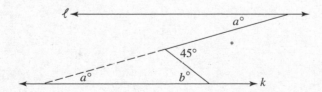

Multiple-Choice Questions

1. In the figure below, what is the value of b?

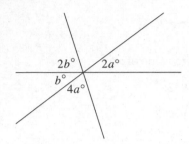

(A) 18
(B) 27
(C) 36
(D) 45

2. In the figure below, what is the value of x if $y:x = 3:2$?

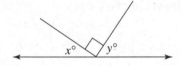

(A) 18
(B) 27
(C) 36
(D) 45

3. What is the measure of the angle formed by the minute and hour hands of a clock at 1:50?

(A) 95°
(B) 105°
(C) 115°
(D) 120°

4. Concerning the figure below, if $a = b$, which of the following statements *must* be true?

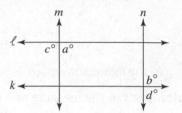

Note: Figure not drawn to scale

  I. $c = d$.
 II. ℓ and k are parallel.
III. m and ℓ are perpendicular.

(A) None
(B) I only
(C) I and II only
(D) I and III only

5. In the figure below, B and C lie on line n, m bisects $\angle AOC$, and ℓ bisects $\angle AOB$. What is the measure of $\angle DOE$?

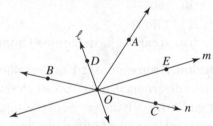

Note: Figure not drawn to scale

(A) 75°
(B) 90°
(C) 105°
(D) 120°

Grid-in Questions

6. In the figure below, what is the value of $\frac{b+a}{b-a}$?

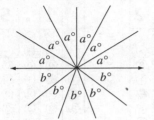

7. In the figure below, $a:b = 3:5$ and $c:b = 2:1$. What is the measure of the largest angle?

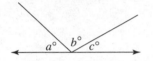

<u>Note</u>: Figure not drawn to scale

8. A, B, and C are points on a line, with B between A and C. Let M and N be the midpoints of $\overline{AB}$ and $\overline{BC}$, respectively. If $AB:BC = 3:1$, what is $AB:MN$?

9. In the figure below, lines k and ℓ are parallel. What is the value of $y - x$?

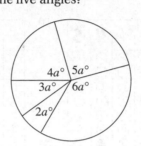

10. In the figure below, what is the average (arithmetic mean) of the measures of the five angles?

Answer Key

1. **C** 2. **C** 3. **C** 4. **B** 5. **B**

6. 1 1
7. 1 0 0
8. 3/2 or 1.5
9. 4 5
10. 7 2

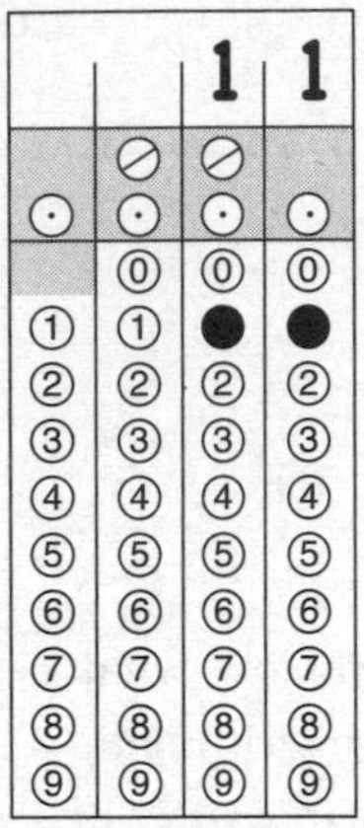

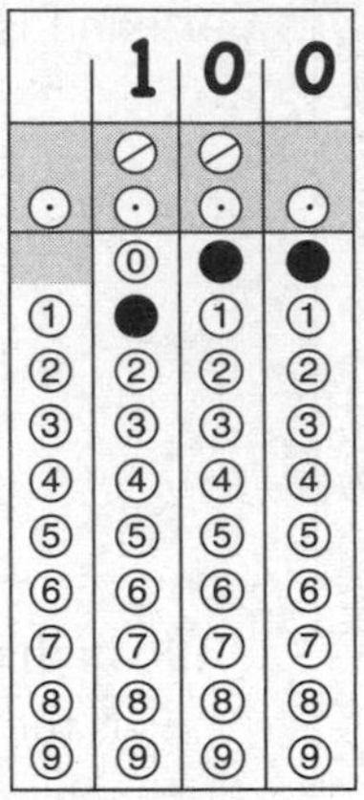

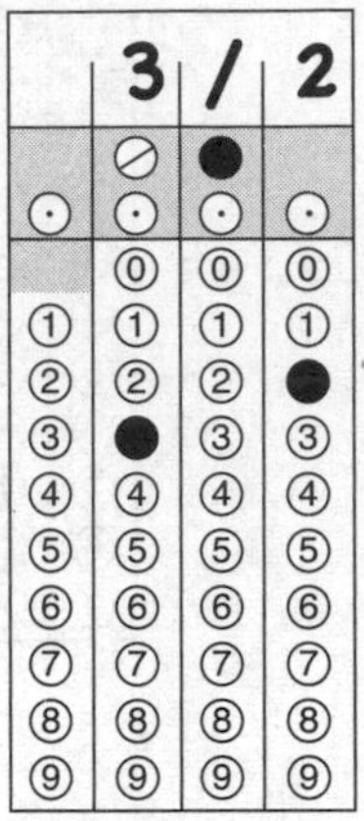

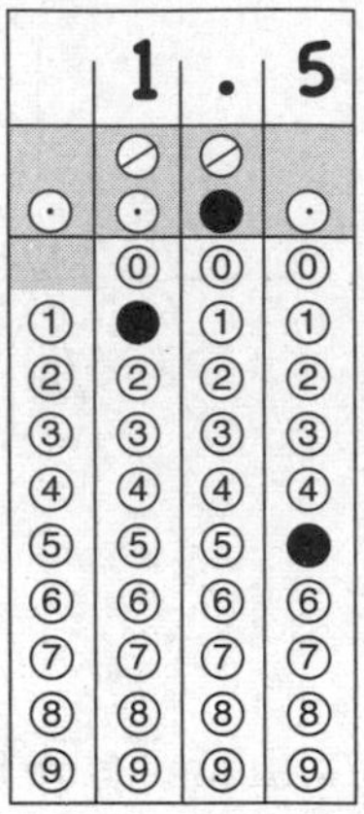

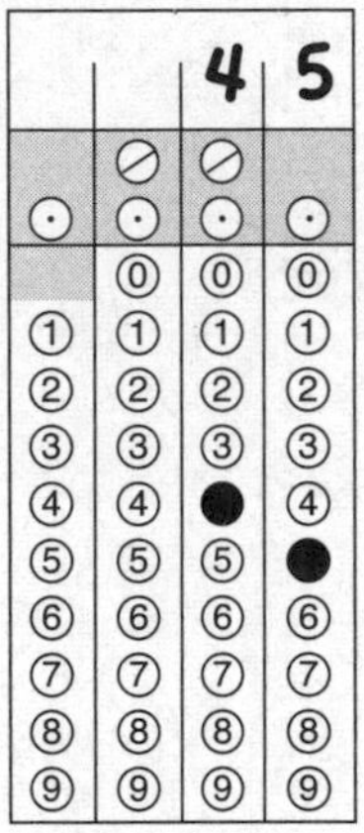

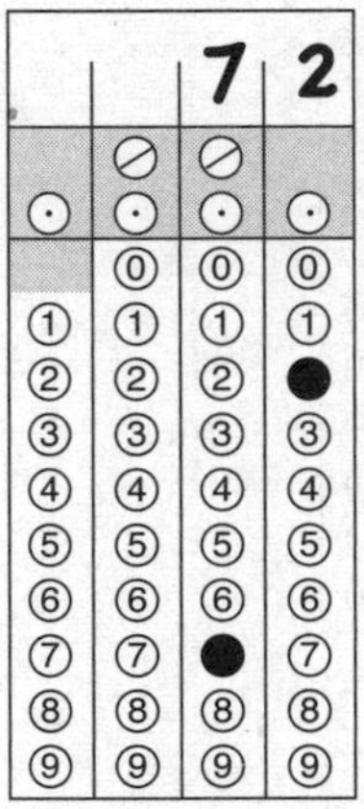

Answers Explained

1. **(C)** Since vertical angles are congruent, the measures of the two unmarked angles are $2b°$ and $4a°$. Also, since the sum of all six angles is 360°:

$$360 = 4a + 2b + 2a + 4a + 2b + b = 10a + 5b$$

Note that since the angles labeled a and $2b$ are vertical angles, $b = 2a$, and so $5b = 10a$. Hence:

$$360 = 10a + 5b = 10a + 10a = 20a \Rightarrow a = 18 \Rightarrow b = 36$$

2. **(C)** Since $x + y + 90 = 180$, then $x + y = 90$. Also, since $y{:}x = 3{:}2$, then $y = 3t$ and $x = 2t$. Therefore:

$$3t + 2t = 90 \Rightarrow 5t = 90 \Rightarrow t = 18 \Rightarrow x = 2(18) = 36$$

3. **(C)** For problems such as this, always draw a diagram. The measure of each of the 12 central angles from one number to the next on the clock is 30°. At 1:50 the minute hand is pointing at 10, and the hour hand has gone $\frac{50}{60} = \frac{5}{6}$ of the way from 1 to 2. Then, from 10 to 1 on the clock is 90°, and from 1 to the hour hand is $\frac{5}{6}(30°) = 25°$, for a total of $90° + 25° = 115°$.

4. **(B)** No conclusion can be drawn about the lines; they could form any angles whatsoever. (II and III are both false.) Statement I is true: $c = 180 - a = 180 - b = d$.

5. **(B)** Let $x = \frac{1}{2} \text{m}\angle AOC$, and $y = \frac{1}{2} \text{m}\angle AOB$. Then,

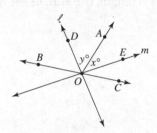

$$x + y = \frac{1}{2} \text{m}\angle AOC + \frac{1}{2} \text{m}\angle AOB =$$

$$\frac{1}{2}(\text{m}\angle AOC + \text{m}\angle AOB) =$$

$$\frac{1}{2}(180°) = 90°$$

6. **11** From the diagram, you see that $6a = 180$, which implies that $a = 30$, and that $5b = 180$, which implies that $b = 36$. Therefore:

$$\frac{b+a}{b-a} = \frac{36+30}{36-30} = \frac{66}{6} = 11$$

7. **100** Since $a:b = 3:5$, then for some number x, $a = 3x$ and $b = 5x$; and since $c:b = 2:1$, then $c = 2b = 10x$. Then: $3x + 5x + 10x = 180 \Rightarrow 18x = 180$.

So, $x = 10$ and $c = 10x = 10(10) = 100$.

8. **$\frac{3}{2}$ or 1.5** If a diagram is not provided on a geometry question, draw one. Since $AB:BC = 3:1$, let $AB = 3$ and $BC = 1$.

From the figure above, you can see that $AB:MN = \frac{3}{2} = 1.5$.

9. **45** Since lines ℓ and k are parallel, the angle marked y in the given diagram and the sum of the angles marked x and 45 are equal: $y = x + 45 \Rightarrow y - x = 45$.

10. **72** The markings in the five angles are irrelevant. The sum of the measures of these angles is 360°, and $360 \div 5 = 72$. If you calculated the measure of each angle, you should have gotten 36, 54, 72, 90, and 108; but you would have wasted time.

More geometry questions on the SAT pertain to triangles than to any other topic. To answer these questions correctly, you need to know several important facts about the angles and sides of triangles. The KEY FACTS in this section are extremely useful. Read them carefully, a few times if necessary, and *make sure you learn them all.*

Key Fact J1

In any triangle, the sum of the measures of the three angles is 180°.

$$x + y + z = 180$$

Figure 1 illustrates KEY FACT J1 for five different triangles, which will be discussed below.

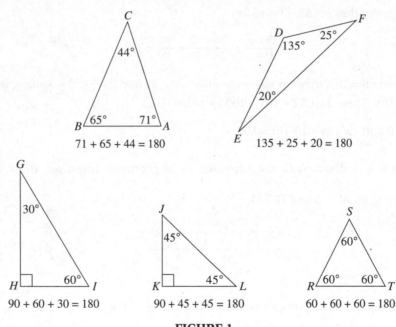

$71 + 65 + 44 = 180$

$135 + 25 + 20 = 180$

$90 + 60 + 30 = 180$

$90 + 45 + 45 = 180$

$60 + 60 + 60 = 180$

FIGURE 1

➡ Example 1

In the figure below, what is the value of x?

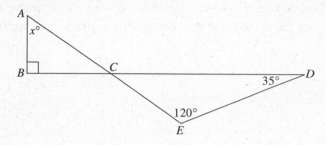

Solution. Use KEY FACT J1 twice: first, for $\triangle CDE$ and then for $\triangle ABC$.

- $m\angle DCE + 120 + 35 = 180 \Rightarrow m\angle DCE + 155 = 180 \Rightarrow m\angle DCE = 25$.
- Since vertical angles are congruent, $m-ACB = 25$ (see KEY FACT I4).
- $x + 90 + 25 = 180 \Rightarrow x + 115 = 180 \Rightarrow x = \mathbf{65}$.

➡ Example 2

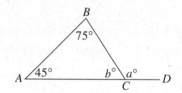

In the figure above, what is the value of a?

Solution. First find the value of b:

$$180 = 45 + 75 + b = 120 + b \Rightarrow b = 60$$

Then, $a + b = 180 \Rightarrow a = 180 - b = 180 - 60 = \mathbf{120}$.

In Example 2, $\angle BCD$, which is formed by one side of $\triangle ABC$ and the extension of another side, is called an ***exterior angle***. Note that, to find a, you did not have to first find b; you could just have added the other two angles: $a = 75 + 45 = 120$. This is a useful fact to remember.

Key Fact J2

The measure of an exterior angle of a triangle is equal to the sum of the measures of the two opposite interior angles.

Key Fact J3

In any triangle:

- **the longest side is opposite the largest angle;**
- **the shortest side is opposite the smallest angle;**
- **sides with the same length are opposite angles with the same measure.**

CAUTION: In KEY FACT J3 the condition "in any triangle" is crucial. If the angles are not in the same triangle, none of the conclusions holds. For example, in the figure on the left below, *AB* and *DE* are *not* equal even though each is opposite a 90° angle; and in the figure on the right, *QS* is not the longest side even though it is opposite the largest angle.

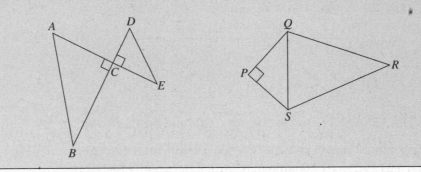

Consider triangles *ABC*, *JKL*, and *RST* in Figure 1 on page 556.

- In △*ABC*: $\overline{BC}$ is the longest side since it is opposite ∠*A*, the largest angle (71°). Similarly, $\overline{AB}$ is the shortest side since it is opposite ∠*C*, the smallest angle (44°). Therefore, *AB* < *AC* < *BC*.
- In △*JKL*: Angles *J* and *L* have the same measure (45°), so *JK* = *KL*.
- In △*RST*: Since all three angles have the same measure (60°), all three sides have the same length: *RS* = *ST* = *TR*.

➡ **Example 3** _____

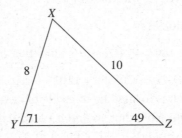

In the figure above, which of the following statements concerning the length of side $\overline{YZ}$ is true?

(A) *YZ* < 8
(B) *YZ* = 8
(C) 8 < *YZ* < 10
(D) *YZ* = 10

Solution.

- By KEY FACT J1, m∠*X* + 71 + 49 = 180 ⇒ m∠*X* = 60.
- Then *Y* is the largest angle, *Z* is the smallest, and *X* is in between.
- Therefore, by KEY FACT J3: *XY* < *YZ* < *XZ* ⇒ 8 < *YZ* < 10.
- The answer is **(C)**.

Classification of Triangles

Name	Lengths of Sides	Measures of Angles	Examples from Figure 1
Scalene	all 3 different	all 3 different	*ABC, DEF, GHI*
Isosceles	2 the same	2 the same	*JKL*
Equilateral	all 3 the same	all 3 the same	*RST*

Acute triangles are triangles such as *ABC* and *RST*, in which all three angles are acute. An acute triangle can be scalene, isosceles, or equilateral.

Obtuse triangles are triangles such as *DEF*, in which one angle is obtuse and two are acute. An obtuse triangle can be scalene or isosceles.

Right triangles are triangles such as *GHI* and *JKL*, which have one right angle and two acute ones. A right triangle can be scalene or isosceles. The side opposite the 90° angle is called the **hypotenuse**, and by KEY FACT J3 it is the longest side. The other two sides are called the **legs**.

If x and y are the measures of the two acute angles of a right triangle, then by KEY FACT J1: $90 + x + y = 180$, and so $x + y = 90$.

This result is our next KEY FACT.

Key Fact J4

In any right triangle, the sum of the measures of the two acute angles is 90°.

➥ Example 4

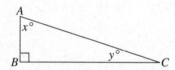

In the figure above, what is the average (arithmetic mean) of x and y?

Solution. Since the diagram indicates that $\triangle ABC$ is a right triangle, then, by KEY FACT J4, $x + y = 90$. Therefore, the average of x and $y = \dfrac{x+y}{2} = \dfrac{90}{2} = \mathbf{45}$.

The most important facts concerning right triangles are the **Pythagorean theorem** and its converse, which are given in KEY FACT J5 and repeated as the first line of KEY FACT J6.

Key Fact J5

Let a, b, and c be the sides of $\triangle ABC$, with $a \leq b \leq c$.

- If $\triangle ABC$ is a right triangle, $a^2 + b^2 = c^2$;
- If $a^2 + b^2 = c^2$, then $\triangle ABC$ is a right triangle.

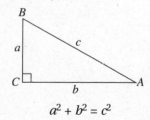

$$a^2 + b^2 = c^2$$

Let *a*, *b*, and *c* be the sides of △*ABC*, with $a \leq b \leq c$.

- $a^2 + b^2 = c^2$ if and only if $\angle C$ is a right angle.
- $a^2 + b^2 < c^2$ if and only if $\angle C$ is obtuse.
- $a^2 + b^2 > c^2$ if and only if $\angle C$ is acute.

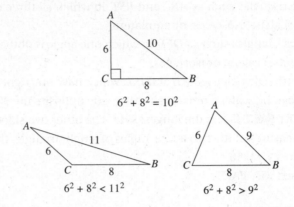

$$6^2 + 8^2 = 10^2$$

$$6^2 + 8^2 < 11^2 \qquad 6^2 + 8^2 > 9^2$$

➡ **Example 5** _____

Which of the following CANNOT be the lengths of the sides of a right triangle?

(A) 3, 4, 5

(B) 1, 1, $\sqrt{2}$

(C) $\sqrt{3}$, $\sqrt{4}$, $\sqrt{5}$

(D) 30, 40, 50

Solution. Just check the choices.

- (A): $3^2 + 4^2 = 9 + 16 = 25 = 5^2$ These *are* the lengths of the sides of a right triangle.
- (B): $1^2 + 1^2 = 1 + 1 = 2 = (\sqrt{2})^2$ These *are* the lengths of the sides of a right triangle.
- (C): $(\sqrt{3})^2 + (\sqrt{4})^2 = 3 + 4 = 7 \neq (\sqrt{5})^2$ These *are not* the lengths of the sides of a right triangle.

Stop. The answer is **(C)**. There is no need to check choice (D)—but if you did, you would find that 30, 40, 50 *are* the lengths of the sides of a right triangle.

Below are the right triangles that appear most often on the SAT. You should recognize them immediately whenever they come up in questions. Carefully study each one, and memorize KEY FACTS J7–J11.

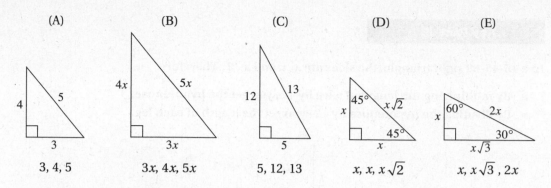

(A)	(B)	(C)	(D)	(E)
3, 4, 5	3x, 4x, 5x	5, 12, 13	x, x, x$\sqrt{2}$	x, x$\sqrt{3}$, 2x

On the SAT, the most common right triangles whose sides are integers are the 3-4-5 right triangle (A) and its multiples (B).

Key Fact J7

For any positive number x, there is a right triangle whose sides are $3x$, $4x$, $5x$.

For example:

$x = 1$	3, 4, 5	$x = 5$	15, 20, 25
$x = 2$	6, 8, 10	$x = 10$	30, 40, 50
$x = 3$	9, 12, 15	$x = 50$	150, 200, 250
$x = 4$	12, 16, 20	$x = 100$	300, 400, 500

NOTE: KEY FACT J6 applies even if x is not an integer. For example:

$x = 0.5$	1.5, 2, 2.5	$x = \pi$	$3\pi, 4\pi, 5\pi$

The only other right triangle with integer sides that you should recognize immediately is the one whose sides are 5, 12, 13 (C).

If x represents the length of each leg, and h represents the length of the hypotenuse of an isosceles right triangle (D), then by the Pythagorean theorem (KEY FACT J5),

$$x^2 + x^2 = h^2 \Rightarrow 2x^2 = h^2 \Rightarrow h = \sqrt{2x^2} = x\sqrt{2}$$

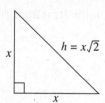

Key Fact J8

In a 45-45-90 right triangle, the sides are x, x, and $x\sqrt{2}$. Therefore:

- By multiplying the length of a leg by $\sqrt{2}$, you get the hypotenuse.
- By dividing the hypotenuse by $\sqrt{2}$, you get the length of each leg.

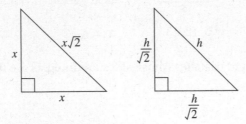

Key Fact J9

The diagonal of a square divides the square into two isosceles right triangles.

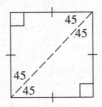

The last important right triangle is the one whose angles measure 30°, 60°, and 90°.

Key Fact J10

An altitude divides an equilateral triangle into two 30-60-90 right triangles.

Let $2x$ be the length of each side of equilateral triangle ABC, in which altitude $\overline{AD}$ is drawn.

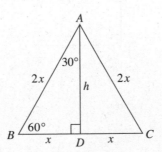

Then $\triangle ADB$ is a 30-60-90 right triangle, and its sides are x, $2x$, and h. By the Pythagorean theorem, $x^2 + h^2 = (2x)^2 = 4x^2 \Rightarrow h^2 = 3x^2 \Rightarrow h = \sqrt{3x^2} = x\sqrt{3}$.

In a 30-60-90 right triangle the sides are x, $x\sqrt{3}$, and $2x$.

If you know the length of the shorter leg (x):

- multiply it by $\sqrt{3}$ to get the length of the longer leg;
- multiply it by 2 to get the length of the hypotenuse.

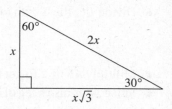

If you know the length of the longer leg (a):

- divide it by $\sqrt{3}$ to get the length of the shorter leg;
- multiply the shorter leg by 2 to get the length of the hypotenuse.

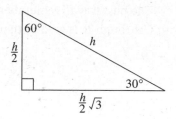

If you know the length of the hypotenuse (h):

- divide it by 2 to get the length of the shorter leg;
- multiply the shorter leg by $\sqrt{3}$ to get the length of the longer leg.

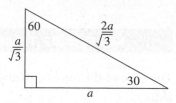

REFERENCE FACT

KEY FACT J11 is one of the facts provided in the "Reference Information" at the beginning of each math section.

➡ **Example 6** _____

What is the area of a square whose diagonal is 10?

Solution. Draw a diagonal in a square of side s, creating a 45-45-90 right triangle.

By KEY FACT J8: $s = \dfrac{10}{\sqrt{2}}$ and $A = s^2 = \left(\dfrac{10}{\sqrt{2}}\right)^2 = \dfrac{100}{2} = \mathbf{50}$

➡ **Example 7** _____

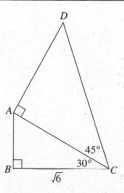

In the diagram above, if $BC = \sqrt{6}$, what is the value of CD?

HELPFUL HINT

If you know some elementary trigonometry, you could use the sine, cosine, and tangent ratios to solve questions involving 30-60-90 triangles and 45-45-90 triangles. But they can all be answered more quickly using KEY FACTS J8 and J11. You should know these facts by heart; but in case you forget, they are given to you in the Reference Information on the first page of each math section.

Solution. $\triangle ABC$ and $\triangle DAC$ are 30-60-90 and 45-45-90 right triangles, respectively. Use KEY FACTS J11 and J8.

- Divide $\overline{BC}$, the length of the longer leg, by $\sqrt{3}$ to get $\overline{AB}$, the length of the shorter leg:

$$\frac{\sqrt{6}}{\sqrt{3}} = \sqrt{2}$$

- Multiply $\overline{AB}$ by 2 to get the length of the hypotenuse: $AC = 2\sqrt{2}$.
- Since $\overline{AC}$ is also a leg of isosceles right triangle DAC, to get the length of hypotenuse $\overline{CD}$, multiply AC by $\sqrt{2}$: $CD = 2\sqrt{2} \times \sqrt{2} = 2 \times (\sqrt{2})(\sqrt{2}) = 2 \times 2 = \mathbf{4}$.

HELPFUL HINT

KEY FACTS J12 and J13 are important. Be sure you understand both of them.

Key Fact J12 Triangle Inequality

The sum of the lengths of any two sides of a triangle is greater than the length of the third side.

The best way to remember this is to see that, in $\triangle ABC$, $x + y$, the length of the path from A to C through B, is greater than z, the length of the direct path from A to C.

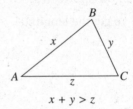

$$x + y > z$$

NOTE: If you subtract x from each side of $x + y > z$, you see that $z - x < y$.

Key Fact J13

The difference between the lengths of any two sides of a triangle is less than the length of the third side.

➡ **Example 8**

If the lengths of two sides of a triangle are 6 and 7, which of the following could be the length of the third side?

   I.   1

   II. 5

   III. 15

(A) None
(B) I only
(C) II only
(D) I and II only

NOTE

If a and b are the lengths of two sides of a triangle with a > b, then any number greater than a − b and less than a + b could be the length of the third side.

Solution. Use KEY FACTS J12 and J13.

- The length of the third side must be *less* than 6 + 7 = 13. (III is false.)
- The length of the third side must be *greater* than 7 – 6 = 1. (I is false.)
- *Any* number between 1 and 13 could be the length of the third side. (II is true.)

The answer is **(C)**.

The following diagram illustrates several triangles, two of whose sides have lengths of 6 and 7.

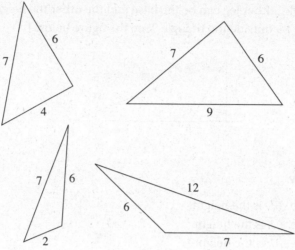

On the SAT, two other terms that appear regularly in triangle problems are ***perimeter*** and ***area*** (see Section 6-K).

➡ **Example 9** _____

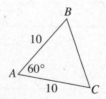

In the figure above, what is the perimeter of $\triangle ABC$?

Solution. First, use KEY FACTS J3 and J1 to find the measures of the angles.

- Since $AB = AC$, m$\angle B$ = m$\angle C$. Represent each measure by x.
- Then, $x + x + 60 = 180 \Rightarrow 2x = 120 \Rightarrow x = 60$.
- Since the measure of each angle of $\triangle ABC$ is 60°, the triangle is equilateral.
- Then, $BC = 10$, and the perimeter is 10 + 10 + 10 = **30**.

Key Fact J14

The area of a triangle is given by $A = \frac{1}{2}bh$, where b = base and h = height.

NOTE:

1. *Any* side of the triangle can be taken as the base.
2. The height is a line segment drawn perpendicular to the base from the opposite vertex.
3. In a right triangle, either leg can be the base and the other the height.
4. The height may be outside the triangle. [See the figure below.]

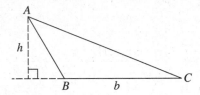

In the figure below:

- If $\overline{AC}$ is the base, $\overline{BD}$ is the height.
- If $\overline{AB}$ is the base, $\overline{CE}$ is the height.
- If $\overline{BC}$ is the base, $\overline{AF}$ is the height.

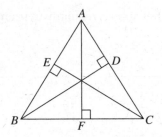

➡ Example 10

What is the area of an equilateral triangle whose sides are 10?

(A) $25\sqrt{3}$

(B) 50

(C) $50\sqrt{3}$

(D) 100

Solution. Draw an equilateral triangle and one of its altitudes.

- By KEY FACT J10, $\triangle ADB$ is a 30-60-90 right triangle.
- By KEY FACT J11, $BD = 5$ and $AD = 5\sqrt{3}$.
- The area of $\triangle ABC = \frac{1}{2}(10)(5\sqrt{3}) = \mathbf{25\sqrt{3}}$ **(A)**.

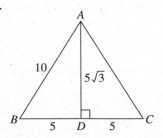

Replacing 10 by s in Example 10 yields a very useful result.

If A represents the area of an equilateral triangle with side s, then $A = \dfrac{s^2\sqrt{3}}{4}$.

Two triangles, such as I and II in the figure below, that have the same shape, but not necessarily the same size, are said to be *similar*.

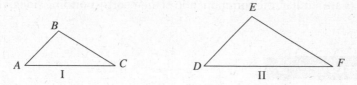

KEY FACT J16 makes this intuitive definition mathematically precise.

Key Fact J16

Two triangles are *similar* provided that the following two conditions are satisfied.

1. **The three angles in the first triangle are congruent to the three angles in the second triangle.**

$$m\angle A = m\angle D, \quad m\angle B = m\angle E, \quad m\angle C = m\angle F$$

2. **The lengths of the corresponding sides of the two triangles are in proportion:**

$$\frac{AB}{DE} = \frac{BC}{EF} = \frac{AC}{DF}$$

NOTE: Corresponding sides are sides opposite angles of the same measure.

An important theorem in geometry states that, if condition 1 in KEY FACT J16 is satisfied, then condition 2 is automatically satisfied. Therefore, to show that two triangles are similar, it is sufficient to show that their angles have the same measure. Furthermore, if the measures of two angles of one triangle are equal to the measures of two angles of a second triangle, then the measures of the third angles are also equal. This is summarized in KEY FACT J17.

Key Fact J17

If the measures of two angles of one triangle are equal to the measures of two angles of a second triangle, the triangles are similar.

➡ **Example 11** _____

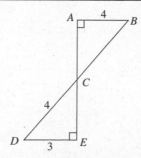

In the diagram above, what is BC?

Solution. Since vertical angles are congruent, m∠ECD = m∠ACB. Also, m∠A = m∠E since both ∠A and ∠E are right angles. Then the measures of two angles of △CAB are equal to the measures of two angles of △CED, and by KEY FACT J17, the two triangles are similar. Finally, by KEY FACT J16, corresponding sides are in proportion. Therefore:

$$\frac{DE}{AB} = \frac{DC}{BC} \Rightarrow \frac{3}{4} = \frac{4}{BC} \Rightarrow 3(BC) = 16 \Rightarrow BC = \frac{16}{3}$$

If two triangles are similar, the common ratio of their corresponding sides is called the ***ratio of similitude***.

Key Fact J18

If two triangles are similar, and if *k* is the ratio of similitude, then:

- **The ratio of all the linear measurements of the triangles is *k*.**
- **The ratio of the areas of the triangles is *k²*.**

In the figure below, △ABC and △PQR are similar with m∠C = m∠R.

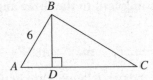

Then $\overline{AB}$ and $\overline{PQ}$ are corresponding sides, and the ratio of similitude is $\frac{6}{2} = 3$. Therefore,

- All the sides are in the ratio of 3:1:

$$BC = \mathbf{3} \times QR \qquad AC = \mathbf{3} \times PR$$

- The altitudes are in the ratio of 3:1:

$$BD = \mathbf{3} \times QS$$

- The perimeters are in the ratio of 3:1:

$$\text{Perimeter of } \triangle ABC = \mathbf{3} \times (\text{perimeter of } \triangle PQR)$$

- The areas are in the ratio of 9:1:

$$\text{Area of } \triangle ABC = \mathbf{9} \times (\text{area of } \triangle PQR)$$

Multiple-Choice Questions

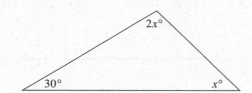

1. In the triangle above, what is the value of x?

   (A) 30
   (B) 40
   (C) 50
   (D) 60

2. What is the area of an equilateral triangle whose altitude is 6?

   (A) 18

   (B) $12\sqrt{3}$

   (C) $18\sqrt{3}$

   (D) $24\sqrt{3}$

3. Two sides of a right triangle are 12 and 13. Which of the following could be the length of the third side?

   I. 5

   II. 11

   III. $\sqrt{313}$

   (A) I only
   (B) I and II only
   (C) I and III only
   (D) I, II, and III

4. What is the smallest integer, x, for which x, $x + 5$, and $2x - 15$ can be the lengths of the sides of a triangle?

   (A) 8
   (B) 9
   (C) 10
   (D) 11

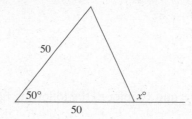

5. What is the value of x in the figure above?

   (A) 100
   (B) 115
   (C) 120
   (D) 130

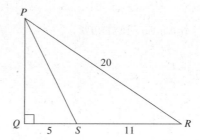

6. What is the value of PS in the triangle above?

   (A) $5\sqrt{2}$
   (B) 10
   (C) 11
   (D) 13

Questions 7 and 8 refer to the following figure.

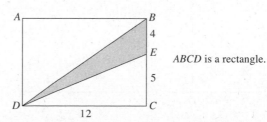

$ABCD$ is a rectangle.

7. What is the area of $\triangle BED$?

   (A) 12
   (B) 24
   (C) 36
   (D) 48

8. What is the perimeter of △BED?

  (A) $19 + 5\sqrt{2}$
  (B) 28
  (C) 32
  (D) 36

12. What is the area of △ABC?

  (A) 108
  (B) $54 + 72\sqrt{2}$
  (C) $54 + 72\sqrt{3}$
  (D) 198

Questions 9 and 10 refer to the following figure.

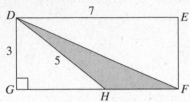

DEFG is a rectangle.

9. What is the area of △DFH?

  (A) 3
  (B) 4.5
  (C) 6
  (D) 7.5

10. What is the perimeter of △DFH?

  (A) $8 + \sqrt{41}$
  (B) $8 + \sqrt{58}$
  (C) 16
  (D) 18

Questions 11 and 12 refer to the following figure.

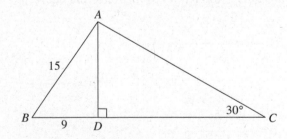

11. What is the perimeter of △ABC?

  (A) 48
  (B) $48 + 12\sqrt{2}$
  (C) $48 + 12\sqrt{3}$
  (D) 72

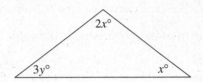

13. Which of the following expresses a true relationship between x and y in the figure above?

  (A) $y = 60 - x$
  (B) $y = x$
  (C) $x + y = 90$
  (D) $y = 180 - 3x$

Questions 14 and 15 refer to the following figure, in which rectangle ABCD is divided into two 30-60-90 triangles, a 45-45-90 triangle, and shaded triangle ABF.

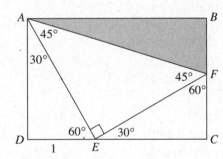

14. What is the perimeter of shaded triangle ABF?

  (A) $\sqrt{2} + 2\sqrt{3}$
  (B) $1 + \sqrt{2} + \sqrt{3}$
  (C) $2 + \sqrt{2} + \sqrt{3}$
  (D) $2\sqrt{2} + 2\sqrt{3}$

15. What is the area of shaded triangle ABF?

(A) $\dfrac{\sqrt{3}}{2}$

(B) 1

(C) $\dfrac{2\sqrt{3}}{3}$

(D) $\dfrac{\sqrt{3}+1}{2}$

Grid-in Questions

16. If the difference between the measures of the two smaller angles of a right triangle is 20°, what is the measure, in degrees, of the smallest angle?

Questions 17 and 18 refer to the figure below.

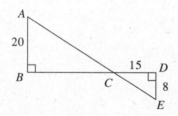

17. What is the perimeter of $\triangle ABC$?

18. What is the area of $\triangle ABC$?

19. Reanna and Jason each drew a triangle. Both triangles have sides of length 10 and 20, and the length of the third side of each triangle is an integer. What is the greatest possible difference between the perimeters of the two triangles?

20. If the measures of the angles of a triangle are in the ratio of 1:2:3, and if the perimeter of the triangle is $30 + 10\sqrt{3}$, what is the length of the smallest side?

Answer Key

1.	**C**	4.	**D**	7.	**B**	10.	**B**	13.	**A**
2.	**B**	5.	**B**	8.	**C**	11.	**C**	14.	**D**
3.	**C**	6.	**D**	9.	**B**	12.	**C**	15.	**B**

16. **3 5**

17. **1 0 0**

18. **3 7 5**

19. **1 8**

20. **1 0**

Answers Explained

1. **(C)** $x + 2x + 30 = 180 \Rightarrow 3x + 30 = 180 \Rightarrow 3x = 150 \Rightarrow x = 50$

2. **(B)** Sketch and label equilateral triangle ABC, and draw in altitude $\overline{AD}$, whose length is given as 6.

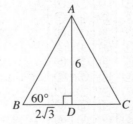

By KEY FACT J11:

$$BD = \frac{6}{\sqrt{3}} = \frac{6}{\sqrt{3}} \cdot \frac{\sqrt{3}}{\sqrt{3}} = \frac{6\sqrt{3}}{3} = 2\sqrt{3}$$

Since $\overline{BD}$ is one-half the base of the triangle, the area is $2\sqrt{3} \times 6 = 12\sqrt{3}$.

3. **(C)** If the triangle were not required to be right, by KEY FACTS J11 and J12 *any* number greater than 1 and less than 25 could be the length of the third side. For a right triangle, however, there are only *two* possibilities.

   - If 13 is the hypotenuse and one of the legs is 12, then the other leg is 5. (I is true.) (If you didn't recognize the 5-12-13 triangle, use the Pythagorean theorem: $12^2 + x^2 = 13^2$, and solve.)
   - If 12 and 13 are the lengths of the two legs, then use the Pythagorean theorem to find the length of the hypotenuse:

$$12^2 + 13^2 = c^2 \Rightarrow c^2 = 144 + 169 = 313$$

So, $c = \sqrt{313}$.

(III is true.)

Since $11^2 + 12^2 \ne 13^2$, an 11-12-13 triangle is not a *right* triangle. (II is false.)

4. **(D)** In a triangle the sum of the lengths of any two sides must be greater than the third side. For $x + (x + 5)$ to be greater than $2x - 15$, $2x + 5$ must be greater than $2x - 15$; but that's always true. For $x + (2x - 15)$ to be greater than $x + 5$, $3x - 15$ must be greater than $x + 5$; but $3x - 15 > x + 5$ is true only if $2x > 20$, which means $x > 10$. The smallest integer value of x is 11.

5. **(B)** Label the other angles:

$50 + a + b = 180 \Rightarrow a + b = 130$, and since the triangle is isosceles, $a = b$. Therefore, a and b are each 65, and $x = 180 - 65 = 115$.

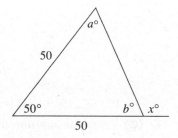

6. **(D)** Use the Pythagorean theorem twice, unless you recognize the common right triangles in this figure (*which you should*). Since $PR = 20$ and $QR = 16$, $\triangle PQR$ is a $3x$-$4x$-$5x$ right triangle with $x = 4$. Then $PQ = 12$, and $\triangle PQS$ is a right triangle whose legs are 5 and 12. The hypotenuse, PS, therefore, is 13. [If you had difficulty with this question, review the material, but in the meantime remember TACTIC 2: trust the diagram. $\overline{PS}$ is longer than $\overline{SR}$, so you can eliminate (A), (B), and (C). The answer must be (D).]

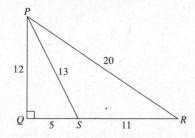

7. **(B)** You *could* calculate the area of the rectangle and subtract the areas of the two white right triangles, but don't. If $\overline{BE}$ is the base of $\triangle BED$, $\overline{DC}$ is the height.

   The area is $\frac{1}{2}(BE)(DC) = \frac{1}{2}(4)(12) = 24$.

8. **(C)** Since both $\overline{BD}$ and $\overline{ED}$ are the hypotenuses of right triangles, their lengths can be calculated by the Pythagorean theorem, but again these are triangles you should recognize: the sides of $\triangle DCE$ are 5-12-13, and those of $\triangle BAD$ are 9-12-15 ($3x$-$4x$-$5x$, with $x = 3$). Therefore, the perimeter of $\triangle BED$ is $4 + 13 + 15 = 32$.

9. **(B)** Since $\triangle DGH$ is a right triangle, whose hypotenuse is 5 and one of whose legs is 3, the other leg, GH, is 4. Since $GF = DE = 7$, $HF = 3$. Now, $\triangle DFH$ has a base of 3 (HF) and a height of 3 (DG), and its area is $\frac{1}{2}(3)(3) = 4.5$.

10. **(B)** For $\triangle DFH$, you already have that $DH = 5$ and $HF = 3$; you need only find DF, which is the hypotenuse of $\triangle DEF$. By the Pythagorean theorem,

    $$3^2 + 7^2 = (DF)^2 \Rightarrow (DF)^2 = 9 + 49 = 58$$

    So, $DF = \sqrt{58}$.
    The perimeter is $3 + 5 + \sqrt{58} = 8 + \sqrt{58}$.

11. **(C)** Triangle ADB is a right triangle whose hypotenuse is 15 and one of whose legs is 9, so this is a $3x$-$4x$-$5x$ triangle with $x = 3$, and $AD = 12$. Now $\triangle ADC$ is a 30-60-90 triangle, whose shorter leg is 12. Hypotenuse AC is 24, and leg CD is $12\sqrt{3}$, so the perimeter is $24 + 15 + 9 + 12\sqrt{3} = 48 + 12\sqrt{3}$.

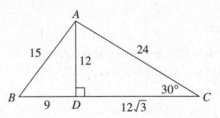

12. **(C)** From the solution to Exercise 11, you have the base ($9 + 12\sqrt{3}$) and the height (12) of $\triangle ABC$. Then, the area is $\frac{1}{2}(\overset{6}{\underset{1}{12}})(9 + 12\sqrt{3}) = 54 + 72\sqrt{3}$.

13. **(A)** $x + 2x + 3y = 180 \Rightarrow 3x + 3y = 180 \Rightarrow x + y = 60 \Rightarrow y = 60 - x$.

14. **(D)**

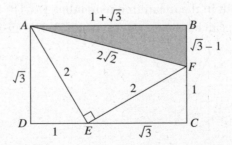

You are given enough information to determine the sides of all the triangles. Both 30-60-90 triangles have sides 1, $\sqrt{3}$, 2; and the 45-45-90 triangle has sides 2, 2, $2\sqrt{2}$. Also, $AB = CD = 1 + \sqrt{3}$, and $BF = AD - CF = \sqrt{3} - 1$.

Then, the perimeter of the shaded triangle is

$$1 + \sqrt{3} + \sqrt{3} - 1 + 2\sqrt{2} = 2\sqrt{2} + 2\sqrt{3}$$

15. **(B)** The area of $\triangle ABF = \frac{1}{2}(\sqrt{3} + 1)(\sqrt{3} - 1) = \frac{1}{2}(3 - 1) = \frac{1}{2}(2) = 1$.

16. **35**

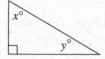

- Draw a diagram and label it. Let x be the measure of the larger angle and y be the measure of the smaller angle. Then, $\quad x + y = \ 90$
- Add the equations:
$$\begin{array}{r} x + y = \ 90 \\ + \ x - y = \ 20 \\ \hline 2x \quad\ = 110 \end{array}$$

Then $x = 55$, and $y = 90 - 55 = 35$.

17. **100** By the Pythagorean theorem,

$$8^2 + 15^2 = (CE)^2 \Rightarrow (CE)^2 = 64 + 225 = 289$$

So, $CE = \sqrt{289} = 17$.

Then the perimeter of $\triangle CDE$ is $8 + 15 + 17 = 40$.

Triangles ABC and CDE are similar (each has a 90° angle, and the vertical angles at C are congruent). The ratio of similitude is $\frac{20}{8} = 2.5$, so the perimeter of $\triangle ABC$ is $2.5 \times 40 = 100$.

18. **375** The area of $\triangle CDE = \frac{1}{2}(8)(15) = 60$.

Since the ratio of similitude for the two triangles (as calculated in Solution 17) is 2.5, the area of $\triangle ABC$ is $(2.5)^2$ times the area of $\triangle CDE$:

$$(2.5)^2 \times 60 = 6.25 \times 60 = 375$$

19. **18** Assume a triangle has sides of length 10, 20, and x. Then, since the sum of the lengths of any two sides of a triangle is greater than the length of the third side,

$$10 + 20 > x \Rightarrow x < 30 \text{ and } x + 10 > 20 \Rightarrow x > 10$$

Since x must be an integer, $11 \le x \le 29$, and the perimeter P satisfies $41 \le P \le 59$. The greatest possible difference then between the two perimeters is $59 - 41 = 18$.

20. **10** If the measures of the angles are in the ratio of 1:2:3, then:

$$x + 2x + 3x = 180 \Rightarrow 6x = 180 \Rightarrow x = 30$$

The triangle is a 30-60-90 right triangle, and the sides are $a, 2a,$ and $a\sqrt{3}$. The perimeter therefore is $3a + a\sqrt{3} = a(3 + \sqrt{3})$, so

$$a(3 + \sqrt{3}) = 30 + 10\sqrt{3} = 10(3 + \sqrt{3})$$

So, $a = 10$.

6-K QUADRILATERALS AND OTHER POLYGONS

A *polygon* is a closed geometric figure made up of line segments. The line segments are called *sides*, and the endpoints of the line segments are called *vertices* (each one is a *vertex*). Line segments inside the polygon drawn from one vertex to another are called *diagonals*.

The simplest polygons, which have three sides, are the triangles, which you studied in Section 6-J. A polygon with four sides is called a *quadrilateral*. The only other names you should know are pentagon, hexagon, and octagon for polygons with 5, 6, and 8 sides respectively.

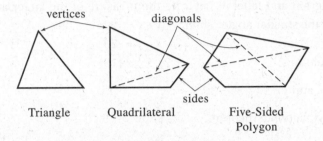

Triangle   Quadrilateral   Five-Sided Polygon

This section will present a few facts about polygons in general and then review the key facts you need to know about three special quadrilaterals.

Every quadrilateral has two diagonals. If you draw in either one, you will divide the quadrilateral into two triangles.

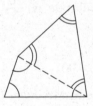

Since the sum of the measures of the three angles in each of the triangles is 180°, the sum of the measures of the angles in the quadrilateral is 360°.

Key Fact K1

In any quadrilateral, the sum of the measures of the four angles is 360°.

In exactly the same way as shown above, any polygon can be divided into triangles by drawing in all of the diagonals emanating from one vertex.

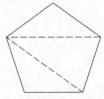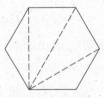

Notice that a five-sided polygon is divided into three triangles, and a six-sided polygon is divided into four triangles. In general, an *n*-sided polygon is divided into (*n* − 2) triangles, which leads to KEY FACT K2.

The sum of the measures of the *n* angles in a polygon with *n* sides is $(n - 2) \times 180°$.

➥ **Example 1**

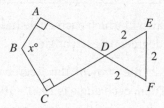

In the figure above, what is the value of *x*?

Solution. Since $\triangle DEF$ is equilateral, all of its angles measure 60°; also, since the two angles at vertex D are vertical angles, their measures are equal. Therefore, the measure of $\angle D$ in quadrilateral *ABCD* is 60°. Also, $\angle A$ and $\angle C$ are right angles, so each measures 90°.

Finally, since the sum of the measures of all four angles of *ABCD* is 360°:

$$60 + 90 + 90 + x = 360 \Rightarrow 240 + x = 360 \Rightarrow x = \mathbf{120}$$

An ***exterior angle*** of a polygon is formed by extending a side. In the polygons below, one exterior angle has been drawn in at each vertex. Surprisingly, if you add the measures of all of the exterior angles in any of the polygons, the sums are equal.

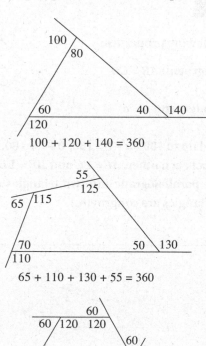

$$100 + 120 + 140 = 360$$

$$65 + 110 + 130 + 55 = 360$$

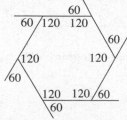

$$60 + 60 + 60 + 60 + 60 + 60 = 360$$

In any polygon, the sum of the measures of the exterior angles, taking one at each vertex, is 360°.

➡ **Example 2**

A 10-sided polygon is drawn in which each angle has the same measure. What is the measure, in degrees, of each angle?

Solution 1. By KEY FACT K2, the sum of the degree measures of the 10 angles is $(10 - 2) \times 180 = 8 \times 180 = 1440$. Then, each angle is $1440 \div 10 =$ **144**.

Solution 2. By KEY FACT K3, the sum of the degree measures of the 10 exterior angles is 360, so each one is 36. Therefore, the degree measure of each interior angle is $180 - 36 =$ **144**.

A *parallelogram* is a quadrilateral in which both pairs of opposite sides are parallel.

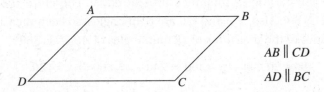

$AB \parallel CD$
$AD \parallel BC$

Parallelograms have the following properties:

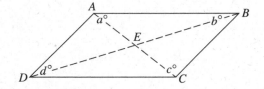

- Opposite sides are congruent: $AB = CD$ and $AD = BC$.
- Opposite angles are congruent: $a = c$ and $b = d$.
- Consecutive angles add up to 180°: $a + b = 180$, $b + c = 180$, $c + d = 180$, and $a + d = 180$.
- The two diagonals bisect each other: $AE = EC$ and $BE = ED$.
- A diagonal divides the parallelogram into two triangles that have exactly the same size and shape. (The triangles are congruent.)

➡ **Example 3**

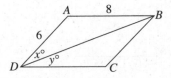

In the figure above, *ABCD* is a parallelogram. Which of the following statements *must* be true?

(A) $x < y$
(B) $x = y$
(C) $x > y$
(D) $x + y < 90$

Solution. Since $\overline{AB}$ and $\overline{CD}$ are parallel line segments cut by transversal *BD*, m∠*ABD* = *y*. In △*ABD*, *AB* > *AD*, so by KEY FACT J3 the measure of the angle opposite $\overline{AB}$ is greater than the measure of the angle opposite $\overline{AD}$. Therefore, ***x* > *y* (C).**

A ***rectangle*** is a parallelogram in which all four angles are right angles. Two adjacent sides of a rectangle are usually called the ***length*** (ℓ) and the ***width*** (*w*). Note that the length is not necessarily greater than the width.

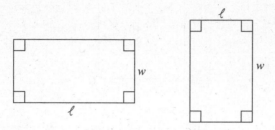

Key Fact K5

Since a rectangle is a parallelogram, all of the properties listed in KEY FACT K4 hold for rectangles. In addition:

- **The measure of each angle in a rectangle is 90°.**
- **The diagonals of a rectangle are congruent: $\overline{AC} \cong \overline{BD}$.**

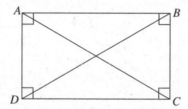

A ***square*** is a rectangle in which all four sides have the same length.

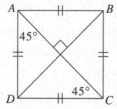

Key Fact K6

Since a square is a rectangle, all of the properties listed in KEY FACTS K4 and K5 hold for squares. In addition:

- **All four sides have the same length.**
- **Each diagonal divides the square into two 45-45-90 right triangles.**
- **The diagonals are perpendicular to each other: $\overline{AC} \perp \overline{BD}$.**

➡ Example 4_____

What is the length of each side of a square if its diagonals are 10?

Solution. Draw a diagram. In square $ABCD$, diagonal $\overline{AC}$ is the hypotenuse of a 45-45-90 right triangle, and side $\overline{AB}$ is a leg of that triangle. By KEY FACT J7,

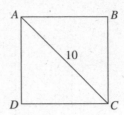

$$AB = \frac{AC}{\sqrt{2}} = \frac{10}{\sqrt{2}} \times \frac{\sqrt{2}}{\sqrt{2}} = \frac{10\sqrt{2}}{2} = \mathbf{5\sqrt{2}}$$

The ***perimeter*** (P) of any polygon is the sum of the lengths of all of its sides. The only polygons for which we have formulas for the perimeter are the rectangle and the square.

Key Fact K7

In a rectangle, $P = 2(\ell + w)$; in a square, $P = 4s$.

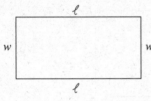

$$P = \ell + w + \ell + w = 2(\ell + w) \qquad P = s + s + s + s = 4s$$

➡ Example 5_____

The length of a rectangle is twice its width. If the perimeter of the rectangle is the same as the perimeter of a square of side 6, what is the square of the length of a diagonal of the rectangle?

Solution. Don't do anything until you have drawn diagrams.

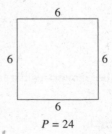

$$P = 24$$

Since the perimeter of the square is 24, the perimeter of the rectangle is also 24. Then $2(\ell + w) = 24 \Rightarrow \ell + w = 12$.

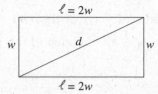

But $\ell = 2w$, so

$$2w + w = 3w = 12 \Rightarrow w = 4 \text{ (and } \ell = 8)$$

Finally, use the Pythagorean theorem:

$$d^2 = 4^2 + 8^2 = 16 + 64 = \mathbf{80}$$

A **_trapezoid_** is a quadrilateral in which exactly one pair of opposite sides is parallel.

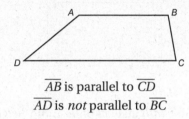

$\overline{AB}$ is parallel to $\overline{CD}$
$\overline{AD}$ is *not* parallel to $\overline{BC}$

The parallel sides are called the **_bases_** of the trapezoid, and the distance between the two bases is called the **_height_**.

If the two nonparallel sides are congruent, the trapezoid is called **_isosceles_**. In that case only, the diagonals are congruent.

Key Fact K8

Isosceles trapezoids have the following properties:

- **The base angles (the angles opposite the congruent sides) are congruent.**
- **The diagonals are congruent.**

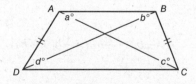

$\overline{AB}$ is parallel to $\overline{CD}$
$\overline{AD} \cong \overline{BC}$
$a = b$ and $c = d$
$\overline{AC} \cong \overline{BD}$

In Section 6-J you reviewed the formula for the *area* of a triangle. The only other polygons for which you need to know area formulas are the parallelogram, rectangle, square, and trapezoid.

■ Parallelogram: Since the area of each of the two triangles formed by drawing a diagonal in a parallelogram is $\frac{1}{2}bh$, the area of the parallelogram is twice as great:

$$A = \frac{1}{2}bh + \frac{1}{2}bh = bh$$

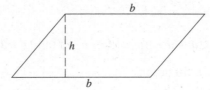

■ Rectangle: In a rectangle the same formula holds, but it is usually written as $A = \ell w$,

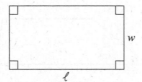

using the terms *length* and *width* instead of *base* and *height*.

■ Square: In a square the length and width are equal; we label each of them s (side), and write $A = s \times s = s^2$.

If d is the diagonal of a square, $d = s\sqrt{2} \Rightarrow d^2 = 2s^2 \Rightarrow s^2 = \frac{1}{2}d^2$.

■ Trapezoid: If b_1 and b_2 are the lengths of the two parallel sides of a trapezoid and h is the height, the area of the trapezoid is the sum of the area of the two triangles formed by drawing in a diagonal:

$$A = \frac{1}{2}b_1h + \frac{1}{2}b_2h = \frac{1}{2}h(b_1 + b_2)$$

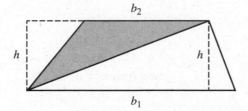

Here are the area formulas you need to know:

- For a parallelogram: $A = bh$
- For a rectangle: $A = \ell w$
- For a square: $A = s^2$ or $A = \frac{1}{2}d^2$
- For a trapezoid: $A = \frac{1}{2}h(b_1 + b_2)$

➡ Example 6

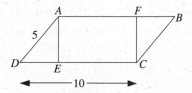

In the figure above, the area of parallelogram $ABCD$ is 40. What is the area of rectangle $AFCE$?

(A) 20
(B) 24
(C) 28
(D) 32

Solution. Since the base, CD, is 10 and the area is 40, the height, AE, must be 4. Then $\triangle AED$ must be a 3-4-5 right triangle with $DE = 3$, which implies that $EC = 7$. The area of the rectangle is $7 \times 4 = \mathbf{28}$ **(C)**.

Multiple-Choice Questions

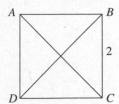

1. In the figure above, the two diagonals divide square *ABCD* into four small triangles. What is the sum of the perimeters of those triangles?

   (A) $2 + 2\sqrt{2}$

   (B) $8 + 4\sqrt{2}$

   (C) $8 + 8\sqrt{2}$

   (D) 16

2. If the length of a rectangle is 4 times its width, and if its area is 144, what is its perimeter?

   (A) 24

   (B) 30

   (C) 60

   (D) 96

3. If the angles of a five-sided polygon are in the ratio of 2:3:3:5:5, what is the degree measure of the smallest angle?

   (A) 40

   (B) 60

   (C) 80

   (D) 90

Questions 4 and 5 refer to a rectangle in which the length of each diagonal is 12, and one of the angles formed by the diagonal and a side measures 30°.

4. What is the area of the rectangle?

   (A) 18

   (B) 72

   (C) $18\sqrt{3}$

   (D) $36\sqrt{3}$

5. What is the perimeter of the rectangle?

   (A) 18

   (B) 24

   (C) $12 + 12\sqrt{3}$

   (D) $18 + 6\sqrt{3}$

6. The length of a rectangle is 5 more than the side of a square, and the width of the rectangle is 5 less than the side of the square. If the area of the square is 45, what is the area of the rectangle?

   (A) 20

   (B) 25

   (C) 45

   (D) 50

Questions 7 and 8 refer to the following figure, in which *M*, *N*, *O*, and *P* are the midpoints of the sides of rectangle *ABCD*.

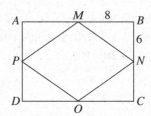

7. What is the perimeter of quadrilateral *MNOP*?

   (A) 24

   (B) 32

   (C) 40

   (D) 48

8. What is the area of quadrilateral *MNOP*?

   (A) 48

   (B) 60

   (C) 72

   (D) 96

Questions 9 and 10 refer to the following figure, in which *M* and *N* are midpoints of two of the sides of square *ABCD*.

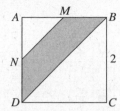

9. What is the perimeter of the shaded region?

   (A) 3
   (B) $2 + 3\sqrt{2}$
   (C) $3 + 2\sqrt{2}$
   (D) 5

10. What is the area of the shaded region?

   (A) 1.5
   (B) 1.75
   (C) $2\sqrt{2}$
   (D) $3\sqrt{2}$

Grid-in Questions

11. In the figure below, *ABCD* is a parallelogram. What is the value of *y* – *z*?

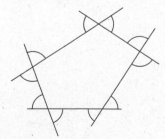

12. In the figure below, what is the sum of the degree measures of all of the marked angles?

13. If, in the figures below, the area of rectangle *ABCD* is 100, what is the area of rectangle *EFGH*?

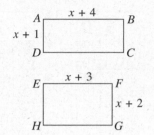

14. How many sides does a polygon have if the measure of each interior angle is 8 times the degree measure of each exterior angle?

15. In quadrilateral *WXYZ*, the measure of ∠*Z* is 10 more than twice the average of the measures of the other three angles. What is the measure, in degrees, of ∠*Z*?

Answer Key

1.	**C**	3.	**B**	5.	**C**	7.	**C**	9.	**B**
2.	**C**	4.	**D**	6.	**A**	8.	**D**	10.	**A**

11. `50` 12. `720` 13. `102` 14. `18`

15. `150`

Answers Explained

1. **(C)** Each of the four small triangles is a 45-45-90 right triangle whose hypotenuse is 2. Therefore, each leg is $\dfrac{2}{\sqrt{2}} = \sqrt{2}$. The perimeter of each small triangle is $2 + 2\sqrt{2}$, and the sum of the perimeters is 4 times as great: $8 + 8\sqrt{2}$.

2. **(C)** Draw a diagram and label it.

Since the area is 144, then:

$$144 = 4x^2 \Rightarrow x^2 = 36 \Rightarrow x = 6$$

The width is 6, the length is 24, and the perimeter is 60.

3. **(B)** The sum of the degree measures of the angles of a five-sided polygon is $(5 - 2) \times 180 = 3 \times 180 = 540$. Then:

$$540 = 2x + 3x + 3x + 5x + 5x = 18x$$

So, $x = 540 \div 18 = 30$.

The degree measure of the smallest angle is $2x$: $2 \times 30 = 60$.

4. **(D)** Draw a diagram and label it. Since $\triangle BCD$ is a 30-60-90 right triangle, BC is 6 (half the hypotenuse) and CD is $6\sqrt{3}$.

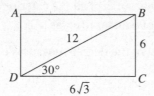

Then the area of rectangle $ABCD$ is $\ell w = 6(6\sqrt{3}) = 36\sqrt{3}$.

5. **(C)** The perimeter of the rectangle is $2(\ell + w) = 2(6 + 6\sqrt{3}) = 12 + 12\sqrt{3}$.

6. **(A)** Let x represent the side of the square. Then the dimensions of the rectangle are $(x + 5)$ and $(x - 5)$, and its area is $(x + 5)(x - 5) = x^2 - 25$. Since 45 is the area of the square, $x^2 = 45$, and so $x^2 - 25 = 20$.

7. **(C)** Each triangle surrounding quadrilateral $MNOP$ is a 6-8-10 right triangle. Then, each side of the quadrilateral is 10, and its perimeter is 40.

8. **(D)** The area of each of the triangles is $\frac{1}{2}(6)(8) = 24$, so together the four triangles have an area of 96. The area of the rectangle is $16 \times 12 = 192$. Therefore, the area of quadrilateral $MNOP$ is $192 - 96 = 96$.

NOTE: Joining the midpoints of the four sides of any quadrilateral creates a parallelogram whose area is one-half the area of the original quadrilateral.

9. **(B)** Since M and N are midpoints of sides of length 2, AM, MB, AN, and ND are each equal to 1. Also, $MN = \sqrt{2}$, since it's the hypotenuse of an isosceles right triangle whose legs are 1; and $BD = 2\sqrt{2}$, since it's the hypotenuse of an isosceles right triangle whose legs are 2. Then, the perimeter of the shaded region is $1 + \sqrt{2} + 1 + 2\sqrt{2} = 2 + 3\sqrt{2}$.

10. **(A)** The area of $\triangle ABD = \frac{1}{2}(2)(2) = 2$, and the area of $\triangle AMN = \frac{1}{2}(1)(1) = 0.5$. The area of the shaded region is $2 - 0.5 = 1.5$.

11. **50** The sum of the degree measures of two consecutive angles of a parallelogram is 180, so

$$180 = (3x - 5) + (2x - 15) = 5x - 20$$

So, $5x = 200 \Rightarrow x = 40$.

Since opposite angles of a parallelogram are equal, $y = 3x - 5 = 115$ and $z = 2x - 15 = 65$. Then $y - z = 50$.

12. **720** Each of the 10 marked angles is an exterior angle of the pentagon. If you take one angle at each vertex, the sum of the degree measures of those five angles is 360; the sum of the degree measures of the other five is also 360: $360 + 360 = 720$.

13. **102** The area of rectangle $ABCD = (x + 1)(x + 4) = x^2 + 5x + 4$. The area of rectangle $EFGH = (x + 2)(x + 3) = x^2 + 5x + 6$, which is exactly 2 more than the area of rectangle $ABCD$: $100 + 2 = 102$.

14. **18** The sum of the degree measures of an interior and exterior angle is 180, so

$$180 = 8x + x = 9x \Rightarrow x = 20$$

Since the sum of the degree measures of all the exterior angles of a polygon is 360, there are $360 \div 20 = 18$ angles and, of course, 18 sides.

15. **150** Let W, X, Y, and Z represent the degree measures of the four angles. Since

$$W + X + Y + Z = 360$$

then

$$W + X + Y = 360 - Z$$

Also:

$$Z = 10 + 2\left(\frac{W+X+Y}{3}\right) = 10 + 2\left(\frac{360-Z}{3}\right)$$

Then:

$$Z = 10 + \frac{2}{3}(360) - \frac{2}{3}Z = 10 + 240 - \frac{2}{3}Z \Rightarrow \frac{5}{3}Z = 250 \Rightarrow Z = 150$$

A *circle* consists of all the points in a plane that are the same distance from one fixed point, called the *center*. That distance is called the *radius* of the circle. The figure below is a circle of radius 1 unit whose center is at point *O*. *A*, *B*, *C*, *D*, and *E*, which are each 1 unit from *O*, are all

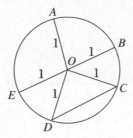

points on circle *O*. The word *radius* is also used to represent any of the line segments joining the center and a point on the circle. The plural of *radius* is *radii*. In circle *O*, above, $\overline{OA}$, $\overline{OB}$, $\overline{OC}$, $\overline{OD}$, and $\overline{OE}$ are all radii. If a circle has radius *r*, each of the radii is *r* units long.

Key Fact L1

Any triangle, such as $\triangle COD$ in the figure above, formed by connecting the endpoints of two radii is isosceles.

➡ **Example 1**_____

If *P* and *Q* are points on circle *O*, what is the value of *x*?

Solution. Since $\overline{OP} \cong \overline{OQ}$ (each is a radius of the circle), $\triangle POQ$ is isosceles. Then $\angle P$ and $\angle Q$ are congruent, so

$$70 + x + x = 180 \Rightarrow 2x = 110 \Rightarrow x = \mathbf{55}$$

A line segment, such as $\overline{BE}$ in circle *O* at the beginning of this section, whose endpoints are on a circle and that passes through the center is called a *diameter*. Since $\overline{BE}$ is made up of two radii, $\overline{OB}$ and $\overline{OE}$, a diameter is twice as long as a radius.

Key Fact L2

If *d* is the diameter and *r* the radius of a circle, then $d = 2r$.

Key Fact L3

A diameter is the longest line segment that can be drawn in a circle.

The total length around a circle, from A to B to C to D to E and back to A in the circle at the beginning of this section, is called the **circumference** of the circle. In every circle the ratio of the circumference to the diameter is exactly the same and is denoted by the symbol π (the Greek letter pi).

Key Fact L4

For every circle:

$$\pi = \frac{\text{circumference}}{\text{diameter}} = \frac{C}{d} \quad \text{or} \quad C = \pi d \quad \text{or} \quad C = 2\pi r$$

Key Fact L5

The value of π is *approximately* 3.14.

CALCULATOR HINT

On almost every question on the SAT that involves circles, you are expected to leave your answer in terms of π, so don't multiply by 3.14 unless you must. If you need an approximation—to test a choice, for example—then use your calculator.

➡ **Example 2**

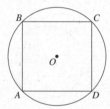

In the figure above, square $ABCD$ is inscribed in circle O. If the area of the square is 50, what is the circumference of the circle?

(A) $\pi\sqrt{50}$
(B) 10π
(C) 50π
(D) 100π

Solution. Since the area of square $ABCD$ is 50, the length of each side is $\sqrt{50}$. Diagonal $\overline{AC}$ divides the square into two isosceles right triangles whose legs are $\sqrt{50}$ and whose hypotenuse is $\overline{AC}$. So, $\overline{AC} = (\sqrt{50})(\sqrt{2}) = \sqrt{100} = 10$. But since $\overline{AC}$ is also a diameter of circle O, the circumference is $\pi d = \mathbf{10\pi}$ **(B)**.

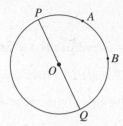

An ***arc*** consists of two points on a circle and all the points between them. If two points, such as P and Q in circle O, are the endpoints of a diameter, they divide the circle into two arcs called ***semicircles***. On the SAT, arc $\overset{\frown}{AB}$ always refers to the small arc joining A and B. To refer to the large arc going from A to B through P and Q, we would say arc $\overset{\frown}{APB}$ or arc $\overset{\frown}{AQB}$.

An angle whose vertex is at the center of a circle is called a ***central angle***.

Key Fact L6

The degree measure of a complete circle is 360.

Key Fact L7

The degree measure of an arc equals the degree measure of the central angle that intercepts it.

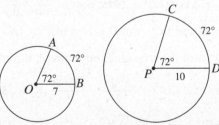

> **CAUTION:** Degree measure is *not* a measure of length. In the circles above, arc $\overset{\frown}{AB}$ and arc $\overset{\frown}{CD}$ each measure 72°, even though arc $\overset{\frown}{CD}$ is much longer.

How long *is* arc $\overset{\frown}{CD}$? Since the radius of circle P is 10, its circumference is

$$20\pi \ [2\pi r = 2\pi(10) = 20\pi]$$

Since there are 360° in a circle, arc $\overset{\frown}{CD}$ is $\dfrac{72}{360}$, or $\dfrac{1}{5}$, of the circumference: $\dfrac{1}{5}(20\pi) = 4\pi$.

Key Fact L8

The formula for the area of a circle of radius r is $A = \pi r^2$.

The area of circle P in Key Fact L7 is $\pi(10)^2 = 100\pi$ square units.

The area of sector CPD is $\frac{1}{5}$ of the area of the circle: $\frac{1}{5}(100\pi) = 20\pi$.

Key Fact L9

If an arc measures $x°$, the length of the arc is $\frac{x}{360}(2\pi r)$; and the area of the sector formed by the arc and two radii is $\frac{x}{360}(\pi r^2)$.

Examples 3 and 4 refer to the circle below.

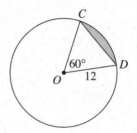

➡ **Example 3**

What is the area of the shaded region?

(A) $144\pi - 144\sqrt{3}$

(B) $144\pi - 36\sqrt{3}$

(C) $24\pi - 36\sqrt{3}$

(D) $24\pi - 72$

Solution. The area of the shaded region is equal to the area of sector COD minus the area of $\triangle COD$. The area of the circle is $\pi(12)^2 = 144\pi$. Since $\frac{60}{360} = \frac{1}{6}$, the area of sector COD is $\frac{1}{6}(144\pi) = 24\pi$. Since $m\angle O = 60$, $m\angle C + m\angle D = 120$; but $\triangle COD$ is isosceles, so $\angle C = \angle D$. Therefore, each measures $60°$, and the triangle is equilateral. Finally, by KEY FACT J15,

$$\text{area of } \triangle COD = \frac{12^2\sqrt{3}}{4} = \frac{144\sqrt{3}}{4} = 36\sqrt{3}$$

so the area of the shaded region is $\mathbf{24\pi - 36\sqrt{3}}$ **(C)**.

➡ **Example 4**

What is the perimeter of the shaded region?

(A) $12 + 4\pi$

(B) $12 + 12\pi$

(C) $12 + 24\pi$

(D) $12\sqrt{2} + 4\pi$

Solution. Since $\triangle COD$ is equilateral, $CD = 12$. Since circumference of circle $= 2\pi(12) = 24\pi \Rightarrow$ arc $CD = \frac{1}{6}(24\pi) = 4\pi$, the perimeter is **12 + 4π** **(A)**.

A line and a circle or two circles are ***tangent*** if they have only one point of intersection. A circle is ***inscribed*** in a triangle or square if it is tangent to each side. A polygon is ***inscribed*** in a circle if each vertex is on the circle.

Line ℓ is tangent to circle O.
Circles O and Q are tangent.

The circle is inscribed
in the square.

The pentagon is inscribed
in the circle.

➤ Example 5_____

A is the center of a circle whose radius is 10, and B is the center of a circle whose diameter is 10. If these two circles are tangent to one another, what is the area of the circle whose diameter is $\overline{AB}$?

(A) 30π
(B) 56.25π
(C) 100π
(D) 225π

Solution. Draw a diagram. Since the diameter of circle B is 10, its radius is 5. Then the diameter, $\overline{AB}$, of the dotted circle is 15, its radius is 7.5, and its area is $\pi(7.5)^2 = $ **56.25π** **(B)**. (Note that you should use your calculator to square 7.5 but not to multiply by π.)

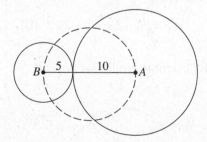

HELPFUL HINT

On multiple-choice questions involving circles, the choices are almost always in terms of π, so you shouldn't multiply anything by 3.14.

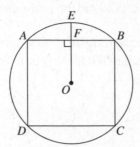

In the figure above, square *ABCD* is inscribed in a circle whose center is *O* and whose radius is 4. If $\overline{EO} \perp \overline{AB}$ at *F*, what is the length of $\overline{EF}$?

(A) $\sqrt{2}$

(B) $2\sqrt{2}$

(C) $4 - \sqrt{2}$

(D) $4 - 2\sqrt{2}$

Solution. Draw diagonal $\overline{AC}$. Then, $\triangle AFO$ is a 45-45-90 right triangle. Since hypotenuse *AO* is a radius, its length is 4; and by KEY FACT J8:

$$OF = \frac{4}{\sqrt{2}} = \frac{4}{\sqrt{2}} \times \frac{\sqrt{2}}{\sqrt{2}} = 2\sqrt{2}$$

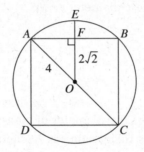

EO = 4 since it is also a radius. Then

$$EF = EO - OF = \mathbf{4 - 2\sqrt{2}} \ \ (\mathbf{D})$$

In the figure below, line ℓ is tangent to circle *O* at point *P*.

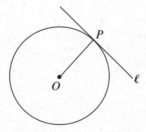

An important theorem in geometry states that radius $\overline{OP}$ is perpendicular to ℓ.

A line tangent to a circle is perpendicular to the radius drawn to the point of contact.

➡ **Example 7**_____

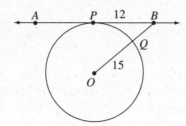

In the figure above, $\overleftrightarrow{AB}$ is tangent to circle O at point P. If $OB = 15$ and $PB = 12$, what is QB?

Solution. Draw in radius $\overline{OP}$, creating $\triangle OPB$. By KEY FACT L10, $\overline{OP} \perp \overline{AB}$, so $\triangle OPB$ is a right triangle. Then, by the Pythagorean theorem,

$$OP^2 + PB^2 = OB^2 \Rightarrow OP^2 + 144 = 225$$

$$\text{So, } OP^2 = 81 \Rightarrow OP = 9$$

Since all radii are equal, $OQ = 9$ and so $QB = 15 - 9 = \textbf{6}$.

HELPFUL HINT

You don't have to take the time to use the Pythagorean theorem if you recognize this as a multiple of a 3-4-5 triangle.

Multiple-Choice Questions

1. What is the circumference of a circle whose area is 100π?

   (A) 10
   (B) 20
   (C) 10π
   (D) 20π

2. What is the area of a circle whose circumference is π?

   (A) $\dfrac{\pi}{4}$

   (B) $\dfrac{\pi}{2}$

   (C) 2π
   (D) 4π

3. What is the area of a circle that is inscribed in a square of area 2?

   (A) $\dfrac{\pi}{2}$

   (B) π

   (C) $\pi\sqrt{2}$

   (D) 2π

4. A square of area 2 is inscribed in a circle. What is the area of the circle?

   (A) $\dfrac{\pi}{2}$

   (B) π

   (C) $\pi\sqrt{2}$

   (D) 2π

5. What is the area of a circle whose radius is the diagonal of a square whose area is 4?

   (A) 2π
   (B) 4π
   (C) 8π
   (D) 16π

Questions 6 and 7 refer to the following figure.

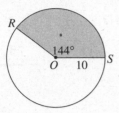

6. What is the length of arc RS?

   (A) 4π
   (B) 8π
   (C) 20π
   (D) 40π

7. What is the area of the shaded sector?

   (A) 4π
   (B) 8π
   (C) 20π
   (D) 40π

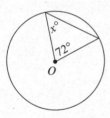

8. In the figure above, what is the value of x?

   (A) 36
   (B) 45
   (C) 54
   (D) 60

9. If A is the area and C the circumference of a circle, which of the following is an expression for A in terms of C?

   (A) $\dfrac{C^2}{4\pi}$

   (B) $\dfrac{C^2}{4\pi^2}$

   (C) $2C\sqrt{\pi}$

   (D) $2C^2\sqrt{\pi}$

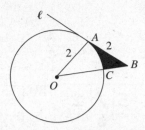

10. In the figure above, ℓ is tangent to circle O at A, and $OA = AB = 2$. What is the area of the shaded region?

(A) $\frac{1}{2}\pi$

(B) $4 - \frac{1}{2}\pi$

(C) $2 - \frac{1}{2}\pi$

(D) $2 - \pi$

Grid-in Questions

11. The circumference of a circle is $a\pi$ units, and the area of the circle is $b\pi$ square units. If $a = b$, what is the radius of the circle?

12. A 9×12 rectangle is inscribed in a circle. What is the radius of the circle?

13. In the figure below, the ratio of the length of arc AB to the circumference of the circle is 2 to 15. What is the value of y?

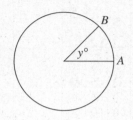

14. If the area of the shaded region is $k\pi$, what is the value of k?

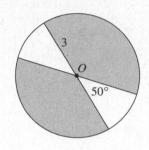

15. If line ℓ is tangent to circle O at point P, if B is a point on ℓ such that $PB = 8$, and if $OB = 10$, what is the radius of the circle?

Answer Key

1. **D**	3. **A**	5. **C**	7. **D**	9. **A**
2. **A**	4. **B**	6. **B**	8. **C**	10. **C**

11. **2**

12. **7.5**   or   **15/2**

13. **48**

14. **13/2**   or   **6.5**

15. **6**

Answers Explained

1. **(D)** $A = \pi r^2 = 100\pi \Rightarrow r^2 = 100 \Rightarrow r = 10$
   $C = 2\pi r = 2\pi(10) = 20\pi$

2. **(A)** $C = 2\pi r = \pi \Rightarrow 2r = 1 \Rightarrow r = \dfrac{1}{2}$

   $$A = \pi r^2 = \pi\left(\dfrac{1}{2}\right)^2 = \dfrac{1}{4}\pi = \dfrac{\pi}{4}$$

3. **(A)** Draw a diagram. Since the area of square $ABCD$ is 2, $AD = \sqrt{2}$. Then, diameter $EF = \sqrt{2}$ and radius $OE = \dfrac{\sqrt{2}}{2}$, so area $= \pi\left(\dfrac{\sqrt{2}}{2}\right)^2 = \dfrac{2}{4}\pi = \dfrac{\pi}{2}$.

   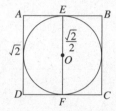

4. **(B)** Draw a diagram. Since the area of square $ABCD$ is 2, $AD = \sqrt{2}$. Then diagonal $\overline{BD} = \sqrt{2} \times \sqrt{2} = 2$. But $\overline{BD}$ is also a diameter of the circle, so the diameter is 2 and the radius is 1.
   Therefore, the area is $\pi(1)^2 = \pi$.

   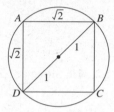

5. **(C)** If the area of the square is 4, each side is 2, and the length of a diagonal is $2\sqrt{2}$. The area of a circle whose radius is $2\sqrt{2}$ is $\pi(2\sqrt{2})^2 = 8\pi$.

6. **(B)** The length of arc $RS = \left(\dfrac{144}{360}\right)2\pi(10) = \left(\dfrac{2}{5}\right)20\pi = 8\pi$.

   [Note that, instead of reducing $\dfrac{144}{360}$, you should use your calculator and divide:

   $144 \div 360 = 0.4$, and $(0.4)(20\pi) = 8\pi$.]

7. **(D)** The area of the shaded sector is

   $$\left(\dfrac{144}{360}\right)\pi(10)^2 = \left(\dfrac{2}{5}\right)100\pi = 40\pi$$

8. **(C)** The triangle is isosceles, so the third (unmarked) angle is also x:

   $$180 = 72 + 2x \Rightarrow 2x = 108 \Rightarrow x = 54$$

9. **(A)** $C = 2\pi r \Rightarrow r = \dfrac{C}{2\pi}$

   Since $A = \pi r^2$, $A = \pi\left(\dfrac{C}{2\pi}\right)^2 = \pi\left(\dfrac{C^2}{4\pi^2}\right) = \dfrac{C^2}{4\pi}$.

10. **(C)** Since ℓ is tangent to circle O at A, $\overline{OA} \perp \ell$ and $\triangle OAB$ is an isosceles right triangle. Then $m\angle O = 45$.
    The area of the shaded region is the area of $\triangle OAB$ minus the area of sector OAC.

The area of $\triangle OAB$ is $\frac{1}{2}(2)(2) = 2$. Since the area of the circle is $\pi(2^2) = 4\pi$, the area of sector OAC is $\frac{45}{360} = \frac{1}{8}$ of 4π, or $\frac{1}{2}\pi$.

Finally, the area of the shaded region is $2 - \frac{1}{2}\pi$.

11. **2** Since $a = b$, then $C = a\pi = b\pi = A$, so

$$2\pi r = \pi r^2 \Rightarrow 2r = r^2 \Rightarrow r = 2$$

12. **7.5 or $\frac{15}{2}$** Draw a diagram. By the Pythagorean theorem (or by recognizing a $3x$-$4x$-$5x$ triangle with $x = 3$), the length of diagonal $\overline{AC}$ is 15. But $\overline{AC}$ is also a diameter of the circle, so the diameter is 15 and the radius is 7.5 or $\frac{15}{2}$.

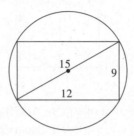

13. **48** Since arc $\overset{\frown}{AB}$ is $\frac{2}{15}$ of the circumference, y is $\frac{2}{15} \times 360 = 48$.

14. **$\frac{13}{2}$ or 6.5** The area of the circle is 9π; and since the white region is $\frac{100}{360} = \frac{5}{18}$ of the circle, the shaded region is $\frac{13}{18}$ of it:

$$\frac{13}{18} \times 9\pi = \frac{13}{2}\pi \text{ or } 6.5\pi$$

15. **6** Draw a diagram and label it.

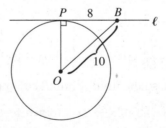

Since radius $\overline{OP}$ is perpendicular to ℓ, $\triangle OPB$ is a right triangle.
By the Pythagorean theorem,

$$OP^2 + 8^2 = 10^2 \Rightarrow OP^2 + 64 = 100$$

So, $OP^2 = 36 \Rightarrow OP = 6$.

(Of course, you should save time by recognizing a 6-8-10 right triangle.)

6-M SOLID GEOMETRY

In this section, we will review all of the formulas you will need to calculate volumes of solid figures on the SAT. Remember, however, that each of these formulas is given to you in the Reference Information box at the beginning of each math section of the test.

A **rectangular solid** or **box** is a solid formed by six rectangles, called **faces**. The sides of the rectangles are called **edges**. As shown in the diagram that follows, the edges are the **length**, **width**, and **height**.

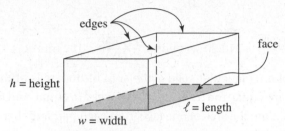

RECTANGULAR SOLID

A **cube** is a rectangular solid in which the length, width, and height are equal, so that all the edges are the same length.

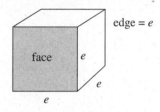

CUBE

The **volume** of a solid, which is the amount of space it occupies, is measured in **cubic units**. One cubic unit is the amount of space occupied by a cube all of whose edges are 1 unit long. In the figure above, if the length of each edge of the cube is 1 inch, the area of each face is 1 square inch, and the volume of the cube is 1 cubic inch.

Key Fact M1

- The formula for the volume of a rectangular solid is $V = \ell wh$, where ℓ, w, and h are the length, width, and height, respectively.
- In a cube, all the edges are equal. Therefore, if e is the length of an edge, the formula for the volume of a cube is $V = e^3$.

REFERENCE FACT

KEY FACT M1 is one of the facts provided in the "Reference Information" at the beginning of each math section.

➡ Example 1

The base of a rectangular tank is 2 feet wide and 4 feet long; the height of the tank is 20 inches. If water is pouring into the tank at the rate of 2 cubic inches per second, how many <u>hours</u> will be required to fill the tank?

Solution. Draw a diagram. Change all the units to inches (2 feet = 24 inches and 4 feet = 48 inches). Then the volume of the tank is 24 × 48 × 20 = 23,040 cubic inches. At 2 cubic inches per second:

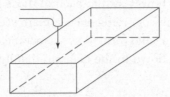

 required time = $\dfrac{23,040}{2}$ = 11,520 seconds = $\dfrac{11,520}{60}$ = 192 minutes = $\dfrac{192}{60}$ = **3.2** hours

The *surface area* of a rectangular solid is the sum of the areas of the six faces. Since the top and bottom faces are equal, the front and back faces are equal, and the left and right faces are equal, you can calculate the area of one face from each pair and then double the sum. In a cube, each of the six faces has the same area.

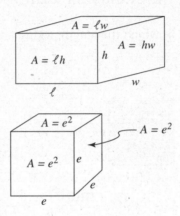

Key Fact M2

- The formula for the surface area of a rectangular solid is $A = 2(\ell w + \ell h + wh)$.
- The formula for the surface area of a cube is $A = 6e^2$.

➡ Example 2 _____

The volume of a cube is v cubic yards, and its surface area is a square feet. If $v = a$, what is the length, in <u>inches</u>, of each edge?

Solution. Draw a diagram. If e is the length of the edge in yards, then $3e$ is the length in feet, and $36e$ is the length in inches.

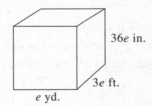

Therefore, $v = e^3$ and $a = 6(3e)^2 = 6(9e^2) = 54e^2$.

Since $v = a$, $e^3 = 54e^2 \Rightarrow e = 54$; the length of each edge is $36(54) = \mathbf{1944}$ inches.

A ***diagonal*** of a box is a line segment joining a vertex on the top of the box to the opposite vertex on the bottom. A box has four diagonals, all the same length. In the box below they are line segments $\overline{AG}$, $\overline{BH}$, $\overline{CE}$, and $\overline{DF}$.

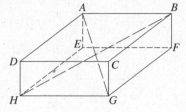

Key Fact M3

A diagonal of a box is the longest line segment that can be drawn between two points on the box.

Key Fact M4

If the dimensions of a box are ℓ, w, and h, and if d is the length of a diagonal, then

$$d^2 = \ell^2 + w^2 + h^2$$

For example, in the box to the right:

$$d^2 = 3^2 + 4^2 + 12^2 = 9 + 16 + 144 = 169 \Rightarrow d = 13$$

This formula is really just an extended Pythagorean theorem. $\overline{EG}$ is the diagonal of rectangular base *EFGH*. Since the sides of the base are 3 and 4, *EG* is 5. Now, $\triangle CGE$ is a right triangle whose legs are 12 and 5, so diagonal $\overline{CE}$ is 13. (The only reason not to use the Pythagorean theorem is that these triangles are so familiar.)

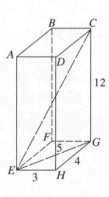

➡ Example 3

What is the length of a diagonal of a cube whose sides are 1?

Solution. Use the formula:

$$d^2 = 1^2 + 1^2 + 1^2 = 3 \Rightarrow d = \sqrt{3}$$

Without the formula you would draw a diagram and label it. Since the base is a 1×1 square, its diagonal is $\sqrt{2}$. Then the diagonal of the cube is the hypotenuse of a right triangle whose legs are 1 and $\sqrt{2}$, so

$$d^2 = 1^2 + (\sqrt{2})^2 = 1 + 2 = 3 \quad \text{and} \quad d = \sqrt{3}$$

A *cylinder* is similar to a rectangular solid except that the base is a circle instead of a rectangle. The volume of a cylinder is the area of its circular base (πr^2) times its height (h). The surface area of a cylinder depends on whether you are envisioning a tube, such as a straw, without a top or bottom, or a can, which has both a top and a bottom.

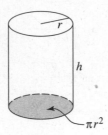

REFERENCE FACT

The formula for the volume of a cylinder is one of the facts provided in the "Reference Information" at the beginning of each math section.

Key Fact M5

- The volume, V, of a cylinder whose circular base has radius r and whose height is h is the area of the base times the height:

$$V = \pi r^2 h$$

- The surface area, A, of the side of the cylinder is the circumference of the circular base times the height:

$$A = 2\pi rh$$

➥ **Example 4**

The volume of a cube and the volume of a cylinder are equal. If the edge of the cube and the radius of the cylinder are each 6, which of the following is the best approximation of the height of the cube?

(A) 1
(B) 2
(C) 3
(D) 6

Solution. The volume of the cube is $6^3 = 216$. The volume of the cylinder is $\pi(6^2)h = 36\pi h$. Then

$$216 = 36\pi h \Rightarrow \pi h = 6 \Rightarrow h = \frac{6}{\pi}$$

Since π is approximately 3, h is approximately **2** **(B)**.

Prisms

Rectangular solids and cylinders are special cases of geometric solids called prisms. A **prism** is a three-dimensional figure that has two congruent parallel **bases**. The (perpendicular) distance between the two bases is called the **height**. Four prisms are depicted in the figure below.

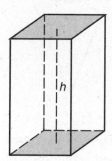 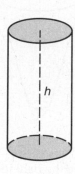 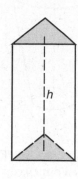 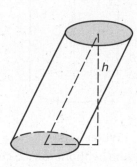

On the SAT, all of the prisms are **right prisms**, which means that any line segment joining corresponding points on the bases is perpendicular to the bases. In the figure above, the first three prisms are right prisms; the fourth one is not. The volume formulas given in KEY FACTS M1 and M5 are special cases of the following formula.

Key Fact M6

The formula for the volume of any right prism is $V = Bh$, where B is the area of one of the bases and h is the height.

➡ Example 5

What is the volume of the triangular prism below?

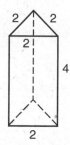

First calculate the area of a base and then multiply it by the height. By KEY FACT J15, the area of an equilateral triangle whose sides are 2 is $\dfrac{2^2\sqrt{3}}{4} = \sqrt{3}$. So the volume of the prism is $(\sqrt{3})(4) = 4\sqrt{3}$.

Cones

Imagine taking a cylinder and shrinking the size of one of the circular bases.

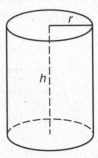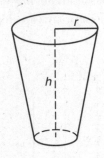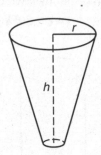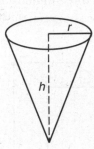

When it shrinks to a point, we call the resulting solid a cone. If you picture an ice cream cone (without the ice cream) or a dunce cap, you have the right idea. Notice that the radius of the circular base and the height of the cone are the same as in the original cylinder.

On the SAT, cones are usually referred to as "right circular cones." This is done to emphasize that the base is a circle and that the height (the line segment joining the vertex and the center of the circular base) is perpendicular to the base.

Key Fact M7

The formula for the volume of a right circular cone is $V = \frac{1}{3}\pi r^2 h$.

➡ Example 6

Assume that the volumes of a right circular cone and a right circular cylinder are equal and that the radius of the cone is twice the radius of the cylinder. How do their heights compare?

Let r be the radius of the cylinder, $2r$ the radius of the cone, and h and H the heights of the cone and the cylinder, respectively. Then

$$\frac{1}{3}\pi(2r)^2 h = \pi r^2 H \Rightarrow \frac{1}{3}\pi \, 4r^2 h = \pi \, r^2 H \Rightarrow \frac{4}{3}h = H$$

Pyramids

A *pyramid* is very similar to a cone. The difference is that the base of a pyramid is a polygon, not a circle. If there is a question concerning a pyramid on the SAT you take, the base will be a rectangle.

The formula for the volume of a pyramid with a rectangular base is $V = \frac{1}{3}\ell wh$, where ℓ and w are the length and width of the base and h is the height.

➡️ **Example 7**

What is the volume of a pyramid whose base is a square of side 3 feet and whose height is 6 feet?

Sketch the pyramid and use the formula given in KEY FACT M8.

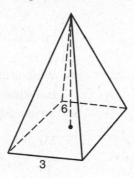

The area of the square base is 9 square feet, and so $V = \frac{1}{3}(9)(6) = 18$ cubic feet.

Spheres

A sphere is the set of all points in space that are a fixed distance, r, from a given point, O. O is called the center of the sphere, and r is the radius.

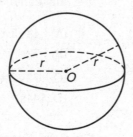

The formula for the volume of a sphere of radius r is $V = \frac{4}{3}\pi r^3$.

➡️ **Example 8**

What is the radius of a sphere whose volume is equal to the volume of a cube whose edges are 2?

By KEY FACT M1, the volume of the cube is $2^3 = 8$. Then by KEY FACT M9,

$$\frac{4}{3}\pi r^3 = 8 \Rightarrow \pi r^3 = 6 \Rightarrow r^3 = \frac{6}{\pi} \Rightarrow r = \sqrt[3]{\frac{6}{\pi}} \approx 1.24$$

Multiple-Choice Questions

1. What is the volume of a cube whose surface area is 150?

   (A)   25
   (B) 100
   (C) 125
   (D) 1000

2. What is the surface area of a cube whose volume is 64?

   (A)   16
   (B)   64
   (C)   96
   (D) 128

3. A solid metal cube of side 3 inches is placed in a rectangular tank whose length, width, and height are 3, 4, and 5 inches, respectively. What is the volume, in cubic units, of water that the tank can now hold?

   (A) 27
   (B) 33
   (C) 48
   (D) 60

4. The height, h, of a cylinder is equal to the edge of a cube. If the cylinder and the cube have the same volume, what is the radius of the cylinder?

   (A) $\dfrac{h}{\sqrt{\pi}}$

   (B) $h\sqrt{\pi}$

   (C) $\dfrac{\sqrt{\pi}}{h}$

   (D) $\dfrac{h^2}{\pi}$

5. If the height of a cylinder is 4 times its circumference, what is the volume of the cylinder in terms of its circumference, C?

   (A) $\dfrac{C^3}{\pi}$

   (B) $\dfrac{2C^3}{\pi}$

   (C) $\dfrac{2C^2}{\pi^2}$

   (D) $\dfrac{\pi C^2}{4}$

6. What is the volume of a pyramid whose base is a square of area 36 and whose four faces are equilateral triangles?

   (A)   36
   (B) $36\sqrt{2}$
   (C) 108
   (D) $108\sqrt{2}$

7. An isosceles right triangle whose legs are 6 is rotated about one of its legs to generate a right circular cone. What is the volume of that cone?

   (A) $48\sqrt{2}\,\pi$
   (B) 72π
   (C) $72\sqrt{2}\,\pi$
   (D) 144π

Grid-in Questions

8. The sum of the lengths of all the edges of a cube is 6 centimeters. What is the volume, in cubic centimeters, of the cube?

9. A 5-foot-long cylindrical pipe has an inner diameter of 6 feet and an outer diameter of 8 feet. If the total surface area (inside and out, including the ends) is $k\pi$, what is the value of k?

	⊘	⊘	
⊙	⊙	⊙	⊙
	⓪	⓪	⓪
①	①	①	①
②	②	②	②
③	③	③	③
④	④	④	④
⑤	⑤	⑤	⑤
⑥	⑥	⑥	⑥
⑦	⑦	⑦	⑦
⑧	⑧	⑧	⑧
⑨	⑨	⑨	⑨

10. What is the number of cubic inches in 1 cubic foot?

	⊘	⊘	
⊙	⊙	⊙	⊙
	⓪	⓪	⓪
①	①	①	①
②	②	②	②
③	③	③	③
④	④	④	④
⑤	⑤	⑤	⑤
⑥	⑥	⑥	⑥
⑦	⑦	⑦	⑦
⑧	⑧	⑧	⑧
⑨	⑨	⑨	⑨

11. A rectangular tank has a base that is 10 centimeters by 5 centimeters and a height of 20 centimeters. If the tank is half full of water, by how many centimeters will the water level rise if 325 cubic centimeters are poured into the tank?

	⊘	⊘	
⊙	⊙	⊙	⊙
	⓪	⓪	⓪
①	①	①	①
②	②	②	②
③	③	③	③
④	④	④	④
⑤	⑤	⑤	⑤
⑥	⑥	⑥	⑥
⑦	⑦	⑦	⑦
⑧	⑧	⑧	⑧
⑨	⑨	⑨	⑨

12. Three identical balls fit snugly into a cylindrical can: the radius of the spheres equals the radius of the can, and the balls just touch the bottom and the top of the can. What fraction of the volume of the can is taken up by the balls?

	⊘	⊘	
⊙	⊙	⊙	⊙
	⓪	⓪	⓪
①	①	①	①
②	②	②	②
③	③	③	③
④	④	④	④
⑤	⑤	⑤	⑤
⑥	⑥	⑥	⑥
⑦	⑦	⑦	⑦
⑧	⑧	⑧	⑧
⑨	⑨	⑨	⑨

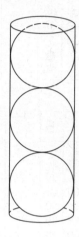

Answer Key

1. **C**   2. **C**   3. **B**   4. **A**   5. **A**   6. **B**   7. **B**

8. 1/8   or   .125

9. 84

10. 1728

11. 6.5

12. 2/3   or   .666   or   .667

Answers Explained

1. **(C)** Since the surface area is 150, each of the six faces of the cube is a square whose area is $150 \div 6 = 25$. Then, each edge is 5, and the volume is $5^3 = 125$.

2. **(C)** Since the volume of the cube is 64, then $e^3 = 64 \Rightarrow e = 4$. The surface area is $6e^2 = 6 \times 16 = 96$.

3. **(B)** The volume of the tank is $3 \times 4 \times 5 = 60$ cubic units, but the solid cube is taking up $3^3 = 27$ cubic units. Therefore, the tank can hold $60 - 27 = 33$ cubic units of water.

4. **(A)** Since the volumes are equal, $\pi r^2 h = e^3 = h^3$. Therefore,

$$\pi r^2 = h^2 \Rightarrow r^2 = \frac{h^2}{\pi} \Rightarrow r = \frac{h}{\sqrt{\pi}}$$

5. **(A)** Since $V = \pi r^2 h$, you need to express r and h in terms of C. It is given that $h = 4C$; and since $C = 2\pi r$, then $r = \dfrac{C}{2\pi}$. Therefore,

$$V = \pi \left(\frac{C}{2\pi}\right)^2 (4C) = \pi \left(\frac{C^2}{4\pi^2}\right)(4C) = \frac{C^3}{\pi}$$

6. **(B)** Sketch the pyramid.

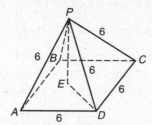

Since the area of the square is 36, each side is 6; and since each triangular face is equilateral, each edge of the pyramid is 6. To find the height, $h = PE$, of the pyramid, use the Pythagorean theorem on $\triangle PED$. Since $\overline{ED}$ is half of diagonal $\overline{BD}$, $ED = \frac{1}{2}(6\sqrt{2}) = 3\sqrt{2}$.

So:

$$(PD)^2 = (PE)^2 + (ED)^2 \Rightarrow (6)^2 = h^2 + (3\sqrt{2})^2 \Rightarrow$$

$$36 = h^2 + 18 \Rightarrow h^2 = 18 \Rightarrow h = \sqrt{18} = 3\sqrt{2}$$

Finally, by KEY FACT M8, the volume of the pyramid is:

$$\frac{1}{3}\ell wh = \frac{1}{3}(6)(6)(3\sqrt{2}) = 36\sqrt{2}$$

7. **(B)** Sketch the triangle and cone.

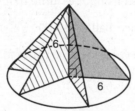

Since the radius and height of the cone are 6, by KEY FACT M7:

$$V = \frac{1}{3}\pi r^2 h = \frac{1}{3}\pi(6)^2(6) = 72\pi$$

8. $\frac{1}{8}$ **or .125** Since a cube has 12 edges:

$$12e = 6 \Rightarrow e = \frac{1}{2}$$

Therefore: $V = e^3 = \left(\frac{1}{2}\right)^3 = \frac{1}{8}$ or .125.

9. **84** Draw a diagram and label it. Since the surface of a cylinder is given by $A = 2\pi rh$, the area of the exterior is $2\pi(4)(5) = 40\pi$, and the area of the interior is $2\pi(3)(5) = 30\pi$. The area of *each* shaded end is the area of the outer circle minus the area of the inner circle: $16\pi - 9\pi = 7\pi$, so

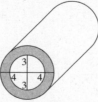

total surface area $= 40\pi + 30\pi + 7\pi + 7\pi = 84\pi \Rightarrow k = 84$

10. **1728** The volume of a cube whose edges are 1 foot can be expressed in either of two ways:

$$(1 \text{ foot})^3 = 1 \text{ cubic foot} \quad \text{or} \quad (12 \text{ inches})^3 = 1728 \text{ cubic inches}$$

11. **6.5** Draw a diagram. Since the area of the base is $5 \times 10 = 50$ square centimeters, each 1 centimeter of depth has a volume of 50 cubic centimeters. Therefore, 325 cubic centimeters will raise the water level $325 \div 50 = 6.5$ centimeters.

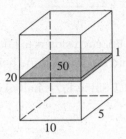

(Note that the fact that the tank was half full was not used, except to be sure that the tank didn't overflow. Since the tank was half full, the water was 10 centimeters deep, and the water level could rise by 6.5 centimeters. Had the tank been three-fourths full, the water would have been 15 centimeters deep, and the extra water would have caused the level to rise 5 centimeters, filling the tank; the rest of the water would have spilled out.)

12. $\dfrac{2}{3}$ **or .666 or .667** To avoid using r, assume that the radii of the spheres and the can are 1. Then the volume of each ball is $\dfrac{4}{3}\pi(1)^3 = \dfrac{4}{3}\pi$, and the total volume of the three balls is $3\left(\dfrac{4}{3}\pi\right) = 4\pi$. Since the volume of the can is $\pi(1)^2(6) = 6\pi$, the balls take up $\dfrac{4\pi}{6\pi} = \dfrac{2}{3}$ of the can. Grid in $\dfrac{2}{3}$ or .666 or .667.

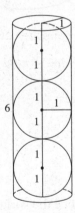

6-N COORDINATE GEOMETRY

The coordinate plane is formed by two perpendicular number lines called the **x-axis** and **y-axis**, which intersect at the **origin**. The axes divide the plane into four **quadrants**, labeled, in counterclockwise order, I, II, III, and IV.

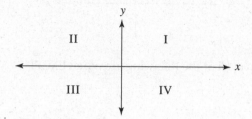

Each point in the plane is assigned two numbers, an **x-coordinate** and a **y-coordinate**, which are written as an ordered pair, **(x, y)**.

- Points to the right of the y-axis have positive x-coordinates, and those to the left have negative x-coordinates.
- Points above the x-axis have positive y-coordinates, and those below it have negative y-coordinates.
- If a point is on the x-axis, its y-coordinate is 0.
- If a point is on the y-axis, its x-coordinate is 0.

For example, point A in the figure below is labeled (2, 3), since it is 2 units to the right of the y-axis and 3 units above the x-axis. Similarly, point B(–3, –5) is in Quadrant III, 3 units to the left of the y-axis and 5 units below the x-axis.

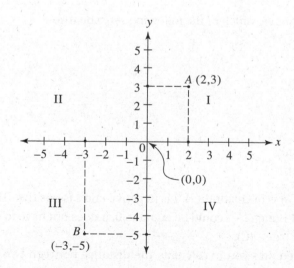

Example 1

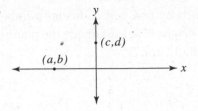

In the figure above, all of the following are equal EXCEPT

(A) ac
(B) ad
(C) bc
(D) bd

Solution. Since (a, b) lies on the x-axis, $b = 0$. Since (c, d) lies on the y-axis, $c = 0$. Each of the choices is equal to 0 except **ad** **(B)**.

Example 2

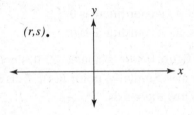

In the figure above, which of the following *must* be true?

 I. $rs < 0$
 II. $r < s$
 III. $r + s = 0$

(A) I only
(B) II only
(C) I and II only
(D) I, II, and III

Solution. Since (r, s) is in Quadrant II, r is negative and s is positive. Then $rs < 0$ (I is true) and $r < s$ (II is true). Although $r + s$ could be equal to 0, it does not have to equal 0 (III is false). **Only I and II** must be true **(C)**.

Often a question requires you to calculate the distance between two points. This task is easiest when the points lie on the same horizontal or vertical line.

Key Fact N1

- **All the points on a horizontal line have the same y-coordinate. To find the distance between them, subtract their x-coordinates.**
- **All the points on a vertical line have the same x-coordinate. To find the distance between them, subtract their y-coordinates.**

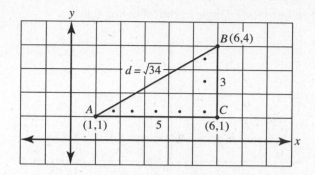

In the graph, the distance from *A* to *C* is $6 - 1 = 5$. The distance from *B* to *C* is $4 - 1 = 3$. It is a little harder, but not much, to find the distance between two points that are not on the same horizontal or vertical line; just use the Pythagorean theorem. For example, in the preceding graph, if *d* represents the distance from *A* to *B*,

$$d^2 = 5^2 + 3^2 = 25 + 9 = 34 \Rightarrow d = \sqrt{34}$$

Key Fact N2

The distance, *d*, between two points, $A(x_1, y_1)$ and $B(x_2, y_2)$, can be calculated using the distance formula:

$$d = \sqrt{(x_2 - x_1)^2 + (y_2 - y_1)^2}$$

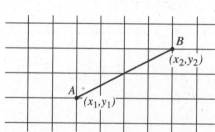

The distance formula is nothing more than the Pythagorean theorem, so you never need to use it. You can always create a right triangle by drawing a horizontal line through one of the points and a vertical line through the other, and then use the Pythagorean theorem. For example, to find the distance between $A(1, 1)$ and $B(5, 4)$, create a right triangle by drawing a horizonal line through *A* and a vertical line through *B*.

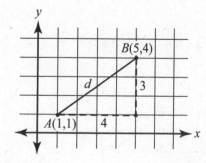

$$3^2 + 4^2 = d^2$$
$$9 + 16 = d^2$$
$$25 = d^2$$
$$d = 5$$

Examples 3 and 4 refer to the triangle in the following figure.

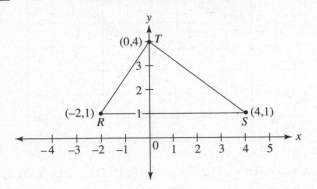

⮕ **Example 3** _____

What is the area of $\triangle RST$?

(A) 6
(B) 9
(C) 12
(D) 15

Solution. $R(-2, 1)$ and $S(4, 1)$ lie on the same horizontal line, so $RS = 4 - (-2) = 6$. Let that be the base of the triangle. Then the height is the distance along the vertical line from T to RS: $4 - 1 = 3$. The area is $\frac{1}{2}(6)(3) = $ **9 (B)**.

⮕ **Example 4** _____

What is the perimeter of $\triangle RST$?

(A) 14
(B) 16
(C) $11 + \sqrt{13}$
(D) $11 + \sqrt{61}$

Solution. The perimeter is $RS + ST + RT$. From the solution to Example 3, you know that $RS = 6$. Also, $ST = 5$, since it is the hypotenuse of a 3-4-5 right triangle. To calculate RT, use either the distance formula:

$$\sqrt{(-2-0)^2 + (1-4)^2} = \sqrt{(-2)^2 + (-3)^2} = \sqrt{4+9} = \sqrt{13}$$

or the Pythagorean theorem:

$$RT^2 = 2^2 + 3^2 = 4 + 9 = 13 \Rightarrow RT = \sqrt{13}$$

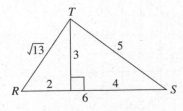

Then the perimeter is $6 + 5 + \sqrt{13} = $ **$11 + \sqrt{13}$ (C)**.

Key Fact N3

If $P(x_1, y_1)$ and $Q(x_2, y_2)$ are any two points, then the midpoint, M, of segment $\overline{PQ}$ is the point whose coordinates are $\left(\dfrac{x_1+x_2}{2}, \dfrac{y_1+y_2}{2}\right)$.

➥ Example 5

$A(2, -3)$ and $B(8, 5)$ are the endpoints of a diameter of a circle. What are the coordinates of the center of the circle?

(A) (3, 1)

(B) (3, 4)

(C) (5, 1)

(D) (5, 4)

Solution. The center of a circle is the midpoint of any diameter. Therefore, the coordinates are $\left(\dfrac{2+8}{2}, \dfrac{-3+5}{2}\right) = \left(\dfrac{10}{2}, \dfrac{2}{2}\right) = \textbf{(5, 1)}$ **(C)**.

The *slope* of a line is a number that indicates how steep the line is.

Key Fact N4

- **Vertical lines *do not have slopes*.**
- **To find the slope of any other line, proceed as follows:**

  1. **Choose any two points, $A(x_1, y_1)$ and $B(x_2, y_2)$, on the line.**

  2. **Take the differences of the *y*-coordinates, $y_2 - y_1$, and the *x*-coordinates, $x_2 - x_1$.**

  3. **Divide: slope $= \dfrac{y_2 - y_1}{x_2 - x_1}$.**

We will illustrate each part of KEY FACT N5 by using the slope formula to calculate the slopes of *RS*, *RT*, and *ST* from Example 3: $R(-2, 1)$, $S(4, 1)$, $T(0, 4)$.

Key Fact N5

- **The slope of any horizontal line is 0:**

$$\text{slope of } \overline{RS} = \frac{1-1}{4-(-2)} = \frac{0}{6} = 0$$

- **The slope of any line that goes up as you move from left to right is positive:**

$$\text{slope of } \overline{RT} = \frac{4-1}{0-(-2)} = \frac{3}{2}$$

- **The slope of any line that goes down as you move from left to right is negative:**

$$\text{slope of } \overline{ST} = \frac{1-4}{4-0} = -\frac{3}{4}$$

➡ Example 6

In the figure to the right, which line has the greatest slope?

(A) m
(B) n
(C) p
(D) q

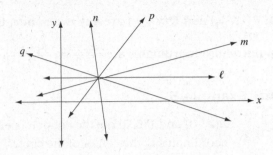

Solution. Since the slope of line ℓ is 0 and the slopes of lines n and q are negative, eliminate choices (A), (B), and (D). Lines m and p have positive slopes, but line p is steeper **(C)**.

The next key fact concerns the relationships between the slopes of parallel and perpendicular lines.

Key Fact N6

- **If two nonvertical lines are parallel, their slopes are equal.**
- **If two nonvertical lines are perpendicular, the product of their slopes is –1.**

If the product of two numbers, r and s, is –1, then

$$rs = -1 \Rightarrow r = -\frac{1}{s}$$

Therefore, another way to express the second part of KEY FACT N6 is to say that, **if two nonvertical lines are perpendicular, the slope of one is the negative reciprocal of the slope of the other.**

➡ Example 7

In the figure to the right, line ℓ passes through points (1, 2) and (3, 5). Line m (not shown) is perpendicular to ℓ. What is the slope of line m?

(A) $-\dfrac{3}{2}$

(B) $-\dfrac{2}{3}$

(C) $\dfrac{2}{3}$

(D) $\dfrac{3}{2}$

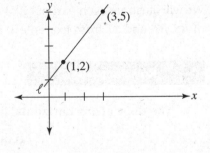

Solution. First use the slope formula to calculate the slope of line ℓ: $\dfrac{5-2}{3-1} = \dfrac{3}{2}$.

Then the slope of line m is the negative reciprocal of $\dfrac{3}{2}$, which is $-\dfrac{2}{3}$ **(B)**.

Note that you can see from the diagram in Example 7 that the slope of ℓ is positive. If you sketch any line perpendicular to ℓ, you can see that its slope is negative. So immediately you know the answer must be (A) or (B).

Every line that is drawn in the coordinate plane has an equation. All the points on a horizontal line have the same y-coordinate. For example, in the following figure, horizontal line ℓ passes through $(-3, 3)$, $(0, 3)$, $(2, 3)$, $(5, 3)$, and $(10, 3)$.

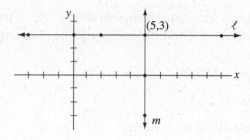

The equation of line ℓ is $y = 3$.

Similarly, every point on vertical line m has an x-coordinate equal to 5, and the equation of m is $x = 5$.

Every other line in the coordinate plane has an equation that can be written in the form $y = mx + b$, where m is the slope of the line and b is the **y-intercept**—the y-coordinate of the point where the line crosses the y-axis. These facts are summarized in KEY FACT N7.

Key Fact N7

- **For any real number a: $x = a$ is the equation of the vertical line that crosses the x-axis at $(a, 0)$.**
- **For any real number b: $y = b$ is the equation of the horizontal line that crosses the y-axis at $(0, b)$.**
- **For any real numbers b and m: $y = mx + b$ is the equation of the line that crosses the y-axis at $(0, b)$ and whose slope is m.**

On the SAT, you won't have to graph a line, but you may have to recognize the graph of a line. In a multiple-choice question, you may be given the graph of a line and asked which of the four choices is the equation of that line; or you may be given the equation of a line and asked which of the four choices is the correct graph.

➡ Example 8

Which of the following is the equation of the line in the figure to the right?

(A) $y = 2x + 4$

(B) $y = \dfrac{1}{2}x + 4$

(C) $y = 2x - 2$

(D) $y = \dfrac{1}{2}x - 4$

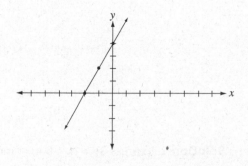

There are two different ways to handle this question.

Solution 1. Since the line is neither horizontal nor vertical, its equation has the form $y = mx + b$. Since the line crosses the y-axis at 4, $b = 4$. Also, since the line passes through $(-2, 0)$ and $(0, 4)$, its slope is $\dfrac{4-0}{0-(-2)} = \dfrac{4}{2} = 2$.

So $m = 2$, and the equation is $y = 2x + 4$ **(A)**.

Solution 2. Test some points. Since the line passes through $(0, 4)$, $y = 4$ when $x = 0$. Plug in 0 for x in the five choices; only in (A) and (B) does y equal 4. The line also passes through $(-2, 0)$, so when $x = -2$, $y = 0$.

Replace x by -2 in choices (A) and (B).

- $2(-2) + 4 = -4 + 4 = 0$, so (A) works.

- $\dfrac{1}{2}(-2) + 4 = -1 + 4 = 3$, so (B) does not work.

Any equation of the form $ax + by = c$, with $b \neq 0$, is the equation of a straight line since it can be rewritten as follows:

$$ax + by = c \Rightarrow by = -ax + c \Rightarrow y = -\frac{a}{b}x + \frac{c}{b}$$

So the graph of $ax + by = c$ is a straight line whose slope is $-\dfrac{a}{b}$ and whose y-intercept is $\dfrac{c}{b}$.

➡ **Example 9**_____

Which of the following is the graph of the line whose equation is $3y = 2x + 6$?

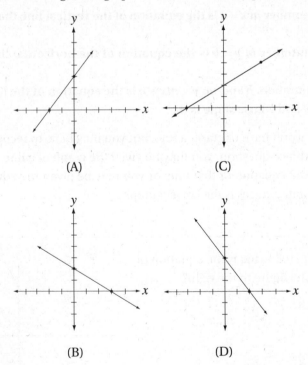

(A)　　　　　　　　(C)

(B)　　　　　　　　(D)

Solution 1. Express $3y = 2x + 6$ in standard form by dividing each term by 3: $y = \dfrac{2}{3}x + 2$. From this equation you see that the y-intercept is 2. Eliminate choices (A) and (D). Since the slope $\dfrac{2}{3}$ is positive, eliminate (B). The answer must be **(C)**.

Solution 2. Test some points.

- When $x = 0$, $3y = 2(0) + 6 = 6 \Rightarrow y = 2$, so $(0, 2)$ is a point on the graph.
- When $x = 3$, $3y = 2(3) + 6 = 12 \Rightarrow y = 4$, so $(3, 4)$ is on the graph.

Only choice **(C)** passes through both $(0, 2)$ and $(3, 4)$.

Occasionally on the SAT, there is a question concerning a linear inequality, such as $y > 2x + 1$. The graph of this inequality consists of all the points that are above the line $y = 2x + 1$. Note that the point $(2, 5)$ is on the line, whereas $(2, 6)$, $(2, 7)$, and $(2, 8)$ are all above the line. We indicate the set of all points satisfying the inequality by shading or striping the region above the line. To indicate that the points on the line itself do not satisfy the inequality, we draw a dotted line. To indicate that the points on a line are included in a graph, we draw a solid line. For example, $(2, 5)$ is not on the graph of $y > 2x + 1$, but it is on the graph of $y \geq 2x + 1$. Similarly, the graph of $y < 2x + 1$ and $y \leq 2x + 1$ are shaded or striped regions below the line $y = 2x + 1$. These inequalities are shown in the following graphs.

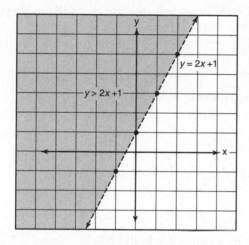
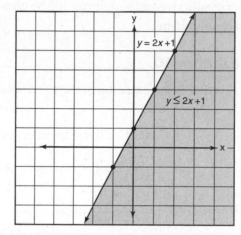

Besides the line, you need to know the equations for two other geometric shapes for the SAT: the circle and the parabola.

Section 6-L discussed the facts you need to know about circles. In this section, we review the standard equation of a circle, which is given in KEY FACT N8.

Key Fact N8

- **The equation of the circle whose center is the point (h, k) and whose radius is r is $(x - h)^2 + (y - k)^2 = r^2$.**

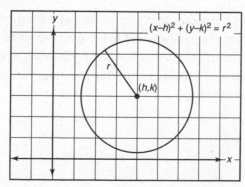

- If the center is at the origin, (0, 0), then $h = k = 0$ and the equation reduces to $x^2 + y^2 = r^2$.

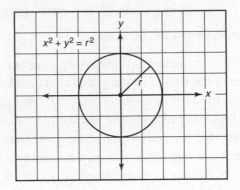

To write the equation of a circle, you need to know its center and its radius. Either they will be specifically given to you or you will be given some other information that will enable you to determine them.

➡ Example 10

What is the equation of the circle whose center is at (–3, 2) and whose radius is 5?

Plug $h = -3$, $k = 2$, and $r = 5$ into the standard equation:

$$(x - (-3))^2 + (y - 2)^2 = 5^2 \Rightarrow (x + 3)^2 + (y - 2)^2 = 25$$

➡ Example 11

In Example 5, we considered the circle in which $A(2, -3)$ and $B(8, 5)$ are the endpoints of a diameter. What is the equation of this circle?

In Example 5, we used the midpoint formula to find that the center is at (5, –1). Now we use the distance formula to get the radius. Either find the distance from the center, O, to A or B, or find the distance from A to B and divide that by 2.

$$OB = \sqrt{(8-5)^2 + (5-(-1))^2} = \sqrt{9+36} = \sqrt{45}$$

Therefore, the equation for this circle is:

$$(x - 5)^2 + (y - (-1))^2 = (\sqrt{45})^2 \Rightarrow (x - 5)^2 + (y + 1)^2 = 45$$

There are many facts about **parabolas** that you do *not* need for the SAT. Basically, you need to know the general equation of a parabola and to recognize that the graph of a parabola is a U-shaped curve that is symmetrical about a line, called the **axis of symmetry**, which passes through the parabola's **vertex**, or **turning point**. Any parabola you see on the SAT will likely have a vertical axis of symmetry.

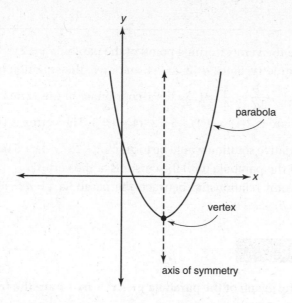

KEY FACT N9 lists the equations you need to know about parabolas.

Key Fact N9

For any real numbers a, b, c with $a \neq 0$:

- $y = ax^2 + bx + c$ is the equation of a parabola whose axis of symmetry is a vertical line.
- Conversely, the equation of any parabola with a vertical axis of symmetry has an equation of the form $y = ax^2 + bx + c$.
- The equation of the parabola's axis of symmetry is $x = \dfrac{-b}{2a}$.
- The vertex of the parabola is the point on the parabola whose x-coordinate is $\dfrac{-b}{2a}$.
- If $a > 0$, the parabola opens upward and the vertex is the lowest point on the parabola.
- If $a < 0$, the parabola opens downward and the vertex is the highest point on the parabola.

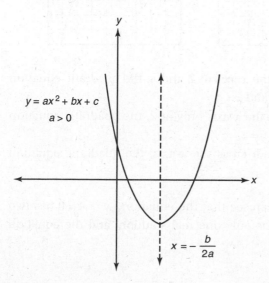

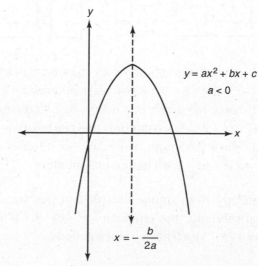

➥ Example 12

To determine the vertex (turning point) of the parabola $y = 2x^2 - 4x + 5$, first find its axis of symmetry. Since $a = 2$, $b = -4$, and $c = 5$, the equation of the axis of symmetry is $x = \dfrac{-b}{2a} = \dfrac{4}{4} = 1$. So the x-coordinate of the vertex is 1 and the y-coordinate is $2(1)^2 - 4(1) + 5 = 2 - 4 + 5 = 3$. The vertex is (1, 3).

Of course, an alternative solution would be to graph $y = 2x^2 - 4x + 5$ on a graphing calculator and to trace along the parabola until the cursor is at the vertex.

There is an important relationship between the parabola $y = ax^2 + bx + c$ and the quadratic equation $ax^2 + bx + c = 0$.

Key Fact N10

The x-intercepts of the graph of the parabola $y = ax^2 + bx + c$ are the (real) solutions of the equation $ax^2 + bx + c = 0$.

Consider the graphs of the following six parabolas.

(i)
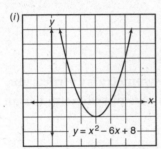
$y = x^2 - 6x + 8$

(ii)
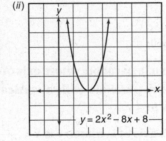
$y = 2x^2 - 8x + 8$

(iii)
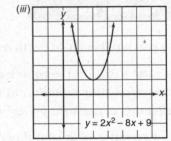
$y = 2x^2 - 8x + 9$

(iv)
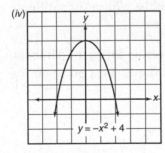
$y = -x^2 + 4$

(v)
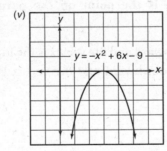
$y = -x^2 + 6x - 9$

(vi)
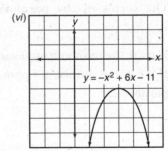
$y = -x^2 + 6x - 11$

I. Since the graph of $y = x^2 - 6x + 8$ crosses the x-axis at 2 and 4, the quadratic equation $x^2 - 6x + 8 = 0$ has two real solutions: $x = 2$ and $x = 4$.

II. Since the graph of $y = 2x^2 - 8x + 8$ crosses the x-axis only at 2, the quadratic equation $2x^2 - 8x + 8 = 0$ has only one real solution: $x = 2$.

III. Since the graph of $y = 2x^2 - 8x + 9$ does not cross the x-axis, the quadratic equation $2x^2 - 8x + 9 = 0$ has no real solutions.

Similarly, from graphs (*iv*), (*v*), and (*vi*), you can see that the equation $-x^2 + 4 = 0$ has two real solutions; the equation $-x^2 + 6x - 9 = 0$ has only one real solution; and the equation $-x^2 + 6x - 11 = 0$ has no real solutions.

EXERCISES ON COORDINATE GEOMETRY

Multiple-Choice Questions

1. If $A(-1, 1)$ and $B(3, -1)$ are the endpoints of one side of square $ABCD$, what is the area of the square?

   (A) 12
   (B) 16
   (C) 20
   (D) 36

2. If $P(2, 1)$ and $Q(8, 1)$ are two of the vertices of a rectangle, which of the following *cannot* be another of the vertices?

   (A) $(2, 8)$
   (B) $(8, 2)$
   (C) $(2, -8)$
   (D) $(-2, 8)$

3. A circle whose center is at $(6,8)$ passes through the origin. Which of the following points is NOT on the circle?

   (A) $(12, 0)$
   (B) $(6, -2)$
   (C) $(16, 8)$
   (D) $(-2, 12)$

4. What is the slope of the line that passes through (a, b) and $\left(\frac{1}{a}, b\right)$?

   (A) 0
   (B) $\dfrac{1-a^2}{a}$
   (C) $\dfrac{a^2-1}{a}$
   (D) Undefined

5. If $c \neq 0$ and the slope of the line passing through $(-c, c)$ and $(3c, a)$ is 1, which of the following is an expression for a in terms of c?

   (A) $-3c$
   (B) $2c$
   (C) $3c$
   (D) $5c$

6. What is the slope of the line that passes through $(3, 2)$ and is parallel to the line that passes through $(-2, 3)$ and $(2, -3)$?

   (A) $-\dfrac{3}{2}$
   (B) $-\dfrac{2}{3}$
   (C) $\dfrac{2}{3}$
   (D) $\dfrac{3}{2}$

7. What is the slope of the line that passes through $(3, 2)$ and is perpendicular to the line that passes through $(-2, 3)$ and $(2, -3)$?

   (A) $-\dfrac{3}{2}$
   (B) $-\dfrac{2}{3}$
   (C) $\dfrac{2}{3}$
   (D) $\dfrac{3}{2}$

8. What is the equation of the line that passes through $(4, -4)$ and $(4, 4)$?

   (A) $x = 4$
   (B) $y = 4$
   (C) $y = 4x$
   (D) $y = 4x + 4$

9. Line ℓ is tangent to a circle whose center is at $(3, 2)$. If the point of tangency is $(6, 6)$, what is the slope of line ℓ?

   (A) $-\dfrac{4}{3}$

   (B) $-\dfrac{3}{4}$

   (C) $\dfrac{3}{4}$

   (D) $\dfrac{4}{3}$

10. What is the equation of the line that crosses the y-axis at $(0, 5)$ and crosses the x-axis at $(5, 0)$?

    (A) $x = 5$
    (B) $y = 5$
    (C) $y = x - 5$
    (D) $y = -x + 5$

Questions 11 and 12 refer to circle O, in which $A(-1, 0)$ and $B(3, -2)$ are the endpoints of a diameter.

11. What is the area of circle O?

    (A) 2.5π
    (B) 5π
    (C) 10π
    (D) 20π

12. Which of the following is the equation of circle O?

    (A) $(x + 1)^2 + (y - 1)^2 = \sqrt{5}$
    (B) $(x - 1)^2 + (y + 1)^2 = \sqrt{5}$
    (C) $(x + 1)^2 + (y - 1)^2 = 5$
    (D) $(x - 1)^2 + (y + 1)^2 = 5$

Questions 13–15 concern the parabola whose equation is $y = x^2 - 20x - 69$.

13. Where does the graph of the parabola cross the y-axis?

    (A) -69
    (B) -3
    (C) 23
    (D) 69

14. What is the sum of the x-coordinates of the points where the graph of the parabola crosses the x-axis?

    (A) -69
    (B) 0
    (C) 20
    (D) 69

15. Which of the following is the parabola's vertex?

    (A) $(-10, 231)$
    (B) $(0, -69)$
    (C) $(10, -169)$
    (D) $(-3, 0)$

Grid-in Questions

16. If the coordinates of $\triangle RST$ are $R(0, 0)$, $S(7, 0)$, and $T(2, 5)$, what is the sum of the slopes of the three sides of the triangle?

17. If the area of circle O below is $k\pi$, what is the value of k?

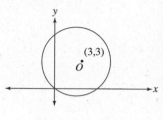

(3,3)
O

Questions 18 and 19 concern parallelogram JKLM, whose coordinates are $J(-5, 2)$, $K(-2, 6)$, $L(5, 6)$, $M(2, 2)$.

18. What is the area of parallelogram JKLM?

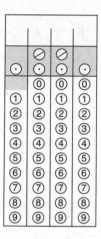

19. What is the perimeter of parallelogram JKLM?

20. What is the area of quadrilateral ABCD?

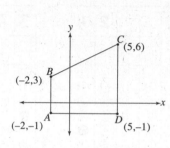

C (5,6)

B (−2,3)

A (−2,−1)

D (5,−1)

Answer Key

1. **C**	3. **D**	5. **D**	7. **C**	9. **B**	11. **B**	13. **A**	15. **C**	
2. **D**	4. **A**	6. **A**	8. **A**	10. **D**	12. **D**	14. **C**		

16.

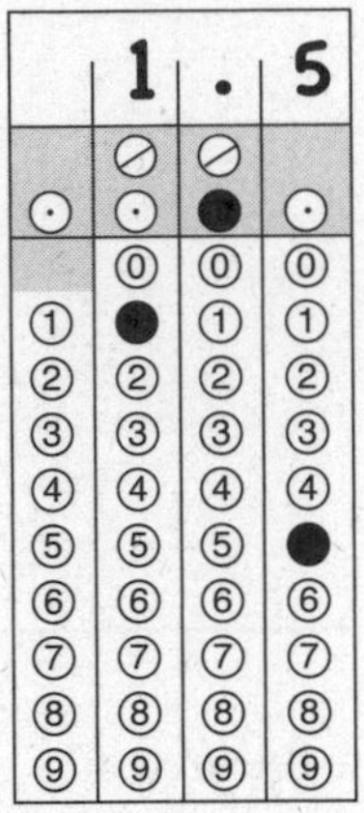

1 . 5

17.

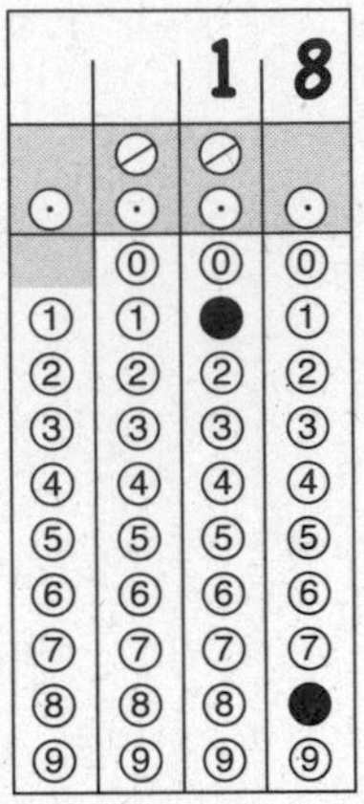

1 8

18.

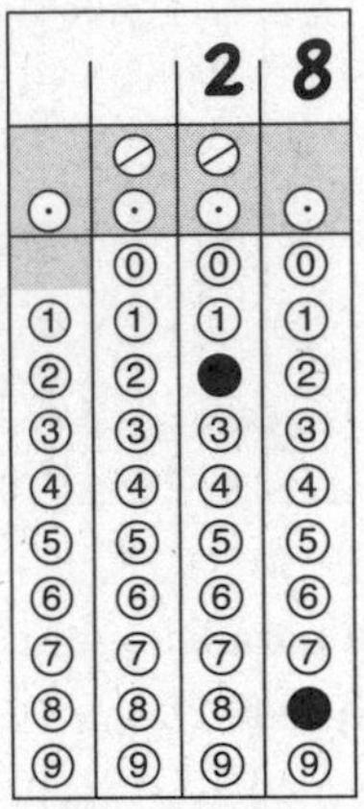

2 8

19.

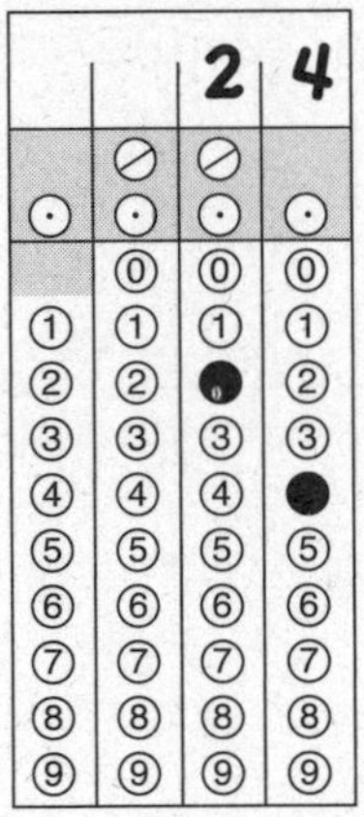

2 4

20.

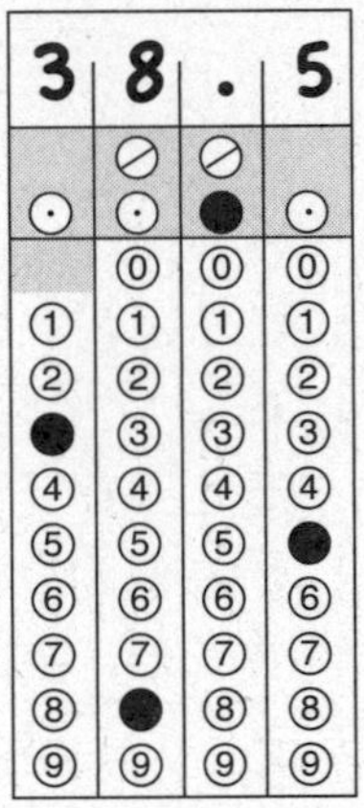

3 8 . 5

or

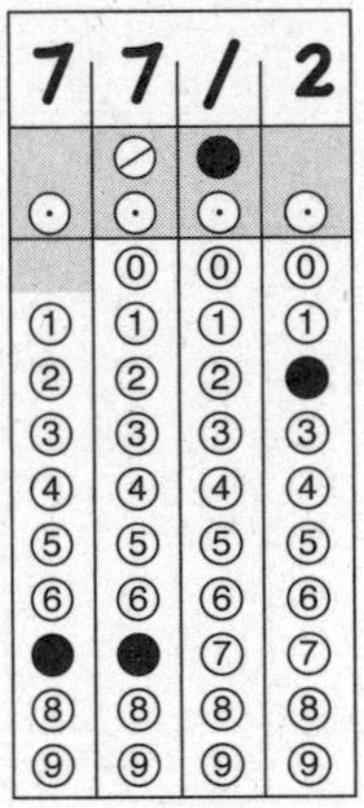

7 7 / 2

Answers Explained

1. **(C)** The area of square $ABCD$ is s^2, where $s = AB$.

   To calculate s, use the distance formula:

   $$s = \sqrt{\left(3-(-1)\right)^2 + (-1-1)^2} = \sqrt{4^2 + (-2)^2}$$
   $$= \sqrt{16+4} = \sqrt{20}$$

   Then $s^2 = 20$.

2. **(D)** Draw a diagram. Any point whose x-coordinate is 2 or 8 could be another vertex. Of the choices, only $(-2, 8)$ is *not* possible.

   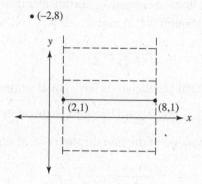

3. **(D)** Draw a diagram. The radius of the circle is 10 (since it's the hypotenuse of a 6-8-10 right triangle). Which of the choices is (are) 10 units from $(6, 8)$?

   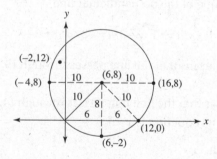

   ■ First, check the easy ones. (C): $(16, 8)$ is 10 units to the right of $(6, 8)$, and (B): $(6, -2)$ is 10 units below it.

   ■ Check (A): $(12, 0)$, which works, and (D): $(-2, 12)$, which doesn't.

   The answer is **(D)**.

4. **(A)** The formula for the slope is $\dfrac{y_2 - y_1}{x_2 - x_1}$; but before using it, look at the question again. Since the y-coordinates are equal, the numerator, and thus the fraction, equals 0.

5. **(D)** The slope is equal to

   $$\frac{y_2 - y_1}{x_2 - x_1} = \frac{a-c}{3c-(-c)} = \frac{a-c}{4c} = 1$$

   So, $a - c = 4c \Rightarrow a = 5c$.

6. **(A)** Use TACTIC 1: draw a diagram. Quickly sketch the line through (–2, 3) and (2, –3) and the line parallel to it that goes through (3, 2).

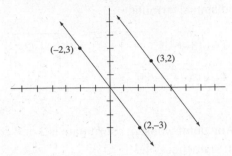

Clearly, the slopes of both lines are negative. The answer must be (A) or (B). By KEY FACT N4, the slope of the line through (–2, 3) and (2, –3) is

$$\frac{-3-3}{2-(-2)} = \frac{-6}{4} = -\frac{3}{2}$$

By KEY FACT N6, nonvertical parallel lines have equal slopes, so the answer is $-\frac{3}{2}$.

Note that it is irrelevant that the second line passes through (3, 2).

7. **(C)** By KEY FACT N4, the slope of the line through (–2, 3) and (2, –3) is

$$\frac{-3-3}{2-(-2)} = \frac{-6}{4} = -\frac{3}{2}$$

By KEY FACT N6, if two nonvertical lines are perpendicular, the product of their slopes is –1. Then, if m is the slope of the perpendicular line,

$$-\frac{3}{2}m = -1 \Rightarrow -3m = -2 \Rightarrow m = \frac{2}{3}$$

As in Exercise 6, it is irrelevant that the line passes through (3, 2).

8. **(A)** A quick sketch shows that the line that passes through (4, –4) and (4, 4) is vertical. Then, by KEY FACT N7, its equation is $x = 4$.

9. **(B)** Draw a rough sketch.

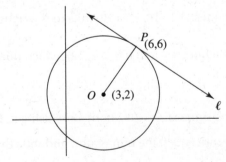

Line segment $\overline{OP}$, joining (3, 2) and (6, –6) is a radius and so, by KEY FACT L10, is perpendicular to line ℓ. The slope of $\overline{OP}$ is $\frac{6-2}{6-3} = \frac{4}{3}$. Therefore, the slope of ℓ is $-\frac{3}{4}$.

10. **(D)** Since the line is neither horizontal nor vertical, its equation has the form $y = mx + b$. Since it crosses the y-axis at $(0, 5)$, $b = 5$. Since it passes through $(0, 5)$ and $(5, 0)$, its slope is $\frac{0-5}{5-0} = \frac{-5}{5} = -1$ and its equation is $y = -1x + 5$ or $y = -x + 5$.

11. **(B)** By the distance formula (KEY FACT L3):

$$AB = \sqrt{(3-(-1))^2 + (-2-0)^2} = \sqrt{4^2 + (-2)^2} = \sqrt{16+4} = \sqrt{20}$$

Since the diameter is $\sqrt{20}$, the radius is $\frac{\sqrt{20}}{2}$. Now use the area formula:

$$A = \pi r^2 = \pi \left(\frac{\sqrt{20}}{2} \right)^2 = \pi \left(\frac{20}{4} \right) = 5\pi$$

**Alternatively, you could have used the midpoint formula (KEY FACT L4) to determine that the center O is at

$$\left(\frac{-1+3}{2}, \frac{0+(-2)}{2} \right) = \left(\frac{2}{2}, \frac{-2}{2} \right) = (1, -1)$$

and then used the distance formula to find the length of radius $\overline{OA}$.

12. **(D)** From the solution to Question 11, above, the radius of circle O is $\frac{\sqrt{20}}{2} = \frac{2\sqrt{5}}{2} = \sqrt{5}$.

From the alternative solution to Question 11, the center is at $(1, -1)$. Finally, by KEY FACT J11, the equation of circle O is:

$$(x-1)^2 + (y-(-1))^2 = (\sqrt{5})^2$$
$$(x-1)^2 + (y+1)^2 = 5$$

13. **(A)** Since the y-intercept of a graph is a point whose x-coordinate is 0, just evaluate the equation when $x = 0$:

$$y = 0^2 - 20(0) - 69 = -69$$

14. **(C)** The x-intercepts of the graph are the solutions of the equation $x^2 - 20x - 69 = 0$.

$$x^2 - 20x - 69 = 0 \Rightarrow (x - 23)(x + 3) = 0 \Rightarrow x = 23 \text{ or } x = -3$$

The sum of the roots is $23 + (-3) = 20$.

15. **(C)** The vertex of the parabola is on the parabola's axis of symmetry, whose equation is $x = \frac{-b}{2a} = \frac{20}{2} = 10$. So the x-coordinate of the vertex is 10; to get the y-coordinate, replace x by 10 in the equation of the parabola:

$$y = (10)^2 - 20(10) - 69 = 100 - 200 - 69 = -169$$

The vertex is $(10, -169)$.

16. **1.5** Sketch the triangle, and then calculate the slopes. Since $\overline{RS}$ is horizontal, its slope is 0.

The slope of $\overline{RT} = \dfrac{5-0}{2-0} = 2.5$.

The slope of $\overline{ST} = \dfrac{5-0}{2-7} = \dfrac{5}{-5} = -1$.

Now add: $0 + 2.5 + (-1) = 1.5$.

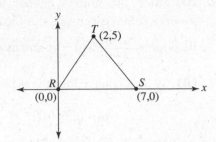

17. **18** Since the line segment joining (3, 3) and (0, 0) is a radius of the circle, the radius equals $3\sqrt{2}$.

Therefore, area $= \pi\left(3\sqrt{2}\right)^2 = 18\pi \Rightarrow k = 18$.

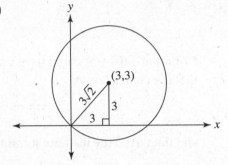

Here is the diagram for solutions 18 and 19.

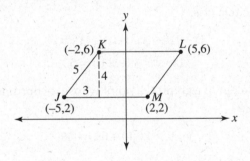

18. **28** The base is 7, and the height is 4. The area is $7 \times 4 = 28$.

19. **24** Sides $\overline{JM}$ and $\overline{KL}$ are each 7. Also, sides $\overline{JK}$ and $\overline{LM}$ are each the hypotenuse of a 3-4-5 right triangle, and so they are 5. The perimeter is $2(7 + 5) = 24$.

20. **38.5 or** $\dfrac{77}{2}$ Draw in line segment $\overline{BE}$, dividing quadrilateral $ABCD$ into rectangle $ABED$ and $\triangle BEC$. The area of the rectangle is $4 \times 7 = 28$, and the area of the triangle is $\dfrac{1}{2}(7)(3) = 10.5$.

The total area is 38.5 or $\dfrac{77}{2}$.

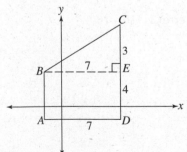

DATA ANALYSIS

6-O INTERPRETATION OF DATA

The SAT has several questions that require you to interpret and/or manipulate the data that appear in some type of table or graph. The graphs will be no more complicated, and probably will be simpler, than the ones that you usually see in newspapers and magazines or in your science or social studies textbooks.

Sometimes you are asked two or three questions based on the same set of data. Some of these questions are quite easy, requiring only that you *read* the information in the table or graph. Others are more challenging and may ask you to *interpret* the data, or *manipulate* them, or *make a prediction* based on them.

The data can be presented in the columns of a table or displayed graphically. The graphs that appear most often are bar graphs, line graphs, circle graphs, and scatter-plot diagrams. This section illustrates each of these and gives examples of the types of questions that may be asked.

Although the second hint is good advice on *all* SAT questions, it is particularly important on table and graph problems because there is so much information that can be used, and so many different questions can be asked.

HELPFUL HINT

Before even reading the questions based on a graph or table, take 10 or 15 seconds to look it over. Make sure you understand the information that is being displayed and the units of the quantities involved.

Line Graphs

A **line graph** indicates how one or more quantities change over time. The horizontal axis is usually marked off in units of time; the units on the vertical axis can represent almost any type of numerical data: dollars, weights, exam grades, number of people, and so on.

Here is a typical line graph:

HELPFUL HINT

After looking over the entire graph, read the first question. Be clear about what is being asked, and circle it in your test booklet. Answer the questions based only on the information provided in the graph.

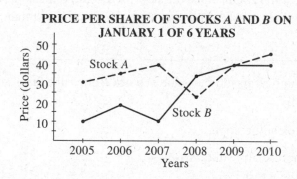

PRICE PER SHARE OF STOCKS *A* AND *B* ON JANUARY 1 OF 6 YEARS

Before reading even one of the questions based on the above graph, you should have acquired *at least* the following information:

(i) The graph gives the values of two different stocks.

(ii) The graph covers the period from January 1, 2005, to January 1, 2010.

(iii) During that time, both stocks rose in value.

There are literally dozens of questions that could be asked about the data in this graph. The next seven examples are typical of the types of questions that could appear on the SAT.

➡ Example 1 _____

What is the difference, in dollars, between the highest and lowest values of a share of stock *A*?

Solution. The lowest value of stock *A* was $25 (in 2005); the highest value was $40 (in 2010). The difference is **$15**.

➡ Example 2 _____

On January 1 of what year was the difference in the values of a share of stock *A* and a share of stock *B* the greatest?

Solution. Just look at the graph. The difference was clearly the greatest in **2007**. (Note that you don't have to calculate what the difference was.)

➡ Example 3 _____

On January 1 of what year was the ratio of the value of a share of stock *A* to the value of a share of stock *B* the greatest?

Solution. From 2008 to 2010 the values of the two stocks were fairly close, so those years are not candidates. In 2007 the ratio was 40:10 or 4:1 or 4. In 2006 the ratio was 35:20 or 7:4 or 1.75. In 2005 the ratio was 30:10 or 3:1 or 3. The ratio was greatest in **2007**.

➡ Example 4 _____

In what year was the percent increase in the value of a share of stock *B* the greatest?

Solution. Just look at the graph. Since the slope of the graph is steepest in **2007** (between January 1, 2007 and January 1, 2008), the rate of growth was greatest then.

➡ Example 5 _____

During how many years did the value of stock *B* grow at a faster rate than that of stock *A*?

Solution. Again, look at the slopes.

- In 2005, *B* rose more sharply than *A*. (✔)
- In 2006, *B* fell while *A* rose.
- In 2007, *B* rose while *A* fell. (✔)
- In 2008, *A* rose more sharply than *B*.
- In 2009, *A* rose; *B* stayed the same.

B grew at a faster rate during **2** years.

➡ Example 6 _____

What was the average yearly increase in the value of a share of stock *A* from 2005 to 2010?

Solution. Over the 5-year period from January 1, 2005, to January 1, 2010, the value of a share of stock *A* rose from $30 to $45, an increase of $15. The average yearly increase was $15 ÷ 5 years or **$3** per year.

➡ Example 7

If from 2005 to 2015 the value of each stock increases at the same rate as it did from 2005 to 2010, what will then be the ratio of the value of a share of stock *B* to the value of a share of stock *A*?

Solution. From 2005 to 2010, the value of stock *A* increased by 50% (from $30 to $45) and the value of stock *B* quadrupled (from $10 to $40). At the same rates, stock *A* will grow from $45 to $67.50 in the years 2010–2015, while stock *B* will grow from $40 to $160. The ratio of the value of a share of stock *B* to the value of a share of stock *A* will be 160 to 67.5, or approximately **2.37**.

HELPFUL HINT

On data interpretation questions ignore the extraneous information you are given. Zero in on exactly what you need.

To answer these seven questions, most (but not all) of the data contained in the graph was used. On the SAT, if you had two questions based on that line graph, you can see that there would be many items of information you would not use.

Bar Graphs

The same information that was given in the preceding line graph, could have been presented in a *table* or in a *bar graph*.

PRICE PER SHARE OF STOCKS *A* AND *B*
ON JANUARY 1 OF 6 YEARS

Stock	Prices (dollars)					
	2005	2006	2007	2008	2009	2010
Stock *A*	30	35	40	25	40	45
Stock *B*	10	20	15	35	40	40

PRICE PER SHARE OF STOCKS *A* AND *B*
ON JANUARY 1 OF 6 YEARS

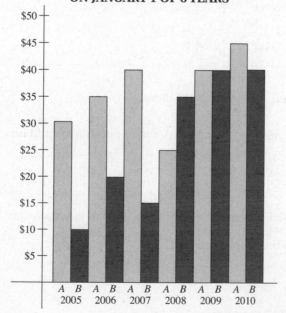

In a bar graph, the taller the bar, the greater is the value of the quantity. Bar graphs can also be drawn horizontally; in that case the longer the bar, the greater is the quantity. You will see examples of each type in the exercises at the end of this section, in the model tests, and, of course, on the SAT.

The following bar graph shows the numbers of students taking courses in the various foreign languages offered at a state college.

**NUMBERS OF STUDENTS ENROLLED IN
LANGUAGE COURSES AT STATE COLLEGE IN 2010**

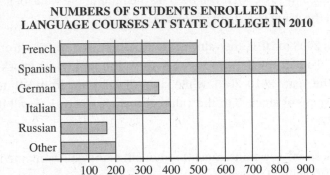

In a slight variation of the horizontal bar graph, the bars are replaced by a string of icons, or symbols. For example, the graph below, in which each picture of a person represents 100 students, conveys the same information as does the preceding bar graph.

**NUMBERS OF STUDENTS ENROLLED IN
LANGUAGE COURSES AT STATE COLLEGE IN 2010**

French

Spanish

German

Italian

Russian

Other

Each ⅄ represents 100 students.

From either of the two preceding graphs, many questions could be asked. Examples 8–10 illustrate a few types.

➡ Example 8

What is the total number of students enrolled in language classes in 2010?

Solution. Just read the graph and add: **2500.**

➡ Example 9

If the "Other" category includes five languages, what is the average (arithmetic mean) number of students studying each language offered at the college?

Solution. There are 2500 students divided among 10 languages (the 5 listed plus the 5 in the "Other" category): $2500 \div 10 = \textbf{250}$.

➡ Example 10

If the number of students studying Italian in 2011 was the same as the number taking Spanish in 2010, by what percent did the number of students taking Italian increase?

Solution. The number of students taking Italian increased by 500 from 400 to 900. This represents a $\dfrac{500}{400} \times 100\% = \textbf{125\%}$ increase.

Circle Graphs

A *circle graph* is another way to present data pictorially. In a circle graph, which is sometimes called a *pie chart*, the circle is divided into sectors, with the size of each sector exactly proportional to the quantity it represents.

For example, the information included in the preceding bar graph is presented in the following circle graph.

**NUMBERS OF STUDENTS ENROLLED IN
LANGUAGE COURSES AT STATE COLLEGE IN 2010**

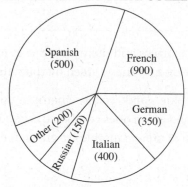

Usually on the SAT, in each sector of the circle is noted the number of degrees of its central angle or the percent of the total data it contains. For example, in the circle graph above, since in 2010, 500 of the 2500 language students at State College were studying French, the sector representing French is exactly $\frac{1}{5}$ of the circle. On the SAT this sector would also be marked either $72° \left(\frac{1}{5} \text{ of } 360° \right)$ or $20\% \left(\frac{1}{5} \text{ of } 100\% \right)$. The SAT graph would look like one of the graphs on the next page.

**DISTRIBUTION OF THE 2500 STUDENTS
ENROLLED IN LANGUAGE COURSES**

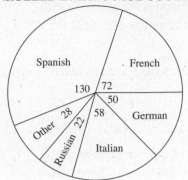

**DISTRIBUTION OF THE 2500 STUDENTS
ENROLLED IN LANGUAGE COURSES**

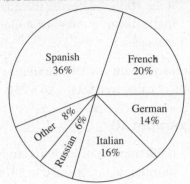

Very often on the SAT, some data are omitted from a circle graph, and it is your job to determine the missing item. Examples 11 and 12 are based on the following circle graph, which shows the distribution of marbles by color in a large jar.

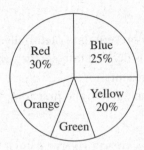

➡ Example 11 _____

If the jar contains 1200 marbles and there are twice as many orange marbles as there are green, how many green marbles are there?

Solution. Since the red, blue, and yellow marbles constitute 75% of the total (30% + 25% + 20%), the orange and green ones combined account for 25% of the total: 25% of 1200 = 300. Then, since the ratio of orange marbles to green ones is 2:1, there are 200 orange marbles and **100** green ones.

➡ Example 12 _____

Assume that the jar contains 1200 marbles, and that all of the red ones are removed and replaced by an equal number of marbles, all of which are blue or yellow. If the ratio of blue to yellow marbles remains the same, how many additional yellow marbles are there?

Solution. Since 30% of 1200 is 360, the 360 red marbles were replaced by 360 blue and yellow ones. To maintain the current blue to yellow ratio of 25 to 20, or 5 to 4, $\frac{5}{9}$ of the new marbles would be blue and $\frac{4}{9}$ would be yellow: $\frac{4}{9}$ of 360 = **160**.

Scatter Plot

A *scatter plot* is a graph that displays the relationship between two variables. It consists of a horizontal axis and a vertical axis (just like the first quadrant of the *xy*-coordinate plane) and a series of dots. Each dot represents an individual data point and is plotted the same way that points are plotted in the *xy*-plane. For example, in the scatter plot below, the horizontal axis represents the number of hours that a group of students studied for their final exam in math and the vertical axis represents the students' scores on the exam.

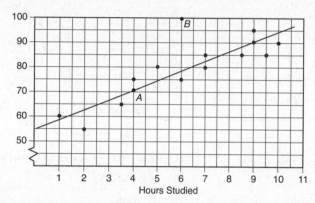

Look at Student *A*. He studied for 4 hours and earned a 70 on the final. Note that in this case, there is a fairly strong *positive correlation* between the two variables. The *general trend* is that more hours of study correlate to higher test scores. However, the correlation is clearly not perfect. Student *B*, for example, is an outlier. She studied for only 6 hours but had the highest score—higher than any of the students who studied 9 or 10 hours.

The line that is drawn on the scatter plot is called the *line of best fit* and can be used to predict the most likely value of one variable given the other. For example, from the line of best fit we see that a student who studies 8 hours would probably have a test score very close to 87. We also see that a student who earned a 60 on the final probably studied for about $1\frac{1}{2}$ hours.

Some scatter plots have a *negative correlation*, and some have no correlation at all. An example of two variables whose scatter plot would likely have a negative correlation is one where the variable along the horizontal axis is a person's weight and the variable on the vertical axis is the speed at which that person can run a 100-meters dash. The general trend would likely show that the heavier the person is, the slower he or she can run. An example of variables whose scatter plot would likely show no correlation is people's height and the number of times per month the people go to the movies.

Be very careful. A strong correlation *does not mean* that there is *causation*. Even if one variable increases whenever a second variable increases, there may be no cause and effect. For example in 2015 in the town of Brest, there was a very high correlation between the number of gallons of ice cream consumed in a week and the number of people who drowned that week. Clearly eating ice cream didn't cause the drownings. Something else was going on. In fact, during the weeks that it was very hot, people ate lots of ice cream. During those same weeks, more people went to the pools and beaches. Hence, there were more drownings. The causative variable was the temperature.

On the SAT, you will not be given a set of data and asked to create a scatter plot, nor will you have to calculate the line of best fit for a given scatter plot. However, you will have to recognize what type of correlation is exhibited. You may also have to make a prediction based on a line of best fit that has been drawn in a scatter-plot graph.

Multiple-Choice Questions

Questions 1–3 refer to the following graph.

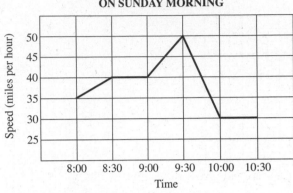

SPEEDS AT WHICH MARC DROVE ON SUNDAY MORNING

1. For what percent of the time was Marc driving at 40 miles per hour or faster?

   (A) 25
   (B) $33\frac{1}{3}$
   (C) 40
   (D) 50

2. How far, in miles, did Marc drive between 8:30 and 9:00?

   (A) 0
   (B) 20
   (C) 30
   (D) 40

3. What was Marc's average speed, in miles per hour, between 8:30 and 9:30?

   (A) 40
   (B) $41\frac{2}{3}$
   (C) 42.5
   (D) 45

Questions 4–6 refer to the following graph.

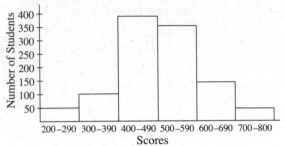

CRITICAL READING SAT SCORES OF ALL THE JUNIORS AT CENTRAL HIGH SCHOOL

4. How many juniors at Central High School took the SAT?

   (A) 1000
   (B) 1100
   (C) 1200
   (D) 1250

5. What percent of the juniors had Critical Reading SAT scores of less than 600?

   (A) $95\frac{5}{11}$
   (B) $83\frac{1}{3}$
   (C) $81\frac{9}{11}$
   (D) It cannot be determined from the information given.

6. How many juniors had Critical Reading SAT scores between 450 and 550?

   (A) 375
   (B) 525
   (C) 750
   (D) It cannot be determined from the information given.

Questions 7 and 8 refer to the following graph.

2010 SMITH FAMILY HOUSEHOLD BUDGET

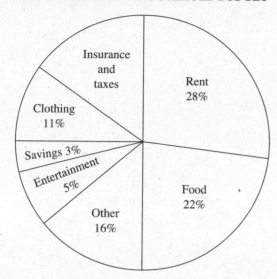

7. If the Smiths' income in 2010 was $40,000, how much more did they spend on insurance and taxes than they did on clothing?

(A) $1,600
(B) $2,000
(C) $3,200
(D) $4,400

8. What is the degree measure of the central angle of the sector representing insurance and taxes?

(A) 45
(B) 54
(C) 60
(D) 72

Grid-in Questions

Questions 9 and 10 refer to the following graph.

DISTRIBUTION OF GRADES OF 500 STUDENTS ON THE FINAL EXAM IN MATH

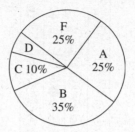

9. How many students earned a grade of D?

10. What percent of the students who failed the exam would have had to pass it, in order for the percent of students passing the exam to be at least 85%?

Answer Key

1.	**D**	3.	**C**	5.	**C**	7.	**A**
2.	**B**	4.	**B**	6.	**D**	8.	**B**

9. **2 5**

10. **4 0**

Answers Explained

1. **(D)** Of the $2\frac{1}{2}$ hours (from 8:00 until 10:30) that Marc was driving, he was going 40 miles per hour or faster for $1\frac{1}{4}$ hours (from 8:30 until 9:45). Therefore, he was driving at 40 miles per hour or faster 50% of the time.

2. **(B)** During the half hour between 8:30 and 9:00, Marc was driving at a constant rate of 40 miles per hour, so he drove $\frac{1}{2} \times 40 = 20$ miles.

3. **(C)** From the graph it is clear that, from 9:00 to 9:30, Marc's speed increased steadily from 40 to 50 miles per hour and that his average speed was 45 miles per hour. From 8:30 to 9:00 his average speed was clearly 40 miles per hour. Then, for the entire hour, he averaged $\frac{40+45}{2} = 42.5$ miles per hour.

4. **(B)** Just read the graph carefully, and add the numbers of juniors who had scores in each range:

$$50 + 100 + 400 + 350 + 150 + 50 = 1100$$

5. **(C)** Of the 1100 students, 900 had scores less than 600, and $\frac{900}{1100} = 81\frac{9}{11}\%$.

6. **(D)** There is no way of knowing. It is possible, though very unlikely, that all of the scores between 400 and 590 were between 400 and 420 or 570 and 590, and that no one scored between 450 and 550. Undoubtedly, some did, but you can't tell how many.

7. **(A)** The total percent for the six categories for which percents are given is

$$28 + 22 + 16 + 5 + 3 + 11 = 85$$

so the percent of their income that the Smiths spend on insurance and taxes is 15%. Since they spend 11% on clothing, the difference between the two categories is 4%. Finally, 4% of $40,000 is $1600.

8. **(B)** Since insurance and taxes take up 15% of the Smiths' income (see solution 7), the sector representing insurance and taxes must be 15% of the circle. The degree measure of the central angle for this sector is 15% of 360 = 54.

9. **25** Since 25% + 35% + 10% + 25% = 95%, 95% of the students earned grades of A, B, C, or F, and the other 5% earned grades of D: 5% of 500 = 25.

10. **40** For the passing rate to have been at least 85%, no more than 75 students (15% of 500) could have failed. Of the 125 students (25% of 500) who actually failed, 50 of them would have had to pass: 50 out of 125 is 40%.

MISCELLANEOUS TOPICS

6-P COUNTING AND PROBABILITY

Some questions on the SAT begin, "How many ...." In these problems you are being asked to count something: how many apples can Maria buy, how many dollars did Jose spend, how many pages did Elizabeth read, how many numbers satisfy a certain property, or how many ways are there to complete a particular task. Sometimes these problems can be handled by simple arithmetic. Other times it helps to use TACTIC 14 and systematically make a list. Occasionally it helps to know the counting principle and other strategies that will be reviewed in this section.

Counting

USING ARITHMETIC TO COUNT

Examples 1–3 require only arithmetic. Be careful, though; they are not the same.

➡ Example 1

John bought some apples. If he entered the store with $113 and left with $109, how much did the apples cost?

➡ Example 2

Kim was selling tickets for the school play. One day she sold tickets numbered 109 through 113. How many tickets did she sell that day?

➡ Example 3

John is the 109th person in a line, and Kim is the 113th person. How many people are there between John and Kim?

Solutions 1–3. It may seem that each of these examples requires a simple subtraction: $113 - 109 = 4$. In Example 1, John did spend **$4** on apples. In Example 2, however, Kim sold **5** tickets; and in Example 3, only **3** people are on line between John and Kim! Assume that John went into the store with 113 one-dollar bills, numbered 1 through 113; he spent the 4 dollars numbered 113, 112, 111, and 110, and still had the dollars numbered 1 through 109; Kim sold the 5 tickets numbered 109, 110, 111, 112, and 113; and between John and Kim the 110th, 111th, and 112th persons—3 people—were on line.

- In Example 1, you just need to subtract: $113 - 109 = 4$.
- In Example 2, you need to subtract *and then add 1*: $113 - 109 + 1 = 4 + 1 = 5$.
- In Example 3, you need to subtract and then *subtract 1 more*: $113 - 109 - 1 = 3$.

Example 1 is too easy for the SAT, but questions such as Examples 2 and 3 are not as obvious and require a little extra thought. *When do you have to add or subtract 1?*

The issue is whether or not the first and last numbers are included. In Example 1, John spent dollar number 113, but he still had dollar 109 when he left the store. In Example 2, Kim sold both ticket number 109 and ticket 113. In Example 3, neither Kim (the 113th person) nor John (the 109th person) should be counted.

To count how many integers there are between two integers, follow these rules:

- If exactly one of the endpoints is included: subtract.
- If both endpoints are included: subtract and then add 1.
- If neither endpoint is included: subtract and then subtract 1 more.

➡ Example 4

From 1:09 to 1:13, Elaine read pages 109 through 113 in her English book. What was her rate of reading, in pages per minute?

(A) $\dfrac{3}{4}$

(B) $\dfrac{4}{5}$

(C) 1

(D) $\dfrac{5}{4}$

Solution. Since Elaine read both pages 109 and 113, she read $113 - 109 + 1 = 5$ pages. She started reading during the minute that started at 1:09 (and ended at 1:10). Since she stopped reading at 1:13, she did not read during the minute that began at 1:13 (and ended at 1:14), so she read for $1:13 - 1:09 = 4$ minutes. She read at the rate of $\dfrac{5}{4}$ pages per minute   **(D)**.

SYSTEMATICALLY MAKING A LIST

When the numbers in a problem are small, it is often better to systematically list all of the possibilities than to risk making an error in arithmetic. In Example 4, rather than even thinking about whether or not to add 1 or subtract 1 after subtracting the numbers of pages, you could have just quickly jotted down the pages Elaine read (109, 110, 111, 112, 113), and then counted them.

➡ Example 5

Blair has 4 paintings in the basement. She is going to bring up 2 of them and hang 1 in her den and 1 in her bedroom. In how many ways can she choose which paintings go in each room?

(A) 4

(B) 6

(C) 12

(D) 16

Solution. Label the paintings 1, 2, 3, and 4, write B for bedroom and D for den, and make a list.

B-D	B-D	B-D	B-D
1-2	2-1	3-1	4-1
1-3	2-3	3-2	4-2
1-4	2-4	3-4	4-3

There are **12** ways to choose (**C**).

For additional examples of systematically making lists, see TACTIC 14 in Chapter 5.

In Example 5, making a list was feasible, but if Blair had 10 paintings and needed to hang 4 of them, it would be impossible to list all the different ways of hanging them. In such cases you need the *counting principle*.

USING THE COUNTING PRINCIPLE

Key Fact P2

If two jobs need to be completed and there are *m* ways to do the first job and *n* ways to do the second job, then there are *m* × *n* ways to do one job followed by the other. This principle can be extended to any number of jobs.

In Example 5, the first job was to pick 1 of the 4 paintings and hang it in the bedroom. That could be done in 4 ways. The second job was to pick a second painting to hang in the den. That job could be accomplished by choosing any of the remaining 3 paintings. There are $4 \times 3 = 12$ ways to hang the 2 paintings.

Now, assume there are 10 paintings to be hung in 4 rooms. The first job is to choose 1 of the 10 paintings for the bedroom. The second job is to choose 1 of the 9 remaining paintings to hang in the den. The third job is to choose 1 of the 8 remaining paintings for, say, the living room. Finally, the fourth job is to pick 1 of the 7 remaining paintings for the dining room. These 4 jobs can be completed in $10 \times 9 \times 8 \times 7 = \mathbf{5,040}$ ways.

➡ Example 6 _____

How many integers are there between 100 and 1,000, all of whose digits are odd?

Solution. You're looking for three-digit numbers, such as 135, 711, 353, and 999, in which all three digits are odd. Note that you are *not* required to use three different digits. Although you certainly wouldn't want to list all of the possibilities, you could count them by listing some of them and seeing whether a pattern develops. In the 100's there are 5 numbers that begin with 11: 111, 113, 115, 117, 119. Similarly, there are 5 numbers that begin with 13: 131, 133, 135, 137, 139; 5 numbers that begin with 15, 5 that begin with 17, and 5 that begin with 19, for a total of $5 \times 5 = 25$ in the 100's. In the same way there are 25 in the 300's, 25 in the 500's, 25 in the 700's, and 25 in the 900's, for a grand total of $5 \times 25 = \mathbf{125}$. You can actually do this calculation in less time than it takes to read this paragraph.

The best way to solve Example 6, however, is to use the counting principle. Think of writing a three-digit number as three jobs that need to be done. The first job is to select one of the five odd digits and use it as the digit in the hundreds place. The second job is to select one of the five odd digits to be the digit that goes in the tens place. Finally, the third job is to select one of the five odd digits to be the digit in the units place. Each of these jobs can be done in 5 ways, so the total number of ways is $5 \times 5 \times 5 = \mathbf{125}$.

COMBINATIONS AND PERMUTATIONS

Some students, by the time they take the SAT, have learned in a math class about combinations and permutations; as a result, they try to use the formulas for them on the SAT. The problem is that there has *never* been a single question on any SAT that requires you to know or use those formulas, and very few SATs have even one question on which you could even use those formulas. The occasional question on which you could use one of the formulas can always be solved as quickly, or even more quickly, without them.

For example, Example 6—*How many integers are there between 100 and 1,000, all of whose digits are odd?*—could *not* be answered using the formula for permutations. That question should be answered using the counting principle: $5 \times 5 \times 5 = 125$. Consider now a slight variation of Example 6: *How many integers are there between 100 and 1,000, all of whose digits are __different__ odd integers?* Here, because the digits have to be different, we can consider each integer as a permutation of the five digits 1, 3, 5, 7, and 9, taken three at a time. On any scientific or graphing calculator we could enter 5, then $_nP_r$, the button for permutations, then 3, and finally the "enter" or "equals" button. That would evaluate $_5P_3$, the number of permutations of 5 things taken 3 at a time, which is equal to 60. The better thing to do would be to again use the counting principle: $5 \times 4 \times 3 = 60$. That is just as fast, and you don't have to worry about whether or not the formula for permutations will work; you can *always* use the counting principle.

Consider the following question: *From a group of 4 students, in how many ways can 2 of them be chosen to attend a conference?* This question can be answered by evaluating $_4C_2$ on a calculator. Enter 4, then $_nC_r$, the button for combinations, then 2, and finally the "enter" or "equals" button. The answer is 6. You could also think of the students as *A, B, C,* and *D,* and in about the same amount of time write *AB, AC, AD, BC, BD, CD* and see that the answer is 6. Or you could use the counting principle: there are 4 ways to choose the first student and 3 ways to choose the second one, so it seems as if there are $4 \times 3 = 12$ ways; however, since each pair of students has been counted twice (*AB* and *BA,* for example), you need to divide 12 by 2 to get 6.

The bottom line is this. On any question on the SAT, you may use anything you know. Just because questions about 30-60-90 right triangles can be answered using trigonometry, doesn't mean they should be. You never need to use the formulas for combinations and permutations. If you don't know them, you certainly shouldn't learn them for the SAT; if you do know them and are sure you know when they can be used and when they can't, and you won't ever use $_nC_r$ instead of $_nP_r$ (or vice versa), then you may use them if you choose to. Of course, if you do, you should *never* actually use the formulas; you should always just use the appropriate buttons on your calculator.

USING VENN DIAGRAMS

A **Venn diagram** is a figure with two or three overlapping circles, usually enclosed in a rectangle, that is used to solve certain counting problems. To illustrate, assume that a school has 100 seniors. The following Venn diagram, which divides the rectangle into four regions, shows the distribution of those students in the band and the orchestra.

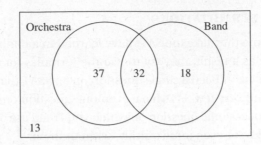

The 32 written in the part of the diagram where the two circles overlap represents the 32 seniors who are in both band and orchestra. The 18 written in the circle on the right represents the 18 seniors who are in the band but not in the orchestra, while the 37 written in the left circle represents the 37 seniors who are in the orchestra but not in the band. Finally, the 13 written in the rectangle outside the circles represents the 13 seniors who are in neither band nor orchestra. The numbers in all four regions must add up to the total number of seniors: $32 + 18 + 37 + 13 = 100$.

Note that there are 50 seniors in the band—32 who are also in the orchestra and 18 who are not in the orchestra. Similarly, there are $32 + 37 = 69$ seniors in the orchestra. Be careful: the 50 names on the band roster and the 69 names on the orchestra roster add up to 119 names—more than the number of seniors. The reason is that 32 names are on both lists and so have been counted twice. The number of seniors who are in band or orchestra is only $119 - 32 = 87$. Those 87, together with the 13 who are in neither band nor orchestra, make up the total of 100.

Although no problem on an SAT *requires* the use of a Venn diagram, occasionally there will be a problem that you will be able to solve more easily if you draw a Venn diagram, as in Example 7.

➡ Example 7 _____

Of the 410 students at Kennedy High School, 240 study Spanish and 180 study French. If 25 students study neither language, how many students study both?

Solution. Draw a Venn diagram. Let x represent the number of students who study both languages, and write x in the part of the diagram where the two circles overlap.

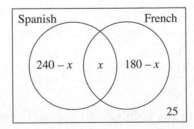

Then the number who study only Spanish is $240 - x$, and the number who study only French is $180 - x$. The number who study at least one of the languages is $410 - 25 = 385$, so

$$385 = (240 - x) + x + (180 - x) = 420 - x$$

So, $x = 420 - 385 = \mathbf{35}$ who study both.

Probability

The *probability* that an *event* will occur is a number between 0 and 1, usually written as a fraction, that indicates how likely it is that the event will happen. For example, for the spinner at the right, there are 4 possible outcomes: it is equally likely that the spinner will stop in any of the four regions. There is 1 chance in 4 that it will stop in the region marked 2, so we say that the probability of spinning a 2 is one-fourth and write $P(2) = \frac{1}{4}$. Since 2 is the only even number on the spinner, we could also say $P(\text{even}) = \frac{1}{4}$. Also, there are 3 chances in 4 that the spinner will land in a region with an odd number in it, so $P(\text{odd}) = \frac{3}{4}$.

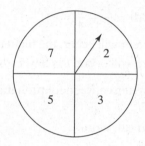

Key Fact P3

If E is any event, the probability that E will occur is given by

$$P(E) = \frac{\text{number of favorable outcomes}}{\text{total number of possible outcomes}}$$

assuming that all of the possible outcomes are equally likely.

NOTE

Although probabilities are defined as fractions, they can also be written as decimals or percents.

In the preceding example, each of the four regions is the same size, so it is equally likely that the spinner will land on the 2, 3, 5, or 7. Therefore:

$$P(\text{odd}) = \frac{\text{number of ways of getting an odd number}}{\text{total number of possible outcomes}} = \frac{3}{4}$$

Note that the probability of *not* getting an odd number is 1 minus the probability of getting an odd number:

$$1 - \frac{3}{4} = \frac{1}{4}$$

Let's look at some other probabilities associated with spinning this spinner once:

$$P(\text{number} > 10) = \frac{\text{number of ways of getting a number} > 10}{\text{total number of possible outcomes}} = \frac{0}{4} = 0$$

$$P(\text{prime number}) = \frac{\text{number of ways of getting a prime number}}{\text{total number of possible outcomes}} = \frac{4}{4} = 1$$

$$P(\text{number} < 4) = \frac{\text{number of ways of getting a number} < 4}{\text{total number of possible outcomes}} = \frac{2}{4} = \frac{1}{2}$$

Let *E* be an event, and let *P(E)* be the probability that it will occur.

- If *E* is **impossible** (such as getting a number greater than 10 in the spinner example), $P(E) = 0$.
- If it is **certain** that *E* will occur (such as getting a prime number in the spinner example), $P(E) = 1$.
- In all cases, $0 \le P(E) \le 1$.
- The probability that event *E* will *not* occur is $1 - P(E)$.
- If two or more events constitute all the outcomes, the sum of their probabilities is 1.

  [For example, $P(\text{even}) + P(\text{odd}) = \dfrac{1}{4} + \dfrac{3}{4} = 1$.]

- The more likely it is that an event will occur, the higher (the closer to 1) its probability is; the less likely it is that an event will occur, the lower (the closer to 0) its probability is.

Even though probability is defined as a fraction, probabilities can also be written as decimals or percents.

Instead of writing $P(E) = \dfrac{1}{2}$, you can write

$$P(E) = .50 \text{ or } P(E) = 50\%$$

➥ Example 8 _____

In 2003, Thanksgiving was on Thursday, November 27, and there are 30 days in November. If one day in November 2003 was chosen at random for a concert, what is the probability that the concert was on a weekend (Saturday or Sunday)?

There are two ways to answer this: either quickly draw a calendar, or reason out the solution.

Solution 1. Make a blank calendar and put 27 in the Thursday column:

S	M	T	W	Th	F	S
				27		

Now just go forward and backward from 27. Enter 28, 29, 30 and then 26, 25, 24, ..., 1.

S	M	T	W	Th	F	S
						1
2	3	4	5	6	7	8
9	10	11	12	13	14	15
16	17	18	19	20	21	22
23	24	25	26	27	28	29
30						

Finally, count (or circle) the Saturdays and Sundays. There are 5 of each for a total of 10, so the probability is $\frac{10}{30} = \frac{1}{3}$.

Solution 2. Since the 27th was a Thursday, the 28th, 29th, and 30th were Friday, Saturday, and Sunday, respectively. Repeatedly subtracting 7, you see that the Saturdays were on November 29, 22, 15, 8, 1 and the Sundays were on November 30, 23, 16, 9, 2 for a total of 10 weekend days. Then $\frac{10}{30} = \frac{1}{3}$.

➡ **Example 9** _____

An integer between 100 and 999, inclusive, is chosen at random. What is the probability that all the digits of the number are odd?

Solution. By KEY FACT O1, since both endpoints are included, there are $999 - 100 + 1 = 900$ integers between 100 and 999. In Example 6, you saw that there are 125 three-digit numbers all of whose digits are odd. Therefore, the probability is

$$\frac{\text{number of favorable outcomes}}{\text{total number of possible outcomes}} = \frac{125}{900} = \frac{5}{36} \approx .138$$

Occasionally, on an SAT there will be a question that relates probability and geometry. The next KEY FACT will help you deal with that type of question.

Key Fact P5

If a point is chosen at random inside a geometrical figure, the probability that the chosen point lies in a particular region is:

$$\frac{\text{area of that region}}{\text{area of the whole figure}}$$

➡ **Example 10** _____

In the figure above, a white square whose sides are 4 has been pasted on a black square whose sides are 5. If a point is chosen at random from the large square, what is the probability that the point is in the black area?

Solution. The area of the large square is $5^2 = 25$, and the area of the white square is $4^2 = 16$. Therefore, the area of the black region is $25 - 16 = 9$, and the probability that the chosen point is in the black area is $\frac{9}{25}$.

Multiple-Choice Questions

1. Let A be the set of primes less than 6, and B be the set of positive odd numbers less than 6. How many different sums of the form $a + b$ are possible if a is in A and b is in B?

   (A) 6
   (B) 7
   (C) 8
   (D) 9

2. Dwight Eisenhower was born on October 14, 1890, and died on March 28, 1969. What was his age, in years, at the time of his death?

   (A) 77
   (B) 78
   (C) 79
   (D) 80

3. There are 27 students in Mr. White's homeroom. What is the probability that at least 3 of them have their birthdays in the same month?

   (A) $\frac{3}{27}$

   (B) $\frac{3}{12}$

   (C) $\frac{1}{2}$

   (D) 1

4. A jar has 5 marbles, 1 of each of the colors red, white, blue, green, and yellow. If 4 marbles are removed from the jar, what is the probability that the yellow marble was removed?

   (A) $\frac{1}{5}$

   (B) $\frac{1}{4}$

   (C) $\frac{4}{5}$

   (D) $\frac{5}{4}$

5. A cafeteria has a lunch special consisting of soup or salad, a sandwich, coffee or tea, and a dessert. If the menu lists 3 soups, 2 salads, 8 sandwiches, and 7 desserts, how many different lunches can you choose?
   (**NOTE:** Two lunches are different if they differ in any aspect.)

   (A) 22
   (B) 280
   (C) 336
   (D) 560

6. A printer that can print 1 page in 5 seconds shuts down for 3 minutes to cool off after every hour of operation. How many minutes will the printer take to print 3600 pages?

   (A)   300
   (B)   312
   (C)   315
   (D) 18,000

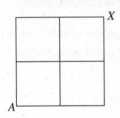

7. In the figure above, how many paths are there from A to X if the only ways to move are up and to the right?

   (A) 4
   (B) 6
   (C) 8
   (D) 9

8. A jar contains 20 marbles: 4 red, 6 white, and 10 blue. If you remove 1 marble at a time, randomly, what is the minimum number that you must remove to be certain that you have at least 2 marbles of each color?

   (A) 10
   (B) 12
   (C) 16
   (D) 18

9. At the audition for the school play, *n* people tried out. If *k* people went before Judy, who went before Liz, and *m* people went after Liz, how many people tried out between Judy and Liz?

(A) $n - m - k - 2$

(B) $n - m - k - 1$

(C) $n - m - k$

(D) $n - m - k + 1$

Note: Figure not drawn to scale

10. In the figure above, each of the small circles has a radius of 2 and the large circle has a radius of 6. If a point is chosen at random inside the large circle, what is the probability that the point lies in the shaded region?

(A) $\frac{7}{9}$

(B) $\frac{2}{3}$

(C) $\frac{1}{3}$

(D) $\frac{2}{9}$

Grid-in Questions

11. There are 100 people on a line. Andy is the 37th person and Ali is the 67th person. If a person on line is chosen at random, what is the probability that the person is standing between Andy and Ali?

12. How many four-digit numbers have only even digits?

13. How many ways are there to rearrange the letters in the word *elation*, if the first and last letter must each be a vowel?

Questions 14 and 15 refer to the following diagram. *A* is the set of positive integers less than 20; *B* is the set of positive integers that contain the digit 7; and *C* is the set of primes.

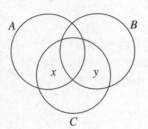

15. What is one number less than 50 that is a member of the region labeled *y*?

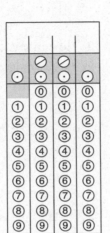

14. How many numbers are members of the region labeled *x*?

Answer Key

1. **B** 3. **D** 5. **D** 7. **B** 9. **A**
2. **B** 4. **C** 6. **B** 8. **D** 10. **A**

11. `.29`

12. `500`

13. `1440`

14. `6`

15. `37` or `47`

Answers Explained

1. **(B)** $A = \{2, 3, 5\}$ and $B = \{1, 3, 5\}$. Any of the 3 numbers in A could be added to any of the 3 numbers in B, so 9 sums could be formed. However, there could be some duplication. List the sums systematically; first add 1 to each number in A, then 3, and then 5: 3, 4, 6; 5, 6̸, 10; 7, 8, 10̸. There are 7 *different* sums.

2. **(B)** President Eisenhower's last birthday was in October 1968. His age at death was $1968 - 1890 = 78$ years.

3. **(D)** If there were no month in which at least 3 students had a birthday, then each month would have the birthdays of at most 2 students. But that's not possible; even if there were 2 birthdays in January, 2 in February, ..., and 2 in December, only 24 students would be accounted for. It is guaranteed that, with more than 24 students, at least 1 month will have 3 or more birthdays. The probability is 1.

4. **(C)** It is equally likely that any 1 of the 5 marbles will be the one that is not removed. Therefore, the probability that the yellow marble is left is $\frac{1}{5}$, and the probability that it is removed is $\frac{4}{5}$.

5. **(D)** You can choose your first course (soup or salad) in 5 ways, your beverage in 2 ways, your sandwich in 8 ways, and your dessert in 7 ways. The counting principle says to multiply: $5 \times 2 \times 8 \times 7 = 560$. (Note that, if you got soup *and* a salad, then, instead of 5 choices for the first course, there would have been $2 \times 3 = 6$ choices for the first two courses.)

6. **(B)** Use the given information to find the rate of pages per hour.

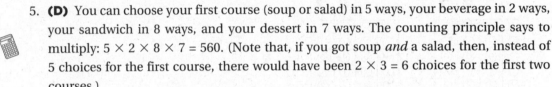

$$\frac{1 \text{ page}}{5 \text{ seconds}} = \frac{12 \text{ pages}}{1 \text{ minute}} = \frac{720 \text{ pages}}{1 \text{ hour}}$$

so 3600 pages will take $3600 \div 720 = 5$ hours, or 300 minutes, of printing time. There will also be 12 minutes (4×3 minutes) when the printer is shut down to cool off, for a total of 312 minutes. Note that there are 5 printing periods and 4 cooling-off periods.

7. **(B)** Either label all the vertices and systematically list the possibilities, or systematically trace the diagram. If you start by going from A to B, there are 3 paths: you can get up to the top by BC, EF, or HX, and once there must proceed to the right. Similarly, there are 3 paths if you start by going right from A to D. In all, there are 6 paths from A to X.

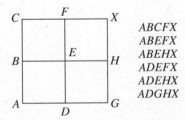

ABCFX
ABEFX
ABEHX
ADEFX
ADEHX
ADGHX

8. **(D)** In a problem like this one, the easiest thing to do is to see what could go wrong in your attempt to get 2 marbles of each color. If you were really unlucky, you might remove 10 blue ones in a row, followed by all 6 white ones. At that point you would have 16 marbles, and you still wouldn't have even 1 red. The next 2 marbles, however, must both be red. The answer is 18.

9. **(A)** It may help to draw a line and label it.

$$(\underset{k+1}{\overset{k}{\longrightarrow}})\underset{}{\overset{J}{\bullet}}(\underset{n-m}{\overset{L}{\longrightarrow}})\overset{}{\overset{}{\bullet}}(\overset{m}{\longrightarrow})$$

Since k people went before Judy, she was number $k + 1$ to try out; and since m people went after Liz, she was number $n - m$ to try out. Then, the number of people to try out between Judy and Liz was $(n - m) - (k + 1) - 1 = n - m - k - 2$.

10. **(A)** Since the formula for the area of a circle is πr^2, the area of each small circle is $\pi(2^2) = 4\pi$. Then the total white area is 8π. The area of the large circle is $\pi(6^2) = 36\pi$. Therefore, the area of the shaded region is $36\pi - 8\pi = 28\pi$, and the probability that a point chosen at random lies in that shaded region is $\frac{28\pi}{36\pi} = \frac{7}{9}$.

11. **.29** There are $67 - 37 - 1 = 29$ people between Andy and Ali. The probability that the person chosen is standing between them is $\frac{29}{100} = .29$.

12. **500** The easiest way to answer this question is to use the counting principle. The first digit can be chosen in any of 4 ways (2, 4, 6, 8), whereas the second, third, and fourth digits can be chosen in any of 5 ways (0, 2, 4, 6, 8). Therefore, the total number of four-digit numbers with only even digits is $4 \times 5 \times 5 \times 5 = 500$.

13. **1440** Again, use the counting principle. How many ways are there to fill in seven blanks, _ _ _ _ _ _ _, with letters from the word *elation*? Think of this as seven jobs to do. The first job is to choose one of the 4 vowels in the word to be the first letter; the second job is to choose one of the remaining 3 vowels to be the last letter. Thus, there are $4 \times 3 = 12$ ways to choose the first and last letters. Since there are no other restrictions, the five other jobs are to place the remaining 5 letters in the five remaining blanks. There are 5 choices for the first blank, 4 for the next, then 3, then 2, and finally 1.

There are $12 \times 5 \times 4 \times 3 \times 2 \times 1 = 1440$ arrangements.

14. **6** In the diagram, the region labeled x contains all of the primes less than 20 that do not contain the digit 7. They are 2, 3, 5, 11, 13, 19—6 numbers in all.

15. **37 or 47** Region y consists of primes that contain the digit 7 and are greater than 20.

A *sequence* is just a list of numbers separated by commas. It can be finite, such as 1, 3, 5, 7, 9; or it can be infinite, such as 5, 10, 15, 20, 25, ... Each number in the list is called a *term* of the sequence. The terms of a sequence don't have to follow any pattern or rule, but on the SAT they always do. The most common type of sequence question presents you with a rule for finding the terms of a sequence, and then asks you for a particular term.

TACTIC
Q1 Never answer a question involving a sequence without writing out at least the first five terms.

➥ **Example 1** _____

A sequence is formed as follows: the first term is 3, and every other term is 4 more than the term that precedes it. What is the 100th term?

Solution. The sequence begins 3, 7, 11, 15, 19, 23 (7 is 4 more than 3, 11 is 4 more than 7, etc.). Clearly, you could continue writing out the terms, and if the question asked for the 10th term, that would be the easiest thing to do. You are not, however, going to write out 100 terms. What you need now is a little imagination or inspiration. How else can you describe the terms of this sequence? The terms are just 1 less than the corresponding multiples of 4 (4, 8, 12, 16, 20, 24, ...): 7, which is the 2nd term, is 1 less than 2×4; 19, which is the 5th term, is 1 less than 5×4. Now you have the solution. The 100th term is 1 less than 100×4: $400 - 1 = \textbf{399}$.

In Examples 2–4, the sequences S_n are formed as follows:
For any positive integer n: the first term of the sequence S_n is n, and every term after the first is 1 more than twice the preceding term.

➥ **Example 2** _____

What is the value of the smallest term of S_5 that is greater than 100?

Solution. Sequence S_5 proceeds as follows: 5, 11, 23, 47, 95, 191, ..., so the smallest term greater than 100 is **191**.

➥ **Example 3** _____

What is the units digit of the 500th term of S_9?

Solution. Of course, you're not going to write out 500 terms of any sequence, but you *always* write out the first five: 9, 19, 39, 79, 159, ...
There's no question about it: the units digit of *every* term is **9**.

Example 4

If one of the first 10 terms of S_{1000} is chosen at random, what is the probability that it is odd?

Solution. For any integer m whatsoever, $2m$ is even and $2m + 1$ is odd. The first term of S_{1000} is 1000, but every other term is odd. The probability is $\frac{9}{10}$.

Two types of sequences that could appear on the SAT are *arithmetic sequences* and *geometric sequences.*

An *arithmetic sequence* is a sequence such as the one in Example 1, in which the difference between any two consecutive terms is the same. In Example 1, that difference was 4. An easy way to find the nth term of such a sequence is to start with the first term and add the common difference $n - 1$ times. In Example 1, the sixth term is 23, which can be obtained by taking the first term, 3, and adding the common difference, 4, five times: $3 + 5(4) = 23$. In the same way, the 100th term is $3 + 99(4) = 3 + 396 = 399$.

Key Fact Q1

If $a_1, a_2, a_3, \dots$ is an arithmetic sequence whose common difference is d, then

$$a_n = a_1 + (n - 1)\, d$$

A *geometric sequence* is a sequence in which the ratio between any two consecutive terms is the same. For example, the sequence, 2, 10, 50, 250, 1250, … is a geometric sequence: the ratios $\frac{10}{2}$, $\frac{50}{10}$, $\frac{250}{50}$ are all equal to 5.

An easy way to find the nth term of a geometric sequence is to start with the first term and multiply it by the common ratio $n - 1$ times. For example, in the sequence 2, 10, 50, 250, 1250, … the fourth term is 250, which can be obtained by taking the first term, 2, and multiplying it by the common ratio, 5, three times: $2 \times 5 \times 5 \times 5 = 2 \times 5^3 = 2 \times 125 = 250$. In the same way, the 100th term is 2×5^{99}.

Key Fact Q2

If $a_1, a_2, a_3, \dots$ is a geometric sequence whose common ratio is r, then $a_n = a_1 (r)^{n-1}$.

Consider the following three sequences:

(i) 1, 7, 13, 19, 25, 31, …

(ii) 6, 3, $\frac{3}{2}$, $\frac{3}{4}$, $\frac{3}{8}$, $\frac{3}{16}$, …

(iii) 1, 2, 3, 5, 8, 13, …

Sequence (i) is an arithmetic sequence in which the common difference is 6. A reasonable SAT question would be: What is the 75th term of this sequence? By KEY FACT P2, the answer is $1 + 74(6) = 1 + 444 = 445$. This could be a multiple-choice or a grid-in question.

Sequence (ii) is a geometric sequence in which the common ratio is $\frac{1}{2}$. A reasonable SAT question would be: What is the 75th term of this sequence? By KEY FACT P3, the answer is $6 \times \left(\frac{1}{2}\right)^{74}$. This could only be a multiple-choice question because there is no way to grid in such an answer. It is likely that one of the answer choices would, in fact, be $6 \times \left(\frac{1}{2}\right)^{74}$. But since

$$6 \times \left(\frac{1}{2}\right)^{74} = 6 \times \frac{1}{2} \times \left(\frac{1}{2}\right)^{73} = 3 \times \left(\frac{1}{2}\right)^{73}$$

the correct answer choice could also be $3 \times \left(\frac{1}{2}\right)^{73}$.

Sequence (iii) is neither an arithmetic sequence nor a geometric sequence: there is no common difference $(13 - 8 \neq 8 - 5)$, and there is no common ratio $\left(\frac{13}{8} \neq \frac{8}{5}\right)$.

Therefore, you have no formula for evaluating the nth term of this sequence, and it would *not* be reasonable to ask for the 75th term. If you were told that the rule for the sequence is that each term is the sum of the two preceding terms $(3 = 1 + 2, 5 = 2 + 3, 8 = 3 + 5, ...)$, then it would be reasonable to ask: What is the smallest term in this sequence that is greater than 100? The answer is 144, which you could get just by calculating five more terms. 1, 2, 3, 5, 8, 13, 21, 34, 55, 89, 144.

A *repeating sequence* is a sequence in which a group of terms repeats in a cyclical pattern.

 TACTIC Q2 **When k numbers form a repeating sequence, to find the nth number, divide n by k and take the remainder r. The rth term and the nth term are the same.**

Examples 5 and 6 refer to the infinite sequence 1, 4, 2, 8, 5, 7, 1, 4, 2, 8, 5, 7, ... , in which the six digits 1, 4, 2, 8, 5, and 7 keep repeating in that order.

➡ **Example 5** _____

What is the 500th term of the sequence?

Solution. When 500 is divided by 6, the quotient is 83 ($6 \times 83 = 498$) and the remainder is 2. Therefore, the first 498 terms are just the numbers 1, 4, 2, 8, 5, 7 repeated 83 times. The 498th term is the 83rd 7 in the sequence. Then the pattern repeats again: the 499th term is 1, and the 500th term is **4**.

In this example, notice that the 500th term is the same as the 2nd term. This occurs because 2 is the remainder when 500 is divided by 6.

➡ Example 6

What is the sum of the 800th through the 805th terms of the sequence?

Solution. Don't waste time determining what the 800th term is. Any six consecutive terms of the sequence consist, in some order, of exactly the same six numbers: 1, 4, 2, 8, 5, and 7. Their sum is **27**.

Some SAT questions could be based on repeating patterns. Questions involving repeating patterns are very similar to those involving repeating sequences, except that the terms don't have to be numbers.

➡ Example 7

In order to divide the campers at a camp into six teams (the reds, whites, blues, greens, yellows, and browns), the director had all the campers form a line. Then, starting with the first person, each camper on line called out a color, repeating this pattern: red, white, blue, green, yellow, brown, red, white, blue, green, yellow, brown, ... What color was called out by the 500th camper?

(A) Red
(B) White
(C) Green
(D) Yellow

Solution. This is exactly the same as Example 5. When 500 is divided by 6, the quotient is 83 and the remainder is 2. Then, by TACTIC Q2, the 500th camper called out the same color as the 2nd camper: **white (B)**.

➡ Example 8

Last year Elaine's birthday was on Friday. If Susan's birthday was 150 days after Elaine's, how many Sundays were there between Elaine's birthday and Susan's birthday?

Solution. The 7 days of the week repeat in cyclical pattern. Using TACTIC Q2, divide 150 by 7, getting a quotient of 21 and a remainder of 3. Thus, the 150th day after Elaine's birthday was Monday, the same as the 3rd day after her birthday. During the 21 full weeks between Elaine's and Susan's birthdays, there were 21 Sundays, and there was 1 more during the last 3 days, for a total of **22**.

EXERCISES ON SEQUENCES

Multiple-Choice Questions

1. In the United States, Thanksgiving is celebrated on the fourth Thursday in November. Which of the following statements is (are) true?

   I. Thanksgiving is always the last Thursday in November.
   II. Thanksgiving is never celebrated on November 22.
   III. Thanksgiving cannot be celebrated on the same date 2 years in a row.

   (A) None
   (B) I only
   (C) II only
   (D) III only

2. A gum-ball dispenser is filled with exactly 1000 pieces of gum. The gum balls always come out in the following order: 1 red, 2 blue, 3 green, 4 yellow, and 5 white. After the fifth white, the pattern repeats, starting with 1 red, and so on. What is the color of the last gum ball to come out of the machine?

   (A) Red
   (B) Blue
   (C) Green
   (D) Yellow

3. The Declaration of Independence was signed in July 1776. What month and year was it 500 months later?

   (A) August 1817
   (B) November 1817
   (C) March 1818
   (D) May 1818

4. If a population that is initially 100 triples every year, which of the following is an expression for the size of the population after t months?

   (A) 100×3^t
   (B) 100×12^{3t}
   (C) $100 \times 3^{\frac{t}{12}}$
   (D) $100 \times 3^{\frac{12}{t}}$

Grid-in Questions

5. Three children guessed the number of jelly beans in a jar. The guesses were 98, 137, and 164. None of the guesses was correct. One guess was off by 12, another by 27, and the third by 39. How many jelly beans were in the jar?

6. The pointer on the dial below moves 3 numbers clockwise every minute. If it starts at 1, what number will it be pointing to in exactly 1 hour?

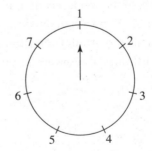

7. A sequence is formed by choosing a number, x, to be the first term. Every term after the first is y more than the preceding term. If the 8th term is 19 and the 12th term is 29, what is xy?

Answer Key

1. **D**   2. **D**   3. **C**   4. **C**

5. **1 2 5**   6. **6**   7. **3 . 7 5**   or   **1 5 / 4**

Answers Explained

1. **(D)** If November 1 is a Thursday, then so are November 8, 15, 22, and 29. Therefore, Thanksgiving could fall on November 22 (II is false); and if it does, it is not the last Thursday in November (I is false). Assume that one year Thanksgiving falls on Thursday, November X. Then exactly 52 weeks (or $7 \times 52 = 364$ days) later it will again be Thursday, but it won't be November X, because November X comes 365 (or 366) days after the preceding November X (III is true).

2. **(D)** Since the pattern repeats itself after every 15 gum balls, divide 1000 by 15. The quotient is 66, and the remainder is 10. Therefore, the 1000th gum ball is the same color as the 10th, which is yellow.

3. **(C)** The 12 months of the year form a repeating sequence.

$$500 \div 12 = 41.666\ldots \text{ and } 41 \times 12 = 492$$

Therefore, exactly 41 years (or 492 months) after July 1776 it will be July in the year $1776 + 41 = 1817$.
Since $500 - 492 = 8$, 500 months after July 1776 is 8 months after July 1817, which is March 1818.

4. **(C)** Since t months is $\frac{t}{12}$ years, the population triples $\frac{t}{12}$ times. After t months, the population will be $100 \times 3^{\frac{t}{12}}$.

5. **125** There are lots of ways to reason this out. Here is one. The number must be over 100; otherwise, the guess of 164 would be off by more than 64, and none of the guesses was that far wrong, Thus, the guess of 98 was too low. If it was 12 too low, there would be 110 jelly beans, but then 164 would be off by 54, which isn't right. If 98 was 27 too low, the number would be 125, which is 12 less than 137 and 39 less than 164. That's it.

6. **6** To see the pattern develop, write out the locations of the pointer for the first few minutes. Advancing 3 numbers per minute, it goes from $1 \to 4 \to 7 \to 3 \to 6 \to 2 \to 5 \to 1$; and when it is back to 1, the whole cycle repeats. To know where the pointer will be in 60 minutes, divide 60 by 7. Since the quotient is 8 and the remainder is 4, after 60 minutes the pointer will be pointing to the same number it pointed to after 4 minutes. Be careful. That number is not 3; it's 6. After 1 minute the pointer is at 4, after 2 minutes it's at 7, and so on.

Alternative solution. Since the pointer advances 3 numbers per minute, it advances $3 \times 60 = 180$ minutes per hour. Dividing 180 by 7 gives a quotient of 25 and a remainder of 5, so the pointer makes 25 complete cycles and then advances 5 more numbers, from 1 to 6.

7. **3.75 or $\frac{15}{4}$** Each term is y more than the preceding term; therefore, the 9th term is $19 + y$, the 10th term is $19 + y + y = 19 + 2y$, the 11th term is $19 + 2y + y = 19 + 3y$, and the 12th term is $19 + 3y + y = 19 + 4y$. But the 12th term is 29, so

$$29 = 19 + 4y \Rightarrow 10 = 4y \Rightarrow y = 2.5$$

You could now count backward from the 8th term to the 1st term, subtracting 2.5 each time. Instead, note that, to get from the 1st to the 8th term, it was necessary to add 2.5 seven times. Therefore:

$$x + (7 \times 2.5) = 19 \Rightarrow x + 17.5 = 19 \Rightarrow x = 1.5$$

Finally,

$$xy = 1.5 \times 2.5 = 3.75 \text{ or } \frac{15}{4}$$

6-R FUNCTIONS AND THEIR GRAPHS

You have undoubtedly studied functions many times in your math classes. However, most of what you learned about functions is *not* tested on the SAT. This section reviews the basic facts about functions and their graphs that you do need for the SAT.

As used on the SAT, a ***function*** is a rule that assigns to each number in one set a number in another set. Functions are usually designated by the letter f, although any letters could be used. The numbers in the first set are labeled x, and the number in the second set to which x is assigned by the function is designated by the letter y or by $f(x)$.

For example, we can write $y = f(x) = 2x + 3$. This function assigns, to each real number x, the number $2x + 3$.

The number assigned to 5 is $2(5) + 3 = 10 + 3 = 13$, and the number assigned to -5 is $2(-5) + 3 = -10 + 3 = -7$.

To express these facts, we write

$$f(5) = 13 \text{ and } f(-5) = -7$$

The proper way to think of the function $f(x) = 2x + 3$ is that f takes *anything* and assigns to it 2 times *that thing* plus 3:

$$f(anything) = 2(that\ thing) + 3$$

- $f(100) = 2(100) + 3 = 203$
- $f(0) = 2(0) + 3 = 0 + 3 = 3$
- $f(a) = 2a + 3$
- $f(a + b) = 2(a + b) + 3$
- $f(x^2) = 2x^2 + 3$
- $f(2x^2 + 3) = 2(2x^2 + 3) + 3 = 4x^2 + 9$
- $f(f(x)) = 2(f(x)) + 3 = 2(2x + 3) + 3 = 4x + 6 + 3 = 4x + 9$

➡ Example 1 _____

If $f(x) = x^2 + 2x$, what is $f(3) + f(-3)$?

Solution. $f(3) = 3^2 + 2(3) = 9 + 6 = 15$,
$\qquad\qquad f(-3) = (-3)^2 + 2(-3) = 9 - 6 = 3$.

Then $\qquad f(3) + f(-3) = \mathbf{15 + 3 = 18}$.

➡ Example 2 _____

If $f(x) = x^2 + 2x$, what is $f(x + 2)$?

(A) $x^2 + 2x + 4$
(B) $x^2 + 2x + 8$
(C) $x^2 + 6x + 4$
(D) $x^2 + 6x + 8$

Solution. $f(x + 2) = (x + 2)^2 + 2(x + 2) = (x^2 + 4x + 4) + (2x + 4) = \mathbf{x^2 + 6x + 8}$ **(D)**.

Sometimes on the SAT, you are asked a question that tests both your understanding of what a function is and your ability to do some basic algebra. The following example does just that.

➡ **Example 3** _____

If $f(x) = 3x + 3$, for what value of a is it true that $3f(a) = f(2a)$?

(A) –3
(B) –2
(C) 2
(D) 3

Solution. $3f(a) = 3(3a + 3) = 9a + 9$,
$\quad\quad\quad f(2a) = 3(2a) + 3 = 6a + 3$.

Therefore, $9a + 9 = 6a + 3 \Rightarrow 3a = -6 \Rightarrow a = -2$ **(B)**.

The **graph** of a function, f, is a certain set of points in the coordinate plane. Point (a, b) is on the graph of f if and only if $b = f(a)$. For example, the graph of $f(x) = 2x + 3$ consists of all points (x, y) such that $y = 2x + 3$. Since $f(5) = 13$ and $f(-5) = -7$, then $(5, 13)$ and $(-5, -7)$ are both points on the graph of $f(x) = 2x + 3$. In Section 6-N, you saw that the graph of $y = 2x + 3$ is a line whose slope is 2 and whose y-intercept is 3.

On the SAT you may have to know whether a certain point is on the graph of a given function, but you won't have to actually graph the function.

➡ **Example 4** _____

Which of the following is NOT a point on the graph of

$$f(x) = x^2 + \frac{4}{x^2} ?$$

(A) $(-1, 5)$
(B) $(2, 5)$
(C) $(-2, -5)$
(D) $(4, 16.25)$

Solution. Test each answer choice until you find one that does NOT work.

- $f(-1) = (-1)^2 + \dfrac{4}{(-1)^2} = 1 + 4 = 5$. So, $(-1, 5)$ *is* a point on the graph.

- $f(2) = 2^2 + \dfrac{4}{2^2} = 4 + 1 = 5$. So, $(2, 5)$ *is* a point on the graph.

- $f(-2) = (-2)^2 + \dfrac{4}{(-2)^2} = 4 + 1 = 5 \neq -5$. So, $(-2, 5)$ is a point on the graph, but **(-2, -5)** is NOT.

The answer is choice **(C)**.

Example 5

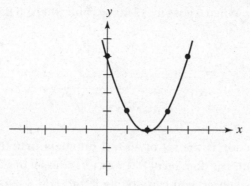

Which of the following could be the equation of the graph shown in the figure above?

(A) $y = -2x + 4$

(B) $y = 2x + 4$

(C) $y = x^2$

(D) $y = x^2 - 4x + 4$

Solution. Since the graph passes through $(2, 0)$, $x = 2$ and $y = 0$ must satisfy the equation. Test each of the five choices in order.

- (A) Does $0 = -2(2) + 4$?   Yes
- (B) Does $0 = 2(2) + 4$?   No
- (C) Does $0 = 2^2$?   No
- (D) Does $0 = 2^2 - 4(2) + 4$?   Yes

The answer is (A) or (D). To break the tie, try another point on the graph, say $(0, 4)$ and test choices (A) and (D).

- (A) Does $4 = -2(0) + 4$?   Yes
- (D) Does $4 = (0)^2 - 4(0) + 4$?   Yes

Unfortunately, that didn't help. Try one more, point $(1, 1)$.

- (A) Does $1 = -2(1) + 4$?   No
- (D) Does $1 = 1^2 - 4(1) + 4$?   Yes

The answer is $y = x^2 - 4x + 4$ **(D)**.

Of course, if you realized that the graphs of the equations in choices (A) and (B) are straight lines, you could have immediately eliminated them and tested only choices (C) and (D).

You can think of a function as a machine. A washing machine performs a function. It cleans clothes: dirty clothes go in and clean clothes come out. In the same way you can think of $f(x) = 2x + 3$ as a machine. When 5 goes in, 13 comes out; when –5 goes in, –7 comes out.

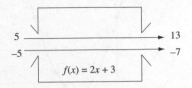

The ***domain*** of a function is the set of all real numbers that can go into the machine without causing a problem. The domain of $f(x) = 2x + 3$ is the set of all real numbers, because, for any real number whatsoever, you can double it and add 3. No number will cause the machine to jam.

If $f(x) = \sqrt{2x+3}$, however, the domain is not the set of all real numbers. Although 5 is in the domain of f, because $f(5) = \sqrt{2(5)+3} = \sqrt{13}$, –5 is not in the domain of f. The reason is that $\sqrt{2(-5)+3} = \sqrt{-10+3} = \sqrt{-7}$, which is not a real number. If you try to evaluate $\sqrt{2(-5)+3}$ on your calculator (a machine that evaluates many functions), you will get an error message.

Since the domain of a function is the set of all real numbers except those that cause problems, you need to know what can cause a problem. Many things can be troublesome, but for the SAT you need to know about only two of them.

Key Fact R1

A number x is *not* in the domain of $y = f(x)$ if evaluating $f(x)$ would require you to divide by 0 or to take the square root of a negative number.

➡ **Example 6** _____

Which of the following numbers is NOT in the domain of $f(x) = \sqrt{4-x}$?

(A) –6
(B) –4
(C) 4
(D) 6

Solution. Since you cannot take the square root of a negative number, the domain of $f(x) = \sqrt{4-x}$ is the set of all real numbers x such that $4 - x \geq 0 \Rightarrow 4 \geq x$. Only **6 (D)** is not in the domain.

Note that 4 is in the domain of $f(x) = \sqrt{4-x}$ because $f(4) = \sqrt{4-4} = \sqrt{0} = 0$. But 4 is *not* in the domain of $g(x) = \dfrac{1}{\sqrt{4-x}}$ because $\dfrac{1}{\sqrt{4-4}} = \dfrac{1}{\sqrt{0}} = \dfrac{1}{0}$, which is undefined. Remember, you can *never* divide by 0.

Again, if a function is thought of as a machine, the **range** of a function is the set of all real numbers that can come out of the machine. Recall that, if $f(x) = 2x + 3$, then $f(5) = 13$ and $f(-5) = -7$, so 13 and -7 are both in the range of $f(x)$. In general, it is much harder to find the range of a function than to find its domain, but you will usually be able to test whether a particular number is in the range.

➡ **Example 7** _____

Which of the following is NOT in the range of $f(x) = x^2 - 3$?

(A) 6
(B) 1
(C −1
(D) −6

Solution. Since for any real number x, $x^2 \geq 0$, then $x^2 - 3 \geq -3$. Therefore, **−6 (D)** is not in the range of $f(x)$.

Note that in the solution to Example 7 you do not have to test each of the choices, but you can. To test whether 6 is in the range of $f(x)$, see whether there is a number x such that $f(x) = 6$: $x^2 - 3 = 6 \Rightarrow x^2 = 9 \Rightarrow x = 3$ or $x = -3$.

Then $f(3) = 6$, and 6 is in the range. Similarly, $f(2) = 1$ and $f(\sqrt{2}) = -1$, so 1 and −1 are also in the range. If you test −6, you see that $f(x) = -6 \Rightarrow x^2 - 3 = -6 \Rightarrow x^2 = -3$.

But there is no real number whose square is −3. Nothing that can go into the machine will cause −6 to come out.

On the SAT, questions such as Examples 6 and 7 may be phrased without using the words "domain" and "range." For example, Example 6 may be expressed as follows:

The function $f(x) = \sqrt{4-x}$ is defined for each of the following numbers EXCEPT

(A) −6
(B) −4
(C) 4
(D) 6

Similarly, Example 7 may be expressed as follows:

For the function $f(x) = x^2 - 3$, which of the following numbers may NOT be the value of $f(x)$?

(A) 6
(B) 1
(C) −1
(D) −6

On the SAT you take, it is possible that there will be a question that shows you a graph and asks you which of four other graphs is related to the original one in a certain way. To answer such a question, you can either test points or use the five facts listed in the following KEY FACT.

If $f(x)$ is a function and r is a positive number:

1. The graph of $y = f(x) + r$ is obtained by shifting the graph of $y = f(x)$ UP r units.
2. The graph of $y = f(x) - r$ is obtained by shifting the graph of $y = f(x)$ DOWN r units.
3. The graph of $y = f(x + r)$ is obtained by shifting the graph of $y = f(x)$ r units to the LEFT.
4. The graph of $y = f(x - r)$ is obtained by shifting the graph of $y = f(x)$ r units to the RIGHT.
5. The graph of $y = -f(x)$ is obtained by reflecting the graph of $y = f(x)$ in the x-axis.

Each part of KEY FACT R2 is illustrated below.

Figure (a) is the graph of the absolute-value function: $y = f(x) = |x|$. Figures (b)–(f) are transformations of the original graph.

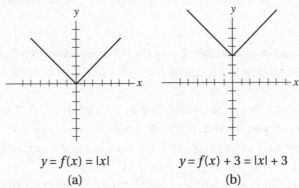

$y = f(x) = |x|$
(a)

$y = f(x) + 3 = |x| + 3$
(b)

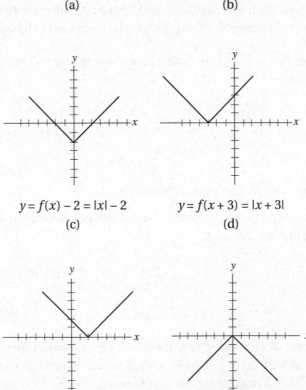

$y = f(x) - 2 = |x| - 2$
(c)

$y = f(x + 3) = |x + 3|$
(d)

$y = f(x - 2) = |x - 2|$
(e)

$y = -f(x) = -|x|$
(f)

➥ Example 8 _____

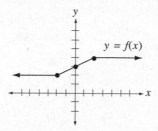

$y = f(x)$

If the figure above is the graph of $y = f(x)$, which of the following is the graph of $y = f(x + 2)$?

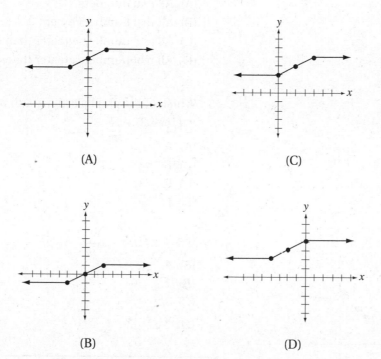

(A)

(C)

(B)

(D)

Solution 1. Since $(0, 3)$ is a point on the graph of $y = f(x)$, $f(0) = 3$. Then $3 = f(0) = f(-2 + 2)$ and so $(-2, 3)$ is a point on the graph of $y = f(x + 2)$. Only choice **(D)** passes through $(-2, 3)$. Note that, if two or three of the graphs passed through $(-2, 3)$, you would test those graphs with a second point, say $(2, 4)$.

Solution 2. By KEY FACT R2, the graph of $y = f(x + 2)$ results from shifting the graph of $y = f(x)$ 2 units to the left. Only choice **(D)** is 2 units to the left of the graph in question.

Multiple-Choice Questions

Questions 1–4 concern the function $y = f(x) = \sqrt{x}$, whose graph is shown below. Choices (A)–(D) are graphs of functions that are somehow related to $f(x)$.

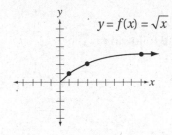

$$y = f(x) = \sqrt{x}$$

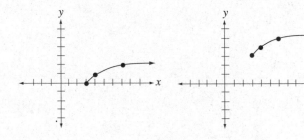

(A)   (C)

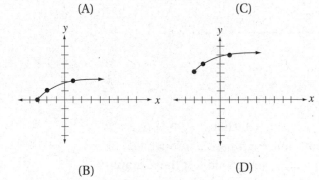

(B)   (D)

1. Which of the graphs is the graph of $y = f(x - 3)$?

   (A) A
   (B) B
   (C) C
   (D) D

2. What is the domain of the function $y = f(x - 3)$?

   (A) All real numbers
   (B) All real numbers except 3
   (C) All real numbers greater than 3
   (D) All real numbers greater than or equal to 3

3. Which of the graphs is the graph of $y = f(x + 3) + 3$?

   (A) A
   (B) B
   (C) C
   (D) D

4. If $g(x) = f(f(x))$, what is $g(4)$?

   (A) 4
   (B) 2
   (C) $\sqrt{2}$
   (D) $2\sqrt{2}$

5. If $f(x) = |x|$, for what value of x does $f(x - 3) = f(x + 3)$?

   (A) –3
   (B) 0
   (C) 3
   (D) No value of x

Grid-in Questions

6. If $f(x) = x^2 - 2^x$, what is the value of $f(3)$?

7. What is the smallest integer that is NOT in the domain of $f(x) = \sqrt{\pi - x}$?

Questions 8 and 9 concern the function $f(x) = 8 - 2x^2$.

8. How many integers satisfy the condition that $f(x)$ is positive?

9. How many positive integers are in the range of $f(x)$?

10. If $f(x) = x + 5$, for what value of x does $f(4x) = f(x + 4)$?

Answer Key

1. **A**   2. **D**   3. **D**   4. **C**   5. **B**

6. **1**

7. **4**

8. **3**

9. **8**

10. **4/3**   or   **1.33**

Answers Explained

1. **(A)** The graph of $y = f(x - 3)$ is the result of shifting the given graph 3 units to the right.

2. **(D)** The domain of $y = f(x - 3) = \sqrt{x-3}$ is the set of all real numbers such that $x - 3 \geq 0$. So, the domain consists of all real numbers greater than or equal to 3.

3. **(D)** To get the graph of $y = f(x + 3)$, you need to shift the original graph 3 units to the left (this is graph (B)). Then, to get the graph of $y = f(x + 3) + 3$, shift graph (B) 3 units up, yielding graph (D).

4. **(C)** $g(4) = f(f(4)) = \sqrt{f(4)} = \sqrt{\sqrt{4}} = \sqrt{2}$

5. **(B)** If $|x - 3| = |x + 3|$, then either $x - 3 = x + 3$, which is impossible, or
$$x - 3 = -(x + 3) \Rightarrow x - 3 = -x - 3$$
Then $x = -x$, and so $x = 0$.

6. **1** $f(3) = 3^2 - 2^3 = 9 - 8 = 1$

7. **4** Since you can't take the square root of a negative number, the domain of $f(x)$ consists of every real number, x, such that $\pi - x \geq 0$. The numbers that are *not* in the domain of $f(x)$ satisfy the inequality $\pi - x < 0 \Rightarrow \pi < x$. The smallest integer greater than π is 4.

8. **3** $f(x)$ is positive $\Rightarrow f(x) > 0 \Rightarrow 8 - 2x^2 > 0$. So, $8 > 2x^2$ and, therefore, $4 > x^2$. The only integers whose squares are less than 4 are -1, 0, and 1; there are 3 of them. Note that $f(2)$ and $f(-2)$ are both 0, which is not positive.

9. **8** Since x^2, and hence $2x^2$, must be greater than or equal to 0, the maximum value of $f(x)$ is 8. This means that 8 is the largest number in the range of $f(x)$. In fact, every number less than or equal to 8 is in the range. There are 8 positive integers in the range: 1, 2, 3, 4, 5, 6, 7, 8. For example, $f(0) = 8$, $f(1) = 6$, $f(\sqrt{2}) = 4$, and $f(\sqrt{2}) = 1$.

10. $\dfrac{4}{3}$ **or 1.33** If $f(x) = x + 5$, then $f(4x) = 4x + 5$ and $f(x + 4) = (x + 4) + 5 = x + 9$.

    Then, $4x + 5 = x + 9 \Rightarrow 3x = 4 \Rightarrow x = \dfrac{4}{3}$ or 1.33.

The SAT that you take will probably have a couple of questions on trigonometry. This section reviews the facts that you need to know in order to answer those questions. If you have studied trigonometry in school, you surely have learned much more trigonometry than is required for the SAT. The few questions you see should present little or no difficulty. If, on the other hand, you are not familiar with trigonometry, you have two choices.

You can study this section carefully and learn what you need to know to answer those questions. Alternatively, you can save the time and effort and just not worry about them. Anytime you encounter a question involving a trigonometric ratio (sine, cosine, or tangent), just take a wild guess and move on. Remember that you don't need to attempt all of the questions to do really well. Correctly answering only 40 of the 58 math questions on the SAT can earn you a score over 600. Correctly answering 50 of the 58 questions can earn you a score over 700! (See page 18 for more information about the number of questions you should attempt.) Certainly if you have a limited time to study, you are better off reviewing what you know rather than trying to learn a brand-new topic about which there will be very few questions.

This section is rather short because it reviews very little of what is taught in a high school trigonometry course. It reviews only the trigonometry that could be the basis of an SAT question. The most important things you need to know for the SAT are the definitions of the trigonometric ratios. The one other thing to know is the definition of a radian and how to convert degree measure to radian measure.

Sine, Cosine, and Tangent

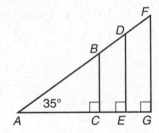

In the figure above, right triangles ABC, ADE, and AFG each have a 90° angle and a 35° angle, so they are all similar to one another. Therefore, their sides are in proportion:

$$\frac{BC}{AB} = \frac{DE}{AD} = \frac{FG}{AF} = \frac{\text{length of the side opposite the 35° angle}}{\text{length of the hypotenuse}}$$

This ratio is called the sine of 35° and is written sin 35°. To evaluate sin 35°, you could very carefully measure the lengths of $\overline{FG}$ and $\overline{AF}$ and divide. In the given figure, $FG \approx 1$ inch, $AF \approx 1.75$ inches, so $\frac{FG}{AF} \approx \frac{1}{1.75} = 0.57$.

Fortunately, you do not have to do this. You can use your calculator. Depending on what calculator you use, you would either enter 35 and then press the $\boxed{\text{sin}}$ button or press the $\boxed{\text{sin}}$ button and then enter 35. Regardless, in a fraction of a second, you will see the answer correct to several decimal places: sin 35° = 0.573576436, far greater accuracy than you need for the SAT.

→ Example 1

In the triangle below, what is the length of hypotenuse $\overline{PQ}$?

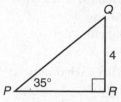

Use the sine ratio (and your calculator):

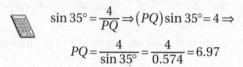

$$\sin 35° = \frac{4}{PQ} \Rightarrow (PQ)\sin 35° = 4 \Rightarrow$$

$$PQ = \frac{4}{\sin 35°} = \frac{4}{0.574} = 6.97$$

The formal definitions of the three trigonometric ratios you need are given in KEY FACT S1.

Key Fact S1

Let θ be one of the acute angles in a right triangle.

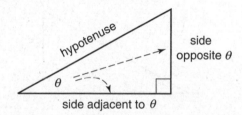

- The formula for the sine of θ, denoted $\sin \theta$, is:

$$\sin \theta = \frac{\text{the length of the side opposite } \theta}{\text{the length of the hypotenuse}}$$

$$= \frac{\text{opposite}}{\text{hypotenuse}}$$

- The formula for the cosine of θ, denoted $\cos \theta$, is:

$$\cos \theta = \frac{\text{the length of the side adjacent to } \theta}{\text{the length of the hypotenuse}}$$

$$= \frac{\text{adjacent}}{\text{hypotenuse}}$$

- The formula for the tangent of θ, denoted tan θ, is:

$$\tan\theta = \frac{\text{the length of the side opposite } \theta}{\text{the length of the side adjacent to } \theta}$$

$$= \frac{\text{opposite}}{\text{adjacent}}$$

- From the definitions of the three trigonometry ratios, it follows immediately that for any acute angle θ, $\tan\theta = \dfrac{\sin\theta}{\cos\theta}$.

For decades, students have remembered these definitions by memorizing the "word" SohCahToa. For example, the "S" in "Soh" stands for "sine" and the "oh" reminds you that sine is Opposite over Hypotenuse.

If you know the value of any one of sin θ, cos θ, or tan θ, you can always find the values of the other two.

➡ Example 2 _____

If $\sin\theta = \dfrac{15}{17}$, what are the values of cos θ and tan θ?

Solution. Draw right triangle *ABC* and label *BC*, the side opposite θ, as 15 and the hypotenuse as 17.

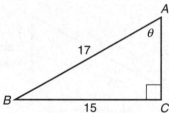

Now use the Pythagorean theorem to find *AC*:

$$(AC)^2 + 15^2 = 17^2 \Rightarrow AC^2 + 225 = 289 \Rightarrow$$
$$(AC)^2 = 64 \Rightarrow AC = 8$$

So, $\cos\theta = \dfrac{8}{17}$ and $\tan\theta = \dfrac{15}{8}$.

If you were given that sin θ = 0.835, you would proceed exactly the same way. Draw a triangle and use the Pythagorean theorem to get

$$x^2 + (0.835)^2 = 1^2 \Rightarrow x^2 + 0.697 = 1 \Rightarrow x^2 = 0.303 \Rightarrow x = 0.55$$

Now use SohCahToa:

$$\cos\theta = \frac{0.55}{1} = 0.55 \text{ and } \tan\theta = \frac{0.835}{0.55} = 1.52$$

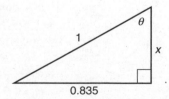

➡ Example 3

What are the values of *a* and *b* in the triangle below?

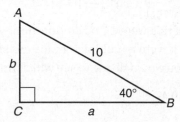

Solution. To find *a* and *b*, you can use the sine and cosine ratios:

$$\sin 40° = \frac{b}{10} \Rightarrow b = 10(\sin 40°) = 10(0.643) = 6.43$$

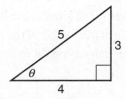 $$\cos 40° = \frac{a}{10} \Rightarrow a = 10(\cos 40°) = 10(0.766) = 7.66$$

Alternatively, you could find either *a* or *b* by using a trigonometric ratio, as above, and then find the other variable by using the Pythagorean theorem. For example, if as above you find that *b* = 6.43, then

$$a^2 + (6.43)^2 = 10^2 \Rightarrow a^2 + 41.34 = 100 \Rightarrow a^2 = 58.66 \Rightarrow a = 7.66$$

You could also be asked to find the measure of an angle θ if you are given the value of the sine, cosine, or tangent of that angle. For example, if you are given that $\sin \theta = 0.8$, to find the value of θ, you use your calculator to evaluate the inverse sine or arcsin of 0.8, written $\sin^{-1}(0.8)$. On most calculators, SIN^{-1} is the second function button above the SIN button. So depending on your calculator, you would either press [2nd] [SIN] [.8] [enter] or [.8] [2nd] [SIN].

➡ Example 4

What is the measure of the smallest angle in a 3-4-5 triangle?

Solution. Draw and label the triangle, which you should immediately recognize as a right triangle.

By KEY FACT J3, the smallest angle is opposite the smallest side. So $\sin \theta = \frac{3}{5}$ and $\theta = \sin^{-1}\left(\frac{3}{5}\right) = 36.87°$. Note that you can convert $\frac{3}{5}$ to 0.6 and take $\sin^{-1}(0.6)$, but that isn't necessary.

Using the inverse sine gives an alternative solution to Example 2, in which you were asked to find the value of cos θ given that $\sin \theta = \frac{15}{17}$. Use your calculator to evaluate:

$$\theta = \sin^{-1}\left(\frac{15}{17}\right) \approx 61.93$$

Then cos (61.93) = 0.4705. If this were a grid-in question, you should bubble in .470 (it's not necessary to round up). If it were a multiple-choice question and if the answer choices were fractions, not decimals, you would divide to see which fraction was equal to (or virtually equal to) 0.4705; in fact, $\frac{8}{17}$ = 0.4705.

➡ **Example 5** _____

A 20-foot ladder is leaning against a vertical wall. If the base of the ladder is 13 feet from the wall, what is the angle formed by the ladder and the ground?

Solution. Of course, you start by drawing a diagram.

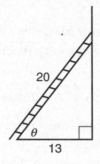

Then:

$$\cos \theta = \frac{13}{20} \Rightarrow \theta = \cos^{-1}\left(\frac{13}{20}\right) = 49.46°$$

Mathematicians sometimes use ***radians*** instead of degrees to measure angles. Since there will be at most one question on the SAT involving radian measure, this is really a topic you can skip if you are not already familiar with the concept.

Recall that an arc of a circle consists of two points on the circle and all the points between them. On the SAT, arc $\overset{\frown}{AB}$ always refers to the smaller arc joining A and B. The ***radian measure*** of a central angle of a circle is the ratio of the length of the arc cut off by the angle to the radius. In the figure below, θ, measured in radians, is equal to the length of the arc, s, divided by the radius, r: $\theta = \frac{s}{r}$.

   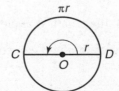

$m\angle COD = 180° = \pi r$ radians

Since the length of the circumference of a circle of radius, r, is $2\pi r$, the length of semi-circular arc $\overset{\frown}{CD}$ in the figure above is πr. So the radian measure of straight angle COD is $\frac{\pi r}{r} = \pi$. Since the degree measure of straight angle COD is 180°, we have the following conversions between radians and degrees:

π radians = 180° $\qquad$ 2π radians = 360° $\qquad$ $\frac{\pi}{2}$ radians = 90° $\qquad$ $\frac{\pi}{4}$ radians = 45°

$$1 \text{ radian} = \left(\frac{180}{\pi}\right)^{\circ} \qquad 1° = \frac{\pi}{180} \text{ radians}$$

If a question on the SAT involves radian measure and if you are determined to answer it, your best strategy would be to convert from radians to degrees. For example, to evaluate $\sin\frac{\pi}{6}$, convert $\frac{\pi}{6}$ radians to $\frac{180}{6} = 30°$ and then use your calculator to evaluate $\sin 30°$: $\sin 30° = 0.5$.

➡ **Example 6** _____

If $\sin\theta = a$, what is the value of $\sin(\pi - \theta)$?

(A) 0
(B) $-a$
(C) a
(D) $\frac{1}{a}$

Solution. The best way to answer a question like this on the SAT is to pick a simple value for θ, measured in degrees, say $\theta = 30°$. Then $\pi - \theta$ radians = 180° − 30° = 150°.

Now use your calculator to evaluate $\sin 30°$ and $\sin 150°$. They are both equal to 0.5, so the answer is choice (**C**).

What You *Don't* Need To Know

We have just reviewed the ONLY trigonometry you need to know for the SAT. Here is a list of several topics in trigonometry that you may have studied in school that are NOT included on the SAT:

- Angles whose measures are negative
- Reference angles
- The reciprocal trigonometric functions: secant, cosecant, and cotangent
- Graphs of the trigonometric and inverse trigonometric functions
- The law of sines and the law of cosines
- The trigonometric formula for the areas of a triangle and parallelogram
- Double-angle formulas and half-angle formulas
- Trigonometric identities

1. In the triangle below, what is the sum of a and b?

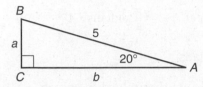

(A) 5
(B) 6.41
(C) 7.17
(D) 8.45

2. A ladder is leaning against a wall, forming an angle of 65° with the ground. If the foot of the ladder is 8 feet from the wall, what is the length of the ladder, in feet?

(A) 7.25
(B) 8.83
(C) 17.15
(D) 18.93

3. If $0° < \theta < 90°$ and $\tan \theta = 5$, what is $\sin \theta + \cos \theta$?

(A) 0.85
(B) 1
(C) 1.18
(D) 5.2

4. What is the measure of the smallest angle in a 5-12-13 right triangle?

(A) 15°
(B) 21°
(C) 22.6°
(D) 45°

5. If $\triangle ABC$ is isosceles and $m\angle C = 90°$, which of the following must be true?

I. $\tan A = 1$
II. $\sin A = \cos A$
III. $\sin A = \cos B$

(A) I only
(B) II only
(C) I and II only
(D) I, II, and III

6. A kite string is tied to a peg in the ground. If the angle formed by the string and the ground is 70° and if there is 100 feet of string out, to the nearest foot, how high above the ground is the kite?

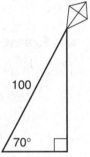

(A) 34
(B) 64
(C) 74
(D) 94

7. If the longer leg of a right triangle is twice as long as the shorter leg, what is the ratio of the measure of the larger acute angle to the measure of the smaller acute angle?

(A) 1.50
(B) 1.78
(C) 2.00
(D) 2.39

8. A car is parked 120 feet from a building that is 350 feet tall. What is the measure of the angle of depression from the top of the building to the car?

(A) 18.9°
(B) 64.2°
(C) 71.1°
(D) 78.6°

Answer Key

1. **B**	3. **C**	5. **D**	7. **D**
2. **D**	4. **C**	6. **D**	8. **C**

Answers Explained

1. **(B)** Use the sine and cosine ratios:

   $$\sin 20° = \frac{a}{5} \Rightarrow a = 5(\sin 20°) = 5(0.342) = 1.710$$

   $$\cos 20° = \frac{b}{5} \Rightarrow b = 5(\cos 20°) = 5(0.940) = 4.700$$

   $$\text{So } a + b = 1.710 + 4.700 = 6.41$$

2. **(D)** First draw a diagram.

   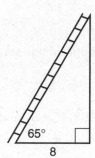

   By using the cosine ratio, we get that $\cos 65° = \dfrac{8}{L}$, where L represents the length of the ladder.

   $$L \cos 65° = 8 \Rightarrow$$
   $$L = 8 \div (\cos 65°) = 18.93$$

3. **(C)** Draw a right triangle. Since $\tan \theta = \dfrac{\text{opposite}}{\text{adjacent}}$, label the side opposite θ as 5 and the side adjacent to θ as 1.

   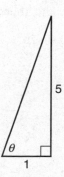

   Then use the Pythagorean theorem to find the hypotenuse:

   $$1^2 + 5^2 = c^2 \Rightarrow c^2 = 1 + 25 = 26 \Rightarrow c = \sqrt{26}$$

So $\sin \theta = \dfrac{5}{\sqrt{26}}$ and $\cos \theta = \dfrac{1}{\sqrt{26}}$. Then:

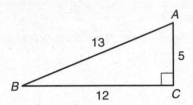

$$\sin \theta + \cos \theta = \frac{5}{\sqrt{26}} + \frac{1}{\sqrt{26}} = \frac{6}{\sqrt{26}} = 1.18$$

Alternatively, you could have found that $\theta = \tan^{-1}(5) = 78.69°$ and then added $\sin 78.69 + \cos 78.69 = 1.18$.

4. **(C)** Draw and label a 5-12-13 right triangle.

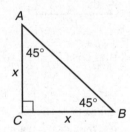

The smallest angle is B, the angle opposite the smallest side. Since $\sin B = \dfrac{5}{13}$, we have $B = \sin^{-1}\left(\dfrac{5}{13}\right) = 22.6°$.

5. **(D)** Sketch isosceles right $\triangle ABC$ with $AC = BC$ and $m\angle A = m\angle B = 45°$.

Then $\tan A = \dfrac{x}{x} = 1$ (I is true). $\sin A$, $\cos A$, $\sin B$, and $\cos B$ are all equal to $\dfrac{x}{AB}$ (II and III are true). Note that $\sin 45° = \cos 45° = 0.707$.

6. **(D)** If x represents the height of the kite, then:

$$\sin 70° = \frac{x}{100} \Rightarrow x = 100 \sin 70° = 100(0.9396) = 93.96 \approx 94$$

7. **(D)** Draw and label a diagram.

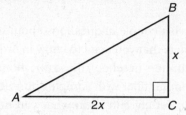

Then:

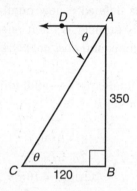

$$\tan B = \frac{2x}{x} = 2 \Rightarrow m\angle B = \tan^{-1}(2) = 63.435°$$

$$\tan A = \frac{x}{2x} = \frac{1}{2} \Rightarrow m\angle A = \tan^{-1}(0.5) = 26.565°$$

$$\text{So } \frac{m\angle B}{m\angle A} = \frac{63.435}{26.565} = 2.39$$

8. **(C)** Draw a diagram and label it.

The angle of depression, $\angle DAC$, is the angle between the line of sight and the horizontal and by KEY FACT I6 is congruent to $\angle C$. Since $\tan C = \frac{350}{120}$, $m\angle C = \tan^{-1}\left(\frac{350}{120}\right) = 71.1°$.

The SAT you take will likely have a couple of questions about imaginary and complex numbers. This section reviews the facts that you need to know in order to answer those questions. If you have studied complex numbers in school, these questions should present no difficulty. If, on the other hand, you are not familiar with complex numbers, you have two choices.

You can study this section carefully and learn what you need to know to answer those questions. Alternatively, you can save the time and effort and just not worry about this topic. Anytime you encounter a question involving the letter i (the imaginary unit), ignore it; *just take a wild guess and move on.* Remember that you don't need to attempt all of the questions to do really well. Correctly answering only 40 of the 58 math questions on the SAT can earn you a score over 600. Correctly answering 50 of the 58 questions can earn you a score over 700! (See page 18 for more information about the number of questions you should attempt.)

Imaginary Numbers

If x is a real number, then x is positive, negative, or zero. If $x = 0$, then $x^2 = 0$; and if x is either positive or negative, then x^2 is positive. So if x is a real number, x^2 CANNOT be negative.

In the set of real numbers, the equation $x^2 = -1$ has no solution. In order to solve such an equation, mathematicians defined a new number, i, called the **imaginary unit**, with the property that $i^2 = -1$. This number is often referred to as the square root of -1: $i = \sqrt{-1}$. Note that i is *not* a real number and *does not correspond to any point on the number line.*

All of the normal operations of mathematics—addition, subtraction, multiplication, and division—can be applied to the number i.

Addition:	$i + i = 2i$	$2i + 5i = 7i$
Subtraction:	$i - i = 0$	$2i - 5i = -3i$
Multiplication:	$(i)(i) = i^2 = -1$	$(2i)(5i) = 10i^2 = 10(-1) = -10$
Division:	$\dfrac{i}{i} = 1$	$\dfrac{2i}{5i} = \dfrac{2}{5}$

Key Fact T1

If x is a positive number, then $\sqrt{-x} = \sqrt{-1}\sqrt{x} = i\sqrt{x}$.

➡ Example 1

$$\sqrt{-16} = \sqrt{16}\sqrt{-1} = 4i \text{ and}$$
$$\sqrt{-12} = \sqrt{-1}\sqrt{12} = \sqrt{-1}\sqrt{4}\sqrt{3} = i \cdot 2 \cdot \sqrt{3} = 2i\sqrt{3}$$

CAUTION

$(\sqrt{-4})(\sqrt{-4}) =$
$(2i)(2i) = 4i^2 = -4$
$(\sqrt{-4})(\sqrt{-4})$ is
not equal to
$\sqrt{(-4)(-4)} = \sqrt{16} = 4$

➧ Example 2

What is $5\sqrt{-25} - 3\sqrt{-64}$?

Solution.

$$5\sqrt{-25} = 5\sqrt{-1}\sqrt{25} = (5i)(5) = 25i \text{ and}$$

$$3\sqrt{-64} = 3\sqrt{-1}\sqrt{64} = (3i)(8) = 24i$$

$$\text{Therefore, } 5\sqrt{-25} - 3\sqrt{-64} = 25i - 24i = i$$

On the SAT, you could be asked to raise i to some positive integer power. In particular, note:

$i^1 = i$ $(a^1 = a$ for *any* number)
$i^2 = -1$ (by definition)
$i^3 = -i$ $i \cdot i \cdot i = (i \cdot i)(i) = i^2 \cdot i = -1(i) = -i$
$i^4 = 1$ $i^4 = i \cdot i \cdot i \cdot i = (i \cdot i)(i \cdot i) = (-1)(-1) = 1$
$i^5 = i$ $i^5 = i^4 \cdot i = 1 \cdot i = i$
$i^6 = -1$ $i^6 = i^5 \cdot i = i \cdot i = i^2 = -1$
$i^7 = -i$ $i^7 = i^6 \cdot i = (-1)i = -i$
$i^8 = 1$ $i^8 = i^7 \cdot i = (-i)(i) = -i^2 = -(-1) = 1$

Note that the powers of i form a repeating sequence in which the four terms, $i, -1, -i, 1$ repeat in that order indefinitely.

As you will see in KEY FACT T2, this means that to find the value of i^n for any positive integer n, you should divide n by 4 and calculate the remainder.

Key Fact T2

For any positive integer n:

- **If n is a multiple of 4, $i^n = 1$.**
- **If n is not a multiple of 4, $i^n = i^r$, where r is the remainder when n is divided by 4.**

➧ Example 3

To evaluate i^{375}, use your calculator to divide 375 by 4:

$$375 \div 4 = 93.75 \Rightarrow \text{the quotient is 93}$$

Then multiply 93 by 4:

$$93 \times 4 = 372 \Rightarrow \text{the remainder is } 375 - 372 = 3$$

So $i^{375} = i^3 = -i$.

NOTE: The concepts of *positive* and *negative* apply only to real numbers. If a is positive, a is to the right of 0 on the number line. Since imaginary numbers do not lie on the number line, you cannot compare them. It is meaningless even to ask whether i is positive or negative or whether $12i$ is greater than or less than $7i$.

Complex Numbers

The imaginary unit can be added to and multiplied by real numbers to form *complex numbers*. Every complex number can be written in the form $a + bi$, where a and b are real numbers. a is called the *real part* and bi the *imaginary part* of the complex number $a + bi$. Two complex numbers are equal if, and only if, their real parts are equal and their imaginary parts are equal.

Key Fact T3

If $a + bi = c + di$, then $a = c$ and $b = d$.

➡ Example 4

If $2(3 + yi) = x + 8i$, what are the values of x and y?

Solution.

$$x + 8i = 2(3 + yi) \Rightarrow x + 8i = 6 + 2yi$$

$$\text{So, } x = 6 \text{ and } 8 = 2y \Rightarrow x = 6 \text{ and } y = 4$$

The *conjugate* of the complex number $a + bi$ is the complex number $a - bi$.

The arithmetic of complex numbers follows all the rules you are familiar with for real numbers. KEY FACT T4, below, gives you these rules and demonstrates each one using the complex numbers $3 + 5i$ and $2 + 3i$.

Key Fact T4

- **To add complex numbers, add their real parts and add their imaginary parts. For example:**

$$(3 + 5i) + (2 + 3i) = 5 + 8i$$

- **To subtract complex numbers, subtract their real parts and subtract their imaginary parts. For example:**

$$(3 + 5i) - (2 + 3i) = 1 + 2i$$

- **To multiply complex numbers, "FOIL" them as if they were binomials and then replace i^2 by -1. For example:**

$$(3 + 5i)(2 + 3i) = 6 + 9i + 10i + 15i^2$$
$$= 6 + 19i + 15(-1)$$
$$= 6 + 19i - 15$$
$$= -9 + 19i$$

- The product of the complex number $(a + bi)$ and its conjugate $(a - bi)$ is the real number $a^2 + b^2$:

$$(a + bi)(a - bi) = a^2 - (bi)^2 = a^2 - b^2(-1) = a^2 + b^2$$

For example: $(2 + 3i)(2 - 3i) = 2^2 + 3^2 = 4 + 9 = 13$

- To divide two complex numbers, write the quotient as a fraction, and multiply the numerator and the denominator by the conjugate of the denominator. For example:

$$(3 + 5i) \div (2 + 3i) = \frac{3 + 5i}{2 + 3i} = \frac{3 + 5i}{2 + 3i} \cdot \frac{2 - 3i}{2 - 3i} = \frac{6 - 9i + 10i - 15i^2}{4 + 9} = \frac{21 + i}{13} = \frac{21}{13} + \frac{1}{13}i$$

1. If a and b are real numbers and if $ai^2 = bi^4$, which of the following must be true?

   I. $a = b$
   II. $a = -b$
   III. $|a| = |b|$

   (A) I only
   (B) II only
   (C) III only
   (D) II and III only

2. Which of the following is a negative number?

   (A) i^{25}
   (B) i^{50}
   (C) i^{75}
   (D) i^{100}

3. Which of the following is equal to $(1 + i)^2$?

   (A) -2
   (B) 2
   (C) $-2i$
   (D) $2i$

4. If a and b are real numbers, which of the following is equal to $(a + bi)(a - bi)$?

   (A) $a^2 - b^2$
   (B) $a^2 + b^2$
   (C) $a^2 + 2abi - b^2$
   (D) $a^2 - 2abi + b^2$

5. If a, b, c, and d are consecutive positive integers, what is the value of $i^a + i^b + i^c + i^d$?

   (A) 0
   (B) -1
   (C) 1
   (D) i

6. If $i^m = i^n$, which of the following must be true?

   I. $m = n$
   II. $m + n$ is even
   III. $n - m$ is a multiple of 4.

   (A) I only
   (B) I and III only
   (C) II and III only
   (D) I, II, and III

7. If $(a + bi)(c + di)$ is a real number, which of the following statements must be true?

   (A) $ac = bd$
   (B) $ac = -bd$
   (C) $ad = bc$
   (D) $ad = -bc$

8. If $(3 + 5i) \div (2 + 3i) = (a + bi)$, then what is the value of $(a + b)$?

   (A) $-\dfrac{8}{13}$
   (B) $\dfrac{8}{13}$
   (C) $-\dfrac{22}{13}$
   (D) $\dfrac{22}{13}$

Answer Key

Answers Explained

1. **(D)** Since $i^2 = -1$ and $i^4 = 1$, $ai^2 = bi^4 \Rightarrow a(-1) = b(1) \Rightarrow -a = b$. Hence $a = -b$ and $|a| = |-b| = |b|$. (II and III are true.) Statement I *could* be true—if a and b were each 0—but does not have to be true: $-2i^2 = 2i^4$, but $-2 \neq 2$. Only statements II and III are true.

2. **(B)** Since 100 and 200 are multiples of 4, $i^{100} = i^{200} = 1$. The remainders when 25, 50, and 75 are divided by 4 are 1, 2, and 3, respectively. Therefore, $i^{25} = i$, $i^{50} = -1$, and $i^{75} = -i$. Of these, only i^{50} is a negative number.

3. **(D)** $(1 + i)^2 = (1 + i)(1 + i) = 1 + 2i + i^2 = 1 + 2i + (-1) = 2i$

4. **(B)** $(a + bi)(a - bi) = a^2 - abi + abi - b^2 i^2 = a^2 - b^2(-1) = a^2 + b^2$

5. **(A)** Since the values of the power of i repeat indefinitely in groups of four, i^a, i^b, i^c, i^d are in some order: $i, -1, -i,$ and 1. So their sum is $i + (-1) + (-i) + 1 = 0$.

6. **(C)** Since $i^4 = i^8 = 1$, I is false. If m is odd and n is even, then i^m equals i or $-i$ and i^n equals 1 or -1, so $i^m \neq i^n$. Similarly, it can't be that m is even and n is odd. Therefore, m and n are both even or both odd. In either case, $m + n$ is even (II is true). In fact, $i^n = i^m \Rightarrow \dfrac{i^n}{i^m} = 1 \Rightarrow i^{n-m} = 1 \Rightarrow n - m$ is a multiple of 4 (III is true). Only statements II and III are true.

7. **(D)** $(a + bi)(c + di) = ac + adi + bci + bdi^2 = ac - bd + (ad + bc)i$
   In order for a complex number to be real, the coefficient of i has to be 0.
   So $ad + bc = 0$ and $ad = -bc$.

8. **(D)** $(3 + 5i) \div (2 + 3i) = \dfrac{3 + 5i}{2 + 3i} \cdot \dfrac{2 - 3i}{2 - 3i} = \dfrac{6 - 9i + 10i - 15i^2}{4 - 9i^2} = \dfrac{6 + i(-15)(-1)}{4 + 9} = \dfrac{21 + 1}{13} = \dfrac{21}{13} + \dfrac{1i}{13}$
   So $a = \dfrac{21}{13}$ and $b = \dfrac{1}{13}$. Therefore $a + b = \dfrac{22}{13}$.

PART SIX
Test Yourself

ANSWER SHEET
Model Test 1

MODEL TEST 1

Section 1: Reading

1. Ⓐ Ⓑ Ⓒ Ⓓ	14. Ⓐ Ⓑ Ⓒ Ⓓ	27. Ⓐ Ⓑ Ⓒ Ⓓ	40. Ⓐ Ⓑ Ⓒ Ⓓ
2. Ⓐ Ⓑ Ⓒ Ⓓ	15. Ⓐ Ⓑ Ⓒ Ⓓ	28. Ⓐ Ⓑ Ⓒ Ⓓ	41. Ⓐ Ⓑ Ⓒ Ⓓ
3. Ⓐ Ⓑ Ⓒ Ⓓ	16. Ⓐ Ⓑ Ⓒ Ⓓ	29. Ⓐ Ⓑ Ⓒ Ⓓ	42. Ⓐ Ⓑ Ⓒ Ⓓ
4. Ⓐ Ⓑ Ⓒ Ⓓ	17. Ⓐ Ⓑ Ⓒ Ⓓ	30. Ⓐ Ⓑ Ⓒ Ⓓ	43. Ⓐ Ⓑ Ⓒ Ⓓ
5. Ⓐ Ⓑ Ⓒ Ⓓ	18. Ⓐ Ⓑ Ⓒ Ⓓ	31. Ⓐ Ⓑ Ⓒ Ⓓ	44. Ⓐ Ⓑ Ⓒ Ⓓ
6. Ⓐ Ⓑ Ⓒ Ⓓ	19. Ⓐ Ⓑ Ⓒ Ⓓ	32. Ⓐ Ⓑ Ⓒ Ⓓ	45. Ⓐ Ⓑ Ⓒ Ⓓ
7. Ⓐ Ⓑ Ⓒ Ⓓ	20. Ⓐ Ⓑ Ⓒ Ⓓ	33. Ⓐ Ⓑ Ⓒ Ⓓ	46. Ⓐ Ⓑ Ⓒ Ⓓ
8. Ⓐ Ⓑ Ⓒ Ⓓ	21. Ⓐ Ⓑ Ⓒ Ⓓ	34. Ⓐ Ⓑ Ⓒ Ⓓ	47. Ⓐ Ⓑ Ⓒ Ⓓ
9. Ⓐ Ⓑ Ⓒ Ⓓ	22. Ⓐ Ⓑ Ⓒ Ⓓ	35. Ⓐ Ⓑ Ⓒ Ⓓ	48. Ⓐ Ⓑ Ⓒ Ⓓ
10. Ⓐ Ⓑ Ⓒ Ⓓ	23. Ⓐ Ⓑ Ⓒ Ⓓ	36. Ⓐ Ⓑ Ⓒ Ⓓ	49. Ⓐ Ⓑ Ⓒ Ⓓ
11. Ⓐ Ⓑ Ⓒ Ⓓ	24. Ⓐ Ⓑ Ⓒ Ⓓ	37. Ⓐ Ⓑ Ⓒ Ⓓ	50. Ⓐ Ⓑ Ⓒ Ⓓ
12. Ⓐ Ⓑ Ⓒ Ⓓ	25. Ⓐ Ⓑ Ⓒ Ⓓ	38. Ⓐ Ⓑ Ⓒ Ⓓ	51. Ⓐ Ⓑ Ⓒ Ⓓ
13. Ⓐ Ⓑ Ⓒ Ⓓ	26. Ⓐ Ⓑ Ⓒ Ⓓ	39. Ⓐ Ⓑ Ⓒ Ⓓ	52. Ⓐ Ⓑ Ⓒ Ⓓ

Section 2: Writing and Language

1. Ⓐ Ⓑ Ⓒ Ⓓ	12. Ⓐ Ⓑ Ⓒ Ⓓ	23. Ⓐ Ⓑ Ⓒ Ⓓ	34. Ⓐ Ⓑ Ⓒ Ⓓ
2. Ⓐ Ⓑ Ⓒ Ⓓ	13. Ⓐ Ⓑ Ⓒ Ⓓ	24. Ⓐ Ⓑ Ⓒ Ⓓ	35. Ⓐ Ⓑ Ⓒ Ⓓ
3. Ⓐ Ⓑ Ⓒ Ⓓ	14. Ⓐ Ⓑ Ⓒ Ⓓ	25. Ⓐ Ⓑ Ⓒ Ⓓ	36. Ⓐ Ⓑ Ⓒ Ⓓ
4. Ⓐ Ⓑ Ⓒ Ⓓ	15. Ⓐ Ⓑ Ⓒ Ⓓ	26. Ⓐ Ⓑ Ⓒ Ⓓ	37. Ⓐ Ⓑ Ⓒ Ⓓ
5. Ⓐ Ⓑ Ⓒ Ⓓ	16. Ⓐ Ⓑ Ⓒ Ⓓ	27. Ⓐ Ⓑ Ⓒ Ⓓ	38. Ⓐ Ⓑ Ⓒ Ⓓ
6. Ⓐ Ⓑ Ⓒ Ⓓ	17. Ⓐ Ⓑ Ⓒ Ⓓ	28. Ⓐ Ⓑ Ⓒ Ⓓ	39. Ⓐ Ⓑ Ⓒ Ⓓ
7. Ⓐ Ⓑ Ⓒ Ⓓ	18. Ⓐ Ⓑ Ⓒ Ⓓ	29. Ⓐ Ⓑ Ⓒ Ⓓ	40. Ⓐ Ⓑ Ⓒ Ⓓ
8. Ⓐ Ⓑ Ⓒ Ⓓ	19. Ⓐ Ⓑ Ⓒ Ⓓ	30. Ⓐ Ⓑ Ⓒ Ⓓ	41. Ⓐ Ⓑ Ⓒ Ⓓ
9. Ⓐ Ⓑ Ⓒ Ⓓ	20. Ⓐ Ⓑ Ⓒ Ⓓ	31. Ⓐ Ⓑ Ⓒ Ⓓ	42. Ⓐ Ⓑ Ⓒ Ⓓ
10. Ⓐ Ⓑ Ⓒ Ⓓ	21. Ⓐ Ⓑ Ⓒ Ⓓ	32. Ⓐ Ⓑ Ⓒ Ⓓ	43. Ⓐ Ⓑ Ⓒ Ⓓ
11. Ⓐ Ⓑ Ⓒ Ⓓ	22. Ⓐ Ⓑ Ⓒ Ⓓ	33. Ⓐ Ⓑ Ⓒ Ⓓ	44. Ⓐ Ⓑ Ⓒ Ⓓ

Section 3: Math (No Calculator)

1. Ⓐ Ⓑ Ⓒ Ⓓ   5. Ⓐ Ⓑ Ⓒ Ⓓ   9. Ⓐ Ⓑ Ⓒ Ⓓ   13. Ⓐ Ⓑ Ⓒ Ⓓ
2. Ⓐ Ⓑ Ⓒ Ⓓ   6. Ⓐ Ⓑ Ⓒ Ⓓ   10. Ⓐ Ⓑ Ⓒ Ⓓ   14. Ⓐ Ⓑ Ⓒ Ⓓ
3. Ⓐ Ⓑ Ⓒ Ⓓ   7. Ⓐ Ⓑ Ⓒ Ⓓ   11. Ⓐ Ⓑ Ⓒ Ⓓ   15. Ⓐ Ⓑ Ⓒ Ⓓ
4. Ⓐ Ⓑ Ⓒ Ⓓ   8. Ⓐ Ⓑ Ⓒ Ⓓ   12. Ⓐ Ⓑ Ⓒ Ⓓ

16.   17.   18.

19.   20.

ANSWER SHEET
Model Test 1

Section 4: Math (Calculator)

1. Ⓐ Ⓑ Ⓒ Ⓓ
2. Ⓐ Ⓑ Ⓒ Ⓓ
3. Ⓐ Ⓑ Ⓒ Ⓓ
4. Ⓐ Ⓑ Ⓒ Ⓓ
5. Ⓐ Ⓑ Ⓒ Ⓓ
6. Ⓐ Ⓑ Ⓒ Ⓓ
7. Ⓐ Ⓑ Ⓒ Ⓓ
8. Ⓐ Ⓑ Ⓒ Ⓓ

9. Ⓐ Ⓑ Ⓒ Ⓓ
10. Ⓐ Ⓑ Ⓒ Ⓓ
11. Ⓐ Ⓑ Ⓒ Ⓓ
12. Ⓐ Ⓑ Ⓒ Ⓓ
13. Ⓐ Ⓑ Ⓒ Ⓓ
14. Ⓐ Ⓑ Ⓒ Ⓓ
15. Ⓐ Ⓑ Ⓒ Ⓓ
16. Ⓐ Ⓑ Ⓒ Ⓓ

17. Ⓐ Ⓑ Ⓒ Ⓓ
18. Ⓐ Ⓑ Ⓒ Ⓓ
19. Ⓐ Ⓑ Ⓒ Ⓓ
20. Ⓐ Ⓑ Ⓒ Ⓓ
21. Ⓐ Ⓑ Ⓒ Ⓓ
22. Ⓐ Ⓑ Ⓒ Ⓓ
23. Ⓐ Ⓑ Ⓒ Ⓓ
24. Ⓐ Ⓑ Ⓒ Ⓓ

25. Ⓐ Ⓑ Ⓒ Ⓓ
26. Ⓐ Ⓑ Ⓒ Ⓓ
27. Ⓐ Ⓑ Ⓒ Ⓓ
28. Ⓐ Ⓑ Ⓒ Ⓓ
29. Ⓐ Ⓑ Ⓒ Ⓓ
30. Ⓐ Ⓑ Ⓒ Ⓓ

31. [grid-in response field]
32. [grid-in response field]
33. [grid-in response field]
34. [grid-in response field]

35. [grid-in response field]
36. [grid-in response field]
37. [grid-in response field]
38. [grid-in response field]

ANSWER SHEET
Model Test 1

Essay

PLANNING PAGE

READING TEST

65 MINUTES, 52 QUESTIONS

Turn to Section 1 of your answer sheet to answer the questions in this section.

Directions: Following each of the passages (or pairs of passages) below are questions about the passage (or passages). Read each passage carefully. Then, select the best answer for each question based on what is stated in the passage (or passages) and in any graphics that may accompany the passage.

Questions 1–11 are based on the following passage.

In this adaptation of an excerpt from An Incident at Owl Creek Bridge, *a short story set in Civil War times, a man is about to be hanged. The first two paragraphs set the scene; the remainder of the passage presents a flashback to an earlier, critical encounter.*

A man stood upon a railroad bridge in Northern Alabama, looking down into the swift waters twenty feet below. The man's
Line hands were behind his back, the wrists
(5) bound with a cord. A rope loosely encircled his neck. It was attached to a stout cross-timber above his head, and the slack fell to the level of his knees. Some loose boards laid upon the sleepers supporting the metals of
(10) the railway supplied a footing for him and his executioners—two private soldiers of the Federal army, directed by a sergeant, who in civil life may have been a deputy sheriff. At a short remove upon the same temporary
(15) platform was an officer in the uniform of his rank, armed. He was a captain. A sentinel at each end of the bridge stood with his rifle in the position known as 'support'—a formal and unnatural position, enforcing an erect
(20) carriage of the body. It did not appear to be the duty of these two men to know what was occurring at the center of the bridge; they

merely blockaded the two ends of the foot plank which traversed it.
(25)   The man who was engaged in being hanged was apparently about thirty-five years of age. He was a civilian, if one might judge from his dress, which was that of a planter. His features were good—a straight
(30) nose, firm mouth, broad forehead, from which his long, dark hair was combed straight back, falling behind his ears to the collar of his well-fitting frock coat. He wore a moustache and pointed beard, but no
(35) whiskers; his eyes were large and dark grey and had a kindly expression that one would hardly have expected in one whose neck was in the hemp. Evidently this was no vulgar assassin. The liberal military code makes
(40) provision for hanging many kinds of people, and gentlemen are not excluded.
     Peyton Farquhar was a well-to-do planter, of an old and highly respected Alabama family. Being a slave-owner, and, like other
(45) slave-owners, a politician, he was naturally an original secessionist and ardently devoted to the Southern cause. Circumstances had prevented him from taking service with the gallant army that had fought the disastrous
(50) campaigns ending with the fall of Corinth, and he chafed under the inglorious restraint, longing for the release of his energies, the larger life of the soldier, the opportunity for distinction. That opportunity, he felt,

GO ON TO THE NEXT PAGE

(55) would come, as it comes to all in war time. Meanwhile, he did what he could. No service was too humble for him to perform in aid of the South, no adventure too perilous for him to undertake if consistent with the character
(60) of a civilian who was at heart a soldier, and who in good faith and without too much qualification assented to at least a part of the frankly villainous dictum that all is fair in love and war.

(65)   One evening while Farquhar and his wife were sitting near the entrance to his grounds, a grey-clad soldier rode up to the gate and asked for a drink of water. Mrs. Farquhar was only too happy to serve him with her own
(70) white hands. While she was gone to fetch the water, her husband approached the dusty horseman and inquired eagerly for news from the front.

    "The Yanks are repairing the railroads,"
(75) said the man, "and are getting ready for another advance. They have reached the Owl Creek bridge, put it in order, and built a stockade on the other bank. The commandant has issued an order, which
(80) is posted everywhere, declaring that any civilian caught interfering with the railroad, its bridges, tunnels, or trains, will be summarily hanged. I saw the order."

    "How far is it to the Owl Creek bridge?"
(85) Farquhar asked.

    "About thirty miles."

    "Is there no force on this side of the creek?"

    "Only a picket post half a mile out, on the
(90) railroad, and a single sentinel at this end of the bridge."

    "Suppose a man—a civilian and a student of hanging—should elude the picket post and perhaps get the better of the sentinel,"
(95) said Farquhar, smiling, "what could he accomplish?"

The soldier reflected. "I was there a month ago," he replied. "I observed that the flood of last winter had lodged a great quantity of
(100) driftwood against the wooden pier at the end of the bridge. It is now dry and would burn like tow."

    The lady had now brought the water, which the soldier drank. He thanked her
(105) ceremoniously, bowed to her husband, and rode away. An hour later, after nightfall, he repassed the plantation, going northward in the direction from which he had come. He was a Yankee scout.

1. As used in line 13, "civil" most nearly means

    (A) polite.
    (B) noncriminal.
    (C) nonmilitary.
    (D) individual.

2. In cinematic terms, the first two paragraphs most nearly resemble

    (A) a wide-angle shot followed by a close-up.
    (B) a sequence of cameo appearances.
    (C) a trailer advertising a feature film.
    (D) two episodes of an ongoing serial.

3. It can most reasonably be inferred from the passage that the man awaiting hanging was

    (A) innocent of any criminal intent.
    (B) an unlikely candidate for execution.
    (C) a victim of mistaken identity.
    (D) purposely assuming a harmless demeanor.

GO ON TO THE NEXT PAGE

1

4. Which choice provides the best evidence for the answer to the previous question?

   (A) Lines 25–27 ("The man . . . age")
   (B) Lines 27–29 ("He was . . . planter")
   (C) Lines 33–38 ("He wore . . . hemp")
   (D) Lines 44–47 ("Being . . . cause")

5. The author's tone in discussing "the liberal military code" (line 39) can best be described as

   (A) approving.
   (B) ironic.
   (C) irked.
   (D) regretful.

6. It can most reasonably be inferred from the passage that Peyton Farquhar would consider which of the following a good example of how a citizen should behave in wartime?

   (A) He should use even underhanded methods to support his cause.
   (B) He should enlist in the army without delay.
   (C) He should turn to politics as a means of enforcing his will.
   (D) He should avoid involving himself in disastrous campaigns.

7. As used in line 59, "consistent" most nearly means

   (A) unchanging.
   (B) compatible.
   (C) logically sound.
   (D) steady and predictable.

8. It can most reasonably be inferred from the passage that Mrs. Farquhar is

   (A) sympathetic to the Confederate cause.
   (B) too proud to perform menial tasks.
   (C) uninterested in news of the war.
   (D) reluctant to ask her slaves to fetch water.

9. Which choice provides the best evidence for the answer to the previous question?

   (A) Lines 56–64 ("No service . . . war")
   (B) Lines 68–70 ("Mrs. Farquhar . . . hands")
   (C) Lines 70–73 ("While she . . . front")
   (D) Lines 104–106 ("He thanked . . . away")

10. From Farquhar's exchange with the soldier (lines 84–102), it can most reasonably be inferred that Farquhar is going to

    (A) sneak across the bridge to join the Confederate forces.
    (B) attempt to burn down the bridge to halt the Yankee advance.
    (C) remove the driftwood blocking the Confederates' access to the bridge.
    (D) undermine the pillars that support the railroad bridge.

11. The main purpose of the concluding sentence of the passage is to

    (A) offer an excuse for Farquhar's failure to destroy the bridge.
    (B) provide context useful in understanding Farquhar's emotional reactions.
    (C) establish that Farquhar has been entrapped into taking an unwise action.
    (D) contrast Farquhar's patriotic behavior with the scout's treachery.

GO ON TO THE NEXT PAGE

MODEL TEST 1

Questions 12–21 are based on the following passage.

The following passage is taken from Franklin Delano Roosevelt's Third Inaugural Address, made on January 20, 1941, nearly a year before the bombing of Pearl Harbor triggered America's entry into the Second World War.

A nation, like a person, has something deeper, something more permanent, something larger than the sum of all its parts.
Line It is that something which matters most to
(5) its future—which calls forth the most sacred guarding of its present.

It is a thing for which we find it difficult— even impossible—to hit upon a single, simple word.

(10) And yet we all understand what it is—the spirit—the faith of America. It is the product of centuries. It was born in the multitudes of those who came from many lands—some of high degree, but mostly plain people, who
(15) sought here, early and late, to find freedom more freely.

The democratic aspiration is no mere recent phase in human history. It is human history. It permeated the ancient life of early
(20) peoples. It blazed anew in the middle ages. It was written in the Magna Carta.

In the Americas its impact has been irresistible. America has been the New World in all tongues, to all peoples, not because this
(25) continent was a new-found land, but because all those who came here believed they could create upon this continent a new life—a life that should be new in freedom.

Its vitality was written into our own
(30) Mayflower Compact, into the Declaration of Independence, into the Constitution of the United States, into the Gettysburg Address.

Those who first came here to carry out the longings of their spirit, and the millions
(35) who followed, and the stock that sprang from them—all have moved forward constantly and consistently toward an ideal which in itself has gained stature and clarity with each generation.

(40) The hopes of the Republic cannot forever tolerate either undeserved poverty or self-serving wealth.

We know that we still have far to go; that we must more greatly build the security
(45) and the opportunity and the knowledge of every citizen, in the measure justified by the resources and the capacity of the land.

But it is not enough to achieve these purposes alone. It is not enough to clothe
(50) and feed the body of this Nation, and instruct and inform its mind. For there is also the spirit. And of the three, the greatest is the spirit.

Without the body and the mind, as all men
(55) know, the Nation could not live.

But if the spirit of America were killed, even though the Nation's body and mind, constricted in an alien world, lived on, the America we know would have perished.

(60) That spirit—that faith—speaks to us in our daily lives in ways often unnoticed, because they seem so obvious. It speaks to us here in the Capital of the Nation. It speaks to us through the processes of governing in the
(65) sovereignties of 48 States. It speaks to us in our counties, in our cities, in our towns, and in our villages. It speaks to us from the other nations of the hemisphere, and from those across the seas—the enslaved, as well as the
(70) free. Sometimes we fail to hear or heed these voices of freedom because to us the privilege of our freedom is such an old, old story.

GO ON TO THE NEXT PAGE

The destiny of America was proclaimed in words of prophecy spoken by our first
(75) President in his first inaugural in 1789—words almost directed, it would seem, to this year of 1941: "*The preservation of the sacred fire of liberty and the destiny of the republican model of government are justly*
(80) *considered . . . deeply, ... finally, staked on the experiment intrusted to the hands of the American people.*"

If we lose that sacred fire—if we let it be smothered with doubt and fear—then we
(85) shall reject the destiny which Washington strove so valiantly and so triumphantly to establish. The preservation of the spirit and faith of the Nation does, and will, furnish the highest justification for every sacrifice
(90) that we may make in the cause of national defense.

In the face of great perils never before encountered, our strong purpose is to protect and to perpetuate the integrity of democracy.
(95) For this we muster the spirit of America, and the faith of America.

We do not retreat. We are not content to stand still. As Americans, we go forward, in the service of our country, by the will of God.

12. As used in line 14, "plain" most nearly means

(A) candid.
(B) ordinary.
(C) homely.
(D) intelligible.

13. The author indicates which of the following about the American belief in freedom?

(A) It lacked any supporters who belonged to the upper classes.
(B) It had its origins at the time of the American Revolution.
(C) It is an ideal that has lost its hold on the public.
(D) It has deep-seated historical roots.

14. Which choice provides the best evidence for the answer to the previous question?

(A) Lines 1–3 ("A nation . . . parts")
(B) Lines 17–21 ("The democratic . . . Carta")
(C) Lines 23–28 ("America has been . . . freedom")
(D) Lines 33–39 ("Those who first . . . generation")

15. The author uses the Mayflower Compact, Declaration of Independence, Constitution, and Gettysburg Address as examples of

(A) subjects of previous inaugural addresses.
(B) expressions of the democratic aspiration.
(C) documents of historical interest.
(D) writings with ongoing legal implications.

GO ON TO THE NEXT PAGE

16. The author recognizes counterarguments to the position he takes in lines 33–39 ("Those who first . . . generation") by

(A) acknowledging that economic injustices must be addressed before democracy can prevail.

(B) admitting that the native-born descendents of our immigrant forebears have lost faith in democracy.

(C) conceding the lack of resources and capacity that hinder the fulfillment of the American dream.

(D) likening the Nation to a human body with physical, mental, and spiritual needs.

17. As used in line 76, "directed" most nearly means

(A) addressed.

(B) ordered.

(C) supervised.

(D) guided.

18. What main effect does the repetition of the phrase "It speaks to us" in lines 62–70 have on the tone of the passage?

(A) It creates a whimsical tone, endowing an abstract quality with a physical voice.

(B) It creates a colloquial tone, describing commonplace activities in ordinary words.

(C) It creates a dramatic tone, emphasizing the point being made and adding to its emotional impact.

(D) It creates a menacing tone, reminding us of our failure to heed the voices of freedom crying for our aid.

19. It can most reasonably be inferred that the experiment to which Washington refers in line 81 is

(A) a scientific investigation.

(B) a presidential inauguration.

(C) democratic government.

(D) national defense.

20. Which choice provides the best evidence for the answer to the previous question?

(A) Lines 56–59 ("But . . . perished")

(B) Lines 60–62 ("That spirit . . . obvious")

(C) Lines 83–87 ("If we . . . establish")

(D) Lines 92–94 ("In the face . . . democracy")

21. It is reasonable to conclude that a major goal of Roosevelt in making this speech was to

(A) inform American citizens of changes of policy in the new administration.

(B) impress his European counterparts with the soundness of America's foreign policy.

(C) encourage American voters to avoid the divisiveness inherent in partisan politics.

(D) inspire the American people to defend the cause of freedom in dangerous times.

GO ON TO THE NEXT PAGE

Questions 22–31 are based on the following passage.

This passage is from Mortal Lessons: Notes on the Art of Surgery, *a classic book written by a contemporary American surgeon about his art.*

One holds the knife as one holds the bow of a cello or a tulip—by the stem. Not palmed nor gripped nor grasped, but lightly, with the
Line tips of the fingers. The knife is not for pressing.
(5) It is for drawing across the field of skin. Like a slender fish, it waits, at the ready, then, go! It darts, followed by a fine wake of red. The flesh parts, falling away to yellow globules of fat. Even now, after so many times, I still marvel at
(10) its power—cold, gleaming, silent. More, I am still struck with dread that it is I in whose hand the blade travels, that my hand is its vehicle, that yet again this terrible steel-bellied thing and I have conspired for a most unnatural
(15) purpose, the laying open of the body of a human being.

A stillness settles in my heart and is carried to my hand. It is the quietude of resolve layered over fear. And it is this resolve that
(20) lowers us, my knife and me, deeper and deeper into the person beneath. It is an entry into the body that is nothing like a caress; still, it is among the gentlest of acts. Then stroke and stroke again, and we are joined by other
(25) instruments, hemostats and forceps, until the wound blooms with strange flowers whose looped handles fall to the sides in steely array.

There is a sound, the tight click of clamps fixing teeth into severed blood vessels, the
(30) snuffle and gargle of the suction machine clearing the field of blood for the next stroke, the litany of monosyllables with which one prays his way down and in: *clamp, sponge, suture, tie, cut.* And there is color. The green
(35) of the cloth, the white of the sponges, the red and yellow of the body. Beneath the fat lies the fascia, the tough fibrous sheet encasing the muscles. It must be sliced and the red beef of the muscles separated. Now there are
(40) retractors to hold apart the wound. Hands move together, part, weave. We are fully engaged, like children absorbed in a game or the craftsmen of some place like Damascus.

Deeper still. The peritoneum, pink and
(45) gleaming and membranous, bulges into the wound. It is grasped with forceps, and opened. For the first time we can see into the cavity of the abdomen. Such a primitive place. One expects to find drawings of
(50) buffalo on the walls. The sense of trespassing is keener now, heightened by the world's light illuminating the organs, their secret colors revealed—maroon and salmon and yellow. The vista is sweetly vulnerable at
(55) this moment, a kind of welcoming. An arc of the liver shines high and on the right, like a dark sun. It laps over the pink sweep of the stomach, from whose lower border the gauzy omentum is draped, and through which veil
(60) one sees, sinuous, slow as just-fed snakes, the indolent coils of the intestine.

You turn aside to wash your gloves. It is a ritual cleansing. One enters this temple doubly washed. Here is man as microcosm,
(65) representing in all his parts the Earth, perhaps the universe.

I must confess that the priestliness of my profession has ever been impressed on me. In the beginning there are vows, taken with
(70) all solemnity. Then there is the endless harsh novitiate of training, much fatigue, much sacrifice. At last one emerges as a celebrant, standing close to the truth lying curtained in the ark of the body. Not surplice and cassock
(75) but mask and gown are your regalia. You hold no chalice, but a knife. There is no wine, no wafer. There are only the facts of blood and flesh.

GO ON TO THE NEXT PAGE

22. The passage is best described as

(A) a definition of a concept.
(B) an example of a particular method.
(C) a lesson on a technique.
(D) a description of a process.

23. It can most reasonably be inferred from the passage that the "wake of red" to which the author refers (line 7) is

(A) a sign of embarrassment.
(B) an infectious rash.
(C) a line of blood.
(D) the blade of the knife.

24. Which choice provides the best evidence for the answer to the previous question?

(A) Lines 1–2 ("One . . . stem")
(B) Lines 2–4 ("Not . . . fingers")
(C) Lines 7–8 ("The flesh . . . fat")
(D) Lines 17–18 ("A stillness . . . hand")

25. As used in line 8, "parts" most nearly means

(A) leaves.
(B) splits.
(C) surrenders.
(D) distributes.

26. As used in line 42, "engaged" most nearly means

(A) betrothed.
(B) engrossed.
(C) hired.
(D) embattled.

27. In lines 49–50, the comment "One expects to find drawings of buffalo on the walls" metaphorically compares the abdominal cavity to

(A) an art gallery.
(B) a zoological display.
(C) a Western film.
(D) a prehistoric cave.

28. The author most likely describes the colors of the internal organs as "secret" (line 52) because

(A) they are beyond ordinary human understanding.
(B) they normally are hidden from sight.
(C) their access is limited to authorized personnel.
(D) they are darker in color than the external organs are.

29. In creating an impression of abdominal surgery for the reader, the author primarily makes use of

(A) comparison with imaginary landscapes.
(B) contrast to other types of surgery.
(C) references to religious imagery.
(D) evocation of the patient's emotions.

GO ON TO THE NEXT PAGE

30. Which choice provides the best evidence for the answer to the previous question?

(A) Lines 36–40 ("Beneath the fat . . . wound")
(B) Lines 44–48 ("The peritoneum . . . abdomen")
(C) Lines 54–57 ("The vista . . . sun")
(D) Lines 62–64 ("It is a . . . washed")

31. One aspect of the passage that may make it difficult to appreciate is the author's apparent assumption throughout that readers will

(A) have qualms about reading descriptions of major surgery.
(B) be already adept at handling surgical tools.
(C) be familiar with the organs and tissues that are named.
(D) relate accounts of specific surgical acts to their own experience of undergoing surgery.

GO ON TO THE NEXT PAGE

Questions 32–42 are based on the following passages.

Passage 1 is taken from a historical study, done in the 1980s, of the relationship between the press and each American president from George Washington to Ronald Reagan. Passage 2 is taken from a 2006 master's thesis on the relationship between the president and the press during the first term of President George W. Bush.

PASSAGE 1

In the shifting relationship between the press and the presidency over nearly two centuries, there has remained one primary
Line constant—the dissatisfaction of one with
(5) the other. No president has escaped press criticism, and no president has considered himself fairly treated. The record of every administration has been the same, beginning with mutual protestations of goodwill,
(10) ending with recriminations and mistrust.

This is the best proof we could have that the American concept of a free press in a free society is a viable idea, whatever defects the media may have. While the Founding Fathers
(15) and their constituencies did not always agree on the role the press should play, there was a basic consensus that the newspaper (the only medium of consequence at the time) should be the buffer state between the rulers
(20) and the ruled. The press could be expected to behave like a watchdog, and government at every level, dependent for its existence on the opinions of those it governed, could expect to resent being watched and having its
(25) shortcomings, real or imaginary, exposed to the public view.

Reduced to such simple terms, the relationship of the presidents to the press since George Washington's first term is
(30) understandable only as an underlying

principle. But this basic concept has been increasingly complicated by the changing nature of the presidency, by the individual nature of presidents, by the rise of other
(35) media, especially television, and by the growing complexity of beliefs about the function of both press and government.

In surveying nearly two centuries of this relationship, it is wise to keep in mind an
(40) axiom of professional historians—that we should be careful not to view the past in terms of our own times, and make judgments accordingly. Certain parallels often become obvious, to be sure, but to assert what an
(45) individual president should or should not have done, by present standards, is to violate historical context. Historians occasionally castigate each other for this failing, and in the case of press and government, the
(50) danger becomes particularly great because the words themselves—"press" and "government," even "presidency"—have changed in meaning so much during the past two hundred years.

(55) It is part of American mythology that the nation was "cradled in liberty" and that the colonists, seeking religious freedom, immediately established a free society, but the facts are quite different. The danger of
(60) an uncontrolled press to those in power was well expressed by Sir William Berkeley, governor of Virginia, when he wrote home to his superiors in 1671: "I thank God there are no free schools nor printing, and I hope
(65) we shall not have these hundred years; for learning has brought disobedience, and heresy, and sects into the world, and printing has divulged them, and libels against the best government, God keep us from both."
(70) There are those in twentieth-century America who would say "Amen" to Berkeley's view of printing and "libels against the best government."

GO ON TO THE NEXT PAGE

Table 1

Solo and Joint Press Conferences by President 1981–2004

President	Total	Solo	Joint	Joint Sessions as Percent of Total
Reagan*	46	46	0	00.0%
George H. W. Bush*	142	83	59	41.5%
Clinton*	193	62	131	67.9%
George W. Bush**	88	20	68	77.3%

*Cited in Kumar, 2003b
**Compiled from *Weekly Compilation of Presidential Documents*

PASSAGE 2

In their analysis of aggressive journalist
(75) behavior in a comparative study of press
conferences held by Presidents Eisenhower
and Reagan, Clayman and Heritage (2002)
developed an original encoding system
according to ten different features of
(80) question design. Their findings showed
significantly greater levels of aggression and
adversarial behavior by the press in dealings
with the more recent president. Clayman,
Elliot, Heritage & McDonald's updated study
(85) (2004) refined the coding process and used a
more continuous sample to test the validity
and reliability of the original study. Their
comparison of journalistic adversarialness
covered each president from Eisenhower to
(90) Clinton and supported original results that
show a long-term decline in deference to the
president. The continuous sample revealed
more volatility than the simpler work on
which it was based but is a further testament
(95) to the increased aggressiveness, sometimes
adversarial treatment prevalent in press
conferences regardless of partisanship or
personal idiosyncrasy.

These findings would suggest that
(100) the increasingly contentious, adversarial
relationship between the press and the
highest ranking executive official has
created a modern press conference where
the president must relinquish more agenda-
(105) setting control than in other communicative
processes. In each session, he subjects
himself to open questioning that is shown to
be significantly less deferential, more direct
and often more aggressive and hostile than
(110) ever before. This would seem an appropriate
justification for the dwindling numbers of
traditional solo press conferences in recent
administrations (Kumar, 2003b).

GO ON TO THE NEXT PAGE

32. The main purpose of Passage 1 is to

(A) examine methods of evaluating the relationship between the press and the president.
(B) argue that the adversarial relationship between the press and the presidency has proven deleterious to both.
(C) present an overview of an inherently conflicted relationship that faces new challenges.
(D) consider a political dilemma created by the mutual antagonism between two major institutions.

33. According to the opening paragraph of Passage 1, all American presidents have experienced

(A) defects in the quality of their press coverage.
(B) goodwill from some reporters in the press corps.
(C) alternating periods of antagonism and harmony with the press.
(D) mutual animosity involving themselves and the press.

34. Which choice provides the best evidence for the answer to the previous question?

(A) Lines 7–10 ("The record . . . mistrust")
(B) Lines 11–14 ("This . . . may have")
(C) Lines 14–20 ("While . . . ruled")
(D) Lines 27–31 ("Reduced . . . principle")

35. As used in line 27, "reduced" most nearly means

(A) decreased.
(B) boiled down.
(C) marked down.
(D) demoted.

36. The authors of Passage 1 caution the reader about judging the actions of long-dead presidents because

(A) historical accounts, when investigated, have proven to be untrustworthy.
(B) contemporary authors have rewritten history to reflect current academic opinions.
(C) readers today cannot fully grasp the significance these actions had in their own time.
(D) history, at best, is an imprecise science.

37. Which choice provides the best evidence for the answer to the previous question?

(A) Lines 1–7 ("In the shifting . . . treated")
(B) Lines 20–26 ("The press . . . public view")
(C) Lines 27–37 ("Reduced . . . government")
(D) Lines 43–54 ("Certain parallels . . . years")

38. In the opening sentence of the final paragraph (lines 55–59) of Passage 1, the authors seek primarily to

(A) define a term.
(B) defend a widely held belief.
(C) correct a misconception.
(D) champion a cause.

39. As used in line 107, "open" most nearly means

(A) receptive.
(B) unrestricted.
(C) unconcealed.
(D) vulnerable.

GO ON TO THE NEXT PAGE

40. Data in the graph about presidential solo and joint press conferences from 1981–2004 most strongly support which of the following statements?

(A) President Clinton held more solo press conferences than President George H. W. Bush did.

(B) Presidents Clinton and George W. Bush held a far higher percentage of joint press conferences than either of their predecessors did.

(C) President Reagan's failure to hold joint press conferences resulted from a reluctance to share the spotlight with other members of his administration.

(D) While President George H. W. Bush held far more press conferences than his son President George W. Bush did, both Presidents Bush held more joint sessions than solo sessions.

41. Which choice best describes the relationship between the two passages?

(A) Passage 2 denies the static nature of the phenomenon described in Passage 1.

(B) Passage 2 evaluates the conclusions drawn from assertions made in Passage 1.

(C) Passage 2 predicts the eventual healing of a breach reported in Passage 1.

(D) Passage 2 critiques the hypotheses proposed by researchers cited in Passage 1.

42. On which of the following points would the authors of both passages most likely agree?

(A) Those who criticize the press for its treatment of the president fail to understand the press's watchdog function.

(B) Members of the press corps are unlikely to prefer joint press conferences to solo sessions.

(C) The relationship between the press and the presidency is inherently adversarial, and likely to remain so.

(D) The president needs to regain agenda-setting control of traditional solo press conferences.

GO ON TO THE NEXT PAGE

MODEL TEST 1

Questions 43–52 are based on the following passage.

The following passage is abridged from Rachel Ehrenberg's "The facts behind the frack" (Science News), an article on the controversies surrounding the hydraulic fracturing method of recovering natural gas from below the Earth's surface.

To call it a fractious debate is an understatement.

Hydraulic fracturing, or fracking,
Line wrenches open rock deep beneath the Earth's
(5) surface, freeing the natural gas that's trapped inside. Proponents argue that fracking-related gas recovery is a game changer, a bridge to the renewable energy landscape of the future. The gas, primarily methane, is
(10) cheap and relatively clean. Because America is brimful of the stuff, harvesting the fuel via fracking could provide the country with jobs and reduce its dependence on foreign sources of energy.

(15) But along with these promises have come alarming local incidents and national reports of blowouts, contamination and earthquakes. Fracking opponents contend that the process poisons air and drinking water and
(20) may make people sick. What's more, they argue, fracking leaks methane, a potent greenhouse gas that can blow up homes, worries highlighted in the controversial 2010 documentary *Gasland*.

(25) Fears that fracking companies are operating in a Wild West environment with little regulation have prompted political action. In June, the group Don't Frack Ohio led thousands of protesters on a march to
(30) the statehouse, where they declared their commitment to halting hydraulic fracturing in the state. Legislation banning the process has been considered but is now on hold

in California. New York—which sits atop a
(35) giant natural gas reserve—has a statewide fracking moratorium; pending policies would allow the process only where local officials support it.

Despite all this activity, not much of
(40) the fracking debate has brought scientific evidence into the fold. Yet scientists have been studying the risks posed by fracking operations. Research suggests methane leaks do happen. The millions of gallons
(45) of chemical-laden water used to fracture shale deep in the ground has spoiled land and waterways. There's also evidence linking natural gas recovery to earthquakes, but this problem seems to stem primarily
(50) from wastewater disposal rather than the fracturing process itself. While the dangers are real, most problems linked to fracking so far are not specific to the technology but come with many large-scale energy
(55) operations employing poor practices with little oversight, scientists contend. Whether the energy payoff can come with an acceptable level of risk remains an open question.

(60) Hydraulic fracturing operations have been linked to some small earthquakes, including a magnitude 2.3 quake near Blackpool, England, last year. But scientists agree such earthquakes are extremely rare,
(65) occurring when a well hits a seismic sweet spot, and are avoidable with monitoring. Of greater concern are earthquakes associated with the disposal of fracking fluid into wastewater wells. Injected fluid essentially
(70) greases the fault, a long-known effect. In the 1960s, a series of Denver earthquakes were linked to wastewater disposal at the Rocky Mountain arsenal, an Army site nearby. Wastewater disposal was also blamed for a

GO ON TO THE NEXT PAGE

(75) magnitude 4.0 quake in Youngstown, Ohio, last New Year's Eve.

A study headed by William Ellsworth of the U.S. Geological Survey in Menlo Park, Calif., documents a dramatic increase in (80) earthquakes in the Midwest coinciding with the start of the fracking boom. From 1970 to 2000, the region experienced about 20 quakes per year measuring at or above magnitude 3.0. Between 2001 and 2008, there (85) were 29 such quakes per year. Then there were 50 in 2009, 87 in 2010 and 134 in 2011. "The change was really quite pronounced," says Ellsworth. "We do not think it's a purely natural phenomenon." However, the (90) earthquakes weren't happening near active drilling—they seemed to be clustered around wastewater wells.

Human-induced earthquakes

After decades of a steady earthquake rate (dotted line) in the central and eastern (95) United States, activity began to rise in about 2009 and jumped to five times the normal rate by 2013, probably due to human activity.

It's hard to look back without pre-quake data and figure out what triggers a single (100) earthquake, notes Ellsworth. There are several pieces of the geology equation that, if toggled, can tip a fault from stable to unstable. A recent study examining seismic activity at wastewater injection wells in (105) Texas linked earthquakes with injections of more than 150,000 barrels of water per month. But not every case fits the pattern, suggesting the orientation of deep faults is important. Ellsworth advises that injection (110) at active faults be avoided. Drill sites should be considered for their geological stability, and seismic information should be collected. (Only about 3 percent of the 75,000-odd hydraulic fracturing setups in (115) the United States in 2009 were seismically monitored.) "There are many things we don't understand," says Ellsworth. "We're in ambulance-chasing mode where we're coming in after the fact."

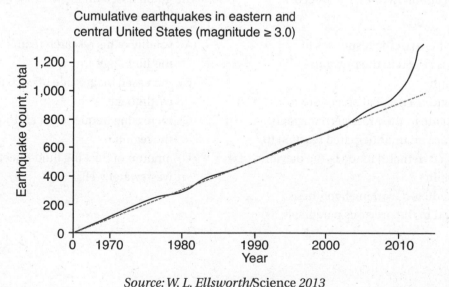

Cumulative earthquakes in eastern and central United States (magnitude ≥ 3.0)

Source: W. L. Ellsworth/Science 2013

GO ON TO THE NEXT PAGE

43. In line 1, the author chooses the word "fractious" (contentious; heated) to create

    (A) a metaphor.
    (B) a play on words.
    (C) an exaggeration.
    (D) a counterargument.

44. To call fracking-related gas recovery "a game changer" (line 7) is to assert that fracking

    (A) has no foreseeable negative consequences.
    (B) will radically alter natural gas production.
    (C) is not taken seriously by its proponents.
    (D) will require active federal regulation.

45. Which choice provides the best evidence for the answer to the previous question?

    (A) Lines 9–14 ("The gas . . . energy")
    (B) Lines 15–20 ("But . . . sick")
    (C) Lines 20–24 ("What's more . . . *Gasland*")
    (D) Lines 51–59 ("While . . . question")

46. What function does the discussion of fracking legislation in lines 32–38 serve in the passage?

    (A) It describes specific responses to concerns raised in the previous paragraph.
    (B) It analyzes theoretical objections to a claim made in the previous paragraph.
    (C) It provides an unanticipated reaction to an explicit demand made in the previous paragraph.
    (D) It contradicts a working hypothesis proposed in the previous paragraph.

47. In line 58, "open" most nearly means

    (A) unresolved.
    (B) vulnerable.
    (C) accessible.
    (D) ajar.

48. The stance that the author takes throughout the passage is best described as that of

    (A) an advocate of technological innovations.
    (B) an opponent of pointless regulatory oversight.
    (C) a legislator concerned about potential danger.
    (D) an observer striving to present a balanced account.

49. Which choice provides the best evidence for the answer to the previous question?

    (A) Lines 25–28 ("Fears . . . political action")
    (B) Lines 32–38 ("Legislation . . . support it")
    (C) Lines 51–59 ("While . . . question")
    (D) Lines 98–100 ("It's hard . . . Ellsworth")

50. The graph based on Ellsworth's figures accentuates the

    (A) validity of his research team's methodology.
    (B) increased magnitude of each individual earthquake.
    (C) increasing frequency of earthquakes in the region.
    (D) amount of fracking fluid injected into wastewater wells.

GO ON TO THE NEXT PAGE

51. In line 87, "pronounced" most nearly means

    (A) noticeable.
    (B) declared.
    (C) decided on.
    (D) articulated.

52. It can be most reasonably inferred from the concluding paragraph that Ellsworth looks on current hypotheses about connections between the recent increases in earthquakes and the start of the fracking boom as

    (A) corroborated by pre-quake data.
    (B) based on insufficient knowledge.
    (C) evidence of seismic activity.
    (D) contradicted by his research findings.

STOP

If there is still time remaining, you may review your answers.

WRITING AND LANGUAGE TEST

35 MINUTES, 44 QUESTIONS

Turn to Section 2 of your answer sheet to answer the questions in this section.

> **Directions:** Questions follow each of the passages below. Some questions ask you how the passage might be changed to improve the expression of ideas. Other questions ask you how the passage might be altered to correct errors in grammar, usage, and punctuation. One or more graphics accompany some passages. You will be required to consider these graphics as you answer questions about editing the passage.
>
> There are three types of questions. In the first type, a part of the passage is underlined. The second type is based on a certain part of the passage. The third type is based on the entire passage.
>
> Read each passage. Then, choose the answer to each question that changes the passage so that it is consistent with the conventions of standard written English. One of the answer choices for many questions is "NO CHANGE." Choosing this answer means that you believe the best answer is to make no change in the passage.

Questions 1–11 are based on the following passage.

Out with the Old and the New

Modernism can be characterized by its complete rejection of 19th-century traditions and values of prudish and proper etiquette. F. Scott Fitzgerald's "Bernice Bobs Her Hair" was written in 1920 and reflects this ❶ embrace of conventional morality most effectively through the character of Marjorie Harvey. Marjorie, an immensely popular and desirable young woman, is plagued by Bernice, her dull cousin who fails to entertain ❷ or be entertained by Marjorie's many social environments. In a desperate attempt to make Bernice more popular and therefore, more bearable, Marjorie teaches Bernice to appear beautifully at ease with ❸ itself in order to gain social favor. Fitzgerald uses Bernice's

1. Which wording is most consistent with the paragraph as a whole?

   (A) NO CHANGE
   (B) ignorance
   (C) rebuff
   (D) significance

2. (A) NO CHANGE
   (B) and entertainment
   (C) with the entertaining of
   (D) of the entertaining for

3. (A) NO CHANGE
   (B) oneself
   (C) themselves
   (D) herself

transformation to embody Modernist ideals of moral relativism and **④ the implementation of mockery of** former Victorian standards of custom.

Marjorie, a quintessential modern girl, represents the destruction of conventional norms and former ideas of femininity. Young and beautiful, she is interested only in having a good time and being good company to the many suitors **⑤ whom** flock to her. Despite her good looks and family wealth, Bernice is disliked for her stifling and overly formal Victorian propriety. **⑥ On the other hand, Bernice is old-fashioned, outdated, and unpopular.**

The "new," modern woman is best denoted by her wit, carelessness, and lack of emotion. Where the dignified nature of Bernice is seen as snobbish and out of style, Marjorie's sardonic and indifferent manner is fresh and exciting. The stark contrast **⑦ between** the Victorian and Modernist eras is even depicted in the girls' taste in literature: Marjorie casts off Bernice's reference to *Little Women* in exchange for the more recent Oscar Wilde.

Still, Modernism isn't let off easy in Fitzgerald's well-liked short story. **⑧ When** Marjorie is preferred socially, she is flagrantly rude and always needing to be entertained. She instructs Bernice in social protocol in a **⑨ few short** sentences, causing the reader to question the frivolous hedonism that dominates the early 20th century. Once Bernice adopts her cousin's apathy, she easily falls into the world of dancing, dating,

4. (A) NO CHANGE
   (B) for the mocking of
   (C) to mock
   (D) mocking

5. (A) NO CHANGE
   (B) who
   (C) whose
   (D) who's

6. Where in this paragraph should the underlined sentence be placed?

   (A) where it is now
   (B) before the first sentence
   (C) before the second sentence
   (D) before the third sentence

7. (A) NO CHANGE
   (B) among
   (C) for
   (D) on

8. (A) NO CHANGE
   (B) While
   (C) Because
   (D) Since

9. (A) NO CHANGE
   (B) short few
   (C) few, short
   (D) short, few

GO ON TO THE NEXT PAGE

and laughing. In fact, never being serious happens to come quite easy.

The equally ❿ <u>kind-hearted natures</u> of both of Fitzgerald's characters come crashing down when Marjorie tricks Bernice into getting her hair bobbed—a style so rebellious that it causes Bernice to faint. Bernice finds revenge in severing off a golden lock of Marjorie's hair while she sleeps. While using Bernice and Marjorie to model both eras, Fitzgerald finds flaws in ⓫ <u>both: the old manner is a lifeless forgery, while</u> the new approach is only relaxed on the surface.

10. Which choice would best be logically placed here to represent the characterizations of Marjorie and Bernice in the paragraph?

(A) NO CHANGE
(B) revolutionary dogmatism
(C) false facades
(D) frivolous piety

11. (A) NO CHANGE
(B) both, the old manner is a lifeless forgery while
(C) both—the old manner is a lifeless, forgery, while
(D) both; the old manner, is a lifeless forgery while

GO ON TO THE NEXT PAGE

Questions 12–22 are based on the following passage and supplementary material.

Extra, Extra (Written in 2015)

If any field has drastically changed in the last two decades, it is journalism. Journalism includes the gathering and distribution of news through a variety of mediums, **❶②** building upon the long-standing professional excellence with which journalism is associated. Whether via print, broadcast, or digital, journalists are responsible for keeping the public informed, and often play a vital role in allowing the general population to participate in the political process. Although the digital age has understandably discouraged popularity in some traditional forms of **❶③** news media the field itself is optimistic, not only is the digital platform more than making up for the moderate declines in traditional news sources, **❶④** but also research shows that Americans are spending more time consuming news than they have since the early 1990s. **❶⑤** The traditional dominance of newspapers has continued unabated.

12. Which choice most specifically elaborates on the first part of this sentence?

   (A) NO CHANGE
   (B) growing its reach to include urban, suburban, and rural population centers.
   (C) which have recently expanded to incorporate smartphones, tablets, and blogs.
   (D) demonstrating that seeking the average public opinion is most objective.

13. (A) NO CHANGE
   (B) news media, the field itself is optimistic, not only
   (C) news media, the field itself is optimistic: not only
   (D) news media the field itself; is optimistic not only

14. (A) NO CHANGE
   (B) and
   (C) for
   (D) since

15. Which choice best concludes this paragraph and transitions to the topic of the next paragraph?

   (A) NO CHANGE
   (B) Journalism isn't dying; the way reporters do their job is changing.
   (C) Journalism is no longer the sort of career that globally minded people would chose.
   (D) With the steady demise of public interest in quality journalism, it is only a matter of time before journalism falls by the wayside.

GO ON TO THE NEXT PAGE

Quite simply, the days of print-only newsrooms are past. Now, one doesn't wait until the 6 P.M. broadcast to hear what's happening around the world, ⓰ nor does one grab the newspaper on Sunday morning for breaking news. The public expects minute-by-minute updates, and media companies meet this demand with 24-7 online newsreels. Journalists can no longer limit themselves to gathering stories or writing articles or speaking publicly—they must be able to do it all and then some. Even entry-level positions require candidates who have had media training and internship experience in addition to a formal education. Internships at most media outlets include everything from copy editing to blogging.

The tough competition and demanding prerequisites for the job market need not be deterrents. Leading journalism ⓱ department's are reassuring that their students leave undergraduate with all the tools necessary for success. For instance, the University of Missouri at Columbia ⓲ —boasting the number one journalism department in the nation according to *The Huffington Post*—offers more than 30 interest areas, incorporating an intensive liberal arts education along with hands-on experience in media labs and internships for academic credit. Ohio ⓳ University also having, a journalism department ranked in the top ten nationwide offers three campus publications plus a broadcasting outlet for students to gain professional experience before graduation, not to mention OU's Institute for International Journalism, which offers opportunities for reporting abroad.

16. (A) NO CHANGE
(B) because
(C) for
(D) while

17. (A) NO CHANGE
(B) departments' are insuring that they're
(C) departments are assuring there
(D) departments are ensuring that their

18. Which choice best connects this sentence to the previous sentence?
(A) NO CHANGE
(B) —located in the geographic near-middle of the United States—
(C) —a university that offers a variety of possible undergraduate majors and minors—
(D) —ranked among the best universities for average starting salary among its graduates—

19. (A) NO CHANGE
(B) University also having a journalism department ranked in the top ten nationwide offers
(C) University, also having a journalism department, ranked in the top ten, nationwide, offers
(D) University, also having a journalism department ranked in the top ten nationwide, offers

Technology and its **20** <u>endless affects</u> on all areas of the job market are tedious subjects for the student and young professional. One cannot consider a career field without hearing how formidable its outlook is and how quickly one could fail in an uncertain economy. Indeed, journalism students have been well informed **21** <u>about the steadily increasing demand for journalists in the recent past</u>, but the truth stands that there will always be a demand for the news, and therefore, a need for journalists. The field **22** <u>is adapting</u> and so are its constituents.

20. (A) NO CHANGE
    (B) endless effects
    (C) endlessly affects
    (D) endlessly effects

21. Which choice offers the most accurate interpretation of the data in the chart?

    (A) NO CHANGE
    (B) about the gradual decline in jobs for journalists in the past decade,
    (C) about the constant level of employment for journalists these past few years,
    (D) about the job market fluctuations in recent years,

22. (A) NO CHANGE
    (B) was adapting
    (C) is adopting
    (D) was adopting

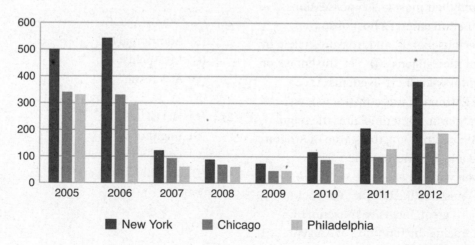

Journalism-Related Job Openings

■ New York   ■ Chicago   ■ Philadelphia

GO ON TO THE NEXT PAGE

Questions 23–33 are based on the following passage.

Parthenon

Of all the ancient, sacred, and truly splendid buildings to visit, the Parthenon may just be the most treasured of all. **㉓** A long time past, the Greeks built their apotheosis over a span of nine years atop the Acropolis of Athens as a tribute to Athena, the city's beloved patron goddess of war and reason. The temple itself was completed in 438 B.C., although decorative sculpting and engraving within the structure went on for several more years. Since then, the structure has served as **㉔** temple, treasury, church, and most recently, tourist attraction.

Pericles—leading politician in 5th century B.C.—recruited the sculptor Phidias to oversee two architects, Iktinos and Kallikrates, in the construction of the Parthenon to house a forty-foot high statue of Athena. **㉕** Honestly and judiciously, the ancient Greeks planned an exceptional monument with a base the size of half a football field and pillars over thirty feet tall. Athenians stored their most lavish possessions inside the Parthenon among a host of statues, sculptures, precious metals, and treasures taken in the conquest of the Persians. **㉖** Yet, the endeavor and all it stood for were short-lived: just seven years after the Parthenon was constructed, war broke out with Sparta. Sometime after the reign of Athens, in 5th century A.D., the statue of Athena was plundered and later destroyed.

Perhaps, even with Athena—the very core of Parthenon—missing, the temple **㉗** could of still served as a great, inclusive museum of Greek history, tracing the founding of Ancient Greece, Athenian democracy, and early western civilization; yet, the Parthenon would endure

23. Which choice would most specifically describe how long ago the Parthenon was constructed?

   (A) NO CHANGE
   (B) More than 2,500 years ago,
   (C) Many decades of ages past,
   (D) In days gone by,

24. (A) NO CHANGE
   (B) temple, treasury church, and most recently, tourist attraction.
   (C) temple treasury, church and most recently tourist attraction.
   (D) temple treasury church, and most recently tourist attraction.

25. What could best be used for the underlined portion to convey the high priority the Greeks placed on completing the Parthenon in a glorious fashion?

   (A) NO CHANGE
   (B) Sparing no expense,
   (C) With artistic patience,.
   (D) Using architectural techniques,

26. (A) NO CHANGE
   (B) Additionally,
   (C) In conclusion,
   (D) As a result,

27. (A) NO CHANGE
   (B) might of
   (C) could have
   (D) should have been

GO ON TO THE NEXT PAGE

many other foes. The Parthenon was first converted to a Christian church, which led to the removal of **28** its' "pagan gods." With the rise of the Ottoman Empire, the monument was used as a mosque until a Venetian attack on Athens destroyed large parts of the building and left its **29** archaeology deserted. By the 18th century, little was left of the Parthenon after decades of European pillaging.

30 In the contemporary world in which we reside, the Parthenon is one of the most popular tourist attractions in the world, enticing millions of people each year and warranting an ongoing restoration project currently in its third decade. Even in its antiquity, its subtle beauty and architectural refinement **31** is uncontested. Its miracle comes not from its magnitude, but from the curvatures between its platform and columns that offer an illusion of symmetry that exceeds its true dimensions, and in the elaborate engravings within its marble surfaces **32** that having to outlast centuries of calamity. Now, architects, engineers, and artists work to recreate the surprisingly balanced and unbelievably precise work of the Athenians. **33** How is it that today's architects are taking forty years to do what they did in less than ten?

28. (A) NO CHANGE
    (B) it's
    (C) it is
    (D) its

29. (A) NO CHANGE
    (B) components
    (C) particles
    (D) remnants

30. (A) NO CHANGE
    (B) In the world of today,
    (C) Contemptuously,
    (D) Today,

31. (A) NO CHANGE
    (B) are
    (C) was
    (D) were

32. (A) NO CHANGE
    (B) which has to outlast
    (C) that have outlasted
    (D) which had outlasted

33. Which of the following would be the most effective conclusion to the essay?

    (A) NO CHANGE
    (B) It is vital that we learn from the past in order to not repeat the mistakes of history.
    (C) Tourism is a growing business worldwide, as people seek out memorable experiences rather than to accumulate possessions.
    (D) The world continues to be haunted by the Venetian attack on the Parthenon, turning a brilliant accomplishment into utter ruins.

GO ON TO THE NEXT PAGE

Questions 34–44 are based on the following passage.

Where Have all the Cavemen Gone?

㉞ All humans have their ultimate genetic roots in Africa. While our own ancestors were battling drought on the coasts of the African sub-continent, ㉟ the icebound north of modern Eurasia experienced the spread of the evolutionarily distinct species *Homo neanderthalensis,* where the Neanderthals developed the tools of flint and bone that have today come to characterize the so-called Mousterian culture of the early Stone Age.

(1) Early hypotheses for their extinction centered, predictably, around the ㊱ climate extreme change of the last Ice Age. (2) However, more recent studies of Neanderthal anatomy and artifacts suggest that they were remarkably well-equipped to deal with the fiercely cold and barren conditions, ㊲ and even thrived within them for nearly 200,000 years. (3) To cope with the glacial conditions, Neanderthals became short in stature—no more than a meter and half tall—and developed short, broad extremities that would

34. Which choice would best function as the introductory thesis of the essay?

(A) NO CHANGE
(B) The defeat of the Neanderthal invaders can only be considered a triumph of human ingenuity.
(C) The disappearance of the Neanderthals is one of the great mysteries in the evolutionary success of modern humans.
(D) In order to cope with the repercussions of possible global climate change, we should look to the example of Neanderthal adaptation.

35. (A) NO CHANGE
(B) the evolutionarily distinct species *Homo neanderthalensis* had spread to the icebound north of modern Eurasia,
(C) the species *Homo neanderthalensis,* being evolutionarily distinct, found itself spread to modern Eurasia in the north icebound,
(D) the north icebound of modern Eurasia experience evolutionarily distinct species spread of the *Homo neanderthalensis,*

36. (A) NO CHANGE
(B) climate, extreme
(C) extreme climate
(D) extreme, climate

37. (A) NO CHANGE
(B) but
(C) for it was the case that they
(D) OMIT the underlined portion.

GO ON TO THE NEXT PAGE

2

have increased the efficiency of circulation, and helped to preserve body heat. **38**

Another popular theory posits that Neanderthals met their extinction through absorption. That is—supposing Neanderthals were *not* a distinct species, but rather a subspecies of *Homo sapiens*—some researchers believe that they disappeared after **39** conflicts with humans when they arrived in Eurasia roughly 80,000 years ago. However, a sample of mitochondrial DNA surviving in the remains of a Neanderthal discovered in the Caucus Mountains demonstrates 3.5 percent genetic divergence from **40** contemporary *Homo sapiens*. While it is possible that some Neanderthals may have become culturally assimilated with our ancestors, it is highly unlikely that their DNA contributed to that of modern humans.

Currently, the most widely held theory to explain the extinction of the Neanderthals boils down quite simply to the processes of natural selection. While Neanderthals appear to have maintained a stable population during the Ice Age, **41** a drastic genetic bottleneck was experienced by our African ancestors, leaving only the strongest and most intelligent to survive and carry on the species. When *Homo*

38. The writer would like to insert this sentence to provide further support to his argument in this paragraph.

"Further, there is strong evidence to suggest that later Neanderthals were capable of creating sophisticated and versatile garments from animal pelts designed to maintain core warmth without inducing perspiration."

Where would it best be placed?

(A) before sentence 1
(B) before sentence 2
(C) before sentence 3
(D) after sentence 3

39. Which choice is the most consistent elaboration on the first sentence of this paragraph?

(A) NO CHANGE
(B) interbreeding
(C) discoveries
(D) commerce

40. Which wording best conveys that the Neanderthals only have a slight genetic divergence from present-day humans?

(A) NO CHANGE
(B) punctual
(C) unique
(D) scientific

41. (A) NO CHANGE
(B) a drastic genetic bottleneck by our African ancestors was experienced,
(C) our African ancestors drastically experienced a bottleneck that was genetic,
(D) our African ancestors experienced a drastic genetic bottleneck,

2

GO ON TO THE NEXT PAGE

neanderthalensis at last met *Homo sapiens*, it is probable that ④② they was outmatched, at the very least, in technology, creativity, and social efficacy. In the several thousand years that followed, competition for resources would have pushed Neanderthals farther and farther to the ④③ oceans of Europe and Asia. The last known remnants of Neanderthal culture issue from the remote location of Gorham's Cave on the Gibraltar coast. By this time—roughly 27,000 years ago—*Homo neanderthalensis* had been displaced by its evolutionary cousin ④④ to the very edge of the land nearly back into Africa itself where our common ancestors, first emerged millions of years prior.

42. (A) NO CHANGE
    (B) they were
    (C) the Neanderthals are
    (D) the Neanderthals were

43. (A) NO CHANGE
    (B) margins
    (C) debris
    (D) remains

44. (A) NO CHANGE
    (B) to the very edge, of the land nearly back into Africa itself, where our common ancestors.
    (C) to the very edge of the land, nearly back into Africa itself, where our common ancestors.
    (D) to the very edge of the land nearly, back into Africa itself where our common, ancestors.

STOP

If there is still time remaining, you may review your answers.

MATH TEST (NO CALCULATOR)

25 MINUTES, 20 QUESTIONS

Turn to Section 3 of your answer sheet to answer the questions in this section.

Directions: For questions 1–15, solve each problem and choose the best answer from the given options. Fill in the corresponding circle on your answer document. For questions 16–20, solve the problem and fill in the answer on the answer sheet grid.

Notes:
- Calculators are **NOT PERMITTED** in this section.
- All variables and expressions represent real numbers unless indicated otherwise.
- All figures are drawn to scale unless indicated otherwise.
- All figures are in a plane unless indicated otherwise.
- Unless indicated otherwise, the domain of a given function is the set of all real numbers x for which the function has real values.

REFERENCE INFORMATION

Area Facts	Volume Facts	Triangle Facts

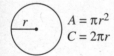

$A = \ell w$

$A = \frac{1}{2} bh$

$A = \pi r^2$
$C = 2\pi r$

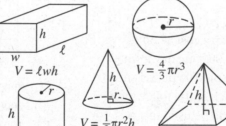

$V = \ell wh$

$V = \pi r^2 h$

$V = \frac{1}{3}\pi r^2 h$

$V = \frac{4}{3}\pi r^3$

$V = \frac{1}{3}\ell wh$

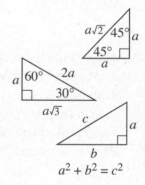

$a^2 + b^2 = c^2$

The arc of a circle contains 360°.

The arc of a circle contains 2π radians.

The sum of the measures of the angles in a triangle is 180°.

1. At the beginning of January, John deposits A dollars into a non-interest-bearing bank account. If John withdraws d dollars from the account every month and makes no additional deposits, how much money, in dollars, will be in the account after m months?

   (A) $A - md$

   (B) $(A - m)d$

   (C) $A - \dfrac{m}{d}$

   (D) $A - \dfrac{d}{m}$

2. If $f(x) = x^2 - 11$, for what values of x is $f(x) < 25$?

   (A) $-6 < x$

   (B) $x < 6$

   (C) $x \le -6$ or $x \ge 6$

   (D) $-6 < x < 6$

3. At Joe's Pizzeria, small pizzas cost $7.50 and large pizzas cost $11.00. One day from 3:00 P.M. to 9:00 P.M., Joe sold 100 pizzas and took in $848. Solving which of the following systems of equations could be used to determine the number of small pizzas, S, and the number of large pizzas, L, that Joe sold during that 6-hour period?

   (A) $\quad S + L = 848$
   $7.5S + 11L = 100$

   (B) $\quad S + L = 100$
   $7.5S + 11L = \dfrac{848}{6}$

   (C) $\quad S + L = 100$
   $7.5S + 11L = 848$

   (D) $\quad S + L = 100$
   $7.5S + 11L = 848 \times 6$

4. Which of the following statements is true concerning the equation below?

$$3(5 - 2x) = 6(2 - x) + 3$$

   (A) The equation has no solutions.

   (B) The equation has one positive solution.

   (C) The equation has one negative solution.

   (D) The equation has infinitely many solutions.

5. The chart below shows the value of an investment on January 1 of each year from 2005 to 2010. During which year was the percent increase in the value of the investment the greatest?

Year	Value
2005	$150
2006	$250
2007	$450
2008	$750
2009	$1,200
2010	$1,800

   (A) 2005

   (B) 2006

   (C) 2008

   (D) 2009

GO ON TO THE NEXT PAGE

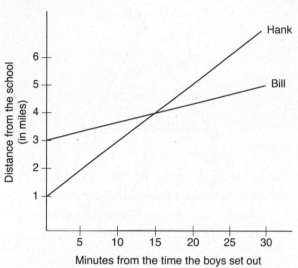

Minutes from the time the boys set out

6. Hank's and Bill's houses are 1 and 3 miles from their school, respectively. Each boy left his house on a bicycle at the same time and rode for 30 minutes. The graph above shows the distance, in miles, each boy was from the school during their rides. Based on this information, which of the following statements, if any, is *not* necessarily true?

(A) Hank is riding faster than Bill for the entire 30 minutes.
(B) The distance that Hank rode is greater than the distance that Bill rode.
(C) Hank and Bill's paths cross exactly once during their 30-minute rides.
(D) Each of the above statements must be true.

7. Which of the following is equivalent to $\dfrac{2x^2-8}{x^2-4x+4}$?

(A) $\dfrac{2(x+2)}{x-2}$

(B) $\dfrac{2(x+4)}{x-4}$

(C) $\dfrac{2x+2}{x-2}$

(D) $\dfrac{6}{4x-4}$

8. If $m \neq 0$, $m \neq 1$, and $f(x) = mx + b$, then which of the following statements concerning the graphs whose equations are $y = f(x) + 3$ and $y = f(x + 3)$ must be true?

(A) The graphs don't intersect.
(B) The graphs intersect in one point.
(C) The graphs intersect in two points.
(D) The graphs intersect in more than two points.

9. For how many positive integers, x, does the function $f(x) = \dfrac{\sqrt{x-3}}{x^2-8x-20}$ have no real values?

(A) 2
(B) 3
(C) 4
(D) Infinitely many

GO ON TO THE NEXT PAGE

MODEL TEST 1

10. If for all real numbers x, $h(5 - x) = x^2 + x + 1$, what is the value of $h(9)$?

    (A) 13
    (B) 21
    (C) 28
    (D) 91

11. A white cube has a volume of 27. If a red circle of radius 1 is painted on each face of the cube, what is the total area of the surface of the cube that is *not* red?

    (A) $27 - 3\pi$
    (B) $27 - 6\pi$
    (C) $54 - 6\pi$
    (D) $54 - 12\pi$

12. Tim's Tennis Camp is open only to teenagers—all campers must be between 13 and 19 years old, inclusive. Which of the following inequalities can be used to determine if a person who is y years old is eligible to attend the camp?

    (A) $|y - 13| \le 6$
    (B) $|y - 13| \le 19$
    (C) $|y - 19| \le 13$
    (D) $|y - 16| \le 3$

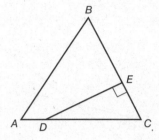

13. In the figure above, line segment $\overline{DE}$ is perpendicular to side $\overline{BC}$ of equilateral triangle ABC. If $AB = 12$ and $BE = 8$, what is the area of quadrilateral $ABED$?

    (A) $14\sqrt{3}$
    (B) $28\sqrt{3}$
    (C) $36\sqrt{3}$
    (D) $72\sqrt{3}$

14. The list price of a certain book is d dollars. Anne bought a copy of the book from an online dealer that offers a discount of 10% off the list price of all books and doesn't collect sales tax. Beth bought the same book at a bookstore, where the book was on sale for 15% off the list price. However, she had to pay 5% sales tax on his purchase. Which of the following statements is true?

    (A) Anne and Beth paid the same price for their books.
    (B) Anne paid more than Beth for the book.
    (C) Anne paid less than Beth for the book.
    (D) Who paid more for her book depends on d, the list price.

15. If the lines whose equations are $y = ax + b$ and $x = cy + d$ are parallel, which statement is true?

    (A) $a = -\dfrac{1}{c}$
    (B) $a = \dfrac{1}{c}$
    (C) $c = a$
    (D) $c = -a$

GO ON TO THE NEXT PAGE

Grid-in Response Directions

In questions 16–20, first solve the problem, and then enter your answer on the grid provided on the answer sheet. The instructions for entering your answers follow.

- First, write your answer in the boxes at the top of the grid.
- Second, grid your answer in the columns below the boxes.
- Use the fraction bar in the first row or the decimal point in the second row to enter fractions and decimals.

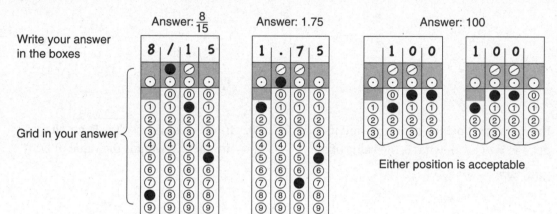

- Grid only one space in each column.
- Entering the answer in the boxes is recommended as an aid in gridding but is not required.
- The machine scoring your exam can read only what you grid, so you **must grid-in your answers correctly to get credit.**
- If a question has more than one correct answer, grid-in only one of them.
- The grid does not have a minus sign; so no answer can be negative.
- A mixed number *must* be converted to an improper fraction or a decimal before it is gridded.

  Enter $1\frac{1}{4}$ as 5/4 or 1.25; the machine will interpret 11/4 as $\frac{11}{4}$ and mark it wrong.

- **All decimals must be entered as accurately as possible.** Here are three acceptable ways of gridding

$$\frac{3}{11} = 0.272727\ldots$$

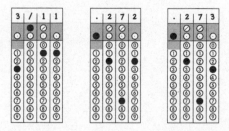

- Note that rounding to .273 is acceptable because you are using the full grid, but you would receive **no credit** for .3 or .27, because they are less accurate.

16. $A(1, 1)$, $B(5, 3)$, and $C(5, 9)$ are three points in the xy-plane. If $\overline{AB}$ is a diameter of Circle 1 and $\overline{BC}$ is a diameter of Circle 2, what is the slope of the line that goes through the centers of the two circles?

17. If a and b are positive constants and if $a(x - y) = b(y - x)$, what is the value of the ratio $\frac{x}{y}$?

18. If c is a real number and if $1 + i$ is a solution of the equation $x^2 - 2x + c = 0$, what is the value of c?

19. If (a, b) and (c, d) are the two points of intersection of the line whose equation is $y = x$ and the parabola whose equation is $y = x^2 - 6x + 12$, what is the value of $a + b + c + d$?

20. If $h(5 - 2x) = \sqrt{x^2 + 3x + 5}$ for all real numbers x, what is the value of $h(3)$?

STOP

If there is still time remaining, you may review your answers.

MATH TEST (CALCULATOR)

55 MINUTES, 38 QUESTIONS

Turn to Section 4 of your answer sheet to answer the questions in this section.

Directions: For questions 1–30, solve each problem and choose the best answer from the given options. Fill in the corresponding circle on your answer document. For questions 31–38, solve the problem and fill in the answer on the answer sheet grid.

Notes:

- Calculators **ARE PERMITTED** in this section.
- All variables and expressions represent real numbers unless indicated otherwise.
- All figures are drawn to scale unless indicated otherwise.
- All figures are in a plane unless indicated otherwise.
- Unless indicated otherwise, the domain of a given function is the set of all real numbers *x* for which the function has real values.

REFERENCE INFORMATION

Area Facts

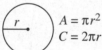

$A = \ell w$

$A = \frac{1}{2}bh$

$A = \pi r^2$
$C = 2\pi r$

Volume Facts

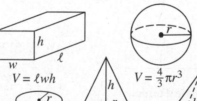

$V = \ell w h$

$V = \pi r^2 h$

$V = \frac{1}{3}\pi r^2 h$

$V = \frac{4}{3}\pi r^3$

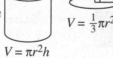

$V = \frac{1}{3}\ell w h$

Triangle Facts

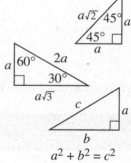

$a^2 + b^2 = c^2$

The arc of a circle contains 360°.

The arc of a circle contains 2π radians.

The sum of the measures of the angles in a triangle is 180°.

1. If Wally's Widget Works is open exactly 20 days each month and produces 80 widgets each day it is open, how many years will it take to produce 96,000 widgets?

(A) fewer than 5
(B) 5
(C) more than 5 but fewer than 10
(D) 10

2. What is the volume, in cubic inches, of a cube whose total surface area is 216 square inches?

(A)   18
(B)   36
(C)   216
(D) 1,296

GO ON TO THE NEXT PAGE

3. If $2 - 3n \geq 5$, what is the greatest possible value of $2 + 3n$?

   (A) −1
   (B) 1
   (C) 4
   (D) 5

4. Which of the following statements concerning the equation $\dfrac{2x^2 - 3}{5 - x^2} = -2$ is true?

   (A) The equation has no solutions.
   (B) The equation has exactly one solution.
   (C) The equation has exactly two solutions.
   (D) The equation has infinitely many solutions.

5. If $f(x) = x^2 - 3x$ and $g(x) = f(3x)$, what is $g(-10)$?

   (A) 390
   (B) 490
   (C) 810
   (D) 990

Questions 6 and 7 refer to the following table.

Class	Number of Students	Number in Band
A	20	5
B	30	7
C	23	5
D	27	6
E	25	6

6. What is the average (arithmetic mean) number of students per class?

   (A) 24
   (B) 24.5
   (C) 25
   (D) 25.5

7. Which class has the highest percent of students in the band?

   (A) A
   (B) B
   (C) D
   (D) E

8. In a class, 20 children were sharing equally the cost of a present for their teacher. When 4 of the children decided not to contribute, each of the other children had to pay $1.50 more. How much, in dollars, did the present cost?

   (A)   50
   (B)   80
   (C) 100
   (D) 120

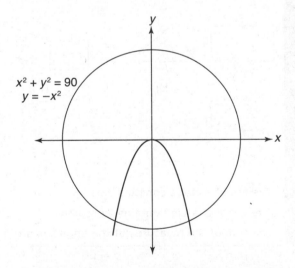

$x^2 + y^2 = 90$
$y = -x^2$

9. A system of two equations and their graphs are shown above. If (a, b) and (c, d) are the points of intersection of the circle and the parabola, what is the value of $a + b + c + d$?

   (A) −18
   (B)   −6
   (C)   6
   (D)   18

GO ON TO THE NEXT PAGE

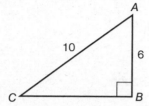

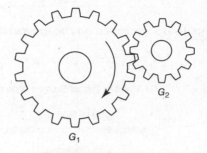

Note: Figure not drawn to scale.

10. In the figure above, what is the value of the cosine of angle C?

(A) 0.4
(B) 0.5
(C) 0.6
(D) 0.8

11. For Jen's birthday, Wes bought her a ring, a bouquet of flowers, and a box of candy, for which he spent a total of $528. If the flowers cost three times as much as the candy, and the ring cost ten times as much as the flowers and candy combined, how much did he pay for the flowers?

(A) $12
(B) $24
(C) $30
(D) $36

12. The diagram above depicts two gears, G_1 and G_2. Gear G_1, which has 48 teeth, turns clockwise at a rate of 60 rotations per second. If gear G_2 has 36 teeth, which of the following statements is true?

(A) Gear G_2 turns clockwise at a rate of 45 rotations per second.
(B) Gear G_2 turns clockwise at a rate of 80 rotations per second.
(C) Gear G_2 turns counterclockwise at a rate of 45 rotations per second.
(D) Gear G_2 turns counterclockwise at a rate of 80 rotations per second.

GO ON TO THE NEXT PAGE

MODEL TEST 1

Questions 13–15 are based on the information in the following graphs.

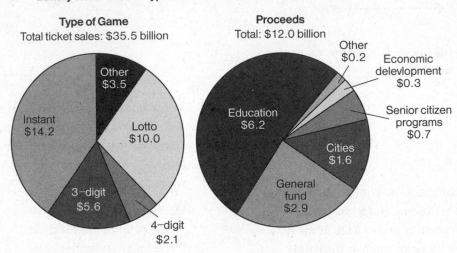

Lottery Ticket Sales – Type of Game and Use of Proceeds: 2009

All figures are in billions of dollars.

13. The revenue from lottery ticket sales is divided between prize money and the various uses shown in the graph labeled "Proceeds." In 2009, approximately what percent of the money spent on tickets was returned to the purchasers in the form of prize money?

(A) 23.5%
(B) 50%
(C) 66%
(D) 74%

14. Approximately what percent of the proceeds that went to the states' General fund would have to be given to the Senior citizen program so that the proceeds for the Senior citizen program and the Cities would be equal?

(A) 0.9%
(B) 9%
(C) 31%
(D) 48%

15. Assume that in 2010 the sales of Lotto were discontinued, and the dollar value of the sales of all other games increased by 10% compared to 2009. If a new circle graph was created to reflect the Lottery Ticket Sales in 2010, which of the following would be closest to the degree measure of the central angle of the sector representing Instant games?

(A) 100°
(B) 150°
(C) 180°
(D) 200°

GO ON TO THE NEXT PAGE

16. Each week, Alice's gross salary is $9.00 an hour for the first 40 hours she works and $15.00 an hour for each hour she works in excess of 40 hours. Her net pay is her gross pay less the following deductions: a flat fee of $20 for her contribution to her health insurance; 8% of her gross salary for payroll taxes, and 15% of her gross pay for withholding taxes. Which of the following expressions represents Alice's net pay in a week that she works x hours where $x > 40$?

(A) $0.23(15x - 240) - 20$
(B) $0.23(15x - 220)$
(C) $0.77(15x - 240) - 20$
(D) $0.77(15x - 220)$

17. If $i = \sqrt{-1}$, which of the following is equal to $(1 + i)^3$?

(A) $-2 + 2i$
(B) $2 - 2i$
(C) 4
(D) $4 + 4i$

18. If the x-intercepts of the graph of $y = 4x^2 - 8x + 3$ are a and b, what is the value of $a + b$?

(A) 0.5
(B) 1
(C) 1.5
(D) 2

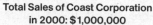

Questions 19–20 are based on the information in the following graph.

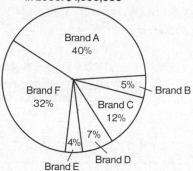

Total Sales of Coast Corporation in 2000: $1,000,000

19. If the above circle graph were drawn to scale, then which of the following is closest to the difference in the degree measurements of the central angle of the sector representing Brand C and the central angle of the sector representing Brand D?

(A) $5°$
(B) $12°$
(C) $18°$
(D) $25°$

20. The total sales of Coast Corporation in 2005 were 50% higher than in 2000. If the dollar value if the sales of Brand A was 25% higher in 2005 than in 2000, then the sales of Brand A accounted for what percentage of total sales in 2005?

(A) 20%
(B) 25%
(C) $33\frac{1}{3}\%$
(D) 50%

GO ON TO THE NEXT PAGE

21. Store 1 is a full-service retail store that charges regular process. Store 2 is a self-service factory-outlet store that sells all items at a reduced price. In January 2014, each store sold three brands of DVD players. The number of DVD players sold and their prices are shown in the following tables.

Number of DVD Players Sold

	Store 1	Store 2
Brand A	10	30
Brand B	20	40
Brand C	20	20

Prices of DVD Players

	Brand A	Brand B	Brand C
Store 1	$80	$100	$150
Store 2	$50	$80	$120

What was the difference between Store 1 and Store 2 in the dollar values of the total sales of the three brands of DVD players?

(A)   80
(B)   140
(C)   330
(D) 1,300

Questions 22 and 23 refer to the figure below, which represents a solid piece of wood being used in the construction of a house. All of the dimensions are in feet.

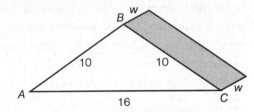

22. What is the area, in square feet, of the triangular face of the solid?

(A) 24
(B) 48
(C) 50
(D) 80

23. If the density of the wood is 3 pounds per cubic foot and if the weight of the solid is 360 pounds, what is the width, w, in feet, of the solid?

(A) 5.0
(B) 2.5
(C) 2.4
(D) 1.5

GO ON TO THE NEXT PAGE

Note: Figure not drawn to scale.

24. In the figure above, both triangles are equilateral. If the area of △ABC is 6 and the area of △DEF is 10, to the nearest hundredth what is the ratio of AB to DE?

   (A) 0.36
   (B) 0.60
   (C) 0.75
   (D) 0.77

25. If $g(x) = (\sin x + \cos x)^2$, what is $g\left(\dfrac{\pi}{3}\right)$?

   (A) 1
   (B) 1.366
   (C) 1.866
   (D) 2

Questions 26–28 are based on the two graphs below.

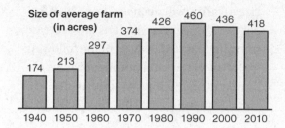

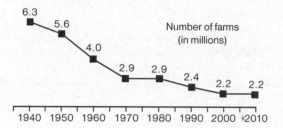

26. In which year was the total acreage of farmland in the United States the smallest?

   (A) 1940
   (B) 1970
   (C) 2000
   (D) 2010

27. In 2010, the states with the most total acres of farmland were Texas, Montana, Kansas, Nevada, and New Mexico. The acreage in each state (measured in millions of acres) was 130, 61, 46, 46, and 43, respectively. Those five states accounted for approximately what percent of the total farm acreage in the country?

   (A) 15%
   (B) 25%
   (C) 35%
   (D) 45%

GO ON TO THE NEXT PAGE

28. If future projections are that the number of farms in the United States will decrease by 5% from 2010 to 2030 and that the average size of farms will decrease from 2010 to 2030 by the same percent as the decrease from 1990 to 2010, which of the following is closest to the total number of acres of farmland, in millions of acres, in the United States in 2030?

(A) 750
(B) 800
(C) 850
(D) 900

29. If $i^2 = -1$, what is the value of $i^{75} - (-i)^{75}$?

(A) $-2i$
(B) $2i$
(C) -2
(D) 0

30. In parallelogram $ABCD$, each side measures 10. If $m\angle A = 45°$, what is the area of the parallelogram?

(A) 50
(B) 64.6
(C) 70.7
(D) 78.2

GO ON TO THE NEXT PAGE

Grid-in Response Directions

In questions 31–38, first solve the problem, and then enter your answer on the grid provided on the answer sheet. The instructions for entering your answers follow.

- First, write your answer in the boxes at the top of the grid.
- Second, grid your answer in the columns below the boxes.
- Use the fraction bar in the first row or the decimal point in the second row to enter fractions and decimals.

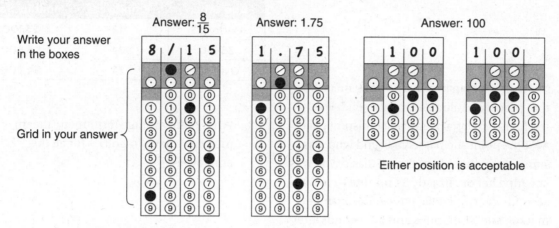

- Grid only one space in each column.
- Entering the answer in the boxes is recommended as an aid in gridding but is not required.
- The machine scoring your exam can read only what you grid, so you **must grid-in your answers correctly to get credit.**
- If a question has more than one correct answer, grid-in only one of them.
- The grid does not have a minus sign; so no answer can be negative.
- A mixed number *must* be converted to an improper fraction or a decimal before it is gridded.

  Enter $1\frac{1}{4}$ as 5/4 or 1.25; the machine will interpret 11/4 as $\frac{11}{4}$ and mark it wrong.

- **All decimals must be entered as accurately as possible.** Here are three acceptable ways of gridding

$$\frac{3}{11} = 0.272727\ldots$$

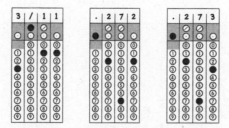

- Note that rounding to .273 is acceptable because you are using the full grid, but you would receive **no credit** for .3 or .27, because they are less accurate.

31. On a particular map of Long Island, one inch represents a distance of 20 miles. One day, Maurice drove from Hauppauge to Riverhead, which are 1.25 inches apart on that map, at an average speed of 40 miles per hour. How many minutes did his drive take?

32. Michelle participated in a 26-mile marathon that proceeded along a straight road. For the first 20 miles, she ran at a constant pace. At some point she passed a friend who was standing on the side of the road and who was cheering her on. Exactly 54 minutes and 36 seconds later, Michelle passed the 12-mile marker, and 31 minutes and 30 seconds after that, she passed the 15-mile marker. How far, in miles, was it from the starting line to the point where her friend was standing?

Base your answer to Question 33 on the information in the following chart that shows the number of employees at Acme Air-Conditioning in three age groups and the average monthly salary of the workers in each group.

Age Group	Number of Employees	Average Monthly Salary
Under 35	12	$3,100
35–50	24	$3,800
Over 50	14	$4,200

33. What is the average (arithmetic mean) monthly salary, in dollars for all the employees?

34. To use a certain cash machine, you need a Personal Identification Code (PIC). If each PIC consists of two letters followed by one of the digits from 1 to 9 (such as AQ7 or BB3) or one letter followed by two digits (such as Q37 or J88), how many different PICSs can be assigned?

GO ON TO THE NEXT PAGE

35. The base of pyramid 1 is a rectangle whose length is 3 and whose width is 2. The base of pyramid 2 is a square whose sides are 3. If the volumes of the pyramids are equal, what is the ratio of the height of pyramid 1 to the height of pyramid 2?

36. On October 20, 2015, one United States dollar was worth 0.88 euros and one Canadian dollar was worth 0.68 euros. On that date, to the nearest whole number, what is the number of Canadian dollars that could be purchased for 100 United States dollars?

Use the following information in answering Questions 37 and 38.

Every day to go to work, Ed drives the 6.3 miles between Exits 17 and 18 on Route 91, always at a constant rate of 60 miles per hour. At 60 miles per hour, Ed's car can go 24.3 miles per gallon of gasoline; at 70 miles per hour, Ed's car can only go 20.8 miles per gallon of gasoline.

37. How much less time, in seconds, would it take Ed to drive those 6.3 miles at 70 miles per hour instead of 60 miles per hour?

38. Last year, Ed drove the 6.3 miles from Exit 17 to Exit 18 a total of 240 times (always at 60 miles per hour). If during the year he paid an average of $3.50 per gallon for gasoline, how much more would it have cost him if he had driven at 70 miles per hour each day? (Express your answer to the nearest dollar, and grid it in without the dollar sign.)

STOP

If there is still time remaining, you may review your answers.

ESSAY (OPTIONAL)

Directions: This assignment will allow you to demonstrate your ability to skillfully read and understand a source text and write a response analyzing the source. In your response, you should show that you have understood the source, give proficient analysis, and use the English language effectively. If your essay is off-topic, it will not be scored.

Only what you write on the lined paper in your answer document will be scored—avoid skipping lines, using unreasonably large handwriting, and using wide margins in order to have sufficient space to respond. You can also write on the planning sheet in the answer document, but this will not be evaluated—no other scrap paper will be given. Be sure to write clearly and legibly so your response can be scored.

You will be given 50 minutes to complete the assignment, including reading the source text and writing your response.

Read the following passage, and think about how the author uses:

- Evidence, such as applicable examples, to justify the argument
- Reasoning to show logical connections among thoughts and facts
- Rhetoric, like sensory language and emotional appeals, to give weight to the argument

---

A Lesson on Commas

"Think left and think right and think low and think high.
Oh, the thinks you can think up if only you try."
—*Dr. Seuss*

1   It was my third year teaching English at Rosinburgh High when the freckled, garrulous Emily of the second row interrupted my comma lesson with an abrupt question, "Mrs. Jensen, why do you write?" I considered telling Emily to stay after class if she wished to converse off topic. Yet, the abridged somnolence in the farthest row and my romantic inclinations to a teaching career somewhat like that of Julia Roberts in *Mona Lisa Smile*—both sparked by the most recent inquisition—conspired my actual response: "Why does one listen to music? Or dance? Or look to the stars?" Amusement, surely. Communication and complex stimulation, absolutely. But mostly, I write in the name of indomitable creativity. I am of the distinct opinion that creativity is the most essential ingredient of erudition, expression, and future success, and being so, must be encouraged inside the classroom.

2   Creativity, contrary to popular belief, is not limited to the milieu of the elite, pedantic, or particularly adept; it is not reserved for the Picassos, the Bachs, or the Austens. Rather it is a gift bestowed to each and every one of us that should be maintained and even bolstered. The failure to include it in the public curriculum is a failure to society it in its entirety, as it indisputably dissuades curiosity, exploration, and activism. Emily, what if I told you that creativity is behind every piece of art, every

new electronic, and every scientific discovery? What if I told you progress would be simply unfeasible without it? If you question its innateness, a moment's reflection on the sublime imagination of any child you have ever come into the briefest contact with will assure you otherwise.

3   As for its consequence, let us first consider personal fulfillment. Where would you suppose yourself most happy: in a desultory, routine job or an engaging, challenging career? While the question may seem puerile, its implications are far from trivial. The number one reason for unhappiness in adults is hating their jobs, and *LinkedIn* places "not being challenged" and "not feeling valued" at the top of the list for workplace dissatisfaction. If we can generalize creativity to the extent Google does, i.e., to the generation and contemplation of new ideas to create something perceived as valuable, then we can arrive at the need for it in our workplaces and domestic spheres. Simply put, humans need creativity to feel gratification. You may venture that the heretic without imagination is yet to be born, but I would add that the contented without imagination is just as uncommon.

4   Shall we move on to its effluence in a broader sense? Higher creativity preludes greater innovation and, thus, success and progress. In fact, a 2010 IBM survey ranked creativity as the single most important factor in corporate success. Let us ruminate for a moment on medical cures, energy alternatives, and space exploration—the need for creativity extends far beyond the recluse artist indeed. Perhaps your aspirations fall short of those of Steve Jobs or Shinya Yamanaka; still, you need to bring problem-solving and critical thinking into your career for the sake of efficiency, diversification, and job security. It is what allows you to see the world as it is, exercise your interest in all that surrounds you, and bring fresh thinking to your circumstance. After all, it was Albert Einstein who said, "Imagination is more important than knowledge."

5   I have convinced you of creativity's import, but my rambling will seem only didactic if I neglect to address the ways that creativity can be nourished within the education system. You'll be surprised to learn how easily it can be incorporated into everyday scholarship. Schools, and teachers more specifically, can cultivate creativity by encouraging questioning and debate. The *why's* and the *how's* are a good place to start. Similarly, classrooms can make a habit of identifying problems and brainstorming solutions: the *what's good, what's bad*, and *how could it be improved*. A next step is in inspiring alternative problem solving—these are the beloved *what if's*. Promoting creativity begins with the generating of new knowledge, in lieu of the passing on of existing knowledge solely. It may be unclear to Emily why I write, particularly when I have so little success at it, but it is apparent to me how valuable her curiosity is, and how paramount that it be nurtured rather than dulled.

> Write a response that demonstrates how the author makes an argument to persuade an audience that creativity should be taught in schools. In your response, analyze how the author uses at least one of the features from the essay directions (or features of your own choosing) to develop a logical and persuasive argument. Be certain that your response cites relevant aspects of the source text.
>
> Your response should not give your personal opinion on the merit of the source text, but instead show how the author crafts an argument to persuade readers.

MODEL TEST 1

Section 1: Reading

1.	C	14.	B	27.	D	40.	B
2.	A	15.	B	28.	B	41.	A
3.	B	16.	A	29.	C	42.	C
4.	C	17.	A	30.	D	43.	B
5.	B	18.	C	31.	C	44.	B
6.	A	19.	C	32.	C	45.	A
7.	B	20.	D	33.	D	46.	A
8.	A	21.	D	34.	A	47.	A
9.	B	22.	D	35.	B	48.	D
10.	B	23.	C	36.	C	49.	C
11.	C	24.	C	37.	D	50.	C
12.	B	25.	B	38.	C	51.	A
13.	D	26.	B	39.	B	52.	C

Number Correct _____

Number Incorrect _____

Section 2: Writing and Language

1.	C	12.	C	23.	B	34.	C
2.	A	13.	C	24.	A	35.	B
3.	D	14.	A	25.	B	36.	C
4.	C	15.	B	26.	A	37.	A
5.	B	16.	A	27.	C	38.	D
6.	D	17.	D	28.	D	39.	B
7.	A	18.	A	29.	D	40.	A
8.	B	19.	D	30.	D	41.	D
9.	A	20.	B	31.	B	42.	D
10.	C	21.	D	32.	C	43.	B
11.	A	22.	A	33.	A	44.	C

Number Correct _____

Number Incorrect _____

ANSWER KEY
Model Test 1

Section 3: Math (No Calculator)

1. **A**   5. **B**   9. **B**   13. **B**
2. **D**   6. **C**   10. **A**   14. **B**
3. **C**   7. **A**   11. **C**   15. **B**
4. **D**   8. **A**   12. **D**

16. **2**   17. **1**   18. **2**   19. **14**

20. **3**

Number Correct _____

Number Incorrect _____

Section 4: Math (Calculator)

1. B	7. A	13. C	19. C	25. C
2. C	8. D	14. C	20. C	26. D
3. A	9. A	15. D	21. D	27. C
4. A	10. D	16. C	22. B	28. B
5. D	11. D	17. A	23. B	29. A
6. C	12. D	18. D	24. D	30. C

31. **37.5**

32. **6.8**

33. **3744**

34. **8190**

35. **3/2 or 1.5**

or

36. **129**

37. **54**

38. **37**

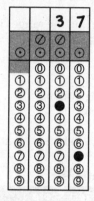

Number Correct _____

Number Incorrect _____

SCORE ANALYSIS

Reading and Writing Test

Section 1: Reading _____ = _____ (A)
                                # correct   raw score

Section 2: Writing _____ = _____ (B)
                                # correct   raw score

To find your Reading and Writing test scores, consult the chart below: find the ranges in which your raw scores lie and read across to find the ranges of your test scores.

_____ + _____ = _____ (C)
range of reading   range of writing   range of reading + writing
test scores   test scores   test scores

To find the range of your Reading and Writing Scaled Score, multiply (C) by 10.

Test Scores for the Reading and Writing Sections

Reading Raw Score	Writing Raw Score	Test Score
44–52	39–44	35–40
36–43	33–38	31–34
30–35	28–32	28–30
24–29	22–27	24–27
19–23	17–21	21–23
14–18	13–16	19–20
9–13	9–12	16–18
5–8	5–8	13–15
less than 5	less than 5	10–12

Math Test

Section 3: _____ = _____ (D)
                 # correct   raw score

Section 4: _____ = _____ (E)
                 # correct   raw score

Total Math raw score: (D) + (E) = _____

To find your Math Scaled Score, consult the chart below: find the range in which your raw score lies and read across to find the range for your scaled score.

Scaled Scores for the Math Test

Raw Score	Scaled Score	Raw Score	Scaled Score
50–58	700–800	20–25	450–490
44–49	650–690	15–19	400–440
38–43	600–640	11–14	350–390
32–37	550–590	7–10	300–340
26–32	500–540	less than 7	200–290

ANSWERS EXPLAINED

Section 1: Reading Test

1. **(C)** Substitute the answer choices in the original sentence. The sergeant is a person who might have been a deputy sheriff before he joined the army—that is, in his civil or *nonmilitary* life.

2. **(A)** Paragraph 1 presents a general picture of the man on the bridge, the executioners and the officer standing nearby, the sentinels at the far ends of the bridge. Cinematically, it is like *a wide-angle shot* of the whole panorama. Paragraph 2 takes a closer look at the man, examining his clothes, his face, his expression. It is as if the camera has moved in for *a close-up* shot.

3. **(B)** You can use the process of elimination to answer this question. Was the man awaiting hanging *innocent of any criminal intent*? No. He was willing to go along with the idea that all was fair in love and war, and would willingly perform a criminal act (assaulting a sentinel and burning down a bridge). Choice (A) is incorrect. Was the man awaiting hanging an *unlikely candidate for execution*? Possibly. Keep choice (B) in mind as you consider the other choices. Was the man awaiting hanging *a victim of mistaken identity*? No. He was caught in the act of attempting to burn down the bridge. Was the man awaiting hanging *purposely assuming a harmless demeanor*? Nothing in the passage suggests that he was putting on the appearance of being harmless. Choice (C) is incorrect. Only choice (B) is left. It is the correct answer.

4. **(C)** To have one's neck "in the hemp" is to have one's neck in a noose, a rope made out of hemp. The author's comment that the man "had a kindly expression that one would hardly have expected in one whose neck was in the hemp" suggests that he is *an unlikely candidate for execution* and that some unusual circumstances must have brought him to this fate.

5. **(B)** In calling the military code "liberal" because it doesn't exclude members of the upper classes from being executed, the author is being highly *ironic*. Generally, people would like regulations to be interpreted liberally to permit them to do the things they want. Here, the liberal military code is permitting the man to be hanged. Clearly, the gentleman facing execution would have preferred the code to be less liberal in this case.

6. **(A)** Farquhar agrees readily with the saying that all is fair in love and war. This implies he is willing to use *underhanded* or unfair *methods to support his* [the Southern] *cause*.

7. **(B)** Look at the context in which the word *consistent* occurs. "(N)o adventure [was] too perilous for him to undertake if [it was] *consistent* with the character of a civilian who was at heart a soldier." Farquhar has no objection to performing humble errands or undertaking dangerous tasks as long as these tasks are appropriate to someone who sees himself as a sort of "undercover soldier," a secret agent of the Confederacy. Anything he does must be consistent or *compatible* with his image of himself in this role.

8. **(A)** The fact that Mrs. Farquhar is married to a man "ardently devoted to the Southern cause," together with her readiness to fetch water for a Confederate soldier, suggests some degree of sympathy on her part for the Confederate cause. Choice (B) is incorrect. Mrs. Farquhar's action, in hospitably fetching water "with her own white hands,"

contradicts the idea that she is too proud to perform menial tasks. Choices (C) and (D) are also incorrect. There is nothing in the passage to suggest either of them.

9. **(B)** The assertion that Mrs. Farquhar "was only too happy" to fetch water for a soldier wearing the grey uniform of the Confederate army provides strong evidence that she is *sympathetic to the Confederate cause.*

10. **(B)** Farquhar wishes to prevent the Yankee advance. To do so, he must somehow damage the railroad, its bridges, its tunnels, or its trains. The soldier tells him that some highly flammable driftwood is piled up at the base of the wooden railroad bridge. Clearly, it would make sense for Farquhar to try to set fire to the driftwood in *an attempt to burn down* the bridge.

11. **(C)** The scout is a Yankee soldier disguised as a member of the enemy. By coming to the Farquhars' plantation in Confederate disguise, he is able to learn they are sympathetic to the enemy. By telling Farquhar of the work on the bridge, stressing both the lack of guards and the abundance of fuel, he is tempting Farquhar into an attack on the bridge (and into an ambush). The scout's job is to locate potential enemies and draw them out from cover. The concluding sentence thus establishes *that Farquhar has been entrapped into taking an unwise action*, an action that will lead to his execution at Owl Creek bridge.

12. **(B)** President Roosevelt mentions two types of people who came to America seeking freedom: "some of high degree, but mostly plain people." The people of high degree were members of the upper classes, those set apart by aristocratic birth or social position; the others were plain, *ordinary* people.

13. **(D)** Roosevelt describes the American spirit as "the product of centuries." In other words, the hope of freedom and the love of liberty go back for centuries; America's democratic ideal *has deep-seated* (firmly established) *historical roots.*

14. **(B)** Choice (B) clearly supports the contention that the American belief in freedom "has deep-seated historical roots." It pointedly asserts that the "democratic aspiration is no mere recent phase in human history" and goes on to mention the Magna Carta or Great Charter of 1215 as a specific example of a historic document that embodies the spirit of democracy.

15. **(B)** Look at the context in which these documents are mentioned. "Its vitality was written into our own Mayflower Compact, into the Declaration of Independence, into the Constitution of the United States, into the Gettysburg Address." To what does the phrase "Its vitality" refer? The answer appears two paragraphs earlier, in the opening sentence "The democratic aspiration is no mere recent phase in human history." The democratic aspiration is Roosevelt's theme, the subject he is discussing. According to Roosevelt, the vitality and strength of democratic aspiration were written into America's founding documents. Thus, he clearly is citing these documents as examples of *expressions of the democratic aspiration.*

16. **(A)** In lines 36–39, Roosevelt asserts that Americans "have moved forward constantly and consistently toward an ideal which in itself has gained stature and clarity with each generation." It is his optimistic contention that we have been coming closer and closer to reaching that ideal and that the democratic spirit has grown stronger. However, he acknowledges that "we still have far to go" before we reach that ideal: the existence of

both "undeserved poverty" and "self-serving wealth" stands in the way of democracy. In other words, *economic injustices must be addressed before democracy can prevail.*

17. **(A)** In his 1789 First Inaugural Address, Washington was directing his words to his contemporaries. In other words, he was *addressing* his words to them, speaking to them in a formal way. To Roosevelt, Washington's words sounded prophetic, as if he *addressed* his words to the people of 1941.

18. **(C)** Repetition is a common, yet effective literary device that strengthens the power of the point being made. One website of popular literary terms describes the effect of repetition as follows: "The aura that is created by the usage of repetition cannot be achieved through any other device. It has the ability of making a simple sentence sound like a dramatic one. It enhances the beauty of a sentence and stresses on the point of main significance." Thus, the main effect of the repetition of the phrase "It speaks to us" is to create a *dramatic tone, emphasizing the point being made and adding to its emotional impact.*

19. **(C)** What experiment was "intrusted to the hands of the American people"? Consider the context. Washington was writing an address that he was to deliver on his inauguration as president of the United States, a new nation founded upon democratic principles. The experiment entrusted to the American people was the radical experiment of *democratic government.*

20. **(D)** Washington's "experiment intrusted to the hands of the American people" is the republican model of government, whose preservation he urges. It is this same model of government that Roosevelt urges Americans to defend when he asserts that "our strong purpose is to protect and to perpetuate the integrity of democracy."

21. **(D)** As we know from the introduction to the passage, Roosevelt delivered his Third Inaugural Address in January of 1941, at a time when Britain and its allies were hard pressed by Hitler's forces but the United States had not yet gone to war. Nonetheless, it was clear that democracy was under attack and that America was facing "great perils never before encountered." The passage's final paragraphs emphasize the need to preserve the sacred fire of liberty. The president exhorts his listeners "to protect and to perpetuate the integrity of democracy." Thus, it is reasonable to conclude that a major goal of Roosevelt in making this speech was to *inspire the American people to defend the cause of freedom in dangerous times.*

22. **(D)** Step by step, the author traces the course of a surgical procedure, from the initial grasping of the scalpel through the opening incision to the eventual sensory exploration of the internal organs. In doing so, he is *describing a process.* Choice (A) is incorrect. Although in the course of the passage the author occasionally defines a term (for example, the term *fascia*), the passage, taken as a whole, describes the process of surgery; it does not define a term. Choice (B) is incorrect. The passage does not provide an example of a particular method of surgery; instead, it describes the process of surgery. Choice (C) is incorrect. This is not a lesson, instructing novice surgeons in the steps they should take to perform a successful abdominal surgery; it is a vivid description of the process of surgery.

23. **(C)** As the surgeon draws the knife across the skin, it leaves a thin *line of blood* in its wake (path or track passed over by a moving object). Choices (A) and (B) are incorrect;

nothing in the opening paragraph supports either choice. Choice (D) is incorrect. The darting knife is *followed* by the fine wake of red; the knife blade is not the wake of red.

24. **(C)** The darting knife is followed by a wake of red. If the meaning of the simile is still unclear at this point, the subsequent sentence, in which the parted flesh reveals yellow blobs of fat below, is a clue that the "fine wake of red" is a bloody incision made by the knife. Choices (A) and (B) are incorrect. They describe the way to hold the knife, not the effect of the knife as it cuts its way through the patient's skin. Choice (D) is incorrect. It has nothing to do with the knife's wake or trail of red.

25. **(B)** To part the flesh is to *split* apart or separate the skin, cutting it apart with the knife. Choice (A) is incorrect. Although in some contexts "parts" means *leaves*, as in "parting from someone at the train station," that is not how it's used here. Choice (C) is incorrect. Although in some contexts "parts" means *surrenders* ("parting with hard-earned cash"), that is not how it is used here. Choice (D) is incorrect. Although in some contexts "parts" means *distributes* ("parting an estate into shares"), that is not how it's used here.

26. **(B)** The simile "like children absorbed in a game" indicates that, in this context, "engaged" means *engrossed* or deeply involved. Choice (A) is incorrect. Although in some contexts "engaged" means *betrothed* or pledged to marry, that is not how it is used here. Choice (C) is incorrect. Although in some contexts "engaged" means *hired* ("engaged as a contractor"), that is not how it is used here. Choice (D) is incorrect. Although in some contexts "engaged" means *embattled* ("engaged forces"), that is not how it is used here.

27. **(D)** Primitive drawings of buffalo and other wild beasts still exist in *caves* in which *prehistoric* humans dwelled. Thus, one might expect to find them in a cavity described as "a primitive place." Choice (A) is incorrect. In "a primitive place," one might expect to find primitive drawings; one wouldn't necessarily expect to find them in an art gallery. Choices (B) and (C) are incorrect. Nothing in the passage suggests that one might expect to find *drawings* of buffalo in either a zoological display or a Western film.

28. **(B)** The colors of the internal organs are secret because, until the peritoneum is opened and the world's light illuminates the abdominal cavity, the internal organs cannot be seen. In other words, the colors of the internal organs *normally are hidden from sight.*

29. **(C)** The author looks on his work as a surgeon as if it were a priestly vocation. The first hint of this comes in lines 32–34: "the litany of monosyllables with which one prays his way down and in: *clamp, sponge, suture, tie, cut.*" The one-word requests that the surgeon makes for a clamp or a sponge are like a litany, a form of prayer made up of a series of invocations or petitions that are usually led by the clergy. The surgeon "prays his way down and in." Clearly, the author is making use of priestly or *religious imagery.* Choice (A) is incorrect. Although the author likens the abdominal cavity to a cavern, he primarily describes the surgery in religious terms. Choice (B) is incorrect. The author never contrasts abdominal surgery with other types of surgery. Choice (D) is incorrect. The author never evokes or suggests the patient's emotions; if anything, he evokes the surgeon's emotions.

30. **(D)** In these two sentences, the author makes explicit his sense of surgery as a religious rite, an impression he continues to develop in the subsequent paragraph ("the priestliness of my profession has ever been impressed on me").

31. **(C)** Consider the various descriptive passages in which the author explores the formerly hidden organs and tissues now exposed to view through surgical intervention.

"The peritoneum, pink and gleaming and membranous, bulges into the wound." "An arc of the liver shines high and on the right, like a dark sun. It laps over the pink sweep of the stomach, from whose lower border the gauzy omentum is draped, and through which veil one sees, sinuous, slow as just-fed snakes, the indolent coils of the intestine." Peritoneum, liver, stomach, omentum, intestine: the author names them, evokes their appearance in a brief descriptive phrase ("peritoneum, pink and gleaming and membranous," "gauzy omentum," "indolent coils of the intestine"). However, he does not bother to define these anatomical terms. Instead, he apparently assumes that his readers will *be familiar with the organs and tissues* to which he refers. Choice (A) is incorrect. The author freely goes into vivid detail about surgical procedures. He would be unlikely to be as free in his imagery if he assumed that his readers had qualms about reading descriptions of surgery. Choice (B) is incorrect. The author carefully describes how to hold a scalpel; he would not do so if he assumed his readers were already adept at handling surgical tools. Choice (D) is incorrect. Nothing in the passage suggests that the author assumes his readers have undergone surgery.

32. **(C)** Throughout Passage 1, the author constantly emphasizes the lengthy time period his book will cover. In the passage's opening sentence he refers to "the shifting relationship between the press and the presidency *over nearly two centuries*"; later he refers to "the relationship of the presidents to the press *since George Washington's first term*." The author is "surveying nearly two centuries of this relationship." In other words, he is presenting *an overview* of a relationship. What sort of relationship is it? It is one of "mutual . . . recriminations and mistrust." There has been one main constant in it, "the dissatisfaction of one with the other. In other words, it is *an inherently conflicted relationship*. Not only that, but this relationship "has been increasingly complicated by the changing nature of the presidency, by the individual nature of presidents, by the rise of other media, especially television, and by the growing complexity of beliefs about the function of both press and government." The inherently conflicted relationship clearly *faces new challenges* and will continue to do so as our institutions and technology continue to change. The correct answer is choice (C).

33. **(D)** The first paragraph of the passage says that the administration of every president has ended with "recriminations and mistrust." Presidents, like everyone else, hate to be criticized in public. Therefore, they all have experienced *animosity involving themselves and the press*. Choice (C) is incorrect. The first paragraph states that, while the initial stage of the relationship between the press and the president may seem harmonious ("beginning with mutual protestations of good will"), the relationship ends in antagonism. The paragraph never suggests that periods of antagonism and harmony alternate.

34. **(A)** If the record of *every* administration has begun with the press and the presidency claiming to feel goodwill toward one another and has ended with them blaming and mistrusting one another, then clearly *all* American presidents have experienced *mutual animosity* (ill will) *involving themselves and the press*.

35. **(B)** To be reduced to simple terms is to be simplified or *boiled down* to its essential, basic nature. Choices (A), (C), and (D) are incorrect. Although reduced can mean *decreased* ("reduced speed"), *marked down* ("reduced prices"), or *demoted* ("reduced in rank"), it is not how the word is used here.

36. **(C)** The author advises the reader to (lines 41–42) "be careful not to view the past in terms of our own times." This advice is an axiom (a statement or proposition regarded as being established, accepted, or self-evidently true) of professional historians. As a professional historian, he gives the reader this advice because *readers today cannot fully grasp the significance these actions had in their own time.*

37. **(D)** To use present standards to judge the actions of past presidents "is to violate historical context." *Because* the words "press," "government," and "presidency" have changed in meaning, because our lives today differ so greatly from the lives of people in earlier times, we cannot fully understand the significance of presidential actions two centuries ago.

38. **(C)** The opening sentence of the final paragraph concludes with the clause "but the facts are quite different." Many Americans believe that the colonists immediately established a free society. The author says that this belief is incorrect. Thus, he is trying to *correct a misconception* or mistaken idea.

39. **(B)** The open questioning to which the author refers (line 107) is the *unrestricted*, no holds barred questioning that the president faces in modern solo press conferences. Choices (A), (C), and (D) are incorrect. Although "open" can mean *receptive* ("open to suggestions"), *unconcealed* ("open carry"), or *vulnerable* ("open to abuse"), that is not how it is used here.

40. **(B)** Use the process of elimination to answer this question. Did President Clinton hold more solo press conferences than President George H. W. Bush did? No. President Clinton held 62 solo press conferences; President George H. W. Bush held 83 solo press conferences. Choice (A) is incorrect. Did Presidents Clinton and George W. Bush hold a far higher percentage of joint press conferences than either of their predecessors did? This seems to be correct. President Clinton's percentage of joint press conferences was 67.9%; President George W. Bush's percentage of joint press conferences was 77.3%. Neither of their predecessors came even close. Choice (B) is most likely the correct answer. Quickly scan the remaining choices to see whether you can find a better answer than choice (B). Choice (C) asks you to draw a conclusion that is unsupported by the data in the graph. True, the graph provides data showing President Reagan held no joint press conferences; however, it provides no information to indicate why he did this. Choice (C) is incorrect. Choice (D) is also incorrect. Unlike his son, President George H. W. Bush held fewer joint press conferences than solo sessions.

41. **(A)** Passage 1 *describes a phenomenon*. This phenomenon is the dissatisfaction of the press and the president with each other. Passage 1 describes it as a constant, that is, an unchanging factor. Passage 2, however, focuses on changes in this relationship. It does not describe the situation as *static*. Instead, it emphasizes the "increasingly contentious, adversarial" nature of the relationship and suggests that this increased aggressiveness from the press may have brought about the shift from solo press conferences, during which the president is more open to direct hostility, to joint press conferences, in which he has more control of the situation. Thus, in focusing on the increases in press aggressiveness and on the changes in the structure of presidential press conferences, *Passage 2 denies the static nature of the phenomenon described in Passage 1.*

42. **(C)** Both authors make a point of the adversarial nature of the relationship between the press and the president. This inherent antagonism is at the heart of the relationship and is likely to influence the actions of both the press and the president for years to come.

43. **(B)** Choice (B) is correct. To describe the debate over fracking or hydraulic fracturing as "fractious" is to make *a play on* the words "fractious" and "fracturing." The author chooses the adjective "fractious" because it begins like "fracturing." The similarity in sound between the two words strengthens the sentence's effect. In contrast, consider the effect of this slight change on the opening sentence: "To call it a heated debate is an understatement." Lacking the word play, the revised sentence feels a bit flat. Choice (A) is incorrect. A metaphor is a figure of speech in which a term or phrase is applied to something to which it is not literally applicable in order to suggest a resemblance, as in "My boss is such a bear today." Choice (C) is incorrect. It is no exaggeration to say that the debate over fracking has become heated or *fractious*. Hydraulic fracturing is a controversial subject, and the discussion about it is contentious. Choice (D) is incorrect. A counterargument is an argument put forward to oppose an idea or theory developed in another argument. It has nothing to do with the author's word choice here.

44. **(B)** Choice (B) is correct. A game changer is an event, idea, or procedure that brings about a significant shift in the current way of doing something. By calling fracking-related gas recovery a game changer, fracking's supporters are asserting that fracking is going to *radically alter natural gas production*. Choice (A) is incorrect. In calling fracking a game changer, its proponents do not assert that fracking has no foreseeable negative consequences. Instead, they assert that its positive benefits (reduced dependence on foreign sources of energy, new jobs, relatively clean energy, etc.) strongly outweigh its possible drawbacks. Choice (C) is incorrect. In calling fracking a game changer, its proponents are not asserting that they fail to take it seriously. Choice (D) is incorrect. Although later portions of the passage mention a need for regulation, fracking's proponents say nothing about any need for *active federal regulation*.

45. **(A)** Choice (A) is correct. In lines 6–14, the author lists the following points made by fracking's supporters:

    1. Compared to natural gas recovered by drilling oil wells, natural gas recovered through fracking is inexpensive (it "is cheap").
    2. Compared to natural gas recovered by drilling oil wells, natural gas recovered through fracking is relatively free from pollutants or unpleasant substances (it is "relatively clean").
    3. The United States contains an abundance of natural gas that can be recovered through fracking. ("America is brimful of the stuff.")

    To have access through fracking to an abundant supply of inexpensive, relatively clean natural gas would *change* our methods of *natural gas production radically*. It would change the entire oil industry. Indeed, it is doing so. None of the remaining choices provide evidence in support of the assertion that fracking is a game changer.

46. **(A)** In lines 15–24, the author relates the public's fears about the dangers of fracking. Media reports of fracking-triggered earthquakes and fracking-caused environmental contamination fuel these fears. In the paragraph immediately following, the author depicts the reaction these fears have produced in the political arena. She mentions protests and legislative attempts to halt or ban fracking in several states. Her discussion of fracking legislation thus *describes specific responses* (marches, moratoriums, policy changes) *to concerns raised in the previous paragraph*.

47. **(A)** Choice (A) is correct. An open question is a matter that has not yet been decided, an issue that remains *unresolved.* Choice (B) is incorrect. Although "open" can mean *vulnerable,* as in the welfare system's being "open to abuse," that is not the sense in which it is used here. Choice (C) is incorrect. Although "open" can mean *accessible,* as in a school program's being "open to all students," that is not the sense in which it is used here. Choice (D) is incorrect. Although "open" can mean *ajar,* as in a door's being "left open," that is not the sense in which it is used here.

48. **(D)** Use the process of elimination to answer this question. Choice (A) is incorrect. Nothing in the passage suggests that its author advocates or supports technological innovations such as fracking; she merely reports the opinions of fracking's advocates. Choice (B) is incorrect. Nothing in the passage suggests that its author either opposes or supports regulatory oversight, whether pointless or not; she merely describes legislative attempts to regulate fracking. Choice (C) is incorrect. Nothing in the passage suggests that its author is a concerned legislator; she merely recounts the actions taken by legislators regarding fracking. Only choice (D) is left. It is the correct answer. The author is *an observer striving* to be objective and *to present a balanced account.*

    Remember to read the italicized introduction. Often it contains useful information. Here, the italicized introduction indicates that the passage comes from a popular science magazine, *Science News.* Such magazines have the task of presenting current research findings in an objective, unbiased manner, weighing both sides of an argument rather than arguing the merits of a particular claim.

49. **(C)** The author acknowledges that the dangers of fracking are real. She also acknowledges that the potential energy payoff is real as well. She is striving to present both sides of the argument objectively.

50. **(C)** The solid line on the graph vividly depicts a sudden, marked jump in the number and frequency of earthquakes from about 2009. This accentuates or emphasizes the *increasing frequency of earthquakes in the region.* Choice (B) is incorrect. The graph plots the increased frequency of earthquakes, not their increased magnitude. Choices (A) and (D) are incorrect. Nothing in the passage supports either answer.

51. **(A)** In stating that the change in the frequency and number of earthquakes was pronounced, Ellsworth is asserting that it was marked or particularly *noticeable.* Choices (B), (C), and (D) are incorrect. Although "pronounced" can mean *declared* ("pronounced dead"), *decided on* ("pronounced on innocence or guilt"), or *articulated* ("correctly pronounced words"), that is not how it is used here.

52. **(C)** Ellsworth indicates that researchers lack pre-quake data (lines 98–100). He advises researchers to collect seismic information about current and potential drilling sites. He concludes the paragraph by stating explicitly that "(t)here are many things we don't understand." All these comments in the passage's concluding paragraph suggest that Ellsworth looks on current hypotheses about connections between the recent increases in earthquakes and the start of the fracking boom as *based on insufficient knowledge.* Geologists simply don't know enough about what actually occurs during fracking to be able to properly test their hypotheses about fracking's possible effects on the increasing frequency of earthquakes.

Section 2: Writing and Language

1. **(C)** The first sentence of the paragraph states that Modernism is characterized by the "complete rejection" of traditions and values, which is consistent with a "rebuff" of conventional morality. Moreover, the remainder of the paragraph mentions moral relativism, which further solidifies the notion of a "rebuff" of mainstream values. Choice (A) is not correct because it is the opposite of an embrace. Choice (B) is not right because it can be reasonably inferred that Fitzgerald must have understood conventional morality since he skillfully wrote about matters concerning it. Choice (D) is incorrect because its connotation is too positive.

2. **(A)** The writer uses an interesting turn of phrase to state that Bernice does not listen to (entertain) or find amusing (be entertained by) Marjorie's social activities. Choice (B) does not work because a transitional word would be needed after "entertainment." Choices (C) and (D) result in nonsensical meanings.

3. **(D)** The underlined portion refers to the female Bernice, so "herself" is appropriate. The other options are not consistent with a third-person singular female.

4. **(C)** "To mock" is parallel with the earlier "to embody" in the sentence and concisely expresses the intended idea. Choices (A) and (B) are too wordy. Choice (D) is not be parallel to the earlier phrasing.

5. **(B)** "Who" is correct since it stands for a subject that is human. Choice (A) is used in reference to objects. Choice (C) shows possession. Choice (D) means "who is."

6. **(D)** This sentence needs to come before the third sentence, which starts with "Despite her good looks. . . ." This sentence provides a transition between a description of Marjorie and a contrasting description of Bernice. The other placements are illogical as they would not allow for a clear transition between the descriptions of the two characters.

7. **(A)** Two eras are being compared, so "between" is the best choice. Choice (B) is wrong because "among" is used for a comparison of three or more things. "Contrast for," which is choice (C), and "Contrast on," which is choice (D), are not idiomatically correct.

8. **(B)** "While" is the only option that provides a contrast within the sentence between how Marjorie is preferred socially and her rudeness.

9. **(A)** When adjectives have to be ordered a certain way to provide a logical meaning, there should be no commas separating them. In this case, it only makes sense to say "few short sentences," not "short few sentences," making choice (A) the only viable option. Choices (B) and (D) change the meaning, and choice (C) has an unnecessary comma.

10. **(C)** The last sentence of the paragraph makes this choice the most clear, stating that both Bernice and Marjorie are quite superficial. So characterizing them as having "false facades" is most logical. With their vengeful dramatics, they are far from being "kind-hearted" as in choice (A). Choice (B) is incorrect since they are not revolutionary ideologues but, instead, more decadent. Choice (D) is not the right answer because being frivolous and pious are contradictory.

11. **(A)** In choice (A), the colon comes after a complete sentence right before the flaws are clarified and the comma comes before the transitional "while." Choice (B) results in a

run-on sentence. Choice (C) has an unnecessary comma after "lifeless." Choice (D) has an unnecessary comma after "manner."

12. **(C)** The first part of the sentence states that journalism gathers and distributes news in a wide variety of ways, and choice (C) gives specific examples of the technology that does this. Choices (A), (B), and (D) are irrelevant to the first part of the sentence.

13. **(C)** This choice places a comma after the introductory dependent clause ending in "media" and puts a colon before a clarification of how the field is optimistic. Choice (A) lacks a necessary comma after "media" and leads to a run-on sentence. Choice (B) leads to a run-on. Choice (D) puts a semicolon between a subject and a verb, which should not be separated.

14. **(A)** "But also" follows "not only" when making a statement like "not only this but also that." None of the other options works with this idiomatic phrasing.

15. **(B)** The current paragraph emphasizes that journalism has undergone major changes, while the following paragraph delves more deeply into concrete explanations of these changes. So choice (B) makes the most sense because it provides both a conclusion to the current paragraph and a transition into the topic of the next. Choices (A) and (C) contradict the information presented in the next paragraph. Choice (D) speaks more to the quality of journalism than to its overall popularity.

16. **(A)** The sentence is stating two things that *do not* happen, so saying "doesn't" in conjunction with "nor" makes sense. Choice (B) shows cause and effect. Choice (C) shows a direct connection between two ideas. Choice (D) shows contrast.

17. **(D)** This choice correctly does not have an apostrophe after "departments" because this word is functioning as the subject, not as a possessive adjective. Choices (A) and (B) incorrectly have apostrophes after "departments." Choice (D)is also correct because "ensuring" means to "make sure," which fits the context. "Assure" means to "reassure," and "insure" has to do with financial transactions.

18. **(A)** The previous sentence refers to "leading journalism departments," so a sentence about the number one journalism department in the country is a logical connection. The other choices may very well give interesting and factual information about this school, but they are not directly connected to the previous sentence.

19. **(D)** This choice correctly places commas around the parenthetical phrase. Choice (A) has a comma at an awkward point, choice (B) lacks the necessary pauses, and choice (C) is too choppy.

20. **(B)** The adjective "endless" is needed to modify the noun "effects." Also, "affect" is generally a verb, and "effect" is generally a noun. The incorrect options either use the adverb "endlessly" and/or use the verb "affect."

21. **(D)** According to the graph, the number of journalism-related job openings has gone up, then down, and then up again in recent years. This variation is best described as a "fluctuation." Choice (A) is incorrect because since the passage was written in 2015, there has not been a steady increase in demand for journalists in recent years, given the big drop from 2006 to 2009. Choice (B) is not right because in recent years, the number of jobs available increased. Choice (C) is not correct because the level of employment has gone up and down, not remained steady.

22. **(A)** To "adapt" is to make something suitable, and to "adopt" is to make something one's own. In this case, the field of journalism is making gradual changes in order to adjust to technological advances, so "adapt" makes sense. Choices (C) and (D) are therefore incorrect. The paragraph is in the present tense, so "is adapting" works (choice (A)) and "was adapting" (choice (B)) does not.

23. **(B)** Giving an approximation of the years is the most precise option. Choices (A), (C), and (D) are too vague.

24. **(A)** This choice gives necessary breaks between all of the listed items and also has a break after the clarifying phrase "most recently." Choices (B), (C), and (D) all change the original meaning because of their comma placements or lack thereof.

25. **(B)** To convey giving a high priority to making the Parthenon glorious, the phrase "sparing no expense" is the best choice. It indicates that the Greeks were willing to put as many economic resources as needed into finishing the Parthenon in a beautiful manner. Honesty and judiciousness, choice (A), do not necessarily relate to making the Parthenon glorious. Although "artistic patience" and the use of "architectural techniques" (choices (C) and (D)) could be loosely related to completing the Parthenon in the glorious fashion, these do not convey that finishing it was a high priority.

26. **(A)** This is the only option that expresses the needed contrast between the previous sentence and the current one since there is a contrast between the glorious construction of the Parthenon and the fact that the glory was very short-lived. The other options do not express the needed contrast.

27. **(C)** "Could've" sounds like "could of," but it is short for "could have." The use of the word "of" in this context is therefore incorrect, making choices (A) and (B) wrong. Choice (C) correctly expresses the verb "have." Choice (D) makes the sentence say "should have been still served," which is nonsensical.

28. **(D)** "Its" correctly refers to the singular Parthenon's possession of "pagan gods." The word "Its'" is always incorrect (choice (A)). Both choice (B) and choice (C) mean "it is."

29. **(D)** "Remnants" means "surviving pieces or traces of something," so logically these refer to the parts of the Parthenon that remained after its destruction. Choice (A) refers to the study of such remains, not the remains themselves. Choices (B) and (C) do not give a precise description of what these are.

30. **(D)** This choice concisely expresses the intended idea. Choices (A) and (B) are too wordy. Choice (C) likely wants to say something along the lines of "contemporary," but the word given actually means "with contempt."

31. **(B)** "Beauty" and "refinement" create a compound subject, which requires the plural "are." In addition, the paragraph is in the present tense, so the verb must be in the present tense. Choices (C) and (D) are in the past tense, and choice (A) is singular.

32. **(C)** The fact that these engravings have lasted for a long time is an essential part of their description, so "that" is needed instead of "which." Choice (C) also uses the proper tense. Choice (A) uses the incorrect verb tense. Choices (B) and (D) use "which," which works for nonessential characteristics of described objects.

33. **(A)** The essay focuses throughout on the impressive feat of the Parthenon's construction, so choice (A) gives a direct connection to this general theme. Choices (B) and (C) are too vague. Choice (D) focuses on only a small part of the passage.

34. **(C)** By examining the topic sentences of the paragraphs, you can see that the essay is presenting various theories about what happened to the Neanderthals. Choice (C) is therefore the most fitting option to introduce the essay's argument. Choice (A) is vague, and choice (B) is disconnected from the essay's argument. Choice (D) contradicts the essay's argument since the Neanderthals were not ultimately successful in adapting.

35. **(B)** Mention of the Neanderthals at the beginning of the underlined portion is necessary to make a logical comparison with "our own ancestors." Choices (A) and (D) make illogical comparisons since they compare geographic regions to ancestors. Choice (C) has confusing word order at the end, placing "icebound" such that it literally means that the Neanderthals were icebound. Choice (B) puts things in a logical order and makes a logical comparison of people to Neanderthals.

36. **(C)** It is necessary to have the words in the order "extreme climate" to express the correct meaning. Since the words must be in this order, no comma is needed to separate them. If the adjectives can be reversed, then a comma between them is necessary (e.g., "the big, tall mountain").

37. **(A)** The last part of this sentence gives more support to the claim in the first part of the sentence, making "and" appropriate. Choice (B) shows contrast, choice (C) is too wordy, and choice (D) removes a needed transition.

38. **(D)** This sentence is best placed at the end of the paragraph since it has the initial transition "further," which indicates that it is building on the previous argument. Moreover, it is logical to have this after sentence 3 since this sentence gives information in support of the idea that Neanderthals had excellent body heat-generating ability. The clothing cited in the sentence builds on this genetic advantage. Choice (A) makes no sense because this sentence cannot function as an introduction. Choice (B) interrupts a logical transition between sentences 1 and 2. Choice (C) inverts the logical sequence of the inserted sentence building upon sentence 3.

39. **(B)** The first sentence of the paragraph states "absorption" may have been the cause of Neanderthal extinction. Therefore, "interbreeding" most logically expresses how this absorption could have taken place. Choice (A) would have resulted in Neanderthal extermination. Choices (C) and (D) do not give the strong explanation that "interbreeding" would.

40. **(A)** "Contemporary" is the only option that clarifies that these are present-day humans to whom the Neanderthals are compared.

41. **(D)** This choice concisely expresses the idea using logical word order. Choices (A) and (B) use passive voice. Choice (C) jumbles the word order such that the meaning is confused.

42. **(D)** Without a clarification of the pronoun, it could be referring to *Homo neanderthalensis* or to *Homo sapiens*. Therefore, choices (A) and (B) are too vague. This took place in the past, so choice (D) is correct. The present tense in choice (C) is wrong.

43. **(B)** "Margins" is the most logical wording, since Neanderthals would have been pushed to the outer reaches of these geographic areas. Choice (A) does not make sense since there are not oceans in Europe and Asia. Choices (C) and (D) do not make sense since human-like species could not live on "debris" or "remains."

44. **(C)** This choice correctly places the clarifying phrase, "nearly back into Africa itself," out of the way using commas. Choice (A) breaks up the phrase "ancestors first emerged." Choice (B) breaks up the phrase "edge of the land." Choice (D) breaks up the phrase "nearly back to Africa."

Section 3: Math Test (No Calculator)

1. **(A)** If John withdraws d dollars every month, the total amount he withdraws in m months is md dollars, and the amount remaining in the account is $A - md$ dollars.

   **Plug in easy-to-use numbers. Assume John's initial deposit is $100 and that he withdraws $10 a month. After 6 months, he will have withdrawn $60 and still have $40 in the account. Which answer choice is equal to 40 when $A = 100$, $d = 10$, and $m = 6$? Only choice (A) works.

2. **(D)** $f(x) < 25 \Rightarrow x^2 - 11 < 25 \Rightarrow x^2 < 36 \Rightarrow -6 < x < 6$

3. **(C)** Since S represents the number of small pizzas sold during that 6-hour period and L represents the number of large pizzas sold during that same period, $S + L$ is the total number of pizzas sold. So $S + L$ must equal 100. Since each small pizza costs 7.5 dollars and each large pizza costs 11 dollars, $7.5S + 11L$ is the total number of dollars Joe took in. So this expression must equal 848. The two equations are $S + L = 100$ and $7.5S + 11L = 848$.

4. **(D)** Note that the left side and the right side of the given equation are equivalent:

   $$3(5 - 2x) = 15 - 6x \quad \text{and} \quad 6(2 - x) + 3 = 12 - 6x + 3 = 15 - 6x$$

   Since every real number is a solution of the equation $15 - 6x = 15 - 6x$, **the equation has infinitely many solutions**.

   **A solution to the equation $3(5 - 2x) = 6(2 - x) + 3$ would be the x-coordinate of the point of intersection of the straight lines $y = 3(5 - 2x)$ and $y = 6(2 - x) + 3$. Since these lines are the same line (they both have the equation $y = 15 - 6x$), *every* point on one line is a point on the other.

5. **(B)** The percent increase in a quantity is $\dfrac{\text{actual increase}}{\text{original}} \times 100\%$ (KEY FACT C5). For *each* year calculate the actual increase and divide. For example, in 2005 the increase was

   $100 (from $150 to $250), so the percent increase was $\dfrac{100}{150} \times 100\% = 66.66\%$. In **2006** the increase was $\dfrac{200}{250} \times 100\% = 80\%$. Check the other choices; this is the greatest.

6. **(C)**

- The slope of each line represents each boy's speed. Since the slope of Hank's line is greater than the slope of Bill's line, Hank is always riding faster than Bill. Choice (A) must be true.
- Since Hank and Bill rode for the same amount of time and since Hank was riding faster, Hank covered a greater distance than Bill. Choice (B) is true.
- After 15 minutes, each boy is the same distance (4 miles) from the school. However, they are not necessarily anywhere near each other. It is possible that Hank's house is 1 mile south of the school and that Hank rode for 30 minutes due south, whereas Bill's house might be 3 miles north of the school and that Bill rode due north. After 15 minutes, they could each be 4 miles from the school but be several miles apart from one another. Choice (C) is not necessarily true.

7. **(A)** $\dfrac{2x^2-8}{x^2-4x+4} = \dfrac{2(x^2-4)}{(x-2)(x-2)} = \dfrac{2(x-2)(x+2)}{(x-2)(x-2)} = \dfrac{2(x+2)}{(x-2)}$

**Use TACTIC 6: Plug in a number for x. For example, if $x = 3$:

$$\frac{2x^2-8}{x^2-4x+4} \text{ is } \frac{2(3^2)-8}{3^2-4(3)+4} = \frac{18-8}{9-12+4} = \frac{10}{1} = 10$$

Only choice (A) is 10 when $x = 3$: $\dfrac{2(3+2)}{3-2} = \dfrac{2(5)}{1} = 10$.

8. **(A)** $y = f(x) + 3 = mx + b + 3$ and $y = f(x+3) = m(x+3) + b = mx + 3m + b$. So both graphs are straight lines whose slopes are m. Therefore, the graphs are either a pair of parallel lines (if their y-intercepts are different) or the same line (if their y-intercepts are equal). The y-intercepts are $b + 3$ and $3m + b$, which are equal only if $3m = 3$. However, it is given that $m \neq 1$, so the intercepts are not equal. The lines are parallel, so **the graphs do not intersect**.

9. **(B)** The function $f(x) = \dfrac{\sqrt{x-3}}{x^2-8x-20}$ is undefined whenever the expression under the

square root sign is negative and whenever the denominator is equal to 0.

- $x - 3 < 0$ whenever $x < 3$. There are 2 positive integers that satisfy this inequality: 1 and 2.
- Since $x^2 - 8x - 20 = (x - 10)(x + 2)$, this expression is equal to 0 only when $x = 10$ and $x = -2$. So there is only 1 positive integer that makes the denominator 0.

In total, there are **3** positive integers for which $f(x)$ has no real values.

10. **(A)** If $9 = 5 - x$, then $x = -4$. So $h(9) = h(5 - (-4)) = (-4)^2 + (-4) + 1 = 16 - 4 + 1 = \mathbf{13}$.

11. **(C)** Since the volume of the white cube is 27 cubic inches, each edge is 3 inches. Then the area of each face is 9, and the total surface of the cube is $6 \times 9 = 54$. Each face has a red circle whose radius is 1, so the area of each circle is $\pi(1^2) = \pi$. Finally, the total red area is 6π, and the total surface area that is NOT red is **$54 - 6\pi$**.

12. **(D)** In questions such as these, first find the midpoint of the eligible values. Here, a value for y is acceptable only if $13 \le y \le 19$; the midpoint of this interval is 16. All of the acceptable ages are within 3 years of 16—anywhere from 3 years less than 16 to 3 years greater than 16. The inequality that expresses this is $|y - 16| \le 3$.

13. **(B)**

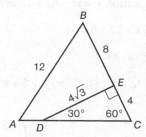

- Since triangle ABC is equilateral, $BC = AB = 12$, and so $EC = 12 - 8 = 4$.

- Since $\overline{DE}$ is perpendicular to $\overline{BC}$, m$\angle E = 90°$. Since triangle ABC is equilateral, m$\angle C = 60°$. So triangle DEC is a 30-60-90 triangle. By KEY FACT J11, $DE = 4\sqrt{3}$.

- By KEY FACT J15, the area of equilateral triangle ABC is $\dfrac{12^2 \sqrt{3}}{4} = \dfrac{144\sqrt{3}}{4} = 36\sqrt{3}$.

- The area of triangle DEC is $\dfrac{1}{2}(4)(4\sqrt{3}) = 8\sqrt{3}$.

- So the area of quadrilateral $ABED = 36\sqrt{3} - 8\sqrt{3} = \mathbf{28\sqrt{3}}$.

14. **(B)** It should be clear that the answer does *not* depend on d. So the easiest thing to do, as in all problems involving percents, is to assume that the list price of the book is \$100. Then Anne paid \$90 after receiving a \$10 discount (\$10 being 10% of \$100). Beth, on the other hand, received a \$15 discount. So she paid \$85 for her copy of the book plus a sales tax of 5% of \$85, which is $0.05 \times \$85 = \$4.25$. So Beth's total cost was \$89.25. Anne paid 75 cents more than Beth.

15. **(B)** By KEY FACT N7, the slope of the line $y = ax + b$ is a. To find the slope of line $x = cy + d$, first solve for y:

$$x = cy + d \Rightarrow cy = x - d \Rightarrow y = \frac{1}{c}x - \frac{d}{c}$$

Since the slope of the line is the coefficient of x, the slope is $\dfrac{1}{c}$. Since parallel lines have equal slopes (KEY FACT N6), $\boldsymbol{a = \dfrac{1}{c}}$.

16. **2** The centers of the two circles are the midpoints of the two diameters.

- The midpoint of $\overline{AB}$ is $\left(\dfrac{1+5}{2}, \dfrac{1+3}{2}\right) = (3, 2)$.

- The midpoint of $\overline{BC}$ is $\left(\dfrac{5+5}{2}, \dfrac{3+9}{2}\right) = (5, 6)$.

- The slope of the line that passes through (3, 2) and (5, 6) is $= \dfrac{6-2}{5-3} = \dfrac{4}{2} = \mathbf{2}$.

17. **1** $a(x - y) = b(y - x) \Rightarrow ax - ay = by - bx \Rightarrow ax + bx = by + ay \Rightarrow x(a + b) = y(a + b) \Rightarrow x = y$. So the ratio $\dfrac{x}{y} = \mathbf{1}$.

18. **2** If $1 + i$ is a solution of the equation $x^2 - 2x + c = 0$, then

$(1 + i)^2 - 2(1 + i) + c = 0 \Rightarrow (1 + 2i + i^2) - (2 + 2i) + c = 0 \Rightarrow 1 + 2i - 1 - 2 - 2i + c = 0$

So $-2 + c = 0$, and $c = $ **2.**

19. **14** Replacing y by x in the equation $y = x^2 - 6x + 12$ gives:

$x = x^2 - 6x + 12 \Rightarrow x^2 - 7x + 12 = 0 \Rightarrow$

$(x - 3)(x - 4) = 0 \Rightarrow x = 3$ or $x = 4$

Since $y = x$, $(a, b) = (3, 3)$ and $(c, d) = (4, 4)$. So $a + b + c + d = $ **14.**

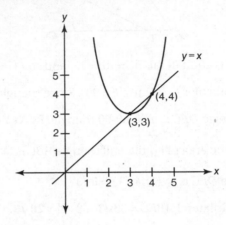

20. **3** If $3 = 5 - 2x$, then $2x = 2$ and $x = 1$.

So $h(3) = h(5 - 2(1)) = \sqrt{(1)^2 + 3(1) + 5} = \sqrt{9} = $ **3.**

Section 4: Math Test (Calculator)

1. **(B)** Wally produces 80 widgets per day × 20 days per month × 12 months per year = 19.200 widgets per year; $96{,}000 \div 19{,}200 = $ **5.**

2. **(C)** If the total surface area of the cube is 216, then the area of each of the 6 faces is $216 \div 6 = 36$. Since each face is a square of area 36, each edge is 6. Finally, the volume of the cube is $6^3 = $ **216.**

3. **(A)** $2 - 3n \geq 5 \Rightarrow -3n \geq 3$. Dividing both sides of this inequality by -3, and remembering to reverse the direction of the inequality gives $n \leq -1$. Therefore, $3n \leq -3$, and $2 + 3n \leq 2 + (-3) = $ **−1.**

4. **(A)** If $\dfrac{2x^2 - 3}{5 - x^2} = -2$, then $2x^2 - 3 = -2(5 - x^2) = -10 + 2x^2$. Subtracting $2x^2$ from both sides of this equation gives $-3 = -10$, which of course is false. So the **equation has no solutions.**

5. **(D)** $g(-10) = f(3(-10)) = f(-30) = (-30)^2 - 3(-30) = 900 - (-90) = 900 + 90 = $ **990**

**$g(x) = f(3x) = (3x)^2 - 3(3x) = 9x^2 - 9x$

Then $g(-10) = 9(-10)^2 - 9(-10) = 900 + 90 = $ **990.**

6. **(C)** The average is just the sum of the number of students in the five classes (125) divided by 5: $125 \div 5 = $ **25.**

7. **(A)** In class **A**, one-fourth, or 25% (5 of 20), of the students are in the band. In each of the other classes, the number in the band is *less than* one-fourth of the class.

8. **(D)** Let x be the amount, in dollars, that each of the 20 children was going to contribute, then $20x$ represents the cost of the present. When 4 children dropped out, the remaining 16 each had to pay $(x + 1.50)$ dollars, so

$$16(x + 1.5) = 20x \Rightarrow 16x + 24 = 20x \Rightarrow 24 = 4x \Rightarrow x = 6$$

So the cost of the present was $20 \times 6 = \mathbf{120}$ dollars.

**Use TACTIC 5: backsolve. Try choice (C), 100. If the present cost $100, then each of the 20 children would have to pay $5. When 4 dropped out, the remaining 16 would have to pay $100 \div 16 = \$6.25$ apiece, an increase of $1.25. Since the actual increase was $1.50, the gift was more expensive. Eliminate (A), (B), and (C). The answer must be (D).

9. **(A)** Since $y = -x^2$, $x^2 = -y$. Replacing x^2 by $-y$ in the equation of the circle, we get:

$$-y + y^2 = 90 \Rightarrow y^2 - y - 90 = 0 \Rightarrow (y - 10)(y + 9) = 0 \Rightarrow y = 10 \text{ or } y = -9$$

A quick glance at the graphs shows that y cannot possibly be equal to 10, so y must equal -9. If you didn't think to check the graphs, plugging in 10 for y into either equation leads to a contradiction. Since x^2 can't be negative, $-x^2$ can't be positive. Also if $x^2 + 10^2 = 90$, then x^2 would be negative.
Then $x^2 + (-9)^2 = 90 \Rightarrow x^2 + 81 = 90 \Rightarrow x^2 = 9 \Rightarrow x = 3$ or $x = -3$. So $(a, b) = (-3, -9)$ and $(c, d) = (3, -9)$.
Finally, $a + b + c + d = -3 + -9 + 3 + -9 = \mathbf{-18}$.

10. **(D)** Since triangle ABC is a right triangle, we can use the Pythagorean theorem to find BC: $6^2 + (BC)^2 = 10^2 \Rightarrow (BC)^2 = 100 - 36 = 64 \Rightarrow BC = 8$.
(Of course, if you immediately realize that triangle ABC is a 6-8-10 right triangle, then you don't have to use the Pythagorean theorem.)

So $\cos C = \dfrac{\text{adjacent}}{\text{hypotenuse}} = \dfrac{8}{10} = 0.8$.

11. **(D)** Let c represent the cost, in dollars, of the candy. Then $3c$ is the cost of the flowers, and $10(c + 3c) = 10(4c) = 40c$ is the cost of the ring. So,

$$528 = 40c + 3c + c = 44c \Rightarrow c = 528 \div 44 = 12$$

Therefore, the candy cost $12, the flowers cost **$36**, and the ring cost $480.

12. **(D)** It should be clear from the diagram that gear G_2 turns in a **counterclockwise** direction. As tooth A pushes against tooth C followed by tooth B pushing against tooth D, the teeth on gear G_2 are turning in the opposite direction as those on gear G_1.

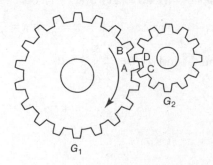

It should also be clear that the fewer the teeth on a gear, the faster it goes. In fact, the number of teeth is inversely proportional to the number of rotations per second:

number of teeth on G_1 × number of rotations per second of G_1 =
number of teeth on G_2 × number of rotations per second of G_2

 So if r represents the number of rotations per second of G_2, we have

$$48 \times 60 = 36r \Rightarrow 2{,}880 = 36r \Rightarrow r = 2{,}880 \div 36 = \mathbf{80}$$

 13. **(C)** The difference between the total ticket sales ($35.5 billion) and the total distribution of the proceeds $12.0 billion) was the amount returned to the purchasers of lottery tickets in the form of prize money: $35.5 billion – $12.0 billion = $23.5 billion. Divide 23.5 by 35.5 to see that approximately **66%** of the ticket sales was allocated to prize money.

 14. **(C)** In order for the amount received by Senior citizens programs to be the same as the amount received by the Cities, an additional $0.9 billion would have to be allocated to the Senior citizen programs: $0.9 billion is approximately **31%** of the $2.9 billion currently going to the General fund.

 15. **(D)** in 2009, the total sales for all games other than Lotto in billions of dollars was 35.5 – 10.0 = 25.5. In 2010, each of the remaining games experienced a 10% increase in sales, so the total sales in 2010 was 25.5 + 10%(25.5) = 25.5 + 2.55 = 28.05. In 2010, the sales of the Instant games was 10% higher than in 2009: 14.2 + 1.42 = 15.62. So in 2010, the percent of the total sales attributed to Instant games was $\frac{15.62}{28.05}$ = .557 = 55.7%.

Finally, the measure of the central angle for the sector representing Instant games is 55.7% of 360° = **200°**.

 16. **(C)** Alice's gross pay in dollars is:

$$40 \times 9 + (x - 40) \times 15 = 360 + 15x - 600 = 15x - 240$$

23% of her gross pay (8% for payroll taxes and 15% for withholding taxes) is deducted from her gross pay. So her net pay is 77% of her gross pay (100% – 23%) minus a $20 contribution for her health insurance premium:

$$\mathbf{0.77(15x - 240) - 20}$$

17. **(A)** $(1 + i)^3 = [(1 + i)(1 + i)](1 + i) = [1 + 2i + i^2](1 + i) = [1 + 2i - 1](1 + i) = [2i](1 + i) = 2i + 2i^2 = 2i - 2 = \mathbf{-2 + 2i}$

18. **(D)** If the graph of a function crosses the x-axis at n, then $(n, 0)$ is a point on the graph. So $(a, 0)$ and $(b, 0)$ are points on the graph. Therefore, a and b are the solutions of the equation $4x^2 - 8x + 3 = 0$. There are a few ways to solve this equation.

■ First solution: Factor $4x^2 - 8x + 3 = (2x - 3)(2x - 1)$. So,

$$2x - 3 = 0 \text{ or } 2x - 1 = 0 \Rightarrow x = \frac{3}{2} \text{ or } x = \frac{1}{2}$$

So a and b are $\frac{3}{2}$ and $\frac{1}{2}$, and $a + b = \frac{3}{2} + \frac{1}{2} = \mathbf{2}$.

- Second solution: Use the quadratic formula on the equation $4x^2 - 8x + 3 = 0$.

$$x = \frac{8 \pm \sqrt{(-8)^2 - 4(4)(3)}}{2(4)} = \frac{8 \pm \sqrt{64 - 48}}{8} = \frac{8 \pm \sqrt{16}}{8} = \frac{8 \pm 4}{8}$$

So $x = \frac{12}{8} = \frac{3}{2}$ or $x = \frac{4}{8} = \frac{1}{2}$.

- Third solution: Use a graphing calculator. Graph $y = 4x^2 - 8x + 3$, and see where the graph crosses the x-axis.

19. **(C)** The central angle of the sector representing Brand C is 12% of 360°:

$$(0.12) \times 360° = 43.2°$$

The central angle of the sector representing Brand D is 7% of 360°:

$$(0.7) \times 360° = 25.2°$$

Finally, $43.2° - 25.2° = \mathbf{18°}$.

**Note this can be done in one step by noticing that the percentage difference between Brands C and D is 5%, and 5% of 360 is $(0.05) \times 360 = 18$.

20. **(C)** Since total sales in 2000 were $1,000,000, in 2005 sales were $1,500,000 (a 50% increase).

In 2000, sales of Brand A were $400,000 (40% of $1,000,000).

In 2005, sales of Brand A were $500,000 (25% or $\frac{1}{4}$ more than in 2000).

Finally, $500,000 is $\frac{1}{3}$ or $\mathbf{33\frac{1}{3}}$ **%** of $1,500,000.

21. **(D)** Store 2 sold 30 DVDs at $50, 40 DVDs at $80, and 20 DVDs at $120.

Store 2: $(30 \times \$50) + (40 \times \$80) + (20 \times \$120) = \$7,100$

Store 1 sold 10 DVDs at $80, 20 DVDs at $100, and 20 DVDs at $150.

Store 1: $(10 \times \$80) + (20 \times \$100) + (20 \times \$150) = \$5,800$

Finally, $\$7,100 - \$5,800 = \mathbf{\$1,300}$.

22. **(B)** The face of the solid is an isosceles triangle whose base is 16. To find its area, draw in altitude $\overline{BD}$ in the diagram below.

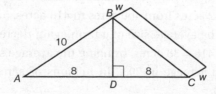

Since the altitude to the base of an isosceles triangle is also a median, $AD = DC = 8$. So triangle ABD is a 6-8-10 right triangle. (If you don't immediately recognize that, use the Pythagorean theorem: $10^2 = 8^2 + (BD)^2 \Rightarrow (BD)^2 = 100 - 64 = 36 \Rightarrow BD = 6$.) The area of triangle ABC is

$$\frac{1}{2}bh = \frac{1}{2}(16)(6) = \mathbf{48}$$

23. **(B)** The solid is a prism whose triangular face has an area of 48 square feet (see the solution to question 22) and whose width is w. So the volume of the solid is $48w$ cubic feet, and its weight is

$$(48w \text{ cubic feet}) \times (3 \text{ pounds per cubic foot}) = 144w \text{ pounds}$$

Then $144w = 360 \Rightarrow w = 360 \div 144 = \textbf{2.5}$.

 24. **(D)** Since they have the same angles, by KEY FACT J16 all equilateral triangles are similar. If k is the ratio of the sides of two similar triangles, then by KEY FACT J18 the ratio of their areas is k^2. Here the ratio of the areas is 6:10, or 0.6, so $k^2 = 0.6$ and $k = \sqrt{0.6} = \textbf{0.77}$.

 25. **(C)** Here are two ways to answer this question.

- You can just put your calculator into radian mode and evaluate:

$$\left(\sin\frac{\pi}{3} + \cos\frac{\pi}{3}\right)^2 = (0.866 + 0.5)^2 = 1.366^2 = \textbf{1.866}$$

- Leave your calculator in degree mode and convert $\frac{\pi}{3}$ radians to degrees:

$$\frac{\pi}{3} \text{ radians} = \frac{180}{3} = 60 \text{ degrees}$$

$$(\sin 60° + \cos 60°)^2 = (0.866 + 0.5)^2 = 1.366^2 = \textbf{1.866}$$

 26. **(D)** For each of the given years, the total acreage of farmland can be calculated by multiplying the number of farms by the average size of a farm. There is no way to answer this question, without doing the calculation for each year.

- 1940: 6.3 million farms × 174 acres per farm = 1,096 million acres
- 1970: 2.9 million farms × 374 acres per farm = 1,085 million acres
- 2000: 2.2 million farms × 436 acres per farm = 959 million acres
- 2010: 2.2 million farms × 418 acres per farm = 919 million acres

 27. **(C)** Find the sum: $130 + 61 + 46 + 46 + 43 = 326$. The sum of the farm acreages for the five states is 326 million acres. In the solution to the previous question, we saw that the total farm acreage in the country in 2010 was 919 million acres, and $326 \div 919 = 0.3547$ or approximately **35%**.

 28. **(B)** It is projected that from 2010 to 2030, the number of farms will decrease by 5%. Since 5% of 2.2 million is 110,000, the number of farms in 2030 will be approximately $2,200,000 - 110,000 = 2,090,000 = 2.09$ million. From 1990 to 2010, the average size of a farm decreased by 42 acres from 460 acres to 418 acres, and $42 \div 460 = 0.091 = 9.1\%$. If from 2010 to 2030 the average size of a farm again decreases by 9.1%, there will be a decrease of $0.091 \times 418 = 38$ acres, bringing the average size to $418 - 38 = 380$ acres. Finally, the total farm acreage in 2030 in millions of acres is projected to be about $2.09 \times 380 = 794 \approx \textbf{800}$.

29. **(A)** By KEY FACT T2, i^{75} is equal to i^r, where r is the remainder when 75 is divided by 4. Since $75 \div 4 = 18.75$, the quotient is 18. Then $18 \times 4 = 72$ and $75 - 72 = 3$. So the remainder is 3.

Therefore $i^{75} = i^3$ and $(-i)^{75} = (-1)^{75}(i)^{75} = (-1)(i)^3 = -i^3$.

Since $i^3 = -i$, then $-i^3 = i$.

Finally, $i^{75} - (-i)^{75} = i^3 - (-i^3) = -i - i = -2i$.

30. **(C)** By KEY FACT K9, the formula for the area of a parallelogram is $A = bh$. Sketch the parallelogram and draw the height.

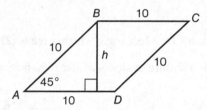

To find h, use the sine ratio (KEY FACT S1):

$$\sin 45° = \frac{h}{10} \Rightarrow h = 10 \sin 45° = 10(0.707) = 7.07$$

An alternative method of finding h is to use KEY FACT J8, which says that in a 45-45-90 right triangle, the length of each leg is equal to the length of the hypotenuse divided by $\sqrt{2}$: $h = \dfrac{10}{\sqrt{2}} = 7.07$.

Either way, $h = 7.07$ and the area of the parallelogram is:

$$A = bh = 10(7.07) = \mathbf{70.7}$$

31. **37.5** First set up a proportion to determine the distance between Hauppauge and Riverhead:

$$\frac{1 \text{ inch}}{20 \text{ miles}} = \frac{1.25 \text{ inches}}{x \text{ miles}}$$

So $x = (1.25)(20) = 25$. Traveling at 40 miles per hour, it takes $\dfrac{25}{40} = \dfrac{5}{8}$ of an hour to drive 25 miles. Finally, $\dfrac{5}{8}$ of an hour is equal to $\dfrac{5}{8}$ (60 minutes) = **37.5** minutes.

32. **6.8** Since Michelle took 31.5 minutes to run the 3 miles from the 12-mile marker to the 15-mile marker, she was running at the constant rate of 1 mile every 10.5 minutes ($31.5 \div 3 = 10.5$). Michelle took 54.6 minutes (36 seconds = $36 \div 60 = 0.6$ minutes) to run from where her friend was standing to the 12-mile marker. So that distance was 54.6 minutes $\div$ 10.5 minutes per mile = 5.2 miles.

Her friend was 5.2 miles from the 12-mile marker, and so was $12 - 5.2 = \mathbf{6.8}$ miles from the starting line.

33. **3744** Use a weighted average:

$$\frac{12(3,100)+24(3,800)+14(4,200)}{(12+24+14)} = \frac{187,200}{50} = \mathbf{3,744}$$

34. **8190** There are $26 \times 26 \times 9 = 6,084$ PICs with two letters and one digit, and there are $26 \times 9 \times 9 = 2,106$ PICs with one letter and two digits, for a total of $6,084 + 2,106 = \mathbf{8,190}$.

35. $\frac{\mathbf{3}}{\mathbf{2}}$ **or 1.5** The formula for the volume of a pyramid with a rectangular base is $V = \frac{1}{3}\,lwh$, where l and w are the length and width of the rectangle, and where h is the height of the pyramid. (Remember that this fact is given to you on the first page of each math section.)

The base of pyramid 1 is a 2 by 3 rectangle whose area is $(2)(3) = 6$.

The base of pyramid 2 is a square of side 3 whose area is $3^2 = 9$. If h_1 and h_2 represent the two heights, then:

$$\frac{1}{3}(6)h_1 = \frac{1}{3}(9)h_2 \Rightarrow 2h_1 = 3h_2 \Rightarrow \frac{h_1}{h_2} = \frac{3}{2}$$

36. **129** Let c, d, and e represent the value of one Canadian dollar, one U.S. dollar, and one euro, respectively. Since $c = .68e$, we have that $e = \frac{c}{.68}$. Then we have:

$$d = .88e = .88\left(\frac{c}{.68}\right) \Rightarrow d = \left(\frac{.88}{.68}\right)c = 1.294c$$

So, one U.S. dollar could have purchased 1.294 Canadian dollars, and 100 U.S. dollars could have purchased 129.40, or approximately **129** Canadian dollars.

37. **54**

- 60 miles per hour = 60 miles per 60 minutes = 1 mile per 1 minute. Driving at 60 miles per hour, Ed takes 6.3 minutes to drive those 6.3 miles.

- 70 miles per hour = 70 miles per 60 minutes = $\frac{7}{6}$ mile per 1 minute. Driving at 70 miles per hour, Ed would take $6.3 \div \frac{7}{6} = 6.3 \times \frac{6}{7} = 0.9 \times 6 = 5.4$ minutes to drive those 6.3 miles.

- So Ed would take $6.3 - 5.4 = 0.9$ minutes less to drive those 6.3 miles at 70 miles per hour.

- Finally, 0.9 minutes = 0.9×60 seconds = **54** seconds.

38. **37**

- 6.3 miles per day $\times$ 240 days = 1,512 miles.

- At 60 miles per hour, Ed used $1,512 \div 24.3 = 62.222$ gallons of gasoline, which cost $62.222 \times \$3.50 = \$217.78$.

- At 70 miles per hour, Ed would have used $1,512 \div 20.8 = 72.692$ gallons of gasoline, which would have cost $72.692 \times \$3.50 = \$254.42$.

- So traveling at 70 miles per hour instead of 60 miles per hour would have cost Ed $\$254.42 - \$217.78 = \$36.64$ more, which to the nearest dollar is **\$37**.

SAT Essay Scoring

SAT Essay Scoring Rubric

	Score: 4
Reading	Excellent: The essay shows excellent understanding of the source.
	The essay shows an understanding of the source's main argument and key details and a firm grasp of how they are interconnected, demonstrating clear comprehension of the source.
	The essay does not misinterpret or misrepresent the source.
	The essay skillfully uses source evidence, such as direct quotations and rephrasing, representing a thorough comprehension of the source.
Analysis	Excellent: The essay gives excellent analysis of the source and shows clear understanding of what the assignment requires.
	The essay gives a complete, highly thoughtful analysis of the author's use of reasoning, evidence, rhetoric, and/or other argumentative elements the student has chosen to highlight.
	The essay has appropriate, adequate, and skillfully chosen support for its analysis. The essay focuses on the most important parts of the source in responding to the prompt.
Writing	Excellent: The essay is focused and shows an excellent grasp of the English language. The essay has a clear thesis. The essay has a well-executed introduction and conclusion. The essay shows a clear and well-crafted progression of thoughts both within paragraphs and in the essay as a whole. The essay has a wide range of sentence structures. The essay consistently shows precise choice of words. The essay is formal and objective in its style and tone. The essay demonstrates a firm grasp of the rules of standard English and has very few to no errors.

	Score: 3
Reading	Skillful: The essay shows effective understanding of the source.
	The essay shows an understanding of the source's main argument and key details.
	The essay is free of major misinterpretations and/or misrepresentations of the source.
	The essay uses appropriate source evidence, such as direct quotations and rephrasing, representing comprehension of the source.
Analysis	Skillful: The essay gives effective analysis of the source and shows an understanding of what the assignment requires.
	The essay decently analyzes the author's use of reasoning, evidence, rhetoric, and/or other argumentative elements the student has chosen to highlight.
	The essay has appropriate and adequate support for its analysis. The essay focuses primarily on the most important parts of the source in responding to the prompt.
Writing	Skillful: The essay is mostly focused and shows an effective grasp of the English language. The essay has a thesis, either explicit or implicit. The essay has an effective introduction and conclusion. The essay has a clear progression of thoughts both within paragraphs and in the essay as a whole. The essay has an assortment of sentence structures. The essay shows some precise choice of words. The essay is formal and objective in its style and tone. The essay demonstrates a grasp of the rules of standard English and has very few significant errors that interfere with the writer's argument.

Score: 2	
Reading	Limited: The essay shows some understanding of the source.
	The essay shows an understanding of the source's main argument, but not of key details.
	The essay may have some misinterpretations and/or misrepresentations of the source.
	The essay gives only partial evidence from the source, showing limited comprehension of the source.
Analysis	Limited: The essay gives partial analysis of the source and shows only limited understanding of what the assignment requires.
	The essay tries to show how the author uses reasoning, evidence, rhetoric, and/or other argumentative elements the student has chosen to highlight, but only states rather than analyzes their importance, or at least one part of the essay's analysis is unsupported by the source.
	The essay has little or no justification for its argument.
	The essay may lack attention to those elements of the source that are most pertinent to responding to the prompt.
Writing	Limited: The essay is mostly not cohesive and shows an ineffective grasp of the English language. The essay may not have a thesis, or may diverge from the thesis at some point in the essay's development. The essay may have an unsuccessful introduction and/or conclusion. The essay may show progression of thoughts within the paragraphs, but not in the essay as a whole. The essay is relatively uniform in its sentence structures. The essay shows imprecise and possibly repetitive choice of words.
	The essay may be more casual and subjective in style and tone. The essay demonstrates a weaker grasp of the rules of standard English and does have errors that interfere with the writer's argument.

Score: 1	
Reading	Insufficient: The essay shows virtually no understanding of the source.
	The essay is unsuccessful in showing an understanding of the source's main argument. It may refer to some details from the text, but it does so without tying them to the source's main argument.
	The essay has many misinterpretations and/or misrepresentations of the source.
	The essay gives virtually no evidence from the source, showing very poor comprehension of the source.
Analysis	Insufficient: The essay gives little to no accurate analysis of the source and shows poor understanding of what the assignment requires.
	The essay may show how the author uses reasoning, evidence, rhetoric, and/or other argumentative elements that the student has chosen to highlight but does so without analysis.
	Or many parts of the essay's analysis are unsupported by the source.
	The support given for points in the essay's argument are largely unsupported or off topic.
	The essay may not attend to the elements of the source that are pertinent to responding to the prompt.
	Or the essay gives no explicit analysis, perhaps only resorting to summary statements.
Writing	Insufficient: The essay is not cohesive and does not demonstrate skill in the English language. The essay may not have a thesis. The essay does not have a clear introduction and conclusion. The essay does not have a clear progression of thoughts. The essay is quite uniform and even repetitive in sentence structure.
	The essay shows poor and possibly inaccurate word choice. The essay is likely casual and subjective in style and tone. The essay shows a poor grasp of the rules of standard English and may have many errors that interfere with the writer's argument.

Top-Scoring Sample Student Response

In the passage, "A Lesson on Commas," the author is presented with an off-topic question from one of her students in regards to why she chooses to write. When faced with a crossroads on whether to continue on with her planned lesson, or go off on a tangent and respond to the student's question, the teacher uses the opportunity to explain why creativity must be taught in the classroom.

As the author looks around the room and notices that her own lesson may be lacking in creativity, specifically in regards to "the abridged somnolence" of the students "in the farthest row," she realizes that she has an opportunity to seize the moment and further explain why this is so important. She first looks to begin her argument by engaging the students with a creative response—Why does one listen to music? Or dance? Or look to the stars? And then goes on to state her belief in regards to the importance of creativity in that it is "the most essential ingredient of erudition, expression, and future success," in order to make an impactful statement to catch her students' attention.

Her next focus is to debunk the concept that the term "creativity" is only applicable to art. To support her belief that creativity "is not reserved for the Picassos, the Bachs, or the Austens," she identifies that it is something that is rooted within all of us, which she bolsters by asking the class to think about the "sublime imagination" of any child that they have ever met. Furthermore, she identifies that creativity is used in every walk of life, as it is the primary driver behind not just art, but also "every new electronic, and every scientific discovery." Statements such as these help to connect students that might not see themselves as "artistic" to the fact that "creativity" is still relevant to them.

Mrs. Jenson then explains the significance that creativity holds, which she does by asking her students a simple question about their future. While alluding to the idea that everyone would prefer a "challenging" job over a "routine" one, she quotes a well-known source, LinkedIn, on the fact that "not being challenged . . . is at the top of the list for workplace dissatisfaction" in order to add validity to her argument. When tied together with the fact that "hating their jobs" is the "number one reason for unhappiness in adults," she is able to make the greater connection between how one's work-life impacts their overall well being.

However, this alone does not explain how creativity directly ties in with feeling challenged at the workplace. While acknowledging that it is easier to see how creativity is used by some of the world's top minds, in fields such as medicine and engineering, she uses a two-step process in order to bring this together for those that may end up in less notable areas. The first is by referencing creativity in a "Google" sense, undoubtedly a concept that students are familiar with. By breaking down the meaning of creativity to its most general terms, "generation and contemplation of new ideas to create something perceived as valuable," we can think of it as something that can be used in almost any setting. And when applied in the context of a working environment, creativity can therefore be thought of in terms of our "problem-solving and critical thinking" abilities, which in turn helps with our "efficiency, diversification, and job security." In this sense, she is explaining how one must use creativity in order to help make their job more challenging, which will in turn help improve their overall happiness in their adult life.

Having stated her belief in the importance of creativity, providing support for how it is a relevant for everyone to practice, and making the connection between it, work, and a healthy sense of self-worth, the author then addresses how this can be taught in school. Whether it be by "encouraging questioning and debate" to get students to think about "the why's and how's," "identifying problems and brainstorming solutions" to help students determine "what's good, what's bad and what can be improved," or by "inspiring alternative problem-solving" to enable students to consider the "what-ifs," she identifies many ways to help foster creativity. And because of her aforementioned statements regarding the importance of creative thinking, her conclusion serves to make a sound argument for the importance of actively teaching creativity in schools.

ANSWER SHEET
Model Test 2

Section 1: Reading

1. Ⓐ Ⓑ Ⓒ Ⓓ   14. Ⓐ Ⓑ Ⓒ Ⓓ   27. Ⓐ Ⓑ Ⓒ Ⓓ   40. Ⓐ Ⓑ Ⓒ Ⓓ
2. Ⓐ Ⓑ Ⓒ Ⓓ   15. Ⓐ Ⓑ Ⓒ Ⓓ   28. Ⓐ Ⓑ Ⓒ Ⓓ   41. Ⓐ Ⓑ Ⓒ Ⓓ
3. Ⓐ Ⓑ Ⓒ Ⓓ   16. Ⓐ Ⓑ Ⓒ Ⓓ   29. Ⓐ Ⓑ Ⓒ Ⓓ   42. Ⓐ Ⓑ Ⓒ Ⓓ
4. Ⓐ Ⓑ Ⓒ Ⓓ   17. Ⓐ Ⓑ Ⓒ Ⓓ   30. Ⓐ Ⓑ Ⓒ Ⓓ   43. Ⓐ Ⓑ Ⓒ Ⓓ
5. Ⓐ Ⓑ Ⓒ Ⓓ   18. Ⓐ Ⓑ Ⓒ Ⓓ   31. Ⓐ Ⓑ Ⓒ Ⓓ   44. Ⓐ Ⓑ Ⓒ Ⓓ
6. Ⓐ Ⓑ Ⓒ Ⓓ   19. Ⓐ Ⓑ Ⓒ Ⓓ   32. Ⓐ Ⓑ Ⓒ Ⓓ   45. Ⓐ Ⓑ Ⓒ Ⓓ
7. Ⓐ Ⓑ Ⓒ Ⓓ   20. Ⓐ Ⓑ Ⓒ Ⓓ   33. Ⓐ Ⓑ Ⓒ Ⓓ   46. Ⓐ Ⓑ Ⓒ Ⓓ
8. Ⓐ Ⓑ Ⓒ Ⓓ   21. Ⓐ Ⓑ Ⓒ Ⓓ   34. Ⓐ Ⓑ Ⓒ Ⓓ   47. Ⓐ Ⓑ Ⓒ Ⓓ
9. Ⓐ Ⓑ Ⓒ Ⓓ   22. Ⓐ Ⓑ Ⓒ Ⓓ   35. Ⓐ Ⓑ Ⓒ Ⓓ   48. Ⓐ Ⓑ Ⓒ Ⓓ
10. Ⓐ Ⓑ Ⓒ Ⓓ   23. Ⓐ Ⓑ Ⓒ Ⓓ   36. Ⓐ Ⓑ Ⓒ Ⓓ   49. Ⓐ Ⓑ Ⓒ Ⓓ
11. Ⓐ Ⓑ Ⓒ Ⓓ   24. Ⓐ Ⓑ Ⓒ Ⓓ   37. Ⓐ Ⓑ Ⓒ Ⓓ   50. Ⓐ Ⓑ Ⓒ Ⓓ
12. Ⓐ Ⓑ Ⓒ Ⓓ   25. Ⓐ Ⓑ Ⓒ Ⓓ   38. Ⓐ Ⓑ Ⓒ Ⓓ   51. Ⓐ Ⓑ Ⓒ Ⓓ
13. Ⓐ Ⓑ Ⓒ Ⓓ   26. Ⓐ Ⓑ Ⓒ Ⓓ   39. Ⓐ Ⓑ Ⓒ Ⓓ   52. Ⓐ Ⓑ Ⓒ Ⓓ

Section 2: Writing and Language

1. Ⓐ Ⓑ Ⓒ Ⓓ   12. Ⓐ Ⓑ Ⓒ Ⓓ   23. Ⓐ Ⓑ Ⓒ Ⓓ   34. Ⓐ Ⓑ Ⓒ Ⓓ
2. Ⓐ Ⓑ Ⓒ Ⓓ   13. Ⓐ Ⓑ Ⓒ Ⓓ   24. Ⓐ Ⓑ Ⓒ Ⓓ   35. Ⓐ Ⓑ Ⓒ Ⓓ
3. Ⓐ Ⓑ Ⓒ Ⓓ   14. Ⓐ Ⓑ Ⓒ Ⓓ   25. Ⓐ Ⓑ Ⓒ Ⓓ   36. Ⓐ Ⓑ Ⓒ Ⓓ
4. Ⓐ Ⓑ Ⓒ Ⓓ   15. Ⓐ Ⓑ Ⓒ Ⓓ   26. Ⓐ Ⓑ Ⓒ Ⓓ   37. Ⓐ Ⓑ Ⓒ Ⓓ
5. Ⓐ Ⓑ Ⓒ Ⓓ   16. Ⓐ Ⓑ Ⓒ Ⓓ   27. Ⓐ Ⓑ Ⓒ Ⓓ   38. Ⓐ Ⓑ Ⓒ Ⓓ
6. Ⓐ Ⓑ Ⓒ Ⓓ   17. Ⓐ Ⓑ Ⓒ Ⓓ   28. Ⓐ Ⓑ Ⓒ Ⓓ   39. Ⓐ Ⓑ Ⓒ Ⓓ
7. Ⓐ Ⓑ Ⓒ Ⓓ   18. Ⓐ Ⓑ Ⓒ Ⓓ   29. Ⓐ Ⓑ Ⓒ Ⓓ   40. Ⓐ Ⓑ Ⓒ Ⓓ
8. Ⓐ Ⓑ Ⓒ Ⓓ   19. Ⓐ Ⓑ Ⓒ Ⓓ   30. Ⓐ Ⓑ Ⓒ Ⓓ   41. Ⓐ Ⓑ Ⓒ Ⓓ
9. Ⓐ Ⓑ Ⓒ Ⓓ   20. Ⓐ Ⓑ Ⓒ Ⓓ   31. Ⓐ Ⓑ Ⓒ Ⓓ   42. Ⓐ Ⓑ Ⓒ Ⓓ
10. Ⓐ Ⓑ Ⓒ Ⓓ   21. Ⓐ Ⓑ Ⓒ Ⓓ   32. Ⓐ Ⓑ Ⓒ Ⓓ   43. Ⓐ Ⓑ Ⓒ Ⓓ
11. Ⓐ Ⓑ Ⓒ Ⓓ   22. Ⓐ Ⓑ Ⓒ Ⓓ   33. Ⓐ Ⓑ Ⓒ Ⓓ   44. Ⓐ Ⓑ Ⓒ Ⓓ

Section 3: Math (No Calculator)

1. Ⓐ Ⓑ Ⓒ Ⓓ   5. Ⓐ Ⓑ Ⓒ Ⓓ   9. Ⓐ Ⓑ Ⓒ Ⓓ   13. Ⓐ Ⓑ Ⓒ Ⓓ
2. Ⓐ Ⓑ Ⓒ Ⓓ   6. Ⓐ Ⓑ Ⓒ Ⓓ   10. Ⓐ Ⓑ Ⓒ Ⓓ   14. Ⓐ Ⓑ Ⓒ Ⓓ
3. Ⓐ Ⓑ Ⓒ Ⓓ   7. Ⓐ Ⓑ Ⓒ Ⓓ   11. Ⓐ Ⓑ Ⓒ Ⓓ   15. Ⓐ Ⓑ Ⓒ Ⓓ
4. Ⓐ Ⓑ Ⓒ Ⓓ   8. Ⓐ Ⓑ Ⓒ Ⓓ   12. Ⓐ Ⓑ Ⓒ Ⓓ

16. [grid-in answer box]

17. [grid-in answer box]

18. [grid-in answer box]

19. [grid-in answer box]

20. [grid-in answer box]

Section 4: Math (Calculator)

1. Ⓐ Ⓑ Ⓒ Ⓓ
2. Ⓐ Ⓑ Ⓒ Ⓓ
3. Ⓐ Ⓑ Ⓒ Ⓓ
4. Ⓐ Ⓑ Ⓒ Ⓓ
5. Ⓐ Ⓑ Ⓒ Ⓓ
6. Ⓐ Ⓑ Ⓒ Ⓓ
7. Ⓐ Ⓑ Ⓒ Ⓓ
8. Ⓐ Ⓑ Ⓒ Ⓓ

9. Ⓐ Ⓑ Ⓒ Ⓓ
10. Ⓐ Ⓑ Ⓒ Ⓓ
11. Ⓐ Ⓑ Ⓒ Ⓓ
12. Ⓐ Ⓑ Ⓒ Ⓓ
13. Ⓐ Ⓑ Ⓒ Ⓓ
14. Ⓐ Ⓑ Ⓒ Ⓓ
15. Ⓐ Ⓑ Ⓒ Ⓓ
16. Ⓐ Ⓑ Ⓒ Ⓓ

17. Ⓐ Ⓑ Ⓒ Ⓓ
18. Ⓐ Ⓑ Ⓒ Ⓓ
19. Ⓐ Ⓑ Ⓒ Ⓓ
20. Ⓐ Ⓑ Ⓒ Ⓓ
21. Ⓐ Ⓑ Ⓒ Ⓓ
22. Ⓐ Ⓑ Ⓒ Ⓓ
23. Ⓐ Ⓑ Ⓒ Ⓓ
24. Ⓐ Ⓑ Ⓒ Ⓓ

25. Ⓐ Ⓑ Ⓒ Ⓓ
26. Ⓐ Ⓑ Ⓒ Ⓓ
27. Ⓐ Ⓑ Ⓒ Ⓓ
28. Ⓐ Ⓑ Ⓒ Ⓓ
29. Ⓐ Ⓑ Ⓒ Ⓓ
30. Ⓐ Ⓑ Ⓒ Ⓓ

31.
32.
33.
34.

35.
36.
37.
38.

Essay

PLANNING PAGE

READING TEST

65 MINUTES, 52 QUESTIONS

Turn to Section 1 of your answer sheet to answer the questions in this section.

> **Directions:** Following each of the passages (or pairs of passages) below are questions about the passage (or passages). Read each passage carefully. Then, select the best answer for each question based on what is stated in the passage (or passages) and in any graphics that may accompany the passage.

Questions 1–11 are based on the following passage.

The following passage is taken from Jane Austen's novel Persuasion. *In this excerpt we meet Sir Walter Elliot, father of the heroine.*

Vanity was the beginning and end of Sir Walter Elliot's character: vanity of person and of situation. He had been remarkably
Line handsome in his youth, and at fifty-four was
(5) still a very fine man. Few women could think more of their personal appearance than he did, nor could the valet of any new-made lord be more delighted with the place he held in society. He considered the blessing of beauty
(10) as inferior only to the blessing of a baronetcy; and the Sir Walter Elliot, who united these gifts, was the constant object of his warmest respect and devotion.

His good looks and his rank had one
(15) fair claim on his attachment, since to them he must have owed a wife of very superior character to anything deserved by his own. Lady Elliot had been an excellent woman, sensible and amiable, whose judgment
(20) and conduct, if they might be pardoned the youthful infatuation which made her Lady Elliot, had never required indulgence afterwards. She had humored, or softened, or concealed his failings, and promoted
(25) his real respectability for seventeen years;

and though not the very happiest being in the world herself, had found enough in her duties, her friends, and her children, to attach her to life, and make it no matter of
(30) indifference to her when she was called on to quit them. Three girls, the two eldest sixteen and fourteen, was an awful legacy for a mother to bequeath, an awful charge rather, to confide to the authority and guidance of a
(35) conceited, silly father. She had, however, one very intimate friend, a sensible, deserving woman, who had been brought, by strong attachment to herself, to settle close by her, in the village of Kellynch; and on her
(40) kindness and advice Lady Elliot mainly relied for the best help and maintenance of the good principles and instruction which she had been anxiously giving her daughters.

This friend and Sir Walter did not marry,
(45) whatever might have been anticipated on that head by their acquaintance. Thirteen years had passed away since Lady Elliot's death, and they were still near neighbors and intimate friends, and one remained a
(50) widower, the other a widow.

That Lady Russell, of steady age and character, and extremely well provided for, should have no thought of a second marriage, needs no apology to the public,
(55) which is rather apt to be unreasonably discontented when a woman *does* marry again, than when she does *not*; but Sir

GO ON TO THE NEXT PAGE

Walter's continuing in singleness requires
explanation. Be it known, then, that Sir
(60) Walter, like a good father (having met
with one or two disappointments in very
unreasonable applications), prided himself
on remaining single for his dear daughters'
sake. For one daughter, his eldest, he would
(65) really have given up anything which he
had not been very much tempted to do.
Elizabeth had succeeded at sixteen to all
that was possible of her mother's rights and
consequence; and being very handsome, and
(70) very like himself, her influence had always
been great, and they had gone on together
most happily. His two other children were
of very inferior value. Mary had acquired
a little artificial importance by becoming
(75) Mrs. Charles Musgrove; but Anne, with an
elegance of mind and sweetness of character,
which must have placed her high with any
people of real understanding, was nobody
with either father or sister; her word had no
(80) weight, her convenience was always to give
way—she was only Anne.

1. The main purpose of the passage is to

    (A) provide an overview of the
        interrelationships of the members of a
        family.
    (B) point out some unfortunate personality
        defects in a main character.
    (C) explain the relationship between a main
        character and his amiable wife.
    (D) describe a main character and a major
        change in his life.

2. As used in line 3, "situation" most nearly
    means

    (A) position of employment.
    (B) physical surroundings.
    (C) state of affairs.
    (D) social standing.

3. Which choice best summarizes the first two
    paragraphs of the passage (lines 1–43)?

    (A) Even though the loss of his admirable
        wife devastates a character, he perseveres
        in caring for their young children.
    (B) A vain and foolish character is left to care
        for three daughters after the death of his
        sensible wife.
    (C) After seventeen years, a character who
        can no longer endure being married to a
        conceited fool abandons her family.
    (D) Largely prompted by a character's good
        looks, an otherwise intelligent woman
        enters into a misalliance.

4. The narrator speaks well of Lady Elliot for all
    of the following reasons EXCEPT

    (A) her concealment of Sir Walter's
        shortcomings.
    (B) her choice of an intimate friend.
    (C) her guidance of her three daughters.
    (D) her judgment in falling in love with Sir
        Walter.

5. Which choice provides the best evidence for
    the answer to the previous question?

    (A) Lines 5–9 ("Few women . . . society")
    (B) Lines 18–23 ("Lady . . . afterwards")
    (C) Lines 23–31 ("She had . . . them")
    (D) Lines 31–35 ("Three . . . father")

GO ON TO THE NEXT PAGE

MODEL TEST 2

6. It can most reasonably be inferred that over the years Lady Elliot was less than happy because of

   (A) her lack of personal beauty.
   (B) her separation from her most intimate friend.
   (C) the disparity between her character and that of her husband.
   (D) her inability to teach good principles to her young daughters.

7. As used in line 33, "charge" most nearly means

   (A) accusation.
   (B) responsibility.
   (C) official instruction.
   (D) headlong rush.

8. The narrator indicates that Lady Elliot's emotions regarding her approaching death were complicated by her

   (A) pious submissiveness to her fate.
   (B) anxieties over her daughters' prospects.
   (C) resentment of her husband's potential remarriage.
   (D) reluctance to face the realities of her situation.

9. Which choice provides the best evidence for the answer to the previous question?

   (A) Lines 23–31 ("She . . . quit them")
   (B) Lines 31–35 ("Three . . . father")
   (C) Lines 35–43 ("She . . . daughters")
   (D) Lines 44–50 ("This friend . . . widow")

10. The phrase "make it no matter of indifference to her when she was called on to quit them" (lines 29–31) is an example of

   (A) ironic understatement.
   (B) effusive sentiment.
   (C) metaphorical expression.
   (D) personification.

11. The "applications" made by Sir Walter (line 62) were most likely

   (A) professional.
   (B) insincere.
   (C) marital.
   (D) paternal.

GO ON TO THE NEXT PAGE

Questions 12–22 are based on the following passage.

The following passage is taken from a book of popular history written in 1991.

The advantage of associating the birth of democracy with the Mayflower Compact is that it is easy to do so. The public loves a
Line simple explanation, and none is simpler than
(5) the belief that on November 11, 1620—the day the compact was approved—a cornerstone of American democracy was laid. Certainly it makes it easier on schoolchildren. Marking the start of democracy in 1620 relieves
(10) students of the responsibility of knowing what happened in the hundred some years before, from the arrival of the Santa Maria to the landing of the Mayflower.

The compact, to be sure, demonstrated
(15) the Englishman's striking capacity for self-government. And in affirming the principle of majority rule, the Pilgrims showed how far they had come from the days when the king's whim was law, and nobody dared say
(20) otherwise.

But the emphasis on the compact is misplaced. Scholarly research in the last half-century indicates that the compact had nothing to do with the development
(25) of self-government in America. In truth, the Mayflower Compact was no more a cornerstone of American democracy than the Pilgrim hut was the foundation of American architecture. As Samuel Eliot Morrison so
(30) emphatically put it, American democracy "was not born in the cabin of the Mayflower."

The Pilgrims indeed are miscast as the heroes of American democracy. They spurned democracy and would have been
(35) shocked to see themselves held up as its defenders. George Willison, regarded as one

of the most careful students of the Pilgrims, states that "the merest glance at the history of Plymouth" shows that they were not
(40) democrats.

The mythmakers would have us believe that even if the Pilgrims themselves weren't democratic, the Mayflower Compact itself was. But in fact the compact was expressly
(45) designed to curb freedom, not promote it. The Pilgrim governor and historian, William Bradford, from whom we have gotten nearly all of the information there is about the Pilgrims, frankly conceded as much. Bradford
(50) wrote that the purpose of the compact was to control renegades aboard the Mayflower who were threatening to go their own way when the ship reached land. Because the Pilgrims had decided to settle in an area
(55) outside the jurisdiction of their royal patent, some aboard the Mayflower had hinted that upon landing they would "use their owne libertie, for none had power to command them." Under the terms of the compact, they
(60) couldn't; the compact required all who lived in the colony to "promise all due submission and obedience" to it.

Furthermore, despite the compact's mention of majority rule, the Pilgrim fathers
(65) had no intention of turning over the colony's government to the people. Plymouth was to be ruled by the elite. And the elite wasn't bashful in the least about advancing its claims to superiority. When the Mayflower
(70) Compact was signed, the elite signed first. The second rank consisted of the "goodmen." At the bottom of the list came four servants' names. No women or children signed.

Whether the compact was or was not
(75) actually hostile to the democratic spirit, it was deemed sufficiently hostile that during the Revolution, the Tories put it to use as "propaganda for the crown." The

GO ON TO THE NEXT PAGE

monarchists made much of the fact that
(80) the Pilgrims had chosen to establish an
English-style government that placed power
in the hands of a governor, not a cleric, and
a governor who owed his allegiance not to
the people or to a church but to "our dread
(85) Sovereign Lord King James." No one thought
it significant that the authorities had adopted
the principle of majority rule. Tory historian
George Chalmers, in a work published in
1780, claimed the central meaning of the
(90) compact was the Pilgrims' recognition of the
necessity of royal authority. This may have
been not only a convenient argument, but a
true one. It is at least as plausible as the belief
that the compact stood for democracy.

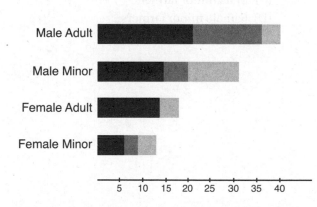

Mayflower Passengers

■ First Rank ("The Elite") — Landed/Professional

■ Second Rank ("Goodmen") — Farmers

▨ Servants

12. The author's attitude toward the general
    public can best be described as

    (A) sympathetic.
    (B) condescending.
    (C) perplexed.
    (D) hostile.

13. The purpose of the first paragraph (lines
    1–13) is to

    (A) present an elaborate speculation.
    (B) develop a chronological summary.
    (C) capture the reader's attention.
    (D) provide a working hypothesis.

14. As used in line 8, "Marking" most nearly
    means

    (A) assessing.
    (B) forming.
    (C) designating.
    (D) manifesting.

15. In stating that "[t]he compact, to be sure,
    demonstrated the Englishman's striking
    capacity for self-government," the author

    (A) concedes a point.
    (B) invokes an expert.
    (C) offers a rationale.
    (D) rejects an assumption.

16. The Pilgrims' attitude toward the concept of
    democracy can best be described as

    (A) complete rejection.
    (B) qualified endorsement.
    (C) marked approbation.
    (D) objective neutrality.

GO ON TO THE NEXT PAGE

17. As used in line 35, "held up" most nearly means

   (A) delayed.
   (B) cited.
   (C) waylaid.
   (D) carried.

18. According to the passage, the compact's primary purpose was to

   (A) establish legal authority within the colony.
   (B) banish non-Pilgrims from the settlement.
   (C) eradicate heretical thinking among the settlers.
   (D) protect each individual's civil rights.

19. Which choice provides the best evidence for the answer to the previous question?

   (A) Lines 41–44 ("The mythmakers . . . itself was")
   (B) Lines 44–49 ("But in fact . . . as much")
   (C) Lines 53–62 ("Because the Pilgrims . . . to it")
   (D) Lines 63–67 ("Furthermore . . . elite")

20. In the passage, the details about the signers of the Mayflower Compact are used to emphasize

   (A) the Pilgrims' respect for the social hierarchy.
   (B) the inclusion of servants among those signing.
   (C) the great variety of social classes aboard.
   (D) the lack of any provision for minority rule.

21. Which choice provides the best evidence for the answer to the previous question?

   (A) Lines 46–49 ("The Pilgrim . . . much")
   (B) Lines 59–62 ("Under . . . it")
   (C) Lines 63–66 ("Furthermore . . . people")
   (D) Lines 69–73 ("When . . . signed")

22. Which category of passenger is least represented on the accompanying graph?

   (A) Male adult servants
   (B) Female adult farmers
   (C) Male minor farmers
   (D) Female minor farmers

GO ON TO THE NEXT PAGE

MODEL TEST 2

Questions 23–32 are based on the following passage.

The following passage is based on Emily Underwood's "Sleep: The Brain's Housekeeper?", published in Science *magazine in 2013.*

Every night since we first evolved, humans have made what might be considered a baffling, dangerous mistake. Despite the
Line   once-prevalent threat of being eaten by
(5)   predators and the loss of valuable time for gathering food, accumulating wealth, or reproducing, we go to sleep. Scientists have long speculated and argued about why we devote roughly a third of our lives to sleep,
(10)   but with little concrete data to support any particular theory. Now, new evidence has refreshed a long-held hypothesis: During sleep, the brain cleans itself.

Most physiologists agree that sleep serves
(15)   many different purposes, ranging from memory consolidation to the regulation of metabolism and the immune system. While the purposes of biological functions such as breathing and eating are easy to
(20)   understand, scientists have never agreed on any such original purpose for sleeping. A new study by Maiken Nedergaard provides what sleep researcher Charles Czeisler calls the "first direct experimental evidence
(25)   at the molecular level" for what could be sleep's basic purpose: It clears the brain of toxic metabolic byproducts. The new work confirms a long-standing hypothesis that sleep promotes recovery—something
(30)   is paid back or cleaned out. It builds on Nedergaard's recent discovery of a network of microscopic, fluid-filled channels that clear toxins from the brain, much as the lymphatic system clears out metabolic waste
(35)   products from the rest of the body. Instead of carrying lymph, this system transports waste-laden cerebrospinal fluid (CSF). Before the discovery of this "glymphatic" system, as Nedergaard has dubbed it, the brain's only
(40)   known method for disposing of cellular waste was breaking it down and recycling it within individual cells, she says.

The earlier study showed that glia, the brain's non-neuronal cells, control the
(45)   flow of CSF through channels in their cell membranes. "If we delete the channels in glial cells, the flow almost stops," Nedergaard says. Because the transport of fluid across cell membranes requires a lot of energy,
(50)   Nedergaard and her team had a hunch that the brain would not be able both to clean the brain and to process sensory information at the same time. Therefore, they decided to test whether the activity of the glymphatic
(55)   system changed during sleep. Lulu Xie, the new study's first author, spent the next two years training mice to relax and fall asleep on a two-photon microscope, which can image the movement of dye through living tissue.
(60)   Once Xie was sure the mice were asleep by checking their EEG (electroencephalogram) brain activity, she injected a green dye into their CSF through a catheter-like device in their necks. After half an hour, she awakened
(65)   them by touching their tails and injected a red dye that the two-photon microscope could easily distinguish from the green. By tracking the movements of red and green dye throughout the brain, the team found that
(70)   large amounts of CSF flowed into the brain during sleep, but not during the waking state, Nedergaard reports.

A comparison of the volume of space between nerve cells while the mice were
(75)   awake and asleep revealed that the glial channels carrying CSF expanded by 60% when the mice were asleep. The team also

GO ON TO THE NEXT PAGE

injected labeled β amyloid proteins into the brains of sleeping mice and wakeful mice (80) and found that during sleep, CSF cleared away this "dirt" outside of the cells twice as quickly—"like a dishwasher," Nedergaard says. Such proteins can aggregate as pathogenic plaques outside cells and are (85) associated with Alzheimer's disease, she says.

Many neurological diseases—from Alzheimer's disease to stroke and dementia—are associated with sleep disturbances. The study suggests that lack of sleep could have (90) a causal role, by allowing the byproducts to build up and cause brain damage.

New scientific results often raise new questions, and this study of sleep is no exception to the rule. Does the need to (95) remove waste products actively regulate sleep? In other words, does the buildup of metabolic byproducts make us sleepy? Is this cleaning function of sleep shared across species? No one role of sleep rules out all (100) others, and sleep presumably has many functions, just as the weekend is variously for shopping, socializing, and cleaning the house. It is possible that different species have evolved different functions of sleep to (105) suit their different habitats.

23. The main purpose of the passage is to

(A) explain why humans sleep more than other mammals.
(B) prove that sleep is in fact beneficial to human beings.
(C) discuss recent experiments regarding brain activity during sleep.
(D) clarify the workings of the lymphatic system.

24. It may most reasonably be inferred from the passage that one function of the lymphatic system is the

(A) relay of sensory information.
(B) regulation of temperature.
(C) transport of cerebrospinal fluid.
(D) drainage of waste.

25. Which choice provides the best evidence for the answer to the previous question?

(A) Lines 21–27 ("A new . . . byproducts")
(B) Lines 27–30 ("The new . . . cleaned out")
(C) Lines 30–35 ("It builds . . . body")
(D) Lines 37–42 ("Before . . . says")

26. The new experiment described indicates that the purpose of sleep is to

(A) build up pathogenic plaques outside cells.
(B) replenish the body's energy stores.
(C) clean the brain and provide other unknown benefits.
(D) reduce the buildup of electrical signals.

GO ON TO THE NEXT PAGE

27. As used in line 29, "promotes" most nearly means

    (A) exchanges a pawn.
    (B) raises in rank.
    (C) fosters.
    (D) publicizes.

28. Why did the scientists consider the fact that glial channels expanded by 60 percent a significant result?

    (A) It suggested that the brain expanded during sleep.
    (B) It suggested that the flow of cerebrospinal fluid increased during sleep.
    (C) It suggested that other organs expanded simultaneously in similar fashion.
    (D) It suggested a peak in the processing of sensory information.

29. As used in line 67, "distinguish" most nearly means

    (A) characterize.
    (B) tell apart.
    (C) make prominent.
    (D) discern.

30. Which statement about the function of Xie's injection of two different colored dyes into the mice's cerebrospinal fluid is best supported by the passage?

    (A) It enabled the researchers to differentiate between different types of molecules in the cerebrospinal fluid.
    (B) It enabled the researchers to differentiate cerebrospinal fluid that entered the brain during a sleeping state from cerebrospinal fluid that entered the brain during a wakeful state.
    (C) It enabled the researchers to differentiate between cerebrospinal fluid and lymph.
    (D) It enabled the researchers to differentiate between fluids that cleared out waste products from the lymphatic system and fluids that cleared out waste products from the glymphatic system.

31. Which choice provides the best evidence for the answer to the previous question?

    (A) Lines 55–59 ("Lulu Xie … living tissue")
    (B) Lines 64–67 ("After half an hour … green")
    (C) Lines 67–72 ("By tracking … reports")
    (D) Lines 73–77 ("A comparison … asleep")

32. The reference to common weekend activities in lines 101–103 ("the weekend … cleaning the house") primarily serves to

    (A) emphasize the importance of leisure time for mental and physical health.
    (B) determine which activities provide the most benefits.
    (C) illustrate by analogy the likely diversity of the roles played by sleep.
    (D) demonstrate the fundamental similarity between recreation and sleep.

GO ON TO THE NEXT PAGE

MODEL TEST 2

Questions 33–42 are based on the following passages.

The first passage is taken from Sojourner Truth's 1851 speech before the Women's Convention in Akron, Ohio. The second passage is adapted from a speech made by Frederick Douglass in 1888, some 23 years after the end of the Civil War.

PASSAGE 1

Well, children, where there is so much racket there must be something out of kilter. I think that 'twixt the negroes of the South
Line and the women at the North, all talking about
(5) rights, the white men will be in a fix pretty soon. But what's all this here talking about?

That man over there says that women need to be helped into carriages, and lifted over ditches, and to have the best place
(10) everywhere. Nobody ever helps me into carriages, or over mud-puddles, or gives me any best place! And ain't I a woman? Look at me! Look at my arm! I have ploughed and planted, and gathered into barns, and no
(15) man could head me! And ain't I a woman? I could work as much and eat as much as a man—when I could get it—and bear the lash as well! And ain't I a woman? I have borne thirteen children, and seen most all sold
(20) off to slavery, and when I cried out with my mother's grief, none but Jesus heard me! And ain't I a woman?

Then they talk about this thing in the head; what's this they call it? [Member of
(25) audience whispers, "intellect."] That's it, honey. What's that got to do with women's rights or negroes' rights? If my cup won't hold but a pint, and yours holds a quart, wouldn't you be mean not to let me have my little half
(30) measure full?

Then that little man in black there, he says women can't have as much rights as men, 'cause Christ wasn't a woman! Where did your Christ come from? Where did your
(35) Christ come from? From God and a woman! Man had nothing to do with Him.

If the first woman God ever made was strong enough to turn the world upside down all alone, these women together ought to be
(40) able to turn it back, and get it right side up again! And now they is asking to do it, the men better let them.

Obliged to you for hearing me, and now old Sojourner ain't got nothing more to say.

PASSAGE 2

(45) Long years ago Henry Clay said, on the floor of the American Senate, "I know there is a visionary dogma that man cannot hold property in man," and, with a brow of defiance, he said, "That is property which
(50) the law makes property. Two hundred years of legislation has sanctioned and sanctified Negro slaves as property." But neither the power of time nor the might of legislation has been able to keep life in that stupendous
(55) barbarism. The universality of man's rule over woman is another factor in the resistance to the woman-suffrage movement. We are pointed to the fact that men have not only always ruled over women, but that they do so
(60) rule everywhere, and they easily think that a thing that is done everywhere must be right. Though the fallacy of this reasoning is too transparent to need refutation, it still exerts a powerful influence. Even our good Brother
(65) Jasper yet believes, with the ancient Church, that the sun "do move," notwithstanding all the astronomers of the world are against him. One year ago I stood on the Pincio in Rome and witnessed the unveiling of the statue

GO ON TO THE NEXT PAGE

(70) of Galileo. . . . One or two priests passed the statue with averted eyes, but the great truths of the solar system were not angry at the sight, and the same will be true when woman shall be clothed, as she will yet be, with all *(75)* the rights of American citizenship. . . . [W]hatever the future may have in store for us, one thing is certain—this new revolution in human thought will never go backward. When a great truth once gets abroad in the *(80)* world, no power on earth can imprison it, or prescribe its limits, or suppress it. It is bound to go on till it becomes the thought of the world. Such a truth is woman's right to equal liberty with man.

33. The author of Passage 1 demonstrates that women are not frail and in need of protection by

    (A) using the example of Northern women who have fought for the right to vote.
    (B) emphasizing the importance of their role as mothers.
    (C) pointing out that women undergo the rigors of childbearing.
    (D) describing her work and treatment as a slave.

34. Which choice provides the best evidence for the answer to the previous question?

    (A) Lines 3–6 ("I think . . . pretty soon")
    (B) Lines 12–18 ("Look at . . . as well")
    (C) Lines 27–30 ("If my cup . . . measure full")
    (D) Lines 37–41 ("If the first . . . up again")

35. As used in line 5, "fix" most nearly means

    (A) repair.
    (B) rut.
    (C) battle.
    (D) predicament.

36. The author of Passage 2 predicts that women will ultimately achieve equal rights because

    (A) the truth cannot be held back.
    (B) the Church supports it.
    (C) they are American citizens.
    (D) people adapt to revolutionary ideas.

37. Which choice provides the best evidence for the answer to the previous question?

    (A) Lines 55–57 ("The universality . . . movement")
    (B) Lines 62–64 ("Though the . . . influence")
    (C) Lines 70–75 ("One or two . . . citizenship")
    (D) Lines 79–81 ("When a great . . . suppress it")

38. As used in line 51, "sanctioned" most nearly means

    (A) authorized.
    (B) penalized.
    (C) prohibited.
    (D) praised.

39. The reference to "the unveiling of the statue of Galileo" in Rome (lines 69–70) serves mainly to

    (A) introduce the scientific basis for the equality of women.
    (B) demonstrate that truth always triumphs despite powerful opposition.
    (C) argue that women's rights are an important issue around the world.
    (D) prove that the teachings of the Church are not always correct.

GO ON TO THE NEXT PAGE

40. Which choice best states the relationship between the two passages?

(A) Passage 2 attacks the political position that Passage 1 strongly advocates.

(B) Passage 2 argues that the political position advocated in Passage 1 will inevitably succeed.

(C) Passage 2 supports the political position that Passage 1 strongly advocates but cautions against moving too quickly.

(D) Passage 2 demonstrates that the political position advocated in Passage 1 has gained increased support.

41. How would the author of Passage 2 most likely react to the arguments of "that man over there," referred to in line 8, Passage 1?

(A) He would agree with the man's arguments about women's need for support and protection.

(B) He would disagree with the man, but also not fully agree with the author of Passage 1.

(C) He would disagree with and be angered by the man's arguments.

(D) He would liken the man's arguments to those of the Church when it rejected Galileo's observation that the Earth revolves around the sun.

42. Where does Passage 2 answer what happened as a result of "the negroes of the South . . . talking about rights" (lines 3–5)?

(A) Lines 50–52 ("Two hundred . . . property")

(B) Lines 52–55 ("But neither . . . barbarism")

(C) Lines 62–64 ("Though the . . . influence")

(D) Lines 76–78 ("[W]hatever . . . backward")

Questions 43–52 are based on the following passage.

The following passage is taken from "Dinosaur metabolism neither hot nor cold, but just right," *an article by Michael Balter that appeared in the 13 June 2014 issue of* Science.

Call it the Goldilocks solution. Paleontologists have struggled for 50 years to determine whether dinosaurs were cold-
Line blooded ectotherms like today's reptiles,
(5) making little effort to control their body temperatures, or warm-blooded endotherms, like most modern mammals and birds, which keep their body temperatures at a constant, relatively high set point. The answer
(10) greatly influences our view of dinosaurs, as endotherms tend to be more active and faster growing.

A recent study concludes that dinosaur blood ran neither cold nor hot but something
(15) in between. Examining growth and metabolic rates of nearly 400 living and extinct animals, the researchers conclude that dinosaurs, like a handful of modern creatures including tuna and the echidna, belonged to an
(20) intermediate group that can raise their body temperature but don't keep it at a specific level. The researchers christen these creatures mesotherms.

Establishing a new metabolic category is
(25) "audacious," admits lead author John Grady, an evolutionary biologist at the University of New Mexico, Albuquerque. And some still think dinosaurs were "just fast-growing ectotherms," as vertebrate physiologist
(30) Frank Paladino of Indiana University–Purdue University Fort Wayne insists. But paleobiologist Gregory Erickson of Florida State University in Tallahassee calls the paper

GO ON TO THE NEXT PAGE

Metabolic Middle Ground
Dinosaurs and some living animals are mesotherms, raising but not maintaining their body temperature.

Ectotherms   Endotherms

Metabolic rate

"a remarkably integrative, landmark study"
(35) that transforms our view of the great beasts.

For the first 150 years after their discovery, dinosaurs were considered ectotherms like today's reptiles. Ectothermy makes some sense: "It requires much less energy from
(40) the environment," explains Roger Seymour, a zoologist at the University of Adelaide in Australia. But it has drawbacks, too: "The animal cannot feed in cold conditions and has a much more limited capacity for
(45) sustained, powerful activity, even if warmed by the sun," he says.

Beginning in the late 1960s, researchers put forward the then-heretical idea of dinosaurs as endotherms, and evidence for
(50) this has accumulated. Annual growth rings in dinosaur bones suggest fast, energy-hungry developmental rates. Birdlike air sacs may have boosted their respiratory efficiency, suggesting rapid movements. And isotopic
(55) data from fossils suggest higher body temperatures (*Science*, 22 July 2011, p. 443).

Giant endotherms pose their own puzzles, however, such as the huge quantities of food needed to sustain them. An endothermic

(60) Tyrannosaurus rex "would probably have starved to death," Grady says.

He and his colleagues tackled the problem by examining the relationship between an animal's growth rate—how fast it becomes
(65) a full-sized adult—and its resting metabolic rate (RMR), a measure of energy expenditure. Earlier studies, based on limited data, had suggested that growth rates scale with metabolic rates. That is, the more energy an
(70) animal can expend, the faster it can grow and the bigger it can get. The team pulled together updated data on 381 living and extinct vertebrates, including 21 species of dinosaurs, and developed mathematical
(75) equations that predict the relationship between metabolic rate, growth rate, and body size in living animals.

These equations show that ectotherms and endotherms fall into distinct clusters
(80) when growth rate is plotted against metabolic rate. High-energy endotherms grow fast and have high metabolic rates, whereas ectotherms have low values of both. Those two categories include most living species,
(85) but the team found that a handful, such as

GO ON TO THE NEXT PAGE

fast-swimming sharks, tuna, reptiles such
as large sea turtles, and a few odd mammals
like the echidna, fall into an in-between
state: mesothermy. These animals use their
(90) metabolism to raise their body temperatures,
but do not "defend" a set temperature.

Using their equations, the team calculated
dinosaur RMRs, plugging in reliable
published data on these extinct animals.
(95) Dino growth rates can be estimated because
rings of bone, which give a measure of
age, were laid down annually, and body
size can be estimated from bone size. The
results placed dinosaurs squarely among
(100) the mesotherms. The earliest birds—direct
descendants of dinosaurs— plotted as
mesotherms, too.

Grady and colleagues think mesothermy
may have allowed dinosaurs to grow
(105) large and active with lower energy costs.
Geochemist Robert Eagle of the California
Institute of Technology in Pasadena agrees:
"In a world that was generally hotter than
today, it wasn't really necessary to be a full
(110) endotherm." Previous studies have suggested
that during the Mesozoic, even mammalian
endotherms kept their bodies at a lower set
point than they do today, he says.

Grady suggests that mesothermy might
(115) even help explain why dinosaurs ruled the
Earth: They could easily outcompete other
reptiles, which were lethargic ectotherms.
And by getting big quickly, they occupied
the large-animal niches, and prevented the
(120) small, energy-hungry endothermic mammals
from getting bigger themselves. Until, of
course, the fateful asteroid struck, and
dinosaurs vanished.

43. The primary purpose of the chart
accompanying the passage is to illustrate that

(A) tyrannosaurs were carnivores that preyed
on mammals and birds.
(B) ostriches are birds that have lost the
ability to fly.
(C) alligators have a lower metabolic rate
than sharks.
(D) in metabolic rate dinosaurs are most
akin to sharks.

44. The passage is written from the perspective
of someone who is

(A) an active participant in evolutionary
biology research.
(B) a supporter of the long-held theory that
dinosaurs were ectotherms.
(C) well-informed about competing theories
regarding dinosaur metabolism.
(D) skilled at developing mathematical
equations.

45. In the opening sentence, the author makes

(A) an allusion to a familiar tale.
(B) a contrast with a literary archetype.
(C) an exaggeration about a theory's
significance.
(D) an exception to a rule.

46. By admitting that the action of establishing a
new metabolic category is "audacious," study
author Grady is

(A) denying the action's validity.
(B) acknowledging its radical nature.
(C) confessing an error in methodology.
(D) refuting a hypothesis.

GO ON TO THE NEXT PAGE

47. What function do the fourth and fifth paragraphs (lines 36–56) serve in the passage as a whole?

    (A) They acknowledge that a theory described by the author of the passage has some limitations.
    (B) They give an overview of previous theories about the body temperature and activity level of dinosaurs.
    (C) They advocate the abandonment of a long-established assumption about the nature of dinosaur metabolism.
    (D) They illustrate the difficulty of reaching any conclusions about the physiology of prehistoric reptiles.

48. It is reasonable to conclude that the main goal of the scientists conducting the research described in the passage is to

    (A) learn the history of classifying dinosaurs as cold-blooded or warm-blooded.
    (B) explore possible ways to predict the body temperatures of mammals and birds.
    (C) characterize dinosaurs according to their metabolic and growth rates.
    (D) determine the role that dinosaur metabolism played in their extinction.

49. Which choice provides the best evidence for the answer to the previous question?

    (A) Lines 13–22 ("A recent . . . level")
    (B) Lines 24–27 ("Establishing . . . Albuquerque")
    (C) Lines 36–38 ("For the first . . . reptiles")
    (D) Lines 106–110 ("Geochemist . . . endotherm'")

50. As used in line 68, "scale" most nearly means

    (A) flake.
    (B) reduce.
    (C) ascend.
    (D) correlate.

51. As used in line 97, "laid down" most nearly means

    (A) rested.
    (B) deposited.
    (C) sacrificed.
    (D) formulated.

52. In line 91, the quotes around the word "defend" indicate that

    (A) the word is being used for ironic effect.
    (B) it has been quoted from an authoritative source.
    (C) the author would prefer a different word in its place.
    (D) the word is being used in an unusual sense.

STOP

If there is still time remaining, you may review your answers.

WRITING AND LANGUAGE TEST

35 MINUTES, 44 QUESTIONS

Turn to Section 2 of your answer sheet to answer the questions in this section.

> **Directions:** Questions follow each of the passages below. Some questions ask you how the passage might be changed to improve the expression of ideas. Other questions ask you how the passage might be altered to correct errors in grammar, usage, and punctuation. One or more graphics accompany some passages. You will be required to consider these graphics as you answer questions about editing the passage.
>
> There are three types of questions. In the first type, a part of the passage is underlined. The second type is based on a certain part of the passage. The third type is based on the entire passage.
>
> Read each passage. Then, choose the answer to each question that changes the passage so that it is consistent with the conventions of standard written English. One of the answer choices for many questions is "NO CHANGE." Choosing this answer means that you believe the best answer is to make no change in the passage.

Questions 1–11 are based on the following passage and supplementary material.

Chiroptera

❶ As insignificant animals, bats make up a quarter of mammal species worldwide. They are the only mammals capable of true flight; their webbed forelimbs—which anatomically resemble the human hand—can sustain flight unlike the "gliding" of squirrels and opossums. ❷ Although often considered pests themselves, most bats feed on insects and share a large part of natural pest control. The remaining percentage of bat species, whose diet doesn't consist of insects, are frugivores, carnivores, or hematophagous. It is the latter bloodsuckers who attract the most attention. The ecological roles of bats ❸ do not end with pest control. They are also responsible for pollinating and

1. Which choice best expresses that bats are not quite the most widespread mammalian species?
   (A) NO CHANGE
   (B) Representing 12 percent of mammals,
   (C) Second only to rodents,
   (D) Far more populous than humans,

2. (A) NO CHANGE
   (B) Because they are
   (C) However
   (D) For this very reason, they are

3. (A) NO CHANGE
   (B) does
   (C) don't
   (D) do's

GO ON TO THE NEXT PAGE

dispersing fruit seeds. In fact, some tropical plants rely solely on bats for reproduction.

Bats are of the order Chiroptera and divided into two suborders: Microchiroptera and Megachiroptera. ❹ The smallest bats are known to have bodies approximately one inch long. And some are known to live up to 30 years. Echolocation is the highly sophisticated sense of hearing in which sound waves bounce off objects and emit echoes that microbats use to detect obstacles. It is this ❺ object that allows the nocturnal microbat to sense where an object is, how big or small that object may be, and even how fast that object is moving. In contrast, megabats have well-developed eyesight and more advanced characteristics in their brains. They often inhabit warm climates and live socially in colonies.

Recently, bat populations have been threatened by the deadly white-nose syndrome. Since the winter of 2007–2008, millions of bats have died as a result of this white fungus that spreads into the ears, muzzle, and wings of hibernating bats. Some estimates show a ❻ 10 percent increase in the brown bat population in United States since the initial spread of the disease through the end of 2010. While the full consequences of such a large population reduction are yet unknown, ❼ and it is clear that farmers will feel the ❽ affect with their best pest controllers now all but absent. Scientists at Michigan Technological University are working hard to prevent further spread of the disease. Using chemical fingerprinting, these scientists are tracing the ❾ bats hibernation sites and movements to detect what areas

4. (A) NO CHANGE
(B) The smallest bats are known, to have bodies approximately one inch long.
(C) The smallest bats are known, to have bodies, approximately one inch long.
(D) The smallest, bats are known to have bodies approximately one inch long.

5. (A) NO CHANGE
(B) material
(C) phenomenon
(D) thing

6. Which choice is best supported by the information in the accompanying graph?
(A) NO CHANGE
(B) 15 percent decline
(C) 40 percent decline
(D) 65 percent decline

7. (A) NO CHANGE
(B) but
(C) or
(D) OMIT the underlined portion.

8. (A) NO CHANGE
(B) effect
(C) affectedness
(D) effectively

9. (A) NO CHANGE
(B) bat's
(C) bat is
(D) bats'

GO ON TO THE NEXT PAGE

Bat Population in Pennsylvania

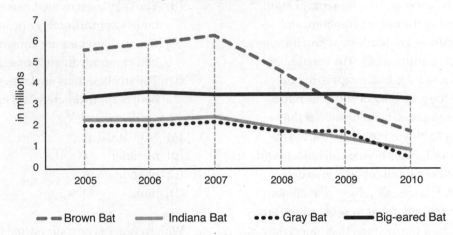

Note: The population numbers are tallied at the *end* of each year.

are infected and how the syndrome is being transmitted. Their research is particularly significant with the disease spreading to the ❿ brown bats of Tennessee—a species that is already on the endangered list. Interestingly, some species have altered their mating and living habits to help protect themselves, and it is through observation of these adaptations that researchers ⓫ so preservationists can make the necessary interventions.

10. Based on the latter part of the sentence and the information in the graph, which bats most likely fit this description?

(A) NO CHANGE
(B) Indiana
(C) gray
(D) big-eared

11. Which choice is most logically inserted at this point in the sentence?

(A) have decided how the species are thriving
(B) are learning which species are in the most danger
(C) are finding the preferred cultural associations of bats
(D) may locate major bat predators

Questions 12–22 are based on the following passage.

The Tyrannical and the Taciturn

The so-called "marriage group" from Geoffrey Chaucer's *The Canterbury Tales* consists of five stories, in each of which marriage is **12** not—as tradition would dictate, the resolution, but instead functions as a central narrative conflict. Generally, the dysfunctional aspects of each married pair **13** are supported by specific textual quotations: an unbalanced distribution of power and ineffective communication between the espoused.

Perhaps nowhere **14** is this timeless marital troubles better illustrated than in the second narrative of the suite, "The Clerk's Tale." **15** In the story of "The Clerk's Tale," we find the greatest power imbalance of any of Chaucer's unhappy couples. A Marquis of Lombardy, Lord Walter, fears that marriage will mean the surrender of his personal freedom, stating **16** "I me rejoysed of my liberte / That seelde tyme is founde in marriage." To ensure that his "liberte" is uncompromised by wedlock, he does not choose for his bride a noblewoman of equal birth but, instead, the daughter of his poorest subject, Griselda.

12. (A) NO CHANGE
    (B) not—as tradition would dictate—the resolution, but
    (C) not as tradition would dictate, the resolution, but
    (D) not, as tradition would dictate—the resolution, but

13. Which of the following would most logically connect to what comes next in the sentence?

    (A) NO CHANGE
    (B) could be said to derive from two critical failings:
    (C) are ironic given the dominant themes in the work:
    (D) contribute to a resolution between the protagonist and antagonist:

14. (A) NO CHANGE
    (B) is these
    (C) are those
    (D) are them

15. (A) NO CHANGE
    (B) In this medieval narrative found in *The Canterbury Tales*,
    (C) Here
    (D) Therefore

16. The author is considering removing the quotation marks in the underlined portion. Should she do so?

    (A) Yes. The underlined portion represents the internal monologue of the narrator.
    (B) Yes. The underlined portion is written in the medieval style, which is consistent with the style of the rest of the essay.
    (C) No. The quotation marks serve to demonstrate the narrator's possession of specific thoughts.
    (D) No. The quotation marks serve to set aside a statement by a character.

GO ON TO THE NEXT PAGE

The disparity of partnership in the marriage inevitably leads Walter to abuse his power. Soon after the couple's first child is born, Walter begins "testing" his wife's devotion through a series of truly mean-spirited pranks, including a false order for the execution of their two children and **17** a renouncement of their marriage. Griselda consents to each demand precisely as she promised on their wedding day, and one begins to imagine that the Marquis is not so much testing his wife's devotion **18** so they are exploring the extent to which his power reaches.

Conversely, Griselda contributes to the complications **19** through her unwillingness to communicate openly with Walter. In Griselda's final test, wherein she is cast out of the castle and replaced by a younger woman of higher birthright, Griselda asks **20** that Walter not send her away naked, once again emphasizing her intent to preserve the dignity of the bodies that fall victim to his wishes. This exchange is notable in that it is the first time Griselda directly asserts her desires to Walter, and although she desists as soon as he raises an objection, she allows herself, finally, at **21** what she believes, to be the end of their marriage, to communicate to him what she feels to be right and honorable.

In any case, Griselda's concern for the physical body **22** becomes somewhat ironic given the tale's conclusion, particularly its invocation of the myth of Echo and Narcissus. Just as Echo could not speak of her own accord but only reflect the words of others, Griselda's inability to communicate with Walter beyond reflection of his immediate will causes her, in some sense, to lose even her physical body as a character, reduced to merely the echo of his desires.

17. (A) NO CHANGE
(B) a marriage of their renouncing.
(C) of their marriage, a renouncing.
(D) with the renouncement of their marital vows.

18. (A) NO CHANGE
(B) when they were
(C) so he was
(D) as he is

19. (A) NO CHANGE
(B) as
(C) since
(D) to

20. Which choice best communicates Griselda's limited request?

(A) NO CHANGE
(B) so that
(C) only that
(D) from that

21. (A) NO CHANGE
(B) what she believes to be the end of their marriage to communicate to him what
(C) what she believes—to be the end of their marriage, to communicate to him what
(D) what she believes to be the end of their marriage, to communicate to him what

22. (A) NO CHANGE
(B) became
(C) had become
(D) have become

GO ON TO THE NEXT PAGE

Questions 23–33 are based on the following passage and supplementary material.

A, B, C—1, 2, 3

Few jobs are as important as that of teachers. A society's quality of life often depends on its economic growth, which is directly affected by its **23** workforce, which, of course, is educated by its school teachers. Take a moment to imagine the ten most influential people in your life—chances are, at least one of them is a teacher or an instructor you have presently or have had in the past. **24** From English class during first period to mathematics as the final period, teachers are those constant guardians molding you into the person you will become, pushing you to do **25** your best and critiquing you when you're falling short of your potential. Many students realize too late that relationships with their teachers, and later with their professors, should be fostered into life-long connections.

26 However, what is it that's so special about being a teacher? It begins with the decision to devote your life to the education of others. Most teachers have, at some point, entertained the idea of a career that requires less personal investment and pays better than **27** an average of approximately $45,000 per year in many cities; yet, when asked, few would take back their decision. The most probable explanation is that

23. (A) NO CHANGE
    (B) workforce which, of course, are educated by its
    (C) workforce, which, of course is educated by its'
    (D) workforce, which of course is educated by it's

24. Which choice would most logically emphasize the wide span of time during which teachers have a direct influence over students?

    (A) NO CHANGE
    (B) From the opening of the school doors to their closing at day's end,
    (C) From schools in the United States to schools located in faraway countries,
    (D) From elementary to middle to high school and beyond,

25. (A) NO CHANGE
    (B) you're best and criticizing you when your
    (C) your best and criticizing one when one's
    (D) you're best and critiquing you when you're

26. (A) NO CHANGE
    (B) So,
    (C) But,
    (D) Further,

27. Which choice offers the most accurate interpretation of the data in the chart that accompanies this passage?

    (A) NO CHANGE
    (B) an average of approximately $50,000 per year
    (C) an average of approximately $55,000 per year
    (D) an average of approximately $60,000 per year

GO ON TO THE NEXT PAGE

despite the negatives, the field of teaching is uniquely rewarding and exceptionally worthwhile. A ㉘ teachers' workday starts and ends with the training and shaping of the next generation; and for many, there's no better way to invest their own training ㉙ compared in the opening of young minds.

Nonetheless, becoming a teacher takes much more than a kind heart and a good dose of patience. All school teachers need to have a bachelor's degree—most commonly in education, but sometimes in the subject that the teacher wishes to teach—and it is increasingly common for teachers to obtain a master's degree. ㉚ Obscuringly, after degree completion, teachers need to acquire a teaching certificate, or a license to teach—most often, this licensing is achieved via teacher-education programs where ㉛ perspective teachers student-teach under more experienced instructors. Many schools prefer that their teachers continue to learn, train, and attend field-related events throughout their employment.

28. (A) NO CHANGE
    (B) teacher's
    (C) teachers
    (D) teacher has a

29. (A) NO CHANGE
    (B) than
    (C) then
    (D) related

30. (A) NO CHANGE
    (B) Given,
    (C) Furthermore,
    (D) Professionally,

31. (A) NO CHANGE
    (B) prospective
    (C) prospecting
    (D) previewing

GO ON TO THE NEXT PAGE

Public School Teacher Salary

■ Median Annual Income in U.S. Dollars

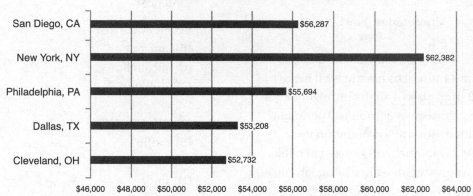

City	Median Annual Income
San Diego, CA	$56,287
New York, NY	$62,382
Philadelphia, PA	$55,694
Dallas, TX	$53,208
Cleveland, OH	$52,732

$46,000 $48,000 $50,000 $52,000 $54,000 $56,000 $58,000 $60,000 $62,000 $64,000

Even then, the job is far from cookie-cutter. Most teachers are expected to be knowledgeable in psychology and counseling in order to provide other support for students. Licensure requirements and salaries can vary based on geography; **32** salaries in many urban school districts can vary by as much as approximately $4,000 based on the city's location. Additionally, if you choose to teach at the secondary level, it is best to be ready to answer questions about college, career planning, and young adult issues. One thing is **33** for sure, a good teacher is there because he or she wants to be.

32. Which choice offers the most accurate interpretation of the data in the chart?

(A) NO CHANGE
(B) salaries in many urban school districts can vary by as much as approximately $7,000 based on the city's location.
(C) salaries in many urban school districts can vary by as much as approximately $10,000 based on the city's location.
(D) salaries in many urban school districts can vary by as much as approximately $13,000 based on the city's location.

33. (A) NO CHANGE
(B) for sure: a good
(C) for sure a good
(D) for a

GO ON TO THE NEXT PAGE

Questions 34–44 are based on the following passage.

Murder Most Fowl

Al Capone, speakeasies, the Saint Valentine's Day Massacre—most of us have at least heard of Chicago's **34** transparent affairs throughout the United States' thirteen-year "noble experiment" with prohibition. But while prohibition was repealed in 1933, another, less renowned noble experiment was inaugurated in Chicago in 2006—a citywide ban on the sale of foie gras, or fatty duck liver. Like veal, foie gras has often been a target of animal rights groups such as PETA **35** because ducks traditionally undergo a technique called "gavage" in order to fatten the liver artificially. **36** Gavage involves, the force-feeding of corn, to ducks through a funnel. Sponsors of the ban cited the raising of foie gras as a particularly heinous act of commercialized animal cruelty—one that overshadows the treatment of chickens, pigs, cows, and other animals raised for slaughter. The ban was passed by **37** Chicago's City Council in an omnibus bill despite the opposition of the city's mayor.

Foie gras is considered a very traditional and desirable ingredient in **38** French cooking, not surprisingly, Chicago's many respected French-style chefs were outraged by the council's decision. Other chefs throughout the city expressed similar

34. Which word is most applicable to the types of "affairs" listed at the beginning of the sentence?

(A) NO CHANGE
(B) ancient
(C) alcoholic
(D) dubious

35. (A) NO CHANGE
(B) while
(C) although
(D) and

36. (A) NO CHANGE
(B) Gavage involves the, force-feeding of corn to ducks through a funnel.
(C) Gavage involves the force-feeding of corn to ducks through a funnel.
(D) Gavage involves the force-feeding, of corn to ducks through a funnel.

37. (A) NO CHANGE
(B) Chicagos City Council
(C) Chicagos' Cities Council
(D) Chicagos Cities Council

38. (A) NO CHANGE
(B) French cooking; not surprisingly, Chicago's many
(C) French cooking: not surprisingly Chicagos many
(D) French cooking not surprisingly, Chicago's many

GO ON TO THE NEXT PAGE

MODEL TEST 2

dismay at what they perceived as everything from artistic censorship to the Orwellian tyranny of an authoritarian state. Restaurant patrons, for the most part, **39** were appalled at the City Council's encroachment on personal dietary choices. In fact, many restaurants reported a tremendous spike in foie gras sales in the months between when the bill was passed and the date on which it took effect.

40 What's more, after the ban became active—much like in the old days of prohibition— enterprising Chicagoan restaurateurs, diners, and chefs found ways around the legislation. Some restaurants, such as Har-De-Har-Har and Copperblue, simply continued to sell foie gras, claiming the **41** enormous livers were sourced either from chickens or from naturally fed ducks. Bin 36 offered a salad of figs, honey, and apricots at what appeared to be the exorbitant price of thirty **42** dollars—until one realized the salad included a "complimentary" serving of foie gras. Bin 36, being the most cavalier of the culinary rebels, was investigated by the Health Department, who nonetheless declined to issue a citation. Following that decision, attempts to enforce the ban essentially **43** vivified, and any restaurant in Chicago wishing to serve foie gras could do so without a serious fear of reprisal.

Two years after the ban was passed, it was repealed. Chefs hailed the action as a victory **44** to personal freedom. Many animal rights advocates decried it as surrender to wealthy special interest groups. Mayor Richard Daley reflected on the council's decision to ban foie gras in the first place as "the silliest thing they've ever done."

STOP

If there is still time remaining, you may review your answers.

39. Which choice best expresses that restaurant patrons had the opposite attitude about the foie gras ban than the chefs described in the previous sentence?

(A) NO CHANGE
(B) considered moving away from this oppressive society.
(C) just wondered what all the fuss was about.
(D) felt that artists should be able to paint whatever they would like.

40. (A) NO CHANGE
(B) Conversely,
(C) However,
(D) In contrast,

41. Which wording gives the most logical and vivid description based on the context of the sentence?

(A) NO CHANGE
(B) suspiciously large and luscious
(C) grotesquely unappetizing
(D) poultry

42. (A) NO CHANGE
(B) dollars, until one, realized the salad
(C) dollars: until one realized, the salad
(D) dollars; until one realized the salad

43. (A) NO CHANGE
(B) congealed,
(C) checked,
(D) froze,

44. (A) NO CHANGE
(B) since
(C) for
(D) on

MATH TEST (NO CALCULATOR)

25 MINUTES, 20 QUESTIONS

Turn to Section 3 of your answer sheet to answer the questions in this section.

Directions: For questions 1–15, solve each problem and choose the best answer from the given options. Fill in the corresponding circle on your answer document. For questions 16–20, solve the problem and fill in the answer on the answer sheet grid.

Notes:

- Calculators are **NOT PERMITTED** in this section.
- All variables and expressions represent real numbers unless indicated otherwise.
- All figures are drawn to scale unless indicated otherwise.
- All figures are in a plane unless indicated otherwise.
- Unless indicated otherwise, the domain of a given function is the set of all real numbers x for which the function has real values.

REFERENCE INFORMATION

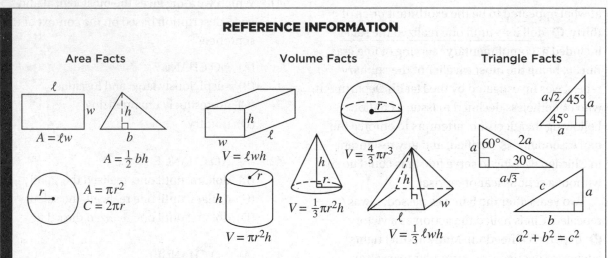

Area Facts · Volume Facts · Triangle Facts

$A = \ell w$

$A = \frac{1}{2} bh$

$A = \pi r^2$
$C = 2\pi r$

$V = \ell w h$

$V = \pi r^2 h$

$V = \frac{4}{3}\pi r^3$

$V = \frac{1}{3}\pi r^2 h$

$V = \frac{1}{3}\ell w h$

$a^2 + b^2 = c^2$

The arc of a circle contains 360°.
The arc of a circle contains 2π radians.
The sum of the measures of the angles in a triangle is 180°.

GO ON TO THE NEXT PAGE

MODEL TEST 2

Year	1990	1991	1992	1993	1994	1995
Number of tournaments	4	5	10	6	9	12

1. The chart above shows the number of tennis tournaments that Adam entered each year from 1990 through 1995. In what year did he enter 50% more tournaments than the year before.

   (A) 1991
   (B) 1992
   (C) 1994
   (D) 1995

2. Which of the following statements is true concerning the equation below?

   $$5(x + 1) + 3 = 3(x + 3)$$

   (A) The equation has no solutions.
   (B) The equation has one positive solution.
   (C) The equation has one negative solution.
   (D) The equation has infinitely many solutions.

3. What is the slope of the line whose equation is $3x + 4y = 24$?

   (A) $-\dfrac{4}{3}$
   (B) $-\dfrac{3}{4}$
   (C) $\dfrac{3}{4}$
   (D) $\dfrac{4}{3}$

4. A, B, and C are three cities in New York State. The distance between A and B is m miles, and the distance between B and C is n miles. If on a map of New York, A and B are c centimeters apart, on that map how many centimeters apart are B and C?

   (A) $\dfrac{cn}{m}$
   (B) $\dfrac{cm}{n}$
   (C) $\dfrac{mn}{c}$
   (D) $\dfrac{c}{mn}$

5. At North Central University, students need at least 120 credits to graduate. Most courses are three credits, but all lab sciences courses, as well as some advanced courses that require more work, are four credits. Which of the following inequalities represents a possible number of three-credit courses, x, and four-credit courses, y, that a student could take to have enough credits to graduate?

   (A) $\dfrac{3}{x} + \dfrac{4}{y} > 120$
   (B) $\dfrac{3}{x} + \dfrac{4}{y} \geq 120$
   (C) $3x + 4y > 120$
   (D) $3x + 4y \geq 120$

6. If at Lake Hollow High School the ratio of boys to girls in the French club is 2:3 and the ratio of boys to girls in the Spanish club is 3:5, which of the following statements must be true?

(A) The number of girls in the French club is equal to the number of boys in the Spanish club.

(B) The number of boys in the Spanish club is greater than the number of boys in the French club.

(C) The percent of Spanish club members who are girls is greater than the percent of French club members who are girls.

(D) If new members join the French club (and no old members leave) and if the ratio of boys to girls among those new members is 3:2, then the club will have an equal number of boys and girls.

7. John and his sister Mary each drove the same route from their uncle's house in Boston to their home in New York, a distance of 200 miles. For the entire trip, John averaged 25 miles per gallon of gasoline and Mary averaged 20 miles per gallon. How far, in miles, was Mary from their home when she had used exactly as much gasoline as John had for his entire trip?

(A) 20
(B) 40
(C) 80
(D) 160

8. If the lines whose equations are $2x + 3y = 4$ and $y = 2x$ intersect at the point (a, b), what is the value of $a + b$?

(A) 1
(B) 1.5
(C) 2
(D) 2.5

9. Container I is a rectangular solid whose base is a square 4 inches on a side, and container II is a cylinder whose base is a circle with a diameter of 4 inches. The height of each container is 5 inches. How much more water, in cubic inches, will container I hold than container II?

(A) $4(4 - \pi)$
(B) $20(4 - \pi)$
(C) $80(\pi - 1)$
(D) $80(1 - \pi)$

GO ON TO THE NEXT PAGE

MODEL TEST 2

10. Pam is a potter who sells the vases she creates to Carl, who then sells them in his crafts boutique for 60% more than he pays Pam for them. To attract customers into his store over the July 4th weekend, Carl runs a special sale on Pam's vases, selling them for 20% less than he pays her for them. A customer who buys one of these vases during the sale is receiving a discount of what percent off Carl's normal selling price?

(A) 25%
(B) 48%
(C) 50%
(D) 80%

$$y = x^2 + 1$$
$$y = -x^2 + 3$$

11. If (a, b) and (c, d) are solutions of the system of equations above, what is the value of $a + b + c + d$?

(A) 1
(B) 2
(C) 3
(D) 4

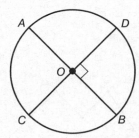

12. In Circle O above with radius r, $\overline{AB}$ and $\overline{CD}$ are a pair of perpendicular diameters. If the area and perimeter of square $ADBC$ (not shown) are a square inches and b inches, respectively, and if $a = b$, what is the length, in inches, of r?

(A) $\sqrt{2}$
(B) 2
(C) $2\sqrt{2}$
(D) $4\sqrt{2}$

13. The members of the varsity baseball team at Meadowlawn High School are all juniors and seniors. There are 5 more seniors on the team than juniors. If 40% of the team members are juniors, how many students are on the team?

(A) 18
(B) 24
(C) 25
(D) 30

GO ON TO THE NEXT PAGE

MODEL TEST 2

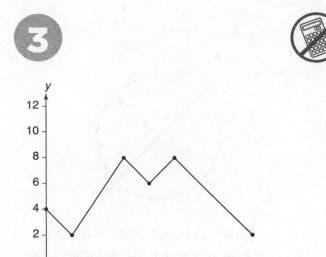

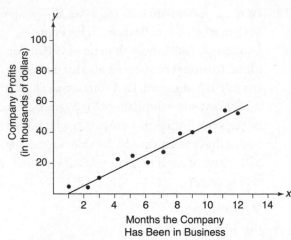

14. The complete graph of $y = f(x)$ is shown above. If $f(3) = a$, what is the value of $f(3a)$?

(A) 3.5
(B) 5.5
(C) 7.5
(D) 10.5

15. The scatter plot diagram above shows the profits of a start-up company during its first year of business. If the company's profits continue to grow at the same rate as predicted by the line of best fit, which has been drawn in, which of the following will be closest to the company's monthly profit after it has been in business for a year and a half?

(A) $40,000
(B) $60,000
(C) $80,000
(D) $85,000

GO ON TO THE NEXT PAGE

Grid-in Response Directions

In questions 16–20, first solve the problem, and then enter your answer on the grid provided on the answer sheet. The instructions for entering your answers follow.

- First, write your answer in the boxes at the top of the grid.
- Second, grid your answer in the columns below the boxes.
- Use the fraction bar in the first row or the decimal point in the second row to enter fractions and decimals.

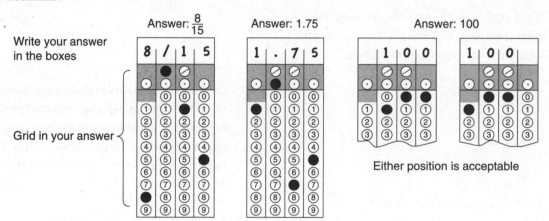

- Grid only one space in each column.
- Entering the answer in the boxes is recommended as an aid in gridding but is not required.
- The machine scoring your exam can read only what you grid, so you **must grid-in your answers correctly to get credit**.
- If a question has more than one correct answer, grid-in only one of them.
- The grid does not have a minus sign; so no answer can be negative.
- A mixed number *must* be converted to an improper fraction or a decimal before it is gridded. Enter $1\frac{1}{4}$ as 5/4 or 1.25; the machine will interpret 11/4 as $\frac{11}{4}$ and mark it wrong.
- **All decimals must be entered as accurately as possible.** Here are three acceptable ways of gridding

$$\frac{3}{11} = 0.272727\ldots$$

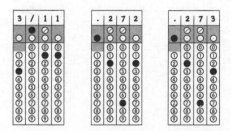

- Note that rounding to .273 is acceptable because you are using the full grid, but you would receive **no credit** for .3 or .27, because they are less accurate.

16. What is the value of $8^{-\frac{1}{3}}$?

17. If the cosine of the larger acute angle in a right triangle is 0.6, what is the cosine of the smaller acute angle in that triangle?

18. If $i = \sqrt{-1}$, what is the value of

$(7 + i\sqrt{7})(7 - i\sqrt{7})$?

19. Based on the following system of equations, what is the value of xy?

$$3x + 4y = 4x + 3y$$
$$x + y = 5$$

20. Consider the parabola whose equation is $y = x^2 - 8x + 16$. If m represents the number of times the parabola crosses the y-axis and n represents the number of times the parabola crosses the x-axis, what is the value of $m + n$?

If there is still time remaining, you may review your answers.

MATH TEST (CALCULATOR)

55 MINUTES, 38 QUESTIONS

Turn to Section 4 of your answer sheet to answer the questions in this section.

Directions: For questions 1–30, solve each problem and choose the best answer from the given options. Fill in the corresponding circle on your answer document. For questions 31–38, solve the problem and fill in the answer on the answer sheet grid.

Notes:

- Calculators **ARE PERMITTED** in this section.
- All variables and expressions represent real numbers unless indicated otherwise.
- All figures are drawn to scale unless indicated otherwise.
- All figures are in a plane unless indicated otherwise.
- Unless indicated otherwise, the domain of a given function is the set of all real numbers x for which the function has real values.

REFERENCE INFORMATION

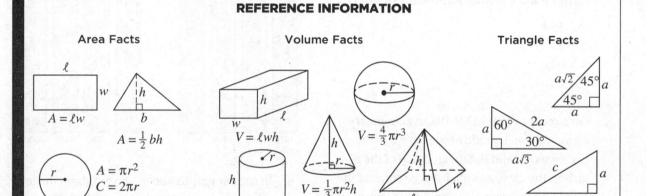

The arc of a circle contains 360°.

The arc of a circle contains 2π radians.

The sum of the measures of the angles in a triangle is 180°.

1. Water is pouring at a constant rate into a tank that is a 4-foot-high rectangular solid. If the water was turned on at 11:00 and if at 11:25 the depth of the water in the tank was 4 inches, at what time was the pool full?

   (A) 3:35
   (B) 4:00
   (C) 4:25
   (D) 5:00

2. Which of the following statements is true concerning the equation below?

   $$\sqrt{x+7} = -4$$

   (A) The equation has no solutions.
   (B) The equation has one positive solution.
   (C) The equation has one negative solution.
   (D) The equation has more than one solution.

GO ON TO THE NEXT PAGE

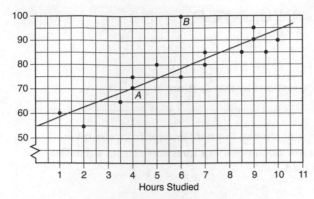

Hours Studied

3. The scatter plot above shows the relationship between the number of hours that a group of high school students studied for their biology midterm and their grades on their tests. The line of best fit has also been drawn. If the equation of the line of best fit is written in the form $y = mx + b$, what is the value of $m + b$?

    (A) 55.4
    (B) 59.0
    (C) 62.4
    (D) 65.0

4. On a recent exam in Mr. Walsh's chemistry class, the mean grade of the b boys in the class was 82, and the mean grade of the g girls in the class was 88. If $b \neq g$, which of the following must be true about the mean grade, m, of all the students in the class?

    (A) $m = 85$
    (B) $m \neq 85$
    (C) $m < 85$
    (D) $m > 85$

5. Brigitte is translating children's books from French into English. On average, it takes her 45 minutes to translate a page. If Brigitte works 8 hours a day for 5 days per week, how many pages can she translate in 6 weeks?

    (A) 180
    (B) 240
    (C) 320
    (D) 480

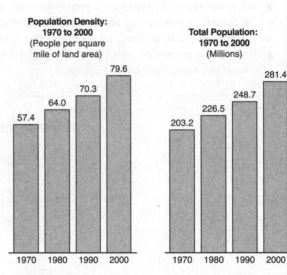

6. In the bar graphs above, the graph on the left gives the population density of the United States (number of people per square mile of land area) from 1970 to 2000. The graph on the right shows the population of the United States in millions for the same period of time. Which of the following is closest to the total land area of the United States, in square miles?

    (A) 2,500,000
    (B) 3,000,000
    (C) 3,500,000
    (D) 4,000,000

GO ON TO THE NEXT PAGE

MODEL TEST 2

Questions 7–8 are based on the following information.

On January 1, 2014, Michael put d dollars into an empty safe deposit box. Then on the first day of every month, he put e dollars into the box. No other money was put into the box, and none was taken out. After 3 monthly deposits, the box contained $175. After 8 monthly deposits, it contained $300.

7. Which of the following equations gives the amount, a, of money in the box, in dollars, after m monthly deposits have been made?

    (A) $a = 100 + 25m$
    (B) $a = 100 + 25(m - 1)$
    (C) $a = 25 + 50m$
    (D) $a = 25 + 50(m - 1)$

8. What was the amount of money, in dollars, in the box on December 25, 2015?

    (A) $650
    (B) $675
    (C) $725
    (D) $750

9. If $f(x) = 4x^4 - 4$, for what value of x is $f(x) = 4$?

    (A) 1
    (B) 1.19
    (C) 1.41
    (D) 1.68

10. A car going 40 miles per hour set out on a 8-mile trip at 9:00 A.M. Exactly 10 minutes later, a second car left from the same place and followed the same route. How fast, in miles per hour, was the second car going if it caught up with the first car at 10:30 A.M.?

    (A) 45
    (B) 50
    (C) 55
    (D) 60

11. If the product of the two complex numbers $a + 4i$ and $9 - bi$ is a real number and if $a = 6$, what is the value of b?

    (A) 3
    (B) 4
    (C) 6
    (D) 9

12. If Eli flips five fair coins and if, for each of them, Max guesses whether it landed heads or tails, what is the probability that Max makes at least one correct guess?

    (A) 0.03
    (B) 0.50
    (C) 0.80
    (D) 0.97

GO ON TO THE NEXT PAGE

Questions 13–15 are based on the information in the following graphs.

College Enrollment, by Age and Gender
1975 and 1995

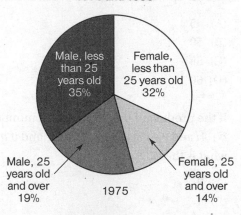

Male, less than 25 years old 35%

Female, less than 25 years old 32%

Male, 25 years old and over 19%

Female, 25 years old and over 14%

1975

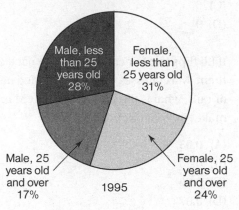

Male, less than 25 years old 28%

Female, less than 25 years old 31%

Male, 25 years old and over 17%

Female, 25 years old and over 24%

1995

13. If there were 10,000,000 college students in 1975, how many more male students were there than female students?

(A) 400,000
(B) 600,000
(C) 800,000
(D) 1,000,000

14. In 1975, approximately what percent of female college students were at least 25 years old?

(A) 14%
(B) 30%
(C) 45%
(D) 76%

15. If the total number of students enrolled in college was 40% higher in 1995 than in 1975, what is the ratio of the number of male students in 1995 to the number of male students in 1975?

(A) 5:6
(B) 6:7
(C) 7:6
(D) 6:5

16. A and B are two points in the xy–plane. If their coordinates are $A(1, 1)$ and $B(5, 5)$, which of the following is the equation of the circle for which $\overline{AB}$ is a diameter?

(A) $(x-3)^2 + (y-3)^2 = 4$
(B) $(x-3)^2 + (y-3)^2 = 8$
(C) $(x+3)^2 + (y+3)^2 = 4$
(D) $(x+3)^2 + (y+3)^2 = 8$

17. At a national educational conference, all of the participants are teachers or administrators. If there are 584 teachers at the conference and 27% of the participants are administrators, how many administrators are attending the conference?

(A) 158
(B) 216
(C) 312
(D) 800

GO ON TO THE NEXT PAGE

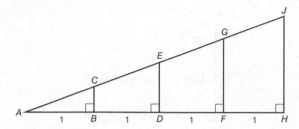

18. In the figure above, what is the ratio of the area of △AHJ to the area of △ABC?

(A) 4:1
(B) 8:1
(C) 12:1
(D) 16:1

The graphs below show the percent of boys and girls in the National Honor Society at Central High School in 2010 and 2015.

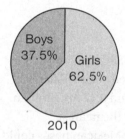 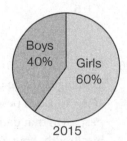

2010   2015

19. If in 2015 there were six more boys and two more girls in the school's National Honor Society than in 2010, how many students in total were in the society in 2015?

(A) 48
(B) 72
(C) 112
(D) 120

20. All general admission tickets for an upcoming concert are the same price and are available only online. The online agency handling ticket sales charges a processing fee for all orders, regardless of how many tickets are purchased. If the charge for four tickets is $107.95 and the charge for seven tickets is $181.45, how much is the processing fee?

(A) $6.95
(B) $7.95
(C) $8.95
(D) $9.95

Use the information below and the data in the following chart in answering Questions 21 and 22.

A survey was conducted of 82,184 citizens of the four Scandinavian countries—Denmark, Sweden, Norway, and Finland—concerning their vacation plans for next summer. The chart below shows where, if anyplace, the people surveyed plan to travel.

Country	Travel within Europe	Travel outside of Europe	Not planning to travel	Total
Denmark	10,321	6,244	5,388	21,953
Sweden	13,644	5,881	4,465	23,990
Norway	11,222	5,369	3,468	20,059
Finland	8,196	2,662	5,324	16,182
Total	43,383	20,156	18,645	82,184

21. According to the survey, in which country did the highest percentage of people say that they would be traveling outside of Europe?

(A) Denmark
(B) Sweden
(C) Norway
(D) Finland

GO ON TO THE NEXT PAGE

MODEL TEST 2

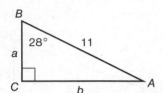

22. When a random sampling of 1,000 of the people who said they planned to travel outside of Europe were asked during a follow-up survey if they planned to visit the United States, 168 said "yes." Based on the data in the chart and the follow-up survey, which of the following statements is most likely to be accurate?

   (A) Of the 82,184 people in the original survey, fewer than 3,000 plan to visit the United States this summer.
   (B) Of the 82,184 people in the original survey, between 3,000 and 5,000 plan to visit the United States this summer.
   (C) Of the 82,184 people in the original survey, between 5,000 and 10,000 plan to visit the United States this summer.
   (D) Of the 82,184 people in the original survey, more than 10,000 plan to visit the United States this summer.

23. What is the total surface area of a cube if the length of each main diagonal is 9?

   (A) 81
   (B) 162
   (C) $27\sqrt{3}$
   (D) $81\sqrt{3}$

Note: Figure not drawn to scale.

24. In the figure above, what is the value of $\dfrac{b}{a}$?

   (A) 0.47
   (B) 0.53
   (C) 0.67
   (D) 0.88

25. If $i^2 = -1$ and if $(1 + 2i) \div (3 + 4i) = (a + bi)$, what is the value of $a + b$?

   (A) 0.25
   (B) 0.52
   (C) 6
   (D) 10

26. On January 2, 2016, the official rate of exchange for one United States dollar was 16.56 Mexican pesos and 9.47 Argentinian pesos. On that date, to the nearest hundredth, how many Mexican pesos could be exchanged for one Argentinian peso?

   (A) 0.57
   (B) 0.75
   (C) 1.57
   (D) 1.75

GO ON TO THE NEXT PAGE

MODEL TEST 2

27. In a large urban high school, all students are assigned to a homeroom. One of those homerooms has 30 students in it, and all the others have 27. In each homeroom with 27 students, three students were chosen at random to participate in a survey. In the one homeroom with 30 students, 4 students were chosen. If the school has exactly 3,000 students, how many of them took part in the survey?

(A) 333
(B) 334
(C) 336
(D) 337

Questions 28–30 are based on the information in the following graph.

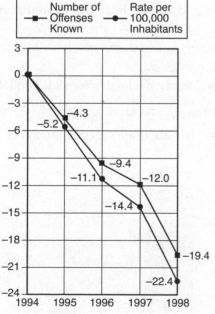

Motor Vehicle Theft in the U.S.
Percent Change from 1994 to 1998

Legend:
- Number of Offenses Known
- Rate per 100,000 Inhabitants

Data points (Number of Offenses Known): 1994: 0, 1995: −5.2, 1996: −11.1, 1997: −12.0, 1998: −19.4
Data points (Rate per 100,000 Inhabitants): 1994: 0, 1995: −4.3, 1996: −9.4, 1997: −14.4, 1998: −22.4

Source: U.S. Department of Justice, Federal Bureau of Investigation.

28. If 1,000,000 vehicles were stolen in 1994, how many were stolen in 1996?

(A) 889,000
(B) 906,000
(C) 940,000
(D) 1,094,000

29. To the nearest tenth of a percent, by what percent did the number of vehicles stolen decrease from 1997 to 1998?

(A) 7.4%
(B) 8.0%
(C) 8.4%
(D) 12.0%

30. To the nearest percent, by what percent did the population of the United States increase from 1994 to 1998?

(A) 1%
(B) 2%
(C) 3%
(D) 4%

GO ON TO THE NEXT PAGE

Grid-in Response Directions

In questions 31–38, first solve the problem, and then enter your answer on the grid provided on the answer sheet. The instructions for entering your answers follow.

- First, write your answer in the boxes at the top of the grid.
- Second, grid your answer in the columns below the boxes.
- Use the fraction bar in the first row or the decimal point in the second row to enter fractions and decimals.

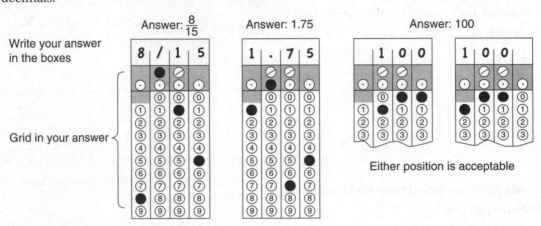

- Grid only one space in each column.
- Entering the answer in the boxes is recommended as an aid in gridding but is not required.
- The machine scoring your exam can read only what you grid, so you **must grid-in your answers correctly to get credit.**
- If a question has more than one correct answer, grid-in only one of them.
- The grid does not have a minus sign; so no answer can be negative.
- A mixed number *must* be converted to an improper fraction or a decimal before it is gridded.

  Enter $1\frac{1}{4}$ as 5/4 or 1.25; the machine will interpret 11/4 as $\frac{11}{4}$ and mark it wrong.

- **All decimals must be entered as accurately as possible.** Here are three acceptable ways of gridding

$$\frac{3}{11} = 0.272727\ldots$$

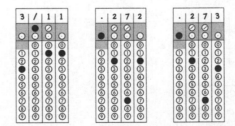

- Note that rounding to .273 is acceptable because you are using the full grid, but you would receive **no credit** for .3 or .27, because they are less accurate.

31. If $-\frac{3}{7} < a - b < -\frac{3}{8}$, what is one possible value of $2b - 2a$?

34. If the graph of $y = 10x^2 + bx + c$ has x-intercepts at 1.4 and 1.5, what is the value of $c - b$?

32. At North Central High School, the only foreign languages taught are Spanish, French, and Chinese, and every student is required to take a language course. The table below shows how many sophomores, juniors, and seniors took classes in those languages last year.

	Sophomores	Juniors	Seniors	Total
Spanish	170	200	190	560
French	125	98	106	329
German	35	42	14	91
Totals	330	340	310	980

What fraction of the juniors and seniors did not take a Spanish class last year?

Use the data in the following diagram in answering Questions 35 and 36.

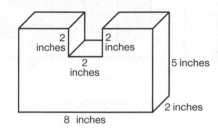

35. The figure above represents a block of wood in the shape of a rectangular solid from which a rectangular groove has been removed. What is the volume, in cubic feet, of the block?

36. Given that the density of Honduran mahogany is 41 pounds per cubic foot and the density of Spanish mahogany is 53 pounds per cubic foot, how much more, in pounds, would the block weigh if it were made of Spanish mahogany than if it were made of Honduran mahogany?

33. To the nearest thousandth, what is the cosine of the angle formed by the line whose equation is $y = 2x$ and the positive x-axis?

GO ON TO THE NEXT PAGE

MODEL TEST 2

Questions 37 and 38 are based on the data in the following graphs that give information about the 500 campers who attended the New England Music Summer Camp for Teens in 2015. The bar graph gives the breakdown by age of the campers, and the circle graph shows the musical specialties of the 15-year-old campers.

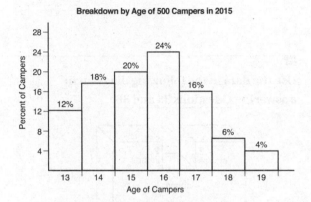

Breakdown by Age of 500 Campers in 2015

Specialties of 15-Year Olds

37. How many of the campers were 15-year-old pianists?

38. In 2015, 12 of the 13-year-olds, 18 of the 14-year-olds, and 12% of the campers aged 16 to 19 were pianists. What percent of all the campers were pianists? (Enter your answer without a percent sign. For example, if the answer were 50%, you should grid in 50.)

STOP

If there is still time remaining, you may review your answers.

ESSAY (OPTIONAL)

Directions: This assignment will allow you to demonstrate your ability to skillfully read and understand a source text and write a response analyzing the source. In your response, you should show that you have understood the source, give proficient analysis, and use the English language effectively. If your essay is off-topic, it will not be scored.

Only what you write on the lined paper in your answer document will be scored—avoid skipping lines, using unreasonably large handwriting, and using wide margins in order to have sufficient space to respond. You can also write on the planning sheet in the answer document, but this will not be evaluated—no other scrap paper will be given. Be sure to write clearly and legibly so your response can be scored.

You will be given 50 minutes to complete the assignment, including reading the source text and writing your response.

Read the following passage, and think about how the author uses:

- Evidence, such as applicable examples, to justify the argument
- Reasoning to show logical connections among thoughts and facts
- Rhetoric, like sensory language and emotional appeals, to give weight to the argument

---

Healthy Is Happy

1   I just don't have the time. An inveterate excuse that has postponed physical activity for decades past, it is commonly used by busy parents, exhausted students, and overworked professionals, along with the mastermind procrastinators themselves. Not to worry—one workout won't make or break you. However, as studies continue to confirm, a lifestyle sans regular physical activity can do irreparable damage, and not just to your body. Get this: there is a definite and direct correlation between sound health and fitness and success in career and personal life. The denizens of the bodybuilding and triathlon worlds are hardly the only ones with something at stake. Physically active persons are more successful in their academic endeavors, career ambitions, and relationships, period.

2   Regular exercise releases endorphins that enhance mood, and increase energy and mental sharpness. Acute minds make for better retainment and prolonged focus, a recipe for improved grades and better career prospects. Take the average college student: stressed, anxious, overworked, and fatigued, grabbing processed foods from convenient stops on the way to and from class. Participating in just 45 minutes of rigorous activity three days a week leaves one with cardiovascular endurance, restored alertness, and appropriate serotonin levels to defend against anxiety and depression. The *Journal of Pediatrics* published a report of 12,000 Nebraska schoolchildren that proved better fitness was linked to higher achievement scores regardless of body type. And in 2010, ABC News detailed a study of students at Naperville Central High School who doubled their reading scores on standardized testing after participating in a dynamic morning exercise regimen. It's not just six pack abs but your intellect that you're working for.

3   Advantages of attentiveness and conviviality extend beyond your years in the classroom. Increased productivity and discipline accompanied by reduced stress ensue the active lifestyle of the boss's favorites. A recent survey found that 75% of executives making six-figures listed physical fitness as critical to their career success. They cited better sleep, diligence, and concentration as their favorite advantages to leading a healthy lifestyle; making better diet choices and maintaining higher attendance rates were just icing on the cake, so to speak. Likewise, the survey didn't only postulate the benefits of the fit and ambitious, but deliberated on the faults of the unhealthy and lax, conceding that obesity is a serious career impediment. The word has spread: many employers are now offering incentives for healthier employees and even investing in at-work gyms and cardio machines. Those who would blame their careers for mitigating their gym time should beware—the former suffers without the latter.

4   Nonetheless, your mediocrity was hardly noticed in school, and your humdrum job doesn't deserve you at your best anyway. At least you have someone special to come home to. Or do you? Physical fitness, in all its breadth, extends to relationships as well. You guessed it: those who are happy with themselves are much better friends and companions. An opposite strength, commitment, is valuable in tough workout routines and tougher intimacies. Not only are the lively and fit elect more likely to communicate better, but they are also known to lead active lifestyles outside the gym and the office, spending time in new activities and hobbies with their loved ones. The *Journal of Personality and Social Psychology* found that couples who maintain a healthy self-image and try new things together, stay together. Yet again, contradiction arises when one lists family as the reason behind his or her physical concession; you invest in your family when you invest in yourself.

5   If health and appearance aren't motivation enough to make time for a jog, hike, or swim, perhaps scholastic, career, and relational aspirations can do the trick. An active lifestyle is vital to rather than incongruous with a swamped day-to-day—it should be, like food and sleep, just another necessity, and an enjoyable one at that. For you weight lifters, a combination of strength training and aerobic exercise is proven to generate the fastest results. For all others, your indignation with the crowded, sweaty gym doesn't have to be a hindrance; you're more likely to continue your routine if you have fun doing it, so get a bike, shoot some hoops, join a challenge, or take a dance class. Do yourself a favor, and pave the way for success.

> Write a response that demonstrates how the author makes an argument to persuade an audience that physical fitness should be a priority. In your response, analyze how the author uses at least one of the features from the essay directions (or features of your own choosing) to develop a logical and persuasive argument. Be certain that your response cites relevant aspects of the source text.
>
> Your response should not give your personal opinion on the merit of the source text, but instead show how the author crafts an argument to persuade readers.

ANSWER KEY
Model Test 2

Section 1: Reading

1.	A	14.	C	27.	C	40.	B
2.	D	15.	A	28.	D	41.	D
3.	B	16.	A	29.	B	42.	B
4.	D	17.	B	30.	B	43.	D
5.	B	18.	A	31.	C	44.	C
6.	C	19.	C	32.	C	45.	A
7.	B	20.	A	33.	D	46.	B
8.	B	21.	D	34.	B	47.	B
9.	B	22.	D	35.	D	48.	C
10.	A	23.	C	36.	A	49.	A
11.	C	24.	D	37.	D	50.	D
12.	B	25.	C	38.	A	51.	B
13.	C	26.	C	39.	B	52.	D

Number Correct _____

Number Incorrect _____

Section 2: Writing and Language

1.	C	12.	B	23.	A	34.	D
2.	A	13.	B	24.	D	35.	A
3.	A	14.	C	25.	A	36.	C
4.	A	15.	C	26.	B	37.	A
5.	C	16.	D	27.	C	38.	B
6.	D	17.	A	28.	B	39.	C
7.	D	18.	D	29.	B	40.	A
8.	B	19.	A	30.	C	41.	B
9.	D	20.	C	31.	B	42.	A
10.	C	21.	D	32.	C	43.	D
11.	B	22.	A	33.	B	44.	C

Number Correct _____

Number Incorrect _____

Section 3: Math (No Calculator)

1. **C**	5. **D**	9. **B**	13. **C**
2. **B**	6. **C**	10. **C**	14. **C**
3. **B**	7. **B**	11. **D**	15. **D**
4. **A**	8. **B**	12. **C**	

16. **1/2 or .5**

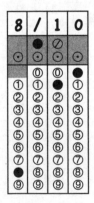

or

17. **4/5 or 8/10 or .8**

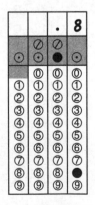

18. **56**

19. **25/4 or 6.25**

2	5	/	4

or

6	.	2	5

20. **2**

			2

Number Correct _____

Number Incorrect _____

Section 4: Math (Calculator)

1. **B**	7. **A**	13. **C**	19. **D**	25. **B**
2. **A**	8. **B**	14. **B**	20. **D**	26. **D**
3. **B**	9. **C**	15. **C**	21. **A**	27. **B**
4. **B**	10. **A**	16. **B**	22. **B**	28. **B**
5. **C**	11. **C**	17. **B**	23. **B**	29. **C**
6. **C**	12. **D**	18. **D**	24. **B**	30. **D**

31. **.8**

		.	8

32. **2/5 or 4/10 or .4**

2	/	5

or

4	/	1	0

or

		.	4

$.75 < x < .857$

33. **.447**

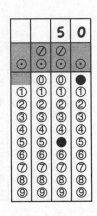

34. **50**

35. **1/2 or .5**

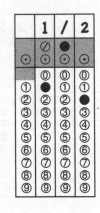

or

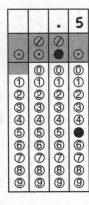

36. **6**

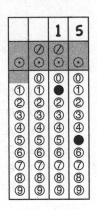

37. **15**

38. **15**

Number Correct _____

Number Incorrect _____

SCORE ANALYSIS

Reading and Writing Test

Section 1: Reading _____ = _____ (A)

correct   raw score

Section 2: Writing _____ = _____ (B)

correct   raw score

To find your Reading and Writing test scores, consult the chart below: find the ranges in which your raw scores lie and read across to find the ranges of your test scores.

_____ + _____ = _____ (C)

range of reading   range of writing   range of reading + writing

test scores   test scores   test scores

To find the range of your Reading and Writing Scaled Score, multiply (C) by 10.

Test Scores for the Reading and Writing Sections

Reading Raw Score	Writing Raw Score	Test Score
44–52	39–44	35–40
36–43	33–38	31–34
30–35	28–32	28–30
24–29	22–27	24–27
19–23	17–21	21–23
14–18	13–16	19–20
9–13	9–12	16–18
5–8	5–8	13–15
less than 5	less than 5	10–12

Math Test

Section 3: _____ = _____ (D)

correct   raw score

Section 4: _____ = _____ (E)

correct   raw score

Total Math raw score: (D) + (E) = _____

To find your Math Scaled Score, consult the chart below: find the range in which your raw score lies and read across to find the range for your scaled score.

Scaled Scores for the Math Test

Raw Score	Scaled Score	Raw Score	Scaled Score
50–58	700–800	20–25	450–490
44–49	650–690	15–19	400–440
38–43	600–640	11–14	350–390
32–37	550–590	7–10	300–340
26–32	500–540	less than 7	200–290

ANSWERS EXPLAINED

Section 1: Reading Test

1. **(A)** In the course of this passage, you learn that Sir Walter is a conceited fool whose late wife, a sensible woman, had tried to protect him and their daughters from the consequences of his foolishness. You learn that he values his oldest daughter (who in looks and snobbery resembles him), but disregards his youngest daughter Anne (who in character and good sense most resembles his late wife). The author's intent here is to give you background information about this family in order to set the stage for the plot developments to come. Thus, the main purpose of the passage is to *provide an overview of the interrelationships of the members of* Sir Walter's *family*.

2. **(D)** The first paragraph opens by stating that Sir Walter was vain about two things: he exhibited both "vanity of person and of situation." The paragraph then goes on to explain both terms. Sir Walter, still handsome in his fifties, prides himself on his personal appearance; that is, his vanity of person. In addition, he takes pride in his baronetcy, the place he holds in society; that is, his vanity of situation. Thus, "situation" here most nearly means *social standing*.

3. **(B)** The first paragraph establishes Sir Walter as a vain and foolish character. The second paragraph establishes Lady Elliot as a sensible woman whose death leaves her three young daughters in their foolish father's care. Thus, *A vain and foolish character is left to care for three daughters after the death of his sensible wife* best summarizes the first two paragraphs of the passage. Choice (A) is incorrect. Nothing in the first two paragraphs suggests that Sir Walter was devastated by his wife's death. Choice (C) is incorrect. Lady Elliot abandons her family by dying, not by running away from a husband she can no longer endure. Choice (D) is incorrect. It sums up part of the story, but it fails to include vital information (Sir Walter's vanity, Lady Elliot's death, the relationship of the daughters with their father, etc.). Thus, it does not provide the *best* summary of the first two paragraphs.

4. **(D)** The narrator does not commend Lady Elliot for falling in love with Sir Walter, calling it a "youthful infatuation." Therefore, choice (D) is correct. The narrator speaks well of Lady Elliot for concealing Sir Walter's shortcomings: she has "promoted his real respectability." Choice (A) is supported by the passage. Therefore, it is incorrect. The narrator commends Lady Elliot for her choice of a friend: she has chosen "a sensible, deserving woman," one who even moves into the neighborhood to be near her. Choice (B) is supported by the passage. Therefore, it is incorrect. The narrator speaks well of the way Lady Elliot guides her daughters: she has given them "good principles and instruction." Choice (C) is supported by the passage. Therefore, it is incorrect.

5. **(B)** In the years following Lady Elliot's unwise marriage, her judgment and conduct demonstrated the superiority of her character; no one had to make any allowances for any foolishness or misbehavior on her part. Her infatuation with Sir Walter and subsequent marriage represent the only misjudgment in her otherwise blameless life.

6. **(C)** The narrator's statement that Lady Elliot was "not the very happiest being in the world herself" is preceded by a list of all Lady Elliot had to do to cover up for her "conceited, silly" husband. Thus we can infer that the cause of her unhappiness was

the difference or *disparity* between her character and that of her husband. Choice (A) is incorrect. Nothing in the passage suggests Lady Elliot lacks beauty. Indeed, we suspect that Sir Walter, so conscious of his own beauty, would not have chosen an unattractive wife. Choice (B) is incorrect. Lady Elliot's best friend had moved to be near her; they were not separated. Choice (D) is incorrect. Nothing in the passage suggests that *over the years* Lady Elliot had been unable to teach her daughters good principles. She regrets being unable to continue teaching them good principles in the years to come.

7. **(B)** The "awful charge" that Lady Elliot must entrust to her foolish husband is his *responsibility* for the guidance of their daughters. Choices (A), (C), and (D) are incorrect. Although "charge" can mean *accusation* ("a charge of attempted murder), *official instruction* ("the judge's charge to the jury"), or *headlong rush* ("a cavalry charge"), that is not how it is used here.

8. **(B)** Choice (B) is correct. The narrator tells little directly of Lady Elliot's feelings about dying. However, such phrases as "Three girls.. . . . was an awful legacy to bequeath" and "anxiously giving her daughters [instruction]" show us something of her mind. Her concern centers not on herself but on those she must leave behind: her daughters. Her emotions as she faces death are complicated by *anxieties over her daughters' prospects*. Choice (A) is incorrect. Nothing in the passage suggests resignation or pious submissiveness on her part. Choice (C) is incorrect. There is no evidence in the passage to suggest that Lady Elliot has any concerns about her husband's possible remarriage. Choice (D) is also incorrect. Lady Elliot clearly has faced the reality of her approaching death: she recognizes its inevitability and realizes that she is leaving her daughters to the care of her conceited, silly husband.

9. **(B)** Worry complicated Lady Elliot's emotions regarding her approaching death. She worried about what would happen to her daughters once she was no longer there to guide them. Which lines best support this answer? Lines 31–35: "Three girls, the two eldest sixteen and fourteen, was an awful legacy for a mother to bequeath, an awful charge rather, to confide to the authority and guidance of a conceited, silly father."

10. **(A)** Lady Elliot in "quitting" her family is not simply taking a trip: she is dying. We expect a person facing death to react strongly, emotionally. Instead, the narrator states that Lady Elliot was merely attached enough to life to make dying "no matter of indifference to her." That is clearly an *understatement*. It is an example of *irony*, the literary technique that points up the contradictions in life, in this case the contradiction between the understated expression and the deeply felt reality.

11. **(C)** Sir Walter's applications have been *marital* ones. In his conceit, he has applied for the hand in marriage of some women who were far too good for him (his applications were *unreasonable*). Sensibly enough, these women have turned him down (he has been *disappointed* in his proposals of matrimony). However, his conceit is undiminished: he prides himself on remaining single for his dear daughters' sake.

12. **(B)** By stating that the public loves a simple explanation and by commenting on how much easier it is for schoolchildren to ignore what happened on the American continent from 1492–1620, the historian-author reveals a *condescending*, superior attitude toward the public at large, who are content with easy answers.

13. **(C)** Throughout this passage, the author is making the point that it is wrong to consider the Mayflower Compact a cornerstone of American democracy. Instead of presenting his thesis immediately, the author uses the opening paragraph to *capture the reader's attention* with some light, humorous comments about why people foolishly continue to harbor this belief.

14. **(C)** Those who mark the start of democracy in 1620 are *designating* or specifying 1620 as the year democracy originated in America.

15. **(A)** Note the phrase set off in commas: "to be sure." It is a synonym for the adverb *admittedly* and is used to acknowledge that something is true. The author has just been lightly casting doubt on the idea of associating the Mayflower Compact with the birth of democracy. Here, he *concedes the point* that the compact did establish a form of self-government and thus had some relationship to democracy.

16. **(A)** According to the author, the Pilgrims "spurned democracy." In other words, they rejected it. Their attitude toward democracy was one of *complete rejection*.

17. **(B)** The democracy-rejecting Pilgrims would have been amazed to find themselves held up or *cited* as defenders of democracy.

18. **(A)** The Pilgrims had been given a royal patent that legally empowered them to settle in a certain area. Because they had decided to colonize a different area, some of the group felt that once they were ashore no laws would bind them. The compact bound the signers to obey the laws of the colony. It thus served to *establish legal authority within the colony*. That was its primary purpose.

19. **(C)** In these two sentences, the author sums up the situation on board the Mayflower that led to the signing of the compact. The Pilgrims had been granted a royal patent to form a colony in a specific area. If they had settled in that particular area, they would have been constrained to follow the terms of that patent; they would have been under the jurisdiction of the British crown, obeying British law. However, they "had decided to settle in an area outside the jurisdiction of their royal patent," and it was unclear what laws and rules would govern them. By signing the compact, the Pilgrims promised to abide by the laws of their new colony. This supports the claim that the compact's primary purpose was to *establish legal authority within the colony*.

20. **(A)** According to the passage, the Pilgrims signed the Mayflower Compact in order of rank: first, the gentlemen; next, the "goodmen" or yeoman-farmers; finally, the servants. In doing so, they showed their *respect for the social hierarchy*.

21. **(D)** These four brief sentences sum up the order in which the Pilgrims signed the compact. They signed in order of their class or rank. They were very aware of their position in the social hierarchy, and showed their *respect for the social hierarchy* by signing in their proper places.

22. **(D)** This bar graph represents the composition of those aboard the Mayflower who went on to found the colony. Look at the different shaded segments of the bar graph. The smaller the segment, the fewer people it represents. Of the four passenger categories given, the smallest is choice (D), *Female minor farmers*. These were children of farming families who had not been indentured as servants.

23. **(C)** The passage reports on *recent experiments regarding brain activity during sleep* and discusses their results and implications. Choice (A) is incorrect. Even though the passage indicates that humans sleep a great deal, it merely explains one reason why they need to sleep. It does not explain why they need to sleep more than other animals. Choice (B) is incorrect. It is well known, and assumed in the passage, that sleep is beneficial to humans. This does not need to be proved. The questions are why and how it is beneficial. Choice (D) is incorrect. The passage focuses on the "glymphatic" system in the brain, not the lymphatic system. In order to explain the function of the glymphatic system, the author compares it to the lymphatic system, but that is a supporting point and not the main focus of the passage.

24. **(D)** The passage indicates that one of the functions of the glymphatic system is the clearing out of toxic metabolic byproducts from the brain. The lymphatic system performs a similar function for the rest of the body: "the lymphatic system clears out metabolic waste products from the rest of the body." Thus, one of its functions is the *drainage of waste.* Choice (A) is incorrect. The *glymphatic* system is associated with the brain; the *lymphatic* system is not. Choice (B) is incorrect. The regulation of temperature is not mentioned in the passage. Choice (C) is incorrect. According to the passage, the *glymphatic* system transports cerebrospinal fluid, while the *lymphatic* system transports metabolic waste products from the rest of the body.

25. **(C)** Scan the passage to find the word "lymphatic." It appears solely in line 34, in which the workings of the lymphatic system in clearing out metabolic waste products from the body are compared to the workings of the so-called glymphatic system in clearing out cellular waste from the brain.

26. **(C)** According to the passage, sleep serves to drain toxic chemical waste products from the brain, in addition to carrying out other functions that are not yet understood fully. Choices (A), (B), and (D) are clearly incorrect because they do not include the cleaning function that is the main consideration described in the passage.

27. **(C)** The passage reports the long-standing hypothesis that sleep *promotes* recovery. In other words, sleep leads to, contributes to, or helps bring about recovery. The term *fosters* best captures this meaning. Choices (A), (B), and (D) are incorrect. Although "promotes" can have the meaning *exchanges a pawn* ("She wanted to promote her pawn into a queen"), *raises in rank* ("promoted to sergeant"), or *publicizes* ("ads promoting products"), that is not how the word is used here.

28. **(D)** The expansion of the glial channels by 60 percent created significantly more room for fluid in the channels. This was a significant result: the increased volume *suggested that the flow of cerebrospinal fluid increased during sleep*, resulting in an increased ability to wash waste chemicals out of the brain. Choice (A) is incorrect. Nothing in the passage suggests that the overall size of the brain increases. Choice (C) is incorrect. No information is provided about the effects of sleep on other organs. Choice (D) is incorrect. Less sensory information is processed during sleep. The scientists hypothesized that the cleaning function and the processing of sensory information are in a sense competing: the brain cannot maximize both at the same time.

29. **(B)** As used in the passage, "distinguish" means to differentiate the two dyed fluids or to *tell* them *apart.* Choices (A), (C), and (D) are incorrect. Although "distinguish" can

mean *characterize* ("Her Brooklyn accent distinguishes her"), *make prominent* ("She distinguished herself on the ski slopes"), or *discern* ("In the dark cellar he couldn't distinguish anything"), that is not how it is used here.

30. **(B)** The passage makes it clear that the point of using the dyed fluids is to differentiate between the fluid that circulates while the mice are asleep from the fluid that circulates while the mice are awake. Choice (A) is incorrect. The passage never mentions any different types of molecules that might make up the cerebrospinal fluid. In addition, the dyes are associated not with different types of molecules, but with different batches of cerebrospinal fluid that are essentially identical in composition. Choice (C) is incorrect. Lymph was not dyed in the experiment. Choice (D) is incorrect. The experiment focused on the glymphatic system exclusively, not on the lymphatic system.

31. **(C)** The sentence: "By tracking the movements of red and green dye throughout the brain, the team found that large amounts of CSF flowed into the brain during sleep, but not during the waking state" reveals the reason the different-colored dyes were used: to differentiate between fluid that flowed into the brain during sleep from fluid that flowed into the brain during the waking state. Choice (A) is incorrect. This sentence merely describes the preliminary work Lulu Xie had to do to make the experiment possible. Choice (B) is incorrect. This sentence reports that the two-photon microscope could distinguish the red dye from the green dye, but it does not explain why that was important for the success of the experiment. Choice (D) is incorrect. This sentence reports a concrete result of the experiment, but it does not reveal the specific logical steps that led the scientists to that conclusion.

32. **(C)** The passage compares what the brain does during sleep to what a human does during the weekend. The point is to suggest not only that cleaning is one function performed by both, but also that both carry out other functions in addition to cleaning. Sleep therefore most likely provides the brain time both to clean itself and to perform several other functions, just as the weekend provides a human the opportunity to clean the house, visit friends, and perform other functions. Choice (A) is incorrect. This statement sounds true. However, even though one could use this comparison to make the point that, just as sleep is essential for the health of the brain, the weekend is essential for the (mental and physical) health of the human, it is not the point the author is making here. Choice (B) is incorrect. There is no suggestion of ranking different activities and deciding which one is most beneficial. Choice (D) is incorrect. As with choice (A), the point sounds plausible, but that is not the focus of the comparison here.

33. **(D)** The primary focus of this passage is the contradiction between traditional beliefs about the frailty of women and the manner in which black women were treated under slavery. Though there may be other examples of women's strength in this passage, the best answer is choice (D) because it reflects the central theme of the passage. Choice (A) is incorrect. Though the passage mentions, "women at the North . . . talking about rights," this is done as an aside and is not a central part of Truth's argument. Choice (B) is incorrect. Though Truth mentioned having, "born thirteen children," she does this as a demonstration of her treatment under slavery, rather than as proof of the hard work that women do as mothers. Choice (C) is incorrect. Though childbirth is certainly physically challenging, Truth makes no mention of this in the passage.

34. **(B)** This is the section of the passage in which Truth recounts many of the details of her hard treatment as a slave, including hard physical labor and beatings. It comes immediately after she cites a man's argument that women need to be "helped into carriages" and is intended as evidence against this argument regarding women's weakness. Choice (A) is incorrect. As the explanation of question 33 states, the actions of northern women are mentioned as an aside; they are not a central part of Truth's argument. Choice (C) is incorrect. This sentence is a request for kindness and makes no mention of the strength of women. In fact, this sentence argues that even if women are weaker than men are, that does not justify denying them rights. Choice (D) is incorrect. Though this sentence does mention the strength of biblical women, it is not as strong an answer as choice (B). Why not? First, the sentence provides only one example of female strength. Second, the example is given in order to urge men to meet women's demands, rather than to contradict traditional depictions of women's frailty.

35. **(D)** "Fix" is used in informal English as a synonym for *predicament*. Though Truth is giving a speech, her style is down-to-earth and casual. One good way to test possible answers is to substitute them in the sentence for the word in question and see if the sentence makes sense with the substitution. In this case, saying that the white men will be in a predicament makes sense. Choice (A) is incorrect. Though repair is one meaning of *fix*, this sentence is not about fixing something that is broken. Additionally, if you substitute the word *repair* in the sentence, it does not make sense. We do not talk about being *in* a repair. Choice (B) is incorrect. While it is common to talk about being "in a rut," this figure of speech refers to being stuck in a particular way of doing things. Talking about rights for women and blacks is not going to cause white men to be unable to change. Choice (C) is incorrect. Although it is common to talk about being *in* a battle, a *battle* is a far more extreme conflict then a predicament or *fix*.

36. **(A)** The primary focus of this passage is the inevitability of progress toward women's rights because the equality of women is a fundamental truth. Douglass begins by pointing out that slavery, which had been legal for 200 years, was ended. He then refers to the ultimate triumph of Galileo's observation that the Earth revolves around the sun, despite the church's insistence to the contrary. Finally, he predicts a victory for women's rights because, "When a great truth gets abroad in the world, no power on earth can imprison it." Choice (B) is incorrect. The church is mentioned in regards to Galileo, not in regards to women. Choice (C) is incorrect. Though Douglass argues that women should receive the "rights of American citizenship," he does not argue that their citizenship is a reason that they will win those rights. Choice (D) is incorrect. Douglass argues that the truth always wins out but he does not explain why this occurs. Choice (D) might explain why, but Douglass does not make that argument.

37. **(D)** In this sentence, Douglass states his primary claim, which is that the truth cannot be stopped. This is for him the fundamental reason that women will be victorious in their struggle for equal rights. Choice (A) is incorrect. This sentence cites a barrier to winning women's suffrage rather than a reason that the movement will succeed. Choice (B) is incorrect. This sentence grants that belief in traditional roles for women is still powerful, despite its obvious falsehood. It states the opposite of Douglass's overall claim. Choice (C) is incorrect. This sentence grants that even when women achieve equal rights, some will still refuse to accept the change.

38. **(A)** *Authorized* is a synonym of "sanctioned." It is the best answer in this case because Douglass is speaking about the legislation that allowed slavery, despite the truth that "man cannot hold property in a man." He is describing Henry Clay's bold claim that the law defines what rights people have, rather than a theory of natural rights. Legislation *authorized* slavery, despite its violation of natural rights. Choice (B) is incorrect. The legislation that Douglass refers to allowed slavery rather than penalizing it. Choice (C) is incorrect. The legislation that Douglas refers to allowed slavery rather than prohibiting it. Choice (D) is incorrect. Douglass makes no mention of whether the legislation in question describes slavery as praiseworthy.

39. **(B)** The story of Galileo's conflict with the Church regarding the Earth's orbit of the sun is one of the most well-known historical examples of an organization's attempting to hold fast to its beliefs despite evidence to the contrary. Douglass uses this example to demonstrate that the truth will always be victorious, despite powerful opposition. Choice (A) is incorrect. Douglass does not believe that there is any basis, scientific or otherwise, for treating women unequally. Choice (C) is incorrect. Though Douglass believes that women's rights are important, he makes no mention of the state of women's rights and their acceptance in other parts of the world. Choice (D) is incorrect. The "unveiling of the statue of Galileo" in a location where the church was very strong demonstrates that the truth will triumph despite powerful opposition, not that this opposition was incorrect.

40. **(B)** In Passage 1, Sojourner Truth makes a strong argument that women should receive the same rights as men. In Passage 2, Douglass, who supports equal rights for women, argues that women will be victorious in the struggle for equal rights because the struggle is based on the truth that women are men's equals. Choice (A) is incorrect. Douglass is a supporter of Sojourner Truth's cause. Choice (C) is incorrect. Douglass takes no position on how rapidly progress should be made on this issue. He simply argues that progress is inevitable. Choice (D) is incorrect. Though Douglass notes that progress was made on the legality of slavery, he does not mention whether any progress has been made toward recognizing equal rights for women.

41. **(D)** "That man" argues that women are weak and require assistance. Douglass disagrees with this argument and likens it to the church's insistence that the sun revolves around the Earth. Both are examples of people vociferously advocating old beliefs despite evidence to the contrary. Choice (A) is incorrect. Douglass does not agree with the man's argument. Choice (B) is incorrect. Douglass does disagree with the man, but he fully agrees with the author of Passage 1. Choice (C) is incorrect. Though Douglass disagrees with the man and *might* be angered by his arguments, there is no evidence in the passage proving that he is angered. As a result, though choice (C) could be correct, choice (D) is the best answer.

42. **(B)** In this sentence, Douglass strongly implies that the "two hundred years of legislation" mentioned previously no longer authorize slavery. These laws were not able to "keep life" in the institution of slavery. Douglass is speaking in 1888, two decades after the Emancipation Proclamation. It is, therefore, a fact, that slavery is no longer legal at the time he is speaking. Choice (A) is incorrect. This is Henry Clay's argument for slavery. Douglass uses it as evidence of a powerful belief or argument that has been defeated by truth. Choice (C) is incorrect. In this sentence Douglass grants that incorrect beliefs still

have significant power. Choice (D) is incorrect. This sentence argues that the march of progress toward equal rights will not be reversed, but it makes no claim about what has occurred in the past.

43. **(D)** Note that the caption on the chart is "Metabolic middle ground." The dinosaurs and the shark are in the middle of the chart. This graphically reinforces the concept that, like sharks, dinosaurs are neither cold-blooded ectotherms nor warm-blooded endotherms, but have metabolisms that fall somewhere in between. Thus, the chief purpose of the chart is to illustrate that *in metabolic rate dinosaurs are most akin to sharks.*

44. **(C)** The author of the passage succinctly summarizes the competing theories that categorize dinosaurs as ectotherms, endotherms, or mesotherms. Clearly he is *well-informed about* these *competing theories* based on studies of dinosaur metabolic rates. Choices (A) and (D) are incorrect. Nothing in the passage suggests that the author is an active researcher or involved in the development of mathematical equations. Choice (B) is also incorrect: his presentation of the ectotherm theory is objective; nothing suggests he has any bias in its favor.

45. **(A)** In both the title of the article ("Dinosaur metabolism neither hot nor cold, but just right") and its opening sentence, the author is alluding or referring to the classic children's tale of Goldilocks and the three bears, with the three bowls of porridge. By calling this latest theory about dinosaurs a Goldilocks solution, he hints that this time the researchers may have gotten things "just right."

46. **(B)** First, the conventional wisdom was that dinosaurs were cold-blooded ectotherms. Then researchers came up with the heretical notion that dinosaurs were hot-blooded endotherms. Now Grady and his fellow researchers have come up with a third idea, in the process establishing an entirely new metabolic category. In admitting that what they have done is audacious (daring), Grady is *acknowledging* how *radical* or revolutionary their suggestion is and how profound a change it makes in the way we think of dinosaurs.

47. **(B)** Note the references to time with which paragraphs four and five open: "For the first 150 years" and "Beginning in the late 1960s." Paragraph 4 describes the theory that dinosaurs were cold-blooded; paragraph 5, the alternate theory that they were warm-blooded. Taken together, the two paragraphs *give an overview of previous theories about the body temperature and activity level of dinosaurs.*

48. **(C)** The scientists conducting this research are trying to figure out into which category dinosaurs fit. Are they cold-blooded ectotherms? Are they warm-blooded endotherms? Is there yet another category into which they can fit? By studying the dinosaurs' metabolic and growth rates, the researchers are attempting to *characterize dinosaurs* as cold-blooded, warm-blooded, or something in-between.

49. **(A)** Lines 13–22 sum up the conclusion reached by Grady and his fellow researchers: dinosaurs "belonged to an intermediate group that can raise their body temperature but don't keep it at a specific level." Their goal was to figure out into which category dinosaurs fit. In discovering that dinosaurs belonged to an intermediate group, they achieved their goal.

50. **(D)** To say that growth rates scale with metabolic rates is to say there is a *correlation* between the two rates. Creatures with a high metabolic rate have more energy to

expend. Thanks to this extra energy, they can reach their adult size faster: they have a high growth rate. Choices (A), (B), and (C) are incorrect. Although scale can mean *flake* ("paint scaling from the banister"), *reduce* ("they scaled back their plans"), or *ascend* ("she scaled a 30-foot flagpole"), that is not how the word is used here.

51. **(B)** To lay down bone is to build up a deposit of bone tissue. Thus, rings of bone were laid down or *deposited* each year. Choices (A), (C), and (D) are incorrect. Although laid down can mean *rested* ("laid down for a nap"), *sacrificed* ("laid down his life"), or *formulated* ("laid down strict rules), that is not how it is used here.

52. **(D)** The *Harbrace College Handbook* states that "[w]ords used in a special sense are sometimes enclosed in quotation marks." What is the usual sense of the word "defend"? Its primary meaning is to protect someone or something from harm, as in defending our country. Here, however, it *is being used in an unusual sense.* The author is not saying that sharks, tuna, and giant sea-turtles do not resist attacks on their body temperature. He's saying that their bodies do not maintain a constant set temperature. Choice (A) is incorrect. Although the word "defend" is not being used in its usual sense, it is not being used to create *an ironic* (satirical or wryly amusing; paradoxical) *effect.*

Section 2: Writing and Language Test

1. **(C)** The key phrase in the question is "not quite the most widespread." Stating that bats are "second only to rodents" means that bats are almost the most widespread but come in second place. Choice (A) does the opposite of what the question asks. Choice (B) gives a percentage without a frame of reference. Choice (D) is too vague because we would need information about the numbers of humans relative to those of other mammals.

2. **(A)** "Although" gives the needed contrast between the first part of the sentence and the second part. Choices (B) and (D) show cause and effect. Choice (C), "however," would work if a contrast was needed between the previous sentence and the current sentence but does not work to provide a contrast within a sentence like this.

3. **(A)** "Do" is numerically consistent with the plural subject "roles." Choice (B), "does," is singular. Choice (C), "don't," causes a double negative given the "not" that follows. Choice (D), "do's," is not a word.

4. **(A)** This is a complete sentence that requires no breaks. The phrase "bodies approximately one inch long" is relatively long, but it should remain a unified phrase without any pauses. The other options unnecessarily break up the sentence.

5. **(C)** This word refers to "echolocation," which is best described as a "phenomenon" since it is a process that allows bats to navigate. The other options are all associated with physical items.

6. **(D)** Notice that the footnote beneath the graph states that the population numbers are tabulated at the end of each year. According to the graph, the bat population decreased from around 6,000,000 at the time of the outbreak of the illness at the end of 2007 to about 2,000,000 in 2010. This is a decrease of roughly $\frac{2}{3}$, which equates to about 65%.

7. **(D)** The word "while" earlier in the sentence already provides the transition needed. So omitting any word at this point makes the most sense.

8. **(B)** "Effect," which is choice (B), is typically a noun. However, "affect" in choice (A) is typically a verb. In this sentence, the farmers are feeling the consequences of these changes, and "consequences" is a noun like "effect." Even though "affectedness" in choice (C) is a noun, it means having a pretentious attitude. Choice (D), "effectively," is an adverb.

9. **(D)** "Bats'" correctly shows possession by plural bats. Choice (A), "bats," is a noun. Choice (B), "bat's," shows possession by a single bat. Choice (C), "bat is," has a noun and a verb.

10. **(C)** The sentence states that this is a species "already on the endangered list." So the most logical choice is the bat species that has the smallest population. Since the paragraph is speaking from a more recent perspective, look at the bat species that has the smallest population in the most recent year, i.e., gray bats.

11. **(B)** Consider what immediately follows the insertion point—"so preservationists can make the necessary interventions." Preservationists would naturally be most interested in helping those species in need of intervention because the species were in danger of becoming extinct. So the statement "are learning which species are in the most danger" most logically connects to this. Choice (A) is the opposite of what is needed. Choice (C) is irrelevant. Even though choice (D) relates a bit to the information that follows, it does not give as strong a connection as choice (B) does. Preservationists would more likely find information about which bat species most need help more useful than information about bat predator locations.

12. **(B)** This choice uses consistent punctuation, dashes, to set aside the parenthetical phrase. Choices (A) and (D) are inconsistent; a parenthetical phrase that begins with one form of punctuation should end with the same type. Choice (C) does not have a needed pause before the start of the parenthetical phrase with the word "as."

13. **(B)** What follows are two general ways that married couples in *The Canterbury Tales* are dysfunctional, so choice (B) gives the best transition. Choice (A) is incorrect because the listed items are not quotations. Choice (C) is incorrect because these themes are consistent with the text, not ironic. Choice (D) is incorrect because the listed items lead to conflict, not resolution.

14. **(C)** The subject comes after the underlined portion. The subject is the plural "marital troubles," so the plural verb "are" works. Choices (A) and (B) are both singular, and choice (D) uses "them" incorrectly.

15. **(C)** There is no need to repeat the name of the story, as choice (A) does, since it is mentioned immediately before this sentence. Choice (B) is not correct because it is wordy and adds no substance to the sentence. Choice (D) is incorrect because the current sentence is simply expanding on the previous one, not showing cause and effect.

16. **(D)** This is a direct quotation from Lord Walter, as indicated by the word "stating" immediately beforehand and by the use of old English spelling. Choices (A) and (B) give factual reasoning, but it is necessary to leave the quotation marks for clarity. Choice

(C) is not correct because these words are not coming from the narrator but from a character.

17. **(A)** This choice is parallel to the structure of the previous phrase "a false order for . . ." and is logical. Choice (B) is illogical, choice (C) is too choppy, and choice (D) is too wordy and is not parallel.

18. **(D)** This phrase completes the idiomatic expression "is not so much . . . as he is." The other options do not connect appropriately to this earlier phrasing.

19. **(A)** It is correct to say "contributes . . . through," making choice (A) correct. The other options do not work in conjunction with "contributes" to make a sensible phrase.

20. **(C)** The key word in this question is "limited." Therefore "only that" makes sense since it minimizes the extent of her request. The other options do not limit the request in any way.

21. **(D)** The entire phrase "at what she believes to be the end of their marriage" is parenthetical. Choice D is the only option that both leaves this phrase intact and places a comma at the end of it so that it is set aside from the rest of the sentence.

22. **(A)** Even though this story is from long ago, the paragraph is referring to the events as though they were read in a present-day perspective. Therefore, choice (A) works to give a present-tense verb that matches the singular subject "concern." Choices (B) and (C) indicate past events, and choice (D) is plural.

23. **(A)** Choices (C) and (D) do not use the required possessive form "its." Choice (B) incorrectly uses the plural verb "are." Choice (A) gives appropriate pauses with the commas, uses the singular "is" to match the singular subject "workforce," and correctly uses the possessive "its" to show that school teachers are a part of the singular society.

24. **(D)** Choices (A) and (B) do not indicate a wide time span since they limit the instructional influence to the confines of a day. Choice (C) refers to places, not time. Choice (D) works best since it indicates that teachers can influence students from the early years of school all the way through postsecondary education.

25. **(A)** The first word in the underlined portion must be "your" since it refers to the reader's possession of "best," making choices (B) and (D) incorrect. Choice (C) is incorrect because it jumps to using "one" partway through instead of being consistent in the use of "you." Choice (A) uses the correct form of "your" to show possession and uses "you're" to stand for "you are."

26. **(B)** "So," gives a logical transition from the previous paragraph to the rhetorical sentence that starts this paragraph. Choices (A) and (C) incorrectly show contrast, and choice (D) shows a causal connection that is too direct.

27. **(C)** You won't have a calculator at your disposal on the Writing and Language section. However, you can estimate the average, especially given that the answer choices are reasonably far apart from one another. Based on the different salaries in each of the five cities, $55,000 comes closest to the average, making choice (C) correct.

28. **(B)** This choice properly indicates that a singular teacher owns a workday. Choice (A) indicates plural teacher ownership. Choice (C) indicates plural teachers as a subject. Choice (D) inserts unnecessary verbs.

29. **(B)** "Than" completes the comparative phrase "better . . . than." Choice (A) can work for comparisons but not in this context. Choice (C) is for time, and choice (D) does not lead to a comparison.

30. **(C)** "Furthermore," provides an appropriate transition into the continued explanation of the education and training of teachers. Choice (A) indicates confusion, choice (B) indicates an assumption, and choice (D) does not provide a transition.

31. **(B)** "Prospective" means "preparing to do so in the future," which applies to teachers who are being trained since they are not yet licensed professionals. "Perspective" in choice (A) indicates a point of view. "Prospecting" in choice (C) indicates searching. "Previewing" in choice (D) does not apply to people in the process of learning their profession, although it could refer to what the trainees themselves will be doing with respect to professional skills.

32. **(C)** The data in the chart give an approximate salary range between $52,000 and $62,000, making the variation about $10,000.

33. **(B)** The colon is appropriate because it indicates a clarification to follow. Choice (A) results in a comma splice, while choices (C) and (D) result in run-on sentences.

34. **(D)** "Dubious," which can mean "suspicious," correctly refers to the unsavory and illegal happenings mentioned in the beginning of the sentence. The activities are not best described as "transparent," choice (A). Since these activities were associated with lawbreaking, they were not likely done in a way that was easily seen. Choice (B) is incorrect since events from just a few decades past could not be accurately characterized as "ancient." Choice (C) is associated with speakeasies but not necessarily with a person or a massacre.

35. **(A)** "Because" functions to show a cause-and-effect relationship between the first part of the sentence and the second part. Choices (B) and (C) show contrast, and choice (D) shows a continuation of the same thought.

36. **(C)** This is the only option that leaves the unified phrase "force-feeding of corn to ducks" completely intact.

37. **(A)** This is the only choice that shows ownership by the singular city of Chicago of the City Council. Choices (B) and (D) do not show possession, and choice (C) shows plural possession.

38. **(B)** A break between the independent clauses in the sentence is needed, which choices (A) and (D) do not have. Choice (C) needs a comma after the introductory phrase "not surprisingly," and also needs to show that "Chicago" possesses the "chefs." Choice (B) uses a semicolon to break up the two independent clauses and uses the correct possessive form of "Chicago."

39. **(C)** The emotions expressed in the previous sentence are extreme and intense, so writing "just wondered what all the fuss was about" demonstrates a clear contrast in attitude. Choices (A), (B), and (D) all indicate some degree of agreement with the attitudes of the chefs mentioned in the previous sentence.

40. **(A)** "What's more" correctly indicates a continuation of the ideas from the previous paragraph. The other options all illustrate a contrast. Sometimes similarities among the answers can help you eliminate choices.

41. **(B)** Choices (A) and (D) do not provide vivid descriptions. Choice (C) is inconsistent with the type of food one wants at a restaurant. Choice (B) is both logical and vivid.

42. **(A)** The dash serves to provide a long pause before the closing thought in the sentence. Choice (B) is too choppy and creates a run-on. Choice (C) has an unnecessary comma. Choice (D) is incorrect because there is not a complete sentence after the semicolon.

43. **(D)** The context indicates that the Health Department stopped enforcing this ban, making "froze" the most logical option. "Vivified," choice (A), conveys an increase in the liveliness of the ban, which is inconsistent with the context. "Congealed," choice (B), means "to take shape." Choice (C), "checked," is illogical. Stating "were checked" could possibly work, but "checked" by itself doesn't make sense.

44. **(C)** The proper idiomatic phrase is "victory for." The other options join "victory" with prepositions that don't agree given the phrasing needed in this context.

Section 3: Math Test (No Calculator)

1. **(C)** Test the choices. In **1994**, Adam entered 3 more tournaments than in 1993, an increase of $\frac{3}{6} = \frac{1}{2} = 50\%$. (From 1990 to 1991 the increase was 25%, from 1991 to 1992 it was 100%, and from 1994 to 1995 it was $33\frac{1}{3}\%$.)

2. **(B)** $5(x + 1) + 3 = 3(x + 3) \Rightarrow 5x + 5 + 3 = 3x + 9 \Rightarrow 5x + 8 = 3x + 9 \Rightarrow 2x = 1 \Rightarrow x = \mathbf{0.5}$

   **A solution to the equation $5(x + 1) + 3 = 3(x + 3)$ is the x-coordinate of the point of intersection of the straight lines $y = 5(x + 1) + 3$ and $y = 3(x + 3)$. Since these lines intersect at the point (0.5, 10.5), the original equation has one solution, $x = \mathbf{0.5}$.

3. **(B)** Rewrite the given equation in $y = mx + b$ form.

$$3x + 4y = 24 \Rightarrow 4y = -3x + 24 \Rightarrow y = -\frac{3}{4}x + 6$$

So the slope, m, is $-\frac{3}{4}$.

   **Find two points on the given line and use the slope formula. For example, when $x = 0$, $y = 6$, and when $y = 0$, $x = 8$. Therefore, (0, 6) and (8, 0) are points on the line, and the slope of the line is $\frac{6-0}{0-8} = \frac{6}{-8} = -\frac{3}{4}$.

4. **(A)** To answer any question about maps or scale drawings, set up a proportion and cross-multiply:

$$\frac{\text{miles}}{\text{centimeters}}: \quad \frac{m}{c} = \frac{n}{x} \Rightarrow mx = cn$$

So $x = \dfrac{cn}{m}$.

5. **(D)** Multiplying (not dividing) the number of courses a student takes by the number of credits each course is worth gives the total number of credits the student earns. (Clearly, taking 5 three-credit courses earns $5 \times 3 = 15$ credits, not $5 \div 3 = 1.66$ credits.) So the answer is either choice (C) or choice (D). Since "at least 120 credits" means "120 credits or more," the desired inequality is "greater than or equal to" 120: $\mathbf{3x + 4y \geq 120}$.

6. **(C)** When you have to determine which of four statements is true, just treat each one as a true-false question.

   - The French club could have 2 boys and 3 girls, and the Spanish club could have 30 boys and 50 girls. Statement (A) is false.
   - The Spanish club could have 3 boys and 5 girls, and the French club could have 20 boys and 30 girls. Statement (B) is false.
   - 3 out of every 5 members of the French club, or 60%, are girls; 5 out of every 8 members of the Spanish club, or 62.5%, are girls. Statement (C) is true.
   - Once you know that Statement (C) is true, you don't have to waste your time testing Statement (D); it must be false. For example, if the French club originally had 2 boys and 3 girls and if among the new members there were 30 boys and 20 girls, then the number of boys and girls would *not* be equal.

7. **(B)** Since John averaged 25 miles per gallon for the 200-mile trip, he used $200 \div 25 = 8$ gallons of gas. At the point that Mary had used 8 gallons of gas, she had traveled $8 \times 20 = 160$ miles. So she was still $200 - 160 = 40$ miles from home.

8. **(B)** If (a, b) is a point on each line, then $2a + 3b = 4$ and $b = 2a$. Replacing b by $2a$ in the first equation, we get $2a + 3(2a) = 4 \Rightarrow 8a = 4 \Rightarrow a = \dfrac{1}{2}$. Since $b = 2a$, $b = 1$. Finally, $a + b = \dfrac{1}{2} + 1 = \dfrac{3}{2} = \mathbf{1.5}$.

9. **(B)** The formulas for the volumes of a rectangular solid and a cylinder are $V = lwh$ and $V = \pi r^2 h$, respectively. (Remember that these formulas are given to you on the first page of every math section.) The volume of container I is $(4)(4)(5) = 80$ cubic inches. Since the diameter of container II is 4, its radius is 2, and so its volume is $\pi(2^2)(5) = 20\pi$. The difference in volumes is $80 - 20\pi = \mathbf{20(4 - \pi)}$.

10. **(C)** The simplest way to answer this type of question is to plug in a simple number. Since this is a question involving percents, the easiest number to use is 100. Assume that Pam sells her vases to Carl for $100. Since 60% of 100 is 60, he sells them for $160. Since 20% of 100 is 20, during the July 4th sale Carl sells the vases for $80, $20 less than he pays for them. Since $80 is exactly half of $160, the customer is receiving a **50%** discount.

If you didn't think to plug in a number, you should have proceeded in exactly the same manner. If Pam sells Carl her vases for x dollars, he normally sells them for $1.6x$ dollars. During the July 4th sale, he sells them for $0.8x$, which is exactly **50% of $1.6x$.

11. **(D)** If $y = x^2 + 1$ and $y = -x^2 + 3$, then $x^2 + 1 = -x^2 + 3 \Rightarrow 2x^2 = 2 \Rightarrow x^2 = 1$. So $x = 1$ or $x = -1$.

If $x = 1$, then $y = 2$. If $x = -1$, then $y = 2$. So the two solutions are (1, 2) and (–1, 2), and $a + b + c + d = 1 + 2 + (-1) + 2 = \textbf{4}$.

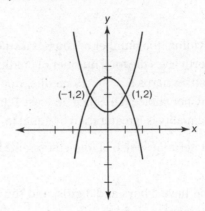

12. **(C)** Each of the four triangles in the diagram below are 45-45-90 right triangles.

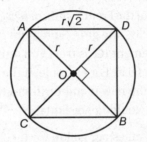

The sides of each triangle are r, r, and $r\sqrt{2}$. So each side of square $ADBC$ is $\sqrt{2}$, and its perimeter, b, is $4r\sqrt{2}$. The area, a, of square $ADBC$ is $(r\sqrt{2})^2 = 2r^2$.

Since $a = b$, we have $2r^2 = 4r\sqrt{2} \Rightarrow r = \textbf{2}\sqrt{\textbf{2}}$.

13. **(C)** Let x represent the number of juniors on the team. Then the number of seniors on the team is $x + 5$, and the total number of students on the team is $2x + 5$. So the fraction of the team that are juniors is $\frac{x}{2x+5}$. However, it is given that the juniors make up 40% or $\frac{4}{10}$ of the team. So,

$$\frac{x}{2x+5} = \frac{4}{10} \Rightarrow 10x = 8x + 20 \Rightarrow 2x = 20 \Rightarrow x = 10$$

So the team consists of 10 juniors and 15 seniors, a total of **25** students.

**You are told that 40% of the team members are juniors and 60% of them are seniors. The 20% difference is due to the fact that there are 5 more seniors on the team than juniors. So those "extra" 5 seniors make up the 20% difference. If those 5 seniors represent 20% or one-fifth of the team, the entire team consists of $5 \times 5 = \textbf{25}$ players.

14. **(C)** The slope of the straight line segment connecting (2, 2) and (6, 8) is

$$\frac{8-2}{6-2} = \frac{6}{4} = \frac{3}{2} = 1.5$$

Therefore, as x goes up 1 from 2 to 3, y goes up 1.5 from 2 to 3.5. Therefore, the point $(3, 3.5)$ is on the graph. So $a = 3.5$, and $3a = 3 \times 3.5 = 10.5$. To evaluate $f(10.5)$, consider the straight-line segment connecting $(10, 8)$ and $(16, 2)$. The slope of that segment is

$$\frac{2-8}{16-10} = \frac{-6}{6} = -1$$

So as x goes up 0.5 from 10 to 10.5, y goes down 0.5 from 8 to **7.5**.

15. **(D)** Since the profit is increasing linearly, we need to find the slope of the line of best fit. The points that are easiest to read exactly are the lattice points. We see that the line passes through $(3, 10)$ and $(9, 40)$. So the slope of the line is $\frac{40-10}{9-3} = \frac{30}{6} = 5$. So the company's profit is increasing by approximately \$5,000 per month. A year and a half is 18 months. In the 9 months from the time the company was in business 9 months to when it will be in business 18 months, the profit is expected to increase by \$45,000 from \$40,000 to **\$85,000**.

16. $\frac{1}{2}$ **or .5** This problem would be trivial if you could use a calculator. But, since this question is in the non-calculator section, you need to know how to manipulate fractional and negative exponents.

$$8^{-\frac{1}{3}} = \frac{1}{8^{\frac{1}{3}}} = \frac{1}{\sqrt[3]{8}} = \frac{1}{2}$$

17. $\frac{4}{5}$ **or** $\frac{8}{10}$ **or .8** Draw a right triangle. Label it ABC, with C as the right angle, and let the cosine of B be $0.6 = \frac{6}{10} = \frac{3}{5}$. Then label the side adjacent to angle B as 3 and the hypotenuse as 5.

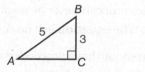

Clearly, this is a 3-4-5 right triangle, so side $\overline{AC}$ is 4, and $\cos A = \frac{4}{5}$ **or** $\frac{8}{10}$ **or .8.**

18. **56** $(7 + i\sqrt{7})(7 - i\sqrt{7}) = 49 - 7i^2 = 49 - 7(-1) = 49 + 7 = 56$

19. $\frac{25}{4}$ **or 6.25** Subtracting $3x$ and $3y$ from both sides of the first equation gives $x = y$. Since $x + y = 5$, we see that $x = y = 2.5$. So $xy = 2.5 \times 2.5 = \mathbf{6.25}$.

**Alternatively, since $x + y = 5$, we have that $x = 5 - y$. Then replacing x by $5 - y$ in the first equation, we get that

$$3(5 - y) + 4y = 4(5 - y) + 3y \Rightarrow 15 + y = 20 - y \Rightarrow 2y = 5 \Rightarrow y = \frac{5}{2}$$

So, $x = 5 - \frac{5}{2} = \frac{5}{2}$. Finally, $xy = \frac{5}{1} \times \frac{5}{2} = \frac{25}{4}$.

20. **2** First of all, every parabola whose equation is of the form $y = ax^2 + bx + c$ crosses the y-axis exactly once, at the point where $x = 0$. Here, it is at the point $(0, 16)$. So $m = 1$.

In general, such a parabola can cross the x-axis once, twice, or not at all. It happens wherever $y = 0$. To know how many times this parabola crosses the x-axis, we have to solve the equation $0 = x^2 - 8x + 16 = (x - 4)(x - 4)$. The equation has only one solution: $x = 4$. The parabola crosses the x-axis once, at the point $(4, 0)$. So $n = 1$ and $m + n = \mathbf{2}$.

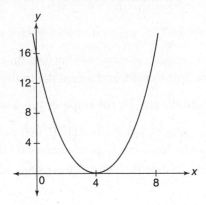

Section 4: Math Test (Calculator)

1. **(B)** Convert 4 feet to 48 inches, and set up a proportion:

$$\frac{\text{depth of water in inches}}{\text{time in minutes}} : \frac{4}{25} = \frac{48}{x}$$

By cross-multiplying, we get $4x = (25)(48) = 1200$, and so $x = 300$. So the tank will be full 300 minutes, or exactly 5 hours, after 11:00, which is **4:00**.

**Equivalently, you could reason that if it takes 25 minutes to fill the tank to 4 inches, it would take 3 times as long (75 minutes) to fill the tank to 12 inches, or 1 foot. So it would take $(4)(75) = 300$ minutes to fill the tank to 4 feet.

2. **(A)** The value of a square root can never be negative So there is no value of x that could make $\sqrt{x+7}$ equal to -4. **The equation has no solutions.**

If you didn't see that, you should have proceeded as follows: If $\sqrt{x+7} = -4$, then squaring both sides gives $x + 7 = 16$. So $x = 9$. So 9 is the only possible solution. However, before choosing choice (B), we have to check that 9 is, in fact, a solution; i.e., it is not extraneous. Does $\sqrt{9+7} = -4$? No, $\sqrt{9+7} = \sqrt{16} = 4$, not -4.

3. **(B)** It appears that the y-intercept of the line of best fit, the grade that would correspond to not studying at all (0 hours), is 55. So $b = 55$. The slope of the line is obtained by using the slope formula. Since the line of best fit passes through the points $(4, 70)$ and $(9, 90)$, the slope of the line is $\frac{90-70}{9-4} = \frac{20}{5} = 4$, and $m = 4$. So $m + b = 4 + 55 = \mathbf{59}$.

4. **(B)** Since the average of 82 and 88 is 85, the only way that the mean grade, m, of all the students in the class could be 85 is if $b = g$. Since it is given that $b \neq g$, m cannot be 85; $\boldsymbol{m \neq 85}$.

**The weighted average, m, of all the students in the class is $\frac{82b+88g}{b+g}$. So if $m = 85$, then $\frac{82b+88g}{b+g} = 85 \Rightarrow 82b + 88g = 85b + 85g \Rightarrow 3b = 3g \Rightarrow b = g$. Since it is given that $b \neq g$, m cannot be 85.

5. **(C)** Since 45 minutes is $\frac{3}{4}$ of an hour, a rate of 1 page per 45 minutes is a rate of 1 page per $\frac{3}{4}$ of an hour, which is equal to $1 \div \frac{3}{4} = \frac{4}{3}$ pages per hour. So in an 8 hour day Brigitte can translate $8 \times \frac{4}{3} = \frac{32}{3}$ pages. In a 5-day week, she can translate $5 \times \frac{32}{3} = \frac{160}{3}$ pages. Finally, in 6 weeks, she can translate $6 \times \frac{160}{3} = \mathbf{320}$ pages.

6. **(C)** Note that (population) ÷ (population per square mile) = area, in square miles.

Since the area of the United States didn't change between 1970 and 2000, subject to rounding errors in approximating both the population density and the population, the answer should be the same for each of the years. For example,

- 1970: 203,200,000 people ÷ 57.4 people per square mile = 3,540,000 square miles ≈ **3,500,000**.
- 2000: 281,400,000 people ÷ 79.6 people per square mile = 3,535,000 square miles ≈ **3,500,000**.

7. **(A)** After m monthly deposits have been made, the box contained $d + me$ dollars. From the given information, we have

$$175 = d + 3e \quad \text{and} \quad 300 = d + 8e$$

Subtracting the first equation from the second one gives $125 = 5e$, and so $e = 25$. Then $175 = d + 3(25) = d + 75$. Therefore, $d = 100$, and we have that $\boldsymbol{a = 100 + 25m}$.

8. **(B)** Since after the initial deposit in January 2014 deposits to the box were made on the first of each month, 11 monthly deposits were made in 2014 (on the first of February through the first of December) and 12 monthly deposits were made in 2015 (on the first of January through the first of December). Therefore on December 25, 2014, the amount in the box was the amount of the initial deposit on January 1, 2014 plus 23 times the amount of the monthly deposits. From the solution to the preceding question, we have that the amount in the box on December 25, 2014 was $100 + 23 × $25 = $100 + $575 = **$675**.

9. **(C)** $f(x) = 4x^4 - 4 = 4 \Rightarrow 4x^4 = 8 \Rightarrow x^4 = 2 \Rightarrow x = \sqrt[4]{2} \approx 1.189$

**Use TACTIC 5: backsolve. Clearly 1, choice (B), doesn't work, so try choice (C). $f(1.19) = 4(1.19)^4 = 4.02$. That is so close to 4 that it must be the answer. The small difference is due to rounding in the answer choices. The real value of x is closer to 1.1892, and $4(1.1892)^4 - 4 = 3.9998$.

10. **(A)** At 10:30 A.M. the first car had been going 40 miles per hour for 1.5 hours, and so had gone $40 × 1.5 = 60$ miles. The second car covered the same 60 miles in 1 hour and 20 minutes, or $1\frac{1}{3} = \frac{4}{3}$ hours. Therefore, its rate was $60 \div \frac{3}{4} = 60 \times \frac{3}{4} = \mathbf{45}$ miles per hour.

11. **(C)** The product $(a + 4i)(9 - bi) = 9a - abi + 36i - 4bi^2 = 9a + 4b + i(36 - ab)$. Since the product is a real number, the coefficient of i must be 0. So $36 - ab = 0$. Then $ab = 36$, and since $a = 6$, b is also equal to **6**.

12. **(D)** For each coin, the probability that Max guesses wrong is $\frac{1}{2}$. So the probability that he guesses wrong 5 times in a row is $\frac{1}{2} \times \frac{1}{2} \times \frac{1}{2} \times \frac{1}{2} \times \frac{1}{2} = \frac{1}{32}$. The probability that he does not guess incorrectly each time (and hence the probability that he is correct at least once) is $1 - \frac{1}{32} = \frac{31}{32} \approx \mathbf{0.97}$.

13. **(C)** From the top graph, we see that in 1975, 54% (35% + 19%) of all college students were male and the other 46% were female. So there were 5,400,000 males and 4,600,000 females—a difference of **800,000**.

14. **(B)** In 1975, of every 100 college students, 46 were female—32 of whom were less than 25 years old, and 14 of whom were 25 years old and over. So, 14 of every 46 female students were at least 25 years old. Finally, $\frac{14}{46} \approx 0.30 = \mathbf{30\%}$.

15. **(C)** From the two graphs, we see that in 1975 54% (35% + 19%) of all college students were male, whereas in 1995 the corresponding figure was 45% (28% + 17%). For simplicity, assume that there were 100 college students in 1975, 54 of whom were male. Then in 1995 after a 40% increase in enrollment, there were 140 college students, 63 of whom were male (45% of 140 = 63). So the ratio of the number of male students in 1995 to the number of male students in 1975 is 63:54 = **7:6**.

16. **(B)** The standard form for the equation of a circle whose center is the point (h, k) and whose radius is r is $(x - h)^2 + (y - k)^2 = r^2$. The center of the circle for which $\overline{AB}$ is a diameter is $(3, 3)$, which is the midpoint of segment $\overline{AB}$. The radius of the circle is the distance from a point on the circle, say $A(1, 1)$ to the center $(3, 3)$.

$r = \sqrt{(3-1)^2 + (3-1)^2} = \sqrt{8}$. So $h = 3$, $k = 3$, and $r^2 = 8$.

The equation of the circle is $\mathbf{(x - 3)^2 + (y - 3)^2 = 8}$.

17. **(B)** If the administrators constitute 27% of the total, then the teachers are 100% – 27% = 73% of the total. So if T is the total number of participants:

$$0.73T = 584 \Rightarrow T = 584 \div 0.73 = 800$$

Therefore, there are 800 – 584 = **216** administrators at the conference.

18. **(D)** Since $\angle A$ is an angle in both $\triangle AHJ$ and $\triangle ABC$ and since each triangle has a right angle, the triangles are similar. Since $AH = 1$ and $AB = 4$, the ratio of similitude is 4:1, which means that the ratio of their areas is $4^2:1 = \mathbf{16:1}$.

**Since $AH = 4 \times AB$, $HJ = 4 \times BC$. Assume $BC = 2$; then $HJ = 8$. Then the area of $\triangle ABC = \frac{1}{2}(1)(2) = 1$, and the area of $\triangle AHJ = \frac{1}{2}(4)(8) = 16$.

19. **(D)** Let x represent the number of students in the society in 2010. Then the number of students in the society in 2015 was $x + 8$. The number of boys in the society in 2010 was $.375x$ and the number of boys in the society in 2015 could be expressed both as $0.375x + 6$ and $.4(x + 8)$. Therefore,

$$0.375x + 6 = 0.4(x + 8) \Rightarrow 0.375x + 6 = 0.4x + 3.2 \Rightarrow 2.8 = 0.025x \Rightarrow x = 112$$

So, in 2010 the society had 112 members. In 2015, it had 112 + 8 = **120**.

20. **(D)** If P represents the processing fee and t is the cost of each ticket, we have

$$107.95 = P + 4t \quad \text{and} \quad 181.45 = P + 7t$$

Subtracting the first equation from the second one gives $73.50 = 3t$. So $t = 24.50$. Then $107.95 = P + 4(24.5) = P + 98$. Therefore, $P = 107.95 - 98 = \textbf{9.95}$.

21. **(A)** For each of the four countries, you can just divide the number in the column headed "Travel Outside of Europe" by the number in the column headed "Total." However, if you notice immediately that the answer can't be Finland since there were fewer than half as many people in Finland planning to travel outside of Europe than people from any of the other countries, then you can just do the division for the other three countries.

- Denmark: $6,244 \div 21,953 = 0.284 = 28.4\%$
- Sweden: $5,881 \div 23,990 = 0.245 = 24.5\%$
- Norway: $5,369 \div 20,059 = 0.268 = 26.8\%$

The answer is (A), **Denmark**.

22. **(B)** Of the 1,000 people in the sample, 16.8% ($168 \div 1,000$) of them plan to travel to the United States. Since the sample was random, it is likely that about 16.8% of all the original respondents who said they planned to travel outside of Europe would travel to the United States: $0.168 \times 20,156 = 3,386$. So it is highly likely that the actual number of people would be **between 3,000 and 5,000**.

23. **(B)** Draw and label a cube with a main diagonal of 9 and a side of s.

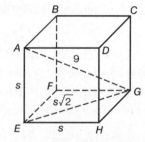

By KEY FACT J8, the length of $\overline{EG}$, a diagonal of the square base, is $s\sqrt{2}$. Then by the Pythagorean theorem (KEY FACT J5), in right $\triangle AEG$:

$$s^2 + (s\sqrt{2})^2 = 9^2 \Rightarrow s^2 + 2s^2 = 81 \Rightarrow 3s^2 = 81 \Rightarrow s^2 = 27$$

Since a cube has 6 faces, each of which has area s^2, the formula for the total surface area of a cube is $A = 6s^2$. So $A = 6 \times 27 = \textbf{162}$.

24. **(B)** In $\triangle ABC$, $\dfrac{b}{a} = \tan 28° = 0.53$.

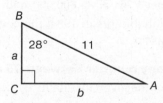

**$\sin 28° = \dfrac{b}{11} \Rightarrow b = 11 \sin 28° = 5.164$.

$\cos 28° = \dfrac{a}{11} \Rightarrow a = 11 \cos 28° = 9.712$.

So $\dfrac{b}{a} = \dfrac{5.164}{9.712} = \textbf{0.53}$.

25. **(B)** Express the quotient as a fraction. Then multiply the numerator and denominator by the conjugate of the denominator:

$$(1+2i) \div (3+4i) = \frac{1+2i}{3+4i} = \frac{1+2i}{3+4i} \cdot \frac{3-4i}{3-4i} = \frac{3-4i+6i-8i^2}{9+16} = \frac{11+2i}{25} = \frac{11}{25} + \frac{2}{25}i$$

So $a = \frac{11}{25}$ and $b = \frac{2}{25}$ and $a+b = \frac{13}{25} = \mathbf{0.52}$.

26. **(D)** 16.56 Mexican pesos and 9.47 Argentinian pesos have the same value (namely, 1 U.S. dollar). Set up a proportion:

$$\frac{\text{Mexican pesos}}{\text{Argentinian pesos}} = \frac{16.56}{9.47} = \frac{x}{1} \Rightarrow x = 1.7486 \approx \mathbf{1.75}$$

27. **(B)** Since $3{,}000 \div 27 = 111.1111\ldots$, the school has 111 homerooms. (110 of the homerooms have 27 students each, which accounts for $27 \times 110 = 2{,}970$ students. The remaining 30 students are in the 111th homeroom.) Since each of the 110 homerooms with 27 students has 3 participating students, there were a total of 330 participants from those homerooms. The total number of students participating in the survey was those 330 students plus the 4 students in the homeroom with 30 students, a total of **334** students.

28. **(B)** From 1994 to 1996 there was a 9.4% decrease in the number of vehicles stolen. Since 9.4% of $1{,}000{,}000 = 94{,}000$, the number of vehicles stolen in 1996 was $1{,}000{,}000 - 94{,}000 = \mathbf{906{,}000}$. If you get stuck on a question such as this, you have to guess. But since the number of stolen vehicles is clearly decreasing, be sure to eliminate choice (D) before guessing.

29. **(C)** For simplicity, assume that 1,000 vehicles were stolen in 1994. By 1997, the number had decreased by 12.0% to 880 (12% of $1{,}000 = 120$, and $1{,}000 - 120 = 880$); by 1998, the number had decreased 19.4% to 806 (19.4% of $1{,}000 = 194$ and $1{,}000 - 194 = 806$). So from 1997 to 1998, the number of vehicles stolen decreased by 74 from 880 to 806. This represents a decrease of $\frac{74}{880} \approx 0.084 = \mathbf{8.4\%}$.

30. **(D)** Simplify the situation by assuming that in 1994 the population was 100,000 and there were 1,000 vehicles stolen. As in the solution to question 29, in 1998 the number of stolen vehicles was 806. At the same time, the number of thefts per 100,000 inhabitants decreased 22.4% from 1,000 to 776. So if there were 776 vehicles stolen for every 100,000 inhabitants, and 806 cars were stolen, the number of inhabitants must have increased.

To know by how much, solve the proportion: $\frac{776}{100{,}000} = \frac{806}{x}$. By cross-multiplying, we get $776x = 80{,}600{,}000$ and $x = 80{,}600{,}000 \div 776 \approx 103{,}900$. Then for every 100,000 inhabitants in 1994, there were 103,900 in 1998, an increase of 3.9% or approximately **4%**.

31. **any number between .75 and .857** Since $2b-2a$ is -2 times $a-b$, multiply each term of the given inequality by -2, remembering to change the order of the inequalities since you are multiplying by a negative number:

$$\frac{6}{7} > -2a+2b > \frac{6}{8} \Rightarrow \frac{6}{8} < 2b-2a < \frac{6}{7} \Rightarrow 0.75 < 2b-2a < 0.857$$

Alternate solution. Pick values for a and b that satisfy the original inequality. Since $-\frac{3}{7} = -0.428$ and $-\frac{3}{8} = -0.375$, let $a = 0$ and $b = 0.4$ so that $a - b = -0.4$. Then $2a - 2b = -0.8$ and $2b - 2a = 0.8$.

 32. $\frac{2}{5}$ **or** $\frac{4}{10}$ **or .4** There are a total of 650 juniors and seniors (340 juniors and 310 seniors). Of those, 260 took a language other than Spanish ($98 + 42 + 106 + 14 = 260$). So, the desired fraction is $\frac{260}{650} = \frac{4}{10} = \frac{2}{5}$.

33. **.447** Sketch the line $y = 2x$. Label two points on the line, such as $(0, 0)$ and $(1, 2)$.

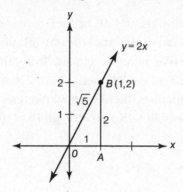

Use the Pythagorean theorem to find the length of $\overline{OB}$, the hypotenuse of $\triangle OAB$:

$$(OB)^2 = 1^2 + 2^2 = 5 \Rightarrow OB = \sqrt{5} \approx 2.236$$

Then $\cos \angle BOA = \dfrac{\text{adjacent}}{\text{hypotenuse}} = \dfrac{1}{2.236} \approx 0.447$.

 34. **50** Since the graph of $y = 10x^2 + bx + c$ has x-intercepts at 1.4 and 1.5, $(x - 1.4)$ and $(x - 1.5)$ are factors of $10x^2 + bx + c$. So $y = 10(x - 1.4)(x - 1.5) = 10(x^2 - 2.9x + 2.1) = 10x^2 - 29x + 21$. Then $b = -29$ and $c = 21$. So $c - b = 21 - (-29) = 21 + 29 = \mathbf{50}$.

 35. $\frac{1}{2}$ **or .5** The volume of the rectangular block is the area of its face multiplied by its length. Of course, we must use consistent units; since we want the volume in cubic feet, we have to convert the dimensions given in inches to feet:

$$8 \text{ inches} = \frac{8}{12} = \frac{2}{3} \text{ feet}; 5 \text{ inches} = \frac{5}{12} \text{ feet}; 2 \text{ inches} = \frac{2}{12} = \frac{1}{6} \text{ feet}$$

The face of the block is a rectangle with a square removed. The area of the rectangle is $\frac{2}{3} \times \frac{5}{12} = \frac{10}{36}$ square feet. The area of the square is $\frac{1}{6} \times \frac{1}{6} = \frac{1}{36}$ square feet. So the area of the face is $\frac{10}{36} - \frac{1}{36} = \frac{9}{36} = \frac{1}{4}$ square feet. So the volume of the solid is $\frac{1}{4}$ square feet $\times$ 2 feet $= \frac{1}{2}$ cubic feet.

 36. **6** Since the density of an object is its weight divided by its volume, the weight of an object is the product of its volume times its density. From the solution to question 37, we know that the volume of the block is $\frac{1}{2}$ cubic feet.

So calculate the densities:

- Spanish mahogany: (0.5 cubic feet) × (53 pounds per cubic foot) = 26.5 pounds.
- Honduran mahogany: (0.5 cubic feet) × (41 pounds per cubic foot) = 20.5 pounds.

So a block made of Spanish mahogany would weigh **6** pounds more than a block made of Honduran mahogany.

37. **15** From the bar graph, we see that 20% of the 500 campers were 15 years old. Since 20% of 500 is 100, there were 100 15-year-old campers at the camp. From the circle graph, we see that 15% of the 15 year olds were pianists. So the number of 15-year-old pianists at the camp in 2015 was 15% of 100, which equals **15**.

38. **15** Since 12 of the 13-year-olds and 18 of the 14-year-olds were pianists, 30 of the campers under the age of 15 were pianists. From the solution to question 35, we know that 15 of the 15 year olds were pianists. Finally, from the bar graph, we know that 24% + 16% + 6% + 4% = 50% of the 500 campers, or 250, were 16 or older. Since 12% of those 250 campers were pianists, there were 30 pianists aged 16 or more. Finally, the total number of pianists was 30 + 15 + 30 = 75. So 75 of the 500 campers were pianists, and 75 ÷ 500 = .15 = **15%**.

SAT Essay Scoring

SAT Essay Scoring Rubric

	Score: 4
Reading	**Excellent:** The essay shows excellent understanding of the source.
	The essay shows an understanding of the source's main argument and key details and a firm grasp of how they are interconnected, demonstrating clear comprehension of the source.
	The essay does not misinterpret or misrepresent the source.
	The essay skillfully uses source evidence, such as direct quotations and rephrasing, representing a thorough comprehension of the source.
Analysis	**Excellent:** The essay gives excellent analysis of the source and shows clear understanding of what the assignment requires.
	The essay gives a complete, highly thoughtful analysis of the author's use of reasoning, evidence, rhetoric, and/or other argumentative elements the student has chosen to highlight.
	The essay has appropriate, adequate, and skillfully chosen support for its analysis. The essay focuses on the most important parts of the source in responding to the prompt.
Writing	**Excellent:** The essay is focused and shows an excellent grasp of the English language. The essay has a clear thesis. The essay has a well-executed introduction and conclusion. The essay shows a clear and well-crafted progression of thoughts both within paragraphs and in the essay as a whole. The essay has a wide range of sentence structures. The essay consistently shows precise choice of words. The essay is formal and objective in its style and tone. The essay demonstrates a firm grasp of the rules of standard English and has very few to no errors.

	Score: 3
Reading	**Skillful:** The essay shows effective understanding of the source.
	The essay shows an understanding of the source's main argument and key details.
	The essay is free of major misinterpretations and/or misrepresentations of the source.
	The essay uses appropriate source evidence, such as direct quotations and rephrasing, representing comprehension of the source.
Analysis	**Skillful:** The essay gives effective analysis of the source and shows an understanding of what the assignment requires.
	The essay decently analyzes the author's use of reasoning, evidence, rhetoric, and/or other argumentative elements the student has chosen to highlight.
	The essay has appropriate and adequate support for its analysis. The essay focuses primarily on the most important parts of the source in responding to the prompt.
Writing	**Skillful:** The essay is mostly focused and shows an effective grasp of the English language. The essay has a thesis, either explicit or implicit. The essay has an effective introduction and conclusion. The essay has a clear progression of thoughts both within paragraphs and in the essay as a whole. The essay has an assortment of sentence structures. The essay shows some precise choice of words. The essay is formal and objective in its style and tone. The essay demonstrates a grasp of the rules of standard English and has very few significant errors that interfere with the writer's argument.

Score: 2	
Reading	Limited: The essay shows some understanding of the source. The essay shows an understanding of the source's main argument, but not of key details. The essay may have some misinterpretations and/or misrepresentations of the source. The essay gives only partial evidence from the source, showing limited comprehension of the source.
Analysis	Limited: The essay gives partial analysis of the source and shows only limited understanding of what the assignment requires. The essay tries to show how the author uses reasoning, evidence, rhetoric, and/or other argumentative elements the student has chosen to highlight, but only states rather than analyzes their importance, or at least one part of the essay's analysis is unsupported by the source. The essay has little or no justification for its argument. The essay may lack attention to those elements of the source that are most pertinent to responding to the prompt.
Writing	Limited: The essay is mostly not cohesive and shows an ineffective grasp of the English language. The essay may not have a thesis, or may diverge from the thesis at some point in the essay's development. The essay may have an unsuccessful introduction and/or conclusion. The essay may show progression of thoughts within the paragraphs, but not in the essay as a whole. The essay is relatively uniform in its sentence structures. The essay shows imprecise and possibly repetitive choice of words. The essay may be more casual and subjective in style and tone. The essay demonstrates a weaker grasp of the rules of standard English and does have errors that interfere with the writer's argument.

Score: 1	
Reading	Insufficient: The essay shows virtually no understanding of the source. The essay is unsuccessful in showing an understanding of the source's main argument. It may refer to some details from the text, but it does so without tying them to the source's main argument. The essay has many misinterpretations and/or misrepresentations of the source. The essay gives virtually no evidence from the source, showing very poor comprehension of the source.
Analysis	Insufficient: The essay gives little to no accurate analysis of the source and shows poor understanding of what the assignment requires. The essay may show how the author uses reasoning, evidence, rhetoric, and/or other argumentative elements that the student has chosen to highlight but does so without analysis. Or many parts of the essay's analysis are unsupported by the source. The support given for points in the essay's argument are largely unsupported or off topic. The essay may not attend to the elements of the source that are pertinent to responding to the prompt. Or the essay gives no explicit analysis, perhaps only resorting to summary statements.
Writing	Insufficient: The essay is not cohesive and does not demonstrate skill in the English language. The essay may not have a thesis. The essay does not have a clear introduction and conclusion. The essay does not have a clear progression of thoughts. The essay is quite uniform and even repetitive in sentence structure. The essay shows poor and possibly inaccurate word choice. The essay is likely casual and subjective in style and tone. The essay shows a poor grasp of the rules of standard English and may have many errors that interfere with the writer's argument.

Top-Scoring Sample Student Response

People these days seem to be busier than ever between work, school, family, and other commitments. This often doesn't leave times for the things we know we SHOULD do, but don't really want to. Other activities seem to get in the way that seem more important. Often, the first objective that drops from our "to-do" lists is exercise. In "Healthy Is Happy," the author argues that time should be made for exercise because there is such a high correlation between being physically active and success. The author relies on citing professional, scientific studies, relatable examples, and a casual tone through diction that appeals to a wide variety of readers, in order to convince them that exercise and success are closely linked.

It's often hard to convince a skeptical reader. Citing professional studies is often a foolproof way to show people that your opinion or idea is, in fact, backed up by science. This is exactly what the author did. The author makes a grand claim that exercise and success are inextricably linked. She then backs this claim with a study published in a well-known journal (The Journal of Pediatrics) which found that "fitness was linked to higher achievement scores regardless of body type." This also speaks to naysayers who may argue that only "fit" children were tested. Another study cited by the author appeared on ABC News and showed that high school students doubled their reading scores on standardized tests if they "[participated] in a dynamic morning exercise regimen." These findings are quite significant when thinking of achievement and success in the classroom.

Just when the reader begins to wonder, "but what about those outside the classroom," the author references a recent study which "found that 75% of executives making six-figures listed physical fitness as critical to their career success." It's hard to argue that health is only related to success in school when high paid business men and women place such a high value on fitness. The executives said fitness helped them across the following areas: sleep, diligence, and concentration.

High paying business executives are great role models, but it may be hard for the average Joe to relate to them. As such, the author made great use of more relatable examples. Throughout the essay, the author seems to speak to the lay reader through problems experienced by people in all walks of life. The author offers up complaints like their careers making it hard to get to the gym, being a stressed out college student, and even someone busy with family commitments. These are pretty universal experiences that allow the reader to put themselves in the shoes of the essay, so to speak. The author draws in the reader, making them think "yeah, that's me!" then gives examples of how fitness could help them improve their lives in a variety of ways.

Relatability can make or break a persuasive paper. If a reader disagrees with your point and also feels like they are being personally attacked, they will often disregard it regardless of the evidence behind the argument. Throughout "Healthy Is Happy," the author maintains a casual tone that is appealing to readers. He/she references widespread roles like "busy parent," "exhausted student," "overworked professional." Additionally, the author uses colloquial phrases like "take the average college student," "six pack abs," "the word has spread," "or do you?" The insertion of these colloquials helps balances out the sometimes verbose, extended vocabulary. This strategy and use of diction allows the essay to appeal to the widest variety of readers, and thereby sways the most amount of people toward exercise.

Many studies have proven the link between exercise and success. Some of these studies have even been published by reputable sources like the The Journal of Pediatrics and ABC News. Scientific studies lend more credibility to arguments than generalized, broad statements. Additionally, using smart diction and applicable examples makes the author seem like a credible, but relatable resource. Overall, the author's use of scientific studies, pertinent examples, and casual tone make for a solid argument.

ANSWER SHEET
Model Test 3

Section 1: Reading

1. Ⓐ Ⓑ Ⓒ Ⓓ
2. Ⓐ Ⓑ Ⓒ Ⓓ
3. Ⓐ Ⓑ Ⓒ Ⓓ
4. Ⓐ Ⓑ Ⓒ Ⓓ
5. Ⓐ Ⓑ Ⓒ Ⓓ
6. Ⓐ Ⓑ Ⓒ Ⓓ
7. Ⓐ Ⓑ Ⓒ Ⓓ
8. Ⓐ Ⓑ Ⓒ Ⓓ
9. Ⓐ Ⓑ Ⓒ Ⓓ
10. Ⓐ Ⓑ Ⓒ Ⓓ
11. Ⓐ Ⓑ Ⓒ Ⓓ
12. Ⓐ Ⓑ Ⓒ Ⓓ
13. Ⓐ Ⓑ Ⓒ Ⓓ

14. Ⓐ Ⓑ Ⓒ Ⓓ
15. Ⓐ Ⓑ Ⓒ Ⓓ
16. Ⓐ Ⓑ Ⓒ Ⓓ
17. Ⓐ Ⓑ Ⓒ Ⓓ
18. Ⓐ Ⓑ Ⓒ Ⓓ
19. Ⓐ Ⓑ Ⓒ Ⓓ
20. Ⓐ Ⓑ Ⓒ Ⓓ
21. Ⓐ Ⓑ Ⓒ Ⓓ
22. Ⓐ Ⓑ Ⓒ Ⓓ
23. Ⓐ Ⓑ Ⓒ Ⓓ
24. Ⓐ Ⓑ Ⓒ Ⓓ
25. Ⓐ Ⓑ Ⓒ Ⓓ
26. Ⓐ Ⓑ Ⓒ Ⓓ

27. Ⓐ Ⓑ Ⓒ Ⓓ
28. Ⓐ Ⓑ Ⓒ Ⓓ
29. Ⓐ Ⓑ Ⓒ Ⓓ
30. Ⓐ Ⓑ Ⓒ Ⓓ
31. Ⓐ Ⓑ Ⓒ Ⓓ
32. Ⓐ Ⓑ Ⓒ Ⓓ
33. Ⓐ Ⓑ Ⓒ Ⓓ
34. Ⓐ Ⓑ Ⓒ Ⓓ
35. Ⓐ Ⓑ Ⓒ Ⓓ
36. Ⓐ Ⓑ Ⓒ Ⓓ
37. Ⓐ Ⓑ Ⓒ Ⓓ
38. Ⓐ Ⓑ Ⓒ Ⓓ
39. Ⓐ Ⓑ Ⓒ Ⓓ

40. Ⓐ Ⓑ Ⓒ Ⓓ
41. Ⓐ Ⓑ Ⓒ Ⓓ
42. Ⓐ Ⓑ Ⓒ Ⓓ
43. Ⓐ Ⓑ Ⓒ Ⓓ
44. Ⓐ Ⓑ Ⓒ Ⓓ
45. Ⓐ Ⓑ Ⓒ Ⓓ
46. Ⓐ Ⓑ Ⓒ Ⓓ
47. Ⓐ Ⓑ Ⓒ Ⓓ
48. Ⓐ Ⓑ Ⓒ Ⓓ
49. Ⓐ Ⓑ Ⓒ Ⓓ
50. Ⓐ Ⓑ Ⓒ Ⓓ
51. Ⓐ Ⓑ Ⓒ Ⓓ
52. Ⓐ Ⓑ Ⓒ Ⓓ

Section 2: Writing and Language

1. Ⓐ Ⓑ Ⓒ Ⓓ
2. Ⓐ Ⓑ Ⓒ Ⓓ
3. Ⓐ Ⓑ Ⓒ Ⓓ
4. Ⓐ Ⓑ Ⓒ Ⓓ
5. Ⓐ Ⓑ Ⓒ Ⓓ
6. Ⓐ Ⓑ Ⓒ Ⓓ
7. Ⓐ Ⓑ Ⓒ Ⓓ
8. Ⓐ Ⓑ Ⓒ Ⓓ
9. Ⓐ Ⓑ Ⓒ Ⓓ
10. Ⓐ Ⓑ Ⓒ Ⓓ
11. Ⓐ Ⓑ Ⓒ Ⓓ

12. Ⓐ Ⓑ Ⓒ Ⓓ
13. Ⓐ Ⓑ Ⓒ Ⓓ
14. Ⓐ Ⓑ Ⓒ Ⓓ
15. Ⓐ Ⓑ Ⓒ Ⓓ
16. Ⓐ Ⓑ Ⓒ Ⓓ
17. Ⓐ Ⓑ Ⓒ Ⓓ
18. Ⓐ Ⓑ Ⓒ Ⓓ
19. Ⓐ Ⓑ Ⓒ Ⓓ
20. Ⓐ Ⓑ Ⓒ Ⓓ
21. Ⓐ Ⓑ Ⓒ Ⓓ
22. Ⓐ Ⓑ Ⓒ Ⓓ

23. Ⓐ Ⓑ Ⓒ Ⓓ
24. Ⓐ Ⓑ Ⓒ Ⓓ
25. Ⓐ Ⓑ Ⓒ Ⓓ
26. Ⓐ Ⓑ Ⓒ Ⓓ
27. Ⓐ Ⓑ Ⓒ Ⓓ
28. Ⓐ Ⓑ Ⓒ Ⓓ
29. Ⓐ Ⓑ Ⓒ Ⓓ
30. Ⓐ Ⓑ Ⓒ Ⓓ
31. Ⓐ Ⓑ Ⓒ Ⓓ
32. Ⓐ Ⓑ Ⓒ Ⓓ
33. Ⓐ Ⓑ Ⓒ Ⓓ

34. Ⓐ Ⓑ Ⓒ Ⓓ
35. Ⓐ Ⓑ Ⓒ Ⓓ
36. Ⓐ Ⓑ Ⓒ Ⓓ
37. Ⓐ Ⓑ Ⓒ Ⓓ
38. Ⓐ Ⓑ Ⓒ Ⓓ
39. Ⓐ Ⓑ Ⓒ Ⓓ
40. Ⓐ Ⓑ Ⓒ Ⓓ
41. Ⓐ Ⓑ Ⓒ Ⓓ
42. Ⓐ Ⓑ Ⓒ Ⓓ
43. Ⓐ Ⓑ Ⓒ Ⓓ
44. Ⓐ Ⓑ Ⓒ Ⓓ

Section 3: Math (No Calculator)

1. Ⓐ Ⓑ Ⓒ Ⓓ   5. Ⓐ Ⓑ Ⓒ Ⓓ   9. Ⓐ Ⓑ Ⓒ Ⓓ   13. Ⓐ Ⓑ Ⓒ Ⓓ
2. Ⓐ Ⓑ Ⓒ Ⓓ   6. Ⓐ Ⓑ Ⓒ Ⓓ   10. Ⓐ Ⓑ Ⓒ Ⓓ   14. Ⓐ Ⓑ Ⓒ Ⓓ
3. Ⓐ Ⓑ Ⓒ Ⓓ   7. Ⓐ Ⓑ Ⓒ Ⓓ   11. Ⓐ Ⓑ Ⓒ Ⓓ   15. Ⓐ Ⓑ Ⓒ Ⓓ
4. Ⓐ Ⓑ Ⓒ Ⓓ   8. Ⓐ Ⓑ Ⓒ Ⓓ   12. Ⓐ Ⓑ Ⓒ Ⓓ

16.

17.

18.

19.

20.

ANSWER SHEET
Model Test 3

Section 4: Math (Calculator)

1. Ⓐ Ⓑ Ⓒ Ⓓ
2. Ⓐ Ⓑ Ⓒ Ⓓ
3. Ⓐ Ⓑ Ⓒ Ⓓ
4. Ⓐ Ⓑ Ⓒ Ⓓ
5. Ⓐ Ⓑ Ⓒ Ⓓ
6. Ⓐ Ⓑ Ⓒ Ⓓ
7. Ⓐ Ⓑ Ⓒ Ⓓ
8. Ⓐ Ⓑ Ⓒ Ⓓ

9. Ⓐ Ⓑ Ⓒ Ⓓ
10. Ⓐ Ⓑ Ⓒ Ⓓ
11. Ⓐ Ⓑ Ⓒ Ⓓ
12. Ⓐ Ⓑ Ⓒ Ⓓ
13. Ⓐ Ⓑ Ⓒ Ⓓ
14. Ⓐ Ⓑ Ⓒ Ⓓ
15. Ⓐ Ⓑ Ⓒ Ⓓ
16. Ⓐ Ⓑ Ⓒ Ⓓ

17. Ⓐ Ⓑ Ⓒ Ⓓ
18. Ⓐ Ⓑ Ⓒ Ⓓ
19. Ⓐ Ⓑ Ⓒ Ⓓ
20. Ⓐ Ⓑ Ⓒ Ⓓ
21. Ⓐ Ⓑ Ⓒ Ⓓ
22. Ⓐ Ⓑ Ⓒ Ⓓ
23. Ⓐ Ⓑ Ⓒ Ⓓ
24. Ⓐ Ⓑ Ⓒ Ⓓ

25. Ⓐ Ⓑ Ⓒ Ⓓ
26. Ⓐ Ⓑ Ⓒ Ⓓ
27. Ⓐ Ⓑ Ⓒ Ⓓ
28. Ⓐ Ⓑ Ⓒ Ⓓ
29. Ⓐ Ⓑ Ⓒ Ⓓ
30. Ⓐ Ⓑ Ⓒ Ⓓ

31.
32.
33.
34.

35.
36.
37.
38.

ANSWER SHEET
Model Test 3

Essay

PLANNING PAGE

START YOUR ESSAY HERE

READING TEST

65 MINUTES, 52 QUESTIONS

Turn to Section 1 of your answer sheet to answer the questions in this section.

> **Directions:** Following each of the passages (or pairs of passages) below are questions about the passage (or passages). Read each passage carefully. Then, select the best answer for each question based on what is stated in the passage (or passages) and in any graphics that may accompany the passage.

Questions 1–11 are based on the following passage.

The following passage is taken from Great Expectations *by Charles Dickens. In it, the hero, Pip, recollects a dismal period in his youth during which he for a time lost hope of ever bettering his fortunes.*

It is a most miserable thing to feel ashamed of home. There may be black ingratitude in the thing, and the punishment
Line may be retributive and well deserved; but,
(5) that it is a miserable thing, I can testify. Home had never been a very pleasant place to me, because of my sister's temper. But Joe had sanctified it and I believed in it. I had believed in the best parlor as a most elegant
(10) salon; I had believed in the front door as a mysterious portal of the Temple of State whose solemn opening was attended with a sacrifice of roast fowls; I had believed in the kitchen as a chaste though not magnificent
(15) apartment; I had believed in the forge as the glowing road to manhood. Now, it was all coarse and common, and I would not have had Miss Havisham and Estella see it on any account.

(20) Once, it had seemed to me that when I should at last roll up my shirt sleeves and go into the forge, Joe's 'prentice, I should be distinguished and happy. Now the reality was in my hold, I only felt that I was dusty

(25) with the dust of small coal, and that I had a weight upon my daily remembrance to which the anvil was a feather. There have been occasions in my later life (I suppose as in most lives) when I have felt for a time as
(30) if a thick curtain had fallen on all its interest and romance, to shut me out from any thing save dull endurance any more. Never has that curtain dropped so heavy and blank, as when my way in life lay stretched out straight
(35) before me through the newly-entered road of apprenticeship to Joe.

I remember that at a later period of my "time," I used to stand about the churchyard on Sunday evenings, when night was falling,
(40) comparing my own perspective with the windy marsh view, and making out some likeness between them by thinking how flat and low both were, and how on both there came an unknown way and a dark mist and
(45) then the sea. I was quite as dejected on the first working-day of my apprenticeship as in that after time; but I am glad to know that I never breathed a murmur to Joe while my indentures lasted. It is about the only thing I
(50) am glad to know of myself in that connection.

For, though it includes what I proceed to add, all the merit of what I proceed to add was Joe's. It was not because I was faithful, but because Joe was faithful, that I never ran
(55) away and went for a soldier or a sailor. It was not because I had a strong sense of the virtue

GO ON TO THE NEXT PAGE

MODEL TEST 3

of industry, but because Joe had a strong
sense of the virtue of industry, that I worked
with tolerable zeal against the grain. It is not
(60) possible to know how far the influence of any
amiable honest-hearted duty-going man flies
out into the world; but it is very possible to
know how it has touched one's self in going
by, and I know right well that any good that
(65) intermixed itself with my apprenticeship
came of plain contented Joe, and not of
restless aspiring discontented me.

What I wanted, who can say? How can I
say, when I never knew? What I dreaded was,
(70) that in some unlucky hour I, being at my
grimiest and commonest, should lift up my
eyes and see Estella looking in at one of the
wooden windows of the forge. I was haunted
by the fear that she would, sooner or later,
(75) find me out, with a black face and hands,
doing the coarsest part of my work, and
would exult over me and despise me. Often
after dark, when I was pulling the bellows for
Joe, and we were singing Old Clem, and when
(80) the thought how we used to sing it at Miss
Havisham's would seem to show me Estella's
face in the fire, with her pretty hair fluttering
in the wind and her eyes scorning me,—often
at such a time I would look towards those
(85) panels of black night in the wall which the
wooden windows then were, and would fancy
that I saw her just drawing her face away, and
would believe that she had come at last.

After that, when we went in to supper,
(90) the place and the meal would have a more
homely look than ever, and I would feel more
ashamed of home than ever, in my own
ungracious breast.

1. The passage as a whole is best described as

    (A) an analysis of the reasons behind a
        change in attitude.
    (B) an account of a young man's reflections
        on his emotional state.
    (C) a description of a young man's
        awakening to the harshness of working
        class life.
    (D) a criticism of young people's ingratitude
        to their elders.

2. Thanks to Joe, the narrator's early image of
    his home can best be described as basically

    (A) miserable.
    (B) modest.
    (C) positive.
    (D) realistic.

3. Which choice provides the best evidence for
    the answer to the previous question?

    (A) Lines 1–5 ("It is a most . . . testify")
    (B) Lines 8–16 ("I had believed . . .
        manhood")
    (C) Lines 23–36 ("Now the reality . . . Joe")
    (D) Lines 37–45 ("I remember . . . the sea")

4. In the passage, Joe is portrayed most
    specifically as

    (A) distinguished.
    (B) virtuous.
    (C) independent.
    (D) coarse.

GO ON TO THE NEXT PAGE

5. Which word could best replace "time" in line 38?

   (A) apprenticeship
   (B) childhood
   (C) sentence
   (D) existence

6. The passage suggests that the narrator's increasing discontent with his home during his apprenticeship was caused by

   (A) a new awareness on his part of how his home would appear to others.
   (B) the increasing heaviness of the labor that his apprenticeship required.
   (C) the unwillingness or inability of Joe to curb his sister's temper.
   (D) a combination of simple ingratitude and human sinfulness.

7. Which choice provides the best evidence for the answer to the previous question?

   (A) Lines 1–2 ("It is . . . home")
   (B) Lines 6–7 ("Home . . . temper")
   (C) Lines 16–19 ("Now, it . . . account")
   (D) Lines 23–27 ("Now the reality . . . feather")

8. According to the passage, the narrator gives himself a measure of credit for

   (A) working diligently despite his unhappiness.
   (B) abandoning his hope of a military career.
   (C) keeping his menial position secret from Estella.
   (D) concealing his despondency from Joe.

9. The author includes the description of the narrator's view from the churchyard (lines 37–45) primarily to

   (A) suggest the narrator's strong prospects for advancement.
   (B) highlight the beauty of the natural setting.
   (C) emphasize the depth of the narrator's gloom.
   (D) foreshadow Joe's eventual demise.

10. As used in line 91, "homely" most nearly means

   (A) plain and unrefined.
   (B) cosy and comfortable.
   (C) proper and domestic.
   (D) commonly known.

11. The description in the next-to-last paragraph indicates that what the narrator fears most about Estella is her

   (A) passionate temperament.
   (B) scornful disposition.
   (C) haunting beauty.
   (D) inquisitive nature.

MODEL TEST 3

Questions 12–21 are based on the following passage.

The following passage is excerpted from a text on Native American history. Here, the author describes how certain major Indian nations related to the European powers during the 1700s.

By the end of the seventeenth century the coastal tribes along most of the Atlantic seaboard had been destroyed, dispersed,
Line or subjected directly to European control.
(5) Yet the interior tribes—particularly those who had grouped themselves into confederations—remained powers (and were usually styled nations) who dealt with Europeans on a rough plane of equality.
(10) Throughout the eighteenth century, the Creeks, Choctaws, Chickasaws, Cherokees, and Iroquois, as well as the tribes of the Old Northwest, alternately made war and peace with the various European powers,
(15) entered into treaties of alliance and friendship, and sometimes made cessions of territory as a result of defeat in war. As the imperial power of France and Great Britain expanded into the interior, those
(20) powerful Indian nations were forced to seek new orientations in their policy. For each Indian nation the reorientation was different, yet each was powerfully affected by the growth of European settlements,
(25) population, and military power. The history of the reorientation of Iroquois policy toward the Europeans may serve as an example of the process that all the interior nations experienced in the eighteenth century.
(30) The stability that had marked the Iroquois Confederacy's generally pro-British position was shattered with the overthrow of James II in 1688, the colonial uprisings that followed in Massachusetts, New York, and
(35) Maryland, and the commencement of King William's War against Louis XIV of France. The increasing French threat to English hegemony in the interior of North America was signalized by French-led or French-
(40) inspired attacks on the Iroquois and on outlying colonial settlements in New York and New England. The high point of the Iroquois response was the spectacular raid of August 5, 1689, in which the Iroquois virtually

Iroquois Confederacy Relations and Treaties with the French & English

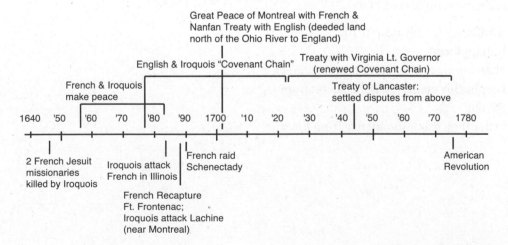

1

(45) wiped out the French village of Lachine, just outside Montreal. A counterraid by the French on the English village of Schenectady in March, 1690, instilled an appropriate measure of fear among the English and their
(50) Iroquois allies.

The Iroquois position at the end of the war, which was formalized by treaties made during the summer of 1701 with the British and the French, and which was maintained
(55) throughout most of the eighteenth century, was one of "aggressive neutrality" between the two competing European powers. Under the new system the Iroquois initiated a peace policy toward the "far Indians," tightened
(60) their control over the nearby tribes, and induced both English and French to support their neutrality toward the European powers by appropriate gifts and concessions.

By holding the balance of power in
(65) the sparsely settled borderlands between English and French settlements, and by their willingness to use their power against one or the other nation if not appropriately treated, the Iroquois played the game of
(70) European power politics with effectiveness. The system broke down, however, after the French became convinced that the Iroquois were compromising the system in favor of the English and launched a full-scale attempt
(75) to establish French physical and juridical presence in the Ohio Valley, the heart of the borderlands long claimed by the Iroquois. As a consequence of the ensuing Great War for Empire, in which Iroquois neutrality was
(80) dissolved and European influence moved closer, the play-off system lost its efficacy and a system of direct bargaining supplanted it.

12. The author's primary purpose in this passage is to

(A) disprove the charges of barbarism made against the Indian nations.
(B) expose the French government's exploitation of the Iroquois balance of power.
(C) describe and assess the effect of European military power on the policy of an Indian nation.
(D) show the inability of the Iroquois nation to engage in European-style diplomacy.

13. As used in line 8, "styled" most nearly means

(A) arranged.
(B) designated.
(C) brought into conformity with.
(D) designed in a particular fashion.

14. In writing that certain of the interior tribes "dealt with Europeans on a rough plane of equality" (lines 8–9), the author

(A) suggests that the coastal tribes lacked essential diplomatic skills.
(B) concedes that the Indians were demonstrably superior to the Europeans.
(C) acknowledges that European-Indian relations were not those of absolute equals.
(D) emphasizes that the Europeans wished to treat the Indians equitably.

MODEL TEST 3

GO ON TO THE NEXT PAGE

MODEL TEST 3 877

15. According to the chart, the years 1684–1700 were characterized by

    (A) a significant easing in relations between the Iroquois and the French.
    (B) roughly neutral relationships between the Iroquois and both the French and the English.
    (C) intermittent warlike raids by the Iroquois against the French.
    (D) a lessening of hostility toward the English by the French.

16. It can be inferred from the passage that the author's attitude toward the Iroquois leadership can best be described as one of

    (A) suspicion of their motives.
    (B) respect for their competence.
    (C) indifference to their fate.
    (D) pride in their heritage.

17. Which choice provides the best evidence for the answer to the previous question?

    (A) Lines 17–21 ("As the imperial . . . policy")
    (B) Lines 25–29 ("The history . . . century")
    (C) Lines 46–50 ("A counterraid . . . allies")
    (D) Lines 57–63 ("Under . . . concessions")

18. The author attributes such success as the Iroquois policy of aggressive neutrality had to

    (A) the readiness of the Iroquois to fight either side.
    (B) the Iroquois' ties of loyalty to the British.
    (C) French physical presence in the borderlands.
    (D) European reliance on formal treaties.

19. Which choice provides the best evidence for the answer to the previous question?

    (A) Lines 10–17 ("Throughout . . . war")
    (B) Lines 30–36 ("The stability . . . France")
    (C) Lines 64–70 ("By holding . . . effectiveness")
    (D) Lines 71–77 ("The system . . . Iroquois")

20. As used in line 73, "compromising" most nearly means

    (A) embarrassing.
    (B) jeopardizing.
    (C) accepting lower standards.
    (D) striking a balance.

21. The final three paragraphs of the passage provide

    (A) an instance of a state of relationships described earlier.
    (B) a modification of a thesis presented earlier.
    (C) a refutation of an argument made earlier.
    (D) a summary of the situation referred to earlier.

GO ON TO THE NEXT PAGE

Questions 22–31 are based on the following passage.

The following passage on the formation of oil is excerpted from Athabasca, *a novel about oil exploration written by Alistair MacLean.*

Five main weather elements act upon rock. Frost and ice fracture rock. It can be gradually eroded by airborne dust. The action
Line of the seas, whether through the constant
(5) movement of tides or the pounding of heavy storm waves, remorselessly wears away the coastlines. Rivers are immensely powerful destructive agencies—one has but to look at the Grand Canyon to appreciate their
(10) enormous power. And such rocks as escape all these influences are worn away over the eons by the effect of rain.

Whatever the cause of erosion, the net result is the same. The rock is reduced to its
(15) tiniest possible constituents—rock particles or, simply, dust. Rain and melting snow carry this dust down to the tiniest rivulets and the mightiest rivers, which, in turn, transport it to lakes, inland seas and the
(20) coastal regions of the oceans. Dust, however fine and powdery, is still heavier than water, and whenever the water becomes sufficiently still, it will gradually sink to the bottom, not only in lakes and seas but also in the sluggish
(25) lower reaches of rivers and where flood conditions exist, in the form of silt.

And so, over unimaginably long reaches of time, whole mountain ranges are carried down to the seas, and in the process, through
(30) the effects of gravity, new rock is born as layer after layer of dust accumulates on the bottom, building up to a depth of ten, a hundred, perhaps even a thousand feet, the lowermost layers being gradually compacted
(35) by the immense and steadily increasing

pressures from above, until the particles fuse together and reform as a new rock.

It is in the intermediate and final processes of the new rock formation that
(40) oil comes into being. Those lakes and seas of hundreds of millions of years ago were almost choked by water plants and the most primitive forms of aquatic life. On dying, they sank to the bottom of the lakes and
(45) seas along with the settling dust particles and were gradually buried deep under the endless layers of more dust and more aquatic and plant life that slowly accumulated above them. The passing of millions of years and
(50) the steadily increasing pressures from above gradually changed the decayed vegetation and dead aquatic life into oil.

Described this simply and quickly, the process sounds reasonable enough. But
(55) this is where the gray and disputatious area arises. The conditions necessary for the formation of oil are known; the cause of the metamorphosis is not. It seems probable that some form of chemical catalyst is involved,
(60) but this catalyst has not been isolated. The first purely synthetic oil, as distinct from secondary synthetic oils such as those derived from coal, has yet to be produced. We just have to accept that oil is oil, that
(65) it is there, bound up in rock strata in fairly well-defined areas throughout the world but always on the sites of ancient seas and lakes, some of which are now continental land, some buried deep under the encroachment
(70) of new oceans.

GO ON TO THE NEXT PAGE

22. The passage is written from the perspective of someone who is

(A) actively engaged in conducting petrochemical research.
(B) an advocate for the production of purely synthetic oil.
(C) a prospector involved in the search for underwater oil deposits.
(D) knowledgeable about oil deposits and the oil-mining industry.

23. As used in line 1, "act" most nearly means

(A) behave.
(B) make a decision.
(C) have a particular effect.
(D) counterfeit.

24. The author uses the Grand Canyon (line 9) as an example of

(A) the urgent need for dams.
(B) the devastating impact of rivers.
(C) the magnificence of nature.
(D) a site where oil may be found.

25. According to the author, our understanding of the process by which oil is created is

(A) adequate.
(B) systematic.
(C) erroneous.
(D) deficient.

26. Which choice provides the best evidence for the answer to the previous question?

(A) Lines 38–40 ("It is . . . being")
(B) Lines 43–49 ("On dying . . . them")
(C) Lines 56–58 ("The conditions . . . not")
(D) Lines 60–63 ("The first . . . produced")

27. It can most reasonably be inferred that prospectors should search for oil deposits

(A) wherever former seas existed.
(B) in mountain streambeds.
(C) where coal deposits are found.
(D) in new rock formations.

28. The author does all of the following EXCEPT

(A) describe a process.
(B) state a possibility.
(C) mention a limitation.
(D) propose a solution.

29. As used in line 56, "conditions" most nearly means

(A) surroundings.
(B) prerequisites.
(C) medical problems.
(D) social positions.

GO ON TO THE NEXT PAGE

30. The author indicates that the cause of the metamorphosis of decayed vegetation and dead aquatic life into oil should be considered

    (A) an historical anomaly.
    (B) an unexplained phenomenon.
    (C) a scientific curiosity.
    (D) a working hypothesis.

31. Which choice provides the best evidence for the answer to the previous question?

    (A) Lines 38–40 ("It is in . . . being")
    (B) Lines 49–52 ("The passing . . . oil")
    (C) Lines 56–60 ("The conditions . . . isolated")
    (D) Lines 60–63 ("The first . . . produced")

Questions 32–41 are based on the following passage.

The following passage is taken from Up from Slavery, *the autobiography of Booker T. Washington.*

Finally the war closed, and the day of freedom came. It was a momentous and eventful day to all upon our plantation. We
Line had been expecting it. Freedom was in the
(5) air, and had been for months. . . . As the great day drew nearer, there was more singing in the slave quarters than usual. It was bolder, had more ring, and lasted later into the night. Most of the verses of the plantation
(10) songs had some reference to freedom. True, they had sung those same verses before, but they had been careful to explain that the "freedom" in these songs referred to the next world, and had no connection with life in
(15) this world. Now they gradually threw off the mask, and were not afraid to let it be known that the "freedom" in their songs meant freedom of the body in this world.

The night before the eventful day, word
(20) was sent to the slave quarters to the effect that something unusual was going to take place at the "big house" the next morning. There was little, if any, sleep that night. All was excitement and expectancy. Early the
(25) next morning word was sent to all the slaves, old and young, to gather at the house. In company with my mother, brother, and sister, and a large number of other slaves, I went to the master's house. All of our master's family
(30) were either standing or seated on the veranda of the house, where they could see what was to take place and hear what was said. There was a feeling of deep interest, or perhaps sadness, on their faces, but not bitterness. As
(35) I now recall the impression they made upon me, they did not at the moment seem to be

GO ON TO THE NEXT PAGE

sad because of the loss of property, but rather because of parting with those whom they had reared and who were in many ways very
(40) close to them. The most distinct thing that I now recall in connection with the scene was that some man who seemed to be a stranger (a United States officer, I presume) made a little speech and then read a rather long
(45) paper—the Emancipation Proclamation, I think. After the reading we were told that we were all free, and could go when and where we pleased. My mother, who was standing by my side, leaned over and kissed her children,
(50) while tears of joy ran down her cheeks. She explained to us what it all meant, that this was the day for which she had been so long praying, but fearing that she would never live to see.

(55)   For some minutes there was great rejoicing, and thanksgiving, and wild scenes of ecstasy. But there was no feeling of bitterness. In fact, there was pity among the slaves for our former owners. The wild
(60) rejoicing on the part of the emancipated colored people lasted but for a brief period, for I noticed that by the time they returned to their cabins there was a change in their feelings. The great responsibility of being
(65) free, of having charge of themselves, of having to think and plan for themselves and their children, seemed to take possession of them. It was very much like suddenly turning a youth of ten or twelve years out
(70) into the world to provide for himself. In a few hours the great questions with which the Anglo-Saxon race had been grappling for centuries had been thrown upon these people to be solved. These were the
(75) questions of a home, a living, the rearing of children, education, citizenship, and the establishment and support of churches. Was

it any wonder that within a few hours the wild rejoicing ceased and a feeling of deep
(80) gloom seemed to pervade the slave quarters? To some it seemed that, now that they were in actual possession of it, freedom was a more serious thing than they had expected to find it. Some of the slaves were seventy or
(85) eighty years old; their best days were gone. They had no strength with which to earn a living in a strange place and among strange people, even if they had been sure where to find a new place of abode. To this class the
(90) problem seemed especially hard. Besides, deep down in their hearts there was a strange and peculiar attachment to "old Marster" and "old Missus," and to their children, which they found it hard to think of breaking off.
(95) With these they had spent in some cases nearly a half-century, and it was no light thing to think of parting. Gradually, one by one, stealthily at first, the older slaves began to wander from the slave quarters back to the
(100) "big house" to have a whispered conversation with their former owners as to the future.

GO ON TO THE NEXT PAGE

32. As used in line 1, "closed" most nearly means

    (A) shut.
    (B) ended.
    (C) grew nearer.
    (D) blocked off.

33. Which choice best summarizes the first two paragraphs of the passage (lines 1–54)?

    (A) Even though a young man has been brought up in slavery, he finds comfort in singing.
    (B) A loving parent attempts to help her children understand the importance of freedom.
    (C) A man recollects an historic moment that changed his life and the lives of everyone he knew.
    (D) The end of the Civil War failed to disrupt the customary routines of plantation life.

34. Which choice provides the best evidence for the answer to the previous question?

    (A) Lines 5–9 ("As the great . . . night")
    (B) Lines 19–22 ("The night before . . . morning")
    (C) Lines 34–48 ("As I now . . . pleased")
    (D) Lines 48–54 ("My mother . . . see")

35. It can most reasonably be inferred from the passage that the mask that the slaves gradually threw off was

    (A) a disguise that they wore in order to conceal their true identity.
    (B) the pretense that the freedom they sang about was purely spiritual.
    (C) an elaborate façade that allowed them to perform at public gatherings.
    (D) a grotesque false face typically worn at a carnival or masquerade.

36. Which choice provides the best evidence for the answer to the previous passage?

    (A) Lines 1–3 ("Finally . . . plantation")
    (B) Lines 5–7 ("As . . . usual")
    (C) Lines 9–10 ("Most . . . freedom")
    (D) Lines 15–18 ("Now . . . world")

37. The "charge" to which the author refers (line 65) can best be characterized as

    (A) a formal accusation.
    (B) a headlong rush forward.
    (C) the price asked for goods or services.
    (D) the duty of being responsible for oneself.

38. As used in line 96, "light" most nearly means

    (A) indistinct.
    (B) pale.
    (C) trivial.
    (D) agile.

39. Throughout the passage the narrator most emphasizes which aspect of the experience?

    (A) The orderliness of the freed slaves' reception of the news.
    (B) The absence of any ill will expressed by either the slaves or their masters.
    (C) The presence of a white stranger on the veranda of the big house.
    (D) The lack of appropriate preparation for events of such great significance.

GO ON TO THE NEXT PAGE

40. During the course of the final paragraph, the focus of the narrator's recollection shifts from

(A) a scene of momentary jubilation to sobering reflection on problems to be faced.

(B) generalizations about newfound freedom to the specifics of his personal situation.

(C) the identification of a change of mood to consideration of current possibilities.

(D) evaluation of factors making the slaves unhappy to recognition of solutions.

41. The final paragraph indicates that the older slaves' stealthy visit to the big house was mainly inspired by their

(A) bitterness at the sudden changes in their lives.

(B) impatience with the noisy rejoicing of the younger slaves.

(C) reluctance to remain in the slave quarters any longer.

(D) apprehensions about their uncertain future.

Questions 42–52 are based on the following passages.

The following two passages explore recent research on the effects of food intake on animal metabolisms.

PASSAGE 1

Fruit flies' brains may be wired to count calories.

Several genes in the brain appear to
Line help the flies learn to distinguish between
(5) normal-calorie and high-calorie foods—and to remember to choose the healthier option later. Feeding the flies a constant diet of high-calorie foods disrupts their ability to make these metabolic memories, researchers
(10) report April 7 in *Nature Communications*.

Preliminary studies suggest that mice make similar metabolic memories, the researchers say. Taken together, the results hint that human brains may also be wired
(15) to do the same thing, which could have implications for weight control and health. But constant exposure to high-calorie foods may have damaged humans' abilities to make metabolic memories, says study
(20) coauthor Dongsheng Cai. Being able to rebuild humans' metabolic memory could help control diseases such as obesity and diabetes, he says.

Cai and his colleagues gave fruit flies
(25) (*Drosophila melanogaster*) a choice between yeast mixed with a moderate amount of a sugar called sorbitol and yeast mixed with an extra amount of this sugar. Flies spent a day in a vial with the moderately sugary yeast and
(30) then a day in a vial with extra-sugary (and therefore higher-calorie) yeast. After cycling through the vials several times, the flies started to eat more of the moderately sugary yeast. The food choices tasted the same, but

GO ON TO THE NEXT PAGE

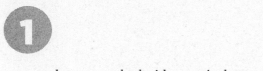

(35) each was matched with a particular smell. Flies put in a container with only the smells that matched the two food options (but no food) preferred the smell associated with the moderate-calorie yeast.

(40) When the flies spent consecutive days in vials with the more sugary yeast, however, they lost their ability to distinguish between the moderate-calorie and high-calorie options. This observation suggests that

(45) access to high-calorie food may damage the flies' ability to make metabolic memories, the researchers say. These flies also had higher levels of sugar and fat accumulated in their bodies, conditions that predispose mammals

(50) to diabetes.

["Brains may be wired to count calories, make healthy choices," by Ashley Yeager, *Science News* blog, 11:00AM, APRIL 7, 2015]

PASSAGE 2

When you eat may determine how long and strongly your heart beats.

Fruit flies that limited eating to 12-hour stints had steadier heartbeats in old age

(55) than flies that ate whenever they wanted, researchers report in the March 13 *Science*. The study adds to a growing body of evidence that the timing of meals may be as important for health as diet composition and calorie

(60) counts are.

The research also "suggests that the body clock is involved in cardiovascular function and risk," says Frank Scheer, a neuroscientist and physiologist at Harvard Medical School.

(65) Scheer was not involved in the fruit fly study, but has shown that disrupting people's daily, or circadian, rhythms can damage their health.

Circadian clocks work in nearly every

(70) cell in the body. They govern a wide variety of body rhythms, such as those associated with body temperature, blood pressure, and sleep. The main timekeeper is located in the brain and is set by light, but other clocks

(75) synchronize themselves according to feeding time.

Previous research in mice had suggested that limiting eating to 12 hours per day could protect rodents from obesity and

(80) other ravages of high-fat diets. Those studies couldn't address heart problems associated with poor diet because mice don't get heart disease the way people do, says Satchidananda Panda, a circadian biologist at

(85) the Salk Institute for Biological Studies.

Fruit flies, on the other hand, develop irregular heartbeats and other heart problems as they age. So Panda set out to test whether limiting the amount of time fruit

(90) flies eat, but not cutting back on calories, could affect the insects' heart health.

One group of flies ate a cornmeal diet around the clock; another group had access to the same food for only 12 hours each day.

(95) Both groups ate about the same amount overall, but the 24-hour group snacked at night.

The groups had similar amounts of activity. The flies with time-restricted feeding

(100) did most of their moving during the day, though, and slept better at night.

At 3 weeks old, flies in both groups had regular, healthy hearts. At 5 weeks—fruit fly middle age—the 12-hour eaters' hearts

(105) maintained a steady rhythm of roughly one beat per second. The hearts of the anytime eaters beat irregularly, sometimes skipping a beat and sometimes quivering. By 7 weeks, the anytimers had badly deteriorated heart

(110) function. Flies on a 12-hour schedule also

GO ON TO THE NEXT PAGE

MODEL TEST 3

Heart function in fruit flies

━━ Flies with unrestricted eating time   ━━ Flies with restricted eating time

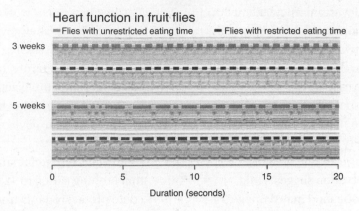

3 weeks

5 weeks

0   5   10   15   20
Duration (seconds)

KEEPING TIME
Fruit flies that eat just 12 hours per day (blue lines) maintain steady heartbeats into
middle age (5 weeks old), whereas the hearts of fruit flies that can eat around the clock
(red) beat irregularly. Each gray or black dash represents the contraction of the heart.

lost a few beats over time, but their heart
problems were not as severe.

Switching anytime flies to a 12-hour
schedule at 5 weeks old improved some
(115) measures of heart function, but not all. In
other experiments, restricting feeding time
also staved off some of the negative heart
effects of high-fat diets.

Improved sleep in the 12-hour eaters
(120) might account for some of the heart benefits,
Scheer says. Lack of sleep is linked to a
variety of diseases in people, including heart
disease. No one knows whether restricting
mealtimes will improve human health, he
(125) says.

[From "For healthy eating, timing matters,"
by Tina Hesman Saey, *Science News*, Vol. 187,
#7, April 4, 2015.]

42. The main purpose of Passage 1 is to

(A) present a recent study with possible
implications for humans.

(B) provide new evidence to support the use
of fruit flies in scientific experiments.

(C) analyze the importance of following a
low-calorie diet.

(D) note a common misconception about
the nature of memory.

43. As used in line 14, "wired" most nearly means

(A) equipped.

(B) tense.

(C) stregthened.

(D) tied.

44. It can most reasonably be inferred from
Passage 1 that metabolic memories

(A) encourage the absorption of sorbitol and
yeast by both mice and fruit flies.

(B) are involved in the process of food
selection.

(C) last longer than other forms of memory
found in laboratory animals.

(D) are solely dependent on the sense of
smell.

GO ON TO THE NEXT PAGE

45. Which choice provides the best evidence for the answer to the previous question?

(A) Lines 3–7 ("Several . . . later")
(B) Lines 11–13 ("Preliminary . . . say")
(C) Lines 17–20 ("But . . . Cai")
(D) Lines 36–39 ("Flies . . . yeast")

46. The author of Passage 2 cites Scheer as

(A) a reporter involved in an ongoing investigation of the eating patterns of fruit flies.
(B) a researcher unconnected with the study being discussed but possessing relevant expertise.
(C) an advocate for heart-healthy, low-fat diets for adults.
(D) an expert on the cardiovascular effects of restricting feeding time.

47. It can most reasonably be inferred from Passage 2 that fruit flies are preferable to mice as subjects for cardiovascular research because

(A) mice seldom suffer any ill effects from eating high-fat diets.
(B) fruit flies, unlike mice, contract cardiac problems as they age.
(C) fruit flies are more prone to obesity than mice are.
(D) fruit flies breed rapidly and therefore are readily available as cardiac research subjects.

48. Which choice provides the best evidence for the answer to the previous question?

(A) Lines 53–56 ("Fruit flies . . . *Science*")
(B) Lines 77–80 ("Previous research . . . diets")
(C) Lines 80–88 ("Those studies . . . age")
(D) Lines 88–91 ("So Panda . . . heart health")

49. As used in line 81, "address" most nearly means

(A) speak to.
(B) protest.
(C) deal with.
(D) call.

50. Which statement about the effect of restricted eating times on fruit flies is best supported by the chart?

(A) Fruit flies whose eating time was restricted to 12 hours per day developed irregular heartbeats at the age of 3 weeks.
(B) Fruit flies limited to eating just 12 hours per day for the most part maintained a one heartbeat per second rhythm into middle age.
(C) The hearts of the fruit flies with restricted eating time frequently skipped a beat or quivered.
(D) Fruit flies with time-restricted feeding slept better at night than their counterparts in the anytime feeding group did.

GO ON TO THE NEXT PAGE

MODEL TEST 3

51. One difference between the experiments described in the two passages is that, unlike the researchers discussed in Passage 1, Panda and his colleagues

   (A) fed one group of fruit flies a more highly calorific diet than they fed the other.
   (B) regulated the amount of time groups of fruit flies had for eating.
   (C) restricted the amount of calories the fruit flies were allowed to consume.
   (D) failed to develop high levels of sugar and fat in their test subjects.

52. The fruit flies given extra sugary yeast in Passage 1 and those following the 24-hour eating schedule in Passage 2 shared which trait?

   (A) They gradually adapted to a high-calorie diet.
   (B) They became unable to remember which food option to select.
   (C) They increasingly grew physically inactive and began to develop sleep problems at night.
   (D) They suffered more severe health problems than fruit flies in their control groups did.

If there is still time remaining, you may review your answers.

WRITING AND LANGUAGE TEST

35 MINUTES, 44 QUESTIONS

Turn to Section 2 of your answer sheet to answer the questions in this section.

> **Directions:** Questions follow each of the passages below. Some questions ask you how the passage might be changed to improve the expression of ideas. Other questions ask you how the passage might be altered to correct errors in grammar, usage, and punctuation. One or more graphics accompany some passages. You will be required to consider these graphics as you answer questions about editing the passage.
>
> There are three types of questions. In the first type, a part of the passage is underlined. The second type is based on a certain part of the passage. The third type is based on the entire passage.
>
> Read each passage. Then, choose the answer to each question that changes the passage so that it is consistent with the conventions of standard written English. One of the answer choices for many questions is "NO CHANGE." Choosing this answer means that you believe the best answer is to make no change in the passage.

Questions 1–11 are based on the following passage.

The Giants of Theater

The great dramatists of the 20th century—Arthur Miller, Tennessee Williams, John Osborne, and Harold Pinter—still owe an enormous creative debt to their 19th-century ❶ forebears, most particularly to the two Scandinavian playwrights Henrik Ibsen and August Strindberg. The hallmarks of modern theater in their present incarnation—from stark realism to surreal expressionism— ❷ from the two mens' works directly derive.

1. (A) NO CHANGE
    (B) elders
    (C) seniors
    (D) historians

2. (A) NO CHANGE
    (B) from the works of these two men directly derive.
    (C) derive directly from the works of these two men.
    (D) come directly from this.

GO ON TO THE NEXT PAGE

Strindberg and Ibsen were themselves not just rivals ❸ but grave enemies. Famously, Strindberg mocked and attacked Ibsen's most successful and enduring play, "A Doll's House," in a short story of the same title and claimed that his ongoing hostilities with Ibsen had cost him his "wife, children, fortune, and career." Ibsen, meanwhile, somewhat more ❹ soberly—though no less venomously—kept a portrait of Strindberg in his study where he worked, naming it "Madness Incipient." He once remarked, "I can't write a line without that madman staring down at me with those crazy eyes."

Strindberg and Ibsen found ways to clash with one another on nearly every issue of their time—politics, society, science, religion, women's rights— ❺ by focusing on how these current events had global implications. But at the core of their rivalry lay something more elemental than mere differences of opinion and competitive antagonism; the characters that populate each writer's ❻ respectedly works are fundamentally

3. Which choice best expresses that the intellectual relationship between Strindberg and Ibsen went far beyond an ordinary rivalry?

(A) NO CHANGE
(B) while being peaceful advocates.
(C) but impassioned artistic adversaries.
(D) and fiercely competitive belligerents.

4. (A) NO CHANGE
(B) soberly; though no less venomously kept
(C) soberly though no less—venomously kept
(D) soberly: though no less venomously, kept

5. The writer would like to express that Strindberg and Ibsen shared their ideas on contemporary issues in both direct and indirect ways. Which choice best conveys this?

(A) NO CHANGE
(B) all of which found either subtle or overt expression in their plays.
(C) through a willingness to both compromise and stick to their guns, depending on the situation.
(D) some of which called for metaphor, some which called for simile.

6. (A) NO CHANGE
(B) respectable
(C) respectful
(D) respective

GO ON TO THE NEXT PAGE

distinct in the way they relate to the world around them. Michael Meyer **7** , a Hollywood screenwriter for many prominent films, once compared the two, writing, "Ibsen's characters think and speak logically and consecutively . . . Strindberg's dart backwards and forwards. They do not think, or speak, ABCDE but AQBZC." These two men—writing in the same genre at the same point in history, and emerging from both the same level of society and corner of the world— **8** nonetheless developed remarkably antithetical worldviews, each powerful enough not only to weather the criticism of the opposition but to develop and grow in spite of it.

Although in life the two considered themselves plenary **9** opposites as drama continues to evolve into the postmodern era, we may begin to realize that the worlds envisioned by Strindberg and Ibsen were perhaps not so different as they believed. Described by playwright Bernard Shaw as **10** "the giants of the theatre of our time," their lingering influences have coexisted and even comingled in drama for more than a century now. The staggering plurality of postmodern theater itself we must attribute, at least in part, to the initial fracturing of the modern drama in its **11** outset state, when refusing to yield to prevailing winds, Strindberg and Ibsen produced a cyclone.

7. The writer wants to insert a brief statement at this point that speaks about Meyer's qualifications to have a worthwhile opinion on this topic. Which, if true, best accomplishes this goal?

(A) NO CHANGE
(B) , a noted scholar on ancient Scandinavian history,
(C) , a contemporary Scandinavian poet,
(D) , translator and biographer of both playwrights,

8. (A) NO CHANGE
(B) consequently
(C) also
(D) divergently

9. (A) NO CHANGE
(B) opposites as drama continues, to evolve into the postmodern era we may
(C) opposites, as drama continues to evolve into the postmodern era, we may
(D) opposites as drama continues to evolve into the postmodern era we may

10. (A) NO CHANGE
(B) the giants of the theatre of our time,
(C) the giants' of the theatre of our time,
(D) 'the giants of the theatre of our time,'

11. (A) NO CHANGE
(B) germinating
(C) floral
(D) germinal

GO ON TO THE NEXT PAGE

Questions 12–22 are based on the following passage.

Gravity, It's Everywhere

His is a household name, and he is most often thought of as a man unearthing the world's most **⑫** <u>imminent</u> mysteries while napping under an apple tree. He is Sir Isaac Newton, an English physicist and mathematician responsible for the law of universal gravitation. More than 300 years ago, the idea was quite **⑬** <u>revolutionary: two objects, regardless of their mass, exert</u> gravitational force toward one another with a force proportional to the product of the two masses and inversely proportional to the square of the distance between them. Newton's equation explained why that apple fell onto his head, **⑭** <u>why on the ground one firmly stays,</u> and how Earth orbits the sun. It also allowed NASA scientists to send a man to the moon many years later. Newton's discovery of gravity wasn't nearly as impressive as his revelation that gravity was universal.

Using Kepler's laws of planetary motion, Newton attempted **⑮** <u>to cast aside all previous scientific discoveries,</u> supposing that planets could move around the Sun because of a force acting between the bodies. The apple, he reasoned, fell **⑯** <u>and</u> it was attracted to Earth, and even if it was much higher in the tree, it would still fall toward Earth. So why didn't the moon fall and crash into Earth? Newton attested that the moon is, **⑰** <u>in fact,</u> in a constant freefall to Earth but is caught in a gravitational field, and Earth's

12. (A) NO CHANGE
    (B) eminent
    (C) complimentary
    (D) complementary

13. (A) NO CHANGE
    (B) revolutionary, two objects regardless of their mass, exert
    (C) revolutionary—two objects regardless of their mass, exert
    (D) revolutionary; two objects, regardless of their mass exert

14. (A) NO CHANGE
    (B) on the ground one firmly stays,
    (C) why one stays firmly on the ground,
    (D) one stays firmly on the ground,

15. Which choice best expresses Newton's scientific journey based on the context of the passage?

    (A) NO CHANGE
    (B) to fill in the blanks,
    (C) to gather more observational data,
    (D) to explore the solar system,

16. (A) NO CHANGE
    (B) because
    (C) but
    (D) from

17. (A) NO CHANGE
    (B) as a matter of fact,
    (C) (can you believe it?),
    (D) based on his accurate theoretical contemplations,

GO ON TO THE NEXT PAGE

movement allows the moon to orbit it without ever hitting the surface. The equation, though simple, accounts for the position of all planets and moons and is partly responsible for ⓲ the paths of astronauts and the successful orbits of satellites.

It wasn't until 1915 that Albert Einstein expanded on Newton's work to impart his theory of general relativity, which states that the gravity of any mass curves the space and time around it. Einstein's theory of relativity is superior to ⓳ Newton because it takes into account special relativity and can be used when great precision is necessary. By creating a metric theory of gravitation, Einstein showed that phenomena in classical mechanics correspond to inertial motion within a curved geometry of space-time. This scientific discovery laid the groundwork in both astrophysics and cosmology for years to come. Not only did the theory help to explain an irregularity in Mercury's orbit, but ⓴ the bending of starlight was also demonstrated by it and set the theoretical foundations for black holes.

㉑ So, when extreme precision isn't a requirement, Newton's law of universal gravitation is still widely used to approximate the effects of gravitation—say, for instance, in physics class. ㉒ While Newton's theory was preeminent for a time, that time is long since gone.

18. The writer wishes to express that Newton's theory can explain the behavior of human-influenced space activities. Which choice best accomplishes this goal?

(A) NO CHANGE
(B) the movements of both comets and asteroids.
(C) the rising of the tides and the occurrence of earthquakes.
(D) Einstein's eventual development of a revolutionary paradigm.

19. (A) NO CHANGE
(B) it
(C) these
(D) Newton's law of universal gravitation

20. (A) NO CHANGE
(B) starlight used it to bend the demonstration
(C) it also demonstrated how starlight bends
(D) demonstrating the starlight

21. (A) NO CHANGE
(B) Additionally,
(C) For this very reason,
(D) Yet,

22. The writer wants to conclude the essay with a sentence that speaks to the lasting relevance of Newtonian theory. Which choice best accomplishes the writer's aim?

(A) NO CHANGE
(B) It's hard to believe that science from the year 1687 is still applicable today.
(C) It is impressive that Newtonian theory could account for irregularities in Mercury's orbit.
(D) Students in today's classrooms still recognize Newton as a brilliant mind.

GO ON TO THE NEXT PAGE

MODEL TEST 3

Questions 23–33 are based on the following passage and supplementary material.

Do the Numbers Lie?

The question of college rankings **㉓** underline continue to be a major player at every level of the university. From the student flipping through college guides, to academics searching for job offerings, to department administrators figuring their next year's budget, the number next to the university can decide quite a bit. The ranking is supposed to be an indicator of the **㉔** institute's performance: its ability to produce excellence. So it makes sense, particularly with the rising tuition costs, that prospective students should weigh the value of their money against the reputation of the education they will receive. **㉕** Furthermore, faculty must consider, like all job seekers, the security of their employment and the

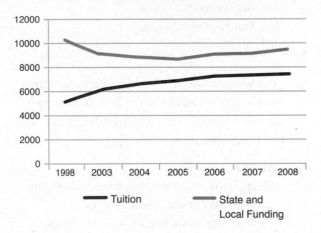

Average Revenues Per Student at Public Universities

Legend: ▬▬ Tuition   ▬▬ State and Local Funding

---

23. (A) NO CHANGE
    (B) continues
    (C) is continue
    (D) are continuing

24. (A) NO CHANGE
    (B) institutes performance—its
    (C) institutes performance; it's
    (D) institute's performance, its'

25. The writer wants to insert a sentence at this point that further develops the argument in the paragraph and incorporates information from the graph. Which choice best accomplishes this goal?

    (A) This trend is diluted by nearly a 20 percent overall drop in state and local governmental support for public universities between 1998 and 2008, making college students bear ever less of the tuition burden.
    (B) This trend is encouraged by nearly a 10 percent overall increase in state and local governmental support for public universities between 1998 and 2008, making college students bear a moderate amount of the tuition burden.
    (C) This trend is exacerbated by nearly a 10 percent overall drop in state and local governmental support for public universities between 1998 and 2008, making college students bear ever more of the tuition burden.
    (D) This trend is worsened by nearly a 30 percent overall drop in state and local governmental support for public universities between 1998 and 2008, making college students bear far too much of the tuition burden.

GO ON TO THE NEXT PAGE

opportunities for career advancement. And more often than not, a university's funding and resources are directly affected by how it measures up in the vast world of rankings. ㉖ Rankings often comprise a variety of important educational factors.

The needs and goals of high school students are far too nuanced to decide on a university by a single number. Could a particular student searching for the best fit for the next four to five years of ㉗ their life ever find all the answers in a college ranking report? While one student may be looking for small class sizes, another may be looking for job placement, while ㉘ in another is in search of a strong study abroad program. When taking into account all the aspects of a successful college experience, the ranking system is oversimplified and ineffective. What works for one may not work for another. Moreover, ranking reports do little to show whether universities are doing a good job at actually educating.

㉙ To counter ranking systems and create a more meaningful college experience, many universities are adopting undergraduate initiatives that incorporate internships, research experiences, study abroad programs, and community outreach

26. Which choice provides the best transition between the current paragraph and the following paragraph?

(A) NO CHANGE
(B) Universities are in dire need of alternative sources of income.
(C) Applicants often consider college rankings, but those numbers provide insufficient information on which to base a choice.
(D) High schools today have become real pressure cookers.

27. (A) NO CHANGE
(B) your
(C) they're
(D) his or her

28. (A) NO CHANGE
(B) from
(C) one
(D) still

29. Which choice provides the most relevant introduction to this paragraph?

(A) NO CHANGE
(B) In order to satisfy federal demands for greater governmental oversight,
(C) So they may attract students from underrepresented demographic groups,
(D) To provide more opportunities for students to acquire financial assistance,

opportunities. The idea is simple: the best undergraduate experience is one that is engaging, challenging, and lifelong. **30** In such programs these experiences just like required classes, are essential to the degree which encourages collaboration between faculty and students, as well as commitment to the community. Often, students are introduced to their university's **31** alumni who have graduated from the school who share their interests and exposed to careers in their field of study. This university approach can be attractive to the student who is looking for more than a number on a page.

The decision of which college to attend is one of the biggest a person will make. While it is important to keep up with which universities are leading the world's research and hiring the most notable experts, it is more important to consider which university will **32** best foster your growth and personal development. College rankings that encourage differentiation between better and worse universities **33** leaves a lot on the table.

30. (A) NO CHANGE
    (B) In such programs, these experiences just like required classes are essential to the degree, which
    (C) In such programs these experiences just, like required classes, are essential to the degree which
    (D) In such programs, these experiences, just like required classes, are essential to the degree, which

31. (A) NO CHANGE
    (B) alumni who are graduates of the educational institution in question
    (C) alumnuses who are proud to have both matriculated and successfully graduated from the school
    (D) alumni

32. (A) NO CHANGE
    (B) well
    (C) better
    (D) good

33. (A) NO CHANGE
    (B) leafs
    (C) lives
    (D) leave

GO ON TO THE NEXT PAGE

Questions 34–44 are based on the following passage and supplementary material.

Draw Your Home

In the third grade, **34** my teacher Mrs. Wabash, asked the class to spend ten minutes sketching our home, specifically the exterior of our house as it appeared to passersby. This prelude was part of a larger exercise that I **35** have long since forgotten. What I remember most was sitting in my desk completely dumbfounded for the majority of that interval, wondering how on earth I had forgotten the space where I spent the majority of my eight years. Surely, I could recall most of my bedroom; I knew my house was blue; of course, there were many windows and a big porch. **36** Consequently what did the door look like? Were there three or four steps leading to it? **37** How could he know this was even a real door? To these questions and many more, I had no answer.

That afternoon, I walked home from the bus stop, sat on my lawn, and meticulously copied what I saw **38** in paper, memorizing every detail. Wounded at my previous inattention, I began studying every structure that I **39** personally visited myself. The obsession resulting from Mrs. Wabash's experiment did not fade with time. By high school, my journal of sketched structures transformed from ones I had seen to ones I had thought up independently. I became transfixed with several iconic **40** buildings: the Guggenheim, Getty Center, Reichstag, Smithsonian, among others. When it came time to fill out college applications, I didn't blink before selecting "Architecture" as my intended major.

34. (A) NO CHANGE
    (B) my teacher, Mrs. Wabash; asked
    (C) my teacher—Mrs. Wabash, asked
    (D) my teacher, Mrs. Wabash, asked

35. (A) NO CHANGE
    (B) had since long forgot.
    (C) has long since forgotten.
    (D) forgot since long.

36. (A) NO CHANGE
    (B) And
    (C) For
    (D) But

37. Which choice logically maintains the flow and focus established by the preceding sentences?

    (A) NO CHANGE
    (B) Was the roof pointed or squared?
    (C) Why should I study architecture?
    (D) I remembered what my neighbor's house looked like.

38. (A) NO CHANGE
    (B) into paper,
    (C) onto paper,
    (D) within paper,

39. (A) NO CHANGE
    (B) witnessed with my own two eyes.
    (C) entered.
    (D) foresaw.

40. (A) NO CHANGE
    (B) buildings; the Guggenheim, Getty Center,
    (C) buildings—the Guggenheim Getty Center
    (D) buildings. The Guggenheim, Getter Center,

The word meant little to me at the time: just that I could eventually be paid to do what I had been doing ineptly for years. An architect is one who plans, designs, and oversees the construction of ㊶ buildings homes and other structures. I researched the course requirements at three universities I was considering and found, to my amazement, a quote from a professor of architectural engineering in one of the programs; he said, "The study of architecture is one grounded in the sciences, but inspired by the arts." I was hooked.

Since then, I have found my work as a professional architect to be ㊷ undoubtedly rewarding and mercilessly demanding. Architects are rarely afforded a regular workweek. Instead, we spend hours upon hours preparing and re-preparing scale drawings, looking into environmental and safety regulations, and meeting with clients. From contracts to design to construction, the architect is there, ㊸ there job never done. It is indeed an occupation that encompasses nearly every field of work—engineering, mathematics, marketing, administration, customer service, law, and public safety are all needed in successful architecture. ㊹ Sometimes I ponder whether all of the time I spend on my architectural projects is truly worth the effort.

41. (A) NO CHANGE
    (B) buildings, homes, and other structures.
    (C) buildings homes, and other structures.
    (D) buildings, homes, and other, structures.

42. If the author wishes to express both the positive and negative nature of architecture, which of the following choices best accomplishes her goal?

    (A) NO CHANGE
    (B) fearsomely boring and drearily trivial.
    (C) moderately enjoyable and somewhat interesting.
    (D) terribly impersonal and pleasantly dispassionate.

43. (A) NO CHANGE
    (B) their job
    (C) our job
    (D) his or her job

44. Which choice most effectively concludes the essay by tying it to the introductory paragraph?

    (A) NO CHANGE
    (B) I look forward to one day fulfilling my dream of becoming an actual architect rather than a starry-eyed student.
    (C) Yet when a job is finished, truly finished, and I look up at it, I thank Mrs. Wabash.
    (D) My dream ever since the third grade of studying architecture was about to become a reality.

STOP

If there is still time remaining, you may review your answers.

MATH TEST (NO CALCULATOR)

25 MINUTES, 20 QUESTIONS

Turn to Section 3 of your answer sheet to answer the questions in this section.

Directions: For questions 1–15, solve each problem and choose the best answer from the given options. Fill in the corresponding circle on your answer document. For questions 16–20, solve the problem and fill in the answer on the answer sheet grid.

Notes:

- Calculators are **NOT PERMITTED** in this section.
- All variables and expressions represent real numbers unless indicated otherwise.
- All figures are drawn to scale unless indicated otherwise.
- All figures are in a plane unless indicated otherwise.
- Unless indicated otherwise, the domain of a given function is the set of all real numbers x for which the function has real values.

REFERENCE INFORMATION

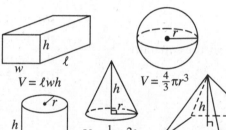

Area Facts

$A = \ell w$

$A = \frac{1}{2} bh$

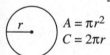

$A = \pi r^2$
$C = 2\pi r$

Volume Facts

$V = \ell w h$

$V = \pi r^2 h$

$V = \frac{4}{3}\pi r^3$

$V = \frac{1}{3}\pi r^2 h$

$V = \frac{1}{3}\ell w h$

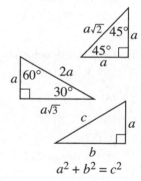

Triangle Facts

$a^2 + b^2 = c^2$

The arc of a circle contains 360°.
The arc of a circle contains 2π radians.
The sum of the measures of the angles in a triangle is 180°.

GO ON TO THE NEXT PAGE

1. Which of the following statements is true concerning the lines whose equations are $2x + 3y = 4$ and $4x + 6y = 8$?

   (A) The lines are the same line.
   (B) The lines are distinct parallel lines.
   (C) The lines are perpendicular.
   (D) The lines intersect, but are not perpendicular.

2. On September 1, Bill deposited d dollars into a non-interest-bearing bank account. He then made weekly deposits of w dollars and made no withdrawals. After 4 weeks, Bill had $60 in his account. After 8 weeks, he had $85. Which of the following equations gives the dollar amount, A, in Bill's account x weeks after his initial deposit?

   (A) $A = 10x + 20$
   (B) $A = 10x + 5$
   (C) $A = 8.25x + 27$
   (D) $A = 6.25x + 35$

3. How many values of x satisfy the equation $x^2 - 8x = -16$?

   (A) None
   (B) 1
   (C) 2
   (D) More than 2

4. On January 1, 2015, the values of Alice's brokerage account and of Barbara's brokerage account were a dollars and b dollars, respectively. During the year, the value of Alice's account increased by 10% and the value of Barbara's account decreased by 10%. If on December 31, 2015 the values of their accounts were equal, what is the ratio of a to b?

   (A) $\dfrac{9}{11}$
   (B) $\dfrac{9}{10}$
   (C) $\dfrac{10}{9}$
   (D) $\dfrac{11}{9}$

5. Which of the following is an equation of a line that has the same x-intercept as the line whose equation is $y = 3x - 6$?

   (A) $y = 3x - 4$
   (B) $y = 2x - 6$
   (C) $y = 6x - 3$
   (D) $y = 2x - 4$

$$y = x^2 + 2$$
$$y = \frac{1}{2}x^2 + 1$$

6. Which of the following is a true statement concerning the graphs of the two equations above?

   (A) The two graphs do not intersect.
   (B) The two graphs have exactly one point of intersection.
   (C) The two graphs have exactly two points of intersection.
   (D) The two graphs have more than two points of intersection.

GO ON TO THE NEXT PAGE

7. For what value of n will the equation

$$3(x+2) + 2(x+3) = 6(x+1) - n(x+5)$$

have no solutions?

(A) −1
(B) 0
(C) 1
(D) 2

8. Which of the following are the solutions of the equation: $x^2 + 2x = 11$?

(A) $1 + 2\sqrt{2}$ and $1 - 2\sqrt{2}$
(B) $-1 + 2\sqrt{2}$ and $-1 - 2\sqrt{2}$
(C) $1 + 2\sqrt{3}$ and $1 - 2\sqrt{3}$
(D) $-1 + 2\sqrt{3}$ and $-1 - 2\sqrt{3}$

9. $\overline{AB}$ and $\overline{CB}$, the two congruent sides of isosceles triangle ABC, are each 5, and the cosine of $\angle A$ is 0.8. What is the area of triangle ABC?

(A) 8
(B) 10
(C) 12
(D) 16

10. Elaine had d dollars. She used 60 percent of her money to buy pencils that cost p cents each. She spent the rest of her money to buy markers that cost m cents each. Which of the following expressions represents the number of markers she bought?

(A) $\dfrac{2d}{5m}$
(B) $\dfrac{5d}{2m}$
(C) $\dfrac{40d}{m}$
(D) $\dfrac{40d}{mp}$

11. Which of the following expresses the area of a circle in terms of C, its circumference?

(A) $\dfrac{C^2}{4\pi}$
(B) $\dfrac{C^2}{2\pi}$
(C) $\dfrac{C}{2\pi}$
(D) $\dfrac{C}{4\pi}$

12. The JFK Middle School select chorus consisted of b boys and g girls. After auditions, the director of the chorus added 3 more boys and 5 more girls. The next day, the director randomly chose one chorus member to sing the first solo at the spring concert. What is the probability that a boy was chosen?

(A) $\dfrac{b}{b+g}$
(B) $\dfrac{b+3}{g+5}$
(C) $\dfrac{b+3}{b+g+5}$
(D) $\dfrac{b+3}{b+g+8}$

13. If $f(x) = 2(ax^2 + bx + c) - 3(2ax^2 + 3bx + 3)$, where a, b, and c are constants, and if $f(x) = xg(x)$, what is the value of c?

(A) 0
(B) 1
(C) 4.5
(D) It depends on what $g(x)$ is.

GO ON TO THE NEXT PAGE

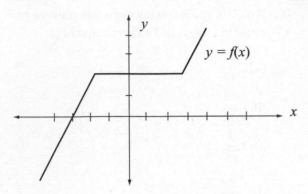

15. A sphere and a cone have equal volumes. If the radius of the cone is twice the radius of the sphere, what is the ratio of the height of the cone to its radius?

(A) .5:1
(B) 1:1
(C) 2:1
(D) π:1

14. The figure above is the graph of the function $y = f(x)$. What are the x-coordinates of the points where the graph of $y = f(x - 2)$ intersects the x-axis?

(A) Only –5
(B) Only –1
(C) –5 and –1
(D) All numbers between –2 and 3

GO ON TO THE NEXT PAGE

Grid-in Response Directions

In questions 16–20, first solve the problem, and then enter your answer on the grid provided on the answer sheet. The instructions for entering your answers follow.

- First, write your answer in the boxes at the top of the grid.
- Second, grid your answer in the columns below the boxes.
- Use the fraction bar in the first row or the decimal point in the second row to enter fractions and decimals.

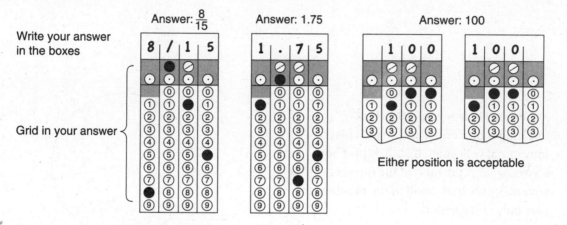

- Grid only one space in each column.
- Entering the answer in the boxes is recommended as an aid in gridding but is not required.
- The machine scoring your exam can read only what you grid, so you **must grid-in your answers correctly to get credit.**
- If a question has more than one correct answer, grid-in only one of them.
- The grid does not have a minus sign; so no answer can be negative.
- A mixed number *must* be converted to an improper fraction or a decimal before it is gridded.

  Enter $1\frac{1}{4}$ as 5/4 or 1.25; the machine will interpret 11/4 as $\frac{11}{4}$ and mark it wrong.

- **All decimals must be entered as accurately as possible.** Here are three acceptable ways of gridding

$$\frac{3}{11} = 0.272727\ldots$$

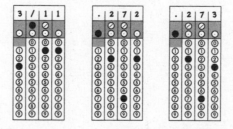

- Note that rounding to .273 is acceptable because you are using the full grid, but you would receive **no credit** for .3 or .27, because they are less accurate.

16. During 2015, the nine members of the Playa Vista Senior Book Club read on average 52 books. When Mary, the oldest member of the club, moved away, the average number of books read in 2015 by the eight remaining members was 42. How many books did Mary read in 2015?

17. At Central High School, 50 girls play intramural basketball and 40 girls play intramural volleyball. If 10 girls play both sports, what is the ratio of the number of girls who play only basketball to the number who play only volleyball?

18. If $-\frac{1}{2} < x - 3 < \frac{1}{3}$, what is one possible value

of $\frac{1}{x}$?

19. If b is a real number and if $2 + i$ is a solution of the equation $x^2 - bx + 5 = 0$, what is the value of b?

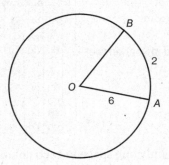

Note: Figure not drawn to scale.

20. In the figure above, what is the radian measure of $\angle AOB$?

If there is still time remaining, you may review your answers.

MATH TEST (CALCULATOR)

55 MINUTES, 38 QUESTIONS

Turn to Section 4 of your answer sheet to answer the questions in this section.

Directions: For questions 1–30, solve each problem and choose the best answer from the given options. Fill in the corresponding circle on your answer document. For questions 31–38, solve the problem and fill in the answer on the answer sheet grid.

Notes:

- Calculators **ARE PERMITTED** in this section.
- All variables and expressions represent real numbers unless indicated otherwise.
- All figures are drawn to scale unless indicated otherwise.
- All figures are in a plane unless indicated otherwise.
- Unless indicated otherwise, the domain of a given function is the set of all real numbers x for which the function has real values.

REFERENCE INFORMATION

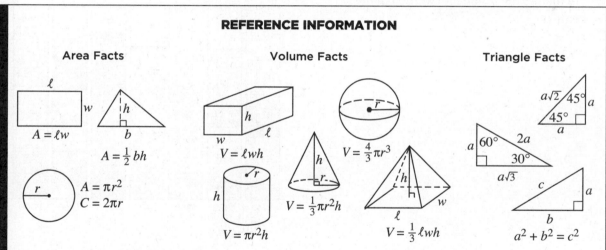

Area Facts

$A = \ell w$

$A = \frac{1}{2} bh$

$A = \pi r^2$
$C = 2\pi r$

Volume Facts

$V = \ell w h$

$V = \pi r^2 h$

$V = \frac{4}{3} \pi r^3$

$V = \frac{1}{3} \pi r^2 h$

$V = \frac{1}{3} \ell w h$

Triangle Facts

$a^2 + b^2 = c^2$

The arc of a circle contains 360°.

The arc of a circle contains 2π radians.

The sum of the measures of the angles in a triangle is 180°.

GO ON TO THE NEXT PAGE

1. After leaving home at 10:30 A.M. and driving at an average speed of 40 miles per hour, Brigitte arrived at her parents' house at 1:30 P.M. How fast, in miles per hour, would she have had to have driven in order to have arrived at 1:00?

(A) 45
(B) 48
(C) 50
(D) 60

2. On the final exam in a university psychology course, the average (arithmetic mean) grade was 86. If the average grades of the m men and w women in the course were 80 and 90, respectively, what is the ratio of the number of men to the number of women in the course?

(A) $\dfrac{3}{5}$

(B) $\dfrac{2}{3}$

(C) $\dfrac{3}{2}$

(D) $\dfrac{5}{3}$

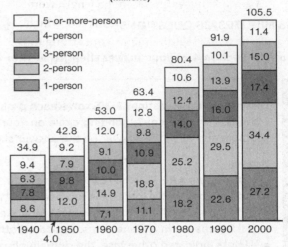

Households by Size: 1940 to 2000
(Millions)

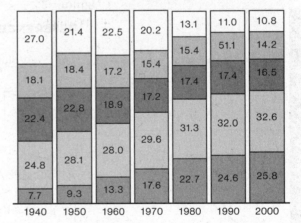

Distribution of Households by Size: 1940 to 2000
(percent)

3. Based on the information in the graphs above, all of the following statements are true except

(A) there were more households with 5 or more persons in 1960 than in 2000.
(B) the percent of 1-person households more than tripled from 1940 to 2000.
(C) the median size of a household in 1970 was 3 people.
(D) the percent of 2-person households increased in every decennial census from 1940 to 2000.

GO ON TO THE NEXT PAGE

4. In rectangle *ABCD*, the length, *AB*, is twice as long as the width, *BC*. If the length were doubled and the width were halved, which of the following statements concerning the perimeter (*P*) and the area (*A*) of the new rectangle would be true?

(A) *P* would not change, and *A* would not change.

(B) *P* would increase by 50%, and *A* would not change.

(C) *P* would not change, and *A* would increase by 50%.

(D) *P* would increase by 50%, and *A* would increase by 100%.

5. The weights, in kilograms, of five students are 48, 56, 61, 52, and 57. If 1 kilogram = 2.2 pounds, how many of the students weigh over 120 pounds?

(A) 1

(B) 2

(C) 3

(D) 4

Questions 6 and 7 are based on the information in the following table.

Team Participation by Class at Central H.S. in 2015

Class	Number of Students	Percent of Students
Freshman	180	15
Sophomore	120	*x*
Junior	*y*	40
Senior	*z*	*w*
Total	*t*	100

6. What is the value of *t*, the total number of students on teams?

(A) 750

(B) 1,200

(C) 1,500

(D) 1,800

7. What is the value of *z*, the number of seniors on teams?

(A) 360

(B) 420

(C) 630

(D) 720

GO ON TO THE NEXT PAGE

8. If $a < -1$, which of the following could be the graph of $y - 1 = \dfrac{a}{a+1}x$?

(A)
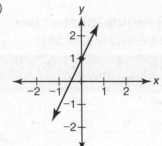

(B)
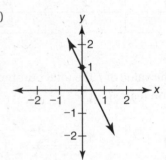

(C)
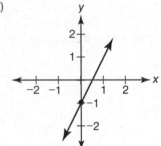

(D)
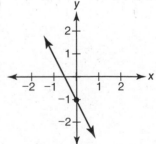

9. If Naveed is riding his bike at a rate of 22 feet per second, how fast is he going in miles per hour? (1 mile = 5,280 feet)

    (A) 10
    (B) 12
    (C) 15
    (D) 16

10. If the average of 5 positive integers is 70, what is the largest possible value of their median?

    (A) 70
    (B) 114
    (C) 116
    (D) 346

11. Susan is a candidate for mayor of a city that has 20 election precincts. She assigned each of her 84 volunteers to work in one of the precincts. Each precinct that has 1,000 or more registered voters has been assigned 5 volunteers, and each precinct that has fewer than 1,000 registered voters has been assigned 3 volunteers. What percent of the precincts have fewer than 1,000 registered voters?

    (A) 25%
    (B) 40%
    (C) 60%
    (D) 75%

12. If the length of a rectangle is three times its width, what is the sine of the angle that the diagonal makes with the longer side?

    (A) 0.316
    (B) 0.333
    (C) 0.500
    (D) 0.866

GO ON TO THE NEXT PAGE

Questions 13–15 are based on the information in the following graphs.

**Sales and Earnings of
XYZ Corporation 1991–1998**

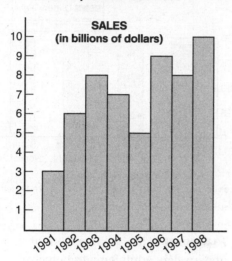

**SALES
(in billions of dollars)**

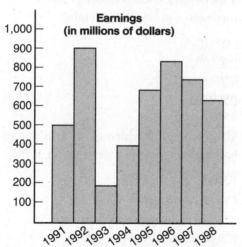

**Earnings
(in millions of dollars)**

**1998 Sales of XYZ Corporation
by Category**

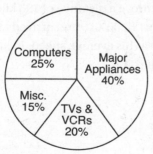

Computers
25%

Major
Appliances
40%

Misc.
15%

TVs &
VCRs
20%

13. What is the average (arithmetic mean) in billions of dollars of the sales of XYZ Corporation for the period 1991–1998?

(A) 5.5
(B) 6.0
(C) 7.0
(D) 8.0

14. For which year was the percentage increase in earnings from the previous year the greatest?

(A) 1992
(B) 1993
(C) 1994
(D) 1995

15. What was the ratio of earnings to sales of XYZ Corporation in 1993?

(A) $\dfrac{40}{1}$

(B) $\dfrac{25}{1}$

(C) $\dfrac{1}{25}$

(D) $\dfrac{1}{40}$

GO ON TO THE NEXT PAGE

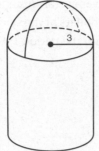

16. The figure above shows a solid formed by placing a hemisphere of radius 3 centimeters onto a cylinder whose height is 6 centimeters and whose radius is 3 centimeters. What is the total volume, in cubic inches, of this solid?

(A) 36π
(B) 54π
(C) 72π
(D) 90π

17. Each week Sally, a salesperson in Eddie's Electronic Emporium, receives a base pay of $300 plus a commission on the dollar amount of her sales. During any week when the total value of her sales is $5,000 or less, her commission is 10%. During those weeks when the total value of her sales exceeds $5,000, her commission is 12% of the entire amount. Last year during the first week of February, she earned $1,080. What was the total value of her sales that week?

(A) $5,400
(B) $6,500
(C) $7,500
(D) $9,000

Questions 18 and 19 are based on the information in the following graph.

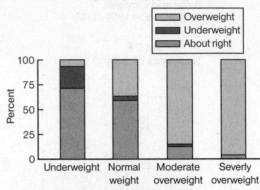

Perceptions of Body Weight Status

Perceived compared with actual weight status of adult females.

Source: U.S. Department of Agriculture.

18. To the nearest 5%, what percent of underweight adult females perceive themselves to be underweight?

(A) 10%
(B) 25%
(C) 35%
(D) 40%

19. The members of which of the four groups had the least accurate perception of their body weight?

(A) Underweight
(B) Normal weight
(C) Moderately overweight
(D) Severely overweight

20. Henry drove a distance of 198 kilometers. If he left at 10:00 A.M. and arrived at 1:40 P.M., what was his average speed, in kilometers per hour?

(A) 45
(B) 54
(C) 60
(D) 65

GO ON TO THE NEXT PAGE

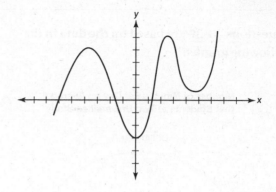
21. On January 1, 2000, the value of a certificate of deposit (CD) was \$765. If the value of the CD increased by 6% each year, what was its value, in dollars, on January 1, 2012?

   (A) 1,316
   (B) 1,370
   (C) 1,498
   (D) 1,539

22. If $i = \sqrt{-1}$ and $(a + bi)(1 + i) = 3 + 5i$, then $a + bi =$

   (A) $-2 + 2i$
   (B) $2 + 2i$
   (C) $1 + 4i$
   (D) $4 + i$

23. For what value of k will the graphs of $3x + 4y + 5 = 0$ and $kx + 6y + 7 = 0$ NOT intersect?

   (A) -8
   (B) 4.5
   (C) 5
   (D) 8

24. Of the 326 children at North Central preschool, 211 have a dog and 174 have a cat. If 83 of the children have neither a cat nor a dog, how many have both?

   (A) 32
   (B) 72
   (C) 112
   (D) 142

25. If the volume of a sphere is equal to the volume of a cube, what is the ratio of the edge of the cube to the radius of the sphere?

   (A) 1.16
   (B) 1.53
   (C) 1.61
   (D) 2.05

26. The figure above shows the graph of $y = f(x)$ for all values of x between -6 and 7. For how many values of x in that interval is $f(x)$ equal to 3?

   (A) 4
   (B) 5
   (C) 6
   (D) 7

27. Assume that 0.1% of the population of the United States has a certain disease. Assume further that there is a test for this disease that is 99% accurate. This means that 99% of the people who have the disease will test positive, and 1% of the people who have the disease will erroneously test negative. Similarly, 99% of the people who do not have the disease will test negative, and 1% of the people who do not have the disease will erroneously test positive. In 2015, 1,000,000 people were given this test. What percent of the people who tested positive actually had the disease?

   (A) 1%
   (B) 9%
   (C) 90%
   (D) 99%

GO ON TO THE NEXT PAGE

Questions 28–30 are based on the data in the following graphs.

Number of Minutes Per Day on Average that Students at Two Universities Study

University A

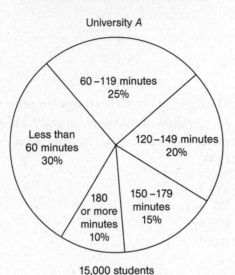

15,000 students

University B

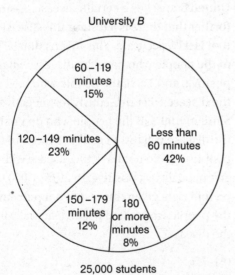

25,000 students

The circle graphs above show the distribution of students at two universities based on how much time on average, in minutes, they studied each day.

28. Which of the following could be the median number of minutes studied per day by the students at University A?

(A) 50
(B) 100
(C) 125
(D) 175

29. Compared with University A, how many more students at University B on average studied less than one hour per day?

(A) 2,200
(B) 3,300
(C) 6,000
(D) 8,500

30. If one student is chosen at random from all the students at Universities A and B, what is the probability, to the nearest ten thousandth, that he or she studies on average at least three hours per day?

(A) 0.0625
(B) 0.0675
(C) 0.0785
(D) 0.0875

GO ON TO THE NEXT PAGE

Grid-in Response Directions

In questions 31–38, first solve the problem, and then enter your answer on the grid provided on the answer sheet. The instructions for entering your answers follow.

- First, write your answer in the boxes at the top of the grid.
- Second, grid your answer in the columns below the boxes.
- Use the fraction bar in the first row or the decimal point in the second row to enter fractions and decimals.

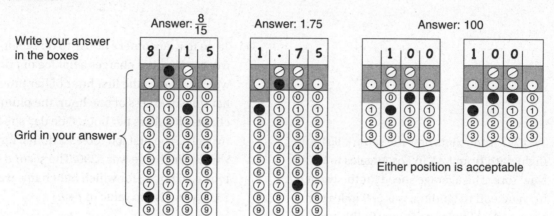

Answer: $\frac{8}{15}$ Answer: 1.75 Answer: 100

Write your answer in the boxes

Grid in your answer

Either position is acceptable

- Grid only one space in each column.
- Entering the answer in the boxes is recommended as an aid in gridding but is not required.
- The machine scoring your exam can read only what you grid, so you **must grid-in your answers correctly to get credit**.
- If a question has more than one correct answer, grid-in only one of them.
- The grid does not have a minus sign; so no answer can be negative.
- A mixed number *must* be converted to an improper fraction or a decimal before it is gridded.

  Enter $1\frac{1}{4}$ as 5/4 or 1.25; the machine will interpret 11/4 as $\frac{11}{4}$ and mark it wrong.

- **All decimals must be entered as accurately as possible.** Here are three acceptable ways of gridding

$$\frac{3}{11} = 0.272727\dots$$

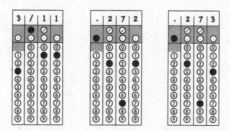

- Note that rounding to .273 is acceptable because you are using the full grid, but you would receive **no credit** for .3 or .27, because they are less accurate.

31. Water enters a vat, whose capacity is 60 liters, through a faucet at the top and leaves the vat through a drain at the bottom. If the vat is empty, the drain is open, and water starts to flow through the faucet at a constant rate of 5 liters per minute, it takes exactly 50 minutes until the vat is full. At what rate, in liters per minute, is water flowing through the drain?

32. Two 747 jumbo jets flew the same 2,954-mile flight path from LAX in Los Angeles to JFK in New York. The average speed for the two jets, from takeoff to landing, was 569 miles per hour and 543 miles per hour. To the nearest minute, how much less time did the faster jet take to complete the flight?

33. To the nearest hundredth, what is the sine of the acute angle formed by the line whose equation is $y = 3x - 3$ and the positive x-axis?

34. To go to a customer's house to do repair work, a plumber charges a flat fee of f dollars, which includes the first hour of her time. For her time in excess of one hour, the plumber charges h dollars per hour. One day she had two jobs. The first job took 3.5 hours, for which her charge was $290. The second job took 4.25 hours, for which her charge was $335. What is the value of $f + h$?

GO ON TO THE NEXT PAGE

Questions 35–36 are based on the graphs below.

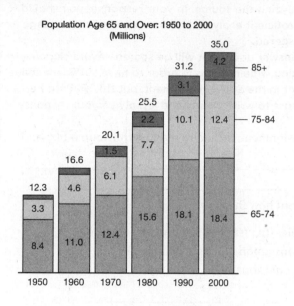

Population Age 65 and Over: 1950 to 2000
(Millions)

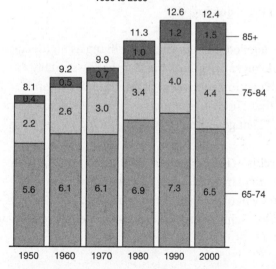

Percent of Total Population Age 65 and Over:
1950 to 2000

35. Based on the information in the graphs above, to the nearest million; how many millions of people lived in the United States in 1950? (For example, if the population in 1950 was 75,126,000, rounded to the nearest million it was 75,000,000, and you should grid in 75.)

36. The number of people age 85 and above living in the United States in 2000 was how many times the number of people age 85 and above living in the United States in 1950?

Questions 37–38 are based on the following information.

In a certain country, all citizens pay an annual tax of 20% of their first $20,000 of income and 30% of all income in excess of $20,000.

37. Michelle is a citizen of this country. If in 2014 her income was N and her tax was $9,250, what is the value of $\dfrac{N}{1,000}$?

38. If in 2014, 20% of Michelle's income had been exempt from taxation, how much less in taxes, to the nearest dollar, would she have had to pay?

STOP

If there is still time remaining, you may review your answers.

ESSAY (OPTIONAL)

Directions: This assignment will allow you to demonstrate your ability to skillfully read and understand a source text and write a response analyzing the source. In your response, you should show that you have understood the source, give proficient analysis, and use the English language effectively. If your essay is off-topic, it will not be scored.

Only what you write on the lined paper in your answer document will be scored—avoid skipping lines, using unreasonably large handwriting, and using wide margins in order to have sufficient space to respond. You can also write on the planning sheet in the answer document, but this will not be evaluated—no other scrap paper will be given. Be sure to write clearly and legibly so your response can be scored.

You will be given 50 minutes to complete the assignment, including reading the source text and writing your response.

Read the following passage, and think about how the author uses:

- Evidence, such as applicable examples, to justify the argument
- Reasoning to show logical connections among thoughts and facts
- Rhetoric, like sensory language and emotional appeals, to give weight to the argument

Dead Presidents Take Precedence

1   Henry David Thoreau, in his seminal piece *Walden*, detailed the years he spent living as an ascetic in a minimalist hut on the pond of the same name. If you can overlook the fact that he actually was just living in his mother's yard (possibly the 19th century equivalent of the basement?) and secretly subsisting on her cooking, you might agree that Thoreau is among our nation's preeminent philosophers. Consider his provocative declaration: "That government is best which governs least."

2   Now—before you brand me with a scarlet A for Anarchist—I will concede that there are certainly flaws within this type of all-or-nothing reasoning, particularly in this age of global terrorism and climate change and Ebola and highway potholes. But, when it comes to the economy, Mr. Thoreau (Patron Saint of Lawn Gnomes) has no shortage of fiscal scholars in his corner—especially relating to his hands-off(!) philosophy on minimum wage laws.

3   But before we analyze the present, it's important to understand the how and the why that have defined U.S. labor law for nearly a century. And, at its core was that three-word ominous behemoth that plunged the country into an economic crisis never seen before and never seen since: The Great Depression. If desperate times truly call for desperate measures, then President Franklin Delano Roosevelt may have been justified when he signed the first minimum wage law into effect in 1933. It should be noted that The Supreme Court overturned this first minimum wage law as unconstitutional, arguing that Congress (and FDR, really) lacked the legislative authority for such a far-reaching mandate. Nonetheless, Congress—in its proud tradition of standard disregard for public opinion and judicial oversight—again passed similar minimum wage legislation in 1938. The

Supreme Court must have had a change of heart (because the Constitution itself hadn't changed), this time upholding the law in a 1941 case. 82 years after FDR's brainchild, the U.S. still embraces similar legislation (updated periodically to reflect changes in the cost of living—$7.25 currently).

4   Now, I'd be remiss if I neglected to mention that I'm no economist (though I am smart enough to recognize that buying mayonnaise by the gallon is a solid deal despite my overwhelming, pervasive fear of commitment). That is why I'll defer to the experts on this one. In 1978, the *American Economic Review* reported that 90% of U.S. economists (as in, people whose job it is to analyze economic theory) believed that a minimum wage actually harmed unskilled laborers, youth, and minorities by leading to higher unemployment for these groups, which are the primary people that the law is designed to help. Since that groundbreaking 1978 survey, the disparity in economist opinion isn't as pronounced, but it is still significant; countless surveys have since been performed, and economists continue to oppose a minimum wage at a 75% clip.

5   Noted Washington think tank The Cato Institute delineates many of these objections held by economic scholars. The principal governmental miscalculation, The Cato Institute argues, is that there is no such thing as the proverbial free lunch; that is, to say, that there is a finite amount of money that businesses budget for labor. So, if a local clothing store now employs six people at $7.25 an hour ($43.50 per hour among the six), a minimum hike to $8.70 would lead to the termination of one of the six employees. Moreover, it would then lead to more scrutiny and a higher workload for the five remaining employees. You see, the Road to Hell really is paved with Good Intentions.

6   Most damaging, however, is the threat of outsourcing. For better or worse, the world is rapidly shedding its Americentric economic focus in deference to a more globalized approach. Corporations are extraditing jobs to countries where labor is cheaper, essentially shipping the dollars spent by American consumers to laborers in Bangladesh and Malaysia and Taiwan. The next time you get dressed, I challenge you to look at the labels on each article of clothing you will wear for the day; I'll bet you dollars to doughnuts that you'll see Botswana and Burundi and Bosnia 100 times each before you see Boston. And, unfortunately, we owe that entirely to the minimum wage.

7   It all comes down to this: we'd never trust the lawyers in Congress to perform open heart surgery. So, why do we trust them to dictate something as paramount as economic policy when the people far better qualified to do so say otherwise?

Write a response that demonstrates how the author makes an argument to persuade an audience that the government should not require a minimum wage. In your response, analyze how the author uses at least one of the features from the essay directions (or features of your own choosing) to develop a logical and persuasive argument. Be certain that your response cites relevant aspects of the source text.

Your response should not give your personal opinion on the merit of the source text, but instead show how the author crafts an argument to persuade readers.

ANSWER KEY
Model Test 3

Section 1: Reading

1.	B	14.	C	27.	A	40.	A
2.	C	15.	C	28.	D	41.	D
3.	B	16.	B	29.	B	42.	A
4.	B	17.	D	30.	B	43.	A
5.	A	18.	A	31.	C	44.	B
6.	A	19.	C	32.	B	45.	A
7.	C	20.	B	33.	C	46.	B
8.	D	21.	A	34.	C	47.	B
9.	C	22.	D	35.	B	48.	C
10.	A	23.	C	36.	D	49.	C
11.	B	24.	B	37.	D	50.	B
12.	C	25.	D	38.	C	51.	B
13.	B	26.	C	39.	B	52.	D

Number Correct   _____

Number Incorrect   _____

Section 2: Writing and Language

1.	A	12.	B	23.	B	34.	D
2.	C	13.	A	24.	A	35.	A
3.	C	14.	C	25.	C	36.	D
4.	A	15.	B	26.	C	37.	B
5.	B	16.	B	27.	D	38.	C
6.	D	17.	A	28.	D	39.	C
7.	D	18.	A	29.	A	40.	A
8.	A	19.	D	30.	D	41.	B
9.	C	20.	C	31.	D	42.	A
10.	A	21.	D	32.	A	43.	D
11.	D	22.	B	33.	D	44.	C

Number Correct   _____

Number Incorrect   _____

Section 3: Math (No Calculator)

1. **A**
2. **D**
3. **B**
4. **A**

5. **D**
6. **A**
7. **C**
8. **D**

9. **C**
10. **C**
11. **A**
12. **D**

13. **C**
14. **B**
15. **A**

16. **132**

17. **4/3 or 1.33**

or

18. **1/3 or .333**

19. **4**

20. **1/3 or .333**

Number Correct _____

Number Incorrect _____

ANSWER KEY
Model Test 3

Section 4: Math (Calculator)

1. **B**	7. **B**	13. **C**	19. **A**	25. **C**
2. **B**	8. **A**	14. **C**	20. **B**	26. **C**
3. **D**	9. **C**	15. **D**	21. **D**	27. **B**
4. **B**	10. **C**	16. **C**	22. **D**	28. **B**
5. **C**	11. **C**	17. **B**	23. **B**	29. **C**
6. **B**	12. **A**	18. **B**	24. **D**	30. **D**

31. **3.8**

32. **15**

33. **.95**

34. **200**

35. **152**

36. **7**

37. **37.5**

38. **2250**

Number Correct _____

Number Incorrect _____

SCORE ANALYSIS

Reading and Writing Test

Section 1: Reading   _____ = _____ (A)
                          # correct   raw score

Section 2: Writing   _____ = _____ (B)
                          # correct   raw score

To find your Reading and Writing test scores, consult the chart below: find the ranges in which your raw scores lie and read across to find the ranges of your test scores.

_____ + _____ = _____ (C)
range of reading   range of writing   range of reading + writing
test scores   test scores   test scores

To find the range of your Reading and Writing Scaled Score, multiply (C) by 10.

Test Scores for the Reading and Writing Sections

Reading Raw Score	Writing Raw Score	Test Score
44–52	39–44	35–40
36–43	33–38	31–34
30–35	28–32	28–30
24–29	22–27	24–27
19–23	17–21	21–23
14–18	13–16	19–20
9–13	9–12	16–18
5–8	5–8	13–15
less than 5	less than 5	10–12

Math Test

Section 3:   _____ = _____ (D)
                  # correct   raw score

Section 4:   _____ = _____ (E)
                  # correct   raw score

Total Math raw score: (D) + (E) = _____

To find your Math Scaled Score, consult the chart below: find the range in which your raw score lies and read across to find the range for your scaled score.

Scaled Scores for the Math Test

Raw Score	Scaled Score	Raw Score	Scaled Score
50–58	700–800	20–25	450–490
44–49	650–690	15–19	400–440
38–43	600–640	11–14	350–390
32–37	550–590	7–10	300–340
26–32	500–540	less than 7	200–290

ANSWERS EXPLAINED

Section 1: Reading Test

1. **(B)** The opening lines indicate that the narrator is *reflecting on his feelings*. Throughout the passage he uses words like "miserable," "ashamed," and "discontented" to describe his emotional state. Choice (A) is incorrect. The narrator does not *analyze* or dissect the reasons for a change in attitude; he dwells on an ongoing attitude. Choice (C) is incorrect. The passage presents an example of emotional self-awareness, not of political consciousness. Choice (D) is incorrect. The narrator criticizes himself, not young people in general.

2. **(C)** Consider the narrator's early beliefs about his home. How does the narrator describe it? Clearly he views it in *positive* terms: "a most elegant salon" (lines 9–10), "the Temple of State" (line 11). Choice (A) is incorrect: it is the narrator's growing feeling of shame about his home that is miserable, not the home itself. Choice (B) is incorrect: to believe in one's home as the Temple of State is to have a somewhat exaggerated image of it, not a modest (humble, unpretentious) one. Choice (D) is incorrect: the narrator's childhood beliefs in his humble home as the Temple of State and his parlor as a most elegant salon are unrealistic rather than realistic.

3. **(B)** The repeated refrain of "I had believed" calls the reader's attention to the positive way in which the narrator looked on his home, with even the humble kitchen described as "a chaste though not magnificent apartment." (*Chaste* here means simple and restrained in style, without unnecessary ornamentation.) Choice (A) is incorrrect. Lines 1–5 provide evidence that the narrator's view of his home was miserable, not positive. Likewise, choices (C) and (D) are incorrrect. Lines 23–36 and 37–45 provide additional evidence that the narrator's view of his home was negative rather than positive.

4. **(B)** Note the adjectives used to describe Joe: "faithful," "industrious," "kind." These are virtues, and Joe is fundamentally *virtuous*. Choice (A) is incorrect. Joe is plain and hardworking, not renowned or distinguished. Choice (C) is incorrect. The passage portrays not Joe but the narrator as desiring to be independent. Choice (D) is incorrect. The narrator thinks his life is coarse; he thinks Joe is virtuous.

5. **(A)** Choice (A) is correct. Consider the sentence "Before achieving the status of master carpenter, John served his time as a journeyman for three years." The "time" to which the narrator refers is the period of his *apprenticeship*. This is supported by the last sentence of the previous paragraph, in which the narrator speaks of his profound gloom as he entered his "apprenticeship to Joe."

6. **(A)** Choice A is correct. As a child, the narrator had no idea how his home might appear to others. Now, however, he has been exposed to Miss Havisham and to Estella, and he has become painfully aware how these others would despise him for the coarseness and commonness of his home and work. Choices (B) and (C) are incorrect. Nothing in the passage suggests that either might be the case. Choice (D) is incorrect. Nothing in the passage suggests that sinfulness has prompted the narrator's discontent. Although ingratitude may play a part in his discontent, shame at his background plays a far greater part.

7. **(C)** The narrator states that he "would not have had Miss Havisham and Estella see (his home) on any account." He is aware that his home would appear coarse and common

in their eyes. (The use of "Now" to introduce the sentence indicates that this is a new awareness for the narrator, who previously viewed his home in a far more positive light.)

8. **(D)** In lines 47–49, the narrator manages to say something good about his youthful self: "I am glad to know that I never breathed a murmur to Joe while my indentures lasted." He gives himself credit for *concealing his despondency from Joe* during the time he was apprenticed. Choices (A) and (B) are incorrect. The narrator gives Joe all the credit for his having worked industriously and for his not having run away to become a soldier. Choice (C) is incorrect. While the narrator struggles to keep his menial position a secret from Estella, he gives himself no credit for doing so; instead, he blames himself for having been so ashamed of his humble origins.

9. **(C)** Choice (A) is incorrect. Nothing in the passage suggests that the narrator has strong prospects for advancement. Choice (B) is incorrect. The natural setting, a "flat and low," mist-shrouded marsh, is bleak rather than beautiful. Choice (D) is incorrect. Nothing in the passage hints that Joe is going to die. Only choice (C) is left. The description of the windy marsh view, with an uncertain path leading only to darkness and the sea, accentuates the reader's sense of the narrator's melancholy mood.

10. **(A)** The narrator is ashamed of his home because it is "homely": *plain and unrefined*, lacking in the elegance and sophistication that would make it acceptable to the elegant and beautiful Estella. Note that, because the narrator is ashamed of his home, he must be using *homely* in a negative sense. You can eliminate any answers that present *homely* in a positive light.

11. **(B)** The narrator fears that Estella would catch him "with a black face and hands, doing the coarsest part of (his) work," and would rejoice to see him in such a lowly, contemptible position. He fears her readiness to despise those she thinks below her status. Thus, he fears her *scornful disposition* (nature; character).

12. **(C)** The opening sentence describes the shattering of the Iroquois leadership's pro-British policy. The remainder of the passage describes how Iroquois policy changed to reflect changes in European military goals. Choice (A) is incorrect. Nothing in the passage suggests that such charges were made against the Iroquois. Choice (B) is incorrect. It is unsupported by the passage. Choice (D) is incorrect. The passage demonstrates the Iroquois were able to play European power politics. Remember: when asked to find the main idea, be sure to check the opening and summary sentences of each paragraph.

13. **(B)** The Europeans *designated* or called these confederations of Indian tribes nations, giving them the same title they used for European states. Choices (A), (C), and (D) are incorrect. Although styled can mean *arranged* ("neatly-styled hair"), *brought into conformity with* ("styled according to *The Chicago Manual of Style*"), or *designed in a particular fashion* ("a conservatively styled gown"), that is not how it is used here.

14. **(C)** In this sentence, "rough" means approximate, as in "a rough guess." The tribes dealt with Europeans as approximate equals, not as exact or *absolute equals*.

15. **(C)** The time line clearly indicates that the period between 1684 and 1700 included many warlike acts involving the Iroquois and the French, acts that ceased only with the Great Peace of Montreal in 1701. This visual impression is supported by lines 37–50, which state that "[t]he increasing French threat to English hegemony in the interior of North America was signalized by French-led or French-inspired attacks on the Iroquois

and on outlying colonial settlements in New York and New England. The high point of the Iroquois response was the spectacular raid of August 5, 1689, in which the Iroquois virtually wiped out the French village of Lachine, just outside Montreal. A counterraid by the French on the English village of Schenectady in March, 1690, instilled an appropriate measure of fear among the English and their Iroquois allies."

16. **(B)** In lines 69–70, the author states that the Iroquois "played the game of European power politics with effectiveness." Thus, he shows *respect for their competence*. None of the other choices is supported by the passage. Remember: when asked to determine the author's attitude or tone, look for words that convey value judgments.

17. **(D)** Look closely at lines 57–63. What is their function? They list what the Iroquois accomplished by means of their system of aggressive neutrality. The Iroquois initiated a peace policy toward the British and the French (and were able to enforce it). The Iroquois won concessions from the British and the French, who had to keep on the tribe's good side by giving the Iroquois gifts. The Iroquois strengthened their dominance over other tribes nearby. In listing all these instances in which "the Iroquois played the game of European power politics with effectiveness," the author plainly shows that the Iroquois were competent in their dealings with the European powers. Thus, his most likely attitude toward the Iroquois leadership is one of respect for their competence.

18. **(A)** The Iroquois shifted their allegiance from one side to the other, depending on which allegiance was most advantageous to the tribes. Playing the British and French against each other, their policy of aggressive neutrality depended on *the readiness of the Iroquois to fight either side*. Choice (B) is incorrect. Ties of loyalty may actually have hampered the Iroquois; the French fear that the Iroquois were compromising the system in favor of the British led to the eventual breakdown of the policy of neutrality. Choice (C) is incorrect. French presence in the borderlands would have been a challenge to Iroquois power. Choice (D) is incorrect. It is unsupported by the passage.

19. **(C)** Lines 66–68 indicate that the Iroquois played the game of power politics with effectiveness "by their willingness to use their power against one or the other nation." In other words, they were ready to fight either side.

20. **(B)** The French believed that the Iroquois were *jeopardizing* or undermining the system of Iroquois neutrality by making decisions that favored the English. Choices (A), (C), and (D) are incorrect. Although "compromising" can mean *embarrassing* ("compromising evidence of an affair"), *accepting lower standards* ("compromising on safety"), or *striking a balance* ("compromising on an issue"), that is not how it is used here.

21. **(A)** The opening paragraph describes the changing state of relationships between the European powers and the tribes of the interior during the eighteenth century. As more and more French and English settlers moved into the interior, the Indian nations had to find new ways of dealing with the encroaching French and English populations. The paragraph concludes by stating: "The history of the reorientation of Iroquois policy toward the Europeans may serve as an example of the process that all the interior nations experienced in the eighteenth century." Thus, the next three paragraphs, which sum up the Iroquois' experience, provide *an instance of a state of relationships described earlier*.

22. **(D)** Use information contained in the italicized introduction to help you with the passage. The introduction tells you that this passage has been taken from a novel. The

novelist-author is not a researcher, a prospector, or an advocate for purely synthetic oil. He simply is someone *knowledgeable about oil deposits and the oil-mining industry.*

23. **(C)** In acting upon rock, the weather elements *have a particular effect* on it, reducing it "to its tiniest possible constituents—rock particles or, simply, dust."

24. **(B)** The author mentions the Grand Canyon while speaking of rivers as "immensely powerful destructive agencies." The dramatic canyon illustrates the *devastating impact* a river can have.

25. **(D)** Use the process of elimination to answer this question. Is our understanding of the process by which oil is created *adequate* (sufficient)? No. There is a "gray and disputatious area" (line 55) about which we do not yet know enough. You can eliminate choice (A). Is our understanding of the process *systematic* (structured or organized according to a fixed plan or system)? Nothing in the passage suggests that it is. You can eliminate choice (B). Is our understanding of the process *erroneous* (incorrect)? Our knowledge is not necessarily false; it is merely incomplete. You can eliminate choice (C). Is our understanding of the process *deficient* (inadequate; lacking)? Yes. We still need to learn more about just what causes decayed vegetation and dead aquatic life to turn into oil. The correct answer is choice (D).

26. **(C)** Lines 56–58 explicitly state that we do not know what causes decomposed organic matter to metamorphose or change into oil. This assertion clearly supports the claim that our understanding of the process by which oil is created is deficient.

27. **(A)** The last sentence states that oil is always found "on the sites of ancient seas and lakes." This suggests that prospectors should search for oil deposits *wherever former seas existed.*

28. **(D)** The author describes several processes (erosion, rock formation, oil formation). He states the possibility that a chemical catalyst is involved in oil formation. He mentions the limitation of our ability to produce oil synthetically. However, he never *proposes a solution* to any problem.

29. **(B)** The "conditions necessary for the formation of oil" are the circumstances that must exist before oil becomes possible. In other words, they are the *prerequisites* for oil's formation.

30. **(B)** The "cause of the metamorphosis (of decayed vegetation, etc., into oil) is not [known]." In other words, it is *an unexplained phenomenon,* an observable fact whose cause remains mysterious.

31. **(C)** In lines 58–60, the author indicates that some form of chemical catalyst may be involved in the metamorphosis of decayed vegetation and dead aquatic life into oil. However, he goes on to state that no one has yet isolated such a catalyst. Until such a catalyst is found or another way to explain oil's metamorphosis can be verified, the cause of the metamorphosis of oil will remain unexplained.

32. **(B)** Choice (B) is correct. The slaves' day of freedom came after the Civil War had *ended.* Choice (A) is incorrect. Although "closed" can mean *shut,* as in "She closed the door," that is not how it is used here. Choice (C) is incorrect. Although "closed" can mean *grew nearer,* as in "Her pursuer was closing fast," that is not how it is used here. Choice (D) is

incorrect. Although "closed" can mean *blocked off*, as in "The road works crew closed the street to traffic," that is not how it is used here.

33. **(C)** Choice (C) is correct. The historic moment is "the day of freedom," the day on which Washington and his family learned they were no longer slaves.

34. **(C)** Lines 34–48 clearly provide evidence that the author is recollecting a historic moment, the day on which a white stranger read the gathered slaves what the author presumes was the Emancipation Proclamation and told them they were free. Note the repeated use of the word *recall*: "As I now recall"; "The most distinct thing that I now recall." This repetition backs up the claim that, in the first two paragraphs, *A man recollects a historic moment that changed his life and the lives of everyone he knew.*

35. **(B)** Look at the context in which the word "mask" appears. The sentence immediately previous states that the slaves "had been careful to explain that the 'freedom' in these songs referred to the next world, and had no connection with life in this world." The slaves' explanation was a pretense, a mask they wore to disguise the fact that these spiritual songs expressed their longing to be physically free of the bonds of slavery. Thus, the mask that the slaves gradually threw off was *the pretense that the freedom they sang about was purely spiritual.*

36. **(D)** By throwing off the mask, the slaves show that they "were not afraid to let it be known that the 'freedom' in their songs meant freedom of the body in this world." This supports the claim that the mask they gradually threw off was *the pretense that the freedom they sang about was purely spiritual.*

37. **(D)** To have charge of themselves is to have *the duty of being responsible for* themselves and for their families. Choices (A), (B), and (C) are incorrect. Although charge can mean *a formal accusation* ("a charge of murder"), *a headlong rush forward* ("a cavalry charge"), or *the price asked for goods or services* ("an admission charge"), that is not how it is used here.

38. **(C)** Look at the context in which the word *light* appears. "Besides, deep down in their hearts there was a strange and peculiar attachment to 'old Marster' and 'old Missus,' and to their children, which they found it hard to think of breaking off. With these they had spent in some cases nearly a half-century, and it was no light thing to think of parting." It was hard for some of these elderly slaves to break away from all they had known. It was not a light or *trivial* (unimportant) thing for them to consider leaving. Choices (A), (B), and (D) are incorrect. Although light can mean *indistinct* ("light handwriting"), *pale* ("light blue"), or *agile* ("light on her feet"), that is not how it is used here.

39. **(B)** Throughout the passage, the narrator is struck by the lack of bitterness displayed on this occasion both by the plantation owner's family and by the newly emancipated slaves. About his master's family, Washington writes, "There was a feeling of deep interest, or perhaps sadness, on their faces, but not bitterness." About the slaves he writes: "For some minutes there was great rejoicing, and thanksgiving, and wild scenes of ecstasy. But there was no feeling of bitterness." Thus, he clearly chooses to emphasize the *absence of any ill will expressed by either the slaves or their masters.*

40. **(A)** The narrator opens the final paragraph by recounting the slaves' initial reactions "great rejoicing," "thanksgiving," "wild scenes of ecstasy"—in other words, *jubilation* (joyous exultation). However, this jubilation does not last: "The wild rejoicing on the

part of the emancipated colored people lasted but for a brief period, for I noticed that by the time they returned to their cabins there was a change in their feelings." It is only *momentary*. What follows this brief rejoicing? It is followed by sober and *sobering reflection* (serious thought) *on problems to be faced*, major problems that include the need to find shelter, the need for a way to make one's living, etc.

41. **(D)** The older slaves who visit their former masters at the big house have begun to think about the problems they now face as free men and women. They have *apprehensions* (fears) *about their uncertain future*. They are accustomed to having their masters tell them what to do. Thus, their fear and uncertainty inspires them to turn to their masters for advice.

42. **(A)** Phrases in the opening paragraphs of Passage 1 ("researchers report April 7 in *Nature Communications*," "the researchers say," "study coauthor") support the claim that the passage's main purpose is to *present a recent study*. The passage later cites the study coauthor's assertion that "[b]eing able to rebuild humans' metabolic memory could help control diseases such as obesity and diabetes." Thus, the recent study has *possible implications for humans*.

43. **(A)** To be wired to count calories is to be *equipped* or prepared biologically to distinguish high-calorie foods from normal-calorie foods. Choices (B), (C), and (D) are incorrect. Although wired can mean *tense* ("wired and edgy"), *strengthened* ("wired papier-mâché sculpture"), or *tied* ("wired bales of hay"), that is not how it is used here.

44. **(B)** As the fruit flies learn to tell apart normal-calorie and high-calorie foods, they become able to remember the type of food they prefer, "the healthier option." Their metabolic memory of their preference for moderate-calorie food enables them to choose this healthier option. Thus, it is reasonable to infer that metabolic memories *are involved in the process of food selection*. Choice (A) is incorrect. Although both mice and fruit flies apparently make metabolic memories, nothing in the passage suggests that these memories encourage the absorption of sorbitol and yeast. Choice (C) is incorrect. The passage says nothing about other forms of memory. Choice (D) is incorrect. Nothing in the passage suggests that metabolic memories are *solely* dependent on the sense of smell.

45. **(A)** Although lines 3–7 do not specifically mention metabolic memories, they do deal with the effects of memories on food selection: the flies learn to distinguish between normal-calorie and high-calorie foods, in process making what the next sentence refers to as metabolic memories. The flies "remember to choose the healthier option later." Thus, lines 3–7 provide evidence that metabolic memories are involved in the process of food selection.

46. **(B)** In line 65, the author specifically states that "Scheer was not involved in the fruit fly study." He was *unconnected with the study being discussed*, but as a neuroscientist and physiologist at Harvard Medical School he possessed *relevant expertise* about the disruption of circadian rhythms in humans.

47. **(B)** If mice do not get heart disease the way people do, then mice would not be good subjects for cardiovascular research on heart problems such as irregular heartbeats. Fruit flies "develop irregular heartbeats and other heart problems" in the course of aging; this suggests that they would be appropriate subjects for such research.

48. **(C)** These two sentences sum up the reasons that fruit flies are preferable to mice as subjects for cardiovascular research. The first points out why mice don't work as subjects for studies about heart problems associated with poor diet. The second states why fruit flies *do* work as subjects for such studies. Note the use of the phrase "on the other hand" to signal the contrast between mice and fruit flies as experimental subjects.

49. **(C)** To address a problem is to begin to *deal with* it or confront it. Choices (A), (B), and (D) are incorrect. Although address can mean *speak to* ("address an audience"), *protest* ("address your complaints to"), or *call* ("Please address him as Doctor Who."), that is not how it is used here.

50. **(B)** Middle age for fruit flies is 5 weeks old. A quick glance at the "Heart function in fruit flies" chart shows that at 5 weeks the heartbeat of the flies with restricted eating time (the lower line) maintained a steady pace, with each beat lasting about a second. In contrast, the heartbeats of the flies with unrestricted eating time varied markedly, with some contractions lasting a full 2 seconds, and others so brief that they barely registered on the chart.

51. **(B)** The opening sentence of the second paragraph states that "Fruit flies that limited eating to 12-hour stints had steadier heartbeats in old age than flies that ate whenever they wanted." These fruit flies did not choose voluntarily to limit their eating time. The researchers in Passage 2 set up a test to see what effect limiting or regulating *the amount of time groups of fruit flies had for eating* would have. Choice (A) is incorrect. Panda and his colleagues were involved in the study described in Passage 2. It was in the study described in Passage 1 that the researchers *fed one group of fruit flies a more highly calorific diet than they fed the other.* Choice (C) is incorrect. Panda and his colleagues did not restrict *the amount of calories the fruit flies were allowed to consume.* Lines 88–91 specifically state that they limited the amount of time the fruit flies ate *without* cutting back on calories. Choice (D) is incorrect. Nothing in the passage suggests that Panda and his colleagues *failed to develop high levels of sugar and fat in their test subjects.*

52. **(D)** Both the fruit flies following the high-calorie diet and the fruit flies following the anytime eating schedule *suffered more severe health problems* than did the fruit flies allowed to follow a moderate-calorie diet or the fruit flies on a 12-hour eating schedule. The fruit flies on the high-calorie diet lost the ability to tell the difference between moderate-calorie and high-calorie foods; their bodies accumulated higher levels of sugar and fat. The fruit flies on the anytime eating schedule developed irregular heart rhythms and slept poorly at night.

Section 2: Writing and Language Test

1. **(A)** The sentence first mentions 20th-century dramatists and then states that they owe a great deal to those who preceded them in the 19th century, making "forebears" the most sensible option. "Elders" in choice (B) and "seniors" in choice (C) refer to older groups of people but without the connotation of paving the way for current generations. "Historians" in choice (D) refers to those who study history, not to those who are studied by historians.

2. **(C)** Choices (A) and (B) have inverted word order, and choice (D) is too vague. Choice (C) puts the words in a logical sequence and uses precise wording.

3. **(C)** To express that this relationship went well beyond a typical rivalry, the phrase "impassioned artistic adversaries" works since it indicates the intensity of Strindberg's and Ibsen's feelings toward one another. Choices (A) and (D) are too violent in meaning, and choice (B) is the opposite of what is required.

4. **(A)** The dashes properly set aside a parenthetical phrase. Choice (B) does not work since a complete sentence does not appear after the semicolon. Choice (C) interrupts the thought right in the middle. Choice (D) uses inconsistent punctuation on either side of the parenthetical phrase.

5. **(B)** "Subtle" indicates "indirect," and "overt" indicates "direct," making choice (B) the best option for the required task. Choices (A), (C), and (D) all give irrelevant possibilities.

6. **(D)** "Respective" means "belonging separately to" different entities, which makes sense in reference to the two different writers. The other options all use some form of "respect" in the sense of "admiration."

7. **(D)** Someone who has both translated the works of these authors and written biographies about them would be intimately familiar with both the writing and histories of them. As such, Meyer would definitely be qualified to assert his opinion on this topic. Choices (A), (B), and (C) all show some familiarity with playwriting or history but do not indicate the level of expertise evident in choice (D).

8. **(A)** "Nonetheless" means "in spite of," which makes sense given the fact that these writers had similar backgrounds yet ended up having very different worldviews. "Consequently," in choice (B), indicates cause and effect. "Also," in choice (C), indicates the continuation of thought. "Divergently," in choice (D), could apply toward the differences in their views but does not work as a transition to show a logical contrast.

9. **(C)** The commas set aside the phrase "as drama continues to evolve into the postmodern era" that leads into the rest of the sentence. Choice (A) lacks a needed comma. Choice (B) breaks up the phrase "continues to evolve." Choice (D) gives no breaks whatsoever.

10. **(A)** This is the only option that puts quotation marks around a direct quote from Bernard Shaw. Choices (B) and (C) have no quotation marks. Choice (D) would work if this phrase were inside another quotation.

11. **(D)** "Germinal" indicates that it is in its earliest stage of development. "Outset," in choice (A), has the right general meaning but is the wrong part of speech since it is a noun instead of an adjective. "Germinating," in choice (B), and "floral," in choice (C), refer to plant life.

12. **(B)** "Eminent" means "noteworthy," which makes sense in reference to a famous concept like that of gravity. "Imminent," choice (A), means "about to happen." "Complimentary," choice (C), is associated with praise. "Complementary," choice (D), is associated with combining things together so they improve the quality of each other.

13. **(A)** The colon sets off the clarification that follows, and the commas set aside the nonessential yet descriptive phrase, "regardless of their mass." Choice (B) causes a run-on sentence. Choices (C) and (D) are both missing needed pauses.

14. **(C)** This is the only choice that is parallel to the other items listed in this sentence. Not only are the other options not parallel, they also have confused word orders.

15. **(B)** The passage indicates that Newton built on the ideas of Kepler, so "filling in the blanks" correctly indicates that Newton was attempting to solve previously mysterious questions. Choice (A) incorrectly indicates that Newton disagreed with all previous findings instead of trying to build on them. Choices (C) and (D) do not work. Newton's discoveries were intellectual in that he came up with revolutionary explanatory systems that were not grounded primarily in observation or exploration.

16. **(B)** Newton is explaining the cause for the apple falling, so "because" is the only option that makes sense. The other options do not indicate cause and effect.

17. **(A)** "In fact" means that Newton's explanation could account for why the moon didn't fall and crash into Earth, demonstrating a contrast between intuitive assumptions and the "fact" of the matter. Choices (B) and (D) are too wordy, and choice (C) is too casual in tone.

18. **(A)** The key phrase in the question is "human-influenced space activities." Astronauts and satellites are clearly human-influenced space activities. Choices (B) and (C) are not associated with human influence. Choice (D) is not a space activity but a theory.

19. **(D)** This is the only option that gives a logical comparison between the theory of Einstein and the theory of Newton. Be sure to compare the same sorts of objects to one another.

20. **(C)** This option uses construction parallel to that in the first part of the sentence and puts the words in a logical order. Choice (A) uses passive voice. Choice (B) confuses the intended meaning. Choice (D) is not parallel.

21. **(D)** "Yet," is the only option that indicates a contrast between the limitations of Newton's theory mentioned in the previous paragraph and the continuing applicability it has to this day.

22. **(B)** This choice most clearly indicates the "lasting relevance" of Newton's theory since it has been relevant for more than three centuries. Choice (A) asserts the irrelevance of Newton's theory. Choice (C) focuses on only a small part of Newton's theory (a part that was actually disproven by experimental observation according to the previous paragraph). Choice (D) is too vague.

23. **(B)** "Continues" matches with the singular subject "question." Choices (A) and (D) are plural. Choice (C) might work if it said "is continuing" instead of "is continue."

24. **(A)** This choice uses the proper singular possessive form of "institute" and uses a colon to give an appropriate pause before the clarification. Choices (B) and (C) do not show possession with "institutes," and choice (D) uses "its'," which is always incorrect.

25. **(C)** According to the graph, in 1998, the amount of state and local funding was roughly $10,000 per student. By 2008, it was a bit more than $9,000 per student. This is best characterized as "nearly a 10 percent" drop.

26. **(C)** The first paragraph introduces the topic of college rankings, and the second goes in-depth into evaluating their shortcomings. Choice (C) gives a highly specific, logical transition between the two paragraphs. Choices (A) and (D) are vague, and choice (B) is not relevant to the topic of rankings.

27. **(D)** "His or her" correctly refers to the singular "student" mentioned earlier in the sentence, given that we do not know the student's gender. Choices (A) and (C) are

plural, and choice (B) is inconsistent with the third-person "student" mentioned in this sentence.

28. **(D)** This is the third item listed in this sentence. To differentiate it from the others, using "still" makes the most sense. The other options do not indicate a third item in this sequence.

29. **(A)** The previous paragraph highlights the problems with college rankings, and the current paragraph highlights ways that colleges are making their programs more appealing beyond easily quantifiable criteria. Choice (A) provides a logical link between these themes. Choice (B) is irrelevant. Choices (C) and (D) are too specific.

30. **(D)** This option places commas such that they lead to a logical meaning. "In such programs" is an introductory phrase, and "just like required classes" is a parenthetical phrase. Choices (A), (B), and (C) do not have needed breaks, making for jumbled meanings.

31. **(D)** Since an alumnus is by definition someone who has graduated from a school, choices (A), (B), and (C) are needlessly repetitive, making choice (D) the best option.

32. **(A)** It is implied that someone would most likely be considering from among more than two universities, so "best" gives the needed superlative. Choices (C) works for comparing. Choices (B) and (D) do not work in the phrase "will . . . foster."

33. **(D)** The subject of the sentence is "rankings," so the plural verb "leave" is needed. Choices (A) and (C) are singular, and choice (B) refers to tree parts.

34. **(D)** This choice uses commas to set aside the appositive since Mrs. Wabash is the same as the "teacher." The other options do not use appropriate punctuation to set aside an appositive.

35. **(A)** This option correctly uses the present perfect tense to indicate that the narrator has forgotten this exercise. Choice (D) incorrectly uses "forgot," choice (C) incorrectly uses "has," and choice (D) is nonsensical.

36. **(D)** "But" gives a logical contrast between what the narrator clearly remembers in the previous sentence and what is more cloudy in this sentence. The other options do not express this contrast.

37. **(B)** This choice maintains the narrator's focus on trying to remember sensory details. Choice (A) is philosophical. Choice (C) is irrelevant. Choice (D) contradicts the feeling of ignorance.

38. **(C)** The proper phrasing is to copy something "onto" paper—one cannot copy something "in," "into," or "within" paper.

39. **(C)** "Entered" concisely expresses the intended idea. Choice (A) is repetitive since the narrator has already indicated that he is the one visiting these places. Choice (B) is too wordy, and choice (D) means "to predict" instead of "to perceive."

40. **(A)** The colon correctly sets off this list of the buildings, and the commas in this choice separate each item. Choice (B) would need a complete sentence after the semicolon. Choice (C) does not have the needed commas. Choice (D) does not have a complete sentence for the second part.

41. **(B)** The commas in this choice separate each item from the next. Choice (A) lacks any commas. Choice (C) requires one to separate "buildings" and "homes." Choice (D) breaks apart the unified "other structures."

42. **(A)** Stating that architecture is both "rewarding" and "demanding" clearly indicates the positive and negative aspects of this field. Choice (B) has two negative adjectives, choice (C) has two positive adjectives, and choice (D) has two neutral adjectives.

43. **(D)** "His or her" is needed to refer to the singular, gender-neutral architect. Choice (A) is wrong, because "there" is used for places. Choices (B) and (C) are both plural.

44. **(C)** Early in the paragraph, the narrator states that he is a "professional architect." Choice (C) ties this professional path to the early inspiration from Mrs. Wabash's class. Choice (A) is far too negative. Choices (B) and (D) are inconsistent with the fact that the narrator is indeed a professional architect.

Section 3: Math Test (No Calculator)

1. **(A)** Since multiplying both sides of the equation $2x + 3y = 4$ by 2 yields $4x + 6y = 8$, **the lines are the same.**

2. **(D)** From the given information, we have that $d + 4w = 60$ and $d + 8w = 85$. Subtracting the first equation from the second gives $4w = 25$. So $w = 6.25$. By replacing $4w$ by 25 in the first equation, we get that $d + 25 = 60 \Rightarrow d = 35$. So Bill's initial deposit was $35, and each week he deposited $6.25 into his account. After x weeks, the value of the account was **$35 + 6.25x$ dollars**.

3. **(B)** $x^2 - 8x = -16 \Rightarrow x^2 - 8x + 16 = 0 \Rightarrow (x-4)(x-4) = 0 \Rightarrow x - 4 = 0 \Rightarrow x = 4$. So the equation has at most one solution. Replacing x by 4 in the given equation confirms that 4 is a solution. So the equation has exactly 1 solution.

4. **(A)** $a + 10\%(a) = a + 0.1a = 1.1a$, and $b - 10\%(b) = b - 0.1b = 0.9b$. Since it is given that $1.1a = 0.9b$, we have $\dfrac{a}{b} = \dfrac{0.9}{1.1} = \dfrac{\mathbf{9}}{\mathbf{11}}$.

   **Note: If after increasing a and decreasing b the results are equal, a must be smaller than b, so *the ratio of a to b must be less than 1*. Eliminate choices (C) and (D). Now test choices (A) and (B). To test (B), pick two numbers in the ratio of 9 to 10 (90 and 100, for example). Then 90 increased by 10% is 99, and 100 decreased by 10% is 90.

   The results are not equal, so eliminate (B). The answer must be (A), $\dfrac{\mathbf{9}}{\mathbf{11}}$. (90 increased by 10% and 110 decreased by 10% are both 99.)

5. **(D)** The x-intercepts of any graph are the points on the graph whose y-coordinates are 0. To find where the line $y = 3x - 6$ crosses the x-axis, let $y = 0$:

   $$0 = 3x - 6 \Rightarrow 3x = 6 \Rightarrow x = 2$$

   Of the four choices, only in (D), $\boldsymbol{y = 2x - 4}$, is $x = 2$ when $y = 0$.

6. **(A)** If (a, b) is a point of intersection of the two graphs, then $b = a^2 + 2$ and $b = \dfrac{1}{2}a^2 + 1$. So $a^2 + 2 = \dfrac{1}{2}a^2 + 1 \Rightarrow \dfrac{1}{2}a^2 = -1$. This is impossible since $\dfrac{1}{2}a^2$ cannot be negative. So there are no points of intersection. **The two graphs do not intersect.**

Note that each graph is a parabola. Even a quick rough sketch will show that one graph is always above the other.

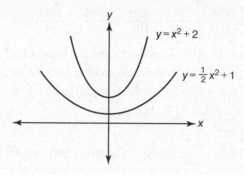

7. **(C)** In order for the equation $ax + b = cx + d$ to have no solutions, it must be that $a = c$ and $b \neq d$.

$$3(x + 2) + 2(x + 3) = 6(x + 1) - n(x + 5) \Rightarrow$$
$$3x + 6 + 2x + 6 = 6x + 6 - nx - 5n \Rightarrow$$
$$5x + 12 = (6 - n)x + 6 - 5n$$

For the given equation to have no solutions, it must be that $5 = 6 - n$. So $n = 1$. When $n = 1$, the last equation becomes $5x + 12 = 5x + 1$, which has **0** solutions.

8. **(D)** Subtract 11 from both sides of the given equation to put it in the standard form for a quadratic equation: $x^2 + 2x - 11 = 0$. Looking at the answer choices should make it clear that this equation cannot be solved by factoring. So use the quadratic formula:

$$x = \frac{-2 \pm \sqrt{4 - (-44)}}{2} = \frac{-2 \pm \sqrt{48}}{2} = \frac{-2 \pm 4\sqrt{3}}{2} = -1 \pm 2\sqrt{3}$$

So the two solutions are $-1 + 2\sqrt{3}$ **and** $-1 - 2\sqrt{3}$.

9. **(C)** In triangle ABC, draw in altitude BD.

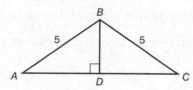

We know that $\cos A = \dfrac{AD}{5}$. Since it is given that $\cos A = 0.8$, we have $\dfrac{AD}{5} = 0.8$. Therefore $AD = 5 \times 0.8 = 4$. Since an altitude to the base of an isosceles triangle is also a median, $DC = AD = 4$, and $AC = 8$. You should see immediately that triangle ABD is a 3-4-5 right triangle. So $BD = 3$. (If you don't recognize the 3-4-5 triangle, use the Pythagorean theorem to get that $BD = 3$.)

Finally, the area of triangle ABC is $\dfrac{1}{2}bh = \dfrac{1}{2}(8)(3) = $ **12**.

10. **(C)** Note that it is irrelevant how much each pencil costs, so the correct answer cannot contain p. Elaine used $\dfrac{60}{100}d$ dollars to buy pencils and $\dfrac{40}{100}d$ dollars to buy markers. To find out how many markers she bought, divide the number of dollars she spent on

markers, $\frac{40}{100}d = \frac{40d}{100}$, by the cost in dollars of each marker. Each marker costs *m cents*

or $\frac{m}{100}$ dollars. Then $\frac{40d}{100} \div \frac{m}{100} = \frac{40d}{100} \times \frac{100}{m} = \frac{\textbf{40d}}{\textbf{m}}$.

**Alternative solution. Plug in numbers. Assume Elaine had \$100 and she spent \$60 on pencils and the other \$40 on markers, which cost \$2 or 200 cents each. Then she bought 20 markers. Which answer choice is equal to 20 when $d = 100$ and $m = 200$? Only choice (C): $\frac{\textbf{40d}}{\textbf{m}} = \frac{40 \times 100}{200} = 20$.

11. **(A)** Since $C = 2\pi r$, then $r = \frac{C}{2\pi}$. Since the formula for the area of a circle is $A = \pi r^2$,

$$\pi r^2 = \pi\left(\frac{C}{2\pi}\right)^2 = \pi\left(\frac{C^2}{4\pi^2}\right) = \frac{C^2}{4\pi}.$$

12. **(D)** The probability that the student chosen was a boy is

$$\frac{\text{the number of boys in the chorus}}{\text{total number of students in the chorus}}$$

After the auditions, the number of boys in the chorus was $b + 3$ and the number of girls was $g + 5$. So the total number of students in the chorus was $b + 3 + g + 5 = b + g + 8$. The desired probability is $\frac{\textbf{b+3}}{\textbf{b+g+8}}$.

13. **(C)** Since $f(x) = xg(x)$, $f(0) = 0g(0) = 0$. From the definition of $f(x)$, we see that

$$f(0) = 2(c) - 3(3) = 2c - 9. \text{ So } 2c - 9 = 0 \Rightarrow 2c = 9 \Rightarrow c = \textbf{4.5}$$

14. **(B)** The graph of $y = f(x - 2)$ is obtained by shifting the graph of $y = f(x)$ 2 units to the right. Therefore the x-intercept $(-3, 0)$ shifts 2 units to $(-1, 0)$; the **only** x-coordinate is **–1**.

15. **(A)** If r represents the radius of the sphere, and R and h represent the radius and height of the cone, respectively, the formulas for the volumes of the sphere and the cone are $V = \frac{4}{3}\pi r^3$ and $V = \frac{1}{3}\pi R^2 h$, respectively. Remember: these formulas are given to you on the first page of every math section. Since it is given that $R = 2r$, we have

$$\frac{4}{3}\pi r^3 = \frac{1}{3}\pi R^2 h = \frac{1}{3}\pi(2r)^2 h = \frac{1}{3}\pi 4r^2 h \Rightarrow r^3 = r^2 h \Rightarrow r = h \Rightarrow h = \frac{1}{2}R \Rightarrow \frac{h}{R} = \frac{1}{2}$$

16. **132** If in 2015, the nine club members read an average of 52 books, then in total they read $9 \times 52 = 468$ books. Since the eight club members other than Mary read an average of 42 books during the year, collectively they read $8 \times 42 = 336$ books. This means that in 2015, Mary read $468 - 336 = \textbf{132}$ books.

17. $\frac{\textbf{4}}{\textbf{3}}$ **or 1.33** Mentally, or by using a Venn diagram, determine the number of girls who play only one sport.

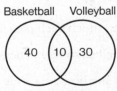

Basketball   Volleyball

40 play only basketball and 30 play only volleyball. The ratio is 40:30. Grid in $\frac{4}{3}$ or **1.33**.

18. $\frac{1}{3}$ **or any number between .3 and .4** Adding 3 to each term of the given inequality

gives:

$$\frac{5}{2} < x < \frac{10}{3} \Rightarrow 2.5 < x < 3.33$$

So a possible value of x is 3, in which case $\frac{1}{x} = \frac{1}{3}$.

**Since $\frac{5}{2} < x < \frac{10}{3}$, we have $\frac{2}{5} > \frac{1}{x} > \frac{3}{10}$. So $0.3 < \frac{1}{x} < 0.4$.

**Pick a value for $x - 3$ that satisfies the original inequality. For example, if $x - 3 = 0$, then $x = 3$ and $\frac{1}{x} = \frac{1}{3}$.

19. **4** If $2 + i$ is a solution of the equation $x^2 - bx + 5 = 0$, then

$(2 + i)^2 - b(2 + i) + 5 = 0 \Rightarrow (4 + 4i + i^2) - 2b - bi + 5 = 0 \Rightarrow 4 + 4i - 1 - 2b - bi + 5 = 0$

So $8 - 2b + (4 - b)i = 0 + 0i$, and so $8 - 2b = 0$ and $4 - b = 0$. So $b = 4$.

20. $\frac{1}{3}$ The relationship between the radian measure of a central angle (θ), the radius (r), and the length of the arc intercepted by the angle (s) is $s = r\theta$. So, $2 = 6\theta \Rightarrow \theta = \frac{1}{3}$.

Section 4: Math Test (Calculator)

1. **(B)** While driving at 40 miles per hour, Brigitte took 3 hours to get to her parents' house. So the distance she drove was $40 \times 3 = 120$ miles. To make the trip in 2.5 hours, she would have had to drive at $120 \div 2.5 = $ **48** miles per hour.

2. **(B)** From the given information, we have that the weighted average of the men's and women's grades was $\frac{80m + 90w}{m + w} = 86$. By cross-multiplying, we get that

$$80m + 90w = 86m + 86w \Rightarrow 4w = 6m \Rightarrow \frac{m}{w} = \frac{4}{6} = \frac{2}{3}$$

**If you got stuck on this, be sure to guess. Make it an educated guess, though. Since the class average was closer to the women's average than to the men's average, there must be more women than men in the course. So the ratio of the number of men to the number of women in the course must be less than 1. Therefore, the answer must be choice (A) or choice (B).

3. **(D)** Test each statement to see if it is true.

■ Choice (A): In 1960, there were 12 million households with 5 or more persons. In 2000 there were only 11.4 million such households. Statement (A) is true.
■ Choice (B): From 1940 to 2000, the percent of 1-person households more than tripled from 7.7% to 25.8%. Statement (B) is true.
■ Choice (C): In 1970, 17.6% of the households had 1 person and 29.6% of the households had 2 people. So 47.2% of the households had 2 or fewer people. Since the median is at the 50th percentile, the median was 3. Statement (C) is true.
■ Choice (D): From the 1950 census to the 1960 census, the percent of 2-person households decreased from 28.1% to 28%. Statement (D) is false.

4. **(B)** The easiest way to answer this question is to assign numbers to the original width and length such that the length is twice the width, say the length is 20 and the width is 10. Then the new length would be 40 and the new width would be 5. The original perimeter would be 60 and the new perimeter would be 90, an increase of 50%. The original area would be $20 \times 10 = 200$, and the new area would be $40 \times 5 = 200$; the area would not change. **So *P* would increase by 50%, and *A* would not change.**

5. **(C)** Set up a proportion:

$$\frac{2.2 \text{ pounds}}{1 \text{ kilogram}} = \frac{120 \text{ pounds}}{x \text{ kilograms}}$$

Then $2.2x = 120 \Rightarrow x = \dfrac{120}{2.2} = 54.54 \ldots$

Therefore, the **3** students weighing more than 120 pounds are the 3 who weigh more than 54.54 kilograms.

**Quickly multiply by 2.2: $56 \times 2.2 = 123.2$, so 56, 57, and 61 kilograms are all more than 120 pounds. The other two weights are less.

6. **(B)** Since the 180 freshmen make up 15% of the total number of students:

$$0.15t = 180 \Rightarrow t = \frac{180}{0.15} = \mathbf{1{,}200}$$

7. **(B)** From the solution to question 6, we know that the total number of students on teams is 1,200. Then there are 480 juniors on teams (40% of 1,200). So z, the number of seniors on teams, is $1{,}200 - (180 + 120 + 480) = 1{,}200 - 780 = \mathbf{420}$.

The sophomores account for $\dfrac{120}{1{,}200} = \dfrac{1}{10} = 10\%$ of the students on teams, so the percentage, w, of seniors is $100 - (15 + 10 + 40) = 100 - 65 = 35$, and finally, 35% of 1,200 is **420.

8. **(A)** Rewrite the given equation as $y = \dfrac{a}{a+1}x + 1$. We see that the graph is a straight line whose y-intercept is 1. So the correct answer choice must be (A) or (B). Since $a < -1$, that means $a + 1 < 0$. So $\dfrac{a}{a+1}$, the slope of the line, is positive (the numerator and denominator are both negative). So the answer is choice (A).

9. **(C)** Just set up a simple proportion:

$$\frac{22 \text{ feet}}{\text{second}} = \frac{22 \times 60 \text{ feet}}{60 \text{ seconds}} = \frac{1{,}320 \text{ feet}}{\text{minute}} = \frac{1{,}320 \times 60 \text{ feet}}{60 \text{ minutes}} = \frac{79{,}200 \text{ feet}}{\text{hour}}$$

Finally, $79{,}200 \div 5{,}280 = 15$. So Naveed's speed is **15** miles per hour.

10. **(C)** By TACTIC E1, if the average of 5 numbers is 70, their sum is $5 \times 70 = 350$. The median of the 5 numbers is the middle one when they are listed in increasing order. To make the third one as large as possible, make the others as small as possible. Since the numbers are not necessarily *different* positive integers, the two smallest could both be 1: 1, 1, ___, ___, ___. That leaves 348 for the remaining 3 integers. Since the fourth and fifth numbers must be at least as large as the third, the most the median could be is $348 \div 3 = 116$. The five numbers could be 1, 1, 116, 116, **116**.

11. **(C)** Let x represent the number of precincts that have fewer than 1,000 registered voters and to which 3 volunteers have been assigned. Let y represent the number of precincts with 1,000 or more registered voters and to which 5 volunteers have been assigned. Then

$$x + y = 20 \quad \text{and} \quad 3x + 5y = 84$$

Multiplying the first equation by 3 gives $3x + 3y = 60$. Subtracting $3x + 3y = 60$ from $3x + 5y = 84$ gives $2y = 24$. So $y = 12$. Therefore, $x = 20 - 12 = 8$. So 8 out of 20, or **40%**, of the precincts have fewer than 1,000 registered voters.

12. **(A)** Of course, you should draw a diagram and label it.

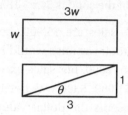

You could label the sides w and $3w$, but it is even easier to label them 1 and 3. Now you have two choices:

(1) Since $\tan \theta = \frac{1}{3}$, $\theta = \tan^{-1}\left(\frac{1}{3}\right) = 18.430$. Then $\sin \theta = \sin(18.430) = 0.316$.

(2) Use the Pythagorean theorem to find the hypotenuse x.

$(x)^2 = 3^2 + 1^2 = 10 \Rightarrow x = \sqrt{10}$. Then $\sin \theta = \dfrac{1}{\sqrt{10}} = \mathbf{0.316}$.

13. **(C)** Read the sales figures in the bar graph on the left for each of the eight years, add them, and then divide by 8. Rather than that, you could visualize the situation. Where could you draw a horizontal line across the graph so that there would be the same amount of gray area above the line as white area below it? Imagine a horizontal line drawn through the 7 on the vertical axis. The portions of the bars above the line for 1993 and 1996–1998 are just about exactly the same size as the white areas below the line for 1991, 1992, and 1994. The answer is **(C)**.

14. **(C)** Looking at the Earnings bar graph, it is clear that the only possible answers are 1992, 1994, and 1995, the three years in which there was a significant increase in earnings from the year before. From 1993 to 1994 expenditures doubled, from $200 million to $400 million—an increase of 100%. From 1991 to 1992 expenditures increased by $400 million (from $500 million to $900 million), but that is less than a 100% increase. From 1994 to 1995 expenditures increased by $300 million (from $400 million to $700 million); but again, this is less than a 100% increase. The answer is **(C)**.

15. **(D)** In answering question 15, observe that earnings are given in millions, while sales are in billions. If you answer too quickly, you might say that in 1993 earnings were 200 and sales were 8, and conclude that the desired ratio is $\dfrac{200}{8} = \dfrac{25}{1}$. You will avoid this mistake if you keep track of units: earnings were 200 *million* dollars, whereas sales were 8 *billion* dollars. The correct ratio is

$$\frac{200{,}000{,}000}{8{,}000{,}000{,}000} = \frac{2}{80} = \mathbf{\frac{1}{40}}$$

16. **(C)**

- The formula for the volume of a cylinder is $V = \pi r^2 h$, where r is the radius and h is the height. The volume of the cylinder is $\pi(3^2)(6) = 54\pi$.

- The formula for the volume of a sphere of radius r is $V = \frac{4}{3}\pi r^3$. The volume of a sphere of radius 3 is $\frac{4}{3}\pi(3)^3 = 36\pi$. Therefore, the volume of the hemisphere of radius 3 is $\left(\frac{1}{2}\right)36\pi = 18\pi$.

- Therefore, the total volume of the solid is $54\pi + 18\pi = \mathbf{72\pi}$.

17. **(B)** If during any week Sally's sales are $5,000, her commission would be 10% of that amount, or $500 and her total earnings would be $800. Since during the week in question, she earned more than $800, her sales exceeded $5,000. So her commission was 12%. Of her earnings of $1,080, $300 was her base pay and the other $780 was her commission. So if V represents the dollar value of her sales, $0.12V = \$780$ and $V = \$780 \div 0.12 = \mathbf{\$6,500}$.

**Note: this is an easy question to answer by backsolving. Start with choice (B) or choice (C). Add 12% of the value you are testing to $300 and see if the total is $1,080. If the total is less than $1,080, try a larger number. If it's more than $1,080, try a smaller number.

18. **(B)** The bar representing underweight adult females who perceive themselves to be underweight extends from about 70% to about 95%, a range of approximately **25%**.

19. **(A)** Almost all overweight females correctly considered themselves to be overweight; and more than half of all females of normal weight correctly considered themselves "about right." But nearly 70% of **underweight** adult females inaccurately considered themselves "about right."

20. **(B)** To find Henry's average speed, in kilometers per hour, divide the distance he went, in kilometers (198), by the time it took, in hours. Henry drove for 3 hours and 40 minutes, which is $3\frac{2}{3}$ hours (40 minutes = $\frac{40}{60}$ hour = $\frac{2}{3}$ hour). Henry's average speed, in kilometers per hour, was $198 \div 3\frac{2}{3} = 198 \div \frac{11}{3} = 198 \times \frac{3}{11} = \mathbf{54}$.

21. **(D)** On January 1, 2001, the value of the CD was $765 + 0.06(765) = (1.06)(765)$. On January 1 of each year, the value of the CD was (1.06) times its value on January 1 of the preceding year. After 12 years, the value of the CD was $(1.06)^{12}(765) = \mathbf{1,539}$.

22. **(D)** $(a + bi)(1 + i) = a + ai + bi + bi^2 = (a - b) + (a + b)i$.

So $(a - b) + (a + b)i = 3 + 5i \Rightarrow a - b = 3$ and $a + b = 5$.

Adding these two equations gives $2a = 8$. So $a = 4$ and $b = 1$. That means $a + bi = 4 + i$.

**$(a + bi)(1 + i) = 3 + 5i \Rightarrow a + bi = \dfrac{3+5i}{1+i} = \dfrac{3+5i}{1+i} \cdot \dfrac{1-i}{1-i} = \dfrac{3-3i+5i-5i^2}{1+1} = \dfrac{8+2i}{2} = 4 + i$

23. **(B)** The two given equations are each the equation of a line. If two lines do not intersect, they are parallel. So by KEY FACT N6, they have equal slopes.

By solving for y to put $3x + 4y + 5 = 0$ into slope-intercept form, we get $y = -\frac{3}{4}x - \frac{5}{4}$. So the slope is $-\frac{3}{4}$. Similarly, by rewriting $kx + 6y + 7 = 0$ as $y = -\frac{k}{6}x - \frac{7}{6}$, we see that its slope is $\frac{k}{6}$. So $-\frac{3}{4} = -\frac{k}{6} \Rightarrow -4k = -18 \Rightarrow k = \textbf{4.5}$.

24. **(D)** Let x = the number of children who have both a dog and a cat. Then $211 - x$ children have a dog but no cat, and $174 - x$ children have a cat but no dog. This is illustrated in the Venn diagram below.

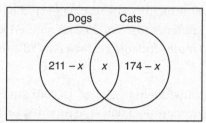

Since 83 children have neither a dog nor a cat, $326 - 83 = 243$ children have a dog, a cat, or both. So $(211 - x) + x + (174 - x) = 243 \Rightarrow 385 - x = 243 \Rightarrow x = 385 - 243 = \textbf{142}$.

25. **(C)** The formula for the volume of a sphere is $V = \frac{4}{3}\pi r^3$.

(Remember that this formula is given to you on the first page of each Math section.) The formula for the volume of a cube is $V = e^3$. So:

$$e^3 = \frac{4}{3}\pi r^3 \Rightarrow \frac{e^3}{r^3} = \frac{4}{3}\pi \Rightarrow \frac{e}{r} = \sqrt[3]{\frac{4}{3}\pi} = \textbf{1.61}$$

26. **(C)** $|f(x)| = 3$ if $f(x) = 3$ or $f(x) = -3$. There is only one value of x for which $f(x) = -3$, namely 0: $(0, 3)$ is the only point on the graph of $y = f(x)$ whose y-coordinate is -3. There are 5 values of x for which $f(x) = 3$, the 5 values where the graph of $y = f(x)$ crosses at the horizontal line $y = 3$. So, in total there are $1 + 5 = 6$ values of x between -6 and 7 for which $|f(x)| = \textbf{3}$.

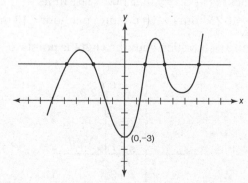

27. **(B)** The disease afflicts 0.1% of the population. Of the 1,000,000 people tested $0.001 \times 1,000,000 = 1,000$ people had the disease and the other 999,000 didn't have it. Of the 1,000 people who had the disease, 990 of them (99% of 1,000) tested positive and the other 10 erroneously tested negative. Of the 999,000 people who didn't have the disease,

989,010 of them (99% of 999,000) tested negative, and 9,990 of them (1% of 999,000) erroneously tested positive. So in total, 9,900 + 990 = 10,980 people tested positive, of whom 990 actually had the disease. Finally, 990 ÷ 10,980 = 0.09 = **9%**. Therefore, even though the test is 99% accurate, only 9% of the people who tested positive for the disease actually had it.

28. **(B)** The median of a set of data is the number for which 50% of the data is smaller than that number and 50% of the data is greater than that number. The students who studied less than 60 minutes per day account for only 30% of the data. Because the students who studied 60 to 119 minutes account for the next 25% of the data, the student at exactly the 50th percentile lies in this second group. Only choice (B) (**100** minutes) lies in this group.

 29. **(C)** At University *A*, 4,500 students (30% of 15,000) studied less than one hour per day. At University *B*, 10,500 students (52% of 25,000) studied less than one hour per day. So 10,500 – 4,500 = 6,000 more students at University (B) studied for less than one hour per day.

 30. **(D)** At University *A*, 1,500 students (10% of 15,000) study at least three hours (180 minutes) per day. At University *B*, 2,000 students (8% of 25,000) study at least three hours (180 minutes) per day. In total, 3,500 of the 40,000 students in both universities study at least three hours per day. Finally, 3,500 ÷ 40,000 = **0.0875**.

Note that since 8% of the students at University *B* study at least three hours per day, if 8% of the students at University *A* also study at least three hours per day, the answer would be 8% = 0.08. Since at University *A* the figure is 10%, the weighted average is raised a little and so the answer must be a bit more than 0.08.

 31. **3.8** In 50 minutes, 5 × 50 = 250 liters of water flow through the faucet into the vat. Since at the end of the 50 minutes the vat is full, there are 60 liters of water in the vat and the other 250 – 60 = 190 liters left the vat through the drain. So the rate of flow through the drain is 190 liters ÷ 50 minutes = **3.8** liters per minute.

 32. **15**

- To go 2,954 miles at 543 miles per hour takes 2,954 ÷ 543 = 5.44 hours.
- To go 2,954 miles at 569 miles per hour takes 2,954 ÷ 569 = 5.19 hours.
- The faster plane took 5.44 – 5.19 = 0.25 hours less time.
- Finally, 0.25 hours = 0.25 hours × 60 minutes per hour = **15** minutes.

33. **.95** Sketch the line *y* = 3*x* – 3, which goes through the points (0, –3), (1, 0), and (2, 3).

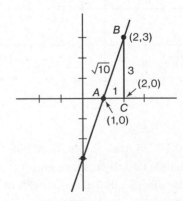

Use the Pythagorean theorem to find the length of AB:

$$(AB)^2 = 1^2 + 3^2 = 10 \Rightarrow AB = \sqrt{10} \approx 3.162$$

Then, $\sin \angle CAB = \dfrac{\text{opposite}}{\text{hypotenuse}} = \dfrac{3}{3.162} = \mathbf{0.95}$.

34. **200** The second job cost $45 dollars more than the first because it took 45 minutes, or 0.75 hours, longer. So the plumber's hourly rate, h, is $45 \div 0.75$ hours = $60 per hour. Her charge of $290 for the first job consisted of her flat fee of f dollars plus $60 per hour for the 2.5 additional hours:

$$290 = f + 2.5(60) = f + 150 \Rightarrow f = 140$$

So $f + h = 140 + 60 = \mathbf{200}$.

**Alternatively, to get the values of f and h, we could have solved the following system of equations:

$$355 = f + 3.25h \quad \text{and} \quad 290 = f + 2.5h$$

Subtracting the second equation from the first gives $45 = 0.75h$. Now proceed as above: $h = 45 \div 0.75 = 60$. Replace h with 60 in either of the equations to get $f = \mathbf{140}$.

35. **152** The two bar graphs show that in 1950, 8.1% of the population was age 65 and over and that the number of people age 65 and above was 12.3 million. So if P represents the total population in 1950, then

$$0.081P = 12,300,000. \text{ So } P = 12,300,000 \div 0.081 = 151,851,852 \approx 152,000,000$$

So grid in **152**.

36. **7** From the top chart, we can just read that in 2000 the number of people living in the United States age 85 and above was 4.2 million, or 4,200,000. In 1950, there were 12.3 million people age 65 and above. Of those, 8.4 million were 65–74 and 3.3 million were 75–84. So 8.4 + 3.3 = 11.7 million people were between 65 and 84 and the remaining 12,300,000 − 11,700,000 = 600,000 were 85 and above. Since 4,200,000 ÷ 600,000 = 7, there were 7 times as many people 85 and above in 2000 than in 1950.

37. **37.5** On her first $20,000 of income, Michelle's tax was $4,000 (20% of $20,000). So $9,250 − $4,000 = $5,250 represents the 30% tax she paid on her income in excess of $20,000.

$$9,250 = 4,000 + 30\%(N - 20,000) \Rightarrow 5,250 = 0.30(N - 20,000) \Rightarrow$$

$$\frac{5,205}{0.30} = N - 20,000 \Rightarrow N = 17,500 + 20,000 = 37,500$$

So $\dfrac{N}{1,000} = \mathbf{37.5}$.

38. **2250** From the solution to question 37, we know that Michelle's income was $37,500. If 20% of that had been exempt from taxation, her taxable income would have been reduced by $7,500 (20% of $37,500). So her tax would have been reduced by **$2,250** (30% of $7,500).

SAT Essay Scoring Rubric

	Score: 4
Reading	Excellent: The essay shows excellent understanding of the source.
	The essay shows an understanding of the source's main argument and key details and a firm grasp of how they are interconnected, demonstrating clear comprehension of the source.
	The essay does not misinterpret or misrepresent the source.
	The essay skillfully uses source evidence, such as direct quotations and rephrasing, representing a thorough comprehension of the source.
Analysis	Excellent: The essay gives excellent analysis of the source and shows clear understanding of what the assignment requires.
	The essay gives a complete, highly thoughtful analysis of the author's use of reasoning, evidence, rhetoric, and/or other argumentative elements the student has chosen to highlight.
	The essay has appropriate, adequate, and skillfully chosen support for its analysis. The essay focuses on the most important parts of the source in responding to the prompt.
Writing	Excellent: The essay is focused and shows an excellent grasp of the English language. The essay has a clear thesis. The essay has a well-executed introduction and conclusion. The essay shows a clear and well-crafted progression of thoughts both within paragraphs and in the essay as a whole. The essay has a wide range of sentence structures. The essay consistently shows precise choice of words. The essay is formal and objective in its style and tone. The essay demonstrates a firm grasp of the rules of standard English and has very few to no errors.

	Score: 3
Reading	Skillful: The essay shows effective understanding of the source.
	The essay shows an understanding of the source's main argument and key details.
	The essay is free of major misinterpretations and/or misrepresentations of the source.
	The essay uses appropriate source evidence, such as direct quotations and rephrasing, representing comprehension of the source.
Analysis	Skillful: The essay gives effective analysis of the source and shows an understanding of what the assignment requires.
	The essay decently analyzes the author's use of reasoning, evidence, rhetoric, and/or other argumentative elements the student has chosen to highlight.
	The essay has appropriate and adequate support for its analysis. The essay focuses primarily on the most important parts of the source in responding to the prompt.
Writing	Skillful: The essay is mostly focused and shows an effective grasp of the English language. The essay has a thesis, either explicit or implicit. The essay has an effective introduction and conclusion. The essay has a clear progression of thoughts both within paragraphs and in the essay as a whole. The essay has an assortment of sentence structures. The essay shows some precise choice of words. The essay is formal and objective in its style and tone. The essay demonstrates a grasp of the rules of standard English and has very few significant errors that interfere with the writer's argument.

Score: 2	
Reading	Limited: The essay shows some understanding of the source.
	The essay shows an understanding of the source's main argument, but not of key details.
	The essay may have some misinterpretations and/or misrepresentations of the source.
	The essay gives only partial evidence from the source, showing limited comprehension of the source.
Analysis	Limited: The essay gives partial analysis of the source and shows only limited understanding of what the assignment requires.
	The essay tries to show how the author uses reasoning, evidence, rhetoric, and/or other argumentative elements the student has chosen to highlight, but only states rather than analyzes their importance, or at least one part of the essay's analysis is unsupported by the source.
	The essay has little or no justification for its argument.
	The essay may lack attention to those elements of the source that are most pertinent to responding to the prompt.
Writing	Limited: The essay is mostly not cohesive and shows an ineffective grasp of the English language. The essay may not have a thesis, or may diverge from the thesis at some point in the essay's development. The essay may have an unsuccessful introduction and/or conclusion. The essay may show progression of thoughts within the paragraphs, but not in the essay as a whole. The essay is relatively uniform in its sentence structures. The essay shows imprecise and possibly repetitive choice of words.
	The essay may be more casual and subjective in style and tone. The essay demonstrates a weaker grasp of the rules of standard English and does have errors that interfere with the writer's argument.

Score: 1	
Reading	Insufficient: The essay shows virtually no understanding of the source.
	The essay is unsuccessful in showing an understanding of the source's main argument. It may refer to some details from the text, but it does so without tying them to the source's main argument.
	The essay has many misinterpretations and/or misrepresentations of the source.
	The essay gives virtually no evidence from the source, showing very poor comprehension of the source.
Analysis	Insufficient: The essay gives little to no accurate analysis of the source and shows poor understanding of what the assignment requires.
	The essay may show how the author uses reasoning, evidence, rhetoric, and/or other argumentative elements that the student has chosen to highlight but does so without analysis.
	Or many parts of the essay's analysis are unsupported by the source.
	The support given for points in the essay's argument are largely unsupported or off topic.
	The essay may not attend to the elements of the source that are pertinent to responding to the prompt.
	Or the essay gives no explicit analysis, perhaps only resorting to summary statements.
Writing	Insufficient: The essay is not cohesive and does not demonstrate skill in the English language. The essay may not have a thesis. The essay does not have a clear introduction and conclusion. The essay does not have a clear progression of thoughts. The essay is quite uniform and even repetitive in sentence structure.
	The essay shows poor and possibly inaccurate word choice. The essay is likely casual and subjective in style and tone. The essay shows a poor grasp of the rules of standard English and may have many errors that interfere with the writer's argument.

Top-Scoring Sample Student Response

All Americans can agree that the lower the unemployment rate, the better. This is the resounding consensus that the author of "Dead Presidents Take Precedence" appeals to throughout his argument to deregulate the minimum wage. In a conversational and often ironic tone, the writer references hoary philosophers, historical contradictions, and economic experts in order to build an argument that the reader cannot help but nod his or her head in agreement. The writer employs a second-person approach that captivates the reader quickly in its direct, but friendly overture—what seems agreeable can, in fact, be detrimental, and I'm going to show you how, he seems to say.

The author seemingly begins astray, providing a highly contested political statement as the basis for the argument to come in Thoreau's, "That government is best which governs least." However, he quickly establishes himself as a more moderate and reliable narrator, turning instead to historical fact and economic expertise. Tracing the minimum wage law from 1933 to 1941, the writer establishes its history in contradiction and illegitimacy, citing presidential overreach, congressional inconsistency, and unconstitutional judiciary oversight as evidence. With the reader now questioning the law's validity, the writer is free to engage in a dramatic and humorous exploration of more recent opinion, albeit one-sided.

Establishing himself as a layperson of economic study, the author installs a compact with the reader: we are both amateurs, so we must refer to the authorities on the subject. With empirical reasoning, the writer furthers his argument stating that "90% of U.S. economists" and "Noted Washington think tank The Cato Institute" found the minimum wage harmful rather than helpful. Instead of creating a more fair and productive workforce, he argues, the law only leads to higher unemployment rates and worse conditions for those who manage to retain employment. Effectively, the writer maintains a dialogue with the reader and offers up a conceivable and straightforward example of how the minimum wage law could easily fail the working public. As collaborative amateurs, we are exposed to a sensible example: a small business is forced to cut an employee because of limited funding when wages are increased.

Finally, the writer persuades any stragglers by introducing "the threat of outsourcing," arguing that our insistence on a minimum wage is ultimately leaving Americans without work and shipping jobs overseas. With a relatable example—that of where your clothes are manufactured—the writer is able to hone in the real-life proof that many companies are indeed outsourcing. Since the reader can undoubtedly remember a thousand "Made in China" stickers plastered all over his or her toys, clothes, and electronics, he/she is easily able to hold on for the author's next big jump: "we owe that entirely to the minimum wage." The argument, though quite possibly strained, becomes entirely believable once the narrator has successfully befriended the reader, provided favorable statistics, and executed accessible examples.

First through historical allusion and then via professional detractors, the author effectively allows the reader to question not only the foundation of the minimum wage but also its implications for national fiscal success. "Can we afford to lose more jobs?" becomes the prominent question—a question linked by the author directly to wage regulation. Perhaps this is why the writer decides to end in a rhetorical question that discredits those without formal training in economic policy. Of course, the reader obliges and is likely to return to the overwhelming statistics of those economists not in favor of federal minimum wage mandates. In allowing the reader to evidently come to his/her own decision to trust the experts, the writer has satisfyingly built a persuasive argument.

ANSWER SHEET
Model Test 4

Section 1: Reading

1. Ⓐ Ⓑ Ⓒ Ⓓ
2. Ⓐ Ⓑ Ⓒ Ⓓ
3. Ⓐ Ⓑ Ⓒ Ⓓ
4. Ⓐ Ⓑ Ⓒ Ⓓ
5. Ⓐ Ⓑ Ⓒ Ⓓ
6. Ⓐ Ⓑ Ⓒ Ⓓ
7. Ⓐ Ⓑ Ⓒ Ⓓ
8. Ⓐ Ⓑ Ⓒ Ⓓ
9. Ⓐ Ⓑ Ⓒ Ⓓ
10. Ⓐ Ⓑ Ⓒ Ⓓ
11. Ⓐ Ⓑ Ⓒ Ⓓ
12. Ⓐ Ⓑ Ⓒ Ⓓ
13. Ⓐ Ⓑ Ⓒ Ⓓ

14. Ⓐ Ⓑ Ⓒ Ⓓ
15. Ⓐ Ⓑ Ⓒ Ⓓ
16. Ⓐ Ⓑ Ⓒ Ⓓ
17. Ⓐ Ⓑ Ⓒ Ⓓ
18. Ⓐ Ⓑ Ⓒ Ⓓ
19. Ⓐ Ⓑ Ⓒ Ⓓ
20. Ⓐ Ⓑ Ⓒ Ⓓ
21. Ⓐ Ⓑ Ⓒ Ⓓ
22. Ⓐ Ⓑ Ⓒ Ⓓ
23. Ⓐ Ⓑ Ⓒ Ⓓ
24. Ⓐ Ⓑ Ⓒ Ⓓ
25. Ⓐ Ⓑ Ⓒ Ⓓ
26. Ⓐ Ⓑ Ⓒ Ⓓ

27. Ⓐ Ⓑ Ⓒ Ⓓ
28. Ⓐ Ⓑ Ⓒ Ⓓ
29. Ⓐ Ⓑ Ⓒ Ⓓ
30. Ⓐ Ⓑ Ⓒ Ⓓ
31. Ⓐ Ⓑ Ⓒ Ⓓ
32. Ⓐ Ⓑ Ⓒ Ⓓ
33. Ⓐ Ⓑ Ⓒ Ⓓ
34. Ⓐ Ⓑ Ⓒ Ⓓ
35. Ⓐ Ⓑ Ⓒ Ⓓ
36. Ⓐ Ⓑ Ⓒ Ⓓ
37. Ⓐ Ⓑ Ⓒ Ⓓ
38. Ⓐ Ⓑ Ⓒ Ⓓ
39. Ⓐ Ⓑ Ⓒ Ⓓ

40. Ⓐ Ⓑ Ⓒ Ⓓ
41. Ⓐ Ⓑ Ⓒ Ⓓ
42. Ⓐ Ⓑ Ⓒ Ⓓ
43. Ⓐ Ⓑ Ⓒ Ⓓ
44. Ⓐ Ⓑ Ⓒ Ⓓ
45. Ⓐ Ⓑ Ⓒ Ⓓ
46. Ⓐ Ⓑ Ⓒ Ⓓ
47. Ⓐ Ⓑ Ⓒ Ⓓ
48. Ⓐ Ⓑ Ⓒ Ⓓ
49. Ⓐ Ⓑ Ⓒ Ⓓ
50. Ⓐ Ⓑ Ⓒ Ⓓ
51. Ⓐ Ⓑ Ⓒ Ⓓ
52. Ⓐ Ⓑ Ⓒ Ⓓ

Section 2: Writing and Language

1. Ⓐ Ⓑ Ⓒ Ⓓ
2. Ⓐ Ⓑ Ⓒ Ⓓ
3. Ⓐ Ⓑ Ⓒ Ⓓ
4. Ⓐ Ⓑ Ⓒ Ⓓ
5. Ⓐ Ⓑ Ⓒ Ⓓ
6. Ⓐ Ⓑ Ⓒ Ⓓ
7. Ⓐ Ⓑ Ⓒ Ⓓ
8. Ⓐ Ⓑ Ⓒ Ⓓ
9. Ⓐ Ⓑ Ⓒ Ⓓ
10. Ⓐ Ⓑ Ⓒ Ⓓ
11. Ⓐ Ⓑ Ⓒ Ⓓ

12. Ⓐ Ⓑ Ⓒ Ⓓ
13. Ⓐ Ⓑ Ⓒ Ⓓ
14. Ⓐ Ⓑ Ⓒ Ⓓ
15. Ⓐ Ⓑ Ⓒ Ⓓ
16. Ⓐ Ⓑ Ⓒ Ⓓ
17. Ⓐ Ⓑ Ⓒ Ⓓ
18. Ⓐ Ⓑ Ⓒ Ⓓ
19. Ⓐ Ⓑ Ⓒ Ⓓ
20. Ⓐ Ⓑ Ⓒ Ⓓ
21. Ⓐ Ⓑ Ⓒ Ⓓ
22. Ⓐ Ⓑ Ⓒ Ⓓ

23. Ⓐ Ⓑ Ⓒ Ⓓ
24. Ⓐ Ⓑ Ⓒ Ⓓ
25. Ⓐ Ⓑ Ⓒ Ⓓ
26. Ⓐ Ⓑ Ⓒ Ⓓ
27. Ⓐ Ⓑ Ⓒ Ⓓ
28. Ⓐ Ⓑ Ⓒ Ⓓ
29. Ⓐ Ⓑ Ⓒ Ⓓ
30. Ⓐ Ⓑ Ⓒ Ⓓ
31. Ⓐ Ⓑ Ⓒ Ⓓ
32. Ⓐ Ⓑ Ⓒ Ⓓ
33. Ⓐ Ⓑ Ⓒ Ⓓ

34. Ⓐ Ⓑ Ⓒ Ⓓ
35. Ⓐ Ⓑ Ⓒ Ⓓ
36. Ⓐ Ⓑ Ⓒ Ⓓ
37. Ⓐ Ⓑ Ⓒ Ⓓ
38. Ⓐ Ⓑ Ⓒ Ⓓ
39. Ⓐ Ⓑ Ⓒ Ⓓ
40. Ⓐ Ⓑ Ⓒ Ⓓ
41. Ⓐ Ⓑ Ⓒ Ⓓ
42. Ⓐ Ⓑ Ⓒ Ⓓ
43. Ⓐ Ⓑ Ⓒ Ⓓ
44. Ⓐ Ⓑ Ⓒ Ⓓ

ANSWER SHEET
Model Test 4

Section 3: Math (No Calculator)

1. Ⓐ Ⓑ Ⓒ Ⓓ   5. Ⓐ Ⓑ Ⓒ Ⓓ   9. Ⓐ Ⓑ Ⓒ Ⓓ   13. Ⓐ Ⓑ Ⓒ Ⓓ
2. Ⓐ Ⓑ Ⓒ Ⓓ   6. Ⓐ Ⓑ Ⓒ Ⓓ   10. Ⓐ Ⓑ Ⓒ Ⓓ   14. Ⓐ Ⓑ Ⓒ Ⓓ
3. Ⓐ Ⓑ Ⓒ Ⓓ   7. Ⓐ Ⓑ Ⓒ Ⓓ   11. Ⓐ Ⓑ Ⓒ Ⓓ   15. Ⓐ Ⓑ Ⓒ Ⓓ
4. Ⓐ Ⓑ Ⓒ Ⓓ   8. Ⓐ Ⓑ Ⓒ Ⓓ   12. Ⓐ Ⓑ Ⓒ Ⓓ

16.   17.   18.

19.   20.

ANSWER SHEET
Model Test 4

Section 4: Math (Calculator)

1. Ⓐ Ⓑ Ⓒ Ⓓ   9. Ⓐ Ⓑ Ⓒ Ⓓ   17. Ⓐ Ⓑ Ⓒ Ⓓ   25. Ⓐ Ⓑ Ⓒ Ⓓ

2. Ⓐ Ⓑ Ⓒ Ⓓ   10. Ⓐ Ⓑ Ⓒ Ⓓ   18. Ⓐ Ⓑ Ⓒ Ⓓ   26. Ⓐ Ⓑ Ⓒ Ⓓ

3. Ⓐ Ⓑ Ⓒ Ⓓ   11. Ⓐ Ⓑ Ⓒ Ⓓ   19. Ⓐ Ⓑ Ⓒ Ⓓ   27. Ⓐ Ⓑ Ⓒ Ⓓ

4. Ⓐ Ⓑ Ⓒ Ⓓ   12. Ⓐ Ⓑ Ⓒ Ⓓ   20. Ⓐ Ⓑ Ⓒ Ⓓ   28. Ⓐ Ⓑ Ⓒ Ⓓ

5. Ⓐ Ⓑ Ⓒ Ⓓ   13. Ⓐ Ⓑ Ⓒ Ⓓ   21. Ⓐ Ⓑ Ⓒ Ⓓ   29. Ⓐ Ⓑ Ⓒ Ⓓ

6. Ⓐ Ⓑ Ⓒ Ⓓ   14. Ⓐ Ⓑ Ⓒ Ⓓ   22. Ⓐ Ⓑ Ⓒ Ⓓ   30. Ⓐ Ⓑ Ⓒ Ⓓ

7. Ⓐ Ⓑ Ⓒ Ⓓ   15. Ⓐ Ⓑ Ⓒ Ⓓ   23. Ⓐ Ⓑ Ⓒ Ⓓ

8. Ⓐ Ⓑ Ⓒ Ⓓ   16. Ⓐ Ⓑ Ⓒ Ⓓ   24. Ⓐ Ⓑ Ⓒ Ⓓ

31.   32.   33.   34.

35.   36.   37.   38.

Essay

PLANNING PAGE

READING TEST

65 MINUTES, 52 QUESTIONS

Turn to Section 1 of your answer sheet to answer the questions in this section.

> **Directions:** Following each of the passages (or pairs of passages) below are questions about the passage (or passages). Read each passage carefully. Then, select the best answer for each question based on what is stated in the passage (or passages) and in any graphics that may accompany the passage.

Questions 1–11 are based on the following passage.

The following passage is an excerpt from Henry James's short story "The Pupil." *In this section, Pemberton, the young British tutor, describes some of the hasty trips around Europe during which he came to know his pupil, Morgan Moreen, and Morgan's family.*

A year after he had come to live with them Mr. and Mrs. Moreen suddenly gave up the villa at Nice. Pemberton had got used
Line to suddenness, having seen it practiced on
(5) a considerable scale during two jerky little tours—one in Switzerland the first summer, and the other late in the winter, when they all ran down to Florence and then, at the end of ten days, liking it much less than they
(10) had intended, straggled back in mysterious depression. They had returned to Nice "for ever," as they said; but this didn't prevent their squeezing, one rainy muggy May night, into a second-class railway-carriage—you
(15) could never tell by which class they would travel—where Pemberton helped them to stow away a wonderful collection of bundles and bags. The explanation of this maneuver was that they had determined to spend the
(20) summer "in some bracing place"; but in Paris they dropped into a small furnished

apartment—a fourth floor in a third-rate avenue, where there was a smell on the staircase and the *portier*[1] was hateful—
(25) and passed the next four months in blank indigence.

The better part of this forced temporary stay belonged to the tutor and his pupil, who, visiting the Invalides[2] and Notre Dame, the
(30) Conciergerie and all the museums, took a hundred rewarding rambles. They learned to know their Paris, which was useful, for they came back another year for a longer stay, the general character of which in Pemberton's
(35) memory today mixes pitiably and confusedly with that of the first. He sees Morgan's shabby knickerbockers—the everlasting pair that didn't match his blouse and that as he grew longer could only grow faded. He remembers
(40) the particular holes in his three or four pairs of colored stockings.

Morgan was dear to his mother, but he never was better dressed than was absolutely necessary—partly, no doubt, by his own fault,
(45) for he was as indifferent to his appearance as a German philosopher. "My dear fellow, so are you! I don't want to cast you in the shade." Pemberton could have no rejoinder for this—the assertion so closely represented
(50) the fact. If however the deficiencies of his own wardrobe were a chapter by themselves he didn't like his little charge to look too

GO ON TO THE NEXT PAGE

poor. Later he used to say "Well, if we're poor, why, after all, shouldn't we look it?" and he
(55) consoled himself with thinking there was something rather elderly and gentlemanly in Morgan's disrepair—it differed from the untidiness of the urchin who plays and spoils his things. He could trace perfectly the
(60) degrees by which, in proportion as her little son confined himself to his tutor for society, Mrs. Moreen shrewdly forbore to renew his garments. She did nothing that didn't show, neglected him because he escaped notice,
(65) and then, as he illustrated this clever policy, discouraged at home his public appearances. Her position was logical enough—those members of her family who did show had to be showy.
(70)   During this period and several others Pemberton was quite aware of how he and his comrade might strike people; wandering languidly through the Jardin des Plantes[3] as if they had nowhere to go, sitting on the
(75) winter days in the galleries of the Louvre, so splendidly ironical to the homeless, as if for the advantage of the steam radiators. They joked about it sometimes: it was the sort of joke that was perfectly within the boy's
(80) compass. They figured themselves as part of the vast vague hand-to-mouth multitude of the enormous city and pretended they were proud of their position in it—it showed them "such a lot of life" and made them conscious
(85) of a democratic brotherhood. If Pemberton couldn't feel a sympathy in destitution with his small companion—for after all Morgan's fond parents would never have let him really suffer—the boy would at least feel it with
(90) him, so it came to the same thing. He used sometimes to wonder what people would think they were—to fancy they were looked askance at, as if it might be a suspected case of kidnapping. Morgan wouldn't be taken

(95) for a young patrician with a tutor—he wasn't smart enough—though he might pass for his companion's sickly little brother.

[1]Hall porter or custodian.
[2]Famous Paris monument; site of the tomb of Napoleon.
[3]Botanical garden.

1. The primary purpose of the passage is to

    (A) denounce the ill treatment of an exceptional child.
    (B) describe a boy's reactions to his irresponsible parents.
    (C) portray a selfish and unfeeling mother and son.
    (D) recount an outsider's impressions of an odd family.

2. It can most reasonably be inferred from the passage that the reason for the Moreens' sudden departure from Nice had to do with

    (A) ill health.
    (B) shifts of mood.
    (C) educational opportunities.
    (D) financial problems.

3. Which choice provides the best evidence for the answer to the previous question?

    (A) Lines 3–11 ("Pemberton . . . depression")
    (B) Lines 11–18 ("They had . . . bags")
    (C) Lines 18–26 ("The explanation . . . indigence")
    (D) Lines 31–36 ("They learned . . . first")

GO ON TO THE NEXT PAGE

4. It can be most reasonably inferred from the passage that the narrator is making these comments about Pemberton's travels with the Moreen family

   (A) on Pemberton's return with the Moreens to Nice.
   (B) in response to visiting Paris for the first time.
   (C) some time after Pemberton's wanderings with the Moreens.
   (D) in an effort to write down his memoirs.

5. Which choice provides the best evidence for the answer to the previous question?

   (A) Lines 31–36 ("They learned . . . the first")
   (B) Lines 42–46 ("Morgan was dear . . . philosopher")
   (C) Lines 59–63 ("He could trace . . . garments")
   (D) Lines 77–85 ("They joked . . . brotherhood")

6. The tone of Morgan's speech to his tutor (lines 46–49) can best be described as

   (A) apathetic.
   (B) bitter.
   (C) teasing.
   (D) self-righteous.

7. As described in lines 42–69, Mrs. Moreen's approach toward Morgan can best be described as

   (A) stern but nurturing.
   (B) fond but pragmatic.
   (C) cruel and unfeeling.
   (D) doting and overprotective.

8. It can most reasonably be inferred from lines 63–69 that Mrs. Moreen most likely ceases to spend money on new clothing for Morgan because

   (A) she and her husband have grown increasingly miserly with the passage of time.
   (B) the child is so small for his age that he needs little in the way of clothing.
   (C) she is unwilling to offend Pemberton by dressing his pupil in finer clothes than Pemberton can afford.
   (D) she has only enough money to buy clothes for the family members who must appear in polite society.

9. As used in line 72, "strike" most nearly means

   (A) appear to.
   (B) run into.
   (C) achieve.
   (D) hit.

10. It can be inferred from the passage that Morgan and Pemberton regard the "hand-to-mouth multitude" of Paris (line 81) with a sense of

   (A) amusement.
   (B) condescension.
   (C) indifference.
   (D) identification.

11. As used in line 96, "smart" most nearly means

   (A) intelligent.
   (B) brisk.
   (C) fashionable.
   (D) impertinent.

GO ON TO THE NEXT PAGE

MODEL TEST 4

Questions 12–22 are based on the following passage.

In this excerpt from an essay on the symbolic language of dreams, the writer Erich Fromm explores the nature of symbols.

One of the current definitions of a symbol is that it is "something that stands for something else." We can differentiate

Line between three kinds of symbols: the
(5) *conventional*, the *accidental*, and the *universal* symbol.

The *conventional* symbol is the best known of the three, since we employ it in everyday language. If we see the word
(10) "table" or hear the sound "table," the letters *t-a-b-l-e* stand for something else. They stand for the thing "table" that we see, touch, and use. What is the connection between the *word* "table" and the *thing* "table"? Is there
(15) any inherent relationship between them? Obviously not. The *thing* table has nothing to do with the *sound* table, and the only reason the word symbolizes the thing is the convention of calling this particular thing by
(20) a name. We learn this connection as children by the repeated experience of hearing the word in reference to the thing until a lasting association is formed so that we don't have to think to find the right word.
(25) There are some words, however, in which the association is not only conventional. When we say "phooey," for instance, we make with our lips a movement of dispelling the air quickly. It is an expression of disgust
(30) in which our mouths participate. By this quick expulsion of air we imitate and thus express our intention to expel something, to get it out of our system. In this case, as in some others, the symbol has an inherent
(35) connection with the feeling it symbolizes.

But even if we assume that originally many or even all words had their origins in some such inherent connection between symbol and the symbolized, most words no longer have this
(40) meaning for us when we learn a language.

Words are not the only illustration for conventional symbols, although they are the most frequent and best known ones. Pictures also can be conventional symbols. A flag, for
(45) instance, may stand for a specific country, and yet there is no intrinsic connection between the specific colors and the country for which they stand. They have been accepted as denoting that particular country,
(50) and we translate the visual impression of the flag into the concept of that country, again on conventional grounds.

The opposite to the conventional symbol is the *accidental* symbol, although they have
(55) one thing in common: there is no intrinsic relationship between the symbol and that which it symbolizes. Let us assume that someone has had a saddening experience in a certain city; when he hears the name of that
(60) city, he will easily connect the name with a mood of sadness, just as he would connect it with a mood of joy had his experience been a happy one. Quite obviously, there is nothing in the nature of the city that is either
(65) sad or joyful. It is the individual experience connected with the city that makes it a symbol of a mood.

The *universal* symbol is one in which there is an intrinsic relationship between
(70) the symbol and that which it represents. Take, for instance, the symbol of fire. We are fascinated by certain qualities of fire in a fireplace. First of all, by its aliveness. It changes continuously, it moves all the time,
(75) and yet there is constancy in it. It remains the same without being the same. It gives the impression of power, of energy, of grace

GO ON TO THE NEXT PAGE

and lightness. It is as if it were dancing, and had an inexhaustible source of energy.

(80) When we use fire as a symbol, we describe the *inner experience* characterized by the same elements which we notice in the sensory experience of fire—the mood of energy, lightness, movement, grace, gaiety,

(85) sometimes one, sometimes another of these elements being predominant in the feeling.

The universal symbol is the only one in which the relationship between the symbol and that which is symbolized is not

(90) coincidental, but intrinsic. It is rooted in the experience of the affinity between an emotion or thought, on the one hand, and a sensory experience, on the other. It can be called universal because it is shared by all

(95) men, in contrast not only to the accidental symbol, which is by its very nature entirely personal, but also to the conventional symbol, which is restricted to a group of people sharing the same convention. The

(100) universal symbol is rooted in the properties of our body, our senses, and our mind, which are common to all men and, therefore, not restricted to individuals or to specific groups. Indeed, *the language of the universal symbol*

(105) *is the one common tongue developed by the human race, a language which it forgot before it succeeded in developing a universal conventional language.*

12. The primary purpose of the passage is to

(A) refute an argument about the nature of symbolism.
(B) describe the process of verbalization.
(C) summarize the findings of a long-term research project.
(D) refine the definition of a technical term.

13. As used in lines 11–12, "stand for" most nearly means

(A) tolerate.
(B) represent.
(C) support.
(D) rise.

14. According to lines 25–35, "table" and "phooey" differ in that

(A) only one is a conventional symbol.
(B) "table" is a more commonly used symbol than "phooey."
(C) "phooey" has an intrinsic natural link with its meaning.
(D) children learn "phooey" more readily than they learn "table."

15. It can be inferred from the passage that another example of a word with both inherent and conventional associations to its meaning is

(A) hiss.
(B) hike.
(C) hold.
(D) candle.

GO ON TO THE NEXT PAGE

MODEL TEST 4

16. Which of the following would the author be most likely to categorize as a conventional symbol?

    (A) a patchwork quilt
    (B) a bonfire
    (C) the city of London
    (D) the Statue of Liberty

17. Which choice provides the best evidence for the answer to the previous question?

    (A) Lines 20–24 ("We learn . . . word")
    (B) Lines 33–35 ("In this case . . . symbolizes")
    (C) Lines 36–40 ("But even . . . language")
    (D) Lines 44–52 ("A flag . . . grounds")

18. According to the author's argument, a relationship between Disneyland and the mood of joy can best be described as

    (A) innate.
    (B) immutable.
    (C) elemental.
    (D) coincidental.

19. Which choice provides the best evidence for the answer to the previous question?

    (A) Lines 36–40 ("But even . . . language")
    (B) Lines 44–48 ("A flag . . . stand")
    (C) Lines 57–63 ("Let us . . . one")
    (D) Lines 68–70 ("The *universal* . . . represents")

20. According to the passage, a major factor that distinguishes a universal symbol from conventional and accidental symbols is

    (A) its origins in sensory experience.
    (B) its dependence on a specific occasion.
    (C) the intensity of the mood experienced.
    (D) its appeal to the individual.

21. By saying "Take . . . the symbol of fire" (line 71), the author is asking the reader to

    (A) grasp it as an element.
    (B) consider it as an example.
    (C) accept it as a possibility.
    (D) assume it as a standard.

22. As used in line 100, "properties" most nearly means

    (A) possessions.
    (B) attributes.
    (C) premises.
    (D) assets.

GO ON TO THE NEXT PAGE

MODEL TEST 4

Questions 23–32 are based on the following passage.

The following passage is taken from a classic study of tarantulas published in Scientific American *in 1952.*

A fertilized female tarantula lays from 200 to 400 eggs at a time; thus it is possible for a single tarantula to produce several
Line thousand young. She takes no care of them
(5) beyond weaving a cocoon of silk to enclose the eggs. After they hatch, the young walk away, find convenient places in which to dig their burrows and spend the rest of their lives in solitude. Tarantulas feed mostly on
(10) insects and millipedes. Once their appetite is appeased, they digest the food for several days before eating again. Their sight is poor, being limited to sensing a change in the intensity of light and to the perception of
(15) moving objects. They apparently have little or no sense of hearing, for a hungry tarantula will pay no attention to a loudly chirping cricket placed in its cage unless the insect happens to touch one of its legs.
(20) But all spiders, and especially hairy ones, have an extremely delicate sense of touch. Laboratory experiments prove that tarantulas can distinguish three types of touch: pressure against the body wall, stroking of the body
(25) hair and riffling of certain very fine hairs on the legs called trichobothria. Pressure against the body, by a finger or the end of a pencil, causes the tarantula to move off slowly for a short distance. The touch excites
(30) no defensive response unless the approach is from above, where the spider can see the motion, in which case it rises on its hind legs, lifts its front legs, opens its fangs and holds this threatening posture as long as the object
(35) continues to move. When the motion stops,

the spider drops back to the ground, remains quiet for a few seconds, and then moves slowly away.

The entire body of a tarantula, especially
(40) its legs, is thickly clothed with hair. Some of it is short and woolly, some long and stiff. Touching this body hair produces one of two distinct reactions. When the spider is hungry, it responds with an immediate and swift
(45) attack. At the touch of a cricket's antennae the tarantula seizes the insect so swiftly that a motion picture taken at the rate of 64 frames per second shows only the result and not the process of capture. But when the spider is not
(50) hungry, the stimulation of its hairs merely causes it to shake the touched limb. An insect can walk under its hairy belly unharmed.

The trichobothria, very fine hairs growing from disklike membranes on the legs, were
(55) once thought to be the spider's hearing organs, but we now know that they have nothing to do with sound. They are sensitive only to air movement. A light breeze makes them vibrate slowly without disturbing the
(60) common hair. When one blows gently on the trichobothria, the tarantula reacts with a quick jerk of its four front legs. If the front and hind legs are stimulated at the same time, the spider makes a sudden jump. This
(65) reaction is quite independent of the state of its appetite.

These three tactile responses—to pressure on the body wall, to moving of the common hair, and to flexing of the trichobothria—are
(70) so different from one another that there is no possibility of confusing them. They serve the tarantula adequately for most of its needs and enable it to avoid most annoyances and dangers. But they fail the spider completely
(75) when it meets its deadly enemy, the digger wasp *Pepsis*.

GO ON TO THE NEXT PAGE

23. The primary purpose of the passage is to

(A) report on controversial new discoveries about spider behavior.
(B) summarize what is known about the physical and social responses of tarantulas.
(C) challenge the findings of historic laboratory experiments involving tarantulas.
(D) discuss the physical adaptations that make tarantulas unique.

24. It can most reasonably be inferred from the opening paragraph that tarantulas

(A) become apprehensive at sudden noises.
(B) depend on their mothers for nourishment after hatching.
(C) must consume insects or millipedes daily.
(D) are reclusive by nature.

25. Which choice provides the best evidence for the answer to the previous question?

(A) Lines 1–6 ("A fertilized . . . eggs")
(B) Lines 6–9 ("After . . . solitude")
(C) Lines 9–12 ("Tarantulas . . . again")
(D) Lines 12–15 ("Their sight . . . objects")

26. As used in line 29, "excites" most nearly means

(A) enlivens.
(B) inflames.
(C) stimulates.
(D) awakens.

27. The author's attitude toward tarantulas would best be described as one of

(A) nervous fascination.
(B) reluctant curiosity.
(C) marked ambivalence.
(D) objective appreciation.

28. The description of what happens when one films a tarantula's reaction to the touch of a cricket (lines 45–49) primarily is intended to convey a sense of the tarantula's

(A) omnivorous appetite.
(B) graceful movement.
(C) quickness in attacking.
(D) indifference to stimulation.

29. As used in line 65, "independent" most nearly means

(A) self-sufficient.
(B) self-governing.
(C) impartial.
(D) regardless.

30. In the passage, the author does all of the following EXCEPT

   (A) deny a possibility.
   (B) define a term.
   (C) correct a misapprehension.
   (D) pose a question.

31. In the paragraphs immediately following this passage, the author most likely will

   (A) explain why scientists previously confused the tarantula's three tactile responses.
   (B) point out the weaknesses of the digger wasp that enable the tarantula to subdue it.
   (C) describe how the digger wasp goes about attacking tarantulas.
   (D) demonstrate how the tarantula's three tactile responses enable it to meet its needs.

32. Which choice provides the best evidence for the answer to the previous question?

   (A) Lines 53–58 ("The trichobothria . . . movement")
   (B) Lines 64–66 ("This reaction . . . appetite")
   (C) Lines 67–71 ("These three . . . them")
   (D) Lines 74–76 ("But . . . *Pepsis*")

Questions 33–42 are based on the following passage.

This passage is adapted from John Locke, Second Treatise of Civil Government, *originally published in 1689. Locke's* Two Treatises of Civil Government *had a profound effect on the framers of the US Declaration of Independence and Constitution.*

[I]t will be said that, the people being ignorant and always discontented, to lay the foundation of government in the unsteady
Line opinion and uncertain humor of the people
(5) is to expose it to certain ruin; and no government will be able long to subsist if the people may set up a new legislative whenever they take offense at the old one. To this I answer: Quite the contrary. People are not so
(10) easily got out of their old forms as some are apt to suggest. They are hardly to be prevailed with to amend the acknowledged faults in the frame they have been accustomed to. And if there be any . . . defects, . . . it is not an
(15) easy thing to get them changed, even when all the world sees there is an opportunity for it. This slowness and aversion in the people to quit their old constitutions has, in the many revolutions which have been seen in
(20) this kingdom, in this and former ages still kept us to, or after some interval of fruitless attempts still brought us back again to, our old legislative of Kings, Lords, and Commons. And whatever provocations have made the
(25) crown be taken from some of our princes' heads, they never carried the people so far as to place it in another line.
   But it will be said, this hypothesis lays a ferment for frequent rebellion. To which
(30) I answer: First, no more than any other hypothesis. For when the people are made miserable, and find themselves exposed to the ill-usage of arbitrary power . . . the same

GO ON TO THE NEXT PAGE

will happen. The people generally ill-treated,
(35) and contrary to right, will be ready upon
any occasion to ease themselves of a burden
that sits heavy upon them. They will wish
and seek for the opportunity, which in the
change, weakness, and accidents of human
(40) affairs seldom delays long to offer itself. He
must have lived but a little while in the world
who has not seen examples of this in his
time, and he must have read very little who
cannot produce examples of it in all sorts of
(45) governments in the world.

Secondly, I answer, such revolutions
happen not upon every little
mismanagement in public affairs. Great
mistakes in the ruling part, many wrong
(50) and inconvenient laws, and all the slips of
human frailty will be borne by the people
without mutiny or murmur. But if a long
train of abuses, prevarications and artifices,
all tending the same way, make the design
(55) visible to the people—and they cannot but
feel what they lie under, and see whither
they are going—it is not to be wondered
that they should then rouse themselves and
endeavor to put the rule into such hands
(60) which may secure to them the ends for which
government was at first erected. . . .

Thirdly, I answer that this power in the
people of providing for their safety anew by
a new legislative when their legislators have
(65) acted contrary to their trust by invading their
property, is the best fence against rebellion,
and the probablest means to hinder it.
For rebellion being an opposition, not to
persons, but authority, which is founded
(70) only in the constitutions and laws of the
government, those whoever they be who
by force break through, and by force justify
their violation of them, are truly and properly
rebels. For when men by entering into society

(75) and civil government have excluded force,
and introduced laws for the preservation
of property, peace, and unity amongst
themselves, those who set up force again
in opposition to the laws . . . are properly
(80) rebels; which they who are in power . . .
being likeliest to do, the properest way to
prevent the evil is to show them the danger
and injustice of it who are under the greatest
temptation to run into it.

33. As used in line 4, "humor" most nearly means

(A) wit.
(B) skepticism.
(C) amusement.
(D) temperament.

34. According to Locke, which of the following
will NOT occur as a result of basing
government on the will of the people?

(A) Governments will be unstable because
the people will rebel whenever they are
dissatisfied.
(B) Governments will be stable because
people are averse to change.
(C) The people will not rebel frequently.
(D) A government will be overturned when a
long history of abuse cannot be tolerated
by the people.

GO ON TO THE NEXT PAGE

MODEL TEST 4

35. Which choice best describes the structure of the first paragraph?

   (A) A principle is stated, an opposing principle is stated, and a synthesis is reached.
   (B) A position is stated, an opposing position is stated, and examples supporting the latter position are given.
   (C) A question is posed, a method of analysis is recommended, and the question is answered.
   (D) A historical period is introduced, and events from the period are reviewed.

36. Locke's primary argument in the second paragraph is that

   (A) rebellion is inevitable, regardless of whether the power to govern is placed in the hands of the people.
   (B) history is filled with examples of rulers using their power to halt rebellions.
   (C) violent rebellion is a poor strategy for changing the government's treatment of the people.
   (D) rebellions will increase if the power to govern is given to the people.

37. Which choice provides the best evidence for the answer to the previous question?

   (A) Lines 30–34 ("First, no more . . . will happen")
   (B) Lines 34–37 ("The people . . . upon them")
   (C) Lines 37–40 ("They will . . . offer itself")
   (D) Lines 40–45 ("He must . . . the world")

38. The author uses "abuses, prevarications and artifices, all tending the same way" (lines 53–54) as examples of

   (A) actions the people take when rebelling against the government.
   (B) historical events.
   (C) things that prevent the government from performing its proper functions.
   (D) government behavior that justifies the people's rebellion.

39. As used in line 60, "ends" most nearly means

   (A) purposes.
   (B) conclusions.
   (C) extremities.
   (D) segments.

40. Locke argues that the best check on rebellion is

   (A) providing the government with absolute authority.
   (B) giving the people the power to replace an abusive government.
   (C) a strong military.
   (D) a divided government made up of Kings, Lords, and Commons.

41. Which choice provides the best evidence for the answer to the previous question?

   (A) Lines 17–23 ("This . . . Commons")
   (B) Lines 34–37 ("The people . . . upon them")
   (C) Lines 62–67 ("this power . . . hinder it")
   (D) Lines 71–74 ("those . . . properly rebels")

GO ON TO THE NEXT PAGE

42. Based on the passage, what is Locke's argument for why the government, rather than the people, should at times be viewed as a rebel?

(A) Government is founded on the will of the people; therefore, the people are always right.

(B) The people will never rise up to overthrow the government because they are afraid of change.

(C) Most governments do not protect the natural rights of the people.

(D) Rebellion is opposition to the authority of the law; therefore, the government is a rebel when it violates the legal limits of its power.

Questions 43–52 are based on the following passages.

Largely unexplored, the canopy or treetop region of the tropical rainforest is one of the most diverse plant and animal communities on Earth. Passage 1 is an excerpt from a 1984 Scientific American *article on the rain forest canopy; in it, the naturalist Donald R. Perry shares his research team's observations of epiphytes, unusual plants that flourish in this treetop environment. Passage 2, "Elucidating Epiphyte Diversity" by Andrew Sugden is taken from the 6 May 2011 issue of* Science.

PASSAGE 1

The upper story of the rain forest, which we investigated, incorporates two-thirds of its volume. This region can be divided
Line arbitrarily into a lower canopy, extending
(5) from 10 to 25 meters above the ground, an upper canopy, reaching a height of 35 meters, and an emergent zone that encompasses the tops of the tallest trees, which commonly grow to heights of more
(10) than 50 meters. The canopy is well lighted, in contrast to the forest understory, which because of thick vegetation above receives only about 1 percent of the sunlight that falls on the treetops. In the canopy all but
(15) the smallest of the rain forest trees put forth their leaves, flowers and fruit. It also contains many plants that exist entirely within its compass, forming vegetative communities that in number of species and complexity of
(20) interactions surpass any others on the earth.

Among the most conspicuous features of vegetation in the canopy of the tropical rain forest are epiphytes. About 28,000 species in 65 families are known worldwide, 15,500
(25) of them in Central and South America; they

GO ON TO THE NEXT PAGE

Layering of environments in the rain forest fosters species diversity. In the understory, or basement, light is dim, humidity rarely drops below 95 percent, and temperature varies little. In the canopy, sunlight is abundant and humidity and temperatures fluctuate. Each level of the forest has its own array of plants and animals, including pollinating insects.

include species of orchids, bromeliads, and arboreal cacti as well as lower plants such as lichens, mosses, and ferns. Thousands more epiphyte varieties remain unidentified.

(30)   The Greek meaning of the word epiphyte is "plant that grows on a plant," and they carpet tree trunks and branches. Epiphytes sprout from seeds borne by the wind or deposited by animals, their roots holding

(35) tight to the interstices of the bark. Yet they are nonparasitic; their hosts provide them with nothing more than a favorable position in the brightly lighted canopy. For nourishment epiphytes depend on soil particles and

(40) dissolved minerals carried in rainwater, and on aerial deposits of humus. The deposits are the product of organic debris, such as dead leaves from epiphytes and other plants, that lodges among epiphyte roots.

(45)   Water is directly available to epiphytes only when it rains; other plants have continuous access to moisture trapped in the soil. As a result many epiphytes have

developed features that collect and retain

(50) rainwater. Some, including orchids and arboreal cacti, have succulent stems and leaves, with spongy tissues that store water, as well as waxy leaf coatings that reduce the loss of moisture through transpiration.[1]

(55) Many orchids have bulbous stem bases; other families of epiphytes impound water in tanks formed by tight rosettes of leaves or in cups shaped by the junctions of broadened petioles[2] and stems. Some species possess

(60) absorbent, spongelike root masses that soak up and hold water. Bromeliads, a Central and South American family, can hold reserves of several gallons within their cisternlike bases, forming "arboreal swamps" that attract

(65) insects of many species, earthworms, spiders, sow bugs, scorpions, tree frogs, and insect-eating birds.

[1]Passage of water through a plant to the atmosphere.
[2]Slender stalks that attach a leaf to the stem.

GO ON TO THE NEXT PAGE

PASSAGE 2

In tropical forests, an important fraction of
the total plant species diversity is composed
(70) of epiphytes: plants that are rooted for part
or all their life on the trunks and branches
of trees and lianas. The patterns of epiphyte
diversity are still poorly understood relative
to those of trees, however, because of
(75) logistical challenges, such as tree height.
Benavides et al. performed a comparative
analysis of the epiphyte communities in
lowland forest in Colombian Amazonia,
aiming to understand how landscape unit
(80) (swamp forest, floodplain forest, and well-
drained upland) and host tree species
influenced the composition of their epiphyte
communities, using a combination of
collecting by tree climbing and binocular
(85) observations. They recorded 154 epiphyte
species on 411 tree species. There were
clear associations between tree/liana
species assemblages and epiphyte species
assemblages, but there were few significant
(90) associations between individual host species
and epiphyte species. The high diversity of
both groups of plants in the sampled plots
made testing for individual host preferences
difficult, suggesting the need for further
(95) studies.

43. The author of Passage 1 characterizes the
    floor or understory of the rain forest as
    relatively

    (A) insignificant.
    (B) voluminous.
    (C) illuminated.
    (D) obscure.

44. Which choice provides the best evidence for
    the answer to the previous question?

    (A) Lines 1–3 ("The upper . . . volume")
    (B) Lines 10–14 ("The canopy . . . treetops")
    (C) Lines 16–20 ("It also . . . earth")
    (D) Lines 21–29 ("Among . . . unidentified")

45. As used in line 18, "compass" most nearly
    means

    (A) a curved arc.
    (B) directions.
    (C) parameters.
    (D) enclosing limits.

46. It can most reasonably be inferred from
    Passage 1 that which of the following is true
    of epiphytes?

    (A) They lack an adequate root system.
    (B) They cannot draw moisture from tree
        trunks.
    (C) They are incapable of transpiration.
    (D) They are hard to perceive in the dense
        rain forest canopy.

47. As used in line 27, "lower" most nearly means

    (A) below average.
    (B) relatively primitive.
    (C) less tall.
    (D) more sparse.

GO ON TO THE NEXT PAGE

MODEL TEST 4

48. Epiphytes have direct access to water only when it rains because

    (A) they lack the ability to collect moisture.
    (B) dead leaves and other organic debris cover their roots.
    (C) the thick canopy protects them from rainstorms.
    (D) they lack connections to water in the ground.

49. In line 64, the quotes around the phrase "arboreal swamps" indicate that

    (A) the author is quoting a standard technical term.
    (B) the term is intended to have a humorous effect.
    (C) the term is being used in a special sense.
    (D) the author means the term literally.

50. What information discussed in Passage 2 is clarified by referring to the infographic accompanying Passage 1?

    (A) The information in lines 68–72 ("In tropical . . . lianas")
    (B) The information in lines 72–75 ("The patterns . . . height")
    (C) The information in lines 85–86 ("They recorded . . . species")
    (D) The information in lines 91–95 ("The high . . . studies")

51. Which choice best states the relationship between the two passages?

    (A) Passage 2 draws alternative conclusions from the observations shared in Passage 1.
    (B) Passage 1 proposes a hypothesis that is confirmed in Passage 2.
    (C) Passage 1 introduces a concept that is elaborated on in Passage 2.
    (D) Passage 2 restates in less vivid terms the information presented in Passage 1.

52. The authors of both passages would most likely agree with which of the following statements about epiphyte studies?

    (A) They are most efficiently conducted by means of binocular observation.
    (B) They need to focus on observations of epiphytes in the understory.
    (C) They necessarily entail certain challenges for researchers.
    (D) They should primarily be considered an untapped resource.

STOP

If there is still time remaining, you may review your answers.

WRITING AND LANGUAGE TEST

35 MINUTES, 44 QUESTIONS

Turn to Section 2 of your answer sheet to answer the questions in this section.

> **Directions:** Questions follow each of the passages below. Some questions ask you how the passage might be changed to improve the expression of ideas. Other questions ask you how the passage might be altered to correct errors in grammar, usage, and punctuation. One or more graphics accompany some passages. You will be required to consider these graphics as you answer questions about editing the passage.
>
> There are three types of questions. In the first type, a part of the passage is underlined. The second type is based on a certain part of the passage. The third type is based on the entire passage.
>
> Read each passage. Then, choose the answer to each question that changes the passage so that it is consistent with the conventions of standard written English. One of the answer choices for many questions is "NO CHANGE." Choosing this answer means that you believe the best answer is to make no change in the passage.

Questions 1–11 are based on the following passage and supplementary material.

The Online Job Hunt

More and more, technology is changing the ways people find jobs and employers select candidates. Think back to the days when the job hunter ❶ chose his or her most precious qualities, wrote them out on one sheet of paper, and sold the best version of ❷ themselves to a prospective employer. No longer is it that simple. Google and various social media sites like Facebook and Twitter mean that your control over exactly how you come across to an employer is very different from the traditional resume model. In fact, research shows that approximately ❸ one-half of all employers are taking to online searches in the hiring process. What does Google say about you?

1. (A) NO CHANGE
    (B) choose
    (C) has chose
    (D) had choose

2. (A) NO CHANGE
    (B) yourself
    (C) himself or herself
    (D) oneself

3. Which choice offers the most accurate interpretation of the data in the chart?

    (A) NO CHANGE
    (B) one-fourth
    (C) two-thirds
    (D) four-fifths

GO ON TO THE NEXT PAGE

The good news is technology can work in your favor **④** if you recognize the challenges of using technology properly. If you approach the World Wide Web as a tool, it can be **⑤** valuable in a way not witnessed heretofore. Indeed, there are more ways than ever to market yourself and your skills, and to network with other professionals in your field. First, you will want to make sure you are competing in the online job hunt. Career websites like LinkedIn, Dice, and Monster make it simple to get started. **⑥** Within your online, profiles it is critical that you include information, about your educational background, previous work experience, intern or research positions, and volunteer efforts. **⑦** Now is not the time to be modest.

What's more—you don't have to stop there. **⑧** Whereas the old resume needed to be concise and fit in the scopes of one or two pages,

4. Which choice provides the most logical and relevant conclusion to the sentence?

(A) NO CHANGE
(B) since technology has made unbelievable strides.
(C) despite the dangers of downloading computer viruses.
(D) just as methodically as it can work against you.

5. (A) NO CHANGE
(B) unprecedentedly valuable.
(C) precious beyond your wildest dreams.
(D) helpful.

6. (A) NO CHANGE
(B) Within your online profiles it is critical that you include information about your educational background, previous
(C) Within your online profiles, it is critical that you include information about your educational background, previous
(D) Within your online profiles, it is critical that you include information about: your educational background, previous

7. Which choice most logically reinforces the statement in the previous sentence?

(A) NO CHANGE
(B) Be careful to keep it short and sweet.
(C) Remember—your application gets accepted, not your personality.
(D) Good things happen to those who wait.

8. (A) NO CHANGE
(B) Since
(C) Because
(D) Moreover

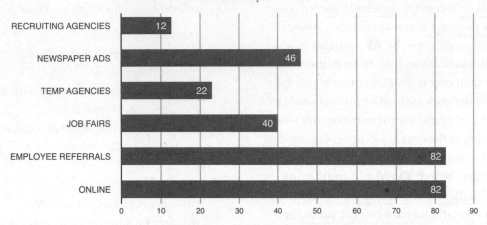

Percent Using Recruiting Methods to Fill Jobs

*100 Human Resource Departments were randomly selected and asked which recruiting methods they currently use to fill their job openings.

■ Percent Using Recruiting Methods to Fill Jobs*

your online profile can be much more thorough. Make sure to post a ❾ professional picture, this allows the employer to see that you are a real person with real skills and makes you more likely to be interviewed. Include any awards or achievements that can relate to the job position and depict your broader talents. Don't forget to mention any particular leadership responsibilities you've been granted in previous experience. Have you taken the initiative to attend conferences or events? Do tell. ❿ Be sure to supplement your job search with the tried-and-true methods of newspaper ads and recruiting agencies.

9. (A) NO CHANGE
(B) professional picture: this
(C) professional; picture this
(D) professional picture this

10. Which choice offers an accurate interpretation of the data in the chart by emphasizing one of the most popular recruiting methods?

(A) NO CHANGE
(B) Additionally, polish your interpersonal networking skills before you head to a job fair to "wow" potential employers.
(C) There is even room in most online career profiles for positive feedback from colleagues, supervisors, or mentors.
(D) And while it may not be ideal, working temporarily at a job in a part-time capacity can be a great way to get your foot in the door.

GO ON TO THE NEXT PAGE

972 NEW SAT

While many argue that job hunting has changed for the worse, it doesn't have to be that way. Never before have recent graduates, career changers, and the unemployed ever had such a plethora of resources at their disposal. **⓫** <u>Employers are able to find prospective candidates at the click of a button, while job hunters can meet and connect with career professionals that were previously unreachable.</u> Don't let Google—in all its magnitude—be your disadvantage.

11. Should the underlined sentence be kept or deleted?

(A) Kept. It provides specific details in support of the paragraph's argument.

(B) Kept. It gives the essay's first statement about the importance of online job hunting.

(C) Deleted. It contradicts information elsewhere in the passage.

(D) Deleted. It distracts from the primary argument of the paragraph.

GO ON TO THE NEXT PAGE

MODEL TEST 4

Questions 12–22 are based on the following passage.

The Glass Menagerie

Among artists living and influential, few rival the famous American classical composer Phillip Glass. He is celebrated for his wide-ranging collaborations with literary figures such as Allen Ginsberg, film directors such as Woody Allen, and **12** David Bowie whom is a producer of records. His broad range in operas, symphonies, and compositions has contributed to his **13** unparalleled popularity within multigenerational audiences. Perhaps no other composer has appealed to such an expansive fan base, allowing Glass's influence in opera houses, dance halls, and popular culture to go uncontested. His operas continue to play internationally and rarely leave an open seat.

With music that is highly repetitive, Glass has been **14** referred to as a minimalist and aligned with the work of other composers like La Monte Young, Terry Riley, and Steve Reich. **15** Minimalism a term that Glass has taken strides to distance himself from, is marked by a nonnarrative and nonrepresentational conception of a work in progress, and represents a new approach to the activity of listening to music by focusing on the internal processes of the music. Tom Johnson **16** , a self-identifying minimalist, defines it this way: "It [minimalism] includes, by definition, any music that works with limited or minimal materials: pieces that use only a few notes, pieces that use only a few words of text, or pieces written for very limited instruments, such as antique cymbals, bicycle wheels, or whiskey glasses." Glass prefers, instead, to refer to himself as a classicist with repetitive structures.

12. (A) NO CHANGE
    (B) David Bowie who is best known as a record producer.
    (C) a person who has the career of being a record producer, like David Bowie.
    (D) record producers such as David Bowie.

13. The author wants to show that Bowie has great popularity. Which word best expresses this notion?

    (A) NO CHANGE
    (B) solid
    (C) decent
    (D) voracious

14. Which word, if inserted at this point, would best express that Glass's music is not universally admired?

    (A) understandably
    (B) logically
    (C) controversially
    (D) repeatedly

15. (A) NO CHANGE
    (B) Minimalism: a term that Glass has taken strides to distance himself from is
    (C) Minimalism—a term from which Glass has taken strides to distance himself—is
    (D) Minimalism, a term from which Glass has taken strides to distance himself—is

16. The writer would like to express that Tom Johnson is a relevant person to provide commentary on this topic. Which choice best accomplishes this?

    (A) NO CHANGE
    (B) , an admirer of all things Phillip Glass,
    (C) , an American historian of the eighteenth and nineteenth centuries,
    (D) , an expert in operatic costume design,

GO ON TO THE NEXT PAGE

17 To his highest achievements, Glass has been nominated for several Academy Awards and won a Golden Globe award in 1999 for his score in *The Truman Show*. He has been the topic of a series of documentaries and has **18** writing more then one autobiography. In his most recent, *Words Without Music*, Glass discusses his influences, beginning with his Jewish father who ran a record shop in Baltimore. His father's love for Schubert, Shostakovich, and Bartok **19** took in Glass a love for music; by the time he was fifteen years old, he had become the classical-music buyer for the record shop. He studied at the University of Chicago and the Julliard School, before moving to Paris to study technique under the infamous Nadia Boulanger. It was only with the success of his opera "Einstein on the Beach" in 1976 that Glass made a prominent name **20** for himself.

Coinciding with his return to New York, Glass formed the Phillip Glass Ensemble, seven musicians whose music is amplified and fed through a mixer. The rest is history. In the last two decades, Glass **21** had composed numerous operas, symphonies, concertos, and soundtracks; his prolific works are so common that **22** they are occasionally encountered by the populace.

17. (A) NO CHANGE
    (B) On
    (C) Between
    (D) Among

18. (A) NO CHANGE
    (B) writing more than
    (C) written more then
    (D) written more than

19. (A) NO CHANGE
    (B) spurred
    (C) used
    (D) inspire

20. (A) NO CHANGE
    (B) through oneself.
    (C) by yourself.
    (D) in oneself.

21. (A) NO CHANGE
    (B) had been composing
    (C) has composed
    (D) have composed

22. Which choice would most clearly and specifically support the statement immediately beforehand in the sentence?

    (A) NO CHANGE
    (B) even a layperson would recognize his tunes.
    (C) one can even find them performed in the elite symphonic halls of high society.
    (D) it is relatively effortless for a nonexpert to recognize their quality.

GO ON TO THE NEXT PAGE

Questions 23–33 are based on the following passage and supplementary material.

For Richer or For Poorer

Everyone is familiar with Robin Hood's plight to take from the rich and give to the poor. However, the debate of economic redistribution is far from archaic and rarely confined to folklore, especially given that between 1980 and 2010, incomes for the **㉓** top 20 percent nearly doubled while incomes in the bottom 10 percent measurably increased. One of the latest arguments for redistribution comes from French economist

23. Which choice gives the most accurate interpretation of the data in the graph?

(A) NO CHANGE
(B) top 10 percent nearly doubled while incomes in the bottom 20% barely changed.
(C) top 10 percent nearly tripled while incomes in the middle 10% barely changed.
(D) top 10 percent nearly quadrupled while incomes in the bottom 20% decreased.

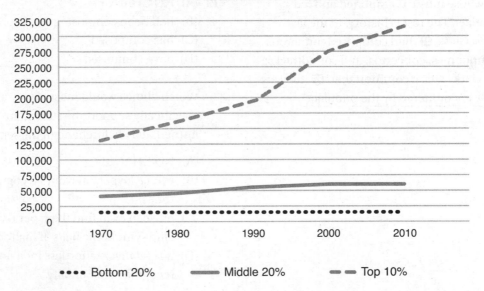

U.S. Median Annual Income

•••• Bottom 20%   —— Middle 20%   – – Top 10%

GO ON TO THE NEXT PAGE

Thomas Piketty, who has gathered and studied tax records over a 200-year span. **㉔** Piketty argues that inequality is an inherent feature of capitalism that threatens democracy.

In his recent best seller, *Capital in the Twenty-First Century*, Piketty uses data gathered from 20 countries to posit that the rate of return in developed countries is **㉕** persistently greater than economic growth—this lasting trend is the main driver of inequality and will only widen the gap further in the future. His work shows that return has been steady even during years of recession when growth has plummeted. While many consider his book esoteric— **㉖** especially given its old age and questionable modern-day applicability—it is indisputably attracting wide attention. Piketty's data on the wealthy elite makes it somewhat pioneering despite its foundations in age-old economics. **㉗** Piketty even offers a solution; economic redistribution through a progressive global tax on wealth.

24. The writer is considering inserting this sentence at this point in the passage:

    "His research considers the questions of long-term inequality, concentration of wealth, and potential economic growth, and ultimately concludes that the ever-rising concentration of wealth is not self-correcting."

    Should she make this insertion?

    (A) Yes. It elaborates on Piketty's background and connects to the next sentence.
    (B) Yes. It provides helpful details about Piketty's research methodology.
    (C) No. It gives irrelevant information to the paragraph's argument.
    (D) No. It repeats the general idea from the previous sentence.

25. (A) NO CHANGE
    (B) chronically more massive
    (C) consistently more expensive
    (D) often large

26. Which choice best elaborates on the first part of this sentence?

    (A) NO CHANGE
    (B) since beautiful illustrations are just as helpful to my understanding as is polished prose
    (C) given the often controversial ideas presented in this work
    (D) a trait that may explain why the 600+ page tome sits unread on library bookshelves

27. (A) NO CHANGE
    (B) Piketty, even offers a solution, economic
    (C) Piketty even offers a solution: economic
    (D) Piketty even offers, a solution economic

Piketty faces many ㉘ observers. Matthew Rognlie, a graduate student at MIT, has become a media sensation with his paper that points out what he sees as several flaws in Piketty's argument. Rognlie argues that, according to the law of diminishing returns, the rate of return will eventually ㉙ decrease; goes on to say that Piketty has an inflated idea of current return and doesn't consider depreciation. Rognlie ㉚ points at housing wealth as the cause of worsening inequality and shows that Piketty's conclusions are based on the assumption that capital can be substituted for the working class, which is untrue in the housing market. According to Rognlie, the solution put forth in *Capital in the Twenty-First Century*, since it will do little to limit ㉛ homeowners' returns on assets, is no solution at all.

But, if Rognlie's argument holds, do all homeowners benefit? Surely not. Working-class families will continue to buy only in neighborhoods where they can afford homes and where home values are unpredictable. ㉜ Unexpectedly, they will face further financial instability; meanwhile, the privileged few who can afford to purchase real estate in New York, Chicago, London, and so on will see their returns peak. ㉝ Whether or not you agree or disagree with Piketty is not as important as whether you recognize the severity and possible implications of his argument.

28. Which word choice is most logically supported by the information in the sentence that follows?

(A) NO CHANGE
(B) scholars.
(C) enemies.
(D) critics.

29. (A) NO CHANGE
(B) decrease, goes
(C) decrease; he goes
(D) decrease, he goes

30. (A) NO CHANGE
(B) points to
(C) points on
(D) point through

31. (A) NO CHANGE
(B) homeowner's
(C) the home owner's
(D) homeowners

32. (A) NO CHANGE
(B) Paradoxically,
(C) Typically,
(D) Hence,

33. (A) NO CHANGE
(B) Whether you agree or disagree with
(C) Whether you are agreeing
(D) OMIT the underlined portion.

Questions 34–44 are based on the following passage.

Hypocrisy of Hippocratic Humorism

Sometimes, scientific paradigm shifts in the name of innovation are anything but innovative. The revolutionary theory of the four bodily humors (i.e., the idea that disease results from a physical imbalance in the bodily "humors") **34** had popularized in 400 B.C.E. in ancient Greece and has been a major obstacle to scientific advancement ever since.

The theory of the humors cannot even be described as a paradigm shift (and certainly not one contributing to medical science) for **35** it revolutionized the way that medical practitioners approached their craft. The couching of the humors in the physical world as opposed to the spiritual world did not make it any less mystical but made it more **36** intellectualized entrenched. We of course know today that humorism is abjectly bunk; one of the four humors—specifically black bile—does not exist in nature but was added to tidily complement classical theories of the four natural elements. From a scientific perspective, black bile has every bit as much to do with cancer as **37** demons do with epilepsy.

Even a cursory **38** analysis of Western medicine's history will reveal that the single greatest obstacle to the advent of evidence-based

34. (A) NO CHANGE
    (B) have
    (C) was
    (D) were

35. Which choice would most logically and relevantly justify the statement made in the first part of the sentence?

    (A) NO CHANGE
    (B) it merely trades one baseless system of mystical superstition for another.
    (C) it does not attempt to provide a theoretical understanding of bodily functions.
    (D) while it was influential in ancient Greece, it did not have influence beyond this limited geographic area.

36. (A) NO CHANGE
    (B) intellectually
    (C) intelligent
    (D) intellectual

37. The writer wants to use an applicable analogy to establish the absurdity of using black bile to justify cancer. Which choice best accomplishes this goal?

    (A) NO CHANGE
    (B) ice does with water.
    (C) cartoons do with teenage violence.
    (D) drugs do with addiction.

38. (A) NO CHANGE
    (B) analyses of Western medicines' history
    (C) analysis of the history of the medicine of the West
    (D) analyzing of the history of medical science in Western society

medical science was not—as has often been posited—religion but Hippocratic humorism itself. **39** One's tendency to linearize progress retrospectively—particularly in the sciences—has contributed to the fallacious belief that the discovery that lightning results not from the fury of an angry God **40** and from an atmospheric electrical discharge, and the transition of the accepted source of epilepsy from mischievous Roman deities to an imaginary bodily fluid are in some way equivalently significant to the development of modern science.

Humorism held medical discovery back for centuries at a time when the pure sciences **41** were conducting medical research; it established a systemic insularity in the field that cut medicine off from discoveries in biology, chemistry, and physics, and generated a remarkably long-lived illusion of comprehensiveness that categorically rejected revision and innovation. **42** Somewhat, humorism was a far more persistent enemy of medical science than was superstition because it wore the guise of

39. (A) NO CHANGE
    (B) Ones
    (C) The
    (D) They're

40. (A) NO CHANGE
    (B) but from
    (C) because of
    (D) with

41. The writer would like to emphasize how humorism prevented medical discovery from advancing. Which choice best accomplishes this goal?

    (A) NO CHANGE
    (B) were shifting from the foreground to the background;
    (C) were about to develop further scientifically;
    (D) were preparing for a renaissance;

42. (A) NO CHANGE
    (B) In contrast,
    (C) Further,
    (D) Because of this,

GO ON TO THE NEXT PAGE

naturalism. By pretending to possess a physical basis for its tenets, humorism **43** contributed to a deep-seeded belief, among physicians well, into the nineteenth century that pathology was not only independent of supernatural influences but of essentially all external influences. This notion of corporeal isolation—established by the theory of humoral imbalances—laid the foundation for the staunch medical opposition encountered by advocates of the germ theory of disease, and **44** conducted a paucity of help to the geometric growth of the sciences.

43. (A) NO CHANGE
    (B) contributed to a deep-seeded belief among physicians, well into the nineteenth century, that pathology was not, only independent
    (C) contributed to a deep-seeded belief among physicians well into the nineteenth century that pathology, was not only independent
    (D) contributed to a deep-seeded belief among physicians well into the nineteenth century that pathology was not only independent

44. Which choice most specifically elaborates on the long-term negative impact that the belief in corporeal isolation had on medical science?

    (A) NO CHANGE
    (B) delayed understanding of microbial pathogens for at least three centuries.
    (C) viral pathogens cannot be treated by antibiotics but must run their natural course.
    (D) germs continue to plague patients and medical practitioners up to the present day.

STOP

If there is still time remaining, you may review your answers.

MATH TEST (NO CALCULATOR)

25 MINUTES, 20 QUESTIONS

Turn to Section 3 of your answer sheet to answer the questions in this section.

Directions: For questions 1–15, solve each problem and choose the best answer from the given options. Fill in the corresponding circle on your answer document. For questions 16–20, solve the problem and fill in the answer on the answer sheet grid.

Notes:
- Calculators are **NOT PERMITTED** in this section.
- All variables and expressions represent real numbers unless indicated otherwise.
- All figures are drawn to scale unless indicated otherwise.
- All figures are in a plane unless indicated otherwise.
- Unless indicated otherwise, the domain of a given function is the set of all real numbers x for which the function has real values.

REFERENCE INFORMATION

Area Facts

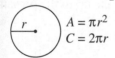

$A = \ell w$

$A = \frac{1}{2} bh$

$A = \pi r^2$
$C = 2\pi r$

Volume Facts

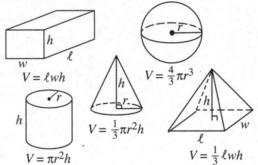

$V = \ell wh$

$V = \frac{4}{3}\pi r^3$

$V = \frac{1}{3}\pi r^2 h$

$V = \pi r^2 h$

$V = \frac{1}{3}\ell wh$

Triangle Facts

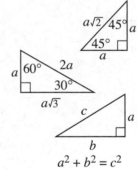

$a^2 + b^2 = c^2$

The arc of a circle contains 360°.

The arc of a circle contains 2π radians.

The sum of the measures of the angles in a triangle is 180°.

GO ON TO THE NEXT PAGE

1. Max purchased some shares of stock at $10 per share. Six months later the stock was worth $20 per share. What was the percent increase in the value of Max's investment?

   (A) 20%
   (B) 50%
   (C) 100%
   (D) 200%

2. The median annual salary of all the employees at Hartley's Home Supplies is $45,000, whereas the range of their salaries is $145,000. Which of the following is the most logical explanation for the large difference between the median and the range?

   (A) Half of the employees earn less than $45,000.
   (B) There is at least one employee who earns more than $150,000.
   (C) The average salary of the employees is between $45,000 and $145,000.
   (D) More employees earn over $100,000 than earn less than $25,000

3. Which of the following expressions is equivalent to $\dfrac{a+b}{3+4}$?

   (A) $\dfrac{a}{3}+\dfrac{b}{4}$

   (B) $\dfrac{a}{7}+\dfrac{b}{7}$

   (C) $\dfrac{a+b}{3}+\dfrac{a+b}{4}$

   (D) $\dfrac{a+b}{7}+\dfrac{a+b}{7}$

4. Two cylindrical tanks have the same height, but the radius of the larger tank equals the diameter of the smaller tank. If the volume of the larger tank is $k\%$ more than the volume of the smaller tank $k=$

   (A) 100
   (B) 200
   (C) 300
   (D) 400

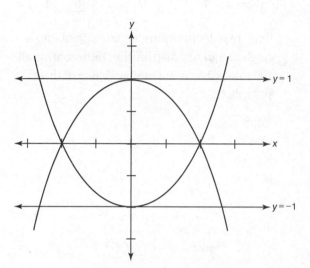

$$y = x^2 - 1$$
$$y = -x^2 + 1$$
$$y = 1$$
$$y = -1$$

5. A system of four equations and their graphs are shown above. How many solutions does this system of equations have?

   (A) 0
   (B) 2
   (C) 4
   (D) 8

GO ON TO THE NEXT PAGE

MODEL TEST 4

6. Barbara and Marc each rolled a single die 50 times. The frequency distributions for each of them are given below.

Distribution of Barbara's 50 Rolls

Number	1	2	3	4	5	6
Frequency	4	10	8	8	8	12

Distribution of Marc's 50 Rolls

Number	1	2	3	4	5	6
Frequency	7	11	13	3	8	8

If the two distributions are combined into a single frequency distribution representing all 100 rolls, what is the median value of those 100 rolls?

(A) 3
(B) 3.25
(C) 3.5
(D) 4

$$[(2x + y) + (x + 2y)]^2$$

7. Which of the following expressions is equivalent to the expression above?

(A) $3(x^2 + y^2)$
(B) $9(x^2 + y^2)$
(C) $3(x + y)^2$
(D) $9(x + y)^2$

8. To get to a business meeting, Joanna drove m miles in h hours, and arrived $\frac{1}{2}$ hour early. At what rate should she have driven to arrive exactly on time?

(A) $\dfrac{2m+h}{2h}$

(B) $\dfrac{2m-h}{2h}$

(C) $\dfrac{2m}{2h-1}$

(D) $\dfrac{2m}{2h+1}$

9. How many points of intersection are there of the graphs whose equations are $y = -(x - 3)^2 + 3$ and $y = (x + 3)^2 - 3$?

(A) 0
(B) 1
(C) 2
(D) More than 2

10. If f and g are functions such that $f(x) = (2x + 3)g(x)$, which of the following statements must be true?

(A) The graph of $f(x)$ crosses the x-axis at $-\frac{2}{3}$.

(B) The graph of $f(x)$ crosses the x-axis at $-\frac{3}{2}$.

(C) The graph of $f(x)$ crosses the x-axis at $\frac{2}{3}$.

(D) The graph of $f(x)$ crosses the x-axis at $\frac{3}{2}$.

GO ON TO THE NEXT PAGE

MODEL TEST 4

11. Lee purchased a 7-year $1,000 certificate of deposit (CD) at his local savings bank. As a special incentive, the bank offered an introductory interest rate of 5% for the first year and then paid its regular 3% interest per year for the next 6 years. Which of the following gives the value V, in dollars, of the CD n years after Lee purchased it, where $1 < n \leq 7$?

(A) $V(n) = 1,050(0.97)^{n-1}$
(B) $V(n) = 1,050(1.03)^{n-1}$
(C) $V(n) = 1,050(0.97)^{n}$
(D) $V(n) = 1,050(1.03)^{n}$

12. If $i = \sqrt{-1}$ and $(1 + i) \div (1 - i) = (a + bi)$, where a and b are real numbers, what are the values of a and b?

(A) $a = 0$ and $b = 1$
(B) $a = 0$ and $b = -1$
(C) $a = 1$ and $b = 0$
(D) $a = 2$ and $b = -2$

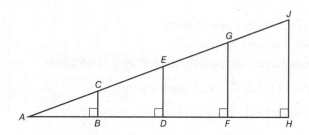

13. In the figure above, what is the ratio of the area of trapezoid $FHJG$ to the area of trapezoid $BCED$?

(A) 2:1
(B) 3:1
(C) 4:1
(D) 7:3

14. If the amount, a, in Alan's retirement account is $\frac{1}{10}$ percent of b, the amount in his boss's retirement account, then b is what percent of a?

(A) 100%
(B) 1,000%
(C) 10,000%
(D) 100,000%

15. If a is a constant, for what values of a does the line whose equation is $x + y = a(x - y)$ have a positive slope?

(A) $a = 1$
(B) $a \neq -1$
(C) $-1 < a < 1$
(D) $a < -1$ or $a > 1$

GO ON TO THE NEXT PAGE

Grid-in Response Directions

In questions 16–20, first solve the problem, and then enter your answer on the grid provided on the answer sheet. The instructions for entering your answers follow.

- First, write your answer in the boxes at the top of the grid.
- Second, grid your answer in the columns below the boxes.
- Use the fraction bar in the first row or the decimal point in the second row to enter fractions and decimals.

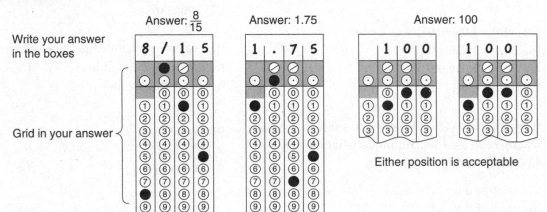

- Grid only one space in each column.
- Entering the answer in the boxes is recommended as an aid in gridding but is not required.
- The machine scoring your exam can read only what you grid, so you **must grid-in your answers correctly to get credit.**
- If a question has more than one correct answer, grid-in only one of them.
- The grid does not have a minus sign; so no answer can be negative.
- A mixed number *must* be converted to an improper fraction or a decimal before it is gridded.

  Enter $1\frac{1}{4}$ as 5/4 or 1.25; the machine will interpret 11/4 as $\frac{11}{4}$ and mark it wrong.

- **All decimals must be entered as accurately as possible.** Here are three acceptable ways of gridding

$$\frac{3}{11} = 0.272727\ldots$$

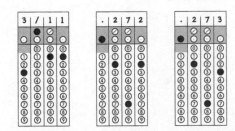

- Note that rounding to .273 is acceptable because you are using the full grid, but you would receive **no credit** for .3 or .27, because they are less accurate.

16. What is the value of $4^{\frac{1}{2}} \times 8^{\frac{1}{3}} \times 16^{\frac{1}{4}}$?

•19. What is the sum of the x-coordinate and y-coordinate of the point where the lines $y = 3x + 2$ and $y = 2x + 3$ intersect?

17. If $f(x) = 3 + \dfrac{5}{x}$, what number CANNOT be a value of $f(x)$?

20. The graph whose equation is

$$(x - 4)^2 + (y - 2)^2 = 4$$

is a circle. If m represents the number of times the circle intersects the y-axis and if n represents the number of times the circle intersects the x-axis, what is the value of $m + n$?

18. For what value of n will the equation $3(x + 2) + 5(x + 3) = 2(x + 5) + n(x + 3) - 7$ have infinitely many solutions?

STOP

If there is still time remaining, you may review your answers.

MODEL TEST 4

MATH TEST (CALCULATOR)

55 MINUTES, 38 QUESTIONS

Turn to Section 4 of your answer sheet to answer the questions in this section.

Directions: For questions 1–30, solve each problem and choose the best answer from the given options. Fill in the corresponding circle on your answer document. For questions 31–38, solve the problem and fill in the answer on the answer sheet grid.

Notes:

- Calculators **ARE PERMITTED** in this section.
- All variables and expressions represent real numbers unless indicated otherwise.
- All figures are drawn to scale unless indicated otherwise.
- All figures are in a plane unless indicated otherwise.
- Unless indicated otherwise, the domain of a given function is the set of all real numbers x for which the function has real values.

REFERENCE INFORMATION

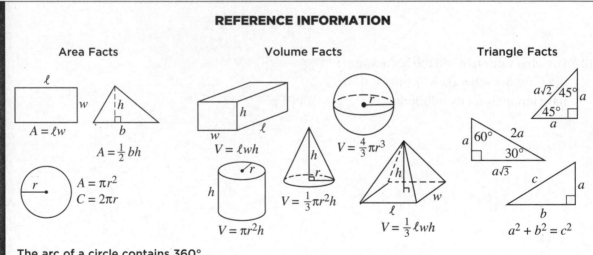

Area Facts   Volume Facts   Triangle Facts

$A = \ell w$

$A = \frac{1}{2}bh$

$A = \pi r^2$
$C = 2\pi r$

$V = \ell wh$

$V = \pi r^2 h$

$V = \frac{4}{3}\pi r^3$

$V = \frac{1}{3}\pi r^2 h$

$V = \frac{1}{3}\ell wh$

$a^2 + b^2 = c^2$

The arc of a circle contains 360°.

The arc of a circle contains 2π radians.

The sum of the measures of the angles in a triangle is 180°.

GO ON TO THE NEXT PAGE

1. The estate of a wealthy man was distributed as follows: 10% to his wife, 5% divided equally among his three children, 5% divided equally among his five grandchildren, and the balance to a charitable trust. If the trust received $1,000,000, how much did each grandchild inherit?

   (A) $10,000
   (B) $12,500
   (C) $20,000
   (D) $62,500

2. Which of the following statements is true concerning the equation below?

$$\sqrt{x+6} = x$$

   (A) The equation has no solutions.
   (B) The equation has one positive solution.
   (C) The equation has one negative solution.
   (D) The equation has more than one solution.

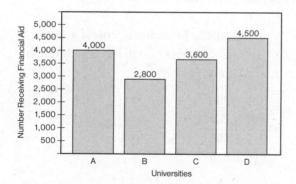

3. The bar graph above shows the number of students in four universities who received financial aid from the university in 2015. The average size of the financial aid package per student at universities A, B, C, and D was $15,500; $21,000; $18,700; and $14,300, respectively. Which university gave out the greatest total amount of financial aid?

   (A) A
   (B) B
   (C) C
   (D) D

4. Marie has a website where she sells CDs and DVDs. She purchases her CDs for $2.75 each and her DVDs for $5.75 each. Marie pays 95¢ to mail each CD and DVD to her customers. She charges $4.99 per CD and $9.99 per DVD plus a postage and handling fee of $1.75 per CD or DVD. Which of the following represents her profit, P, in dollars, on the sale of x CDs and y DVDs?

   (A) $P = 3.04x + 5.04y$
   (B) $P = 2.24x + 4.24y + 0.80$
   (C) $P = 2.24x + 4.24y + 0.80xy$
   (D) $P = 3.00(x + y) + 0.80(x + y)$

5. There are 25 students in Mrs. Wang's first period algebra class. On Monday, five students were absent and the other 20 students took a test. The average grade for those students was 86. The next day after the five absent students took the test, the class average was 88. What was the average of those five students' grades?

   (A) 90
   (B) 92
   (C) 94
   (D) 96

GO ON TO THE NEXT PAGE

Question 6 is based on the information below.

A survey of 500 registered voters in a certain state was taken to ascertain the number of Democrats, Republicans, and Independents who supported a certain ballot initiative called Proposition 8. The results of that survey are tabulated below.

	Support Proposition 8	Opposed to Proposition 8	Undecided	Total
Democrats	113	32	40	185
Republicans	35	145	30	210
Independents	44	41	20	105
Total	192	218	90	500

6. On Election Day, all of the voters in the survey who had expressed support for the proposition voted for it and all of the voters who had been opposed to the proposition voted against it. If in addition, 80% of those who had been undecided voted for the proposition and 20% voted against it, what percent of the 500 people in the survey voted for the proposition?

   (A) 42.7%
   (B) 47.2%
   (C) 52.8%
   (D) 58.2%

Questions 7–8 are based on the following information.

According to the United States Census Bureau, on average there is a birth in the United States every 8 seconds, a death every 12 seconds, and a net increase of one person due to immigration and emigration every 30 seconds.

7. Which of the following is closest to the average daily increase in the population of the United States?

   (A) 2,280
   (B) 4,260
   (C) 6,480
   (D) 9,520

8. The population of the United States reached 320,000,000 in January of 2015. According to the Census Bureau's analysis, in what year should the country's population reach 350,000,000?

   (A) 2017
   (B) 2022
   (C) 2027
   (D) 2032

GO ON TO THE NEXT PAGE

MODEL TEST 4

9. In $\triangle ABC$, C is a right angle and $\tan A = 1$. What is the value of $\sin A + \cos A$?

(A) $\dfrac{\sqrt{2}}{2}$

(B) 1

(C) $\sqrt{2}$

(D) $2\sqrt{2}$

10. The members of the French Club conducted a fund-raising drive. The average (arithmetic mean) amount of money raised per member was $85. Then Jean joined the club and raised $50. This lowered the average to $80. How many members were there before Jean joined?

(A) 5

(B) 6

(C) 7

(D) 8

11. The cost of renting a van from ABC Rentals is d dollars per day plus c cents per mile. In June, Samantha rented a van for three days and drove it 200 miles. The rental fee was $210. In July, she paid $245 to rent a van for one day and drove it 300 miles. What would be the total cost, in dollars, if she were to rent a van for five days during which time she drove 480 miles?

(A) $430

(B) $440

(C) $450

(D) $460

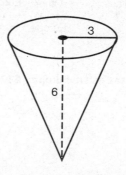

12. The diagram above represents a conical tank whose radius is 3 feet and whose height is 6 feet. If the tank is full of water and if exactly half the water in the tank is poured out, what is the height, to the nearest inch, of the water remaining in the tank?

(A) 36

(B) 48

(C) 54

(D) 57

GO ON TO THE NEXT PAGE

Questions 13–15 are based on the information in the following graphs.

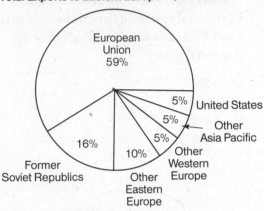

1993
Total Exports to Eastern Europe = $98 Billion

European Union 59%

5% United States
5% Other Asia Pacific
5% Other Western Europe
10% Other Eastern Europe
16% Former Soviet Republics

1996
Total Exports to Eastern Europe = $174 Billion

European Union 64%

13% Former Soviet Republics
12% Other Eastern Europe
5% Other Western Europe
4% Other Asia Pacific
United States 2%

13. Which of the following statements concerning the value of exports to Eastern Europe from other Eastern European countries from 1993 to 1996 is the most accurate?

(A) They increased by 12%.
(B) They increased by 20%.
(C) They increased by 50%.
(D) They increased by 100%.

14. France is one of the countries in the European Union. If in 1996 France's exports to Eastern Europe were four times those of the United States, then what percent of the European Union's exports to Eastern Europe came from France that year?

(A) 8%
(B) 12.5%
(C) 20%
(D) 25%

15. If from 1996 to 2000 the percent increase in total exports to Eastern Europe was the same as the percent increase from 1993 to 1996, and the percent of exports from the European Union remained the same as in 1996, to the nearest billion, what was the value, in dollars, of exports from the European Union to Eastern Europe in 2000?

(A) 188
(B) 198
(C) 208
(D) 218

GO ON TO THE NEXT PAGE

MODEL TEST 4

4

16. The following table shows the hourly wages earned by the 16 employees of a small company and the number of employees who earn each wage.

Wages per Hour	Number of Employees
$6	3
8	5
10	4
13	4

What is the average (arithmetic mean) of the median, the mode, and the range of this set of data?

(A) 4.5
(B) 8
(C) 8.5
(D) 9

17. Alan's allowance is three times as much as Bob's and one-third as much as Carol's? If their average (arithmetic mean) allowance is $26, what is Bob's allowance?

(A) $6
(B) $13
(C) $18
(D) $26

Questions 18–19 are based on the information in the following graphs.

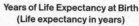

Years of Life Expectancy at Birth
(Life expectancy in years)

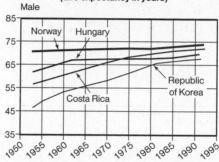

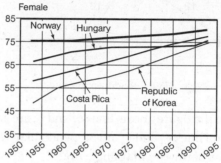

Source: U.S. Bureau of the Census, Center for International Research.

18. For how many of the countries listed in the graphs is it true that the life expectancy of a female born in 1955 was higher than the life expectancy of a male born in 1990?

(A) 1
(B) 2
(C) 3
(D) 4

19. By sex and nationality, who had the greatest increase in life expectancy between 1955 and 1990?

(A) Korean females
(B) Korean males
(C) Costa Rican females
(D) Costa Rican males

GO ON TO THE NEXT PAGE

MODEL TEST 4

20. If for all real numbers x, $g(3 - x) = x^2 + x + 1$, what is the value of $g(7)$?

(A) 13
(B) 21
(C) 57
(D) 111

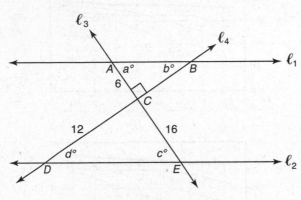

Note: Figure not drawn to scale.

21. In the figure above, lines ℓ_1 and ℓ_2 are parallel and lines ℓ_3 and ℓ_4 are perpendicular. What is the perimeter of triangle ABC?

(A) 18
(B) 24
(C) 36
(D) 48

22. If $i = \sqrt{-1}$ and if $i^n = i$, which of the following could be equal to n?

(A) 45
(B) 55
(C) 75
(D) 95

23. How many pounds of peanuts must be added to a mixture of 20 pounds of peanuts and 50 pounds of cashews if the resulting mixture is to be 60% peanuts by weight?

(A) 30
(B) 42
(C) 52
(D) 55

24. If a sphere and a right circular cone have the same radius and equal volumes, what is the ratio of the height of the cylinder to its radius?

(A) 4
(B) $\dfrac{1}{3}\pi$
(C) $\dfrac{3}{4}\pi$
(D) $\dfrac{4}{3}\pi$

25. In 2000, Jennifer invested $1,000 in a seven-year Certificate of Deposit (CD) that paid 2% interest, compounded annually. When that CD matured in 2007, she invested all of the money in another seven-year CD, also paying 2% compounded annually, that matured in 2014. To the nearest dollar, how much more money did Jennifer earn from 2007 to 2014 than she did from 2000 to 2007?

(A) $22
(B) $44
(C) $149
(D) $171

GO ON TO THE NEXT PAGE

26. In a survey of 500 families, each family has at least one child. If 345 of the families have at least one boy and 245 of the families have at least one girl, how many families have only one boy?

(A) 245
(B) 255
(C) 265
(D) 275

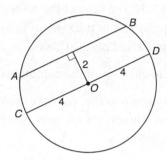

27. In the figure above, chord $\overline{AB}$ is parallel to diameter $\overline{CD}$. If $CD = 8$ and the distance between $\overline{AB}$ and $\overline{CD}$ is 2, to the nearest hundredth what is the length of AB?

(A) 2.83
(B) 3.46
(C) 5.66
(D) 6.93

Questions 28–30 are based on the information in the following graphs.

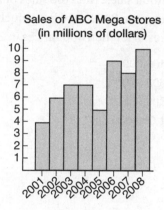

Sales of ABC Mega Stores
(in millions of dollars)

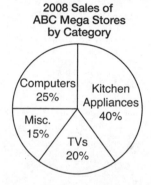

2008 Sales of
ABC Mega Stores
by Category

Computers 25%
Kitchen Appliances 40%
Misc. 15%
TVs 20%

28. In how many years from 2001 through 2008, inclusive, did the sales of ABC Mega Stores exceed the average of the annual sales during that period?

(A) 3
(B) 4
(C) 5
(D) 6

GO ON TO THE NEXT PAGE

MODEL TEST 4

29. If the retail sales of ABC Mega Stores were 20% higher in 2009 than in 2008 and if in 2009 kitchen appliances accounted for 30% of the total sales, then the sales of kitchen appliances in 2009 were how much less than the sales of kitchen appliances in 2008?

(A) $400,000
(B) $600,000
(C) $800,000
(D) $1,000,000

30. In 2010, the total sales of ABC Mega Stores were exactly the same as in 2008. However, compared with 2008, in 2010 sales of kitchen appliances and TVs were each up by 5% and sales of computers decreased by 10%. Which of the following statements must be true?

(A) In 2010, the sales of TVs were greater than the sales of computers.
(B) In 2010, the sales of miscellaneous items were less than in 2008.
(C) In 2010, the ratio of the sales of kitchen appliances to the sales of TVs was greater than it had been in 2008.
(D) If in 2010, $\frac{2}{3}$ of the computers sold were laptops and the rest were desktops, then the sales of laptops were twice the sales of desktops.

Grid-in Response Directions

In questions 31–38, first solve the problem, and then enter your answer on the grid provided on the answer sheet. The instructions for entering your answers follow.

- First, write your answer in the boxes at the top of the grid.
- Second, grid your answer in the columns below the boxes.
- Use the fraction bar in the first row or the decimal point in the second row to enter fractions and decimals.

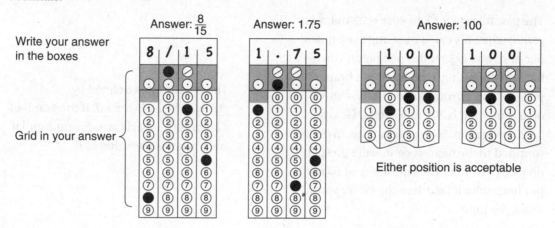

Write your answer in the boxes   Answer: $\frac{8}{15}$ Answer: 1.75   Answer: 100

Grid in your answer

Either position is acceptable

- Grid only one space in each column.
- Entering the answer in the boxes is recommended as an aid in gridding but is not required.
- The machine scoring your exam can read only what you grid, so you **must grid-in your answers correctly to get credit.**
- If a question has more than one correct answer, grid-in only one of them.
- The grid does not have a minus sign; so no answer can be negative.
- A mixed number *must* be converted to an improper fraction or a decimal before it is gridded.

  Enter $1\frac{1}{4}$ as 5/4 or 1.25; the machine will interpret 11/4 as $\frac{11}{4}$ and mark it wrong.

- **All decimals must be entered as accurately as possible.** Here are three acceptable ways of gridding

$$\frac{3}{11} = 0.272727\ldots$$

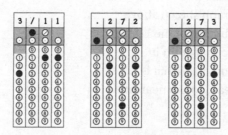

- Note that rounding to .273 is acceptable because you are using the full grid, but you would receive **no credit** for .3 or .27, because they are less accurate.

31. A supermarket just increased the price at which it sells a quart of milk by 20%. How many quarts of milk can now be purchased for the amount of money that used to buy 30 quarts of milk?

32. The gas mileage for Ken's car is 22 miles per gallon when his car is traveling at 60 miles per hour and is 25 miles per gallon when his car is traveling at 50 miles per hour. Ken will be driving from Boston to New York on a route that is 209 miles long. Gas costs $3.20 per gallon. How much more, in dollars rounded to the nearest cent, will Ken spend on gas if he drives the entire way at 60 miles per hour than if he drives the entire way at 50 miles per hour?

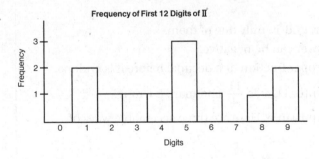

33. The decimal expansion of π begins 3.141592653589. The bar graph shown above shows the frequency distribution of the 12 digits to the right of the decimal point in this portion of the expansion of π. What is the average (arithmetic mean) to the nearest tenth of those digits?

34. John is transferring 128 files of various sizes from his computer to a colleague's computer. If the average size of his files is 256 megabytes and he can transfer 1 gigabyte of data every 12 minutes, how long will it take, in hours, to transfer all of the files? (1 gigabyte = 1024 megabytes)

35. The function f is defined by $f(x) = ax^3 + bx^2 + cx + d$. If the graph of f crosses the x-axis at 1, 2, and 3 and if $a = 1$, what is the value of c?

36. What is the cosine of the smallest angle in a right triangle whose smallest side is 5 and whose hypotenuse is 10?

GO ON TO THE NEXT PAGE

MODEL TEST 4

Questions 37–38 are based on the data in the following graphs, which give information about the 800 participants at last year's Conference of New England Educators.

Distribution of Home State of Participants

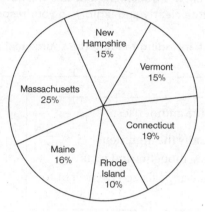

New Hampshire 15%
Vermont 15%
Massachusetts 25%
Connecticut 19%
Maine 16%
Rhode Island 10%

Distribution of Grade Level Taught by Participants from Massachusetts

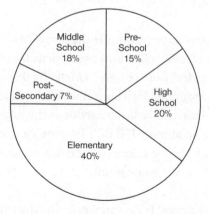

Middle School 18%
Pre-School 15%
Post-Secondary 7%
High School 20%
Elementary 40%

37. How many of the conference's participants were high school teachers from Massachusetts?

38. If $\frac{4}{15}$ of the participants from states other than Massachusetts were elementary school teachers, what percent of all the participants at the conference taught at the elementary level? (Note: Grid in your answer without the percent sign. For example, if your answer is 15.3%, you should grid in 15.3 on your answer sheet.)

STOP

If there is still time remaining, you may review your answers.

Directions: This assignment will allow you to demonstrate your ability to skillfully read and understand a source text and write a response analyzing the source. In your response, you should show that you have understood the source, give proficient analysis, and use the English language effectively. If your essay is off-topic, it will not be scored.

Only what you write on the lined paper in your answer document will be scored—avoid skipping lines, using unreasonably large handwriting, and using wide margins in order to have sufficient space to respond. You can also write on the planning sheet in the answer document, but this will not be evaluated—no other scrap paper will be given. Be sure to write clearly and legibly so your response can be scored.

You will be given 50 minutes to complete the assignment, including reading the source text and writing your response.

Read the following passage, and think about how the author uses:

- Evidence, such as applicable examples, to justify the argument
- Reasoning to show logical connections among thoughts and facts
- Rhetoric, like sensory language and emotional appeals, to give weight to the argument

Breaking Down Borders

1   Sitting in my first International Business course among some three hundred other students, I was surprised at the surplus of hands that shot up when the professor asked how many of us had traveled abroad. *How many of you have visited more than five countries? Ten? Twenty? Thirty?* By this time, only a handful of my peers kept their hands raised. Yet, surrounded by a cohort who wished to pursue careers in global markets, it was not those few avid travelers who stood out as the exception, but the four of us—myself included—who had never traveled abroad. It didn't take me long to see what I was missing; the very next summer I studied abroad. The experience is one that cannot be overstated, and everyone, regardless of major, should pursue it at some point.

2   At the forefront of my mandate to spend a semester or two abroad is personal growth. The evidence is empirical: a survey by the Institute for the International Education of Students found that studying abroad was a defining moment in a young person's life that continues to impact them long after their domestic return. In fact, 98% of the 3,400 respondents allowed that their experience abroad had left them with a better understanding of themselves, their cultural values, and their biases. Increased tolerance, compassion, and confidence are a few of the advantages. The individual change that occurs when studying abroad is a dynamic that works from the inside out—you become a better human being and opportunity arises for a better world.

3   This has broader relevance. Students who study abroad develop lifelong friendships and learn to embrace difference, along with fostering a crucial tendency to be skeptical of their own predispositions. Likewise, they are more likely to volunteer and work abroad in the future. World

news and politics, human rights advocating, and environmental conservation are just a few of the areas that students tend to become more active after visiting foreign countries. It is these humanitarians whose concern is with the world's welfare that are best equipped in the philanthropic and civic spheres. The importance of these "global citizens" can be imagined most clearly in contrast with the rocky diplomatic relations between today's nations. Study abroad experiences help to train and mold future leaders who can promote universal peace, empathy, and well-being.

4   The implications for professional growth are just as impressive. In the above referenced survey, 87% of respondents stated that their study abroad influenced future educational and career experiences. Not only does study abroad help students to find their career path, but it also makes them more appealing to employers. Among the marketable benefits are language skills, an extensive network, cultural adaptability, self-reliance, open-mindedness, and an appreciation for diversity. With the job market becoming increasingly global, these abilities are in high demand, and the job-seeker cannot afford to come to the table empty-handed.

5   Many who are hesitant to the rapid changes of a global world argue that there are plenty of opportunities for work and volunteer experience within our own borders. And while this may be true, the suggestion that this retracts value from visiting other countries and other peoples is absurd. The well-rounded and ambitious student will have taken measures to differentiate themselves at home and abroad. Concern at the high cost for travel abroad is equally as viable. Yet, more and more, programs are being initiated to fund, or help fund, studying abroad. Entire departments within colleges nationwide are devoted solely to study abroad opportunities and the funding thereof, not to mention the vast grants and independent scholarships available for the determined. Another surprisingly fruitful option is fundraising—hundreds of websites are designed principally with the goal of making fundraising convenient. It can be as simple as asking for the help of friends and family.

6   In the end, increased studying abroad is better for society as a whole. Its popularity coincides with the emergence of an educated, progressive, and thoughtful youth. The expansion of a globally-inclined culture, despite its challenges, is an unmatched occasion for collective welfare and benevolence. The student who says *yes* to experience abroad is investing in him/herself personally and professionally.

Write a response that demonstrates how the author makes an argument to persuade an audience that studying abroad is valuable. In your response, analyze how the author uses at least one of the features from the essay directions (or features of your own choosing) to develop a logical and persuasive argument. Be certain that your response cites relevant aspects of the source text.

Your response should not give your personal opinion on the merit of the source text, but instead show how the author crafts an argument to persuade readers.

ANSWER KEY
Model Test 4

Section 1: Reading

1.	D	14.	C	27.	D	40.	B
2.	D	15.	A	28.	C	41.	C
3.	C	16.	D	29.	D	42.	D
4.	C	17.	D	30.	D	43.	D
5.	A	18.	D	31.	C	44.	B
6.	C	19.	C	32.	C	45.	D
7.	B	20.	A	33.	D	46.	B
8.	D	21.	B	34.	A	47.	B
9.	A	22.	B	35.	B	48.	D
10.	D	23.	B	36.	A	49.	C
11.	C	24.	D	37.	A	50.	D
12.	D	25.	B	38.	D	51.	D
13.	B	26.	C	39.	A	52.	C

Number Correct _____

Number Incorrect _____

Section 2: Writing and Language

1.	A	12.	D	23.	B	34.	C
2.	C	13.	A	24.	A	35.	B
3.	D	14.	C	25.	A	36.	B
4.	D	15.	C	26.	D	37.	A
5.	B	16.	A	27.	C	38.	A
6.	C	17.	D	28.	D	39.	C
7.	A	18.	D	29.	C	40.	B
8.	A	19.	B	30.	B	41.	D
9.	B	20.	A	31.	A	42.	C
10.	C	21.	C	32.	D	43.	D
11.	A	22.	B	33.	B	44.	B

Number Correct _____

Number Incorrect _____

Section 3: Math (No Calculator)

1. **C**	5. **A**	9. **A**	13. **D**
2. **B**	6. **A**	10. **B**	14. **D**
3. **B**	7. **D**	11. **B**	15. **D**
4. **C**	8. **D**	12. **A**	

16. **2**   17. **3**   18. **6**   19. **6**

20. **1**

Number Correct _____

Number Incorrect _____

MODEL TEST 4

Section 4: Math (Calculator)

1. **B**	7. **C**	13. **D**	19. **A**	25. **A**
2. **B**	8. **C**	14. **B**	20. **A**	26. **B**
3. **C**	9. **C**	15. **B**	21. **A**	27. **D**
4. **A**	10. **B**	16. **B**	22. **A**	28. **A**
5. **D**	11. **D**	17. **A**	23. **D**	29. **A**
6. **C**	12. **D**	18. **A**	24. **A**	30. **B**

31. **25**   32. **3.65**   33. **4.8**   34. **6.4**

35. **11**   36. **.866**   37. **40**   38. **30**

Number Correct _____

Number Incorrect _____

SCORE ANALYSIS

Reading and Writing Test

Section 1: Reading   _____ = _____ (A)
    # correct   raw score

Section 2: Writing   _____ = _____ (B)
    # correct   raw score

To find your Reading and Writing test scores, consult the chart below: find the ranges in which your raw scores lie and read across to find the ranges of your test scores.

_____ + _____ = _____ (C)
range of reading   range of writing   range of reading + writing
test scores   test scores   test scores

To find the range of your Reading and Writing Scaled Score, multiply (C) by 10.

Test Scores for the Reading and Writing Sections

Reading Raw Score	Writing Raw Score	Test Score
44–52	39–44	35–40
36–43	33–38	31–34
30–35	28–32	28–30
24–29	22–27	24–27
19–23	17–21	21–23
14–18	13–16	19–20
9–13	9–12	16–18
5–8	5–8	13–15
less than 5	less than 5	10–12

Math Test

Section 3:   _____ = _____ (D)
    # correct   raw score

Section 4:   _____ = _____ (E)
    # correct   raw score

Total Math raw score: (D) + (E) = _____

To find your Math Scaled Score, consult the chart below: find the range in which your raw score lies and read across to find the range for your scaled score.

Scaled Scores for the Math Test

Raw Score	Scaled Score	Raw Score	Scaled Score
50–58	700–800	20–25	450–490
44–49	650–690	15–19	400–440
38–43	600–640	11–14	350–390
32–37	550–590	7–10	300–340
26–32	500–540	less than 7	200–290

ANSWERS EXPLAINED

Section 1: Reading Test

1. **(D)** The narrator is *recounting* what the tutor Pemberton, who is not related to the Moreens and is therefore an outsider to the family, has told him about *his impressions of an odd family.*

2. **(D)** The Moreens' sudden shifts are apparently motivated by *financial problems*, for the class they travel in and the apartments they stay in vary with their financial state.

3. **(C)** The word *indigence* (extreme poverty) in choice (C) is an immediate clue that financial problems may have caused the Moreens to depart suddenly from Nice. Lines 18–26 reveal that, although the Moreens rationalized their move from Nice as based on a decision to spend the summer in someplace healthful and refreshing, they wound up in Paris staying in cramped, unwholesome lodgings four flights up a malodorous staircase. Clearly, their lack of money has caused them to abandon the villa at Nice until they can recover from their financial difficulties.

4. **(C)** Throughout the passage the narrator describes event after event, all of them set in the past. Thus, it seems reasonable to infer that he is making these comments *some time after Pemberton's wanderings with the Moreens.*

5. **(A)** Lines 33–36 state that the Moreens "came back another year for a longer stay, the general character of which in Pemberton's memory today mixes pitiably and confusedly with that of the first." The narrator's reference to "Pemberton's memory *today*" indicates that he is speaking *some time after* the events recounted in this tale. The narrator is telling the story of events his friend Pemberton remembers from years past.

6. **(C)** In telling his tutor that he does not wish to outshine him or cast him in the shade by dressing better than he does, Morgan is affectionately *teasing* Pemberton.

7. **(B)** Mrs. Moreen loves Morgan ("Morgan was dear to his mother"), but she shrewdly refrains from buying him new clothes when she realizes that nobody "important" will see how he is dressed. Her attitude is *fond* (loving) *but pragmatic* (practical).

8. **(D)** Mrs. Moreen does not spend money for new clothes for Morgan because he does not make public appearances, that is, does not appear in "polite society." She does spend money on new clothes for the family members who move in polite circles. She loves Morgan and does not neglect him intentionally. This suggests that *she has only enough money to buy clothes for the family members who must appear in polite society.*

9. **(A)** Appearances matter to Pemberton. He is highly conscious of his and Morgan's shabbiness and general appearance of poverty. He is extremely aware of how the two of them might *appear to* people. Choices (B), (C), and (D) are incorrect. Although strike can mean *run into* ("striking the curb"), *achieve* ("strike a compromise"), or *hit* ("strike the first blow"), that is not how it is used here.

10. **(D)** Morgan and Pemberton consider themselves "part of the vast vague hand-to-mouth multitude of" Paris and feel conscious of being part of a "democratic brotherhood." Thus, on some levels, even if partly in jest, they *identify* with the poor.

11. **(C)** A young patrician is the child of an aristocratic family. Given Morgan's shabby clothing, he does not look smart or *fashionable* enough for people to consider him a member of the aristocracy. Choices (A), (B), and (D) are incorrect. Although smart can mean *intelligent* ("a smart student"), *brisk* ("a smart pace"), or *impertinent* ("Don't get smart with me!"), that is not how it is used here.

12. **(D)** The author begins by giving a definition of the technical term "symbol" and proceeds to analyze three separate types of symbols. Thus, he is *refining* or further defining his somewhat basic original description.

13. **(B)** For a group of letters to "stand for" an object, the letters must in some way *represent* that object to the people who accept the letters as a conventional symbol for the object. Choices (A), (C), and (D) are incorrect. Although "stand for" can mean *tolerate* ("I won't stand for this nonsense!"), *support* ("I stand for human rights."), or *rise* ("All stand for the honorable Judge!"), that is not how the word is used here.

14. **(C)** In describing the associations of the word "phooey," the author states that "the symbol has an inherent connection with the feeling it symbolizes." In other words, there is a built-in *intrinsic natural link* between the symbol and its meaning.

15. **(A)** When we say "hiss," we expel air in a sibilant manner, making a sharp "s" sound as we thrust our tongue toward the tooth ridge and dispel the air quickly. Thus we express our disapproval of something, our desire to push it away from us, so that the meaning of "hiss" has both inherent and conventional associations.

16. **(D)** To the author, *the Statue of Liberty* would be a conventional symbol, for it is a symbol that has been agreed upon by a group of people to represent the abstract idea of freedom.

17. **(D)** Discussing the flag, the author states that, "there is no intrinsic connection" between the flag's colors and the country it represents. In the same way, there is no intrinsic connection between a statue of a woman holding a lighted torch and the abstract idea of liberty. However, this statue has "been accepted as denoting" or being a sign of that particular abstract idea. Thus "we translate the visual impression of" the statue into the concept of that abstraction, "again on conventional grounds." This discussion of the flag as a conventional symbol supports the claim that the author would consider the Statue of Liberty to be a conventional symbol.

18. **(D)** If by some accident you were to have a memorably joyful time at a theme park, such as Disneyland, it might come to have some symbolic value for you, so that thoughts of Disneyland might bring a sense of joy to your mind. However, the relationship between Disneyland and your joyful mood is not an inherent, built-in one; instead, it is purely *coincidental.*

19. **(C)** Lines 57–63 consider how a city might accidentally take on symbolic value for someone because that person had had a saddening experience there. In the same way, Disneyland might take on symbolic value for someone because that person had had a memorably joyful experience there. There is nothing inherently joyful about Disneyland; one can have happy times there and one can have sad times there. If one associates Disneyland with joy, therefore, the relationship is purely coincidental.

20. **(A)** The author describes how one's inner experience of a universal symbol is rooted in or grows out of one's *sensory experience.*

21. **(B)** The author offers fire as *an example* of a universal symbol and asks the reader to *consider it.*

22. **(B)** The "properties" mentioned here are our body's *attributes* or characteristics. Choices (A), (C), and (D) are incorrect. Although "properties" may mean *possessions* ("stolen property"), *premises* ("commercial properties"), or *assets* ("valuable property"), that is not how it is used here.

23. **(B)** Rather than covering new ground or challenging historic theories, the passage *summarizes* general knowledge.

24. **(D)** Since the passage states that female tarantulas abandon their offspring in cocoons to hatch on their own and that young tarantulas go off to spend their lives in solitude, it follows that tarantulas must be *reclusive* or solitary by nature.

25. **(B)** The statement that "the young walk away, find convenient places in which to dig their burrows and spend the rest of their lives in solitude" supports the claim that tarantulas are *reclusive* or solitary.

26. **(C)** To excite a defensive response is to *stimulate* that kind of reaction. "Excite" here is a technical physiological term, as in "exciting a nerve." Choices (A), (B), and (C) are incorrect. Although "excites" can mean *enlivens* ("live music excites dancers"), *inflames* ("kissing excites him"), or *awakens* ("exciting someone's curiosity"), that is not how it is used here.

27. **(D)** The author's presentation of factual information about tarantulas is evidence of a scientifically *objective* or impartial attitude toward them. In addition, he *appreciates* them, acknowledging their delicacy of touch, swiftness of reaction time, etc. His attitude thus can best be described as one of *objective appreciation.*

28. **(C)** The key words here, "seizes the insect so swiftly," describe the spider's *quickness in attacking.*

29. **(D)** Under the conditions described here, the spider will jump whether or not it is hungry. Thus, its reaction occurs quite *regardless* of the state of its appetite. Choices (A), (B), and (C) are incorrect. Although independent can mean *self-sufficient* ("independent and self-reliant"), *self-governing* ("a fully independent country"), or *impartial* ("an independent investigation"), that is not how it is used here.

30. **(D)** Use the process of elimination to answer this question. In lines 67–71 the author denies the possibility that the viewer could confuse the spider's three tactile responses. You can eliminate choice (A). In lines 53–54, the author defines trichobothria as very fine hairs growing from disklike membranes on the spider's legs. You can eliminate choice (B). In lines 53–57, the author corrects the misapprehension that the trichobothria might be hearing organs. You can eliminate choice (C). Only choice (D) is left. At no time does the author *pose* or ask *a question.* By elimination, choice (D) is the correct answer.

31. **(C)** The concluding sentence of the passage states that the tarantula's tactile responses do not help it when it meets (that is, is attacked by) its deadly enemy, the digger wasp. It follows that subsequent paragraphs will discuss *digger wasp attacks* in more detail.

32. **(C)** Choices (A) and (D) are incorrect. By the end of the passage the author no longer is discussing the spider's three tactile responses. Choice (B) is incorrect. If the spider's three tactile responses fail the spider when it is attacked by digger wasps, then it is unlikely that the spider would be able to subdue the digger wasp, whether or not it was aware of the digger wasp 's weaknesses. Only choice (C) is left. The spider's three tactile responses prove unequal to meet the challenge of attacks from digger wasps.

33. **(D)** When Locke writes of concerns regarding the "unsteady opinion and uncertain humor" of the people, he is discussing the fear that some have that the mood of the people will change too frequently to provide a stable basis for government. In this case, "humor" is a synonym for mood or *temperament,* as it is in another common phrase, "ill humor" (a mood of bad temper or irritability). Choice (A) is incorrect. Though some witty comments may be humorous, *wit* is not a synonym for *humor,* nor is it the way the word "humor" is used here. Choice (B) is incorrect. Though some skeptical comments may be humorous, *skepticism* is not a synonym for "humor," nor is it the way the word "humor" is used here. Choice (C) is incorrect. Though the word "humor" often refers to comedy or amusement, there is nothing in the context of this passage to suggest that government might be unstable because of the people's sense of humor.

34. **(A)** Locke's main point in this passage is that the people should have the power to govern and that they should be able to rid themselves of a government that is oppressive. Locke would, therefore, not agree that basing government on the will of the people would cause instability. Choice (B) is incorrect. Locke specifically mentions the "slowness and aversion in the people to quit their old constitutions." In other words, the people are averse to change. Choice (C) is incorrect. Locke specifically mentions that such revolutions happen not upon every little mismanagement in public affairs." In other words, the people will not rebel often, even when the government is performing poorly. Choice (D) is incorrect. Locke agrees that the people will rebel at times. He specifies that this will occur after "a long train of abuses." In other words, it will take a long history of abuse by government to move the people to rebel.

35. **(B)** This passage begins with the straw man (a sham argument set up to be defeated) that the people will overthrow the government whenever the mood takes them. Locke answers immediately, "Quite the contrary," and goes on to make arguments and give examples supporting this position. Choice (A) is incorrect. Though the passage begins with two conflicting propositions, Locke spends the rest of the passage disproving the first proposition and supporting the second. Choice (C) is incorrect. No question is asked, and no method of analysis is proposed. Choice (D) is incorrect. Though Locke discusses history throughout the passage, he does not begin the passage with history.

36. **(A)** In this passage, Locke grants that there will be occasional rebellions. He argues, however, that they will be no more frequent if the people have the power to govern than they are when the people do not have that power. This is what he means when he writes, "no more than any other hypothesis." Choice (B) is incorrect. Locke does not cite any examples of rulers successfully stopping popular rebellions. Choice (C) is incorrect. Locke does not assess the effectiveness of violent rebellion in replacing oppressive governments. Choice (D) is incorrect. Locke argues the contrary; that rebellion will decrease if government knows that the people can replace it if they are abused.

37. **(A)** As stated above, in this passage, Locke grants that there will be occasional rebellions. He argues, however, that such rebellions will be no more frequent if the people have the power to govern than they are when the people do not have that power. Choice (B) is incorrect. This sentence argues that people will rebel against oppressive government, but it does not make the comparison between people with the power to govern and powerless people that is made in choice (A). Choice (C) is incorrect. Like choice (B), it predicts popular rebellion but does not make the comparison found in choice (A). Choice (D) is incorrect. This sentence indicates that historical examples of rebellion are plentiful, but as in choices (B) and (C) above, it makes no comparison between people with the power to govern and people who lack that power.

38. **(D)** Locke uses this language to describe government behavior that justifies popular rebellion. Rebellion is not justified for every individual incidence of mistreatment by government. However, when repeated incidents demonstrate a pattern of abuse, as indicated by the words, "all tending the same way," then rebellion is justified. Choice (A) is incorrect. Locke does not describe the actions that the people can take in attempting to overturn the government. Choice (B) is incorrect. Locke does not point to any specific examples from history. These are generalizations. Choice (C) is incorrect. Locke does not discuss in this passage how popular rebellion might prevent government from fulfilling its proper functions.

39. **(A)** When Locke writes about "the ends for which government was at first erected," he is referring to the reasons or *purposes* for which he believes government was created. The use of the word "for" is an important clue because we often discuss the reasons *for* a thing. Choices (B), (C), and (D) are incorrect. Though "ends" can mean *conclusions* ("beginnings and ends"), *extremities* ("the top and bottom ends"), or *segments* ("all ends of the political spectrum"), that is not how it is used here.

40. **(B)** Locke argues that placing the power to govern in the hands of the people is the best check on rebellion because he believes that the government is more likely to rebel than the people are. He claims that those in power are the most likely to use force in violation of the law and that the best way to prevent this is to show them the danger of violating the law, which is that the people may overturn their power to rule. Choices (A) and (C) are incorrect. Locke's main argument in this passage is that the people should have the power to govern and that this will create the most responsive and stable government. Giving the government absolute power would increase rebellion and decrease stability, according to Locke. Choice (D) is incorrect. Though Locke mentions a government made up of Kings, Lords, and Commons, he uses this as an example of an enduring form of government to which Britain keeps returning, despite rebellions. Locke does not argue that this form of government prevents or discourages rebellion.

41. **(C)** In this sentence Locke argues that the power of the people to replace an abusive government with a "new legislative" is the "probablest" (most likely) means to stop rebellion. Choice (A) is incorrect. This sentence describes the people's aversion to change and preference for returning to familiar forms of government. Choice (B) is incorrect. This sentence argues that the people will attempt to overturn abusive governments regardless of whether they have the authority to do so. Choice (D) is incorrect. In this section Locke attempts to change the reader's understanding of what a rebel is by arguing that when the government violates the law, it is the rebel.

42. **(D)** Locke argues that rebellion is not opposition to government but opposition to the rule of law. When the government acts "contrary to their trust" by violating the rights of the people, the government, rather than the people, should be understood to be rebels. Choice (A) is incorrect. Though Locke argues that government should be based on the will of the people, he never argues that the people cannot be wrong. Choice (B) is incorrect. Though Locke argues that the people do not like (are averse to) change, he also argues that they have risen up against abusive rulers repeatedly throughout history. Choice (C) is incorrect. Though Locke makes frequent reference to governments violating the rights of the people, including a specific reference to their right to property, he never makes any claims as to the extent of this problem. It is unclear, based on this passage, whether some, most, or all governments are guilty of this abuse.

43. **(D)** The shadowy, gloomy understory is dimly lit or *obscure*. Remember, words can have multiple meanings. *Obscure* often means unclear or ambiguous: think of "an obscure sentence." It also can mean not well known or important: think of "an obscure minor poet." Here it means lacking illumination, dark, or dim.

44. **(B)** The key phrase here is "in contrast to the forest understory." Although lines 10–14 begin by mentioning the upper story of the rainforest, the greater part of the sentence describes the understory, stating it "receives only about 1 percent of the sunlight that falls on the treetops." Clearly this supports the claim that the understory is relatively dimly lit or *obscure*.

45. **(D)** The plants that exist only within the compass of the canopy live within its boundaries or *enclosing limits*. Choice (A) is incorrect. A pair of compasses may be used in drawing *a curved arc*; however, that is not how the word is used here. Choice (B) is incorrect. Although a magnetic compass is an instrument for determining *direction*, "compass" does not mean *directions*. Choice (C) is incorrect. *Parameters* are limits or boundaries that define the scope of a process or activity. "Compass" here refers to limits or boundaries that define the scope of a physical space or area.

46. **(B)** The tree trunks provide the epiphytes only with a good location up in the canopy. Because they are nonparasitic, epiphytes *cannot draw moisture* (or any nourishment whatsoever) *from tree trunks*.

47. **(B)** Compared to orchids and bromeliads, the "lower" plants (lichens, mosses, and ferns) are *relatively primitive*. Choices (A), (C), and (D) are incorrect. Although "lower" can mean *below average* ("lower attendance than usual"), *less tall* ("a lower fence"), or *more sparse* ("supplies were even lower"), that is not how it is used here.

48. **(D)** Because epiphytes do not sink their roots into the earth, *they lack connections* to the earth and thus do not have direct access *to water in the ground*. They have direct access to water only when it rains.

49. **(C)** Both desert cacti and arboreal cacti grow in environments in which access to moisture is difficult to achieve. The desert cacti lack access to moisture because the amount of rainfall in desert regions is minimal and little moisture exists in the soil. The arboreal cacti lack access to moisture because they grow high up in the canopy with no root connections to the soil. Thus, both kinds of cacti have had to develop *features to cut down* or reduce *the loss of moisture*.

50. **(D)** The author of Passage 2 speaks of the logistical challenges scientists face when they attempt to observe epiphytes in their native habitats. Among these logistical challenges, the author specifically singles out tree height: the taller the tree, the harder it is for scientists to observe the epiphytes rooted on its topmost branches. The infographic accompanying Passage 1 makes it extremely clear just how hard it would be for scientists to observe epiphytes located in the canopy's upper story or in the emergent layer (the tops of trees that poke up above the rainforest canopy). As the infographic shows, these emergent trees tower as much as 50 meters (roughly 165 feet) above the ground.

51. **(D)** In describing the canopy of the tropical rainforest, the author of Passage 1 expresses himself in vivid, sometimes eloquent language: he writes of plants "forming vegetative communities that in number of species and complexity of interactions surpass any others on the earth." He lists colorful details (succulent stems and leaves, bulbous stem bases, tight rosettes of leaves), and metaphorically describes epiphytes as carpeting trees and branches. The author of Passage 2, in contrast, cites scholarly studies, reporting their specific numerical findings ("154 epiphyte species on 411 tree species"). He is far more analytical than evocative. Both passages convey information about epiphytes, but *Passage 2* clearly *restates in less vivid terms the information presented in Passage 1.*

52. **(C)** In both passages, the authors mention the challenges they face in studying epiphytes. Epiphytes are incredibly numerous: Perry states that "[a]bout 28,000 species in 65 families are known worldwide" and goes on to assert that "[t]housands more epiphyte varieties remain unidentified." Sugden points out the logistical challenges researchers face, "such as tree height." Clearly these authors would most likely agree that epiphyte studies *necessarily entail* or inevitably involve *certain challenges for researchers.*

Section 2: Writing and Language Test

1. **(A)** This option gives the only correct use of a past form of the verb. Choice (B) is in the present tense. Choices (C) and (D) should say "chosen" instead of "chose" or "choose."

2. **(C)** This needs to refer to the singular, gender-neutral "job hunter" making "himself or herself" appropriate. The other options are not consistent with "job hunter."

3. **(D)** The chart states that 82 percent of employers use online methods to fill jobs. This equates to roughly four-fifths since 4 divided by 5 is 0.8, which is close to 82 percent if expressed as a percentage.

4. **(D)** The first paragraph of the essay emphasizes the potential problems that your online presence can have with respect to the job search. The current paragraph emphasizes ways that you can take control of online resources to seek out job opportunities. Therefore, the contrast that choice (D) provides is most appropriate. Choices (A), (B), and (C) are all loosely related to the essay topic but do not provide the needed transition.

5. **(B)** This choice maintains the original meaning while being concise. Choice (A) is too wordy, choice (C) subtly changes the original intent, and choice (D) is too vague.

6. **(C)** This choice separates the introductory phrase, "Within your online profiles" from the independent clause that follows. Choice (A) has confused word order. Choice (B) lacks a comma after the introductory phrase. Choice (D) inserts an unnecessary colon, creating a far too abrupt pause.

7. **(A)** The previous sentence encourages readers to include detailed descriptions of their job qualifications when applying for new positions. Stating that job seekers should not be modest is therefore a logical follow-up. Choice (B) encourages concise wording instead of description. Choices (C) and (D) are irrelevant.

8. **(A)** "Whereas" is the only option that provides a contrast within the sentence between the ideas that a resume should be concise and that an online profile can be more thorough.

9. **(B)** The colon serves to give a needed pause between the independent clause before the colon and the clarifying independent clause after the colon. Choices (A) and (D) each produce a run-on sentence. Choice (C) interrupts "professional picture."

10. **(C)** According to the chart, employee referrals and online searching are the two most popular ways for employers to recruit. Choice (C) is the only option that ties directly to one of these methods, in this case, online searching.

11. **(A)** This sentence gives details to support the statement in the previous sentence, that there is now a "plethora" of resources available to the unemployed. So this sentence should be kept, making choices (C) and (D) incorrect. Choice (B) is incorrect because the second paragraph gives quite a bit of evidence that online job hunting is worthwhile.

12. **(D)** This is the only option that is parallel to the other listed phrases in the sentence: "literary figures such as Allen Ginsberg" and "film directors such as Woody Allen." The other options all violate parallelism in their phrasing, and choice (C) is too wordy.

13. **(A)** To say that something is "unparalleled" emphasizes its excellence since nothing can parallel it. So to show great popularity, this is the best option. Choices (B) and (C) are too mild. Choice (D) more fittingly describes an appetite rather than popularity.

14. **(C)** If there is controversy over this assertion, then there must be detractors who do not believe that Glass is a significant composer. The other options all indicate that these characterizations are widespread.

15. **(C)** The dashes set aside the parenthetical phrase, and the word choice in choice (C) is logical. Choices (A) and (B) do not set aside the parenthetical phrase. Choice (D) uses inconsistent punctuation to set aside the phrase.

16. **(A)** The theme of the paragraph is the minimalism of Glass's compositions. So if Johnson is a minimalist, that would make him more qualified to express his views on this topic. Choice (B) does not directly relate to the quotation that follows. Choice (C) indicates too broad of a background. Choice (D) describes a loosely related field but one that is not directly applicable to speaking authoritatively on musical minimalism.

17. **(D)** "Among" indicates that Glass has multiple awards, which is supported by the rest of the sentence. Choices (A) and (B) give illogical introductions to the sentence. Choice (C) is appropriate for a comparison of only two things.

18. **(D)** "Has written" is the present perfect tense. "Has writing" is incorrect, making choices (A) and (B) wrong. Choice (C) incorrectly uses "then," which refers to time. Choice (D) properly uses the comparative "than."

19. **(B)** Based on the context, "spurred" is most logical since it means "inspired." Choice (D) is in the incorrect tense, and choices (A) and (C) do not convey the precise meaning needed.

20. **(A)** This is the only option that correctly refers to the singular male "Glass."

21. **(C)** Since these actions happened "in the last two decades," they are continuing up to the present day. So the present perfect "has composed" is most logical. Choice (D) is also in the present perfect but is not consistent with the singular subject "Glass." Choices (A) and (B) are not in the present perfect tense and indicate events in the distant past.

22. **(B)** If an ordinary person who is not a music enthusiast recognizes Glass's compositions, that would support the idea that the works are common. Choices (A), (C), and (D) do not indicate widespread recognition.

23. **(B)** Between 1980 and 2010, the median annual incomes of those in the top 10 percent rose from approximately $160,000 to approximately $320,000, which is a doubling. During that same time interval, the median annual incomes of those in the bottom 20 percent remained at around $15,000.

24. **(A)** Having a clear understanding of Piketty's research goals helps make the connection between the two sentences. Choice (B) is not correct because this sentence focuses on Piketty's goals, not on his methods. Choice (C) is not right because the information is relevant. Choice (D) is incorrect; it is not repetitive.

25. **(A)** It is most sensible to use "greater" when referring to economic rates of return. Choice (B) refers to physical objects, choice (C) refers to prices, and choice (D) is too vague.

26. **(D)** The word "esoteric" means "intended for understanding by a select few people." So choice (D) gives a logical elaboration stressing that few people find this book accessible. The other options do not relate to the text being esoteric.

27. **(C)** This option correctly uses a colon to set off a clarification. Choice (B) uses a comma, which does not provide a sufficiently significant pause. Choice (D) has a pause in an awkward spot. Choice (A) needs a complete sentence after the semicolon.

28. **(D)** The paragraph goes on to cite Rognlie as an example of someone who found flaws in Piketty's arguments. Rognlie is best described as a "critic." Choice (A) is too neutral. Choice (B) is true but not specific in describing Rognlie's views. Choice (C) is too negative.

29. **(C)** This option both clarifies the subject and uses a semicolon to give a clear break between the independent clauses. Choice (A) does not have the necessary independent clause after the semicolon. Choice (B) does not give a parallel construction. Choice (D) creates a run-on.

30. **(B)** When referring to ideas, the phrase "points to" is fitting. Choice (A) is for pointing at physical objects, and choices (C) and (D) are not idiomatically correct.

31. **(A)** "Homeowners'" correctly indicates that there are multiple homeowners who possess returns on assets. Choices (B) and (C) are singular, and choice (D) does not indicate possession.

32. **(D)** "Hence" is the only option to indicate a cause-and-effect relationship.

33. **(B)** This option gives a clear statement of the two possible opinions. Choice (A) is too repetitive. Choice (C) improperly uses "agreeing," which is not parallel. Choice (D) makes the sentence illogical, comparing Piketty himself to an understanding of his argument.

34. **(C)** "Was" correctly indicates singular past tense. Choices (A) and (B) need to be used in conjunction with another verb in this context, and choice (D) is plural.

35. **(B)** The overall position of the author is that the theory of the humors has been a major obstacle to scientific advancement. To finish the current sentence, a statement as to the absurdity of the theory is most sensible. Choice (A) has a more positive connotation. Choices (C) and (D) are inconsistent with information elsewhere in the passage.

36. **(B)** This is the only option that properly uses an adverb, "intellectually," to modify the adjective "entrenched."

37. **(A)** The idea behind the analogy is that a mystical, unscientific cause for an illness is not helpful in developing useful cures. Choice (A) is the most applicable since it takes an unscientific cause for an illness and connects it to the illness itself. Choices (B), (C), and (D) all offer analogous reasoning but are irrelevant.

38. **(A)** This choice concisely expresses the needed idea, using the singular possessive apostrophe correctly. Choice (B) uses the plural "analyses." Choices (C) and (D) are too wordy.

39. **(C)** The author is making a general statement about a way of thinking, so "the" is most appropriate. Choice (A) is inconsistent because the passage lacks the word "one." Choices (B) and (D) use incorrect spellings to indicate possession.

40. **(B)** This option finishes the phrase "not from . . . but from." The other options are idiomatically incorrect.

41. **(D)** A "renaissance" is a "rebirth." So choice (D) properly emphasizes the fact that the theory of humors held back society, especially given the advances in science alluded to immediately after this. Choice (A) does not logically lead into the context that follows. Choices (B) and (C) are vague.

42. **(C)** "Further" correctly indicates that what follows in this sentence will build upon the argument already presented. Choice (A) does not make a strong tie to the argument, choice (B) shows contrast, and choice (D) shows cause and effect.

43. **(D)** Although this is a really long phrase, it needs no interruptions from commas. The phrase must remain unified to convey the entire idea.

44. **(B)** The lack of an understanding of germ theory (for which this notion of "corporeal isolation" is partly responsible) is most specifically elaborated upon by choice (B)—holding back medicine for three centuries is quite significant. Choice (A) uses awkward phrasing. Choice (C) is irrelevant. Choice (D) makes an obvious, unhelpful statement.

Section 3: Math Test (No Calculator)

1. **(C)** The percent increase of an investment is $\frac{\text{actual increase}}{\text{original value}} \times 100\%$. Each of Max's share was originally worth $10, and the actual increase in value of each share was $10. Max's percent increase in value was $\frac{10}{10} \times 100\% = \mathbf{100\%}$.

2. **(B)** Since the range is the difference between the highest and lowest salaries, the most logical explanation is that at least one employee (perhaps the president of the company)

makes a very high salary. For example, the lowest salary could be $20,000, but the president could earn $165,000. Each of the other statements could be true. In fact by definition of the median, choice (A) must be true. However, choices (A), (C), and (D) do not provide an explanation for the large value of the range.

3. **(B)** $\dfrac{a+b}{3+4} = \dfrac{a+b}{7} = \dfrac{a}{7} + \dfrac{b}{7}$

   **The solution is straightforward. However, if you aren't confident that you would do it correctly, plug in numbers and test the choices. For example, if $a = 3$ and $b = 4$, then $\dfrac{a+b}{3+4} = \dfrac{3+4}{3+4} = 1$. Only choice (B) is equal to 1 when $a = 3$ and $b = 4$.

4. **(C)** The volume of the small tank is $\pi r^2 h$, and the volume of the large tank is $\pi(2r)^2 h$, which equals $4\pi r^2 h$, so the large tank is 4 times the size of the small one. *Be careful!* This is an *increase* of 300%, not 400%. (4 is 3 more than 1, so is 300% more than 1.) Therefore, $k = $ **300**.

5. **(A)** Solutions to a system of equations are those points that lie on each of the graphs. Since the lines whose equations are $y = 1$ and $y = -1$ are parallel, they do not intersect. So no point can lie on all four graphs. Note that each line intersects each parabola and the two parabolas intersect each other in two points. However, 0 points lie on all four graphs.

6. **(A)** Write out the combined frequency distribution.

   Combined Distribution of all 100 rolls

Number	1	2	3	4	5	6
Frequency	11	21	21	11	16	20

   Since the combined distribution consists of 100 numbers, the median is the average of the middle two, the 50th and 51st numbers. From the distribution above, we see that there are $11 + 21 = 32$ numbers less than 3 (11 ones and 21 twos) and 21 threes, so the 33rd through the 53rd numbers are all 3. In particular, the 50th and 51st numbers are both 3. So the median is **3**.

7. **(D)** $[(2x+y) + (x+2y)]^2 = [3x+3y]^2 = [3(x+y)]^2 = 9(x+y)^2$

   **Questions such as this one can always be answered by plugging in numbers. For example, if x and y were each 1, then the given expression would be equal to $[3+3]^2 = 6^2 = 36$. Of the four choices, only $9(x+y)^2$, choice (D), is equal to 36 when x and y are each equal to 1.

8. **(D)** Joanna needed to drive the m miles in $h + \dfrac{1}{2}$ hours. Since $r = \dfrac{d}{t}$, to find her rate, you divide the distance, m, by the time, $\left(h + \dfrac{1}{2}\right)$: $\dfrac{m}{h + \dfrac{1}{2}} = \dfrac{2m}{2h+1}$.

9. **(A)** The graphs of the two equations are each parabolas. Even a rough sketch should indicate that they don't intersect. So there are 0 points of intersection.

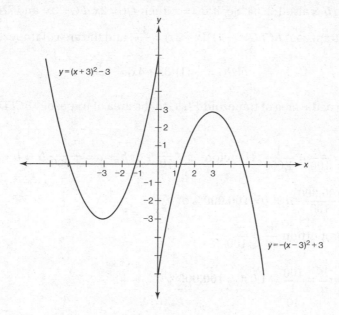

$y = (x+3)^2 - 3$

$y = -(x-3)^2 + 3$

**Alternatively, you can solve the system of equations:

$$-(x-3)^2 + 3 = (x+3)^2 - 3 \Rightarrow$$
$$-(x^2 - 6x + 9) + 3 = x^2 + 6x + 9 - 3 \Rightarrow$$
$$-x^2 + 6x - 6 = x^2 + 6x + 6 \Rightarrow -2x^2 = 12 \Rightarrow x^2 = -6$$

Since x^2 cannot be negative, the system of equations has no solution, and so the two graphs do not intersect.

10. **(B)** The graph of $f(x)$ crosses the x-axis whenever $f(x) = 0$. We have no way of knowing how many times this happens, However, it happens at least once—when $2x + 3 = 0$— which happens when $x = -\dfrac{3}{2}$. In fact, $f\left(-\dfrac{3}{2}\right) = (0)g\left(-\dfrac{3}{2}\right) = 0$.

11. **(B)** During the first year after Lee purchased the CD, the value of the CD increased $50 (5% of its original value of $1,000). So at the end of the first year, the CD was worth $1,050. During each of the next n years, the value of the CD increased by 3%. For example, at the end of the second year, the CD was worth 1.03% of what it was worth at the end of the first year: $1,050(1.03). At the end of the third year, it was worth 1.03% of that: $1,050(1.03)(1.03) = $1,050(1.03)^2$. At the end of n years, it was worth **$1,050(1.03)$^{n-1}$**.

12. **(A)** Express the quotient as a fraction. Then multiply the numerator and denominator by the conjugate of the denominator:

$$(1 + i) \div (1 - i) = \frac{1+i}{1-i} = \frac{1+i}{1-i} \cdot \frac{1+i}{1+i} = \frac{1+i+i+i^2}{1+1} = \frac{2i}{2} = i = 0 + 1i$$

So, $a = 0$ and $b = 1$.

13. **(D)** Since $\angle A$ is an angle in each of the four triangles, and since each triangle has a right angle, all the triangles are similar. Since the ratio $AB{:}AD{:}AF{:}AH = 1{:}2{:}3{:}4$, the ratio $BC{:}DE{:}FG{:}HJ$ is also $1{:}2{:}3{:}4$. So, if $BC = x$, then $DE = 2x$, $FG = 3x$, and $HJ = 4x$. Therefore, the area of trapezoid $BCED = \frac{1}{2}(1)(x+2x) = \frac{3x}{2}$, and the area of trapezoid

$$FHJG = \frac{1}{2}(1)(3x+4x) = \frac{7x}{2}$$

So the ratio of the area of trapezoid $FHJG$ to the area of trapezoid $BCED$ is $\frac{7x}{2}:\frac{3x}{2} = \textbf{7:3}$.

14. **(D)** $\frac{1}{10}\% = \frac{\frac{1}{10}}{100} = \frac{1}{1{,}000}$. Therefore, $a = \frac{1}{10}\%$ of $b \Rightarrow a = \frac{1}{1{,}000}b \Rightarrow b = 1{,}000a$

Then, $b = \frac{100{,}000}{100}a \Rightarrow b = \textbf{100{,}000\% of } a$.

**Use the proportion $\frac{\text{is}}{\text{of}} = \frac{\%}{100}$.

$\frac{a}{b} = \frac{\frac{1}{10}}{100} \Rightarrow \frac{b}{a} = \frac{100}{\frac{1}{10}} = 1{,}000 = \textbf{100{,}000\%}$

**Let $b = 100$. Then $a = \frac{1}{10}\%$ of $100 = \frac{1}{10} = 0.1$. So 100 is what percent of 0.1?

$100 = x\%$ of $0.1 \Rightarrow 100 = \frac{x}{100}(0.1) \Rightarrow 10{,}000 = 0.1x \Rightarrow x = \textbf{100{,}000}$

15. **(D)** $x + y = a(x - y) \Rightarrow x + y = ax - ay \Rightarrow ay + y = ax - x \Rightarrow y(a+1) = (a-1)x \Rightarrow y = \frac{a-1}{a+1}x$

So the slope of the line is $\frac{a-1}{a+1}$, which will be positive if the numerator and the denominator are both negative (which is true whenever $a < -1$) or if the numerator and the denominator are both positive (which is true whenever $a > 1$). So the slope is positive when $\textbf{\textit{a} < -1 or \textit{a} > 1}$.

16. **2** This problem is trivial with a calculator. Since this is in the noncalculator section, you need to know how to manipulate fractional and negative exponents.

- $4^{\frac{1}{2}} = \sqrt{4} = 2$

- $8^{\frac{1}{3}} = \sqrt[3]{8} = 2$

- $16^{-\frac{1}{4}} = \frac{1}{16^{\frac{1}{4}}} = \frac{1}{\sqrt[4]{16}} = \frac{1}{2}$

So, $4^{\frac{1}{2}} \times 8^{\frac{1}{3}} \times 16^{\frac{1}{4}} = 2 \times 2 \times \frac{1}{2} = \textbf{2}$

17. **3** $f(x) = 3 \Rightarrow 3 + \frac{5}{x} = 3 \Rightarrow \frac{5}{x} = 0$, which is impossible, so **3** cannot be a value of $f(x)$. (A fraction can equal 0 only if its numerator is 0.) Note that x cannot be 0, but $f(x)$ can be: $f(x)$ is 0 if $x = -\frac{5}{3}$.

18. **6** In order for the equation $ax + b = cx + d$ to have infinitely many solutions, it must be that $a = c$ and $b = d$.

$$3(x + 2) + 5(x + 3) = 2(x + 5) + n(x + 3) - 7 \Rightarrow$$

$$3x + 6 + 5x + 15 = 2x + 10 + nx + 3n - 7 \Rightarrow$$

$$8x + 21 = (2 + n)x + (3 + 3n)$$

For the given equation to have infinitely many solutions, it must be that $8 = 2 + n$ and $21 = 3 + 3n$, which is true if $n = 6$. Note that if $n = 6$, the last equation becomes $8x + 21 = 8x + 21$, which is true for every value of x.

19. **6** Since $y = 3x + 2$ and $y = 2x + 3$, then $3x + 2 = 2x + 3 \Rightarrow x = 1$. So the x-coordinate of the point of intersection is 1. To find the y-coordinate, plug $x = 1$ into either equation, say $y = 3x + 2$: $y = 3(1) + 2 = 5$. So the point of intersection of the two lines is $(1, 5)$, and the sum of the x- and y-coordinates is $1 + 5 = 6$.

20. **1** Since the x-coordinate of each point on the y-axis is 0, the circle intersects the y-axis when $x = 0$. By replacing x by 0 in the equation of the circle, we get:

$$(0 - 4)^2 + (y - 2)^2 = 4 \Rightarrow 16 + (y - 2)^2 = 4 \Rightarrow (y - 2)^2 = -12$$

However, $(y - 2)^2$ cannot be negative. So the circle does not touch the y-axis, and $m = 0$. Since the y-coordinate of each point on the x-axis is 0, the circle intersects the x-axis when $y = 0$. By replacing y by 0 in the equation of the circle, we get:

$$(x - 4)^2 + (0 - 2)^2 = 4 \Rightarrow (x - 4)^2 + 4 = 4 \Rightarrow (x - 4)^2 = 0 \Rightarrow x - 4 = 0 \Rightarrow x = 4$$

So the only point where the circle intersects the x-axis is the point $(4, 0)$ and $n = 1$. So $m + n = 0 + 1 = 1$.

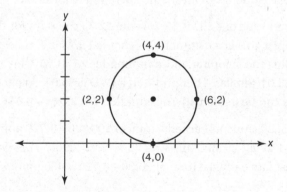

Section 4: Math Test (Calculator)

1. **(B)** The trust received 80% of the estate (10% went to the man's wife, 5% to his children, and 5% to his grandchildren). If E represents the value of the estate, then

$$0.80E = 1,000,000$$

$$E = 1,000,000 \div 0.80 = 1,250,000$$

Each grandchild received 1% (one-fifth of 5%) of the estate, or **$12,500**.

2. **(B)** If $\sqrt{x+6} = x$, then squaring both sides gives $x + 6 = x^2$. So,

$$x^2 - x - 6 = 0 \Rightarrow (x-3)(x+2) = 0 \Rightarrow x = 3 \text{ or } x = -2$$

It appears as if the equation has two solutions. However, one or both of them could be extraneous. So check each of them.

- Since $\sqrt{3+6} = \sqrt{9} = 3$, 3 is a solution.
- Since $\sqrt{-2+6} = \sqrt{4} = 2 \neq -2$, -2 is *not* a solution.

The equation has one positive solution.

**Since a square root can never be negative, choice (C) can be eliminated immediately. Once we determine that the only possible solutions are 3 and –2, we have to test only 3; –2 could not possibly be a solution.

3. **(C)** The total amount of financial aid that each university gave out is the product of the number of students receiving financial aid and the average amount of financial aid per student. To compare the universities, make a table.

	A	*B*	*C*	*D*
Number Receiving Financial Aid	4,000	2,800	3,600	4,500
Average Size of Financial Aid	$15,500	$21,000	$18,700	$14,300
Total Amount of Financial Aid	$62,000,000	$58,800,000	$67,320,000	$64,350,000

So university *C* gave out the greatest amount of financial aid.

4. **(A)** Marie's cost to sell one CD is $3.70—the $2.75 she pays for the CD plus the $0.95 she pays to ship it to her customer. On that sale, Marie collects $6.74—her selling price of $4.99 plus the shipping and handling fee of $1.75. This represents a profit of $6.74 – $3.70 = $3.04. Similarly, her profit on a DVD is $5.04. So her profit on the sale of *x* CDs and *y* DVDs can be found with the equation ***P* = 3.04*x* + 5.04*y*.**

5. **(D)** The original 20 students earned a total of $20 \times 86 = 1,720$ points. The total number of points earned by all 25 students was $25 \times 88 = 2,200$. Therefore, the five students who took the test late earned a total of $2,200 - 1,720 = 480$ points. So their average was $480 \div 5 = 96$.

**Let *x* be the average of the five students, and treat this as a weighted average problem:

$$\frac{20(86)+5x}{25} = 88 \Rightarrow 1,720 + 5x = 2,200 \Rightarrow 5x = 480 \Rightarrow x = \mathbf{96}$$

6. **(C)** Of the 192 people who supported the proposition in the survey, all 192 of them voted for the proposition as did 80% of the 90 people who had been undecided. Since 80% of 90 is 72, the total number of people from the survey who voted for the proposition was $192 + 72 = 264$. Finally, $264 \div 500 = 0.528 = \mathbf{52.8\%}$.

7. **(C)** The least common multiple of 8, 12, and 30 is 120. So every 120 seconds:

- The population increases due to births by $120 \div 8 = 15$ people.
- The population decreases due to deaths by $120 \div 12 = 10$ people.
- The population increases due to net immigration by $120 \div 30 = 4$ people.

So every 120 seconds = 2 minutes, the population increases by $15 - 10 + 4 = 9$ people. Therefore, the population increases by 4.5 per minute, $60 \times 4.5 = 270$ per hour, and $24 \times 270 = \mathbf{6,480}$ per day.

8. **(C)** The solution to question 7 says that the country's population increases by about 6,480 per day. So the annual increase in population is about

$$6,480 \times 365 = 2,365,200$$

For the population to reach 350,000,000, it has to increase by 30,000,000, which should take

$$30,000,000 \div 2,365,200 = 12.68 \text{ years}$$

So the population should reach 350,000,000 about 12.68 years after January 2015, sometime in 2027.

9. **(C)** Draw right triangle ABC.

Since $\tan A = 1$, and by KEY FACT S1,

$$\tan A = \frac{\text{opposite}}{\text{adjacent}} = \frac{BC}{AC}, \text{ then } AC = BC$$

Assume AC and BC are each 1; then by KEY FACT J8, $AB = \sqrt{2}$.
So, again by KEY FACT S1:

$$\sin A + \cos A = \frac{1}{\sqrt{2}} + \frac{1}{\sqrt{2}} = \frac{2}{\sqrt{2}}$$

Since $\frac{2}{\sqrt{2}}$ is not an answer choice, you can either:

- Rationalize the denominator:

$$\frac{2}{\sqrt{2}} \times \frac{\sqrt{2}}{\sqrt{2}} = \frac{2\sqrt{2}}{2} = \sqrt{2}, \text{ or}$$

- Use your calculator: $\frac{2}{\sqrt{2}} = 1.414$.

Only choice (C), $\sqrt{2}$, equals 1.414.

10. **(B)** Let n represent the number of members of the club before Jean joined. These members raised a total of $85n$ dollars (KEY FACT E1). After Jean was in the club, the total raised was $85n + 50$, the average was 80, and the number of members

was $n + 1$:
$$\frac{85n + 50}{n + 1} = 80$$

Cross-multiply: $\qquad\qquad 85n + 50 = 80(n + 1)$

Distribute: $\qquad\qquad 85n + 50 = 80n + 80$

Subtract $80n$ and 50
from each side: $\qquad\quad 5n = 30$

Divide by 5: $\qquad\qquad n = \mathbf{6}$

**Backsolve, starting with 6, choice (B). If there were 6 members, they would have raised $6 \times \$85 = \$510$. After Jean joined and raised $50, there would have been 7 members who raised a total of $\$510 + \$50 = \$560$. And $\$560 \div 7 = \$80$. Choice (B) works.

11. **(D)** First of all, we have to keep the units consistent. Keeping everything in dollars, we have that the rental rate is d dollars per day, and the mileage rate is $\frac{c}{100}$ dollars per mile. Then we have:

$$3d + 200\left(\frac{c}{100}\right) = 210 \quad \text{and} \quad d + 300\left(\frac{c}{100}\right) = 245$$

So $3d + 2c = 210$ and $d + 3c = 245$.

From the second equation, we have that $d = 245 - 3c$. Replacing d by $245 - 3c$ in the first equation gives

$$210 = 3(245 - 3c) + 2c = 735 - 9c + 2c = 735 - 7c \Rightarrow 7c = 525 \Rightarrow c = 75$$

Then $3d + 2(75) = 210 \Rightarrow 3d + 150 = 210 \Rightarrow 3d = 60 \Rightarrow d = 20$.

Finally, the cost for Samantha to rent a van for five days during which time she drives 480 miles is

$$5(20) + 480\left(\frac{75}{100}\right) = 100 + 480\left(\frac{3}{4}\right) = 100 + 360 = 460$$

12. **(D)** The formula for the volume of a cone is $V = \frac{1}{3}\pi r^2 h$, so the volume of this cone is $\frac{1}{3}\pi 3^2(6) = 18\pi$ cubic feet. When half the water in the tank is poured out, the volume of the remaining water is 9π cubic feet. In the diagram below, the two triangles are similar. If h represents the height of the water, $r = \frac{1}{2}h$.

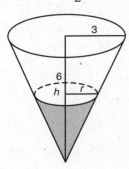

So 9π cubic feet, the volume of the water still in the tank, is equal to

$$\frac{1}{3}\pi\left(\frac{h}{2}\right)^2 h = \frac{1}{12}\pi h^3 \text{ cubic feet}$$

Then,

$$9\pi = \frac{1}{12}\pi h^3 \Rightarrow h^3 = 108 \Rightarrow h = \sqrt[3]{108} = 4.76$$

Finally, 4.76 feet = 4.76×12 inches = 57.12 inches.

13. **(D)** Exports to Eastern Europe from other Eastern European countries increased from $9.8 billion (10% of $98 billion) to $20.88 billion (12% of $174 billion)—an increase of slightly more than **100%**.

14. **(B)** If France's exports to Eastern Europe were four times those of the United States, then France accounted for 8% of the total exports. Since 8% is $\frac{1}{8}$ of 64%, France accounted for $\frac{1}{8}$ or **12.5%** of the exports from the European Union.

15. **(B)** The percent increase in total exports to Eastern Europe from 1993 to 1996 was

$$\frac{\text{the actual increase}}{\text{original amount}} \times 100\% = \frac{174-98}{98} \times 100\% = \frac{76}{98} \times 100\% = 77.55\%$$

So, in billions of dollars, the increase in total exports to Eastern Europe from 1996 to 2000 was $0.7755 \times 174 = 134.94$, making total exports $174 + 135 = 309$ billion dollars. The value of exports from the European Union was 64% of $309 = 197.76$ billion dollars. To the nearest billion, the figure was **198**.

16. **(B)** The mode is 8, since more people earn $8 an hour than any other salary. Since there are 16 employees, the median is the average of the 8th and 9th items of data: $8 and $10, so the median is 9. The range is the difference between the greatest and least values: $13 - 6 = 7$. Finally, the average of 8, 9 and 7 is **8**.

17. **(A)** Let A, B, and C represent Alan's, Bob's, and Carol's allowances, respectively. Then $A = 3B$ and $A = \frac{1}{3}C$. So $C = 3A = 3(3B) = 9B$. Then

$$26 = \frac{A+B+C}{3} = \frac{3B+B+9B}{3} = \frac{13B}{3}$$

So $13B = 3 \times 26 = 78 \Rightarrow B = \textbf{6}$.

**Test the answers starting with choice (C). If $B = 18$, then $A = 54$ and $C = 162$. The average of 54, 18, and 162 is 78, which is too big. Eliminate choices (C) and (D) and try choices (A) and (B). Since choice (C) was much too big, try (A), which works.

18. **(A)** In Norway, the life expectancy of a female born in 1955 was 75 years, which is greater than the life expectancy of a male born in 1990. In Hungary, the life expectancy of a female born in 1955 was 66 years, whereas the life expectancy of a male born in 1990 was greater than 67. In the other two countries, the life expectancy of a female born in 1955 was less than 65 years, and the life expectancy of a male born in 1990 was greater than 65. The answer is **1**.

19. **(A)** The life expectancy of **Korean females** born in 1955 was about 51 and in 1990 it was about 74, an increase of 23 years. This is greater than any other nationality and sex.

20. **(A)** If $7 = 3 - x$, then $x = -4$. So $g(7) = g(3 - (-4)) = (-4)^2 + (-4) + 1 = 16 - 4 + 1 = 13$.

21. **(A)** Since ℓ_1 and ℓ_2 are parallel, $a = c$ and $b = d$ (KEY FACT I6). If the measures of two angles in one triangle are equal to the measures of two angles in another triangle, the two triangles are similar (KEY FACT J17). In addition, since ℓ_3 and ℓ_4 are perpendicular, both triangles are right triangles. Then either by using the Pythagorean theorem or by recognizing that triangle EDC is a $3x$-$4x$-$5x$ triangle with x equal to 4, we get that $DE = 20$. Therefore, the perimeter of triangle EDC is $12 + 16 + 20 = 48$. Since side AC in triangle ABC corresponds to side CE in triangle EDC, the ratio of similitude is $6{:}16 = 3{:}8$. So the perimeter of triangle ABC is $\frac{3}{8}$ of the perimeter of triangle EDC, and $\frac{3}{8}(48) = 18$.

22. **(A)** The powers of i form a repeating sequence:

$i^1 = i$ ($a^1 = a$ for *any* number)

$i^2 = -1$ (by definition)

$i^3 = -i$ $i \cdot i \cdot i = (i \cdot i)(i) = i^2 \cdot i = -1(i) = -i$

$i^4 = 1$ $i^4 = i \cdot i \cdot i \cdot i = (i \cdot i)(i \cdot i) = (-1)(-1) = 1$

$i^5 = i$ $i^5 = i^4 \cdot i = 1 \cdot i = i$

$i^6 = -1$ $i^6 = i^5 \cdot i = i \cdot i = i^2 = -1$

$i^7 = -i$ $i^7 = i^6 \cdot i = (-1)i = -i$

$i^8 = 1$ $i^8 = i^7 \cdot i = (-1)(i) = -i^2 = -(-1) = 1$

Note that the powers of i form a repeating sequence in which the four terms i, -1, $-i$, 1 repeat in that order indefinitely.

So if $i^n = i$, then n is 1 more than a multiple of 4. Only choice (A) satisfies this condition: **45** = 44 + 1, whereas 55, 75, and 95 are each 3 more than a multiple of 4.

23. **(D)** If x pounds of peanuts are added to the existing mixture, the result will be a mixture whose total weight will be $(70 + x)$ pounds, of which $(20 + x)$ pounds will be peanuts. Then, by expressing 60% as $\frac{6}{10}$, we have

$$\frac{20 + x}{70 + x} = \frac{6}{10} \Rightarrow 200 + 10x = 420 + 6x \Rightarrow 4x = 220 \Rightarrow x = \mathbf{55}$$

24. **(A)** By KEY FACTS M9 and M7, the volume of a sphere is $\frac{4}{3}\pi r^3$ and the volume of a right circular cone is $\frac{1}{3}\pi r^2 h$. (Remember that both of these formulas are given to you on the first page of each math section.) Then:

$$\frac{4}{3}\pi r^3 = \frac{1}{3}\pi r^2 h \Rightarrow 4r^3 = r^2 h \Rightarrow 4r = h \Rightarrow \frac{h}{r} = 4$$

**Use TACTIC 3. Plug in a number for the radius, say $r = 1$. Then the volume of the sphere is $\frac{4}{3}\pi(1)^3 = \frac{4}{3}\pi$, and the volume of the cone is $\frac{1}{3}\pi r^2 h = \frac{1}{3}\pi h$. So $\frac{4}{3}\pi = \frac{1}{3}\pi h \Rightarrow h = \mathbf{4}$.

MODEL TEST 4

25. **(A)** At the end of the first year, Jennifer's CD was worth:

$$\$1,000 + 0.02(\$1,000) = 1.02(\$1,000)$$

During the second year, that money earned 2% interest. At the end of the second year, the CD was worth $1.02(1.02(\$1,000)) = (1.02)^2(\$1,000)$. When her first CD matured after 7 years, it was worth $(1.02)^7(\$1,000) = \$1,148.69$. Jennifer then deposited all of that money into a second CD. When it matured in 2014, that CD was worth $(1.02)^7(\$1,148.69) = \$1,319.48$. From 2000 to 2007, Jennifer earned $\$148.69$. From 2007 to 2014, she earned $\$1,319.48 – \$1,148.69 = \$170.79$. So the second CD earned $\$170.79 – \$148.69 = \$22.10$ more than the first one did. To the nearest dollar, the answer is **$22**.

26. **(B)** Let x represent the number of families that had at least one boy and at least one girl, and draw a Venn diagram to illustrate the situation.

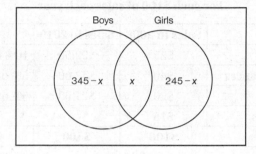

So, $345 – x$ families have only boys and $245 – x$ families have only girls. Therefore $(345 – x) + x + (245 – x) = 500 \Rightarrow 590 – x = 500 \Rightarrow x = 90$. So, $345 – 90 = \textbf{255}$ familes had only boys.

27. **(D)** Since the diameter of the circle is 8, its radius is 4. In the diagram below, OE is 2 and radius OB is 4.

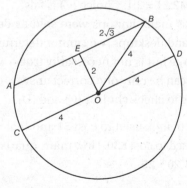

There are several ways to get that $EB = 2\sqrt{3} = 3.464$. Once you have that information you double it to get that $AB = 4\sqrt{3} = 6.928 \approx \textbf{6.93}$. How do you find EB?

- You could use the Pythagorean theorem: $2^2 + (EB)^2 = 4^2$. So $(EB)^2 = 16 – 4 = 12$, and $EB = \sqrt{12} = 3.464$.
- You could use the fact that if one leg of a right triangle is half the hypotenuse, then that leg is the shorter leg of a 30-60-90 right triangle. To get the length of the longer leg, you multiply the length of the shorter leg by $\sqrt{3}$.
- You could use trigonometry: $\sin B = \dfrac{2}{4} = 0.5$ and $\sin^{-1}(0.5) = 30°$.

Then $\cos 30 = .866 = \dfrac{EB}{4}$. So $EB = 4(0.866) = 3.464$.

28. **(A)** To find the average of the annual sales from 2001 through 2008, add up the sales (in millions) for each year and divide by 8:

$$(4 + 6 + 7 + 7 + 5 + 9 + 8 + 10) \div 8 = 56 \div 8 = 7$$

The number of years that sales were greater than $7,000,000 is **3** (2006, 2007, and 2008).

 29. **(A)** From the chart we see that in 2008 total sales were $10,000,000. In 2009, after a 20% increase, total sales were $12,000,000. From the circle graph we see that in 2008 sales of kitchen appliances were $4,000,000 (40% of $10,000,000). In 2009, sales of kitchen appliances were $3,600,000 (30% of $12,00,000)—a decrease of **$400,000**.

 30. **(B)** The simplest way to check the truth of each statement is to make a chart comparing the sales in 2008 and 2010.

For each $100 of sales each year

Category	Sales in 2008	Sales in 2010	
Computers	$25	$22.50	10% of 25 = 2.50
Kitchen Appliances	$40	$42.00	5% of 40 = 2.00
TVs	$20	$21.00	5% of 20 = 1.00
Miscellaneous	$15		
Total	**$100**	**$100**	

- From the chart we see that for every $21 of sales of TVs, there were $22.50 of sales of computers. Choice (A) is false.
- In 2010, the total sales in the three categories other than miscellaneous was $85.50, so the sales of miscellaneous items was $14.50. Choice (B) is true.
- In 2008, the ratio of the sales of kitchen appliances to the sales of TVs was 40:20 = 2:1. In 2010, the ratio was 42:21 = 2:1. Choice (C) is false.
- We know that twice as many laptops were sold as desktops, but without knowing the prices of laptops and desktops, we cannot determine how their sales compared. Choice (D) could be true but is not necessarily true.
- Note that since there can be only one correct answer, once you know that choice (B) is tue, you do not have to check choices (C) and (D).

 31. **25** Assume that a quart of milk used to cost $1 and that now it costs $1.20 (20% more). Then 30 quarts of milk used to cost $30. How many quarts of milk costing $1.20 each can be bought for $30? 30 ÷ 1.20 = **25**.

 32. **3.65**

- If Ken drives the 209 miles at 60 miles per hour, his gas mileage will be 22 miles per gallon. So he will use 209 ÷ 22 = 9.5 gallons of gas.
- If Ken drives the 209 miles at 50 miles per hour, his gas mileage will be 25 miles per gallon. So he will use 209 ÷ 25 = 8.36 gallons of gas.
- When driving at 60 miles per hour, Ken will use 9.5 – 8.36 = 1.14 gallons more and will spend 1.14 × $3.20 = $3.648 ≈ **$3.65** more than if had he driven at 50 miles per hour.

MODEL TEST 4

33. **4.8** What we want here is the weighted average of the first 12 digits to the right of the decimal point in the expansion of π. The weights are the heights of the bars in the graph.

$$\frac{0\times0+2\times1+1\times2+1\times3+1\times4+3\times5+1\times6+0\times7+1\times8+2\times9}{12}$$

$$= \frac{0+2+2+3+4+15+6+0+8+18}{12} = \frac{58}{12} = \mathbf{4.83}$$

Note that since you are given the expansion, you don't need to use the graph at all. You could just add the 12 digits to the right of the decimal point in the expansion and divide by 12.

$$(1+4+1+5+9+2+6+5+3+5+8+9) \div 12 = 58 \div 12 = \mathbf{4.83}$$

34. **6.4** Since the average size of his 128 files is 256 megabytes, the total amount of data John has to transfer is $128 \times 256 = 32{,}768$ megabytes, which is equal to $32{,}768 \div 1024 = 32$ gigabytes. Since it takes 12 minutes to transfer 1 gigabyte of data and since 12 minutes is one-fifth of an hour, John can transfer 5 gigabytes of data per hour. So it will take $32 \div 5 = \mathbf{6.4}$ hours to transfer all the data.

35. **11** If the graph of a function crosses the x-axis at n, then $(n, 0)$ is a point on the graph, $f(n) = 0$, and $x - n$ is a factor of $f(x)$. So $(x - 1)$, $(x - 2)$, and $(x - 3)$ are all factors of $f(x)$, as is their product:

$$(x-1)(x-2)(x-3) = (x^2 - 3x + 2)(x-3) = x^3 - 6x^2 + 11x - 6$$

Since $a = 1$, $f(x)$ has to be equal to $x^3 - 6x^2 + 11x - 6$. Thus $b = -6$, $c = \mathbf{11}$, and $d = -6$.

36. **.866** Let x be the length of the third side and use the Pythagorean theorem to find the value of x:

$$5^2 + x^2 = 10^2 \Rightarrow x^2 = 100 - 25 = 75 \Rightarrow x = \sqrt{75} \approx 8.66$$

Then the side opposite the smallest angle is 5, the side adjacent to the smallest angle is 8.66, and the hypotenuse is 10.

So the cosine of the smallest angle $= \dfrac{\text{adjacent}}{\text{hypotenuse}} = \dfrac{8.66}{10} = \mathbf{.866}$.

37. **40** From the first graph, we see that 25% of the conference's 800 participants came from Massachusetts. From the second graph, we see that 20% of the Massachusetts participants were high school teachers. So the number of high school teachers from Massachusetts was

$$20\% \text{ of } 25\% \text{ of } 800 = 0.20 \times 0.25 \times 800 = \mathbf{40}$$

38. **30** Of the 800 participants, 25% of them, or 200, came from Massachusetts. The other 600 participants came from states other than Massachusetts. Of those 600 non-Massachusetts participants, $\frac{4}{15}(600) = 160$ of them were elementary school teachers. In addition, 80 of the delegates from Massachusetts (40% of 200) were elementary teachers. So in total, $160 + 80 = 240$ of the 800 conference delegates were elementary school teachers, and $240 \div 800 = 0.30 = \mathbf{30\%}$.

SAT Essay Scoring

SAT Essay Scoring Rubric

	Score: 4
Reading	Excellent: The essay shows excellent understanding of the source.
	The essay shows an understanding of the source's main argument and key details and a firm grasp of how they are interconnected, demonstrating clear comprehension of the source.
	The essay does not misinterpret or misrepresent the source.
	The essay skillfully uses source evidence, such as direct quotations and rephrasing, representing a thorough comprehension of the source.
Analysis	Excellent: The essay gives excellent analysis of the source and shows clear understanding of what the assignment requires.
	The essay gives a complete, highly thoughtful analysis of the author's use of reasoning, evidence, rhetoric, and/or other argumentative elements the student has chosen to highlight.
	The essay has appropriate, adequate, and skillfully chosen support for its analysis. The essay focuses on the most important parts of the source in responding to the prompt.
Writing	Excellent: The essay is focused and shows an excellent grasp of the English language. The essay has a clear thesis. The essay has a well-executed introduction and conclusion. The essay shows a clear and well-crafted progression of thoughts both within paragraphs and in the essay as a whole. The essay has a wide range of sentence structures. The essay consistently shows precise choice of words. The essay is formal and objective in its style and tone. The essay demonstrates a firm grasp of the rules of standard English and has very few to no errors.

	Score: 3
Reading	Skillful: The essay shows effective understanding of the source.
	The essay shows an understanding of the source's main argument and key details.
	The essay is free of major misinterpretations and/or misrepresentations of the source.
	The essay uses appropriate source evidence, such as direct quotations and rephrasing, representing comprehension of the source.
Analysis	Skillful: The essay gives effective analysis of the source and shows an understanding of what the assignment requires.
	The essay decently analyzes the author's use of reasoning, evidence, rhetoric, and/or other argumentative elements the student has chosen to highlight.
	The essay has appropriate and adequate support for its analysis. The essay focuses primarily on the most important parts of the source in responding to the prompt.
Writing	Skillful: The essay is mostly focused and shows an effective grasp of the English language. The essay has a thesis, either explicit or implicit. The essay has an effective introduction and conclusion. The essay has a clear progression of thoughts both within paragraphs and in the essay as a whole. The essay has an assortment of sentence structures. The essay shows some precise choice of words. The essay is formal and objective in its style and tone. The essay demonstrates a grasp of the rules of standard English and has very few significant errors that interfere with the writer's argument.

	Score: 2
Reading	Limited: The essay shows some understanding of the source. The essay shows an understanding of the source's main argument, but not of key details. The essay may have some misinterpretations and/or misrepresentations of the source. The essay gives only partial evidence from the source, showing limited comprehension of the source.
Analysis	Limited: The essay gives partial analysis of the source and shows only limited understanding of what the assignment requires. The essay tries to show how the author uses reasoning, evidence, rhetoric, and/or other argumentative elements the student has chosen to highlight, but only states rather than analyzes their importance, or at least one part of the essay's analysis is unsupported by the source. The essay has little or no justification for its argument. The essay may lack attention to those elements of the source that are most pertinent to responding to the prompt.
Writing	Limited: The essay is mostly not cohesive and shows an ineffective grasp of the English language. The essay may not have a thesis, or may diverge from the thesis at some point in the essay's development. The essay may have an unsuccessful introduction and/or conclusion. The essay may show progression of thoughts within the paragraphs, but not in the essay as a whole. The essay is relatively uniform in its sentence structures. The essay shows imprecise and possibly repetitive choice of words. The essay may be more casual and subjective in style and tone. The essay demonstrates a weaker grasp of the rules of standard English and does have errors that interfere with the writer's argument.
	Score: 1
Reading	Insufficient: The essay shows virtually no understanding of the source. The essay is unsuccessful in showing an understanding of the source's main argument. It may refer to some details from the text, but it does so without tying them to the source's main argument. The essay has many misinterpretations and/or misrepresentations of the source. The essay gives virtually no evidence from the source, showing very poor comprehension of the source.
Analysis	Insufficient: The essay gives little to no accurate analysis of the source and shows poor understanding of what the assignment requires. The essay may show how the author uses reasoning, evidence, rhetoric, and/or other argumentative elements that the student has chosen to highlight but does so without analysis. Or many parts of the essay's analysis are unsupported by the source. The support given for points in the essay's argument are largely unsupported or off topic. The essay may not attend to the elements of the source that are pertinent to responding to the prompt. Or the essay gives no explicit analysis, perhaps only resorting to summary statements.
Writing	Insufficient: The essay is not cohesive and does not demonstrate skill in the English language. The essay may not have a thesis. The essay does not have a clear introduction and conclusion. The essay does not have a clear progression of thoughts. The essay is quite uniform and even repetitive in sentence structure. The essay shows poor and possibly inaccurate word choice. The essay is likely casual and subjective in style and tone. The essay shows a poor grasp of the rules of standard English and may have many errors that interfere with the writer's argument.

Top-Scoring Sample Student Response

While it was initially the author's intention to expand her knowledge of the global marketplace that drove her to study abroad in the passage "Breaking Down Borders," she quickly realized that there is a much greater humanitarian benefit that stands to be gained by everyone who chooses to pursue such ventures. As such, she primarily relies on her first-hand experience to help persuade her audience of the value of studying abroad. However, she also combines this with statistics-based, survey-driven data, in order to help aid her opinion and bolster its value above that of mere hearsay or anecdotal evidence.

In opening the passage by telling the story of her class, the reader is immediately invested in what the author has to say. By reflecting on one's own experiences, and imagining where they fall in the pecking order of the number of countries visited, the reader is immersed in the scene that the author is describing. However, romanticism such as this can be fleeting, which is a detail that the writer seems to be well aware of as she quickly switches gears to present factual data that helps to back her claim that the primary benefit of studying abroad is for "personal growth." By quoting a survey from the Institute for the International Education of Students, the author identifies that an overwhelming 98% of respondents experienced both an increased level of self-awareness, as well as a better understanding of the manner in which the cultural implications can impact the way each person sees the world around them. Furthermore, the survey states that this experience helped to promote character traits of "increased tolerance, compassion, and confidence." Factual claims of this nature, along with a statistic as glaring as the one provided, help to establish credence in the writer's beliefs and paves the way for a certain amount of trust with her claims moving forward.

The writer goes on to make some logical connections between how the increased understanding that students obtain of the world around them, in conjuncture with the traits that studying abroad helps to develop, plays a large role in making the travelers better "global citizens." Many examples of this are pointed out, which include: developing lifelong friendships, embracing difference, volunteering, traveling, as well as actively participating in world news and politics, human rights advocating, and environmental conservation. In turn, these activities can lead to the development of future leaders, whose worldly understanding can help to strengthen the bonds and decrease "the rocky diplomatic relations" that currently exists "between today's nations." Bold statements such as these may hold little weight if not for the level of faith that the writer had previously achieved from her readers.

In perhaps a bit of realization that the potential prospects identified to this point may have begun to become a bit too grandiose, the writer reins back in her readers by making claims in regards to "professional growth" in general, which are sure to connect with most of the populace at large. By once again quoting the aforementioned survey, the author states that "87% of respondents stated that their study abroad influenced future educational and career experiences." Furthermore, the author goes on to explain how the traits associated with studying abroad directly correlate to the same types of skills that employers are looking for when hiring. This list of characteristics, becoming ever more important in an "increasingly global" market, includes "language skills, an extensive network, cultural adaptability, self-reliance, open-mindedness, and an appreciation for diversity."

The author completes her passage by combating the notion that traveling abroad somehow takes away from, or is mutually exclusive to, performing similar charitable works domestically. On the contrary, she retorts that those who perform such works abroad are actually more likely to perform them locally as well, because the "well-rounded and ambitious student will have taken measures to differentiate themselves at home and abroad." This is yet another of a seemingly endless array of reasons why the author advocates for us to study abroad, in an attempt to improve ourselves, our future, and our world as a whole. But it is the statistical facts that she presents that helps her appease to not just our heart, but our mind as well, and is why she makes a strong and persuasive argument in regards to the value of studying abroad.

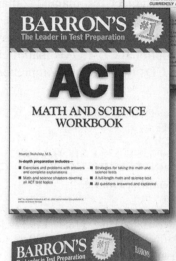
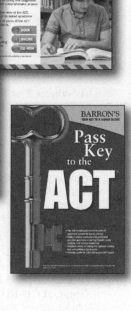

PRONUNCIATION KEY*

ă	as in pat	ĕ	as in pet and cherry	oi	as in point and toy
ā	as in play and maid	ē	as in see	ə	as in a<u>bo</u>ve and cac<u>tus</u>
ah	as in bother and hot	ēr	as in ear and peer	û(r)	as in purr and pert
ahr	as in car	ĭ	as in pit	o͞o	as in school and mule
â(r)	as in Mary and fair	ī	as in pie and my	o͝o	as in full and good
aw	as in paw	ō	as in toe and grow	ng	as in Ping-Pong
ow	as in how and cloud				

*<u>Note</u>: Pronunciation often tends to be regional and you may find that you pronounce a word differently than what is shown. These guidelines are meant to give you a general idea of the pronunciation (to distinguish between the adjective, verb, or noun forms of the word, for example), and are based primarily on the first-listed pronunciation in *Merriam Webster's Collegiate Dictionary*, Eleventh Edition.

Fold along perforation before detaching cards.

abstract
(ab STRĂKT)

academic
(ă kə DĔ mĭk)

accommodation
(ə kah mə DĀ shən)

acute
(ə KYŌŌT)

adverse
(ĂD vərs)

abridge
(ə BRĬJ)

acclaim
(ə KLĀM)

adopt
(ə DAHPT)

adversary
(ĂD vû(r) sĕr ē)

adj. related to education; not practical or directly useful.

When Sharon applied for the faculty post, the dean asked about her academic qualifications.

Seismologists' studies about earthquakes are not of purely academic interest, for these studies enable us to assess the danger of potential earthquakes.

adj. theoretical; not concrete; nonrepresentational.

To him, hunger was an abstract concept; he had never missed a meal.

v. condense or shorten.

Because the publishers felt the public wanted a shorter version of War and Peace, they proceeded to abridge the novel.

adj. quickly perceptive; keen; brief and severe.

The acute young doctor realized immediately that the gradual deterioration of the patient's previously acute hearing was due to a chronic illness, not an acute one.

n. provision of housing; settlement or compromise.

We used the cottage for the accommodation of visiting relatives. In 1949–1950, a chance existed for the Chinese Communist Party and the United States to reach an accommodation or, at least, to avoid a confrontation.

v. applaud; announce with great approval. also n.

The NBC sportscasters acclaimed every American victory in the Olympics and decried every American defeat.

adj. unfavorable; preventing success.

The recession had a highly adverse effect on Father's investment portfolio: he lost so much money that he had to sell our summer cottage.

n. opponent.

The young wrestler struggled to defeat his adversary.

v. legally take a child as one's own; choose to follow; assume an attitude; formally accept (a suggestion or report).

Tom and Joan adopted a daughter. I just adopted a new weight-loss plan. Don't adopt such a patronizing tone when you talk to me! Was the committee's report adopted unanimously, or did anyone abstain?

Fold along perforation before detaching cards.

adversity
(ăd VÛ(R) sə tē)

advocate
(ĂD və kāt)

aesthetic
(ĕs THĔ tĭk)

affirmation
(ă fər MĀ shən)

afford
(ə FAWRD)

alleviate
(ə LĒ vē āt)

ambiguous
(ăm BĬ gyə wəs)

ambivalence
(ăm BĬ və lən(t)s)

amplify
(ĂM plə fī)

adj; artistic; dealing with or capable of appreciation of the beautiful. aesthete, n.

The beauty of Tiffany's stained glass appealed to Esther's aesthetic sense.

---

v. urge; plead for.

The abolitionists advocated freedom for the slaves.

---

n. poverty; misfortune.

We must learn to meet adversity gracefully.

---

v. relieve.

This should alleviate the pain; if it does not, we shall have to use stronger drugs.

---

v. have enough money to pay for; provide.

Although Phil is not sure he can afford a membership at the yoga studio, he wants to sign up because of the excellent training the studio affords.

---

n. positive assertion; confirmation; solemn pledge by one who refuses to take an oath.

Despite Tom's affirmations of innocence, Aunt Polly still suspected he had eaten the pie.

---

v. increase in volume or intensity; add details to clarify or broaden (a story or report).

Lucy used a loudspeaker to amplify her voice, drowning out poor Charlie Brown's attempt to amplify his earlier remarks.

---

n. the state of having contradictory or conflicting emotional attitudes.

Torn between loving her parents one minute and hating them the next, she was confused by the ambivalence of her feelings.

---

adj. unclear or doubtful in meaning.

His ambiguous instructions misled us; we did not know which road to take.

Fold along perforation before detaching cards.

appreciate
(ə PRĒ shē āt)

assertion
(ə SƏR shen)

autonomous
(aw TAH nə məs)

application
(ă plĭ KĀ shən)

articulate
(ahr TĬ kyə lət)

attribute
(Ă trĭ byōōt)

antithesis
(ăn TĬ thə səs)

arbitrary
(ÄHR bə trĕr ē)

astute
(ə STŌŌT)

v. be thankful for; increase in worth; recognize.

Little Orphan Annie truly *appreciated* the stocks Daddy Warbucks gave her, which *appreciated* in value over the years. While I *appreciate* the artistry that went into Lucian Freud's paintings, I still dislike them.

n. confident statement; demand for other people's acceptance or respect.

Malcolm made the *assertion* that his brother Reece always acted like a wimp. Reece's lack of self-*assertion* made him a target for every bully in town.

adj. self-governing, autonomy, *n.*

Although the University of California at Berkeley is just one part of the state university system, in many ways Cal Berkeley is *autonomous*, for it runs several programs that are not subject to outside control.

n. request; act of putting something to use; diligent attention; relevance.

Jill submitted her scholarship *application* to the financial aid office. Martha's research project is purely academic; it has no practical *application*. Aunt Polly praised Tom for his *application* to his homework. Unfortunately, John's experience in book publishing had little or no *application* to the e-publishing industry.

adj. effective; distinct.

Her *articulate* presentation of the advertising campaign impressed her employers.

n. inherent quality; characteristic.

The resort has always had one outstanding *attribute*: an excellent location on one of the best ocean-sports bays along the Kohala Coast.

n. direct opposite.

Stagnation is the *antithesis* of growth.

adj. capricious; randomly chosen; tyrannical.

Tom's *arbitrary* dismissal angered him; his boss had no reason to fire him.

adj. wise; shrewd; keen.

The painter was an *astute* observer, noticing every tiny detail of her model's appearance.

Fold along perforation before detaching cards.

benevolent
(bə NĔV e lənt)

capacity
(kə PĂ sə tē)

civil
(SĬ vəl)

benign
(bə NĪN)

censure
(SĔN(T) shər)

coercion
(ko Û(R) zhən)

brevity
(BRE və tē)

cite
(SĪT)

commemorate
(ke MĔ mə rāt)

n. conciseness.

Brevity is essential when you send a telegram or cablegram; you are charged for every word.

---

adj. gentle in manner; not malignant.

Although her *benign* smile made Miss Marple seem to be a sweet little old lady, in reality she was a tough-minded, shrewd observer of human nature. We were relieved that Tom's tumor turned out to be *benign*.

---

adj. generous; charitable.

Mr. Fezziwig was a *benevolent* employer who wished to make Christmas merrier for young Scrooge and his other employees.

---

v. refer to or quote, especially to justify a position; praise; summon someone before a court.

When asked to say why she supported vaccinating children against polio, Rosemary *cited* several reports of dangerous new outbreaks of this once nearly eliminated disease. The mayor *cited* the volunteers of Hook & Ladder Company 1 for their heroism in extinguishing the recent fire. Although Terry was *cited* for contempt of court, he never went to jail.

---

v. blame; criticize.

The senator was *censured* for behavior inappropriate to a member of Congress.

---

n. volume; amount that something can produce; ability; role or position.

This thermos container has a one-liter *capacity*. Management has come up with a plan to double the factory's automobile production *capacity*. I wish I had the mental *capacity* to understand Einstein's theory of relativity. Rima traveled to Japan in her *capacity* as director of the Country Dance & Song Society.

---

v. honor the memory of.

The statue of the Minute Man *commemorates* the valiant soldiers who fought in the Revolutionary War.

---

n. use of force to get someone to obey.

The inquisitors used both physical and psychological *coercion* to force Joan of Arc to deny that her visions were sent by God.

---

adj. pertaining to ordinary citizens, as opposed to the church or military; courteous and polite.

Although Internal Revenue Service agents are *civil* servants, they are not always *civil* to suspected tax cheats.

Fold along perforation before detaching cards.

compliance
(kəm PLī ən(t)s)

compound
(KAHM paund)

compound
(kəm PAUND)

concede
(kən SĒD)

concentration
(kahn sən TRĀ shən)

conciliatory
(kən SĬL yətawr ē)

concise
(kən SĪS)

concrete
(kahn KRĒT)

condone
(kən DŌN)

v. compose; combine ingredients; make something bad worse. Her style was *compounded* of elements drawn from Silverstein, Carroll, and Lear, whose verses she imitated. Once, doctors *compounded* their own medicines, using a mortar and pestle to grind the ingredients. Trying to run away from fear only *compounds* the problem; the only way to overcome fear is to tackle the problem head-on.

n. something composed of the union of separate parts or elements; walled-in area containing separate buildings. As a chemical *compound*, a water molecule contains one oxygen and two hydrogen atoms linked by covalent bonds. The Kennedy *Compound* consists of three houses on six acres of waterfront property on Cape Cod.

n. readiness to yield; conformity in fulfilling requirements. Bullheaded Bill was not noted for easy *compliance* with the demands of others.

adj. reconciling; soothing. She was still angry despite his *conciliatory* words.

n. focusing one's total attention; gathering; cluster; relative amount of a substance. As Ty filled in the bubbles on his answer sheet, he frowned in *concentration*. Oakland has one of the largest *concentrations* of Tagalog-speakers in California. Fertilizers contain high *concentrations* of nitrogen to help promote the growth of crops.

v. acknowledge something to be true; admit defeat; grant; award. Despite all the evidence Monica had assembled, Mark refused to *concede* that she was right. Although it was clear that his opponent had won, for two weeks after the election Senator Foghorn refused to *concede* defeat. When were American women finally *conceded* full voting rights?

v. overlook; forgive; give tacit approval; excuse. Unlike Widow Douglass, who *condoned* Huck's minor offenses, Miss Watson did nothing but scold.

adj. physical or material in nature, as opposed to abstract; real; specific. The word *boy* is *concrete*; the word *boyhood* is abstract. Unless the police turn up some *concrete* evidence of his guilt, we have no case against him. I don't have time to listen to vague pitches; come up with a *concrete* proposal, and then we can talk.

adj. brief and compact. When you define a new word, be *concise*; the shorter the definition, the easier it is to remember.

Fold along perforation before detaching cards.

consensus
(kən SĔN(T) səs)

consistency
(kən SĬS tən(t) sē)

constraint
(kən STRĀNT)

contend
(kən TĔND)

contention
(kən TĔN(T) shən)

conviction
(kən VĬK shən)

corroborate
(kəRAH bərāt)

credulity
(krĭ DYŌŌ lətē)

criterion
(krī TĪR ē ən)

n. compulsion; repression of feelings. constrain, *v.*

There was a feeling of *constraint* in the room because no one dared to criticize the speaker.

---

n. judgment that someone is guilty of a crime; strongly held belief.

Even her *conviction* for murder did not shake Peter's *conviction* that Harriet was innocent of the crime.

---

n. standard used in judging.

What *criterion* did you use when you elected this essay as the prizewinner?

---

n. absence of contradictions; dependability; degree of thickness.

Sherlock Holmes judged explanations on their *consistency,* preferring them to include no improbabilities. Show up every day and do your job; *consistency* in performance is the mark of a good employee. If the pea soup is too thick, add some stock until it reaches the *consistency* you want.

---

n. angry disagreement; point made in a debate or an argument; competition.

Some people are peacemakers; others seek out any excuse for quarrels and *contention.* It is our *contention* that, if you follow our tactics, you will boost your score on the SAT. Through his editor, Styron learned that he was in *contention* for the National Book Award.

---

n. belief on slight evidence; gullibility; naïveté

Con artists take advantage of the *credulity* of inexperienced investors to swindle them out of their savings.

---

n. general agreement.

The *consensus* indicates that we are opposed to entering into this pact.

---

n. argue earnestly; struggle in rivalry.

Sociologist Harry Edwards *contends* that some colleges exploit young African-American athletes, supporting them as athletes *contending* against one another in sports but failing to support them as students working toward a degree.

---

v. confirm; support.

Though Huck was quite willing to *corroborate* Tom's story, Aunt Polly knew better than to believe either of them.

Fold along perforation before detaching cards.

cryptic
(KRĬP tĭk)

cursory
(KÛ(R) sə rē)

definition
(dĕ fə NĬ shən)

delineate
(dĭ LĬ nē āt)

denounce
(dĭ NOWN(T)S)

deprecate
(DĔ prĭ kāt)

deride
(dĭ RĪD)

determination
(dĭ tər mə NĀ shən)

deterrent
(dĭ TÛ(R) ent)

n. statement of a word's exact meaning; clarity of sound or image being reproduced; distinctness of outlines, boundaries.

This word list gives three *definitions* for the word *definition*. The newest flat screen monitors have excellent resolution and amazing color *definition*. The gym's fitness program includes specific exercises to improve *definition* of the abdominal muscles.

v. express disapproval of; protest against; belittle.

A firm believer in old-fashioned courtesy, Miss Post *deprecated* the modern tendency to address new acquaintances by their first names.

n. something that discourages; hindrance.

Does the threat of capital punishment serve as a *deterrent* to potential killers?

adj. casual; hastily done.

Because a *cursory* examination of the ruins indicates the possibility of arson, we believe the insurance agency should undertake a more extensive investigation of the fire's cause.

v. condemn; criticize. denunciation, *n.*

The reform candidate *denounced* the corrupt city officers for having betrayed the public's trust.

n. firmness of purpose; calculation; decision.

Nothing could shake his *determination* that his children would get the best education that money could buy. Thanks to my calculator, my *determination* of the answer to the problem took only seconds. In America's system of government, the president and Congress must heed the Supreme Court's *determination* of constitutional issues.

adj. mysterious; hidden; secret.

Thoroughly baffled by Holmes's *cryptic* remarks, Watson wondered whether Holmes was intentionally concealing his thoughts about the crime.

n. portray.

He is a powerful storyteller, but he is weakest when he attempts to *delineate* character.

v. ridicule; make fun of. derision, *n.*

The critics *derided* his pretentious dialogue and refused to consider his play seriously.

Fold along perforation before detaching cards.

discerning
(dĭ SÛ(R) nĭng)

discrepancy
(dĭs KRĔ pən sē)

disinclination
(dĭ sin klə NĀ shən)

diminution
(dĭ mə NOŌ shən)

discount
(DĬS kaunt)

disdain
(dĭs DĀN)

digression
(dĭ GRĔ shən)

discordant
(dĭs KAWR d(ə)nt)

discriminating
(dĭs KRĬ mə nā tĭng)

adj. mentally quick and observant; having insight.

Though no genius, the star was sufficiently *discerning* to tell her true friends from the countless phonies who flattered her.

n. lessening; reduction in size.

Old Jack was as sharp at eighty as he had been at fifty; increasing age led to no *diminution* of his mental acuity.

n. wandering away from the subject. digress, v.

Nobody minded when Professor Renoir's lectures wandered away from their official theme; his *digressions* were always more fascinating than the topic of the day.

n. lack of consistency; difference.

The police noticed some *discrepancies* in his description of the crime and did not believe him.

v. minimize the significance of; reduce in price.

Be prepared to *discount* what he has to say about his ex-wife; he is still very bitter about the divorce. Sharon waited to buy a bathing suit until Macy's fall sale, when the department store *discounted* the summer fashions.

adj. not harmonious; conflicting.

Nothing is quite so *discordant* as the sound of a junior high school orchestra tuning up.

n. unwillingness.

Some mornings I feel a great *disinclination* to get out of bed.

v. view with scorn or contempt.

In the film *Funny Face*, the bookish heroine *disdained* fashion models for their lack of intellectual interests.

adj. treating people of different classes unequally; able to see subtle differences.

The firm was accused of *discriminating* hiring practices that were biased against women. A superb interpreter of Picasso, she was sufficiently *discriminating* to judge the most complex works of modern art.

Fold along perforation before detaching cards.

disparity
(dǐ SPĂR ə tē)

divergent
(də VÛ(R) jənt)

eloquence
(Ě lə kwən(t)s)

disparage
(dǐ SPĂR ĭj)

disseminate
(dǐ SĚ mə nāt)

economy
(ǐ KAH nə mē)

dismiss
(dǐs MǏS)

disperse
(dǐ SPÛ(R)S)

dogmatic
(dawg MĂ tǐk)

n. difference; condition of inequality.
Their *disparity* in rank made no difference at all to the prince and Cinderella.

adj. differing; deviating.
After medical school, the two doctors took *divergent* paths, one becoming a surgeon, the other dedicating himself to a small family practice.

n. expressiveness; persuasive speech.
The crowds were stirred by Martin Luther King's *eloquence*.

v. belittle.
A doting mother, Emma was more likely to praise her son's crude attempts at art than to *disparage* them.

v. distribute; spread; scatter (like seeds).
By their use of the Internet, propagandists have been able to *disseminate* their pet doctrines to new audiences around the globe.

n. national condition of monetary supply, goods production, etc.; frugality; thrift; efficiency or conciseness in use of words, etc.
The President favors tax cuts to stimulate the *economy*. I need to practice *economy* when I shop; no more impulse buying for me! After reading the epigrams of Alexander Pope, I admire the *economy* of his verse; in few words, he conveys worlds of meaning.

v. let go from employment; refuse to accept or consider.
To cut costs, the store manager *dismissed* all the full-time workers and replaced them with part-time employees at lower pay. Because Tina believed in Tony's fidelity, she *dismissed* the notion that he might be having an affair.

v. scatter.
The police fired tear gas into the crowd to *disperse* the protesters.

adj. opinionated; arbitrary; doctrinal.
We tried to discourage Doug from being so *dogmatic*, but never could convince him that his opinions might be wrong.

Fold along perforation before detaching cards.

emulate
(ĔM yə lāt)

enigma
(ĭ NĬG mə)

euphemism
(YŌŌ fə mĭ zem)

embellish
(ĭm BĔ lĭsh)

enhance
(ĭn HĂN(T)S)

erudite
(ĔR yə dīt)

elusive
(ē LŌŌ sĭv)

engage
(ĕn GĀJ)

equivocal
(ĭ KWĬ və kəl)

v. imitate; rival.

In a brief essay, describe a person you admire, someone whose virtues you would like to *emulate*.

n. puzzle; mystery.

"What do women want?" asked Dr. Sigmund Freud. Their behavior was an *enigma* to him.

n. mild expression in place of an unpleasant one.

The expression "he passed away" is a *euphemism* for "he died."

v. adorn; ornament.

The costume designer *embellished* the leading lady's ball gown with yards and yards of ribbon and lace.

v. increase; improve.

You can *enhance* your chances of being admitted to the college of your choice by learning to write well; an excellent essay can *enhance* any application.

adj. learned; scholarly.

Though his fellow students thought him *erudite*, Paul knew he would have to spend many years in serious study before he could consider himself a scholar.

adj. evasive; baffling; hard to grasp.

Trying to pin down exactly when the contractors would be finished remodeling the house, Nancy was frustrated by their *elusive* replies.

v. pledge to do something (especially, to marry); hire; attract and keep (attention); induce someone to participate; take part in; attack (an enemy).

When Tony and Tina became *engaged*, they decided to *engage* a lawyer to write up a prenuptial agreement. Tony's job *engages* him completely. When he's focused on work, not even Tina can *engage* him in conversation. Instead, she *engages* in tennis matches, fiercely *engaging* her opponents.

adj. ambiguous; intentionally misleading.

Rejecting the candidate's *equivocal* comments on tax reform, the reporters pressed him to state clearly where he stood on the issue.

Fold along perforation before detaching cards.

exemplary
(ĭg ZĔM plə rē)

expedient
(ĭk SPĒ dē ənt)

extraneous
(ĕk STRĀ nē əs)

execute
(ĔK sə kyōōt)

exonerate
(ĭg ZAH nə rāt)

expository
(ĭk SPAHZ ə tawr ē)

exacerbate
(ĭg ZĂ sər bāt)

exhaustive
(ĭg ZAW stiv)

explicit
(ĭk SPLĬ sət)

adj. serving as a model; outstanding.
At commencement, the dean praised Ellen for her *exemplary* behavior as class president.

adj. suitable; practical; politic.
A pragmatic politician, he was guided by what was *expedient* rather than by what was ethical.

adj. not essential; superfluous.
No wonder Ted can't think straight! His mind is so cluttered up with *extraneous* trivia, he can't concentrate on the essentials.

v. put into effect; carry out; put to death (someone condemned by law).
The Agency for International Development is responsible for *executing* American policies regarding foreign assistance. The ballet master wanted to see how well Margaret could *execute* a pirouette. Captured by the British while gathering military intelligence, Nathan Hale was *executed* on September 22, 1776.

v. acquit; exculpate.
The defense team feverishly sought evidence that might *exonerate* their client.

adj. serving to clarify or interpret something; explanatory.
The manual that came with my iPhone was no masterpiece of *expository* prose; the explanations it provided were so inadequate that I had trouble figuring out how to synchronize my contacts.

v. worsen; embitter.
The latest bombing *exacerbated* England's already existing bitterness against the IRA, causing the prime minister to break off the peace talks abruptly.

adj. thorough; comprehensive.
We have made an *exhaustive* study of all published SAT tests and are happy to share our research with you.

adj. totally clear; definite; outspoken.
Don't just hint around that you're dissatisfied; be *explicit* about what's bugging you.

Fold along perforation before detaching cards.

extricate
(EK strə kāt)

facility
(fə SĬL ə tē)

fanaticism
(fə NĂ tə sĭ zəm)

exuberance
(ĭg ZŌŌ b(ə) rən(t)s)

faculty
(FĂK əl tē)

feasible
(FĒ zə bəl)

fabricate
(FĂB rə kāt)

fallacious
(fə LĀ shəs)

flagrant
(FLĀ grənt)

v. manufacture or build; make up to mislead or deceive; falsify.

Motawi Tileworks *fabricates* distinctive ceramic tiles in the Arts and Crafts style. The defense lawyer accused the arresting officer of *fabricating* evidence against her client.

adj. false; misleading.

Your reasoning must be *fallacious* because it leads to a ridiculous answer.

adj. conspicuously wicked; blatant; outrageous.

The governor's appointment of his brother-in-law to the State Supreme Court was a *flagrant* violation of the state laws against nepotism.

n. overflowing abundance; joyful enthusiasm; flamboyance; lavishness.

I was bowled over by the *exuberance* of Amy's welcome. What an enthusiastic greeting!

n. inherent mental or physical power; teaching staff.

As he grew old, Professor Twiggly feared he might lose his *faculties* and become unfit to keep his position on the *faculty*.

adj. capable of being done; practical.

Without additional funding, it may not be *feasible* to build a new stadium for the team on the city's highly developed West Side.

v. free; disentangle.

Icebreakers were needed to *extricate* the trapped whales from the icy floes that closed them in.

n. natural ability to do something with ease; ease in performing; something (building, equipment) set up to perform a function.

Morgan has always displayed a remarkable *facility* for playing basketball. Thanks to years of practice, he handles the ball with such *facility* that as a twelve-year-old he can outplay many students at the university's recreational *facility*.

n. excessive zeal; extreme devotion to a belief or cause.

The leader of the group was held responsible even though he could not control the *fanaticism* of his followers.

Fold along perforation before detaching cards.

frugality
(froo GĂ lə tē)

furtive
(FÛ(R) tĭv)

genre
(ZHAHN rə)

graphic
(GRĂ fĭk)

gravity
(GRĂ və tē)

guile
(GĪ(ə)L)

hamper
(HĂM pər)

heresy
(HĔR ə sē)

hierarchy
(HĪ (ə) rahr kē)

n. particular variety of art or literature.

Both a short story writer and a poet, Langston Hughes proved himself equally skilled in either *genre*.

n. deceit; duplicity; wiliness; cunning.

Iago uses considerable *guile* to trick Othello into believing that Desdemona has been unfaithful.

n. arrangement by rank or standing; authoritarian body divided into ranks.

To be low man on the totem pole is to have an inferior place in the *hierarchy*.

adj. stealthy; sneaky.

Noticing the *furtive* glance the customer gave the diamond bracelet on the counter, the jeweler wondered whether he had a potential shoplifter on his hands.

n. seriousness.

We could tell we were in serious trouble from the *gravity* of the principal's expression.

n. opinion contrary to popular belief; opinion contrary to accepted religion.

He was threatened with excommunication because his remarks were considered to be pure *heresy*.

n. thrift; economy. frugal, *adj.*

In economically hard times, anyone who doesn't learn to practice *frugality* risks bankruptcy.

adj. pertaining to visual art; relating to visual images; vividly portrayed.

The illustrator Jody Lee studied *graphic* arts at San Francisco's Academy of Art. In 2016, the SAT began to include reading questions that required students to interpret *graphic* information from charts and diagrams. The description of the winter storm was so *graphic* that you could almost feel the hailstones.

v. obstruct.

The new mother didn't realize how much the effort of caring for an infant would *hamper* her ability to keep an immaculate house.

Fold along perforation before detaching cards.

homogeneous
(hō mə JĒ nē us)

hypocritical
(hǐ pə KRǏ tǐ kəl)

hypothetical
(hī pə THĔ tǐ kəl)

immutable
(ǐ(m) MYOO̅ tə bəl)

impair
(ǐm PÂ(R))

impede
(ǐm PĒD)

incite
(ǐn SĪT)

incongruous
(ǐn KAHNG grə wəs)

incorrigible
(ǐn KAWR ə jə bəl)

adj. based on assumptions or hypotheses; supposed.
Why do we have to consider *hypothetical* cases when we have actual case histories that we may examine?

v. hinder; block; delay.
A series of accidents *impeded* the launching of the space shuttle.

adj. not correctable.
Miss Watson called Huck *incorrigible* and said he would come to no good end.

adj. pretending to be virtuous; deceiving.
Believing Eddie to be interested only in his own advancement, Greg resented his *hypocritical* posing as a friend.

v. injure; hurt.
Drinking alcohol can *impair* your ability to drive safely; if you're going to drink, don't drive.

adj. not fitting; absurd.
Dave saw nothing *incongruous* about wearing sneakers with his tuxedo.

adj. of the same kind.
Because the student body at the prep school was so *homogeneous*, they decided to send their daughter to a school that offered greater cultural diversity.

adj. unchangeable.
All things change over time; nothing is *immutable*.

v. arouse to action.
He *incited* his fellow students to go on strike to protest the university's anti-affirmative action stand.

Fold along perforation before detaching cards.

induce
(ĭn DŌŌS)

inference
(ĬN fə rən(t)s)

ingenious
(ĭn JĒN yəs)

inherent
(ĭn HĔR ənt)

innate
(ĭ NĀT)

innocuous
(ĭ NAH kyə wəs)

innovation
(ĭ nə VĀ shən)

instigate
(ĬN(T) stə gāt)

intrepid
(ĭn TRĚ pəd)

adj. clever; resourceful.

She admired the *ingenious* way that her computer keyboard opened up to reveal the built-in CD-ROM below.

adj. harmless.

An occasional glass of wine with dinner is relatively *innocuous* and should have no ill effect on you.

adj. fearless.

For her *intrepid* conduct nursing the wounded during the war, Florence Nightingale was honored by Queen Victoria.

n. deduction; conclusion.

From the glazed looks on the students' faces, it was easy for me to draw the *inference* that they were bored out of their minds.

adj. inborn.

Mozart's parents soon recognized young Wolfgang's *innate* talent for music.

v. urge; start; provoke.

Rumors of police corruption led the mayor to *instigate* an investigation into the department's activities.

v. persuade; bring about. inducement, *n.*

After the quarrel, Tina said nothing could *induce* her to talk to Tony again.

adj. firmly established by nature or habit.

Katya's *inherent* love of justice caused her to champion anyone she considered treated unfairly by society.

n. change; introduction of something new. innovate, *v.*

Although Richard liked to keep up with all the latest technological *innovations*, he didn't always abandon tried and true techniques in favor of something new.

Fold along perforation before detaching cards.

levity
(LĔ və tē)

materialism
(mə TĬR ē ə lĭ zəm)

mitigate
(MĬ tə gāt)

ironic
(ī RAH nĭk)

material
(mə TĬR ē əl)

meticulous
(mə TĬ kyə ləs)

inundate
(Ĭ nən dāt)

malicious
(mə LĬ shəs)

medium
(MĒ dē əm)

n. lack of seriousness; lightness.

Stop giggling and wriggling around in the pew; such *levity* is improper in church.

n. preoccupation with physical comforts and things.

By its nature, *materialism* is opposed to idealism, for where the materialist emphasizes the needs of the body, the idealist emphasizes the needs of the soul.

v. appease; moderate.

Nothing Jason did could *mitigate* Medea's anger; she refused to forgive him for betraying her.

adj. resulting in an unexpected and contrary outcome.

It is *ironic* that his success came when he least wanted it.

adj. relating to physical matter; bodily; of great importance or relevance.

Newton firmly based his hypotheses on his observations of the *material* world. We have to meet our *material* needs for food and shelter before we can begin to think about satisfying our emotional or intellectual needs. The police department reported that they had uncovered new evidence that might be *material* to the investigation.

adj. excessively careful; painstaking.

Martha Stewart was a *meticulous* housekeeper, fussing about each and every detail that went into making up her perfect home.

v. overwhelm; flood; submerge.

This semester I am *inundated* with work: you should see the piles of paperwork flooding my desk. Until the great dam was built, the waters of the Nile used to *inundate* the river valley like clockwork every year.

adj. hateful; spiteful. malice, n.

Jealous of Cinderella's beauty, her *malicious* stepsisters expressed their spite by forcing her to do menial tasks.

n. means of doing something; substance in which an organism lives; form or material employed by an artist, an author, or a composer.

M.I.T.'s use of the Internet as a *medium* of education has transformed the university into a global enterprise. Ty's experiment involved growing bacteria in a nutrient-rich *medium*. Johnny's favorite artistic *medium* is photography; he hopes to become a photojournalist.

Fold along perforation before detaching cards.

mundane
(mən DĀN)

nurture
(NÛ(R) chû(r))

objective
(əb JĔK tĭv)

objective
(əb JĔK tĭv)

oblivion
(ə BLĬ vē ən)

opaque
(ō PĀK)

ostentatious
(ahs tən TĀ shis)

pacifist
(PĂ sə fĭst)

partial
(PAHR shəl)

adj. not influenced by personal feelings or prejudices; unbiased; able to be perceived by the senses; verifiable.

Andrea loved her little son so much that it was impossible for her to be *objective* about his behavior. Nurses directly gather *objective* data by taking the patient's temperature or measuring the patient's height and weight.

adj. dark; not transparent.

The *opaque* window shade kept the sunlight out of the room.

adj. not complete or whole; favoring one side over another; particularly fond of.

John's first movie review was only a *partial* success. Although many readers praised his review, others felt he had presented a very *partial* view of Bergman's film *Wild Strawberries*. Of course, John was always *partial* to strawberries.

v. nourish; educate; foster.

The Head Start program attempts to *nurture* prekindergarten children so they will do well when they enter public school.

n. obscurity; forgetfulness.

After a decade of popularity, his works had fallen into *oblivion*; no one bothered to read them anymore.

n. one opposed to force; antimilitarist.

Shooting his way through the jungle, Rambo was clearly not a *pacifist*.

adj. worldly as opposed to spiritual; everyday. Uninterested in philosophical or spiritual discussion, Tom talked only of *mundane* matters such as the daily weather forecast.

n. something aimed at, which takes effort to attain.

Morgan's *objective* is to play basketball so well that he can be a starter on the varsity team.

adj. showy; pretentious; trying to attract attention.

Trump's latest casino in Atlantic City is the most *ostentatious* gambling palace in the East.

Fold along perforation before detaching cards.

pervasive (pər VĀ sĭv)	**philanthropist** (fĭ LĂN(T) thrə pĭst)	**pragmatic** (prăg MĂ tĭk)
peripheral (pə RĬ f(ə) rəl)	**phenomena** (fĭ NAH mə nah)	**ponderous** (PAHN d(ə) rəs)
partisan (PAHR tə zən)	**pessimism** (PĔ sə mĭ zəm)	**placate** (PLĀ kāt)

adj. pervading; spread throughout every part.

Despite airing them for several hours, Martha could not rid her clothes of the *pervasive* odor of mothballs that clung to them.

adj. marginal; outer.

We lived, not in central London, but in one of those *peripheral* suburbs that spring up on the outskirts of a great city.

adj. one-sided; prejudiced; committed to a party.

On certain issues of principle, she refused to take a *partisan* stand, but let her conscience be her guide.

n. lover of mankind; doer of good.

In his role as a *philanthropist* and public benefactor, John D. Rockefeller, Sr. donated millions to charity.

n. pl. observable facts; subjects of scientific investigation. (singular form, *phenomenon*.)

Among the most beautiful natural *phenomena*, auroras, also known as northern and southern lights, are natural light displays in the sky.

n. belief that life is basically bad or evil; gloominess.

Considering how well you have done in the course so far, you have no real reason for such *pessimism* about your final grade.

adj. practical; concerned with the practical worth or impact of something.

The coming trip to France should provide me with a *pragmatic* test of the value of my conversational French class.

adj. weighty; unwieldy.

His humor lacked the light touch; his jokes were always *ponderous*.

v. pacify; conciliate.

The store manager tried to *placate* the angry customer, offering to replace the damaged merchandise.

Fold along perforation before detaching cards.

presumptuous
(prǐ ZeM(P) che wes)

profound
(pre FOWND)

prolific
(pre Lǐ fǐk)

precocious
(prǐ KŌ shes)

prodigal
(PRAH dǐ gel)

proliferation
(pre lǐ fe RĀ shen)

preclude
(prǐ KLŌOD)

prevalent
(PRĚ ve lent)

profusion
(pre FYŌO zhen)

adj. overconfident; impertinently bold; taking liberties.

Matilda thought it was *presumptuous* of the young man to have addressed her without first having been introduced. Perhaps manners were freer here in the New World.

adj. deep; not superficial; complete.

Freud's remarkable insights into human behavior caused his fellow scientists to honor him as a *profound* thinker.

adj. abundantly fruitful.

My editors must assume I'm a *prolific* writer; they expect me to revise six books this year.

adj. advanced in development.

Listening to the grown-up way the child discussed serious topics, he couldn't help remarking how *precocious* she was.

adj. wasteful; reckless with money, also *n.*

Don't be so *prodigal* spending my money; when you've earned some money yourself, you can waste it as much as you want!

n. rapid growth; spread; multiplication. proliferate, *v.*

Times of economic hardship inevitably encourage the *proliferation* of countless get-rich-quick schemes.

v. make impossible; eliminate.

The fact that the band was already booked to play in Hollywood on New Year's Eve *precluded* their accepting the New Year's Eve gig in London.

adj. widespread; generally accepted.

Reed had no patience with the conservative views *prevalent* in the America of his day.

n. overabundance; lavish expenditure.

Seldom have I seen food and drink served in such *profusion* as at the wedding feast.

Fold along perforation before detaching cards.

qualified
(KWAH lə fīd)

random
(RĂN dəm)

redundant
(rĭ DəN dənt)

prudent
(PRŌŌ dənt)

rancor
(RĂNG kər)

rectify
(RĚK tə fī)

proximity
(prahk SĬ mə tē)

quandary
(KWAHN d(ə) rē)

rebuttal
(rĭ Bə t(ə)l)

adj. made fit (by training, experience) to do a specific job; limited in some manner.

Was the candidate for tax collector a *qualified* accountant? Unable to give the candidate full support, the mayor gave him only a *qualified* endorsement.

adj. without definite purpose, plan, or aim.

Although the sponsor of the raffle claimed all winners were chosen at *random*, people had their suspicions when the grand prize went to the sponsor's brother-in-law.

adj. superfluous; repetitious; excessively wordy.

The bottle of wine I brought to Bob's was certainly *redundant*; how was I to know he owned a winery?

---

adj. cautious; careful. prudence, *n.*

A miser hoards money not because he is *prudent* but because he is greedy.

n. bitterness; hatred.

Thirty years after the war, she could not let go of the past but was still consumed with *rancor* against the foe.

v. set right; correct.

You had better send a check to *rectify* your account before American Express cancels your credit card.

---

n. nearness.

Blind people sometimes develop a compensatory ability to sense the *proximity* of objects around them.

n. dilemma.

When both Harvard and Stanford accepted Laura, she was in a *quandary* as to which school she should attend.

n. refutation; response with contrary evidence.

The defense lawyer confidently listened to the prosecutor sum up his case, sure that she could answer his arguments in her *rebuttal*.

Fold along perforation before detaching cards.

reflect
(rĭ FLĔKT)

refute
(rĭ FYOOT)

relegate
(RĔ le gāt)

renounce
(rĭ NOWN(T)S)

reprehensible
(rĕ prĭ HĔN(T) sə bəl)

reprimand
(RĔ prə mănd)

reprove
(rĭ PROOV)

repudiate
(rĭ PYOO dē āt)

reticence
(RĔ tə sən(t)s)

v. banish to an inferior position; delegate; assign.

After Ralph dropped his second tray of drinks that week, the manager *relegated* him to a minor post, cleaning behind the bar.

v. reprove severely; rebuke. also n.

Every time Ermengarde made a mistake in class, she was afraid that Miss Minchin would *reprimand* her and tell her father how badly she was doing in school.

n. reserve; uncommunicativeness; inclination to silence.

Fearing his competitors might get advance word about his plans from talkative staff members, Hughes preferred *reticence* from his employees to loquacity.

v. disprove.

The defense called several respectable witnesses who were able to *refute* the false testimony of the prosecution's sole witness.

adj. deserving blame.

Shocked by the viciousness of the bombing, politicians of every party uniformly condemned the terrorists' *reprehensible* deed.

v. disown; disavow.

On separating from Tony, Tina announced that she would *repudiate* all debts incurred by her soon-to-be-ex-husband.

v. think seriously about; represent faithfully; show a physical image; create a good or bad impression.

Mr. Collins *reflected* on Elizabeth's rejection of his proposal. Did it *reflect* her true feelings, he wondered. While looking at his image *reflected* in the mirror, he refused to believe that she could reject such a fine-looking man. Such behavior *reflected* badly upon her.

v. abandon; disown; repudiate.

Joan of Arc refused to *renounce* her belief that her voices came from God.

v. censure; rebuke.

The principal severely *reproved* the students whenever they talked in the halls.

Fold along perforation before detaching cards.

sanction
(SANG(K) shən)

scrutinize
(SKRŌŌt(ə)n īz)

substantiate
(səb STĔN(T) shē āt)

rhetorical
(rĭ TAWR ĭ kəl)

scrupulous
(SKRŌŌ pyə ləs)

stagnant
(STĂG nənt)

retract
(rĭ TRĂKT)

satirical
(sə TĬR ĭ kəl)

skeptic
(SKĔP tĭk)

v. approve; ratify.
Nothing will convince me to *sanction* the engagement of my daughter to such a worthless young man.

v. examine closely and critically.
Searching for flaws, the sergeant *scrutinized* every detail of the private's uniform.

v. establish by evidence; verify; support.
These endorsements from satisfied customers *substantiate* our claim that Barron's *How to Prepare for the SAT* is the best SAT-prep book on the market.

adj. pertaining to effective communication; insincere in language.
To win his audience, the speaker used every *rhetorical* trick in the book.

adj. conscientious; extremely thorough.
Though Alfred is *scrupulous* in fulfilling his duties at work, he is less conscientious about his obligations at home.

adj. motionless; stale; dull.
Mosquitoes commonly breed in ponds of *stagnant* water.

v. withdraw; take back.
When I saw how Fred and his fraternity brothers had trashed the frat house, I decided to *retract* my offer to let them use our summer cottage.

adj. mocking.
The humor of cartoonist Gary Trudeau is often *satirical*.

n. doubter; person who suspends judgment until the evidence supporting a point of view has been examined. skepticism, *n.*
I am a *skeptic* about the new health plan; I want some proof that it can work.

Fold along perforation before detaching cards.

superfluous
(sŏo PÛ(R) flŏo əs)

taciturn
(TĂ sə tû(r)n)

turbulence
(TÛ(R) byə lən(t)s)

superficial
(sŏo pər Fĭ shəl)

synthesis
(SĬN thə sĭs)

transient
(TRĂN(T) sh(ē) ənt)

succinct
(sək SĬNG(K)T)

surpass
(sər PĂS)

terse
(TÛ(R)S)

adj. unnecessary; excessive; overabundant.

Betsy lacked the heart to tell June that the wedding present was *superfluous*; they had already received five toasters.

adj. habitually silent; talking little.

The stereotypical cowboy is a *taciturn* soul, answering lengthy questions with a "Yep" or "Nope."

n. state of violent agitation.

Warned of approaching *turbulence* in the atmosphere, the pilot told the passengers to fasten their seat belts.

adj. trivial; shallow.

Since your report gave only a *superficial* analysis of the problem, I cannot give you more than a passing grade.

n. combination of different parts to create a connected whole; chemical production of a more complex substance from simpler substances; electronic production of sounds.

Combining their masters' Catholicism with their own West African beliefs, Haitian slaves created a *synthesis* now known as Voodoo. The *synthesis* of aspirin involves the reaction of salicylic acid and acetic anhydride in the presence of a catalyst.

adv. momentary; temporary; staying for a short time.

Lexy's joy at finding the perfect gift for Phil was *transient*; she still had to find presents for all the cousins. Located near the airport, this hotel caters to a largely *transient* trade.

adj. brief; terse; compact.

Don't bore your audience with excess verbiage: be *succinct*.

v. exceed.

Her SAT scores *surpassed* our expectations.

adj. concise; abrupt; pithy.

There is a fine line between speech that is *terse* and to the point and speech that is too abrupt.

Fold along perforation before detaching cards.

undermine (əN dû(r) mīn)	**usurp** (yo͞o SəRP)	**vacillate** (VĂ sə lāt)
venerate (VĔ nə rāt)	**verbose** (vû(r) BŌS)	**vilify** (vĭ lə fī)
virtuoso (vû(r) cho͞o Ō sō)	**volatile** (VAH lə t(ə)l)	**zealot** (ZĔ lət)

v. waver; fluctuate.

Uncertain which suitor she ought to marry, the princess *vacillated*, saying now one, now the other.

v. slander.

Waging a highly negative campaign, the candidate attempted to *vilify* his opponent's reputation.

n. fanatic; person who shows excessive zeal.

Though Glenn was devout, he was no *zealot* who tried to force his beliefs on friends.

v. seize another's power or rank.

The revolution ended when the victorious rebel general succeeded in his attempt to *usurp* the throne.

adj. wordy.

Someone mute can't talk; someone *verbose* can hardly stop talking.

adj. changeable; explosive; evaporating rapidly.

The political climate today is extremely *volatile*; no one can predict what the electorate will do next.

v. weaken; sap.

The recent scandals have *undermined* many people's faith in the government. The heavy rains have washed away much of the cliffside, threatening to *undermine* the pillars supporting several houses at its edge.

v. revere.

In Tibet today, the common people still *venerate* their traditional spiritual leader, the Dalai Lama.

n. highly skilled artist.

The child prodigy Yehudi Menuhin grew into a *virtuoso* whose violin performances thrilled millions.